THE FORGOTTEN BATTLE OF THE KURSK SALIENT

7th Guards Army's Stand Against Army Detachment Kempf

Valeriy Zamulin

Translated & edited by Stuart Britton

Helion & Company

Helion & Company Limited
Unit 8 Amherst Business Centre
Budbrooke Road
Warwick
CV34 5WE
England
Tel. 01926 499619
Email: info@helion.co.uk
Website: www.helion.co.uk
Twitter: @helionbooks
Visit our blog at http://blog.helion.co.uk/

Published by Helion & Company 2018. Published in paperback 2023
Designed and typeset by Mach 3 Solutions Ltd (www.mach3solutions.co.uk)
Cover designed by Paul Hewitt, Battlefield Design (www.battlefield-design.co.uk)

Text © Valeriy Zamulin 2017. English edition translated and edited by
Stuart Britton, © Helion & Company Limited 2017.
Images © as individually credited
Maps drawn by George Anderson © Helion & Company Limited 2017

Parts of this book have been published in Russian with the title *Krax nastupleniia Generala Kempfa* (Veche, 2016).

Front cover: An artillery battalion of the 7th Guards Army's 265th Cannon Artillery Regiment shells the enemy's bridges across the Northern Donets River; July 1943. (Author's personal archive).
Rear cover: The commander of the 6th Panzer Division Major General W. von Hünersdorff (in a Sd.Kfz.250/3 halftrack) listens to a report from the commander of II/Panzergrenadier Regiment 114 Captain Necknauer in the vicinity of Belinskaia in the valley of the Razumniaia River; 7 July 1943. (Bundesarchiv, Bild 101I-022-2923-29A, photo: Kipper).

Every reasonable effort has been made to trace copyright holders and to obtain their permission for the use of copyright material. The author and publisher apologize for any errors or omissions in this work, and would be grateful if notified of any corrections that should be incorporated in future reprints or editions of this book.

ISBN 978-1-804512-47-0

British Library Cataloguing-in-Publication Data.
A catalogue record for this book is available from the British Library.

All rights reserved. No part of this publication may be reproduced, stored in a retrieval system, or transmitted, in any form, or by any means, electronic, mechanical, photocopying, recording or otherwise, without the express written consent of Helion & Company Limited.

For details of other military history titles published by Helion & Company Limited contact the above address, or visit our website: http://www.helion.co.uk.

We always welcome receiving book proposals from prospective authors.

Contents

List of Photographs	iv
List of Maps	ix
List of Tables	x
Introduction	xi
1 "We didn't anticipate even a quarter of what the Russians had prepared here"	21
2 In the shadow of the main attack – Army Detachment Kempf's role in Operation Citadel	107
3 5 July 1943 – The beginning of the end of a tragicomedy	135
4 The 7th Guards Army's main defensive belt crumbles	241
5 Breith's III Panzer Corps reaches the line of the 69th Army, 7-8 July 1943	301
6 The fall of the Belgorod bastion, 9-10 July 1943	404
7 "The beast is badly wounded, but still very dangerous." Breith's III Panzer Corps' dashing foray into the 69th Army's rear	487
8 The pinning counterattack: 7th Guards Army and the events of 12 July	529
9 "The operation's failure turned into a tragedy"	564
Index	592

List of Photographs

In Plate Sections

The commander of the 64th Army (subsequently the 7th Guards Army) Lieutenant General M.S. Shumilov in Stalingrad, before departing to the Belgorod area; end of February 1943. (RGAFKD)   i

The spring of 1943 came early: This is how the roads in the region of the Kursk bulge looked. (RGAKFD)   i

The city of Belgorod after the March 1943 fighting came to an end. (Captured files of the RGAKFD)   ii

The commander of the 7th Guards Army Lieutenant General M.S. Shumilov washes up in the village of Protopopovka, Kursk Oblast, on a sunny April 1943 morning. (A photo from an issue of the *Krasnaia znamia* newspaper in the files of the "Stalingradskaia bitva" ("Battle of Stalingrad") State Historical Park Museum)   iii

In moments of calm, even army commanders had no objection to a little mischief. Lieutenant General M.S. Shumilov (on the right) has a little fun at the expense of a major on his 7th Guards Army headquarters staff, who is showing his "booty" to correspondents of the *Krasnaia znamia* army newspaper; village of Protopopovka, Kursk Oblast, April 1943. (A photo from an issue of the *Krasnaia znamia* newspaper in the files of the "Stalingradskaia bitva" State Historical-Memorial Park Museum)   iii

The Commander-in-Chief of the Voronezh Front General of the Army N.F. Vatutin (in the center) receiving a report from one of his subordinate commanders during one of his trips to the front; spring of 1943. (RGAKFD)   iv

A major, a battalion commander in one of the 81st Guards Rifle Division's regiments, addresses his subordinate commanders; Voronezh Front, 7th Guards Army, May 1943. (Files of the "Stalingradskaia bitva" State Historical-Memorial Park Museum)   iv

Commanders of the 27th Guards Tank Brigade study a mock-up of the terrain in its sector, June 1943. (RGAKFD)   iv

T-34 radio operators of the 7th Guards Army's 27th Guards Tank Brigade in training: Sergeant Major Babushkin maintains contact with a tank battalion commander, May 1943. (Shebekino Historical-Art Museum)   v

The training of driver-mechanics in the 201st Separate Tank Brigade to overcome artificial obstacles. The tanks are Lend-Lease British Matilda tanks.   v

A training brochure issued on the eve of the Battle of Kursk to anti-tank gun, tank and artillery crews entitled "The most vulnerable and damage-prone places on the German Pz-VI tank and the means to counter them". The page on the right states, "Fire at the fuel tanks and forward wheels".   vi

Tank company commander Senior Lieutenant F. Martekhov (first from the right) of the 7th Guards Army's 27th Guards Tank Brigade, who for his exploits in the Belgorod area on 12 July 1943 was deemed worthy of the title "Hero of the Soviet Union", in conversation with a group of the brigade's officers and soldiers at his dugout during a moment of rest; village of Voznesenovka, May 1943.   vi

LIST OF PHOTOGRAPHS

The commander of the 7th Guards Army Lieutenant General M.S. Shumilov (third from the right) and the chief of the Army's motorized transport pool Lieutenant Colonel Ia.T. Savchenko (fourth from the right) talk with a group of commanders of the motorized transport service. In the background on the left, a sector of barbed wire in a defensive belt is visible; June 1943. (Archive of the "Kurskaia bitva. Belgorodskoe napravlenie" ("Battle of Kursk. Belgorod axis") Museum-Diorama.	vii
A Soviet leaflet calling upon grenadiers of the 168th Infantry Division to surrender, found near Belgorod in 2007. (Author's personal archive)	vii
Soldiers of one of the first-echelon divisions of the 7th Guards Army head out for their shift to man a combat outpost in the basin of the Northern Donets River; June 1943. (RGAKFD)	viii
The commander of Army Detachment Kempf General W. Kempf. (Captured photo. Author's personal archive)	viii
The commander of the III Panzer Corps General H. Breith; February 1943. (Captured photo. Author's personal archive)	viii
General-Instructor of Panzer Troops Colonel General H. Guderian (in the first row, second from the left) during a meeting in II SS Panzer Corps' SS Panzergrenadier Division *Leibstandarte Adolf Hitler* of Hoth's Fourth Panzer Army. Standing next to Guderian on his left is the commander of the SS Panzergrenadier Division *Das Reich* Lieutenant General G. Keppler. It was the II SS Panzer Corps that was supposed to act in close cooperation with Army Detachment Kempf. Khar'kov, April 1943. (Bundesarchiv, Bild 101III-Wiesebach-152-11A, photo: Wiesebach)	ix
H. Guderian (second from the right) examines the new Pz.Kpf. VI Tiger tanks equipping SS Panzergrenadier Division *Leibstandart Adolf Hitler*'s heavy panzer company. This particular tank is a *Panzerbefehlswagen* command tank carrying the tactical number 100). SS Captain Heinrich Kling, the commander of the heavy panzer company (on the right) is giving an explanation. Khar'kov, April 1943. (Bundesarchiv, Bild 101III-Wiesebach-152-14A, photo: Wiesebach)	ix
Senior Lieutenant V.M. Moiseev, the commander of one of 7th Guards Army's artillery batteries, conducts observation with the use of a BSD scissors telescope on the Belgorod axis; Voronezh Front, July 1943. (RGAKFD)	x
General of Panzer Troops E. Raus, the commander of Korps Raus, during Operation Citadel. Belgorod area, July 1943. (Bundesarchiv, Bild 146-1984 019-28, photo: Wolff/Altvater)	x
An artillery battalion of the 7th Guards Army's 265th Cannon Artillery Regiment shells the enemy's bridges across the Northern Donets River; July 1943. (Author's personal archive)	xi
A crew of a German 150mm howitzer fires at positions of the Guardsmen; Belgorod area, July 1943. (Captured photo, RGAKFD)	xii
The commander of the 25th Guards Rifle Corps Lieutenant General G.B. Safiulin; a 1944 photograph. (TsAMO RF)	xii
The commander of the 78th Guards Rifle Division Major General A.V. Skvortsov. (TsAMO RF)	xii
Assistant platoon commander Senior Sergeant I. Artem'ev of a submachine gun company of the 7th Guards Army's 78th Guards Rifle Division in firing positions with his company in the area of the village of Solomino; July 1943. (RGAKFD)	xiii
The commander of the 81st Guards Rifle Division Major General I.K. Morozov; a 1945 photograph. (TsAMO RF)	xiii
The commander of the 235th Guards Rifle Regiment G.T. Skiruta; a 1945 photograph. (TsAMO RF)	xiii

The explosion of a German tank in a minefield. In the foreground is a case for bottles containing an incendiary mixture that was hurled aside by the explosion; July 1943. (TsAMO RF) xiv

Sergeant N.N. Ivanov's anti-tank rifle squad in positions on the Northern Donets River; July 1943. (RGAKFD) xiv

The commander of the 72nd Guards Rifle Division Major General A.I. Losev at a forward observation post; July 1943. (RGAKFD) xiv

A crew of a 37mm M1943 Flak gun, which has been mounted on a truck, fires at Soviet ground assault aircraft in the vicinity of bridges across the Northern Donets River in the Belgorod area. July 1943. (Bundesarchiv, Bild 101I-022-2926-38, photo: Wolff/Altvater) xv

A Kazakh member of the Russian Liberation Army serving in a company of III Panzer Corps, which was used in the course of Operation Citadel in order to destroy Soviet command posts and communications, clarifies a combat task with a German Sergeant. July 1943. (Bundesarchiv, Bild 101I-022-2916-13A, photo: Wolff/Altvater) xv

The commander of the 3rd Battalion of the 73rd Guards Rifle Division's 214th Guards Rifle Regiment; a photograph that was touched up with an airbrush after the war. (RGAKFD) xvi

Tankers of one of the companies of III Panzer Corps' Heavy Panzer Battalion 503 examines the location of a hull hit in their Tiger tank from an armor-piercing shell fired by a Soviet gun. July 1943. (Bundesarchiv, Bild 101I-022-2935-25A, photo: Wolff/Altvater) xvi

A Maksim heavy machine-gun crew of a tank brigade's motorized rifle battalion provides supporting fire for a company that is defending a village somewhere in the sector of the 7th Guards Army; July 1943. (RGAKFD) xvi

The Commander-in-Chief of the Voronezh Front General of the Army N.F. Vatutin on a trip to the front; July 1943. (RGAKFD) xvii

The chief of staff of the Voronezh Front Lieutenant General S.P. Ivanov discusses a document with the Front's Military Council member Lieutenant General N.S. Khrushchev (on the left) outside the Front headquarters; area of Rzhava Station, July 1943. (Photography by F. Kislova, RGAKFD) xvii

The commander of the 35th Guards Rifle Corps Lieutenant General S.G. Goriachev; a July 1943 photograph. (RGAKFD) xviii

The commander of the 92nd Guards Rifle Division Colonel V.F. Trunin; a 1945 photograph. (TsAMO RF) xviii

The commander of the 94th Guards Rifle Division Colonel I.G. Russkikh; a June 1943 photograph. (TsAMO RF) xviii

A truck carrying infantry of one of Army Detachment Kempf's infantry divisions moving through the captured village of Sevriukovo; July 1943. (A captured photograph, RGAKFD) xix

The commander of the 6th Panzer Division Major General W. von Hünersdorff (in a Sd.Kfz.250/3 halftrack) listens to a report from the commander of II/Panzergrenadier Regiment 114 Captain Necknauer in the vicinity of Belinskaia in the valley of the Razumniaia River; 7 July 1943. (Bundesarchiv, Bild 101I-022-2923-29A, photo: Kipper) xix

Near Belinskaia, the commander of the 6th Panzer Division Major General W. von Hünersdorff (second from the left) together with a group of his officers observing the fighting in the area of the villages of Sevriukovo and Miasoedovo; 7 July 1943. (Bundesarchiv, Bild 101I-022-2923-19A, photo: Kipper) xx

Colonel A. Schulz, the commander of the 6th Panzer Division's Panzer Regiment 11 (in the foreground on the left) issues an order to a subordinate commander in the Sevriukovo area. In the background is a Pz.Kpf. III command tank. 7 July 1943. (Bundesarchiv, Bild 101I-022-2922-13, photo: Kipper) xx

LIST OF PHOTOGRAPHS

Colonel A. Schulz, commander of Panzer Regiment 11 at a crossing site on the Razumniaia River. In front of him is the armor skirt of a passing tank. 8 July 1943. (Bundesarchiv, Bild 101I-022-2922-09, photo: Kipper)	xxi
German trucks of one of Army Detachment Kemp's divisions move toward the front across a rebuilt bridge in the village of Iastrebovo. In the foreground is the remnants of the previous bridge that had been blown up by retreating troops of Shumilov's army. 8 July 1943. (Bundesarchiv, Bild 101I-022-2925-15, photo: Wolff/Altvater)	xxi
An RSO prime mover tows a 50mm anti-tank gun. On the left front of the vehicle is the tactical insignia of the 168th Infantry Division, painted in white. Area of Iastrebovo, 8 July 1943. (Bundesarchiv, Bild 101I-022-2925-06, photo: Wolff/Altvater)	xxii
A panzerjäger unit of one of Army Detachment Kempf's divisions rolls past a destroyed Soviet prime mover that had been towing a 76mm ZiS-3 M1939 divisional gun. Area of Sevriukovo, July 1943. (Bundesarchiv, Bild 101I-022-2924-15, photo: Kipper)	xxii
A group of soldiers and officers of the 201st Separate Tank Brigade aboard a captured German Sd.Kfz.8 Daimler Benz heavy half-tracked prime mover moving toward the area of combat operations in the 7th Guards Army's sector on 9 July 1943. (Files of the "Stalingradskaia bitva" State Historical Park Museum)	xxiii
Mark II Matilda tanks of one of the 201st Separate Tank Brigade's companies moving out with tank riders aboard toward the front.	xxiii
The commander of the 201st Separate Tank Brigade's 201st Motorized Rifle Battalion Captain D.A. Dziubin; a 10 July 1943 photograph. (TsAMO RF)	xxiv
Senior Lieutenant A.S. Kuskin's bloody Party card. He was the commander of the 201st Separate Tank Brigade's 296th Tank Battalion.	xxiv
Junior Lieutenant V.A. Vlasov, an anti-tank rifle platoon commander of the 201st Separate Tank Brigade's 201st Motorized Rifle Battalion; a 10 July 1943 photograph. (TsAMO RF)	xxiv
A German aerial reconnaissance photograph of the two major villages in the interfluvial area between the Northern Donets and Razumniaia Rivers, Melekhovo and Shliakhovoe, through which Army Detachment Kempf's assault wedge broke through toward Prokhorovka; a July 1943 photograph. (NARA US)	xxv
The commander of the 69th Army Lieutenant General Kriuchenkin (on the right) and his chief of operations Colonel D.N. Surzhits at a forward observation post on the Korocha axis; a July 1943 photograph. (Photograph by I. Ozersky, RGAKFD)	xxvi
The commander of a rifle company (second from left in foreground, with binoculars) observes the start of an attack. To his right, the crew of a 50mm mortar prepares to support the attack; a July 1943 photograph. (RGAKFD)	xxvi
A dug-in Red Army soldier awaits the completion of an attack by Il-2 ground assault aircraft against German positions; Voronezh Front, July 1943. (RGAKFD)	xxvii
Elements of the 69th Army taking up new positions in the basin of the Northern Donets River; Korocha axis, July 1943. (RGAKFD)	xxvii
Medic V. Kameneva of one of the Guards rifle divisions dragging a wounded soldier from the battlefield; Voronezh Front, July 1943. (Given the cleanliness of her uniform and face, this is likely a staged photograph). (RGAKFD)	xxviii
The commander of the 305th Rifle Division Colonel A.F. Vasil'ev (in the center) discusses recent combat results with a group of subordinate commanders at his forward outpost in Shliakhovoe. Judging from the smiles, the news was good. Korocha axis, July 1943. (RGAKFD	xxviii

An armored group of one of the panzer divisions of Breith's III Panzer Corps waits for the start of an attack. On the left in the background are Pz.Kpfw. VI Tigers, and on the right are Pz.Kpfw. III and IV tanks. In the foreground is the gun barrel of another Tiger tank. Sector of the 69th Army, July 1943. (Bundesarchiv, Bild 101I-022-2950-15A, photo: Kipper)   xxix

A column of prisoners, consisting of soldiers and officers of the 69th Army captured by troops of Army Detachment Kempf, moving to the rear. July 1943. (Bundesarchiv, Bild 101I-022-2925-05, photo: Wolff/Altvater)   xxix

Army Detachment Kempf's chief of staff Major General H. Speidel (on the left) meets with the commander of the 198th Infantry Division's Grenadier Regiment 305 Major J. Grassman in the area east of Belgorod. July 1943. (Bundesarchiv, Bild 101I-022-2933-05, photo: Heinz Mittelstaedt)   xxx

The commander of the 6th Panzer Division Major General W. von Hünersdorff (in the center) in a Sd.Kfz.250/3 halftrack in the area of Rzhavets. July 1943. (Bundesarchiv, Bild 101I-022-2912-13A, photograph: Horster)   xxx

A tank-riding company of the 7th Guards Army's 27th Guards Tank Brigade waits for the signal of attack; 12 July 1943. (RGAKFD)   xxxi

The commander of the 111th Rifle Division Colonel M.A. Bushin; a 1945 photograph. (TsAMO RF)   xxxi

Soldiers of the 73rd Guards Rifle Division in combat in the area of the "Batratskaia Dacha" State Farm; a July 1943 photograph. (Author's personal archive)   xxxii

The burial ceremony for fallen soldiers and commanders of the 7th Guards Army's 73rd Guards Rifle Division; July 1943. (Author's personal archive)   xxxii

Senior Lieutenant G.M. Kozhar (third from left and in the inset), the commander of the 1st Tank Company of the 201st Separate Tank Brigade's 295th Tank Battalion, stands together with his crew in front of his Matilda tank; a May 1943 photograph. (TsAMO RF)   xxxii

List of Maps

In Color Section

1. "Vatutin's Plan": The 7th Guards Army in the system of the Voronezh Front's defense and the anticipated directions of the enemy's attack. — a
2. The sector of the 7th Guards Army's main and second defensive belts on 1 July 1943 (minus the 15th Guards and 36th Guards Rifle Divisions). — b
3. Combat operations in the 7th Guards Army's sector, 5 July 1943. — c
4. The course of combat operations in the 7th Guards Army's sector on 6 July 1943. — d
5. III Panzer Corps' breakthrough at the boundary between the 6th Guards and 7th Guards Armies on 7 July 1943 and the combat in the Melikhovo area on 8 July 1943. — e
6. The 81st and 92nd Guards Rifle Divisions' combat against III Panzer Corps, 9 July 1943. — g
7. Breakthrough of the 69th Army's second army-level defensive belt by III Panzer Corps in the course of 11 July and the night of 11-12 July 1943. — g
8. Encirclement of the 35th Guards Rifle Corps' 94th Guards Rifle Division on 11 July 1943 and the 7th Guards Army's participation in the 12 July 1943 counteroffensive. — h

List of Tables

1	Combat strength of the 7th Guards Army's armored forces on 1 July 1943	33
2	Combat strength of the Voronezh Front's 7th Guards Army as of 5 July 1943	34
	a) Manpower and horses	34
	b) Small arms	35
	c) Mortars and Guns	36
	2) Vehicles, tanks, rocket launchers and anti-aircraft guns	38
3	Condition of the materiel of the 7th Guards Army's armored forces at 2000 4 July 1943	72
4	The Voronezh Front's armies' supply with obstacles and tools as of 1 April and 5 July 1943	74
5	Initial AFV strength for the formations of Army Detachment Kempf on 4 July 1943	116
6	Manpower and strength of Army Group South's formations in terms of tanks and assault guns, field artillery and rocket artillery	121
7	Casualties taken by the units of the 213th Rifle Division over the period between 5 and 11 July 1943	200
8	Manpower losses of the 72nd Guards Rifle Division in the course of combat operations on 5 and 6 July 1943	229
9	Availability of armored fighting vehicles in the 7th Guards Army's tank brigades and regiments from 5 to 16 July 1943 (according to combat reports from the units and operational summaries of the headquarters of the 7th Guards Army's Armored and Mechanized Forces	243
10	Number of operational assault guns in Army Detachment Kempf's separate assault gun units and operational self-propelled guns in the 7th Guards Army's self-propelled artillery regiments from 5 until 16 July 1943	264
11	Casualties of Army Detachment Kempf and the Fourth Panzer Army during Operation Citadel (5 to 16 July 1943)	298
12	Information on meteorological conditions in the sector of the Voronezh Front between 1 and 16 July 1943	418
13	Availability of tanks in the panzer divisions of Army Detachment Kempf's III Panzer Corps on 5 July and between 9 and 21 July 1943	436
14	Manpower and combat equipment of the 7th Guards Army as of 10 July 1943	456
15	Amount of personnel and weapons in the rifle divisions of the 7th Guards Army's shock and auxiliary groupings, formed for the counterattack on 12 July 1943	533
16	Casualties of the 7th Guards Army between 1 and 10 July 1943	568
17	Casualties of the 7th Guards Army between 5 and 16 July 1943	570
18	Casualties of the 6th Guards Army between 5 and 16 July 1943	571

Introduction

In your hands is the third monograph that completes the series of works planned by me about the combat operations of the Voronezh Front to repulse the Wehrmacht's offensive within the framework of Operation Citadel during the Battle of Kursk. The first two works came out in Russian in 2007: *Kurskii izlom. Reshaiushchaia bitva Otechestvennoi Voiny* [*Kursk turning point. Decisive battle of the Patriotic War*][1] and *Zasekrechennaia Kurskaia bitva. Zasekrechennye dokumenty svidetel'stvuiut* [*Classified Battle of Kursk: Classified documents bear witness*].[2] Respectively, they were dedicated to the events on the Oboian' direction [XXXXVIII Panzer Corps' offensive sector] and in the vicinity of Prokhorovka Station. This book was first published in 2008, but work on the issues that arose while writing it continued. Over the time that has since passed, a significant number of new important sources – Soviet and captured documents, plus the recollections of veterans of the combat operations on the Korocha axis – have been disclosed in Russian and Western archives. In addition, concerned readers have sent me interesting material. All this taken together enabled me to clarify certain events and data given in the 1st Edition, as well to provide a deeper analysis both on the course of events as a whole, and on a number of key moments. Thus the need arose to write a corrected and expanded version of the original manuscript, which I in fact did.

The place that the battle, which developed east and northeast of Belgorod after Army Detachment Kempf went on the offensive against the 7th Guards Army on 5 July 1943, occupies in the historiography of the Battle of Kursk doesn't equal the significance that it had for our eventual victory in this colossal battle. If an enormous amount of scholarly books and memoirs have been published in both Russia and the West about the combat operations on the axis of Army Group South's main attack, which at least in general outlines presents an image of what happened there, then in the case of the events near Belgorod, not much is known. Considering the difficult terrain, as well as the circumstance that from the end of March 1943 the trenches of the opposing sides were separated by the Northern Donets River,[3] both the Soviet and German command from the beginning viewed this sector as only allowing the possibility of launching a secondary attack. Until recently it was considered that it was just this circumstance that determined the fact that right up to the present day, historians haven't shown any particular interest in the events in this area.

However, in the course of my work on the two preceding monographs it became clear that there were significantly more weighty factors that became the reason for the silence over the battle near Belgorod that was both large in scale (a total of approximately 150,000 men on both sides took part in the fighting) and important in significance. The disclosed documents of the opposing sides speak to the fact that the events on the left flank of the Voronezh Front had a very important influence on the failure of Operation Citadel, but at the same time reveal that the actions of the Soviet forces in this area were less than successful. Thus, in order to conceal the failures and blunders, after the war the opposing sides sought to hush up what actually happened on this sector of the

---

1   Published in Moscow by Iauza/EKSMO in 2007, and republished in 2008 and 2013.
2   Published in Moscow by Iauza/EKSMO in 2007, and republished in 2008, 2010 and 2013.
3   Editor's note: On Soviet military maps of 1943, this river was labeled the "Severnyi Donets", or "Northern Donets" River. Today it is known as the Severskii Donets River. I have chosen the conventional name for it in Western military literature, the Northern Donets River.

front in the July days of 1943 as far as this was possible. Therefore, despite the seemingly exhaustive study of the Battle of Kursk, neither the broad reader nor the specialist had much knowledge about the fighting on the Korocha axis. At the same time, the deeper you penetrate into the events at the Kursk Bulge, the more you recognize that without having examined what happened in the sector of Army Detachment Kempf's offensive, it is impossible to grasp the scale of the fighting in the course of those two weeks and properly assess the plans of the Soviet and German commands, to set forth the internal logic of the key moments, to determine the main factors that affected the taking of one or another important decision, and finally, to see the entire enormous mechanism that worked for Voronezh Front's success in this colossal battle. The recognition of this mutual relationship became for me the decisive motivation for taking on the research and writing of this book. In addition, one of the key tasks of this work is to preserve the memory of those soldiers and officers of the Red Army that sacrificed their lives in this "unknown" fighting.

The Voronezh Front's leadership worked out a plan for the Kursk defensive operation that was complex and multi-tiered. It had not one, but at a minimum two primary objectives. First it was to stop and grind down the enemy forces within the deeply-echeloned defensive lines of the armies. Second was to prepare the optimal conditions (including the creation of a suitable staging area) for launching a counteroffensive toward Khar'kov and further on toward the Dnieper River. The whole point of the plan was Voronezh Front Commander-in-Chief General of the Army N.F. Vatutin's idea to split the combat spearhead of Army Group South, directed toward Kursk, by means of creating a powerful knot of resistance on the inner flanks of Field Marshal E. von Manstein's two shock groupings – Colonel General H. Hoth's Fourth Panzer Army (on the Oboian'-Prokhorovka direction) and General W. Kempf's Army Detachment (on the Korocha axis). The fortified ground in the confluence of the Northern Donets and Lipovyi Donets Rivers, which was located behind the boundary between the 6th Guards and 7th Guards Armies, was to be this knot. In the estimation of the Soviet command, these two armies were located on the enemy's most likely directions of attack. In the sectors of their adjoining divisions on the flanks of the armies, it was proposed to create a strong foci of resistance, which having received the antagonist's initial attack would serve as a breakwater to split the solid combat wedge of Army Group South into several pieces. Behind this defensive bulwark, it was also planned to deploy an entire army – the 69th Army – in the confluence of the Northern and Lipovyi Donets Rivers, which after the divergence of the enemy's attacking spearheads, was to hold this area and prevent a deep penetration into Voronezh Front's defenses by means of launching flank attacks against Hoth's and Kempf's advancing forces. After the German forces were stopped, it was proposed to commit the main forces of the *Stavka* of the Supreme High Command's strategic reserve – the Steppe Military District (later Front) in the confluence between the two rivers, in order first to isolate the enemy forces that were operating in the direction of Oboian', and then destroy them. After this was accomplished, both *fronts*, Voronezh and Steppe, were to launch a crushing attack through Belgorod toward Khar'kov and beyond.

However, in the course of the Kursk defensive operation, Vatutin's forces were unable to fulfill these two tasks. Despite every effort, Army Detachment Kempf was able to overcome the defensive sectors held by the 7th Guards and 69th Armies, and having emerged in the area south of Prokhorovka, it was able to seize the ground between the Northern and Lipovyi Donets Rivers jointly with the Fourth Panzer Army, which was operating to the north. In the process the enemy deprived the Soviet side of a suitable staging area for launching the planned counteroffensive. The causes for this were many, including a mistake made by the Soviet Supreme High Command when determining the area out of which the Wehrmacht would launch the main attack against the Kursk salient, as well as an underestimate by the leadership of the Voronezh Front's regarding the strength of Army Group South and an overassessment of the capabilities of its own forces that were operating on the Korocha axis.

There were also failures in the course of other strategic operations, of course, but the events at Kursk are a special case. In the official Soviet history, the defeat of the Wehrmacht at the Kursk bulge was called (not without justification) "*the fundamental turning point in the war*" and together with the Battles of Moscow and Stalingrad became the cornerstone in propaganda work to validate the thesis regarding the resilience of the socialist regime and the glorification of the leading role of the Communist Party in the defeat of Nazism. Accordingly, to allow a conspiratorial thought about the miscalculations of Soviet commanders in the course of such a significant event of the war was inadmissible. Thus for long years in domestic historical literature only the first two "victorious" days of the Voronezh Front's battle near Belgorod were more or less clearly illuminated, while the following days seemingly fell under the shadow of the "unparalleled battle at Prokhorovka", and thus have never been studied in detail.

For the Germans, the events on the axis of Army Group South's secondary attack had more serious consequences. E. von Manstein's underestimation of the time needed by the forces of Army Detachment Kempf to break through the 7th Guards Army's defenses in parallel with the Fourth Panzer Army's breaching of the 6th Guards Army's defensive belt for the success of Citadel as a whole became that small pebble over which the offensive of his entire army group stumbled. Kempf's troops already on the first day of the offensive was to break through the main belt of defenses of Shumilov's 7th Guards Army, and having overrun the 81st Guards Rifle Division, was to arrive on the right flank of the Fourth Panzer Army in order to cover it. Accordingly, on 5 July 1943 both of von Manstein's shock groupings had to overcome the most heavily fortified sectors of the 6th Guards and 7th Guards Armies' defenses and create a continuous breakthrough front, but this didn't happen. Not on the first day, nor on the second day, and not even on the third day of active combat operations could Army Detachment Kempf break through the line of the 7th Guards Army to its entire depth and establish shoulder-to-shoulder contact with the Fourth Panzer Army. From the very first minutes of the operation, the Guardsmen forced both enemy shock groupings to advance in diverging directions. This was a most important factor in the Voronezh Front's success in the course of the defensive phase of the Battle of Kursk.

Mistakes were also made already in the stage of planning Army Detachment Kempf's offensive. Indeed, the command of Army Detachment Kempf was aware of them, as was von Manstein personally, but there was no attempt to make any drastic decisions to eliminate them. In addition, the miscalculations were worsened by the strange passivity of the Field Marshal over the first two days of Operation Citadel. As a result, Army Detachment Kempf's offensive didn't gather the necessary momentum, and its divisions began to grind in place and suffer heavy losses. Meanwhile the Fourth Panzer Army already on 6 July 1943 reached the Prokhorovka axis, yet had nothing with which to screen its extended right flank. Hoth had no other option but to weaken his shock group and direct the relieved forces to screen his flank. Moreover, the forces diverted to buttress the flank were not small – entire divisions, including a panzergrenadier division. Right up to the official cessation of Operation Citadel, there was no success in finding any other means to resolve this problem. Therefore, not only objective factors brought about the failure of Operation Citadel, but also subjective ones; the inadequately elaborated plan for the operation and the unsatisfactory command over the troops on the part of Army Group South's headquarters.

Reflection on the results of the major strategic operations of the Second World War began in the West already at the end of the 1940s, but by military men, not historians. The Cold War provided the main impetus to begin the resurrection of West Germany and its armed forces as a forward outpost against the growing influence of the USSR. A significant portion of the command cadres of the West German Bundeswehr was comprised of former officers and generals of the Wehrmacht; there was simply no other choice. For this purpose, already in 1947 many generals and senior officers, including some of those who had fought at Kursk, were released from British and American military prisons. Two problems rose immediately. First, for the public, how to form an army that would include these former generals and officers who once served Nazi Germany, which had been condemned by the Nuremburg tribunal as an aggressor? Second, how could their authority be maintained as representatives of a leading military school of thought after the shattering defeat in the Second World War?

Primarily, mass media was directed to resolve this problem. In addition, already in the early 1950s, the memoirs of the defeated Nazi war dogs began to be published, through which a certain thesis ran like a red line: "*The soldiers of Germany honorably did their duty; a crazy Gefreitor [Hitler] was the primary guilty party in this tragedy.*" At this time, books by active participants in the Battle of Kursk came out, including ones by Field Marshal E. von Manstein and General E. Raus. In them, just as in the case of the memoirs of their colleagues, there was no honest depiction of the course of fighting, including near Belgorod, much less any deep analysis of the difficulties and problems that arose; in contrast the subject of a search for the guilty parties among the political leadership of Germany responsible for its defeat ran like a leitmotif.

Naturally in the situation of the Cold War, there could not be any talk of an objective approach to the study even of such a major battle. At this time, both in the West and the USSR the principle of historical truth didn't dominate in the periodical, memoir or academic research literature, but a clash between the two systems. At the same time, European and American scholars who in fact wanted to explore objectively the failure of Operation Citadel not only ran up against an impenetrable wall of the subjective assessments of its former veterans on the German side, but also the hyper-secrecy of the Soviet archives. With the passage of time, the topicality of the subject of the war declined in the public life of European countries. The Battle of Kursk also passed into distant history. As American historians D. Glantz and J. House relate, today on the whole it appears to the reader as a series of "myths and misperceptions."[4] What can be said about those of its events like, for example, the fighting near Belgorod, which has never been studied even by historians?

It fell to Shumilov's 7th Guards Army, which had previously gained fame in the fighting at Stalingrad, to play "first violin" in the defense of the Korocha direction. I will mention that it was to his army that Field Marshal F. Paulus had surrendered. At the end of March 1943, at the conclusive stage of the Red Army's unsuccessful defensive operation to retain possession of Khar'kov, it together with the 6th Guards Army (at the time still the 21st Army) played the key role in stabilizing the situation in Voronezh Front's sector. At the beginning of July 1943, its divisions, being the first to meet Kempf's assault formations, did everything to make sure Vatutin's plan worked out and inflicted maximal damage to the foe. The present research is the first attempt to analyze the combat operations in the sector of the 7th Guards Army in the course of Operation Citadel and to assess the combat performance of its leaders and troops on the basis of captured and recently declassified materials of the Central Archives of the Russian Federation's Ministry of Defense [TsAMO].

The book examines four main stages, through which Shumilov's Guards army passed when preparing for and conducting the Kursk defensive operation. The first consisted of devising a defensive plan, reorganizing and refitting the army (bringing its divisions up to establishment strength and training the arriving personnel), and setting up the two belts of the army's defense. The second stage was the combat to hold the main defensive belt. The third stage was the defense of the second defensive belt and the fighting on the boundary between the 6th Guards and 7th Guards Armies. Finally, the fourth and final stage was the army's participation in the frontal

---

4 Glantz, D. and House, J., *Kurskaia bitva: Reshaiushchaia povorotnyi punkt vtoroi mirovoi voiny* [*Battle of Kursk: The Decisive Turning Point of the Second World War*] (Moscow: Astrel', 2006), p. 9. This is the Russian translation of the book by Glantz and House, *The Battle of Kursk*, published by the University Press of Kansas in 1999.

counterattack of 12 July 1943. At each stage, the course of the combat operations and the participation of the army's formations in them have been described in sufficient detail. However, in turn each of them contained key moments, which required particularly deep analysis and a more detailed description of the events. These are the plans of the opposing sides for the summer of 1943; the fighting for bridges over the Northern Donets on 5 July 1943; the retention of the Mikhailovka – Blizhniaia Igumenka – Staryi Gorod area; the eventual withdrawal of the 81st Guards Rifle Division and a portion of the 92nd Guards Rifle Division out the forming pocket; the impetuous lunge made by the shock formation of Army Detachment Kempf – the III Panzer Corps – through the defensive lines of the 69th Army; and finally the preparation and conducting of the so-called "pinning attacks" by the forces of the 7th Guards Army within the framework of the 12 July frontal counterattack. The high degree of detail when describing the events that took place on the left wing of the Voronezh Front helps not only to form an overall picture of how the process of disrupting Operation Citadel went on the secondary axis, but also, I hope convincingly, to demonstrate the influence of 7th Guards Army's stubborn defense on the eventual failure of the offensive by von Manstein's forces on the main axis of attack.

In our country, the point of view has taken root that the Battle of Kursk was first of all a head-to-head struggle between the armored forces of the Soviet Union and Germany, and thus the tankers played the primary role in the victory. I consider this viewpoint not quite correct; each of the types of troops had a substantial influence on the course of the battle. In this respect, the picture of the combat operations outside of Belgorod laid out in this book gives a clear example of how heroically the Soviet rifle divisions fought against the adversary and the significant contribution they made to the enemy's defeat. Army Detachment Kempf's panzer divisions here were opposed by the formations of two combined-arms armies, first Lieutenant General M.S. Shumilov's 7th Guards Army, and then Lieutenant General V.D. Kriuchenkin's 69th Army. Despite significant problems with the preparation for the battle and the command and control during the battle, they demonstrated tenacity and courage. The first, most visible success of Shumilov's Guardsmen was the frustration of the plan by the III Panzer Corps' command to get three panzer divisions across the Northern Donets River on the offensive's first day. Because of the stubborn resistance on the army's right flank, one-third of Breith's panzer corps – the 6th Panzer Division – stood inactive on the western bank of the Donets for 24 hours at a time when every battalion and company mattered. Only on 6 July did it enter the fighting. This failure together with the inability of the Fourth Panzer Army's XXXXVIII Panzer Corps, which was operating on the axis of the main attack by Army Group South, to break through the forward edge of the 6th Guards Army on 5 July 1943, augured the failure of Operation Citadel on the southern face of the Kursk salient.

The combat that developed in the Staryi Gorod – Blizhniaia Igumenka area was both heavy and costly for both sides. The reinforced 81st Guards Rifle Division that was occupying the defenses here withstood the onslaught of two panzer divisions and one infantry division for five days. The reason for such a lengthy defense was not only the strongly-fortified positions, but primarily the stubbornness and courage of its defenders. The Guardsmen fought not only self-sacrificingly, but also effectively, something which is very important. The peak of the fighting in this area took place on 9 July 1943. According to the most conservative German data, in two panzer divisions of the III Panzer Corps alone almost 100 tanks were knocked out of action on this day while fighting to break through the line of the 81st Guards Rifle Division and two regiments of the 92nd Guards Rifle Division. For comparison, some historians believe that in the course of the famous battle at Prokhorovka on 12 July 1943, which four tank corps of Rotmistrov's tank army collided with three divisions of the II SS Panzer Corps in a fierce clash, not more than 150-160 German combat machines were knocked out or destroyed.

Unfortunately, our side also didn't escape heavy losses. In addition, serious miscalculations and shortcomings were committed by a number of senior commanders, which cost the troops dearly. For example, when moving up to the axis of the main attack of Breith's panzer corps, the command of the 92nd Guards Division lost control over its subordinate regiments that were advancing to the front on foot. Things only became worse; over a week of fighting, because of the incompetent actions of the division commander and poor supervision by the leadership of the 35th Guards Rifle Corps, the 92nd Guards Rifle Division lost more than 60% of its men. The story about these and other, no less dramatic, but forgotten episodes of that colossal battle will be told in the given research.

As in my previous works, in this book all the events of the spring and summer of 1943 are analyzed on the basis of three blocks of resources: materials of the Soviet formations and armies from the Russian Ministry of Defense's Central Archives; the operational documents and accounts produced by Army Detachment Kempf and its headquarters, which can be found in the US National Archives; as well as veterans' recollections and recent publications by domestic and foreign historians. Although all sources in their own way are important and irreplaceable, nevertheless the archival documents of the combat formations were taken as the basis for analysis. Their particular value stems from the fact that from the beginning, they were prepared for combat work, and thus they are virtually spared of the ideological sheen and heroic airs, which mar the books by the "instigators" of the history of the past war, both in Russia and the West. An enormous crust of legends and myths has formed around the Battle of Kursk over the past 70 years. Thus, in order to understand how that epochal event unfolded in reality, what problems the opposing sides encountered in the process, and what cost our people had to pay for the fundamental turning point in the war against a strong and well-prepared aggressor, original documents are irreplaceable assistants.

If to compare the bases of sources gathered when writing this book and my previous publications, then it should be noted that rather serious difficulties arose when collecting and organizing the archival materials about the fighting between the 7th Guards Army and Army Detachment Kempf. The experience of many years of work in the TsAMO RF testifies to the fact that in whatever the complex situation that the Soviet forces found themselves in, the most complete information can normally be found in the army-level documents. This is connected with the fact that the information from all the units and formations came together here, and secondly, the officers that served in the headquarters of armies had more work experience and a higher level of staff "culture" than did the officers at the corps, or more especially, the division level. Unfortunately, with respect to the headquarters of the 7th Guards Army in the April – July period of 1943, this is impossible to say. The army arrived from Stalingrad after bloody, heavy fighting and immediately underwent a large turnover in its command and staff cadres. In April it began the process of converting into a Guards formation, and some of its staff officers were sent to help make up the command staff of its forming two rifle corps. Key figures in the army headquarters also changed – its chief of staff and chief of operations. Some of its commanders departed due to promotions or additional training. As a result, although for objective reasons, nevertheless the professional level of the officers of the army headquarters dropped for a certain period. This, naturally, affectedd the results of everyday work. The quality of the documents and the depth of analysis of operational information perceptibly decreased even in comparison with the 69th Army, which had formed up only in February 1943. This also concerns the account documents. For example, the account on the results of the Battle of Kursk was prepared by the 7th Guards Army's Operations Department only in October 1943, and it laid out the course of the fighting schematically, while the analysis of the combat operations was superficial. When working on this book, this factor not only substantially complicated the depicting of the course of the army's combat operations, but something which is significantly more important, obscured the understanding of the motivations that governed the army commander when reaching one decision or another.

The situation is worsened by the absence of documents for a whole array of units and formations over the period of the Battle of Kursk in the archives. Ordinarily, the shortage of information in the files of the armies and corps can be compensated by the information from the headquarters of divisions, regiments and even battalions. In the given case it is impossible to use this approach, since a significant batch of documents of the units and formations of the 7th Guards Army never reached the TsAMO RF for preservation and are considered lost. This includes the papers of the 81st Guards Rifle Division's and 78th Guards Rifle Division's regiments, which wound up in encirclement. The files of the headquarters of these divisions are also sparse. Thus I had to turn to a broader circle of archival sources from other collections: the documents from the headquarters of the Voronezh Front, the headquarters of the commander of other troop types, and the headquarters of armies that flanked the 7th Guards Army, as well as from lower, smaller formations – the tank, self-propelled gun and artillery regiments and brigades of Shumilov's army, as well as from engineer units and the intelligence and counterintelligence service at all levels. This helped offset the lack of documents.

Serious problems also arose with German sources. As a rule, the course of the combat operations is laid out more concisely and clearly in the journals of combat operations of the Wehrmacht's combat formations that took part in them. Although these were prepared already after the events happened, in them the course of the battle, the decisions made by the commander and the general outlines of the motivations behind them are written up on an hourly basis through the use of original documentary material. In addition, this document as a rule has appendices, which contain all the orders, summary reports and a printed record of telephone conversations between the command and higher headquarters. The corps-level journals are the most detailed and interesting for research. In the offensive toward Kursk, two of the three corps of Army Detachment Kempf took part: the III Panzer Corps and Korps zbV Raus [which on 20 July became XI Corps]. Unfortunately, I was unable to acquire fully the journal of combat operations of the XI Corps, while that of the III Panzer Corps is thought to be lost. Only its appendices have been preserved: operational orders, summaries, messages and orders to the rear, and in part pages with the decoded conversations between the division commanders and the corps. In addition, in the US National Archives I managed to find the journal of combat operations of Army Detachment Kempf, although the appendices were missing. This interesting and very important material has never before been published in Russia and has not been used by Russian historians. Although everything that happened in the sector of Army Detachment Kempf's offensive has not been described in detail in the collected documents, and moreover consists of dry military language, nevertheless these sources seriously eased my work and provide rich material for a comparative analysis. Especially useful are the combat orders, messages and command discussions, which allow an understanding of the intentions of the German side and the essence of what happened not only on a tactical, but also on an operational level.

The search for recollections by eyewitnesses and participants in those events, which for any serious scholar plays a substantial role, also took quite a bit of effort. At the beginning of the 1960s, the well-known Soviet writer and frontline correspondent K.M. Simonov appealed to war veterans with a request to submit their memoirs and recollections to archives of all levels as eyewitness testimony of the tragedy and heroism of the Soviet people in that terrible war. However, Simonov's initiative received a sharp reaction from the Main Political Directorate of the Soviet Army. Its leadership rightly supposed that these materials would constitute a "delayed-action mine", and if historians managed to gain access to them, stone by stone they would refute the ideologically calibrated (or more accurately, fabricated) history of the Great Patriotic War, and cast many "outstanding commanders and military chiefs" in an unfavorable light. However, chiefly these memoirs and recollections would dispel the myth about the "wisdom and sagacity of the Communist Party". In 1965 during one of the conferences dedicated to the problems of studying the history of the Great Patriotic War, then chief of the Main Political Directorate of the Soviet Army General of the Army A.A. Epishev concisely laid down the position of the country's leadership: "Give them the black bread of truth. Why the devil is this necessary, if it isn't beneficial for us?!"[5] This principle for many long years became the guiding one in the work not only of the TsAMO RF, but also in civilian archives of the entire country. As a result an enormous seam of "living truth" about the war never made its way to historians, writers and journalists, and this also means it never reached a wider audience of readers. There were exceptions; for example, the archive of the Belgorod Oblast Committee of the Communist Party of the Soviet Union, and today the State Archive of Latest History of Belgorod Oblast, has been collecting most valuable material down to morsels – manuscripts written by veterans. Primarily, however, Russian authors who wrote about the Great Patriotic War had to use only authorized sources, which meant thoroughly purged and sterilized sources.

In part museums offset this situation. With no restrictions, they were receiving manuscripts from former frontline veterans for preservation. Thanks to this, today not only in capital city museums, but also in regional museums rich memoir material has accumulated, but not everywhere, and only in museums dedicated to major battles or clashes, which in the 1960s to 1980s were "known by ear". There were no such events near Belgorod, and thus the collections of unpublished memoirs by veterans of the 7th Guards Army in the museums of Belgorod Oblast are modest. Unfortunately, in addition key figures of the 7th Guards Army, including its commander General M.S. Shumilov, didn't leave behind any memoirs or manuscripts. As veterans of the 7th Guards Army, who happened to know the army commander personally, later told me, by his nature Shumilov was not given to boasting and made no effort to puff up his contributions to the victory after the war, but held to the conviction: "They won't allow me to tell the truth, and even without me so many lies have already been written about the war."

With all that said, when collecting the materials for this book I also made several unexpected discoveries. In the TsAMO RF I managed to uncover a collection of manuscripts by captured Wehrmacht generals, who, just like members of a group under the leadership of the former Chief of Staff of Army Group South T. Busse in the USA, prepared studies for the General Staff of the Red Army about the participation of their divisions and corps in major operations and battles of the Soviet – German front. Among those who wrote recollections were several former commanders of divisions and corps that took part in the Battle of Kursk. In particular, this collection preserves a study that was translated into Russian in 1949, entitled "Forcing of the Donets River by the forces of the 7th Panzer Division in July 1943 (Operation Citadel)". Its author General von Funck was the commander of this panzer division in the fighting near Belgorod. Until recently, this document was held in a secret archive, and thus it has never been published in the open press. In my view, it has two important qualities. Firstly, it was written by a direct participant in the Battle of Kursk, and thus contains information that is hard to find in other sources. Secondly, the document contains both the author's attitude toward the described events and his assessment of them, and he was an important figure in the leadership of Army Detachment Kempf. Moreover, the study is virtually deprived of the propaganda rhetoric from the Cold War period, because it was written for a narrow circle of professionals and was never intended for publication. However, it must be remembered that when H. von Funck was writing it, he had no access to archival documents, and because of this his description of the combat operations is somewhat superficial. Because of this, the essay proved useful as supplementary material when analyzing the III Panzer Corps' offensive on the first days of the operation.

The book also makes wide use of other captured materials, which have already been published by me, for example "Description of the combat operations of the 19th Panzer Division 5-19 July 1943", as well as those being first put into academic circulation. For example, the accounts written

---

5   *Voenno-istoricheskii zhurnal* [*Military history journal, or VIZh*], No. 8 (2009), p. 69.

by the command of the artillery units of the *Waffen SS*, which describes the tactical experience of using certain weapons systems in the Battle of Kursk, including the new self-propelled gun-carriages, the Hummel and Wäspe.

The book includes illustrative material – rare photographs collected over the course of several years of work in the collections of a number of domestic museums, the State Archive of Film and Photographic Documents (in Krasnogorsk) and the TsAMO RF (in Podol'sk). There are also a significant number of tables, which help the reader to ponder more deeply that which has been laid out in the main body of text.

I consider it my obligation to express my gratitude to everyone who helped me in the work on this book, and primarily, the leadership of Kursk State University. I felt the special support in this period from its provost, a talented academic organizer, a man drawn to the history of Russia and a Doctor of Science, Professor Vitalii Alekseevich Kudinov. The outstanding scholar and Doctor of Science, Professor Aleksei Borisovich Shevelev gave me great, comradely assistance in processing the collected material. Thanks to the indefatigable energy, persistence and painstaking work of this excellent man, the captured material that was used when revising this research manuscript was translated and processed. I am also grateful to Candidate of History A.S. Isaev for his assistance in preparing the maps for the book.

The work on this manuscript continued for several years. Just the preparation and editing of the text required two years. I spent more than a year working in the TsAMO RF, seeking relevant archived documents, and twice crossed the Atlantic in order to visit the US National Archives. I questioned more than a hundred veterans of the Battle of Kursk in various cities of Russia. Over all this period, my wife Svetlana Zamulina shared the burden of partings and painstaking labor with me. I want to express my sincere gratitude to her for her great patience, understanding and support at difficult moments, and the substantial practical assistance she gave me in work over the manuscripts.

I hope that this book, like my previous research works, will be received with interest by a wide audience of readers. Anyone who wants to share their impressions of it, ask a question or seek clarification regarding details in it are welcome to contact me at valeriy-zamulin@yandex.ru.

Valeriy Zamulin, June 2016

1

"We didn't anticipate even a quarter of what the Russians had prepared here"

The above quote is what the command of Army Detachment Kempf's 19th Panzer Division wrote in its account of Operation Citadel regarding the fortified lines of the 7th Guards Army. The decision by the *Stavka* of the Supreme High Command[1] to go over to a pre-meditated defense and created deeply-echeloned belts of field fortifications for the two *fronts* [Central and Voronezh Fronts] that were holding the Kursk salient, together with the formation of a major strategic reserve – the Steppe Military District, later Steppe Front – were the most important factors that enabled the Red Army to stop the Wehrmacht's final strategic offensive on the Soviet-German front. Thus the first chapter of this work will be dedicated to the place of Shumilov's 7th Guards Army in the plan of Voronezh Front's Kursk defensive operation, the system of defenses built by its troops in April-June 1943, and the process of restoring the combat capabilities of its subordinate formations after the winter campaign.

The stabilization of the Soviet-German front in the southwestern sector arrived around 27 March 1943. By this time the opposing sides had exhausted their potential for active operations, and the weather to a significant degree contributed to this. The spring thaw took over, and flood water covered all the roads and fields and filled the ravines and balkas; the European part of the Soviet Union turned into a sea of mud. On this same day, a notable event took place in an ordinary village hut in Oboian', 60 kilometers north of Belgorod, where the headquarters of the Voronezh Front was established: in place of Colonel General F.I. Golikov, the new Front commander-in-chief General of the Army N.F. Vatutin arrived and assumed command. Nikolai Fedorovich took over at a time when the subordinate troops were in a difficult situation. In the course of the Khar'kov offensive, and later the defensive operation its formations had suffered heavy losses and were extremely depleted. Over the last month they'd been forced to fall back to the east with bloody fighting, abandoning to the enemy Ukrainian territory that they had already liberated. By the end of March 1943, the main forces of the Voronezh Front were digging in along new lines, but Red Army troops and commanders, in groups and alone, were continuing to make their way

---

1 The *Stavka* of the Supreme High Command was created on 23 June 1941 and was the highest organ of the strategic leadership of the Soviet Union's armed struggle in the Great Patriotic War. It was located in Moscow and initially was named the *Stavka* of the Main Command. The USSR People's Commissar of Defense Marshal of the Soviet Union S.K. Timoshenko headed it. However, in connection with a change in the system of command of the acting armies of the Workers' and Peasants' Red Army on 10 July 1941, its name was changed. On 16 July 1941, I.V. Stalin became the People's Commissar of Defense, and from 8 August 1941, the Supreme Commander-in-Chief. The main working organ of the *Stavka* was the General Staff of the Red Army.

out of deep enemy encirclement even in the middle of April. Opposite the center and left flank of the Voronezh Front (in the Tomarovka – Belgorod area), an enemy panzer group was operating, and no continuous front line had been able to be created, because a significant portion of the rifle divisions of the 21st and 64th Armies, which were arriving from Stalingrad and beginning to take up combat sectors here, was still on the way. Even so, by this time the Germans had become played out. Together with their own rather heavy losses, the spring thaw underway was bogging them down. Thus three exceptionally complex tasks, which demanded an immediate resolution, were now confronting the new Commander-in-Chief of the Voronezh Front.

First, he had to organize the gathering and assembly of the personnel and equipment of the rifle divisions (of the combined-arms armies that constituted the Front's main force) that were arriving from the territory of Khar'kov Oblast, and have them dig in along the current line, including with the deployment of minefields on the tank-vulnerable directions and the construction of elaborate field fortifications in the sectors they were holding. Second, he had to determine the adversary's immediate objectives and taking into account the Front's capabilities, in the shortest possible amount of time devise a plan for a stubborn defense and begin to implement it without delay. Third, he had to work out a complex program of measures to rebuild the forces through the arrival of *Stavka* reserves and to evacuate the population from the territory occupied by the Front, primarily from areas of Kursk Oblast.

At the end of March 1943, the Voronezh Front's forward edge ran through: Snagost', Bliakhova, Alekseevka, Molotov State Farm, Volkov, Bititsa, Ol'shanka, Dibrova, Glybnia, along the right bank of the Syrovatka River as far as [excl.] Krasnopol'e, [excl.] Novo-Dmitrievka, Vysokii, Zavertiachii, Nadezhda, Novaia zhizn', Trefiliovka, Berezovka, Trirechnoe, Dragunskoe, Zadel'noe, [excl.] Blizhniaia Igumenka, Staryi Gorod and further along the left bank of the Northern Donets River as far as First Sovetskoe, with a total length of 245 kilometers (following the trace of the frontline). Its boundary lines on the right (with Central Front and 60th Army): Staryi Oskol, Dezhevka, Verkhnii Reutets, Lokinskaia Station, Kornevo, Krovolets (all for the Voronezh Front); on the left (with Southwestern Front and the 57th Army): Volokonovka, Volchansk, Khar'kov. Thereby, its troops were taking on the defense of the southwestern, southern and southeastern parts of the Kursk salient.

On this same day, 27 March 1943, N.F. Vatutin signed Order No. 0087, according to which his subordinate troops were to immediately begin fortifying the territory, reconnoiter the ground and create a system of defense. At this moment, the 64th Army, 38th Army and 40th Army comprised the Front's first echelon. Within two months, the 69th Army would be deployed behind the boundary between the 64th and 21st Armies;[2] at that moment, its strength was in fact equivalent to that of a rifle corps, even though formally it was considered an army. It was from this document [Order No. 0087] that the working up of a short-term plan for the Front's actions (1 to 1.5 months) began. At the end of March, in order to assess the existing operational situation and prepare proposals for conducting the spring-summer campaign, the Deputy of the Supreme Commander-in-Chief Marshal of the Soviet Union G.K. Zhukov and the Chief of the General Staff Marshal of the Soviet Union A.M. Vasilevsky arrived at Vatutin's headquarters. Over the next several days they visited the front together with General of the Army Vatutin, inspected in detail the line of deployment of the 21st and 64th Armies, and listened to his proposals regarding the primary measures to erect a defense on the southern face of the Kursk salient. The opinion and assessments of the Marshals of the Soviet Union on the key questions that formed in the course of these trips, the reports from the commands of the Central and Voronezh Fronts, as well as reports

---

2   In the middle of April 1943, the 21st Army would be transformed into the 6th Guards Army, and the 64th Army – into the 7th Guards Army.

from front and strategic intelligence lay at the basis of the three principal decisions taken at a conference with I.V. Stalin on 12 April 1943:

1. The Kursk salient was recognized as the most suitable sector of the Soviet-German front both for the enemy's summer offensive and for the following counteroffensive by the Red Army.
2. The Central and Voronezh Fronts were supposed to go over temporarily to a pre-meditated defense, to begin planning the defensive operation quickly, and to initiate the construction of belts of defense with an intricate and dense system of artificial obstacles and fortifications. Wherever it was impossible to do this work because of the spring thaw, they were to conduct promptly the mining of tank-vulnerable sectors and concentrate anti-tank means along the main roads.

    The first three lines of defense, called respectively the main, second and rear defensive belts, were to be prepared by the forces of the armies of the first and second echelon, while the construction of the third, rear defensive belt would include the local population. In addition, it was also planned to throw up a Front-level defensive line and a State-level defensive belt along the Don River, which were to be built by the engineers of the Fronts, the Steppe Military District and the commands of defensive works construction. Taking into account the preliminary analysis of the condition of the enemy's forces and the short time thought possible before they would go on the offensive, deadlines for completing the primary fortification work was set for 15 April 1943 (in fact, this work continued until the end of the month). This related to the construction of the main defensive fortifications, which secured a system of fire and the combat dispositions of the troops on the occupied line (rifle pits, trenches, earth-and-timber bunkers, mortar and artillery sites, and so on), as well as the mining of the main tank-vulnerable directions. Fortunately, Order No. 0087 gave artificial obstacles particular attention, and just a bit later, on 9 April 1943, as work was already underway, a follow-on, special order was signed "On the creation of practical obstacles on the Front's territory". In part, it stated: "… in addition to the zones of minefields connected with the defensive belts, the creation of obstacles and demolitions in important populated locations, and on rivers and roads in the interval between the belts, which have as their aim the restriction of the enemy's operational maneuver and the slowing of his advance into the depth of our defenses."
3. To continue to assemble the *Stavka*'s strategic reserves, consolidated into a Reserve Front,[3] in the rear of the *fronts* that were holding the Kursk salient. The Reserve Front was created on 6 April 1943 and it consisted of six combined-arms armies and one tank army. It was centered on Voronezh. This strategic *front* was given an assignment: in the event of a breakthrough of the lines of the Central or Voronezh Fronts, it was to occupy a defense along the Kshen' and Oskol Rivers between the towns of Livny and Novyi Oskol and prevent the enemy from advancing into the depth of the country, as had happened in the summer of 1942.

When planning the Kursk defensive operation, which, I will mention, was shared by both the Central and Voronezh Fronts, N.F. Vatutin had to resolve several extremely difficult tasks. First, he had to determine the directions of the enemy's main and secondary attacks, and second, he had to devise a framework for assembling his forces and creating defensive lines to block them. At the end of March 1943, immediately after assuming command and familiarizing himself with the state

---

3   On 13 April 1943 it was re-named the Steppe Military District.

of affairs in his subordinate forces, he sent a directive to the headquarters of the armies: Within two weeks, to present the plans for fortifying their own lines of defense for the spring-summer period and an assessment of the operational situation and the enemy's intentions once the ground and roads dried out. I will cite an excerpt from 69th Army's plan of defense. This document is interesting for the fact that already on 14 April it was confirmed by the Voronezh Front's Military Council practically without any changes, which means N.F. Vatutin fully shared the proposals regarding possible enemy actions that were expressed in it:

1. The most likely operational objective of the enemy in the forthcoming spring-summer offensive should be considered the encirclement and destruction of the Kursk grouping with a subsequent emergence on the line of the Don River.
    The enemy's main directions [of the offensive] might be:
    a. Belgorod – Kastornoe (an outer enveloping attack), Belgorod – Kursk (an inner enveloping attack);
    b. Orel – Kastornoe (an outer enveloping attack), Orel – Kursk (inner enveloping attack).
2. The most probable operational directions for the enemy's Belgorod grouping:
    a) Tomarovka – Oboian' – Kursk;
    b) Belgorod – Skorodnoe – Tim or Belgorod – Korocha – Staryi Oskol;
    c) Volchansk – Novyi Oskol or Volchansk – Volokonovka.
4. The enemy's Belgorod grouping has essentially ended its operational deployment, and his offensive should be expected once the roads improve following the end of the spring muddy season, which means the end of April – first half of May 1943.[4]

Accordingly, for the Soviet command even at the army level, the objectives and assignments of Operation Citadel as set in Operational Order No. 6, which Hitler was to sign only on 15 April 1943, were fully obvious even before its official adoption. At the same time, the headquarters of the 69th Army accurately determined both the directions of the main attacks by Army Group South that opposed the Voronezh Front, as well as the time for the initiation of its active operations. I will remind the reader that in Order No. 6, Hitler directed that all the forces assigned to the operation be brought up to full combat readiness by 28 April 1943, and set the earliest time for the start of the offensive – 3 May. I am far from the opinion that the Soviet generals, and in particular the commander of the 69th Army Lieutenant General V.D. Kriuchenkin, supposedly had some special capabilities of clairvoyance. I believe that for a person familiar with the main principles of conducting major offensive operations and the capabilities of the German Army at this time (even if only in general outlines), the configuration of the front lines in the area of the Kursk salient and the conditions of the ground in front of the Voronezh Front were suggesting the most likely variants of developments at the moment the ground dried out. It was only difficult to determine on the fly whether Germany was capable (by virtue of its economic potential), and its leadership ready, to conduct a major offensive operation or whether a "defensive mood" predominated in Berlin, and if the former, what forces would be committed for an offensive.

When working out the plan for the defensive operation N.F. Vatutin also decided to take as a guiding principle the account's conjecture that Army Group South's main objective was Kursk, and the most suitable place for a breakthrough by the enemy's armor on his Front's sector was along the Belgorod – Oboian' highway (the Oboian' highway) and between the Northern Donets and Razumnaia Rivers. Thus, he expressed the opinion that most likely, Manstein would attempt

---

4   Central Archive of the Russian Federation's Ministry of Defense [TsAMO RF], F. 69A, op. 10753, d. 410, ll. 17-18.

to overrun the line of Lieutenant General I.M. Chistiakov's 6th Guards Army (main attack) and Lieutenant General M.S. Shumilov's 7th Guards Army (secondary attack, most likely out of the Mikhailovka bridgehead) with his *panzerkiel* [bell-shaped panzer formations]. Accordingly, the general width of the most probable (and essentially possible) sectors of the German offensive in the sector of the Voronezh Front might amount to 46% (100 kilometers) of its line of defense. Based upon this consideration, the General of the Army proposed the following option for allocating his strength. He calculated to direct his main efforts to strengthening the left flank (a sector of 164 kilometers), by deploying three combined-arms armies here, one rifle corps (in the second echelon) and all of the Front's mobile and anti-tank reserves. Thereby, of the Front's 35 rifle divisions, he was proposing to position 22 on the likely direction of Army Group South's attack, plus his anti-tank and mobile (two tank corps) reserves. Both G.K. Zhukov and A.M. Vasilevsky approved this plan.

I will note that even though subsequently the plan of the Front's defense underwent a number of changes and several options for it were devised due to the changing operational situation and incoming intelligence, nevertheless Vatutin never changed his opinion regarding the direction of Army Group South's main attack right up until the start of the fighting, and this assessment remained the sole framework for arranging the primary scheme of the Front's defense and for allocating his forces prior to the Kursk defensive operation.

There followed the need to resolve two more important questions. First: How to prevent a deep penetration in the Front's defenses in the first several days of the offensive and to keep the still fresh German panzer divisions contained within the system of the army-level defensive belts? Second: How to reduce their penetrative power not only by means of the physical destruction of his armored equipment, but also compel the enemy command to disperse his forces across the entire front, and not allow their concentration at the point of the main attack?

According to N.F. Vatutin's calculations, Army Group South would most likely launch the main attack with the Fourth Panzer Army out of the Belgorod area to the north in the Oboian' – Kursk direction, or strictly to the northeast between Oboian' and Prokhorovka, while the secondary attack (Army Detachment Kempf) would be delivered out of approximately the same area, but in the direction of Korocha, strictly to the northeast. The principle outline for blocking the adversary's main grouping, as he proposed, appeared as follows. For the successful advance of the forward formations, it was extremely important for the enemy that both shock groupings maintained "shoulder to shoulder" contact between them as they advanced, which meant they would make progress at the same speed. This would allow them to conserve their forces, complicate maneuver for the defending side, and thereby, create conditions for the rapid overcoming of the 6th Guards and 7th Guards Armies' defenses and the expansion of the breakthrough corridor. In the first days of the offensive, the enemy would be striving to accomplish this. Subsequently, it was necessary to keep von Manstein's main grouping within the positions of the 6th Guards Army's divisions of the first, and in the extreme case, second defensive belts while knocking out primarily the German armored equipment. To achieve this, Vatutin planned several measures.

First, he decided to allocate to the army the largest share of artillery and anti-tank assets, and to cram its sector as much as possible with all kinds of artificial obstacles and booby traps, and thereby create a model of a contemporary field fortification system while taking into account combat experience and leading analyses. Second, considering that the enemy's first attack would be the strongest, and the threat existed that the divisions of the 6th Guards Army's first echelon would be unable to hold their positions, the Front command with the agreement of the General Staff planned already on the second or at least third day of the operation to move up Lieutenant General M.E. Katukov's 1st Tank Army to the second belt of the 6th Guards Army. Its two tank corps and one mechanized corps were to strengthen the defenses in the bend of the Pena River and like an "armored shield" block the main tank-passable "corridor" between the basins of the Pena and Lipovyi Donets Rivers, through which it was assumed that the Germans would advance out of the Belgorod area either to the north (toward Oboian') or to the northeast (toward Prokhorovka).

In addition, the commander of the 40th Army Lieutenant General K.S. Moskalenko was instructed to prepare several counterattacks on his left flank in the direction of the 6th Guards Army. As soon as the enemy broke through the defenses of the first echelon of Chistiakov's army, his formations were to strike the left flank of the Germans' main grouping. It was for this purpose that K.S. Moskalenko was given a significant amount of artillery and infantry support tanks. By their amounts, the 40th Army stood in third place among the Front's six armies.[5] Simultaneously with Moskalenko's forces, Lieutenant General V.D. Kriuchenkin's 69th Army would be prepared to launch a counterattack against the right flank of von Manstein's main grouping (the Fourth Panzer Army) from out of the second echelon.

Thus, according to Vatutin's conception, at the start of the operation the Germans' assault wedge on the Oboian' direction would bump up against the "armored shield" of Katukov's 1st Tank Army, while its flanks would be caught in the "jaws" created by Moskalenko's and Kriuchenkin's forces. At the same time, the Germans would still be engaged in heavy fighting with Chistiakov's 6th Guards Army as well.

Even if despite this, the Fourth Panzer Army managed to make a noticeable advance forward, for example, by also breaking through the 6th Guards Army's second echelon, it would still wind up in no condition to develop this success into operational space, given the circumstance that the Soviet defenders managed to stop the offensive on the secondary direction, which is to say, from Belgorod to the north or northeast. Two main factors would bring this about: the losses when breaking through the main defensive belt and the need to detach substantial forces in order to cover the continually extending flanks as the advance continued. These unfavorable factors for Army Group South might help the Soviet forces retain the army-level defensive belts, but only in the case that von Manstein couldn't commit powerful reserves into the battle after the initial breakthrough. N.F. Vatutin and the General Staff conceded such a possibility and analyzed it, and thus to counter it they planned to create their own substantial reserves. Even so, such an option was extremely unfavorable for the Soviet side. If together with the approach of enemy reserves the secondary German offensive hadn't been stopped, the dispersal of the operational and possibly even the strategic reserves would begin. In this case the Front's defensive operation would begin to develop according to a worse scenario and lead to serious consequences. Thus for the Soviet side it was extremely important not to allow both of von Manstein's assault groupings to join into a single fist, but instead already from the first days of the operation keep them separate, so as to force the enemy command to expend forces to cover not two flanks (in the event the attack groupings linked up), but four.

Consequently, for a successful completion of the defensive operation, keeping Army Detachment Kempf within the system of the army-level fortified belts had no less significance than in the main sector of the German attack. N.F. Vatutin believed that this could be accomplished in the following manner. First, it was necessary to fortify the 7th Guards Army's reliably in order to

---

5   In recent times, in publications dedicated to the Great Patriotic War, as assertion has appeared that the presence of the large quantity of strength and means in the 40th Army testifies to the fact that the Front's leadership wasn't able to determine precisely where the German main attack would fall, and so it distributed its forces on all of the most probable tank-vulnerable directions. However, this conjecture (it is impossible to call it otherwise) is based upon ignorance of Voronezh Front's plan of defense. Moskalenko's 40th Army from the outset had a major task (together with defending its own sector of the front): it had to contribute to containing the enemy's main grouping, which would be delivering its main attack against the neighboring 6th Guards Army (both through counterattacks and detaching formations from its own sector to reinforce Chistiakov's army).

prevent the enemy from making progress through its defenses at the same pace with which the enemy's main grouping, the Fourth Panzer Army, might advance in the event that it secured a breakthrough into the depth of the 6th Guards Army's defenses. Second, there would have to be a virtually impenetrable obstacle on the boundary between the 6th Guards and 7th Guards Army. Thus, Vatutin planned to repulse the attack by the enemy's secondary grouping with the forces of the 7th Guards Army and the 69th Army (or possibly with Front reserves counterattacking out of their positions).

When on the offensive, an attack against the boundaries of units or formations is a most common and effective means for achieving a breakthrough. N.F. Vatutin decided to make use of this practice when setting up his defenses. He arranged them so that in the rear, backing the first-echelon divisions of Chistiakov's and Shumilov's armies, there would be swampy terrain – the confluence of the Northern and Lipovyi Donets Rivers. So it was here that he established the boundary between the two armies, and then planned to strengthen this sector with a significant quantity of artillery, mortars and machine guns. Skipping ahead in the events, I will note that by the start of the offensive, the two divisions of the 6th Guards and 7th Guards Armies that were holding the boundary here (the 375th and 81st Guards Rifle Divisions) had a density of 19-23 artillery pieces per kilometer of front alone. No other single sector of the front would have such a high saturation with artillery. In addition, Vatutin positioned the 69th Army between the basins of these two rivers, in order to cover the very same boundary between the 6th and 7th Guards Armies. As a result, a natural obstacle, the interfluvial area between the Northern and Lipovyi Donets Rivers, which appeared like a wedge pointed toward the front and would be packed with the forces of the 69th Army would be converted into an arrowhead-shaped, well-fortified nest of resistance, while in front of its tip (at the boundary between the 6th and 7th Guards Armies) there would be a powerful artillery grouping. Because of this, as N.F. Vatutin presumed, at the start of the operation the enemy would be unable to make headway against the 375th and 81st Guards Rifle Divisions and would be forced to try to go around them. Consequently, Army Group South's unified offensive front would diverge into two independent directions. Moreover, if the Germans still made an attempt to break through into the depth of the 6th Guards and 7th Guards Armies, then the right flank of the main grouping and the left flank of the secondary grouping would still come under the fire and counterattacks from the 69th Army out of the Donets interfluvial area.

Considering that the 7th Guards Army had to withstand the attack of the secondary grouping, and that it also had a natural obstacle – the Northern Donets River – in front of it, N.F. Vatutin allocated noticeably less artillery to it than he did to 6th Guards Army, but at the same time gave it considerably more infantry support tanks (numbering almost a corps), and planned to shift his mobile and anti-tank reserve to its sector. With respect to the available information about the enemy strength opposite the Voronezh Front before the Battle of Kursk, Shumilov's army received sufficient forces to meet the goals given to it. Only later in the course of the operation would it become clear that this information proved to be not fully accurate.

We will discuss the numerical strength and combat effectiveness of the 7th Guards Army a bit below. In the meantime, however, I will dwell on the tasks and condition of the 69th Army, which in the course of Army Detachment Kempf's offensive would play a very important role, just like the 7th Guards Army. In May 1943 it was withdrawn to the rear army-level belt, which ran behind the sectors of two armies: the 6th Guards Army, along the Borogodetskoe – Vypolzovka – Alekseevka – Nechaevka line; and the 7th Guards Army, along the Belyi Kolodez' – Bol'she Troitskoe – Belianka – Efremovka line. Its line had a total extent of 120 kilometers of frontage and by the beginning of July consisted of 58 battalion regions. The ground that it crossed was primarily like that in front of it and the approaches to the rear belt. A significant portion of it was loaded with natural obstacles like balkas and streams (tributaries of the Northern Donets), and groves and woodlots. The most likely directions of a breakthrough by enemy tanks were the following: Iakovlevo – Prokhorovka, Petropavlovskii – Sabynino – Prokhorovka, Shliakhovoe – Korocha, Repnoe – Bekhteevka Repnoe – Khoroshevatoe, Voznesenovka – Popovka, and Staraia Tavolzhanka – Terezovka.

Back in the middle of April, the Voronezh Front's Military Council, when reviewing the army's defensive plan, gave it three main tasks: a) repel possible enemy attacks and maintain possession of its line; b) in the event of a breakthrough of the 6th Guards and 7th Guards Armies' main defensive belt to its entire depth or the withdrawal of their flank divisions to secondary positions, in cooperation with the troops of these armies and Front reserves, to destroy the attacking enemy; c) in the event of a successful repulse of the enemy's attack by the armies standing in front of it, to be ready for an offensive in order to exploit the success in three directions: Tomarovka – Graivoron – Akhtyrka; Belgorod – Khar'kov; or Volchansk – Khar'kov.

Despite the great exertions made by the Front command and N.F. Vatutin personally, by 5 July 1943 Kriuchenkin's army was the weakest one in the Voronezh Front. Five rifle divisions comprised its basis: the 107th, 111th, 183rd, 270th and 305th Rifle Divisions. By the start of the fighting, it had a total of 41,601 men, or 1.5 times fewer than in the 7th Guards Army. Not a single one of its rifle divisions numbered 8,000 men. All of its divisions were arrayed into a single echelon; on average each division had a frontage of 22 to 28 kilometers, depending on the importance of the axis and the terrain. Moreover it should be added that when Army Group South kicked off its offensive, 69th Army was in the process of regrouping, and just 24 hours before the start of the German offensive, its troops were being taken from their positions and being moved to replace the 7th Guards Army. The headquarters of one of its two corps, the 48th Rifle Corps, would arrive only in the first few days of July. Corps commander Major General Z.Z. Ragoznyi would take command of his three subordinate divisions (107th, 183rd and 305th Rifle Divisions) and corps' units just a day before the start of the German offensive. The commander of the second corps, the 49th Rifle Corps, Major General G.N. Terent'ev, faced an even worse situation. He would receive just two understrength divisions (the 111th and 270th Rifle Divisions) without any means of reinforcement, but neither the army nor the Front were in a condition to detach more to him due to objective factors.

Army commander V.D. Kriuchenkin received no tank or howitzer artillery units as assets, nor did he have any rocket artillery. With regards to anti-tank units, he had only a single destroyer anti-tank artillery regiment and three separate anti-tank rifle battalions. The reason for this was the fact that N.F. Vatutin could only use whatever the *Stavka* provided to him. At this time, the formation of the *Stavka* reserve, the Steppe Military District, was underway, which was planned to be the primary instrument for an offensive into Ukraine in the summer campaign. Thus, substantial forces and significant reserves were being sent to it. In addition, in Moscow at this time the opinion held sway that the German main grouping was in the Orel bulge, opposite the Central Front. Fearing a German offensive toward Tula and further on to Moscow, I.V. Stalin directed that if by the middle of July the enemy hadn't launched his offensive, the Central Front was to be the first to attack in cooperation with the Briansk Front and part of the Western Front. For this reason, the Central Front received significantly more artillery (by 2,000 pieces) than did the Voronezh Front when it was given control of the *Stavka*'s 4th Breakthrough Artillery Corps. It would in fact play a key role in the course of repulsing the German offensive within the framework of Operation Citadel.

N.F. Vatutin anticipated such a development, and thus at the end of April he decided to offset it by ordering Lieutenant General S.G. Goriachev, the commander of the 35th Guards Rifle Corps (which had just been formed and added to the Front reserve) to get close cooperation with the headquarters of Kriuchenkin's army up and running, so that his forces at any moment could come under Kriuchenkin's command. The 35th Guards Rifle Corps' line lay 15-25 kilometers behind the 69th Army's positions and seemingly comprised its second defensive belt. It had three rifle divisions (92nd Guards, 93rd Guards and 94th Guards Rifle Divisions) that had formed up in April 1943 on the basis of separate rifle brigades. It hadn't yet seen any fighting, but its brigades were nearly fully staffed and well-equipped. By the start of July among the Front's divisions, they had the greatest numerical strength – on average 9,462 men. In addition, already in the course of the operation, given need it was slotted to assign additional forces to the 69th Army.

Thus, N.F. Vatutin did everything within his capabilities to strengthen Kriuchenkin's army, and was hoping that having received the enemy's initial attacks, the 6th and 7th Guards Armies together with the 1st Tank Army would inflict heavy losses on the Germans, and so the 69th Army's troops would encounter the enemy's formations already in a badly battered condition. Therefore it would be capable of carrying out the tasks it had been given: to be a firm barrier on the boundary between the 6th and 7th Guards Armies and a flanking battering ram in the event of an enemy breakthrough of their lines. Unfortunately, this portion of his plan proved to be the most weakly developed. The hopes placed on the tenacity of V.D. Kriuchenkin's and S.G. Goriachev's troops weren't justified, while the command staff of their divisions, which in their majority had only been appointed to their posts in the spring of 1943 (including senior officers of the headquarters and regiments) proved not only unable to handle the combat tasks they'd been given, but in a number of cases even unable to carry out fundamental duties.

Now let's return to the Belgorod area in the latter half of the month of March 1943 and examine how Shumilov's army arrived in the Voronezh Front and the sort of shape it was in. At this moment, the 7th Guards Army had just wound down the unsuccessful and very costly Khar'kov defensive operation. An order to the troops of General P.S. Rybalko's 3rd Tank Army,[6] the main forces of which had been defending Khar'kov, reached its headquarters at 1600 on 15 March 1943, and later that night they began to break out to friendly lines. On 18 March *kampfgruppen* of the SS Panzergrenadier Divisions *Leibstandarte Adolf Hitler* and *Das Reich* not only took the city, but having reached the eastern bank of the Northern Donets River, captured the large village of Mikhailovka, in which incidentally a portion of the Belgorod railroad station's infrastructure was located (the depot and other buildings). Considering that the SS troops were operating in armored combat groups (panzergrenadiers mounted in halftracks and reinforced with panzers), the danger that they might make a further successful advance to the north and northeast was real. The Front command tried to organize a defense along the Northern Donets River with hastily-gathered rifle and cavalry divisions, but lacked sufficient strength for this. The leadership of the General Staff itself was busy with the creation of a defensive line near Belgorod, and it created an auxiliary command post in Oboian' in order to resolve operational questions. At the order of I.V. Stalin, Marshal of the Soviet Union G.K. Zhukov traveled to Oboian'. He faced the task not only of stopping von Manstein's forces that were keen to reach Kursk, but also one of holding the tactically advantageous line of the Northern Donets River until the arrival of the 21st and 64th Armies that were already on their way from Stalingrad. Thus in addition to Major General V.A. Badanov's 2nd Guards "Tatsinskaia" Tank Corps that was operating here, Major General I.A. Vovchenko's still only partially re-formed 3rd Guards "Stalingrad" Tank Corps had been shifted hastily by railroad and unloaded in Shebekino. According to the plan of the Soviet side, these mobile formations were to tie up the SS *kampfgruppen* and the XXXXVIII Panzer Corps with fighting and gain time for the infantry and cavalrymen to dig in along the river until the arrival of Chistiakov's and Shumilov's armies.[7]

---

6   After the completion of the fighting for Khar'kov, a group of the senior command staff of the 3rd Tank Army led by the army commander and the tank formations were withdrawn into the reserve, and on the basis of its remaining headquarters staff and troops the 57th Army was formed, which took up a defense on the left flank of Shumilov's army (extending from Shebekino to the south).
7   The order about the transfer of the 64th Army by railroad was received by its headquarters on 1 March

At the moment the SS troops rolled into Belgorod, the following forces of the 69th Army were taking up a defense along the eastern bank of the Northern Donets River: the 2nd Guards Motorized Rifle Brigade of the 2nd Guards Tank Corps, the 160th Rifle Division and the 183rd Rifle Division in the sector between Mikhailovka and Krutoi Log, and the 6th Guards Cavalry Corps[8] (8th Cavalry Division) further along to Shebekino. In addition, some of the 64th Army's own forces were also already deployed in these positions (in the first echelon), but judging from archival sources available today, the command of the 64th Army officially took over the defense of this sector only on 24 March 1943. According to Special Order No. 0233[9] from the 64th Army's commander M.S. Shumilov,[10] Major General A.S. Kositsyn took command of the Mikhailovka – Krutoi Log combat sector.[11] In addition to the divisions mentioned above, the 213th Rifle Division that was arriving in that area at that moment became subordinate to him. It was the first division of the 64th Army that not only arrived in the Belgorod area, but also took up a combat sector here. On 19 March a second division of Shumilov's army, the 73rd Guards Rifle Division, began

---

1943, and that of the 21st Army (which was to move by rail and foot), according to I.M Chistiakov's testimony, was received over the telephone on the night of 10/11 March 1943.

8   In the documents this cavalry corps often appears as "Cavalry Corps Sokolov" under the name of its commander, Major General S.K. Sokolov.
9   TsAMO RF, F. 341, op. 5312, dD. 225, l. 1.
10 Mikhail Stepanovich Shumilov, Colonel General (1943), born on 5 November 1895 in Kurgan Oblast's village of Verkhniaia Techa to a peasant family. In 1916 after completing a normal school, he was sent to the Chuguev Infantry School. Between October 1916 and March 1917 he served in the 109th Reserve Regiment. Then until December 1919 he took part in the fighting on the Western Front as a member of the 32nd Infantry Regiment as a warrant officer. He joined the Red Army in 1918. During the Russian Civil War he commanded a platoon, followed by a company and a regiment on the Eastern and Southern Fronts. After the end of the Civil War, he remained in the Red Army as a battalion commander. In 1924 he completed command and political courses, and in 1929, the "Shot" courses, after which he took command of a rifle regiment. Between 1933 and 1937 he was the chief of staff of the 95th Rifle Division, and from June 1937 he commanded the 7th Rifle Division. From February 1938 to May 1938 he served in Spain, and when he returned he was awarded the Order of the Red Banner. In March 1939 he was appointed commander of the Belorussian Military District's 11th Rifle Corps. With the corps he took part in the annexation of Western Ukraine and the Winter War with Finland. From June 1940 his corps became part of the Baltic Military District's 8th Army, but after the German invasion in June 1941, the army joined the Northwestern Front. He participated in the heavy fighting in the Baltic region. In November 1941 the corps was disbanded, and Major General M.S. Shumilov became the deputy commander of the Leningrad Front's 55th Army. Between January and July 1942 he was commander of the Southwestern Front's 21st Army, and in July he replaced V.I. Chuikov as the commander of the 64th Army. He remained in this post until the war's end. On 26 October 1943 he was awarded the title "Hero of the Soviet Union". By the start of the Battle of Kursk, Lieutenant General M.S. Shumilov was an experienced army commander. His direct superiors described him as a commander with high organizational skills who could quickly orient himself in a complex situation, confidently take the correct decisions and resolutely put them into action. No less important, the general was "a chief who was attentive to the needs of subordinates", a quality he preserved until the end of his life. His calm, poised nature helped him command troops successfully. During study in higher academic courses, their directors described him as follows: "Relates to his studies with exceptional diligence. He did all his assignments with great precision, clarity, in full and in depth. He superbly knows the basics of combined-arms combat. He crisply organizes the cooperation of all types of troops and combined-arms formations in combat and operations. He has studied the new organization of the rifle division and rifle corps and properly uses them in combat and operations. On examinations of the tactics of higher formations he received a top score. He successfully passed the entire course and tests on the tactics of higher formations, and passed the comprehensive set of tactics with an "Excellent" grade. He knows how to work out and conduct operational-tactical military courses and maneuvers. He mastered the higher academic courses. Health is weak." Although this assessment relates to 1948, the many qualities, like responsibility and a nuanced approach to readying operations and the crispness in organizing matters were inherent qualities of the commander already in 1943. He passed away in Moscow on 28 June 1975.
11 At that moment Major General A.S. Kositsyn was the commander of the 183rd Rifle Division.

to assemble in the Shebekino – Miasoedovo area. The combat formations of the 7th Guards Army fully took over the Staryi Gorod – Bezliudovka – Volchansk sector only in the first half of April.

When the 64th Army began to arrive in the Voronezh Front from Stalingrad, almost all of its divisions already had the Guards honorific title. On 1 March 1943 by an order of the USSR's People's Commissariat of Defense, its 29th, 38th, 422nd and 204th Rifle Divisions, for their tenacity and courage demonstrated in the fighting on the Volga, were converted into the 72nd Guards, 73rd Guards, 78th Guards and 81st Guards Rifle Divisions respectively. The 15th Guards and 36th Guards Rifle Divisions received this lofty title earlier, in 1942. Only the 213th Rifle Division was an ordinary rifle division. The 73rd Guards Rifle Division had a special status. Having satisfied a request from the Don Front's Military Council and the local organs of authority of Stalingrad Oblast, Moscow bestowed upon it the honorific title "Stalingrad"; in addition, one of its rifle regiments (the 209th) received the honorific title "Abgonerovo", a second (the 211th) received the honorific title "Basargino", and the third (the 214th) – "Voroponovo". Its artillery regiment (the 153rd) received the honorific title "Urazovo". The army itself became a Guards army on 17 April 1943, having received the numeric designation 7th Guards Army. From this moment the process of reforming began, both at the army level and in those formations subordinate to it. Of the seven divisions, six had to be brought up to the TO&E of a Guards division. In addition, the Voronezh Front, just like the entire acting army, began to return to the previously abolished system of command over the troops, a distinctive feature of which was at the corps level. By the middle of May, when all the main changes had completed, the combat roster of the 7th Guards Army was as follows:

    24th Guards Rifle Corps (Major General N.A. Vasil'ev):
        15th Guards Rifle Division (Major General E.I. Vasilenko)
        36th Guards Rifle Division (Major General M.I. Denisenko)
        72nd Guards Rifle Division (Major General A.I. Losev)

    25th Guards Rifle Corps (Major General G.B. Safiulin)
        73rd Guards Rifle Division (Colonel S.A. Kozak);
        78th Guards Rifle Division (Colonel A.V. Skvortsov)
        81st Guards Rifle Division (Major General I.K. Morozov)

The 7th Guards Army's reserve was Colonel I.E. Buslavev's 213th Rifle Division.

By this time the Front Command had also finally determined the boundaries between the armies of the first echelon. The left flank of the 7th Guards Army was the boundary between the Voronezh and Southwestern Fronts. The boundary line between the 24th Guards Rifle Corps and the 57th Army's 19th Rifle Division ran along the line: Volokonovka (7th Guards Army) – Volchansk (57th Army) – Khar'kov (57th Army), while the boundary between the right-flank 25th Guards Rifle Corps and its neighbor on the right, the 6th Guards Army's 375th Rifle Division, was Ushakovo (7th Guards Army) – Chernaia Poliana (6th Guards Army). The boundary between the 7th Guards Army's corps themselves (the right flank of the 24th Guards Rifle Corps and the left flank of the 25th Guards Rifle Corps passed through Repnoe, Pentsevo, Nizhnii Ol'shanets and Brodok.

From the beginning of 1943, a Guards Army, in addition to its two rifle corps, was supposed to have (or have operationally subordinate) a separate tank corps, but the 7th Guards Army had neither. This was connected with the fact that the *Stavka* was directing its main resources to the formation of strategic reserves, while the replenishment of the armies that were reforming directly at the front took the back seat. Because of this, for example, before the start of the fighting the 1st Tank Army, which became part of Voronezh Front on 28 April, had also not been brought back up to establishment strength, even though I.V. Stalin had personally promised to send a motorized rifle brigade, destroyer anti-tank artillery regiment and a number of other units directly to its 31st Tank Corps. Moreover, the ground in the sector of the 7th Guards Army was broken, and made the use of compact large tank formations difficult. Therefore N.F. Vatutin assigned two infantry support tank brigades, three infantry support tank regiments and two self-propelled artillery regiments, including one heavy one, to M.S. Shumilov's army. By list these units had a total of 257 tanks and self-propelled guns, not only more than a regular tank corps had, but also more than that of a mechanized corps of the Red Army. The combat and numerical strength of the armored and mechanized forces of the 7th Guards Army on 1 July 1943 is given in Table 1.

Given the correct use (which, unfortunately, rarely happened), this was a sufficient amount of armor, together with the mobile anti-tank reserve of the army commander and corps commanders, to conduct an active defense successfully. However, considering that the enemy was planning to break through the army's line with panzer divisions, which was no secret to the Soviet side, the 7th Guards Army needed a major mobile formation, which the army commander could use for launching powerful counterattacks against the enemy's flanks in the event of a deep enemy penetration. N.F. Vatutin was aware of this problem, and in the period of preparing for the Battle of Kursk, he planned a maneuver (given a sharpening of the situation) by the 2nd Guards "Tatsinskaia" Tank Corps out of the Korocha area, where it was located at the time, to the 7th Guards Army's sector. Jumping somewhat ahead in the events, I'll note that unfortunately already in the first days of the fighting, this plan was superseded by events; because of the strong pressure on the line of the 6th Guards Army, already on 5 July N.F. Vatutin would be forced to switch the 2nd Guards Tank Corps to the Oboian' direction.

In addition, Shumilov's army had two separate battalions of armored trains, but by the beginning of 1943 this type of weapon had already become outdated. Therefore, they weren't used directly in the fighting against Army Detachment Kempf, but the 34th Separate Armored Train Battalion[12] was located in the area of Belyi Kolodez' (in the reserve of the 24th Guards Rifle Corps), while the 38th Separate Armored Train Battalion that arrived in the middle of May (in place of the 26th Separate Armored Train Battalion, which had been sent for re-formation) was included in the army commander's reserve and parked at Prikolotnoe Station.

With respect to artillery, as reinforcements the army received three regiments of 152mm howitzers (the 109th Guards, 161st Guards and 265th Guards Cannon Artillery Regiments); four separate destroyer anti-tank artillery regiments (114th Guards, 115th Guards, 1669th and 1670th Destroyer Anti-tank Artillery Regiments); the 30th Separate Destroyer Anti-tank Artillery Brigade; five battalions of anti-tank rifles; as well as the 290th Mortar Regiment and the 97th Guards and 315th Guards Mortar Regiments of rocket launchers. The combat and numerical strength of the 7th Guards Army on 5 July 1943 are shown in Table 2.

For the forthcoming defensive operation, the Voronezh Front command decided to concentrate the bulk of its anti-aircraft artillery in three armies of the first echelon: the 40th, 6th Guards and 7th Guards Armies. The anti-aircraft gunners had the primary task of covering the combat positions against enemy airstrikes, followed by protecting the main supply depots and warehouses. Each army received one anti-aircraft artillery division.[13] For the struggle against the *Luftwaffe* in the remaining sectors of the armies, in addition to the anti-aircraft means of the units and formations, each army was also given two anti-aircraft artillery regiments. The 7th Guards Army

---

12 It consisted of two armored trains of one coal-fired locomotive, eight armored railcars and 2 platform cars mounted with anti-aircraft guns. (TsAMO RF, F. 203, op. 2851, d. 25, l. 353.)
13 Typically, one anti-aircraft artillery division was responsible for covering an area with a width of 15-20 kilometers and a depth of 5-7 kilometers.

Table 1 Combat strength of the 7th Guards Army's armored forces on 1 July 1943[1]

Tank brigade or regiment		Personnel			Arms								Tanks						SP guns	Vehicles
		Command	Jr. command	Enlisted men	Total	Rifles	PPSh	Anti-tank Rifles	Light/heavy machine guns	A-A Machine guns	Guns/mortars	Total	Mk II, III	KV-1	T-34	T-60	T-70	Su-76/Su-122		
167 STR	Table	101	211	212	524	145	145	18	2	–	–	40	–	–	32	–	8	–		74
	Actual	96	225	206	527	165	145	8	2	–	–	43	–	–	32	–	11	–		71
148 STR	Table	101	211	212	524	145	145	18	2	–	–	39	–	–	32	–	7	–		74
	Actual	97	235	211	543	163	145	18	2	–	–	47	–	–	33	1	13	–		75
201 STB	Table	242	455	475	1172	502	156	24	20/4	9	4/6	?	?	–	?	–	–	–		125
	Actual	232	424	530	1186	437	255	37	14	1	8/2	52	18/31	–	3	–	–	–		57
262 HTR	Table	80	99	72	251	54	57	–	–	–	–	21	–	21	–	–	–	–		38
	Actual	75	141	33	249	38	45	–	–	–	–	24	–	24	–	–	–	–		38
27 GTB	Table	216	455	475	1146	489	170	24	20/4	9	4/6	52	–	–	48	–	4	–		125
	Actual	212	520	495	1227	466	220	21	27/6	–	4/7	54	–	–	50	–	4	–		128
1438 SPR	Table	72	68	132	272	70	75	–	–	–	–	–	–	1	–	–	–	12/9		48
	Actual	56	88	121	265	131	–	–	–	–	–	–	–	–	–	–	–	12/9		23
1529 HSPR	Table	72	68	132	272	70	75	–	–	–	–	1	–	1	–	–	–	12 SU–152		48
	Actual	71	74	129	274	87	95	–	–	–	–	1	–	1	–	–	–	12 SU–152		36
Total	Table																			
	Actual	839	1707	1725	4271	1387	905	84	51	1	12/9	223	18/31	25	118	1	28	42/12		428

Notes
1 For manpower, arms and motorized transport, as of 20 June 1943; for tanks and self-propelled guns – for 4 July 1943. Source: TsAMO RF, f. 203, op. 2843, d. 341, ll. 199-208.

Acronyms: STR – Separate Tank Regiment; STB – Separate Tank Brigade; HTR – Heavy Tank Regiment; GTB – Guards Tank Brigade; SPR – Self-propelled Artillery Regiment; HSPR – Heavy Self-propelled Artillery Regiment.

34 THE FORGOTTEN BATTLE OF THE KURSK SALIENT

Table 2 Combat strength of the Voronezh Front's 7th Guards Army as of 5 July 1943

a) Manpower and horses

Units	Personnel				Horses, total
	Command staff	Jr. Command staff	Rank and file	Total	
Rifle forces					
15 GRD	832	2462	5390	8684	996
36 GRD	866	2437	5315	8618	498
72 GRD	853	1884	5931	8668	863
73 GRD	840	2354	5423	8617	864
78 GRD	849	2317	5180	8346	824
81 GRD	864	2104	5734	8702	870
213 RD	795	2532	5538	8865	1063
Total	5899	16090	38511	60500	6038
Armored forces					
27 GTB	214	538	487	1239	-
262 HTR	68	143	32	243	-
148 STR	95	233	212	540	-
201 STB	243	448	531	1222	-
167 STR	97	227	206	530	-
34 S. Armored 2Train Battalion	26	99	82	207	-
38 S. Arm. Train Battalion	21	85	68	174	-
Total	764	1773	1618	4155	-
Artillery					
265 GCAR	101	240	734	1075	15
161 GCAR	90	181	463	734	-
109 GCAR	99	224	628	951	-
114 GDATAR	50	168	232	450	-
115 GDATAR	52	152	271	475	3
30 SDATAB	165	325	840	1330	10
1669 ADATAR	44	104	335	483	-
1670 ADATAR	49	100	329	478	-
290 AMR	65	190	420	675	-
1438 SPAR	62	91	114	257	-
1529 HSPAR	67	74	129	270	-
1 ATRBn	24	90	149	263	
2 ATRBn	25	68	148	241	3
4 ATRBn	23	113	143	279	9
5 ATRBn	27	79	151	257	3
Total	957	2266	5276	8499	49
Guards Mortar forces					
97 GMtrR	80	213	447	740	–
315 GMtrR	84	210	430	724	–

Units	Personnel				Horses, total
	Command staff	Jr. Command staff	Rank and file	Total	
	Anti-air Defense forces Of the 5th Anti-Air Defense Division				
670 AAR	40	83	229	352	–
743 AAR	37	114	290	441	–
1119 AAR	39	101	232	372	–
1181 AAR	39	78	246	363	–
	Separate				
162 GAAR	36	93	187	316	–
258 GAAR	40	114	215	369	–
Total	231	583	1399	2213	–
Grand total for the 7th Guards Army	8015	21135	47681	76831	6087

b) Small arms

Unit	Rifles	PPD, PPSh SMGs	Machine guns			Anti–tank Rifles
			Light	Heavy	Anti–Air	
		Rifle troops				
15 GRD	3778	2408	420	140	5	252
36 GRD	5777	2425	436	139	5	242
72 GRD	4360	2358	403	133	1	178
73 GRD	3675	2241	441	140	1	165
78 GRD	4766	2287	387	137	2	199
81 GRD	5730	2474	418	139	–	277
213 RD	5080	2003	426	111	3	213
Total:	33166	16196	2931	939	17	1526
		Armored Forces				
27 GTB	466	220	27	6	–	21
262 HTR	17	45	–	–	–	–
148 STR	163	145	2	–	–	18
201 STB	437	255	14	1	–	37
167 STR	165	145	2	–	–	18
34 S. Armored Train Battalion	125	3	38	8	5	3
38 S. Armored Train Battalion	73	40	21	8	5	2
Total:	1446	853	104	23	10	94
		Artillery Forces				
265 GCAR	698	74	–	–	3	21
161 GCAR	441	66	2	–	–	21
109 GCAR	501	159	13	–	1	18
114 GDATAR	299	72	8	–	–	13

36 THE FORGOTTEN BATTLE OF THE KURSK SALIENT

Unit	Rifles	PPD, PPSh SMGs	Machine guns			Anti–tank Rifles
			Light	Heavy	Anti–Air	
115 GDATAR	206	53	7	–	–	10
30 SDATAB	620	436	10	–	–	21
1669 ADATAR	241	48	10	–	–	10
1670 ADATAR	241	48	10	–	–	10
290 AMtrR	415	73	–	–	–	–
1438 SPAR	131	94	7	–	–	–
1529 SPAR	87	92	–	–	–	–
1 ATR Bn	92	100	–	–	–	71
2 ATR Bn	65	35	6	–	–	56
4 ATR Bn	71	100	4	–	–	70
5 ATR Bn	63	72	–	–	–	71
Total:	4206	1672	80	1	4	462
Guards Mortar forces						
97 GMtrR	370	16	7	–	–	21
315 GMtrR	423	25	18	–	3	24
Total:	793	41	25	–	3	45
Anti-Air Defense forces Of the 5th Anti-Aircraft Division						
670 AADR	70	20	–	–	15	–
743 AADR	27	13	–	–	1	–
1119 AADR	69	22	–	–	16	–
1181 AAD	60	22	–	–	16	–
Separate						
162 GAAR	139	29	–	–	17	–
258 GAAR	137	41	–	–	16	–
Total:	502	147	–	–	81	–
Grand total for 7th Guards Army	40113	18909	3140	963	115	2428

c) Mortars and Guns

	Mortars			Guns				
	120mm	82mm	50mm	152mm	122mm	76mm long range	76mm field artillery	45mm
Rifle forces								
15 GRD	27	86	14	–	12	24	12	48
36 GRD	24	92	58	–	12	23	12	48
72 GRD	25	71	54	–	12	24	12	46
73 GRD	20	64	48	–	11	21	12	45
78 GRD	18	81	54	–	11	19	12	43
81 GRD	24	87	61	–	12	24	12	41

	Mortars			Guns				
	120mm	82mm	50mm	152mm	122mm	76mm long range	76mm field artillery	45mm
213 RD	21	82	56	–	12	19	12	48
Total:	159	563	345	–	82	154	84	319
Armored forces								
27 GTB	–	7	–	–	–	4	–	–
262 HTR	–	–	–	–	–	–	–	–
148 STR	–	–	–	–	–	–	–	–
201 STB	–	8	–	–	–	–	–	2
167 STR	–	–	–	–	–	–	–	–
34 S. Armored Train Bn	–	–	–	–	–	4	–	3
38 S. Armored Train Bn	–	–	–	–	–	6	–	5
Total:	–	15	–	–	–	14	–	10
Artillery forces								
265 GCAR	–	–	–	17	–	–	–	–
161 GCAR	–	–	–	17	–	–	–	–
109 GCAR	–	–	–	18	–	–	–	–
114 GDATAR	–	–	–	–	–	20	–	–
115 GDATAR	–	–	–	–	–	20	–	–
30 SDATAB	–	–	–	–	–	24	–	20
1669 ADATAR	–	–	–	–	–	20	–	–
1670 ADATAR	–	–	–	–	–	4	–	–
290 AMtrR	36	–	–	–	–	–	–	–
1438 SPAR	–	–	–	–	12	9	–	–
1529 HSPAR	–	–	–	12	–	–	–	–
1 ATR Bn	–	–	–	–	–	–	–	–
2 ATR Bn	–	–	–	–	–	–	–	–
4 ATR Bn	–	–	–	–	–	–	–	–
5 ATR Bn	–	–	–	–	–	–	–	–
Total	36	–	–	64	12	97	–	20
Guards Mortar troops								
97 GMtrR	–	–	–	–	–	–	–	–
315 GMtrR	–	–	–	–	–	–	–	–
Total:	–	–	–	–	–	–	–	–
Anti-aircraft forces **Of the 5th Anti-Aircraft Division:**								
670 A-AR	–	–	–	–	–	–	–	–
743 A-AR	–	–	–	–	–	–	–	–
1119 A-AR	–	– –	–	–	–	–	–	–
1181 A-AR	–	–	–	–	–	–	–	–
Separate								
162 GA-AR	–	–	–	–	–	–	–	–
258 GA-AR	–	–	–	–	–	–	–	1

	Mortars			Guns				
	120mm	82mm	50mm	152mm	122mm	76mm long range	76mm field artillery	45mm
Total	–	–	–	–	–	–	–	1
Guards Mortar forces								
97 GMR	–	–	–	–	–	–	–	–
315 GMR	–	–	–	–	–	–	–	–
Total:	–	–	–	–	–	–	–	–
Anti-Air Defense forces Of the 5th Anti-Air Division:								
670 AAR	–	–	–	–	–	–	–	–
743 AAR	–	–	–	–	–	–	–	–
1119 AAR	–	–	–	–	–	–	–	–
1181 AAR	–	–	–	–	–	–	–	–
162 GAAR	–	–	–	–	–	–	–	–
258 GAAR	–	–	–	–	–	–	–	–
Grand Total for the 7th Guards Army	195	378	345	64	94	265	84	349

d) Vehicles, tanks, rocket launchers and anti-aircraft guns

Unit	Vehicles	Tanks	Rocket launchers	Anti-aircraft guns	
				76, 85 mm	20, 25, 37 mm
Rifle forces					
15 GRD	153	–	–	–	–
36 GRD	164	–	–	–	–
72 GRD	91	–	–	–	–
73 GRD	103	–	–	–	–
78 GRD	103	–	–	–	–
81 GRD	130	–	–	–	–
213 RD	96	–	–	–	–
Total:	840				
Tank forces					
27 GTB	128	54	–	–	4
262 HTR	33	24	–	–	–
148 STR	75	47	–	–	–
201 STB	48	50/2	–	–	–
167 STR	71	46	–	–	–
34 S. Armored Train Bn	3	–	–	–	–
38 S. Armored Train Bn	2	–	–	–	–
Total:	360	221/2	–	–	4

"ANTICIPATING WHAT THE RUSSIANS HAD PREPARED" 39

Unit	Vehicles	Tanks	Rocket launchers	Anti-aircraft guns	
				76, 85 mm	20, 25, 37 mm
Artillery forces					
265 GCAR	30	–	–	–	–
161 GCAR	39	–	–	–	–
109 GCAR	87	–	–	–	–
114 GDATAR	33	–	–	–	–
115 GDATAR	34	–	–	–	–
30 SDATAB	57	–	–	–	–
1669 DATAR	26	–	–	–	–
1670 DATAR	16	–	–	–	–
290 AMtrR	38	–	–	–	–
1438 SPAR	24	–	–	–	–
1529 SPAR	37	1	–	–	–
1 ATR Bn	5	–	–	–	–
2 ATR Bn	3	–	–	–	–
4 ATR Bn	4	–	–	–	–
5 ATR Bn	1	–	–	–	–
Total:	437	1	–	–	–
Guards Mortar troops					
97 GMtrR	75	–	23	–	–
315 GMtrR	90	–	24	–	–
Total	165	–	47	–	–
Anti-aircraft forces of the 5th Anti-Aircraft Division:					
670 A-AR	22	–	–	0	16
743 A-AR	36	–	–	16	0
1119 A-AR	24	–	–	0	16
1181 A-AR	26	–	–	0	16
Separate:					
162 GA-AR	49	–	–	0	12
258 GA-AR	33	–	–	0	17
Total:	190	–	–	16	77
Grand total for the 7th Guards Army	1992	222/2	47	16	81

received the 5th Anti-Aircraft Artillery Division (consisting of four regiments), and the 62nd Guards and 258th Anti-Aircraft Artillery Regiments. On 5 July 1943 they had a combined total of 77 37mm anti-aircraft cannons, 16 85mm anti-aircraft cannons, and 81 anti-aircraft machine guns. Shumilov positioned five of these regiments directly among the combat positions, while one was responsible for covering the army's supply station in Volokonovka.[14]

By 22 April around the entire Kursk salient, the process of fortifying the front, the drawing (and re-drawing) of the combat sectors, and establishing the boundary lines for the forces that had arrived here at the end of March and early April was primarily completed. The detailed work then began to survey the ground, map out the lines of defense, and to determine firing positions, including those in the second echelon. The main defensive belt of the Central and Voronezh Fronts (which was also called the "first army-level belt"), formed an enormous arc with a total length of approximately 550 kilometers, at the base of which ran the main Belgorod – Orel rail line. Its forward edge primarily ran along the slopes of ridges and hills that faced the enemy, and partially on reverse slopes. With the exception of the Northern Donets River (the left flank of Voronezh Front), there were no significant natural obstacles. By this time, a total of 37 rifle divisions of 9 combined-arms armies (including four divisions of the 7th Guards Army) had been deployed along the front, and they received an order to set up a total of more than 350 battalion defensive regions. The divisional sectors on average occupied 14 kilometers of frontage, but those on the most vulnerable directions were significantly fewer.

The second army-level defensive belt was positioned at a distance of 10-15 kilometers behind the main belt and had a total length of 450 kilometers. As a rule, forces of the first-echelon armies occupied it, but not only rifle divisions (for example, in Voronezh Front's 38th Army there was one tank brigade and one destroyer anti-tank artillery brigade in the second army-level belt), and at the same time almost everywhere they had lengthier sectors of defense. For example, on the Central Front the 70th Army had 4 rifle divisions occupying the main belt and 4 rifle divisions in the second belt, while 13th Army had respectively 4 and 3. On the Voronezh Front, the 6th Guards and 7th Guards Armies had 4 rifle divisions in the main belt and 3 in the second, while the 40th Army had respectively 3 and 2 rifle divisions.

The defensive sectors of the first echelon forces of both *fronts* were constructed on the basis of the document "Instruktsiei po rekognostsirovke i polevomu oboronitel'nomu stroitel'stvu" ["Instructions on surveying and on field defensive construction"] which had been adopted by the Red Army's General Staff on 27 April 1943. The combat experience of preceding years had been accumulated in it. According to this document, the armies were to construct three defensive belts: a main, secondary and rear army-level belt. In addition, the first two belts, which comprised the tactical zone and were occupied by the divisions of the first and second echelons of the rifle corps, were to be the most heavily fortified and improved through the use of engineers. In addition, the army commanders each received an additional rifle division as a combined-arms reserve, and these divisions were also to prepare their own defensive line and include it in the army's overall system of defense. The principal distinctions of the new system of field defenses, which would be embodied around the Kursk salient, relative to those that had been built previously, were as follows: first, the depth of each of the belts was significantly increased, and accordingly the armies' tactical zones expanded; second, their structure was improved – the number of defensive positions in the belt increased; third, the nature of the artificial fortifications changed: continuous lines of trenches

---

14 In contrast, the 6th Guards Army received only five anti-aircraft artillery regiments: three were covering the positions of the 23rd Guards Rifle Corps along the Belgorod – Oboian' highway, one was protecting an airfield in the army's sector, and one was guarding the 6th Guards Army's supply station in Prokhorovka.

appeared, and obstacles became more diverse and improved; finally, the insistence on mandatorily knitting all of their elements into a single, balanced system of defense increased.

The primary distinctive feature of the 7th Guards Army's combat sector was the fact that its forward edge ran along the left-hand (eastern) bank of the Northern Donets River. Only in one location – in the village of Mikhailovka – did the enemy manage to gain a foothold on the eastern bank back at the end of March and create a small bridgehead. A defense along a river was a substantial advantage for Shumilov's army. As the 7th Guards Army's chief of engineers General V. Pliaskin recalled:

> Having reached the line of the Northern Donets River, the 64th Army's divisions were forced first of all to liquidate small bridgeheads that had been seized and were being held by the enemy directly outside Belgorod (especially the Mikhailovka bridgehead), as well as opposite the villages of Pushkarnoe, Dal'nie Peski, Solomino, Karnaukhovka, Bezliudovka and Maslova Pristan'. Thanks to the heroism of the units of our Guards divisions, all of the bridgeheads except for the one at Mikhailovka were eliminated. In these battles, the engineer units played a large role.
>
> The weather was cloudy and humid, and nighttime temperatures dropped well below freezing. Exhausted by the previous fighting, the enemy hadn't had time to dig in firmly within the bridgeheads they had seized. Our sappers decided to take advantage of this – a group of sappers of the 329th Engineer-Sapper Battalion under the command of Lieutenant Vasil'ev. Using the darkness of night and the reduced vigilance of the German sentries, on 26 March it stealthily made its way to a point beneath the bridge in the village of Karnaukhovka, wired it with demolition charges, and blew it up. Simultaneously with the sudden explosion of the bridge, our infantry attacked the stunned enemy. Some of the Germans were killed, and the rest fled in panic to the western bank.
>
> On the night of 27-28 March, two more bridges were successfully destroyed in the area of Dorogobuzheno. A group of sappers led by Lieutenants Berezovsky and Kadyrov conducted this mission.
>
> The task to destroy enemy-held bridges in the area of Solomino and Pushkarnoe was resolved in particularly difficult conditions. Sappers under the command of the miner and scout Lieutenant Golovkin, who was widely-known in the army, managed to steal its way through the enemy's pickets and blow up a bridge literally right under the enemy's nose without taking any casualties.[15]

Skipping ahead of the events, I'll note that the river became one of the main reasons why the 7th Guards Army was able to hold its positions in the first days of Army Detachment Kempf's offensive, inflict significant damage to the enemy, and thereby frustrate the plan of Army Group South's command to cover the right flank of the Fourth Panzer Army with Army Detachment Kempf's divisions. On the fronts of remaining armies of Voronezh Front, the distance between the Soviet and German frontline trenches was around 900 to 1400 meters.

In the Red Army, the moment when a commander received an order to adopt a defensive posture was considered the starting point for the organization of his unit's or formation's defense. Under the organization, a system of measures was understood, which included the consideration of the order from higher command; the decisions for the defense made by the commander; the issuance of tasks to subordinate formations and units and the allocation of reinforcements; the organization

---

15 *Na belgorodskom napravlenii. Vospominaniia uchastnikov boev* [*On the Belgorod direction. Recollections of veterans of the fighting*] (Belgorod: Belgorodskoe knizhnoe izdatel'stvo, 1963), p. 96.

of command and control and the arrangement of cooperation; the creation of defensive works designed by engineers on the ground occupied by the troops; the arrangement of a system of fire; and political and educational work among the men. Parallel with these steps, a complex of measures is worked out to monitor the fulfillment of the commander's decisions (orders and directives) and to help subordinates implement them. A system of control was an inseparable and important part of the concept of "organizing a defense".

The commander's first step after the fighting ended was to take steps to fortify the ground gained and to issue immediate tasks to subordinates. Only then, after receiving and giving consideration to an order for a defense, would he start to implement it. In March 1943, Shumilov's army didn't arrive in an empty place. At the moment that the 7th Guards Army's divisions took over the sectors of defense from the 69th Army that was occupying them, the initial steps to fortify the ground had already been completed. This concerned the defense directly along the basin of the Northern Donets River. By the beginning of April, the network of trenches, rifle pits and dugouts here was already partially ready even in the second echelon. In particular, the 69th Army's 183rd Rifle Division had actively engaged in this work (at Solomino and Dorogobuzheno), but not for long, before it turned over its sector to the 213th Rifle Division. Nevertheless, in various places the quality of this work varied. Thus, up until around 15-20 April, all the efforts of the army's command were directed at strengthening the first (and at that moment main) defensive belt, and at creating at least a minimal transportation infrastructure. The work on fortifying the ground by the frontline battalions not only at Belgorod, but also around the entire Kursk salient, was done under extremely difficult conditions, in direct contact with the enemy. The adversary (primarily his artillery) always took advantage of any opportunity to hinder or prevent this work.

It should also be noted that one of the features of the operational situation that existed in the sector of the 7th Guards Army right up until the latter half of April was the uncertain situation on its right flank. The Front command was persistently demanding from Shumilov to drive the Germans out of Mikhailovka and thereby deprive the Germans of their important bridgehead. In order to carry out this task, Shumilov launched several unsuccessful assaults against it. The last attempt was made on 16 April 1943 with the forces of two regiments of the 73rd Guards Rifle Division and also ended in failure; the enemy managed to retain possession of the village.[16] Thus only in the latter half of April did the construction of a system of defense according to the same plans as the rest of the army get underway in this area.

A key moment for the organization of a system of defense was when the commander of an army reached his own decisions. An action plan comprised its basis, which determined the sequence of opening fire against the enemy with the available weapons on the directions where the adversary would most likely go on the attack; the areas (sectors) of terrain, which directly influenced the resilience of the entire system of defense; the layout of the defenses given consideration of the terrain; and the maneuvering with forces.

According to the new field manual adopted for the infantry in 1942 (BUP-1942), the resilience of a defense and the length of resistance in certain positions depended first of all on how thoroughly fortified were the most important (or traversable) sectors of the ground, villages or towns, and even separate buildings or structures (homes, barns, crossroads, etc.). The document emphasized that only by creating powerful strongpoints and nests of resistance, reinforced by minefields was it possible to count on success. Control over these key pieces of terrain or villages blocked the enemy's path into the depth of the formation's or unit's positions, and in the event of a penetration, restricted the enemy's possibility of maneuver, while it simultaneously helped the command of the defending troops ensconced in them to restore a lost position with fire and counterattacks. Given

---

16 TsAMO RF, F. 211 gv. sp., op. 145061, d. 3, l. 21.

an absence of adequate strength for an active defense, such strongpoints enabled a defender to block the enemy's further expansion into the depth of a combat position. It followed to assign most of the personnel, weapons and engineer assets in order to strengthen the sectors identified as key. The commanders of regiments, divisions, corps and even armies were to be personally engaged in determining the significance of these sectors and areas. Only after thorough map study, the reconnoitering of the ground by the commander, and the confirmation of decisions taken by higher command was the initiation of large-scale work on fortifications allowed. Such an approach helped reduce to a minimum the possibility of mistakes and contributed to a more rational expenditure of labor exerted by the units and elements when doing heavy work in the fields. Nevertheless, of course, in practice, divergences from the practice laid out in the field manual were often observed in the troops, which led first of all to mistakes in siting permanent firing positions and establishing fields of fire.

Thus, in the 7th Guards Army as well, the main construction on the defensive line began only after a thorough study of the ground and the issuance of tasks. Immediately after Moscow reached the key decision to go over temporarily to a pre-meditated defense around the entire Kursk salient, the Voronezh Front's Military Council set a main task in front of its chain of command: once the enemy launched the attack, to wear down his strength in prepared positions and to prevent a breakthrough of both army-level belts of defenses, especially on the flanks. Considering that N.F. Vatutin was viewing the option of a German offensive out of the Belgorod area in the direction of Korocha (and further on toward Skorodnoe) as very likely, but only secondary, the main reinforcements that the Front would send to M.S. Shumilov would be engineer assets (equipment), artillery and infantry support tanks. Therefore the army's main instrument for meeting its objectives was to be a well-constructed and elaborate system of field fortifications.

On 4 April 1943 the 7th Guards Army's Military Council sent Order No. 00147 to its subordinate corps, which contained the basic principles for constructing a cohesive defense and a set of measures for rolling out the work on the fortifications. The document required the division commanders by 7 April to conduct a detailed survey of the ground together with the command staff of subordinate units; to check whether or not the sectors of each of the rifle regiments were properly chosen; and to present an assessment of the decisions of their command regarding the organization of a system of fire and the screening of boundaries.

According to Voronezh Front's plan of defense, Shumilov's army was given the responsibility to prepare the main and second army-level belts, while the 69th Army was to construct the rear belt, which was to become its own main defensive belt. Meanwhile, the forces of the 7th Guards Army were expected to occupy fully the first two defensive belts.

Battalion defensive zones, anti-tank strongpoints and anti-tank areas, as well as a complex system of artificial obstacles, were to comprise the basis of all three belts on the Korocha axis, as was the case in the other armies. Relying on the demands and recommendations of the Front's command staff, the headquarters of the 7th Guards Army worked out two typical schemes of defense separately for the divisions of the first and second echelon. They were very similar; adjustments were made depending on the terrain in which one or another division was deployed. The main details of the defensive scheme for the main belt of defenses were:

- The echeloning of the units of the rifle divisions (which was not done even in the 6th Guards Army), which meant the rifle regiments in the divisions would be arranged in two lines, with two regiments up front and a third regiment in the second line, buttressing the boundary between the frontline regiments. The battalions also had just such an arrangement. This decision substantially strengthened the defense, giving it great resilience and elasticity.
- Reinforcing the forward edge of the main defensive belt (relative to the second defensive belt) with artificial obstacles (mine fields, ditches, cheval-de-frise, etc.)

- The presence in each division in its own combat sector of no less than two (as a rule) or three defensive strongpoints in each of its two trench lines, and the mining of all tank-passable directions in the depth of the main belt.
- The mandatory reinforcement of the frontline regiments with combined-arms and anti-tank reserves (and on especially important directions, the reinforcement of even their battalions) through the operational subordination of penal companies (there were five penal companies in the 7th Guards Army), anti-tank rifle battalions, artillery battalions, mortar battalions and even infantry support tank units from the armies to these divisions. The strengthening of the sectors with fortifications was practically the same in every division, and thus the assignment of such units and elements from the army's reserve was the main, and in essence, the only tool available to the army commander (not including the planning of the actions of the mobile reserve and anti-tank reserves of the army) in order to strengthen vulnerable sectors realistically. This showed most visibly when preparing the lines of the divisions that were holding the army's flanks.

The divisions of the second echelon (by the start of the battle, these were the 15th Guards, 73rd Guards and 213th Rifle Divisions) were considered the reserve of the army commander and corps commanders; their main assignment consisted in preparing counterattacks along previously determined directions. Nevertheless, they were also preparing their positions in the second belt of defenses. The only difference was the fact that their regiments weren't echeloned in depth, but arrayed in a single line, and the ground in front of the forward edge wasn't as densely saturated with mines.

As of 1 July 1943, the total length of the main belt of defenses amounted to 53 kilometers, or 21.6% of the entire line of the Voronezh Front according to the trace of the forward edge (245 kilometers), and it was being occupied by:

a. 81st Guards Rifle Division (on the army's right flank), which was holding the sector: grove 1 kilometer east of Chernaia Poliana – Staryi Gorod – labor correction camp – Iastrebovo – Andreevskie (8 kilometers of frontage);
b. To its left, the 78th Guards Rifle Division was occupying the sector: (excl.) correction labor camp – Dorogobuzheno – Nizhnii Ol'shanets – Krutoi Log, Generalovka (10 kilometers of frontage);
c. Further to the left, the 72nd Guards Rifle Division was in the sector: (excl.) Nizhnii Ol'shanets – Maslova Pristan' – (excl.) Point 104.2 – western fringe of the Dacha Shebekinskaia wooded ravine (15 kilometers of frontage);
d. On the army's left flank, the 36th Guards Rifle Division was defending the sector: Point 104.2 – 1-Gatishche, 2-Gatishche – (excl.) 1st Sovetskoe – western portion of Volchansk – Timovka (20 kilometers of frontage).

The army's second belt of defenses had a length of 46 kilometers, or 21.3% of the length of the Voronezh Front's entire second belt. Three divisions were occupying it; two constituted the reserve of the corps commanders and one – the reserve of the army commander:

a. 73rd Guards Rifle Division (the 25th Guards Rifle Corps' reserve): (excl.) Sheino – Miasoedovo – "Solov'ev" collective farm – Korenskaia Dacha wooded ravine – (excl.) Nikol'skoe;
b. 213th Rifle Division (the 24th Guards Rifle Corps' reserve): Gremiachii [Gremiachee] – "Poliana" State Farm – Shebekino – Nezhegol – Churaevo;

c. 15th Guards Rifle Division (the 7th Guards Army's reserve): Shebekino State Farm – Plebenevka (?) State Farm – Gerlegovka – 2-Zavody, Volchansk settlements – Point 156.2 (a frontage of 25 kilometers).

Unlike the 6th Guards Army, the divisions of the 7th Guards Army's first line didn't push forward a reinforced combat security screen in the form of forward outposts; the Northern Donets River obviated the need for this. Nor did it even organize reinforced listening posts. In order to screen the forward edge and guard the minefields at nighttime, each forward rifle company sent out patrols. The company commanders determined their size and weapons. For example, in the 1st Battalion of the 72nd Guards Rifle Division's 224th Guards Rifle Regiment, each company sent three men (armed with a light machine gun, two PPSh submachine guns and 6 grenades) out on nightly patrol. Because of the fact that the forward edge was located almost on the edge of a swampy river basin, the patrols didn't go out very far – not more than 100 meters from the front-line trench. This was very close and didn't allow the patrols to ensure security in full measure. A relatively large distance, approximately 350-400 meters, remained to the river channel itself, and this would allow the enemy's assault groups the possibility to cross the river stealthily at night, and concealed by the swamp's vegetation, to reassemble and launch one sudden charge to wipe out the pickets and break into the first line of trenches. The Soviet side realized this threat, and sought to take steps to set up outposts close to the river in order to keep watch over the river's surface and interdict enemy attempts to cross it. For example, the command of the 72nd Guards Rifle Division ordered the fashioning of facsimile rifle pits out of several barrels (one atop the other), which were then submerged in the swamp, but this scheme had no success.

The forward edge of the 7th Guards Army's main line of defense, as in the case of the other armies, was fortified as follows: attacking Germans would first run into embedded anti-tank mines, then anti-personnel mines. Next they would come up against a single row of cheval-de-frise made from wood (in order to slow up the infantry), followed by concertina wire, coils of trip wire, and then three bands of barbed wire (spaced 60-70 centimeters apart). All of this was densely covered by the fire of rifles and machine guns, as well as mortar fire. In certain divisions, in front of the forward edge of a regiment of the second echelon, in addition to mines there were cleared fields of fire covering constricted avenues of advance. Such an obstacle, for example, was covering the entire forward edge of the 1st Battalion of the 81st Guards Rifle Division's 233rd Guards Rifle Regiment. The clearing extended for 2 kilometers and covered the entire ground between the road running from Hill 153.2 to the railroad tracks and the road running between Hill 156.6 and Staryi Gorod.

General Pliaskin recalled:

> While preparing the defenses of the Kursk salient, several hundred thousand anti-tank mines, anti-personnel mines and roadside bombs were planted by the engineers, and a large number of bridges and other important sites were prepared for demolition. At Belgorod each kilometer of the front had more than 2,000 anti-tank mines and more than 2,600 anti-personnel mines. In connection with this I want to talk about the heroism and self-sacrifice with which this system of obstacles was created. In the period of the spring thaw, several railcars of anti-personnel and anti-tank mines requested by the Front arrived at the Belyi Kolodez' railroad station, which was located in the sector of the neighboring army of the Southwestern Front. But how and by what means could this valuable cargo be transported to the 7th Guards Army? It would have to go at great risk. We asked the station's commandant and the locomotive's engineer to convey the railcars to the railroad station in Volchansk, where the 15th Guards Rifle Division was defending. The town and railroad station were being shelled by enemy artillery. It was necessary to act decisively and boldly. Having explained the situation, the commandant ordered the engineers (it is a pity that I can't remember their names) to run

the train to Volchansk under the cover of darkness, where a battalion of infantry and Major D. Ushakov's 48th Engineer-Sapper Battalion would be waiting for it. Deftly and quickly, observing complete silence, under the cover of the night the soldiers unloaded the deadly load from the railcars, and then the engineers started up the train and headed back. Among the railcars loaded with mines, we discovered a railcar carrying Molotov cocktails! They came in handy for us when repelling enemy tank attacks. Soon the mines were loaded on wagons for the divisions. Everything turned out well. But after all, just one hit on a railcar, and nothing would have been left of them or us! However, we had no other way around the situation.[17]

By the start of the Battle of Kursk, the army-level defensive belts of Shumilov's forces had three defensive strongpoints in the main line, and two strongpoints in the second line. In the main line of defense, these positions were spaced 1,200 to 2,000 meters apart from each other (depending on the terrain). Standard fighting trenches and communication trenches formed the basis of the constructed fieldworks done on the belts. Each strongpoint had 2-3 lines of trenches, while the main defensive belt had 6 to 9 lines of trenches and the second defensive belt had 4-6 lines of trenches. As military historians later calculated, each kilometer of the 7th Guards Army's front contained up to 8 kilometers of a continuous line of standard trenches and communication trenches. On the Central Front, during the construction of the 13th Army's main defensive belt, this figure rose to up to 10 kilometers.[18]

The former chief of engineers of the Steppe Front General A.D. Tsirlin wrote:

> Up until the end of 1942, our views on the construction of fieldworks for defensive belts and positions were governed by the theory and practice of preparing fortified areas. Battalion defensive strongpoints were furnished with a system of earth-and-timber firing positions in the form of casemates, which had mutually supporting fields of fire. The units and formations at this time didn't always have the necessary quantity of weapons in order to ensure the effectiveness of the system of fire in such a battalion strongpoint. The overlapping fields of fire between the earth-and-timber bunkers were not supported by communication trenches, and as a result the companies and platoons couldn't maneuver with their weapons within the strongpoint during a battle and stay concealed. The system of trenches, the switch to which began on a number of *fronts* at the initiative of the troops back in 1942 – and everywhere on the basis of the General Staff's directives from the spring of 1943 – in combination with strong obstacles gave new qualities to our defense.
>
> The use of trenches eliminated the well-known inflexibility of a system of fire ... based on immobile firing positions with restricted fields of fire. Trenches facilitated the mobility of the infantry, which had acquired the possibility to make wide use of concealed maneuver on the battlefield. ... The enemy lost the possibility of placing targeted fire on the elements that were positioned in trenches and other shelters.[19]

In addition, the complex of trenches included firing positions for heavy artillery, as well as tanks and self-propelled guns dug into the ground as immobile, armored firing positions. This was to increase the resilience, activity and maneuverability of the defending troops. In order to break through such a system, the enemy would need significantly more weapons, gear and ammunition. This novelty accelerated the fortification work in the divisions and eased the work to build the

---

17 *Na belgorodskom napravlenii*, pp. 100-101.
18 TsAMO RF, F. 240, op. 2779, d. 453, l. 118.
19 Parot'kin, Major General I.V. (ed.), *Kurskaia bitva* [*Battle of Kursk*] (Moscow: Nauka, 1970), p. 242.

lines, since the number of permanent (which means costly) firing positions that had to be built by hand decreased. The freed up labor went to building a large number of lightly-built (anti-fragmentation) shelters for the infantry, which together with camouflage and dummy positions reduced casualties, which preserved the combat-capability of the elements.

In addition, the use of a continuous line of standard trenches improved command and control in the divisions and contributed to combat cohesion, since there appeared the greater possibility of interpersonal communication between senior commanders and subordinates. It became a rule for the commanders of units and formations, their deputies, senior political officers, and even corps commanders and the army commander when preparing an operation, to visit the combat positions. This raised the morale of the soldiers and junior commanders, and strengthened the belief that with their concerted efforts, the enemy would be defeated. Such thoughts seem far-fetched at first glance, but more than once they were heard from the lips of combat veterans of the war.

The most widespread cover for the machine gunners was bunkers with embrasures and mounts for their machine guns. Riflemen prepared shrapnel-proof shelters, while the commanders of elements and units had command and observation posts, or more often, a combined command and observation post. All of these constructed positions were very similar and built from two basic materials – wood logs and earth. The bunkers were fashioned into the form of timber blockhouses (usually 2.2 meters by 2.2 meters), with a height of 2 meters, which were fully dug into the ground. The cover (roof) consisted of two layers of logs, with 50-60 centimeters of dirt packed between them. One embrasure (typically) with a width of 60 centimeters was cut out in the direction of the enemy, and inside the bunker were crudely-shaped mounts for setting up the machine guns. Machine-gun nests were as a rule positioned in a chessboard fashion, in order to cover the flanks of neighboring machine-gun positions. The ideal cover for a firing position was a brick structure (more accurately a semi-basement), but in the sector of the 7th Guards Army there were few; primarily they were located in Staryi Gorod (the 81st Guards Rifle Division's sector) in buildings of the railroad depot. The majority of the villages and hamlets within the main and secondary defensive belt had already been seriously damaged in the course of preceding fighting, and thus even very few wooden homes and outbuildings were still standing.

The anti-shrapnel shelters for the infantry were four-walled (sometimes three-walled) log constructions, prepared from timber with a thickness of 18-20 centimeters and raised above the soil level. Its walls were typically camouflaged with pieces of turf and they were covered with dirt, and in order to strengthen it on steep slopes, braced with wattling made from vines and branches. The roofs were laid in two layers, but consisted of thinner logs than, for example, on the machine-gun nests and bunkers. These shelters would have 1-2 embrasures.

In order to direct the platoons and fire, each rifle company commander (and higher) was equipped with two observation posts or command-observation posts. They were prepared like ordinary bunkers, but with several embrasures for observation (mounts for observation devices), no less than two entrances (main and alternate) and three lines of communication (main, alternate and reserve). The observation posts and command-observation posts of commanders of various ranks were distinguished only by the number of log layers covering them – a company commander ordinarily had two layers of logs, while a regiment commander had no less than three or more layers.

Already at the end of March 1943, all the villages in the 7th Guards Army's tactical zone began to be adapted for a defense, and on 30 April the Voronezh Front's Military Council signed off on a special directive, No. 00914, which demanded:

> All populated places in the tactical, rear and army defensive zones are to be converted into strongpoints and anti-tank areas, assigning them to Group "B" for defensive construction

work. In addition, the following villages are to be prepared for defense and are assigned to Group "A" for the work:

> 6th Guards Army – Ol'khovka, Gostishchevo, Dal'niaia Igumenka, Shakhovo, Shliakhovoe, Sheino, Lomovo and Oboian'.
> 7th Guards Army – Miasoedovo, Shebekino, Volchansk, Zavody-1 and Zavody-2, Nezhegol and Voznesenovka.
> 69th Army – Aleksandrovskii [Prokhorovka Station – author], Alekseevka, Korocha, Bol'she-Troitskoe.

Construct an outer ring of works around the populated places according to the scheme of Fortified Areas, and in the villages and hamlets themselves create a system of fortified positions and obstacles.

... Get to work immediately to fortify the populated places listed above in the given directive.

... The deadline for the preliminary preparation of the populated places for a defense is 25 May 1943. The deadline for the completion of the fortifications is 10 June 1943.

... Report through the Chief of Fortified Areas every five days on the work being done according to the given directive, with an indication of the number of buildings and embrasures by type of weapon that has been made ready in each place.[20]

So that the reader might grasp the difference Groups "A" and "B", I'll discuss this question in a bit more detail. The system of an outer ring of works included a continuous, branching line of regulation trenches with fortified firing positions (earth-and-timber bunkers) and prepared artillery and mortar positions, the mining of the forward edge, barbed wire in three staked strands, and the creation of major artificial obstacles on tank-vulnerable directions like anti-tank ditches, scarps and counter-scarps. Parallel with this work, within the village or town itself, a network of trenches was prepared; all of the buildings (semi-basements) were converted into permanent firing positions with an all-round field of fire; and communication trenches and ramps for tanks that were designated to defend the village were dug (for example, the tank crews of the 167th Separate Tank Regiment in Miasoedovo built firing emplacements for their combat machines).

The decision about fortifying the villages and hamlets substantially increased the burden on both the troops and the civilian population, but it proved to be far-sighted. By the beginning of July 1943, the directive's demands had essentially been carried out. Indeed, as subsequent events would show, all the anti-tank strongpoints and anti-tank defense areas located in the villages of the tactical zone played an important role in constraining the German armored groups in the course of Operation Citadel. The defense of the strongpoints in Krutoi Log, Razumnoe and Maslova Pristan' was organized particularly successfully. Of the 15 villages in the sector of the 6th Guards and 7th Guards Armies that had been prepared according to the scheme of Fortified Areas, 7 were taken by the enemy, but it took anywhere from a day to 72 hours to storm them, and required the participation of significant forces, not only of panzergrenadiers, but also armor. In the process, the enemy suffered substantial losses in the fighting.

Correctly assuming that enemy panzer groups would be the main problem in the course of the defensive operation, the command of the 7th Guard Army from the very first days of organizing the defense attached particular significance to fortifying the defenses against German tanks. However, the execution of this task was complicated by the terrain conditions. The ground where

---

20 TsAMO RF, F. 203, op. 2843, d. 301, ll. 200-201.

its troops had dug in proved difficult for the use of anti-tank artillery as the main element of the defense. The eastern bank of the Northern Donets River was lower than the western bank, which rose 1 to 1.5 meters above the water. Kempf's forces held all the commanding heights in the area, and thus, as was noted in the documents of its artillery headquarters, from ground observation posts the Germans could survey the Soviet defenses out to a depth of 5-8 kilometers. Even so, the commander of the 7th Panzer Division Major General H. von Funck complained that not all the elevations could be used for setting up an observation post, since the hills were too low and covered with forests.

From the observation posts on the eastern bank, the enemy positions could be viewed only out to a distance of 1-3 kilometers, and only on separate sectors out to 5-6 kilometers. At the same time, all the balkas on the eastern bank ran perpendicular to the river channel, because of which it was impossible to set up concealed observation posts for the artillery in them. Only in one area, the Rzhavets – Titovka area, did dense woods approach almost right up to the eastern bank of the Northern Donets River, which allowed the concealed regrouping of units. In addition, a serious problem arose with the sandy soil, which was prevalent in the 7th Guards Army's sector, since it didn't provide the needed stability for fortifications and required their continuous improvement. Sectors between the Northern Donets and Razumnaia Rivers, and also along the eastern bank of the latter (with a total width of 5-8 kilometers) were open, which during the enemy breakthrough allowed the Germans to launch an attack with panzer groups to the northeast. The III Panzer Corps during the course of Operation Citadel successfully took advantage of this.

At the same time, a number of natural obstacles also gave the Soviet side substantial advantages when organizing an anti-tank defense. The Northern Donets River was the primary obstacle. Although the river was not particularly deep, it had a rather broad, swampy basin (extending up to 200 meters from the river channel on both the western and eastern banks). In addition, the Koren' and Korocha Rivers that flowed from north to south, as well as the presence of the thickly wooded areas around them, reduced the possibility of a maneuver by enemy armor through the right flank and center of the 7th Guards Army to the east. Relying on a detailed analysis of the defensive area, the army headquarters determined six tank-vulnerable directions in its sector, three of which were particularly dangerous, including two in the sector of the 25th Guards Rifle Corps and one in the sector of the 24th Guards Rifle Corps: The first (main) direction – out of the Mikhailovka bridgehead (in the sector of the 81st Guards Rifle Division; the second: toward Korocha (in the sector of the 81st Guards and 78th Guards Rifle Divisions); and the third, the Volchansk – Volokonovka direction (in the sector of the 36th Guards Rifle Division).

Taking this into account, along the forward edge of the main defensive belt, 12 divisional anti-tank strongpoints were set up, and in the secondary belt, 15 army-level anti-tank areas. In comparison, the 6th Guards Army created a total of 28 anti-tank strongpoints, including 18 in the main belt of defenses and 10 in the secondary belt. According to the scheme of the Front's artillery commander, with the aim of achieving the greatest effectiveness of the anti-tank strongpoints, they were to be as "self-sufficient" as possible. Even though the fire of anti-tank guns and anti-tank rifles provided the basis of their firepower, it was mandatorily planned to cover the strongpoints with rifle elements and to bolster them with mortars and a mobile mining group. This was necessary so that its garrison: a) could independently frustrate attempts by enemy sappers to clear passages in the minefields; b) separate the attacking infantry from the tanks and kill enemy submachine gunners as they attempted to infiltrate directly into the firing positions; and c) block attempts by the enemy's panzer groups to bypass the strongpoints from the flanks (by means of moving up mining detachments to likely directions of advance).

The command of the 7th Guards Army not only supported this suggestion by the Front's chief of artillery, but also persistently pursued it when setting up its defenses. Each day, the 7th Guards Army's artillery commander Lieutenant General A.N. Petrov drove out to visit the troops, where he explained the idea's positive sides, and resolved on the spot arising questions with each artillery commander of the divisions and corps. Commandants – artillery officers – were put in charge of the anti-tank strongpoints, and each anti-tank gun had a telephone connection and a messenger. Signals for calling in artillery fire by rifle elements in the event of the appearance of German tanks were worked out and established. In order to prevent the premature disclosure of the gun positions, specific guns and crews were determined, which had the right to open fire at small groups of enemy infantry and tanks. On the army's right flank, heavy KV tanks of the 262nd Heavy Tank Regiments were dug in as immobile firing positions in the anti-tank strongpoints. At the same time, all of the concealed positions of the howitzer artillery (of the battalions and regiments of reinforcement) prepared to fire over open sights at enemy armor, and in case this was impossible, alternate firing positions were set up nearby.

Despite the obvious plusses of the new scheme of reinforcing the anti-tank strongpoints, it provoked a lot of arguments, misunderstanding and even resistance on the part of infantry commanders, and not only them. Officers of Voronezh Front's artillery headquarters wrote in an account:

> It is necessary, however, to note that when putting this idea into practice, a lot of difficulties were encountered. The main one was the lack of understanding of the need of binding all the measures that would create a reliable, strong anti-tank defense into a single whole, even among artillery officers. The lack of understanding was connected with the fact that artillery fire lays at the basis of the anti-tank defense, and because of this, it was an artillery chief that was to resolve questions about the need for supplementing the artillery fire with other measures. It goes without saying that when organizing the anti-tank defense, each artillery chief took as his point of departure the basic plan of defense, which had been received by the combined-arms commanders responsible for the defense of a given sector. A lot had to be done … it was required to send around several directives/coded messages/ from the Front's Military Council and the artillery headquarters.[21]

If to switch from the elliptic and carefully-worded statements from the account of General S.S. Varentsov's headquarters[22] and to formulate the essence of the problem concisely, then it sounded this way: The resistance was due to the narrow-mindedness and professional illiteracy of a significant portion of the officer staff. A majority of both the infantry and artillery commanders were content to fight "in the old way", and they placed their petty self-interests above their service duties. It boiled down to the fact that up until this moment, the rifle battalion commander was the senior chief responsible for holding a battalion defensive zone, but now responsibility for the anti-tank defense and fortification of the positions (in essence, for the strength of the position) was placed upon artillerymen. The infantry commanders became jealous (quarrels began about who was more important), and the arguments ran as follows: "The 'gunners' know their business, but their knowledge is too narrow; we'll be the first to meet the Fritzes, but they, standing behind our backs, are to decide the main questions of the defense (where to mine, where to dig ditches and scarps, etc.)." The novelty was not to the taste of the artillerymen either – they now had too much responsibility, and the fuss and bother would be many times greater. However, all of these squabbles, without which not a single new idea or practice can get by, subsided as soon as the fighting began, and the organized, I will say directly, sensible system of anti-tank areas demonstrated its reliability and effectiveness.

---

21 TsAMO RF, F. 203, op. 2843, d. 421, l. 15.
22 General Varentsov was the Voronezh Front's artillery commander.

The reinforcement of the defensive benefits offered by the Belgorod – Titovka railroad bed had great significance.[23] This railroad branch ran through the army's entire sector, from the left flank of the 36th Guards Rifle Division to the left flank of the 81st Guards Rifle Division (the Kreida siding track), lay almost parallel with the forward edge, and connected such villages, which had been converted into anti-tank strongpoints, as 1-Gatishche, Bezliudovka, Maslova Pristan' and Razumnoe. In places, swampy ground bordered the railroad embankment, which added to the defensive qualities of the railroad bed in these sectors. In essence, the embankment had already been prepared with fortifications to a significant extent, so it was only necessary to fit it into the general system of defense properly, and this the Guardsmen did rather successfully throughout the spring. As a result, on the first two days of the Battle of Kursk, the railroad bed, densely mined and bristling with booby traps and firing positions, played a major role in enabling the first-echelon divisions of both rifle corps to hold their positions. It would become a unique bulwark, which neither the infantry of Korps Raus nor the *kampfgruppen* of III Panzer Corps would be able to overcome from the march.

Now we'll take a more detailed look at how the construction of the defenses went within the frontline rifle divisions. Considering the entire difficult complex of tasks that stood in front of the army, and primarily the main task – to prevent Army Detachment Kempf from linking up with Fourth Panzer Army's main forces, the leadership of the 7th Guards Army strove to form a balanced defense with its available forces. At the decision of G.K. Zhukov, who in March and April 1943 often visited the Voronezh Front and together with N.F. Vatutin reconnoitered the ground in the sector of the 7th Guards Army, the forward edge of the main belt of defenses on the right flank of the 25th Guards Rifle Corps (the sector of the 81st Guards Rifle Division) and the left flank of the 24th Guards Rifle Corps (the sector of the 36th Guards Rifle Division) was more strongly fortified. At M.S. Shumilov's suggestion, in each of the corps a third division was to occupy a line in the second echelon behind the boundary of the two divisions in the first echelon. However, the Marshal of the Soviet Union Zhukov demanded to echelon in depth the forces on the flanks and to position the third division of each of the corps behind the outer flanking divisions of the frontline. In the process, the commanders of the second-echelon divisions received an order to prepare positions along the entire second army-level belt of defenses, and to work out plans for counterattacks in the event of an enemy breakthrough both on the boundary between the frontline divisions of each corps and on the boundary between the two rifle corps themselves. Pursuant to Zhukov's directions, by the start of the Battle of Kursk, the 73rd Guards Rifle Division was backing up the 81st Guards Rifle Division, and the 15th Guards Rifle Division was positioned behind the 36th Guards Rifle Division. The 213th Rifle Division, which had gone by this time into M.S. Shumilov's reserve, was directed at the boundary between the two corps. The army commander also ordered for routes to be prepared for the maneuvering of the forces of the corps' second echelons: both to the area of the boundary between the two corps, and to the sectors of their flanking divisions. In addition, the frontline flanking divisions of the army (the 81st Guards Rifle Division and the 36th Guards Rifle Division) were to receive the bulk of the artillery and tank reserves assigned by the Front in order to reinforce the 7th Guards Army. G.K. Zhukov's demand for the substantial strengthening of the armies' and Front's flanks was dictated by the woeful experience of the summer fighting of 1942, including in this area as well, when the

---

23 This railroad branch linked the two district centers of Belgorod and Volchansk, and it would be logical to call it the Belgorod – Volchansk railroad. However, in the combat documents of the opposing sides, it was often called the Belgorod – Titovka railroad. Probably this is because Volchansk lay outside the sector of the 7th Guards Army's defense and was located outside the zone of Army Detachment Kempf's actions. I will therefore retain the name "Belgorod – Titovka railroad" in the present research.

Germans ruptured the Soviet defenses with powerful panzer attacks directed at the boundaries of divisions and armies.

The 81st Guards Rifle Division arrived at the Voronezh Front back in the first half of March. Having unloaded at Printsevka Station and having conducted a 100-kilometer march, on 15 March it occupied a defense near Belgorod in the second echelon and began throwing up fortifications. But a little more than a month later, on the night of 4-5 May, a planned rotation was conducted on the army's right flank and Morozov's division took over the positions of Colonel S.A. Kozak's 73rd Guards Rifle Division in the first echelon. This was done not only with the aim of allowing the men of the 73rd Guards Rifle Division to rest and to conduct combat training exercises with them. The point was that the 73rd Guards Rifle Division was covering the tantalizing northeastern direction for the enemy, and at the same time had the only direct contact with the enemy: opposite the center of its combat positions was the main "sore point" on the eastern bank of the Northern Donets River, the village of Mikhailovka that was being held by the Germans. The bridgehead wasn't large; including the river basin it covered approximately 10.5 square kilometers (but only around 9 square kilometers offered firm ground). Nevertheless, this space was sufficient for the deployment of a strong assault group of up to 40 tanks, which was of great concern to the Soviet side. Kozak's 73rd Guards Rifle Division, like all of the 7th Guards Army's divisions, had arrived from Stalingrad in a weakened condition, and in the course of April engaged in heavy, but unsuccessful fighting for possession of Mikhailovka. Therefore by the beginning of May it was the numerically weakest division in the 7th Guards Army (on 5 May 1943 it had just 6,824 men).[24] Thus having received the first intelligence warning about a possible German attack prior to 10 May, the Front command assigned this important sector of defense to the numerically stronger 81st Guards Rifle Division.

When turning over its line, the 73rd Guards Rifle Division left behind all its means of reinforcement in their positions. In addition, in June the 81st Guards Rifle Division received additional reinforcements, and already in May the work on fortifications in its positions had begun with great diligence. By the beginning of the Battle of Kursk Morozov's division had completely prepared two defensive strongpoints in the main belt of defenses: the first of three trench lines, the second (alternate) of two lines of trenches, which were positioned along the western fringe of the Belinskaia woods, the village of Sevriukovo and a hill 300 meters north of Sevriukovo. Five anti-tank strongpoints had been set up: on the right flank – Staryi Gorod; on the left flank – the Kreida siding track; on the boundary with the 78th Guards Rifle Division – the corrective labor camp; and in the depth of the defenses – the villages of Blizhniaia Igumenka and Belinskaia. In addition, M.S. Shumilov was aiming the 73rd Guards Rifle Division and a tank group out his mobile reserve toward the tank-vulnerable (northeastern) direction.

In the frontline positions of the 81st Guards Rifle Division were the full-strength 235th Guards Rifle Regiment under the command of Major G.T. Skiruta and the 238th Guards Rifle Regiment under the command of Major T.F. Kriuchikhin with attached assets. Major Skiruta was made responsible for the boundary between the two regiments. Considering that the boundary was directly opposite Mikhailovka, the division command subordinated the 65th Separate Army Penal Company to him, which the regiment commander placed on the left flank of his 1st Rifle Battalion. In the depth of the main belt of defenses (behind the boundary between the frontline regiments), in the sector Blizhniaia Igumenka – Machine Tractor Station hamlet – (excl.) "Day of Harvest" collective farm was Major S.I. Titarenko's 233rd Guards Rifle Regiment with attached assets.

---

24 TsAMO RF, F. 203, op. 2843, d. 426, l. b/n information of the armies for 5 May 1943.

Relative to the other frontline divisions, the 81st Guards Rifle Division's system of defense had a number of distinctive features. First, its sector was minimal, just 8 kilometers wide (9 kilometers following the trace of the front line) and 6 kilometers in depth. Thus, each frontline regiment received a sector (on average) of 4 to 4.5 kilometers, just as the 1942 Infantry Field Manual dictated. However, considering features of the terrain and the importance of individual directions, Major General I.K. Morozov decreased the 238th Guards Rifle Regiment's sector of the front relative to that of the 235th Guards Rifle Regiment. In addition, assuming that the Germans would launch their main attack with panzers out of Mikhailovka against the left-flank 238th Guards Rifle Regiment, he ordered its battalions to be echeloned in depth, with two battalions deployed in the first trench line and one in the second, while in the 235th Guards Rifle Regiment, all of the battalions were arrayed into a single line in the first trench.

Second, in the second line position of the first-echelon regiments (the third line of trenches), the 81st Guards Rifle Division's third regiment – the 233 Guards Rifle Regiment – was deployed, together with anti-tank strongpoints that had been set up on this same line. The division commander's combined-arms reserve, Major Medvedev's separate training rifle battalion, was also positioned here. Each battalion of Titarenko's regiment had fortified its own sector according to the same scheme used by the forward regiments. Such a significant density of the 81st Guards Rifle Division's troops in the main defensive belt to a great extent pre-ordained its great resilience and stubbornness in the course of Operation Citadel, even given the prolonged, systematic attacks by panzer divisions.

Third, several regiments of the army's artillery were made operationally subordinated to I.K. Morozov. Combined, they had 34 152mm howitzers, 36 120mm mortars, 20 76mm ZIS-3 anti-tank guns, 48 BM-13 rocket launchers and 71 anti-tank rifles. Thus, by 5 July 1943 the division had received an artillery group which by its number and firepower was unrivaled in any other division of the 7th Guards Army. In total, (including the 81st Guards Rifle Division's inherent artillery), it consisted of 57 122mm and 152mm howitzers, 65 76mm ZIS-3 anti-tank guns, 12 short-barreled 76mm regimental guns, 41 45-mm anti-tank guns, 87 82mm mortars, 60 120mm mortars, 48 BM-13 rocket launchers and 348 anti-tank rifles. Such a significant amount of guns and mortars allowed the division commander to reinforce substantially not only the first echelon, but also the second echelon with both anti-tank guns (76mm anti-tank batteries of the 114th Guards Destroyer Anti-tank Artillery Regiment) and field guns of medium and large caliber. On its sector, a second divisional artillery regiment was deployed – the 153rd Guards Artillery Regiment of the 73rd Guards Rifle Division. From his own and the attached units, Morozov formed several groups: a long-range artillery group (the 161st Guards Cannon Artillery Regiment), an infantry support artillery group (five battalions), and an anti-tank reserve (a separate destroyer anti-tank artillery battalion and company of tank hunters). In addition to all the above, a subgroup of the army's artillery group (the 265th Guards Cannon Artillery Regiment and the 290th Mortar Regiment) was also located in the 81st Guards Rifle Division's sector.

An interesting detail that the commander of the 81st Guards Rifle Division wrote about in his memoirs: in his division, even the Katiusha rocket launchers were adapted for conducting close-range fire. The crews of two battalions of the 97th Guards Mortar Regiment dug several shelters in the railroad embankment of the Belgorod – Titovka railroad branch so that it was possible to drive the trucks transporting the BM-13 rocket launchers into them and fire at pointblank range at the enemy attacking out of the Mikhailovka bridgehead.

Fourth, M.S. Shumilov moved up the 262nd Breakthrough Heavy Tank Regiment out of his reserve into the division's sector. It was equipped with 24 KV tanks and was subordinated to the division commander as a tank reserve. With the aim of reacting efficient to the unfolding situation, one command-observation post was prepared for the division commander and regiment commander. Some of the tanks were incorporated into the 235th Guards and 238th Guards Rifle

Division's system of defense, and in the initial phase of the battle they were to be used as immobile armored firing positions. The 1st Tank Company (4 KV) took up a position in the area of the Kleida railroad side track. The 2nd Tank Company (4 KV) was deployed in the woods south of Mikhailovka. The 4th Tank Company (2 KV) was dug-in on the southeastern outskirts of Staryi Gorod. The remaining tanks (5 KV of the 3rd Tank Company, 1 KV of the 2nd Tank Company, 3 KV of the 4th Tank Company, 2 reserve KV tanks and the command tank) were located in the reserve of the division commander in the woods 1 kilometer west of Belinskaia.

As a result, the average density of anti-tank artillery and tanks (dug-in) per kilometer of the division's front (if you put the length at 8 kilometers) amounted to 23.1 gun barrels; of artillery with a caliber between 45mm and 152mm (disregarding the 14 reserve KV tanks of the 262nd Heavy Tank Regiment), rocket launchers and 82mm and 120mm mortars – 24.3; and of anti-tank rifles – 34.8.

Fifth, in the 81st Guards Rifle Division, as in the other divisions, a mobile blocking detachment was formed out of sapper elements. However, assuming that the main events would take place on the right flank of his rifle corps, Major General G.B. Safiulin also concentrated his corps' blocking detachment in the sector of Morozov's division. This proved to be a very far-sighted decision, and in the course of repulsing the III Panzer Corps' attacks, this detachment rendered substantial assistance to the Guardsmen.

I.K. Morozov gave the foremost significance to the system of fire of the rifle elements. The most important requirements for it were its density, rate of fire and the provision of reliable cover to the strongpoints. With this aim, the battalions that were located on the most threatened directions were given smaller sectors than those on secondary directions. Firing positions for all the light and heavy machine guns of the frontline regiments were set up on the forward edge. In particular, the 1st and 3rd Battalions of the 235th Guards Rifle Regiment, which were defending the eastern and northeastern outskirts of Mikhailovka, had corresponding frontages of 1.1 and 1.5 kilometers, while the 2nd Battalion of the 235th Guards Rifle Regiment held a sector of 2.5 kilometers. As a result, by the start of the fighting, opposite the forward edge of the 81st Guards Rifle Division a zone of continuous fire had been created that extended out to 400 meters. The average density of fire for the division was 8.8 bullets per linear meter, and on the most important sectors (for example, 1/235th Guards Rifle Regiment) up to 11 bullets per linear meter. This was a very high indicator in comparison with not only the army's other divisions, but also the entire Voronezh Front.

According to an order from the division commander, in each battalion together with the planned machine-gun nests, no less than four heavy earth-and-timber bunkers covered by 6-8 layers of logs with a thickness of 20-25 centimeters should be constructed. A significant number of the machine-gun positions were emplaced in the brick buildings of Staryi Gorod, in structures of the railroad facilities and in two semi-destroyed grain elevators at the Kreida siding track. They were better protected than by the earth-and-timber bunkers and really belonged to the category of permanent emplacements.

The following data testify to the impressive scale of the fortification work done by Morozov's division. By 20 June 1943:

- 39 kilometers of trenches and communication trenches had been dug, which connected the first three trench lines, a reserve position and observation posts for the commander from the company level to the division commander;
- foxholes and emplacements had been dug: 222 for riflemen, 486 for machine guns, 148 for mortars, 136 for anti-tank rifles, and 143 for anti-tank guns;
- 16 tanks had been dug in;
- 56 brick buildings had been converted into firing positions;

- 48 earth-and-timber bunkers had been constructed;
- 64 observation posts had been created;
- 228 timber bunkers for the men had been erected;
- 35 kilometers of terrain had been mined, particularly densely on tank-vulnerable directions, including 13.5 kilometers of anti-tank mines, while 24,789 anti-personnel mines had been emplaced.[25]

Incidentally, these figures were generated over two weeks before the start of the Battle of Kursk, and by 5 July 1943 they would be even greater.

It should be noted that all the above-listed measures to strengthen the positions of the 7th Guards Army's right-flank division were connected primarily with inspections by the Voronezh Front's headquarters, which took place at the end of April. They revealed a number of substantial shortcomings with the strengthening of the boundaries between the divisions, corps and armies across the entire front. At the personal order of N.F. Vatutin, special commissions were created to eliminate them. For example, in order to analyze the terrain and work out the optimal measures regarding the strengthening the boundary between the 6th and 7th Guards Armies, a commission was created that consisted of Major General P.F. Lagutin, the deputy commander of the 6th Guards Army; Major General D.I. Turbin, the 6th Guards Army's artillery commander; Colonel A.A. Funtikov, the chief of staff of the 7th Guards Army's 25th Guards Rifle Corps; Colonel S.A. Kozak, the commander of the 73rd Guards Rifle Division; Colonel P.D. Govorunenko, commander of the 375th Rifle Division; the artillery commanders of the 6th Guards Army's 23rd Guards Rifle Corps and 7th Guards Army's 25th Guards Rifle Corps; divisional engineers of the 81st Guards and 375th Rifle Divisions; and a number of other responsible commanders. A Red Army journal that contained articles that sought to assimilate the war's experience stated:

> According to the decisions of this commission, in order to guard the boundaries the following units were withdrawn from the 6th Guards Army: 93rd Cannon Artillery Regiment, 493rd Destroyer Anti-tank Artillery Regiment, the 375th Rifle Division's 932nd Artillery Regiment, the 16th Guards Mortar Regiment, and the 265th Mortar Regiment. From the 7th Guards Army, the following units were withdrawn: the 81st Guards Rifle Division's 173rd Guards Artillery Regiment, the 114th Guards Destroyer Anti-tank Artillery Regiment, the 161st Guards Cannon Artillery Regiment and the 1st Battalion of the 290th Mortar Regiment. In addition, the commission's decision involved all the weapons positioned in the anti-tank strongpoints of Shishino, Dalniaia Igumenka, Blizhniaia Igumenka, Postnikov and Staryi Gorod.
>
> The commission also worked out all the measures for the use of the second echelon. Thus, in the event of an enemy breakthrough by infantry and tanks at the armies' boundary between the 375th Rifle Division and 73rd Guards Rifle Division, the enemy was to be held up with fire and counterattacks on the line: Petropavlovka, Dal'niaia Igumenka, Miasoedovo, Iastrebovo, Razumnoe. The 6th Guards Army's 89th Guards Rifle Division (with two regiments) and the 96th Separate Tank Brigade after assembling in the Khokhlovo – Dal'niaia Igumenka area were to counterattack in the direction of Staryi Gorod. Two artillery regiments and the 16th Guards Mortar Regiment were to support the division.
>
> In the event of an enemy breakthrough at the boundary between the 6th and 7th Guards Armies, the 81st Guards Rifle Division, after concentrating in the area of the "Batratskaia Dacha" State Farm, had the assignment to counterattack the Germans in the Staryi Gorod

---

25 TsAMO RF, F. 477, op. 188378, d. 2, ll. 22-59.

– "Batratskaia Dacha" – Razumnoe direction. The 167th Separate Tank Regiment, the 30th Separate Destroyer Anti-tank Artillery Regiment, the 265th Guards Army Cannon Artillery Regiment and the 1438th Self-propelled Artillery Regiment were to support the division. Thus, the concentric attacks by the 89th Guards and 81st Guards Rifle Divisions with their attached assets were to encircle and destroy the enemy that had broken through at the boundary and restore the situation on the armies' joint flanks in cooperation with the first-echelon units.

Engineer units were given the responsibility to lay mines on the approaches to Dal'niaia Igumenka; the southern outskirts of Melikhovo; the western outskirts of Sheino; the paved road in the Staryi Gorod sector and the woods north of there; and the ravine northwest of Hill 212.1 and the road north of there. Communications by radio, telephone and through liaison officers were established in order to facilitate cooperation between the armies.

It should be pointed out that all this work to secure the boundaries went on in the first half of May 1943. Subsequently, certain changes were made: a number of the divisions that had been occupying a defense on the main belt (for example, the 73rd Guards and 15th Guards Rifle Divisions) were replaced by new divisions. By the beginning of July certain changes in the artillery grouping on the boundaries also took place. However, despite these changes and others, the general desire of the command of the Voronezh Front and of the armies at all levels to secure the boundaries reliably remained unchanged. The Front commander-in-chief and the commanders of the armies, as well as their representatives, repeatedly drove to the front and checked the organization of the defensive works on the boundaries.[26]

To the above I will add that the Front command also got involved in the work to secure the boundary between the 6th Guards and 7th Guards Armies. In May, two rifle divisions of the 69th Army (the 107th and 305th Rifle Divisions) were deployed in the rear defensive belt on the axis of the boundary between these two armies, and behind them in the depth of the first Front-level line – the 92nd Guards Rifle Division.

In addition to the objective need to strengthen the boundary of the armies and Front (always the most vulnerable spot in any defense), N.F. Vatutin had other weighty reasons to pay particular attention to this matter in the 7th Guards Army. As already noted, the area of Staryi Gorod was playing a special role in his plan to split Manstein's two assault groupings. Thus, the General of the Army, having received information from inspections that neither army commander was paying adequate attention to their boundaries, not only insisted on the creation of a commission, but starting in May and up to the start of the battle he more than once personally visited this area and not only monitored the implementation of the decisions and the quality of work to fortify the belts (he even personally visited frontline regiments), but he also gave valuable advice. For example, in the middle of June he and Military Council member Lieutenant General N.S. Khrushchev were once again inspecting the 81st Guards Rifle Division's defensive arrangements, and during this inspection he suggested to the division commander an original way to use the Maxim machine guns in the river basin. I.K. Morozov recalled:

> The Germans might force a crossing of the Donets; its banks were high, 1.5 to 2 meters, and the water's surface wasn't exposed to fire. There was a lot of dead space. [Vatutin recommended] to set up the machine guns lower, make wells, and in them – platforms, with embrasures just 16-20 centimeters above the water's surface, and to knock away the dirt covering the

---

26 "Sbornik po obobshcheniiu opyta voiny" [Collection on accumulating the war's experience], No. 11 (Moscow: Voenizdat, 1944), pp. 105-106.

"ANTICIPATING WHAT THE RUSSIANS HAD PREPARED" 57

machine gun's barrel whenever this became necessary. Dig communication trenches to the wells and from the rear ... bring up the machine-gun platforms you've made to bring fire on the defiladed approaches and position them like whiskers. Do the work at night, and camouflage it by morning. In this way, it is necessary to increase the amount of raking machine-gun fire sweeping the water's surface.[27]

On 15 June 1943 the division command sent a scheme of the division's improved defense to the headquarters of the 7th Guards Army with an explanatory note, which laid out the organization of fire across the river's surface in the two frontline regiments in particular detail:

1. In the sector of the 235th Guards Rifle Regiment, the 2nd and 3rd Rifle Battalions are occupying the defense close to the Northern Donets River. In order to bring fire on the water's surface, in front of the forward edge earth-and-timber bunkers for heavy and light machine guns have been set up. There are 10 such bunkers for heavy machine guns in the 2nd Rifle Battalion, of which 2 have been fitted into homes. The other 8 are newly-built bunkers covered with 3-4 layers of logs. For the light machine guns, earth-and-timber bunkers of the light type, covered by a single layer of logs, have been built.

    In the 3/235th Guards Rifle Regiment, 3 bunkers have been built for heavy machine guns, 2 of which are in the basements of buildings and 1 – an earth-and-timber bunker covered by layers of logs. For the light machine guns, 5 bunkers of the light type have been built, covered by a single layer of logs.

    As the crow flies, the distance from the bunkers to the river is 150 meters to 750 meters. The banks of the Northern Donets River are obstructed in the majority of cases by shrubs and reeds. In order to keep watch over the river's water surface, two observation posts have been set out.

2. In the sector of the 238th Guards Rifle Regiment, the 3rd Rifle Battalion is occupying the defense closest to the river. In order to bring fire down on the water's surface, 3 fire teams have been created:
    1st team – firing out of 3 bunkers with heavy machine guns;
    2nd team – one bunker with a heavy machine gun, a light machine gun on a platform and a rifle pit;
    3rd team – 1 earth-and-timber bunker with a heavy machine gun, a light machine gun on a platform and a rifle pit

    All the earth-and-timber bunkers have three layers of logs with a diameter of 20-30 centimeters. The direct distance to the river is 250-500 meters and the entire water surface isn't visible, because the river's basin out to 200-1,000 meters is overgrown with grass, reeds and bushes. The entire basin of the Northern Donets River (eastern and western banks) is exposed to fire from the arranged system of fire.

    Communication trenches from the regiment commander with the battalion commanders have been finished. Communication trenches from the battalion commanders with the company commanders are incomplete. The communication trenches from the regiment commander to the division commander has been dug in the 233rd Guards Rifle Regiment, but haven't been completed in the remaining regiments.[28]

More than once, even G.K. Zhukov traveled to the 7th Guards Army to make an inspection. In June, he again visited the army and M.S. Shumilov and N.F. Vatutin received a directive from

---

27 Morozov, I.K. *Polki srazhalis' po-gvardeiski* [*Regiments fought like Guardsmen*] (Volgograd, 1962), p. 135.
28 TsAMO RF, F. 25 gv. sk., op. 1, d. 12, ll. 56-57.

him: together with the command of the 57th Army and the Southwestern Front to strengthen the defense between the two Fronts. The Marshal, like the Commander-in-Chief of the Southwestern Front Colonel General R.Ia. Malinovsky believed that a great possibility existed that the Germans would in fact strike the boundary between the two Fronts. In June, Stalin almost became convinced of this as well, so he authorized Malinovsky to conduct a partial regrouping of his forces to his right flank, while an order followed to N.F. Vatutin regarding a deeper echeloning of his forces on his left flank. A special commission was also created to oversee this, but its level of authority was significantly higher. In addition to both army commanders, their artillery commanders, their chiefs of engineers, and the commanders of their armored and mechanized forces, the Deputy Chief of Staff of the Voronezh Front also was a member of it. I will dwell on its decisions in more detail below.

In the 24th Guards Rifle Corps, during the period of preparing for the Battle of Kursk, the system of defense also underwent substantial changes and improvements, relative to the original scheme, especially on its left flank, and took on its final form only after 20 June. The reason for this was that the Soviet side had no practical experience in creating such powerful and deep defensive belts. Moreover, periodically contradictory intelligence came in. The leadership of the Voronezh Front and of the 7th Guards Army sensed the great responsibility that lay on their shoulders, and so time and again they analyzed the state of affairs in the troops, especially the ones holding tank-vulnerable directions and the flanks of the armies, and strove to strengthen them with every possibility that was available to them at that moment.

In the sector of Vasil'ev's 24th Guards Rifle Corps, eight probable axes of enemy panzer attacks were determined:

1. Maslova Pristan' – "Poliana" State Farm – Churaevo;
2. Maslova Pristan' – Ustinka;
3. Timovka – Shebekino;
4. Novaia Tavolzhanka – Shebekino Station – Logovoe;
5. Novaia Tavolzhanka – Pletnevka State Farm and further on toward Voznesenovka or the Volchansk hamlets;
6. Ogurtsovo – 2-Gatishche – northern portion of Volchansk;
7. Staritsa – Volchansk – Rubezhnoe;
8. 1-Krasnoarmeiskoe – Volchansk.

In order to block the directions that offered good ground for tanks, his troops set up 14 anti-tank regions and strongpoints: Karnaukhov, Maslova Pristan', Kar'ernaia switch track, Bezliudovka, Novaia Tavolzhanka, 1-Gatishche, 2-Gatishche-2, Prilipy, southwestern sector of Volchansk, Sinel'nikovo, Oktiabr'skoe, Pletnevka State Farm, and Hills 167.3 and 162.3.

Of the above-listed directions, five passed through the left flank of Vasil'ev's rifle corps, and thus he gave particular attention to strengthening the Nezhegol River – Prilipy sector. Up until the end of May, the 15th Guards Rifle Division was positioned on the left flank of 24th Guards Rifle Corps' sector. Of the four rifle divisions on the army's first line, it had the most extended sector – 20 kilometers – yet with modest attached assets: the 115th Guards Destroyer Anti-tank Artillery Regiment, the 1st and 2nd Battalions of the 109th Guards Army Cannon Artillery Regiment, and the 5th Anti-tank Rifle Battalion. In June, according to G.K. Zhukov's orders (with the consideration that the left flank of the 7th Guards Army was the boundary between the Voronezh and Southwestern Fronts), intense work began to get underway here. At the decision of the composite special commission for a more reliable protection of the boundary between the Voronezh and Southwestern Fronts, N.F. Vatutin was supposed to provide the main forces. M.S. Shumilov received an order to direct the 36th Guards and 15th Guards Rifle Divisions, the 27th

Guards Tank Brigade, four artillery regiments, the 34th Separate Armored Train Battalion and a mobile anti-tank reserve (the 148th Separate Tank Regiment, the 1670th Separate Destroyer Anti-tank Artillery Regiment and a company of engineers) to secure the boundary. On its part, the Front command positioned the 270th Rifle Division in the 7th Guards Army's rear belt of defenses and told it also to keep an eye on the boundary between the 7th Guards Army and the 57th Army.

Between 29 and 31 May, Major General M.I. Denisenko's[29] 36th Guards Rifle Division was moved up into the army's first echelon on the line: Nezhigal' – 1-Gatishche – Prilipy – northern sector of Volchansk. In the process, the departing division left behind all of its previous assets. After the rotation, striving to firm up the 24th Guards Rifle Corps' left flank and increase the amount of weapons on this division's forward edge, M.S. Shumilov with the Front's authorization first transferred the 15th Guards Rifle Division's 43rd Guards Artillery Regiment to the 36th Guards Rifle Division; and second, moved up part of the 36th Guards Rifle Division (in the western part of Volchansk – Oktiabr'skoe – Point 133.6 area in the division's rear) to the division's front, replacing it with the 15th Guards Rifle Division's 44th Guards Rifle Regiment. Even so, the density of artillery with a caliber between 45mm and 152mm in Denisenko's division remained rather low – 8 artillery pieces per kilometer of front (not including the guns of the armored trains of the 34th Separate Armored Train Battalion).

Shumilov had only one possibility left to resolve the problem – by giving the division part of his mobile reserve, which he in fact did. In early June, the 36th Guards Rifle Division's commander received operational control of the 148th Separate Tank Regiment (33 T-34, 13 T-70 and 1 T-60). This allowed the density of artillery to be brought up to 10.5 guns per kilometer of front. M.I. Denisenko immediately shifted its main forces from the anti-tank defense region at Volchanskie Vyselki to the division's left flank. He concentrated three companies of the 148th Separate Tank Regiment in the area of Zavody-2 (Volchansk), and sent one T-34 tank company to his right flank (the boundary with the 72nd Guards Rifle Division), to a machine-tractor station lying 1.5 kilometers southeast of Titovka. The tank regiment received the assignment to prepare for counterattacks together with the units that were holding the flank.

Between 31 May and 1 June 1943 the 1529th Heavy Self-propelled Artillery Regiment arrived in the 7th Guards Army; it received an order to set up its main positions west of Hill 171.8, which was located in the center, behind the combat positions of the 36th Guards Rifle Division. In addition, the 7th Guards Army's Armored and Mechanized Forces command had worked out a

---

29 Mikhail Ivanovich Denisenko, Major General. Born on 27 July 1899 in Suma Oblast's village of Ol'shana. After completing the third year at a parochial school, he was gainfully employed in the village. He joined the Red Army in 1919 and took part in the Russian Civil War. From 1920, he served as the political instructor of a company. In 1921 he was sent for training in the Uman Infantry Courses, and after their termination until 1925 he studied in the Poltava Regular Infantry School. As a drill instructor, he was repeatedly promoted until he became the commander of a rifle battalion, including 11 months spent commanding the 40th Rifle Division's unauthorized parachute battalion. In April 1936 he was appointed chief of staff of the 1st Airborne Regiment, and a year later in May 1937 he became its commander. In October 1938 the regiment was converted into the 202nd Airborne Brigade, and M.I. Denisenko became the brigade commander. In October 1941, he was transferred to the post of chief of staff of the 10th Airborne Corps, but in April 1942 he took command of the 9th Airborne Corps, which three months later was converted into the 36th Guards Rifle Division. He served in the acting Red Army from August 1942. With the division as part of the 64th and 57th Armies he took part in the Battles of Stalingrad and Kursk, in the liberation of Kirovograd and in the forced crossing of the Dnepr River. For his personal courage and skillful leadership of the division when seizing and holding a bridgehead across the Dnepr River, on 20 December 1943 he was awarded the title "Hero of the Soviet Union". In January 1944 he was transferred to the equivalent post in the 12th Airborne Division, which in December 1944 was converted into the 105th Guards Rifle Division. He ended the war in Vienna as the commander of this division. After the war, he remained in the army. Denisenko passed away on 7 April 1946.

plan for a possible counterattack with the left-hand group of the army commander's tank reserve (the 201st Separate Tank Brigade and the 1529th Heavy Self-propelled Artillery Regiment) out of the Bochkovo area against either flank or in the center of the 36th Guards Rifle Division's sector. Those forces designated for defending the boundary received the following tasks:

1. 15th Guards Rifle Division:
   - Prevent an accumulation of enemy forces on the western bank of the Northern Donets River at the bridges opposite 1-Sovetskoe and Pisarevka with the fire of no less than two battalions;
   - Destroy enemy tanks and infantry that attempt to cross the Northern Donets River in the 1-Sovetskoe – Pisarevka sector with the fire of artillery and mortars;
   - Prepare the fire of two battalions at 1-Sovetskoe, 1-Krasnoarmeiskoe, and the fire of two battalions at the northern outskirts of Sherstirivka and Petrovka;
   - Support a counterattack by the second echelons (36th Guards Rifle Division) and tanks toward Ukrainskoe with the fire of two heavy artillery battalions;
   - Bring forward two rifle battalions, reinforced with anti-tank guns and rifles, to defend the southwestern and southern approaches to Volchansk (in the 57th Army's sector of defense);
   - Ready one reinforced rifle battalion for the Sinel'nikovo – Oktiabr'skoe – Point 147.6 anti-tank defense region;
   - Occupy the (excl.) bridge across the Vol'chia River – Point 137.2 – Point +6, Point 133.6 area with one reinforced rifle battalion for an anti-tank defense;
2. 36th Guards Rifle Division and 148th Tank Regiment:
   - Prepare for a counterattack in two directions: Kim State Farm – Ukrainskoe and Volchanskie Vyselki – Belyi Kolodez';
   - Ready the fire of the division's artillery regiment on the northern exits from Zemlianoi Iar and on the northern slopes of Hill 182.7 and 189.7;
3. Prepare the 27th Guards Tank Brigade for counterattacks in the Volchanskie Vyselki – Ukrainskoe and Pokalianoe – Belyi Kolodez' directions.[30]

The intensive strengthening of the 7th Guards Army's left flank continued for more than a month, but despite this, the desired result wasn't achieved. Indeed, the situation here was continuing to make the Soviet command uneasy. This is in fact understandable; so far the sector still hadn't been strengthened much in terms of an anti-tank defense – there was still too little artillery and the operational density of the rifle units was low. However, by the middle of June Shumilov's army had exhausted its own possibilities to reinforce the defense. At the same time, Vatutin had fallen ill and was bed-ridden, but despite this, he continued to wrestle with this problem. Having given thought to it once again, on the evening of 19 June he summoned his chief of staff Lieutenant General S.P. Ivanov and directed him to give his decision over the telephone to the 7th Guards Army's commander:

Ivanov: Comrade Nikolaev[31] believes that your measures to strengthen the defense are inadequate, and has ordered you to do the following:

1. It is necessary to strengthen and concentrate the 36th Guards Rifle Division's combat positions, and thereby create a high density of fire and a tougher defense on the forward

---

30 "Sbornik po obobshcheniiu opyta voiny", No. 11 (Moscow: Voenizdat, 1944), pp. 105-106.
31 Vatutin's code name for discussions over the telephone.

edge. For this, deploy one regiment of the 15th Guards Rifle Division in the front line [and give it its own sector]; decide for yourself the most suitable position for it. In place of the 15th Guards Rifle Division's Regiment, so as to fill the denuded space it leaves behind and not weaken the second echelon, replace it with a regiment of the 213th Rifle Division.

2. Make provisions for and in the most diligent manner work out the following measures: We are thinking about shifting the 10th Destroyer Brigade[32] from Kriuchenkin to the right flank of your army, and to move the 8th Destroyer Brigade[33] to your army's left flank. Form and fully man and equip these brigades with the calculation to make them continuously ready for battle. Direct the draft that we are giving to you into two regiments, and then form up the rest. You prepare the regrouping of the brigades, but you will conduct it only with our authorization according to the situation.
3. The 148th Mortar Regiment will arrive on your left flank no later than day's end on 21 June.
4. Conduct the regrouping of the rifle regiments and the strengthening of the 36th Guards Rifle Division's density by the morning of 21 June. That is all.

Stepnoi:[34] I request that you report to Comrade Nikolaev to approve the following: To have the entire 36th Guards Rifle Division in a single echelon, and move up a regiment of the 15th Guards Rifle Division out of the army's second echelon to replace the second-echelon regiment of the 36th Guards Rifle Division, without shifting the 213th Rifle Division's regiment. All the rest is understood. That is all.

S.P. Ivanov: As far as I understand you, you don't want the 15th Guards Rifle Division's regiment to move up to the forward edge. Is that the case?

Stepnoi: I now have the 36th Guards Rifle Division occupying a defense, with two regiments in the first echelon and one regiment in the second echelon. In order to thicken the combat positions and increase the density of fire, I ask to have the 36th Guards Rifle Division arrayed in a single echelon, and to replace the reserve regiment of the 36th Guards Rifle Division with a regiment from the 15th Guards Rifle Division's second echelon, without touching the 213th Rifle Division's units. Thereby, the 15th Guards Rifle Division will be left without a second echelon. That is all.

S.P. Ivanov: No, since Comrade Nikolaev doesn't agree. Given your option, in the event of the slightest breakthrough by the enemy of the 36th Guards Rifle Division's front, the commander of this division will no longer be in a position to battle the enemy; he'll have nothing to maneuver. To subordinate a regiment of a different division to him means to break up the 15th Guards Rifle Division, and to do this is senseless. It is better to have in view to assign a piece of ground to a single regiment of the 15th Guards Rifle Division, which will firmly defend it. Consider also that you have no right to weaken the boundary with your neighbor on the left and also not to spoil what Comrade Iur'ev[35] has approved. Now, given the option, if it is your firm opinion that to move up a regiment of the 213th Rifle Division is

---

32   This was the 31st Destroyer Anti-Tank Artillery Brigade from the Front commander-in-chief's mobile reserve; at this time it was still in the process of forming and was located in the town of Korocha.
33   The 30th Destroyer Anti-Tank Artillery Brigade; at the time it was positioned in the center of the 7th Guards Army's defense.
34   The code name for M.S. Shumilov.
35   The code name for G.K. Zhukov.

not reasonable, then it is possible there will be agreement. After you've looked into the decision you've received, in accordance with your received orders, report by 1200 20 July 1943.[36]

I especially cited this entire transcript of the phone call, which touches upon this matter. First, the document gives a plain image of the process of reaching decisions when building the lines of the Voronezh Front. Second, it demonstrates the meticulousness with which N.F. Vatutin arranged the Front's system of defense. Third, it shows on what high level the question about positioning a single regiment was resolved. To this I might add that when working in the TsAMO RF with the files of the 6th Guards Army, I came across documents in which N.F. Vatutin raised the issue of shifting even separate rifle battalions around within the Front's main line of resistance. Possibly, it isn't the job of a *front* commander-in-chief to concern himself with such questions, but that was the reality, and we must be aware of it, in order to understand and truly grasp the problems of the history of the Battle of Kursk. Finally, relying on the transcript, it is possible to picture the rigid framework that constricted the army commander (and not only him), even when taking a decision that triggered only a tiny change in the system of defense. A similar process was used as well when making decisions already in the course of the Kursk defensive operation, even though at that moment the army commanders (and corps commanders) were more free in their decision-making, because of the demands of the dynamics of combat.

In this connection, I want to appeal to scholars of the Battle of Kursk: before tossing accusations at Red Army commanders of all levels for blunders and mistakes, picture yourself in their place and try at first to understand the motivations that were governing them when reaching one or another decision. After all, even generals, who were endowed with high authority, were only the executors of the will of higher command and held within rigid constraints, both formal and real. It isn't even worth mentioning the control and pressure that N.F. Vatutin himself was under from Moscow, like the other *front* commanders-in-chief.

So now let's return to the events in the 7th Guards Army at the end of June 1943. After conducting the regrouping, by the start of the Battle of Kursk the 36th Guards Rifle Division was occupying a sector of defense that stretched from the mouth of the Nezhegol River to the Nezhegol railroad station. As a result, in the first trench line of the main belt of defense there were seven rifle battalions arrayed in a single line, while backing them on the left flank were two more rifle battalions (also formed into a single line). The 7th Guards Army hadn't yet received the 148th Mortar Regiment, but the decision to send it Lieutenant Colonel S.V. Shmanov's 31st Separate Anti-tank Artillery Brigade proved to be far-sighted. Already on the second day of the German offensive, the brigade was committed into the fighting in the 7th Guards Army's sector and played a key role in the struggle against the III Panzer Corps' assault grouping, which had broken through from Razumnoe to the Iastrebovo – "Solov'ev" collective farm area. As is known today, the enemy limited itself to conducting only a reconnaissance-in-force against the 36th Guards Rifle Division on 5 July, and didn't conduct any active combat operations in the division's sector, as the Soviet side expected. Thus, on the first day of the German offensive, the 7th Guards Army commander would be forced to send a significant amount of its assets in order to block the breakthrough of the lines of the neighboring 72nd Guards Rifle Division, which by noon on 5 July would be shattered into several pieces.

However, in war it is impossible to anticipate everything; G.K. Zhukov, N.F. Vatutin and M.S. Shumilov weren't clairvoyant in the given situation, despite their high-ranking posts, and didn't solve all the problems, but simply tried conscientiously to implement the order based not only on the needs of the subordinate troops, but also the Voronezh Front's capabilities, and they weren't

---

36 TsAMO RF, F. 203, op. 28423, d. 461, l. 91.

boundless. In the situation regarding the 72nd Guards Rifle Division, judging from the available information, the Front command to a significant degree was relying on the difficulty of the terrain (the river and its swampy basin) and the fortification of the 7th Guards Army's sector. Nevertheless, when planning the 7th Guards Army's defenses, a German attack against the boundary between the 24th and 25th Guards Rifle Corps was viewed on every level of command as being one of the most likely directions of attack. Therefore, despite the fact that the 72nd Guards Rifle Division was deployed behind a swampy area, it was given not the longest sector to defend – 15 kilometers of frontage, while the neighboring 78th Guards Rifle Division was given an even narrow sector of the front – 10 kilometers. In addition, corps commander General Safiulin ordered the preparation of a possible maneuver and a pivot of the facing of the 81st Guards Rifle Division's artillery assets (given the need) toward the sector of the left-flank 78th Guards Rifle Division (the neighbor of the 72nd Guards Rifle Division). The combat formations of the 78th Guards and 72nd Guards Rifle Divisions were arrayed in two echelons, but according to the amount of assets received, the 72nd Guards Rifle Division was standing in third place in the army. In addition to three artillery battalions (28 guns ranging from 76mm to 152mm), and the army's 101st Anti-tank Rifle Battalion (59 anti-tank rifles and 262 men), the division commander received operational control of 1/175th Guards Engineer Battalion (70 men), the army's 66th Separate Penal Company (234 men) and the army's 185th Blocking Detachment (199 men). Even so, it must be recognized that this was not a very substantial assistance in the struggle against enemy tanks. The figures are indisputable – the center of the 7th Guards Army's defense was the strongest. In Losev's and Skvortsov's rifle divisions, against which the III Panzer Corps of Army Detachment Kempf would strike on 5 July, the average density of artillery with a caliber ranging from 45mm to 152mm per kilometer of front was the lowest; in the 78th Guards Rifle Division, this indicator was only 9 guns per kilometer of front, and in the 72nd Guards Rifle Division, even less, just 8 guns per kilometer of front. However, this doesn't mean that the Soviet side here had committed an obvious blunder.

Considering that the 78th Guards Rifle Division would receive Army Detachment Kempf's main attack, it is worth dwelling in more detail on its combat formation. By the start of the Battle of Kursk, Skvortsov's division was the smallest of all the army's divisions. It had 8,346 men on its roster, including 849 officers, 2,317 non-commissioned officers and 5,180 soldiers.[37] It received the assignment to defend a sector with its forward edge running from a point 1 kilometer southwest of the corrective labor camp through Dal'nie Peski to Nizhnii Ol'shanets. The terrain here had a number of distinctive features that hindered the creation of a strong defense. Major General A.V. Skvortsov reported:

> The steep slopes on the western bank of the Northern Donets River and the system of ridges, covered by woods to a depth of 2-3 kilometers from the forward edge, as well as the villages that run along the western bank, gave the advantage to the enemy to position his troops in concealment, while the presence of improved roads running toward the frontlines and parallel to the front enabled the adversary to concentrate his strength and means efficiently for an offensive in any direction and to conduct the concealed maneuver with reserves opposite the division's front. The ground on the eastern bank was low, gradually rising to the east and deprived of natural cover. The open terrain was exposed to enemy surveillance to the entire depth of the defense and made it difficult to camouflage our positions or maneuver with reserves, and complicated the actions of counterattacking elements. The absence of commanding heights made it difficult to set up observation posts and prevented us from scanning the enemy's combat positions. The lack of paved and improved roads in the division's

---

37 TsAMO RF, F. 203, op. 2843, d. 426, pages without numbers.

sector and the distant location of the supply base in Volokonovka, 100 kilometers away, didn't allow the timely and complete supply of the troops with materiel for conducting battle.[38]

The division's sector of defense was constructed just like it was for the entire army; it consisted of main (three trench lines) and reserve (two trench lines) positions, the latter running along the Belgorod – Titovka railroad bed. The regiments were arranged in two echelons, with Major I.A. Khitsov's 228th Guards Rifle Regiment and Major D.S. Khorolenko's 225th Guards Rifle Regiment forward, and Major S.A. Arshinov's 223rd Guards Rifle Division in reserve. They were given unequal sectors. The right-flank 228th Guards Rifle Regiment (reinforced by two companies of the 4th Anti-tank Rifle Battalion and two batteries of a destroyer anti-tank artillery battalion – 8 45mm anti-tank guns) was deployed along a line stretching from a point 1 kilometer south of the corrective labor camp to Dorogobuzheno, a length of approximately 5 kilometers. The regiment's primary objective was to prevent an enemy breakthrough on its left flank to the villages of Razumnoe and Generalovka. Like his neighbor, I.A. Khitsov received one artillery battalion (2/158th Guards Artillery Regiment) as a reinforcement, which prepared its main firing positions 1 kilometer northeast of Razumnoe. This village was located behind the boundary of the 228th Guards and 225th Guards Rifle Regiments' adjacent flanks, and the strongpoint positioned here was supposed to carry out the role of an obstacle in the event of an enemy attempt to rupture the rifle regiments' joint defense.

The left-flank 225th Guards Rifle Regiment (with one company of the 4th Anti-tank Rifle Battalion) was defending a 7-kilometer sector running from (excl.) Dorogobuzheno to Nizhnii Ol'shanets. The attached 1/158th Guards Artillery Regiment, which was deployed together with the 3/158th Guards Artillery Regiment in the anti-tank strongpoint of Krutoi Log (behind the 225th Guards Rifle Division's reserve positions, was prepared to support it. In addition, to the left of Krutoi Log but still within the 225th Guards Rifle Regiment's sector, the 3/671st Artillery Regiment of the 213th Rifle Division, which had been transferred to the 78th Guards Rifle Division's commander as a personal reserve, was dug into positions.

The 223rd Guards Rifle Regiment (minus one battalion) was defending the Generalovka – Krutoi Log – Hill 164.7 sector. It received the assignment to hold its line along the Razumnaia River, and in the event of an enemy breakthrough of the division's first echelon, it was to counter it and destroy it with a counterattack together with the division's combined-arms reserve (1/223rd Guards Rifle Division and a battery of the 80th Separate Destroyer Anti-tank Artillery Battalion).

Already when allocating the sectors, and then when arranging the combat positions of the 225th Guards Rifle Regiments, two important details factored in reducing the resilience of its line even relative to that of its right-hand neighbor. First, its forward battalions were holding a line that extended for 3.5 kilometers, while those of the 228th Guards Rifle Regiment were holding a sector that extended for just 2 to 2.5 kilometers. Second, although the battalions of both rifle regiments had been echeloned in depth, in the 228th Guards Rifle Regiment the 3rd Battalion was positioned compactly in a reserve position behind the boundary between the two forward battalions, while the 3rd Battalion/225th Guards Rifle Regiment had been dispersed by company. For example, the 7th Rifle Company was defending the Razumnoe double-track section, which was located in a secondary position, while the 8th and 9th Rifle Companies were somewhat to the east, in the Krutoi Log anti-tank strongpoint. In certain specialized publications that came out during the Soviet era, attention is also given to the low density of strength on the left wing of the 78th Guards Rifle Division. For example, the book *Taktika v boevykh primerakh:Diviziia* [*Tactics*

---

38 TsAMO RF, F. 1225, op. 1, d. 11, l. 108.

in combat examples: Division], written under the general editorship of General of the Army A.I. Radzievsky, observes;

> The nature of the terrain didn't allow the enemy to launch the main attack along the Razumnaia River … the presence of villages within the sector of this regiment [the 228th Guards Rifle Regiment – author] and on its forward edge that had been prepared for defense and the unsuitable ground for the actions of attacking troops enabled the creation of a strong defense even with fewer troops. Because of this it would have been more sensible to organize significant densities of guns on the division's left flank.[39]

Theoretically, it would have been more logical to use a substantial portion of the guns that had been attached to the 228th Guards Rifle Division to reinforce instead the 225th Guards Rifle Regiment. Even without these assets, the conditions for creating an impenetrable line were almost ideal: the boundary between the two regiments ran along the swampy basin of the Razumnaia River; the village of Razumnoe itself had been converted into an anti-tank strongpoint; two villages extended in a line along the forward edge (which itself ran for not more than 5 kilometers); and the rest of the ground was in part swampy, in part planted with orchards. However, when constructing the line of the 228th Guards Rifle Regiment, theoretical considerations weren't first and foremost for the division commander General Skvortsov. Judging from available documents, the allocation of the regiment's sectors (which means the issuance of preliminary orders for this) was checked not only by the division commander and corps commander (as was due under regulations), but also personally by M.S. Shumilov and N.F. Vatutin. The reason for such fixed attention was the special system of arranging the Voronezh Front's defenses ("Vatutin's Plan") to split von Manstein's assault groupings and force them to advance in diverging directions. The 228th Guards Rifle Regiment was intentionally strengthened with some excess of forces and means (in view of the available strength), in order to guarantee (as far as this was possible) the security of the 81st Guards Rifle Division's left flank, which together with the 375th Rifle Division was occupying a special place in the system of the main line of resistance. From this follows the narrow sector given to the 228th Guards Rifle Regiment, the greater amount of attached artillery relative to its neighbor, the preparation to shift the fire of the 2/290th Mortar Regiment from the 81st Guards Rifle Division's sector to the sector of the 228th Guards Rifle Regiment, and so forth.

In this connection there is an appropriate question: "Did the Front command get carried away with reinforcing the 81st Guards Rifle Division, and when creating the impenetrable fortress in the Staryi Gorod area, did it overlook weaknesses in other, albeit less significant sectors?" In reality, if N.F. Vatutin and M.S Shumilov understood that the situation on the left flank of the 78th Guards Rifle Regiment was fraught with serious consequences, then why didn't they react as happened, for example, in the 6th Guards Army? Here, the regiments of all the divisions that were holding the main belt of defenses were arranged into a single line, even though there was insufficient strength in the 67th Guards and 52nd Guards Rifle Divisions to cover certain dangerous sectors, and thus with the agreement of the Front's Military Council, I.M. Chistiakov gave their commanders operational control over several artillery battalions (like in the 7th Guards Army also) from second-echelon divisions (the 90th Guards and 51st Guards Rifle Divisions), plus two rifle battalions each. In the 7th Guards Army, only the 36th Guards Rifle Division was reinforced in a similar manner at the expense of the 15th Guards Rifle Division. The impression forms that

---

39 *Taktika v boevykh primerakh: Diviziia* [*Tactics in combat examples: Division*] (Moscow: Voenizdat, 1976), p. 202.

the Front command either underestimated the danger in the center of the 7th Guards Army's defenses, or did this intentionally.

Several scholars express the opinion that N.F. Vatutin, understanding that the Germans' initial attack would be very powerful and that a penetration of the forward edge of his Front was unavoidable, deliberately left weakly protected sectors on the probable directions of the German main attack in the lines of each army of the first echelon (at least in two of them). It was in these sectors that the defense would first begin to crack, and the enemy would persistently seek to commit fresh forces into these breaches, but discover the route of advance to be a dead-end, since immediately after creating this breach, a deadfall set by the Soviet forces was waiting for them – difficult terrain filled with a multitude of artificial "surprises" or a powerful flanking counterattack (or both taken together). However, this plan supposedly didn't work out fully.

As an example one can cite the example of the 6th Guards Army's 52nd Guards Rifle Division.[40] Despite the fact that it was covering the primary direction for tanks – the Belgorod – Oboian' highway – its defense was unable to withstand the powerful assault already on 5 July, and after 17 hours of fighting the II SS Panzer Corps overran it.

At first glance, there was a very similar situation with the 78th Guards Rifle Division as well. In reality, during the war years when conducting major operations there were cases when the Soviet side used various types of ruses and trickery in order to confuse the enemy: diversionary attacks, feigned crossings of rivers at places where there was no intention to commit the main forces, etc. A number of facts support this inference with respect to the plans to use such methods when defending the Kursk salient as well. The Voronezh Front command viewed such alternatives when discussing the future operation. However, thus far all the transcripts of the discussions of N.F. Vatutin with the General Staff and the *Stavka* of the Supreme High Command have not been de-classified, so it is premature to come to any final conclusions. Today, however, relying on documents that are available to scholars, one can say with confidence that so far there is no indisputable evidence that such a plan ever existed and was put into practice. In addition, the nervous atmosphere in the Red Army General Staff and on the *fronts* in June 1943, because the painful memories of the failure in Ukraine in February – March 1943 (just like the Germans had after Stalingrad) were still fresh, speaks against this hypothesis. Of course, it is impossible to put these catastrophes in the same category, but they were comparable in their psychological effect. However, Stalingrad didn't teach Hitler anything and only prompted him to take a new gamble at Kursk. The Soviet side by this time had more lost battles and defeats on its ledger, so when preparing for the summer campaign of 1943, the decision-making was more prudent, for example, despite the enormous reserves that had been accumulated – it was better to wait and go over to a pre-meditated defense. N.F. Vatutin better than anyone else knew the weaknesses of his Front's forces, the low level of the soldiers' training, the poor preparation of the command staff up to the corps level inclusively, the problems with mobility, etc. In this situation he had no wish to trifle with the Nazis, and Moscow was strictly demanding one thing – to create a strong defense out of the available forces and means, which would guarantee against the setbacks and failures of 1942. Thus he counted first of all on a powerful defensive belt on the main line of resistance and counterattacks in its depth. As for the miscalculations that became apparent already in the course of the fighting, no one is insured against them, and the General of the Army at that moment had no strength for all sorts of plans.

By the start of the Battle of Kursk, the Voronezh Front command not without justification believed that the line of the 81st Guards Rifle Division had been thoroughly fortified. Thus, the 73rd Guards Rifle Division that was located in the second echelon was aimed at restoring the

---

40 Lopukhovsky, L., *Prokhorovka bez grifa sekretnosti* [*Prokhorovka without the seal of secrecy*] (Moscow: Iauza/Eksmo, 2012), p. 156.

situation (in the event of a breakthrough) and at ensuring the 78th Guards Rifle Division could hold its sector. The decision to regroup Kozak's division to the left flank of the 25th Guards Rifle Corps (in the second echelon behind the 78th Guards Rifle Division), to the Hill 205.5 – Hill 191.8 – "Solov'ev" collective farm – "Batratskaia Dacha" State Farm – Hill 210.4 line by the end of 2 July 1943 testifies to this. By 2300 the division had assembled in the woods 4 kilometers east of Iastrebovo without its artillery regiment and had begun to move into the indicated line. However, on 3 July an order arrived from the 25th Guards Rifle Corps: "Be ready to march to the northeast", which is to say, closer to the positions of the 78th Guards Rifle Division's reserve regiment.[41] Accordingly, at the final moment the Soviet side had fully figured out the enemy's intention and had created the greatest density of forces and means opposite the Army Detachment Kempf's main point of attack. The 81st Guards Rifle Division had the maximally possible quantity of reinforcing units, and a density of artillery per kilometer of front greater than anywhere else along the army's front (not to mention the elaborate and strong fortifications of its line), while an entire rifle division had deployed behind the 78th Guards Rifle Division! After this it is hard to agree with authors of works on the Battle of Kursk, even with such authorities as Marshal of the Soviet Union K.K. Rokossovsky,[42] who accuse N.F. Vatutin of miscalculations and mistakes that he supposedly made when readying his system of defense and positioning his Front's forces before the start of the battle.

As is known, the basis for a successful, lengthy defense is the presence of full-value reserves, especially artillery and mobile (armored and mechanized) reserves, under the control of a formation or army commander. Thanks to them, the defending rifle units have the possibility to eliminate the enemy's advantage on the directions where he launches his strongest attacks. While preparing for the Battle of Kursk, for the first time in the war, operational mobile reserves and reserves of anti-tank guns began to be formed not only in armies and corps, but they were also transferred to divisions and even rifle regiments. In the 7th Guards Army, in comparison with its right-hand neighbor (the 6th Guards Army), these reserves were rather modest. Nevertheless, the divisions that were holding its main defensive belt also received supplementary artillery, mortar and even tank regiments.

By the start of the Battle of Kursk, Shumilov's army (with the inclusion of the rifle divisions' artillery regiments) had a total of 158 howitzers and howitzer-cannons, including 12 122mm howitzers, 52 152mm howitzer-cannons (of the 161st Guards, 265th Guards and 109th Guards Cannon Artillery Regiments), 12 122mm self-propelled artillery guns (of the 1438th Self-propelled Artillery Regiment) and 12 152mm self-propelled artillery guns (of the 1529th Heavy Self-propelled Artillery Regiment). Only the 6th Guards Army had a larger number of artillery pieces in the Voronezh Front; however, for holding a 53-kilometer sector of the front, even this proved insufficient. Replenishments weren't expected, so the M.S. Shumilov, based upon a tactical assessment of the terrain and the approximate strength of the enemy, decided to use his reserves for reinforcing primarily the right flank, because here was located the Mikhailovka bridgehead and the boundary with the 6th Guards Army. He concentrated the bulk of his artillery reserves – two cannon artillery regiments (34 152mm howitzer-cannons) and the army's heavy mortar regiment (36 120mm mortars) in the 81st Guards Rifle Division's sector. The third cannon artillery regiment was divided between two other divisions; two of its battalions (12 152mm howitzer-cannons) went to the 36th Guards Rifle Division on the left flank, and the third – to the 72nd Guards Rifle Division.

---

41 TsAMO RF, F. 73 gv. sd, op. 1, d. 33, l. 36.
42 Rokossovsky, K.K., *Soldatskii dolg* [*Soldier's duty*] (Moscow: Veche, 2013), p. 251.

In addition, as already mentioned above, in order to increase the density of the artillery fire in the main defensive belt, Shumilov was forced to subordinate to the commanders of the first-echelon divisions from two battalions up to an artillery regiment from the second-echelon divisions. Moreover, for the struggle against the heavy German Tiger tanks, which the Front's troops had already encountered during the February and March 1943 fighting around Khar'kov, with the permission of the Front's Military Council he directed that 12 122mm howitzers be positioned in the sector of the 72nd Guards Rifle Division and the preparation of firing positions for 152mm cannon-howitzers to fire over open sights. I will remind the reader that at this time, howitzers were regarded as a precious weapon, and there was a categorical ban against their use directly on the forward edge. In the event that this order was violated and a howitzer was lost, its commander would be turned over for trial before a military tribunal. Only at a critical moment of the Battle of Kursk, on 9 July 1943 would the leadership of the Voronezh Front be compelled to authorize the deployment of the howitzer regiments for pointblank firing in the sector of the 6th Guards Army as well. Thus, by the start of the fighting the first-echelon divisions of the 7th Guards Army had the following units of reinforcement:

> *81st Guards Rifle Division* – 161st, 265th Cannon Artillery Regiments, 153rd Guards Artillery Regiment (from the 73rd Guards Rifle Division), 290th Mortar Regiment, 114th Guards Destroyer Anti-tank Artillery Regiment, the 97th Guards and 315th Guards Mortar Regiments (of Katiusha rocket launchers), the 262nd Separate Tank Regiment, and the 2nd Anti-tank Rifle Battalion;
> *78th Guards Rifle Division* – 3/671st Artillery Regiment (from the 213th Rifle Division) and the 4th Anti-tank Rifle Battalion;
> *72nd Guards Rifle Division* – 3/109th Guards Cannon Artillery Regiment; 1 and 2/671st Artillery Regiment (from the 213th Rifle Division) and the 1st Anti-tank Rifle Battalion;
> *36th Guards Rifle Division* – 43rd Guards Artillery Regiment (from the 15th Guards Rifle Division), 1 and 2/109th Guards Cannon Artillery Regiment, 115th Guards Destroyer Anti-tank Artillery Regiment, 5th and 6th Anti-tank Rifle Battalions, the 148th Separate Tank Regiment and the 34th Separate Armored Train Battalion

In the event that the calculations proved not quite accurate and the enemy launched his main attack not where it was expected or might break through in a less protected sector, the 7th Guards Army's artillery headquarters in its fire plan envisioned a maneuver and shift of the facing of the attached cannon and mortar units, as well as its own battalions of artillery regiments, to a neighbor's sector. For example:

> a. It was planned to pivot the facing of the 161st Guards Cannon Artillery Regiment to the north (to 90 degrees) toward the sector of its neighbor on the right (the 6th Guards Army's 375th Rifle Division), to 180 degrees in the event of a breakthrough of the 78th Guards Rifle Division's lines, or a maneuver in order to support the 73rd Guards Rifle Division whenever it launched a counterattack toward Sabynino;
> b. The 265th Guards Cannon Artillery Regiment had a contingency plan to pivot its facing by 90 degrees to the south toward the sector of the 78th Guards Rifle Division;
> c. The 2/290th Mortar Regiment had a contingency plan to pivot its facing by 90 degrees to the south toward the sector of the 78th Guards Rifle Division, or to move to the area of Nizhnii Ol'shanets;
> d. The 1st and 2nd Battalions of the 109th Guards Cannon Artillery Regiment had a contingency plan to pivot their facing by 90 degrees to the south or make a maneuver to support its neighbor on the left (the 57th Army's 19th Rifle Division);

e. The 97th Guards Mortar Regiment was to be ready to maneuver along the entire front in order to support all of the frontline divisions.

In Shumilov's anti-tank reserve were the 30th Destroyer Anti-tank Artillery Brigade, the 1669th Destroyer Anti-tank Artillery Regiment and the 1670th Destroyer Anti-tank Artillery Regiment. The 30th Anti-tank Artillery Brigade had two of its regiments (the third had no guns) deployed along the Starikovo, Kupino, Krasnaia Poliana line. The 1669th Anti-tank Artillery Regiment had firing positions in the area of Hill 133.6, the Arbuzovskii double-track section, and on the outskirts of Volchanskie Vyselki (two batteries were deployed on the southern outskirts of Volchansk). The 1670th Destroyer Anti-tank Artillery Regiment had only 4 serviceable anti-tank guns and was not combat-capable.

The anti-tank brigade was located in the center of the second army-level belt, but in the case of an enemy breakthrough by tanks on the flanks, it was to be ready to move to threatened sectors. For this purpose, firing positions had been prepared on tank-vulnerable directions – gun emplacements, slit trenches for the personnel, and shell storage excavations – and automobile ramps set up. Analogous work was done in the 1669th Anti-tank Artillery Regiment as well, which was planned to be used both for active operations on the left flank (including providing support for the adjacent 57th Army), and in the army's center. In addition, N.F. Vatutin when working out the plan for using his own mobile anti-tank reserves anticipated their maneuver from Korocha (the assembly area prior to the battle) to the right flank and center of Shumilov's army.

Back in May, the commanders of all the artillery regiments together with the subordinate commanders reconnoitered the routes of movement for a maneuver, and ordered the preparation of secondary firing positions and observation posts for the pivot of the facing toward adjacent sectors. Unfortunately, in the first two days of the operation the plans for switching the fire, especially of the artillery forces of the 81st Guards Rifle Division to the 78th Guards Rifle Division's sector, didn't pan out, with the exception of 2/290th Mortar Regiment. The artillery regiments and the Katiusha rocket-launcher regiments had been deployed too remotely from the front of the 78th Guards Rifle Division and turned out to be unable to place effective fire on the enemy's bridges and bridgeheads. Therefore, for example, the 25th Guards Rifle Corps' command already on the morning of 5 July was compelled to make a decision about shifting the guns of a number of regiments out of the 81st Guards Rifle Division's sector to the corps' left flank.

Since boundaries are always the most vulnerable point in the defense of formations and armies, back in April M.S. Shumilov before planning the system of covering the boundaries had ordered that the artillery commanders of the divisions and corps personally conduct a reconnaissance to determine the force and means necessary to protect them, and also to select personally the combat positions for their subordinate units. In addition, the army commander wanted direct telephone communications to be established between all the division commanders. A large amount of work was done in order to secure the army's boundaries with artillery fire. For this purpose the 7th Guards Army's artillery headquarters established telephone and radio contact with the command of both the Southwestern Front's 57th Army and with the 93rd Cannon Artillery Regiment of the 6th Guards Army's 27th Heavy Cannon Artillery Brigade (which were to secure the boundary from the direction of the 6th Guards Army); rolled out a direct telephone line between the 93rd Cannon Artillery Regiment and the 81st Guards Rifle Division's 161st Guards Cannon Artillery Regiment; and set up joint observation posts. The 36th Guards Rifle Division was sharing observation posts with the 57th Army's 19th Rifle Division.

The 7th Guards Army's Military Council determined the main task for the armored and mechanized forces in the forthcoming operation with Order No. 00143 from 1 April 1943. It demanded that they be used only "as a mobile reserve for launching counterattacks against enemy penetrations".[43] The employment of the mobile reserves was planned with due regard for G.K. Zhukov's instructions to strengthen the flanks. All of the self-propelled artillery regiments, tank regiments and tank brigades available in the army were included in it, with the exception of the 262nd Heavy Tank Regiment and the 148th Separate Tank Regiment; although they were given to the frontline divisions in order to reinforce them, they continued to be counted as part of the army commander's reserve. M.S. Shumilov nominally split all of the tank units and formations into two groups (there was no formal order for this), attached a self-propelled artillery regiment to each group, and directed each of the groups to cover the army's flanks. Five most probable directions of counterattacks were determined for each of the mobile groups.

The right-flank group, which consisted of two tank regiments and a composite self-propelled artillery regiment (a total of 69 tanks and 21 self-propelled guns) was assembled in the Blizhniaia Igumenka – Miasoedovo – Postnikov area. Lieutenant Colonel A.A. Verba's 167th Separate Tank Regiment and the 1438th Self-propelled Artillery Regiment[44] were equipping two anti-tank areas, the first in the village of Postnikov (1st Tank Company of T-34 tanks, a company of submachine gunners and the 1438th Self-propelled Artillery Regiment), and the second in the Miasoedovo area (the 3rd Tank Company and the 167th Separate Tank Regiment's anti-tank rifle company). Lieutenant Colonel A.A. Verba was appointed as the senior chief of both anti-tank strongpoints. The tankers and self-propelled artillery gunners had the assignment to destroy German panzers that were approaching Postnikov and Miasoedovo, and given the need, to operate jointly with the 73rd Guards Rifle Division in the army's second echelon. Colonel I.I. Aizenberg's 262nd Heavy Tank Regiment (equipped with KV tanks) was transferred to the 81st Guards Rifle Division's reserve.

The left-flank group – two tank brigades, a tank regiment and a heavy self-propelled artillery regiment (154 tanks[45] and 12 self-propelled guns) – was located in the Voznesenovka – Bochkovo area. Colonel M.V. Nevzhinsky's 27th Guards Tank Brigade was occupying defensive positions in the Voznesenovka anti-tank area and had a supplementary task to be ready both independently and jointly with the 213th Rifle Division and 1529th Heavy Self-propelled Artillery Regiment to operate against enemy panzer wedges that were breaking into the depth of the 24th Guards Rifle Corps' lines. Colonel I.A. Taranov's 201st Separate Tank Brigade was positioned in the Viaz'min – (excl.) brick factory anti-tank strongpoint on the northern outskirts of Bochkovo and in the forested area 1 km outside of Chainovka, ready to launch short counterattacks both independently and in conjunction with the 15th Guards Rifle Division and the 1529th Heavy Self-propelled Artillery Regiment. The latter was the last of the armored and mechanized units to arrive in the army and was assembled in the woods 1.5 kilometers southeast of the Krasnianskii State Farm. At the beginning of June its personnel began to set up main firing positions in the area of Hills 167, 171.8 and 184.4, and reserve firing positions southeast of the Stalin State Farm. During the active operations of the army's armored and mechanized forces, the regiment was ready to support both tank brigades with its fire. Colonel A.M. Lifits' 148th Separate Tank Regiment was positioned in the Volchanskii Khutor anti-tank region before the beginning of June, and then was passed to the subordination of the 36th Guards Rifle Division's commander.

The armored fighting vehicles were split unequally between the two tank groups in order to maintain the balance of the firepower on the flanks and to facilitate maneuver. The 7th Guards Army's command believed both flanks to be vulnerable to enemy tanks, but the likelihood that the Germans would launch the main attack against the right flank was considered greater. Therefore

---

43 TsAMO RF, F. 203, op. 2851, d. 25, l. 54.
44 This regiment's files in the TsAMO RF are very sparse, so I had no success in identifying the commander of it at this time.
45 Including one KV-1 tank in the 1529th Heavy Self-propelled Artillery Regiment.

the 81st Guards Rifle Division received considerably more artillery than the 36th Guards Rifle Division, but given a need, it was possible to shift Nevzhinsky's and Taranov's tank brigades and Lifits' tank regiment on the fly to the right flank (whereas the heavy cannon and mortar regiments couldn't move as quickly). In addition, as already mentioned, the plan of action for the Front's mobile reserves included the idea of maneuvering the 2nd Guards "Tatsinskaia" Tank Corps out of the Korocha area to the right flank or center of the 7th Guards Army.

In the spring, alongside the setting up of combat positions, the elaboration of plans and the training of arriving replacements, the repair of all the worn-out tanks began in all the tank regiments and brigades. However, this work went slowly. Lieutenant Colonel Pavlov, the assistant commander of the army's armored and mechanized forces recalled:

> The planning of the repair work under the conditions facing the army was exceptionally complicated by the lack of spare parts, which arrived only from the Front's stockpiles or were scrounged in places. The repair means were used primarily for the brigades that were brought up to the repair station. Such an organization of work leads to lengthy repairs, but it was prompted by the lack of recovery and evacuation vehicles.[46]

The army acutely needed repair capabilities and evacuation means; up until the end of June, it had only three repair units: one army-level recovery company (AEC No. 119), one army-level collection point for broken-down machines (119th SPAM), and one mobile repair base (PBR No. 62). By TO&E, all these units were allotted limited means for recovering disabled tanks, but they weren't even equipped to the authorized level with tractors and prime movers. For example, in the army's repair units, there were only a total of 15 authorized towing vehicles. The same problems existed in the repair elements of the units and formations. The 1438th Self-propelled Artillery Regiment and the 1529th Heavy Self-propelled Artillery Regiment each had only two tractors; the other units got by however they could. I will remind the reader that an order existed that banned even using knocked-out tanks as source of parts to get other tanks up and running. Thus, the command of regiments and brigades was compelled to use only derelict tanks, abandoned on the battlefield, in the role of towing vehicles, but first they had to be found and repaired. For example, in the 201st Tank Brigade with the authorization of the command, only three prime movers were prepared to serve 50 combat machines, two on the basis of turretless Mark III tanks and one combat Mark III, while the 27th Guards Tank Brigade and 148th Separate Tank Regiment had only one prime mover each, built on the basis of a repaired T-34. Only just before the start of the fighting, the 78th Mobile Tank Repair Base arrived from the 4th Field Tank Repair Factory. The fact that the troops of Shumilov's army were unable to recover someone else's tanks even behind their own lines speaks to the difficult situation with recovery and evacuation vehicles. Therefore between 10 and 14 May, the repair company of the 96th Separate Tank Brigade, which was occupying a defense in the 6th Guards Army's second echelon (in the Dal'niaia Igumenka – Postnikov area), searched for tanks that had been abandoned in Staryi Gorod by Soviet units after the winter battles, and evacuated two T-34 tanks back to its own collection point for disabled machines, which were then repaired and returned to service in the summer fighting.[47]

Even so, by the start of the battle the army's tank forces were in a high state of readiness. On 4 July 1943, only 14 combat machines of the total of 224 that were counted on the lists were under repair: 2 in the 27th Guards Tank Brigade (1 a surplus tank), 2 in the 201st Separate Tank Brigade, 2 in the 262nd Heavy Tank Regiment, 1 in the 148th Separate Tank Regiment, and 7 in the 167th

---

46 TsAMO RF, F. 203, op. 2851, d. 25, l. 60 obr.
47 TsAMO RF, F. 96tbr, op. 3191, d. 3, l. 7obr.

Separate Tank Regiment (all surplus). For more detail on the condition of the 7th Guards Army's armored and mechanized forces as of 2000 on 4 July 1943, see Table 3.

Table 3 Condition of the materiel of the 7th Guards Army's armored forces at 2000 4 July 1943[48]

a. Combat units

Unit	Personnel		Tanks						Self-propelled Guns						Tow
	Table	By roster					Under repair						Under repair		
			Type	Table #	On list	In service	Maintenance/ light overhaul	Major overhaul	Type	Table #	On List	In service	Maintenance/ Light overhaul	Major overhaul	T-34/Mk III
27 GTB	1146	1227	T-70		4	4									1/-
			T-34		50	48	–/2								
			Total	53	54	52									
201 STB	1172		Mk II		18	16[1]	2/–								–/3
			Mk III		31	31									
			T-34		3	3									
			Total	46	52	50									
148 STR	524	543	T-60		1	1									1/–
			T-70		13	13									
			T-34		33	32	–/1								
			Total	39	47	46									
167 STR	524	527	T-60		2		2/–[2]								
			T-70		11	7	4/–								
			T-34		33	32	1/–								
			Total	39	46	39									
262 HTR	251	?	KV-1	21	24	22[3]	1[4]	1							
1438 SPR	272	265							SU–76	12	12	12			
									SU–122	9	9	5	–/4		
1529 HSPR	272	274	KV-1	1	1	1			SU–152	12	12	12[5]			
Total				199	224	210	14	1		33	33	29	4		2/3

b. Repair services

Unit	Establishment number of personnel	Mobile repair shops "A" and "B"	Prime movers	
			ChTZ-60, ChTZ-65	STZ-NATI
Airfield Service Co. 119[6]	51	–	10	2
Field Weapon and Vehicle Workshop 119	29	–	3	–
Mobile Repair Base 62	69	5	–	–
Mobile Repair Base 78	72	7	–	–
Total:	141	12	13	2

---

48 TsAMO RF, f. 341, op. 5312, d. 246, l. b/n

Notes
1 Operational summary for 1500 4 July 1943
2 4 T-70 and 2 T-60 were considered unfit for combat due to the absence of shatterproof glass for the driver-mechanic's vision port.
3 By 5 July 1943 one KV tank was on assignment in the village of Novoselovka.
4 In the village of Batratskaia Dacha.
5 1 SU-152 on the morning of 5 July 1943 was at a tactical training exercise in the area of the railroad at Rzhava Station.
6 The 7th Guards Army's armored repair services were located at the Krasnianskii State Farm and in the villages of Bol'she-Troitskoe and Titovka.

As is known, even the most brilliant plan is worth nothing as long as it hasn't been implemented, and thus for an objective assessment of the degree of readiness of the 7th Guards Army's sector to repulse Army Detachment Kempf's attack, it is important to understand how much of the Soviet command's plan remained on paper and accordingly how much the troops had done by the beginning of July. In the order of the 7th Guards Army's Military Council on 4 April 1943, one of the main tasks assigned to the troops was the immediate initiation of systematic work to fortify the positions, not only in the first echelon, but also the second. The order emphasized:

> As the first order of business, assign to the works the digging and camouflaging of main and reserve standard entrenchments for all the weapons; the construction of anti-tank obstacles (especially in the system of anti-tank regions); the exploitation of natural obstacles like flooded and swampy areas; and the construction of barricades in built-up areas, and felled trees entanglements and abatis in wooded areas.
> Make widespread use of the available reserve of mines on tank-vulnerable directions.
> Also as the first order of business, construct observation posts, command posts and earth-and-timber bunkers on the most important directions, and dig communication trenches on exposed terrain. Adapt built-up areas for a defense and mine the places of possible enemy river crossings.
> I forbid the digging of solitary rifle pits that have no connection between themselves.
> As the second order of business: continue to strengthen and improve the works of the first order of business, develop a system of communication trenches, construct machine-gun bunkers and shelters, and improve the camouflage everywhere. Over the entire period, keep the roads in a trafficable condition.[49]

Prior to this moment, the Red Army had never before erected such a powerful zone of field defenses. Usually, the men of the combat units and the organic combat engineers had the time to prepare a defensive line for fighting. Not infrequently, the local population was also called upon to contribute labor to the work. Now, when the need arose to move hundreds of thousands of cubic meters of soil over a relatively short period of time, while simultaneously doing the work to mine large areas, repair bridges and fashion logs for firing positions, command posts and observation posts, a different organization was necessary. Even a cursory assessment of the plan to build the fortifications and artificial obstacles made it clear that such an ambitious plan would require a colossal expenditure of manual labor and an enormous quantity of tools: pickaxes, axes, handbarrows, etc. For the army this was really a major problem, since the count of just the shovels necessary for the work reached the tens of thousands. Thus it was decided to call upon all of the army's construction personnel to build the defensive works, and to take steps to acquire tools from the Front's stockpiles and to make them on the spot. The provisioning of the Voronezh Front's armies with hand tools and obstacles is given in Table 4 for both 1 April 1943 and by the start of the Battle of Kursk:

---

49 TsAMO RF, F. 262ttp, op. 32956, d. 2, l. 64.

Table 4 The Voronezh Front's armies' supply with obstacles and tools as of 1 April and 5 July 1943[50]

Items	As of 1 April 1943						
	6 Gds Army	7 Gds Army	38 Army	40 Army	69 Army	1 Tank Army	Total
AP mines	15135	5398	7400	5093	50	7992	41068
AT mines	–	3389	3430	2981	2206	9854	21590
Artillery shells	1933	–	–	–	–	–	1933
Explosives (metric tons)	–	8	22	6	–	3	39
Rolls of barbed wire	58	2	45	23	11	–	139
Mine detectors	37	440	136	299	25	180	1117
Clippers for barbed wire	–	726	167	950	162	860	2865
Spades	–	18805	10695	12454	750	15112	57816
Shovels	4681	12543	4378	6410	1163	9045	38221
Axes	6180	7443	3571	3648	635	4910	26387
Pickaxes	1224	2618	1830	1189	347	1477	8685
Crowbars	703	2107	1822	1604	141	1958	8340
Saws	635	2158	1093	969	88	1572	6515
	Issued between 1 April and 5 July 1943						
AP mines	97227	73110	54080	78837	30502	1496	335212
AT mines	86520	91039	76947	84244	27033	2977	368760
Artillery shells	14531	10102	15957	9112	10781	–	60483
Explosives (metric tons)	51	27.1	75	36	36	9	234.1
Rolls of barbed wire	380	357	435	342	53	9	1576
Mine detectors	381	85	152	55	100	140	913
Clippers for barbed wire	1661	37	57	446	510	485	3196
Spades	36587	25610	22222	25850	29538	68	139875
Shovels	9099	2700	6253	7500	6868	533	32953
Axes	1642	1477	2429	2350	2900	750	11548
Pickaxes	2656	2200	2488	1200	1962	365	1067
Crowbars	499	557	400	460	460	108	2484
Saws	767	950	405	770	1008	413	4313
	As of 5 July 1943						
AP mines	112362	78508	61480	83930	30552	9448	376280
AT mines	86520	94428	80377	87225	29239	12561	390350
Artillery shells	16464	10102	15957	9112	10781	-	62416
Explosives (metric tons)	51	35.1	97	42	36	12	273.1
Rolls of barbed wire	438	359	480	365	64	9	1715
Mine detectors	418	525	288	354	125	320	2030
Clippers for barbed wire	1661	763	224	1395	672	1345	6061
Spades	36587	44415	32917	38304	30288	15180	19791
Shovels	13780	15243	10631	13910	8031	9579	71174
Axes	7822	8920	6000	5996	3535	5660	37935
Pickaxes	3880	4818	4318	2389	2309	1841	19555
Crowbars	1202	2664	2222	2069	601	2066	10824
Saws	1402	3108	1498	1739	1096	1985	10828

---

50 TsAMO RF, f. 203, op. 2845, d. 227, l. 10

The presence of the river in front of the 7th Guards Army's frontline divisions and especially the hundreds of meters of the river basin overgrown with shrubs and sedge grass substantially eased the work to set up the positions, even though the presence in the direct proximity of the enemy made the work constantly known to the enemy. If the Germans noticed even a small cluster of soldiers or identified field works, they automatically reacted with machine-gun fire at them, or struck them with a mortar or artillery barrage. Thus, in order to keep the system of fortifications and obstacles concealed and to protect the personnel, the 7th Guards Army command issued an order back in March 1943 for all the work on the fortifications to be done between 2200 and 0600. In the daylight hours, the troops were to rest, go through training, or in the extreme case, do work that was out of the enemy's line of sight (work on the interiors of bunkers and dugouts, build hand tools, etc.).

In connection with this I want to dwell on a matter that I consider important and share my point of view, relying on the information I've collected in the archives. More than once I've happened to hear from scholars, museum staff and foreign historians the assertion that when building the defenses at Kursk, the Red Army actively used not only the troops of the acting army and the local population, but also prisoners of war and even convicts. This is confirmed, for example, by the recollections of the former commander of the Heavy Panzer Battalion 503 Captain *Graf Kageneck*. As evidence, I will offer the fact that supposedly in order to build the fortifications of the armies' rear belt of defenses (or the first Front-level belt of defenses) on the Central Front, two prisoner camps were specially created and it was these prisoners, not the civilian population of the Kursk region, who dug the trenches, communication trenches and bunkers. The Germans maintain that in the captured trenches of Soviet units, they reportedly found the letters of German soldiers, and from this they drew the conclusion that they had been dug by prisoners of war. In fact, at that time the Soviet Union did make widespread use of forced labor, both by convicts and prisoners of war, including when ensuring the operation of military industries and when building military sites. Thus, it is possible that such was the case here. However, I've managed to spend a long time working in various archives regarding the Battle of Kursk, and so far I've never come across any documents that would directly or even indirectly give any confirmation of this. On the contrary, revealed sources testify that the Soviet command at the army and Front level demanded not to use prisoners of war to build the army-level belts of defenses, in particular those of the Voronezh Front, and even not to use them as an auxiliary labor force, which was widely practiced in the Wehrmacht (the *Hiwi*). As an example, I will give an excerpt from an order issued by the commander of the 7th Guards Army on 19 April 1943:

> At 0800 this morning, a foreign-manufactured truck belonging to the 662nd Aerial Surveillance Company and being driven by a German prisoner of war as a result of a breakdown rolled down a hill in reverse in the vicinity of my bunker[51] and struck a prisoner of war and a sergeant of the security company, injuring the latter. The senior in the truck was the assistant commander of a supply company Senior Lieutenant Borisov. Such an incident can happen only due to the exceptional lack of discipline in the company, since vehicular passage in the area of the command post is forbidden. Travel in a defective vehicle to the units, which need to make use of vehicles, is also not permissible. In addition, the keeping of a prisoner of war, a German, in a company and putting him to work as a driver is a crude violation of

---

51 From March to the middle of April 1943, the army's headquarters was located in the village of Protopopovka, and then after 15 April moved into a bunker that had been prepared in a forested area between the villages of Krasnaia Zaria and Ternovaia. (*Na belgorodskom napravlenii: Vospominaniia uchastnikov boev* [*On the Belgorod axis: Recollections of veterans of the fighting*] (Belgorod: Belgorodskoe knizhnoe izdatel'stvo, 1963), p. 95.

my order, since all prisoners must be sent immediately to a prisoner of war camp. This violation of the order at the same time shows the complete lack of vigilance in the 622nd Aerial Surveillance Company. I hereby order:

1. All combat formation and units, where for whatever reason a prisoner of war is still being held, are to send them immediately under escort to a prisoner of war camp, and in the future they are not to be kept in the units and made to work.[52]

Further on in the document, a reprimand was given to a deputy commander of anti-aircraft artillery Lieutenant Colonel Sergeev, while the commander of the 622nd Aerial Surveillance Company Captain Khomenko, the company's deputy commander for political affairs Lieutenant Amusov, and the company's assistant commander Senior Lieutenant Borisov were ordered to be held under arrest for five days and to be deprived of 50% of their wages over this period of detention. The order was to be announced to the entire command staff down to the level of company commander inclusively, and was plainly intended for routine use, since it was distributed to the troops for implementation (the cited copy was found in the files of the 290th Mortar Regiment). Thus there is no basis to disbelieve the army commander's sincerity, when he demanded prisoners to be sent immediately to prisoner of war camps, nor is there any reason to doubt it.

I related in detail how the Voronezh Front's defensive belts were built in my book *Kurskii izlom: Reshaiushchaia bitva Otechestvennoi voiny* [*Kursk turning point: Decisive battle of the Patriotic War*], and so not to repeat it I will direct the reader's attention to this book, and to Table 4 that I've already presented above. The data in it will plainly demonstrate the scale of the work being done by the troops of the 7th Guards Army to fortify their lines between 1 April and 5 July 1943. To these data I will add that the Voronezh Front's line was also amply strewn with mines and explosive devices, both on the forward edge and in depth. In addition to the formed pool of engineers in each rifle division (1-2 platoons with 400-500 anti-tank mines each) and the squadrons for constructing obstacles in the rifle corps (for example, in the 25th Guards Rifle Corps there were 206 such squadrons) and armies, reserve anti-tank battalions were prepared as well by the Front command. For example, the 47th Engineer-Sapper Battalion (3 vehicles, 10 wagons, 4,700 anti-tank mines and 500 kilograms of explosives) that was located in the city of Korocha was sent into the sector of the 7th Guards Army and to its boundary with the 6th Guards Army. In order to support the battalions of the Front's anti-tank reserve, a stockpile of 100,000 mines and 10 vehicles was kept constantly ready with the 5th Engineer-Sapper Brigade that was assembled in Zhuravka. In addition, by 5 July 1943 another 82,300 anti-tank mines arrived in the Front's stockpiles in the villages of Saraevka, Kholki and Chernianka and in the city of Ostrogozhsk. Incidentally, the artillery shells mentioned in Table 4 were large caliber German shells that had been captured in the course of the winter fighting, which the Soviet sappers used to make roadside bombs, having modified the triggering mechanisms, or as a source of explosive materials in order to wire bridges and buildings for demolition.

The construction of the field defenses proceeded with no small amount of difficulty in all the armies. The point here was not only the colossal amount of work to be done and the parallel need to bring the divisions back up to strength and to train the replacements. Subjective factors also played a role, primarily the regiment or division commander's personality, his motivation to work toward a result, and his ability to forge a hard-working collective of like-minded individuals out of his subordinate officers, ready to carry out the assigned tasks. By this time N.F. Vatutin had served 23 years in the army; he had a large amount of practical experience, both in staff work

---

52 TsAMO RF, F. 290mp, op. 20928s, d. 4, l. 199.

and a commander's work, and knew all the ins and outs of military service. Thus he was perfectly aware of the fact that in a large army collective, an important factor for success in any task was strict control over the execution of orders. The General of the Army gave primary significance to this aspect of his job. Starting in April the Front headquarters, parallel with the command of the armies, conducted monthly (and sometimes even more frequent) inspections of the lines of the regiments and divisions. This practice was very useful and effective. The inspections checked a wide array of matters: the degree of readiness of the trench network in the main belt; the fortification of firing positions; the keeping of records; the depth and density of minefields and obstacles; the patterns of rifle and artillery fire; communications at every level; and so forth. Inspection trips by specialists of various services and their independent evaluations produced an image of the real state of affairs in the troops; revealed bottlenecks in the work to build the field fortifications and to organize the fire; and yielded assessments of the performance and productivity of commanders, and primarily those who had recently been appointed to their posts. Today the documents that contain the results of the work of these commissions, and the orders that were generated on their basis, allow historians to see a real picture of what was happening in the positions of the Voronezh Front's forces in the course of preparing for the Battle of Kursk, including in the 7th Guards Army.

At the beginning of May (prior to 10 May), the Front headquarters conducted its first complex inspection of the army-level defensive belts. The prompt for this was a *Stavka* directive from 5 May 1943 that arrived at the Central, Voronezh and Southwestern Front commands, which stated:

> In recent days, the significant movements of enemy troops and transports to the areas of Orel, Belgorod and Khar'kov and the approach of enemy troops to the forward edge have been spotted. This forces us to anticipate active operations on the part of the enemy in the near future. The *Stavka* of the Supreme High Command demands that you pay attention to the following:
>
> 1. The full execution of the plan to use the Fronts' aviation in order to destroy enemy aircraft and disrupt traffic along the railroads and unsurfaced roads.
> 2. Pay maximal attention to all types of intelligence in order to reveal the enemy's groupings and his intentions.
> 3. Once again, inspect the condition of your defense, the vigilance of outposts and the readiness of all forces and means, including the troops and the reserves of the armies and Fronts to repulse the attack being prepared by the enemy. Use each and every hour to strengthen the defense. Organize inspections personally and through responsible representatives of your headquarters.[53]

In the course of a week of inspections by the commissions, the average level of the defense's readiness (which corresponded to approximately 35-40% of the needed work) was determined and a wide range of problems were revealed. On the basis of the collected information, the Voronezh Front headquarters made the necessary revisions and efficiently designated steps to eliminate the revealed mistakes and shortcomings. This also concerned the 7th Guards Army, which in the beginning of May conducted a major regrouping of forces with the aim of increasing the density of forces in the main defensive belt and increasing the strength of the lines to resist enemy tanks. In order for the reader to get a mental image in at least general outlines of the condition of the defenses of Shumilov's army in this period, I will cite an excerpt from the "Kratkoe taktiko-tekhnicheskoe opisanie sektora oborony Voronezhskogo fronta po sostoianiiu na 12 May 1943" [Brief

---

53 TsAMO RF, F. 3, op. 11556, d. 13, l. 160.

tactical-technical description of Voronezh Front's defensive sector as of 12 May 1943"], which was compiled by the Department of Fortified Areas of Voronezh Front's headquarters. For purpose of comparison, in the parentheses I have provided the relevant figures for the 6th Guards Army on this same date:

1. The main defensive belt extends for 50 (64) kilometers along the left bank of the Northern Donets River and consists of 28 (31) battalion regions. On the right flank [the 81st Guards Rifle Division] battalion zones are echeloned to the depth of regimental sectors. On the left flank, at the junction with the Southwestern Front, the battalion sectors are echeloned to the depth of the divisional belt.

    The most important directions are: Belgorod, Dal'niaia Igumenka; Belgorod, Iastrebovo, Nikol'skoe; Belgorod, Razumnoe, Miasoedovo; Murom, Maslova Pristan', Churaevo; Murom, Staraia Talvozhanka, Nevizheno; and Murom, Volchansk, Baikovo. The tank-vulnerable routes are covered by anti-tank obstacles [ditches and scarps], mines and timber obstructions [fallen trees in forests]. The available number of units that occupy the defense and the establishment quantity of weapons are protected by fortifications.

    The average saturation of the main defensive belt, per kilometer of front, is:

Anti-tank mines	170 (375)
Anti-personnel mines	280 (182)
Anti-tank obstacles	0.10 (0.28) km
Anti-personnel obstacles	0.30 (1.0) km
Machine-gun areas	12 (14)
Bomb shelters and pillboxes	10.5 (3.2)
Mortar positions	10 (5)
Anti-tank rifle positions	12 (5.5)
Artillery emplacements	8.3 (7.7)
Communication trenches	1.6 (2.2) km

2. The second defensive belt traverses forested terrain from the right flank to Shebekino, and open terrain from Shebekino to the left flank. The belt extends along a front of 55 (70) kilometers and consists of 22 (30) battalion zones. All the battalion zones are functional and fortified. Populated places within the boundaries of the belt have been prepared for defense. Important directions are covered by obstacles. The average saturation of the second defensive belt, per kilometer of front, is:

Anti-tank mines	11 (25)
Anti-personnel obstacles	0.33 (0.30) km
Machine-gun areas	12.5 (4.5)
Bomb shelters and pillboxes	4 (1.0)
Mortar positions	8.3 (4.0)
Anti-tank rifle positions	8.5 (5.0)
Artillery emplacements	5.5 (3.0)
Communication trenches	0.55 (2.6) km[54]

The analysis of the documents produced by the inspections that were conducted in the middle of June 1943 revealed particularly significant shortcomings in the units with respect to organizing the fire and fortifying the positions in the army's system of defensive belts (primarily in the main and second defensive belts). Some divisions were ignoring the demands contained in a number

---

54 Glantz, D. and House, J., *Kurskaia bitva: Reshaiushchii povorotnyi punkt vtoroi mirovoi voiny* [*Battle of Kursk: Decisive turning point of the Second World War*] (Moscow: AST, 2006), pp. 402-408.

of the Front's and army's orders, sometimes because of inexperience, but more often because of negligence and idleness. Even the battalion zones were fortified in a slipshod manner, the fire was organized incompetently, and in certain places the Germans had lifted a portion of the minefields without being noticed, right under the nose of negligent commanders, who didn't even have any inkling about what the Germans had done. Even though the elimination of shortcomings and flagrant disgraces proceeded at a feverish pace, this task wasn't finished before the end of June. In the 7th Guards Army, most of the problems concerned Major General A.P. Losev's 72nd Guards Rifle Division. Between 18 and 20 June, its 224th Guards Rifle Regiment underwent an inspection. As a result, the Front's leadership and the army's Military Council were presented with a report that was peppered with unpleasant facts in the regiment, which was positioned in the main defensive belt. Here is just one excerpt from this report:

> The organization and security of the forward edge: All of the weapons of the 2nd Company have been moved up to the forward edge. According to the report of the 1st Guards Rifle Battalion's commander Captain Ragulin regarding the density of fire amounts to 4 bullets per meter in a zone out to 400 meters from the forward edge. The distance from the forward edge to the river is more than 500 meters. The approaches to the forward edge of defense are covered by indirect and flanking fire. Fire cannot be placed on the river's surface. Weapons haven't been adapted for firing at night. Schemes of fire showing the allocated sectors of fire, the positions of machine guns, and alternate firing positions are absent in the platoons and squads. … A battle plan has been worked out in the regiment, but the subordinate battalion commanders and company commanders don't know it well.
> Fortifications:
> 1. The present communication trenches aren't being secured by the maneuver of elements. In the 1st and 2nd Companies, the platoons aren't linked by communication trenches, so in order to reach the 1st Rifle Company one must cross not less than 400 meters of open ground that is exposed to enemy fire. Not all of the firing positions (even the machine-gun positions) aren linked by communication trenches. The communication trenches that exist are shallow, narrow and also unsupported by the maneuver of elements. The steepness and lack of support for the walls for the most part leads to their collapse (the soil is sandy). Communication trenches, for the most part, have not been set up for a defense in depth.
> 2. There are no earth-and-timber bunkers in all the battalions. In the 2nd Rifle Company there are incompetently constructed anti-fragmentation nests. The primary shortcomings of the anti-fragmentation nests are:
>   a) Large, interior gaps in the framework of the embrasures;
>   b) In certain firing positions, the mounts for the machine guns have been built too large (2/2nd Rifle Battalion);
>   c) [Some bunkers have] low ceilings, which hinder the conducting of fire (1/2nd Rifle Battalion – in Junior Sergeant Krylov's squad, a light machine gun can't even be fired from the position);
>   d) The absence of frameworks for the embrasures in many firing positions;
>   e) The high positioning of the embrasures, which leads to large dead zones;
> 3. There are no alternative sites for the majority of machine guns and anti-tank rifles.

4. There are no compact rifle entrenchments for organizing resistance by gunfire (the rifle emplacements are primarily separate rifle pits, scattered in a system of communication trenches at a distance of 80 meters from each other.
5. The men have been fully provided with dugouts, but the entrances to them face the enemy and they lack antechambers.

   The status of communications: The primary means of communication is wire telephony, which is duplicated by mobile means. Radios don't transmit, but only receive; the checking of radio contact is done by signals. The survivability of the wire communications is insufficient – the scheme is inadequately developed and there are no alternate channels. It is necessary to have at least two routes of communications. Lateral communications are lacking in the battalion. The laying out of the telephone lines in the area of the command post and observation post and the wiring of stations are unsatisfactory (lines are tangled and have not been buried underground).[55]

It is possible that the cited excerpt is too lengthy, but it clearly testifies to the state of affairs in the 72nd Guards Rifle Division, which just two weeks later would take on the main attack by Army Detachment Kemp's *kampfgruppen*. Indeed all of the shortcomings indicated above, which had been tolerated because of the slovenliness and inertia at the command level, would put the division in a difficult situation. It would virtually fall apart into several pieces, command and control would be lost, and in the course of 12 hours the division commander Major General Losev would be unable to establish the location of his units or their condition (this in particular goes back to the question of the survivability of the communication lines).

Thus, as a result of the absence of a plan for the engineering work and the necessary monitoring of it (both general and technical) on the part of the command at the regiment and division level, the 224th Guards Rifle Regiment's line wound up weakly fortified; in its 1st Rifle Battalion, there was not a single properly constructed firing position. As a matter of urgency, the inspection team recommended the immediate construction of four earth-and-timber bunkers in the vicinity of the tactically important Hill 110.1. In addition, a number of shortcomings were also revealed in the 224th Guards Rifle Regiment's artillery and mortar units. However, in this case there was more order, because a commission created by the army's artillery headquarters and the artillery commander himself, General A.N. Petrov, were systematically checking the state of affairs in its "jurisdiction", including in such small elements as a regimental mortar battery. Nevertheless, problems remained, which were primarily objective in nature and similar to those revealed in their neighbors: the poor training of the crews, the lack of knowledge to use an azimuth instrument, and the ignorance of the markings on shells. The training agenda was vague and the exercises were disrupted because a majority of the soldiers and commanders were constantly being diverted to dig trenches and were distant from the works, which often required a 30-minute march to reach them.

A bit earlier, on 17 June, an order from the Front's Military Council regarding the results of the inspection of other frontline divisions reached M.S. Shumilov. I will cite several points from this order, so that the reader might acquire a more complete image of the degree of readiness of the 7th Guards Army's sector of defense at that moment, the level of training and cohesion of the divisions, as well as the level of responsibility of the 7th Guards Army's division commanders for the assigned work:

---

55 TsAMO RF, F. 203, op. 2843, d. 365, ll. 56-57.

As a result of an inspection of the 36th Guards Rifle Division, it has been established:

...

2. The mid-level command staff doesn't know their own men, and certain platoon commanders think of their squads only in terms of numbers.
3. Select soldiers and officers aren't being chosen to man the outposts of the 1/106th Guards Rifle Regiment; a platoon commander from even a different company is being put in charge of the outposts – in rotation. The outpost positions are not being set up properly and are not screened by anti-tank and anti-personnel obstacles.
4. Weapons have not been prepared for night combat. Little lubrication material is being issued in the elements, and as a result there are rusty weapons. The fire of infantry weapons is as a rule only toward the front with a density of 2-4 bullets per linear meter. Weapons haven't been zeroed in on lines, and there are no reference points for conducting fire.... Positions for firing machine guns at enemy aircraft haven't been prepared.
5. In the 104th Guards Rifle Regiment there is no plan of the engineer works. The constructed earth-and-timber bunkers only offer protection against 75mm shells and have limited fields of fire with no overlapping fields of fire between them. The trenches are narrow and haven't been prepared for defense.

    In the 106th Guards Rifle Regiment, trenches and obstacles haven't been developed in depth. The masking of the obstacles is unsatisfactory and there are no dummy positions.

    In the depth of the 104th Guards Rifle Regiment, abatis are being formed by the haphazard cutting of trees; the fallen tree isn't being trimmed of branches and isn't being strengthened.
6. The command posts, observation posts and artillery firing positions are poorly constructed. Overhead protection is weak and the bunkers have been built superficially.[56]

All the above-listed shortcomings in Denisenko's division were found like a carbon copy in Skvortsov's division. In addition:

> In the 78th Guards Rifle Division: maneuvering and the directing of fire haven't been fully worked out in the companies. The machine gunners of the heavy machine guns haven't been trained to fire from enclosed or semi-sheltered positions. The coordination of the fire to take advantage of the artificial obstacles hasn't been sufficiently worked out. In the division's sector, there are regions that haven't been adequately obstructed with obstacles.[57]

There were quite a few problems in the 81st Guards Rifle Division as well, although it should be emphasized that its headquarters was actively engaged in checking the results of the fortification works in the regiments. For this task, the headquarters used personal visits by officers to the forward edge of the battalions and overflights in Po-2 aircraft. From Major General I.K. Morozov's Order No. 081/op from 2 July 1943:

> Through a personal inspection by the deputy chief of staff for intelligence Guards Major Padalko, it has been established that in the 5th Company of 2/235th Guards Rifle Regiment, the 1st Platoon's defenses have been arranged so that the ground lying in front of them can't be covered by fire; there is a dead space of 200-300 meters in front of the rifle pits and firing positions of the light machine guns. Moreover, because of the nature of the ground the

---

56 TsAMO RF, F. 203, op. 2843, d. 301, l. 228.
57 TsAMO RF, F. 203, op. 2843, d. 301, l. 229.

company has the possibility to shift the defense forward and move it closer to the Northern Donets River by 150-200 meters, which will make it possible to observe and bring fire to bear on the river's surface. In addition, in this company buildings that stand in direct proximity to the Northern Donets River haven't been converted into firing positions …

Company commander Guards Senior Lieutenant Kozyrenko and the platoon commander don't know where the minefields and obstacles are located in front of their defense. When checking on them it was found that in certain sectors of the minefield, the anti-personnel fragmentation mines had been cleared, and in essence a passage for the enemy had been opened.

…

The inspection also established that despite the fact that there are 57,300 bullets at the battalion ammunition supply point, there isn't enough bullets in the platoons to fill one drum each for the light machine guns. The heavy machine guns are in an analogous situation with ammunition.

The above-listed disgraceful facts exist because the company commander Guards Senior Lieutenant Kozyrenko and the battalion commander Guards Captain Goshtenar[58] aren't seriously engaged in questions of creating an impenetrable defense and criminally, nonchalantly regard their own direct responsibilities. These commanders have forgotten that the Motherland has entrusted them to defend our holy ground. These facts also became possible because the regiment commander Guards Major Skiruta and the chief of staff Guards Major Sokolenko aren't monitoring the work of their subordinates, and aren't showing strict insistence in the carrying out of orders.[59]

In the course of three months, without exaggeration, titanic exertions were made to implement the plan of fortification works. However, unfortunately, far from everything was transferred from paper into reality, and to a significant extent, this was due to objective reasons. Thus by the start of the Battle of Kursk, the 7th Guards Army's sector of defense wasn't fully organized and fortified, as had been intended back in the springtime. Nevertheless, the bulk of the plan had been carried out, which became the main reason for the generally successful combat work of its troops when fighting to repel Operation Citadel.

Now let's return to the recently declassified archival documents and take a look at the process of restoring the combat capabilities of Shumilov's forces and the training of the personnel. Considering that this discussion relates to the defensive operation of a combined-arms army, I consider it necessary to dwell briefly on the TO&E of Soviet rifle divisions at the beginning of 1943. The rifle division was the basic combined-arms tactical formation in the Red Army's infantry forces. Prior to the start of the Great Patriotic War, it was organizationally part of a rifle corps, which in turn was subordinate to a combined-arms army, but already on 15 July 1941 the *Stavka* changed the structure. Because of the high losses, including at the command level, and the impossibility of quickly replenishing them, almost all of the rifle corps were phased out (of the 62 that existed, by the end of the year there were only 6), and accordingly the command structure changed. All of the units and formations that had been earlier united in a corps (typically 5-6 rifle divisions, although sometimes a cavalry division; one or two tank brigades; and more rarely separate tank battalions or artillery regiments) were made directly subordinate to an army headquarters.

---

58 As documents discovered in the archives reveal, this officer also had disciplinary problems in the future. Less than two weeks later, due to the unsanctioned withdrawal of the battalion because of the imaginary threat of an enemy tank attack, he was turned over for trial in front of a military tribunal and only survived it by some miracle.
59 TsAMO RF, F. 81 gv. sd, op. 1, d. 5, l. 274.

For the same reason, already in the war's second month there arose an acute need to bring the tables of both the divisions and regiments into line with the government's possibilities. A sharp decrease affected not only the supporting elements, but also the combat units. According to the TO&E adopted in July 1941, the authorized number of men in a division shrank by 25%, guns and mortars by 52%, and motorized transport by 64%. A howitzer regiment, a destroyer anti-tank artillery battalion and a headquarters' battery were eliminated from the table of organization. A platoon of 45mm anti-tank guns and the mortar batteries were dropped from the rifle battalions; the mortar companies in the battalions and regiments were reduced to two mortar platoons; and in the regimental artillery batteries, the authorized number of four 76mm guns was cut to just two. As a result, the firepower of a rifle division dropped substantially. To wit, if prior to these changes it could fire 297,460 bullets a minute, then after the reduction it could fire only 140,470 bullets a minute. The weight of its artillery salvoes also decreased substantially, by 74%, and of its mortars – by 53%.[60]

The reduction in the rifle division's firepower immediately and negatively affected its combat performance, and their losses increased. Thus already in October 1941 the tables of organization began to be reviewed in order to improve the organization and enhance the firepower. In order to struggle against the German tanks, the separate destroyer anti-tank artillery battalion returned to the rifle division, and a company of anti-tank rifles was added. In addition, the division commander received a totally new unit – a battalion of eight Katiusha rocket launchers, and a platoon of submachine gunners appeared in each regiment. With the increase in the production of military items by the factories that had been evacuated to the Urals, already in 1942 the possibility appeared to improve the TO&E of the Red Army's rifle divisions more quickly. As a result, by the end of 1942 there were rifle divisions in the acting army that had been formed according to three different tables (December 1941, March 1942 and July 1942). In addition in the latter half of 1941 and throughout 1942, separate rifle brigades were used as independent tactical rifle formations in the Red Army, in parallel with the rifle divisions.

However, already in the latter half of 1942, serious problems in command and control became obvious without the corps level of command, and substantial minuses also became clear when using the separate rifle brigades, the chief one being their weak fire and shock power. Having synthesized the acquired experience, the *Stavka* at the end of 1942 conducted a number of substantial restructuring measures. Their objective was first to improve command and control at the army level; second, considering the perceptible reduction in the country's human resources and the increase in the production and supply of weapons and equipment, to optimize the TO&E of the rifle divisions by reducing the number of men in them and increasing the firepower (primarily anti-tank and artillery means). In addition, it was decided to abolish the bulk of the rifle brigades. On their basis, divisions began to be formed, while some were converted into motorized rifle brigades for the tank corps. Several Guards divisions, which were formed in the spring of 1943 out of separate rifle brigades, would take part in the Battle of Kursk as part of the Voronezh Front; in particular, these were the 92nd Guards, 93rd Guards and 94th Guards Rifle Divisions, which became part of the 35th Guards Rifle Corps.

In December 1942, all of the previous TO&E were officially abolished, and two new ones introduced, one for the regular rifle division and the other for the Guards rifle division. As the experience of future combat operations would show, they proved optimal not only for executing combat assignments, but also answered the possibilities of the government at that moment, as well as the level of training to command the divisions possessed by the bulk of the senior officers' staff of the acting army. From 1 January 1943, all of the rifle divisions began to be organized and replenished

---

60 *Taktika v boevykh primerakh: Diviziia*, pp. 7-8.

according to the new TO&E, including those that would take part in the Battle of Kursk. Their main feature was a reduction in manpower and an increase in firepower. Indicative in this respect are the figures for the total weight of a salvo by the artillery tubes and mortar tubes of a division formed according to the December 1941 table and the December 1942 table: the former was 547.8 kilograms, and the latter was 1,100.7 kilograms. The amount of the primary anti-tank weapons also perceptibly increased: up until July 1941, the total number of anti-tank guns was 12, but according to the December 1942 TO&E, this became 48, plus 212 anti-tank rifles. In addition, in order to improve the command over the artillery, the post of a division's artillery commander appeared.

I will remind the reader that a new field manual for the infantry was introduced in the Red Army in 1942, which revised the tasks of a division. In order to resolve them, an ordinary rifle division was to have a maximum number of 9,435 men, while the Guards rifle division was to have 10,670 men.[61] However, as a rule, in the acting army these standards were rarely observed, so on average a rifle division might have no more than 7,000 to 7,500 men. The recruitment for the combined-arms army was uniform. Even though when positioned on a defense, replacements were first directed into the frontline divisions, nevertheless as a rule (throughout a calm period) all of the divisions were brought up approximately to the same manpower level. In the event that a division was given particularly important assignments, like for example the mission to hold a tank-vulnerable sector, as was the case with the 7th Guards Army's 81st Guards Rifle Division, the higher command would usually reinforce it, but not with manpower (this did happen, but rarely), but with firepower.

A Guards rifle division consisted of 18 units (regiments or separate battalions) and separate elements [the number in parentheses gives the typical manpower in each] : a headquarters (116), three rifle regiments (each 2,713) and one artillery regiment (991), a separate engineer battalion (164), a separate destroyer anti-tank artillery battalion (204), a separate reconnaissance company (79), a separate signals company (154), a separate chemical defense company (34), a separate motorized transport company (83), a field mobile bread bakery (54),[62] a medical-sanitation battalion (90), a veterinarian hospital (9), a divisional workshop (11), a SMERSH counterintelligence department (22), and a field pay-office of the USSR State Bank.[63]

Back in March 1942, in order to train junior command staff, a separate training battalion (392 men), sometimes a company, was added to the division's table of organization. This unit remained in the December 1942 TO&E. The training battalion was viewed as a combined-arms reserve of the division commander and during battles it was usually located not far from his command post. Often the battalion prepared its own positions in the division's second echelon on a particularly dangerous axis and guarded the division commander's command post and command-observation post.

If all the above-mentioned units and elements were fully staffed, then the division's establishment manpower reached 10,542. A rifle regiment (a total of 2,558 men, including 236 command staff, 750 junior command staff and 1,673 enlisted men) was the primary tactical infantry unit. When defending in the first echelon, it was supposed to have a sector that was 4-kilometers wide, but in practice they were 5-6 kilometers wide or even more, while in the second echelon, the rifle regiment's sector reached 9-12 kilometers in width. It consisted of (the numbers in parenthesis

---

61 The units and elements that were part of the homogenous divisions had various table strengths (simple and reinforced), and therefore, for example, two Guards divisions might have a different numerical strength according to the table.
62 The typical output of a division's mobile bread bakery was 12-15 metric tons of baked bread per 24 hours.
63 The table of organization of the 6th Guards Army's 71st Guards Rifle Division was taken for this example.

show the manpower):[64] a headquarters (command staff, political apparatus and chiefs of various services, a total of 21 men) and five platoons: headquarters (13), chemical defense (12), engineer (20), mounted (12) and on-foot (23) scouts, and a signals company (50); two submachine gun companies (100 men each), an anti-tank rifle company (69), three rifle battalions (544 in each), a battery of 45mm M1937 or M1942 anti-tank guns (6 anti-tank guns, 44 men), a battery of 76mm M1927 or M1943 regimental guns (4 guns, 58 men), a battery of 120mm mortars (8 tubes, 62 men), an administrative unit (10), a sanitary company (33), a veterinarian hospital (3), an ammunition supply shop (11), a clothing and equipment supply shop (3), a transport company (18) and a labor detail (24).[65] In addition, when occupying a defense, an anti-aircraft platoon (2 DShK-39 machine guns), a separate penal company and one battalion of a divisional artillery regiment were also attached to the Guards regiments.

The horse served as the main transport means of the rifle regiment. The total number of them varied just a little; for example, according to one of the TO&Es, a Guards regiment was supposed to have 363 equestrian, artillery and draft horses and only three trucks. Most of the horses belong to the artillerymen and medical service: the 45mm anti-tank battery had 26 horses, the 76mm battery had 49 horses and there were 16 horses in the medical-sanitation battalion. In reality even these services in the best case received only 60% of the establishment beasts of burden.

The rifle battalion[66] was the infantry's highest tactical element. Organizationally it was only part of a rifle regiment; thus, a fully-staffed rifle division was to have 9 battalions. It consisted of: a command (4), an anti-tank platoon (2 45mm anti-tank guns, 17), a signals platoon (4), a supply platoon (12) and a sanitary platoon (5); three rifle companies (150 each), a machine-gun company (12 heavy machine guns, 73 men) and mortar company (8 82mm mortars, 67 men), and a company of anti-tank rifles (9 anti-tank rifles, 46 men). When preparing for fighting, the battalions were usually reinforced with mortar and artillery elements depending upon their availability.

The rifle company was the infantry's basic tactical element. It had five platoons: four rifle and a mortar platoon (3 50mm mortars), as well as a machine-gun section (2 Maxim machine guns) and sanitary squad. Given a full-strength Guards division, its rifle companies had 8 members of the command staff, 44 junior commanders and 98 enlisted men.

The rifle platoon was a tactical element that consisted of four rifle squads. The squads possessed varying firepower. For example, in addition to the rifles and submachine guns, the 1st and 3rd Squads each had one light machine gun, while the 2nd and 4th Squads had two light machine guns. Such an organization enabled the platoon to operate not only as part of the company, but also independently.

The rifle squad was the lowest tactical element. In addition to the squad leader, it included a machine gunner and an assistant, riflemen, and submachine gunners. Independently a squad was able to handle such independent tasks as going on patrols, providing security on the march or manning outposts, although in the latter case it was as a rule equipped with 50mm mortars, and on the most important directions, a heavy machine gun.

In order to counter enemy armor, destroy enemy firing positions, command posts and observation posts, inflict casualties and demolish infrastructure in the enemy rear, in addition to the battalion and regimental artillery the division commander had powerful divisional artillery – an artillery regiment and a separate destroyer anti-tank artillery battalion. The artillery regiment

---

64 In the parentheses are the number of personnel and weapons according to one of the tables of organization for a Guards rifle regiment (the 229th Guards Rifle Regiment of the 7th Guards Army's 72nd Guards Rifle Division); TsAMO RF, F. 5 gv.A, op. 4852, d. 38, ll. 72, 72obr.
65 TsAMO RF, F. 5 gv.A, op. 4852, d. 38, ll. 72, 72obr.
66 The table of the 1st Battalion of the 229th Guards Rifle Regiment of the 7th Guards Army's 72nd Guards Rifle Division was taken for this example.

was the primary organizational unit of organic artillery in the Red Army. Each rifle division had one artillery regiment that consisted of three artillery battalions, with three batteries in each (according to the Guards TO&E). When the division adopted a defensive posture, each rifle regiment received an artillery battalion as a basic reinforcement (the regimental artillery group), while the separate destroyer anti-tank artillery battalion remained in the division commander's mobile reserve. At the beginning of 1943 a Guards artillery regiment had nearly 1,000 men (988), 24 ZiS-3 M1942 76mm guns, and 12 M1938 122mm howitzers, while the artillery regiment of a regular rifle division had 8 batteries with 4 cannons and howitzers in each, for a total of 32 pieces of artillery. In order to tow the guns and transport the shells, the regiment possessed not less than 28 ZiS-5, ZiS-6 and GAZ-AA trucks and 15 STZ-5, ChTZ-65 or S-60 Stalinets artillery tractors (the latter for moving the howitzers). Already in the middle of July it was planned to shift all of the divisional artillery (starting with the Guards divisions) to motorized tow, which meant to equip them with Studebaker and Chevrolet trucks.

By the start of the Battle of Kursk, a number of the Guards rifle divisions had already received their imported trucks, however, in the overwhelming majority of the artillery regiments, the horse continued to serve as the primary means for towing and transport. By TO&E, a Guards artillery regiment had 684 horses, including 464 artillery horses (of a special, smallish, draught breed) and 53 wagon train horses. However, there was a catastrophic shortage of them, especially after the troops emerged from winter. In the spring of 1943, the deficit of animals in the acting army reached such dimensions that despite the enormous efforts expended (including the great assistance rendered by our ally, Mongolia), the troops were unable to replenish even half the needed number of horses. For example, in the divisions of the 5th Guards Army, which arrived in the Voronezh Front out of the *Stavka* reserve already in the course of the Battle of Kursk, the artillery regiments had an overall shortage of horses of 76%, and of artillery draught horses – 65%. When moving the division to a new area, each division commander moved out his formation in varying ways, but as a rule used one universal procedure – he collected all of the division's available trucks and handed it over to the artillerymen. Not rarely before a march to the front, each of the division's enlisted men were issued 1-2 artillery shells each to carry, since there was simply no other way to transport the ammunition to the new destination.

In this connection it should be emphasized that the lack of Dodge and Studebaker trucks and Willys jeeps, which best matched the needs of the artillery and were widely used as tow trucks, was one of the main problems in the 7th Guards Army's artillery as well. Thus its command was forced to delegate even the sluggish ChTZ-65 tractors to towing guns, even for the ZiS-3 76mm anti-tank guns, including in the anti-tank units, like for example the 114th Guards and 1669th Destroyer Anti-tank Artillery Regiments. However, whereas these slow tractors were authorized for the howitzer and cannon regiments (considering the weight of the guns and the way they were used), in the anti-tank artillery mobility was one of the main qualities. It is understandable that if a tractor is towing an anti-tank gun, then there can be no talk of any maneuverability or stealth of the destroyer anti-tank artillery regiment. This substantially complicated the combat work of the troops and reduced its effectiveness. In addition to their slow speed, the tractors provided an excellent target on the battlefield because of their tall silhouette.

A destroyer anti-tank artillery battalion (200 men) was not supposed to have any horses; it was equipped with 16 45mm M1942 anti-tank guns (in a regular rifle division, just 12) and 17 heavy vehicles (as a rule, of domestic manufacture). Understanding that the battalion was a "fire brigade" the division commander always kept it at full combat readiness.

From the end of 1942, significantly more corps headquarters began to enter the acting army, especially in the spring of 1943. For example, prior to April 1943 there were just 34 of them, but by July 1943, already 64. This additional command structure significantly reduced the burden on the army headquarters (first of all, regarding ongoing matters) and allowed them to focus more deeply on the operational situation, to organize command and control over the troops more effectively and concisely, and to get cooperation up and running during a battle. The TO&E for the rifle corps was also of two types – a regular one and a Guards one. They had a similar structure, but differed in their numerical strength and quantity of heavy weapons. Each rifle corps consisted of a headquarters, a separate signals battalion, an engineer battalion, a SMERSH counterintelligence department, a separate counterintelligence rifle platoon, a military prosecutor's office, a military tribunal, a military post office, and an artillery battery of the headquarters of the artillery commander. Upon arriving at their place of formation or at the front, the corps headquarters received three rifle divisions, a destroyer anti-tank artillery regiment, and a mortar regiment, but the Guards corps received an additional Guards mortar regiment of Katiusha rocket launchers and one more destroyer anti-tank artillery regiment.

By the end of March 1943, the Voronezh Front's rifle divisions (like, incidentally, the formations of other troop types) were in an exceptionally difficult situation. Here is just one indicator that testifies to their condition, an excerpt from a staff report by its headquarters Department of Staffing:

> By 1 April 1943, after the Voronezh Front's winter offensive, of the 29 divisions under its command:
>
> 7 rifle divisions have a numerical strength of 1,500 to 2,000 men,
> 5 rifle divisions – between 3,500 and 4,500 men,
> 2 rifle divisions – between 4,500 and 5,000 men,
> 4 rifle divisions – between 5,000 to 6,000 men,
> 7 rifle divisions – between 6,000 and 7,500 men,
> 4 rifle divisions – between 8,000 and 10,000 men
>
> In the divisions with a strength between 8,000 and 10,000 men, a significant portion of the soldiers were from among those mobilized on liberated territory and have no uniforms.[67]

The situation with human resources in the Soviet Union grew ever more difficult with each passing year of the war. Because of the heavy casualties at Rzhev [Operation Mars] and in the Battle of Stalingrad, as well as in the course of the subsequent counteroffensive, the situation with respect to manpower in the acting army and especially in the troops of the southwestern direction substantially deteriorated. The population that had been evacuated to the eastern regions was quickly diminishing, while the territory of the most heavily populated European part of the country with more than 60 million people was still under enemy occupation. Thus Moscow was insistently demanding of the Fronts' Military Councils to organize a replenishment of the troops already in February 1943 from local resources, having authorized a call-up of the entire male population near the front between the ages of 17 and 50 inclusively (both those fit and unfit for combat duties). I will remind the reader that at this time, according to law at that time, only citizens who had reached 18 years of age were eligible for call-up into service. However, no one was taking into account those youth who still had several months before reaching the age of eligibility, who had signed up for training in reserve regiments and then sent on into the acting army. The older age groups and people unfit for combat service were supposed to be used in rear service and support units, while those personnel already serving in them were to be transferred to the combat units.

---

67 TsAMO RF, F. 203, op. 2843, d. 301, l. 3.

In the spring of 1943, mobilization was to encompass the entire population, and first of all those people living on territory where the Central, Voronezh and Southwestern Fronts were operating. In February and March, these *fronts* had liberated a portion of Kursk and Orel Oblasts, and all of Voronezh and Rostov Oblasts, as well as certain areas of Ukraine. However, on the Voronezh Front this work didn't get under way right away, including for subjective reasons: on the one hand, it was caused by the sluggishness of the armies' rear apparatus, and on the other, something that must be recognized in all honesty – the population on the liberated territory wasn't rushing to sign up. From Order No. 095/OU from the Voronezh Front's Military Council on 6 March 1943:

> Despite the order about conducting a mobilization of Soviet citizens on the liberated territory … and using former military servicemen who've been freed from imprisonment or encirclement in the areas of Voronezh, Kursk and Khar'kov Oblasts, this contingent hasn't been fully caught by the mobilization and haven't been called up into reserve regiments. A portion of those liable for military service and former military servicemen who've been located in imprisonment or encirclement who are due to be called up are sitting it out in towns and villages, and after our units advance, they'll seek to make their way deeper to the rear, so once again they can be idle and sit things out ….
>
> Appropriate measures haven't been taken on the part of certain army headquarters to gather up the remnants of the designated contingent and establish connection with the district military enlistment centers, and no clear instructions have been given to the enlistment centers about the schedule of sending the indicated contingent to the reserve regiments. Thus it isn't surprising that despite the presence of significant resources on the liberated territory, the 8th, 177th and 236th Reserve Army Regiments have a limited number of enlisted men and junior command staff.
>
> The same thing is observed regarding the round-up of captured horses and sending them to the units. For just the Valuiskii District alone, 200 mules and 100 captured horses have been registered at the district military enlistment center [but haven't been sent on to the army]. Yet this is happening during the springtime thaw, when each unit is experiencing an acute deficit of horses.[68]

At the end of March and beginning of April 1943 the problem with replacements was urgent for the 7th Guards Army as well, even though at the moment of its arrival near Belgorod it was the numerically strongest of all of Voronezh Front's armies. On 5 April 1943 it had a total of 49,729 men,[69] including 42,464 in the combat units.[70] The average strength of one division was 5,975 men. The numerically weakest division was the 81st Guards Rifle Division, which had only 4,834 soldiers and officers (45.9% of its table strength), while the most fully staffed was the 73rd Guards Rifle Division – 7,204 soldiers and officers (68.3%)[71] For comparison's sake, at this time the 6th Guards Army had 37,395 men with an average division strength of 5,981 men.[72] Its 71st Guards Rifle Division had 4,924 soldiers and officers, while its 325th Rifle Division (from April 1943, the 90th Guards Rifle Division) had a total of 7,609 men.[73] The 40th Army had a strength of 25,187

---

68 TsAMO RF, F. 69A, op. 10757, d.1, l. 48.
69 TsAMO RF, F. 203, op. 2870, d. 37, l. 317obr.
70 Ibid., l. 317.
71 Ibid.
72 At this moment the 6th Guards Army had only 6 rifle divisions and 3 ski battalions, while the 7th Guards Army had 7 divisions.
73 TsAMO RF, F. 203, op. 2870, d. 37, l. 315.

men; its numerically weakest division was the 161st Rifle Division, with just 3,080 soldiers and officers, while its strongest was the 237th Rifle Division, with 8,684 men.[74]

Immediately upon assuming his post, N.F. Vatutin became personally occupied with the search for a way out of the manpower problem, and threw himself into it with great energy. Already on 2 April 1943, just six days after his arrival at the front, he held a meeting of the Military Council, which produced a plan of priority measures to replenish the rifle divisions, motorized rifle brigades and artillery units with personnel. The prepared directive demanded the following results:

2. With the receipt of this directive, immediately set about bringing rifle, tank, Guards mortar and artillery units back up to strength.

   Staff the rifle divisions with up to 7,000-8,000 men, the rifle brigades up to 5,000 men, and single out the best enlisted men and junior commanders for the tank, Guards mortar and artillery units.

3. The commander of the 64th Army is to transfer 6,000 men from the number of arriving replacements to the 21st Army.

4. The commanders of the 38th and 40th Armies, after fleshing out all of the formation and units are to transfer all of the excess replacements from their reserve regiments to the 69th Army. Report to me by code the number of those that will be transferred by 4.4.43.

5. The commanders of all the armies when bringing their troops up to strength are not at all to be limited by the number indicated in the plan, but are to take every measure so that the numerical strength of the rifle divisions will be brought up to 8,000 men in the shortest time possible, for which purpose use every inherent possibility to find men and horses, weapons and other gear.

   Simultaneously I am announcing that measures have been taken for the speediest movement of the 21st and 64th Armies' reserve regiments, weapons, combat equipment and rear services.[75]

On 20 April 1943, in order to implement this directive, the Front headquarters determined administrative areas for the armies, wherein they should conduct the house-to-house mobilization of the male population. In dependence on the staffing levels of the divisions and the approximate size of the civilian population, each army was given two to five frontal zone areas of Kursk Oblast. In particular, the Shebekino and Prispeshnik areas were assigned to the 7th Guards Army. According to the Front's plan, in the springtime it was necessary to direct approximately 84,000 conscripts into the armies, including 39,000 "march replacements" (who had a certain amount of prior training), 11,000 from army and Front hospitals (who were already seasoned veterans and comprised the most highly-qualified contingent), and 34,000 raw conscripts from the liberated territory.

The mobilization of the latter category proved to be the most labor-intensive task, while the results were difficult to predict. First, it was necessary to find these several tens of thousands of men (after all, the plan's goal was only the minimum needed for the troops). Second, the new conscripts had to be fed and nourished up to a point where they could meet the rigorous physical standards of a soldier – under German occupation many were famished or had even died from starvation – before they could begin basic training. The territory of Kursk Oblast, where the main forces of Voronezh Front was deployed, had been in German possession between October 1941 and February 1943; many of the young and physically-strong males had been shipped to Germany

---

74 Ibid., l. 314.
75 TsAMO RF, F. 69A, op. 10757, d. 1, l. 49.

for slave labor, while some had been called up by the Red Army's field enlistment offices[76] in 1941 and 1942 in order to replenish the 21st and 40th Armies and had perished in the course of the Kursk – Oboian' and two Khar'kov operations in early 1943. The population had been left physically emaciated by the occupation, and many of the new conscripts were sick, including with infectious diseases like typhus, tuberculosis, syphilis and others. According to the data of the Front's medical board, in certain populated places at this time the number of infected individuals approached 60-65% of the population, and because of infectious outbreaks entire villages had to be strictly quarantined for several weeks. Even before the start of the Battle of Kursk, when the epidemiological situation had somewhat stabilized (corpses had been cleared from the Front's territory, the population had gone through cleansing and disinfecting, and the Front's and armies' infectious disease medical facilities had begun to operate), not a few cases of infectious diseases had been registered in an entire array of villages, particularly on Voronezh Front's right flank. For example, on 26 June 1943 the headquarters of the 90th NKVD Regiment, which had been assigned to secure the Voronezh Front's rear area in the sector of the 6th Guards Army, reported in Operational Summary No. 00177 that in its area of responsibility over the indicated time, 36 people had been found with typhus in Verkhopen'e, 61 in Noven'koe, 24 in Kruglik, 53 in Bobrovo, and 50 in Bogatoe. As M.E. Katukov recalled, in the area of Oboian' where his 1st Tank Army was deployed in March 1943, the epidemiological situation was so strained that it required great efforts by the Red Army in order to eliminate a significant number of foci of typhus.[77]

In order to bring up the conscripts to the determined physical standards, time and high-caloric foods were required, which meant a reduction in the program of combat training, but the situation with food supplies was also difficult. In addition, in the period of the springtime lull in fighting at the front, the commanders of the combat units were broadly involved in conducting large-scale fortification work. All of this taken together seriously and negatively affected the level of individual training of the replacements. M.E. Katukov wrote:

> In the formal, bureaucratic language the "raising of the army to establishment strength" sounds colorless and neutral. But how many troubles and concerns does it conceal?! The duty of the commander and headquarters is to prepare this entire mass of men – as thoroughly as possible – for those most dramatic hours and minutes, which are covered by the word "combat".
>
> The better each soldier is trained, the fewer the losses and the greater the payoff at the front. Only from the side does combat seem to be the chaos of fire, thunder, smoke, cries and the rumble of engines. In reality – it is a combination of intellect, creativity, experience, high organization and skill. Yes, skill emerges as the victor! Arduous, taxing, but all the same skill![78]

The problems with the quality of the training of the command staff at the tactical level were even greater. The bulk of the replacements that entered the rifle divisions at this time, all the way up to regiment commander inclusively had weak and not infrequently simply superficial professional knowledge and expertise in organizing a battle and handling units. The cause was the stunning decline in command staff, including because of regulations that didn't correspond to the

---

76 These were hastily-formed offices in the acting army's formations in order to mobilize the civilian population at the front, relying on martial law.
77 Katukov, *Na ostrie glavnogo udara*, p. 255.
78 Ibid., p. 270.

realities of battle. A veteran of the war, an artilleryman and a well-known Belorussian novelist V. Bykov recalled:

> Once regiments and battalions had been whittled down to the core and the division had been withdrawn to the rear for re-forming, the surviving commanders were put up for decorations – for their unswerving execution of an order: Such was the expression written in their commendations … War, however, was a teacher. Not the former, pre-war military science, not the military academies, much less the short-term and accelerated courses of the military schools, but only individual combat experience, which formed the basis of commanders' combat skill. Gradually combat actions, especially on the lower level, began to acquire an element of soundness. Very quickly it turned out that the combat manuals, written on the basis of the experience of the Civil War, poorly corresponded to the nature of the new war, and in the best case were useless, if not harmful, in their literal application.
>
> In reality, what alone did their precept on the proper place of the commander in a battle (in front of the attacking line) cost, which more often than not led to the rapid death of the commander, while at the same time the unit, left leaderless, quickly lost any combat effectiveness. Relying on the manual's call for attacking in an echeloned formation brought about unjustified losses, especially from enemy mortar fire. These and many other absurdities were patently obvious. Stalin was compelled to overhaul the manuals, and already during the war a new infantry combat manual appeared – Part 1 and Part 2. Meanwhile as any remark regarding any superiority of German tactics or a German weapon was strictly banned in the troops, somewhere up above, in the General Staff this superiority was acknowledged in secret and certain unspoken conclusions were drawn from it. With the sanction of the Supreme Commander-in-Chief, a thing or two took root in the troops.[79]

However, by 1943 the half-measures were yielding an increasingly diminishing effect and human resources were melting away, to a significant extent at the fault of all those poorly-trained commanders. To resolve the problem of raising the level of professionalism of the command staff required not only summarizing the combat experience and setting it down in regulation documents, but also the strict selection of candidates and their thorough and lengthy training (not less than 9 to 12 months), and subsequently by on the job combat training as well. The Red Army leadership and the country as a whole had no understanding of the essence of the problem. Nevertheless, by the start of the Battle of Kursk there had been no cardinal changes in the situation, and again they took the simplest path. At first they called up reserve officers (as a rule of older ages, even if they were totally unseasoned), while a portion of the commanders arrived from hospitals and military schools, and in the autumn of 1942 they began to retrain commissars at every level.

I will remind the reader that the institution of the military commissar had been abolished by an order of the People's Commissar of Defense on 9 October 1942, in which it was noted that it was necessary "to promote more decisively those political workers who have military training to command posts, especially at the company to battalion level."[80] Already within two weeks, starting on 20 October, two-month courses became operational at the fronts "to prepare company commanders from the political workers who have the most military schooling", and on 1 January 1943 200 regiment commanders and 600 battalion commanders who had passed through two months of training began to arrive in the acting army. As a result of this practice, the troops received

---

79 Bykov, V., "Za Rodinu! Za Stalina!" ["For the Motherland! For Stalin!"] *Rodina*, No. 5 (1995), pp. 31-32.
80 *Stalingradskaia bitva* [*Battle of Stalingrad*] (Moscow: Zvonnitsa-MG, 2003), p. 423.

a lot of "unripen fruit" (as they called such commanders at the front), which is to say commanders who were tactically illiterate, who had little ability to find their bearings on the ground and at times didn't even know how to read a map, and who lost control over their elements and units even when engaged in just skirmishes. It was understandable that it was impossible over 60 days to make a specialist in shaping a battle from a man who had only seen combat from the sidelines. The problem was made even worse by the fact that little time was given to the requalification process even for a man who had already mastered a profession, let alone the significant number of the commanders who had little prior education. As veterans recalled, a man who had already completed a full course of ten years in the acting army was viewed as a very well-educated man, and usually he was directed into staff work, not into a command post. The semi-illiteracy greatly reduced a candidate officer's possibility in quickly assimilating theoretical knowledge and grasping the essence of his new profession. However, the front was demanding replacements each and every passing day, and there wasn't a single period when the army didn't have vacancies, so the personnel officers were adhering to the "iron" principle that justified everything – "better a far from stellar commander, than not one at all". Thus the "conveyor belt" to produce command cadres continued to operate, and in order to "familiarize" the freshly-baked battalion commanders and company commanders with their duties, or more precisely to teach them the fundamentals of the military profession "from scratch", this had to take place on the spot. Thus a number of political officers were even appointed as commanders of rifle divisions, who like the overwhelming majority of commissars lacked the knowledge or experience for this. The consequences of such experiments proved very costly for the troops; the case of the 35th Guards Rifle Corps' 92nd Guards Rifle Division, which in the course of trying to stop Army Detachment Kempf's offensive at the fault of the division commander lost two-thirds of its men in just a week of fighting, can serve as an example of this.

The problem of training commanders at the tactical level and raising their qualifications also stood acutely before 7th Guards Army's Military Council in the spring of 1943. After wrapping up the fighting on the Volga River, its divisions had been deprived of a significant portion of its experienced, combat-seasoned officers and generals. For example, there had been changes in the command of the 72nd Guards and 213th Rifle Division, and in the 78th Guards Rifle Division all of the commanders of its rifle regiments and their deputies for political affairs had been sent for further studies or promotions, while some of the battalion and company commanders had also been replaced. A similar situation was observable in other divisions.

Considering this circumstance, the leadership of the Voronezh Front and of all its armies immediately once the front became stabilized directed the entire command staff toward organizing intensive and comprehensive training of the personnel. Intensive training got under way in the 7th Guards Army as well. In the first order after the fighting subsided, its Military Council obligated the division commanders to begin preparing commanders at all levels quickly (within the course of three days). The exercises with the command staff of the regiments, battalions and artillery battalions were devoted to such themes as "Defense of a reinforced rifle battalion" (Parts 1 and 2 of the 1942 Infantry Combat Manual); they were to conduct them personally; the regiment commanders, commanders of divisional artillery and the division's engineers were to conduct them with the commanders of machine-gun, mortar and anti-tank rifle companies. The training was to be organized in two stages: a theoretical stage, followed by working out such practical questions on the ground as:

- The proper reconnoitering of the terrain for the selection of the positions of companies and platoons;
- The organization of battalion foci of resistance;

- The selection of firing positions for machine-gun nests and anti-tank guns, as well as determining the tasks both for their own crews of the machine guns, anti-tank rifles and artillery batteries, as well as for those crews attached as reinforcements;
- The creation of a system for directing a battalion (the choice of a location and setting up main and alternative command posts and observation posts, and a network of communications (both a main line and alternative means of communication);
- The details of the defense of a village or town (strength and means, their distribution, the commander's place in a battle and the organization of cooperation, the creation of a reserve and its positioning, and the selection of directions for counterattacks).

I think the reader will be curious to find out from the mouth of an eyewitness how a similar process was implemented in practice in the neighboring 6th Guards Army. G.A. Sereda, who at the time was a major and the commander of the 89th Guards Rifle Division's 267th Guards Rifle Regiment, recalled:

> In the afternoon we were called to order before the army commander Lieutenant General I.M. Chistiakov (who was being accompanied back then by the chief of staff Major General Pen'kovsky). Reviewing the assembly, Chistiakov asked the officers about the regulations for a regiment's combat formation when on the attack according to the new Infantry Combat Manual. By this time the 1942 Infantry Combat Manual, Parts 1 and 2 had already come out, which directed that the combat formation ensure the maximal concentration of weapons in the first echelon in order to launch a decisive attack against the enemy. Prior to this, our formations had been deeply echeloned, and most of the heavy weapons and manpower had been doomed to inactivity, plodding along in the rear while taking casualties from enemy fire and rendering almost no influence on the outcome of the battle. At the time, the new combat manual for us was like the second discovery of America. Engaged in constant fighting throughout the winter and early spring, we knew nothing about the new combat manual. Having received some inarticulate mumbling instead of a clear answer, General Chistiakov said:
>
> "Well, Guardsmen, how do you plan to fight?"
>
> General Pen'kovsy, who was standing next to General Chistiakov, blurted out a reply: "In the same old way."
>
> We had nothing to say. The army commander, addressing the chief of staff as well by his first and last name (which certain contemporary commanders greatly fear, thinking if they address their subordinates in such a way, their authority will suffer): "Shall we give them time to think about it? At 0500 we'll collect the answers from them. Organize assistance and consultation for them."
>
> There was no choice. We were obliged to study and to teach our subordinates how to fight in a new way. Promptly at 0500 the army commander and chief of staff, having split us into groups, questioned us. Chistiakov himself took the regiment commanders. Even now I recall his question, "What is a direct and reinforced combat outpost?"[81]

It must be said that the training of the command staff was on one hand very important, but on the other a more problematic direction of the combat work in the 7th Guards Army, as incidentally it was in other armies as well. As one can clearly imagine, the officers' corps in the acting army

---

81 Sereda, G.A., *Pervyi saliut Rodiny* [Motherland's first salute] (Saransk: Mordovskoe knizhnoe izdatel'stvo, 1993), p. 35.

wasn't unified and well-cemented, as the Soviet ideological machine tried to depict it. It was genuinely stratified both according to rank and social relations, as well as by the level of knowledge. It isn't a secret, for example, that the platoon leader was closest to the soldiers, while the company commander was already a "high ranker"; the battalion commander was even more so, and was rarely seen in the trenches.

At the same time, the junior command staff in its mass up to the battalion commander inclusively was the least-prepared category of the command staff in a professional sense. This was also because of their ordinarily high casualty rates in the course of the fighting. Senior officers, from the regiment commander and above, were a more stable group, and correspondingly were more highly educated in an elementary way and in a professional sense, and had relatively better preparation. However, according to regulations, they had little to do with the main body of troops; their task was to direct only the command staff of the units and elements. However, not every commander knew how to impart his knowledge and experience, and many were simply lazy and didn't want to burden themselves with excess concerns; they simply passed this task off to less qualified officers, who didn't have the ability to refuse. In addition, as already mentioned, parallel with the combat training the troops were constructing extensive defensive works, and thus each of the soldiers and junior commanders were also carrying a substantial physical load. At the same time, the leadership of the Voronezh Front and the armies were frequently more meticulous about fulfilling the plan of fortification works than to preparing the soldiers for battle.

Moreover, some of the senior officers and generals of the acting army were unfit for their own posts, not only because of a lack of professionalism, but primarily due to low moral and ethical standards. General intoxication, outrages against subordinates and civilians, beatings and murders in a drunken rage, and social degradation of the command staff of separate battalions, regiments and even entire divisions was a rather widespread phenomenon, putting it gently, including within the Voronezh Front. Here is just one example from one explanatory note to a petition about rehabilitating the former commander of the 94th Guards Rifle Division[82] Colonel I.G. Russkikh:

> Former Colonel I.G. Russkikh, commanding a division between April and November 1943, over this time squandered a large amount of food items for personal purposes, which inflicted damage to the government in the amount of 444,169 rubles. Having repeatedly warned him about ceasing his shenanigans, he ignored the warnings and continued to perpetrate them on even a large scale. In the process he callously disregarded the needs of officers, sergeants and the rank and file, got drunk on a regular basis, and reached a point of expending bags of flour in order to make moonshine. The food items he took were from the rations for the division's men. In connection with the fact that the given warnings had no effect on him, the 2nd Ukrainian Front's Military Council was forced to dismiss him from his post and turn him over to trial before a military tribunal.
>
> For the committed crimes, as prescribed by the Legal Code from 7 August 1932, Russkikh was sentenced by the military tribunal to 10 years in a labor corrective camp and stripped from his rank of colonel. He served his time in prison until April 1945, at which point the sentence was commuted and Russkikh was sent to the front. However, in connection with the end of the war, he took no part in combat operations.

---

82 This division was formed in April 1943 as part of the 35th Guards Rifle Corps, a reserve of Voronezh Front's commander-in-chief, and would take active part in the combat operations against Army Detachment Kempf in the 7th Guards Army's sector, then subsequently in the sector of the 69th Army.

A rather important detail: the 35th Guards Rifle Corps' command knew about the disgraces going on in the division (after all, it warned him repeatedly), but were closing their eyes to them, because to one degree or another, similar cases were being uncovered in almost every division. Even so, I.G. Russkikh's case was rather rare, if after receiving the sentence from the military tribunal this senior officer and also a division commander, who'd distinguished himself at Stalingrad, who'd been decorated with Orders, and who had been wounded four times and concussed once, was sent to serve his time in prison, and not to the front. Likely, the scale of the harm done primarily played a role in the sentence. So that the reader can compare the value of the harm done cited in the document with the real values of that time, as an example I'll give the official salary for the commander of an artillery regiment in the acting army; for 1943 it amounted to 1,200 rubles. Moreover, in the documents it is shown that the division commander particularly drank a lot, and more than once he was found in a "non-functioning state" even by the corps commander Lieutenant General S.G. Goriachev while preparing for the Battle of Kursk and during the following offensive toward Khar'kov. What can be said about the training of the regiment commanders, who'd been promoted from the post of battalion commander during the period of the 94th Guards Rifle Division's formation, if the man who was supposed to tutor them drank like a fish while simultaneously pilfering rations?!

Now we'll drop down to the level of the rifle regiment and familiarize ourselves with the account written by a commission of the Front headquarters after inspecting the combat training of the 72nd Guards Rifle Division's 224th Guards Rifle Regiment as of the end of June 1942:

> The training plan for the personnel for the period between 6 and 20 June 1943 was based on the calculation of 4 hours per day. The execution of the plan is unsatisfactory. Only 35% of the plan of exercises with the battalion commanders has been carried out, and just 60% of the training exercises with the company commanders. Exercises regarding the tactical training of the enlisted men and junior command staff are being conducted. The methodology of the classes is incorrect; it all boils down to reading aloud Part 1 of the Infantry Combat Manual, despite the fact that there are the opportunities for withdrawing the companies to the rear to rehearse the dynamics of offensive combat. The junior command staff is being poorly prepared; there is no weapons training. The leaders are not preparing for the exercises. Exercises with the command staff of both the regiment and the battalion haven't been organized.[83]

A difficult situation with the training of the personnel and the executive discipline of the officers formed in the artillery units of the 7th Guards Army as well, especially in those that had arrived in the army from the Front's own artillery or from the reserve as a means of reinforcement. Primarily this concerned the 290th Mortar Regiment and the 1112th Cannon Artillery Regiment.[84] It reached the point that the commander of the 1112th Cannon Artillery Regiment was not only derelict in his own direct duties to organize the fire and prepare his subordinates, but was also openly dissembling in personal reports to the artillery commander about the number of guns that were deployed in firing positions. From Order No. 014 on 23 May 1943 from the 7th Guards Army's artillery commander Lieutenant General A.N. Petrov:

> 2. On 21 May at my direction, an inspection of the regiment's readiness to open fire on the Solomino area was conducted by the senior assistant of the chief of operations Captain Shvarev. The inspection revealed that despite the fact that the regiment had moved into

---

83 TsAMO RF, F. 203, op. 2843, d. 365, l. 56.
84 On 26 June 1943, the 1112th Cannon Artillery Regiment was reformed into the 265th Guards Cannon Artillery Regiment.

its firing positions back on 12.5.43, to the present time it has not completed the process of registering the fire. From the observation post, the bridges and fords across the Northern Donets River are not visible, while mobile observation posts haven't been deployed everywhere. Communications are working exceptionally poorly. Telephone operators haven't been trained to maintain speech discipline. The battery commanders of the 3rd Artillery Battalion when opening up planned fire are not using regulation commands and when observing the fire tolerate a lot of excess chatter on the lines. The gun platoons of the 8th and 9th Batteries haven't been trained and work exceptionally slowly. The battery commanders of the 3rd Artillery Battalion have made poor study of the ground on the enemy's forward edge. Not a single battery commander of this battalion can give a precise and confident answer to the inspecting officers as to where Solomino is located. Means of target indication haven't been worked out by the commander of the 3rd Artillery Battalion Captain Il'iashenko with his battery commanders. As a result of the above-listed shortcomings, the commander of the 8th Battery Senior Lieutenant Krivorukov was unable to open fire at SO-121 (the bridge across the Northern Donets River in Solomino) for 50 minutes and he was dismissed from gunnery. After this, the same task was given to the commander of the 9th Battery Lieutenant Tikhomirov. The battery opened fire only 40 minutes later.

After the inspection, Captain Shvyrev arrived at the regiment headquarters to give a report on his inspection to its commander. Regiment commander Lieutenant Colonel Mel'nikov refused to hear out the report in full and retreated into his quarters; when the inspecting officer called Lieutenant Colonel Mel'nikov over the telephone in order to pass along the results of his inspection, the regiment commander again refused to hear the report, and answered: "I do not want to hear your report; you are an undisciplined captain." To Captain Shvyrev's question to the regiment commander, "How many serviceable guns do you have, and now many are standing in firing positions?" the regiment commander replied "Fourteen serviceable guns, 12 guns in firing positions." Evidently he believes that it isn't necessary to place all the guns in firing positions, in view of the insufficient quantity of shells in the regiment. At the same time, at a presentation in my own presence Lieutenant Mel'nikov reported that 14 guns were in firing positions, and within a day, 2 more, so that 16 guns would be in firing positions, which means he gave a false report. I am ordering:
1. Re-examine the location of the observation posts and move them closer to the forward edge by 2-4 kilometers.
2. By 24.5.43, place 14 guns in firing positions.[85]

It must be said that M.S. Shumilov, like his superior, had one valuable quality. He approached officers, even those who had committed infractions, with understanding and sought every possibility not to remove the subordinate from his post right away, but to work with him, educate him and allow him the possibility to straighten up. At the same time while insisting on patience and persistence, he taught his deputies and staff officers the same. However, if the army commander saw that an officer was rejecting the criticism, he would become hard as nails, because he put the good of the cause above all else. This is probably why at first the artillery regiment commanders mentioned in the above order received rather gentle treatment: Lieutenant Colonel Mel'nikov was given a reprimand and a note about service incompetence, while Captain Il'iashenko was arrested for 10 days and deprived of 50% of his pay for this period.

---

85 TsAMO RF, F. 290 mp, op. 20928s, d. 4, ll. 197-198.

However, it soon became clear that the regiment's leadership was in need of change. In June the chief of artillery of the Voronezh Front's 167th Rifle Division Major V.F. Prokhorov took charge of it. Indeed, it was only after this through the efforts of the new commander and the army's artillery headquarters, as well as Lieutenant General A.N. Petrov himself, that discipline in the artillery regiment was brought up to standards, while the batteries' crews were not only meeting the normative standards when opening fire and regarding its accuracy, but in a number of cases exceeding them. Already in the first days of the Battle of Kursk, the 265th Guards Cannon Artillery Regiment of the Supreme Command Reserve would wind up on the axis of the enemy's main attack and would fall into a precarious situation, but its troops stood their ground and would show courage and tenacity when battling the foe. The tale of their exploit lies ahead. Even so, it must be honestly acknowledged that such fixed attention of the higher command to training a regiment was in general not a typical case for the Front's forces. In the best case everything boiled down to reprimands for the unit commanders and superficial inspections of the performance criteria by the artillery staff officers, and in the worst case ended with tongue lashings at conferences of the command staff and a demand to root out the disgraces.

It is possible to cite a lot of documents similar to the ones presented above. Yet they all testify to one and the same thing: although for a long time after the war Soviet historians persistently insisted that "… thanks to the concern of the Communist Party, the officers' staff acquired rich combat experience, while the soldiers learned to fight and win," such an assessment of the command staff of the acting army prior to the Battle of Kursk must be considered exaggerated. After all, those who were supposed to organize the training and conduct the exercises needed first of all to study the fundamentals themselves, at the very least, for two months, and especially not in a slapdash manner over a matter of days, as the 6th Guards Army commander I.M. Chistiakov practiced. However, unfortunately there was neither the time nor trained cadres for this, but also often simply not even the desire.

Even so, one must give N.F. Vatutin credit; as we ourselves would say to today, he was a workaholic and a total abstainer; he struggled mercilessly with drunkards, loafers and thieves both high and low, who were hindering the creation of combat-effective units and formations, and thereby aiding and abetting the enemy. However, unfortunately, it was beyond the power of General of the Army Vatutin and his subordinate commanders to raise the level of training and get the enormous army mechanism running smoothly, so that it ensured an acceptable degree of cooperation among the different types of troops in battle and kept them supplied with everything necessary. Why? It was because the roots of almost all the army's troubles were embedded in that monstrous political system of the state, which the "Father of all Peoples" had erected. Thus, at its basis both the rank and file and the commanders at the tactical level of the Voronezh Front had low professional training and practical skills. The same assessment could be given to the senior officers, right up to the division commanders inclusively (with rare exceptions). This was one of the main reasons for the rather high losses in all of the armies in the course of the Battle of Kursk.

As the former chief of staff of the Voronezh Front General S.P. Ivanov recalled, in conversations with the Front commander-in-chief, the latter more than once spoke about the situation before the summer fighting, and particularly emphasized that it turned out easier to beat the foe than it was to overcome the indolence, laziness, lack of understanding and even opposition on the part of his own subordinate commanders at every level. I will only add that in the matters of staffing the troops, the functioning of their rear services, and the training of the men, the obstacles that Vatutin mentioned were more prominent.

The process of deploying the active work to mobilize the conscripts and bringing the combat formations up to establishment strength went with loud creaks and groans in all the armies, but especially badly (in the opinion of the Front's leadership) in the 40th and 7th Guards Armies. As follows from the documents, the work was launched haphazardly not only in the divisions, but elementary control over the execution of the orders was lacking on the army level as well. Examples of howling disgraces were uncovered. For example, at a time of virtual peace at the front (at this moment the Voronezh Front wasn't conducting even limited operations), the command of the 40th Army lost track of several thousand men, equivalent to half of a division, in its own rear, and for a week knew nothing about them, until the Front leadership looked into the matter. From the deputy chief of staff's Order No. 0025/OU from 20 May 1943: "Despite the fact that the headquarters of the armies were informed well in advance about the batch of replacements that were allotted to them and the time of its arrival, they failed to organize a proper reception and escorts for the replacements. For example, the 40th Army's headquarters failed to organize a reception and escort for 6,500 replacements from frontal zone hospitals, as a result of which 4,000 of them are wandering around in the rear and the army headquarters still doesn't know where these 4,000 men are."[86]

Although there wasn't such a large-scale screw-up in the other armies, the reception and work with the replacements was also done poorly. It reached a point where the Military Council and N.F. Vatutin personally, having exhausted all forms of persuading the formation commanders and army headquarters, were forced to resort to disciplinary measures. I will present two documents, which were signed on one and the same day of 14 June 1943.

From the command of Voronezh Front's Order No. 00151/OU:

> In the 7th Guards Army, trained replacements numbering 4,470 men were held for 6 days in the army's reserve rifle regiment and weren't sent on to the divisions. Between 9 and 12 June the army couldn't send out reception officers to the Front's 234th Reserve Rifle Regiment in order to pick up 2,500 men. In the army's 190th Reserve Rifle Regiment there are 700 men ready to be sent on as replacements, but they aren't heading to a division, because the reserve regiment is 80 kilometers distant from the army headquarters.
>
> In the 36th Guards Rifle Division, the work to realize the Front's Order No. 0090/OU[87] hasn't been rolled out. On 8.6.43, redundant personnel were being held in the division's rear headquarters and by the commander of the 108th Guards Rifle Regiment.
>
> Several chiefs of staff and army Military Councils aren't adequately monitoring the fulfillment of such an important measure. The 7th Guards Army stands out for the worse.
>
> I am ordering:
>
> 4. The armies' reserve regiments are to be shifted closer to the headquarters of the armies and to be kept at a distance no greater than 25 kilometers from the army headquarters. The Front's 234th Reserve Rifle Regiment is to deploy in the Babrovy Dvory – Skorodnoe – Belyi Kolodez' area.
> 6. The chief of staff of the 7th Guards Army Major General Lukin is to be given a reprimand for failing to take steps to reveal inherent resources and timely dispatch replacements to the troops.[88]

From the Voronezh Front commander-in-chief's Order No. 00152/OU:

> By 10 July of this year the armies and rifle divisions faced the task of replenishing the rifle companies of the 8,000-strong divisions with up to 120 men each, and of the 9,000- strong

---

86 TsAMO RF, F. 69A, op. 10757, d. 1, l. 87.
87 In this order, the task was given to bring the divisions up to 9,000 men each, and the companies in them up to 130 men.
88 TsAMO RF, F. 69A, op. 10757, d.1, l. 101.

divisions with up to 130 men each. A number of rifle division commanders carried out this task precisely and on time … but alongside them are rifle division commanders who up to the present time are idling and not taking adequate steps to flesh out the rifle companies; are continuing to hold attached soldiers at headquarters at the expense of the companies and other elements, and whose rear areas are holding men in excess of the establishment number.

For example, in Major General Losev's 72nd Guard Rifle Division, Major General Vasilenko's 15th Guards Rifle Division and Major General Denisenko's 36th Guards Rifle Division, the rifle companies had fewer than 80 men on their roster on 10.6.1943.

On their part the army commanders haven't shown the proper exactingness to their division commanders. Of all the armies, the 7th Guards Army stands out for the worse on this matter.

2. The commanders: 72nd Guards Rifle Division Major General A.P. Losev
15th Guards Rifle Division Major General E.I. Vasilenko
36th Guards Rifle Division Major General M.I. Denisenko

who have shown negligence in carrying out my order to bring the rifle companies back up to strength and complete inactivity in this matter – I am announcing a reprimand and warning that if by 20 June the rifle companies haven't been brought back up to the strengths I've specified in men, harsher disciplinary measures will be taken against them.[89]

However, the situation in the 7th Guards Army wasn't as simple as it seems at first glance. Let's turn to the statistics. If, for example, you compare the figures of the manning levels of the companies of two divisions of this army as of 17 June: 36th Guards Rifle Division – 67-101 men and the 73rd Guards Rifle Division – 121 men, then it is hard not to agree with N.F. Vatutin's assessment of the results of the work by the two division commanders, which he gave in his order. In reality it seems that the leadership of both the 24th Guards Rifle Corps and of the 7th Guards Army itself had washed their hands of the matter and turned over the resolution of this important problem to the division commanders. How else to explain the fact that Colonel S.A. Kozak, whose 73rd Guards Rifle Division was positioned in the second echelon, was able to carry out the order, while M.I. Denisenko, whose 36th Guards Rifle Division was defending a more important sector in the main defensive belt (the boundary between two *fronts*), wasn't?

However, if we check the status of the companies in the 81st Guards Rifle Division on 10 June, the sector of which was viewed as the most tank-vulnerable axis in the army, then it turns out that only one of its 27 rifle companies had more than 90 men (the 2nd Rifle Company of the 233 Guards Rifle Regiment), while the rest just had 65-89 men each! Even so, there is not a single mention of division commander Morozov and his division in a single document. What reasons the Front command had to bypass a more troubled situation in a frontline division isn't clear, but it is clear that this had to involve some intrigue. Here is one more not quite clear detail: On 5 May 1943 according to the average manning level of the divisions, the 7th Guards Army stood in second place among the Voronezh Front's armies (the top three were the 6th Guards Army – 7,665, the 7th Guards Army – 7,599 and the 40th Army – 7,076),[90] but by the start of the Battle of Kursk stood in first place (7th Guards Army – 8,642, 40th Army – 8,561 and the 6th Guards Army – 8,506).[91] If to compare the number of personnel that arrived in this period as replacements for the divisions, then here too Shumilov didn't lag behind the others. Between 5 May and 5 July the 40th

---

89 TsAMO RF, F. 69A, op. 10757, d. 1, ll. 102, 102obr.
90 TsAMO RF, F. 203, op. 2843, d. 426, information on the armies as of 5 May 1943.
91 Ibid.

Army received a total of 8,702 men, the 38th Army – 5,636, the 7th Guards Army – 4,638 and the 6th Guards Army – 2,997.[92] It is difficult to say why, then, its commanders and even the chief of staff figured more often than the others in the orders of the Front's leadership as slackers and idlers.

I assume that the chief of staff Major General G.S. Lukin, who had only recently replaced Major General I.A. Laskin in the post, was taking the rap for the shortcomings of his predecessor. He had only had time to look into the essence of the new problem, and still hadn't had time to get the process flows of the army's mechanism up and running properly under his direction.

Summing up, I will present the main indicators of the strength of the 7th Guards Army and the manning levels of its divisions by the start of the Battle of Kursk. On 5 July 1943, the 7th Guards Army had 78,831 men on its roster, including 60,500 in its seven rifle divisions. The average strength of each division was 8,643; the 213th Rifle Division had the most men, 8,865, while the 78th Guards Rifle Division had the fewest – 8,346. Overall, the army possessed 856 guns (not including anti-aircraft guns) with a caliber between 45mm and 152mm (including 349 45mm, 84 regimental guns, 97 anti-aircraft guns and only 33 self-propelled guns) and 2,428 anti-tank rifles. It also had 1,215 mortars of which 345 were 50mm, 578 were 82mm and 195 were 120mm, and 97 rocket launchers. In the army's five tank regiments and brigades there were a total of 224 domestically-produced T-60, T-70, T-34 and KV-1 tanks and British-produced Mk-II and Mk-III tanks. In order to deliver to the troops everything necessary, the 7th Guards Army received 1,992 trucks and vehicles of all brands, including almost half, 840, which were turned over directly to the divisions.[93] See Table 2 for a more detailed look at the army's combat composition.

A most important component of an acting army's success is the smooth performance of its rear services. Unfortunately, it must be acknowledged that in the period of preparations for the Battle of Kursk and in the course of it, the quartermaster service in the divisions of the Voronezh Front, and the supply of the troops with food and ammunition were not functioning smoothly. This problem was acute and seriously affected the morale of the men.

It all began back at the end of the winter of 1943. In the course of the decisive advance by the Front's troops from Stalingrad almost to the Dnepr River, the combat divisions had become separated from their own supply bases by 300-400 kilometers. The arriving spring thaw, and the loss of a lot of vehicles due to breakdowns or combat damage, virtually paralyzed the work of the rear services. As a result, from March 1943 Voronezh Front's troops began to experience very serious difficulties with rations. In April, the rations of the soldiers and commanders of the combat units were reduced to a minimum, both in volume and according to the calories. At critical moments, even Po-2 airplanes were delivering hardtack and salt and dropping them in bags on prepared areas in the vicinity of the divisions' command posts. The 73rd Guards Rifle Division's combat diary, for example, mentions this means of delivering supplies.[94] As veterans recalled, at this time in many of the divisions, the soldiers began to experience night blindness due to the extreme hunger and lack of nutrition. A man suffering with this illness had difficult seeing in low light conditions, and at night became virtually blind. As experience demonstrated, practically everyone suffered with these symptoms, but night blindness struck the conscripts from the Central Asian republics particularly hard, and at this time there were a lot of them in the army. In separate units the problem became so acute, that only Russians, Belorussians and Ukrainians could be sent out to man the combat outposts at night, without relief, night after night, even though they were also becoming emaciated. Addressing a conference in the headquarters of the 69th Army in the middle of April, the newly-appointed member of the Voronezh Front's Military Council Lieutenant General N.S.

---

92   Ibid., information on the armies as of 5 May and 5 July 1943.
93   Ibid., page without a number.
94   TsAMO RF, F. 73 gv. sd, op. 1, d. 33, page without a number.

Khrushchev recommended to the division commanders to organize the collection of nettles and wild sorrel in order to prepare a vitamin-rich borsch. This was a half-measure caused by the lack of alternatives. Treatment required systematic, high-caloric meals that included animal fats, and this was extremely difficult to organize at that moment.[95]

Because of this, in the villages that were situated near the front that spring, there were not isolated cases of looting, the illegal abduction of livestock from peaceful residents, and even armed attacks by groups of servicemen against the residents of collective farmers, some of which led to murder. Even so, at this time the hungry, gaunt Soviet civilians of the villages, who'd been picked clean by the occupiers, were doing everything to help their own army. After the war, M.S. Shumilov wrote, "We were deeply grateful to the people, the residents of the Korocha, Velikaia Mikhailovka, Shebekino, Volokovka area, and of the Volchansk and Belgorod areas, who came to help us in these hard days. The rear laborers were constructing defensive fortifications of the second army-level belt, roads and bridges with enthusiasm, and repairing vehicles and doing light repairs to tanks and guns.[96] In the spring thaw, in the difficult conditions of the lack of roads, they were bringing us ammunition and food in carts."[97]

It shouldn't be said that the wave of crimes washed over all of the populated places where troops were located. Nevertheless, the scale of the crimes was such that the command of a number of armies, in particular of the 40th Army, and even the Front command was forced to issue specific orders that demanded the immediate restoration of order in the divisions. The illegal activities of servicemen in the tactical zone not only brought about the unjustified losses, bitterness and suffering of the people, but also surreptitiously undermined the soldiers' collectives and sapped the Red Army's authority in the eyes of the people, which meant these servicemen were in fact working to benefit the enemy. Thus their activities were viewed by the Soviet command not only as simple criminal acts, but as military crimes which carried harsh punishments. The entire structure of both the Red Army and the NKVD were directed at eradicating them.

In addition to the objective difficulties that led to interruptions in food supplies, subjective factors had a great influence: the negligence and disorganization of the rear echelon at every level of command. Having received information about the difficult situation with food, N.F. Vatutin quickly created and sent special commissions to investigate what was happening, and they revealed a dismal picture of thieving and outrages in the rear. From the Voronezh Front commander-in-chief's Order No. 00173:

> The deputy commander of the 167th Rifle Division for rear services Major Kardopolov and the chief of the PAX [mobile field bakeries] 1st Quartermaster-Technician Naradovich over the course of three days supplied the division's men with low-quality bread, prepared with an addition of un-milled oat kernels. Knowing that the bread they had delivered to the units was unsuitable for consumption, and that part of it was being thrown out or used as feed for horses, they continued to prepare and deliver plainly inedible bread to the soldiers, leaving a significant number of Red Army men without bread, forcing them to eat a plainly bad product. Altogether, 15,614 kilograms of this bread was prepared and sent by them to the units.[98]

---

95 In practice it was noted that people recovered more quickly with the consumption of animal liver.
96 It is known that the repair of motorized and armored vehicles, and the fabrication of simple spare parts, equipment and tools was centered in Shebekino.
97 Parot'kin, *Kurskaia bitva*, p. 296.
98 TsAMO RF, F. 288 gv. sp, op. 47024s, d. 4, l. 39. For these offences, both officers were sent into a penal battalion for a three-month period.

I will stress that not simply rank and file servicemen were perpetrating such outrages, but also senior officers (like the deputy division commander), while at the same time the troops and the general population were going hungry. The scale of abuses was demoralizing, thus measures to reform the services were implemented quickly in almost every army and yielded a positive effect. Nevertheless, even before the start of the Battle of Kursk, the situation with food supplies still wasn't fully corrected. For example, M.S. Shumilov on 20 June 1943 personally requested emergency aid from Lieutenant General S.P. Ivanov, the Voronezh Front's chief of staff: "… the Army presently lacks sufficient flour or hardtack, tinned meat or meat, and sugar in its stockpiles; I can feed the divisions a full assortment [of products] only tomorrow, but for 21 June the 36th Guards and 81st Guards Rifle Divisions won't have meat, while the 36th, 73rd and 78th Rifle Divisions won't have flour or hardtack, and there is still nothing in the pipeline. I ask that you take urgent measures."[99]

The sanitary and quartermaster services were no less neglected. On 1 June 1943, N.F. Vatutin in his Order No. 01268a on the results of an inspection of the 35th Guards Rifle Corps, N.F. Vatutin wrote to its commander:

> …
> 2. I'm astonished, extremely so, when all the inspectors note that the regimen, training and work in a Guards corps is worse than in the regular divisions of your neighbor, the 69th Army. It is totally intolerable and criminal, considering that we have enough uniforms now, but you haven't taken any steps to re-clad the soldiers in summer uniforms."
> 3. It is totally intolerable and criminal, when after our visit and considering that we now have an adequate number of uniforms, that you didn't take any steps to redress the soldiers in summer uniforms.[100]

One must pay due respect to the restraint and correctness of General of the Army Vatutin, although likely it was difficult for him to be so tactful. It wasn't easy to restrain one's emotions to see how "father-commanders" in other Guards formations and not only them (in the very same 7th Guards Army and 38th Army) bullied and mistreated subordinates, who were daily shoveling dozens of cubic meters of earth, erecting defensive lines, while being half-starved, unwashed for several weeks, and drenched in sweat in winter tunics and trousers. An excerpt from an account about the situation in the 78th Guards Rifle Division as of 17 June: "Bandaging material is extremely insufficient – in 2nd Battalion of the 225th Guards Rifle Regiment there are just 60 individual packets [for more than 400 soldiers!] The soldiers rarely bathe and without soap [Can such be called a bath at all?]. Because of the lack of water, the soldiers don't regularly wash up. There is insufficient patching material in the units."[101]

What is more, such a depressing situation was noted everywhere, in all the armies. From an order of Voronezh Front's Military Council to the commander of the 38th Army on 17 June 1943:

> 167th Rifle Division – the supply of uniforms is extremely unsatisfactory. Many men lack uniforms, and the majority of the soldiers don't have underwear. They take weekly baths, but there are still lice infestations. The soldiers have no portable food available. The regiment lacks 1,091 mess kits, and there are also no buckets for bringing up food and water …. The majority of the men are unshaven and unshorn.

---

99   TsAMO RF, F. 203, op. 2843, d. 461, l. 91.
100 TsAMO RF, F. 203, op. 2843, d. 301, l. 268.
101 TsAMO RF, F. 203, op. 2843, d. 301, l. 229.

The 340th Rifle Division – In the 1142nd Rifle Regiment, the PFS [food and forage service] doesn't bother putting together a menu. The division's PFS isn't checking on the regiments and isn't bothering to improve the soldier's nutrition. The inspection of individual loaves of bread in the 1144th Rifle Regiment's 3rd Rifle Battalion by means of weighing them has established that the soldiers are being shorted 75-100 grams of bread on average per day. In the 1142nd Rifle Regiment's 3rd Rifle Battalion, the distribution of the food to the soldiers is being implemented in a criminal manner. A significant portion of the battalion is leaving the front and heading 1 kilometer to the rear as single individuals. As a result of this, the defense of the forward edge is weakened for a certain time. A significant number of the soldiers of the 1144th Rifle Regiment have no spoons, and the soldiers get their chow straight out of a kettle.

Items of the clothing allowance for the division's regiments weren't supplied on 12 June 1943; underwear and foot wrappings are particularly lacking. There are up to 500 men walking around in the division's regiments in quilted trousers and hats with earflaps [in the middle of June!], wearing hand-crafted baste shoes [crafted from interwoven bark] or going barefoot. The situation is particularly bad in the 1142nd Rifle Regiment: 185 men are going around wearing quilted trousers; 274 men in hoods and hats with earflaps; 29 are barefooted; 80 men require immediate replacement of their footgear; and 513 pairs require repair. Repairs aren't being made because of the absence of cobbler's material. The soldiers take weekly baths. Lice infestations reach 3% of the men in the 1144th Rifle Regiment. The soldiers aren't shaving and haircuts aren't being organized. In the 1142nd Rifle Regiment, bunkers and communication trenches are in an unsanitary state. There are not specially-equipped toilets.[102]

Reading such documents, you get to understand why frontline veterans, when recalling the war, often called those who served in the rear echelon units "rear rats". It is difficult to refrain from such an evaluation, when because of slovenliness, tens of thousands of men each day who were under the stress of mortal danger at the front were unable to receive the most basic needs – a clean uniform and a decent meal.

It should be particularly noted that the Voronezh Front was no sort of anomaly; ordinary people served in its rear area, and the problems there were typical for the entire Red Army. Order No. 053 from the Deputy People's Commissar of Defense Lieutenant General A.S. Shcherbakov dated 24 January 1943 testifies to the fact that this was a significant problem in the acting army:

> An inspection conducted by the Main Political Directorate of the Red Army has established:
>
> 1. In the units of the Kalinin, Western, Trans-Caucasus and of a number of other Fronts, as well as in the Volga Military District there is evidence of a large number of cases testifying to the callous, bureaucratic attitude of many political organs, commanders and political workers toward the living conditions of the soldiers. Individual political chiefs, commanders, their deputy commanders for political affairs and other political workers show criminal indifference to the everyday life of the soldiers; they show no concern for keeping them fed and uniformed or about heating their dugouts and bunkers, providing medical aid to the wounded and sick, or sanitary-hygienic servicing of the soldiers (washing up in a bathhouse and replacing underwear). At the same time there are cases, when at the fault of commanders and political workers a large amount of food and articles of uniforms, designated for the soldiers, become unsuitable, spoil or rot because of the poor organization of storage and preservation.

---

102 TsAMO RF. F. 203, op. 2843, d. 301, ll. 237-238.

2. The feeding of the troops in a number of units, despite the full availability of food products in the stockpiles and supply bases, is organized badly. For example, the soldiers of the Kalinin Front's 238th and 262nd Rifle Divisions over 3-5 days while on the march each received just 200-250 grams of hardtack a day. The soldiers of the 32nd and 306th Rifle Divisions and the 48th Mechanized Brigade over a course of 5 days didn't receive even bread. As a result of the acute hunger, many of the soldiers had various illnesses, while the 279th Rifle Division in November 1942 even had 25 men who died of hunger.
3. Certain political organs and commanders do not concern themselves with the soldiers' uniforms. In the 25th Rifle Regiment of Briansk Front's 6th Guards Rifle Division, the Red Army soldiers of one of the platoons continued to go around in forage caps and ragged greatcoats, or were standing at post in them in -25 C. weather. In other platoons of this same regiment, the new replacement soldiers didn't receive tunics for 1 to 1.5 months and wore greatcoats as undergarments.[103]

As General A.I. Eremenko, who took command of the Kalinin Front in the spring of 1943, wrote in his diary, in the first three months of 1943, there were 76 cases of death by extreme emaciation in his troops, for which on 25 April 1943 its former commander General M.A. Purkaev was given a reprimand and dismissed from his post, while a member of the Military Council was turned over for trial in front of a military tribunal.[104]

A most difficult situation also developed in February-March 1943 in the Central Front, which was holding the northern face of the Kursk salient. Here in the troops of the 70th Army, because of the thoughtless organization of marches and the rear services, there were also simultaneous cases of death by hunger of Red Army soldiers in several divisions, for which its commander Major General G.F. Tarasov was removed from his post, while two members of the Military Council were given reprimands.[105] Even in May, reporting on the implementation of Order No. 0053, the chief of the Political Department of the Central Front's 60th Army Major General K. Isaev wrote:

> The situation in the units of the army with uniforms and footgear for the personnel was exceptionally stressful. Up to the present time, some of the soldiers of the new batch of replacements don't have a Red Army uniform and are going around in the same garb that they were wearing before being called up into the army. There are a number of soldiers who haven't been equipped with leather footgear and are still wearing felt boots. The supply of the soldiers and officers with summer uniforms is bad.[106]

However, although the above-listed disgraces were due to a significant extent to the army commanders in the field, nevertheless it should be said that there were also objective causes. The main one of them was that this sphere of everyday life in the Red Army was always a matter of secondary and often even tertiary significance. Formally the commander of a unit or formation answered for everything that concerned the personnel, although in reality his superior primarily demanded the implementation of combat orders. In the event that an officer failed to carry out a combat order several times, he wasn't kept long in his post and the reasons for failing to carry them

---

103 *Russkii arkhiv. Velikaia Otechestvennaia: Prikazy Narodnogo komissara oborony SSSR (1943-1945)* [*Russian archive. Great Patriotic War: Orders of the USSR People's Commissar of Defense (1943-1945)*] Vol. 13[2-3] (Moscow: TERRA, 1997), p. 36.
104 Eremenko, A.I., *Dnevniki, zapiski, vospominaniia, 1939-1946* [*Diaries, notes, recollections, 1939-1946*] (Moscow: ROSSPEN, 2013), p. 146.
105 TsAMO RF, F. 62, op. 321, d. 5, l. 118.
106 TsAMO RF, F. 62, op. 321, d. 24, l. 67.

out, as a rule, didn't play a substantial role. In contrast, if he could make his subordinates toe the line and achieve the desired results, he was excused much, including problems with supplies. Even if the entire rear service was in disarray and this fact was identified by a high-ranking commission, the commander in the best case might only receive a verbal rebuke and an order to put things in order. According to frontline standards, this was practically nothing.

Reading the archival documents, not rarely you encounter paradoxical cases, when a drunkard and poor commander in a professional sense, who takes a hill or village at a heavy cost in blood, or who lost dozens of armored vehicles in a single combat ends up decorated with an Order. At the same time, a sensible officer, who cared for his subordinates, and who strove to bypass knots of resistance to avoid excessive casualties, but who didn't always achieve his objective according to the plan, seemed in the eyes of the command to be an irresponsible slacker, and as a rule he would be dismissed from his post in essence over a mere trifle.

The second chronic problem in the Red Army was the lack of motorized transport, and a rear service without wheels is like a soldier without a gun. An acting army is a city in the field (or in the mountains or swamps), and everything that is needed by tens of thousands of men must be delivered daily and year-round, with no discounting due to mud or blizzards. At the front the men joked, "One can come to terms even with the Fritzes, but not with the belly." Stockpiles and supply bases were located dozens of kilometers behind the front, and one couldn't get by without one or two one-and-a-half ton trucks in order to deliver food or supplies, for example, for a battalion of 450-500 men. If you recall that shortage of mechanized tow and horses even of the artillery reached 60% and more, then when planning the use of motorized transport, the needs of the rear services were of secondary importance to a commander.

Wrapping up the brief story about the preparations of the 7th Guards Army for the summer campaign, one should particularly emphasize that the three months of, without exaggeration, titanic work yielded very significant results. First, over a rather short period of time in the difficult conditions of the spring thaw, an entire army was moved from Stalingrad to the Belgorod area, which managed to stabilize the front and substantially strengthened the sector of defense running between Belgorod and Volchansk. Second, over this time the infrastructure on the territory where the 7th Guards Army's troops deployed was not only fully restored, but significantly developed, and a repair and maintenance base was created virtually from scratch. Third, enormous work was done to fortify the sectors of defense of two armies, which at that time became a model for field fortifications. The most important elements of these was a tightly organized system of fire, the primary principle of which was the concentrated use of all weapons on the main axis, and an elaborate system of fortifications and obstacles. Fourth, after the significant losses suffered in the winter of 1943, all of the rifle divisions and the artillery and tank units were not simply replenished, but were practically brought back up to establishment strength, while the arriving replacements received a certain amount of combat training directly at the front. Finally, on the basis of an analysis of the terrain and the intelligence that arrived through various channels, a well-considered plan of defense for the army's combat sector was worked out, and later events would show it to be fully justified. At the same time, it was not only made known to each rifle battalion commander (at least the parts that concerned him) and was reviewed in detail with him, but its main elements were rehearsed by the commanders and elements.

Despite the enormous quantity of problems and difficult tasks which the leadership of the 7th Guards Army and all its personnel encountered, by the start of the summer fighting it was one of the top combined-arms armies of the Voronezh Front judging by the manning levels of the divisions, the training of the men and officers, and the degree of fortification of the lines. The 7th Guards Army's commander Lieutenant General M.S. Shumilov personally made a substantial contribution to the organization and fulfillment of such large-scale work. He was not only an experienced military commander, who had forged his skill in the furnace of Stalingrad, but also a wise man who worked calculatingly and tirelessly, with enthusiasm and verve over the forming and improvement of a large army mechanism, largely from scratch. Jumping somewhat ahead in the events, I'll note that thanks to his initiative, far-sightedness and large capacity for work, the 7th Guards Army would conduct the Kursk defensive operation in a worthy manner.

2

In the shadow of the main attack – Army Detachment Kempf's role in Operation Citadel

Even before the end of March 1943, the frontlines at the southern half of the Soviet-German front had become stabilized, while in Berlin the Wehrmacht command staff had already begun planning a future offensive. The Commander-in-Chief of Army Group South Field Marshal E. von Manstein, whose recent counteroffensive that had recaptured Belgorod had made him the "hero of the day", had no small role in this. It was he who had the idea of an attack toward Kursk. However, immediately after the German forces had seized Belgorod and the area southwest of there, the German offensive had run out of steam, so the decision was made to go over to a defense.

Before laying out the essence of the plan for Army Detachment Kempf's offensive, I will mention the Wehrmacht's overall attack toward Kursk. According to Hitler's Operation Order No. 6, the objective of the general 1943 offensive, which on 31 March received the official code name of Operation *Zitadelle* [Citadel], was the encirclement of the Voronezh and Central Fronts in the Kursk salient by means of meeting attacks by two major German groupings: Army Group South out of the area of Belgorod in the direction of Kursk, and Army Group Center (the Ninth Army) out of the area south of Orel to the south. It was assumed that as a result of the destruction of Vatutin's and Rokossovsky's armies, the Wehrmacht could ultimately dig in along the Nezhegal' – Korocha River – Skorodnoe – Tim – east of Shchigry – Sosna River line. Manstein's troops were assigned the leading role:

> Army Group South with its assembled forces would launch an attack from the Belgorod – Tomarovka line, break through the front at the Prilepy – Oboian' line, and link up at Kursk and east of there with the attacking army of Army Group Center. In order to provide cover for the offensive from the east it was necessary to reach the Nezhegal', Korocha River, Skorodnoe, Tim line as quickly as possible without weakening the forces on the Prilepy, Oboian' axis. In order to screen the offensive from the west, it was planned to use some of the forces which were simultaneously given the task to launch an attack against the encircled enemy grouping.[1]

The Field Marshal selected Colonel General H. Hoth's Fourth Panzer Army to serve as his group's assault wedge, which was supposed to rupture the line of the Voronezh Front and link up east of Kursk with Army Group Center in order to create the inner ring of encirclement. The plan anticipated positioning the panzer army's forces west of the Belgorod – Oboian' highway.

---

1 Parot'kin, Major General I.V. (ed.), *Kurskaia bitva* [*Battle of Kursk*] (Moscow: Nauka, 1970), p. 521.

Indeed, according to its initial conception, Hoth's panzer army was to attack directly to the north in the direction of Oboian', but after an adjustment of the operation's plan in May 1943, its main attack was shifted to the northeast toward Prokhorovka Station. Two of its panzer formations, the XXXXVIII and II SS Panzer Corps, were supposed to breach the Soviet defenses and break into operational space. It was planned to deploy General of Panzer Troops W. Kempf's[2] army detachment, which consisted of three corps (III Panzer Corps, XXXXII Army Corps and Korps "Raus", which was named after its commander General of Panzer Troops Erhard Raus) to the right of it, in the vicinity of Belgorod and to the south. It was to operate along a secondary axis and create the outer ring of encirclement. In order to cover the outer flanks of Hoth's and Kempf's troops, it was planned to bring forward three army corps, consisting of 2-3 infantry divisions each, reinforced with artillery and elements of assault guns, but without tanks. They were to resolve an entire array of extremely complicated tasks: to consolidate the captured ground, cover the flanks of the breakthrough and in emergency situations act as "donors" to the panzer corps in order to plug gaps in the line and cover boundaries. On the left flank of the Fourth Panzer Army was the LII Army Corps (57th, 255th and 322nd Infantry Divisions), and on the right flank of Army Detachment Kempf was General of Infantry Franz Mattenklott's XXXXII Army Corps (the 39th, 161st and 282nd Infantry Divisions).

Army Detachment Kempf faced one more, albeit very important task – from the first day of the offensive to its conclusion, he was supposed to screen the Fourth Panzer Army's right flank (II SS Panzer Corps) securely, and by keeping pace with the latter's advance it was to create an outer ring of encirclement around the Russian forces in the Kursk salient while simultaneously conducting an active defense of its own right flank. In the offensive's first stage, the axis of advance was determined to be Belgorod – Korocha – Skorodnoe, which extended for approximately 65 kilometers. In a revamped order for Operation Citadel on 1 June 1943, W. Kempf wrote:

2. … Fourth Panzer Army breaches the enemy's defenses in the direction toward Kursk, advances across the line Mar'ino – Oboian' and establishes contact as quickly as possible with the Ninth Army attacking from the north.
3. Kempf's operational group has the task to secure the entire operation, conducting an offensive toward the east. For this it holds a line on the Donets River from the right flank to the mouth of the Nezhegal' River and seizes a line: Nezhegol, Korocha.

---

2   Werner Kempf, General of Panzer Troops (01.04.1941). He was born on 09.03.1886 in Königsberg. Already as an officer he participated in the First World War, ending the war as a captain. He served in staff posts in the inter-war period, including as an inspector of motorized units. After being promoted to colonel on 01.04.1935, he was appointed in command of the 4th Panzer Brigade. In early 1939 he received his first general's rank – major general – and became the commander of Division "Kempf" (which was subsequently transformed into the 10th Panzer Division), which took part in the invasion of Poland. On 01.10.1939, he was transferred to the equivalent post in the XXXXI Panzer Corps' 6th Panzer Division. In this role he distinguished himself in the capture of France. When forcing the Maas River, the 6th Panzer Division destroyed the French 102nd Division. For his successful command of the panzer division, on 03.06.1940 he was awarded the Knight's Cross, and on 31.07.1940 he was promoted to lieutenant general. On 06.01.1941 he took command of the XXXXVIII Panzer Corps. With the start of Germany's invasion of the Soviet Union, the XXXXVIII Panzer Corps was part of General E. Kleist's *Panzergruppe* 1 and took part in the encirclement of Southwestern Front's forces near Kiev. On 10.08.1942 he was awarded the Oak Leaves to the Knight's Cross; this was his final high honor. On 30.09.1942 he took command of Army Detachment Kempf, but on 16.08.1943 he was dismissed from this post by Hitler and was located in the command reserve until the spring of 1944. Between 6.10 to 4.12 1944 he commanded the forces in the Vosges Mountains (France). From November 1944 he was in retirement. He died on 6 January 1964 in the Federal Republic of Germany.

> Together with panzer forces it launches an attack in the overall direction of Skorodnoe, in order to provide for itself a flank cover in the sector: Korocha, bend of the Seim River, south of Manturovo ….[3]

The preparation of the army detachment's offensive plan, like incidentally that of the Fourth Panzer Army, went smoothly and was ultimately finalized in the first half of June. This was connected with important decisions made at a conference between Hoth and von Manstein in Bogodukhovo on 10-11 May 1943. Back then, in the course of two days of discussion at the headquarters of the Fourth Panzer Army regarding the plan for the actions of the Fourth Panzer Army in Operation Citadel, Colonel General Hoth was able to persuade the Field Marshal that in order to obtain at least some sort of tangible results from the offensive, which Hoth didn't consider very promising, it was necessary to prepare the first stage of the operation from the ground up and meticulously. In his opinion, first it was essential to resolve two important tasks: to breach the Russian defenses as far as the Teterevino – Noven'koe line and then destroy the Russsians' mobile reserves in the vicinity of Prokhorovka Station. According to Hoth's calculations, as his panzer army advanced into the depth of the Voronezh Front's defenses, on the third or fourth day of the offensive the Russians would bring up the tank and mechanized formations that had been formed and equipped back in the spring to the area of Prokhorovka. By this moment, two of the German assault formations – the XXXXVIII Panzer Corps and II SS Panzer Corps – were to have broken through the Russian fortifications, inflicted a heavy defeat to the 1st Tank Army that was deployed south of Oboian', and arrived at Prokhorovka Station. Hoth wrote:

> One can assume that after the breakthrough of both of the enemy's defensive belts, the Fourth Panzer Army's task would consist in defeating the Russians' 1st Tank Army, since without its destruction the continued conducting of the operation is unthinkable. By that time the Russian motorized and tank forces located east of the Kursk salient would collide with Kempf's group. According to the evidence available today, the size and strength of these formations were such that Kempf's group alone would not be able to destroy them. Probably, this would require pivoting the Fourth Panzer Army with both of its panzer corps to the east to take part in the tank battle, while securing its rear with infantry divisions. It would be incorrect to detach just one panzer corps of the Fourth Panzer Army for this, and leave the other to attack toward the north [toward Oboian']. It was necessary to destroy as much of the enemy's offensive means as possible. This was possible only in the event that all of the panzer forces of Kempf's army detachment and the Fourth Panzer Army would be turned for an attack in close cooperation against the enemy's eastern flank [toward Prokhorovka]. Only after conducting this part of the operation would it become possible to execute the link-up with the Ninth Army.[4]

According to the results of the conference in Bogodukhovo, substantial changes were made in the plan of Citadel, which directly concerned W. Kempf. If the operation began as initially planned, on 4 May, then primarily it would have to be Kempf's forces that would have to resolve the main task of the first stage of Operation Citadel: to seize Prokhorovka and crush the Soviet mobile formations with the support of the Fourth Panzer Army. Now, according to Hoth's proposal, this task would be shifted onto the shoulders of his panzer army, and Kempf received an order to cover the Fourth Panzer Army's flank securely, and in the course of the anticipated tank

---

3   Parot'kin (ed.), *Kurskaia bitva*, p. 518.
4   Parot'kin, *Kurskaia bitva*, p. 514.

battle at Prokhorovka, to support it from the south, having diverted part of the strength of the Voronezh Front onto itself, and possibly even the Russians' strategic reserves.

Today, comparing the strength of the Voronezh Front's sector of defense with the strength and means in von Manstein's shock groups, this decision seems both optimal and far-sighted. One must pay respect to H. Hoth's ability to assess the existing situation soberly, without reference to the higher command's opinion, and to put his plan into action persistently.

Based on his received objectives, W. Kempf allocated his forces in the following manner: Two corps would comprise his attack grouping: the III Panzer Corps (as the battering ram) – for a breakthrough in the direction of Skorodnoe; and Korps Raus with the aim of seizing the lines of the Nezhegol and Korocha Rivers and to create a defensive line along the right bank of the Korocha River. The XXXXII Army Corps would hold in place, in order to guard the right flank along the Northern Donets River. Of the six divisions that were to break through the defenses of the 7th Guards Army, two (Major General Gustav Schmidt's 19th Panzer Division and Major General Chales de Beaulieu's 168th Infantry Division) had suffered very substantial losses during the March battles and by July 1943 hadn't been fully brought up back to strength with men and armored vehicles. If you consider a number of factors, such as the acute lack of forces and means (especially infantry divisions) in the Fourth Panzer Army in order to resolve such grandiose tasks; the insignificant effective combat strength of Army Detachment Kempf and the low staffing and equipping of its divisions, primarily with tanks; the significant numerical strength of the operational and strategic reserves, which had been accumulated by the Soviet side and could be directed into Voronezh Front's sector; the level of fortifications in the 7th Guards Army's sector of defense, which the Northern Donets River made even stronger; then the task standing in front of Kempf's army detachment was not only very important, but at the same time extremely difficult.

With the start of April 1943 the command of Army Group South had to put its formations back into order, and form the shock groupings for Operation Citadel. While infantry divisions took their place in the line, the panzergrenadiers were withdrawn to the rear for rest and refitting, before being assembled in a compact force for the offensive. Work to reorganize the Fourth Panzer Army and Army Detachment Kempf went on parallel with this. By this time they were rather motley. For example, in the course of the battle for Khar'kov, the army corps of General E. Raus,[5] in addition to three infantry divisions (the 167th, 168th and 320th Infantry Divisions) had under its command the SS Grenadier Regiment *Thule* from the SS Motorized Division *Totenkopf*[6] and motorized, panzer and artillery units and elements of the *Grossdeutschland* Division. At the same time in the Fourth Panzer Army, in addition to the SS Corps (SS Divisions *Liebstandarte Adolf*

---

5 Erhard Raus, General of Panzer Troops (01.05.1943). He was born on 08.01.1889 in Wolframitz in Austria-Hungary's Margraviate of Moravia (today Olbramovice in the Czech Republic's South Moravian Region). On 18.08.1909 he joined the Austrian-Hungarian Army and served in infantry units; in 1912 he earned his first officer's rank – lieutenant. After the end of the First World War, he remained in the Austrian Army. Colonel E. Raus switched to the Wehrmacht only after the *Anschluss*; nevertheless, he quickly climbed the career ladder. On 15.07.1940 he was appointed commander of the 4th Motorized Regiment, and already on 15.04.1941, he took command of the 6th Motorized Infantry Brigade. From the summer of 1941 until the end of the war, Raus took part only in the fighting against the Red Army. In September 1941 he received the rank of major general, and a month later he was awarded the Knight's Cross. On 01.04.1942 he took command of the 6th Panzer Division. On 01.03.1943 (in the words of Raus himself this occurred on 10.02.1943), he assumed command of Lieutenant General H. Cramer's Korps zbV [loosely meaning "for special purpose"], after which until 20 July 1943 it was called Korps zbV Raus, before being renamed as the XI Corps. The corps was formed up at the end of December 1942 and was subordinated to the 2nd Hungarian Army. In the course of the severe winter fighting and the long withdrawal after Stalingrad, the corps was badly tattered.

6 Ed. note: the SS divisions, as well as the Grossdeutschland Division, wouldn't be renamed as panzer grenadier divisions until May 1943 after they received halftracks.

Hitler, *Das Reich* and *Totenkopf*) had the XXXXVIII Panzer Corps (6th Panzer Division, 11th Panzer Division and 106th Infantry Division) and the LVII Panzer Corps (17th Panzer Division and the 15th Infantry Division). Now all of this rather disjointed and cumbersome structure was abolished, the regiments returned to their own divisions, and the corps received a different structure. The panzer corps were organized according to an identical table (three panzer or motorized divisions [which had a TO&E equivalent to a panzer division] and one infantry division) and were distributed unequally among Army Group South's armies. Considering that it was planned for the Fourth Panzer Army to launch the main attack, two of the panzer corps, the XXXXVIII Panzer Corps and the II SS Panzer Corps were transferred to it. Meanwhile, Army Detachment Kempf received the III Panzer Corps commanded by General Hermann Breith,[7] which consisted of the 6th, 7th and 19th Panzer Divisions, as well as the 168th Infantry Division. The shakeup in the tables of organization and the regrouping was finished by the end of April, while the replenishment with equipment and men continued right up to the beginning of July.

Prior to the start of Operation Citadel, the III Panzer Corps was to take its place on Army Detachment Kempf's left flank and in the course of the offensive it was to screen the right flank of the II SS Panzer Corps as it advanced. Its 168th Infantry Division had been holding the Mikhailovka bridgehead (and its two small bridges) on the left bank of the Northern Donets River since March. This small piece of earth offered the command of Army Detachment Kempf tantalizing prospects. In a directive from its chief of staff Major General G. Speidel, issued to the panzer corps as part of the plan of actions for Operation Citadel, it was noted that Breith's panzer corps was to launch the main attack with all three of its panzer divisions out of the Mikhailovka bridgehead and across the two bridges which would need to be constructed south of there, at Dorogobuzheno and Solomino. In Kempf's opinion, in those circumstances this option was the most optimal. First, the positioning of the strongest corps on the left flank made it easier for the army detachment to resolve its main assignment – covering the right flank of Hoth's combat wedge. Second, from Mikhailovka lay the shortest path to the main objective – the village of Skorodnoe.

However, when planning the actions of the III Panzer Corps, especially in the first stage of the operation, this setup placed its leadership in a difficult situation. Considering that three panzer divisions had to be moved up simultaneously to the jumping-off line, it was extremely important to figure out the problem regarding the bridges and to strengthen the panzer divisions with infantry, which on the eastern (left) bank of the river would enable a normal crossing of the panzer

---

7   Hermann Breith, General of Panzer Troops (01.03.1943) was born on 07.05.1892 in Pirmasens. He became a cadet in 1910 and took part in the First World War, serving in the infantry and ending the war as a lieutenant. In the inter-war period he served in the Reichswehr, then in the Wehrmacht. In 1930 he switched to the panzer forces. On 01.01.1939 he was promoted to the rank of colonel. Breith entered the Second World War as the commander of Panzer Regiment 36. On 15.02.1940 he was appointed as commander of the 5th Panzer Brigade, and on 22.10.1941, now as a major general, took command of the 3rd Panzer Division. Between 3 January and 30 October 1943, then from 9 January to 31 May 1944, and finally between 30 June 1944 to the end of the war he commanded the III Panzer Corps. In the Wehrmacht, Breith had the reputation as a successful tank commander. Already on 03.06.1940 he received the Knight's Cross. On 31.01.1942 he received the Knight's Cross with Oak Leaves, and on 21.02.1944 – the Knight's Cross with Oak Leaves and Swords. During the Battle of Kursk his panzer corps suffered heavy losses and was withdrawn for refitting. From 1944 the panzer corps was conducting defensive fighting in Ukraine as part of the First, and then Fourth Panzer Armies. In the autumn of 1944 it was subordinate to the Sixth Army, with which it operated in Hungary. From October 1944 the III Panzer Corps received the name Group (panzer) Breith and was retreating with the forces of the 3rd Hungarian Army, but then again became subordinate to the Sixth Army. On 08.05.1945, Breith surrendered together with his formation to the Allies in the Alps. Two years later he was freed from prison and took up residence in the FRG. He died on 9 March 1964 in the town of Wachtberg.

divisions and the deployment of its significant amount of armor and vehicles. Intelligence information revealed that the Russians had thrown up powerful fortifications around the Mikhailovka bridgehead, and indeed the bridgehead itself was not large. Therefore Breith decided to give both of the existing bridges only to the 6th Panzer Division, while the 7th and 19th Panzer Divisions, as well as two infantry divisions of Korps Raus, the 320th and 106th Infantry Divisions, would have to force a crossing of the Northern Donets River from the march, using their organic bridging equipment and whatever improvised means that was available.

A rather unusual solution was proposed to strengthen the *kampfgruppen* of the panzer divisions. In the conditions of an acute deficit of infantry, the corps command suggested splitting up the 168th Infantry Division and allocating a grenadier regiment, an artillery battalion and an engineer company to each of the panzer divisions. The panzer divisions were supposed to create assault groups out of these units and elements, as well as the battalions of the panzer divisions' own motorized infantry regiments, which would be the first to cross the river with the task of expanding the bridgehead in the 6th Panzer Division's sector, and establishing bridgeheads for the 7th and 19th Panzer Divisions. Only after these assault groups' grenadiers shoved the Russians back into the depth of the 7th Guards Army's main belt of defenses would it become possible to cross the armor and heavy weapons to the eastern bank of the Northern Donets River. *Kampfgruppen* of Hünersdorff's,[8] Schmidt's[9] and von Funck's own panzer divisions were to take direct part in the opening assaults. In order to support the assault groups on the eastern bank in the first hours of the offensive, Breith decided to move up a battalion of assault guns to the area of the 6th Panzer Division's bridges, and to give the 19th Panzer Division a company of Tiger tanks. He believed that these attached assets would be used to destroy enemy firing positions directly on the forward edge of the main belt of defenses, and then, after the Russian defenses were penetrated, they would move on in the wake of the first wave of grenadiers that crossed the river and suppress any enemy resistance encountered by the advancing infantry.

Breith presented his plan at a command staff map exercise, which took place on 3 July 1943 with the participation of the leadership of Army Detachment Kempf and Army Group South. The American scholar S. Newton writes:

---

8   Walther von Hünesdorff (Lieutenant General) was born on 28 November 1898 in Cairo, Egypt. He became a cadet in 1915, and after acquiring the officer's rank of lieutenant, entered service in a Hussar regiment. He served in the Reichswehr in staff posts. At the start of the Second World War, von Hünersdorf was serving in the Operations Department of the 253rd Infantry Division, but on 25.10.1939 he was transferred to an equivalent position in the II Army Corps. On 15.02.1941, he became the chief of staff of General H. Hoth's *Panzergruppe* 3. In this role he took part in Operation Barbarossa (the invasion of the Soviet Union). On 01.07.1942 he was appointed to an independent command post as commander of the 6th Panzer Division's Panzer Regiment 11, and on 07.02.1943 he took command of the 6th Panzer Division. On 22.12.1942, he was awarded the Knight's Cross. During the preparations for the Battle of Kursk, he spoke negatively about Operation Citadel, saying the future operation violated the basic principles of leadership and emphasized that Germany didn't have sufficient strength to realize such an ambitious project.

9   Gustav Schmidt (Lieutenant General from 01.01.1943) was born on 24 April 1894 in Carsdorf. He became a cadet in 1913 and served in the infantry. On 10.10.1939 in the rank of colonel he was transferred from the post in command of Infantry Regiment 216 to become the commander of Infantry Regiment 74. On 01.10.1940 he took command of a brigade, and then on 01.04.1942 became the commander of the 19th Panzer Division. On 22.04.1942 he was awarded the German Cross in Gold. In 1943 his panzer division was sent to the south of the Soviet-German front, and as part of the III Panzer Corps took part in fighting near Rostov. For his successful leadership of the troops under his command, on 06.03.1943 Schmidt received the Knight's Cross with Oak Leaves.

Kempf wondered if the regiments of the 168th Infantry Division, even supported by assault guns, Tigers, and corps artillery assets, would have the strength to penetrate the first Soviet defensive line quickly enough to expand the existing bridgeheads for the commitment of the main bodies of the 6th and 19th Panzer Divisions. He questioned Breith's decision not to attach a Tiger company to the 6th Panzer Division and mandated an increase in the infantry attachment to 7th Panzer Division (Breith had originally allocated von Funck only a single battalion). Field Marshal von Manstein expressed his own doubts about a tactical plan that required the 168th Infantry Division to be dismantled and then reassembled in the middle of the battle; he pointed to the absolute necessity of having that division available to relieve the pressure on II SS Panzer Corps's eastern flank.[10]

In addition, the Field Marshal expressed reservations about Breith's plan for only a brief artillery barrage immediately prior to the attack, and not a length artillery preparation, arguing that the Russian camouflage and broken terrain "made identification of enemy positions difficult in spite of careful reconnaissance". However, Breith countered by saying that "under such circumstances a long artillery preparation would have been a complete waste of ammunition, without producing concrete results".[11]

Unquestionably, all the concerns were based on legitimate justifications, and possibly the commander of the III Panzer Corps realized this. However, at the same time all of those present at the map exercise understood that the plan of actions was being worked out under a severe constraint of a deficit of force. Opposite Army Detachment Kempf's front, the Soviet side had constructed a multi-echeloned, powerful defense, the strength of which the Northern Donets River would substantially bolster in the opening hours of the offensive, and German intelligence had already identified numerous tactical reserves in the depth of the Soviet defenses. Neither von Manstein nor Kempf had the possibility of strengthening the III Panzer Corps. Thus, Breith's plan was accepted without any substantive changes. Thereby the leaders of Army Detachment Kempf and Army Group South demonstrated their attitude toward the discussed problems – in the existing situation, the corps commander had the best view of how best to arrange his forces; after all, ultimately he would lead the troops into battle and also be responsible for it.

The greatest weakness in the plan of Army Detachment Kempf's offensive, like that incidentally of the Fourth Panzer Army, was the lack of reserves for both their commanders and the subordinate corps commanders. This gave rise first of all to a lack of confidence on the German side that the available forces could even break through the Russians' powerful field fortifications in a relatively short period of time. Therefore all of the available forces were being committed to the opening attack, even to the detriment of sober calculation. In a number of sectors, it was proposed to deploy the forces so densely that they wouldn't be able to help each other, but would more likely get in each other's way. Not only the command of Army Detachment Kempf and its subordinate corps were wrestling with these problems, but also their neighbors. In particular, the XXXXVIII Panzer Corps faced a very similar situation.

Hermann Breith was considered one of the experienced and most successful panzer commanders in the Wehrmacht, and thus he couldn't help but realize that the absence of reserves would substantially limit his influence on the operational situation, and even given a successful breakthrough by one of his divisions, he wouldn't be able to exploit this tactical success. Nevertheless, he didn't

---

10 Newton, S. *Kurskaia bitva. Nemetskii vzgliad* [*Kursk: The German View*] (Moscow: Iauza/Eksmo, 2006), p. 503. This is the Russian translation of Newton's book, which was published by De Capo Press in 2002. The relevant quote can be found on page 399 of the text.
11 Ibid.

protest the position of Spiedel's staff about committing all three panzer divisions simultaneously into the battle. Even so, he clearly expressed his thoughts regarding other, less significant problems, and in general his recommendations were accepted. At the same time, General Breith had to realize that these decisions would result in an extremely high concentration of forces in the breakthrough sector designated for his panzer corps (four divisions, three of them panzer, within a front of 16 kilometers), and thus difficulties both with the command and maneuver even of insignificant forces would be unavoidable. In addition, the introduction of the 6th Panzer Division into the Mikhailovka bridgehead didn't offer anything promising. As a professional, he had to know that the Soviet side viewed this area as the most likely place for an enemy attack, and thus it would fortify this sector better than any other sector of the front. All these considerations had to lead to the thought that moving the 6th Panzer Division up to the front on 5 July wasn't the most promising decision, and it would be better to keep it in the second echelon, so it could serve as an operational reserve.

In addition, when analyzing the combat deployment of Kempf's forces before the start of the battle, it is impossible not to call attention to the following, rather important, detail. The concept of "an axis of main attack" was concisely expressed only at the level of the army detachment, whereas on the level of III Panzer Corps it was neglected. Breith's panzer divisions were to be arrayed in a single line and received an order to operate essentially in parallel directions. Thus, in the III Panzer Corps there was no concentration of forces for a main attack. Such a balanced distribution of effort allowed the Soviet side, exploiting details of the terrain and the system of its defenses, to shift the fire of heavy artillery and to maneuver tactical reserves to reinforce the most critical sectors, wherever a German breakthrough was threatened. In their turn Breith's division commanders couldn't count on the assistance of a stronger neighbor or the commitment of corps reserves (there simply weren't any), and would have to count only on their own forces and means. This tactical blunder in combination with the objective problem – the absence of reserves – would substantially and negatively affect the operations of Kempf's army detachment, especially in the first, most difficult 48 hours of the operation.

In addition, when working out the offensive plan, the command of Army Group South planned to send all the forces of the VIII Fliegerkorps to the axis of the main attack on the first day of the operation. The bombers were directed into the sector of the II SS Panzer Corps, while the fighters would cover the airspace above the Fourth Panzer Army. As a result, the secondary axis, in essence, was left exposed, and Kempf's troops, which faced the task of crossing a water barrier while under heavy Russian fire, would have to rely only on their own modest means of flak artillery, and it wasn't clear how best to use it, either in a ground role against enemy firing positions, or in an anti-aircraft role. Even the allocation of a squadron of tank-hunting aircraft, which was planned for the support of Kempf's forces on the second day of the operation (or on the first day in the event of a powerful Russian tank counterattack already on 5 July), didn't go smoothly, in part because of bureaucratic waffling. From Army Detachment Kempf's journal of combat operations for 4 July 1943:

> 0945: A call from Army Group South's Operations Department. The army group's Operations Department has announced that according to an order from Luftwaffe headquarters, the tank-hunting squadrons have been detained in Zaporozh'e. The reason for this is being discussed with General Jeschonnek. However, the Army Group is planning that these squadrons will be used for conducting Citadel.
>
> 1100: A call from the commander of the Army Detachment to Field Marshal von Manstein. The commander of the Army Detachment pointed out the great complications arising from the delay of the tank-hunting squadrons. In response General-Field Marshal von

Manstein promised absolutely to pass along these arguments to General Jeschonnek, with whom he should be in contact in the nearest time.[12]

Taken all together, the obvious errors in Breith's plan and the lack of strength and focus, together with the 7th Guards Army's powerful defensive system and the lack of necessary air support for the offensive became the main reasons for the high losses and setbacks experienced by Army Detachment Kempf. Such losses would affect both the manpower and equipment already from the very first minutes of the operation.

In addition to making the final adjustments to the plan of attack, Hermann Breith faced one more quite substantial problem: restoring his panzer corps' combat capabilities. All of his panzer divisions were well below establishment strength in tanks and weapons, and the refitting was going very slowly. The Reich's industry was struggling to keep up with the Wehrmacht's need for armored vehicles. Therefore the command of Army Group South gave Hoth and Kempf the new Panther and Tiger tanks with their reinforced armor and powerful cannons, in order to reinforce the assault groups. However, for the sake of justice it should be noted that in comparison with the Fourth Panzer Army, Army Detachment Kempf received only "crumbs" of this equipment – Army Group South received 249 Panthers and Tigers, while Army Detachment Kempf received only 45! Thus, in spite of all the requests and the justified appeals, the III Panzer Corps was not brought back up to establishment strength in either tanks or artillery before the start of the battle. By 5 July 1943, the 7th Panzer Division had the most tanks – 112, while the 6th Panzer Division had 106 tanks. The weakest was the 19th Panzer Division, which had only 81 tanks. The quality of the arriving replacement tanks wasn't particularly good either. By the start of the fighting, of the total number of tanks in the 6th and 19th Panzer Divisions, Pz.Kpfw. III and Pz.Kpfw. IV tanks comprised just 60% and 57% respectively; the rest were flame-throwing tanks or outdated Pz.Kpfw. II tanks. Thus, in order to break through the Soviet defenses, these panzer divisions could only use half of their available tank pool. They didn't even receive the battalion of self-propelled artillery (6 Hummel 150mm howitzers and 12 Wäspe 105mm howitzers) that had been promised to each of them, while only 12 of the self-propelled artillery arrived in the 7th Panzer Division, instead of the full 18.

Striving to increase the shock power of the III Panzer Corps, the leadership of Army Detachment Kempf transferred to it the attached Heavy Panzer Battalion 503 (45 Tigers) and the StuG [*Sturmgeschütz*, or Assault Gun] Battalion 228 (22 StuG G and 9 StuG H). This was a substantial reinforcement, especially for the troops of the attacking first wave, and in addition the total number of tanks and self-propelled guns in the III Panzer Corps grew by 67. Also very important was the fact that these tanks and assault guns had 75mm or 88mm long-barreled guns. However, skipping ahead in the events, I will note that the capabilities of both the Panthers and the Tigers were plainly overestimated. The Pz.Kpfw. VI, not to mention the Pz.Kpfw. V, were new tank models for the German Army, which hadn't seen wide use prior to this. The tactics for using the units that had been especially created for them – separate heavy battalions – still hadn't been worked out adequately and implemented in the troops. Thus already on the first day of the offensive, this powerful unit would be rendered combat-ineffective because of its mishandling, without producing any noticeable results. For a more detailed look at the equipment of the panzer divisions of Army Detachment Kempf on 4 July 1943, see Table 5:

---

12 National Archives and Records Administration USA (NARA USA), t. 312, r. 54, f. 7569601.

Table 5 Initial AFV strength for the formations of Army Detachment Kempf on 4 July 1943[13]

	Pz-i	Pz-II	Pz-III	Pz-IV	Pz-VI Tiger	T-34/76	Flammpanzer	Total tanks	Marder	Stug G/ Stug H	Hummel	Wäspe	Total SPGs1
III Panzer Korps													
6 Panzer	–	13	52	28	–	–	13	106	14	–	–	–	14
7 Panzer	–	12	62	38	–	–	–	112	6	–	6	6	18
19 Panzer	3	2	38	38	–	–	–	81	12	–	–	–	12
503 Hvy Panzer Battalion	–	–	–	–	45	–	–	45	–	–	–	–	–
228 SP Gun Battalion	–	–	–	–	–	–	–	–	–	22/9	–	–	31
Total for III Panzer Corps	3	27	152	104	45	–	13	344	32	22/9	6	6	109
Army Korps Raus													
905 Assault Gun Battalion	–	–	–	–	–	–	–	–	–	23/9	–	–	32
393 Assault Gun Battery	–	–	–	–	–	–	–	–	–	12/–	–	–	12
Total for Korps Raus	–	–	–	–	–	–	–	–	–	35/9	–	–	44
Total for Army Detachment Kempf	3	27	152	104	45	–	13	344	32	57/18	6	6	109

Note
1 The Wäspe (105mm) and Hummel (155mm) were self-propelled howitzers. The Marder was a self-propelled tank destroyer. The StuG G/H were self-propelled guns for providing direct support to the infantry, but in the Battle of Kursk (and elsewhere) they were used as anti-tank self-propelled guns.

Directing the army detachment toward a struggle with Soviet mobile formations (the tactical and operational reserves) already when entering a breach of the 7th Guards Army's defensive belts, and subsequently in the area of Prokhorovka as well (with the strategic reserves), the command of Army Group South realized that the three incomplete panzer divisions assigned to Army Detachment Kempf were insufficient. Thus from the outset it was decided to compensate their lack of armor with the latest models of tank destroyers, the *Panzerjäger Hornisse* [Hornet] (subsequently renamed the *Nashorn* [Rhinoceros] by Hitler in 1944) Sd. Kfz. 164 mounting the 8.8cm PaK 43/1 L/71 anti-tank gun, which equipped the Heavy Panzerjäger Battalion 560 in the spring of 1943. At the end of May, this unit arrived under von Manstein's operational control, and he handed it to Kempf, who then gave it to the XXXXII Army Corps. However, subsequently events took place regarding this battalion, which viewed from the sideline seem more like a joke. All day long on 4 July 1943, Kempf, his headquarters, the headquarters of Army Group South, von Manstein personally and even the OKH were intensively engaged in a discussion of the problem of the Hornisse, which in my view, shouldn't have been on their minds before the start of such a major offensive. From Army Detachment Kempf's journal of combat operations:

---

13   Zetterling, N., and Frankson, A., Kursk 1943: A statistical analysis (London, Portland: FRANK CASS, 2000), Table 3.22.

1040: A call from the Operations Department of the Army Group regarding the Hornisse. A proposal to withdraw this gun arose simultaneously in the OKH and in Army Group South. General-Field Marshal von Manstein once again raised the question of responsibility in the event of the loss of mobility of these weapons during an attack. The Operations Department of the Army Group promised to take this question under review right away.

1100: A call from the commander of the Army Detachment to Field Marshal von Manstein. The commander of the Army Detachment … declared that at present the Hornisse was being tested for their possible use as immobile firing positions. Discussing the possibility of the failure with the use of this new equipment, he pointed to the presence of a large number of mechanical problems with it, as well as the need to build special alternative routes.[14]

Fifteen minutes after the discussion between Kempf and von Manstein ended, H. Speidel contacted Army Group South's Operations Department and announced the results of the tests and the discussion with the commander of the Heavy Panzerjäger Battalion 560 regarding how best to use this powerful, but fragile weapon. The result was a conclusion: "The use of the battalion in the form of dug-in firing positions is senseless because problems arise with the gun carriage's lack of a trail support, as was established when conducting the latest test firing; when firing, the self-propelled gun sinks deeply into the ground, which noticeably reduces the accuracy of fire: the declination when firing the next round amounts to 2.5 meters when firing from a range of 1,000 meters." However, this wasn't the main point. In conclusion the chief of staff emphasized that "… at present only one company [14 tank destroyers!] is combat-ready in the battalion. All the remaining machines are under repair, in a disassembled state."[15]

However, this wasn't the end of the discussion. At 1700 Army Detachment Kempf sent an official document to Army Group South, a radio telegram that not only repeated the previous arguments, but also emphasized that in its opinion, "the use of this armor for local attacks is also not sensible in view of the high degree of risk of losing valuable personnel and the armor."[16]

Judging from the captured documents, von Manstein attentively followed the resolution of this insignificant (relative to the level of his post), but extremely prickly question considering Berlin's fixed attention on the Hornisse. Prior to this, he had already been under constant nervous tension because of the delays in launching Citadel due to problems with Hitler's brainchild – the Panther tanks, which weren't ready for combat. The Field Marshal was aware of the rather unflattering reviews of these machines and realized that if the operation failed (and the likelihood of this was high), then heavy losses in Panthers (because of mechanical breakdowns, the high concentration of Russian mines, etc.) would only worsen the situation and an angry exchange with the Führer couldn't be avoided.

Now, however, another unpleasant situation had arisen with the new self-propelled guns, over which the OKH was persistently showing great unease. Although it was obvious to everyone that they, like the Panthers, weren't ready for combat; in addition the command of the troops at every level didn't know how or where to use them sensibly. The Field Marshal acted like an ordinary bureaucrat, who saw the danger of a conflict with his superior on his horizon. He ignored the possible positive effect of the use of the tank destroyer in practice, and deemed it right and proper to halt the discussion about their direct use during Operation Citadel. On that same day, he signed an order to assemble all three companies of the Panzerjäger Battalion 560, which were

---

14 NARA USA, t. 312, r. 54, f. 7569601.
15 NARA USA, t. 312, r. 54,
16 NARA USA, t. 312, r. 54, f. 7569603.

located in Belgorod, Chuguev and Liptsy, and to reassemble them in Khar'kov "for the defense of the city's perimeter as immobile firing positions."[17] In other words, von Manstein opted to hide this powerful weapon, which had been hastily produced for Operation Citadel, in the rear to avoid losses of them. Kempf and his headquarters were not only satisfied with this decision, but in an equally veiled form, though one fully clear for those involved in the problem, recommended sending them not to Khar'kov, but back to the Reich, to those who had manufactured the Hornisse. At 1730 Speidel contacted the Operations Department of Theodor Busse's headquarters staff of Army Group South and reported: "The Army Detachment isn't ready to take responsibility for the combat use of this costly weapon, which isn't ready for battle. He [Kempf] also expressed his reservations against the means of using the Hornisse that was prescribed by the Army Group's order [as immobile firing positions]. He asked to pass these considerations up to the high command."[18]

Thus, less than 24 hours before the launching of Operation Citadel, at a time when hundreds of thousands of men and thousands of armored vehicles and guns were poised to go on the attack, all of the Wehrmacht's command ladder, from the XXXXII Army Corps all the way up to Berlin spent the entire day discussing how to use 14 self-propelled tank destroyers in this operation! The question arises: "Didn't they have anything more to do at that moment?" After all, the Panzerjäger Battalion 560 had arrived in Kempf's army detachment not on 4 July, but back at the end of May. Why then did everyone from the OKH down to the headquarters of Army Detachment Kempf begin to address the question about using the battalion just 24 hours before Operation Citadel? Really, did anyone else not know about these problems with the tank destroyer prior to this? Why then was it necessary to distract the officers of the army detachment and of the XXXXII Army Corps and burden the channels of communication with this matter literally just hours before the operation?

Formally, the bureaucratic approach of OKH (and of the Army Group South) to the forming of this battalion and bringing it up to combat readiness was very similar to the slipshod manner in which the brigade of Panther tanks was made ready for Operation Citadel. The difference was only in the fact that Hitler himself periodically inquired about the fate of the Panthers, and this somewhat prodded the contractors and administrators in the Reich's Armament Ministry who were responsible for creating the tank, but no one showed any particular concern about the Hornisse. The decision to form the battalion was taken on 3 April 1943. In May, striving to report more quickly about the fulfillment of Hitler's order regarding the delivery of new equipment to the troops by 12 June (the next start date designated for Operation Citadel after several postponements), the OKH sent a battalion headquarters and 45 Hornisse tank destroyers authorized for it by railroad to Army Detachment Kempf, which assigned it to the XXXXII Army Corps. Having transferred responsibility for the future fate of the unit to Army Detachment Kempf, Berlin forgot about it for a month, even though the battalion was completely unready for combat. Army Group South also attempt to put some distance between itself and this matter. At this time, the Hornisse, like any new equipment, had a full array of teething problems, and the command of the battalion, the corps and the army detachment had no understanding about how best to use this rather heavy (24 metric tons), ponderous and very obvious weapon (it was no less than 3 meters tall) on the battlefield. Indeed, it was its tall silhouette that was its primary shortcoming. The barrel of its 88mm gun was mounted 2.24 meters above the ground, which was 0.6 meters higher than the

---

17 NARA USA, t. 312, r. 54, f. 7569603.
18 Ibid.

standard placement of this gun on its former fixed mount.[19] At the same time its superstructure and gun shield were only lightly armored.

On 17 June 1943 the battalion commander sent the OKH a letter, in which he made it clear that his unit was unready for combat operations because of the large number of mechanical problems with the tank destroyers. For almost two weeks, there was silence. According to Army Detachment Kempf's plan for the offensive, the Hornisse battalion was supposed to move up into the sector of the III Panzer Corps on the second day of the operation in order to beef up the anti-tank defenses of its left flank and the boundary with Korps Raus. However, it was only at the beginning of June that everyone, including the OKH, recalled that the unit wasn't ready for combat.

At that point a feverish search for a solution to the problem began, the stress grew, the lines of communication began to heat up, and everything reached a peak just 24 hours before the offensive. At the same time, all of the calls, discussions and directives at Kempf's address boiled down to one thing: "According to the Führer's order, we've given you a wonder weapon; use it, although we believe that it is best not to deploy it directly on the battlefield so as not to lose them by chance to enemy fire. It is better to dig them in somewhere in the tactical zone." So von Manstein deemed it right and proper not to risk this expensive "gift" from Berlin and took heed of the OKH's recommendation. Thus the battalion remained with the XXXXII Army Corps and took no part in Operation Citadel. Subsequently, in 1944 the Germans nevertheless learned how to use this weapon, and the Nashorn became a powerful component in their arsenal of anti-tank weapons. I've deliberately gone into this episode in such detail, in order to contrast the realities through a concrete example of how the Germans went about preparing for Kursk with the image later created by the German generals regarding the process of preparing for Citadel. This is how in reality those generals, who after the war would stridently accuse Hitler of both the failure of Operation Citadel and the loss of the war in the effort to save the reputation of the Wehrmacht elite, went about resolving problems.

Considering their meagre possibility of breaking through the forward edge of the main belt of the Soviet defenses, the command of Army Detachment Kempf was placing great hopes on the artillery, including the anti-aircraft artillery, even though it didn't have an ample amount of it. By the start of the Battle of Kursk, the Artillery Kommando 3, which was subordinate to Breith's panzer corps, had II/Artillery Regiment 62 (105mm howitzers), II/Artillery Regiment 76 (150mm howitzers), the Separate Heavy Artillery Battalion 875 (210mm howitzers), and Flak Regiments 99 and 153; in addition, already at the start of the operation the headquarters of Artillery Regiment 612 would be attached to it. Korps Raus received a more substantial reinforcement. Its Artillery Kommando 153 had the I/Artillery Regiment 21 (105mm howitzers), I/Artillery Regiment 77 (105mm howitzers), II/Artillery Regiment 54 (105mm howitzers), Flak Regiments 4, 7 and 48 (72 88mm guns), the StuG Battalion 905 (31 StuG) and StuG Battery 393 (12 StuG).

As E. Raus recalled, the basic portion of the reinforcements planned for his army detachment began to arrive at the end of April:

> The three flak regiments, fielding a total seventy-two 88mm guns and approximately 90 smaller flak guns, had been attached to XI Corps [Korps Raus] to serve as a substitute for missing medium artillery. According to Luftwaffe policy, the subordination of flak officers to army unit commanders was forbidden; the corps artillery officer therefore depended on the

---

19 Kholiansky, G.L. (compiler), *Polnaia entsiklopediia tankov mira, 1915-2000* [*Complete encyclopedia of the world's tanks, 1915-2000*] (Moscow, 1998), p. 238.

voluntary cooperation of the senior flak commander. This led to repeated minor frictions but worked out quite well in general.[20]

As for the process of reorganizing the units in preparation for the offensive, Erhard Raus wrote:

> The *Armeeabteilung* [Army Detachment] placed reorganizing units in the vicinity of Kharkov or to the west. Units committed at the front rotated one-third of their strength (one reinforced regimental *Kampfgruppe*) at a time for purposes of reorganizing near the front. Since the original attack date had been set for 4 May, maximum efforts were made to move up required personnel and material.[21]

However, Hitler postponed the attack toward Kursk that had been planned for early May, so Army Group South had the opportunity to continue preparing its forces. By the start of July, W. Kempf was able to gather a total number of fewer than 100,000 servicemen for Citadel, of which only 32,000 to 34,000 were direct combatants.[22] Together, Brieth's III Panzer Corps and Korps Raus had 36 infantry battalions, 344 tanks, 75 assault guns, 32 Marder tank destroyers, 317 pieces of field artillery, 216 Flak guns (including 72 motorized 88mm guns), and 216 Nebelwerfer rocket launchers. For a more detailed look at the combat strength and weapons of Army Detachment Kempf's divisions by the start of Operation Citadel, see Table 6.

Judging from the recollections of the German generals that took part in the Battle of Kursk, it was already clear to the majority of them from the outset of preparing for Operation Citadel that it would be very difficult to reach its objectives. The Red Army had already tasted a great victory, the skill of its generals had noticeably grown, the soldiers' morale had been strengthened, and equipment and armaments were flowing to the front from the Urals in a torrent. There were no doubts that the Russians were striving to use the lull in the fighting at the front not only to refit their forces, replenish their troops and train them for the looming battle, but also to create powerful defensive positions. The first German aerial reconnaissance photographs, which began to arrive at the end of April, only strengthened their convictions.

This circumstance forced the leadership of Army Group South to initiate large-scale and meticulous work to prepare its own troops to overcome a deeply-echeloned defense. It should be noted that according the war's standards, the opposing sides had ample time to prepare for the summer campaign. The only real difference was the fact that the German assault formations that were assigned to Citadel didn't have to busy themselves with building fortifications, like the Soviet troops. Breith's and Raus's combat units spent all spring and early summer conducting combat training, and thus it wasn't surprising that the individual training of their soldiers and officers on the whole was noticeably higher than that of the bulk of the 7th Guards Army. Like Shumilov, Kempf was personally engaged in this work and was directing his subordinate commanders to teach the troops primarily everything they would need to know for the forthcoming offensive.

Special attention was given so that the command staff explained the tasks facing the units and formations, and each officer in his role included in the process the teaching of the most effective approaches and methods for meeting the objectives. Conferences, map studies and tactical games on maps were conducted in each division, and the layout of the Soviet defenses were discussed

---

20 Raus, E., *Tankovye srazheniia na Vostochnom fronte* [Tank battles on the Eastern Front] (Moscow: AST, 2005), p. 295. This is a Russian translation of Raus's book *Panzer Operations: The Eastern Front Memoir of General Raus, 1941-1945*, which was compiled and translated by Steve Newton and published by Da Capo Press in 2003. The cited passage can be found on page 201.
21 Ibid., page 294.
22 Newton, S. *Kurskaia bitva: Nemetskii vzgliad* [Kursk: The German View] (Moscow: Iauza, 2006), p. 500.

Table 6 Manpower and strength of Army Group South's formations in terms of tanks and assault guns, field artillery and rocket artillery

		Number					
		Ration strength	Combat strength	Infantry battalions	Tanks and assault guns	Field artillery	Rocket artillery
Fourth Panzer Army							
LII AK[1]		51638		12		91	
XXXXVIII PzK		61692[2]		29	674	244	39
II SS PzK		73380		21	494	179	138
Total:		223907		62	1168	514	177
Army Detachment Kempf							
III Panzer Korps	6 PzD	16702		21	375	200	54
	7 PzD	15394[3]					
	19 PzD	13780					
	168 ID	?	5515[4]				
	198 ID	?	5572				
Korps Raus	106 ID	15099[5]	6577	18	44	117	72
	320 ID	14494	5995				
	39 ID			6	?	33	
	161 ID			8	?	48	
	282 ID			9	?	36	
Total:				62	419	?	126
Grand total:				124	1508	831(?)	303

Notes
1 As of 1 July 1943
2 As of 1 July 1943
3 As of 27 June 1943
4 Combat strength of the 106th, 168th and 320th Infantry Divisions as of 4 July 1943
5 Including 503 "Hiwi"; this figure doesn't include the 900 men in the reserve infantry battalion, which during the Battle of Kursk was located in Germany.

in detail on the basis of reconnaissance and aerial photographs, with the aim of revealing their strengths and weaknesses. At the same time, as participants in those events recall, possible alternatives in following up a success were envisioned, and the officers were presented with the problems they might encounter under much less favorable circumstances. Already after the war, while being held in Soviet imprisonment, the commander of the 7th Panzer Division H. von Funck[23] wrote:

---

23 Hans von Funck (General of Panzer Troops 1 March 1944) was born on 23 December 1891 in Aachen, Rhine Province. He participated in the First World War, first as a cadet and then as a lieutenant. He was retained in the Reichswehr after the war, commanding cavalry units and serving in staff posts. In the 1930s he transferred to the panzer troops, and on 15.10.1939 he was appointed as commander of Panzer Regiment 5. After this, his career took off. On 13.11.1940 he became the commander of the 3rd Panzer Brigade. On 01.01.1941 he was promoted to the rank of major general, and a month later on 14.2.1941 he was appointed as commander of the 7th Panzer Division, which at that time was located in France. From

Tactical games were conducted on the scale of the Army Group, its subordinate corps, and particularly often in the III Panzer Corps. During these games, the concrete situation was discussed. The right flank of the panzer group, which would attack as a wedge to the northeast out of the Belgorod area and south of there, could come under a threat if the forces adjacent to it on the south [Korps Raus] proved unable to hold an expansive bridgehead on that side of the river. In connection with this, the need appeared to divert a significant portion of the panzer divisions that were intended for launching an attack into the depth (primarily the 7th Panzer Division, which was located on the right flank) to screen the flank. This weakening of the forces on the axis of the main attack was particularly dangerous, because it was well known on the basis of the experience of previous battles that the Russian command would not limit itself only to organizing a stable (positional) defense on the Donets River and in the areas adjacent to it, but would also prepare major mobile reserves in the rear area for launching counterattacks.

Practical training for the operation was prepared on the basis of the theoretical exercises. Training proceeded on the following basic elements:

1. Forcing the river
   a. silently and suddenly under the cover of darkness or a smoke screen.
   b. after a powerful artillery preparation and with all types of heavy weapons, and the broad use of aviation.
2. Combat in the circumstances of a deeply-echeloned enemy defense with an elaborate system of fortifications of the latest type, with the consideration of various types of ground obstacles (balkas, anti-tank ditches, embankments, woods, swamps, minefields etc.).
3. Fighting in open terrain with enemy tank formations, especially reinforced with various types of weapons.
4. Active aerial reconnaissance and reconnoitering on the ground, their cooperation, as well as delaying fighting with the use of secondary forces in order to screen flanks, including reconnoitering as well.[24]

Together with the general questions that touched upon all types of troops, Brieth's and Raus's headquarters worked out individual programs of training for them with consideration of the specifics of their troops and assignments. For example, knowing that the Soviet side made wide use of anti-personnel mines in order to strengthen their lines, in Korps Raus emphasis was placed on training the infantry elements to clear them. The technology for overcoming mines and explosive obstacles had been worked out in the Wehrmacht long before and was used successfully in practice. Commonly the clearing of passages through the minefields proceeded according to the following scheme. Before an offensive, the Germans would thoroughly study the sector of the

---

the first days of Operation Barbarossa, his panzer division as part of the XXXIX Motorized Corps, and then as part of *Panzergruppe* 3, took active part in the fighting in Belorussian (at Minsk), in the Smolensk battles and in front of Moscow. Already on 15.07.1941, for his successes on the Eastern Front, von Funck was one of the first division commanders to be awarded the Knight's Cross. In the winter of 1941-1942, the 7th Panzer Division took heavy losses and it was withdrawn to France for refitting. In the autumn of 1942, von Funck participated in the seizure of the unoccupied portion of France. His panzer division was transferred back to the Eastern Front to a point near Rostov at the beginning of 1943. H. von Funck, like a significant number of the commanders in the divisions of the III Panzer Corps, thought critically of the plan for Operation Citadel and considered it an operation without any prospects, particularly after the offensive was postponed several times.

24 TsAMO RF, F. 15, op. 11600, d. 1539, ll. 4-6.

enemy's defense where a breakthrough was designated, paying particular attention to the location of minefields. Then, if conditions allowed it, sappers at night, using folds in the ground in weakly defended sectors would remove some of the mines, while simultaneously studying the pattern of mining. The clearing of passages through the minefields for the forward units would take place already in the course of the attack under the cover of the fire of tanks and artillery.

In Operation Citadel, it was impossible to use this approach. Since the Soviet frontline trenches ran several hundred meters from the riverbank and the ground was flat and entirely registered with fire, there was nowhere for the sappers to find cover against the fire. In addition, because of the river, in a full number of places the Germans were unable to determine the precise location of these minefields on the eastern bank of the Northern Donets River. Thus, their locations were estimated according to the principle, "Where would we deploy mines, if we were in the place of the defenders?" Thus in the infantry divisions, they were attempting to devise a new method for overcoming the obstacles. However, according to E. Raus, they weren't able to come up with anything reasonable. They stopped on the simplest method, albeit the most labor-intensive as well – teaching all the grenadiers of the assault groups the basic means of detecting and lifting mines. Meanwhile, in the rear artificial ponds and reservoirs were specially constructed, where the assault groups worked out ways to make a forced crossing of water obstacles at fords and in boats, seize bridgeheads in no-man's land, and create the conditions for the rapid laying of light bridges for the infantry and heavy weapons to cross.

It must be noted that even though the infantry divisions were given a rather important role, the staffing of them followed the principle of scrounging, with respect to the both the number and quality of personnel. For example, while the panzergrenadier regiments of the panzer divisions consisted primarily of Germans with a sprinkling of Poles, in contrast soldiers of non-German nationality comprised 25-30% of the men in the infantry divisions or even higher. There were even Red Army servicemen, who'd gone over to the German side, in the combat units, as well as young men conscripted from the occupied territories of the USSR. Such a means of finding replacements was in particular practiced by the leadership of Korps Raus. The German command nevertheless gave preference not to Russians, but to member of other nationalities of the Soviet Union: Ukrainians, natives of the Central Asian republics, and especially Cossacks. Naturally, this couldn't help but effect the level of training, and hence, the combat capability of the divisions. However, this was a compulsory measure – after more than three years of war, Germany was experiencing an acute deficit of males eligible for combat service.

The command staff of III Panzer Corps also had to deal with a multitude of complex tasks. Primarily this concerned getting the tanks, including the heavy Tiger tanks, across a river that was 70-80 meters wide, and working out tactical methods for employing the armor in the first operational echelon when breaking through a deeply-echeloned defense that was saturated with anti-tank obstacles. The troops began to work to become familiar with the portable and pontoon bridging equipment, training while measuring the time it took to lay the bridges, both across water obstacles and across deep balkas and ravines. In order to cross the main body of troops, it was initially planned to use ferries, but considering that the river channel in the sector of the intended breakthrough was narrow (on average 40-60 meters wide) and shallow (with a depth of 1.25 to 2.5 meters), the Germans were forced to reject this idea and use instead rubber boats, trestle bridges, collapsible metal bridges and fords.

The planning and preparation to cross the Tiger battalion was very complicated. Considering the swampy river basin and the heavy weight of the machines, all the means of crossing the river – from using fords to improvising with whatever material was at hand – were tested. Major General H. von Funck recalled,

For the Tiger tanks, particularly heavy bridging equipment was necessary, which was lacking in the division. In case the Army Detachment couldn't put it at the division's disposal, and also if entry into the operation might require getting these tanks across water obstacles, balkas and so on, tests were conducted, and rather successfully so, to build heavy bridges out of the K-type bridging equipment that was organic in the division. The linking of two ordinary bridge beams into one double bridge beam achieved an increase in the load-bearing capacity of the bridge.

In order to quickly overcome anti-tank ditches with steep sides, dug into firm ground and presenting a difficult obstacle, the engineers of the panzer divisions created an effective means that consisted in collapsing the walls of the ditch with explosive charges. This created gently sloping places across which the tanks could descend and climb, as long as the gun barrel was swung around to face the rear.[25]

Meanwhile, organizational issues were also being settled. In order to increase the firepower and maneuverability of the panzer division's artillery regiment, a battalion of self-propelled artillery was added to its table of organization. It consisted of a battery of 6 Hummel 150mm heavy field howitzers and two batteries with a total of 12 Wäspe 105mm light field howitzers. In the spring, the forces of Army Group South began to receive this armament. However, by July Breith's panzer corps couldn't be fully equipped with this self-propelled artillery, nor had instructions regarding their use arrived. As already noted in the III Panzer Corps, only the 7th Panzer Division received a self-propelled artillery battalion. This required a detailed study of the new weapon, after which such questions as the techniques of using the self-propelled artillery to accompany panzer attacks; methods of commanding the battalion when firing from main firing positions and during the movement of the *panzerkiel*; communications between the battalion commander and the artillery regiment's command and the division's artillery chief; supplying the battery with ammunition on the battlefield; and other practices had to be worked out in practice.

The above-listed problems and issues throughout the entire period of preparation for the battle received constant and careful scrutiny in the III Panzer Corps. However, the main accent was nevertheless given to planning and preparing the operation's opening phase, or in other words, ensuring success in the first several hours of the offensive. The aerial photographs of the Soviet lines that were systematically arriving gave a distinct image of their depth and their degree of saturation with anti-tank guns and artificial obstacles. The corps headquarters believed that without the seizure of bridgeheads with a depth of no less than 2-3 kilometers, it would be impossible to begin laying down the bridges and transferring the heavy weapons and equipment to the eastern bank. Thus, Breith's exerted his main efforts to working out measures that might ensure a rapid crossing of the Northern Donets by the assault groups of the first wave without excessive losses, and providing them cover and support in the course of breaching the forward edge of the Soviet main belt of defenses.

Reliable cover fire for the first assault wave was considered the plan's main element. For this, given the lack of the necessary air support for the initial assault across the river, it was extremely important to coordinate the artillery fire at every level. The command of the panzer divisions thoroughly organized, and then worked out a system of command over three groups of artillery on training areas: first that of the panzer division's organic artillery; secondly, that of the company of Tigers, self-propelled guns and battalions of the 168th Infantry Division's artillery regiment (which were included in the lead assault groups); and finally of the corps' and army detachment's artillery and mortar units. H. von Funck wrote that the availability of such powerful and well

---

25 TsAMO RF, F. 15, op. 11600, d. 1539, ll. 6-7.

controlled artillery fire in the hands of the division commander on one hand, and the close coordination of his headquarters with the Luftwaffe's airbase on the other, was viewed as the most important condition for resolving not only and not so much the initial tasks – forcing the river and breaching the Russians' main defensive belt, but mainly during the assault wedge's advance into the depth of the 7th Guards Army's defenses for the first 20-25 kilometers.

The crispness of the command and control system rested upon the uninterrupted flow of communications along the main and alternative channels at every level of the artillery command and along the line to the division headquarters and the Luftwaffe command. Thus, as the first order of business the signal units received equipment and trained personnel.

Throughout the entire extent of preparations for Operation Citadel, the German command placed great significance on matters involving the concealment of its own intentions and keeping secret the forces that were assigned to the offensive. In June, after the making the final decision regarding the offensive's start date, this work increased significantly. Now over a relatively short period of time it was necessary to secure the hidden movement of an enormous quantity of men and material up to their staging areas for the offensive. E. Raus wrote:

> As far as possible, the enemy had to be kept from detecting the movement of German forces into their assembly areas. By spacing the assembly areas far apart and occupying them at staggered intervals, the *Armeeabteilung* [Army Detachment] attempted to deceive the enemy about the attack's timing and the locations of contemplated crossing sites.
>
> In the Chuguev area additional and extensive deception measures attempted to convince the Russians that we contemplated attacking in the Donets bend toward the line Izium-Kupiansk. Motorized columns advanced toward the front lines in daylight, artillery moved into positions and conducted registration fire, and simulated reserves practiced river crossings.[26]

It is hard to agree with the general's optimistic outlook; facts speak to the contrary. In actual fact, the level of the professional training of the intelligence organs and staff officers of the German formations, which were occupied with disguising the plans and organization for Operation Citadel, was rather high. They worked conscientiously. A significant number of staff and intelligence offers were devoted to this task, and the misinformation circulated through various channels. On paper they created non-existent formations, while in discussions and correspondence the real divisions were given different numerical designations. Any movement made by units and formations received diligent preparation. False radio stations were set up in areas where there were no troops, with the aim of creating the appearance that a large combat formation was located there.

However, if these efforts are assessed using the disclosed documents of the Voronezh Front, then it is possible to assert with confidence that the adversary didn't manage to achieve the desired goal. By the start of the offensive, Soviet intelligence had established the approximate number of panzer divisions and their precise assembly areas by the end of June, and had identified the location of the Fourth Panzer Army's headquarters, as well as those of the 6th and 7th Panzer Divisions. The forward edge of Hoth's and Kempf's forces had been examined in greater detail. Thanks to the difficult, dangerous and exhausting work of scouts, sectors of defense of the German divisions had been identified along the entire front. However, it should be recognized that the most reliable and interesting information came from turncoats and captured prisoners. I will cite several excerpts from operational briefings from the headquarters of the Voronezh Front.

---

26 Raus, E., *Tankovye srazheniia na vostochnom fronte*, p. 70.

At midnight on 20 June:

> According to the indications of a deserter from the 11th Panzer Division's reconnaissance battalion, who came over to our side in the area south of Sar. Salmovo, on 16.6.1943 all of the SS panzer divisions and the 6th and 7th Panzer Divisions were located in Khar'kov. Only separate SS panzer units are in the Belgorod area. The 11th Panzer Division, consisting of the 110th Panzergrenadier Regiment 110, Panzergrenadier Regiment 111, the panzer regiment and artillery regiment has been located in the Kolomak area since 10 April, while one of the panzer battalions has been sent to France in order to receive Pz.Kpfw. VI tanks.
>
> According to the prisoner's testimony, Artillery Battalion 52 consisting of three batteries has been attached to the 168th Infantry Division. In the middle of June, he saw elements of the SS *Totenkopf* Division in the Pokrovka area and heard about the preparations for limited operations by the 168th Infantry Division with SS *Totenkopf* elements to seize the patch of woods southwest of Krasnaia Poliana.
>
> Two deserters belonging to the 168th Infantry Division's Mortar Battalion 52 have been detained in Iachevnyi Kolodez'.
>
> In the area 1 kilometer outside of Soldatskii a Polish soldier of the 332nd Infantry Division's Infantry Regiment 676 has been captured.

At midnight on 22 June:

> On the night of 21-22.6, a reconnaissance patrol in the area south of Zaiats (2 kilometers northeast of Russkaia Berezovka) captured an Senior Lance-Corporal of the 255th Infantry Division's Infantry Regiment 465.

At midnight on 29 June:

> A reconnaissance patrol in the area of Novo-Dmitrievka took documents from an executed prisoner of the 57th Infantry Division's Infantry Regiment 164. When repelling an enemy reconnaissance patrol in company-strength at 0700 on 29.6 in the area of Zagodskii (12 kilometers north of Belgorod), a wounded soldier of the SS *Totenkopf* Division's Panzer Regiment 3 was captured, and under preliminary interrogation he indicated that on 2 June, the SS *Totenkopf* Division had moved up to the front and replaced units of the SS *Adolf Hitler* Division.

The Voronezh Front's headquarters had accurate information that the Fourth Panzer Army's 167th Infantry Division was holding the line of defense opposite the 6th Guards Army. Thus, right up to the start of the operation, the Soviet combat intelligence was monitoring the situation with sufficient confidence and was reporting the requisite information about the enemy formations in the sector where they would most likely launch the main attack. Immediately prior to the start of combat operations, the movement of enemy tank and motorized divisions to a point in the rear of the infantry division's combat positions opposite the front of the 6th and 7th Guards Armies was revealed. On the night of 4-5 July, the Military Council of the Voronezh Front reported to Stalin: "Radio intelligence had established the deployment of the 6th Panzer Division and the three SS Panzer Divisions *Adolf Hitler*, *Grossdeutschland* [sic] and *Das Reich* in the Novaia Gorianka – Belgorod sector."[27] If you consider that at the end of June the presence of the SS *Totenkopf* Division

---

27 TsAMO RF, F. 203, op. 2843, d. 431, l. 12.

was identified opposite the left wing of the 6th Guards Army through a captured prisoner, then by the beginning of July the Soviet intelligence service had not only disclosed the panzer grouping located in the Khar'kov area and to the north of it, but also detected the approach of its forces to the front immediately prior to the Battle of Kursk.

Even so, for the sake of justice it should be emphasized the command of the armies (including that of the 7th Guards Army) and of the Voronezh Front regarded this information from the intelligence organs with a great deal of suspicion. When studying the archival sources, I developed the impression that of the Voronezh Front's leading individuals from the army level on up, only N.F. Vatutin was confident that the Germans would launch the offensive on 5 July, even after information began to come in on the results of combat in the 6th Guards Army's sector on the evening of 4 July and from their own intelligence headquarters.

Skipping ahead of the events, I'll note that in the first days of the defensive operation, there was only confusion regarding three panzer divisions. First, even on 6 July, the Front's intelligence believed the 11th Panzer Division was in the German reserve and assembled in the Bogodukhovo area. Second, the exact location of the 19th Panzer Division couldn't be pinpointed within the combat formation of von Manstein's attacking forces, even though it would become evident that it was conducting combat operations on the Front's sector. Third, the presence of the 7th Panzer Division would be determined only on 6 July through prisoner testimony and battlefield documents.

So that the reader can picture the full volume of information that the command of the 7th Guards Army's divisions had about the opposing enemy, I will cite a briefing paper from the headquarters of the 72nd Guards Rifle Division:

> Opposite the division's front, the enemy is defending [1-5 July 1943] with:
> 106th Infantry Division and 34 tanks in the sector /excl./Solomino, Grafovka. The line: / excl./Solomino – Puliaevka, with the Infantry Regiment 240; /excl./Pristen' – Grafovka, with Infantry Regiment 241; and Infantry Regiment 239 in the second echelon on the Hill 210.5, /excl./200.9 line.
> 320th Infantry Division – Grafovka, Bugrovka. On the line: Grafovka, Arkhangel'skoe –Infantry Regiment 562; in the second echelon, the Infantry Regiment 585 in the sector: Zabirovka, Shalino State Farm, Murom.
> Tank grouping: Toplinka – 15 tanks; woods, 2 kilometers southwest of Pristen' – 2 tanks; Grafovka – 25 tanks; Nikol'skoe – 8 tanks; Zabirovka – 5 tanks. All the tanks presumably belong to the 6th Panzer Division.[28]

I will emphasize that the document accurately reflects the enemy's strength, exact identities and the sectors held by their regiments.

The command of Army Detachment Kempf paid great attention to conducting reconnaissance in the tactical zone, first of all in order to reveal the system of defense and to study the terrain (especially the Northern Donets's basin and channel) in the sectors of the forthcoming offensive. The intensity of this work particularly picked up in the latter half of June. The Luftwaffe, patrols and observation posts played the main role in this work. The intelligence departments of the corps served as the coordinator. However, in the III Panzer Corps' sector, this reconnaissance work had its own particular features. In order to mask the presence of its panzer divisions opposite the 7th Guards Army's front, their men were prohibited from appearing at the front to take direct part in capturing prisoners. Patrols were conducted by the infantry divisions that were holding the line of

---

28 TsAMO RF, F. 72 gv. sd, op. 1, d. 60, l. 2.

defense along the river's western bank; they coordinated their activity with the headquarters of the panzer divisions. H. von Funck recalled:

> From the middle of June, increased reconnaissance was conducted by us with the aim of acquiring the necessary information for organizing and conducting the designated operation. By this time it was already known that the 7th Panzer Division was supposed to launch the offensive from the western bank of the Donets River along both sides of the community of Solomino…
>
> It was necessary to conduct reconnaissance with great caution in order not to disclose the presence of fresh forces and the preparation for offensive operations to the enemy. It followed to take all measures to keep the black uniforms of the panzer troops concealed from the enemy and not to give him the opportunity to capture one of our soldiers. Even the intensive movement of machines and the shifting of units that was taking place might alone prompt the enemy's suspicion. Therefore the division was ensuring unified leadership over all of the reconnaissance operations, coordinating them in time and space, and giving thought to their size and nature.
>
> … It was necessary to conduct thorough reconnaissance of the terrain with the aim of revealing the available cover, as well as to ensure that artificial obstacles were timely kept out of enemy observation. Reconnaissance by engineers had especially great significance.
>
> Reconnaissance of the terrain on the opposite bank and the assessment of the enemy were implemented:
> a. by means of the careful scrutiny of maps and aerial photographs;
> b. by means of systematic observation conducted from our positions by elements of all types of troops that were especially assigned for this;
> c. by conducting reconnaissance patrols on that side of the river.[29]

In essence, the general was recognizing the weakness of Army Detachment Kempf's operational and tactical intelligence, which was based only on prisoner testimony, observation and the study of aerial photographs. Unquestionably, such methods yielded a certain amount of information, but it was far from complete and not always accurate. Considering also that the Soviet side was using a rather effective system of misinformation and camouflage, which included well-prepared dummy positions especially for the benefit of German aircraft, the enemy had little knowledge of the army's system of defense, and even less knowledge of the Front's defenses in depth. Direct participants in those events subsequently acknowledge these facts. As the chief of staff of the XXXXVIII Panzer Corps General von Mellenthin later wrote, "Air photos were available for every square meter of the Kursk salient. But though these photographs showed the depth and size of the Russian positions, they did not reveal the details or give any information of the strength of their forces, for the Russians are masters in the art of camouflage. Inevitably, their strength was considerably underestimated."[30]

As for the movement and assembly of reserves, the Soviet side conducted these at night, so prior to the start of the operation the enemy had only a sketchy notion about them. So the enemy, relying on incomplete and not always accurate information from their intelligence and reconnaissance services when calculating the strength and potential of both the 7th Guards Army and the

---

29 TsAMO RF, F. 15, op. 11600, d. 1539, ll. 9-10.
30 Mellenthin, F., *Bronirovannyi kulak vermakhta* [*Wehrmacht's armored fist*] (Smolensk: Rusich, 1999), p. 325. This is the Russian translation of the English-language book *Panzer Battles*, which was published by University Press of Oklahoma in 1956. The relevant passage can be found on page 219 of that book.

Voronezh Front as a whole committed substantial blunders. The Germans underestimated the Soviet side and correspondingly overestimated the breakthrough power of their own forces assembled near Belgorod.

At the same time, it must be acknowledged that the German intelligence had to operate in very difficult conditions against an enemy that was quickly gathering strength and experience. H. von Funck's assertion that his reconnaissance patrols were working on the eastern bank of the Donets River as well corresponds to actual fact, but they were failing to penetrate any further than the sectors of the first-echelon divisions, and even then only on several occasions. The Northern Donets River ran in front of the entire line of the 7th Guards Army, so the sending out of reconnaissance patrols was loaded with significant difficulties. Reports from the Guards divisions of the first echelon are sprinkled with messages about the attempts by the Nazis to penetrate their forward edge. In the overwhelming majority of cases, they resulted only in fleeting combat actions with our own combat outposts. However, undoubtedly there were also on occasion successful infiltrations. In addition, the enemy often relied in this activity on prisoners who had gone over to the Wehrmacht's side. According to documents from Voronezh Front's intelligence headquarters and SMERSH departments, there was a special unit in Army Detachment Kempf (probably, this was Abwehr Kommando 204, about which there will be further discussion), which ran agents recruited from Ukrainians and local residents of the Russian Federal Socialist Republic who lived along the administrative border with Ukraine and who knew the Ukrainian language and details of their lifestyles. The Soviet special services, especially the organs of frontline intelligence, weren't sitting around with their arms folded. They had agents in fine positions in the enemy's intelligence schools and were to a significant degree monitoring the German process of infiltrating reconnaissance and sabotage teams into the operational rear, including into the rear of the forces holding the Kursk bulge. Directive No. 10437 from the Commander-in-Chief of the Voronezh Front dated 25 May 1943 reveals:

> On the night of 22-23 May 1943, on the front of the 7th Guards Army the enemy sent a reconnaissance patrol consisting of 13 men, of which one was a lieutenant and one a senior lieutenant. The entire group consisted of Red Army soldiers and commanders who were captured by the Germans. The patrol members were wearing Red Army uniforms and equipped with Red Army weapons. The group was given the assignment to penetrate the positions of the Red Army's troops and to scout the forward edge, artillery firing positions, and the locations of tanks and minefields. They were to destroy bunkers and dugouts with demolition charges and to capture prisoners. The group's method was to move up to our forward edge at night, and when challenged, pose as a Red Army squad. The patrol demonstrated:
>
> 1. The enemy is conducting wide recruitment of agents among [Red Army] servicemen, creating groups of 10-15 men, and sending them into the dispositions of our forces with reconnaissance and sabotage tasks.
> 2. In the sector of the Voronezh Front, the enemy in the nearest time should send out 3-4 reconnaissance patrols.[31]

Not having substantial success with infiltrating reconnaissance and sabotage groups, the enemy was paying great attention to using strong patrols to scout the front of the 7th Guards Army. These patrols were systematically conducted in the sectors of all the divisions of the first echelon, but

---

31 TsAMO RF, F. 1163, op. 1, d. 52, l. 125.

most often from out of the Mikhailovka bridgehead. Here is one example from a report generated by the headquarters of the 25th Guards Rifle Corps at 1800 on 1 July 1943:

> At 0100 on 1.07.1943 a tank approached the forward edge of the 81st Guards Rifle Division's 238th Guards Rifle Regiment from out of the Mikhailovka area and opened fire at close range; with return fire, our units forced the tank to retreat. At 0220 from the southern outskirts of Mikhailovka, the enemy attempted to probe our line with up to a platoon of infantry, covered by artillery and mortar fire, but it was met by fire from a combat outpost of the 238th Guards Rifle Regiment, as well as by approaching units, and it was thrown back to its jumping off positions. The soldier's booklet was removed from one German corpse; the identity of his unit still hasn't been established.[32]

However, there were also cases when the Germans captured our soldiers, and when Red Army troops positioned in a combat outpost went over to the side of the Germans. One such case happened on the afternoon of 4 July on the right wing of the 24th Guards Rifle Corps. From the operational summary of the 72nd Guards Rifle Division for 0400 5 July: "At 1715 out of the area of an orchard southeast of Toplinka, enemy infantry appeared in strength of up to a company; 10-12 Fritzes crossed the river and reached the forward edge of defense of the 66th Penal Company. With rifle and mortar fire the enemy was thrown back across the river. Meanwhile, 3 [of our] soldiers disappeared; an investigation has been launched."[33] I will note that judging from the fact of how quickly the offensive by the 106th Infantry Division developed through the sector of the 66th Separate Penal Company on the morning of 5 July, as well from a number of circumstantial pieces of evidence, that the Germans probably obtained valuable information about the system of fire and the defenses in this sector from these deserting members of the penal company.

The intelligence organs of Army Detachment Kemp assigned no less significance to activity to undermining the morale of the troops of Shumilov's army. This work was conducted fastidiously and on a large scale. Great emphasis was placed on the friction between the different nationalities. Striving to sow discord and distrust between the soldiers of differing nationalities, the Nazis persistently and assiduously conducted undermining work among the soldiers called up from different republics of the Soviet Union (Uzbeks, Kazakhs, Tatars, Ukrainians, etc.). E. Raus recalls that prior to the start of the Battle of Kursk, his subordinates supposedly managed to persuade an entire company of Uzbeks from the 15th Guards Rifle Division to come over to their side. The general complained, "Part of the company, unfortunately, ran into Russian minefields, suffering considerable losses from exploding mines as well as fire from the alerted enemy artillery." He added, however, "The result of this undertaking was that, having become unreliable, the 15th Uzbek Rifle Division was immediately withdrawn from the front, disciplined, and committed elsewhere."[34]

Although Erhard Raus was a participant in those events, it is hard to agree with his statements. In fact, there was such a shameful manifestation as desertion from the 7th Guards Army's units, although relative to the other Soviet armies, it was on a smaller scale. Indeed, the influence of the enemy's propaganda can be considered one of the reasons for these desertions, especially against the backdrop of the unfavorable situation with food in the Soviet troops. It is possible that such an exceptional case (the desertion of an entire company!) did in fact take place, but when studying the documents in the TsAMO RF, I never came across a confirmation of this. In conversations with me (as well as in a number of publications), counterintelligence veterans asserted that the

---

32 TsAMO RF, F. 25 gv. sk, op. 1, d. 28, l. 51.
33 TsAMO RF, F. 72 gv. sd, op. 1, d. 17, l. 399.
34 Raus, *Tankovye srazheniia na Vostochnom fronte*, p. 286.

SMERSH Department staff that oversaw the rifle regiments had informal plans to recruit an average of 50-70 informants per battalion, which meant 450-600 men per regiment. Considering that in the course of fighting there were many casualties, the Special Department officers sought to raise this number of informants as high as possible; often, they recruited up to a 100 informants per battalion. However, as the popular saying "Even a marksman may miss the target" goes, the special service officers were also human and were fully able to make mistakes. Nevertheless, given such a system of control, is it doubtful that a scheme involving not 10-15 men, but an entire company of not less than 100 men, would remain unknown to the division command. Regarding Raus's assertion that an entire division was withdrawn from the front due to the betrayal of a group of men, and was ultimately disbanded, this is just pure fiction.

General E.I. Vasil'enko's 15th Guards Rifle Division was a tough, well-seasoned formation which was never re-formed, and according to the official documents of the 7th Guards Army its withdrawal from the front to the second echelon was simply a planned rotation of forces, which incidentally the Wehrmacht also practiced. Judging from everything, the episode with the deserters as described by the general was simply based on rumor. Soviet generals in their memoirs also sinned in a similar way, when in order to embellish a described situation written on the basis of what really happened, they would contrive a story, but one that took place elsewhere and on not such a large scale. It is possible that an incident that did occur, but in a different division of the 7th Guards Army, served as the basis for this story. Let's turn to Directive No. 00648 from the Red Army's Chief of the General Staff, dated 25 May 1943: "On 12 May 1943 in the 7th Guards Army's 213th Rifle Division, 12 soldiers led by a squad commander went over to the enemy's side; this crossing wasn't timely prevented."[35]

The reasons for this extraordinary occurrence were written up in more detail in an order from the Front Commander-in-Chief:

> On the night of 11-12 May of this year, a group of servicemen went over to the enemy's side from the forward edge of the 213th Rifle Division's 793rd Rifle Regiment. An investigation has established that the specific guilty parties who allowed the group to go over to the enemy's side include the commander of the 5th Rifle Company Lieutenant Kleimenov, the deputy commander for political affairs Senior Lieutenant Sammarov and squad commander Santagaliev.
>
> Kleimanov and his deputy Sammarov did not bother to keep watch on the men of the company; didn't check the outposts at the forward edge; took no measures to terminate the reading of fascist leaflets that were widely circulating in the company; failed to react to instances of the soldiers' negative attitudes toward fulfillment of duties; failed to ensure the monitoring of these men; and didn't conduct the necessary work with them. Squad commander Santagaliev who directly witnessed the men of his squad that were going over to the enemy's side didn't open fire at the traitors and didn't try to foil the crossing by any other means.[36]

I will note that judging from the archival documents available today, this was the only incident involving a large number of troops of the Voronezh Front that went over to the enemy's side during the run-up to the Battle of Kursk. In response to the idleness and indifferent attitude to their service duties shown by the officers listed in the above order, they were sentenced by a military

---

35 TsAMO RF, F. 426, op. 10753, d. 84, l. 97.
36 TsAMO RF, F. 288 gv. sp, op. 47024, d. 4, l. 36.

tribunal to 10 years of imprisonment, with a commutation of this sentence in exchange for a three-month period of service in a penal battalion.

I'll now turn to another passage in General E. Raus's book. Those readers who are familiar with it have probably noticed that when describing the preparation of his corps for the largest battle, the author in essence limited it to something unusual for a general of his rank: complaints about bloodthirstiness of the Russians and their cynical attitude not only to the lives of their soldiers, but also to their children. In particularly he asserts that in the sector of his corps, the Soviet special services were actively using children and adolescents of 8 to 14 years of age in order to gather intelligence, and it wasn't a simple matter to track these unusual agents. In the area of Belgorod alone, several dozen children were arrested. Because of this the German command had to evict all the citizens from the frontal zone. However, despite its unfeeling attitude with respect to the children, both sides used this form of gathering intelligence. However, if the actions of the Soviet intelligence officers can be morally justified to a certain degree, because after all they were young citizens of the Soviet Union who were struggling against the occupiers for the freedom of their country, then the reproaches of the diehard war dog Raus can't be called anything other than propagandistic blathering from the Cold War period. For an example, I'll cite a recently disclosed document from the NKVD office in Kursk Oblast:

> On the territory of Tim District ... 4 adolescents were detained, who were going through villages and begging. The detained youth were:
>
> 1) Kaverin, Viktor, 1931 year of birth, a native of Kursk Oblast;
> 2) Kaverin, Gennadii, 1930 year of birth, Viktor's brother;
> 3) Azarov, Ivan, 1929 year of birth, a native of Kursk Oblast;
> 4) Azarov, Nikolai, 1928 year of birth, native of Kursk Oblast and Ivan's brother.
>
> According to the testimony of Viktor and Gennadii Kaverin, not long before the Germans' retreat from the Cheremisinovo District, in the winter of 1943, while studying in a school, they and other adolescents were used by the Germans as scouts.
>
> Gennadii Kaverin testified that a German officer (name unknown) selected up to 20 youth from among those enrolled in the school, who seemed most suited to serve as scouts, and together with their teacher Lidia Nikolaevna (surname unknown; she fled with the Germans), they taught them how to identify and distinguish Soviet tanks, guns and vehicles from their German counterparts.
>
> After a short period of training, a group of adolescents consisting of V. Kaverin, G. Kaverin, A. Ermakov (age 13) and I. Lazykin (age 12) was sent to the railroad switch near the city of Shchigry, to the village of Dubrovka and to Cheremisinovo Station with intelligence-gathering tasks. They spent four days collecting intelligence before returning, and reported that Germans were holding these locations and provided the number of tanks, guns and vehicles that they observed. Apparently, this mission along the designated route served as training for the adolescents, since German troops were in these locations.
>
> Two days before the German retreat, the group of adolescents, replenished with additional youth, was taken by car to Shchigry by an officer and there made contact with a certain "Uncle Vania". We have a counterintelligence officer of the NKVD posted in Shchigry.[37]

---

37 Archive of the UFSB for Kursk Oblast, F. 10, op. 3, d. 2, l. 19-19obr.

It must be said that in order to break through the Soviet defenses, especially in the first days of the operation, the German command was placing certain hopes on the work of their sabotage and diversionary groups directly in the tactical zone. I will remind the reader that by the start of Germany's invasion of the Soviet Union, Germany had formed Abwehr I (operational intelligence collection), Abwehr II (sabotage and subversion) and Abwehr III (counter-espionage) divisions within its armed forces, which received the name "Abwehr Kommando". Initially it was planned to have one Abwehr Kommando for each army group, but then their number increased. Abwehr intelligence teams were given numerical designations, starting with the number 100 (for example, Abwehr Kommando 104 was subordinate to Army Group South, and was better known as "Saturn"), sabotage teams with the number 200, and counterintelligence teams with the number 300. All the Kommando had their own special schools and centers that served to receive and transmit reports and as an advanced base from which agents could be passed into their area of operation ("Meldekopfe"). For example, Abwehr II had eight such centers along the entire Eastern Front. Organizationally the Abwehr Kommando teams were split into groups that were attached to the headquarters of the field and panzer armies, where they engaged in the direct organization of subversive measures and sabotage. The Abwehr operated continuously between June 1941 and 14 February 1944; the leadership of the intelligence and sabotage work on the Eastern Front was handled by several structures that replaced each other, like Stab Walli and Stab Ost, but all of them contained sabotage departments and services.

In May 1943 Army Detachment Kempf received Abwehr Kommando 204, which during the period when preparing and conducting Operation Citadel engaged in sabotage work in first the 7th Guards Army's sector, and then that of the 69th Army. The main task of its intelligence and sabotage groups was to infiltrate the tactical zone and disrupt the command and control over the defending troops by destroying headquarters and cutting communication lines and capturing or killing the commanders of units or the commandants of garrisons of major hubs of resistance, but also worked to prevent the demolition of key infrastructure points like bridges and dams in the sector of advance of their own combat groups. Skipping somewhat ahead, in the first few hours after the start of the offensive by Army Detachment Kempf, the forces of the 7th Guards Army that were holding the main line of defense were subjected to a powerful attack by raiding parties of Abwehr Kommando 204 against the headquarters of their battalion and regiments, and in the afternoon against even the command post of one of the rifle divisions. However, fortunately the Guardsmen were able to thwart the Nazis plans.

Summing up the results of what has been said I can assert the following points with confidence: First, by the start of Operation Citadel, Army Detachment Kempf was noticeably inferior to the Fourth Panzer Army in both the level of staffing and equipment, as was well as in the level of its troops' training. Yet it was supposed to cooperate closely with panzer army throughout the extent of the offensive. Meanwhile, considering that the army-level belts of defense of the Voronezh Front, which Army Detachment Kempf would have to overcome, were comparable in the degree of fortifications to those that Hoth's panzer army faced, and were moreover reinforced by the channel of the Northern Donets River, the task it faced of making a deep penetration all the way to Skorodnoe was from the outset unattainable for it. Even so, W. Kempf did have adequate strength to carry out its assignment in the first stage of Operation Citadel: not simply to cover the Fourth Panzer Army's right flank, but also to give it substantial assistance in the fighting for Prokhorovka, which Hoth and von Manstein had planned back in May 1943.

Second, there were two conditions in the first stage of the offensive that would have made it possible for Army Detachment Kempf to achieve success. The first was a more thorough planning for the offensive (especially for that of the III Panzer Corps). During the preparations for Citadel, the command of both Army Detachment Kempf and of Breith's III Panzer Corps plainly underestimated the strength of the Soviet defense. Indeed, it lacked the proper knowledge of it.

The absence of a *schwerpunkt* (a point of main emphasis) for the III Panzer Corps' attack is clear evidence of this, given the dissimilar terrain conditions it faced and the strength of the 7th Guards Army's positions, as well as the demonstrably disastrous plan of attack out of the Mikhailovka bridgehead, which would require the use of bridges that were well-known to the Soviet side. In addition, a serious mistake was made when planning the air support for the operation; as is known, the main forces of the VIII Fliegerkorps were directed to support the II SS Panzer Corps' attack. This despite the fact that Kempf's troops, which were preparing to make a forced crossing of the Northern Donets River, were in acute need for this. It was essential that Army Detachment be given air support during the process of breaching the deeply-echeloned belts of defense when breaking through the 7th Guards Army's main line of resistance, and also for destroying the powerful knot of resistance on the joint flanks of Hoth's and Kempf's groupings in Staryi Gorod (the positions of the 81st Guards Rifle Division). As subsequent events would show, it was on the right flank of the 7th Guards Army and its boundary with the 6th Guards Army that the attacking German troops (of the 168th Infantry Division) would meet the strongest rebuff, and even be forced to retreat.

Finally, having become familiar with the process of planning and preparing Army Group South's summer offensive, including that of Army Detachment Kempf, on the basis of captured documents, the impression arises that the leadership of the Army Group, as incidentally that of the OKH, was on the one hand objectively unable to help the Army Detachment meet its important objectives (for example, by providing it with additional infantry), and on the other was mesmerized by the desire to create a "super-penetrating" wedge out of the Fourth Panzer Army. Plainly, they underestimated the influence this would have on the entire course of Operation Citadel and the failure of the offensive.

In general, during the run-up to the Battle of Kursk, one senses nervous tension and growing alarm in the actions of the German generals (especially in the latter stage). Taking a cue from the Führer, they were plainly losing the grasp of what was real and rational. The situation with reserves, for example, speaks to this. Abandoning all principles and the practical experience of the war, they strove with admirable stubbornness to hurl all of the available panzer divisions into the battle on 5 July 1943. Even Hoth, who was famous for his cool head and "unshakeable fortitude" when defending his own point of view, having planned initially to keep the 3rd Panzer Division in reserve and to introduce it into the battle only on 6 July, abruptly altered this decision already when preparing his amended plan at the end of May. There was also the desire to concentrate more than 400 armored fighting vehicles in the hands of the commander of one division (the *Grossdeutschland* Panzer Grenadier Division), when it could have gotten by with 200, while leaving its neighboring army (Army Detachment Kempf) with panzer divisions that were equipped no more than 60% up to establishment strength. All this is hard to explain strictly by the decisions of the "insane corporal" and the desire of the generals to be merely executors of his will. Fortunately, I didn't have to pass through the furnace of that war, but as veterans have told me, death is a constant companion during war, and a high combat morale and a belief in the rightness of your cause are the most important elements of success at the most critical moments of a battle. Through them they mobilize hidden resources, muster their willpower and strength, and thus it seems they can do genuine wonders in a hopeless situation. However, those who introduced their armies and corps onto the battlefields near Belgorod and Orel were not inspired by these lofty feelings. Fear and a sensation of an approaching catastrophe, which meant retribution for that which they had sown, was weighing on them and dulling their senses of reason and feeling. Indeed, they themselves didn't hide this in their memoirs and books published after the war. It didn't take a soothsayer to realize that the war had already been lost, and Kursk was a lunge into oblivion. I hope the reader won't judge me for this somewhat lengthy and pretentious author's digression, but now let's return to the main topic of discussion.

3

5 July 1943 – The beginning of the end of a tragicomedy

From the middle of June, the tension among the troops positioned around the Kursk salient began to rise precipitously. Indeed, a situation uncommon for the war had arisen: the commanders of the opposing sides on the southern face of the Kursk salient had nearly simultaneously posed the question about going over to active operations to the military and political leadership of both countries, Germany and the USSR. All of Moscow's planning for the summer had been based on the supposition that the enemy would be the first to go on the offensive. Yet already at the end of spring 1943, N.F. Vatutin was proposing to launch a powerful preemptive attack against the enemy's Belgorod – Khar'kov grouping, motivated by the fact that the Germans hadn't fully been able to recover from the losses suffered in the course of the winter and early spring campaign. However, his idea found no support in either the General Staff or the *Stavka*. I.V. Stalin stuck to the opinion that in the existing situation, greatest success could be achieved only by meeting the enemy on prepared lines. However, time had passed, and already the second week of summer was slipping away – summer was the most valuable time of year for conducting combat operations, and yet the Wehrmacht wasn't showing any sign of activity. The situation was plainly hanging in balance; not understanding what was going on, N.F. Vatutin began to show nervousness. The level of readiness of the troops of the Voronezh Front at that moment was as high as possible, and the primary problems of refitting and replenishing the armored formations with tanks, heavy weapons and personnel had been resolved. Thus, fearing that a favorable moment would be missed, on 21 June he again raised the question about going on the attack in front of the *Stavka*. The General of the Army wrote:

> According to all available information the enemy is perfecting his defenses, apparently preparing a second defensive belt, and bringing his infantry and tank divisions up to strength. The enemy's intentions aren't discernible. I assume that the enemy is presently expecting and fearing our offensive.
>
> The enemy is plainly anticipating our offensive along the Bogodukhovo – Valki axis … It is necessary to launch the main attack in order to make a deeper envelopment of the Sumy, Mirgorod, Poltava area with the aim of not only encircling and destroying the enemy's Belgorod – Khar'kov grouping in conjunction with the forces of the Southwestern Front, but also simultaneously to encircle and destroy the Sumy – Akhtyrka and Poltava groupings, to reach the western bank of the Vorskla River, and to encircle all the enemy's forces located east of the Vorskla River.
> …

The depth of the operation on the main directions is 300 kilometers. The time required to conduct the operation is 10-15 days, with a preparatory period of 25-30 days. The operation can begin in the middle of July.[1]

The assessments and conclusions of the commander-in-chief of the Voronezh Front about the enemy and his plans fully corresponded to the situation of that time. However, on this occasion as well, under the influence of Marshals G.K. Zhukov and A.M. Vasilevsky, Stalin remained firm.

At this time, von Manstein was acting in approximately the same way. Throughout the entire spring, intensive deliberations and meetings went on regarding the question of a general offensive in the East. The Wehrmacht's pinnacle of command and the political leadership of Germany were split into two groups – supporters and opponents of Operation Citadel. As evidence of the fact that this undertaking was excessively risky and that there was a serious danger that enormous unpleasantness would be the outcome instead of a great victory, the most various forms of proof were offered: intelligence information, aerial reconnaissance photographs, and the deliberations of headquarters, but nothing could persuade Hitler to cancel the implementation of his idea. Even at the May 1943 conference and subsequently, he more than once repeated that he considered this operation as the Wehrmacht's main task for the current year. The colossal mechanism for preparing the offensive was put into full motion, and gained momentum with each passing day. Trains carrying fuel, weapons and equipment, and soldiers that had been mobilized not only in Germany, but in all the occupied countries of Europe, were constantly leaving the Reich and heading to the east. If you don't count the promised Panther tanks and the shortage of infantry, then Army Group South already by the middle of June had received practically everything that Berlin had promised. It would seem that the arguments had ended, the decision made, the troops were ready, and so the next step would be the offensive. However, Berlin was still dragging its feet; over the past one and a half months, it had postponed the start date for the offensive three times. Already all the conceivable dates had passed, the valuable summertime days were passing, and meanwhile the Russians were digging ever deeper into the ground and building up reserves. The image of the Stalingrad catastrophe increasingly surfaced in the discussions of the senior officers. Once the offensive, set for 12 June, was again postponed, a point of view consolidated among the commanders of Army Group South: further delay with conducting Operation Citadel was senseless. Even W. Kempf was nervous. E. Raus recalled:

> The *Armeeabteilung* [Army Detachment] repeatedly voiced grave concerns over ensuing postponements of the operation. The last time, this concern was evidenced by a particularly urgent manifestation, in the form of a verbal report from General Kempf to Colonel General Kurt Zeitzler, Chief of the Army General Staff. Kempf argued that the enemy would make use of the time not only to regroup his units and fortify his defenses in depth, but also to assemble a strategic reserve that could be utilized to repulse our assault, launch diversionary attacks or even spearhead a planned counteroffensive. Nevertheless, the operation was repeatedly postponed.[2]

Realizing that he had no other option, Field Marshal von Manstein sent a letter to Berlin, in which he expressed his sharp disagreement with the repeated postponements of the offensive. His chief of staff General of Infantry T. Busse recalled, "He believed that any additional delay would

---

1   TsAMO RF, F. 16, op. 1720, d. 14, l. 8.
2   Newton, *Kurskaia bitva. Nemetskii vgliad*, p. 82.

lead to the loss of the most important prerequisites for the success of this offensive; finally, Hitler set the start for Operation Citadel on 5 July."[3]

Let's return, however, to the events directly in the troops of the opposing sides at the end of June 1943. Despite the sizeable difficulties that the scouts and patrols faced in their work, the Army Detachment Kempf command and those of its subordinate divisions had nevertheless been able to accumulate a sufficient amount of information about the 7th Guards Army. The main task of the enemy's tactical reconnaissance was to reveal the Soviet system of defensive fortifications, determine the sectors held by the first-echelon divisions (especially the location of boundaries), and the assembly location of operational reserves. Judging from the information available today, the enemy studied the forward defenses of the main line of resistance that extended between the channel of the Northern Donets River back to the railroad embankment, which ran almost parallel to the river, most intensively. As for how the 7th Guards Army had arranged its defenses further in the depth, the Army Detachment Kempf had only a vague notion. Ehrard Raus recalled that the areas of defense of the four rifle divisions of the first echelon, which were holding a line along the eastern bank of the river, had been determined. Thus all of the initial attacks by the corps' *kampfgruppen* on the day of 5 July precisely struck their boundaries and the boundaries between their rifle regiments. In addition, the enemy command analyzed separate sectors in detail, particularly of the 72nd Guards Rifle Division, and accurately established the location of main firing positions. All of this information, unquestionably, helped Raus' troops when assaulting the main line of resistance.

On 28 June, the forces of both of the German assault groupings in the area of the Kursk bulge began moving into their staging areas for the attack. The movement went according to the previously determined plan and along set routes. In the final days of May, the divisions that had received an order to take part in Citadel had sent reconnoitering groups to the Belgorod area in order to determine the movement routes for the tanks and vehicles, and the places of deployment for the forward units. At the same time the engineer elements were analyzing the river's basin and channel. Then, in the beginning of June, work began to improve the unpaved roads leading directly to the front, repair bridges, and widen the paths and firebreaks through the wooded areas, which might be used for the movement of forces. In addition, in certain places German engineers began the stealthy construction of trestle bridges across the Donets River, including in the area of the Mikhailovka bridgehead.

Although a significant area of the ground on the western bank was covered by woods, it lacked sufficient depth in order to conceal the large mass of troops and equipment that was moving toward the front. H. von Funck wrote:

> When selecting the jumping-off positions for the offensive, it was necessary to conduct thorough reconnaissance of the terrain with the aim of revealing the available cover on it, as well as to provide artificial screens against enemy observation in good time. The troops were to deploy into their jumping-off positions in a dispersed order. The terrain on both sides of the Belgorod – Brodok road [the main road assigned to the 6th Panzer Division] lacked any natural screens that would block enemy observation, especially by enemy aircraft. The road itself, which ran along high ground, was visible from the depth of the enemy's positions. Thus, movement along this most important artery could take place only after sunset or in conditions of poor visibility.[4]

---

3   Ibid., p. 26.
4   TsAMO RF, F. 15, op. 11600, d. 1539, l. 11.

Each unit and element that was designated for the offensive received a specially-assigned march route and a timetable for the passage of its columns. All of the forces, which had previously not been located in the Belgorod area, were to observe complete radio silence until receipt of a special order. Because of this, incidentally, two days prior to the start of the offensive, Voronezh Front's radio traffic intelligence "lost track" of the radios of the 6th, 7th and 11th Panzer Divisions and some of the Flak regiments of Army Group South on the Belgorod axis, which prior to this point had been appearing systematically in the radio traffic. Now they had disappeared, and this was quickly reported to N.F. Vatutin. This was one of the signals about the start of the enemy's assembly of forces at the front, since a similar manner of masking large troop movements was widely practiced in the Red Army as well.

The first to move out were the sapper units; just a bit before this, special work teams (which included prisoners of war) arrived in the woods in front of the Donets River and began chopping down trees in order to erect and repair bridges and crossing sites in the event of their damage; logs were cut and cleared of branches, and then transported to clearings. Light bridging equipment and some of the rubber boats were being hidden in thickets along the riverbanks and on the fringes of woods. However, the bulk of the rubber boats were being stockpiled in villages; for instance, the 7th Panzer Division was storing them in damaged buildings in Solomino. Heavy bridging sections were located on transports that were parked in woods at full readiness in response to a command to drive up to the points where bridges were to be laid. The 7th Panzer Division commander recalled:

> In direct proximity of the river, especially in a sector that was covered by a meadow and bushes in the Solomino area, there were favorable conditions for bringing up and preparing crossing means and materials at night time for the construction of bridges. In other sectors, it was necessary to arrange suitable camouflage for this work. In general and on the whole it can be said that on our bank, the 7th Panzer Division had fully favorable conditions for the sudden crossing of troops on a broad front.[5]

In separate sectors that were deprived of trees, where Korps Raus was to attack, his specialized units themselves were forced to create small "woodlots" for camouflage purposes. However, this means sometimes worked against the Germans and revealed their intentions. The deputy commander of the 1st Artillery Battalion of the 72nd Guards Rifle Division's 155th Guards Artillery Regiment T.Z. Vinogradov recalled:

> Early one morning in the final days of June, the intelligence chief of our battalion Viazovets, who was observing the enemy through a scissors telescope, suddenly called out to his commander, "Comrade Captain, take a look at what the Germans created over the night. N.I. Savchenko nestled up against the scissors telescope, before summoning me. Now that was a wonder! Beyond the Donets, a patch of forest had appeared overnight at right angles across the Toplinka balka. This handcrafted thicket was screening the previously clearly exposed balka to our observation. This fact became one more piece of evidence that the enemy was preparing for a looming offensive.[6]

Day after day, the Front's intelligence was scrupulously monitoring the traffic on the main railroad routes and main roads leading toward Khar'kov and Belgorod. This was being done for the purpose of the average number of loaded railcars and vehicles moving at a given interval of time,

---
5   TsAMO RF, F. 15, op. 11600, d. 1539, l. 12.
6   Vinogradov, T.Z., *Dorogoe – navsegda* [*Dear – forever*] (Moscow: Voenizdat, 1977), p. 80.

5 JULY 1943 – THE BEGINNING OF THE END OF A TRAGICOMEDY

as well as to estimate the amount of troops and cargo being transported to the front over a certain period of time. The enemy was aware of this methodology, which given a thorough rechecking of the information from the air and the analysis of other information yielded rather accurate results. Thus the assembly of forces in the first days of July went with all precautionary measures: the artillery and armor was being brought up only at night, while the infantry, ammunition and bridging equipment moved in daylight hours, but only in small groups of vehicles, on wagons or on foot.

In order to prevent traffic jams and commotion directly at the front in the offensive's first hours, when the bridges still weren't ready and the staging areas were only in the process of forming, the III Panzer Corps command planned to move up its tanks in two stages. First, on the night of 3-4 July, the Tiger tanks of the Separate Heavy Panzer Battalion 503 were brought up on special prime movers, while at the same time assault guns drove up and moved into the woods. In the attack's first minutes, they were to offer direct fire support to the assaulting groups of grenadiers as they crossed the river. Meanwhile the bulk of the panzer regiments of the divisions were located several kilometers distant from the assembled assault guns, ready at any moment to move out toward the bridges.

In addition, from the beginning of July the Soviet side noted a new detail in the enemy's behavior. Every day in various places, the enemy was unexpectedly opening up vigorous artillery fire for no apparent reason. For example, in the operational summary of the Voronezh Front's headquarters for 1000 on 2 July, it was noted that over the night the Germans had fired a total of 160 shells and mortar rounds of various calibers on the positions of the 6th Guards Army, up to 400 on the 38th Army, up to 450 on the 40th Army, and up to 2,000 shells on the fortifications of the 7th Guards Army. At the same time as the barrages were taking place, villages in this area were subjected to intense artillery shelling. Usually, the substantially increasing activity of artillery could testify to several things. First, the thunder of the cannonade was supposed to muffle the sound of engines and tracks of tanks, and thereby divert attention from the assembly of forces. Second, a sudden and intensive barrage inflicted harm to personnel and destroyed shelters and firing positions. Third, the nighttime shelling exhausted and enervated the troops at the front. All of this was part of the plan of Army Group South's command, but were not the main point. During the preparation for Operation Citadel, a plan of camouflage measures was worked out in order to confuse the Soviet side. One of its points demanded the conducting of unexpected, powerful artillery barrages along the entire front of Army Group South from the beginning of July, but most of all on the left wing, with the aim of confusing the enemy about where the main attack was being prepared. There is also the interesting detail testifying to the fine organization of camouflage and skillful cover of the 7th Guards Army's troops. Despite the intense barrage conducted by the enemy artillerymen on 2 July on specially-identified targets, the losses of the divisions of the first echelon were insignificant: 7 men were killed and 20 wounded.

Although the western bank was higher than the eastern bank of the Northern Donets River, and it was here that all of the commanding heights in the district were located, it proved impossible to set up satisfactory observation posts for the artillery and the command of the assaulting groups of grenadiers because of the tall trees. Considering the careful camouflaging of the lines of Shumilov's army, this detail presented a substantial problem to the command of the 6th and 7th Panzer Divisions. I will remind that Hoth's situation was similar. In order to resolve the problem of positioning the artillery observation posts, he was forced on the day of 4 July to launch a limited attack to seize an elevated sector of ground in front of the two Guards divisions of the 6th Guards Army.

Kempf, on the other hand, had to operate differently. Radio operators and specialized elements of the panzer divisions moved up into the combat positions of the 168th Infantry Division, which was holding the front in the sector where the panzer divisions of III Panzer Corps were to be committed, in order to set up forward observation posts directly among the infantry positions.

Indeed, it was only after this that the combat groups of grenadiers and artillery began to deploy in small columns. Skipping somewhat ahead, I will say that despite all the efforts, in the opening hours of the offensive Kempf's artillery would remain blind and to a significant extent fire randomly.

Schematically, the final plan of actions for the first day of the offensive by Army Detachment Kempf to overcome the Northern Donets River and breach the 7th Guards Army's main belt of defenses, which were necessary in order to achieve 5 July's final objective – to emerge in the Dal'niaia Igumenka – Iastrebovo, "Batratskaia Dacha" State Farm area, consisted of two main stages. The first was to force a crossing of the river and establish bridgeheads for the passage of the main forces, primarily the armor. The second stage was the capture of several larger towns along the river (0.5 to 2.5 kilometers from the main channel), which the Soviets had converted into powerful nests of resistance covering the river itself and constituted strongpoints in the main line of resistance. These were Staryi Gorod,[7] Razumnoe, Krutoi Log, Nizhnii Ol'shanets,[8] Maslova Pristan'[9] and Bezliudovka.[10] In order to attain this objective, forces were distributed evenly along the front. Opposite each Guards division, Breith arrayed approximately one and a half panzer divisions and 1/3 of an infantry division: against the 81st Guards Rifle Division (Staryi Gorod) – the 6th Panzer Division, part of the 19th Panzer Division and 1/3 of the 168th Infantry Division; against the 78th Guards Rifle Division (Razumnoe, Krutoi Log) – the 7th Panzer Division, part of the 19th Panzer Division, and 1/3 of the 168th Infantry Division. Korps Raus assigned the 106th and 320th Infantry Divisions to target the 72nd Guards Rifle Division (Nizhnii Ol'shanets, Maslova Pristan' and Bezliudovka). In addition, in the morning hours Kempf had already planned a reconnaissance-in-force on the flanks of Shumilov's Guards army with regimental groups of the XXXXII Army Corps on the Soviet extreme left flank in the sector of the 36th Guards Rifle Division (Nezhigal' area) and of the 168th Infantry Division at the boundary between the 6th and 7th Guards Army in the sector of the 375th Rifle Division (Chernaia Poliana area) on the right. The distribution of forces and means evenly across the entire sector of the intended breakthrough (as well as the over-confidence and underestimation of the strength of the 81st Guards Rifle Division's defense) was a plain mistake and was one of the main reasons for the failure of both the plan for 5 July and of the entire Operation Citadel on the whole.

Breith's panzer corps was poised to attack two divisions of Major General G.B. Safiulin's 25th Guards Rifle Corps, the 81st Guards Rifle and 78th Guards Rifle Divisions, simultaneously with three panzer divisions and the attached combat units of the 168th Infantry Division in the Staryi Gorod – (excl.) Nizhnii Ol'shanets sector, which extended for approximately 15 kilometers. Major General W. von Hünersdorff's 6th Panzer Division was supposed to operate on the left flank. It had the task to attack out of the Mikhailovka bridgehead in the center of the 81st Guards Rifle Division's line and against its right flank (Staryi Gorod), and having breached it, was to emerge on the left flank of the 6th Guards Army's 375th Rifle Division, where together with the forces of the II SS Panzer Corps it was to crush this division and establish shoulder-to-shoulder contact with the II SS Panzer Corps' right-flank SS Panzergrenadier Division *Totenkopf*. In addition, a *kampfgruppe* of von Hünersdorff's 6th Panzer Division was to maintain constant contact with the 19th Panzer Division on its right, which was to operate out of the southern portion of the same bridgehead at Mikhailovka.

In order to implement this plan, von Hünersdorff decided to launch a simultaneous, initial attack with two *kampfgruppen*, which were formed out of elements of the 168th Infantry Division

---

7   In modern times a neighborhood of Belgorod.
8   As of 1.1.1932, it had 1,425 residents.
9   As of 1.1.1932, it had 1,846 residents.
10   As of 1.1.1932, it had 1,379 residents.

(Reconnaissance Battalion 248, II/Grenadier Regiment 417, a company from Engineer Battalion 248 and II, III/Artillery Regiment 248). The left-flank group headed by the commander of Grenadier Regiment 417 Barkmann was to operate out of Belgorod along the western bank of the Donets in the direction of the village of Chernaia Poliana (into the flank of the 6th Guards Army), while the second *kampfgruppe* under the command of Arthan was to attack out of the bridgehead toward Staryi Gorod. Before the start of the attack, a *kampfgruppe* that had already been formed out of elements of the 6th Panzer Division under the command of K.R. von Bieberstein (I/Panzergrenadier Regiment 114 and a company from Engineer Battalion 57) was supposed to move together with StuG Battalion 228 to the area of Mikhailovka in order to reinforce the latter *kampfgruppe*. As the bridgehead expanded, at first all the assault guns, and then a second *kampfgruppe* of the 6th Panzer Division headed by the commander of Panzergrenadier Regiment 4 Colonel M. Unrein[11] was to follow von Bieberstein's *kampfgruppe* into the bridgehead. These forces were to sweep the bridgehead clear of mines and to expand it sufficiently so that a *panzerkampfgruppe* under the command of Lieutenant Colonel von Oppeln-Bronikowski[12] [often shortened to von Oppeln in texts] could assemble in it, consisting of Major F. Bäke's II/Panzer Regiment 11 and Captain Roebke's II/Panzergrenadier Regiment 114 mounted in halftracks, in order to launch an attack with the aim of linking up with the right flank of the 2nd SS Panzergrenadier Division *Totenkopf* on the right wing of the II SS Panzer Corps.

The 19th Panzer Division was positioned in the center of the III Panzer Corps' combat formation. It received the assignment to launch an attack at the boundary between the 81st Guards Rifle Division's left flank and the 78th Guards Rifle Division's right flank and break through their defenses in the sector between the southern portion of the Mikhailovka bridgehead and Dal'nie Peski. Subsequently it was to cooperate with the 6th Panzer Division in destroying the Russians in Mikhailovka, before advancing onward toward the village of Razumnoe in order to link up with the 7th Panzer Division on its right. Like its neighbors, an assault group comprised of attached elements of the 168th Infantry Division (Grenadier Regiment 429, I/Artillery Regiment 248 and a company of the Engineer Battalion 248) were to lead the initial attack. The 19th Panzer Division commander G. Schmidt already had one bridge available, which he planned to use in order to cross a *kampfgruppe* of Lieutenant Colonel Richter's Panzergrenadier Regiment 74 into the southern portion of the Mikhailovka bridgehead on the night of 4-5 July in order to reinforce the grenadiers of Infantry Regiment 168. With the start of the fighting, this composite forward group was to be supported by fire from a Tiger company of Colonel Graf C. von Kageneck's Heavy Panzer Battalion 503. After destroying the Russians' forward outposts and beginning the assault on the positions of Safiulin's rifle corps, the 19th Panzer Division's combat engineers were to begin the construction of a 60-tonne bridge, over which it was planned to cross first the Tiger tanks, and then Lieutenant Colonel H. Becker's entire Panzer Regiment 27.

---

11 Martin Friedrich Karl Unrein, Lieutenant General (1.07.1944) was born in Weimar on New Year's Day of 1901. He served in the cavalry and became a lieutenant in 1922. In September 1939 he was appointed as the adjutant of the IX Army Corps in the rank of major. Later he was promoted to lieutenant colonel and received assignment to the OKW. On 15.09.1941 Lieutenant Colonel M. Unrein received a combat command and took command of the 6th Panzer Division's motorcycle battalion, and on 1.04.1942, he became the commander of Panzergrenadier Regiment 4.
12 Hermann von Oppeln-Bronikowski (Major General 01.01.1945) was born in Berlin on 2.01.1899. He joined the German Imperial Army in 1917 and served in the cavalry. In 1937 he took command of II/10th Cavalry Regiment, and on 14.01.1942 Lieutenant Colonel von Oppeln-Bronikowski assumed command of Panzer Regiment 35. On 5.10.1942, he was transferred to take command of Panzer Regiment 204. For his successful command of the regiment, on 01.01.1943 he was awarded the Knight's Cross. In the spring of 1943, he took over command of the 6th Panzer Division's Panzer Regiment 11.

The 7th Panzer Division on the right flank was to force the Donets River in the Dal'nie Peski – Solomino sector, and having created a bridgehead, was to attack along both sides of the Razumnaia River. After seizing Razumnoe Station, it was to advance along the eastern bank in the direction of the heights to the northeast of the village of Miasoedovo (25 kilometers from the Northern Donets River). The panzer division faced a more difficult situation than that of the rest of the III Panzer Corps' divisions, having been allocated for its offensive a narrow 4-kilometer sector (to the south of which lay Solomino) that had no bridgeheads, while all the bridges had been blown up. Moreover, its offensive sector was bifurcated by the Razumnaia River, which flowed in a southwesterly direction before joining the Northern Donets River near Razumnoe. Thus before initiating its direct assault on the 72nd Guards Rifle Division's positions, in the initial minutes after completing the artillery preparation von Funck would have to send a reinforced assault group using inflatable boats across the river's channel out of the Solomino area. As in the other panzer divisions, the assault group formed in the 7th Panzer Division was based on the attached elements of the 168th Infantry Division (a battalion of Grenadier Regiment 429, the IV and V Battalions of Artillery Regiment 248[13] and a company from Engineer Battalion 248). Also as in the case of the other panzer divisions, the cross-river assault by the grenadiers of the 168th Infantry Division was to be covered by the fire from the western bank of one of the Tiger companies of Separate Heavy Panzer Battalion 503; subsequently, after the heavy tanks' own crossing (at a ford), they were to continue providing fire support for the grenadiers' advance. In the wake of these forces, it was planned to advance the regimental groups of the division itself: Colonel W. Gläsemer's Panzergrenadier Regiment 7[14] along the left bank of the Razumnaia River, and Lieutenant Colonel A. Schülz's[15] armored group along the right bank (Panzer Regiment 25, a battalion of Artillery Regiment 78, a half-track mounted battalion of Panzergrenadier Regiment 6, units of the Panzerjäger Battalion 42 and Motorized Engineer Battalion 58).

Breith was assuming that the heaviest and costliest fighting would take place on the ground between the crossing sites out to the area of Hills 209.0 and 216.1. On the basis of information gleaned from aerial reconnaissance photographs, it was clear that the most heavily-fortified section of the Soviet defenses was located here. This circumstance was disturbing; General Breith was concerned that the two infantry divisions of Korps Raus would not be able to keep pace with the panzer divisions while breaking through the Russian lines, which is indeed what happened already by 6 July. Therefore he cautioned Major General von Funck that in the event that Korps

---

13   IV Battalion was equipped with 150mm howitzers, while the V Battalion was equipped with Nebelwerfer rocket launchers.
14   Wolfgang Gläsemer, Colonel (1.01.1942) was born in Rimberg on 14.03.1899. Commander of Panzergrenadier Regiment 7, between 17.08.1943 and 20.08.1943, and again between 28.01.1944 and 30.01.1944, he temporarily commanded the 7th Panzer Division. He was awarded the Knight's Cross (12.02.1943) and the German Cross in Gold (21.02.1942). He passed away on 10 April 1999.
15   Adelbert Schülz, Major General (01.01.1944) was born on 20.12.1903 in Berlin. In 1925 he voluntarily served in the Prussian police force, and in 1934 he received the rank of Police lieutenant. A year later, as an 1st Lieutenant he transferred to the German Army and served in the panzer troops. From 1937 to the start of the Second World War, Schülz was a company commander. Later he received a promotion to major ahead of schedule, and on 06.06.1940 he was appointed commander of a panzer battalion in Panzer Regiment 25, which from 18.10.1939 was subordinate to the 7th Panzer Division. He stood out in the fighting on the Western Front, and on 29.09.1940 he was awarded the Knight's Cross. From June 1941 he served on the Eastern Front with the division. On 31.12.1941, he received the Oak Leaves to the Knight's Cross. On 5.03.1943 he took command of Panzer Regiment 25, and on 1.04.1943 received promotion to the rank of lieutenant colonel. On 6.08.1943 he received the Swords to his Knight's Cross and was promoted to the rank of colonel. On 9.01.1944 he received his Diamonds to his Knight's Cross, was promoted to major general, and made commander of the 7th Panzer Division. He received a mortal wound on 28 January 1944 and died the same day.

Raus's attack bogged down, he would have to assume the responsibility for screening the III Panzer Corps' right flank. The commander of the 7th Panzer Division himself anticipated such a course of events, and therefore without waiting for a crisis situation to develop for his neighbor, he paid appropriate attention to arranging close cooperation with Korps Raus. Von Funck wrote:

> The commander of the artillery regiment in good time organized cable and radio communications with the neighboring division's [the 106th Infantry Division] chief of artillery. The fire plans for supporting the work on the bridges and the subsequent advance into the depth of the enemy's defenses were thoroughly coordinated. The possibility of concentrated fire of a large number of batteries on the most important targets was prepared with the calculation that it could be opened at any moment in response to the established signal.
>
> All the most important questions concerning the designated course of the operation, the targets that needed to be suppressed, as well as ensuring air cover for the crossing sites and construction of bridges by fighters and Flak regiments were worked out with the Luftwaffe. Each division headquarters was assigned a Luftwaffe signals officer equipped with a radio set. Contact or prearranged signals were timely made over the radio, which allowed the panzer divisions to be informed quickly of the enemy's appearance. For example, purple flares dropped from an aircraft meant that enemy tanks had been spotted.[16]

In addition to the means of reinforcement mentioned above, the 6th Panzer Division also received III/Mortar Regiment 54, while the 19th Panzer Division received the rest of Mortar Regiment 54. The six-barreled rocket launchers that armed the Mortar Regiment 54 were already from the opening minutes of the offensive to join in the destruction of enemy firing positions, first of all in the sectors where the assault groups of the 168th Infantry Division's grenadiers were crossing the Donets.

Korps Raus's designated breakthrough sector was 2-kilometers wider than that of Breith's panzer corps and amounted to 17 kilometers. Its objectives for D-day were to seize the area on both sides of Hill 207 (6 kilometers west of Pentsevo), which lay approximately 7 kilometers from the river channel. With its two divisions it was to launch an attack against the positions (primarily striking the regimental boundaries and their flanks) of just one of the rifle divisions of Major General N.A. Vasil'ev's 24th Guards Rifle Corps – the 72nd Guards Rifle Division. Lieutenant General W. Forst's 106th Infantry Division on the left and Major General G. Postel's 320th Infantry Division on the right were to make a forced crossing of the river in the Nizhnii Ol'shanets – Bezliudovka sector. A battalion of all three regiments of each division were to jump off first on the attack. In the initial stage of the offensive (after crossing the river), the main task of the 106th Infantry Division's *kampfgruppen* was to seize two villages: the larger village of Nizhnii Ol'shanets (by Grenadier Regiment 240) and the smaller village nearby of Karnaukhovka (by Grenadier Regiment 241), while for the 320th Infantry Division, the objectives were Bezliudovka (Grenadier Regiment 585) and Rzhavets (Grenadier Regiment 587). Meanwhile, Maslova Pristan', which was located on the boundary between the two divisions, was to be assaulted by a regiment from each division: the 106th Rifle Division's Grenadier Regiment 239 on the left, and 320th Infantry Division's Grenadier Regiment 586 on the right. Korps Raus' headquarters believed that only after consolidating their hold on these villages and driving the enemy out of their positions along the railroad embankment that the divisions would have the possibility of building the necessary number of bridges and transferring a sufficient amount of infantry and heavy weapons to the eastern bank for a subsequent push forward.

---

16 TsAMO RF, F. 15, op. 11600, d. 1539, l. 16.

After consolidating its foothold on the eastern bank, the 106th Infantry Division was to launch an attack toward Krutoi Log, and after its capture, to pivot to the north toward Hills 216.1 and 207.9, strictly coordinating its actions with the 7th Panzer Division. The 320th Infantry Division was supposed to advance at approximately the same pace. Grenadier Regiment 587's order reveals: "… On the right the reinforced Grenadier Regiment 585, in the center the reinforced Grenadier Regiment 587, and on the left Grenadier Regiment 586 on 5 July breaches the enemy's forward edge of defense and on this same day penetrates to the line: Nezhegol – Koren', by means of creating a bridgehead east of Ustinka; with its right flank it holds the right bank of the Nezhegol as far as Koren', while the center and left reaches the Korocha line and holds it."[17]

When breaking through the forward edge of the 24th Guards Rifle Corps, Raus was planning to use a significant amount of Flak artillery in the ground support role. For this purpose his corps alone had 72 88mm guns. Ehrard Raus recalled:

> The flak regiments' first mission was to take part in the artillery preparation under the direction of the corps artillery commander. For this purpose the Flak regiments were echeloned in depth and committed in three waves. The first echelon was positioned within the main line of resistance and closely behind it; its mission was to place direct fire on enemy heavy weapons and pillboxes. In addition, it had to form Flak assault detachments for anti-tank combat to give close support to the advancing infantry. Together with the corps artillery, the two other regiments were to shatter the enemy's first line of defense and paralyze his infantry by delivering sustained concentrations of fire. After that, elements of the first echelon, with the exception of the assault detachments, as well as the entire second echelon, were to support the advancing infantry. The third echelon was to take over the anti-aircraft protection of the entire artillery area and was also to participate in counterbattery missions.[18]

As is known, in Operation Citadel there was no element of either operational or tactical surprise. For the Soviet Supreme Command, the enemy's plans, the location of the assault groupings, and even the start date for the offensive were not a secret. As combat documents of the Voronezh Front testify, even the details of the steps taken by the Germans to bring their forces up directly to the forward edge of the armies of the first echelon and the preparation of the ground for their deployment didn't remain unnoticed. This particularly concerned the German preparations on the western bank of the Northern Donets River. At the beginning of July, the Front's chief of intelligence Major General I.V. Vinogradov reported that the Germans had already assembled not less than two additional panzer divisions in the Belgorod area. Together with this, the engineer headquarters was providing interesting and no less important reliable information. Information from the Front's and armies' engineer scouts and observation posts, in combination with the analysis of aerial reconnaissance photographs, which the 2nd Air Army was systematically producing, was describing an accurate picture of the enemy's preparations for an offensive along the entire front. A particularly large amount of information was coming from the enemy force's preparations of routes and lines of communication opposite the 7th Guards Army's front, which unquestionably testified to their attacking plans. The Front's chief of engineers Major General Iu.V. Bordzilovsky reported:

---

17 TsAMO RF, F. 203, op. 2845, d. 227, l. 23.
18 Newton, *Kurskaia bitva: Nemetskii vzgliad*, p. 72.

> The Northern Donets River was taken under particularly thorough surveillance by us … as a result, the enemy's assembly of bridging material in the areas north of Solomino, Toplinka, Andreevka /west of Toplinka/ was revealed.
> In the period of the enemy's direct preparations for the offensive, increased work to construct bridges in close proximity to the forward edge and across the river was revealed:
>> On 10.6 the Germans built an underwater bridge in the Toplinka area [the sector of the 72nd Guards Rifle Division];
>> On 13.6 repair work on a bridge in the Pushkarnoe area was spotted [the left flank of the 81st Guards Rifle Division];
>> On 13.6 the presence of a wooden, low-water truss bridge was detected in the Mikhailovka, Suprunovka area [the 81st Guards Rifle Division];
>> On 20.6 the analysis of aerial photographs of Mikhailovka revealed two intact bridges across the Northern Donets;
>> 20-26.6 bridging material consisting of 20 pontoons on vehicles and one pontoon section arrived in the Andreevka area.[19]

Together with this information, at the beginning of summer, evidence began to arrive about the Germans' preparation of the ground directly along the forward edge for the passage of troops, including along the edge of the western river bank. For example, on 15 June a patrol that had penetrated into the rear of the 168th Infantry Division established that barbed wire and a large minefield along the railroad in the area of Pokrovka (north of Belgorod) had disappeared. Four days later, on the night of 19-20 June opposite the front of the 36th Guards Rifle Division in the area of the village of Ogurtsevo, a group of engineer scouts that had approached the trenches of the 320th Infantry Division found flattened sectors of barbed wire, while a previously existing minefield here had been cleared. On 22 June, on the southeastern outskirts of Arkhangel'skoe (the right flank of the 36th Guards Rifle Division), German combat engineers attempted to remove mines, while two days later an observation outpost spotted the same activity, but now in the sector of the 6th Guards Army's 375th Rifle Division (between Kondyrevo and the House of Invalids).

The collected information on the forward edge and in the enemy's tactical zone was not only being sent on to Voronezh Front command. It was being accumulated, supplemented and analyzed in its headquarters, after which it was being released down the chain of command in the form of orders, directives and recommendations. For example, a special map of the fortifications of Army Group South was being kept in the engineer headquarters, which was being fleshed out with information from the daily reports that arrived over the telephone from the frontline armies and divisions, as well as every three days by intelligence summaries that contained information from aerial reconnaissance flights, prisoner testimonies and the network of agents. Once or twice a month, this map was reproduced in 200-300 copies and send down the engineers' chain of command (down to the division's chief engineer inclusively) as well as to the troop commanders (down to the level of the rifle regiment commander).

As a result, by the beginning of July an analysis of the available information allowed one to draw several conclusions. First, the Voronezh Front's leadership was convinced that the enemy was going to follow through on its intentions to go on the offensive, and moreover, would do so on those directions that it had already predicted. Second, based on the reports from Bordzilovsky's intelligence service, it was possible to determine precisely those places in the sector of the 7th Guards Army where the Germans intended to make forced crossings of the Northern Donets River: the Mikhailovka bridgehead, and in the areas of Toplinka and Solomino. A number of

---

19 TsAMO RF, F. 203, Op. 2845, d. 277, l. 19.

special measures were taken in the indicated sectors in order to strengthen the defense: the number of observation outposts increased; additional mining of the banks and ground in those sectors where there had once been bridges, which the enemy might use in order to rebuild the bridges. In addition, a special group was sent to Toplinka in order to destroy a bridge that had been rebuilt by the Germans.

With the aim of inflicting maximum damage to the enemy's manpower and equipment at the moment when they were assembled on their start lines for the offensive, N.F. Vatutin planned two important measures: the conducting of a counter artillery preparation by the armies of the first echelon against established areas of aggregations of enemy forces, and air strikes by ground attack aircraft on German airfields in the area. The preemptive artillery strike, which was called a counter artillery preparation, in the sector of the 7th Guards Army, was an important element of the defensive plan of both *fronts* that were defending the Kursk salient, both Rokossovsky's and Vatutin's. According to documents, it main purpose was to foil the enemy's initial attack, although in reality the Soviet side realized that this was impossible, and therefore it was to inflict maximal damage to the troops that were poised to move out on the attack. The targets selected for the preemptive barrage would be those most reliably identified, since the Front command had set an ammunition limit for the preemptive attack – half of a standard combat load. In its initial scheme, the 7th Guards Army's artillery headquarters planned to conduct fire on eight directions. The multiplicity of targeted directions wasn't the plan's strongest aspect, but there wasn't much choice in the matter. First, there was no experience in organizing such a counter artillery preparation, because this was going to be its first use in practice. Second, when preparing it, the headquarters had to consider primarily the enemy's actions and the degree of reliability of the collected intelligence.

Around 2200 on 4 July, a conversation took place over the Baudot device between N.F. Vatutin and M.S. Shumilov:

> At the apparatus Nikolaev [Vatutin]. Greetings. Briefly report how your day ended today.
>
> At the apparatus Stepnoi [Shumilov]. Greetings. I report: From Belgorod to Maslova Pristan', an ordinary artillery and mortar duel; from Maslova Pristan' to Kolchansk, the enemy has been conducting fire attacks since 1830 against Maslova Pristan', Priiutovka, Novaia Tavolzhanka, Gastishche-1 and Sinel'nikov. Fire attacks against Maslova Pristan', Priiutovka, and into the depth as far as the western fringe of the woods east of Maslova Pristan' /4 kilometers/ continues even now. By 2200 the enemy had fired more than 2,500 shells, and in the sector between Maslova Pristan' and Karnaukhovka, and between Toplinka and the woods west of Karanaukhovka, there were enemy attempts to cross up to a company to our bank in each sector, but with the fire of infantry and mortars the enemy's crossing attempt failed with the exception of 10 men. These 10 men turned back, leaving behind two dead in Toplinka. At 1900 the approach of 6 tanks and up to a company from Brodok was spotted. Aerial reconnaissance dispatched to this area reported the movement of up to 10 vehicles in the area of Toplinka toward Brodok and small groups of enemy north of Toplinka and Puliaevka; no tanks were spotted. That's all I can report as of 2200.
>
> Nikolaev: Where do you believe is the enemy's largest aggregation [of force]?
>
> Stepnoi: As before, the enemy's largest aggregation remains in the Belgorod area; in the Toplinka, Ivanovka, Volkovo and Grafovka area. I am so far assessing these fire attacks that the enemy is conducting as cover for a rotation of units; I haven't observed a large reinforcement of infantry in this area, but only the movement of small groups of infantry in platoon-strength or rarely up to company strength to and from the forward edge. Yesterday at 2000 we observed the chopping of trees in the woods north of Toplinka and in the Korovinskaia Woods. I assume that these woods are being cut down in order to build defensive works, and not for bridges, since throughout today and this evening we haven't seen logs being lowered

from the heights down to the river in the Arkhangel'skoe – Staritsa area. I haven't seen any buildup of enemy forces. Over.[20]

It is difficult to agree with the army commander that a situation, when the enemy over the course of several hours fired 2,500 shells at the forward edge, could be considered "ordinary", since over the preceding days and months, they counted 600-800 rounds per day. Moreover, on 4 July the intensive fire was being conducted in daylight hours and was targeting primarily artillery positions and observation posts. For example, the Germans were systematically firing with heavy guns out of the western outskirts of Belgorod at two grain elevators at the Kreida railyard where the forward observation posts of the 81st Guards Rifle Division and the 167th Tank Regiment had been set up. Fire didn't cease until these two tall buildings had been reduced to piles of ruins. With the same sort of exactingness and persistence, the enemy gunners "smashed" other buildings and structures suitable for use by the Soviet side.

Even the testimony of a deserting combat engineer, who came over to our side in the sector of the 25th Guards Rifle Corps, didn't alarm the army commander, even though he was reporting that the offensive would begin on the night of 4-5 July and also provided interesting details. The commander of the 25th Guards Rifle Corps General G.B. Safiulin recalled:

> I hadn't even managed to enter my command post when I was summoned to the telephone. The corps' chief of intelligence Major I.A. Vorontsov was calling:
> "Comrade Dobrovol'sky (this was my code name), a soldier has come over from the other side. He says he has important information. What are your orders?"
> "Report immediately to me!"
> Soon my political deputy Colonel O.P. Kolesnik, the corps' chief of staff Colonel A.A. Funtikov, I.A. Vorontsov and an interpreter were sitting behind a table with me. We were facing a lanky soldier, his face covered with reddish stubble. He was wearing a dirty, threadbare uniform and worn boots.
> We asked him, "Who are you?"
> Without waiting for the interpreter, he rapidly blurted, "I'm a sapper of the 168th Infantry Division."
> His accent sounded German.
> "What caused you to come here? What is it that you want to report?"
> This time too he didn't wait for the interpreter, and immediately began to tell us. This caught our attention. How did he happen to know the Russian language?
> "We were ordered to clear a minefield and to remove barbed wire obstacles," the deserter said. "They gave us dry rations for five days, and also ponied up some schnapps. Tomorrow the offensive will begin."
> "Tomorrow?"
> "Yes, 5 July."
> "How do you know the Russian language?"
> "I can simply understand it."
> "But you can speak it?"
> "Badly."
> "Are you a German?"
> "No, I'm Slovenian."

---

20 TsAMO RF, F. 203, Op. 2843, d. 461, l. 17.

I wanted to trust his words. Moreover, according to our own intelligence, the start of the offensive was expected between 3 and 6 July. …. I turned over the rest of the interrogation to my chief of staff Funtikov, and ordered my adjutant to feed the Slovenian well, before heading back to my bunker. There I immediately called the army commander and told him word for word what I had heard from the deserter.

"Send him here," the army commander requested, "while on my part I will immediately warn the unit commanders not to let slip any visitors."

Unquestionably, if we examine this incident separately from the other events that were taking place in the neighboring armies and in front of the 7th Guards Army, then it could be justly viewed as a possible provocation by the *Abwehr*. But if taken together with the other information, including that arriving from the Central Front, then a rather clear picture began to emerge.

However, the conversation with N.F. Vatutin testifies to the fact that the army commander, even though he'd been alerted by Moscow about the enemy's possible launching of an offensive between 3 and 6 July, hadn't seen any obvious signs of the preparations for it by Kempf's troops opposite his army's sector by the end of 4 July, or possibly considered it excessive to offer his own speculation in an extremely complex and tense situation. N.F. Vatutin regarded M.S. Shumilov with respect, valued his experience and knowledge, but at this moment he possessed a large amount of information about what was happening, both in the sector of Shumilov's army (and opposite his army), as well as in his neighbor's sector on the right [the 6th Guards Army]. Thus, Vatutin didn't react to the army commander's words, but ordered: if the situation didn't sharply change in the next several hours, to open the preemptive fire according to plan. The counter artillery preparation in the 7th Guards Army was supposed to take place between 0300 and 0325 on 5 July according to three options. It was planned to place the heaviest fire on the Mikhailovka bridgehead and the area of Belgorod adjacent to it, as well as on the areas of the villages of Pushkarnoe, Solomino, Ivanovka, Volkovo, Grafivka and Arkhangel'skoe. When planning the preemptive fire, not only the intelligence about aggregations of enemy troops and any natural cover, where personnel and equipment could be concealed were considered, but also those places of the most likely crossing attempts. For this preemptive barrage, N.F. Vatutin authorized the expenditure of the following number of shells per gun: 76mm – not more than 40; 122mm – not more than 20; 152mm – not more than 10; 120mm mortars – not more than 10; 82mm mortars – not more than 20; 45mm fragmentation shells – as many as could be fired over the allotted time. It was also recommended to fire one salvo of rockets from each rocket-launching battalion at enemy concentrations.

When wrapping up the conversation, the Front commander demanded that Shumilov establish increased monitoring of the fords and the areas where the enemy might attempt to build a bridge. He also ordered all the formation and unit commanders to be at their command posts, to check communications with the covering aviation units, and finally, to synchronize their watches over the radio to that there would be no confusion when issuing missions and executing orders.

The corps commanders G.B. Safiulin and N.A. Vasil'ev received the preliminary order about implementing the plan for the counter artillery preparation over the telephone two and a half hours before the signal by telephone to open fire. In order to monitor the execution of the order and render assistance in the event of need, the 7th Guards Army's artillery commander Lieutenant General A.N. Petrov sent his deputy to the 25th Guards Rifle Corps and his chief of staff to the 24th Guards Rifle Corps.

At the end of June, when information began to come in about the movement of enemy forces toward the front, several adjustments were made to the counter artillery preparation's plan. Considering that the preemptive fire was supposed to begin simultaneously on several directions, the commanders of the 6th and 7th Guards Armies decided to concentrate all of their artillery fire only in the sector of their own armies, and not to redirect their fire to targets opposite their

5 JULY 1943 – THE BEGINNING OF THE END OF A TRAGICOMEDY

neighbor's front, as had been initially planned. Only at the boundary between the armies, in order to reinforce the artillery fire of his own 23rd Guards Rifle Corps, did I.M. Chistiakov ask M.S. Shumilov to contribute the fire of the 120mm mortars of 1/290th Mortar Regiment on German positions opposite the 375th Rifle Division's left flank. Within the 7th Guards Army, a number of artillery regiments and the artillery of separate battalions received fresh missions (within the framework of the previously prepared plan). For example, all of the 36th Guards Rifle Division's artillery was now to deploy in the sector of the 72nd Guards Rifle Division, in order to work over the enemy opposite its positions more thoroughly, while the army's 265th Guards Cannon Artillery Regiment was to shell targets on the western bank of the Northern Donets River opposite the 78th Guards Rifle Division's sector.

On the afternoon of 4 July, scattered rain showers developed over the Voronezh Front, but the temperature remained steady. By 2230, twilight began to gather, and the darkening sky cleared to reveal a multitude of stars; however, after midnight a light fog settled here and there in the river bottomlands. As veterans of the Battle of Kursk recalled, the night of 4-5 July in the sector of the 7th Guards Army was unusually warm and relatively quiet.[21] After several volleys of Katiusha rockets prior to midnight and a bit later at the areas of Pushkarnoe, Suprunovka and Mikhailovka, where the 6th and 19th Panzer Divisions were assembled, it again became quiet, and a fragrant cool breeze wafted from the Shebekinskaia Dacha Woods. Even the chatter of machine guns ceased for a time. Only the neighboring 6th Guard Army's front continued to "breathe" and rumble; an intensive exchange of fire and the explosions of shells and mortar rounds could be heard coming from that direction. However, these minutes of quiet on their front didn't relieve those soldiers and officers crouched in their trenches and at their command posts along both sides of the river. They all sensed that within a matter of hours, Death would again begin stalking these fields and patches of woods. Even so, they all very much didn't want to believe that these peaceful, according to the war's standards, three months had flown by so quickly, and that they again would have to face death. The commander of the 25th Guards Rifle Corps G.B. Safiulin recalled:

> The orange glow of the approaching dawn appeared on the horizon. I was greeting the dawning day of 5 July in my observation post in the village of Blizhniaia Igumenka. The scissors telescope was pointed at the opposite bank of the Northern Donets. There were no signs of life. Beneath a steep cliff, the surface of the water was glass calm. Not a single ripple or splash. Only airy curtains of light mist were floating here and there above the river. However, I was weight down by the burden of expectations. Suddenly, the shroud of silence was ripped apart by the thunder of artillery salvoes. The river and ground began to seethe and mix with the sky …
>
> Suddenly the telephone rang loudly and alarmingly … I rushed to the handset.
>
> "Alert everyone: we will begin precisely according to plan" – I heard the voice of the army commander say. Within 10 minutes, everything was at the ready.[22]

Promptly at 0330 (Moscow time), the artillery barrage ruptured the silence, and against the backdrop of the night sky, the first Katiusha rockets soared like flaming arrows toward the positions of Army Detachment Kempf's forces in Pushkarnoe, Solomino, Toplinka, Volkovo and Arkhangel'skoe. Towering columns of flame, smoke and dust erupted in the villages and hamlets,

---

21 Kozinsky, A.F., *Na korochanskom napravlenii: V ogne Kurskoi bitve; iz vospominanii uchastnikov bitvy* [*On the Korocha axis: in the fire of the Battle of Kursk; from the recollections of veterans of the battle*] (Kursk: Kurskoe knizhnoe izdatel'stvo, 1963), p. 276.

22 Safiulin, G.B., *Dorogami pobedy* [*Along the roads of victory*] (Kazan': Tatarskoe knizhnoe izdatel'stvo, 1987), p. 139.

on the fringes of woods, and along the western bank of the river above the assembly areas of the forward units that were poised to launch the attack, and an enormous, slate-gray cloud with dark fringes, periodically lit from within by more and more explosions, rose above them. The water of the Donets began to boil from the multitude of impacting shells and rounds. There was an unimaginable roar all around, and the ground was shaking beneath the Germans' feet.

The 78th and 81st Guards Rifle Division's artillery operated particularly successfully. At that time in front of their positions, an opportune situation that was in general rather rare had come together for us: the Germans had concentrated their assault groups for the dash across the Donets River precisely in those areas that were known to the Soviet side (in fact, the Germans had no real choice in the matter), and the Guardsmen had not only revealed the locations of enemy troop aggregations, but having a real opportunity to inflict substantial damage to them, took full advantage of it. Division commander Morozov on the night of 4-5 July (up until morning) made full use of his reserve Katiusha regiment – the 97th Guards Mortar Regiment. Its three battalions began to hit the assembly areas of the combat groups and engineer elements of the 168th Infantry Division and of the 6th and 19th Panzer Divisions even before midnight, and continued to fire at short intervals practically until noon on 5 July. Here is the information from only the first six hours of its combat work:

> 2330: a divisional salvo (390th Guards Mortar Division) at the bridging equipment and personnel on the western fringe of Pushkarnoe; 101 TS-13 were launched;
> 2400: a divisional salvo (389th Guards Mortar Division) on the balka southwest of Suprunovka; 113 TS-14 were launched;
> 0230: a divisional salvo (389th Guards Mortar Division) at the area of Mikhailovka; 104 T-13 were launched;
> 0400: a divisional salvo at Mikhailovka (390th Guards Mortar Division); 106 T-13 were launched;
> 0430: a divisional salvo (389th Guards Mortar Division) at the crossroads on the southeastern outskirts of Mikhailovka; 45 TS-13 were launched;
> 0600: a salvo from two rocket launchers (390th Guards Mortar Division) at the road junction south of Mikhailovka; 26 TS-13 were launched;
> 0600: a divisional salvo at the Mikhailovka area (388th Guards Mortar Division); 94 TS-13 were launched.[23]

At the same time, the 36 heavy mortars of the 290th Mortar Regiment and the howitzers of the 161st Guards Cannon Artillery Regiment were intensively shelling the same areas. Thus, over this time period 375 rocket shells alone were launched at the Mikhailovka bridgehead, where the crowded infantry of the 168th Infantry Division and the panzergrenadiers of the 6th Panzer Division were positioned. Meanwhile at 0800, a rocket-launching regiment began directly to bombard the Belgorod – Mikhailovka bridge over which the movement of German troops was fully under way, as well as at the Dorogobuzheno and Dal'nie Peski bridgeheads. Naturally in such circumstances, it was impossible for Breith's troops to avoid heavy casualties in the forward battalions. At 0405 (Moscow time), Kempf phoned Speidel and reported: "At 0300 (Moscow time) the enemy opened up a hurricane of artillery fire on our positions in the Belgorod area. The Mikhailovka bridgehead came under particularly heavy fire."[24]

---

23 Information from the Operational Summary No. 142 (TsAMO RF, F. 97 gv. md, op. 18715, d. 5, l. 248, 248obr).
24 NARA US, t. 312, r. 54, fr. 7569605.

5 JULY 1943 – THE BEGINNING OF THE END OF A TRAGICOMEDY

However, the commander of the 81st Guards Rifle Division wasn't able to make full use of his available artillery. For example, the 114th Guards Destroyer Anti-tank Artillery Regiment, which was armed with 76mm ZiS-3 cannons, didn't fire at the crossing sites and aggregations of enemy troops, because its designated firing positions were located outside of effective firing range and the probability of a hit was too remote. Therefore at the last moment, it was decided not to reveal either the regiment's main or alternative firing positions. For the very same reasons, the attached 153rd Guards Artillery Regiment from the 73rd Guards Rifle Division wasn't used in full. In its journal of combat operations it is given that "… since 0300 5.07.1943, the regiment fired at the enemy's revealed assembly areas; 306 76mm shells and 87 122mm shells were expended."[25] Nevertheless, the activated artillery when striking the crossing sites and the Mikhailovka bridgehead itself proved fully sufficient to disrupt Army Detachment Kempf's plan to move the 6th Panzer Division into the Mikhailovka bridgehead. At this moment, the assault groups of the 19th Panzer Division were also caught in a very difficult situation.

The commander of the 78th Guards Rifle Division Major General A.V. Skvortsov[26] concentrated all of his artillery fire on Solomino, where like his neighbors, the first wave of the 7th Panzer Division's *kampfgruppen* were already crossing to the river's eastern bank. He directed the fire of the entire 158th Guards Artillery Regiment, the battalion and regimental artillery of the 78th Guards Rifle Division's 228th Guards and 225th Guards Rifle Regiments, and the attached 3/671st Artillery Regiment from the 213th Rifle Division on the village of Solomino. Over ten minutes his division alone fired 1,700 76mm and 122mm shells. In addition, the artillery of the 25th Guards Rifle Corps was simultaneously working over the same area. The bombardment of Solomino was also very effective, which the Germans themselves recognized.

This preemptive barrage also had a stunning effect on the troops of Korps Raus. As prisoners later recalled, in particular those soldiers of the 106th Infantry Division that were taken prisoner while fighting for possession of Toplinka Station, the Russian artillery strike was a complete surprise for them.

A bit earlier, the XXXXII Army Corps was also bombarded by Soviet artillery, although I didn't find any mention of this in the domestic historiography of the Battle of Kursk. From a briefing written by its chief of staff:

> Between 0200 and 0230 (Berlin time), the enemy conducted a heavy mortar attack on the corps' northern flank. Our *kampfgruppe,* which had been assigned to conduct a reconnaissance-in-force in the Botkino area, was forced to fall back because of the enemy's strong

---

25 TsAMO RF, F. 153 gv. ap, op. 1, d. 4, l. 38.
26 Skvortsov, Aleksandr Vasil'evich (Major General from 07.12.1942) was born on 17 August 1901 in Yaroslavl' Oblast's village of Sanino. Until 1917, he worked in agriculture and animal husbandry. He began service in the Russian Civil War in 1919. In 1921 he completed the Armavir infantry courses and became a rifle platoon leader, before being promoted to company commander. Subsequently he was in charge of administrative duties and was elected as an at-large Party secretary. Between 1931 and 1940, Skvortsov engaged in military-political work in the Far East as a labor battalion's commissar, instructor of a political department, and deputy political commander of the Khabarovsk garrison. After completing the "Shot" courses, on 31.07.1940 he was appointed as the acting commander of the 70th Rifle Regiment of the 2nd Separate Red Banner Far Eastern Army's 3rd Rifle Division, and on 24.01.1942 became the deputy commander of this division. On 13.07.1942, he received appointment as the commander of the 204th Rifle Division, first of the Southeastern, then of the Don Front. After the Battle of Stalingrad Skvortsov's rifle division was converted into a Guards formation, while the division commander was awarded the Order of the Red Banner. Skvortsov had a chronic illness. In January and February 1943 he was receiving treatment in Moscow. He passed away on 19 December 1948 in Kostroma.

resistance. Another one of our *kampfgruppen,* which had been assigned to conduct a reconnaissance-in-force north of Nezhegol Station failed to send a report.[27]

The counter artillery preparation continued until 0410 (Moscow time), which meant it was went on parallel with the opening barrage on the Guardsmen's positions conducted by Army Detachment Kempf's artillery and the initial storming of the Northern Donets River's eastern bank by the assault groups. As soon as the enemy shifted his fire into the depth of the 7th Guards Army's defenses, staff officers of its artillery contacted the artillery units and rifle divisions in order to check on the situation, and they found out that not a single gun had been knocked out by the opening German barrage. At the same time, the Germans had thoroughly worked over an entire number of dummy and reserve firing positions. Judging from archival records, the Soviet divisional artillery began to take its first losses in guns only after 0700, when the Germans had finally located the precise coordinates of separate firing positions. For example, the 153rd Guards Artillery Regiment (which was positioned south of the orchard near Blizhniaia Igumenka) had only two cannons and one howitzer knocked out over the course of the entire day by enemy artillery fire, although two 76mm Model 1939 guns had already been damaged that morning at 0700 and 1000.[28]

Precise data on the losses of the divisions of Kempf's army detachment in the course of the counter artillery preparation, as incidentally those of Hoth's panzer army as well, are unknown, though even absent them it is clear that it was more effective in the sector of the 7th Guards Army than that of the neighboring 6th Guards Army. There were two reasons for this. First, the bulk of Army Detachment Kempf's troops were strictly tied down to specific sectors, where it had been planned to construct bridges, and the command of the 7th Guards Army's artillery had been able to identify these places accurately. Second, the time to begin the preemptive barrage was perfectly chosen; the Soviet artillery fire caught the German assault groups at the very moment they were crossing the river. Army Detachment Kempf's combat journal recorded, "0325 (Moscow time): the Army Detachment, according to plan, has initiated the crossing of the Donets with the forces of Korps Raus and the III Panzer Corps."[29]

Approximately at this same time, Soviet air force units began executing their strikes, including against field bases in the Belgorod area; for example, on the Mikoianovka airfield, where the forward command post of the VIII Fliegerkorps was located. A supplement to Army Detachment Kempf's morning report noted, "The enemy air activity prior to 0330 (Moscow time) was sporadic; after this time, it sharply increased. The main attacks struck the sector of the XXXXII Army Corps, as well as the Khar'kov area. Several waves of bombers purposefully bombed the airbases in the Khar'kov area."[30] However, this plan had no success; its failure was recognized to one or another degree by many commanders and military chiefs that took part in the Battle of Kursk. The essence of their assessments, which were subsequently given in accounts and memoirs, coincides with the opinion of a senior officer of the General Staff with the headquarters of the Voronezh Front Colonel M.N. Kostin: "The airstrike by our air forces against the enemy's bases didn't bring the desired result, since by the time they were delivered, the enemy's aircraft were already in the air, so at their airfields the enemy had only written-off aircraft and a few reserve replacement aircraft."[31]

At the same time, the losses suffered by the units of Voronezh Front's 2nd Air Army and Southwestern Front's 17th Air Army in the course of the attacks upon the Khar'kov airbase

---

27 NARA US, t. 312, r. 54, fr. 7569605.
28 TsAMO RF, F. 153 gv. ap, op. 1, d. 4, l. 38obr.
29 NARA US, t. 312, r. 54, f. 7569605.
30 NARA US, t. 312, r. 54, f. 7569606.
31 *Russkii arkhiv. Velikaia Otechestvennaia voina* [*Russian archive. Great Patriotic War*] Vol. 15 (Moscow: Terra, 1997), p. 381.

complex and airfields of the German *Luftflotte* IV were substantial,[32] which noticeably reduced their activity later on the morning of 5 July, when their assistance to the ground forces, including those of the 7th Guards Army, would have been extremely important. Nevertheless, as we will see ahead, Kempf's troops thought highly of the Soviet air activity in the course of this day.

Like all of his subordinate commanders, M.S. Shumilov spent the night of 4-5 July at his command post. Approximately 20 minutes after the opening enemy barrage subsided, reports from the corps began to arrive. Major General G.B. Safaulin was the first to contact him over the Baudot device and he reported that the enemy had gone on the offensive along his corps' entire front; the 81st Guards Rifle Division was the first to become engaged, when German infantry in strength of more than two battalions with the support of a small quantity of tanks attacked its positions out of the Mikhailovka bridgehead in the direction of Staryi Gorod. Both of Morozov's forward regiments were tied up in combat. In front of Skvortsov's sector, the enemy had generated a smoke screen and was attempting to build bridges. Some of the enemy infantry was already fighting on our bank, and our cannon and mortar regiments had opened fire at the vicinities of the crossing sites. In conclusion the commander of the 25th Guards Rifle Corps reported that the situation was still murky, but according to the words of the 81st Guards Rifle Division commander Morozov, it was likely that one bridge in the Mikhailovka area had been completely destroyed, but in spite of this the Germans were persistently trying to make a forced crossing of the river using inflatable rafts and by fording.

At some time later, information arrived from the 24th Guards Rifle Corps. Major General N.A. Vasil'ev's report essentially replicated G.B. Safaulin's report. The Germans under the cover of artillery fire on the corps' right flank (in the sector of the 72nd Guards Rifle Division) had crossed some infantry and combat engineers to the eastern bank using light bridges and bungee bridges. Despite the fire that was opened and the minefields, they had gained a foothold on the bank's edge and were trying to advance. The corps commander emphasized that the buildup of enemy infantry was proceeding very quickly at Karnaukhovka. He suggested that one underwater bridge hadn't been located and now the Germans were using it to cross the river.

The 7th Guards Army commander must have sighed with relief; at last, the burden of the unknown that he had carried over the preceding months had fallen away – the enemy had launched a major offensive. He glanced at the map, upon which the operational situation had been drawn just recently, and realized that so far nothing out of the ordinary was happening. The offensive's opening hour had shown that the Germans were continuing to adhere to a time-worn tactic: a strong artillery barrage, smokescreens, the intensive work of engineer units and a surge across a river. Then, most likely, a second stage would follow: the breakthrough and envelopment of the defending divisions by powerful tank groups. However, right now a very important moment for the Soviet side had arrived at dawn – the battle at the bridges. It was precisely at this moment when the enemy's attacking units were most vulnerable and the greatest damage could be inflicted to them.

Having received the initial reports about the operational situation along the entire front, M.S. Shumilov contacted the Front commander-in-chief and reported the situation. It is known that a conversation ensued between 0410 and 0500, but so far I've been unable to find the transcript of it. I've only been able to locate the transcript of discussions between the Front's deputy chief of staff Major General S.I. Teteshkin and the commander of the 2nd Guards "Tatsinskaia" Tank Corps Colonel A.S. Burdeinyi, which lays out in brief fashion the information that the Voronezh Front's leadership had at approximately 0630 (Moscow time) and the first steps taken by its Military Council. The discussions began at 0700 (Moscow time):

---

32 However, some of the IL-2s and their crews that failed to return from their combat missions on 5 July 1943 later showed up on other airbases or made forced landings.

Teteshkin: At Comrade Nikolaev's order I am informing you regarding the situation in Chistiakov's sector:

1. The enemy in strength of up to two divisions with 80 tanks by 2400 4.7, having broken through the combat outposts, reached the forward edge of defense on the front: Novaia Gorianka, Berezovka, Butovo, /excl/ Dragunskoe. In certain sectors the enemy made penetrations, but by morning the situation had been reestablished.

    At 0430 the enemy in strength of up to three battalions attacked in the sector of Hill 228.6 (2 kilometers northwest of Iakhontov). The fighting reached the point of hand-to-hand combat. The enemy has been thrown back to his jumping-off position. On Chistiakov's entire front, up to 300 aircraft have been incessantly working over the forward edge of defense.

    In Shumilov's sector, the enemy at 0600 in strength of up to three infantry battalions attacked out of Mikhailovka in the direction of Staryi Gorod. The offensive has been stopped by fire and the enemy has become pinned down before reaching our forward edge. Up to four infantry battalions have crossed to the eastern bank in the Solomino area, up to two infantry battalions in the Karnaukhovka area, up to three infantry battalions in the Priiutovka area, and up to a regiment in the Bezliudovka area. Across Shumilov's entire sector of defense, the enemy has become pinned down by our fire in the valley of the Northern Donets River.

It has been ordered:

Using every available weapon and the Front's aviation, destroy the enemy units that have crossed and throw the remnants back to the western bank.

Nikolaev has ordered you:

1. Bring your units to combat readiness. [Your] headquarters is to contact Chistiakov's and Shumilov's headquarters, where you are to receive accurate information about the situation. Bring your communications means to combat readiness. All commanders must fully take up positions in their indicated sectors.
2. Organize the reconnoitering of routes for the actions of your enterprise [code word for corps] in Chistiakov's sector, as well as in Shumilov's sector.
3. Inform the commander of the Front's anti-tank reserve in Korocha about the situation, and have in mind possible actions together with him.
4. Immediately report the steps you have taken. I am giving you of additional information: The enemy's air force is also actively working over Shumilov's combat positions. That is all.

Do you have any questions?

Burdeinyi: Everything is clear. My units are at full combat readiness. I have contact with Shumilov, but I'm now restoring it with Chistiakov. I have my reconnaissance in the sector between Shumilov and Chistiakov. I will follow the situation. That is all.

Teteshkin: It is necessary to have your commanders at Shumilov's and Chistiakov's headquarters assess the situation. That is all. Over.[33]

---

33 TsAMO RF, F. 203, op. 2843, d. 461, l. 29.

5 JULY 1943 – THE BEGINNING OF THE END OF A TRAGICOMEDY

I will add that in his morning report to the *Stavka*, N.F. Vatutin reported that according to the outcomes of his conversations with the commanders of the 6th and 7th Guards Armies, he had sent one regiment of Katiusha rocket launchers to each of them from out of his reserve. The 309th Guards Mortar Regiment became operationally subordinate to M.S. Shumilov.

Before midnight on 4 July, W. Kempf and his operational group had arrived at an observation post south of Belgorod. From this observation post, he was to observe and direct the troops, which faced launching the final German strategic offensive on the Eastern Front.

The III Panzer Corps' divisions planned to force a crossing of the Donets River by two means: the leading assault groups were to cross in rubber boats and over small bridges together with the combat engineers, and pushing onward, were to tie up the Guards divisions' combat outposts directly in combat and divert their fire onto themselves. Meanwhile the main forces of infantry, artillery and panzers would cross the river over specially constructed Type-K metal bridges that had been built. For this purpose, Breith's panzer corps had two motorized bridge-building battalions, the 531 and 925, and five motorized engineer battalions to sweep the ground of mines and explosive obstacles: the Engineer Battalions 70, 127 (minus one company), 601, 651 and 674.

However, these options weren't suitable for crossing the 57-tonne Tiger tanks, and therefore a ford was found for the attached Tiger companies of the 7th Panzer Division in the Solomino area, while the Tiger companies in the 6th and 19th Panzer Divisions were to cross over a 60-tonne bridge that would be constructed out of three 24-tonne bridges. The use of pontoon bridges was planned only in the sector of Korps Raus, but the matter never reached this point. Besides metal-construction and bungee bridges, the construction of wooden (pile trestle) bridges of varying load-bearing capacities was anticipated in order to cross wagons, vehicles, prime movers towing artillery pieces, and ammunition. Smokescreens were to be generated in order to conceal the bridges, but not everywhere (as a rule only in the areas of large bridges), so as not to hinder the fire of artillery, panzers and anti-aircraft weapons.

Before turning to the description of the beginning of the first stage of Army Detachment Kempf's combat actions with the creation of bridgeheads across the Northern Donets River, I want to dwell briefly on one important detail, the explanation of which can help genuinely assess the difficult problem that the Army Detachment's command was facing before the operation. In a number of domestic publications on the Battle of Kursk, one comes across the assertion that supposedly Kempf's forces had not the one bridgehead at Mikhailovka at the start of the forced crossing of the Northern Donets River, but several: opposite Pushkarnoe (called "at Pushkarnoe"), in the area of Toplinka, and in some sources, also at Dal'nie Peski. An analysis of the 7th Guards Army's system of defense that I conducted with the use of the frontline battalions' documents allows me to assert with confidence that this information is far from true. I will cite two archival sources that not only refute the presence of bridges on the river in those places (except the two in the area of the Mikhailovka bridgehead), but also entire bridgeheads. The first document is entitled "Legenda k karte 'Kharakteristika mostov na r. Northern Donets [sic] v polose oborony 72 gv. sd po sostoianiiu 3 iulia 1943'" [Legend to the map entitled "Characteristics of the bridges on the Northern Donets River in the 72nd Guards Rifle Division's sector of defense as of 3 July 1943"], which was written by an engineer of this division, Major Bystrov:

Bridge No. 1: in the area of Toplinka. The bridge has been completely demolished. The banks are sloping, the approach is concealed.
Bridge No. 2: in the area of the Puliaevka road, completely demolished; two pilings have been completely splintered. The approaches are concealed, the banks steep.
Bridge No. 3: in the Maslova Pristan' area. The bridge has been completely destroyed; 3 pilings and wooden footings remain; approaches are exposed, and the road is good.

Bridge No. 4: in the Maslova Pristan' area. The bridge has been blown up by our side. From the enemy's direction, 13 pilings with joist supports remain.

Bridge No. 5: in the village of Priiutkova. The bridge has been demolished, the approaches are swampy.

Bridge No. 6: in the village of Bezliudovka. The bridge has been demolished, the banks are eroded.[34]

After the launching of the offensive, the adversary moved infantry across the river too quickly in the Toplinka area. This raised suspicions among the 24th Guards Rifle Corps' command that the Germans had built an underwater bridge, that is to say, a crossing submerged at a shallow depth. However, I've been unable to find any reliable confirmations of this conjecture.

Now let's turn to the combat report from the drill instructor of the 238th Guards Rifle Regiment, Major Znamensky, which was sent on 11 July 1943 at the behest of division commander I.K. Morozov:[35]

> In fulfillment of your Order No. 063 from 10.06.1943, a scout party ... conducted a reconnaissance with the aim of ascertaining whether or not the enemy has a crossing site on the Northern Donets River in the Mikhailovka area (the 238th Guards Rifle Regiment's sector of defense).
>
> As a result of personal observation and the information from the commander of the 7th Rifle Company Senior Lieutenant Trusov, a sniper of the 7th Rifle Company, and platoon commander Junior Lieutenant Shpeinis it has been established that there is a crossing site in the Mikhailovka area, which confirms the information from artillerymen and reconnaissance aircraft about it. Personal observation from a sniper's position of the 7th Rifle Company, 3rd Battalion of the 238th Guards Rifle Regiment has revealed:

---

34 TsAMO RF, F. 72 gv. sd, op. 1, d. 60, l. 5.
35 Morozov, Ivan Konstantinovich (Major General 01.03.1943) was born on 6 January 1905 in Rostov Oblast's Kagalnitsky Station. In 1914 he graduated from a parochial school. Morozov joined the Red Army in 1918 and was a participant in the Russian Civil War. He was twice wounded. In 1924 he completed the courses for Red commanders, and in 1930, the North Caucasus Cavalry School for highland nationalities. He served in the cavalry, with a short break, until the end of the 1930s; his final post in the cavalry was commander of the 79th Cavalry Regiment of the Separate Red Banner Far Eastern Army's 31st Cavalry Division. In March 1941, he was appointed commander of the 29th Separate Reconnaissance Battalion of the Far Eastern Front's 30th Mechanized Corps. In January 1942, Morozov was transferred to the post of deputy commander of the 66th Rifle Division of the Far Eastern Front's 35th Army, but three months later on 01.03.1942, he assumed command of the same army's 422nd Rifle Division. At this moment, he had served four years in the post of regiment chief of staff (of both a cavalry regiment and rifle regiment) and three years in the post of regiment commander. At the time of this promotion, the commander of the 35th Army General Zaitsev described Morozov in the following manner: "Overall and political development are both satisfactory. He works above his level of command. He is a capable, energetic and decisive commander. He is insufficiently prepared tactically for the post he occupies. He works insufficiently in this direction. He stubbornly insists on the units' combat training and combat readiness. Shortcoming: He sometimes allows himself to become quick-tempered and short with subordinates, he is swift to anger and brusque in his relations with subordinates. He corresponds to his post, but needs to increase his operational and tactical training." On 26.07.1942, the division arrived at the Stalingrad front, and on 08.08.1942 it was transferred to Major General M.S. Shumilov's 57th Army (Southeastern Front), with which it participated in the fighting on the Volga. His superiors regarded him as a "firm and demanding commander". For his successful leadership of the division, in March 1943 Colonel I.K. Morozov was twice awarded the Order of the Red Banner. He was twice wounded, once severely. On 15.02.1955 he was discharged from the Soviet Army due to illness. He lived in Stalingrad and Voronezh and wrote several books of recollections. Morozov passed away on 11 July 1979.

The crossing consists of two bridges across the Northern Donets River's previous and new channel on piling supports of a joist system. The bridge rises 0.5 meters above the water and has lateral planking. The bridges have a width of 4 meters and a length of up to 8 meters, while the bridge across the channel flowing at Pushkarnoe has smaller dimensions. Both bridges across the former and new channel are linked by corduroy planking across a swamp; the bridge extends into Mikhailovka on one side, at the coordinate points (…) and on the other side ends at a white building (the building with half the roof torn off), where it branches and turns into roads: the first leading to the church in Suprunovka and the second – toward Pushkarnoe. The actual load-bearing capacity of the bridge is 6-7 metric tons, which allows the passage of vehicles at night time and presumably allows the crossing of light tanks.

The bridge is intact. During the day of 10 June 1943, work was being conducted to make partial adjustments and strengthen the bridge, but after the work of snipers of the 7th Rifle Company, who picked off 2 Germans, the work was halted.

The second crossing site in the northern portion of Mikhailovka isn't visible from the regiment's area of defense. Only the embankment of the approach road to it is visible. The serviceability of the bridge is confirmed by the presence of vehicle movement toward it. Other than these two bridges, there are no other across the Northern Donets in the area of the 238th Guards Rifle Regiment. The right flank of the 7th Rifle Company, from the firing position of a sniper, which affords a splendid view of the entire bridge, offers the best vantage point for correcting artillery fire to destroy the first bridge.[36]

The bridge that was largely out of sight linked the eastern portion of Belgorod directly with Mikhailovka, and remained intact right up to the start of the offensive. A *kampfgruppe* of the 6th Panzer Division used it on the night of 4-5 July to cross into the bridgehead, after which it collapsed under the weight of assault guns. The other bridge that was located in front of the 238th Guards Rifle Regiment (and which could be clearly seen from the sniper's position), however, was targeted for destruction by the command of the 81st Guards Rifle Division. It was decided to employ artillery for this purpose, and not only a plan for its destruction was worked out, but also a plan for keeping it under systematic artillery fire with the aim of preventing the Germans from rebuilding it. When the bridge was destroyed isn't clear: whether it was planned for some date in June or designated for the morning of 5 July is unknown. There is a basis to assume that artillery fire destroyed it in the first minutes of the offensive, when German infantry was crossing it.

However, other than bridges, there were several fords on the Northern Donets, places where not only soldiers, but also armored vehicles could cross the river across the bottom without any special modifications. German engineers prior to the operation scrupulously studied the river channel and revealed the precise locations of these fords. For example, in the sector of the 25th Guards Rifle Corps, where the III Panzer Corps would be attacking, there were four such fords: on the northern outskirts of Dal'nie Peski, on the northern outskirts of Solomino, 250 meters south of the bridge in Solomino, and on the southern outskirts of Nizhnyi Ol'shanets.[37] It was precisely thanks to this knowledge that Kempf's troops in the first hours of the offensive would efficiently be able to move a significant portion of the heavy weapons and armor to the eastern bank in order to expand rapidly the bridgeheads seized by the assault groups. However, if to judge from the accounts written after the battle, the Soviet command believed that the main merit in this was the work of the German sapper elements, who worked under artillery fire with unbelievable speed, erecting or newly restoring dozens of bridges in the matter of hours.

---

36 TsAMO RF, F. 7 gv. A, op. 5312, d. 220, l. 78.
37 TsAMO RF, F. 25 gv. sk, op. 1, d. 27, l. 3.

The first phase of the offensive of both of Kempf's subordinate corps on 5 July (crossing the Northern Donets River and gaining a foothold on the eastern bank) began even before the opening of artillery fire by both sides. Certain divisions in Breith's panzer corps, in particular the 19th Panzer Division, began to move assault groups across the river in inflatable boats and on rafts at approximately 0230 (Moscow time). At this time, in the pre-dawn darkness on the Northern Donets River, six infantry and panzer divisions were assembled in expectation of a thrust into the sector between Mikhailovka and the mouth of the Nezhegol River, which extended for approximately 32 kilometers, and it was these German divisions that faced attacking the positions of six reinforced Guards rifle regiments.

The first to move out against the line of the 81st Guards Rifle Division at 0300 were two *kampfgruppen* of the 6th and 19th Panzer Divisions. The right-hand group under the command of Major von Bieberstein (a company of Engineer Battalion 57, II/Grenadier Regiment 417 and I/Grenadier Regiment 114) on the night of 4-5 July crossed the bridge into the bridgehead and from Mikhailovka attacked the line of Major G.T. Skiruta's[38] 235th Guards Rifle Regiment in the direction of Staryi Gorod. An intelligence summary from the 81st Guards Rifle Division's Long Range Artillery Group at 0800 on 5 July 1943 observes, "At 0600 up to 500 intoxicated enemy soldiers attempted to attack the forward positions out of the northwestern outskirts of Mikhailovka; the attack was driven back with heavy losses for the enemy."[39] There then followed a fresh attack at the boundary between the 1st and 3rd Rifle Battalions with the support of armor. The enemy was attempting to split the regiment into two pieces. The boundary marked the most suitable place (in essence, the only place) for a breakthrough by tanks in the direction of Staryi Gorod; the only problem was that it was necessary to breach the regiment's well-fortified forward edge. Under the cover of artillery fire and the fire of the six-barreled Nebelwerfers, the grenadiers and combat engineers moved up toward the forward edge, and only after the engineers with great difficulty managed to clear several passages through the minefields did the infantry resume the advance. However, before even advancing 100 meters, they were pinned to the ground in front of a roll of concertina wire by dense machine-gun fire. It was at this moment that the 81st Guards Rifle Division's heavy artillery again spoke up. The point is that as division commander Morozov recalled, from the intelligence reports that he received on the evening of 4 July and night of 4-5 July, he was aware that the trenches in the Mikhailovka bridgehead were crowded with German infantry. Therefore 30 minutes after the completion of the German artillery preparation, when von Bieberstein's *kampfgruppe* was tied up in combat in front of the 235th Guards Rifle Division's first trench line, he issued an order for the howitzers and heavy mortars to open up with shifting blocking fire at the enemy trenches in Mikhailovka and at the area of the bridges, in order first to destroy the second wave of attackers in the bridgehead and second to destroy the reserves on the western bank that were approaching the bridges. In combination with the rifle and machine-gun fire of the 3rd Battalion of Skiruta's regiment, this barrage had a substantial effect – the attack by the 6th Panzer Division's first *kampfgruppe* was broken up.

---

38   Skiruta, Grigorii Trofimovich, Lieutenant Colonel (1943). He was born on 4 December 1912 in Kiev Oblast's village of Velikopolovetskoe. Skiruta was a Ukrainian. After completing primary school, he worked as a timekeeper in one of the State farms of Chernigov Oblast. He joined the Red Army in 1932. In 1936 he completed the courses for junior commanders and became a member of the acting army on 26.07.1942. He was a veteran of the Battle of Stalingrad. On 26.10.1943 for his skillful leadership of the regiment and his personal courage demonstrated when forcing a crossing of the Dnepr River, he was awarded the title Hero of the Soviet Union. In October 1944 he was sent to study in the Frunze Military Academy, and after graduating from it he took command of a regiment. He continued to serve in the army after the war, and taught at the "Shot" higher tactical courses. Skiruta went into the reserve in 1961. He passed away on 20 July 1999 in the town of Solnechnogorsk (Moscow Oblast).
39   TsAMO RF, F. 10974, op. 1, d. 3, l. 95.

The commander of the 64th Army (subsequently the 7th Guards Army) Lieutenant General M.S. Shumilov in Stalingrad, before departing to the Belgorod area; end of February 1943. (RGAFKD)

The spring of 1943 came early: This is how the roads in the region of the Kursk bulge looked. (RGAKFD)

The city of Belgorod after the March 1943 fighting came to an end. (Captured files of the RGAKFD)

The commander of the 7th Guards Army Lieutenant General M.S. Shumilov washes up in the village of Protopopovka, Kursk Oblast, on a sunny April 1943 morning. (A photo from an issue of the *Krasnaia znamia* newspaper in the files of the "Stalingradskaia bitva ("Battle of Stalingrad") State Historical Park Museum)

In moments of calm, even army commanders had no objection to a little mischief. Lieutenant General M.S. Shumilov (on the right) has a little fun at the expense of a major on his 7th Guards Army headquarters staff, who is showing his "booty" to correspondents of the *Krasnaia znamia* army newspaper; village of Protopopovka, Kursk Oblast, April 1943. (A photo from an issue of the *Krasnaia znamia* newspaper in the files of the "Stalingradskaia bitva" State Historical-Memorial Park Museum)

The Commander-in-Chief of the Voronezh Front General of the Army N.F. Vatutin (in the center) receiving a report from one of his subordinate commanders during one of his trips to the front; spring of 1943. (RGAKFD)

A major, a battalion commander in one of the 81st Guards Rifle Division's regiments, addresses his subordinate commanders; Voronezh Front, 7th Guards Army, May 1943. (Files of the "Stalingradskaia bitva" State Historical-Memorial Park Museum)

Commanders of the 27th Guards Tank Brigade study a mock-up of the terrain in its sector, June 1943. (RGAKFD)

T-34 radio operators of the 7th Guards Army's 27th Guards Tank Brigade in training: Sergeant Major Babushkin maintains contact with a tank battalion commander, May 1943. (Shebekino Historical-Art Museum)

The training of driver-mechanics in the 201st Separate Tank Brigade to overcome artificial obstacles. The tanks are Lend-Lease British Matilda tanks.

A training brochure issued on the eve of the Battle of Kursk to anti-tank gun, tank and artillery crews entitled "The most vulnerable and damage-prone places on the German Pz-VI tank and the means to counter them". The page on the right states, "Fire at the fuel tanks and forward wheels".

Tank company commander Senior Lieutenant F. Martekhov (first from the right) of the 7th Guards Army's 27th Guards Tank Brigade, who for his exploits in the Belgorod area on 12 July 1943 was deemed worthy of the title "Hero of the Soviet Union", in conversation with a group of the brigade's officers and soldiers at his dugout during a moment of rest; village of Voznesenovka, May 1943.

The commander of the 7th Guards Army Lieutenant General M.S. Shumilov (third from the right) and the chief of the Army's motorized transport pool Lieutenant Colonel Ia.T. Savchenko (fourth from the right) talk with a group of commanders of the motorized transport service. In the background on the left, a sector of barbed wire in a defensive belt is visible; June 1943. (Archive of the "Kurskaia bitva. Belgorodskoe napravlenie" ("Battle of Kursk. Belgorod axis") Museum-Diorama.

Lesen und weitergeben!

GRENADIERE der 168. ID!

Man hat Euch überzeugt, daß die Kriegsgefangenen in russischer Gefangenschaft hungern. In Wirklichkeit sieht es anders aus!

TÄGLICHE RATION DER KRIEGSGEFANGENEN:

700 Gramm Brot   500 Gramm Kartoffeln
250 Gramm Gemüse   40 Gramm Fett
150 Gramm Fleisch   30 Gramm Zucker
100 Gramm verschiedener Hülsenfrüchte, zweimal warmes Essen, morgens und abends Tee; 20 Gramm Tabak, sowie monatlich 150 Gramm Seife.

A Soviet leaflet calling upon grenadiers of the 168th Infantry Division to surrender, found near Belgorod in 2007. (Author's personal archive)

Soldiers of one of the first-echelon divisions of the 7th Guards Army head out for their shift to man a combat outpost in the basin of the Northern Donets River; June 1943. (RGAKFD)

The commander of Army Detachment Kempf General W. Kempf. (Captured photo. Author's personal archive)

The commander of the III Panzer Corps General H. Breith; February 1943. (Captured photo. Author's personal archive)

General-Instructor of Panzer Troops Colonel General H. Guderian (in the first row, second from the left) during a meeting in II SS Panzer Corps' SS Panzergrenadier Division *Leibstandarte Adolf Hitler* of Hoth's Fourth Panzer Army. Standing next to Guderian on his left is the commander of the SS Panzergrenadier Division *Das Reich* Lieutenant General G. Keppler. It was the II SS Panzer Corps that was supposed to act in close cooperation with Army Detachment Kempf. Khar'kov, April 1943. (Bundesarchiv, Bild 101III-Wiesebach-152-11A, photo: Wiesebach)

H. Guderian (second from the right) examines the new Pz.Kpf. VI Tiger tanks equipping SS Panzergrenadier Division *Leibstandart Adolf Hitler*'s heavy panzer company. This particular tank is a *Panzerbefehlswagen* command tank carrying the tactical number 100). SS Captain Heinrich Kling, the commander of the heavy panzer company (on the right) is giving an explanation. Khar'kov, April 1943. (Bundesarchiv, Bild 101III-Wiesebach-152-14A, photo: Wiesebach)

General of Panzer Troops E. Raus, the commander of Korps Raus, during Operation Citadel. Belgorod area, July 1943. (Bundesarchiv, Bild 146-1984-019-28, photo: Wolff/Altvater)

Senior Lieutenant V.M. Moiseev, the commander of one of 7th Guards Army's artillery batteries, conducts observation with the use of a BSD scissors telescope on the Belgorod axis; Voronezh Front, July 1943. (RGAKFD)

An artillery battalion of the 7th Guards Army's 265th Cannon Artillery Regiment shells the enemy's bridges across the Northern Donets River; July 1943. (Author's personal archive)

A crew of a German 150mm howitzer fires at positions of the Guardsmen; Belgorod area, July 1943. (Captured photo, RGAKFD)

The commander of the 25th Guards Rifle Corps Lieutenant General G.B. Safiulin; a 1944 photograph. (TsAMO RF)

The commander of the 78th Guards Rifle Division Major General A.V. Skvortsov. (TsAMO RF)

Assistant platoon commander Senior Sergeant I. Artem'ev of a submachine gun company of the 7th Guards Army's 78th Guards Rifle Division in firing positions with his company in the area of the village of Solomino; July 1943. (RGAKFD)

The commander of the 81st Guards Rifle Division Major General I.K. Morozov; a 1945 photograph. (TsAMO RF)

The commander of the 235th Guards Rifle Regiment G.T. Skiruta; a 1945 photograph. (TsAMO RF)

Sergeant N.N. Ivanov's anti-tank rifle squad in positions on the Northern Donets River; July 1943. (RGAKFD)

The commander of the 72nd Guards Rifle Division Major General A.I. Losev at a forward observation post; July 1943. (RGAKFD)

The explosion of a German tank in a minefield. In the foreground is a case for bottles containing an incendiary mixture that was hurled aside by the explosion; July 1943. (TsAMO RF)

A crew of a 37mm M1943 Flak gun, which has been mounted on a truck, fires at Soviet ground assault aircraft in the vicinity of bridges across the Northern Donets River in the Belgorod area. July 1943. (Bundesarchiv, Bild 101I-022-2926-38, photo: Wolff/Altvater)

A Kazakh member of the Russian Liberation Army serving in a company of III Panzer Corps, which was used in the course of Operation Citadel in order to destroy Soviet command posts and communications, clarifies a combat task with a German Sergeant. July 1943. (Bundesarchiv, Bild 101I-022-2916-13A, photo: Wolff/Altvater)

Tankers of one of the companies of III Panzer Corps' Heavy Panzer Battalion 503 examines the location of a hull hit in their Tiger tank from an armor-piercing shell fired by a Soviet gun. July 1943. (Bundesarchiv, Bild 101I-022-2935-25A, photo: Wolff/Altvater)

The commander of the 3rd Battalion of the 73rd Guards Rifle Division's 214th Guards Rifle Regiment; a photograph that was touched up with an airbrush after the war. (RGAKFD)

A Maksim heavy machine-gun crew of a tank brigade's motorized rifle battalion provides supporting fire for a company that is defending a village somewhere in the sector of the 7th Guards Army; July 1943. (RGAKFD)

Hünersdorff anticipated such a development. To counter it, he gave the StuG Battalion 228 a special mission; it was to cross the river into the bridgehead over the already prepared bridge in the wake of the assault groups and immediately after the start of the attack it was to support it with fire, knocking out fortified firing points. Then after breaching the Russians' defenses and the construction of a bridge for the heavy panzers, Captain Heitman's company of Tiger tanks from the Separate Heavy Panzer Battalion 503 was to assemble in Mikhailovka. As a result, an armored fist was to be formed out of the assault gun battalion and the company of Tigers in order to break through into the depth of the right flank of Morozov's division in the direction of Staryi Gorod.

However, this plan practically collapsed immediately because of problems that arose as the offensive got underway. The first attack out of the Mikhailovka bridgehead sputtered to a stop, and in the course of the second the German infantry fought their way forward for several hundred meters toward Staryi Gorod, before being pinned down by a storm of fire from the defending Guardsmen and a strong system of minefields. It became clear that without the support of panzers, it was going to be extremely difficult to achieve even modest results. There was armor in the bridgehead, but not much. When the first group of assault guns of StuG Battalion 228 was rolling across the bridge, it couldn't withstand their weight and collapsed, so the crossing came to a standstill. The command of the 6th Panzer Division wasn't ready for such a turn of events. For a certain amount of time, the situation was hanging by a thread. At 0500 the III Panzer Corps headquarters sent an update to Army Detachment Kempf's Operations Department:

> The attack out of the bridgehead at Mikhailovka to the southeast was stopped by stubborn enemy resistance. Already Mikhailovka's prepared bridge cannot be used because of the incessant shelling of enemy artillery. The 6th Panzer Division with its right-hand *kampfgruppe* launched an attack from the bridgehead at Mikhailovka to the north and stormed into Staryi Gorod. West of the Donets, a *kampfgruppe* [of the 168th Infantry Division – author] fought its way into the woods 2 kilometers northwest of Chernaia Poliana. General impression of the enemy: He is defending exceptionally stubbornly. The enemy's main artillery grouping is assembled in Blizhniaia Igumenka.[40]

The assault group of the 6th Panzer Division was trying to breach one of the most strongly fortified sectors of the 235th Guards Rifle Regiment – the positions of the 1st Rifle Battalion's 1st Rifle Company and of the 3rd Rifle Battalion's 9th Rifle Company, which were heavily armed and saturated with defensive positions, including concealed machine-gun nests. Therefore each meter gained by the Germans came with great difficulty and substantial losses. At 0610 (Moscow time) Kempf again contacted Speidel, and having heard his report, provided fresh and unsettling news: "The enemy isn't weakening the artillery barrage on the Belgorod staging area; poor visibility is complicating the command and control of our artillery."[41] These words plainly testify to the fact that despite all the efforts, the Army Detachment's artillery command failed to create the sufficient conditions necessary for its crews to conduct fire. Because of this, at a most important moment its effectiveness proved low.

In this situation the commander of Panzergrenadier Regiment 114 Major von Bieberstein attempted to rely on the two battalions of the 168th Infantry Division's Artillery Regiment 248 and III Battalion of Nebelwerfers from Werfer [Engineer Mortar] Regiment 54. From the 6th Panzer Division headquarters' morning report to the III Panzer Corps:

---

40 NARA US, t. 312, r. 54, f. 7569605.
41 Ibid.

During the night, strong, disruptive artillery fire on the front line and on the area of the bridges, especially north of Bolkhovets (1.5 kilometers north of Belgorod). Pursuant to the division's orders, von Bieberstein's *kampfgruppe* (II/417) went on the offensive at 0325 across the railroad and with its forward units advanced toward Staryi Gorod, overcoming wire obstacles together with Artmann's *kampfgruppe*. Bieberstein's *kampfgruppe* was forced to halt its attack, because the 24-tonne bridge collapsed under the weight of the assault guns and thereby the assault guns had no way to support II/417 with their fire.

It is anticipated that the 19th Panzer Division will resume the offensive after the Tigers and the 1st Battery of assault guns cross the 60-tonne bridge, and once the 24-tonne bridge has been repaired.[42]

The attack launched by Barkman's *kampfgruppe* (I/Grenadier Regiment 417, the reconnaissance battalion of the 168th Infantry Division, and a battery of StuG Battalion 228) was going no better; it moved out of Belgorod to the north with the assignment to break through the defenses at the boundary between the 6th and 7th Guards Armies (the left flank of the 375th Rifle Division, northwest of Chernaia Poliana) and make contact with the right flank of the II SS Panzer Corps (SS Panzer Grenadier Division *Totenkopf*). In the vicinity of the woods (the shape of which suggested a circle) west of Chernaia Poliana, it was met by the fire of 3rd Battalion/1241st Rifle Regiment of the 375th Rifle Division and Lieutenant Moiseev's 2nd Tank Company of the 331st Tank Battalion of the 6th Guards Army's 96th Separate Tank Brigade. According to the brigade's headquarters, the fighting began already at 0345 and repeatedly flared up, before subsiding almost at the day's end. Already after sunrise, striving at whatever the cost to overrun the line of Govorunenko's 375th Rifle Division, in addition to assault guns the Germans threw panzers into the fighting as well. Taking advantage of folds in the ground and their well-camouflaged positions, the Soviet tankers knocked out one assault gun and two Pz.Kpfw. VI Tigers. During the attempt to resume the offensive, the enemy encountered not only a dense curtain of fire; the Germans were also forced to repel Soviet counterattacks launched by the commander of the 1241st Rifle Regiment Major N.A. Karklin with the forces of the 3rd Rifle Battalion. By evening the 6th Panzer Division reported that its left-hand *kampfgruppe* was located 2 kilometers northwest of Chernaia Poliana. This meant Barkmann had managed to advance not more than 1 kilometer before getting stuck.

The offensive also started badly in the center of Breith's panzer corps – in the sector of the 19th Panzer Division. Its main forces were assembled opposite the eastern bank of Mikhailovka as far as (excl) Dal'nie Peski. It intended to launch an attack against the left flank of the 81st Guards Rifle Division and right flank of the 78th Guards Rifle Division[43] with two *kampfgruppen* across bridges in the southern and northern parts of Pushkarnoe. Before dawn, Panzergrenadier Regiment 73 together with 27 panzers (according to prisoner testimony) was located in the woods south of Pushkarnoe. Lieutenant Colonel Richter's Panzergrenadier Regiment 74 and 30 panzers, including a Tiger company, was assembled on the northern outskirts of Pushkarnoe in front of the bridge there, as was reported by the scouting party of the 238th Guards Rifle Regiment back in the beginning of June. Since that time, this area had been zeroed in by the batteries of the 161st Guards Cannon Artillery Regiment and 2/290th Mortar Regiment, as well as by the mortar company of the 238th Guards Rifle Regiment.

---

42 NARA US, rg. 242, t. 314, r. 197, f. 001054.
43 At 2200 on 4 July 1943, the 78th Guards Rifle Division had a total of 8,346 men, including 3,030 riflemen, 792 submachine gunners, 962 machine gunners, 490 mortar men, 1,397 artillerymen, and 337 anti-tank riflemen. (TsAMO RF, F. 1225, op. 1, d. 15, l. 12obr.) The average manpower of the rifle regiments was 2,060 soldiers and officers (TsAMO RF, F. 1225, op. 1, d. 11, l. 110).

5 JULY 1943 – THE BEGINNING OF THE END OF A TRAGICOMEDY

According to the testimony of the captured Senior Lance-Corporal O. Esselman from the headquarters company of Panzergrenadier Regiment 74, both *kampfgruppen* were to begin crossing infantry using inflatable boats before the initiation of the artillery preparation, while the tanks were to move across bridges that were to be built after the start of the attack. Planning to make a forced crossing of the river even before the start of the artillery preparation, the enemy command was counting on the element of surprise, which possibly might have helped avoid losing men when crossing the river, but this idea came to naught. On 3 July the commander of the 81st Guards Rifle Division issued an order: in addition to the combat outposts, each battalion of the forward regiments and of the 65th Separate Penal Company was to form a group of up to 7 men, and on each night up to including 6 July, they were to push forward these groups to the river's edge with the aim of keeping watch over the enemy and capture a prisoner for identification purposes. All of these groups were located in their positions on the night of 4-5 July as well. Thus, having crossed the river partway, the inflatable boats carrying the combat engineers and grenadiers came under the fire of the 238th Guards Rifle Regiment's combat outposts and three observation groups.

In addition, just as soon as the report arrived at the division command post that the combat outposts were engaging the enemy, which was trying to cross the river, the attached artillery units began to fire. The assault groups of II/Panzergrenadier Regiment 74 and of the 168th Infantry Division's Infantry Regiment 429 that was attached to the 19th Panzer Division, which at that moment were located at the bridge under construction in the northern section of Pushkarnoe or were already in the process of crossing the river in their inflatable boats were caught in a particularly bad situation. The areas of the crossing sites had been pre-registered by the Soviet artillery, so the heavy shells and mortar rounds were landing right on target. From the 19th Panzer Division's account:

> In order to lay down bridges for the tanks, a staging area at Belgorod was used. Over the course of several weeks, everything was made ready ... heavy metallic sections had been dragged up right to the riverbank and concealed in the bulrushes. Under the cover of darkness on the night of 4-5 July, the hands of hundreds of sappers were to assemble the framework of a cantilever bridge for the Tigers in complete darkness. Meanwhile, everything was ready at the southern crossing site for the laying of a 24-tonne bridge. ... The bridge for the Tiger tanks was half-ready. At this moment the Russians began the well-organized fire of artillery, mortars and flanking machine guns on the crossing site. Despite the nighttime darkness, the fire was very accurate. Thus one of the inflatable rafts, which had been loaded to the maximum, was sunk by a direct hit. The combat engineers were also taking serious losses, since 40-60 men were standing clustered under each of the bridge's girders.[44]

Here's how the former commander of the Heavy Panzer Battalion 503 Captain von Kageneck, who before dawn was positioned not far from the bridge that was being built by the pioneers of the 19th Panzer Division for the Tiger tanks of his company, described offensive's difficult start:

> On 4 July the battalion marched to an assembly area northeast of Belgorod, near the Donets. We were attached directly to *Armee-Abteilung Kempf*. After I had arrived, it was clear to me that Kempf would ignore Guderian's maxim of "*Nicht Kleckern, sondern Klotzen*" [Boot 'em, don't spatter 'em]. He had distributed our three heavy panzer companies on a broad front among his three attacking divisions. I immediately reported to General Breith and asked him

---
44 TsAMO RF, F. 38A, op. 9027, d. 46, l. 151, 151obr.

to persuade higher levels of command to undo that folly. He did exactly that, and was successful, but it took several days before the battalion was reassembled.

And so I experienced the beginning of "*Zitadelle*" more or less as a spectator with the comrades of the Headquarters Company. I stood on the bank of the Donets in the gray light of dawn on 5 July to watch the crossing of our tanks into the bridgehead. The engineers had worked feverishly during the night and the bridge was 80% completed. Then, suddenly, a "red sunrise" arose on the far side as hundreds of Stalin organs [Katiusha rocket-launchers] hurled their rockets exactly onto the crossing site. The bridge was totally demolished and the engineers, unfortunately, suffered heavy losses. Never had I hugged the dirt so tightly as when those terrible shells sprayed their thin fragments just above the ground.[45]

Today it isn't simple to lay out the chronology of events in the course of 5 July in detail in the sector of the 81st Guards Rifle Division,[46] because few of its combat documents remain. For example, I found only two pieces of information in the files of the 238th Guards Rifle Regiment: a combat report at 0600 and an operational summary at 1200. All the rest were likely burned up during the retreat from the Staryi Gorod area on the night of 9-10 July. There are more documents in the files of the division headquarters itself, but the information in them is very sparse, because the operational summaries and orders were plainly put down on paper by officers who were working from memory, while the command and control in these days went primarily through personal meetings of the division commander with subordinates and over the radio. Therefore, any information about the situation on the right flank of the 25th Guards Rifle Corps is of particular interest. I will cite Operational Summary No. 9 from the headquarters of the 238th Guards Rifle Regiment at 0600 on 5 July:

1. The enemy at 0330 launched an offensive, conducting strong artillery and mortar fire along the entire forward edge of the regiment's sector of defense, as well as in its depth. The enemy broke into the line of defense of the neighbor on the left and in the strength of two companies is fighting in the trenches. At 0500 up to a platoon of enemy infantry also broke into the trenches in our sector in the "Zorka" area. The enemy air force is thus far is operating weakly. Our losses: no materiel; personnel losses are unknown.
2. The regiment's elements are occupying the previous line of defense.[47]

I will remind the reader that the right flank of Kruchikhin's regiment was located almost in the center of the division's defense, and in the table of signal codes received the code name "Zorka" – hence "Zorka's sector". It was precisely here that Artmann's grenadiers had made their way up to the first trench line, but there became stuck. The 238th Guards Rifle Regiment was positioned on the 81st Guards Rifle Division's left flank at the boundary between it and the 78th Guards Rifle Division. Here, the situation from the German offensive's very first minutes developed quickly and not in the favor of the Guardsmen.

The positions of Major I.A. Khitsov's 228th Guards Rifle Regiment, which was holding the 78th Guards Rifle Division's right flank, was located in sector of ground favorable for a defense,

---

45 Dr. Lochmann, Richard Freiherr von Rosen and Afred Rubbel, *The combat history of Schwere Panzer-Abteilung 503* [Winnipeg, Canada: J.J. Fedorowicz Publishing, Inc., 2000], p. 90.
46 On 29 June 1943, the 81st Guards Rifle Division had a total of 8,461 men, including 2,207 junior commanders and 5,430 servicemen. Of these, 3,204 were riflemen, 750 were submachine gunners, 1,319 were machine gunners (729 light machine gunners and 589 heavy machine gunners), 479 were anti-tank riflemen, 761 were mortar men, and 1,035 were artillerymen.
47 TsAMO RF, F. 238 gv. sp, op. 20914, d. 7, l. 27.

especially that of its central 3rd Rifle Battalion commanded by Captain P.G. Iastrebov (southern outskirts of Dal'nie Peski – Dorogobuzheno). The regiment was covering the rather large and tactically-important village of Razumnoe that was located behind the railroad. There, the 7th Guards Army's Anti-tank Area No. 5 (18 anti-tank guns) had been set up. The regiment's sector was being viewed by the command of the III Panzer Corps as a serious obstacle to linking the flanks of the 7th and 19th Panzer Divisions, and it was planning to envelop it with the flanking *kampfgruppen* of Schmidt's 19th Panzer Division (from the north) and of von Funck's 7th Panzer Division (from the south).

Despite heavy blocking artillery fire, the 19th Panzer Division's *Kampfgruppe* Köhler (Panzergrenadier Regiment 73), which had the mission to break through to the Belgorod – Titovka railroad bed, and then attack in the direction of the "Day of Harvest" collective farm, managed quickly to get across the Northern Donets River north of Dal'nie Peski, and in a matter of 1.5 hours it had managed to penetrate the forward edge of 1/228th Guards Rifle Regiment and take this village. Dal'nie Peski sat next to the river, and previously a wooden bridge had stood on its western outskirts, and here was a satisfactory exit from the bottom land onto firm ground. Thus it was here that the 19th Panzer Division had launched one of its first attacks in this area, so that it could quickly create a bridgehead in order to construct a bridge. From the 78th Guards Rifle Division's combat diary:

> At 0320 the enemy opened up intense artillery and mortar fire from the Pushkarnoe – Solomino line on the combat positions of the division's units. Under this cover at 0345 up to a battalion of infantry attempted to force a crossing of the Northern Donets River in the sector: (excl.) Pushkarnoe – northern outskirts of Dal'nie Peski. However, the attack was driven back by the fire of 1st Battalion/228th Guards Rifle Regiment. Having concentrated the fire of up to 8 rocket-launchers on the 1st Rifle Battalion, the Germans again hurled now up to two infantry battalions against this sector of defense. With the support of concentrated fire, the second attack was successful. The enemy penetrated the defenses of 1/228th Guards Rifle Regiment and shoved back the 2nd and 3rd Rifle Companies, emerging at Point 126.3.[48]

In the pre-dawn twilight, Köhler's *kampfgruppe* had split up: its submachine gunners and machine gunners diverted the enemy fire onto themselves and were covering the combat engineers, who on their part not only successfully cleared passages through the minefields, but having penetrated in several places to the first trench line, began blowing up several earth-and-timber bunkers with their establishment 3-kilogram demolition charges, thereby creating conditions for the advance of the main forces into the depth of the 228th Guards Rifle Regiment's defenses. By 0500 the 1st Rifle Battalion had fallen back to the line: 2nd Rifle Company – northeastern slopes of Hill 126.3; 1st Rifle Company – eastern slopes of Hill 126.3; and 3rd Rifle Company – southeastern slopes of Hill 126.3.

In order to cover the withdrawal, the 3rd Rifle Battalion commander ordered a company to leave behind several Maksim machine-gun teams. Sergeant Ziiamat Ustinovich Khusanov commanded one of them. He continued to keep his machine-gun firing and carried out his order faithfully, while the company retreated – it not only managed to withdraw, but also had time to dig in at a new position. When Khusanov's team had exhausted its ammunition and his No. 2 had been killed, Ziiamat was no longer able to move and continued to fight off the Germans with grenades. However, he was badly wounded, and having lost consciousness, was left behind in the trench. In the battalion he was thought to have been killed-in-action, and a recommendation was sent to

---

48 TsAMO RF, F. 78 gv. sd, op. 1, d. 16, l. 20, 20obr.

Moscow, signed by the Voronezh Front Commander-in-Chief, regarding the awarding of the Gold Star of the Hero of the Soviet Union to the machine gunner. However, the valiant soldier survived. The former director of the Belgorod Regional Museum P. Goncharenko, who personally knew the Guardsman, recalled the unusual fate of this brave man:

> On the days of the 40th Anniversary of the liberation of Belgorod, in August 1983 I conducted an excursion for the veterans who had arrived from various areas of the country to the places of the former battles of the 7th Guards Army. After talking about the events of those long ago days, I suggested honoring the memory of the heroes buried in Razumnoe. When I mentioned Khusanov's name, a man walked up to me and through tears informed me, "I am Khusanov". Then the veteran told me what had happened with him. He'd been wounded by an explosion from his own grenade. He wound up in Ukraine in a prisoner concentration camp. From there, he escaped to Bulgaria with a group of Bulgarians. There they formed a partisan detachment. The detachment was encircled by the Germans in the foothills of the Carpathians [according to other information, the ensuing battle of the partisan detachment took place in Chernogoria (Montenegro)]. The partisans decided to fight to the last man. Khusanov decided to steal up to the Germans and toss a grenade. He reached a machine-gun nest without being spotted. Having killed the crew with his submachine gun, Khusanov took position behind the machine gun and opened fire at the Germans from the rear. It created a panic that lasted for 40 minutes. Meanwhile, taking advantage of this, the detachment escaped the pocket and fled into the mountains. For a long time, the partisans could hear machine-gun fire, followed by the explosions of grenades, and then everything fell silent. The Germans, believing Khusanov had been killed, collected their dead and wounded from the explosions of Khusanov's grenades, and left. In the morning Bulgarian women came to bury their own dead partisans and came upon the badly-wounded Khusanov. They gave him whatever aid they could, and then carried him on stretchers to Yugoslavia, to partisans in the mountains. For three days, they carried him from village to village, changing the stretcher bearers.
>
> He was given medical aid in a partisan hospital, but an urgent operation was necessary, and the hospital had no doctors who could perform it. Then they took Khusanov to the coastline and crossed the Adriatic Sea to Italy to a hospital run by Italian partisans. After recovering, Khusanov joined the Italian resistance and continued to fight against fascism. At the end of 1944, the advancing Allies linked up with the Italian partisan detachment in which Khusanov served, and Americans took him back to the United States.
>
> After the war ended, Khusanov returned to the Motherland and after passing through verification and checks, he arrived in Tashkent, from whence he had left for the front years before. Having arrived at his home, Ziiamat Ustanovich saw that the windows and door were boarded over. Ziiamat went to his neighbors to find out what had happened and to locate his father. However, his neighbors called him a traitor and refused to receive him. At the same time it became clear to him that his father, unable to withstand his son's "betrayal", had died from grief. Khusanov wasn't able to determine who had brought the false tale of his surrender to his near and dear ones, nor was he able to prove that he wasn't a traitor and hadn't voluntarily surrendered to the Germans. Khusanov traveled to Chimkent Oblast, where he managed to find a job as a teacher in one of the schools.
>
> In 1970 the former commander of the 25th Guards Rifle Corps G.B. Safiulin arrived in Tashkent for the unveiling of a monument to one of its heroes. The General took an interest in whether his fellow natives knew about Khusanov's exploit, but they told him what had happened. Having found out the address of the hero's new place of residence, the General traveled to Chimkent Oblast and met with Khusanov. Having learned the details

of Khusanov's military life, Safiulin returned to Moscow, where he found the Decree of the Presidium of the Supreme Soviet about posthumously awarding Khusanov with the title Hero of the Soviet Union, and established Khusanov had been awarded the title "People's Hero of Bulgaria" (again posthumously) for the valiant feat he had performed on Bulgarian soil, having saved the partisan detachment from certain death. Justice prevailed. As a sign of gratitude for the heroism he had shown in the Battle of Kursk, the Belgorod City Council of People's Deputies made Z. Khusanov an honorary citizen of Belgorod.[49]

To the above I will add that Captain N.M. Chibisov and Lieutenant A.V. Beliakov, members of security organs, played an important role in clearing the name of the former frontline veteran from insinuations and slander.

However, clearing the elements of Khitsov's regiment out of the first line of trenches still didn't mean a clean breakthrough of the main line of resistance. After the withdrawal of the 1st Rifle Battalion's 2nd and 3rd Companies from Dal'nie Peski, the commander of the 3rd Rifle Battalion's 7th Company shifted his 3rd Rifle Platoon to his left flank via communication trenches. As a result, here the enemy offensive toward Razumnoe was brought to a stop. As noted in the documents of the 25th Guards Rifle Corps, Khitsov's regiment was not only putting up stiff resistance to Köhler's grenadiers with fire, but was also launching furious counterattacks, which shocked the enemy. We can find the echoes of these impressions in the documents of General Schmidt's headquarters:

> What little we knew about these fortifications prior to the offensive, we didn't even guess one-fourth of what the Russians had set up here. Each clump of bushes, each collective farm, every patch of woods and the heights had been converted into fortresses. They stretched in all directions from the well-camouflaged rifle pits and trenches, with a depth of 2 meters and a width of 40-50 centimeters, which led to bunkers that were covered by thick logs and railroad rails. Everywhere, reserve positions had been equipped. The artillery fire had little effect on these fortifications, unless you expended an enormous quantity of shells. However, it was hardest of all to imagine the tenacity with which the Russians at times defended each gun pit and each trench line.
>
> A regiment-sized enemy group, reinforced with a battalion of mortars [2/290th Mortar Regiment], offered particularly bitter resistance, and the woods south of the labor correction camp were dense with positions [of the 1st and 3rd Battalions of the 228th Guards Rifle Regiment].[50]

In the morning summary to the headquarters of the III Panzer Corps, the command of the 19th Panzer Division reported that *Kampfgruppe* Köhler when attacking the woods south of the labor corrective camp had run into bitter resistance and was locked in heavy fighting, while the attack of *Kampfgruppe* Richter [Panzergrenadier Regiment 74] had been stopped by concentrated Russian artillery fire on the area of the Mikhailovka bridgehead. It was impossible to support its attack with tanks, because the 60-tonne bridge still hadn't been completed and it wasn't clear when it would be ready. The situation here began to turn in favor of the Germans under the influence of the 7th Panzer Division's unequivocal successes.

---

49 Goncharenko, P., "Zemlia politaia krov'iu" ["Ground soaked with blood"] *Belgorodskie Izvestiia*, 12 July 2003, p. 3.
50 TsAMO RF, F. 38A, op. 9027, d. 46, l. 152.

Simultaneously with the loss of Dal'nie Peski, by 0500 the situation on the left flank of the 228th Guards Rifle Regiment south of Dorogobuzheno had sharply deteriorated. Here, the 7th Panzer Division had launched a strong attack against Major D.S. Khorolenko's neighboring 225th Guards Rifle Regiment. In the morning, the 7th Panzer Division had two *kampfgruppen* in the first echelon. The first moved toward the river south of Solomino. At 0425 it attempted to cross the river in the area of Hill 123.0 in the sector of Captain I.A. Matsokin's 2nd Battalion of the 225th Guards Rifle Regiment, which was holding a line between (excl.) Dorogobuzheno and (excl.) Nizhnii Ol'shanets. Its assault elements (Infantry Regiment 442 and Engineer Battalion 19) used a bridge laid across inflatable boats to cross the Donets; they had the mission to seize a bridgehead and clear the mines from the sector for a future bridge. The attempt proved unsuccessful; under the fire from the Guardsmen, the grenadiers retreated, but thereupon the Germans began to generate a smoke screen. Subsequently, approximately 30 minutes later two companies managed to break through to the first trench line of 2nd Battalion/225 Guards Rifle Regiment, where hand-to-hand combat erupted. From the 78th Guards Rifle Division's journal of combat operations:

> At 0500 the enemy in strength of up to two battalions with the support of artillery fire attempted to force a crossing of the Northern Donets at Solomino in the sector of 2/225th Guards Rifle Regiment. The attack was repulsed with the fire from 2/225th Guards Rifle Regiment, but the enemy continued to bring up infantry and tanks to the river. At 0655, despite heavy losses while laying down a bridge in the area east of the church in Solomino and having crossed two battalions of infantry, the enemy launched a fresh attack against the 225th Guards Rifle Regiment.[51]

At 0500 the III Panzer Corps' Operations Department briefed Speidel's headquarters and reported that "7th Panzer Division has seized a bridgehead in the Solomino area and might break through from there to Dal'nie Peski, having taken the woods to the east of there. At present the division is busy with the construction of a bridge."[52] The bridge was being built east of the church in Solomino for Panzer Regiment 25 and the division's artillery regiment. A captured engineer of 3./Motorized Engineer Battalion 58, Alfred Kunaid testified:

> Our battalion consists of three companies, and each company of three platoons. In order to build a bridge, the battalion has motorized pile drivers, as well as the necessary quantity of power saws, axes and other carpenter's tools. The battalion has 54 vehicles ... Each platoon has three portable flame throwers, each with an effective range of about 25 meters. The company is equipped with explosives (standard charges of 3 kilograms and small TNT blocks of 100 grams), which are used by the engineers to destroy enemy firing points and to build ramps for tanks, which allow them to overcome scarps and ditches. For the offensive I personally received 6 small blocks of TNT; not all the engineers receive the standard demolition charges, but only one in six.
> The crossing of the tanks and infantry was conducted in the Solomino area. Sections of the bridge were prepared in good time and brought to the construction site on the night of 3-4 July 1943. On the night before the offensive, the river was scouted and places were designated for the crossing of tanks. Infantry and engineers crossed the completed bridge with the assignment to begin clearing mines. At first it was impossible to cross only the engineers, because the enemy was conducting heavy fire. I personally took part in clearing two

---

51 TsAMO RF, F. 1225, op. 1, d. 16, l. 20obr, 21.
52 NARA US, t. 312, r. 54, f. 7569605.

minefields in the Solomino area, and then east of Razumnoe. Altogether approximately 300 mines were removed. I don't know of any cases of explosions when the engineers are lifting mines, although it is well-known that it is dangerous to handle Russian mines.

When the infantry crossed to the eastern bank, I watched how 10 men got blown up simultaneously. When the mine exploded, the damage came not from fragments (interrogator's note: it can be assumed that the explosion resulted from PMD-6 or PMD-7 mines[53]). Two hours after the start of the artillery preparation, the bridge was finished [approximately at 0600] and the light and medium tanks began to cross it, while the heavy tanks crossed using a ford. The bridge for the passage of tanks was built on support pilings, and they were driven in with a manual metal ram weighing 60 kilograms. Four men did the pile driving. The bridge extended for 12 meters and was built in the course of two and a half hours by a team of engineers numbering 30-35 men. The tanks were moving in a single-file column, because after the explosion of 6 tanks (which I saw personally) immediately after crossing the bridge, the tankers probably feared moving in a deployed formation.

The engineers, after completing the assignment to clear minefields, were attached to the infantry, and they operated as riflemen. In order to counter tanks, the engineers had anti-tank grenades and bottles containing a smoke-generating mixture, which acted on a tank crew, disabling them. The anti-tank grenades have three strong magnets, thanks to which they stick to the tank's armor. In our platoon, four men were equipped with the grenades and bottles, and they were given the task to take on the enemy tanks whenever they made an appearance.[54]

The company of Tigers of Heavy Panzer Battalion 503 that was attached to the 7th Panzer Division was also unable get across the Donets at the ford near Solomino. Here's how Gerd Niemann, the gunner of Tiger 311, recalled this episode:

5 July 1943: At 0200 hours the tanks were ready to depart; the crews assembled for the briefing. By flashlight, 1st Lieutenant Scherf read the order of the day for the attack on the Russian positions east of the Donets between Belgorod and Orel. Thirty minutes later, simultaneously with the first artillery and rocket-launcher strikes, the Tigers rolled through a narrow defile in the woods onto the plain of the Donets. The river crossing was to be by a ford, not far from the village of Solomino.

We had run through that phase of the operation several times on the sand tables at Kharkov: 2nd Platoon in the lead, then the command tank, followed by the 1st Platoon and then the 3rd Platoon. We approached the crossing in that order on this morning as well. Lieutenant von Rosen's Tiger 321 approached the ford directly. The others remained a bit to the side in covered positions. Tensely, we followed the crossing. Slowly, until the water rose over the track guards, the Tiger made its way through the Donets, apparently without any problems. Just a few meters more and the next tank could follow. But that was not to happen. Tiger 321 remained stuck on the far bank. In spite of repeated approaches, it could not get firm ground under its tracks. It had no return. The fording operation was scuttled.

What was to be done? A bit further upstream was a provisional bridge. At the moment Panzer Regiment 25 was crossing it. Why couldn't we just follow it? No passage for vehicles over thirty tons! A new crossing would have to be arranged for the Tigers. Instead of "Tanks to the front!" the cry was now, "Engineers get to work!" In the meantime, the Russian artillery had found the range of the crossing. The shells burst everywhere, as did the unpredictable

---

53 Anti-personnel wooden mines triggered by pressure.
54 TsAMO RF, F. 7 gv. A, op. 5332, d. 31, ll. 48-49.

salvoes of the Stalin Organs [Katiusha rocket launchers]. The combat engineers did not let that faze them. They dragged the heavy bridging materials forward, drove piles into the riverbed and laid planks on timbers.

The Tigers remained widely dispersed on the open Donets plain. The sun blazed down mercilessly on the steel armor. In the fighting compartment it was as hot as the inside of an incubator. Wounded infantry, returning from the fight, could not understand that the Tigers were unable to move forward. Again and again they called to us, "Move on forward! Move on forward! Your comrades are waiting for you!"

Finally we had reached the point of no return: "Company, March!" After a few hundred meters we were in contact with the enemy.[55]

Thus, just three hours after the fighting began on the line of the 225th Guards Rifle Regiment, the panzers of the 7th Panzer Division had reached the eastern bank of the Northern Donets River. The bulk of them had assembled in order to break through along the Solomino – Razumnoe dirt road across Hill 108.9, while a small group was supporting the infantry, which was trying to roll up the defense of the 6th Company of 2/225th Guards Rifle Regiment from south to north and emerge on the flank of the 3rd Rifle Battalion of Khitsov's regiment. A certain time later, the construction of a 16-tonne Type K bridge was completed for vehicles and the artillery. The 6th Company repelled the enemy's onslaught three times, and even went over to counterattacks. It was only after bitter fighting, in which two of its platoons were completely wiped out, that the Germans broke into the communication trenches and moved along them toward the flank of the 228th Guards Rifle Regiment. The commander of the 8th Rifle Company of 3/228th Guards Rifle Regiment Senior Lieutenant B.N. Kalmykov shifted a heavy machine gun and two anti-tank rifle teams from his right flank to his left, while the 3rd Rifle Battalion commander P.G. Iastrebov sent a platoon of submachine gunners to the threatened flank. As a result, the enemy was stopped.

After the grenadiers of the southern *kampfgruppe* attacked 2/225th Guards Rifle Regiment a second time, assault elements of the 7th Panzer Division's northern *kampfgruppe* forced a crossing of the river in the Dorogobuzheno area (the left flank of 3/228th Guards Rifle Regiment). From the 78th Guards Rifle Division's combat diary:

> At 0700 the Germans began to lay down a bridge southwest of Dorogobuzheno. The lack of artillery didn't allow us to place simultaneous, concentrated fire on all the bridges that the enemy had managed to build by this time. At 0725 with the support of artillery fire, up to two battalions of infantry and 15 tanks crossed over the completed bridge and advanced toward Dorogobuzheno. Meanwhile another 20 tanks remained on the opposite [western] bank in the vicinity of the bridge, supporting the advance of the group that had crossed with their fire. Heavy Pz.Kpfw. VI tanks were located in the first echelon.[56]

According to some information, the group that made the forced crossing of the river consisted of units of the 7th Panzer Division's Panzergrenadier Regiments 6 and 7. It attacked Dorogobuzheno, which was being defended by the 8th Rifle Company of 3/228th Guards Rifle Regiment, reinforced by two platoons of anti-tank rifles and a platoon of heavy machine guns, as well as by two batteries of the 81st Guards Separate Destroyer Anti-tank Artillery Regiment. However, the first attack had no success; the Guardsmen already at the battle's outset set six tanks ablaze and the enemy rolled back, even though the grenadiers were being supported by the intense fire not only

---

55 Lochmann, Rubbel, and von Rosen, *The Combat History of Schwere Panzer-Abteilung 503*, p. 110.
56 TsAMO RF, F. 1225, op. 1, d. 16, l. 20obr, 21.

of tanks from the chalk hills on the western bank, but also from artillery firing from defilade positions. H. von Funck recalled:

> To the east of the southern outskirts of Solomino, in the vicinity of Hill 108.9 and on the road to Dorogobuzheno, two small bridgeheads had been created, which gradually began to expand. In the area of Dal'nie Peski, initially the offensive was checked. In a small patch of woods, located to the southwest of the village, the Russians were putting up rather stubborn resistance. [This was a company of submachine gunners, a platoon of anti-tank rifles from the 2nd Anti-tank Rifle Company of the 4th Guards Separate Anti-tank Rifle Battalion, a platoon of heavy machine guns of 3/228th Guards Rifle Regiment, and a platoon of the 81st Guards Separate Destroyer Anti-tank Artillery Battalion, which were positioned on the right flank of the 8th Rifle Company.] Strong reconnaissance that had been sent ahead confirmed that the passages in the swamps in the direction of Razumnoe Station and the village of Dorogobuzheno had been heavily mined and were being swept by enemy fire. The swamp itself posed a difficult obstacle.[57]

As the participants in those battles from the German side recalled, they had the impression that in the offensive's first moments, the defenders were in a state of shock, and their resistance was light, although the artillery kept shelling the bridges. Even so, its fire wasn't as effective as it became after dawn, and it was uncoordinated. In fact, the absence of operational efficiency in the work of the 7th Guards Army's artillery and its scantiness in the first hours of the offensive were important reasons why the assault groups of von Funck's panzer division, having rather quickly forced a crossing of the river, were able to assemble on the eastern bank not only combat engineers and covering infantry, but also infantry main forces with heavy infantry weapons, and then force the forward battalions of the 78th Guards Rifle Division out of the first trench line in several places. Here is what the headquarters of the 7th Panzer Division reported to the III Panzer Corps headquarters in a morning summary:

> Over night, intensive fire of hostile artillery. At 0425 (Moscow time) the division went on the offensive on a broad front with strong artillery support. The attacking battalions successfully overcame the river and are presently developing the attack against strongly fortified infantry positions and artillery. Resistance on the eastern bank of the river is light. The forward detachment at 0630 (Moscow time) is on the road from Ol'shanets to Dorogobuzheno. The construction of the bridge on the northern outskirts of Solomino is making good progress. Minefields were discovered on an elevation in the center of Solomino, which against army orders hadn't been disarmed, leading to a significant delay. Intensive work of the enemy air force, including bombing of the assembly areas.[58]

However, after dawn the situation began to change sharply. The enemy in the bridgeheads plainly lacked the forces and means for a decisive attack. The assault groups that had crossed to the eastern bank, having created a small bridgehead, began to run out of steam and get bogged down in the Guards divisions' well-organized defenses. The Soviet artillery fire on the 7th Panzer Division's main crossing sites noticeably increased. Several 4-tonne bridges employing rubber boats as supports were smashed to pieces by the Russian heavy mortars. One report after another began to come in to the headquarters of the 7th Panzer Division that because of the poor work

---

57 TsAMO RF, F. 15, op. 11600, d. 1539, l. 18.
58 NARA US, t. 314, r. 197, f. 001055.

of the engineers in the bridgeheads and directly at the bridges, the explosive demolition of equipment and men had begun. The commandant in charge of crossing halted it for a time and again summoned the mine-clearing sappers. Incidentally, there were lots of complaints with respect to the negligence of the sappers in the sectors of other divisions of Breith's panzer corps as well. For example, at the 19th Panzer Division's crossing site that morning, two trucks loaded with infantry were blown up by mines. These incidents were understandable in that situation, and their main cause was the hastiness of work due to the intense Soviet artillery fire. Because of the powerful blocking fire being laid down by the Soviet artillery and heavy mortars, the engineer elements attached to the assault groups were not numerous (approximately a platoon for each), and even though they were working as hard as possible, already in the first minutes of the offensive they suffered painful losses.

At the moment when the resistance of the defenders began to increase, while the 7th Panzer Division's forces on the eastern bank still lacked the strength for a decisive attack, its neighbor, Korps Raus, or more precisely its left-flanking 106th Infantry Division under the command of Lieutenant General W. Forst,[59] played a substantial role in helping von Funck's 7th Panzer Division break free into the depth of the 78th Guards Rifle Division's defenses. Between 0500 and 0530, almost two battalions of the 106th Infantry Division's Infantry Regiment 240 forced a crossing of the river in the Karnaukhovka area and struck the left flank of the 78th Guards Rifle Division, striving to break through to Nizhnii Ol'shanets. The primary task for von Funck was to crush Captain I.A. Matsokin's 2/225th Guards Rifle Regiment as quickly as possible, in order to expand the bridgeheads in the center of the 78th Guards Rifle Division and deploy his main panzer and artillery forces in them. Thus he made use of the standard tactical approach of pincers; taking advantage of the pressure exerted by the soldiers of the 106th Infantry Division on the defenses at Nizhnii Ol'shanets (the left flank of 2/225th Guards Rifle Regiment), he struck the right flank of 2/225th Guards Rifle Regiment with his forces in order to envelop it and link up with the 106th Infantry Division.

At 0830 two *kampfgruppen* of the 7th Panzer Division and 106th Panzer Division on their adjoining flanks launched an attack toward Nizhnii Ol'shanets. The 2/225th Guards Rifle Regiment, fighting in the sector running from (excl.) Dorogobuzheno to (excl.) Nizhnii Ol'shanets, was caught in a difficult situation. Having held out for a bit more than an hour, I.A. Matsokin under the pressure of superior forces was forced to issue an order to the battalion to retreat to a dirt road running along the river basin west of Hill 126.3 between Dorogobuzheno and Belgorod. Around 0930, soldiers of the 106th Infantry Division began to infiltrate into the southern outskirts of Nizhnhii Ol'shanets. Hope rose in von Funck that the 7th Panzer Division's main bridgehead east of Solomino (Hill 108.9 – (excl.) Nizhnii Ol'shanets) would be expanded in the nearest time up to the size required to insert his primary panzer and artillery forces. He recalled:

---

59 Werner Forst (Lieutenant General from 01.01.1943) was born on 21 December 1892 in Magdeburg. He joined the army in 1911. As a junior officer (a lieutenant) he took part in the First World War. For his standout performances, he was awarded the Iron Cross, 1st and 2nd Class. In the inter-war period he served in the artillery, commanding an artillery battalion (1934-1935) and regiment (1936-1940), then for a short time (1940-1941) he was located in the reserve pool of the High Command. Between 18.01 and 22.12.1941 he headed Artkommando 146. On 22.12.1941 Forst became the acting commander of the 293rd Infantry Division, and on 01.03.1942 he was confirmed in this post. On 10.01.1943 Forst took over command of the 106th Infantry Division. For his successful leadership of the division in the course of the summer fighting on the Kursk salient and at Khar'kov, on 29.08.1943 Forst was awarded the Knight's Cross. On 20.02.1944 Forst was withdrawn into the command reserve. Between 01.06.1944 and until the end of the war, Forst served as the inspector of the Reserve Army's artillery command. On 09.05.1945 he was captured by the Allies and was held in prison until June 1947, when he was released. He lived in West Germany and died on 3 February 1971 in Wiesbaden-Sonnenberg.

The right-hand neighbor [the 106th Infantry Division] broke into Verkhnii Ol'shanets, thanks to which favorable conditions arose for an offensive by the 7th Panzer Division's shock force from the south along a path in the swamp in the direction of the Razumnoe railroad station that had been scouted. In the area of the northern outskirts of Solomino, the Tiger company with great difficulty managed to get across the river at a ford. The rest of the panzers couldn't cross the river, because the river bottom and banks had been churned up by shells. The company of heavy tanks was brought up to the path in the swamp, located east of Hill 108.9. However, because of minefields it was forced to stop there, until sappers could clear passages through the minefields. While the engineers worked, it gave them effective support.[60]

The 1st Battalion of the 225th Guards Rifle Regiment under the command of the 23-year-old Captain A.Ia. Belovitsky was holding the anti-tank strongpoint of Nizhnii Ol'shanets. On this day, his Guardsmen had to withstand the enemy's furious attacks. The battalion's sector had been duly fortified, but superior enemy forces were attacking the village. In addition, because of the retreat of Captain I.A. Matsokin's 2nd Battalion to a reserve position, Belovitsky's right flank was exposed. As a result, the Germans were squeezing the 1st Rifle Battalion in a semi-encircled position with the flanking units of the 106th Infantry Division and 7th Panzer Division. Fierce street fighting broke out in the southern portion of the village. Having received a report about a German breakthrough to Nizhnii Ol'shanets, A.V. Skvortsov got in touch with the commander of the reserve 223rd Guards Rifle Regiment Major S.A. Arshinov, and ordered him to prepare his 1st Rifle Battalion immediately for a counterattack toward the threatened village. At this time the division commander received a fresh report: the enemy was assembling tanks on the road leading from Hill 108.9 to the Razumnoe railyard, situated 1 kilometer south of Razumnoe (the alternate position of the 78th Guards Rifle Division, being defended by the 223rd Guards Rifle Regiment). The situation in the sector of the 78th Guards Rifle Division on the morning of 5 July was laid out in detail in an operational summary of its headquarters, which was sent to the corps at 1000. Here is an excerpt from this document:

1. The enemy at 0330 on 5.7.1943 in strength of up to five battalions went on the offensive against the division's front under the cover of strong artillery fire and a smokescreen, and forced a crossing of the Northern Donets River in the areas west of Hill 126.3 [the sector of 1/228th Guards Rifle Regiment], Dal'nie Peski [1/228th Guards Rifle Regiment]; in the vicinity of Hill 108.9 [2/225th Guards Rifle Regiment]; and in the area of Hill 117.4. Simultaneously the enemy was bringing up men in vehicles out of Solomino and laying down a bridge west of the southern outskirts of Nizhnii Ol'shanets.
2. The 78th Guards Rifle Division is locked in combat with the attacking enemy in its defensive sector:
    228th Guards Rifle Regiment is fighting against more than two infantry battalions and offering stiff resistance.
    1/228th Guards Rifle Regiment, offering heavy resistance by fire against more than a battalion of enemy infantry, fell back with its center to the line of the western slopes of Hill 126.3. At 0600 with a reserve company it attempted to restore the situation and to take possession of a nameless height …
    3/228th Guards Rifle Regiment at 0600 was fighting an enemy infantry battalion that had crossed the river, and was holding its lines.

---

60 TsAMO RF, F. 15, op. 11600, d. 1539, ll. 18-19.

225th Guards Rifle Regiment at 0600 was fighting against three enemy infantry battalions along the eastern bank of the Northern Donets River:

2/225th Guards Rifle Regiment, offering stubborn resistance with its right flank, fell back from its main positions to reserve positions.

1/225th Guards Rifle Regiment, repulsing frontal attacks is locked in heavy fighting in semi-encirclement in the area south of Nizhnii Ol'shanets since 0600.

223rd Guards Rifle Regiment – situation unchanged in readiness to stage a counterattack.[61]

Meanwhile at this same time, this is how the situation appeared to the chief of staff of III Panzer Corps in the sector of its divisions' offensive; at 0910 he gave the following briefing to Army Detachment Kempf's headquarters:

The panzer corps has for the most part crossed the Donets. At present time it has been able on the whole to dig in between the Donets and the railroad. The construction of the bridge in the 19th Panzer Division's sector still hasn't been finished. The 7th Panzer Division is battling for Dorogobuzheno. The 19th Panzer Division with forward detachments is attacking toward the labor corrective camp. The enemy is placing strong fire on the Mikhailovka bridgehead. The forces located here are suffering heavy losses. The situation of the 6th Panzer Division is unchanged. Assessment of the enemy: Stubborn resistance can be expected.[62]

The document appears to be rather paradoxical – it seems everything is going well, but the results are quite modest. It is understandable that Brieth's command staff wanted to save face, and that is why it was hiding the failure of the 6th Panzer Division to get across the river, the lack of progress by the 19th Panzer Division, and the difficult situation of the 7th Panzer Division behind the meaningless words "for the most part" and "on the whole".

It may seem strange, but Korps Raus's assault grouping, which was significantly inferior in strength to the III Panzer Corps and lacked the support of tanks (it only had StuG Battalion 905 and StuG Company 328), operated more successfully in the beginning of the first day of the operation than did Brieth's shock formation. At the very least, it reached the railroad embankment more quickly and seized a large sector of ground in the Russian main defensive belt. The high activity and dash of the two infantry divisions of the provisional corps forced M.S. Shumilov already on the afternoon of the first day to introduce both of his mobile and combined-arms reserves into the fighting.

Korps Raus was supposed to provide secure cover for III Panzer Corps' right flank and divert part of the Soviet side's reserves onto itself. The modest capabilities it possessed forced the corps command to carry out its assignments by means of thoroughly arranging close cooperation both within the corps and with its neighbor on the left, and by concentrating its available forces and means on the main directions and against knots of resistance. The 320th Infantry Division with its right flank was to strike through Bezliudovka and the southern portion of the Shebekinskaia Dacha Woods in the direction of Shebekino, thereby drawing Shumilov's tactical reserves onto itself. The 106th Infantry Division received the order to attack with its left-flank *kampfgruppe* through Karnaukhovka toward Nizhnii Ol'shanets, and to seize this strongpoint of the 78th Guards Rifle Division as quickly as possible. Two regiments on the inner flanks of the 320th

---

61   TsAMO RF, F. 1225, op. 1, d. 15, l. 13.
62   NARA US, t. 312, r. 54, f. 7569606.

and 106th Infantry Divisions were to resolve the most important mission – to break the Russian resistance in the triangular area comprised by the strongly-fortified villages of Maslova Pristan', Priiutovka[63] and Rzhavets.[64] Thereby it was to create the conditions for the capture of the tactically-important Hill 207 (8 kilometers east of Maslova Pristan') and the ground east of there (where the positions of the 72nd Guards Rifle Division's second echelon were located), for a subsequent breakthrough to the Koren' River. Forst's and Postel's two central regiments where supposed to augment the attack by the flanking units, in accordance with the operational situation. Thus, by the end of 5 July, Korps Raus was supposed to breach the main belt of the 7th Guards Army in the sector of the 72nd Guards Rifle Division[65] to its entire depth. However, in order to accomplish this it first had to crush the regiments of the first echelon in the main positions between the basin of the Northern Donets River and the embankment of the Titovka – Belgorod railroad. It was here that the bitterest and most costly fighting developed between Raus's divisions and the troops of the 24th Guards Rifle Corps on the first day of the offensive.

The main forces of the 106th and 320th Infantry Divisions were assembled in the Toplinka – Priiutovka sector that extended for 12-13 kilometers. The divisions forced a crossing of the Donets simultaneously with all three regiments arrayed in two echelons: two battalions up, one battalion back. Over a short period of time the assault groups made their way across the river channel and created several small bridgeheads in order to lay down bridges using rubber boats as supports. Despite the strong resistance of the Guardsmen, at dawn both divisions were advancing at approximately the same pace, and already by 0500 they were breaking through the forward edge of both regiments of the 72nd Guards Rifle Division (on the flanks and in the center); in addition, as already mentioned above, the 106th Infantry Division had penetrated the positions of the left-flank regiment of the 78th Guards Rifle Division. Recalled T.Z. Vinogradov (at the time a senior lieutenant), the former deputy political commander of the 1st Battalion of the 72nd Guards Rifle Division's 155th Guards Artillery Regiment that was attached to the 229th Guards Rifle Regiment:

> When the sun rose, the division's entire sector was enveloped in such a dense cloud of smoke and dust from the explosions that the forward edge wasn't visible. On the high bank of the Northern Donets – to the right of us – somewhere in the Solomino area the Nazis had raised an observation balloon. Already several times, the German artillery had blanketed the positions of the 1st Battalion with shells, but to that point there'd been no losses, because we had provided excellent cover for the men and guns.
>
> Somewhere out in front, in the vicinity of the first trench line, battalion field guns and mortars were barking: the enemy had begun to cross the river. The commander of the 229th Guards Rifle Regiment was incessantly asking for fire on the bridges in the Maslova Pristan' area … the 1st Battery focused its fire on the infantry that had accumulated on the eastern bank of the river. The 2nd Battery was placing direct fire on vehicles, halftracks and the

---

63 According to the 1932 Census of the Population, it had 570 residents.
64 According to the 1932 Census of the Population, it had 403 residents.
65 On the morning of 5.07.1943, the 72nd Guards Rifle Division had a total of 8,658 men, including 3,324 in the rifle companies, including 162 men in the submachine gun companies, 406 men in the machine-gun companies, 359 men in the anti-tank rifle companies, 480 mortar men, 1,481 artillerymen in the division's artillery regiments, 361 men in a training battalion, 145 men in a separate engineer battalion, 153 in a separate signals company, 44 sappers, 62 chemical defense personnel, and 135 scouts. In attached elements it had 262 men in the 101st Anti-tank Rifle Battalion, 199 men in the 135th Army Blocking Detachment, 70 men in 1/175 Guards Army Engineer Battalion. It also had 6 152mm howitzers in 3/109th Guards Cannon Artillery Regiment and 14 76mm guns and 122mm howitzers in 1,2/671st Artillery Regiment.

enemy's bridging equipment. Boats were blowing apart into fragments, prime movers and trucks were burning, and soldiers were falling … Yet despite the losses, the enemy under the cover of a wall of artillery fire crossed the river in large groups. A mass of soldiers using whatever means available and by swimming were moving toward our defenses in a constant flow. … The foe's main attack struck the sector of the 229th Guards Rifle Regiment.[66]

The units of the 106th Infantry Division crossed the river in the sector between Toplinka and (excl.) Ivanovka, which extended for approximately 7 kilometers, and launched their main attack against the right flank of Losev's[67] 72nd Guards Rifle Division: Infantry Regiment 240 struck the left flank of the 229th Guards Rifle Regiment commanded by Major G.M. Batalov[68] (through the positions of the 66th Separate Penal Company, which was positioned on the boundary with the 78th Guards Rifle Division) in the direction of Nizhnii Ol'shanets, while Infantry Regiments 239 and 241 struck the main forces of the 229th Guards Rifle Regiment and the 222nd Guards Rifle Regiment, which were defending Karnaukhovka and Maslova Pristan'. The chief of staff of the 72nd Guards Rifle Division Colonel G.K. Volodkin reported, "After the bridges were completed at 0515, the enemy broke into the forward edge of our defense in the area of Karnaukhovka and Priiutovka, as well as south of Toplinka."[69] With an impetuous attack, *kampfgruppen* of Infantry Regiment 240 (a battalion in each) already at 0820 had overwhelmed the 66th Separate Penal Company; the left-flank *kampfgruppe* then broke into Nizhnii Ol'shanets and engaged the 78th Guards Rifle Division's 1st Battalion/225th Guards Rifle Regiment in combat, while the right-flank

---

66 Vinogradov, T.Z., *Dorogoe – navsegda* [*Dear – forever*] (Moscow: Voenizdat, 1977), pp. 83-84.
67 Losev, Anatolii Ivanovich (Major General from 2.3.1943) was born on 19 October 1906 in Kiev to a family of workers. After completing six years of schooling, he took a job, and in 1924 he joined the Red Army. In 1928 Losev graduated from the Kiev Artillery School. Between November 1933 and February 1938, he studied in the Budennyi Military-Technical Academy. In September 1939, after completing the six-month course of study for commanders of long-range artillery regiments, he became the commander of the 155th Rifle Division's 306th Artillery Regiment. He participated in the Soviet-Finnish Winter War in this role. Losev served in the acting army from the very first day of the Great Patriotic War. In September 1941, he was dropped from the rolls of the Communist Party by a Party commission of Briansk Front's 13th Army "for fleeing from the battlefield and leaving his subordinates without leadership", but he refused to acknowledge his guilt. Together with the army's forces, Losev fell into encirclement in the Trubchevsk – Sevsk area. In 1943 he was again admitted into the Communist Party, and in 1945 his years of Party membership were restored. Between December 1941 and March 1942, Losev served as the chief of intelligence of the 28th Army's artillery headquarters, and in May 1942 he became chief of artillery of the 38th Rifle Division of Southwestern Front's 28th Army. Between June and October 1942 he served as the acting commander of this division. On 18.10.1942 Losev was appointed as commander of the 29th Rifle Division, which after the Battle of Stalingrad was converted into a Guards formation. On 16.11.1942 the commander of the 64th Army wrote: "Over his time of command of the division, he showed himself to be a willful, aggressive and combat-wise commander. He is capable of resolving complex combat tasks independently. He skillfully organizes cooperation between all types of troops." On 18.11.1942, Losev was awarded the Order of the Red Star for his skillful leadership over the troops and his personal courage when defending Abganerovo Station and Railyard 74. In 1954 he went into the reserve and took up residence in Kiev. Losev passed away on 21 September 1970.
68 Batalov, Grigorii Mikhailovich (Lieutenant General) was born on 28 January 1915 in Vitebsk, into a family of workers. He was Belorussian. After finishing primary school, he worked as a machinist. He joined the Red Army in 1934. In 1937 he completed the Minsk Military School, and in 1942 – the accelerated courses at the Frunze Military Academy. For forcing the Dnepr on 26.10.1943, he was awarded the title Hero of the Soviet Union. After the war ended, he remained in the Soviet Army. In 1952 he graduated from the Frunze Military Academy, and in 1959, the Academy of the General Staff. He retired in 1971 and lived in Kiev, where he worked as the deputy director of the Institute of Cybernetics of the Ukraine Soviet Socialist Republic's Academy of Sciences.
69 TsAMO RF, F. 72 gv. sd, op. 1, d. 17, l. 400.

kampfgruppe, having encountered stiff resistance from 3rd Battalion/229 Guards Rifle Regiment in Karnaukhovka, went around its left flank (through the positions of the penal company), and having penetrated 1.5 kilometers into the depth of the defenses, broke through to the area of two lakes. As noted in a combat report from the 24th Guards Rifle Corps, "… without encountering serious resistance, the enemy began to exploit the success in the direction of Hill 146.8, thereby creating a threat to the division's right flank."[70]

The right-hand *kampfgruppe* of Infantry Regiment 240, directed to drive into the depth of defense of the 72nd Guards Rifle Division's right flank, was steadily advancing toward the Titovka – Belgorod railroad (the reserve position of Losev's division), where two battalions of the 229th and 222nd Guards Rifle Regiments were located. The seizure of the railroad embankment would signify that the first, most difficult half of the day's objective – an advance of 4 kilometers to the railroad embankment had been accomplished – and now the road to the first stage's main objective, Hill 207 – would be open. At 0520 (Moscow time) Korps Raus reported:

> Situation at 0430 (Moscow time): the 320th Infantry Division with its right-flank regiment is located between the Donets and the railroad; east of Priiutovka, it broke through around a dike and reached the outskirts of Maslova Pristan'. The 106th Infantry Division has broken through to the northern outskirts of Maslova Pristan' and the eastern outskirts of Nizhnii Ol'shanets. The division is laying down bridges. The enemy air force has conducted only isolated attacks.[71]

However, the enemy still lacked the strength to make a decisive breakthrough. Therefore, after breaching the initial positions on the right flank of Balatov's regiment, the Germans halted the attack in order to gather strength, while simultaneously exchanging fire with the 3rd Rifle Battalion and remnants of the 66th Separate Penal Company. At this same time, having broken through the line of the 229th Guards Rifle Regiment's 2nd and 3rd Rifle Battalions and passed through the northeastern and northern outskirts of Maslova Pristan', troops of Infantry Regiment 239 were advancing toward the railroad.

An hour later, approximately at 0930, elements of both regiments of the 106th Infantry Division (a *kampgruppe* of Infantry Regiment 240 from the right, and Infantry Regiment 239 from the left), having encircled 3rd Battalion/229th Guards Rifle Regiment in Karnaukhovka, had reached the area of the railroad embankment while trying to envelop the 1st Battalion/229 Guards Rifle Regiment that was holding it. Meanwhile Infantry Regiment 241 had walled up the 2nd Battalion/229th Guards Rifle Regiment in Maslova Pristan' from the south and reached the railroad on the left flank of 2nd Battalion/229th Guards Rifle Regiment (the reserve regiment of the 72nd Guards Rifle Division), and was attempting to break through to Rzhavets. The commander of Maslova Pristan's garrison Senior Lieutenant V.A. Dvoinyi (the commander of the 2nd Rifle Battalion) contacted Major G.M. Batalov and having reported that his battalion had fallen into semi-encirclement and taken up an all-round defense, requested fire support.

The commander of the 229th Guards Rifle Regiment was in an exceptionally difficult situation; the defense of the forward battalions, which had been prepared over 3 months, had begun to collapse already within the first several hours of combat, yet he seemed unable to influence the situation. His calculations based on support from the division's artillery were proving to be unjustified; the "gunners" were firing on the attacking enemy, but only lightly and often wide of the mark. The Germans, as if on a training exercise, having generated a smokescreen and having

---

70 TsAMO RF, f. 24 gv. sk, op. 1, d. 14, l. 52.
71 NARA US, t. 312, r. 54, f. 7569605.

quickly thrown up light bridges, had crossed not only infantry but also field guns to the eastern bank and had begun to reduce the bunkers methodically. In addition, after sunrise, German assault guns appeared at Maslova Pristan'. Even though there was just a few of them, and observers had reported that three self-propelled guns had immediately been disabled by mines, and one had been knocked out by the artillerymen, this meant that a bridge for the heavy equipment was now ready, and that tanks could be expected to appear at any moment. Incidentally, the mentioned assault gun was knocked out by the crew of a howitzer, which was firing over open sights. Officers of the 7th Guards Army artillery headquarters reported:

> On the northern outskirts of Maslova Pristan', three self-propelled guns blew up on mines, and when they began to retreat, anti-tank guns set ablaze another six. The fire of the 122mm howitzers, acting as anti-tank guns, had a large effect on the enemy's morale. According to prisoners, when the soldiers saw how a self-propelled gun was turned into wreckage by a hit from a single 122mm shell, this strongly affected them.[72]

Thus, Raus's forces over approximately 7 hours overcame all of the artificial obstacles on the forward edge of the first line and made a penetration of 1.5 to 3.5 kilometers into the defenses of the 72nd Guards Rifle Division's right flank. In the process two forward battalions of the 229th Guards Infantry Regiment and the attached penal company had been cut up into several pieces, which were subsequently encircled, while *kampfgruppen* of the 106th Infantry Division had reached the reserve echelon of Losev's division and were trying to overwhelm it from the march. Simultaneously, Infantry Regiment 240 had driven a hole in the defenses of the 78th Guards Rifle Division's left-flank regiment and was tied up in fighting for possession of the major nest of resistance in Nizhnii Ol'shanets, and had even taken the southern end of the village. Raus's forces on the right were operating just as aggressively against Losev's division. Here, the 320th Infantry Division under the command of Major General G. Postel[73] launched a strong attack, having crossed the Northern Donets in the sector between Priiutovka and the mouth of the Nezhegol River. According to captured documents,[74] two of its regiments crossed the river practically side by side with the 106th Infantry Division (Infantry Regiment 586 – at Priiutovka, Infantry Regiment 587 – out of the Volkovo area) and closely cooperated with it. In the first hours of the offensive, they were supposed to take Priiutovka, and then having crossed the railroad embankment, they were to capture Rzhavets together with Infantry Regiment 241. At the same time Postel's third regiment (Infantry Regiment 585) was supposed to take the strongpoint of Bezliudovka. An account of Voronezh Front's engineer headquarters notes:

---

72 TsAMO RF, F. 7 gv. A, op. 5312, d. 539, l. 144.
73 Postel, Georg Wilhelm (Lieutenant General 01.09.1943) was born on 23 April 1896 in Zittau. He became a cadet on 20.08.1914 and received the rank of lieutenant on 29.09.1915. He took part in the First World War and was awarded the Iron Cross 1st and 2nd Class. In the inter-war period he continued to serve in the Reichswehr, then in the Wehrmacht; he commanded first an infantry company and then a battalion, and also served as an instructor in a military school in Munich. Between 5.07.1940 and 24.08.1942, he commanded Infantry Regiment 365. On New Year's Day of 1943, he took command of the 320th Infantry Division. The division arrived on the Eastern Front in January 1943, but in February it fell into encirclement at Khar'kov, but having quickly arranged closed cooperation with the headquarters of the SS corps outside the pocket, the pocket was breached rather quickly. For his skillful leadership of the troops during the fighting in Ukraine, Major General G. Postel on 28.03.1943 was awarded the Oak Leaves. On 10.07.1944 he turned over command of the division and led the XXX Army Corps for six days. At the end of the war he was captured by Soviet troops. He died on 20 September 1953 in a prison camp in Shakhty.
74 The order to the 320th Infantry Division's Infantry Regiment 587 for the offensive.

The 320th Infantry Division forced a crossing of the Northern Donets River … in two echelons: two battalions up and one back. The battalions were reinforced with a platoon of light guns and a detachment of anti-tank guns (three 75mm, 50mm and 45mm guns, a platoon of engineers from the division's Engineer Battalion 320 with two squads of minesweepers and one flamethrower team. The bridging equipment had been distributed among the first-echelon battalions. Each received 15 large inflatable boats, 13 small inflatable boats, 1 short bridge, and 1 inflatable raft. In addition, the II Battalion received an inflatable deck bridge with a 4-tonne load-bearing capacity, while the III Battalion received an inflatable deck bridge with an 8-tonne capacity. The time established for laying down the 4-tonne bridge was 2-2.5 hours, and 6-7 hours for the 8-tonne bridge.[75]

Before crossing the assault guns of Postel's infantry division to the eastern bank of the river, all of the regimental artillery and attached Flak guns were to work over the designated sectors intensively: "Drop the inflatable boats into the water simultaneously with a salvo from all types of weapons."[76] After the infantry moved out, three battalions of Artillery Regiment 320 shifted their fire to the east of where the assault groups were crossing the river, while 14 Panzerjäger Kompanie's anti-tank guns would open flanking fire on previously revealed firing positions. A bluish-gray cloud of propellant fumes, smoke and dirt hung in the air above the crossing sites, while smoke pots were lit in certain sectors with the aim of concealing the bridges from enemy observation. This hindered targeted fire by our artillery. Nevertheless, as archival documents testify, the 320th Infantry Division was unable as planned to complete the construction of bridges for crossing the anti-tank artillery in the first 3-4 hours of the offensive.

The actions of Postel's troops weren't distinguished by originality; like Raus's other formations, it operated according to a well-established routine. After a concentrated artillery barrage, with strong attacks the *kampfgruppen* split apart the defenses of the Soviet divisions "at seams" – at the boundaries, while tactically important places, like for example Rzhavets, although small in size and located already beyond the railroad embankment, were assaulted from the march or simply encircled by flanking units of the *kampfgruppen*. According to an operational summary of the 24th Guards Rifle Corps, the infantry of Infantry Regiments 586 and 587, accompanied by the intense fire of artillery and Nebelwerfers, already at 0920 had completely encircled Priiutovka, and from the south had reached the Rzhavets area through the boundary between 2nd Battalion/229th Guards Rifle Regiment and 1st Battalion/224th Guards Rifle Regiment, and was even fighting for possession of a cemetery in the southern portion of Maslova Pristan'. Thereby, by 1000 the pressure on Senior Lieutenant V.A. Dvoinyi's 2nd Rifle Battalion in Maslova Pristan' had substantially increased, and pincers were clearly forming out of the flank battalions of the 106th and 320th Infantry Divisions around the first company strongpoint in the reserve positions of the 72nd Guards Rifle Division.

It should be noted that the German breakthrough to Rzhavets and its ensuing capture were largely due to the cowardice of individual commanders that were holding important defensive sectors. A report from the chief of the SMERSH Counterintelligence Department of the Voronezh Front General Osetrov reveals:

> Kuznetsov, the commander of a machine-gun company of the 72nd Guards Rifle Division's 222nd Guards Rifle Regiment, demonstrated cowardice, abandoned his unit and fled to the rear. As a result of this, the machine-gun company's men were completely wiped out by the

---

75 TsAMO RF, F. 203, op. 2845, d. 227, l. 25.
76 Ibid.

enemy, and the Germans captured 12 intact Maxim heavy machine guns. The interrogation of eyewitnesses established that when fleeing to the rear, Kuznetsov tore off his epaulets.[77]

A dozen heavy machine guns positioned in bunkers were capable of breaking up more than one enemy attack in strength of up to two battalions of infantry. Deprived of such powerful fire support, the regiment's 2nd Rifle Battalion under the pressure of superior enemy forces was compelled to abandon Rzhavets.

Events developed swiftly on the left flank of Losev's division as well. Here, the troops of Korps Raus needed even less time to reach the division's second echelon. According to information found in the 24th Guards Rifle Corps' journal of combat operations, already within 30 minutes of the attack's opening, two battalions of Infantry Regiment 585 overran the positions of 3rd Battalion/224th Guards Rifle Regiment. At 0450 (Moscow time), the headquarters of Korps Raus reported: "Bezliudovka has been captured. Return enemy fire is not particularly intensive. The enemy has managed to cling only to the outskirts of Maslova Pristan'."[78] Having from the march taken the southeastern outskirts of Bezliudovka, Postel's grenadiers were blockading the village from the north and south, and after sunrise broke through the railroad embankment to the positions of 1st Battalion/222 Guards Rifle Regiment. It became clear – the Germans were striving to reach the southeastern fringe of the Shebekinskaia Dacha Woods through the battalion's right flank. The 24th Guards Rifle Corps commander N.A. Vasil'ev reported:

> At 0600 the enemy in strength of up to two infantry companies launched a human wave attack against the battalion's right flank. After two hours of a stubborn fire fight, which turned into close combat with hand grenades and hand-to-hand fighting in the trenches, the remnants of the enemy infantry fell back and took cover in the woods east of Bezliudovka. After a certain amount of time, the enemy, having worked over the 1st Battalion/222 Guards Rifle Regiment's area of defense with a 20-minute artillery barrage, focusing particularly on its right flank, again launched an attack with the forces of up to two battalions, which was successfully repulsed.[79]

On the first day of the offensive, in the course of overcoming the 7th Guards Army's main defensive belt, the German command attempted to make wide use not only of the standard measures for a breakthrough – concentrated fire and panzer attacks – but also special measures. One of them consisted in the fact that immediately after making a penetration, specially prepared groups of submachine gunners trained by Abwehr Kommando 204, led by experienced commando officers, infiltrated through the gap that had been created. Not uncommonly, they included former soldiers and commanders of the Red Army, who had gone over to the enemy's side. They were given a mission: without getting tied up in combat with forward elements, they were to reach command posts and observation posts of battalions, regiments and even divisions and wipe them out, thereby paralyzing the command and control of the defending units. On 5 July such an approach was tested by the enemy on the entire sector of Army Detachment Kempf's offensive, but the first to experience the widespread attacks by infiltrators were the forces on the left flank and center of Shumilov's 7th Guards Army.

---

77 *Ognennaia duga: Kurskaia bitva cherez glazami Lubianki* [Bulge of fire: Battle of Kursk through the eyes of the Lubianka] (Moscow, 2003), p. 51.
78 NARA US, t. 312, r. 54, f. 7569605.
79 TsAMO RF, F. 24 gv. sk, op. 1, d. 21, l. 14obr.

Early in the morning, at 0630 two groups of submachine gunners clad in Red Army uniforms in a number of up to two platoons each, bypassing fortified sectors, made their way into the rear of the 72nd Guards Rifle Division's left wing: one in the direction of the 224th Guards Rifle Regiment's command post; the other, having crossed the Nezhegol River (at the boundary between the 72nd Guards and 36th Guards Rifle Divisions), attempted to reach Titovka – a large, fortified village and railroad station located in the sector of the 36th Guards Rifle Division, but this latter group was met by fire from the 36th Guards Rifle Division's 106th Guards Rifle Regiment in the woods west of Titovka. These infiltrators were specialized elements of the XXXXII Army Corps. At 1740 (Moscow time), its operations department reported to Speidel's headquarters: "Our group for a reconnaissance-in-force had success in the area north of Nezhegol Station: 12 destroyed bunkers, 70 accurately counted enemy dead, 11 prisoners, 3 deserters and two machine guns. Our losses: 4 killed, between 16 and 20 wounded."[80] In the documents of the 36th Guards Rifle Division's headquarters there is also mention of this incident, but completely different data are given: over the day, the division lost just 34 killed and wounded.[81]

Two more groups of enemy infiltrators failed to score a substantial success, even though initially they posed a serious threat. The infiltrators encircled the command post of the 224th Guards Rifle Regiment on Hill 145.4 together with the regiment commander Major A.I. Ulosovets, and cut all the telephone lines. The regiment command switched to radio communications, and the personnel of the headquarters elements took up an all-round defense. A fierce battle began. A bit earlier, a different enemy group attacked the forward command post of the 1st Artillery Battalion of the 72nd Guards Rifle Division's 155th Guards Artillery Regiment, which was located closer to the combat positions of the 229th Guards Rifle Regiment. Deputy division commander T.Z. Vinogradov recalled:

> A similar situation arose at the observation post of our battalion commander N.I. Savchenko. Enemy submachine gunners appeared in the rear and isolated the command from their troops. Nikolai Ivanovich organized an all-round defense. Communications with the subordinate batteries was lost. Savchenko led his men to break out to the alternative observation post. Covering the withdrawal of his comrades, Private Kagirov tossed grenades at the charging Nazis, and then later, finding himself at the railroad embankment, spotted a machine gun. A dead soldier was lying next to it. Kagirov crouched down behind the machine gun and began to pour fire into groups of fascists, but soon ran out of ammunition ... Seeing a 45mm gun not far away, he rushed over to it and started to load it. There were enough shells to fire several rounds. Next Kagirov returned to our observation post, but several hours later he was sent to a hospital with a severe wound. In this battle, scout Anatolii Ivanovich Kagirov killed approximately 70 fascist solders, for which he was put up for the Order of the Red Star. Incidentally, Nikolai Ivanovich himself told me about his heroic actions.[82]

On 9 July 1943 the chief of the Voronezh Front's SMERSH Counterintelligence Department Major General N.A. Osetrov reported to Moscow:

> From the testimonies of prisoners captured in the area of the 7th Guards Army's 213th Rifle Division [the 72nd Guards Rifle Division's sector] it has been established that the infantry companies have groups consisting of 8-10 Ukrainians, and in addition in separate sectors

---

80 NARA US, t. 312, r. 54, f. 7569609.
81 TsAMO RF, F. 36 gv. sd, op. 1, d. 1, ll. 107-108.
82 Vinogradov, *Dorogoe – navsegda*, pp. 86-87.

[of the army's defense] groups of Russian Liberation Army soldiers dressed in Red Army uniforms are operating. The counterintelligence departments of the divisions have been given instructions to check this information through the unit commanders and to take steps to capture the traitors serving in the "Russian Liberation Army".[83]

A bit later, on 14 July, a reconnaissance patrol of the 69th Army captured an Senior Lance-Corporal of the 6th Panzer Division's Panzergrenadier Regiment 4, who provided information that a group of Ukrainians and Cossacks numbering up to 100 men were operating as part of his regiment. Under the direction of a German officer, they were engaged in reconnaissance and sabotage in the operational rear of the Soviet forces.[84] Thus, gradually the Soviet side began to get a clear picture of the significant scale of the use of these groups for the breakthrough by the Wehrmacht forces on this direction.

Striving to plug the expanding gap in his defenses, A.I. Losev decided to launch a counterattack with the forces of the second echelons of the forward regiments and of the division's reserve in the direction of the three main strongpoints of Maslova Pristan', Rzhavets and Bezliudovka, where the garrisons were holding out in encirclement. The counterattack's objective was to liberate the units of the 229th Guards and 224th Guards Rifle Regiments, and having pinned down the German units that had crossed at these villages, to prevent them from expanding the attack into the depth of the defenses. Considering the significant size of the village and its tactical importance (the main bridges of the 106th Infantry Division had been built here), the strongest counterattack was going to target Maslova Pristan'.

Losev made his intentions known to his corps commander and asked him to issue an order to the commander of the 78th Guards Rifle Division to launch a synchronized attack from the northeast against the enemy that had sealed off Karnaukhovka. N.A. Vasil'ev approved this decision and promised to help with an attack on the right flank, but emphasized that the forces from the army's reserve, which were assembled in the area of the Shebekinskaia Dacha Woods, would be ready for a counterattack to restore the situation in the sector of his division only between 1200 and 1300.

The division commander, having summoned Major Balatov to the radio, informed him that he was giving him the Dvoinyi's 3rd Rifle Battalion of the 222nd Guards Rifle Regiment, and the ordered him to counterattack along both sides of the road running between the "Poliana" State Farm and Maslova Pristan' and take the village with his 1st Rifle Battalion and the attached 3rd Rifle Battalion. Next, together with Dvoinyi's battalion he was to free the 229th Guards Rifle Regiment's 3rd Rifle Battalion that was trapped in Karnaukhovka.

The organization of the counterattack toward Bezliudovka was more difficult. Major A.I. Ulosovets was still at the regiment's encircled command post and fighting off the besieging enemy submachine gunners. Even though he continued to direct his subordinate units over the radio, this means of communication had known limitations. Therefore, despite the fact that the main forces of his regiment were fighting in the Bezliudovka area, in order to organize the counterattack toward the village the General Losev was forced to entrust this task to Major I.F. Popov, the commander of the 222nd Guards Rifle Regiment. He was supposed to move out 224th Guards Rifle Regiment's 2nd Battalion from the north and the 224th Guards Rifle Regiment's 3rd Battalion from the east, while the 222nd Guards Rifle Regiment's 1st Battalion was to strengthen their attack.

From the 24th Guards Rifle Corps' journal of combat operations:

---

83 *Ognennaia duga: Kurskaia bitva cherez glazami Liubanki*, p. 38.
84 TsAMO RF, F. 69A, op. 10765, d. 13, l. 11.

The 3rd Battalion/222nd Guards Rifle Regiment successfully advanced under strong enemy artillery fire, crossed the line of the railroad and pushed forward to the area of the church [in Maslova Pristan'], where it was counterattacked by a force of up to a battalion of infantry out of the direction of Karnaukhovka. Fighting off the enemy's counterattack, the battalion went over to a defense, anchoring its flanks on the railroad.

Units of the 78th Guards Rifle Division failed to launch the planned counterattack in the direction of Maslova Pristan', despite the repeated reports from the commander of the 78th Guards Rifle Division about the readiness, assembly and arrival of units. This significantly complicated the situation on the corps' right flank. By noontime, the units of the 72nd Guards Rifle Division were experiencing an acute lack of ammunition, especially in artillery shells. The commands of the division and corps took urgent steps in order to deliver ammunition supplies to the division's units.[85]

A.V. Skvortsov, the commander of the 78th Guards Rifle Division, was unable to render assistance to the neighboring 72nd Guards Rifle Division due to fully objective reasons. A very difficult situation was developing in the area of Nizhnii Ol'shanets: the Germans had already taken a third of this major strongpoint, and in the division's center and on its right flank several strong counterattacks were undertaken with the use of armor. However, the attempt by the division commander to stop the expansion of the bridgehead east of Solomino with the forces of 2nd Battalion/225th Guards Rifle Regiment brought no success. The division's defense was quickly losing operational stability, and it no longer had any reserves in order even to prop it up, not to mention to launch counterattacks in the sector of its neighbor. In addition to that, the 106th Infantry Division was able rather quickly to scatter the two attacking battalions of the 72nd Guards Rifle Division.

By this time, the 7th Panzer Division had already crossed a significant amount of its armor to the eastern bank. Sensing that the Russian counterattack was being conducted without tank support and only from one direction, Forst decided to cut off and destroy the 3rd Rifle Battalion that was tied up in heavy street fighting in Maslova Pristan'. Two companies of panzergrenadiers accompanied by 12 panzers rolled over the railroad embankment, and getting around the right flank of the 229th Guards Rifle Regiment 1st Battalion, pounced on it from the rear. However, this maneuver didn't dislodge the 1st Rifle Battalion. The Guardsmen didn't flinch and having adopted an all-round defense continued fighting, although their attack toward Maslova Pristan' had to be stopped. This perceptibly weakened the attack and left the company of the 222nd Guards Rifle Regiment 3rd Rifle Battalion that had broken through to the village center in a difficult situation.

The Guardsmen were fighting valiantly; Junior Lieutenant Sarsibai Tatiev, a platoon leader in 1st Battalion/229th Guards Rifle Regiment who was in the trenches in Maslova Pristan' back then remembered:

> Since the morning we had fought off several attacks, but when German self-propelled guns crossed the trenches to the right of my platoon, I had only 7 combat-capable men left. At this time two crews of Maxim heavy machine guns from a different unit drifted into my platoon area. This strengthened our positions, and they helped us repel four more attacks. Then the Germans opened up a concentrated artillery fire on our sector; several exploding shells almost simultaneously blanketed both machine-gun crews and killed some of my remaining guys as well. There were just two of us left, but when the Germans came at us again, there didn't seem to be as many of them either, so we fought off two more attacks with submachine guns. Thin lines of Germans were pinned down 10-15 meters from us and they began to hurl grenades; I

---

85 TsAMO RF, F. 24 gv. sk, op. 1, d. 21, l. 13.

replied, but to be honest, I was tossing anti-tank grenades at them, because they were all I had left. Our bullets also began to run out, and my partner began to load a drum. At this moment a German stick grenade landed between us. I rolled into a dugout in the wall of the trench, and thus grenade fragments only split my lip and embedded themselves in my leg and arm, but I remained alive. However, the soldier who'd been loading the drum was killed. My face was covered with blood, dirt had gotten into my eyes, but I knew my pistol was laying somewhere on the parapet, so I began to feel around for it, intending to shoot myself, but at that moment a German struck my head with a rifle butt and I was knocked unconscious. I came back to my senses that evening, when it felt like someone was kicking me in the side. It was a German officer; at first he pointed his pistol at me, likely planning to finish me off, but then he saw that I had opened my eyes and ordered his soldiers to load me on a stretcher and take me to a prisoner camp across the river, near Belgorod. That's how I wound up as a prisoner.[86]

To the above I might add that Junior Lieutenant S. Tatiev was lucky. Passing through several fascist prisoner camps, he survived. At the end of the war the Red Army liberated him, and in 1945, after the checking that was done on every person who returned to the Soviet Union from captivity, he was demobilized. Until the end of his days, he lived in Samarkand Oblast. Like hundreds and thousands of other former Soviet military prisoners, he experienced everything: the distrust of bosses when applying for jobs, restrictions in the professions he could pursue, side glances of his neighbors, hopelessness, special monitoring by the security organs with nighttime checks, periodic interrogations, the shouts of "Traitor!" and humiliations. However, he never became embittered, and steadfastly endured all the "burdens and deprivations", just as he once did at the front. After the first edition of this book came out, his daughter, Berdnikova Oktiabrina Sarsybaevna got in touch with me and told me about her father's hard fate. She sent me a copy of a letter they had sent to the USSR Ministry of Defense, the lines from which I have cited above.

During the fighting for Nizhnii Ol'shanets, the German command also attempted to use deserters and saboteurs dressed in Red Army uniforms in order to destroy unit command posts and cut lines of communication, but had no success. Then they were seated on assault guns as tank riders and used during so-called "psycho" attacks. After the assault guns reached the forward edge, the deserters in Red Army uniforms would leap from them, and when attacking the Guardsmen, would shout: "Russians surrender!", "Brothers, don't shoot, we're friendlies" and other such things. In addition, knowing that the units of the 72nd Guards Rifle Division had a significant number of men from the Central Asian republics, the enemy would use primarily Kazakhs, Tadzhiks and Kirghiz in such assault groups.

Even so, not all of Kempf's divisions succeeded in carrying out the assignments of the first stage (forcing a crossing of the river and seizing adequate bridgeheads in order to deploy the shock grouping on the eastern bank) as anticipated by 1100. Of all three panzer divisions and three infantry divisions (including the 168th Infantry Division) that took part in the initial assault, only half of them had success. The offensive of the 6th Panzer Division out of the Mikhailovka bridgehead and of the 168th Infantry Division at the boundary between Shumilov's and Chistiakov's armies were fully rendered abortive, as well as that of the left-hand *kampfgruppe* of the 19th Panzer Division out of the northern portion of Pushkarnoe. Indeed, if the failures of the other divisions of III Panzer Corps had an adverse effect on the progress primarily of only Army Detachment Kempf, then the failure of von Hünersdorff's 6th Panzer Division had more substantial consequences, particularly for the Fourth Panzer Army. All four attacks conducted by von Bieberstein's and Artmann's *kampfgruppen* out of the bridgehead against the positions of Morozov's Guardsmen

---

86 Author's personal collection.

resulted only in heavy losses. Even so, the division command still nurtured the hope of developing the insignificant success in the Staryi Gorod area, given the condition that armor could be shifted to that point. The attempt by Richter's *kampfgruppe* to split the 81st Guards Rifle Division's 238th Guards Rifle Regiment virtually accomplished nothing. To put it concisely, the concentrated fire by Soviet artillery on the crossing sites, including on the 60-tonne bridge that had been built for the Tiger tanks, thwarted Breith's scheme to shift the 6th Panzer Division's armor to this point. This was a major success for the 7th Guards Army, but unfortunately also a temporary one. Thanks to the proper organization of the defense and the tenacity of Morozov's Guardsmen, when at the most important and tense moment each unit mattered on the axis of the enemy's main attack, an entire panzer division and a substantial portion of a second were effectively rendered *hors de combat*.

Alongside this, only on the morning of 5 July did the command of Army Detachment Kempf begin to recognize that it didn't have sufficient knowledge of the 7th Guards Army's system of defenses, and therefore could make no prediction regarding how the offensive would go in the future. A briefing that Speidel sent to Army Detachment Kempf at 0925 noted: "The defensive line along the Donets, which extends back to the railroad, has primarily been breached. However, the impression is forming [!] that another strong defensive position runs along the railroad, which can be considered either the main line of resistance or a second defensive belt."[87]

This problem in turn gave rise to another one. After dawn it became clear that because of the serious underestimation of the elaborate system of Russian defenses and the stubbornness of their defenders, the calculations made to keep the artillery supplied with ammunition proved incorrect. At 1000 W. Kempf, who was still located near Belgorod,[88] informed his Operations Department over the telephone that "the expenditure of ammunition is extremely high; the artillery of III Panzer Corps has already fired off more than a standard combat load."[89] Fifteen minutes later, officers of the headquarters, who got in touch with the *Oberquartermeister*, related the information to him about the excessive expenditure of shells and the commander-in-chief's order to organize the in-time delivery of them. However, even in those places where certain progress was noted, as for example in the 7th Panzer Division's sector, the units that had broken through toward Razumnoe were in acute need for artillery support. This forced Army Detachment Kempf's headquarters at 1025 to make an unplanned request to VIII Fliegerkorps to assign dive bombers for a second attack in the area of Krutoi Log and Generalovka, since the Russians were conducting heavy fire on the bridges and the attacking *kampfgruppen* of von Funck's 7th Panzer Division from out of those areas. However, Seideman's headquarters of the VIII Fliegerkorps had to refuse this request, pointing to the fact that all if its aircraft had been sent to strike the area of the Oboian' highway.

Today, it is rather difficult to determine the time when each of Army Detachment Kempf's divisions undertook specific actions. This is not only because access to the combat documents of the Wehrmacht is rather difficult for Russian scholars. The point is that even though Operation Citadel's plan was well-prepared and had been intensively studied by the troops, especially its initial stage – the forced crossing of the Donets – nevertheless, reality forced significant corrections. During combat, the unit and formation commanders when making decisions didn't consider the plans and timetables as set down on paper, but primarily the real operational situation as it existed in the sector of offensive. There are also large problems with the Soviet archival sources.

---

87 NARA US, t. 312, r. 54, f. 7569605.
88 At this time, between 0700 and 1200 (Moscow time), the headquarters of Army Detachment Kempf was moving from the Novaia Bavariia railroad station (in the Khar'kov area) to Dolbino (in the Belgorod area) in order to be closer to the front.
89 NARA US, t. 312, r. 54, f. 7569605.

Operational information in them is often of a superficial nature. In addition, mistakes and slips of the pen were often made in the ongoing documentation on almost every level from the regiment right up to the *front* command. In a combat situation this isn't unusual, but in the summaries and combat reports for 5 July 1943 there is significantly more unreliable information than for typical days. The Operations Department of the 7th Guards Army was particularly guilty in this sense. By this time its chief had been replaced; Major General S.G. Lukin had become the chief of staff, and Major Vasil'ev had arrived to take over the Operations Department, along with several new officers. The "reseating" of the staff in the department didn't end with this. The abrupt change from the "tranquil period" in the army's life to the stressful combat routines also had a noticeable and detrimental impact on the accuracy of the headquarters' work. After three months of lull in the fighting, the first day of the defensive operation had passed, and the men in the headquarters began to stray from their routines and lose their sharpness due the stress of the round-the-clock fighting. That evening the Voronezh Front's chief of staff Major General S.I. Teteshkin admonished Major Vasil'ev:

> The results of the day with respect to the work of your department aren't stellar. The enemy is operating in mobile groups, the situation is dynamic, and ignorance of the real situation doesn't allow our command to take corresponding measures in order to counter the enemy … The information passed on by you doesn't show the enemy's final position or that of our forces. … The information is tardy and the contents leave something to be desired.[90]

Considering this circumstance, for the analysis of the combat operations I've been forced to use a significant quantity of not only direct sources, but also secondary ones. It is difficult to figure out at what time on 5 July how many tanks (or assault guns) of each division of the III Panzer Corps had managed to cross to the eastern bank of the Northern Donets River. It is known from a report of the 25th Guards Rifle Corps, which was later duplicated by the 7th Guards Army headquarters[91] that after 1100 up to 90 enemy tanks moved out of the Solomino – Nizhnii Ol'shanets bridgehead and penetrated into the depth of the 78th Guards Rifle Division's defenses. However, other documents – both Soviet (reports from the front) and German – testify that at this moment von Funck couldn't have assembled such significant forces here. From a report transmitted by a German reconnaissance aircraft that was intercepted by the Voronezh Front's 313th Separate Radio-Intelligence Battalion: "0625 (Moscow time): Our troops have reached the eastern outskirts of Nizhnii Ol'shanets, 500 meters east of the southern outskirts of Mikhailovka, and have forced a crossing of the Donets River 1.4 kilometers southwest of Dorogobuzheno."[92] As we can see, at this time there is still no mention of tanks that have crossed. Indeed, what tanks could have crossed, if the bridges still hadn't been completed? The first information approaching the truth that enemy armor had appeared on the eastern bank, and more importantly at what time, is revealed in Combat Report No. 194 from the Voronezh Front headquarters at 1235:

> By 1100 the enemy had crossed 6 tanks and 200 men to the eastern bank of the Northern Donets River from the Pushkarnoe area. The enemy has made no further advance from here. In the vicinity of Solomino up to 30 tanks crossed the river, 16 of which continued on in the

---

90 TsAMO RF, F. 203, op. 3834, d. 461, l. 22.
91 TsAMO RF, F. 7 gv. A,
92 TsAMO RF, F. 203, op. 2843, d. 452, l. 14.

direction of Dorogobuzheno and the rest toward the Razumnoe railyard. Six enemy tanks were disabled in the Solomino area [likely, they had triggered mines in their own minefield].[93]

The 78th Guards Rifle Division's combat diary gives similar figures: "By 1030 up to 30 tanks were operating in front of the division's sector" and "by 1135 the enemy had crossed 50 tanks."[94]

Thus the avalanche of armor, which Safiulin's headquarters reported, could not have been even according to Soviet records. The figure of "90 tanks" likely arose because the commanders often reported only one number – the total number of tanks that attacked his unit several times successively. For example, if there were three combat actions involving 15-20 attacking enemy machines, in a subsequent report they were transformed at a stroke: "The enemy, committing up to 60 tanks in the battle, broke through the regiment's (or division's) line of defense …" When laying out the course of events in this matter, it happened that the figures didn't appear out of thin air, and the commander wasn't lying, but the essence of the event has been twisted beyond recognition.

Relying on the documents found today in the Russian Federation's Central Archives of the Ministry of Defense, one can assert the following: Skvortsov's Guardsmen had joined in combat with panzers of von Funck's 7th Panzer Division, which attacked out of their bridgehead east of Solomino and at Dorogobuzheno, by approximately 0730. At this moment, up to 15 German armored fighting vehicles were operating on the eastern bank, possibly including several assault guns and Tigers. Relying on this armor support, with brief, strong attacks the German grenadiers gradually drove the battalions of the 228th and 225th Guards Rifle Regiments out of the first line of trenches to the second defensive line – the railroad embankment. Up until 1000 the 78th Guards Rifle Division continued to contain the simultaneous attack of three enemy divisions, but with increasing difficulty, and its strength was melting away. The assault groups of the 7th Panzer Division had already merged the two separate bridgeheads (at Solomino and Dorogobuzheno) into one, into which a constant stream of reinforcements were streaming across two major bridges and several light bridges, even though they were kept under Soviet artillery fire. The 7th and 19th Panzer Divisions in close cooperation with the 106th Infantry Division had seized the first trench line of the forward battalions of Skvortsov's division in four sectors (on the flanks and in the center of the 78th Guards Rifle Division, and in some places had even forced them to fall back to reserve positions, thereby creating the conditions for an attack by 19th Panzer Division's Panzergrenadier Regiment 73 and the 106th Infantry Division's Infantry Regiment 240 now into the flank of its neighbors – the 81st Guards and 72nd Guards Rifle Divisions.

Between 1000 and 1100, as was in fact planned, von Funck had succeeded in creating the conditions for a breakthrough into the depth of the 78th Guards Rifle Division on the axis of his panzer division's main attack, having formed an armored fist at Solomino, and set it in motion. Simultaneously, dozens of armored vehicles (panzers, assault guns, and halftracks) began moving out of two areas to the east with the support of infantry. Judging from an order issued by the commander of the 25th Guards Rifle Corps, already around 1030 Lieutenant Colonel Schülz (the commander of 7th Panzer Division's Panzer Regiment 25) launched an attack from Hill 108.9 along the road leading to the Razumnoe railyard (2 kilometers south of Razumnoe) with the forces of 20-25 panzers (possibly including a few assault guns) and not less than two battalions of infantry. The railyard was part of the line of reserve positions of the 78th Guards Rifle Division's first-echelon regiments, and was being held by one company of the 225th Guards Rifle Regiment and elements of 2nd Battalion/225th Guards Rifle Regiment that had fallen back.

---

93 TsAMO RF, F. 203, op. 2843, d. 431, l. 15.
94 TsAMO RF, F. 1225, op. 1, d. 16, l. 22.

The 78th Guards Rifle Division's commander was ordered to move the 3rd Battalion of the 223rd Guards Rifle Regiment to the railyard and to set up all the guns for conducting direct fire. The first German attack was thrown back, albeit with difficulty, and 17 armored vehicles were left smoking on the battlefield.

At the same time, the 6th and 19th Panzer Divisions were increasing their pressure on the flanks of the 228th Guards Rifle Regiment. Elements of Captain P.G. Iastrebov's 3rd Rifle Battalion (the 9th Rifle Company) were locked in heavy fighting in Dorogobuzheno with Gläsemer's *kampfgruppe* (7th Panzer Division's Panzergrenadier Regiment 7), which was reinforced by 16 panzers. Thus, the first massed panzer attack in the sector of the central panzer division of Breith's panzer corps in the course of Operation Citadel took place right after 1000. This tactical achievement was brought about by a number of factors. The primary one was the defenders' inadequate amount of anti-tank artillery and artillery to counter the enemy's superior forces. The command of the 78th Guards Rifle Division didn't have the capability to destroy the bridges right away either, which were being rapidly built in two main areas – the southern portion of Pushkarnoe to Dal'nie Peski, and at Solomino, while simultaneously battling with the enemy in Nizhnii Ol'shanets, which had broken through to the railroad and were now in the area of the Razumnoe railyard.

It isn't clear whether the company of Tigers that was attached to the 7th Panzer Division took part in the first panzer attack. According to von Funck's recollections, the Tigers (possibly, only some of them) were already on the eastern bank early that morning and were covering the sappers that were trying to clear a narrow passage between two swampy sectors, the Riaski Woods (south of Dorogobuzheno) and the ground north of Hill 108.9, through which Schülz's armored group in fact advance to make the attack on the railyard. However, the book of the British historian R. Cross *Operation Citadel* cited the recollections of a gunner in the crew of a Pz.Kpfw. VI of the Separate Heavy Panzer Battalion 503, who asserts that the Tiger company attached to von Funck's panzer division went on the attack only after noontime. Possibly, several Pz.Kpfw. VI tanks, which crossed at a ford together with the combat engineers, did take part in the first massed panzer attack, but the company's main forces were committed into the fighting only later that afternoon. This conjecture is supported by the fact that in the recollection of German tankers there is mention of clashes with T-34s, and Soviet tanks didn't appear in the 78th Guards Rifle Division's sector until between 1730 and 1800.

At 1040 (Moscow time) III Panzer Corps headquarters reported to Army Detachment Kempf:

> Presently the following bridges are ready: one bridge each with a 24-tonne capacity at Solomino and Pushkarnoe (south), and one 50-tonne bridge at Mikhailovka. Additional bridges should be completed by 1100. The 7th Panzer Division has reached the Razumnoe railyard. As a result of stubborn street fighting, Dorogobuzheno was left in our possession. The 19th Panzer Division is planning to advance from the labor corrective camp toward the railroad embankment, after which it will pivot to the north and seize the Kreida railyard.[95]

Pushing the 3rd Rifle Battalion's elements out of the Dorogobuzheno area still didn't mean that the 6th and 19th Panzer Division's *kampfgruppen* had fully broken the 228th Guards Rifle Regiment's resistance. Major I.A. Khitsov ordered Captain P.G. Iastrebov to withdraw his battered battalion to the reserve positions along the railroad to the sector: (excl.) southwestern outskirts of Razumnoe – railroad hut. Around 1330 the battalion arrived in the indicated area and took up a defense, with its 7th Rifle Company on the right, the 9th Rifle Company in the center, and the 8th Rifle Company on the left. At this moment, Gläsemer's units (up to a battalion

---

95 NARA US, t. 312, r. 54, f. 7569607.

of panzergrenadiers with 16 panzers), following on the foot heels of the companies that were withdrawing from the Dorogobuzheno area, attempted to break through to Razumnoe from the march, but the Guardsmen held fast. With rifle and machine-gun fire the German infantry was pinned to the ground, while the anti-tank guns of the anti-tank strongpoint under the command of Senior Lieutenant D.O. Grishin knocked out the first five tanks. As a result, the attack faltered and the Germans rolled back into the woods near Dorogobuzheno.[96]

One must pay due credit to A.V. Skvortsov and his neighbor I.K. Morozov; in a very difficult situation, they managed to retain command and control over all of their subordinate units, which enabled them to keep the situation under control, including on the left flank of the 81st Guards Rifle Division as well. However, they didn't get by without "costly" decisions either. From the account of the 78th Guards Rifle Division about its combat actions between 5 and 12 July 1943:

> Having met the stubborn resistance of the Dorogobuzheno garrison, at 1020 15 tanks and up to a battalion of infantry, bypassing the village, moved on toward the Razumnoe railyard, and reaching a bend in the road, attacked the left flank of 2/225th Guards Rifle Regiment. At 1025 17 tanks crossed the bridge west of Dorogobuzheno and attacked in the same direction. At 1040, both of the enemy combat groups reached the railyard. The intense machine-gun and mortar fire from our infantry prevented the enemy's motorized infantry from advancing behind the tanks, and this temporarily checked the armored fist, with which the Germans were striving to launch their main attack on this axis. At an order from the division commander, 3/223rd Guards Rifle Regiment was sent to reinforce the defenders of the Razumnoe railyard, and was given the assignment to launch a counterattack in cooperation with 2/225th Guards Rifle Regiment in order to regain the 225th Guards Rifle Regiment's initial position. At 1100 both battalions launched a counterattack from the line of the railroad at the railyard along the road toward Solomino, but the counterattack failed. Meanwhile, enemy tanks and vehicles loaded with infantry were continuing to approach the bridges in Solomino.[97]

Even this frontal attack by infantry against tanks, or the counterattacks launched earlier by the forces of Captain I.A. Matsokin's 2nd Rifle Battalion, from the outset had no hope to accomplish the missions they'd been given. The attacks were conducted without adequate supporting artillery fire against the bridgehead, where the enemy had concentrated significantly superior forces. Did the command of the 78th Guards Rifle Division recognize this? Unquestionably so, but it fundamentally it couldn't change anything. The order from superior command boiled down to one thing: to hold a position at any cost and the counterattacks testified to the resolve to carry it out. That was the entire logic of the situation. Indeed, it mattered that it was no less costly for them to hold a line, taking advantage of the elaborate network of trenches and fortifications.

After the breakthrough by Schülz's *panzerkampfgruppe* to the Razumnoe railyard and the seizure of Dorogobuzheno by Gläsemer's *kampfgruppe*, the situation on the left flank of the 78th Guards Rifle Division became critical. At 1105 10 tanks with up to a company of tank riders aboard reached the orchard next to the railroad 1 kilometer east of Nizhnii Ol'shanets. The pressure on the defenses in the area of the northern outskirts of this village intensified. Considering that according to information of the 78th Guards Rifle Division's scouts, the Germans at Solomino had already crossed up to 50 tanks and 4 batteries of rocket-launchers to the eastern bank by 1135, this threatened not only the fall of Nizhnii Ol'shanets and the reserve positions along the railroad, but also an enemy breakthrough to Krutoi Log. Around 1400 under the

---

96 TsAMO RF, F. 78 gv. sd, op. 1, d. 37, l. 21.
97 TsAMO RF, F. 1225, op. 1, d. 11, l. 104.

increasing pressure of superior enemy forces, the 78th Guards Rifle Division was forced to go over to a mobile defense.[98]

Until the middle of the day, Korps Raus continued stubbornly to push ahead. Shrugging off heavy casualties, by 1200, relying on the support of the Flak regiments and assault guns, the 106th and 320th Infantry Divisions had fractured the defenses of both forward regiments of the 72nd Guards Rifle Division in several places. Having isolated company and battalion strongpoints in the villages of the main line of resistance, they were pushing toward the reserve positions along the railroad, and in certain places had even broken into the system of trenches here. The situation in the Nizhnii Ol'shanets – Karnaukhovka – Maslova Pristan' sector was particularly critical for the Soviet side. This area contained the boundary between the 25th and 24th Guards Rifle Corps, and a breach had been formed in the main line of resistance here already in the first two hours of the offensive. According to the intelligence of the 7th Guards Army's engineer headquarters, by 1100 the Germans had managed to complete the construction of 26-30 bridges of varying load capacities along a 25-kilometer sector, where their main forces were crossing the river. Thanks to this, by 1135 not only a substantial amount of the armor of the 7th Panzer Division had assembled in the bridgehead east of Solomino, including the company of Tigers, but also some of the artillery. Almost simultaneously, the assault guns of StuG Battalion 905 began crossing the 24-tonne pontoon bridge of the 106th Infantry Division at Maslova Pristan'. Thus the German command already had the possibility to expand the breach in the 7th Guards Army's first defensive belt substantially, and subsequently the bridgeheads would only continue to grow.

Thus, summing up the results of Army Detachment Kempf's first 8-10 hours of the offensive, particular attention should be paid to two important problems that stood before its leadership. First, the cost of the tactical successes that had been achieved in this period of time was high. Judging from captured documents, both for Kempf and his subordinates this was a definite surprise. Already the initial reports from the combat units were festooned with information about heavy casualties. Unquestionably the main reason for this was the effective system of defense constructed by the Soviet side along the main line of resistance. Secondly, it was obvious that a sweeping advance hadn't happened and was not yet even in the picture. For the *kampfgruppen* of Breith's panzer corps and Korps Raus, even for those that had seized the first line of trenches of the Guards regiments, the Russians' stubborn resistance came as a shocking surprise. It was totally clear that so far combat was underway with only the Soviet division's first echelons that were holding the main defensive belt, and the Germans could expect all-out fighting in the depth of these division's positions, as well as at the second army-level defensive belt. Indeed, the main surprise by the Soviet command was the counterattacks made by tanks and infantry. Raus's troops would feel their effect already on the afternoon of 5 July.

M.S. Shumilov possessed significant combat experience and a well-developed intuitive sense; he perfectly understood the strong and weak aspects of his forces's defenses, and likely had already determined for himself several most likely alternatives for the way the situation might develop. Thus in the pre-dawn hours while at his command post, he attentively analyzed the information that was coming in, trying to determine which one of the anticipated scenarios the offensive would follow. Having familiarized himself with the initial reports, Shumilov understood that the Germans were launching an attack with significant forces on a front of approximately 30 kilometers, and thus he couldn't contain them only with the corps' own reserves. At this moment, the main thing was to determine accurately which of the corps commanders needed priority help. Already at 0430 he issued an order to the chief of his Operations Department Major Vasil'ev to

---

98 TsAMO RF, F. 25 gv. sk, op. 1, d. 27, l. 3.

get in touch with Colonel I.E. Buslaev, the commander of his combined-arms reserve – the 213th Rifle Division, and to pass along an order to him to bring his division to full combat-readiness. An hour later, at 0530, the commander of the 213th Rifle Division received an order regarding his subordination to Major General N.A. Vasil'ev, the commander of the 24th Guards Rifle Corps. Several conversations between M.S. Shumilov and his subordinate corps commanders preceded this decision.

The following picture had emerged from these discussions. As was anticipated, the Germans were putting heavy pressure on the army's right flank and center with significant forces. However, thanks to the artillery grouping on the right wing, all of the bridges opposite the 81st Guards Rifle Division had been sealed off, and the German infantry that were attempting to cross the Donets River in boats were being decimated by the forward battalions of Morozov's 81st Guards Rifle Division. In contrast, the army commander was alarmed by the situation on the boundary between the two rifle corps, and especially on the right flank of the 24th Guards Rifle Corps. Major General A.I. Losev's 72nd Guards Rifle Division had a minimum of reinforcements, and therefore the enemy was quickly crossing significant forces of infantry with light guns and mortars not only in boats, but also across light bridges that had been quickly thrown up opposite his front. Six bridges alone had been discovered at Toplinka and Karnaukhovka. As a result, already after two hours pincers had clearly formed, with which the Germans were trying to encircle the 72nd Guards Rifle Division. Its forward edge had been breached on its flanks, and street fighting was going on in the villages of Nizhnii Ol'shanets and Bezliudovka; the enemy had also scored a clear success in the area of Maslova Pristan'.

The German advances on the right flank of the 24th Guards Rifle Corps had aggravated the situation in the sector of the 78th Guards Rifle Division that was difficult even without this. A bridgehead had been created at Solomino, in which significant infantry forces had already accumulated, while groups of submachine gunners along the river's basin had spread out along the entire front opposite the 78th Guards Rifle Division; fighting was underway in Dorogobuzheno and Dal'nie Peski. In separate sectors, the regiment commanders were launching counterattacks with their reserves, in order to drive the Germans out of the first series of trenches. In this situation only one thing was encouraging – there had been no sign of any large enemy activity opposite the 36th Guards Rifle Division and at the boundary with the 57th Army. This allowed Shumilov to hope that it was still possible to use the army's reserves. In so doing, with respect to his left flank Shumilov decided to hedge his bets and left the 15th Guards Rifle Division in its positions as part of the 24th Guards Rifle Corps, supposing that this quiet on the left might be deceiving and in the nearest future the Germans would nevertheless strike the boundary between the Voronezh and Southwestern Fronts. Moreover, at dawn they were already probing the sector of the 36th Guards Rifle Division.

Thus at 0630 M.S. Shumilov issued a preliminary order to the commander of the 24th Guards Rifle Corps N.A. Vasil'ev to withdraw the 213th Rifle Division from its area of defense on the western and southwestern fringes of the Shebekinskaia Dacha Woods to the Ustinka – Rzhavets road and to ready it for a counterattack together with the 27th Guards Tank Brigade and units of the 72nd Guards Rifle Division's second echelon with the aim of restoring the corps' front. The situation in the 7th Guards Army's sector finally became clear for the army commander around 1000. By this time, the axis of the main attack of Army Detachment Kempf had clearly materialized – against the line of the 78th and 72nd Guards Rifle Divisions. Thus the decisions made by the army command and its subordinate corps commands at this moment were directed primarily at blocking the attempt by the 7th and 19th Panzer Divisions to breach completely the reserve positions (along the Titovka – Belgorod railroad) in the sector of Skvortsov's 78th Guards Rifle Division and destroying the forces of Korps Raus that had already crossed this line in the sector of Losev's 72nd Guards Rifle Division.

It should be particularly emphasized that the success of Morozov's 81st Guards Rifle Division, which not only repulsed the attack by the 6th and 19th Panzer Division's assault groups, but also had completely thwarted the crossing attempt by von Hünersdorff's 6th Panzer Division, was very important for the command of the 7th Guards Army and especially for that of the 25th Guards Rifle Corps. G.B. Safiulin used the fruits of this success already during the morning hours of 5 July, having begun to regroup his reserves from the corps' right flank to its left.

The 7th Guards Army commander remained in constant contact with the operational headquarters groups of both of his subordinate corps commanders. Between 1000 and 1100 he made contact over the Baudot device with Safiulin, who informed him that the situation on the right flank of his 25th Guards Rifle Corps was stable, and that Morozov's 81st Guards Rifle Division had thrown back every attack, while the German bridges had been destroyed (according to his information, there had been four of them). The situation was developing much more adversely for Skvortsov; enemy combat groups in strength of up to a battalion of infantry had shoved back the right flank of the 78th Guards Rifle Division and bitter fighting was underway on the boundary with the 81st Guards Rifle Division. Its division commander Morozov was ready to shift some of his own reserves and those of his regiments to his left flank, but so far he'd been unable to do so because despite the heavy fire, the Germans were continuing to attack out of Mikhailovka at the boundaries of his forward regiments. Several dozen German tanks out of the Solomino area had broken through to the Razumnoe railyard, and the battalion of the 225th Guards Rifle Regiment that was holding Nizhnii Ol'shanets was fighting in semi-encirclement. If Skvortsov couldn't be helped with artillery, then in the near future the enemy might reach the reserve positions along the railroad embankment, at which point it would be difficult to hold the division's sector without the commitment of substantial reserves.

Next, the 25th Rifle Corps' commander reported on the steps he'd taken to straighten out the situation. The relatively stable situation on the right flank allowed him first to redirect some of the heavy artillery and mortars (the 265th and 161st Guards Cannon Artillery Regiments and 2/290th Mortar Regiment) to target and destroy the bridges in the Dal'nie Peski – Dorogobuzheno – Solomino sector, and second to regroup the 73rd Guards Rifle Division into the 78th Guards Rifle Division's sector, depending on how the situation developed, either to launch a counterattack against the German grouping in the Solomino – Dorogobuzheno area (which had been planned back when preparing for the battle), or to create a strong backstop behind Skvortsov's 78th Guards Rifle Division along the Generalovka – Gremiachii line, because according to his assessment, that was where the Germans might concentrate significant armor forces in the next several hours. By this moment, Kozak's 73rd Guards Rifle Division had already assembled on the line running from the woods north of the "Batratskaia Dacha" State Farm to the woods south of there. The army commander approved these decisions and in turn informed the 25th Guards Rifle Corps commander that he was to receive operational control of the 309th Guards Mortar Regiment of Katiusha rocket-launchers, which had been given to the 7th Guards Army from out of Voronezh Front's reserve.

The air forces at the disposal of the Voronezh Front command should have been an important instrument in preventing Kempf's forces from crossing the river and to inflict heavy losses on them during the attempt. However, due to a number of reasons, this didn't happen. First, in the morning hours because of the heavy consequences of the unsuccessful strikes against the enemy airfields, its forces couldn't be used in full. After dawn, some of the aviation regiments of Lieutenant General S.A. Krasovsky's 2nd Air Army were bringing themselves back to order and counting up their losses while the rest of them were on missions to the Fourth Panzer Army's sector. Before noontime, Lieutenant General V.A. Sudets, the commander of the Southwestern Front's 17th Air Army, received an order to prepare two aviation corps for operations in the sector of the neighboring Voronezh Front on the right, against the bridges on the Northern Donets River. At 1200 Sudets sent a preliminary order to the commanders of the 3rd and 9th Composite Aviation Corps about assigning crews and issuing orders for a mission to destroy the bridges in the Maslova Pristan' – Solomino – Volkovo – Karnaukhovka – Ivanovka – Bezliudovka area. An hour later, the green light was given for the mission by the 17th Air Army's chief of staff. In the confirming order, he emphasized that because of the unclear operational situation in the 7th Guards Army's sector, the bombers could only strike the western bank of the Northern Donets and the bridges themselves; the crews were to view the eastern bank as the line of friendly forces. In order to carry out this mission, in addition to the two composite aviation corps (the 209th, 305th and 306th Storm Aviation Divisions, plus 18 bombers of the 244th Bomber Aviation Division), which were to be covered by groups of fighters from the 207th and 295th Fighter Aviation Divisions, one formation of the 2nd Air Army would also take part in the mission – the 266th Storm Aviation Division of the 1st Storm Aviation Corps.

At 2000 that same evening, the chief of staff of the 1st Storm Aviation Corps Colonel Il'in noted in his Operational Summary No. 102 that 37 individual combat sorties were flown in the course of 5 July to the sector of the 7th Guards Army, of which 17 were carried out by the 266th Storm Aviation Division. Subsequently, he wrote: "During operations against tanks and bridges in the sector of the 7th Guards Army in the Krutoi Log – Razumnoe – Solomino – Bezliudovka area, 10 tanks and around 30 vehicles were destroyed or damaged; the fire of 4 anti-aircraft artillery guns was suppressed[and 3 bridges and 8 bunkers were destroyed. One Il-2 failed to return from the mission and one Il-2 had to make a forced landing."[99] According to information from the 17th Air Army command, its air groups destroyed four bridges, and knocked out 2 tanks and 42 vehicles. To this it should be added that the pilots of Colonel I.S. Polbin's 1st Bomber Aviation Corps of the 2nd Air Army flew 117 aircraft sorties against the attacking enemy in the course of the day. They were able to drop their lethal loads primarily on villages occupied by Hoth's *kampfgruppen*, although some of the Pe-2 bomber crews worked over the 19th Panzer Division's assembly area – the village of Pushkarnoe.

The reaction from the headquarters of Kempf's forces to the growing activity of the Soviet pilots and crews as found in captured documents became discernable only between 1600 and 1700 (Moscow time); both of its subordinate corps reported about this at almost the same time. However, judging from these reports, the situation for them wasn't critical, much less catastrophic, since despite the efforts made by the aviation corps, they were not only unable to disrupt the plans of Breith and Raus, but even to stop the crossing of the Northern Donets River for a sufficiently long time. The reasons for this were several.

In the first place, by this time the bulk of the enemy's attacking forces had already crossed the river and was advancing into the depth of the Guardsmen's defenses of the main belt of resistance, and bridgeheads had been established for the accumulation of strength on the eastern bank. In some places not only major load-bearing bridges had been completed, but the armor and heavy weapons had already crossed them.

In the second place, realizing how defenseless troops were on the march against enemy airstrikes, the German command provided serious Flak cover for their places of assembly on the eastern bank and the bridges themselves. Moreover, some of the Flak units had shifted to the eastern bank as a matter of top priority, where for the rest of the entire day they were used as intended, as anti-aircraft guns, as well as to destroy fortified firing positions. In this respect, the German command wasn't acting according to routine. For example, according to Korps Raus' offensive plan, after the creation of the bridgeheads, Flak Regiment 7 was supposed to pull out of its positions and already at 1300 (Moscow time) such an order was received. However, the situation was developing in a way

---

99 TsAMO RF, F. 1 gv. shak, op. 1, d. 20, l. 6.

that was far from that which had been anticipated. Thus, in a briefing to Speidel's headquarters, Raus noted that "because of the order about transferring Flak Regiment 7, at present the air and ground defenses can't be fully guarded."[100] After this message arrived, 90 minutes later the regiment was returned to him, though it was now intended for carrying out different tasks. However, Army Detachment Kempf managed to work out this problem quickly with the headquarters of the Luftwaffe's 10th Flak Artillery Division.

In the third place, the 17th Air Army's aviation formations that had been assigned to fly missions to the 7th Guards Army sector were staffed by men who had very few hours of flight time, not to mention any combat experience. For example, in the 306th Storm Aviation Division's 951st and 995th Storm Aviation Regiments, only a total of 7 men had flown combat missions, and the results of an inspection conducted on 3 July 1943 speaks eloquently about the level of professional training of the 995th Storm Aviation Regiment:

> Over its time in the reserve, the aviation regiment conducted no aerial gunnery, bombing, or aerial combat training, nor did it even rehearse formation flying or cross-country flights, while 8 pilots were sent back to a front airbase aboard a Douglas airplane because they were unable to fly an Il-2 independently. The rest of the pilots hadn't fully completed the first stage of the program for retraining in the Il-2 aircraft, but having on average 2 flights in a zone and 25 flights in a circle, they were sent on to the front.[101]

In addition, ground attack aircraft alone couldn't carry out the assigned mission, but the number of bombers that appeared above the battlefield was clearly inadequate. From the first day of the defensive operation, the 1st Bomber Aviation Corps, because of the lack of covering fighters in the 2nd Air Army, took part in few raids. This substantially reduced the effectiveness of the work of Krasovsky's air army, and prevented the launching of concentrated bombing strikes, including against the western bank of the Donets River in the first several days of the battle.

As already seen, over the first nine hours of Army Detachment Kempf's offensive, combat actions primarily unfolded in the main positions (between the river channel and the railroad embankment) of the divisions that were holding the main defensive belt. Only on the left flank of the 72nd Guards Rifle Division did a combat group of the 320th Infantry Division cross the railroad embankment by mid-day, where it attempted to crush the 1st Battalion/222 Guards Rifle Regiment that was positioned in the second series of trenches. Raus still didn't have enough strength on the eastern bank to drive back even half of the forward battalions to the reserve positions. His corps and the entire Army Detachment Kempf first began to contemplate a decisive drive into the depth of the 7th Guards Army's defenses between approximately 1000 and 1100, when the possibility appeared to use panzers and assault guns. Even so, at first these were only probing attacks in small groups, and the first massed attack using tanks would be launched only that afternoon. Yet it was at that time that the ground attack aviation division would be able to make weighty assistance to the Guardsmen.

Around noontime, savage fighting erupted at Rzhavets (1 kilometer south of Maslova Pristan'), which was located beyond the railroad, and Raus, fearing that the Russians would hurl tanks that had been spotted in the area of Titovka (the 148th Separate Tank Regiment) against the infantry that were assaulting the village, immediately directed some of the self-propelled guns to Rzhavets. The journal of combat operations of the 24th Guards Rifle Corps notes: "… at 1300 the enemy completed a bridge in Karnaukhovka as well, after which infantry, artillery, mortars and

---
100 NARA US, t. 312, r. 54, f. 7569607.
101 TsAMO RF, F. 306 shad, op. 1, d. 14, l. 25.

The commander of the 64th Army (subsequently the 7th Guards Army) Lieutenant General M.S. Shumilov in Stalingrad, before departing to the Belgorod area; end of February 1943. (RGAFKD)

The spring of 1943 came early: This is how the roads in the region of the Kursk bulge looked. (RGAKFD)

The city of Belgorod after the March 1943 fighting came to an end. (Captured files of the RGAKFD)

The commander of the 7th Guards Army Lieutenant General M.S. Shumilov washes up in the village of Protopopovka, Kursk Oblast, on a sunny April 1943 morning. (A photo from an issue of the *Krasnaia znamia* newspaper in the files of the "Stalingradskaia bitva ("Battle of Stalingrad") State Historical Park Museum)

In moments of calm, even army commanders had no objection to a little mischief. Lieutenant General M.S. Shumilov (on the right) has a little fun at the expense of a major on his 7th Guards Army headquarters staff, who is showing his "booty" to correspondents of the *Krasnaia znamia* army newspaper; village of Protopopovka, Kursk Oblast, April 1943. (A photo from an issue of the *Krasnaia znamia* newspaper in the files of the "Stalingradskaia bitva" State Historical-Memorial Park Museum)

The Commander-in-Chief of the Voronezh Front General of the Army N.F. Vatutin (in the center) receiving a report from one of his subordinate commanders during one of his trips to the front; spring of 1943. (RGAKFD)

A major, a battalion commander in one of the 81st Guards Rifle Division's regiments, addresses his subordinate commanders; Voronezh Front, 7th Guards Army, May 1943. (Files of the "Stalingradskaia bitva" State Historical-Memorial Park Museum)

Commanders of the 27th Guards Tank Brigade study a mock-up of the terrain in its sector, June 1943. (RGAKFD)

T-34 radio operators of the 7th Guards Army's 27th Guards Tank Brigade in training: Sergeant Major Babushkin maintains contact with a tank battalion commander, May 1943. (Shebekino Historical-Art Museum)

The training of driver-mechanics in the 201st Separate Tank Brigade to overcome artificial obstacles. The tanks are Lend-Lease British Matilda tanks.

A training brochure issued on the eve of the Battle of Kursk to anti-tank gun, tank and artillery crews entitled "The most vulnerable and damage-prone places on the German Pz-VI tank and the means to counter them". The page on the right states, "Fire at the fuel tanks and forward wheels".

Tank company commander Senior Lieutenant F. Martekhov (first from the right) of the 7th Guards Army's 27th Guards Tank Brigade, who for his exploits in the Belgorod area on 12 July 1943 was deemed worthy of the title "Hero of the Soviet Union", in conversation with a group of the brigade's officers and soldiers at his dugout during a moment of rest; village of Voznesenovka, May 1943.

The commander of the 7th Guards Army Lieutenant General M.S. Shumilov (third from the right) and the chief of the Army's motorized transport pool Lieutenant Colonel Ia.T. Savchenko (fourth from the right) talk with a group of commanders of the motorized transport service. In the background on the left, a sector of barbed wire in a defensive belt is visible; June 1943. (Archive of the "Kurskaia bitva. Belgorodskoe napravlenie" ("Battle of Kursk. Belgorod axis") Museum-Diorama.

> Lesen und weitergeben!
>
> **GRENADIERE der 168. ID!**
>
> Man hat Euch überzeugt, daß die Kriegsgefangenen in russischer Gefangenschaft hungern. In Wirklichkeit sieht es anders aus!
>
> TÄGLICHE RATION DER KRIEGSGEFANGENEN:
>
> 700 Gramm Brot   500 Gramm Kartoffeln
> 250 Gramm Gemüse   40 Gramm Fett
> 150 Gramm Fleisch   30 Gramm Zucker
> 100 Gramm verschiedener Hülsenfrüchte, zweimal warmes Essen, morgens und abends Tee; 20 Gramm Tabak, sowie monatlich 150 Gramm Seife.

A Soviet leaflet calling upon grenadiers of the 168th Infantry Division to surrender, found near Belgorod in 2007. (Author's personal archive)

Soldiers of one of the first-echelon divisions of the 7th Guards Army head out for their shift to man a combat outpost in the basin of the Northern Donets River; June 1943. (RGAKFD)

The commander of Army Detachment Kempf General W. Kempf. (Captured photo. Author's personal archive)

The commander of the III Panzer Corps General H. Breith; February 1943. (Captured photo. Author's personal archive)

General-Instructor of Panzer Troops Colonel General H. Guderian (in the first row, second from the left) during a meeting in II SS Panzer Corps' SS Panzergrenadier Division *Leibstandarte Adolf Hitler* of Hoth's Fourth Panzer Army. Standing next to Guderian on his left is the commander of the SS Panzergrenadier Division *Das Reich* Lieutenant General G. Keppler. It was the II SS Panzer Corps that was supposed to act in close cooperation with Army Detachment Kempf. Khar'kov, April 1943. (Bundesarchiv, Bild 101III-Wiesebach-152-11A, photo: Wiesebach)

H. Guderian (second from the right) examines the new Pz.Kpf. VI Tiger tanks equipping SS Panzergrenadier Division *Leibstandart Adolf Hitler*'s heavy panzer company. This particular tank is a *Panzerbefehlswagen* command tank carrying the tactical number 100). SS Captain Heinrich Kling, the commander of the heavy panzer company (on the right) is giving an explanation. Khar'kov, April 1943. (Bundesarchiv, Bild 101III-Wiesebach-152-14A, photo: Wiesebach)

General of Panzer Troops E. Raus, the commander of Korps Raus, during Operation Citadel. Belgorod area, July 1943. (Bundesarchiv, Bild 146-1984-019-28, photo: Wolff/Altvater)

Senior Lieutenant V.M. Moiseev, the commander of one of 7th Guards Army's artillery batteries, conducts observation with the use of a BSD scissors telescope on the Belgorod axis; Voronezh Front, July 1943. (RGAKFD)

An artillery battalion of the 7th Guards Army's 265th Cannon Artillery Regiment shells the enemy's bridges across the Northern Donets River; July 1943. (Author's personal archive)

A crew of a German 150mm howitzer fires at positions of the Guardsmen; Belgorod area, July 1943. (Captured photo, RGAKFD)

The commander of the 25th Guards Rifle Corps Lieutenant General G.B. Safiulin; a 1944 photograph. (TsAMO RF)

The commander of the 78th Guards Rifle Division Major General A.V. Skvortsov. (TsAMO RF)

Assistant platoon commander Senior Sergeant I. Artem'ev of a submachine gun company of the 7th Guards Army's 78th Guards Rifle Division in firing positions with his company in the area of the village of Solomino; July 1943. (RGAKFD)

The commander of the 81st Guards Rifle Division Major General I.K. Morozov; a 1945 photograph. (TsAMO RF)

The commander of the 235th Guards Rifle Regiment G.T. Skiruta; a 1945 photograph. (TsAMO RF)

Sergeant N.N. Ivanov's anti-tank rifle squad in positions on the Northern Donets River; July 1943. (RGAKFD)

The commander of the 72nd Guards Rifle Division Major General A.I. Losev at a forward observation post; July 1943. (RGAKFD)

The explosion of a German tank in a minefield. In the foreground is a case for bottles containing an incendiary mixture that was hurled aside by the explosion; July 1943. (TsAMO RF)

A crew of a 37mm M1943 Flak gun, which has been mounted on a truck, fires at Soviet ground assault aircraft in the vicinity of bridges across the Northern Donets River in the Belgorod area. July 1943. (Bundesarchiv, Bild 101I-022-2926-38, photo: Wolff/Altvater)

A Kazakh member of the Russian Liberation Army serving in a company of III Panzer Corps, which was used in the course of Operation Citadel in order to destroy Soviet command posts and communications, clarifies a combat task with a German Sergeant. July 1943. (Bundesarchiv, Bild 101I-022-2916-13A, photo: Wolff/Altvater)

Tankers of one of the companies of III Panzer Corps' Heavy Panzer Battalion 503 examines the location of a hull hit in their Tiger tank from an armor-piercing shell fired by a Soviet gun. July 1943. (Bundesarchiv, Bild 101I-022-2935-25A, photo: Wolff/Altvater)

The commander of the 3rd Battalion of the 73rd Guards Rifle Division's 214th Guards Rifle Regiment; a photograph that was touched up with an airbrush after the war. (RGAKFD)

A Maksim heavy machine-gun crew of a tank brigade's motorized rifle battalion provides supporting fire for a company that is defending a village somewhere in the sector of the 7th Guards Army; July 1943. (RGAKFD)

tanks began increasingly to cross the Northern Donets River. The forced crossing of the river was conducted particularly rapidly in the Toplinka – Ivanovka sector."[102]

At 1230, both of Raus's infantry divisions completed the encirclement of the company and battalion strongpoints of Karnaukhovka, Maslova Pristan', Bezliudovka and in the woods north of Bezliudovka, and also took possession of two fortified villages in the reserve positions of the 72nd Guards Rifle Division, Rzhavets and the whistle stop of Kar'ernaia. However, they couldn't completely stamp out the resistance of the isolated garrisons, even having strengthened the supporting artillery grouping. The German combat groups were tied down in heavy fighting and had no success in developing the breakthrough into the depth of the 72nd Guards Rifle Division's line, even though isolated groups of German infantry were already "roaming" in the division's rear. The command post of the 224th Guards Rifle Regiment was still isolated. It became possible to free it only that afternoon, when Major A.I. Ulosovets called down artillery fire on his own location.

The elements of the 229th Guards Rifle Regiment that were defending the major village of Karnaukhovka[103] fell into a particularly difficult situation. In the first minutes of the offensive, the main attack of two battalion-sized groups of the Infantry Regiment 240 struck the village, which was being defended only by one reinforced company of the 3rd Rifle Battalion. The Guardsmen were fighting self-sacrificingly, and only thanks to their tenacity and resolve was the strongpoint held. However, in war, anything can happen and does. At a most difficult and critical moment, the nerves of one of the platoon commanders gave out, and he not only fled the battlefield, he issued an order for his entire platoon to retreat. The Voronezh Front's SMERSH Counterintelligence Department later reported: "Commander Pavlov (1922 year of birth, a native of Moscow and member of the VLKSM [All-Union Leninist Youth League]), a platoon commander in the 7th Rifle Company of the 72nd Guards Rifle Division's 229th Guards Rifle Regiment withdrew his platoon to the rear without an order from higher command, willfully abandoning the occupied line of defense. Under interrogation Pavlov recognized his complete guilt, explaining his crime by his personal cowardice."[104] In the conditions of bitter fighting with a superior foe, the loss of an entire platoon and the enemy's unexpected penetration into the interior of the company's defense through the abandoned sector had heavy consequences. The Germans occupied the abandoned trenches and attacked the neighboring platoon's flank through the communication trenches. Ferocious hand-to-hand combat erupted in the trenches with grenades, cold steel and rifle butts.

It must be recognized that the overwhelming majority of Losev's subordinate commanders at the tactical level were resolute and aggressive leaders. Thus, for example, in the morning the commander of a company of the 229th Guards Rifle Regiment's 1st Battalion that was holding the small Toplinka Station[105] (on the northeastern outskirts of Maslova Pristan') was killed, and his unit was shaken. Having received information about this, the battalion commander immediately sent his deputy Senior Lieutenant V.G. Kuznetsov[106] to take over the company. Despite the extremely critical situation, the officer kept his cool, and having quickly halted the company's retreat, organized heavy fire at the attacking enemy. As soon as the infantry of the 106th Rifle Division became pinned down, in order to prevent the enemy from digging in, he personally led the company on a counterattack. In the course of the heaviest fighting, which often transformed

---

102 TsAMO RF, F. 24 gv. sk, op. 1, d. 21, l. 13.
103 According to the 1932 Census of the Population, 1,010 people were living in Karnaukhovka.
104 *Ognennaia duga: Kurskaia bitva cherez glazami Lybianka*, p. 50.
105 According to the 1932 Census of the Population, just 15 men were living here.
106 Kuznetsov, Vasilii Grigor'evich, born on 16 June 1916 in Kalinin Oblast's village of Petrovo, into a peasant's family. In 1936, he competed two courses of the Leningrad Engineer-Construction Training School. He joined the Red Army in 1937. In 1938 he graduated from the Tambov Cavalry School. He served in the acting army from July 1942. Kunznetsov was killed in action in Germany on 6 May 1945.

into hand-to-hand fighting and bayonet combat, the Guardsmen regained the line they'd abandoned. A short time later, though, self-propelled guns rolled toward the company's positions. With accurate fire from an anti-tank rifle, V.G. Kuznetsov personally disabled three assault guns. He continued to command this rifle company until the conclusion of the 7th Guards Army's defensive operation, and after the Battle of Kursk ended, on 27 August 1943 he was awarded the country's highest honor for his personal courage and skillful leadership of his men in a difficult situation – the Gold Star of a Hero of the Soviet Union.

By mid-day N.A. Vasil'ev knew about the 72nd Guards Rifle Division's precarious position and realized that without decisive measures, which meant a powerful counterattack, its situation couldn't be eased. A preliminary order to prepare one was sent to the 213th Rifle Division that morning, and around 1000 it was repeated and clarified, but the division still hadn't reached its jumping-off positions. Before noon, the corps commander drove to the command post of the 213th Rifle Division in his Willys jeep, in order to find out the reasons for the delay, and in face of the situation that was rapidly becoming acute, personally gave an order to the division commander to get moving on the attack. Before leaving, he got in touch with the commander of the 36th Guards Rifle Division Major General D.I. Denisenko and directed him to send a company of submachine gunners from the 106th Rifle Regiment to the division's right flank in order to destroy the enemy grouping in the Titovka area.

In fact, the movement into the indicated areas for launching the counterattack and the preparation for it didn't go easily for Buslaev's 213th Rifle Division, nor incidentally did the counterattack itself, even though he had rehearsed it more than once before the start of the operation. From the journal of combat operations of the 213th Rifle Division's 793rd Rifle Regiment:

> At 0700 the regiment received an order to assemble two battalions in a forested area on the western bank of the Koren' River with the mission: to be prepared to hurl the enemy back to the western bank of the Northern Donets River. At 1000 a verbal order was received to move out the regiment, minus the 1st Battalion, to a jumping off position for the offensive: the western fringe of the Shebekinskaia Dacha Woods at Point 187.0. The order informed that tanks from one of the battalions of the 27th Guards Tank Brigade would cooperate in the attack. The regiment's assembly was completed at 1200, with the 2nd Rifle Battalion on the fringe of the woods west of Point 187.0 and the 3rd Rifle Battalion on the southern fringe in the area south of Point 187.0. The failure of the tanks to appear at this time, as well as the absence of a signal for the counterattack that had been established by the division's deputy commander Lieutenant Colonel Kaplun (a green flare), forced the regiment to remain in its jumping-off position for two hours while taking heavy losses from enemy artillery fire.[107]

The delay was connected with the fact that the 702nd Rifle Regiment failed to assemble in the area indicated for it on time. According to the plan, the 213th Rifle Division was to launch the main attack with its left flank, with the forces of five rifle battalions in the Rzhavets – Maslova Pristan' direction. The 1st Battalion of the 793rd Rifle Regiment remained in the army's anti-tank region of the "Poliana" State Farm, while the 2nd Battalion of the 585th Rifle Regiment remained in the Shebekino area, in order to defend the bridges there and to repulse possible enemy tank attacks toward Shebekino from the direction of Titovka and Novaia Tavolzhanka.[108] By 1200 the

---

107 Archive of the State Publicly-Funded Cultural Facility, the Museum-Diorama "Battle of Kursk: Belgorod Axis" (further AGBK MD "KBBN"); the journal of combat operations of the 793rd Rifle Regiment of the 213th Rifle "New Ukraine" Division, p. 9.
108 TsAMO RF, F. 24 gv. sk, op. 1, d. 21, l. 14.

5 JULY 1943 – THE BEGINNING OF THE END OF A TRAGICOMEDY

main forces of Lieutenant Colonel A.A. Vashkevich's 793rd Rifle Regiment and arrived at the line of deployment along the western and southwestern fringes of the Shebekinskaia Dacha Woods, while elements of Major N.V. Zaikovsky's 585th Rifle Regiment were to the south; a half hour later, they moved out in the direction of Rzhavets through the woods southeast of that village. Meanwhile Colonel M.V. Nevzhinsky's[109] 27th Guards Tank Brigade at this time had just finished assembling in the Shebekinskaia Dacha Woods in the area of the Ustinka – Rzhavets road.

Thus, the 213th Rifle Division's commander Colonel Buslaev failed to organize a solid "fist", and shortly after 1200 the 213th Rifle Division and the 27th Guards Tank Brigade went on the counterattack in several disjointed groups. This was the first active measure with such major forces by the Soviet command to repulse the German offensive that was launched on 5 July 1943, not only in the sector of the 7th Guards Army, but also around the entire Kursk bulge.

If to judge from the 24th Guards Rifle Corps' combat diary, the 702nd Rifle Regiment approached its jumping-off positions only at 1300, at a time when the 793rd and 585th Rifle Regiments were already in combat contact with German infantry in the woods southeast of Rzhavets (although the documents of the 793rd Rifle Regiment indicates that two of its battalions entered combat only at 1400). The reason for the discrepancy in times is due to the fact that the regiment's headquarters didn't want to call attention in the documents to the loss of an entire rifle company that had been wiped out in the first unsuccessful attack (prior to 1400) by a German ambush. Therefore its documents indicate that it joined combat with forward groups of the 320th Infantry Division only after 1400. The headquarters of the 24th Guards Rifle Corps notes:

> The 793rd Rifle Regiment with two battalions made contact with the enemy west of Hill 145.4, where it became engaged in a stubborn meeting battle. Having lost almost the entire 5th Rifle Company, which was operating on the regiment's right flank and fell into an enemy ambush and encirclement by enemy submachine gunners, the regiment made slow progress along the Ustinka – Rzhavets road. It was only after the tanks of the 27th Guards Tank Brigade with tank riders of the 6th Rifle Company aboard were sent along the fringe of the woods in the direction of Rzhavets that the enemy's resistance was finally broken, and began falling back with heavy losses in the direction of Rzhavets and Maslova Pristan'.[110]

The 27th Guards Tank Brigade's Operational Summary No. 54 for 2300 5 July 1943 states:

> The brigade had the assignment to attack the enemy in the direction of Maslova Pristan' and to regain the former position. At 1220 one company of T-34 tanks [of the 2nd Tank

---

109 Nevzhinsky, Mikhail Vasil'evich (Colonel) was born in 1901 in Chernigov Oblast's village of Siniaevka. He joined the Red Army in 1919 and participated in the Russian Civil War, where he was wounded. In 1921 he completed the 70th Infantry Courses, and in 1922, the Saratov Infantry Courses. In 1923 he graduated from the Kazan Infantry School, and in 1941, two correspondence courses of a department of the Frunze Military Academy. Between 1926 and 1932, Nevzhinsky served successively as a platoon commander, an adjutant, and the commander of a penal battalion of the Urals Military District. In May 1932 he began staff work in the rifle and mechanized units, and his last post was as the deputy chief of staff of the Kiev Special Military District's 41st Tank Division. On 19.03.1941, he was appointed as the assistant for technical matters for the commander of the 41st Tank Division. On 28.09.1941, Nevzhinsky became the chief of staff of the 7th Tank Brigade, and in November 1942 he transferred to the same post in the 6th Guards Tank Brigade. On 16.07.1942, Nevzhinsky became the acting commander of the 121st Tank Brigade and subsequently took part in the Battle of Stalingrad. On 07.02.1943 the brigade was converted into the 27th Guards Tank Brigade. On 18.08.1943 he was badly wounded near Khar'kov, and after recovering, from 25.04.1944 he commanded the 8th Training Tank Brigade. On 31.12.1945 he went into the reserve, and became a resident of Kiev.
110 TsAMO RF, F. 24 gv. sk, op. 1, d. 21, l.18.

Battalion] in cooperation with the 793rd Rifle Regiment attacked the enemy in the direction of Maslova Pristan'. By 1400 the tanks reached the southern outskirts of the village, as well as an area of minefields where they were met by strong artillery fire coming out of Maslova Pristan'. They engaged in combat to destroy enemy infantry and artillery. By 1440 they fell back to the infantry's positions.

At 1530 the 1st Tank Battalion was introduced into the fighting [in addition to the company of the 2nd Tank Battalion; it was sent into the sector of the 793rd Rifle Regiment that was attacking toward Rzhavets]; by 1800 the tank battalions had reached the northwestern outskirts of Rzhavets, where it engaged in combat with enemy infantry and began destroying their firing positions. At 2130 the brigade's tanks broke through to the southeastern and northeastern outskirts of Maslova Pristan', where it engaged in stubborn fighting until sunset and the arrival of the infantry.[111]

When attempting to break through to Maslova Pristan' from the march, the crew of a T-34 under the command of Lieutenant I.U. Butyrin was killed. A decree of the Presidium of the Supreme Soviet on 26 October 1943 posthumously awarded Ivan Ul'ianovich with the title of "Hero of the Soviet Union". In the commendation list there is no mention of a specific exploit; he was recommended for the award due to a combination of merits; however, the actions of his tank crew when assaulting this village received particular notice. He became the first tanker in the Battle of Kursk to be awarded the Gold Star.

From the 793rd Rifle Regiment's combat diary:

> At 1400 after receiving an order from the division commander about going on the attack, the battalions were given an order over the radio and by staff officers to launch the attack without waiting for the general signal for it. The 2nd Rifle Battalion had the immediate task of hurling the enemy back to the northwest, to seize the woods east of Rzhavets, and subsequently to emerge at Toplinka Station. The 3rd Rifle Battalion was to take Rzhavets and subsequently reach the northwestern outskirts of Maslova Pristan'.
>
> When jumping off from the start line, our battalions collided with the enemy numbering up to two battalions of the 320th Infantry Division's 585th Regiment, and a meeting battle erupted in the area of Rzhavets. Thanks to a group of 9 tanks [from the 27th Guards Tank Brigade] carrying tank riders of the 6th Rifle Company that dismounted in the area of a group of sheds and a resolute attack by the battalions' men, the enemy, taking heavy losses in manpower, began to retreat in the direction of Rzhavets and Maslova Pristan'. Pursuing the foe, the 2nd and 3rd Rifle Battalion took full possession of Rzhavets by 1900, and by 2100 separate groups of the 2nd Rifle Battalion reached the railroad in the woods east of Maslova Pristan', while the 3rd Rifle Battalion reached the crossroads at the railroad hut. By this time an order arrived at regiment headquarters over the telephone for the regiment to go over to the defense on the achieved lines and to establish shoulder-to-shoulder contact with the neighbor. In connection with the shortage of telephone cable and the fact that the radio was working only with great interruptions (due to the lack of power supply), the order was sent by letter using couriers on foot. The battalions received the order by 0300.[112]

---

111 TsAMO RF, F. 3108, op. 1, d. 10, l. 59.
112 AGBUK MD "KBBN", journal of combat operations of the 793rd Rifle Regiment of the 213th Rifle Division, p. 10.

Judging from the available documents, at first Raus didn't take the 213th Rifle Division's attack seriously. Even after three hours of the counterattack, he was exerting efforts to organize a breakthrough on the adjacent flanks of Postel's and Forst's infantry divisions, although it is possible that he didn't have complete information about the situation at the front. A daily operational briefing written by Korps Raus's chief of staff as of 1705 (Moscow time) gives evidence of this:

> The 320th Infantry Division has essentially seized ground right up to the railroad embankment, and with separate units has almost broken through beyond the line of the railroad. The 106th Infantry had its main success on its left flank. At the present time the units there are pushing quickly toward the railroad embankment with the aim of taking it. By 1700 (Moscow time) the divisions are to concentrate their shock groupings on their inner flanks in order to seize the hill northeast of Maslova Pristan' [Point 207] with a concentric attack. Both divisions have suffered heavy casualties, around 800-900 men each. The enemy's air force is increasing its activity.[113]

However, Raus was being forced to react more aggressively in pace with the progress made by Buslaev's and Nevzhinsky's formations, and by evening he had brought up part of StuG Battalion 905 to this area. His headquarters' informational briefing at 1900 (Moscow time) observes, "The 320th Infantry Division's center regiment [Infantry Regiment 587], as a result of a heavy counterattack by the enemy with major infantry forces and the support of 24 tanks was thrown back to the woods east of Priiutovka. At present there is a plan to direct a combined unit of assault guns [and infantry] to this point from the area of Maslova Pristan' for an attack to the southeast. The 320th Infantry Division's center regiment has been given the order to hold Priiutovka under any circumstances."[114]

With the combined efforts of Postel's 320th Infantry Division and the assault guns, the further advance by the 27th Guards Tank Brigade was stopped, after which the attacking infantry was also pinned down. By 2200 the 793rd Rifle Regiment had reached Maslova Pristan' and further along the railroad with a front to the west. Its right flank was exposed and hadn't been able to establish shoulder-to-shoulder contact with its neighbor. Thus a submachine gun company was moved up to plug this gap, while a T-34 tank company of the 27th Guards Tank Brigade was left on the left flank as a reinforcement.

The other two regiments of the 213th Rifle Division operated disjointedly. From the 24th Guards Rifle Corps' journal of combat operations:

> The 702nd Rifle Regiment with two battalions reached Point 145.4, and moving to the south of the graded Ustinka – Maslova Pristan' road ran into a meeting battle in the woods with an enemy in strength of up to a battalion of the 587th Infantry Regiment and one battalion of the 585th Infantry Regiment. The 3rd Battalion of the 702nd Rifle Regiment, having lost its battalion commander, strayed from its axis of advance in the woods and at 1800 linked up with the 793rd Rifle Regiment. By 2200 the battalion had reached the northwestern fringe of the woods 1 kilometer southeast of Rzhavets and dug in there. By 2200 the regiment, making slow progress, reached the northwestern fringe of the woods south of Rzhavets and the railroad, with a front facing to the west.
>
> The 585th Rifle Regiment, with two battalions that had deployed from the march, conducted an energetic attack with one battalion toward Kar'ernaia Station and with the

---

113 NARA US, t. 312, r. 54, f. 7569607.
114 NARA US, t. 312, r. 54, f. 7569609.

other battalion into the woods southeast of Bezliudovka, with the assignment to reach the eastern bank of the Northern Donets [sic] River, having seized the northwestern portion of Bezliukdovka and the woods southeast of Bezliudovka. Under a storm of enemy artillery fire that was falling on the forward units of the 585th Infantry Regiment on the line of the railroad, the regiment reached the northern outskirts of Bezliudovka, the woods north of Bezliudovka and the woods east of Bezliudovka on the heels of the retreating enemy. Together with 3rd Battalion/224th Guards Rifle Regiment and 2nd Battalion/224th Guards Rifle Regiment, the regiment engaged in heavy fighting in the trenches with the enemy, and by the end of the day had completely mopped up and taken the trenches.[115]

Thus, over 10 hours of fighting the 24th Guards Rifle Corps' counterattack force had re-gained possession of a significant portion of the main line of resistance in the sector of the 72nd Guards Rifle Division and had pushed back the enemy in Bezliudovka to the river basin, and had taken the second line of trenches of the main defensive belt in the area of Maslova Pristan'. In the process, it had inflicted significant damage to the foe, which was acknowledged by Raus's headquarters. This rather weighty success was basically pre-determined by three main factors.

First, the counterattack was launched with significant forces and caught the enemy's combat groups as they were on the march. They hadn't yet been able to dig in on the ground they'd seized.

Second, the forward battalions of the 320th Infantry Division that had surged ahead, like incidentally those that had dug in around Bezliudovka, were experiencing an acute deficit of anti-tank artillery and shells, because the majority of the bridges at Bezliudovka at this moment had either been destroyed or badly damaged by Soviet artillery fire, and thus the division command hadn't succeeded in reinforcing the units on the eastern bank in good time. Evidence of this is the contrasting fighting in the Rzhavets area. As soon as the adversary moved up assault guns to this area, the counterattack's pace of advance slowed dramatically. This fact is confirmed as well in operational documents of Korps Raus. At 1433 (Moscow time), its headquarters reported: "Problems have arisen in the 320th Infantry Division, connected with the fact that enemy has taken the bridges under increased artillery fire and the division has no possibility to counter the hostile artillery. On the left flank the enemy launched a counterattack with the support of several tanks."[116]

Third was the presence of armor in the counterattack grouping and its tactically-correct use by the command of the 27th Guards Tank Brigade. The attack was conducted in a compact shock group; strong defensive screens were overrun by the tanks, and the Germans put up an insignificant amount of fire. This was due to the close cooperation between the infantry and the tank units: the tanks were covered by small arms' fire, and the infantry was protected by the tanks' armor and the fire of the main guns. This had a substantial effect: over the period of combat actions during the counterattack, Buslaev's 213th Rifle Division and Nevzhinsky's 27th Guards Tank Brigade pushed forward up to 7-8 kilometers.

The shortcomings must be mentioned as well. Already when organizing the moving out of the 213th Rifle Division, a number of significant mistakes were made. The division command, and that of the 702nd and 793rd Rifle Regiments, knowing that the Germans had broken through the forward edge of the 72nd Guards Rifle Division and the great likelihood that enemy groups had penetrated into the depth of the defenses, failed to organize suitable reconnaissance and security while on the march, which resulted in significant losses. In addition, during the counterattack the lack of supporting artillery was perceptible, but for an objective reason. Just before the start of the

---

115 TsAMO RF, F. 24 gv. sk, op. 1, d. 21, l. 18.
116 NARA US, t. 312, r. 54, f. 7569607.

counterattack, two artillery battalions of the 213th Rifle Division's 671st Artillery Regiment had been transferred to the 72nd Guards Rifle Division and one to the 78th Guards Rifle Division. Thus, at this moment the 24th Guards Rifle Corps' commander didn't have any artillery. He only had the possibility of switching supporting fire from the neighboring 36th Guards Rifle Division's artillery into the sector of the 72nd Guards Rifle Division, which he in fact did. However, the commander of the 213th Rifle Division had no direct contact with the artillery headquarters of the 36th Guards Rifle Division, and thus General Denisenko's subordinate artillerymen concentrated their fire on villages occupied by the enemy within range of the howitzers.

By the way, the correlation between the level of losses of the 213th Rifle Division's regiments in these sectors and whether or not the enemy had sufficient artillery available is clearly discernible in the data. For example, over the entire day of fighting, Buslaev's 213th Rifle Division lost a total of 794 men, including 406 in the 585th Rifle Regiment, 143 in the 702nd Rifle Regiment, 199 in the 793rd Rifle Regiment and 6 in the 671st Artillery Regiment, which incidentally was the highest daily casualty rate in his division over the entire period of defensive fighting.[117] According to the 793rd Rifle Regiment's combat diary, on this day both of its battalions lost approximately 300 soldiers and officers killed or wounded. The regiment suffered particularly heavy losses among the command staff; four rifle company commanders, one machine-gun company commander and the deputy political commander of the 3rd Rifle Battalion were killed in action, while the 9th Rifle Company lost its company commander and all of its platoon commanders (see Table 7 for a more detailed look at the losses of the 213th Rifle Division between 5 and 11 July 1943.)

As can be seen from the table, after the rifle company (120 men) was wiped out in the ambush and the tanks were committed into the fighting, the 793rd Rifle Regiment's subsequent loss of men was fewer, even after the regiment advanced up to 8 kilometers from the Shebekinskaia Dacha Woods and seized Rzhavets, which had already been prepared for defense. At the same time, the 585th Rifle Regiment, which launched an attack toward Bezliudovka – the main strongpoint of the 320th Infantry Division on the eastern bank, where bridges were located that were naturally covered by substantial artillery forces – suffered the highest combat losses, even though two more rifle battalions of the neighboring 72nd Guards Rifle Division's 224th Guards Rifle Regiment were also fighting for this village.

The second stage of the III Panzer Corps' offensive began more successfully on 5 July, even though Breith still faced enough serious problems. These inspired no confidence that the panzer corps would reach the day's objective. Thus, for example, the situation in the Mikhailovka bridgehead, where the panzergrenadiers of the 6th Panzer Division were operating, still hadn't improved in any fundamental way. Several attacks undertaken after sunrise made no headway. The 19th Panzer Division's offensive was struggling to get going. Only Köhler's *kampfgruppe* was able to gain a foothold on the eastern bank and drive the Russians off of Hill 126.3. The fighting here was extremely bitter. Gradually the panzergrenadiers pushed ahead, but they lacked the strength to tip the balance in their favor and seize the initiative. They couldn't count on Richter's *kampgruppe* for help, because the bridge for the Tiger tanks was still under construction. Striving to exploit the tactical success north of Dal'nie Peski, Lieutenant General Gustav Schmidt decided to send Colonel Becker's armored group (II/Panzer Regiment 27 and I/Panzergrenadier Regiment 74) across the 24-tonne bridge in the area of Koloniia Dubovoe and assemble it in the rear of Köhler's *kampfgruppe*. General Breith approved this decision, but cautioned that it was necessary to continue the attempts to create a bridgehead south of Mikhailovka in order to commit the Tiger tanks into it.

---

117 TsAMO RF, F. 24 gv. sk, op. 1, d. 16, l. 62.

Table 7 Casualties taken by the units of the 213th Rifle Division over the period between 5 and 11 July 1943[118]

Unit	Casualties
5 July	
586th Rifle Regiment	406
702nd Rifle Regiment	143
793rd Rifle Regiment	199
671st Artillery Regiment	6
Total:	754
6 July	
586th Rifle Regiment	153
702nd Rifle Regiment	211
793rd Rifle Regiment	257
671st Artillery Regiment	14
180th Separate Signals Company	2
Total:	637
7 July	
586th Rifle Regiment	32
702nd Rifle Regiment	275
793rd Rifle Regiment	314
671st Artillery Regiment	8
387th Separate Sapper Battalion	2
Total:	631
8 July	
586th Rifle Regiment	54
702nd Rifle Regiment	108
793rd Rifle Regiment	118
453rd Separate Anti-tank Artillery Regiment	16
Total:	296
9 July	
702nd Rifle Regiment	182
793rd Rifle Regiment	238
671st Artillery Regiment	1
301st Separate Reconnaissance Company	8
453rd Separate Anti-tank Artillery Regiment	1
Total:	431
10 July	
585th Rifle Regiment	4
702nd Rifle Regiment	6
671st Artillery Regiment	8
Total:	18
11 July	
585th Rifle Regiment	4
702nd Rifle Regiment[1]	3
793rd Rifle Regiment	1
Total:	8
Grand Total:	2775[2]

Notes
1 In the 702nd Rifle Regiment over the entire period of time, 358 men who had been counted as missing in action returned to the regiment.
2 Including 43 commanders, 234 junior commanders and 476 rank and file

118 TsAMO RF, f. 24 gv. sk, op. 1, d. 16, ll. 62-64.

To the south, the units of the 7th Panzer Division hadn't yet been able to overcome the railroad embankment either. Nevertheless, von Funck's panzer division had scored the clearest success in comparison with the other panzer divisions of Breith's III Panzer Corps. The troops of von Funck forced a crossing of the river rather quickly and a considerable amount of troops, including a significant portion of the panzer regiment, were already on the eastern bank. The ground stretching from Hill 108.9 all the way up to the railroad embankment (a distance of approximately 2 kilometers) had been completely cleared of its Russian defenders, and the panzer division's left *kampfgruppe* was engaged in street fighting in Dorogobuzheno, trying to expand the bridgehead for an attack toward Razumnoe, even though the prospects for one were still murky. As the *kampfgruppe* command reported, the artillery fire and Nebelwerfer rocket fire had little effect on the elaborate system of trenches and the well-fortified bunkers – panzers and assault guns were needed in order to destroy the firing positions with their direct fire. Resistance on the 7th Panzer Division's right flank in Nizhnii Ol'shanets hadn't been completely suppressed yet, although the flanking artillery fire out of this area had noticeably diminished. The neighbor on the left was rendering substantial assistance here. The III Panzer Corps' situation was succinctly laid out in its headquarters operational briefing for 1440 (Moscow time):

> 7th Panzer Division: The right-hand *kampfgruppe* is launching an attack toward Razumnoe; the other *kampfgruppe* is also attacking toward Razumnoe.
> 19th Panzer Division has had no great successes, since progress in its sector is extremely complicated by the swampy terrain.
> 6th Panzer Division with the support of Tigers is attacking toward Staryi Gorod.
> 168th Infantry Division's *kampfgruppe* has been forced to retake ground that it had previously abandoned.

According to von Funck, his panzer division faced two important tasks. The main one was to rupture the Russian defenses between the major villages of Razumnoe and Krutoi Log with an attack of the armored wedge out of the bridgehead east of Solomino through Razumnoe Station toward the east. This was to help destroy (or at the least, isolate) these two major strongpoints and to seize enough ground in order to cross the entire 7th Panzer Division to the eastern bank of the Northern Donets River. The second task, flowing from the first one, was the use of panzers with the anticipated engineer support for the attack and the powerful support of artillery. There was still no problem with the combat engineers; the central group had received everything necessary. The command had also organized support from a battalion of field artillery and partially from assault guns for the next attack. However, it was still impossible to count on the full-fledged accompaniment of the attack with the entire panzer artillery regiment. Its main forces, just as before, were still positioned on the western bank, and new observation posts hadn't been prepared either. Considering this circumstance, as well as the strength of the fire coming from the fortified villages that the Russians had prepared for an all-round defense and the likelihood of flanking counterattacks, the risk of the next attack's failure was rather high.

General von Funck recalled, "The command had focused its main attention on crossing the artillery. The crossing had to be conducted in the shortest amount of time as possible, which required the particularly strict observation of the timetable for movement along roads and directly at the bridges. This was a rather complex task, but the crossing was conducted across both bridges quickly and precisely."[119]

---

119 TsAMO RF, F. 15, op. 11600

However, far from everything was going smoothly for von Funck as well. The command of the 25th Guards Rifle Corps and of the 78th Guards Rifle Division clearly recognized the menacing danger. The Germans had pushed armor across the river, which meant in the nearest future it would launch a concentrated attack. Thus, the main task was to hold the enemy in front of the division's reserve position – the railroad embankment – for as long as possible. Having been unable to destroy the bridges, G.B. Safiulin was striving to inflict maximal damage to the enemy within the bridgeheads. By this time he had traveled to A.V. Skortsov's command post in order to be closer to the epicenter of the main events and to be able to take the necessary decisions rapidly and efficiently. At the same time, it was important to strengthen the morale and confidence of the division's personnel through his personal example on the verge of a critical battle. On his part, the division commander sent the senior officers of his headquarters and the Political Department to the regiments and battalions, striving to prevent disruptions in command and control or manifestations of panic when attempting to repel possible panzer attacks. This was urgent for the division; in the period of the springtime pause in operations, its ranks had been replenished with a large number of totally unseasoned conscripts. Even though all of these soldiers had been "overrun" by tanks in training sessions, there were still doubts that tank fright wouldn't make a return appearance.

It should be especially stressed that the success of Morozov's Guardsmen, which not only repulsed the attack by the assault groups of the 6th and 19th Panzer Division, but also completely disrupted the crossing of von Hünersdorff's 6th Panzer Division, was quite valuable for the command of the 7th Guards Army and especially for the 25th Guards Rifle Corps itself. G.B. Safiulin took advantage of this already in the morning of 5 July. First, he had redirected some of his heavy artillery and mortars in order to destroy the bridges of the 19th and 7th Panzer Divisions. Second, he had begun the regrouping of the 73rd Guards Rifle Division into the sector of the 78th Guards Rifle Division, so that in accordance with how the situation developed it could either launch a counterattack against the German grouping in the Solomino – Dorogobuzheno area, which was showing the most activity, or create a strong line of defense behind Skvortsov's division between Generalovka and Gremiachii, where the Germans might strike with tanks. Meanwhile the army commander, thanks to the tenacious defense of the 81st Guards Rifle Division, also had the possibility to send some of his reserves to this threatened area.

Judging from archival documents and the recollections of eyewitnesses on the German side, by the middle of the day the Russian artillery fire on the areas of the bridges had increased significantly, especially in the sector of the 25th Guards Rifle Corps. At this time, the army's howitzer and mortar regiments had shifted their fire from the sector of the 81st Guards Rifle Division to the 78th Guards Rifle Division's sector. In addition, the "Stalin's organs", which the Germans called the famous Katiusha rocket launchers, had begun to work over the areas of the 7th Panzer Division's bridges particularly intensively. In this difficult situation, the crews of the 97th Guards Mortar Regiment acted particularly decisively. By 1100 all three of its battalions had assembled in Krutoi Log, which by this time was already under intense shelling by German artillery, and by 1300 they had launched three successive battalion salvoes (6-8 rocket launchers) at the bridges first in the area of Dal'nie Peski, and then at area of Dorogobuzheno. In total, the M-13 rocket launchers had fired 276 rockets. Considering that the German bridgeheads were still not large, while the troop concentration in them was rather high, the losses from the barrages proved substantial not only in men, but also in equipment. I will cite the story from the political chief of the 78th Guards Rifle Division Colonel B.I. Mutovin, an eyewitness of how these attacks on the bridgehead at Dorogobuzheno were organized:

> Having passed the bottomland, we drove to the outskirts of the village of Razumnoe, where the headquarters of the 228th Guards Rifle Regiment was located. Setting out on foot along

5 JULY 1943 – THE BEGINNING OF THE END OF A TRAGICOMEDY

a trenchline, we reached the observation post of the regiment's commander, I.A. Khitsov. His observation post offered a splendid view of the division's defenses. So we spotted a mass of tanks, self-propelled artillery and halftracks in a bridgehead that the enemy had seized from us, which were deploying into a combat formation, ready to move out to assault our defensive positions.

Exchanging opinions with the regiment commander, we decided that the regiment lacked enough weapons to counter such a large number of tanks. I called the division commander and reported to him about the situation in the regiment's sector, the measures that had been taken, and requested help with anti-tank artillery.

Soon I returned to the division's observation post. By this time, the commander of a regiment of rocket artillery had arrived there. We asked him to fire a salvo at the aggregation of enemy armor. He agreed, but requested the authorization from the army commander General M.S. Shumilov for this. We called the army commander. He gave his authorization. In a matter of minutes, two volleys of rockets, one after the other, blanketed the German tanks, self-propelled guns and armored halftracks.

There was a thunder of explosions and a solid sea of flame. Tanks were in flames, the shells and bullets inside them were cooking off, and the crews inside were being consumed with flames together with the tanks. Our forward battalions immediately launched a counterattack and drove back the enemy infantry. That's how the enemy's next attack was thwarted.[120]

According to the account by Skvortsov's headquarters, the defense of the first-echelon regiments in their reserve positions along the railroad embankment began to crumble after mid-day: "At 1330 the enemy managed to take the northern outskirts of Nizhnii Ol'shanets with two battalions … at 1400 70 tanks and self-propelled guns [Schülz's *panzerkampfgruppe* of the 7th Panzer Division] escorted by two battalions of infantry moved out of the area east of Solomino toward Krutoi Log, and at 1420 38 tanks and up to a company of infantry neared the northeastern outskirts of Krutoi Log."[121] In the course of an hour-long combat, Schülz's panzer regiment, having lost several armored vehicles, bypassed the position of the 7th Company of 3/225th Guards Rifle Regiment and the 2nd Battalion of the 225th Guards Rifle Regiment at the Razumnoe railyard from the south, and having crossed the railroad embankment, slowly moved on to the east toward Hill 160.8, toward the 78th Guards Rifle Division's second echelon, and the railyard's garrison wound up encircled. The commander of the 7th Panzer Division von Funck recalled:

> On the axis of the main attack, a sufficient of force had been assembled in order to provide screening of the flanks and to develop the offensive quickly into the depth of the Russian defenses. However, it was necessary to overcome the enemy's numerous defensive lines and clear minefields. All this significantly slowed the pace of the offensive. In the middle of the day, the central combat group [Schülz's] cut the Krutoi Log – Generalovka road. The enemy opened up powerful blocking fire. At this time the situation still wasn't clear in the center of Krutoi Log. From the neighbor on the right [the 106th Infantry Division] information had just arrived that fighting was underway in the vicinity of the railroad and that progress had just been made in several sectors. Later it was reported that between Maslova Pristan' and Krutoi Log, the offensive was continuing to develop and that in the area to the southeast of this place, the troops had run into bitter enemy resistance.

---

120 Mutovin, B.I., *Cherez vse ispytaniia* [*Through all trials*] (Moscow: Voenizdat, 1986), p. 85.
121 TsAMO RF, F. 1225, op. 1, d. 11, l. 103.

On the left flank of the 7th Panzer Division, the Razumnoe railyard, which the central group had bypassed to the south, was still being held by the enemy. However, there were already signs of the evacuation of Russian troops from there.

Our northern *kampfgruppe* [Gläsemer's], moving out from the Dal'nie Peski area, had cut the road leading to the north from Razumnoe, and was exploiting the offensive to the east.[122]

The excerpt above somewhat accelerates the events; the offensive by Schülz's panzer regiment was grinding its way forward for several hours. At 1530 (Moscow time), a German reconnaissance pilot transmitted: "The lead tanks have reached 1 kilometer west of Krutoi Log and is being shelled by enemy artillery", and 1542: "Our tanks are at the eastern end of Razumnoe."[123]

In the documents of the 78th Guards Rifle Division's headquarters, it is indicated that the Germans took the company-sized strongpoint at the Razumnoe railyard by around 1400. This means that between 1100 and this time, intense combat was taking place there and only by 1400 did the last defenders pull out. After this, Schülz's *panzerkampfgruppe* split up, with one portion moving toward Razumnoe (into the flank of the 228th Guards Rifle Regiment), and the second (30 tanks and a company of motorcyclists) reaching the approaches to Hill 160.8, north of Krutoi Log, an hour later with a rapid dash. However, just as the tanks appeared beyond the unpaved Krutoi Log – Razumnoe road, they were greeted by intense artillery fire – the main forces of the 78th Guards Rifle Division's 158th Guards Artillery Regiment had joined battle. Its 1st and 3rd Artillery Battalions were positioned in the anti-tank strongpoint of Krutoi Log, while its 2nd Artillery Battalion was covering the route from Razumnoe to Generalovka (2 kilometers northeast of Razumnoe) and the terrain southwest of it. The heavy fire of these two anti-tank strongpoints (Razumnoe and Krutoi Log) was blocking the path across Hill 160.8 to Schülz's tankers. The account by Skvortsov's headquarters continues, "Having met strong resistance, the Germans stopped. The tanks pivoted away from the hill and approaching Krutoi Log began to place direct fire on the village [together with other panzers that had previously broken through to Krutoi Log from Nizhnii Ol'shanets]. By this time the 225th Guards Rifle Regiment was already defending on the line: Hill 160.8, northwestern outskirts of Krutoi Log."[124] However, this doesn't mean von Funck had abandoned his advance further to the east. The second portion of the 7th Panzer Division's armored group, which was fighting with the 228th Guards Rifle Regiment in Razunoe, continued the assault.

G.B. Safiulin, who was observing this attack from its very first minutes from the forward outpost of the 78th Guards Rifle Division made contact with M.S. Shumilov around 1100, and having reported about the initial German breakthrough, requested authorization to use a portion of his mobile reserve for the planned counterattack – Lieutenant Colonel Verba's armored group (the 167th Separate Tank Regiment and the 1438th Self-propelled Artillery Regiment). Shumilov gave his approval and added that the order would be sent straightaway to the group. At 1100 the corps commander contacted Lieutenant Colonel Verba over the telephone and gave him his order: "The enemy has rolled over the Razumnoe railyard with a force of up to 50 tanks in the direction of Krutoi Log. Immediately transfer the "households" 167, 1438 and 262 to the area of Batratskaia Dacha."

Literally just 5 minutes later, the headquarters of the 167th Separate Tank Regiment received a coded order from the 7th Guards Army's commander of Armored and Mechanized Forces Colonel

---

122 TsAMO RF, F. 15, op. 11600, d. 1539, l. 21.
123 TsAMO RF, F. 203, op. 2843, d. 452, l. 14.
124 TsAMO RF, F. 1225, op. 1, d. 1, l. 103.

5 JULY 1943 – THE BEGINNING OF THE END OF A TRAGICOMEDY

A.A. Bogdanov: "Together with Zatylkin[125] and the unit that is located with Aizenberg[126] assemble in Batratskaia Dacha. Maintain contact with Kozak. Attack toward Razumnoe. Be ready at 1200. Maslov."[127, 128]

An hour later, at 1200, an order from the commander of the 25th Guards Rifle Corps arrived at the headquarters of the 73rd Guards Rifle Division about the immediate preparation of a counterattack: "The 73rd Guards Rifle Division with the 167th Separate Tank Regiment, the 1438th Self-propelled Artillery Regiment and the 30th Separate Destroyer Anti-tank Artillery Brigade are to assemble on the line: 'Batratskaia Dacha' State Farm, sheds 2 kilometers south of Batratskaia Dacha, Hill 209.6, Machine Tractor Station, Gremiachii, in readiness to launch a counterattack in the direction of Krutoi Log and the Razumnoe railyard, further according to the situation, in order to restore the positions of the 78th Guards Rifle Division."[129] In addition to the above-mentioned reinforcements, division commander S.A. Kozak received the operational control of the 161st Guards Cannon Artillery Regiment and the 315th Guards Mortar Regiment, which up to that moment were positioned in firing positions in the sector of the 81st Guards Rifle Division.

There was no set time for launching the counterattack against von Funck's forces that had broken through; it was anticipated to act according to the situation. The main thing at this moment was to assemble the forces on the jumping-off lines as quickly as possible. It should be noted that the 7th Guards Army command had the thought to launch one single strong counterattack between 1300 and 1400 in the sector of both the 72nd Guards and 78th Guards Rifle Divisions with the forces of two groups. It was anticipated to include the 73rd Guards Rifle Division and the above-listed units of reinforcement in the first group, while the second group would include the 213th Rifle Division and the 27th Guards Tank Brigade. However, it wasn't possible to implement this plan because of the rapid advance made by the 320th Infantry Division and the problems encountered by the 213th Rifle Division when on the march.

The assembly of Kozak's group of forces went slowly, even that of its mobile units, mostly due to objective reasons. Thus, according to the order, the 167th Separate Tank Regiment, with subordinate units in Miasoedovo (10 kilometers from the jumping-off positions) and in Postnikov (20 kilometers distant) had to gather its command staff, give them their assignments, get their tanks moving on the march, and reach the area of Hill 209.6, all within the course of just one hour. At the moment of receiving the order, the regiment was already at combat readiness, but nevertheless its main forces couldn't reassemble in their designated area for the attack until 1400, while some of the tanks of the 167th Separate Tank Regiment (the ones located in Postnikov) didn't arrive until an hour later, along with the 1438th Self-propelled Artillery Regiment. The situation with the remaining units was even worse. The composite company of the 262nd Separate Tank Regiment under the command of Senior Lieutenant Kosenkov (5 KV-1 tanks) only set out from the "Batratskaia Dacha" State Farm at 1515, but didn't arrive in time to join Verba's group. By the time it arrived, the group had already gone on the attack. Moreover, while en route, one of the KV tanks broke down with an overheated engine. At 1500 the battalion columns of the 209th Guards and 214th Guards Rifle Regiments were only nearing the "Batratskaia Dacha" State Farm, and they still had more than 5 kilometers left to cover on foot. Lieutenant Colonel M.G. Sapozhnikov's 30th Separate Destroyer Anti-tank Artillery Brigade and the other howitzer and mortar regiments never in fact arrived in the 73rd Guards Rifle Division's sector, even by 1900.

---

125 Major F.A. Zatylkin, commander of the 1438th Self-propelled Artillery Regiment.
126 This statement is referring to the reserve KV tanks of the commander of the 262nd Separate Tank Regiment Lieutenant Colonel I.I. Aizenberg.
127 Code name for Colonel Bogdanov
128 TsAMO RF, F. 925 sap, op. 1, d. 3, l. 108obr.
129 TsAMO RF, F. 73 gv. sd, op. 1, d. 33, l. 25obr.

Meanwhile, as Kozak's troops were moving up into their jumping-off positions, von Funck's panzer division kept advancing, as a result of which after 1500 combat was already going on in the depth of the 78th Guards Rifle Division's defenses. So far, the combat actions had unfolded between the basin of the Donets River and the Belgorod-Titovka railroad, and the initiative had been in Safiulin's hands, since the Germans had to contend with the most heavily fortified sector of his corps while fighting their way out of shallow bridgeheads. The situation began gradually to change to the worse between 1200 and 1600, and by 1700 reached a breaking point. From the account of the 78th Guards Rifle Division's headquarters:

> At 1605 15 enemy tanks, bypassing the village of Razumnoe, reached the southern outskirts of Generalovka and moved off in the direction of the woods 2.5 kilometers northeast of Krutoi Log, where the command post of the division commander was located. At 1655, 20 German tanks advancing along the road between Maslova Pristan' and Krutoi Log emerged in the area of Hill 157.1. Vehicles carrying infantry and towing artillery continued to roll to the east along the roads running from Solomino and Dorogobuzheno.[130]

Thus far, the 25th Guards Rifle Corps was continuing to operate only with its first echelon, the troops of which had already suffered substantial losses in men and equipment, while the artificial obstacles of the first and even reserve positions of the main belt of defenses had been destroyed. The advance of the 7th Panzer Division's *kampfgruppen* was similar to the action of a trebuchet. The central one, Schülz's *panzerkampfgruppe* by 1700 had completely ruptured the line of the 78th Guards Rifle Division's forward regiments and had penetrated approximately 6 to 6.5 kilometers into the depth of its defenses (2/3 of the depth of the division's positions). Nizhnii Ol'shanets was completely isolated, and the enemy's panzer jaws were closing around the most powerful knot of resistance, Krutoi Log. However, just as before, the heavy fire from the artillery battalions of the 158th Guards Artillery Regiment and 3rd Battalion/265th Guards Cannon Artillery Regiment from out of the area northeast of the village and the woods east of there was continuing to slow them up. Nevertheless, exploiting this success and relying on the armor, the panzergrenadiers of the left-hand group (Panzergrenadier Regiments 6 and 7) broke into the southwestern portion of Razumnoe, while the right-hand group (including a regimental group of Infantry Regiment 442) also with the support of panzers was locked in combat on the southern and southwestern outskirts of Krutoi Log. The hole torn into the center of the 78th Guards Rifle Division's defenses was expanding rapidly, while at the same time a breakthrough of its reserve positions also took place at the boundary with the 81st Guards Rifle Division, where Köhler's *kampfgruppe* of the 19th Panzer Division was persistently attacking.

Meanwhile, as the 7th Panzer Division was completely isolating the Razumnoe railyard, the armored group of the 19th Panzer Division and 14 Tigers of Captain Heilmann's company from the Separate Heavy Panzer Battalion 503, which were supposed to augment the attack by Köhler's *kampfgruppe* that was advancing out of Dal'nie Peski toward the labor corrective camp (on the left flank of the 81st Guards Rifle Division), were nearing the bridge in Koloniia Dubovoe. However, most of Heilmann's 2nd Tiger Company failed even to reach the eastern bank of the Northern Donets River as was intended. The reasons for this disaster (which in Breith's opinion pre-determined the failure of Schmidt's 19th Panzer Division's entire offensive in the course of Citadel), were fully predictable in that situation. This was the absence of close cooperation between the command of the 19th Panzer Division's panzer regiment and the support units, and the 19th Panzer Division's poor handling of the introduction of such a powerful, important and valuable

---

130 TsAMO RF, F. 1225, op. 1, d. 11, l. 102.

unit, upon which such great hopes had been placed on the opening day of the offensive. On 6 July the commander of the Heavy Panzer Battalion 503 Captain Graf von Kageneck offered the following explanation for the high losses in Heilmann's 2nd Tiger Company:

1. From the beginning, no map showed where German mines laid when the bridgehead was being established were located. There were two maps that could be consulted but they contradicted each othere and both were inaccurate. Moreover two of our Tigers were directed towards our own mines that had just been primed. Then two other Tigers hit mines when crossing terrain that was thought to be safe.
2. The mines were cleared negligently. Three other Tigers were damaged by mines even though they had been assured that there weren't any where they were going.
   (During the morning, two cannon from Pz. Art. Reg. 74 also ran over mines although the road they were on was also supposed to have been cleared).
3. The eighth Tiger headed straight for an enemy minefield because the sappers told them it was quite safe to go ahead. The ninth Tiger also ran over a minefield when it wanted to change positions when Russian tanks attacked.[131]

Thus, of the 14 Tigers of the 2nd Company ready at the outset of the fighting, only 6 joined combat, and more than half were lost due to elementary carelessness that resulted in trouble for the driver mechanics.

However, let's return to the events in the sector of the 78th Guards Rifle Division. The line of Major I.A. Khitsev's 228th Guards Rifle Regiment on the its right flank, like the forward edge of the entire division, had strongly fortified and was covered by a substantial amount of heavy weapons, including the corps' artillery (considering that it shared the boundary with the 81st Guards Rifle Division). Safiulin directed the fire of 2/290th Mortar Regiment (120mm mortars) and an artillery battalion of the 265th Guards Cannon Artillery Regiment (152mm howitzers) to its front. The Guardsmen successfully employed all this supporting fire to counter the advancing enemy. Thus the fighting was stubborn and bloody; the account by staff officers of the 19th Panzer Division stated: "It might be hardest of all to picture the stubbornness of the Russians, with which they defended each foxhole and trench. An enemy group in strength of up to one regiment, reinforced by a mortar battalion, in elaborately fortified woods [south of the labor corrective camp] offered the fiercest resistance."[132]

However, that morning, albeit with great difficulty, Köhler's *kampfgruppe* managed to drive Captain V.T. Osis's 1st Battalion/228th Guards Rifle Regiment from the first line of trenches on Hill 126.3, which allowed the crossing of armor at Koloniia Dubovoe to begin. After the panzers of Becker's panzer regiment began to appear on the eastern bank, the collapse of the defense on the 78th Guards Rifle Division's right flank was unavoidable and hastened the tragic events in the division's center sector – the German seizure of the Razumnoe railyard and breakthrough to the village of the same name, where two important points of command over the troops of the division's right wing were located – the headquarters of the 228th Guards Rifle Regiment, and the command post and observation post (in a grain elevator) of the 2nd Artillery Battalion of the 158th Guards Artillery Regiment.

At this time, a certain synchronicity is discernible in the actions of the *kampfgruppen* of von Funck's and Schmidt's panzer divisions. The III Panzer Corps command was plainly trying to disperse the defender's strength and reserves. The offensive that had begun at 1400 in the Mikhailovka – Dorogobuzheno sector looked like a unified attack by two panzer divisions in an

---

131 NARA US, t. 314, r. 197, f. 001123.
132 TsAMO RF, F. 38A, op. 9027, d. 46, l. 152.

overall direction to the east. Becker's Panzer Regiment 27 of the 19th Panzer Division advanced out of the area of Dal'nie Peski toward Generalovka (along the left bank of the Razumnaia River), while *kampfgruppen* of the 7th Panzer Division's Panzergrenadier Regiments 6 and 7 attacked to the right from the Dorogobuzheno area along the right bank of the river. Already within two hours, the motorized infantry of von Funck's 7th Panzer Division, supported by strong fire from Nebelwerfers, were directly breaking into the outskirts of Razumnoe. The village itself was being held by the 2nd and 3rd Battalions of the 228th Guards Rifle Regiment. When Schülz's panzer regiment, advancing from out of the bridgehead east of Solomino, approached the Razumnoe railyard, Major Khitsov brought up Major Dudin's 2/158th Artillery Regiment to this place. The intense fire of all three of its batteries foiled the enemy's intention to break into the village of Razumnoe from the south immediately after capturing the railyard at Razumnoe Station. Schülz's panzers continued to penetrate to the Razumnoe – Krutoi Log road, and having crossed it, split into two parts: the first continued the attack toward Generalovka and the second in the direction of Krutoi Log.

After street fighting began in the village of Razumnoe, command and control in the 228th Guards Rifle Regiment became disrupted when a group of Germans in halftracks reached the regiment's command post, which was located in the village. Colonel B.I. Mutovin recalled:

> The chief of staff Guards Major V.S. Solianko ordered the headquarters guard, a platoon of combat engineers, signalers and a reserve company of anti-tank rifles to take up an all-round defense in order to repulse the enemy's attack, and directed the fighting himself. Pinned down by fire, the fascist submachine gunners were lying prone on the ground. Tanks and armored halftracks came to a stop and opened fire from their guns. Solianko rose up from a trench in order to take a look at the battlefield and was severely wounded by a shell explosion. Sergeant I.P. Savchenko picked up the officer and began to make his way out of the zone of fire. Having reached a shell crater, he stopped and bandaged the officer's wounds. Major Solianko forbade the sergeant from evacuating him to the medical sanitation battle and continued to direct the fighting. In the evening he lost consciousness. The soldiers under the cover of our tanks that had come up carried him to an aid station. Meanwhile Savchenko, having returned to the front, together with the regiment headquarters' security personnel, continued to fight off the Nazis' attacks. Suddenly on the right, from behind a hill, an armored halftrack emerged at full speed and began to close on our trenches. Enemy submachine gunners also rose and launched an attack. The halftrack was now right in front of our trench. Rising, Savchenko tossed a grenade at it. An explosion rang out, the halftrack rocked, and it slowed for a moment, but continued to roll onward. The sergeant's second grenade was on target. Smoke enveloped the halftrack. However, the halftrack spat out a burst of machine-gun fire. I.P. Savchenko was cut down and fell to the bottom of the trench. That's how my combat friend, with whom I'd already traveled a long path of the war's roads, was killed heroically.[133]

Over the entire first half of the day, Breith was attentively following how his troops got across the Northern Donets River and broke through the Russians' first line of defense. However, in the afternoon it finally became clear to him that despite the tactical successes in separate sectors of the offensive, the plan for 5 July was falling apart at the seams. The main problem was on the left flank. The 6th Panzer Division, despite the repeated attacks by its panzergrenadiers both out of the Mikhailovka bridgehead (even with the support of assault guns) and from the river's western bank, had achieved no success, and its main forces had still not crossed the river. The attack of

---

133 Mutovin, *Cherez vse ispytaniia*, pp. 94-95.

the 19th Panzer Division had also not started well and had resulted in heavy losses. By the middle of the day, its left-flank *kampfgruppe* under Richter was still spinning its wheels in place. Events on the right flank were developing more dynamically. The initial attempts by Köhler's *kampfgruppe* to penetrate the defenses of the 78th Guards Rifle Division with the use of the assault gun battalion that morning yielded no results, but after the panzers had crossed the river, the situation began gradually to change for the better. Even though Becker's armored group had also met stiff Russian resistance, by 1600, having driven a corridor that extended for 4 kilometers into the Russian defenses, it had overcome the railroad embankment and continued, albeit slowly, to advance toward Hill 139.9, while simultaneously trying to expand the breach. Only the 7th Panzer Division's successes were encouraging, but it, even with the support of the 19th Panzer Division, had been unable to change the situation in a fundamental fashion. The failure of the 6th Panzer Division to carry out its assignment was a serious blow to the offensive's plan on the first day of the operation; after all, virtually one-third of the III Panzer Corps had failed to leave the start line from the very first hours of Citadel.

Indeed, von Hünersdorff's troops had been given the panzer corps' main assignment: to create a breach in the Russian defenses on Army Detachment Kempf's left flank, and having made contact with the II SS Panzer Corps, to cover securely the right flank of the Fourth Panzer Army that was operating on the main axis of attack. Thus, its lack of success could complicate the entire course of combat operations on the primary axis of the entire Army Group South. Time was passing, but the 6th Panzer Division's efforts in the first half of the day led to nothing. Thus for Breith at that moment a decisive penetration on his corps' left flank was exceptionally important, even if it would have to take place in a different sector. If not through the Mikhailovka bridgehead, then to the south of it, bypassing the (excl.) Mikhailovka – Staryi Gorod knot of resistance from the east with a breakthrough to the II SS Panzer Corps' flank through Blizhniaia Igumenka. Although this was a longer path, it had a certain hope for success, since the 7th Panzer Division had not only created a suitable bridgehead east of Solomino, it had created an actively opereating set of bridges in the area. Therefore, Breith decided to mass his panzer forces in the sector of the 7th Panzer Division, where a certain tactical success had already been scored, with the aim of punching a way through the 7th Guards Army's main defensive belt. The 7th Panzer Division commander von Funck recalled:

> In the area to the east of the bridgehead fortifications of Belgorod, an attack by panzers and other motorized means was exceptionally difficult, because the ground had been heavily mined. In connection with this, the III Panzer Corps made the decision to withdraw all of the units under the 6th Panzer Division's control [which hadn't been activated in the fighting] and to send it across the Donets in the wake of the combat formations of the 7th Panzer Division. Afterward the division was again supposed to pivot to the left [to crush the 81st Guards Rifle Division] and regain its sector of advance.[134]

There exists a point of view, according to which the decision about regrouping the 6th Panzer Division behind the 7th Panzer Division's combat formations was made in haste and based on superficial consideration. In the afternoon, when it became clear that the attempts to cross the 6th Panzer Division across the river had fully failed, it would have been more effective to transfer it to the Fourth Panzer Army. This would have allowed the assembly of the 2nd SS Panzergrenadier Division *Totenkopf* on the direction of the main attack not on 9 July, when this actually happened, but two days earlier, which might have helped the SS men force a crossing of the Psel River

---

134 TsAMO RF, F. 15, op. 11600, d. 1539, l. 22.

more quickly, and accordingly make a significantly deeper penetration into the defenses of the Voronezh Front. The 6th Panzer Division might also have been used together with the 2nd SS Panzergrenadier Division *Totenkopf* in order to overcome the 375th Rifle Division's line of defense. The American scholar S. Newton, who was the first to propose this option, writes:

> By midafternoon on 5 July, when it had become obvious that the 6th Panzer Division was not going to force its way out of the Mikhailovka bridgeheads, someone (the record is unclear whether this was Breith or Kempf) decided to redeploy Huenersdorff's division (reinforced by a Tiger company) behind the more successful 7th Panzer Division on the III Panzer Corps' right flank. Inching its way along the crowded roads east of the Donets, *Kampfgruppe* Oppeln-Bronikowski did not manage to reach the bridge feeding into the 7th Panzer Division's sector until 1300 on 5 July and did not enter battle until 1430. Thus the strongest division in III Panzer Corps did not effectively engage the Russians until thirty-six hours after Operation Citadel commenced, and it did so at the cost of completely abdicating the *Armeeabteilung*'s responsibility for guarding Fourth Panzer Army's right wing.
>
> …
>
> Transferring one-third of Kempf's understrength armor to Hoth's army was a decision that would have had to be made by von Manstein himself. No substantive evidence has been found to suggest this option was even considered. Fourth Panzer Army's war diary and Friedrich Fangohr's account [Fangohr was the chief of staff of the Fourth Panzer Army] of the battle both suggest that Hoth's headquarters did not have a clear idea of just how badly the battle had developed for *Armeeabteilung* Kempf until the middle of 6 July or even the following morning. The war diary kept at Kempf's command post implies, though it does not state conclusively, that the decision to move the 6th Panzer Division was made internally: Von Manstein and Busse seem to have been informed, rather than consulted. Even if that supposition is correct, however, it does not relieve Army Group South of the responsibility for the decision. Given the slow progress that *Kampfgruppe* Oppeln-Bronikowski made moving toward 7th Panzer Division's sector, ample time existed for von Manstein to countermand the orders had he been so inclined.[135]

From the above-cited excerpt it follows that all of the generals (the "German command") who were involved in the regrouping committed a tactical blunder. However, it is difficult to agree with Newton's assertion that the decision by the III Panzer Corps command, supported by Army Detachment Kempf, had been superficially considered at the moment of taking it. For a clear understanding of the problem, it is necessary briefly to present the main tasks that each of the military chiefs – Breith, Kempf and von Manstein – faced at that moment, even though the Field Marshal was the last to find out about it. For the panzer corps commander, this maneuver at that moment was an ordinary matter and in my view there was no mistake in it, since, as S. Newton put it he was relying on "a basic of German armored doctrine that success should be reinforced."[136] Breith was proposing a real way out of the predicament, and judging from everything, his direct superior Kempf understood this. Thanks to the regrouping there appeared not only prospects for covering the flank of Hoth's Fourth Panzer Army, but also, which was no less important, for III Panzer Corps to resolve its own problems by shattering the Russian defense on the left flank of the 25th Guards Rifle Corps and opening a path to the east for the entire Army Detachment Kempf. At the very least, to accuse Kempf of giving no thought to Hoth's situation also appears strange.

---

135 Newton, *Kurskaia bitva: Nemetskii vzgliad*, pp. 506-507.
136 Ibid., p. 506.

The commander of the *Armeeabteilung* was first of all vitally concerned with carrying out the mission to cover the Fourth Panzer Army's right flank, a task for which he carried direct responsibility (and which at that moment wasn't going well), while it was von Manstein's job to worry about the situation with the entire Army Group South's offensive.

Yet with respect to Field Marshal von Manstein, S. Newton is completely correct when he accuses von Manstein of procrastination and being uninformed. Unquestionably, it is hard to understand the actions of the Commander-in-Chief of Army Group South in that situation. The most difficult stage of the operation was underway, as the troops were trying to break through the Russians' most powerful defensive belt. Meanwhile he, while knowing full well how important it was for him to react quickly to situations as the coordinating figure between two assault groupings, and aware that the usual system of passing information from corps headquarters to the headquarters of an army group didn't always ensure this, remained in his headquarters and didn't once make an appearance at the army command posts. Thus Hoth had no knowledge of the real situation in Kampf's sector for more than 24 hours, while the Field Marshal himself remained unaware of the subject of the regrouping of von Hünersdorff's 6th Panzer Division until the end of 5 July. In this connection it must be noted that the Soviet generals and marshals, like the Chief of the General Staff A.M. Vasilevsky and N.F. Vatutin himself acted with more foresight. At the most critical moments they found the time and believed it important to visit the headquarters of an army or even that of a corps, in order to get a report in person from the army commander about the operational situation and his decisions – and when it was necessary, to back them up on the spot.

It is impossible not to agree with the military historians G.A. Koltunov and B.S. Solov'ev, who when assessing the actions of the German command at the end of the first day of Citadel, remarked:

> When analyzing the results of the first day of the offensive, the enemy could see a number of alarming signs for him. However, the Nazi strategy both on this and on subsequent days didn't wish to deal with facts. Documents with all their certainty show that in the battle that had started at Kursk, the German-fascist command, carried away by the inertia of the taken decisions, proved unable soberly to assess the course and prospects of the battle as it was unfolding.[137]

Although the authors of this citation have in mind the incapability of the German command to react adequately to a situation happening in Army Group South's entire sector of offensive, this same consideration applies to the assessment of Breith's own difficult situation.

However, let's return to the combat operations on the front of the 7th Guards Army. After 1700 Colonel von Oppeln-Bronikowski's Panzer Regiment 11 of the 6th Panzer Division received an order to march to the 7th Panzer Division's sector in order to move across the bridges there. The rapid assembly of the panzer regiment at the bridges, much less their appearance on the eastern bank, couldn't be counted upon when all the roads were jammed with vehicles and troops. Thus Breith in the meantime decided to operate with his available forces, and taking advantage of the weight of the 19th and 7th Panzer Division's *kampfgruppen* compressed in the (excl.) Hill 126.3 – western outskirts of Razumnoe – Dorogobuzheno sector, made an attempt to envelop the left flank of the 81st Guards Rifle Division. At 1650 the positions of Major M.F. Kriuchikhin's 238th Guards Rifle Regiment was attacked by Richter's *kampfgruppe* (of the 19th Panzer Division) out of the southern outskirts of Mikhailovka, while von Bieberstein's *kampfgruppe* (of the 6th Panzer Division) struck the boundary between the 235th Guards Rifle Regiment and the 238th Guards

---

137 Koltunov, G.A. and Solov'ev, B.G., *Kurskaia bitva* [*The Battle of Kursk*] (Moscow: Voenizdat, 1970), p. 144.

Rifle Regiment. At the same time, the line of 1 and 2/228th Guards Rifle Regiment (woods, south of the labor corrective camp – southern slopes of Hill 139.9 – (excl.) Generalovka), which were covering the left flank of the 238th Guards Rifle Regiment, were subjected to a strong attack out of the Dal'nie Peski area. Two *kampfgruppen* also moved out against them, both from the 19th Panzer Division: *Kampfgruppe* Köhler toward the labor corrective camp, and Becker's armored group toward Belinskaia.

The attack of the panzergrenadiers out of the area south of Mikhailovka had no success. The 81st Guards Rifle Division broke it up with Katiusha rocket fire. Only in the sector of the 235th Guards Rifle Regiment did *Kampfgruppe* Bieberstein succeed in making something of an advance and reach the western outskirts of Staryi Gorod, but here it was firmly stopped. Becker's armored group operated more successfully. Having reached the southern slopes of Hill 139.9, it split into two groups: the left-hand group attempted to bypass the hill and penetrate into the rear of the 238th Guards Rifle Regiment in the area of the "Day of Harvest" collective farm; while the right-hand group attempted to drive to the southern outskirts of Generalovka.

Having received information that the Germans were bringing up tanks to the north of Dal'nie Peski, I.M. Morozov issued an order to reinforce the division's left flank. Already at 1240, Captain Slivin's 3rd Tank Company of the 262nd Tank Regiment had been sent from the areas of Generalovka and Razumnoe in order to cover the sectors north of Hill 139.9. By 1600 5 KV tanks had taken up a defense along the southern fringes of the collective farm, and already within an hour joined combat with the spearhead of Becker's armored group. At the same time, at 1700, 15 panzers of this same armored group closed to within direct fire range of Generalovka. The first combat of Becker's tankers on the approach to the "Day of Harvest" proved fleeting. The flanking fire of the KV tanks came as a surprise for them and struck the flanks of the lead tanks. Thirty minutes later 8 German tanks were left smoking on the battlefield, and the remaining tanks began to withdraw. However, a group of submachine gunners infiltrated the southern outskirts of Belinskaia along the river channel and attacked the 233rd Guards Rifle Regiment (the 81st Guards Rifle Division's reserve).

Köhler's panzergrenadiers had more success; they took Hill 126.3 and broke into the woods south of the Kreida railyard, though here they were stopped by the stubborn opposition of Captain V.T. Osis's 1/228th Guards Rifle Regiment. The commander of the 81st Guards Rifle Division Major General I.K. Morozov later recalled:

> The enemy attacked from the south toward Belinskaia and from Mikhailovka toward the Kreida railyard and the labor corrective camp. At 1500 Comrade Akhimov's and Captain Zavodsky's battalions [1/238th Guards Rifle Regiment and Slivin's KV-1 tanks], Captain Sushchitsky's tank hunters [of a separate destroyer anti-tank artillery battalion] and the artillerymen of Captain Gakhokidze's 3rd Artillery Battalion [of the 173rd Artillery Regiment] repelled up to 6 attacks by enemy infantry and tanks, destroying up to a battalion of infantry and up to 30 tanks and assault guns. The fighting grew more intense by the minute, and at 1800 the adversary hurled up to 110 tanks and assault guns and up to a division of infantry, supported by artillery and 50 bombers, against the left flank and center of the 81st Guards Rifle Division. It seemed that the 238th Guards and 233rd Guards Rifle Regiments, and the tankers and artillerymen, wouldn't be able to withstand such an avalanche of enemy forces. The troops fought fearlessly and courageously.[138]

---

138 TsAMO RF, personal files of Major General I.K. Morozov, autobiography, ll. 45-46.

5 JULY 1943 – THE BEGINNING OF THE END OF A TRAGICOMEDY

During the attack by Köhler's *kampfgruppe* and Becker's armored group, the 2nd Battalion of the 290th Mortar Regiment fell into a critical situation. Even so, unfortunately, as they said at the front, it was not without "opportunism". It wasn't the soldiers and junior commanders that succumbed to feelings of panic, but senior commanders. From Combat Report No. 5 produced by the 290th Mortar Regiment at 1800 on 7 July 1943:

1. Because of an offensive launched by the enemy on 5 July 1943 against the sector of the 228th Guards Rifle Regiment; following a stubborn stand by the regiment, at 1800 it fell back in the direction of Belinskaia, thereby leaving the left flank of the 238th Guards Rifle Regiment and the firing positions occupied by 2/290th Mortar Regiment exposed.[139]

2. The 2nd Battalion (commanded by Major S.P. Sannikov) was subjected to an enemy attack from the flank and rear. Senior Lieutenant Rusin's 6th Battery was the first to be struck. Having fired off all its shells at the closing enemy, the battery's personnel went over to self-defense. Under the pressure of superior enemy forces, at an order the men fell back to the 5th Battery's firing positions, having first blown up or completely disabled the remaining mortars that had survived the enemy's artillery fire.

   The 5th Battery (commanded by Lieutenant Chiniakov) and 4th Battery (commanded by Lieutenant Silkin), being encircled, also went over to a self-defense with our infantry, having first fired off all their shells. The mortars of the 2nd Battalion were knocked out by the enemy's artillery and mortar attacks. The men brought off 5 120mm mortars of the 4th Battery by hand without their base plates.

   The men of the 2nd Battalion in view of their knocked-out mortars and because of the lack of ammunition took up a defense together with the infantry of the 228th and 238th Guards Rifle Regiments until 1200. Altogether, the 2nd Battalion had 13 120mm mortars knocked out. Five 120mm mortars of the 4th Battery were brought out by hand.[140]

Now let's turn to a report from the Voronezh Front's SMERSH Counterintelligence Department, which lays out the reasons for the loss of almost half the regiment's mortars: "In the period of active combat operations, the commander of the 290th Mortar Regiment Major Znamensky and the commander of the 2nd Battalion of this same regiment Sannikov showed cowardice. Having fallen into a difficult situation, Znamensky and Sannikov fled the battlefield with all of the 2nd Battalion's motorized transport, as a result of which some of the battalion's materiel during the retreat was destroyed, at a time when it was possible to save it and bring it out."[141]

The report from the counterintelligence agents isn't contrived. The command of both the regiment and 2nd Battalion really did panic, and abandoning their subordinates to the will of fate, hastily saved their own lives. Even before the regiment arrived in the Voronezh Front, the situation in it was not good. In the spring it had been located in Rybinsk for forming up, and already back then Major S.K. Znamensky hadn't been able (or had no desire) to instill the proper order and discipline, and paid little attention to organizing training and keeping the men supplied with everything necessary. When the unit departed to join the acting army, the leadership of the

---

139 On 5 July 1943, the 290th Mortar Regiment had 653 men, including 80 command staff, 187 junior commanders and 386 enlisted men; 36 120mm mortars, 36 anti-tank rifles, 415 rifles, 73 TT pistols and Nagan revolvers, three 13-R radio sets, one light automobile, 36 GAZ-AA trucks and 1 ZiS-5 truck (TsAMO RF, F. 290mp, op. 20928c, d. 6, l. 252).
140 TsAMO RF, F. 290 mp, op. 20928c, d. 6, l. 172, 172obr.
141 TsA FSB RF, f. 14, op. 5, d. 112, l. 80-81obr.

training center and the local NKVD organs thereupon sent a recommendation that he be brought to criminal responsibility for the fact that his men had totally trashed the barracks and classrooms (breaking windows and doors, pulling up floorboards, etc.). Yet the regiment command at the same time wrote award recommendations for the command staff "for successes in training the regiment for future battles", including one for his own sidekick Major S.P. Sannikov. One must pay tribute to the 7th Guards Army's artillery commander, who quickly looked into these "heroes" and crossed out these "bogus" pieces of paper with a red pencil. Even during the period of training for the Battle of Kursk, the 290th Mortar Regiment didn't get high marks, and with the start of the fighting the situation in it deteriorated.

The five 120mm mortars indicated in the report as being brought out by hand also had to be destroyed by the crews because of the absence of motorized transport at the firing positions. I will add that on 11 July the mortar regiment passed to the operational control of the 69th Army, but even here it managed right away to "stand out". On 13 July it was assembled and transported to the area of Sviridovo, and on the very next day three of its batteries fled the front and were stopped by a blocking detachment in the village of Samoilovka in the army's rear. The report about cowardice probably became the last drop that overflowed the Voronezh Front command's cup of patience; after the Battle of Kursk, the regiment would be withdrawn for replenishment, and on 15 September 1943 Major S.K. Znamensky was dismissed from his post.[142] I've deliberately dwelled on this unsavory story in such detail in order to show the reader through a concrete example how important and significant is the proper choice of a commander for a unit's combat effectiveness, and how much depended on just a single man in the war.

Now let's return to the events on the boundary between the 78th and 81st Guards Rifle Divisions. By 1800 the situation on the 78th Guards Rifle Division's extreme right flank had substantially deteriorated. Despite the bitter resistance of the 228th Guards Rifle Regiment, the 7th and 19th Panzer Divisions' assault groups had been able to make a rather deep penetration into its line, and were now striking the flank of the reserve regiment. At the same time, an Abwehr special commando group attached to Korps Raus tried to use the same approach it had used in the sector of the 72nd Guards Rifle Division here, during *Kampfgruppe* Köhler's attempt to outflank the line of the 238th Guards Rifle Regiment, by attacking the headquarters of Captain V.T. Osis' 1st Battalion of the 228th Guards Rifle Regiment and attempting to paralyze the actions of its units. Even though the commando team of Abwehrkommando 204 managed to infiltrate through the woods and bushes into the woods south of the labor corrective camp, it failed to destroy the battalion command post and disrupt its lines of communication. Everyone in the area of the 1st Battalion's command post joined battle in response to an alert. The clerk Private N.K. Rybalkin at first killed around a dozen of the attackers with fire from his PPSh submachine gun, and when it ran out of bullets, he entered hand-to-hand combat. By nature he was a strong and compact man, and making quick work with his Finnish knife, he killed another four Nazis in this action. The other soldiers of the specialized headquarters' element fought just as valiantly, thanks to which the main force of the enemy group that had broken through to the command post was wiped out, and the rest fled. Pursuing them, N.K. Rybalkin was killed by a burst of submachine gun fire. For the courage that he demonstrated while fighting to repel the attack against the battalion headquarters, the command of the 7th Guards Army awarded him posthumously the Order of the Red Banner.[143]

Concerned by the infiltration of submachine gunners from his neighbor's sector, the commander of the 238th Guards Rifle Regiment Major T.F. Kriuchikhin earlier that morning had sent an

---

142 Major L.S. Kazarinov assumed command of the 290th Mortar Regiment.
143 Mutovin, *Cherez vse ispytaniia*, p. 94.

attached company of the 4th Battalion/233rd Guards Rifle Regiment to the area of the labor corrective camp. It strengthened the defenses of the 3rd Rifle Battalion and gave the battalion commander a greater possibility to maneuver after the German breakthrough at the boundary between the divisions. Timber slashing and incendiary booby traps set by the 104th Flamethrower Company were used particularly effectively on the right flank of the 238th Guards Rifle Division; the Germans called these improvised devices "incendiary mines". However, the primary factor for the success of the 81st Guards Rifle Division remained its "system of defense" – the smooth cooperation of all the units in combination with the skillful use of a variety of previously prepared artificial obstacles. This allowed its command to hold its line for more than another day.

By 1900 the *kampfgruppen* of Schmidt's 19th Panzer Division had driven a slender, 6.5 to 7-kilometer-long penetration into the defenses of the 25th Guards Rifle Corps, but was finally stopped by the fire of dug-in tanks and the anti-tank guns of two anti-tank strongpoints at the "Day of Harvest" collective farm and in Generalovka, which were covering the approaches to the southern outskirts of Belinskaia. The first day of the 19th Panzer Division's combat on the boundary between the 81st and 78th Guards Rifle Divisions cost its units heavily, especially its panzer regiment. Not less than 32 panzers were destroyed, knocked-out, or disabled by mines, including practically all the Tiger tanks of Heilmann's company. Working from the commander of Heavy Panzer Battalion 503 Captain Graf von Kaganeck's account, Steve Newton writes:

> The heavy tanks had been intended "to advance in direct contact" with the assault troops, "directly behind the mine-detecting sections", but faced by extraordinarily heavy Russian fire, the grenadiers lagged back, and "by the evening of 5 July, four Tigers stood 50 to 80 meters in front of the infantry elements", where they became the target of massed anti-tank fire. By nightfall only one of the fourteen Tigers committed to support 19th Panzer Division remained undamaged. "The loss of the *Tiger-Kompanie*, which was the *Schwerpunkt* of the attacking division," admitted Breith two weeks later, "was very detrimental to directing the battle." When 100 vehicles from the division's own Panzer Regiment 27 executed their own attack at 1300, Red Army anti-tank gunners destroyed nineteen Pz.Kpfw. IIIs and IVs. The best that could be said for Schmidt's division by day's end was that the 19th Panzer Division had paid heavily to shatter the 228th Guards Rifle Regiment and had expanded its bridgehead by an unimpressive two kilometers.[144]

In the difficult situation that had formed by 1500, for the 7th Guards Army's command it was important to block the further expansion of the Germans into the depth of the 25th Guards Rifle Corps quickly. It was possible to achieve this only if the Soviets could retake the initiative on the right flank of the 24th Guards Rifle Corps and reserves brought up quickly to the breakthrough area. Judging from M.S. Shumilov's decisions, he had anticipated such a development of events. Thanks to the counterattack launched by the 213th Rifle Division and 72nd Guards Rifle Division, the advance of Korps Raus had not only been stopped, but on the left flank and in the center Losev's division it had even managed to drive the Germans back to the villages located immediately on the bank of the Donets River. Thus by 1700, the opportunity had appeared as well to localize the penetration made by the Germans into the main belt of defenses of the 25th Guards Rifle Corps: the 73rd Guards Rifle Division was completing its assembly, while Lieutenant Colonel Verba's tank group already by 1500 had assembled in the rear of the 78th Guards Rifle Division. Thus Shumilov was continuing to gather strength on the boundary between the two Guards rifle corps. As insurance, around 1500 he issued an order to Colonel Bogadnaov, the

---

144 Newton, *Kurskaia bitva: Nemetskii vzgliad*, p. 505.

commander of his armored and mechanized forces, to move out the 201st Tank Brigade to the Gremiachii – Machine Tractor Station – "Poliana" State Farm area with the assignment: "Prevent the enemy's expansion out of the area of Maslova Pristan' and Krutoi Log, and in cooperation with the 73rd Guards Rifle Division, check his progress in the Gremiachii, Machine Tractor Station, "Poliana" State Farm area; in the future, drive the enemy back to their jumping-off positions – the western bank of the Sev. Donets River."[145] At 1625 Colonel I.A. Taranov's tank brigade moved to the indicated area.

At the moment that the 7th Panzer Division's armored group (Schülz's panzer regiment) reached the Razumnoe – Krutoi Log road, the 73rd Guards Rifle Division's commander S.A. Kozak[146] was already located at A.V. Skvortsov's forward observation post on Hill 209.6 (2.5 kilometers northeast of Gremiachii). German tanks had penetrated the forward edge of Skvortsov's 78th Guards Rifle Division, and Kozak's 73rd Guards Rifle Division was moving up at the double quick in order to block the breakthrough. However, his regiments were marching on foot, and therefore were late in reaching their jumping-off positions. The atmosphere in the Skvortsov's command post was strained, tensions were rising, and it was being increased by the absence of precise information about the course of the battle in his division's sector. Both rifle division commanders were monitoring closely the operational situation in the sector of Skvortsov's division, striving to determine the line of contact and to find out how much longer the 225th Guards Rifle Regiment that was defending the Generalovka – Hill 164.7 – Krutoi Log line could hold out. Kozak sent out several reconnaissance and observations teams in the western, southwestern and southern directions. Around 1600 information arrived that the Germans had taken Krutoi Log, and 25 tanks mounted with submachine gunners had arrived on the eastern outskirts of this village (at Point 176.0), while another group of tanks was moving toward Hill 164.7 (southeast of Generalovka). This meant that the defense of the 78th Guards Rifle Division's second echelon had been broken and that the enemy was advancing into the rear of the 81st Guards Rifle Division, toward Belinskaia. However, this information proved not quite accurate, but at that moment Kozak didn't realize this. Therefore on the basis of it, he made a number of important decisions. The 73rd Guards Rifle Division's

---

145 TsAMO RF, F. 201 tbr, op. 1, d. 145, l. 89.
146 Kozak, Semen Antonovich (Lieutenant General from 29.04.1945) was born on 10 May 1902 in Zhitomir Oblast's village of Iskoros'. After completing two grades in a rural school, he worked on a railroad, and then switched to Party work. In 1924 in response to a Party mobilization, he was called up into the Red Army. In 1928 he simultaneously completed the 10th grade (as a non-resident student) and the Kiev Artillery School, before being appointed as the commander of an artillery battery in the 51st Rifle Division in Odessa. In 1932 and 1933 he participated in the Leningrad armored warfare courses, and then taught in the Leningrad Tank-Technical School. Between 1936 and 1938, he studied (by correspondence) in the Frunze Military Academy and after completing his studies remained at the academy to teach tactics. In 1939 as chief of the Southern Group of Force's Operations Department, he took part in the absorption of western Ukraine. Between July 1941 and September 1942, he served as a senior inspector of the Main Directorate for Forming and Staffing the RKKA's Forces of the USSR People's Commissariat of Defense. In the autumn of 1941 while forming the Tula Rifle Division, he took part in organizing the defense of Tula. In September 1942 at his personal request he was placed at the disposal of Stalingrad Front's Military Council. From February 1943 he occupied the post of deputy commander of the 64th Army's auxiliary command post, chief of staff of the 7th Rifle Corps, and commander of the 36th Guards Rifle Division. On 25 November 1942, the army's chief of staff Major General Laskin wrote the following about Kozak: "Comrade Kozak is a well-prepared commander tactically speaking. He can organize battle at the scale of a corps and can competently handle all types of troops. He knows how to organize and maintain command and control over all types of troops, and is a snappy staff commander. In combat conditions, he showed himself to be courageous and bold. He corresponds to his assigned post." In February 1943 Kozak assumed command of the 73rd Guards Rifle Division. For his skillful leadership when forcing the Dnepr and Danube Rivers, he was twice awarded the title Hero of the Soviet Union. He passed away on 24 December 1953 in Moscow.

combat diary observes, "Having assessed the current situation, the division commander makes an independent decision: the 209th Guards Rifle Regiment with the 167th Tank Regiment and 1438th Self-propelled Artillery Regiment is to block the path to Belinskaia and through a counterattack is to gain time for the 214th Guards and 211th Guards Rifle Regiments – in the assembly area, in readiness to repel an enemy attack to the east and northeast."[147]

It isn't simple to follow the subsequent events precisely; information about them is almost entirely lacking in the archival documents, but the consequences of S.A. Kozak's decision proved tragic for the 167th Separate Tank Regiment. It isn't known what happened over the following hour, but already at 1700 Lieutenant Colonel Verba, who at 1500 had received the order to prepare a group for an attack jointly with the 211th Guards and 214th Guards Rifle Regiments out of the area of the woods 1 kilometer northeast of Hill 167.4 in the Razumnoe – Krutoi Log direction, was given a fresh assignment. From the 167th Separate Tank Regiment's journal of combat operations:

> Having received an order from the 73rd Guards Rifle Division's commander, the regiment commander at 1730 gave a signal over the radio for the tanks to attack. The tanks moved out on the attack without preliminary artillery preparation, and the tanks were unsupported by infantry or artillery in the fighting. Altogether 27 T-34 and 5 T-70 went out on the attack. Upon reaching the eastern outskirts of Razumnoe and the Razumnoe railyard, our tanks had penetrated the enemy's defense and joined combat with enemy artillery located in Razumnoe and with enemy heavy tanks on the southwestern outskirts of Krutoi Log. The combat lasted for 2 hours and 30 minutes. Despite the Germans' advantage in tanks and artillery, the regiment carried out its assignment; the tankers showed courage and valor, and there wasn't a single instance of shirking. In this fierce combat action, the regiment suffered losses: 20 T-34 and 4 T-70, which were destroyed or knocked out in the depth of the enemy's defenses. The evacuation of the combat machines was impossible because of the fact that many were burned out, and the majority of them were deep behind enemy lines.
>
> Losses in personnel: 7 of the command staff and 12 of the junior commanders were killed; 12 of the command staff and 15 junior commanders were wounded. In this battle the commander of the 2nd Tank Company Senior Lieutenant Ruvim L'vovich Dogman, and T-70 platoon commander of the 4th Tank Company Lieutenant Timofei Osinovich Shenderovsky fell as heroes. Since all the company commanders had been knocked out of action, a platoon commander of the 1st Tank Company Junior Lieutenant N.I. Trekhglazov assumed command of the composite company.[148]

I'll especially note that there is not a single mention of the 1438th Self-propelled Artillery Regiment's participation in this attack in any of the documents I've come across, even though it was part of Verba's group of armor. However, all of these documents relate to the 167th Separate Tank Regiment, which A.A. Verba commanded, and in them he was acting not as commander of the armored group, but as the regiment's commander. Possibly that's why he in fact didn't point to any combat work done by the self-propelled artillery regiment on this day. The recommendation documents of the self-propelled artillery regiment's commander Major F.A. Zatylkin prompts the thought that the 1438th Self-propelled Artillery Regiment never took part in the counterattack; in them there is the note that the regiment between 5 and 14 July 1943 was constantly repelling enemy attacks in the Krutoi Log – "Batratskaia Dacha" State Farm area, and that the major was

---

147 TsAMO RF, F. 73 gv. sd, op. 1, d. 33, l. 25obr, 26.
148 TsAMO RF, F. 167 otp, op. 168101, d. 3, l. 47obr, 48.

wounded on 5 July,[149] but remained at his post and continued to direct his units. It isn't clear where this wound occurred, in the area of the staging positions, or at some moment when the crews of the self-propelled guns were in fact supporting the tanks' attack.

What forced the division commander to send the handful of tanks into a frontal attack against the 7th Panzer Division's armored wedge without reconnaissance or artillery support isn't clear: Was it urgent need, inaccurate intelligence, or ignorance about how tank units should be employed? What prompted Kozak to order this "cavalry charge"? Were the costs justified? We'll make an attempt to answer these difficult questions, relying on combat documents that are today accessible for scholars.

I'll begin from the fact that the operational situation for Kozak wasn't clear. Information that the 7th Panzer Division had managed in places to breach not only the regiments of the first echelon, but also the 78th Guards Rifle Division's second echelon with tanks and had reached the approaches to Generalovka and were heading into the rear of the 25th Guards Rifle Corps was in fact accurate. As already noted, submachine gunners of Becker's armored group had even broken through to the southern outskirts of Belinskaia. As concerns Krutoi Log, its capture was still far away. The 73rd Guards Rifle Division's artillery still wasn't in place: two howitzer regiments and the Katiusha rocket-launchers still hadn't arrived from the 25th Guards Rifle Corps' right flank, and only one not fully-equipped anti-tank regiment (12 anti-tank guns) had arrived from the 30th Destroyer Anti-tank Artillery Brigade in the division's sector, while the 73rd Guards Rifle Division's 153rd Guards Artillery Regiment at that moment was still subordinate to the 81st Guards Rifle Division. The 3rd Artillery Battalion of the 265th Guards Cannon Artillery Regiment was deployed in the sector northeast and east of Generalovka, and judging from the documents, this was the only artillery unit (not including destroyer anti-tank artillery regiments) that the division commander could activate. Accordingly, having received a report about a tank breakthrough, and when preparing to counter it, Colonel S.A. Kozak could count upon only the division's own regimental artillery, 12 guns, and Verba's group of armor, which at 1700 consisted of 39 serviceable tanks of the 167th Separate Tank Regiment[150] and 21 self-propelled guns of the 1438th Self-propelled Artillery Regiment.

In an unclear situation, the first option that comes to mind is to "tread carefully"; to wait things out and adopt a mobile defense, having created several knots of resistance consisting of several tanks, combat engineers and rifle companies, reinforced by anti-tank guns on a front (excl.) Razumnoe – (excl.) Krutoi Log. Kozak had enough strength for holding a line by such means. The rifle regiments had essentially already arrived in their designated areas and had begun to take up a defense of them. In general, the commander of the 73rd Guards Rifle Division did have options, but he acted otherwise, and issued the order for a limited counterattack out of the area of Hill 164.7 with the assignment to tie down the 7th Panzer Division's armored group east of the Razumnoe – Krutoi Log road with an unsupported counterattack by a handful of tanks. In so doing, he decided not to include the rifle elements in the battle, but left them on the lines they occupied, for insurance in the event of a further advance by the Germans.

This decision in that particular situation was suicidal for the tankers. Lieutenant Colonel A.A. Verba, not having any information about the enemy's strength or about the location of his firing means, issued an order "to attack in the general direction of …" Thus the adopted combat formation was unsuccessful. Thirty armored vehicles struck not in a "clenched fist" on a narrow sector,

---

149 TsAMO RF, F. 33, op. 690155, ed. khr. 933, entry number 31421340.
150 On the morning of 5 July 1943, the 167th Separate Tank Regiment had a total of 40 tanks, including 33 T-34 and 7 T-70, as well as 2 BA-64 armored cars. While on the march, a crankshaft had fractured in one of the T-34s, and it was left behind in the woods 3 kilometers southeast of Miasoedovo for recovery and repair (TsAMO RF, F. 925 sap, op. 1, d. 3, l. 108, 108obr).

but in "spread fingers" on a front of 3 kilometers. The tank companies advanced in a fanned-out formation across smooth terrain in three directions: toward Razumnoe, toward the Razumnoe railyard, and toward Krutoi Log. With the start of the fighting, the command post lost contact with the company commanders of the 167th Separate Tank Regiment, and accordingly it was impossible to exert centralized command and control.[151] Thus each tank crew wasn't working to carry out any common tactical assignment, but was trying to struggle with whatever enemy that wound up in the sector of fire of its guns while moving "in a general direction …" The III Panzer Corps' command made wide use of aerial reconnaissance, and thus when Verba's tanks were approaching the line of contact, the forward elements of the 7th Panzer Division arranged its firing means in a "bell-shaped" formation. From the account of the 167th Separate Tank Regiment:

> During our forces' actions in the Krutoi Log – Razumnoe area, the enemy employed the following tactic. Some of the tanks, primarily the Pz.Kpfw. VI, using folds in the ground, were deployed on the flanks, while a small number of tanks with infantry were committed into the fighting in fits and starts, advancing and falling back, drawing the attention of our tanks. As a result, our tanks were lured into the depth of his defenses, engaging his infantry and firing positions, while at this time heavy tanks opened up out of ambush positions and fired at our flanks and rears, inflicting heavy damage to the regiment. Artillery fire added to all this.[152]

As a result, over two-and-half hours 75% of Verba's tank group was destroyed. According to our data, over this same time his tankers managed to brew up or knock out seven Pz.Kpfw. VI, one Pz.Kpfw. IV, one Pz.Kpfw. III, three self-propelled guns and two field guns, 10 machine-gun nests and destroy up to two companies of enemy infantry. These figures are suspicious, especially with respect to the Tigers, even though there is a special note in the journal of combat operations that a special reconnaissance patrol numbering 20 men was sent out that night under the command of Lieutenant Murmantsev, which "found 18 tanks [of the Red Army], of which 15 were burned out and 3 knocked out, but also confirmed the enemy losses in tanks."[153] In the area where the 167th Separate Tank Regiment was operating, the patrol might have found 10-15 German tanks standing motionless on the battlefield, but who in the darkness could check whether they'd been disabled by mine explosions, which was the most frequent occurrence, or knocked out by tank fire?

Now we'll touch upon the most important question: "What influence did the counterattack have on the subsequent course of combat operations in the 78th Guards Rifle Division's sector?" It is rather difficult to answer this question. A very evasive combat report from the 73rd Guards Rifle Division to the 25th Guards Rifle Corps at 1900 that evening doesn't bring any clarity either:

1. As a result of the day's combat, the enemy managed to penetrate to and consolidate on the southern outskirts of Razumnoe, the Razumnoe railyard, and the southwestern outskirts of Krutoi Log.
2. On the right, the units of the 81st Guards Rifle Division are continuing to defend. On the left, units of the 213th Rifle Division are operating.
3. By 1900 on 5.07.1943, the division together with the 167th Separate Tank Regiment and the 1438th Self-propelled Artillery Regiment, having destroyed 7 enemy tanks in Generalovka and having driven his tanks and submachine gunners out of the northern

---

151 TsAMO RF, F. 925 sap, op. 32788, d. 3, l. 136obr.
152 TsAMO RF, F. 925 sap, op. 1, d. 3, l. 109obr.
153 TsAMO RF, F. 167 otp, op. 168101, d. 3, l. 48. Emphasis added.

portion of Krutoi Log, took up a jumping-off position for a counterattack from the directions of Razumnoe, Krutoi Log and Nizhnii Ol'shanets.

    a) The 209th "Abgonerovo" Guards Rifle Regiment with the 167th Separate Tank Regiment and the 1438th Self-propelled Artillery Regiment has assembled for the counterattack on the line: Generalovka, Hill 164.7, southwestern fringe of woods lying 1.5 kilometers northeast of Krutoi Log, Hill 191.2 with a front facing to the southwest.

    b) The 214th "Voroponovo" Guards Rifle Regiment with a regiment of the 30th Destroyer Brigade (12 guns) has assembled for the counterattack on the line: (excl.) Hill 191.2, Hill 197.4, "K", which is 1 kilometer northeast of Koren'skaia Dacha.

    c) The 211th "Bassargino" Guards Rifle Regiment has assembled on the line: "K", Machine Tractor Station, Gremiachii with a front facing the southwest and south (the regiment is waiting for the arrival of regiment from the 30th Separate Destroyer Anti-tank Artillery Brigade).

    d) The 153rd "Urazovo" Guards Artillery Regiment is in firing positions in the sector of the 81st Guards Rifle Division.

    e) My reserve – the training battalion and a battery of the 80th Separate Destroyer Anti-Tank Artillery Battalion are in the area of Hill 209.6.

4. I'm waiting for the arrival of the 315th Guards Mortar Regiment, the 161st Cannon Artillery Regiment and the 265th Cannon Artillery Regiment.[154]

In the first place, it isn't clear: Did the enemy break through to the northern outskirts of Krutoi Log during the day of fighting, or to the southwestern outskirts? In the second place, it isn't clear which of the rifle regiments took direct part in the fighting together with the tankers and self-propelled gunners, and who indeed knocked out 7 tanks in Generalovka. Finally, why isn't there any mention that the 167th Separate Tank Regiment was attacking the enemy's panzer wedge and had already been engaged in heavy fighting in the depth of the German defenses for the previous 90 minutes?

It is possible that by this time, Kozak had recognized his blunder and was trying to put the decision he had made without the agreement of his corps commander, which hadn't proved very effective, on the back burner. At the same time when the report was ready, the combat between the 167th Separate Tank Regiment and the anti-tank guns and panzers of the 7th Panzer Division had reached its logical conclusion. A portion of Schülz's armored group was already located 4.5 kilometers to the east of where the battle with Verba's tankers had taken place, which means in the Russian rear, where the German panzers had overrun combat positions and had nearly stumbled over the headquarters of the 225th Guards Rifle Regiment. The 73th Guards Rifle Division headquarters reported:

> At 1850 enemy tanks approached the balka southeast of Hill 160.8, where the command post of the 225th Guards Rifle Regiment was located. At an order from the division commander, the regiment commander is changing the location of his command post and is moving it into the church in Krutoi Log. At this moment the 228th Guards Rifle Regiment is digging in on the line: northern outskirts of Generalovka – western outskirts of Belinskaia. The units of the division held their occupied lines until the onset of darkness, having repulsed three attacks, each more fierce than the preceding one.[155]

---

154 TsAMO RF, F. 1212, op. 1, d. 28, l. 1.
155 TsAMO RF, F. 1225, op. 1, d. 11, l. 102.

In addition, other units of von Funck's 7th Panzer Division had captured Hill 164.7, while several panzers had even rolled into Generalovka. In the existing situation, the commander of the 73rd Guards Rifle Division was again forced to commit his last reserve against them: the remaining tanks of the 167th Separate Tank Regiment and Captain Malinin's 3rd Battalion of the 209th Guards Rifle Regiment. From the division's combat diary: "By 2100 enemy tanks and submachine gunners had been driven out of Generalovka, leaving behind 4 tanks on the battlefield … Under cover of artillery and mortar fire by 2200 [a different time, 2000, was given in the account] the 3rd Company and the anti-tank rifle company of the 209th Guards Rifle Regiment had driven the enemy off of Hill 164.7 and with their fire supported the advance of the 209th Guards Rifle Regiment's units to the line: Generalovka – southeastern slopes of Hill 164.7."[156]

Thus, the main task that stood before Colonel Verba[157] and his tank group to regain the position of the 78th Guards Rifle Division's units and to "prevent the enemy's further advance" went unfulfilled. Unquestionably, some of the 7th Panzer Division's strength was tied up in fighting with his tank crews, which allowed the commanders of the retreating elements of the 78th Guards Rifle Division, primarily the 225th Guards Rifle Regiment, to rally and organize a mobile defense in a new place. At the same time, the counterattack by the 167th Separate Tank Regiment disrupted the preliminary plans of the 7th Panzer Division's command to break through to the "Batratskaia Dacha" State Farm – Iastrebovka line by day's end, although the enemy was able to make some headway after Verba's counterattack. At 1945 (Moscow time) during discussions between Kempf and Breith, the latter reported: "Razumnoe was taken around 1600. A counterattack by 30 tanks from Generalovka toward Razumnoe will be stopped soon. Our nearest plans include taking the "Batratskaia Dacha" State Farm – Iastrebovka line with our panzers. The enemy is launching another attack with tanks [262nd Heavy Tank Regiment] to the west from the direction of the "Day of Harvest" collective farm."[158]

Two hours later, at 2235 (Moscow time), Spiedel informed Busse:

> 7th Panzer Division has knocked out 10 hostile machines in the Razumnoe area. The remaining elements of enemy tanks are virtually *hors de combat*. As a result of this, the 7th Panzer Division's panzer regiment has cut the road between Krutoi Log and Generalovka. The 19th Panzer Division is engaged in stubborn fighting with enemy tanks on the approaches

---

156 TsAMO RF, F. 73 gv. sd, op. 1, d. 33, l. 26.
157 Verba, Andrei Afanas'evich (Colonel, 20.4.1944) was born on 30 October 1906 in Vinnitsa Oblast's village of Kushchintsy. He joined the Red Army in 1928. In 1933 he passed a non-resident course of seven classes of the Moscow Military District's courses for combat and transport vehicles, and in June 1939 he completed a nine-month course of training at the Red Army's Stalin Academy of Mechanization and Motorization; in November 1942 he completed another two-month course of training at the same academy. On 15.12.1940 he became the assistant commander of the fighting troops of the Kiev Special Military District's 252nd Auto-Armored Battalion. On 25.12.1941 he was appointed commander of a tank battalion in the 132nd Tank Brigade, and then assumed command of a battalion of the 4th Tank Brigade. In February 1942 he took command of a tank group of the Southern Front's 12th Army (after the commander of the 1st Tank Battalion was demoted and reduced in rank and sent into the Front's reserve). On 16.05.1942, Verba became the deputy commander of Southern Front's 3rd Tank Brigade. In November 1942, he received a light wound in the left leg near Demiansk. On 23.01.1943 he was appointed commander of the 167th Tank Regiment of the Supreme Command Reserve. On 25.03.1943 Losev was awarded the Order of the Red Banner. On 02.08.1943 Losev received a severe concussion near Belgorod. Between 30.11.1943 and the end of the war, he commanded the 2nd Ukrainian Front's 20th Guards Tank Regiment. On 15.01.1955, he went into the reserve and took residence in Kiev.
158 NARA US, t. 312, r. 54, f. 7569609.

to the "Day of Harvest" collective farm, while the panzergrenadier regiments are attacking toward the Kreida railyard.[159]

Of course, a certain amount of damage was inflicted on the enemy in manpower and equipment, but it was incomparable with the losses taken and the possible fruits given a more thoughtful approach to planning the battle. According to orders from the Supreme High Command and the regulations of the Red Army, senior commanders and chiefs when issuing orders to the troops were obligated to create the necessary conditions for carrying them out. In the opposite case, the combat potential of the units and formations had to be used differently in the struggle against the foe. That means if the division commander couldn't provide artillery support for the tank group, and knowing that significant armored forces were advancing toward the division, he was obligated to provide reconnaissance to reveal the flanks of the enemy's armored wedge, and only then decide the sector in which to launch the attack, or else deploy the tanks on the defense as armored firing points. The 73rd Guards Rifle Division's commander couldn't but be aware of these maxims, since they had been set in stone by Order No. 57 of the *Stavka* of the Supreme High Command from 22 January 1942, which had been passed down the line of command down to battalion commanders inclusively. Incidentally, this order detailed the typical mistakes made by the commanders of rifle formations, which in fact Kozak had committed as if by carbon-copy:

> Infantry commanders are issuing vague and hasty orders. The attacks of tanks our not being supported by our artillery fire, field guns are not being used in order to accompany the tanks, as a result of which combat machines are being destroyed by enemy anti-tank artillery fire. The combined-arms chiefs are extremely hasty in the use of tanks – they throw them into combat directly from the march, without setting aside time even for conducting elementary reconnoitering of the enemy and the terrain.[160]

Judging from the available records, the 73rd Guards Rifle Division's commander really was in haste, or was simply at a loss about what to do, though it can't be excluded was well that A.V. Skvortsov's request to help the units of his 78th Guards Rifle Division that were retreating under the attacks made by the 7th Panzer Division dig in on a new line seriously influenced his decision. Thus he wasn't able to handle the armor under his command prudently and competently, or to realize its significant potential, as had been done, for example in the course of the earlier attack made by the 213th Rifle Division and 27th Guards Tank Brigade. In violation of the demands, at the very least, of NKO Order No. 325 and *Stavka* Order No. 057, Kozak had launched a head-on strike against the armored wedge of von Funck's panzer division, probably hoping by this means to stop it. As a result, more than 30 tanks of the 167th Separate Tank Regiment were destroyed and almost 200 men perished without carrying out the given order. In addition, the destruction of the 167th Separate Tank Regiment also negatively affected the outcomes of the combat actions on 6 July, when the 73rd Guards Rifle Division joined combat with the armored groups of von Funck's and Hünersdorff's two panzer divisions simultaneously, and Kozak would then acutely feel the lack of the mobile armored reserve that had been destroyed on 5 July.

Although at first glance this can seem cynical, even so, despite the mistakes Colonel S.A. Kozak handled his first battle as a division commander not so badly. In the first place, the further advance of the 7th Panzer Division into the depth of the 25th Guards Rifle Corps' defense was nevertheless stopped, and the tank group played not the least important role in this. In the second place,

---

159 NARA US, t. 312, r. 54, f. 7569611.
160 RGVA, f. 4, op. 11, d. 69, l. 121-122.

in the war the unit and formation commanders of the Red Army acquired combat experience and skill primarily on the basis of blood shed by their men, and often a very large amount of blood. There were not a few cases in the course of the Battle of Kursk as well when over two days on the defensive, entire divisions perished, including because of the inherent incompetence of a division commander, and only after this were they sent to study military affairs in the Frunze or Voroshilov Military Academies. Unfortunately, such was the reality.

Active combat operations on 5 July 1943 ended by approximately 2300 in the sector of the Voronezh Front, although in separate sectors, for example in the vicinity of Cherkasskoe (6th Guards Army's sector) and in Bezliudovka, fierce fighting continued throughout the entire night. What were the initial results of the defensive operation of Vatutin's forces? There were mainly two outcomes.

First, the Soviet side gained clarity with respect to the German plans; as presumed, the enemy launched a decisive offensive exactly in those places where the Voronezh Front had prepared to meet it. Thus, the decision made by the *Stavka* on 12 April 1943 about going over to a pre-meditated defense proved correct, and all the enormous work to prepare the defensive lines, conducted during the pause in operations, proved not to be in vain.

Second, the system of army-level defensive belts demonstrated its high degree of sturdiness, both on the axis of the enemy's main attack (6th Guards Army) and on the axis of the auxiliary attack (7th Guards Army). At the same time, it is important to stress that N.F. Vatutin's scheme to split the front of Hoth's and Kempf's groupings, once they had gone on the attack, began to be realized from the outset. Despite great exertions, the Germans throughout 5 July failed to penetrate even the main line of resistance at the boundary between the 6th Guards and 7th Guards Armies. In addition, despite the heavy pressure on their flanks, thanks to the thorough preparation of the positions and the high saturation of artillery means both of the flanking divisions – the 375th Rifle Division (primarily) and the 81st Guards Rifle Division (completely) managed to hold their lines.

Yet together with these successes, the first day of the defensive operation also brought worrisome news. As was in fact anticipated, in order to overrun the defense the enemy resorted to a direct and already well-tested method of attack – panzer attacks with strong air support, which had already proven to be highly effective. Thanks to this, by the end of the first day of Citadel, the 6th Guards Army's main resistance belt had been breached to its entire depth (in the sector of the 52nd Guards Rifle Division), and two of its divisions, the 52nd Guards and 67th Guards Rifle Divisions had suffered heavy losses. Even though I.M. Chistiakov committed only his anti-tank and mobile reserve in order to stabilize the situation, without involving the main forces of the second echelon, the situation on Army Group South's main axis of attack remained unstable and was fraught with serious complications.

An exceptionally serious situation had developed in the sector of the 7th Guards Army as well. Here, the enemy had also assembled major forces and was using them relatively effectively. According to M.S. Shumilov's report, although the main line of resistance in the center of his army hadn't been entirely breached, because of the fact that two of the divisions that had taken on the enemy's main attack here had suffered substantial losses by evening it was now being held primarily by troops of the second echelon (the 73rd Guards Rifle Division) and the army's reserve (the 213th Rifle Division), which were reinforced by armored brigades (27th Guards Tank Brigade) and regiments (167th Separate Tank Regiment and the 1438th Self-propelled Artillery Regiment.

By the end of the day on the left flank of the 72nd Guards Rifle Division, the woods south of Rzhavets and the village itself had been mopped up of elements of the 320th Infantry Division, the front line had been stabilized roughly along the Titovka – Belgorod railroad line, and at Bezliudovka the enemy had even been thrown back from the railroad embankment and squeezed up against the eastern bank of the river, having captured a significant portion of the village. However, on the right flank the situation was deteriorating by evening; the 106th Infantry Division was continuing to expand the breach it had created. While maintaining possession of the key villages of Nizhnii Ol'shanets and Maslova Pristan', it was doggedly advancing into the depth of the 24th Guards Rifle Corps' defenses. According to the combat journal of the 73rd Guards Rifle Division's 211th Guards Rifle Regiment, which by 1700 had taken up a defense behind the 72nd Guards Rifle Division on the line between the hill 1.2 kilometers west of Korenskaia Dacha (marked "K" on the maps) and the road fork south of the "Poliana" State Farm, already at 1800 18 tanks and assault guns with the support of infantry of the 106th Infantry Division was attacking its combat outposts (reinforced by a company of the 1st Rifle Battalion) on the northwestern fringe of the woods on Hill 167.7 (2 kilometers south of the southern outskirts of Krutoi Log). Having lost two tanks and one assault gun, the enemy fell back, but already two hours later attacked again and even broke through to the woods on the hilltop. However, the Germans were thrown back from there by a counterattack made by the regiment's submachine gun company.[161] Thus, the defense of Losev's 72nd Guards Rifle Division at the boundary between the 7th Guards Army's two rifle corps had been penetrated to its entire depth.

The situation of the 78th Guards Rifle Division was prompting the greatest concern among the 7th Guards Army command. First, here the enemy had already massed two strong panzer groups on the eastern bank of the Northern Donets River, and having attacked with them along both sides of the Razumnaia River, they had split the 78th Guards Rifle Division's defense almost to its entire depth. Second, the Germans' arrival on the approaches to Generalovka and Belinskaia placed the left flank and rear of the 81st Guards Rifle Division under threat. If in the nearest future they managed with their already available forces (the strength of which the 7th Guards Army headquarters placed at not less than 100 tanks) to overrun the defenses of the 25th Guards Rifle Corps through Belinskaia to Blizhniaia Igumenka or even further (across the Northern Donets) to Gostishchevo, then Morozov's 81st Guards Rifle Division would be able to maintain its line all it wanted, but it would fall into encirclement as a result, and both of von Manstein's assault groupings that were attacking toward Kursk would be able to link their flanks.

Closely monitoring the course of combat operations on 5 July, M.S. Shumilov observed an important detail in them: the sharp contrast in the Germans' use of the Luftwaffe directly over the battlefield on the front of the 6th Guards and 7th Guards Armies. Despite the fact that east of Belgorod Army Detachment Kempf was forced to make a river crossing, and then break through a main belt of resistance that was just as strongly fortified as the one on the axis of Army Group South's main attack, the aerial support provided for the attacking Germans here was little both in the morning and throughout the entire day. This unquestionably helped the 7th Guards Army prevent a deep penetration like its neighbor experienced. The enemy divisions that were attacking the 7th Guards Army were primarily supported by artillery. A report from the Aviation Department of the 7th Guards Army headquarters observes:

> Enemy aircraft started their activity from the sunrise on 5 July 1943. Throughout the day the enemy conducted 1,223 individual sorties, and primarily bombed our combat positions in the areas of Miasoedovo, Blizhniaia Igumenka, Staryi Gorod, Iastrebovo, Belinskaia and Krutoi Log, while conducting a small number of missions against the area of the Shebekinskaia Dacha Woods. … The enemy believed that on 5 July his air force would have a large effect on the effectiveness of his offensive. However, it should be noted that the 1,223 individual sorties were conducted by the enemy primarily in the morning on 5 July 1943 and inflicted almost no harm to our troops, with the exception of injuring several of our soldiers and doing completely insignificant damage to equipment. … Beginning on 6 July, the enemy reduced

---

161 TsAMO RF, F. 211 gv. sp, op. 145061, d. 3, l. 24obr.

its aerial activity; for example, over 6 July only 247 individual sorties were flown, and just 274 on 7 July. All of these missions were primarily directed by the enemy to repel the strikes by our ground attack aircraft and bombers.[162]

Thus, in addition to the problems that arose on the main axis of attack (6th Guards Army), which had been previously predicted and were to be resolved by advancing the 1st Tank Army and two separate tank corps up to the second belt of defenses, already on the afternoon of 5 July two other complex problems were placed in front of the Voronezh Front command, which were connected with the need to regroup the 69th and 7th Guards Armies, as well as a portion of the Front's reserves. The plan of maneuver with the Front's forces, including the reinforcing of these armies, had been worked out long before, and it was gradually put into practice throughout the day of 5 July as the situation grew more acute.

On the morning of 5 July, N.F. Vatutin signed Special Order No. 008/op, which contained instructions to the commander of his all-arms reserve – Lieutenant General S.G. Goriachev and his 35th Guards Rifle Corps – to become subordinate to the 69th Army and by 0800 6 July to move up the 94th Guards Rifle Division to Prokhorovka, and the 92nd and 93rd Guards Rifle Divisions to the Korocha area. As subsequent events would show, this decision proved timely and far-sighted. The place of the assembly of the Guards rifle divisions gave evidence that the General of the Army was more concerned by the situation on the Front's left flank than on its center, even though the enemy had launched an attack with significantly stronger panzer formations against the 6th Guards Army. Having formed an armored shield of five tank and mechanized corps in the rear of Chistiakov's 6th Guards Army, he justifiably reasoned that these thousand tanks and self-propelled guns would be adequate to block the Germans' path into the depth of the Front's defenses. M.S. Shumilov didn't have such powerful means, and there was no possibility to reinforce his army with tank units even at the Front's expense, even though an enemy panzer division had already appeared on the eastern bank of the Northern Donets River and it was difficult for the infantry to hold up against it without the support of strong mobile formations. Thus, by bringing up two Guards rifle divisions to the Korocha area, N.F. Vatutin was guarding himself in case the situation sharply deteriorated first of all in the sector of the 7th Guards Army. The 93rd Guards Rifle Division that had been moved up to Prokhorovka had been initially planned to be activated for launching a counterattack from the Prokhorovka direction on 6 July together with the tank corps against the right flank of the Fourth Panzer Army. However, the situation changed by then.

N.F. Vatutin thought rather highly of the actions of the 7th Guards Army's command and the results of the combat work done by its forces throughout 5 July. Keeping the enemy within the system of the main army-level belt of defenses was a serious achievement and had a substantial influence on the successful implementation of the Front's defensive operation. At the same time, he recommended to the 7th Guards Army commander to strengthen the pressure on the strongest enemy grouping, which was moving out of the area east of Solomino and Dorogobuzheno, by means of launching a counterattack against its flanks. He also began to reinforce the 7th Guards Army already on the morning of 5 July, though not directly so.

Considering G.K. Zhukov's order to keep two echelons continuously on the boundary within Voronezh Front's defense, N.F. Vatutin decided that this was not only the army commander's concern and that he shared equal responsibility for it. He therefore issued an order for Colonel M.A. Bushin's 111th Rifle Division from the 49th Army to move into the second echelon on the left flank of the 24th Guards Rifle Corps in order to replace the 15th Guards Rifle Division, which together with the 213th Rifle Division would go into the army commander's reserve. As a

---
162 TsAMO RF, F. 7 gv.A, op. 5312, d. 539, l. 201.

result, M.S. Shumilov had the possibility to use his army's forces fully for an active defense. At the same time, having operationally subordinated the 111th Rifle Division to the 7th Guards Army (Shumilov could only use it on the defense in the former sector of the 15th Guards Rifle Division, and elsewhere, only with the Front's authorization), the General of the Army was plainly making it understood that Shumilov was obliged to rely only on his own strength, which in Vatutin's view was fully sufficient for holding the 7th Guards Army's line of defense.

Now let's dwell in detail on the situation as it stood by the end of 5 July east of Belgorod. What results did the first day of this major battle fought by Shumilov's army bring, which even though it was positioned on the direction of Army Group South's auxiliary attack, still played a significant role in Voronezh Front's defensive operation?

It is difficult to determine the precise line, along which the front stabilized by 2400, especially in the 78th Guards Rifle Division's sector, since fighting continued almost all night in the village of Razumnoe and at Krutoi Log. According to the information of 7th Guards Army's headquarters, by 1900 its divisions that had been attacked by Army Detachment Kempf were defending the line: (excl.) Mikhailovka – area of Hill 126.3 – Razumnoe – southwestern outskirts of Krutoi Log – 800 meters east of Bezliudovka – eastern outskirts of Nizhnii Ol'shanets – 2 kilometers east of Karnaukhovka -- 800 meters east of Maslova Pristan' – (excl.) Bezliudovka, and further along just as before. Thus, of the four rifle divisions of the first echelon, only two were fully holding their positions – the 81st Guards and 36th Guards Rifle Divisions. Moreover, Kempf's forces hadn't undertaken any active operations opposite Denisenko's 36th Guards Rifle Division, except for the morning's reconnaissance-in-force conducted by the XXXXII Army Corps' 282nd Infantry Division. However, by midnight, if to judge from the records of the Front command, the situation of the Soviet side improved somewhat. An intelligence summary at 0700 on 6 July has been preserved, in which the Front's chief of staff Lieutenant General S.P. Ivanov noted in pencil that "by the end of day [5 July], the enemy was holding the Riaski woods, southwestern portion of Razumnoe and Karnaukhovka, while having been thrown back to the western bank from all the remaining points."[163] It is possible that the 7th Guards Army's leadership was counting upon driving the enemy back from that very same Maslova Pristan', for example, by the end of the day, using the significant forces of the army's reserve and knowing that fighting was going on in the village itself had hastily reported this as an established fact. For example, in Combat Report No. 50 at 1800, N.A. Vasil'ev succinctly stated, "I've decided on the night of 5-6 July 1943 with the combined efforts of the 213th Rifle Division and 72nd Guards Rifle Division to drive the enemy out of the northern portion of Maslova Pristan', Priiutovka and Bezliudovka and thereby regain the 72nd Guards Rifle Division's position."[164]

However, there is doubt that Shumilov resorted to open exaggeration and reported that in the sector of the substantially weakened 78th Guards Rifle Division, where in the daytime no counterattack had been launched (with the exception of the 167th Separate Tank Regiment's forlorn counterattack) and there was no plan to launch one on the night of 5-6 July, Shumilov's forces had driven the Germans out of Dal'nie Peski and Dorogobuzheno. I believe it was the Front headquarters that touched up the day's picture, since the information written on the intelligence summary by S.P. Ivanov diverges from the combat reports submitted by the 24th and 25th Guards Rifle Corps. They state that despite all the efforts, the enemy was holding Nizhnii Ol'shanets, Dal'nie Peski and Priiutovka; most of Maslova Pristan' and Razumnoe; and was digging in on the southern and southwestern outskirts of Krutoi Log. One must pay due respect to the tenacity of the men of the 223rd Guards Rifle Regiment, its 3rd Rifle Battalion, and the 8th and 9th Companies of 3/225th

---

163 TsAMO RF, F. 203, op. 2843, d. 452, l. 18.
164 TsAMO RF, F. 24 gv. sk, op. 1, d. 14, l. 53.

Guards Rifle Regiment, along with the batteries of the 1st and 3rd Battalions of the 155th Guards Artillery Regiment that despite the strong German pressure on Krutoi Log, they were keeping firm possession of the majority of this most powerful anti-tank strongpoint in the sector of the 78th Guards Rifle Division. With a certain amount of confidence one can say that by midnight, only Bezliudovka had been partially mopped up of the enemy. The 24th Guards Rifle Corps' journal of combat operations states, "The 585th Rifle Regiment [of the 213th Rifle Division] with two battalions, having thrown back the forward units of the 585th Infantry Regiment, and on the heels of the enemy reached the northern outskirts of Bezliudovka and the woods north and east of Bezliudovka. Together with 2 and 3/224th Guards Rifle Regiment, it engaged in heavy trench combat with the enemy and by the end of the day had fully mopped up and seized the trenches."[165]

From this citation, it isn't clear about what trenches in which part of the village are being discussed – the northern or eastern trench sectors, or else the entire line of the regiments' main positions in the area of this village. There is evidence that the 320th Infantry Division didn't fully fall back from Bezliudovka to the western bank of the river, and that some of its elements had dug in on the western and southwestern outskirts of the village, in the river's basin, and in the patches of woods around the village. The Germans did manage to hold the units of 3/224th Guards Rifle Regiment, in particular the 9th Rifle Company, in this village in encirclement until 6 July. Thus, Postel's division had nevertheless managed to maintain a bridgehead at Bezliudovka, and that night began to rebuild the damaged bridges and construct new crossing sites and bridges.

Incidentally, on 5 July 1943 Soviet troops captured more than two platoons of prisoners from the 320th Infantry Division (30 by the 72nd Guards Rifle Division, 12 by the 27th Guards Tank Brigade). Under interrogation they revealed that the division had suffered painful losses; in particular among company commanders. In addition, a battalion commander in Infantry Regiment 585 had been put out of action (according to other information, two battalion commanders, including the commander of III/Infantry Regiment 586). At the same time, the Red Army Lieutenant I.D. Taranenko came back over to our side, whom the Germans had been using as a nurse in a casualty clearing station of Infantry Regiment 585. He reported that when crossing the Northern Donets, the headquarters company of Infantry Regiment 585 alone had lost 7 killed and 12 wounded.[166]

However, despite this the situation that Losev's 72nd Guards Rifle Division faced continued to remain difficult. Even though the enemy had operated primarily with infantry units supported by artillery and self-propelled guns, he had managed to achieve a substantial success. Already by the afternoon, practically all of the battalion and company strongpoints in the main belt of resistance (Karnaukhovka, Maslova Pristan', Rzhavets, the Kar'ernaia railyard, Priiutovka and Bezliudovka) were in a tight ring of encirclement. Thanks to the fact that all of these villages had been prepared for an all-round defense, the garrisons of Karnaukhovka, Maslova Pristan' and Priiutovka couldn't be destroyed from the march and continued to engage in bloody fighting even in encirclement until evening. In fact, even though the foe had been shoved back to the second line of trenches with a counterattack at 2130, and the frontline positions had almost been fully regained on the left flank, the Soviet troops weren't able to save everyone who had wound up in the pocket. According to an explanatory note added to the report on losses according to Form No. 8 (a 10-day reporting period, over the period between 1 and 10 July 1943), when coming out of encirclement in the area of Bezliudovka, only 150 men remained in the 3rd Battalion of the 224th Guards Rifle Regiment; the rest were missing in action, including the entire 9th Company that had been located in the village itself.[167] However, toward the end of July 1943 some of the soldiers

---

165 TsAMO RF, F. 24 gv. sk, op. 1, d. 21, l. 19.
166 TsAMO RF, F. 72 gv. sd, op. 1, d. 60, l. 26.
167 TsAMO RF, F. 7 gv. A., op. 5317, d. 11, l. 348.

and commanders returned to the regiment and with their assistance the identity of the dead was determined. According to a report from the 7th Guards Army's Personnel Department for 31 July, only 23 men in the 224th Guards Rifle Regiment in Bezliudovka on 5 July were still listed as missing-in-action.[168]

The 3rd Battalion of the 229th Guards Rifle Regiment that was encircled that morning in Karnaukhovka was completely wiped out and as noted in the 24th Guards Rifle Corps' combat diary, no information about it whatsoever arrived in the corps headquarters. The fate of the 2nd Battalion of the 229th Guards Rifle Regiment was also tragic. After the war, an exquisite legend about its battle was contrived in domestic literature: "For 36 hours the Guardsmen of the 2nd Battalion of the 72nd Guards Rifle Division's 229th Guards Regiment under the command of Senior Lieutenant V.A. Dvoinyi fought in encirclement in Maslova Pristan'. Indeed, they held out until the arrival of reinforcements."[169] However, in the documents of the 24th Guards Rifle Corps, the situation is laid out differently, more realistically and callously. The Guardsmen really did fight courageously, but not for 36 hours, and virtually no one was left to wait for the reinforcements. Thanks to the persistence of the 27th Guards Tank Brigade, the tanks of which in the face of heavy fire managed to break through to the northeastern and southeastern outskirts of Maslova Pristan', on the evening of 5 July only 17 soldiers of the 2nd Battalion, led by the battalion commander, came out of the encirclement; of the more than 500 men that reported for duty that morning, the rest were killed or captured. According to the archival documents that I managed to uncover in the files of the 72nd Guards Rifle Division, its headquarters reported that in the course of 5-6 July 1943, of the two battalions of the 229th Guards Rifle Regiment in Karnaukhovka and Maslova Pristan', 686 soldiers and officers, including 169 of the 2nd Battalion and 517 of the 3rd Battalion, went missing in action and never returned to the regiment.[170] If you take into consideration that on 6 July these villages still remained in German possession, then the number of missing-in-action can be assigned with confidence to the losses for 5 July alone.

Together with the units of the 229th Guards Rifle Regiment, the 4th Anti-tank Rifle Battalion also fell into encirclement in the area of Maslova Pristan'. On 8 July it had 17 men missing-in-action. However, after the Soviet troops went in pursuit of the retreating German forces in the latter half of July, soldiers and commanders who had escaped captivity or had hidden from the Germans on occupied territory began to arrive in the forward elements. For example, on 20 July 1943, soldiers of this battalion N.S. Pivovarov and A.I. Berezhnoi returned to the 72nd Guards Rifle Division. Under questioning they reported that on 5 July, when they'd been captured, the Germans gathered approximately another 30 Red Army soldiers together with them on the outskirts of Maslova Pristan' and marched them under escort to the western bank of the Donets to Ziborovka, where a special camp only for Russian prisoners of war had been established. At the moment the group arrived in the camp, it already held 130 prisoners. A provost corps was also located there. At first the prisoners were used as burial teams, but around 8-9 July, when the German offensive toward Kursk began to bog down, they were used to rebuild the Soviet trench lines in the rear of Korps Raus.

Together with a significant number of men from the combat elements, a number of commanders of the 72nd Guards Rifle Division's headquarters failed to come out of encirclement in Maslova Pristan'. For example, a staff group from its Political Department, which was busy with undermining the morale of enemy troops, was in Maslova Pristan' on the morning of 5 July. As a

---

168 Ibid., l. 379.
169 *Ogennaia duga: Belgorod – Kursk – Orel* [*Ring of fire: Belgorod – Kursk – Orel*] (Moscow: ID "Zvonnitsa-MG", 2003), p. 281.
170 TsAMO RF, F. 7 gv. A., op. 5317, d. 11, l. 379.

result, Senior Instructor for Organizational-Party Work Captain V.D. Kharitonov, Instructor for Work among Enemy Troops and Population Senior Lieutenant Ia.P. Belik, and a number of other commanders went missing from it.

By midnight, the headquarters of Losev's 72nd Guards Rifle Division with great difficulty managed to make contact with the command of its regiments. However, the majority of their headquarters didn't have accurate information on the losses and the condition of the units, since wire communications with the battalions had been cut almost immediately after the start of the German artillery preparation, and the majority of the radio sets had been knocked out already by mid-day. Thus, precise figures for the loss of men for 5 July haven't been found. Information about the losses of the 72nd Guards Rifle Division over two days of fighting are presented in Table 8:

Table 8 Manpower losses of the 72nd Guards Rifle Division in the course of combat operations on 5 and 6 July 1943[171]

Unit	Killed or mortally wounded			Wounded			Missing in action			Total			Grand Total
	Command	NCOs	Enlisted	Command	NCOs	Enlisted	Command	NCOs	Enlisted	Command	NCOs	Enlisted	
222 GRR	5	21	96	72	239	390	1	9	96	78	269	582	929
224 GRR	5	19	36	10	40	242	1	4	184	16	63	482	541
229 GRR	6	20	70	7	73	162	84	224	496	98	317	728	1143
155 GAR	–	2	5	3	1	13	–	–	14	3	3	32	38
Separate Guards training bn	–	–	7	2	2	7	–	–	1	2	2	15	19
78 Gds A-T Bn	–	2	1	1	3	7	–	–	25	1	5	33	39
Separate reconnaissance company	–	2	3	1	5	4	–	–	–	1	7	7	15
81 Gds Sapper Battalion	1	–	2	4	–	5	–	–	–	5	–	7	12
Separate signals company	–	2	5	–	–	4	–	–	–	–	2	9	11
Total	17	68	225	100	363	834	86	237	816	204	668	1875	2747
4th Army ATR Bn	1	5	8	6	13	14	–	5	12	8	30	43	81[1]

Notes
1 In addition to the battalion's indicated losses, it lost 17 soldiers and commanders that were captured, including one commander, one junior commander and 9 enlisted men.

In the files of the TsAMO RF, different figures have been preserved, which give a certain image of the condition of the 72nd Guards Rifle Division by the end of the first day of the defensive operation; this is the quantity of weapons left on the battlefield behind enemy lines or disabled. The division lost 4,352 rifles, 2,304 PPSh submachine guns, 400 light machine guns, 133 heavy

---

171 TsAMO RF, f. 72 gv. sd, op. 1, d. 70, l. 235.

machine guns, 53 50mm mortars, 69 82mm mortars, 23 120mm mortars, 36 76mm guns, 46 anti-tank guns, 12 122mm howitzers and 6,823 gas masks.[172]

Regarding the gas masks, it is understandable that the soldiers usually tossed them aside in combat, because they were cumbersome and awkward to carry. The remaining figures speak to the fact that the division lost a significant number of men, not less than 1,500 to 1,700. In addition, even if conditionally speaking 60-70% of the so-called "active bayonets" [fighting troops] had survived, they were not combat-capable, because the possibility to arm the remaining men had been deprived. Finally, the loss of so many arms and weapons is connected with the fact that a significant portion of division's soldiers and officers were in operational encirclement, and of them, only around 700 were listed as missing-in-action. In the afternoon, Losev reported that the troops were experiencing an acute lack of ammunition and there was no possibility to bring up more. Having run out of ammunition, the Red Army troops were simply dropping their weapons and picking up whatever German weapons they came across. Of course, there were also instances of panic and "skedaddling". It has already been noted above that because of the cowardice of the commander of a machine-gun company, the enemy seized 13 fully-operational Maksim machine guns at once.

The situation in the 78th Guards Rifle Division shaped up to be even worse. Two panzer divisions and one infantry division had struck its defenses simultaneously, and thus it also proved helpless to withstand such an onslaught. In the afternoon of 5 July, units of the 25th Guards Rifle Corps' second echelon and Shumilov's mobile reserve already entered combat in its sector. Thanks to their efforts, the enemy's two panzer groups managed to take only the positions of the first-echelon regiments and to capture the battalion strongpoints of Nizhnii Ol'shanets, Dal'nie Peski, and the railroad station and village of Rzhavets. The frontline stabilized along the line: woods south of the labor corrective camp – southwestern slopes of Hill 139.9 – (excl.) southern outskirts of Belinskaia – ground south of Hill 164.7 – southwestern outskirts of Krutoi Log – Nizhnii Ol'shanets. Because of the continued functioning of communications with the regiments that were defending the main belt of defenses and the sharp work of its headquarters, command and control wasn't disrupted in the 78th Guards Rifle Division, and thus it managed to avoid the loss of entire battalions in encirclement, as happened in the 72nd Guards Rifle Division. The 1st Batalion of the 225th Guards Rifle Regiment, which had been isolated in Nizhnii Ol'shanets, even managed to break out of the encirclement. This substantially affected its level of irreplaceable losses, which proved to be almost twice that of Losev's 72nd Guards Rifle Division. According to a summary report released by its headquarters without delay, the 78th Guards Rifle Division had 383 killed and 53 that were missing-in-action.[173] The 225th Guards Rifle Regiment, which was positioned on the axis of the 7th Panzer Division's main attack, suffered worst of all; it had 1,278 killed and wounded (including 271 dead and 1,006 who received wounds of varying severity).[174]

What were the reasons why the army's central sector yielded to the German attack, despite the well-prepared system of defense of the main belt of resistance, which was moreover strengthened by a natural obstacle like the Northern Donets River? There were several reasons for this, and almost all of them have been mentioned above, although in various contexts. Thus I will summarize and supplement them with fresh information from archival sources.

In the first place, the 7th Guards Army command when preparing for the operation wasn't able to determine accurately the direction of the enemy's possible main attack, and therefore didn't properly allocate its forces and means. However, it must be recognized that M.S. Shumilov wasn't

---

172 TsAMO RF, F. 72 gv. sd, op. 1, d. 71, l. 4.
173 TsAMO RF, F. 1225, op. 1, d. 15, l. 74.
174 Ibid., l. 75.

free in determining the sectors where he should concentrate his strength and sources of fire; G.K. Zhukov and N.F. Vatutin made these decisions for him. The army commander, in essence, became the hostage of two points of view as to how it was necessary to construct his defenses. Carrying out the decisions of his superiors, M.S. Shumilov concentrated his main forces, especially artillery, on the flanks, just as the Marshal of the Soviet Union and the Front Commander-in-Chief insisted, though the calculations of Vatutin, who I will remind you strove first and foremost to reinforce the boundary between the 6th and 7th Guards Armies, proved to be more accurate. It was precisely there where Army Detachment Kempf focused the attack of its III Panzer Corps in order to break through the boundary between the armies. Not a single other division of Shumilov's 7th Guards Army positioned where the Germans succeeded in breaching the main defensive belt had such a high density of artillery and anti-tank guns as had Morozov's 81st Guards Rifle Division. This was the main reason for the failure of the attack of Breith's troops on the right flank of the 7th Guards Army and at the same time for their discernible success in the sector of the army's other divisions. Thanks to the powerful preemptive artillery barrage, the 81st Guards Rifle Division already in the opening hours of the offensive deprived the 6th Panzer Division of the possibility to conduct an offensive: it not only destroyed all the bridges, but also prevented them from being rebuilt, while the infantry that made its way across the river was destroyed. Because of this (the division's tremendous firepower), its defenses remained firm even after the armored vehicles of the 19th Panzer Division appeared on its left flank.

The second reason to a large extent flows from the first, and first of all this concerns the 78th Guards Rifle Division. Skvortsov's division was the only one of all the divisions of the first line struck simultaneously by three enemy divisions, including two that attacked within a sector of just 4.5 kilometers. At the same time, it didn't have the necessary amount of artillery to disrupt the crossing of the 19th and 7th Panzer Divisions. I'll remind you that by the morning of 5 July, the 78th Guards Rifle Division received as reinforcements only the 4th Anti-tank Rifle Battalion and 3rd Battalion/671st Artillery Regiment (from the 213th Rifle Division). The shifting of the 81st Guards Rifle Division's artillery fire into the sector of the 78th Guards Rifle Division couldn't cardinally change the situation with the German river crossing, because first, in the morning, the cannon and mortar regiments had been firing on the bridges in Belgorod and the southern end of Pushkarnoe in the interests of the 81st Guards Rifle Division; and secondly, some of the artillery regiments didn't have the necessary range to target the bridges and risked hitting friendly troops. By the time the artillery fire had been shifted into the 78th Guards Rifle Division's sector (after sunrise), the 7th Panzer Division had already crossed *kampfgruppen* to the eastern bank, while some of its panzers had even crossed at fords. In addition, the Soviet artillery fire was conducted from defilade positions, without artillery spotters, so the most part it was blind. Even so, in a number of instances it proved rather effective. Thus the 78th Guards Rifle Division didn't have a real possibility to withstand such heavy pressure for a lengthy period of time on its own – especially when you consider that during the afternoon, when the 19th Panzer Division's Panzer Regiment 27 entered the fighting, aircraft of the German VIII Fliegerkorps struck its positions.

The reasons for the swift advance of Korps Raus' *kampfgruppen* into the depth of the 72nd Guards Rifle Division's defenses are similar to those that applied to the 78th Guards Rifle Division. Losev's Guards division was holding an extended front of 15 kilometers (the 78th Guards Rifle Division's sector stretched for 10 kilometers) and had the lowest density of artillery in the 7th Guards Army, just 8 artillery tubes per kilometer of front. At the same time, a number of important, additional factors were operating here. Relying on the archival documents with which I've become familiar (some of which were cited above), I can state with confidence that the quality of the engineer works in the sector of the 72nd Guards Rifle Division was noticeably lower than in the 78th Guards Rifle Division's sector, not to mention those of the 81st Guards Rifle Division, which could be called model in this sense. The blame for this shortcoming to a great degree lies on the shoulders of Major General A.I. Losev, who although had been commanding the division from the end of 1942, was in essence still a young, relatively inexperienced commander. He had recommended himself with his ability to organize offensive combat and for his ability to forge cooperation among different types of troops (here, his experience as an artilleryman was telling), but when the pause in operations arrived, the resolution of defensive tasks – training troops, working out a system of fire, building fortifications, monitoring and demanding the exact execution of orders – was difficult for him. His rather gentle nature and a number of negative traits affected this. In the combat description of Losev given by his superior N.A. Vasil'ev on 30 June 1943, the corps commander wrote:

> When adopting a defensive posture the division didn't manage well with the fortification of its sector of defense and poorly organized a system of fire – this was the result of the insufficient insistence on high standards and the weak control shown by the division commander. Weapons and ammunition stockpiles in the majority of cases are kept in order, but during inspections, the poor maintenance and protection of weapons was found in a number of separate elements – weapons were dirty and even rusty. …. By his nature, Losev is not demanding – he is open to everyone and exerts little and gentle control over subordinates, and all this has an effect on discipline.[175]

The comments given above are not the product of intrigue on the part of the corps commander, although the career of a division commander rarely went by without them. There is an endorsement on this document: "Agreed. 4/7.43 Shumilov", and it is hard to suspect the army commander of not being objective. It was M.S. Shumilov who had recommended that A.I. Losev be promoted to the rank of major general after the latter's strong performance at Stalingrad, then put him up for the title "Hero of the Soviet Union" for his successful forced crossing of the Dniepr River, and just a bit later would recommend him for the post of rifle corps commander. The documents of the division itself show that when constructing the 72nd Guards Rifle Division's line of defense, its command often put the regiment commanders on record for evident shortcomings, or strictly demanded that the shortcomings be eliminated. As a result of the low demandingness and even the nonchalance in the frontline regiments, the situation in them that formed by the start of the Battle of Kursk was rather woeful. Order No.0103 from the 72nd Guards Rifle Division's chief of staff dated 2 July 1943 decried:

An inspection by a commission of the division headquarters regarding the camouflaging of the troops and defensive works in the division's sector has revealed the following:

1. Some of the communication trenches in 1/229th Guards Rifle Regiment have been camouflaged with thatch. The embrasures of the bunkers are completely unmasked in daylight hours. The camouflage needs changing in many firing positions, and there are no dummy firing positions.

    2/229th Guards Rifle Regiment has communications trenches and weapon pits that are not concealed, and the embrasures of firing positions require clearance. In the area of Priiutovka, the firing positions that have been moved up closer to the channel of the Northern Donets haven't been completely set up, and in certain places aren't connected by communication trenches. There are no dummy firing positions.

    3/229th Guards Rifle Regiment – the majority of the firing positions of the 7th and 9th Rifle Companies aren't camouflaged. There are no dummy firing positions.

---

175 Author's personal archive.

2. 1/224th Guards Rifle Regiment – communication trenches have not been brought up to standard, firing positions for light machine guns haven't been set up, and alternate positions are lacking. The same applies to the 50mm mortars. Camouflaging of the communication trenches and weapon pits is lacking; the firing positions for the 82mm mortars and anti-tank guns are an exception. Only the 2nd and 3rd Platoons of the 2nd Rifle Company, which are occupying natural cover, have concealment against ground observation. The firing positions and artificial obstacles have no concealment from aerial observation, with the exception of the company of 82mm mortars. Only the mortar company also has dummy firing positions. Slit trenches for protection against tanks are absolutely absent in the area of a battalion's defense.

2/224th Guards Rifle Regiment has no concealment of the primary and alternate firing positions from either ground or aerial observation. There are no dummy firing positions or equipped sites.

3/224th Guards Rifle Regiment – paths aren't camouflaged. Firing positions for the most part are concealed with locally improvised material. In the regiment's mortar battery, the main and alternate firing positions are camouflaged. There are routes of retreat, but no dummy firing positions.[176]

The 222nd Guards Rifle Regiment, which was in reserve, was in a similar situation.

At the same time, serious problems existed in the division with respect to the hardiness of the troops. According to reports from the Front's SMERSH counterintelligence, the rank and file for the most part on 5 July 1943 demonstrated high tenacity and courage, and no panicked flights or massed retreats from the forward edge were observed, even during attacks by German armor. Yet a number of unit commanders who were located on the axis of Korps Raus' main attack often lost their composure and sometimes showed open cowardice. Already above, I've cited several examples of flight from the battlefield by a number of junior commanders of the 222nd and 229th Guards Rifle Regiment, as a result of which the enemy managed to achieve a certain tactical success. Unfortunately, there were more than a few such cases in the 72nd Guards Rifle Division on the opening day of the German offensive. Three platoon commanders alone were shot on the spot for abandoning positions without an order together with their men, and this doesn't include Lieutenant Pavlov, who was turned over to trial in front of a tribunal for this same action.

Consideration should be given as well to instances of betrayal before the start of the battle, which also played a negative role in the opening hours of the fighting. Over the days before the German offensive began, several of the 72nd Guards Rifle Division's servicemen went over to the enemy's side, and judging from the evidence, provided the Germans with accurate information about the lay out of the defenses on the forward edge, the locations of the combat outposts, and the zones of fire. This allowed the command of Korps Raus to determine the precise locations of the firing positions of the forward battalions in order to target them with artillery and correctly plan the opening attack. I managed to find echoes of these acts of betrayal in an evening report of its headquarters for 5 July: "The picture given to us by a turncoat in the days prior to the offensive has been fully confirmed."[177] The above-listed subjective factors in combination with the low saturation with artillery led to the fact that the 72nd Guards Rifle Division fought the two German infantry divisions much worse than the 78th Guards Rifle, which also didn't receive significant artillery strength, but which took on the simultaneous attack of two panzer divisions reinforced by regiments of the 168th Infantry Division plus the 106th Infantry Division.

---

176 TsAMO RF, F. 72 gv. sd, op. 1, d. 14, l. 229.
177 NARA US, t. 312, r. 59, f. 7574638.

Now we'll try to assess how the German command viewed the start of Citadel, and how it evaluated the actions of its troops. I think it won't be a surprise to the reader if the leadership of both Army Group South and Army Detachment Kempf weren't delighted by how the first day of this colossal battle ended. Just as the pessimists expected, and this included a number of commanders of Army Detachent Kempf's divisions (including von Funck himself), the operation's plan began to fall apart already in the first hours of implementing it. Of the four corps of Army Group South that stepped off toward Kursk, only the II SS Panzer Corps, which wasn't the strongest corps, managed to break through the first belt of defenses to its entire depth, and did so with difficulty. All of the remaining corps, including the XXXXVIII Panzer Corps that was reinforced with the Panther brigade, upon which Hitler had staked great hopes, had become bogged down in the very first line of defenses, losing men and materiel. General of Infantry Theodor Busse, the chief of staff of Army Group South, later wrote:

> In slugging their way through the enemy defense system, German troops experienced great difficulty. Clinging tenaciously to their positions, the Russians everywhere defended themselves stubbornly. The lack of a sufficient number of infantry divisions in the attack – which had been pointed out repeatedly by army and army group headquarters – became painfully evident on the very first day as our troops began fighting their way through the Soviet defenses.[178]

However, if on the axis of the main attack by Fourth Panzer Army there were at least small achievements that promised certain positive dynamics on 6 July due to the high activity of the II SS Panzer Division, the massing of panzers on a narrow axis and the effects of the VIII Fliegerkorps' strikes, then in the sector of Army Detachment Kempf, the day ended in disappointment and frustration. Thus to a certain extent it was necessary to start all over again. One couldn't speak about the execution of the main task to cover the right flank of the Fourth Panzer Army with the forces of III Panzer Corps. The Russians had even prevented von Hünersdorff's 6th Panzer Division from even crossing to the eastern bank, and so it (one-third of the panzer corps!) spent the entire day inactive, waiting for the opportunity to cross (if you don't count the fruitless attempts by the two *kampfgruppen* to break through to Staryi Gorod and Chernaia Poliana). Only toward evening was the decision made to send its panzer regiment over the bridges of the 7th Panzer Division in the area of Dal'nie Peski and to assemble the rest of its units on the eastern bank of the river after the 168th Infantry Division turned over its sector. Meanwhile the successes of the 7th and 19th Panzer Divisions, which nevertheless managed to get their armor across the river and introduce it into the fighting, proved rather modest. At the very least, the first day's objectives weren't reached. A bridgehead was seized that extended along the river for 10 kilometers and had a depth of up to 7 kilometers, but even it wasn't continuous. Even by the end of the day, Schmidt's and von Funck's *kampfgruppen* had been unable to drive the fiercely resisting Russian units from out of the major villages of Razumnoe and Krutoi Log, in order to close the adjacent flanks of Panzer Regiment 25 and Panzer Regiment 27, or link the right flank of III Panzer Corps with the left flank of Korps Raus.

Even so, no matter how strangely, von Manstein in his memoirs "forgot" to mention all of these problems, and when describing the results of the first day of Citadel emphasized only Raus's failure, the situation in whose sector of offensive was undoubtedly much worse.[179] Rather successfully

---

178 S. Newton, *Kurskaia bitva: Germanskii vzgliad*, p. 35. This quote is on page 19 of the original English-language edition.
179 Manstein, *Uteriannye pobedy*, p. 536.

having started the river crossing and the offensive on the east bank, the assault groups of his divisions, battling their way forward against fierce resistance of the Guardsmen and bypassing major strongpoints, by noon had made only an approximate 2-kilometer advance and reached the railroad embankment, although the forward elements of the reconnaissance detachments had penetrated into the depth of the 24th Guards Rifle Corps by 4.5 to 5 kilometers. However, already at 1230 the Russians counterattacked the 320th Infantry Division with significant infantry forces that were supported by tanks. The German forward elements, having had no time to dig in and relying only on artillery support, began to fall back to the river. The situation in the sector of Korps Raus at 2000 (Moscow time) was laid out in some detail in the evening report from its headquarters:

1. Korps Raus on 5.7 after forcing a crossing of the Donets River in savage and bloody fighting step by step, subsequently focusing fire and the attack against key points, overcame the enemy's deep positions east of the Donets and in an offensive outburst in several places crossed the Titovka – Belgorod railroad. The enemy was fiercely defending between the Donets and Titovka – Belgorod railroad and east of it, clinging to fortifications in its positions and launching a multitude of counterattacks, including with tanks. At the moment of dispatching this report (1800 Berlin time), the corps is attacking out of the Maslova Pristan' area and to the north toward Hill 207 (4 kilometers northeast of Tsigel'tsy – Toplinka).

    The 320th Infantry Division with its right-flank Infantry Regiment 585 has taken Bezliudovka, seized the railroad embankment at B.B. (2 to 2.5 kilometers east of Bezliudovka), while the regiment's left-flank battalion entered the woods immediately north of Bezliudovka and drove back enemy counterattacks. The regiment in the center (Infantry Regiment 587) in the afternoon reached an exit from the woods 3 kilometers southeast of Rzhavets (the main road) and Sh. (1 to 1.5 kilometers east of Rzhavets). An enemy tank attack (at least 25 of them) forced the regiment to retreat beyond the line of the railroad and to dig in again in the woods east of Priiutovka and further to the east. The regiment didn't have enough anti-tank weapons, because all of the previously planned bridges with the exception of the just destroyed K – the bridge at Bezliudovka, couldn't be built due to the enemy's strong artillery fire.

    A repeat request for air support to attack the enemy artillery batteries that are out of range of our own artillery went unfulfilled on the part of VIII Fliegerkorps.

    The left-hand Infantry Regiment 586 after heavy fighting took the hill with the cemetery in the southern part of Maslova Pristan' and thereby reached the line of the railroad. StuG Battalion 905 is still fighting with enemy tanks at Rzhavets.

    In the 106th Infantry Division, the Infantry Regiments 239 and 241 broke through the northern end of Maslova Pristan', Karnaukhovka and the woods east of Toplinka and reached the railroad line. Here, the construction of a bridge is also being significantly held up by strong enemy artillery fire. The regiment on the left (Infantry Regiment 240) reached the railroad with its right flank early in the morning, while its left flank became tied up in heavy street fighting in Nizhnii Ol'shanets, and thus here the railroad line still hasn't been reached. A subsequent counterattack at mid-day out of Krutoi Log was successfully repulsed by Infantry Regiment 240's left-flank battalion.

    Toward evening the corps, after bringing its units back into order, again went on the offensive with the intention of taking the day's objective (the area of hills on both sides of Hill 207).

    …

> The number of prisoners at the present moment is around 500 (already counted). Our own losses are around 700 wounded per division; the number of dead, of which there are many, still hasn't been accurately established.[180]

The situation deteriorated after 1800. The sector of the riverbank that remained in the possession of Forst's and Postel's divisions stretched up to 15-17 kilometers and had a depth of 1.5 to 4.5 kilometers. The 106th Infantry Division managed to achieve the most success. Thanks to the support of the 7th Panzer Division on its left, it managed to take complete possession of Nizhnii Ol'shanets and Karnaukhovka, and despite the Soviet tank attacks, retained possession of part of Maslova Pristan'. Because of this, it was getting its artillery and main infantry forces across the river more successfully than was the 320th Infantry Division. By the evening, its combat groups had even broken through to the vicinity of Hill 167.7, which lay 7 kilometers in the depth of the 24th Guards Rifle Corps' defenses, but they were forced to fall back by an attack from the Russians' second echelon.

In the briefings and reports of Speidel's headquarters, and particularly of its subordinate divisions, throughout the day of 5 July there was an assessment of the Soviet troops, their actions and the system of defense, which unquestionably were a vital factor for their successes and failures. In Army Detachment Kempf's combat diary there is a supplement to the daily report at 2300, in which all of these comments were summarized. The document is fairly unvarnished, and I think it will be interesting and useful for the reader to become familiar with it in order for a deeper understanding of the events of 5 July. German officers observed:

> The army detachment's offensive ran into a powerful, fully-prepared enemy that is occupying deeply-echeloned, thoroughly prepared positions covered by minefields between the Donets and the railroad, which he is stubbornly defending. Previously received evidence about the enemy's grouping has basically been confirmed. The enemy concentrated his main efforts in the defense around the Belgorod bridgehead. A powerful counterattack was directed against the southern flank and center of the 320th Infantry Division with the support of 57 tanks. Major enemy forces with tanks that crossed to the northern bank of the Nezhigal' River managed to be stopped south of Bezliudovka.
>
> Situation in the air. Enemy aircraft have shown high activity throughout the day. At dawn it bombed primarily the areas of Khar'kov and Belgorod. Subsequently it gradually intensified attacks against the attacking troops, bridges, and the immediate rear areas.[181]

Unfortunately, documents that would give a full-fledged assessment of Army Detachment Kempf's command regarding the actions of its troops on the first day of the offensive haven't been found. There is little information as well in the journal of combat operations of its shock formation, Breith's III Panzer Corps. It is difficult to call this a document, since it contains no continuous text that would lay out the command's plan, the course of its implementation, or summarize the combat actions – in general, everything that a journal of combat operations recorded by a combat formation normally contains. At its basis are morning, daytime and evening reports of the panzer divisions to the corps, arranged in chronological order, as well as orders of the III Panzer Corps and its summary reports to the army detachment. It also contains transcripts and various telegrams with orders, primarily, regarding the fortification of seized terrain and logistical matters. However, in the pile of these combat documents, two small typewritten pages have been preserved. This is

---

180 NARA US, t. 312, r. 59, f. 7574638.
181 NARA US, t. 312, r. 54, f. 7569611.

a note by the corps' chief of staff entitled "Notes for the combat journal". It was created at 1845 on 6 July and contains the essence of a dialog with W. Kempf that took place in the III Panzer Corps headquarters about the results of the day of 5 July and the tasks that the corps faced on 6 July. Its contents plainly reveal that on the opening day of the offensive, friction regarding major tactical questions had arisen between the leadership of Army Detachment Kemp and that of the III Panzer Corps. Here is a brief excerpt from this document: "General Kempf announced to the corps commander in person, and to me over the telephone in the presence of General Speidel, that the corps' actions were incorrect; it had advanced in the wrong direction – too far to the east."[182]

The document was prepared for internal use and it is difficult for an outside person to fathom all the nuances of the discussion. Nevertheless, the position of the army detachment's commander is rather obvious. He believed that the 19th and 7th Panzer Divisions with their breakthrough in the direction of Generalovka had strayed too far from the proper direction of advance, instead of crushing the powerful knots of resistance in the villages of Razumnoe and Krutoi Log, and General Breith had made no effort to correct this. As a result of these supposedly improvised steps, the offensive front of not only III Panzer Corps but also of the entire Army Detachment Kempf had split into fragments, and on 6 July unanticipated efforts and time would be necessary to create a unified bridgehead. However, if so far there was enough strength for this (the 6th Panzer Division was coming up), the time for this was catastrophically short. In connection with the advance of Hoth's Fourth Panzer Army, it was necessary to resolve the main task as quickly as possible – the screening of its right flank. In addition, the situation was demanding that Breith give help to Raus in destroying the Russian grouping opposite the latter's front, which had forced Forst's and Postel's divisions to make no headway at the railroad all day. In the opposite case, Korps Raus would again get stuck and wouldn't be able to cover the right flank of III Panzer Corps' combat wedge, which means the resolution of the main task standing in front of the army detachment would become completely disrupted. According to Kempf's thoughts, III Panzer Corps had been able to resolve all of these questions on 5 July, but its command had improperly handled its forces.

The strong Russian counterattack against Raus and the difficult situation that emerged in his corps in its wake was making Kempf very uneasy at this moment, possibly even more than Breith's situation did, because the III Panzer Corps had significantly greater combat potential than did its neighbor Korps Raus. Thus in a conversation with von Manstein at 2205, who had called him first of all to find out why von Hünersdorff's 6th Panzer Division had spent the entire day standing in place, Kempf had nevertheless pointed at this problem as the most difficult one at the given moment:

> General-Field Marshal von Manstein wanted to find out why instead of attacking, the 6th Panzer Division had been shifted laterally to the rear of the 7th Panzer Division. The commander of the army detachment replied that the situation in the 19th Panzer Division's sector was completely unclear. The absence of bridges remained the main problem. The most suitable bridges for crossing troops were in the sector of the 7th Panzer Division. The 6th Panzer Division as a result of the movement to its new sector was to plug the gap that had arisen between the 19th and 7th Panzer Divisions. General-Field Marshal von Manstein, having familiarized himself with the situation, demanded that this panzer division be introduced into the fighting as quickly as possible. This was especially important in view of the fact that enemy aircraft at the present time had the full opportunity to concentrate its efforts in any areas most advantageous for it. In response the army detachment commander indicated that the situation in the sector of Korps Raus was giving rise to serious concerns. His front,

---

182 NARA US, t. 314, r. 197, f. 001098.

which at the start of the offensive amounted to 17 kilometers, had expanded at the present time to 35 kilometers. At the same time, the corps had suffered exceptionally painful losses.[183]

However, both Breith and his headquarters were seeing the reasons for the failure to reach the day's objectives and the overall situation in its sector in a completely different way. They were asserting that their troops had operated according to the orders they'd received. Indeed, they had done everything within their capabilities to create a solid bridgehead. The Russians were defending tenaciously and thus the capture of Razumnoe and Krutoi Log with an attack from the south and west was an extremely difficult and time-consuming matter. Meanwhile, the impetuous advance by 7th Panzer Division's panzer groups in the direction of Generalovka was connected with the fact that Lieutenant Colonel Schülz was reporting that the Russians in front of him had begun to retreat, and the capture of Generalovka seemed to be an established fact. Indeed, in the first phase these hopes were confirmed – several of his combat machines had broken into its outskirts. Meanwhile, control over Generalovka would enable the encirclement of the village of Razumnoe. In addition, by pushing to the east, von Funck's panzer division was simultaneously expanding the bridgehead in depth. In the note, these arguments are laid out in the following manner:

> As concerns the actions of the 7th Panzer Division, it had the objective of launching an attack through the "W" woods[184] (2 kilometers northeast of Krutoi Log) toward Hill 216.1. The commander of Panzer Regiment 25 who splendidly showed himself in the fighting, around 1015 (Moscow time) reported: "The edge of the "W" woods is occupied by strong enemy forces, while around 1010 the enemy's retreat from the wooded sectors west of Hill 209.6 was observed." Each commander of a mobile unit in this situation would strive to take the positions of a weakened adversary. What did it mean to the mobile units to make one more lunge of 3 kilometers? [This is the distance between Razumnoe and Generalovka.] Only someone who lacks any conception of the tactics of mobile units can assert that this choice [the pursuit of the retreating units of the 78th Guards Rifle Division in the direction of Generalovka and Hill 164.7] was incorrect and meant only the splitting of the wedge of the corps' offensive. Thanks to this advance to the east, the necessary ground for deploying the forward group of the 6th Panzer Division between the other panzer divisions was taken.
>
> The corps is convinced that the correctness of its actions will be confirmed by future successes. In any case, the negative assessment [of its actions on 5 July] by the commander of the army detachment is completely incomprehensible for the corps. In the telephone conversation between the army detachment's chief of staff and me that I mentioned at the start, in which I laid out the above cited thoughts, General Speidel was unable to offer any retort to my conclusions.[185]

The arguments of the III Panzer Corps' command and the weighty results (relative to Korps Raus) that two of its panzer divisions managed to achieve on 5 July leads one to think that it is difficult to call Kempf's assessment objective. Its categorical nature (and even the certain irritation expressed by Kempf) was prompted first of all by the failure of the entire army detachment to carry out its orders for the day and the thought of how this would be perceived by the command of Army Group South. Putting it simply, Kempf was plainly seeking a scapegoat for the failure of the

---

183 NARA US, t. 312, r. 54, f. 7569605.
184 The woods northeast of Hill 164.7 by their outline suggested the Latin letter "W"; in Soviet documents, they are called the "Sapog grove".
185 NARA US, t. 314, r. 197, f. 001098.

opening day's offensive of Army Detachment Kempf. This is confirmed by his further judgements as to how it was necessary for Breith's troops to operate on 6 July:

> The corps' task for 6 July demands among others the taking of the hills east of Miasoedovo in cooperation with the forces of the southern sector [Korps Raus]. The enemy:
>
> 1) Is firmly holding the obviously commanding heights near Blizhniaia Igumenka.
> 2) Has well-constructed positions on the line Miasoedovo – Hill 216.1 – Hill 209.6 and south of there, with a shown front to the west. This position is being occupied by the 73rd Guards Rifle Division, which still has not been smashed during this operation. It dominates the northern section of the Razumnoe valley.
>
> The neighboring Korps Raus on the right yesterday, although making something of an advance, remains at the railroad embankment despite the advance of our 7th Panzer Division.
>
> In order to carry out the task to take the hills east of Miasoedovo, it is necessary:
> - either to seize the heights near Blizhniaia Igumenka and north of it, in order then to take the hilly area east of Misasoedovo with an outflanking maneuver from the north;
> - or to break through the flanking Miasoedovo – Hill 209.6 position and south of there, since an outflanking maneuver from the south is possible only through the deeply wooded area of the Shebekinskaia Dacha Woods; the question remains whether or not enemy positions are there, that haven't been revealed by aerial reconnaissance photographs.
>
> A decision "to sweep to the north" [an attack through the left flank of the 81st Guards Rifle Division toward Dal'niaia Igumenka] – is purely theoretical. If would force us to cross the Razumnaia River in view of the enemy, because of which he might bring up other, possibly operational, reserves. It is necessary to avoid this.
>
> Should we conduct a flanking attack … to Sevriukovo, so as to next "break off the corner posts" at Iastrebovo, or should the enemy's position be breached further to the south, in order then to advance from the south and southeast? Without a doubt, the latter option [to launch an attack against the deep right flank of the 72nd Guards Rifle Division and subsequently into the rear of the 24th Guards Rifle Corps] is preferable. In any event the simultaneous decisive advance of the 19th Panzer Division from Blizhnaia Igumenka is exceptionally important.[186]

As is apparent from Kempf's rather wide-ranging thoughts, it wasn't the situation on the adjacent flanks of the 19th and 7th Panzer Divisions, for which he had just raked Breith over the coals that was now agitating him. Indeed, he even considered the encirclement of Razumnoe (with an attack across the river), an offensive toward Dal'niaia Igumenka with the main forces (in the direction of the Fourth Panzer Army's right flank, or toward Sevriukovo (the corps' objective for 5 July) to be "purely theoretical". Having blown off steam, General Kempf gave III Panzer Corps a fully pragmatic objective – to close the flanks of both corps of his army detachment by sending the 6th and 7th Panzer Divisions crashing through the front of the 73rd Guards Rifle Division, which was standing in the path of Korps Raus and simultaneously hanging over the right flank of III Panzer Corps itself.

---

186 NARA US, t. 314, r. 197, f. 001098.

The logic of Army Detachment Kempf command's assessment of the situation in the sector of its shock formations' offensive at the end of 5 July demands as well the unveiling of the essence of the plan of combat actions on 6 July. We will discuss this in the next chapter. In conclusion of my discussion of the events of 5 July, I want to make a brief digression. The documents available to researchers today clearly testify that by the end of the first day of Operation Citadel, the command of Army Group South and those of its armies had collided with such serious problems that they not only hadn't been considered when planning the operation, they hadn't even been foreseen by the Wehrmacht's sharpest mind. This was the unexpected stubbornness of the Soviet troops on the defensive, and the incapability of Panzergrenadier Division *Grossdeutschland* and Hitler's brainchild, the brigade of Panther tanks, to break through the 6th Guards Army's main defensive belt at the village of Cherkasskoe from the march, or the collapse of the 6th Panzer Division's bridges, or a number of other "surprises". The underestimation of the Soviet side, the overestimation of their own capabilities, and even outright arrogance was one of the characteristic mistakes of the political and military leadership of Nazi Germany in the course of the war against the USSR. However, the entire array of miscalculations made when resolving the questions connected with the start of the 1943 summer campaign became the most obvious and far-reaching blunder not only of the war's second stage, but of its entire 1,418 days.

4

The 7th Guards Army's main defensive belt crumbles

The III Panzer Corps headquarters issued its order to the divisions containing the tasks for 6 July just before midnight. Here is its almost complete text:

1. The enemy is defending in his positions, supported by powerful artillery and rocket launcher fire. In the future, reinforcement with reserves and numerous tanks is possible. The 7th and 19th Panzer Divisions have achieved a breakthrough of the hostile positions north of Krutoi Log and south of the Kreida railyard.
2. III Panzer Corps on 6.7 continues to achieve success on the offensive's right flank in a northeastern direction.
3. Tasks:

    7th Panzer Division on 6.7 shifts to the northeast, making the 6th Panzer Division's crossing of the Donets River possible. Here with this order the division gives 6th Panzer Division two bridges across the Donets, including the 50-tonne bridge. Coordinate the passage of the 7th Panzer Division's vehicles at the bridges with the 6th Panzer Division, and subsequently [on the eastern bank] the 7th Panzer Division takes control over the traffic, and at sunrise resumes the offensive, advancing east of Razumnoe around the village of Zaiach'e. Reconnaissance Battalion 78 again becomes subordinate to the division.

    19th Panzer Division seizes the "Day of Harvest" collective farm and the Kreida railyard, and destroys the enemy artillery grouping in the vicinity of Blizhniaia Igumenka. Then the division should be prepared to advance quickly to Dal'niaia Igumenka.

    6th Panzer Division halts its offensive and at 0000 6.7 yields its former sector to the 168th Infantry Division. From this moment, all the former sectors of the 6th Panzer Division without exception, as well as the units of the 168th Infantry Division and I/StuG Battalion 208 that were committed into the fighting there pass to the control of the 168th Infantry Division's commander. The 6th Panzer Division, minus Headquarters Battery 76 (which remains subordinate to Artkommando 3), shifts on the night of 5-6.7 to the Kolonia Dubovoe area and the bridges across the Donets in the Solomino and Dorogobuzheno area, and pursuant to the corps' order, occupies the Krutoi Log (excl.) – Generalovka – Razumnoe – Solomino sector. The division must be ready to attack behind the 7th Panzer Division, in the sector: Razumnoe (along both sides of Miasoedovo) to Melikhovo. In the event of success, join the fighting in the area of Blizhniaia Igumenka in support of 19th Panzer Division's shock group.

    168th Infantry Division in accordance with this order takes over the former sector of 6th Panzer Division at 0000 and defends the attained line … The division overcomes weak enemy resistance, joining the attack of the 19th Panzer Division with its right flank and seizes Staryi Gorod and in like manner Chernaia Poliana, and pushes further to the northwest.

4. Artkommando 3 supports the offensive of the 7th and 19th Panzer Divisions in the direction of Blizhniaia Igumenka. It also supports the actions in the center and on the right flank of the 168th Infantry Division.
5. The command of the corps' pioneer units retains and in the future builds (strengthens) bridges, as well as auxiliary bridges in cooperation with the command of Pioneer Regiment 601.
6. Anti-aircraft artillery
   a. The corps' Flak artillery assumes responsibility for covering the bridges across the Donets and the troops on the axis of the main attack in the Solomino – Dorogobuzheno area. For this, the 1st Battery of II/Flak Regiment 43 passes through the 7th Panzer Division as quickly as possible to the eastern bank of the Donets.
   b. For join combat work detach:
      I/Flak Regiment 38 for the 6th Panzer Division, I/Flak Regiment 61 for the 7th Panzer Division.
7. The corps headquarters remains near Novo-Nikolaevka.[1]

As is visible from the document, all of W. Kempf's wishes were taken into consideration. The main forces of Breith's III Panzer Corps were given two primary tasks. First, the destruction of the 25th Guards Rifle Corps' second echelon – Colonel S.A. Kozak's division and the mobile group (201st Separate Tank Brigade, 167th Separate Tank Regiment and the 1529th Heavy Self-propelled Artillery Regiment) that M.S. Shumilov had moved up to the area of the "Poliana" State Farm by the end of the day. The available combat machines in the tank regiments and tank brigades of the 7th Guards Army between 5 and 16 July 1943 are given in Table 9:

Incidentally, according to von Funck's recollections, his intelligence by the end of 5 July had detected the assembly of an armored grouping on the boundary between III Panzer Corps and Korps Raus. Secondly, it was to penetrate into the depth of the second army-level defensive belt to the area of Miasoedovo. In addition, the command of III Panzer Corps sought not to forget about other problems, for example, the dispersal of the operational reserves of the Soviet side, and was striving to shatter the 7th Guards Army's defenses in the direction of Fourth Panzer Army. With this aim, one-third of the panzer corps (19th Panzer Division) was directed to break through into the rear of 81st Guards Rifle Division, although judging from how the 6th Panzer Division's task was formulated to support the 19th Panzer Division, Breith wasn't placing any great hope on its success.

Now let's take a look at the decisions taken by the command of the 7th Guards Army and its subordinate formations prior to midnight in order to frustrate the enemy's plans, once the main fighting had ended and the line upon which the enemy had been stopped was determined. M.S. Shumilov began to prepare the plan of actions for 6 July already on the afternoon of 5 July, and it consisted of two parts. The first included bolstering the anti-tank defenses on the axis of the 19th and 7th Panzer Divisions' main attack, and the second was devoted to the formation of two strong attack groupings for conducting an active defense, i.e. Shumilov planned to launch counterattacks in several directions.

The army commander considered the line of the 78th Guards Rifle Division and the deep left flank of the 81st Guards Rifle Division to be the sector under the greatest threat. Considering that the enemy's panzer grouping (according to the army headquarters' intelligence, one panzer and

---

1   NARA US, t. 314, r. 242, f. 001067, 001068.

THE 7TH GUARDS ARMY'S MAIN DEFENSIVE BELT CRUMBLES

Table 9 Availability of armored fighting vehicles in the 7th Guards Army's tank brigades and regiments from 5 to 16 July 1943 (according to combat reports from the units and operational summaries of the headquarters of the 7th Guards Army's Armored and Mechanized Forces)

Date and time	148th Separate Tank Regiment[1]				167th Separate Tank Regiment				262nd Separate Tank Regiment						27th Guards Tank Brigade				201st Separate Tank Brigade					
	T-70/T-60		T-34		T-70/T-60		T-34		T-70/T-34/T-60		SU-76/SU-122		KV-1		T-70		T-34		Mk II		Mk III		T-34	
	In service	Under repair	In service	Under repair	In service	Under repair	In service	Under repair	In service	Under repair	In service	Under repair	In service	Under repair	In service	Under repair	In service	Under repair	In service	Under repair	In service	Under repair	In service	Under repair
5.7 2000					2/2	5[2]	12	1					20	1	4		41	4	16	2	31		3	
6.7 2000	11/1		32	1	2/2	4/-	7	3					13	2	5		35	11						
7.7 2000	9/1		29	4	-/2	4/-	3	3					11	2	5		36[3]	10	18		15	3[4]	3	
8.7 2000	8/1	1/-	19	10	2/-	1[5]	5	2					6	3	5		38	9	18		15	6[6]	3	
9.7 2000	8/1	1/-	19	12	2/-	1/-[7]	5	2					6	3	5		41	6	18[8]		14		3	
10.7 2000	6/-	7/1	12	4[9]	2	1[10]	5	2					7	2	5		41	6	17[11]	1	17	5	2	1
11.7 2000	2		5		All remaining tanks transferred to the 262nd Tank Regiment				2/5		5/1		7	1	5		45		16[12]	1	14	8	2	1
12.7 2000	1/-		3				4/2	2	1/5	1/1	4/1		8	1	5		21	3[13]	7	1	10	6	2	1
13.7 2000	1/-		3				1/-	2	¼	1/-	4/1		8	1[14]	5		17	26	6	5[15]	11	9	2	1
14.7 2000	2/-		5		1/-			2	4/4	2/-	5/1		8	1	4		18	23	3	4[16]	11	5	1	1
15.7 2000	2/-		5		1/-			2	4/4	1/-/2	5/1		8	2	4		26	18	3	4	10	6	4[17]	1
16.7 2000	2/-		5		1/-			2	4/4	1/-/2	5/1		8	2	4		30	14	3	4	11	5	4	1

Notes)
1 According to an order from the commander of the 7th Guards Armored and Mechanized Forces, on 10.7.1943 this tank regiment became subordinate to the 69th Army's commander.
2 Including 3 T-70 without protective glass for the driver's view slit, which were considered unsuitable for combat.
3 In addition to the serviceable 36 T-34, 1 T-34 with a jammed turret took part in combat.
4 Five Mk III were located on the battlefield and were due for evacuation.
5 Three T-70 and two T-60 were without protective glass for the driver-mechanic's view slit.
6 Two Mk III were located on the battlefield and were due for evacuation.
7 Three T-70 and two T-60 were without protective glass for the driver-mechanic's view slit.
8 One operational Mk II was away on assignment.
9 Four tanks had lagged behind on the march.
10 As before, 3 T-70 and 2 T-60 lacked protective glass for the driver-mechanic's view slit.
11 One serviceable Mk II was away on assignment, and one German self-propelled gun based on the Pz-IV that had been evacuated from the battlefield had been turned over for repair.
12 In addition, this includes 2 operational Mk III tanks that were still en route to the battlefield.
13 Nine T-34 were due for evacuation from the battlefield.
14 One KV tank was due for evacuation from the battlefield.
15 Two Mk 11 and three Mk III were due for evacuation from the battlefield.
16 At 2100 on 14.7, 5 Mk II, 4 Mk III and 1 T-34 of the brigade were counted as missing
17 Three T-34 tanks had arrived from the 62nd Mobile Repair Base.

two infantry divisions were operating here) had penetrated the 25th Guards Rifle Corps' defenses in a rather narrow sector and was also divided by the Razumnaia River, he decided to arrange a system of defense in the area according to the "hammer and anvil" principle. Lieutenant General M.E. Katukov a day later would apply the same principle on the Prokhorovka direction against two divisions of the II SS Panzer Corps. The firm defense of the 238th Guards and 233rd Guards Rifle Regiments of the 81st Guards Rifle Division, and the front directly at the spearhead of 7th Panzer Division's attack was chosen as the "anvil". On the night of 5-6 July in order to strengthen the anvil, he moved up 3/173rd Guards Artillery Regiment to the "Day of Harvest" collective farm (it was digging in with a front to the south) to join 1/114th Guards Destroyer Anti-tank Artillery Regiment that was already positioned there; Major Kazarinov's 2/114th Destroyer Anti-tank Artillery Regiment from the area of Blizhniaia Igumenka to the Kreida railyard; and deployed two regiments of Lieutenant Colonel M.G. Sapozhnikov's 30th Separate Anti-tank Artillery Brigade to the Belinskaia (south of Belovskaia) – southeastern fringe of the woods 1.5 kilometers northeast of Krutoi Log sector.[2] In addition, I.K. Morozov moved up his 2nd Battalion/233rd Guards Rifle Regiment (from the 81st Guards Rifle Division's second echelon) to the Kreida – "Day of Harvest" collective farm sector in order to reinforce the 238th Guards Rifle Regiment's left flank.

For the counterattacking group, the "hammer", Shumilov intended to use the forces that had assembled on the right flank of III Panzer Corps on the afternoon of 5 July. I will remind the reader that G.B. Safiulin had intended to launch a counterattack with the 73rd Guards Rifle Division and Verba's tank group against the 7th Panzer Division, and for this purpose they had assembled in the Generalovka – Hill 209.6 – Gremiachii sector. However, the situation had abruptly changed because of the retreat of the 78th Guards Rifle Division's forward regiments, and by 1630 a portion of 7th Panzer Division's armored group had reached the outskirts of Generalovka. Simultaneously, panzergrenadiers of the 19th Panzer Division had broken through toward Belinskaia. The attempt made by Kozak to stop the enemy with an attack made by the 167th Separate Tank Regiment had resulted in disaster, and his 73rd Guards Rifle Division had gone over to a strict defense. At 2300 an order arrived from the 25th Guards Rifle Corps about cancelling the preliminary order for a counterattack on 5 July, since it was assumed that it would be launched on the next day. From the 25th Guards Rifle Corps' account:

> At a decision from the army commander, by the morning of 6.07.1943 a shock group was created consisting of the 73rd Guards Rifle Division, the 30th Separate Destroyer Anti-Tank Artillery Brigade, the 167th Separate Tank Regiment, 12 KV tanks, the 262nd Tank Regiment, the 1438th Self-propelled Artillery Regiment, the 309th and 97th Guards Mortar Regiments, the 265th Guards Cannon Artillery Regiment and the 329th Engineer Battalion, all subordinate to the 25th Guards Rifle Corps commander, in order to repulse the enemy's attack. The group's task – having formed on the line: (excl.) Belinskaia – western and south-western fringe of the woods lying 3 kilometers east of Generalovka – western slopes of Point 209.6, to be ready to repel enemy tank attacks and to launch a counterattack. Simultaneously with this, a mobile group consisting of the 201st Tank Brigade and the 1529th Heavy Self-propelled Artillery Regiment was created in the Gremiachii, "Poliana" State Farm area with the task: in the event that enemy tanks developed an offensive in the northern or northeastern

---

2   The movement took place at night, which was one of the reasons why one tractor of Major Kazarinov's artillery battalion toppled into a ravine together with the 76mm cannon it was towing. The tractor couldn't be repaired, and the gun was sent to the 7th Guards Army's mobile artillery workshop.

THE 7TH GUARDS ARMY'S MAIN DEFENSIVE BELT CRUMBLES

directions, to launch a counterattack into their flank from the direction of Krutoi Log and Nizhnii Ol'shanets.[3]

By the end of 5 July 1943, the 7th Guards Army no longer had a second echelon, including on the axis of the III Panzer Corps' attack. Thus even though the gathered forces on the left flank of the 25th Guards Rifle Corps were impressive, M.S. Shumilov wasn't confident that they could hold up against an armored grouping numbering more than 100 panzers and assault guns that was concentrated between Krutoi Log and Razumnoe. He was most alarmed by the paucity of his artillery, the backbone of his defense, on this axis. The 73rd Guards Rifle Division's 153rd Guards Artillery Regiment was still being retained in the sector of the 81st Guards Rifle Division, and the 30th Separate Destroyer Anti-tank Artillery Brigade had only two regiments, one of which was equipped only with the weak 45mm anti-tank guns. At this same time, a mobile anti-tank formation – Lieutenant Colonel S.V. Shmanov's 31st Separate Destroyer Anti-Tank Artillery Brigade – was located in the Korocha area. The army commander shared his concerns regarding his relatively feeble artillery that evening with the Front commander-in-chief, probably calculating that N.F. Vatutin would after all subordinate Shmanov's anti-tank brigade to him. Back at the end of June, the General of the Army had promised to transfer it to him out of his own reserve and had even had informed Shumilov of this through S.P. Ivanov, but then for some reasons, Vatutin kept it under his control. At the start of the German offensive, it was still located in the Voronezh Front reserve and was considered operationally subordinate to the commander of the neighboring 69th Army. By the end of 5 July Vatutin was more concerned about the situation on the Oboian' direction than he was about the situation near Belgorod. In the estimates of his headquarters, on the first day of the offensive the Germans had introduced up to six panzergrenadier divisions into the fighting on the Oboian' direction. The 1st Tank Army, 2nd Guards "Tatsinskaia" Tank Corps and the 5th Guards "Stalingrad" Tank Corps stood ready to launch a counterattack against this German grouping on the morning of 6 July. So it was planned to reinforce the 2nd Guards Tank Corps, which had received an order to crush the Fourth Panzer Army's right flank and seize the Belgorod – Oboian' highway, with the 31st Separate Destroyer Anti-tank Artillery Brigade. At 1800 on 5 July, it began moving out of Korocha toward Lomovo, and two hours later it had assembled in the latter village.

However, an incident brought corrections to these plans. A phone call from I.V. Stalin to the headquarters of the 1st Tank Army decided the fate of the intended counterattack. M.E. Katukov, in the course of the conversation with the Supreme Leader, openly laid out his view of the situation and declared that if he launched a frontal attack against the attacking enemy, the losses of his tank army would be enormous, and it was impossible to say with confidence whether it could carry out its assignment. Stalin agreed that the conditions weren't ready for such a major measure, and the counterattack was thus postponed.

This decision was a key one for understanding the development of the operational situation in the sector of the Voronezh Front on 6 July, and it has therefore drawn the fixed attention of scholars of the Battle of Kursk. However, nowhere in the sources is the precise time indicated for when this discussion took place, with the sole exception of the transcript of N.F. Vatutin's discussions with Moscow, which is still classified. Possibly, the situation with the re-subordination of Shmanov's anti-tank artillery brigade and the chain of decisions connected with this might bring certain clarity to this matter. In the combat diary of the 148th Separate Tank Regiment, which was positioned in the area of Pentsevo and subordinate to the 15th Guards Rifle Division's commander, there are the following lines:

---

3   TsAMO RF, f. 25 gv. sk, op. 1, d. 27 , l. 3.

At 0040 Order No.0020/op was received from the 7th Guards Army's commander of Armored and Mechanized Forces about transferring the 148th Separate Tank Regiment to the 31st Separate Destroyer Anti-tank Artillery Brigade, about assembling its units in the area of Hill 209.6 (800 meters north of the "Solov'ev" collective farm (on the 1:50,000 map) and the organization of an anti-tank defense together with the brigade with the task to prevent the breakthrough of enemy tanks to the northeast. With the arrival of the 94th Guards Rifle Division, the regiment would become subordinate to it. At 0420 the regiment set out from its area of dispositions and by 0800 it was assembled along the western fringe of the woods east of Iastrebovo and Sevriukovo, where it took up a defense.[4]

If the order really was received by the regiment headquarters around 0100 on 6 July, accordingly, considering the time it took for the order about transferring the brigade to the 7th Guards Army to reach the army from the Voronezh Front, the counterattack was probably cancelled by I.V. Stalin no later than 2200 to 2230 on 5 July. Skipping somewhat ahead in the events, I'll note that the 31st Separate Destroyer Anti-tank Artillery Brigade received this order almost 14 hours after it had arrived in the headquarters of the 148th Separate Tank Regiment. The reason for this delay isn't clear, but it almost became a reason for tragic events in the 7th Guards Army's sector. It is possible, though, that these two orders from the Front headquarters were deliberately dispatched at different times. Having delayed the transfer of the 31st Separate Destroyer Anti-tank Artillery Regiment the Front Commander-in-Chief might have wanted to wait until the enemy went on the attack and see how events were starting to unfold on the Oboian' direction.

Having failed to obtain artillery reinforcements from the Voronezh Front, M.S. Shumilov again pondered the army's own artillery units and decided that the 153rd Guards Artillery Regiment was more needed by the 73rd Guards Rifle Division's commander, so he decided to return it to the division. At the same time, considering the difficulty of maneuvering artillery regiments (in the event that the Germans broke through the left flank of the 81st Guards Rifle Division), he decided to leave I.K. Morozov with two battalions of the 265th Guards Cannon Artillery Regiment and the entire 161st Guards Cannon Artillery Regiment (in the sector of the 81st Guards Rifle Division), which Safiulin on the eve before had transferred to Kozak, and ordered that these artillery units fire both to support the 81st Guards Rifle Division's left flank and in the interests of the 73rd Guards Rifle Division.

In order to strengthen his division's sector in an anti-tank respect, S.A. Kozak also made a number of decisions. At 24.00 5 July he ordered the remaining armor of the 167th Separate Tank Regiment after the unsuccessful attack (12 T-34[5] and 1 T-70) and the self-propelled guns of the 1438th Self-propelled Artillery Regiment to dig in on the southern and southwestern fringe of the woods lying 1 kilometer north of Krutoi Log, by which to create from them an anti-tank region in the positions of the 209th Guards and 214th Guards Rifle Regiments (opposite the front of the 7th Panzer Division). In the event that the adversary attempted to break through into the rear of the 81st Guards Rifle Division along the bottomlands of the Razumnaia River (toward the villages of Iastrebovo and Sevriukovo) through the woods east of Generalovka, the anti-tank region would take on the main attack.

At the same time, despite the fatigue of the men of the 201st Tank Brigade under the command of Colonel I.A. Taranov,[6] which had arrived on the left flank of the 73rd Guards Rifle Division

---

4 TsAMO RF, f. 148 otp, op. 661360, d. 3, l. 77.
5 In addition to the 7 T-34 that remained after the attack, the division commander ordered Lieutenant Colonel A.A. Verba to deploy as well his five reserve T-34s on the defense.
6 Taranov, Ivan Afanas'evich (Major General, 1943) was born on 11 November 1895 in Don Oblast's village of Taranovka. He joined the Red Army in 1918 and served in the Russian Civil War in the cavalry,

at 2300 together with the artillery regiments (the 1669th Destroyer Anti-tank Artillery Regiment and the 1529th Heavy Self-propelled Artillery Regiment) that had been attached to Kozak's 73rd Guards Rifle Division, it began to set up a second anti-tank region in the area of the "Poliana" State Farm, which was to form a strong seal between the 73rd Guards and 213th Rifle Divisions – at the boundary (in the depth) between Safiulin's and Vasil'ev's corps. Thus, the positions of the 25th Guards Rifle Corps' counterattack group were chosen quite successfully; it could be used both to repel the attack by von Funck's and von Hünersdorff's panzer divisions, and for launching a counterattack against the adjoining flanks of Breith's III Panzer Corps and Korps Raus.

However, M.S. Shumilov's first step that can be related to the plan of preparing the combat actions on 6 July was nevertheless the decision he took about resurrecting his all-arms reserve and directing it into the 24th Guards Rifle Corps' sector, which he made early on the morning of 5 July. I will remind the reader that as soon as it became clear that the situation was beginning to deteriorate on the right flank of Vasil'ev's corps, the army commander transferred the reserve 213th Rifle Division and 27th Guards Tank Brigade to the corps commander. Thus, already in the opening hours of the operation he'd been deprived of a most important lever of influence on the operational situation. He only had left his anti-tank and mobile reserve. However, after the morning report to N.F. Vatutin, Shumilov received operational control of Colonel M.A. Bushen's 111th Rifle Division from the 49th Rifle Corps, which around 0500 was assembled in the Volchansk area. Moreover, as already noted, the Front Commander-in-Chief emphasized that the division should be deployed in the sector of the 15th Guards Rifle Division and not be touched without his authorization, although Shumilov could use the 15th Guards Rifle Division as he saw fit. After this, M.S. Shumilov got in touch with the commander of the 24th Guards Rifle Corps and gave him an order to make contact with the 111th Rifle Division's commander, direct this division into the corps' second echelon, and having used it to replace the 15th Guards Rifle Division by 0100 6 July, to send the latter to the Shebekino, Ustnika, woods in the vicinity of Ustnika area, into the former positions of the 213th Rifle Division as the army's reserve. From Combat Order No.056/op from the headquarters of the 15th Guards Rifle Division:

3. The 47th Guards Rifle Regiment after replacement by the units of the 399th Rifle Regiment ... goes over to a defense in the sector: woods (700 meters west of Ustnika), railroad bridge (800 meters west of Shebekino) with a front to the west. Forward edge:

---

including in the 1st Cavalry Army. He was wounded twice. In 1933 Taranov completed the Moscow motorized and mechanized courses, then spent time serving in the mechanized units of the cavalry formations. In 1937 and 1938, Taranov was enrolled in the Leningrad armored courses. On 20.01.1940 he was transferred from the post of commander of Siberia Military District's 51st Tank Brigade and became the chief of the Auto-Armored and Mechanized Department of the Finnish Front's 9th Army. On 26.04.1940 Taranov became the commander of the Trans Caucasus District's 41st Light Tank Brigade. Between November 1940 and March 1941, he took courses in the Frunze Military Academy. On 12.03.1941 Taranov became the deputy commander of the 28th Mechanized Corps' 54th Tank Division, which at the start of the war was sent to Iran. From 28.09 to 30.10.1941 he commanded Western Front's 25th Tank Brigade. The tank brigade operated near the Mozhaisk highway as part of the 5th Army. In November 1941 he became the deputy commander for the tank troops of the Western Front's 1st Guards Cavalry Corps. Because of a conflict with the corps commander P.A. Belov, he was called back into the Front's reserve and became the acting commander of the 201st Separate Tank Brigade that was then forming up, and on 25.02.1942 became its fully-authorized commander. In March 1945 Taranov was appointed commander of the 231st Separate Self-propelled Artillery Brigade under the 7th Mechanized Corps, with which he took part in the war with Japan. He later served as the deputy commander of the 7th and 31st Mechanized Divisions and the assistant commander of the 3rd Mountain Rifle Corps. He retired on 08.02.1955 and eventually passed away in August 1972 in Dnepropetrovsk.

three firebreaks west of Ustnika. Anti-tank strongpoint – in the center of the Rzhavets – Ustnika sector of defense.

Conduct reconnaissance along the Ustinka – Rzhavets and Shebekino – Hill 105.7 roads and make contact with the 213th Rifle Division. Artillery support group – 1/43rd Guards Artillery Regiment. Regiment command post – western outskirts of Ustinka.

4. The 50th Guards Rifle Regiment goes over to the defense in the sector: bridge across the Nezhegol River 800 meters south of Ustinka, western outskirts of Shebekino as far as Hill 135.6. Reconnoiter toward Titovka. Regiment command post: sugar factory in Shebekino. Artillery support group: 3/43rd Guards Artillery Regiment.
5. 44th Guards Rifle Regiment takes up a defense in the sector: Shebekino – Nekliudovo road, southeastern outskirts of Shebekino (northern flank 600 meters east of the brick factory). Forward edge: along the western and southern outskirts of Shebekino (north of the Nezhegol River). Artillery support group: 2/43rd Guards Artillery Regiment. Regiment command post: 1 kilometer east of the brick factory.
6. My reserve: training battalion, engineer battalion, reconnaissance company, chemical defense company assembles in the Ustinka area. Take up a defense along the western outskirts of Ustinka.

20th Destroyer Anti-tank Artillery Battalion – at the direction of the artillery commander.
7. Commander of the reserve – the training battalion commander.
8. The division's units are to be occupying a defense by 0500 5.7.43; conduct the march at double-time.[7]

At 1300 5 July, the battalion commanders of the 111th Rifle Division began to arrive in the 15th Guards Rifle Division's sector in order to determine movement routes and to inspect the combat positions and artificial obstacles. At 1800 Colonel L.-A.M. Lifits's 148th Separate Tank Regiment,[8] which had been assigned by M.S. Shumilov to the 15th Guards Rifle Division commander as a reinforcement, assembled in the woods east of Pentsevo. Simultaneously with the order about going into the reserve, Major General E.I. Vasilenko received two verbal preliminary orders: the first about preparing the division to launch a counterattack in the sector of the 24th Guards Rifle Corps, and the second about its possible movement to block the enemy's expansion at the boundary between the two corps.

The day's end and the first half of the night is a very stressful time for staff officers of combat formations in any acting army. At this moment, the intensive collection of information is going on to determine the location of units and their condition. Summaries are being prepared with an account about the results of the fighting in order to sum up the results of the day. Decisions are being made and orders are being prepared, and lower-ranking commanders are being informed of them in difficult night conditions, often given poor communications.

While Safiulin's corps headquarters was arranging the 78th and 73rd Guards Rifle Division's system of defense, division commander Morozov was strengthening his left flank, the 15th Guards Rifle Division was being replaced; and Verba's and Taranov's crews were digging in their combat

---

7   TsAMO RF, F. 15 gv. sd, op. 1, d. 8, ll. 127-128.
8   The regiment was formed on the basis of NKO Order No.11224070 from 10 January 1943 out of the 148th Tank Brigade, which in turn had been created in August-September 1941 on the basis of the 109th Tank Division. On 10.03.1943, Colonel Leib-Aizik Mendel' Lifits was appointed as the regiment commander. It arrived as part of the 7th Guards Army from the 9th Mechanized Corps at the end of March and beginning of April 1943.

machines together with the "self-movers";[9] in parallel no less feverish work was underway in Breith's panzer corps and Korps Raus. The night of 5-6 July 1943 was hectic and exceptionally stressful for the command staff of Army Detachment Kempf. In addition to the usual concerns, they were executing a significant regrouping of forces. The overall main task for both corps was to repair the damaged bridges as quickly as possible and build new ones. Already before daybreak, elements to replenish the thinned combat ranks of the grenadier regiments were to be on the eastern bank; heavy weapons, ammunition and combat supplies had to be moved across the river; and hundreds of wounded and badly concussed men had to be evacuated to the western bank for transportation to a hospital. At the same time each corps had its own specific problems. For example, for the command of Korps Raus it was vitally important at this moment for the 320th Infantry Division to retain its foothold on the eastern bank at Bezliudovka. This would allow under the cover of darkness to lay several 10- to 15-tonne capacity bridges across the river in order to cross its artillery. The deficit of artillery and ammunition on the first day of the offensive became one of the main reasons why Raus' divisions had to abandon the ground they had gained under the pressure of Soviet forces, and in the process suffered significant losses.

The III Panzer Corps command had its own difficulties, but they were more significant. On the afternoon of 5 July, its headquarters had sent an order to Major General von Hünersdorff to withdraw all of his units from the forward edge and to yield his sector to the 168th Infantry Division before midnight, while Major General Chales de Beaulieu was supposed to gather his battalions efficiently, allocate new combat sectors to them, and send them to take up positions along the line: Mikhailovka – (excl.) western outskirts of Staryi Gorod – Pokrovka (north of Belgorod). After this the 6th Panzer Division was to assemble in the Koloniia Dubovoe area and begin the movement of Lieutenant Colonel von Oppeln-Bronikowski's Panzer Regiment 11 into the 7th Panzer Division's start positions to cross the river. After completing the crossing, the panzer regiment was going to become operationally subordinate to the commander of the 7th Panzer Division von Funck. I will note that by the end of 5 July, the 7th Panzer Division had also not yet gotten all of its elements across the Donets. Thus, after Panzer Regiment 11's passage across the bridges, they were to return again to the 7th Panzer Division so it could continue the crossing of its units. In the morning summaries Breith's subordinate divisions reported:

> 6th Panzer Division: The withdrawal from combat is proceeding normally, without enemy pursuit. The order was received in the old sector. The division's units are assembling in the Koloniia-Dubovoe area.
> 168th Infantry Division: The night passed quietly, with the exception of light harassing artillery fire and small arms fire. At 0000 the division received an order regarding the sector from the bridgehead's fortifications (inclusively) to the corps' left boundary. The alignment according to the received order:
> - Group Wollmer [commander of Infantry Regiment 429]: II/Infantry Regiment 249 and II/Infantry Regiment 247 in the bridgehead at the bridge with elements of III/Infantry Regiment 429: on the eastern outskirts of Belgorod up to the northern outskirts of Pokrovka;
> - Group Barkmann [commander of Infantry Regiment 427]: I/Infantry Regiment 417 and elements of the reconnaissance battalion – from the eastern outskirts of Pokrovka to the division's left boundary.

---

9   At the front, this is the somewhat ironic nickname that was applied to the self-propelled gun crews.

The combat possibilities of the battalions assigned for the offensive have been substantially weakened by heavy losses.[10]

By sunrise the main steps to regroup von Hünersdorff's forces had been successfully implemented. Having completed the rotation without any particular complications, its units assembled in the area of the 7th Panzer Division's bridges. The fact that the 11th Panzer Division had been held out of the fighting and had received an order to march to a new area on the western bank contributed to this. In addition, the 7th Guards Army didn't undertake any active operations that night, and this also helped bring the troops back to order and prepare them for the next day's fighting as planned.

As for von Funck's panzer division, it is difficult to call this time "quiet". In the first place, its Panzer Regiment 25 had spent the entire day in combat and had suffered losses, and it was important to consolidate thoroughly on ground that hadn't yet been cleared of mines in places, bring up fuel and ammunition, and evacuate damaged combat machines for repair. In the second place, the plan of actions for Schülz's *panzerkampfgruppe* had changed – it's direction was now turning strictly to the east, and thus it was necessary to conduct reconnaissance in the new direction, assemble the combat elements, give them new tasks, and supply them with everything necessary. As von Funck recalled:

> It was impossible for all the units of the division's panzer group to develop the offensive into the depth because of the rising threat on the flank from the area of Hill 209, where large enemy tank formations had now appeared [the 201st and 27th Guards Tank Brigades]. It was impossible to count upon an attack, which might have effectively diverted them, on the part of the neighbor on the right [Korps Raus]. Thus the division decided to conduct a make-do frontal attack only with the panzergrenadier units [*Kampfgruppe* Gläsemer], and to use the reinforced panzer regiment to launch an attack in the direction of Hill 209; after the destruction of the enemy there, it was to thrust across the open ground in the direction of Hill 216.1 and further to the west; having pivoted, it was to link up with the panzergrenadier units attacking from the west, which is to say it was to clear a path for them from the flank.[11]

In the third place, before the morning attack, the forward edge of the Soviet defense was to be worked over by artillery, and this meant that it was necessary to prepare data for the fire plan, which wasn't a very simple thing to do in the nighttime hours.

Finally, on the night of 5-6 July Soviet bombers of the 17th Air Army were actively targeting the area of the bridges at Solomino and Dorogobuzheno, as well as the sector of the breakthrough between Razumnoe and Krutoi Log. In the course of the night, the 244th Bomber Aviation Division and the 262nd Night Bomber Aviation Division flew 123 individual sorties.[12] Their activity noticeably interfered with the regrouping of the 6th and 7th Panzer Divisions, though they were unable to stop its implementation. General von Funck's headquarters in the morning reported, "… over the night the necessary regrouping for the further offensive was conducted. Lively enemy activity in the air. Strikes by bombers on the bridges across the Donets."[13]

Prior to sunrise, active and very strenuous work was continuing in the headquarters of the 25th Guards Rifle Corps. At last, the troops of the assembled grouping were ready for the counterattack

---

10 NARA US, t. 314, r. 197, f. 001086.
11 TsAMO RF, f. 15, op. 11600, d. 1539, l. 23.
12 Gorbach, V., *Nad ognennoi dugoi: Sovetskaia aviatsiia v Kurskoi bitve* [Over the bulge of fire: Soviet aviation in the Battle of Kursk] (Moscow: Iauza, 2007), p. 135.
13 NARA US, t. 314, r. 197, f. 001086.

THE 7TH GUARDS ARMY'S MAIN DEFENSIVE BELT CRUMBLES

against the significant enemy forces that had penetrated the defenses between Krutoi Log and Razumnoe, but Safiulin, who was supposed to conduct it, had no confidence in the advisability of the forthcoming attack. After the war, the 25th Guards Rifle Corps' commander recalled:

> Most of the artillery had just changed positions and likely still wasn't ready to open fire. In addition, we didn't have accurate information on the enemy's location … Our attack grouping had one rifle division and 80 tanks and self-propelled guns. Meanwhile even by rough estimates, the enemy had forces that were four times larger. As a rule, the attacker's losses are greater – even a schoolboy knows this. That is why I was thinking: "What effect would this attack have? It would be better if it [the 73rd Guards Rifle Division] took up a defense there, which it had been ordered to occupy earlier that evening."
>
> Dawn was beginning to break, but despite the early-morning hour, I decided to call the army commander to share my thoughts with him. My words apparently left Shumilov somewhat perplexed, and he was quiet for a few moments. Then he curtly ordered: "Don't launch the counterattack. Use the artillery, tanks, self-propelled guns and division for repulsing enemy attacks."
>
> I immediately made the army commander's order known to Colonel Kozak.[14]

The morning of 6 July was gloomy; cumulous clouds stretched across the sky and here and there it was drizzling rain. This immediately affected activity in the air, and it sharply fell. Artillery fire on the front of the 7th Guards Army hadn't ceased all night; both sides were conducting so-called harassing fire to prevent the enemy's men from getting normal rest and keeping their nerves on edge. However, around 0400 the Germans initiated a powerful artillery preparation with the use of a significant amount of heavy artillery and Nebelwerfers against the left flank of the 81st Guards Rifle Division and the sector of the 78th and 73rd Guards Rifle Divisions; the barrage lasted for almost two hours. In its daily summary, III Panzer Corps reported:

> The corps artillery dueled with anti-tank batteries and enemy mobile artillery batteries in Belinskaia, Iastrebovo and Blizhniaia Igumenka [II/Artillery Regiment 62 (105mm howitzers)]. Next the enemy's jumping-off positions in the woods north of the "Day of Harvest" collective farm were taken under fire; the light guns there were suppressed by 150mm heavy field howitzers [s.F.H.]. Together with Artillery Regiment 19 [of the 19th Panzer Division], fire was concentrated on the Kreida railyard. The mortar battalion [Heavy Mortar Battalion 857 equipped with 210mm mortars] conducted harassing fire on Kreida, firing 95 shells.

It became clear to the Soviet command that a strong attack was in the offing. The 19th Panzer Division was the first to go on the attack against the positions of the 25th Guards Rifle Corps. As before, it had the assets of I/Infantry Regiment 429 of the 168th Infantry Division, Nebelwerfer Regiment 54 (minus III Battalion) and a company of Tiger tanks. Its three *kampfgruppen* were to draw the attention of as much of the defenders as possible that were defending in the sector where the 7th Panzer Division and *panzerkampfgruppe* of the 6th Panzer Division were ready to launch the main attack. The day's objective for the 19th Panzer Division was to break through the line of the 81st Guards Rifle Division in the direction of Blizhniaia Igumenka. The Germans viewed this village as the main knot of resistance of Morozov's division. Given the difficult terrain, Schmidt back on 5 July had decided that there was only one way to seize Blizhniaia Igumenka, by launching two coordinated attacks, one out of the Mikhailovka bridgehead and the other out

---
14 Safiulin, G.B., *Dorogami pobedy,* pp. 154-155.

of the area north of Dal'nie Peski. The initial attempt to close the pincers around Major M.F. Kriuchikhin's left-flank 238th Guards Rifle Regiment on the evening of 5 July had failed because of the Guardsmen's stubborn resistance. Nevertheless, General Schmidt refused to abandon this plan and decided to implement it on the following day.

Three anti-tank regions were the key strongpoints in this sector: the Kreida railyard, the "Day of Harvest" collective farm, and the village of Belinskaia. Although the latter place was in fact significantly larger than the others, the first two were the most important, since they were shielding the approach to Belinskaia, and without their capture it was impossible to launch an attack with the 19th Panzer Division's main forces. In addition, as long as the Russians were controlling the railyard and collective farm, there was no way to gather the panzer division into a fist, which was presently scattered in three isolated (or weakly connected) areas: on the western bank of the Northern Donets River, in the bridgehead at Mikhailovka, and south of the corrective labor camp – Hill 139.9 line. In addition, the Soviet troops were still holding the area of the large and well-fortified village of Razumnoe. Its final capture was one of the main objectives for the day that Kempf had assigned to Breith.

However, before planning the breakthrough into the depth of the 81st Guards Rifle Division's defenses, it was necessary to crush the Russians' fortified positions north and northeast of Hill 139.9. *Kampfgruppe* Becker had repeatedly attempted to break through to this hill all day on 5 July, but hadn't been able to accomplish this; by late evening, it had only reached the southwestern slopes of Hill 139.9. Thus, early that morning Schmidt ordered a storm of fire to be opened on the hill, and only after it was taken to concentrate the panzer division's main efforts toward the Kreida railyard, the "Day of Harvest" collective farm and Razumnoe. Of the 19th Panzer Division's three *kampfgruppen*, Becker's was the strongest, and it was directed to take the collective farm. General Schmidt was counting upon the fact that *Kampfgruppe* Becker would take it by noon, and at this time the neighbor on the right, 6th Panzer Division's panzer regiment, would move out toward Generalovka. Thereby the two panzer wedges, having attacked side-by-side along the Razumnaia River, would smash through the boundary of the 81st Guards Rifle Division with the 78th Guards and 73rd Guards Rifle Divisions right up to the Belinskaia – Iastrebovo line and emerge at the second army-level belt of defenses. Meanwhile, panzergrenadiers would take the village of Razumnoe, where combat was already underway at dawn on the village's outskirts.

According to intelligence data, the Russians had brought up significant amounts of artillery and tanks to the "Day of Harvest" collective farm and the approaches to it had been densely mined. Thus assuming that the storming of it would be difficult, and the fact that time was pressing, Schmidt, striving to resolve this problem before von Oppeln-Bronikowski's tanks had time to come up, was the first in III Panzer Corps to kick off the attack. At 0445 (Moscow time), after the completion of the artillery preparation, the combat group of I/Infantry Regiment 429 launched a strong attack out of the Mikhailovka bridgehead against the 238th Guards Rifle Regiment's line. It was striving to cut off Kriuchikhin's regiment from the rest of the 81st Guards Rifle Division, and so the attack was directed to the southeast toward the labor corrective camp; *Kampfgruppe* Köhler (I/Panzergrenadier Regiment 73) jumped off on the attack just a bit later from the south. At the same time, Becker's panzers with the attached II/Panzergrenadier Regiment 74[15] were holding on the southwestern slopes of Hill 139.9 in expectation of the grenadiers' breakthrough of the Guards regiment's forward edge, only after which it planned to commit its armor into battle in the direction of the "Day of Harvest" collective farm. Thereby it was assumed that as a result,

---

15 Previously, *Kampfgruppe* Richter had been formed on its basis, but on the night of 5-6 July 1943, it was disbanded and I Battalion was transferred to the 19th Panzer Division's Panzer Regiment 27.

the left-flank 238th Guards Rifle Regiment (and possibly the entire 81st Guards Rifle Division) would be crushed.

Simultaneously, units of the 19th Panzer Division's right wing were ready to increase pressure on Razumnoe from the west and help the 6th Panzer Division take Generalovka with an attack from the north. At dawn the panzergrenadiers of Hünersdorff's panzer division initiated a reconnaissance-in-force in the direction of a collective farm (which on the 1:100000 map isn't labeled, but on other maps it is marked as the "New World" collective farm) that was located east of Hill 139.9 in the bottomlands of the Razumnaia River, and being defended by elements of 2/228th Guards Rifle Regiment of the 78th Guards Rifle Division, in order to determine the possibility of breaking through to the river channel and seizing the bridges across it opposite Generalovka.

Approximately two hours after the attack's start, I/429th Infantry Regiment, having penetrated the forward edge of Major Kriuchikhin's 238th Guards Rifle Regiment, began slowly advancing in the direction of the Kreida railyard. However, at this moment Schmidt's plan suffered its first hitch, not only because of the Guardsmen's strong resistance, but also because of the poor organization of the attack. Pioneers of *Kampfgruppe* Becker had failed to discover an extensive minefield in front of the "Day of Harvest" collective farm, and at the start of the initial attack, a significant number of its tanks rolled right into it. From the 19th Panzer Division's daily report:

> *Kampfgruppe* Becker's attack in the early morning hours toward the "Day of Harvest" collective farm came to a stop east of Hill 139.9 in a wide and deep minefield. Fourteen of its tanks were lost on mines, and four – due to enemy fire. A second attack by *Kampfgruppe* Köhler along the road toward the Kreida railyard was stopped to the south of it at 1400 because of our own heavy losses due to strong Russian flanking fire from all types of weapons from positions on the hills northwest of the "Day of Harvest" collective farm, which hadn't been suppressed with the help of our own artillery. An enemy counterattack from the north was repulsed.[16]

As mentioned in the report, in addition to the minefields, the German breakthrough to the collective farm was hampered by flanking fire from Hill 139.9. This hill had the reserve positions of the 238th Rifle Regiment's regimental battery and the 2/87th Guards Separate Destroyer Anti-tank Artillery Battalion of the 81st Guards Rifle Division. The anti-tank battalion, although equipped with 45mm anti-tank guns, had received armor-piercing discarding sabot shells together in addition to armor-piercing and high explosive shells, which substantially increased its ability to take on enemy armor.[17]

The attack by von Funck's 7th Panzer Division went more successfully. The crossing of the 6th Panzer Division had been designated for 0800 (Moscow time), and prior to this he planned to resolve three "preliminary", but no less important tasks. In the first place, it was necessary, as the German staff officers put it, "to chop down the flanking posts", which meant using Schülz's *panzerkampfgruppe* to help the neighbor on the right take Krutoi Log, and using *Kampfgruppe* Gläsemer to take the village of Razumnoe together with the 19th Panzer Division. These two villages, occupied by a powerful anti-tank artillery grouping, were splitting the offensive of Kempf's two corps just like a breakwater, and its flanking fire was greatly hampering the advance of the 7th and 19th Panzer Division's *kampfgruppen*. Thus their capture was extremely important in order to realize the tasks that were standing in front of Army Detachment Kempf on 6 July.

---

16 NARA US, t. 314, r. 197, f. 001098.
17 In the TsAMO RF, the files of the 238th Guards Rifle Regiment contain one interesting document – an order from the commander of the 81st Guards Rifle Division, in which he notes that cases had become more frequent when the Soviet gunners had used discarding sabot shells against enemy firing positions, and categorically bans their use against any other target than armored vehicles.

Second, von Funck wanted to use artillery fire and strong probes by reconnaissance groups to crack the defenses in the center and on the right flank of the 73rd Guards Rifle Division – there, where the main attack by the forces of two panzer regiments would fall.

Krutoi Log was located in the 106th Infantry Division's sector. Forst had given the assignment to take it to the commander of Infantry Regiment 240 on his left flank. Early that morning, after the lines of Major D.S. Khorolenko's 225th Guards Rifle Regiment and Major S.A. Arshinov's 223rd Guards Rifle Regiment, the main forces of which had fallen back on 5 July from their main positions to this anti-tank strongpoint, had been thoroughly worked over by artillery and Nebelwerfer fire, two of Infantry Regiment 240's *kampfgruppen* were to go on the attack toward the village's southeastern, southern and southwestern outskirts. Meanwhile, Schülz's Panzer Regiment 25 stood ready to launch an attack against Krutoi Log's western and northeastern outskirts. Simultaneously, a detachment of the 7th Panzer Division's Panzer Regiment 25 was to attack the positions of the 73rd Guards Rifle Division in the direction of Hill 191.2. Even before sunrise, *Kampfgruppe* Gläsemer (of the 7th Panzer Division) had become tied up in heavy fighting in Razumnoe with elements of Major I.A. Khitsov's 228th Guards Rifle Regiment and had slowly begun to fight its way through to the northwestern outskirts. In this difficult situation, A.V. Skvortsov got in touch with Major Khitsov and gave him an order to move the 1st and 2nd Rifle Battalions' main forces to the right bank of the Razumnaia River and deploy with a front facing to the southeast, in order to prevent the troops of the two enemy divisions from linking up.

From 0530 to 0710 (Moscow time) on 6 July 1943 on the axis of the III Panzer Corps' main attack (which extended up to 12 kilometers in the sector: southern outskirts of Razumnoe – 1 kilometer south of Generalovka (excl.) – northeastern, western, southwestern, southern and southeastern outskirts of Krutoi Log,), *kampfgruppen* of the 7th Panzer Division and 106th Infantry Division went on the attack. Almost simultaneously, several dozen panzers accompanied by 1 to 1.5 battalions of infantry appeared on the battlefield in each of those areas. The first attack struck the Krutoi Log anti-tank strongpoint (defended by the 78th Guards Rifle Division's 225th Guards Rifle Regiment) with the *kampfgruppen* of two divisions simultaneously. Schülz's panzer regiment attacked through the western and northeastern outskirts of the village in the direction of Hill 191.2, while grenadiers of the 106th Infantry Division accompanied by assault guns attacked the southern and southeastern outskirts. A short time later, the 209th Guards and 214th Guards Rifle Regiments of Kozak's division joined combat in the sector: (excl.) Generalovka – (excl.) Hill 164.7 – (excl.) Hill 191.2. A former machine gunner of the 8th Rifle Company of the 3rd Rifle Battalion of the 73rd Guards Rifle Division's 214th Guards Rifle Regiment V.E. Kvashin remembered:

> In the area east of Krutoi Log, fighting had gone on all day on 5 July. It was unbearably hot. We had to carry everything that we needed: ammunition, water for ourselves and the heavy machine guns [the water-cooled Maksim heavy machine guns], K-rations, bottles of compressed gas and grenades, as well as entrenching tools. On the march our columns were struck by enemy artillery and strafed by Me-109 fighters. The driver of one of the vehicles of our regiment was killed by a burst of machine-gun fire from an aircraft, and the commander of the 211th Guards Rifle Regiment Petrov received a wound.
>
> Our regiment took up a defense [by 2000] on exposed ground because the Germans were occupying the forward edge of the first defensive belt, and the second defensive belt was behind us [which means the 73rd Guards Rifle Division had deployed on ground lying between the fortified belts, which the commander of the 214th Guards Rifle Regiment also recalled after the war].[18] The battalions were arrayed as follows: our 3rd Battalion under Captain A.A.

---

18   *Voenno-istoricheskii zhurnal*, No. 6 (1963), p. 48.

THE 7TH GUARDS ARMY'S MAIN DEFENSIVE BELT CRUMBLES

Bel'gin was in the center, which later turned out to be on the axis of the German tanks' main attack; Captain V.I. Razgel'deev's 2nd Battalion was on our right; to our left was Captain Bobrov's 1st Rifle Battalion. North of our regiment (on our flank), the 209th Guards Rifle Regiment of our division was digging in; to the left, behind the 211th Guards Rifle Regiment, ran the positions of the 72nd Guards Rifle Division. In a patch of woods behind us was the 1438th Self-propelled Artillery Regiment [approximately 1.5 to 2.5 kilometers behind the 3rd Battalion's forward edge], and on the left was a battalion of 76mm guns [2/153rd Guards Artillery Regiment]. At the regiment commander's disposal were tanks and Katiusha rocket launchers, but they were designated for an attack and stood behind us. Immediately upon arriving and receiving orders, we began to dig trenches and set up firing positions for the machine guns, anti-tank rifles and cannons. In the combat positions of our battalion, 45mm and 76mm anti-tank guns took up a defense. My machine-gun crew and I began to dig in on the left flank of the 8th Rifle Company, on the boundary with the 2nd Rifle Battalion. Battalion commander Bel'gin, his deputy Vladimirov, the battalion chief of staff Senior Lieutenant Pereskokov and our company commander Il'iasov were supervising our work.[19]

After sunrise, Schülz's armored group first conducted a brief reconnaissance-in-force against the center of the combat positions of Lieutenant Colonel V.I. Davydenko's 214th Guards Rifle Regiment. However, after receiving a sharp rebuff, the Germans quickly reeled back to their start line. Next, both regiments were attacked. The right-flank 209th Guards Rifle Regiment under Lieutenant Colonel G.P. Slatov was struck by 30 combat machines and up to a battalion of infantry in the direction of Generalovka. The defending regiment had a powerful artillery grouping that consisted of 2/153rd Artillery Regiment and one regiment of the 30th Separate Destroyer Anti-tank Artillery Brigade. Tanks of the 167th Tank Regiment and self-propelled guns of the 1438th Self-propelled Artillery Regiment had also been dug in among its positions, and Major Orlov's 2/265th Guards Cannon Artillery Regiment had deployed in the woods behind the second line of trenches. Thus this attack was repulsed as well by Captain V.M. Malinin's 3rd Battalion of the 209th Guards Rifle Regiment. Lieutenant A.A. Verba wrote in his account:

> At 0800 12 Pz.Kpfw. VI tanks with a battalion of submachine gunners emerged on Hill 164.7 and went on the attack against the woods occupied by the 209th Guards Rifle Regiment and us. Having allowed the enemy tanks to approach within 400 meters, our tank crews at a command from Comrade Trekhglazov opened fire from fixed positions with their main guns, while the company of anti-tank rifles added its fire. As a result of the combat, the enemy was repulsed and the Germans fell back, leaving behind 3 knocked-out tanks and up to a company of dead submachine gunners on the battlefield.[20]

When you read such documents, you comprehend the word "exploit" in a completely different way – it no longer conveys unreasonable pomposity and heroic glitter. You gain recognition of the laborious work and the large amount of blood shed expended by our fathers and forefathers to achieve success against a foe that was well-trained and armed with the latest combat equipment. Indeed, a costly price was paid for the three knocked-out tanks in this relatively brief combat that saw the Germans retreat – the commander of the composite tank company Junior Lieutenant Trekhglazov was killed and a number of other tank commanders wounded, and 5 T-34 tanks were

---

19 From the personal archive of A.I. Il'iasov, the son of the 8th Rifle Company's commander Captain I.V. Il'iasov.
20 TsAMO RF, f. 925, op. 1, d. 3, ll. 108obr, 109

left burning and one 76mm anti-tank gun was destroyed. But what was the price Slatov's 209th Guards Rifle Regiment had to pay in this specific combat action? No one bothered to track such information.

The second attack against the combined line of the two Guards rifle regiments was very strong. According to the information from the headquarters of the 73rd Guards Rifle Division, there were 96 tanks in the German panzer wedge that were distinctly rolling toward the hills that included Hill 191.2 (the line of defense of the 211th Guards Rifle Regiment and its boundary with the 214th Guards Rifle Regiment). The first three waves consisted only of tanks, and Tiger tanks were spearheading them. The tension in the ranks of the defenders grew with each passing minute; everyone understood that the outcome of this battle would depend on the gunners. As veterans recalled, at this moment it was important for the artillerymen to maintain their poise as the enemy tanks approach (or as they said at the front, "to show character"), and allow the tanks to approach as closely as possible, without disclosing the locations of their positions by firing prematurely. If this method worked, and the guns opened fire simultaneously from close range, then simultaneously several enemy tanks would lurch to a stop and begin to smoke, or spin in place due to damaged tracks. This would quickly take the steam out of the panzer wedge's attack, and the tanks would instantly come to a stop with the "cough" of dozens of engines at the same time, before spreading out and targeting the brief flashes of the firing anti-tank guns.

That's approximately how things went during this second massed panzer attack, although there was one nuance – it wasn't the anti-tank guns that first went into action, but 3/265th Guards Artillery Regiment, the 1438th Self-propelled Artillery Regiment, followed by the 97th Guards Mortar Regiment and the 315th Guards Mortar Regiment. Having put down concentrated, shifting blocking fire, the howitzer crews separated the panzergrenadiers from the tanks, while the tanks, protected by their strong armor, continued to advance – but not for long. Within a matter of minutes, 1 and 3/158th Guards Artillery Regiment and the artillery of the 225th Guards Rifle Regiment from out of Krutoi Log, and the crews of 2/153rd Guards Artillery Regiment and the batteries of the 1438th Self-propelled Artillery Regiment from the positions of the 73rd Guards Rifle Division joined the cacophony of fire. Just as the enemy began to concentrate forces on the boundary between the 209th Guards and 214th Guards Rifle Regiments, a firestorm rose above this area, raised by the Katiusha rocket launchers. V.E. Kvashin, the machine gunner of the 8th Rifle Company of the 214th Guards Rifle Regiment's 3rd Rifle Battalion who participated in the fighting on 6 July 1943 recalled:

> Early in the morning, around 0400, when the dawn had just begun to break and we were putting our final touches on our preparations, the Germans opened artillery fire. Their tanks had just begun to gather on the northern outskirts of Krutoi Log. Then this avalanche of armor moved out primarily in the direction of the 214th Guards and 209th Guards Rifle Regiments. We counted approximately 100 tanks; behind them, protected by the armor, submachine gunners were running, without helmets, their sleeves rolled up to their elbow, their uniforms disheveled, their submachine guns at their bellies, intoxicated by strong spirits or the battle itself. The tanks, painted in camouflage colors, were rumbling toward the battalion's positions. The lead Tiger tank's turret was draped with a red flag that had a swastika in the middle of a white circle. An officer in a uniform was standing in an open hatch up to his waist. They were confident in victory, rolling forward as if on parade. I've already passed 33 years of age, but even now, when I see this image in my dreams, I break out into a cold sweat. However, we met them like Guardsmen. The lead tank and the one next to it, before reaching our battalion's trenches, stopped short, and immediately Captain Razgel'deev's fighting men

THE 7TH GUARDS ARMY'S MAIN DEFENSIVE BELT CRUMBLES 257

opened fire in support of us. Having lost 13 tanks, the Germans reeled back, but not for long. Attacks began one after the other.[21]

According to S.A. Kozak's report, the fierce morning combat of two of his regiments against the *kampfgruppen* of von Funck's panzer division lasted for a total of five hours. Between 0600 and 0700 alone, the battalions of Slatov's regiment repulsed four fierce attacks.

The bitter fighting flared up, and an especially critical situation took shape in the area of Hill 187.4. A group of 28 armored vehicles had broken through to this hill. The commander of the 214th Guards Rifle Regiment Lieutenant Colonel V.I. Davydenko ordered for the self-propelled guns of the 1438th Self-propelled Artillery Regiment to come up. At 1000 the self-propelled gun batteries went into action. After an hour, the attack was repulsed. Several knocked-out enemy tanks were left on the battlefield. The self-propelled guns also took losses. One SU-76 burst into flames from a direct hit by a tank shell. Schülz's panzer regiment, which had attacked the 73rd Guards Rifle Division's front, fell back, but the onslaught against Krutoi Log continued. At this time, the infantry of Infantry Regiment 240 simultaneously broke into the village from several directions.

According to the information from the artillery headquarters of the 7th Guards Army, the Germans made two strong attacks with panzers against the anti-tank strongpoint that morning. In the course of the first attack, the German assault wedge blundered into a minefield, and having lost 7 tanks disabled, the armored group withdrew, while the grenadiers dropped to the ground and continued to exchange fire. The second attack that started right after 0900 was heavier and bloodier. The veterans of the 225th Guards Rifle Regiment who survived in that furnace of fire recalled the feeling that the Germans had decided at any cost, ignoring their heavy losses, to smash the strongpoint. In the documents of the 25th Guards Rifle Corps there are comments that from the side it seemed that the enemy infantry was totally numb to everything and were advancing literally head-on, with no regard for losses. In several sectors, savage hand-to-hand combat flared up in the trenches, and only after prisoners were taken did it become clear that a significant portion of the enemy's soldiers were in a state of alcoholic intoxication. By 1000, the artillery of the 78th Guards Rifle Division had knocked out or destroyed 19 tanks on the approaches to the village.

However, subsequent events are very murky as presented in the archival documents. It isn't easy to figure out just when the Soviet troops abandoned Krutoi Log. In a special note sent to I.V. Stalin on the evening of 6 July, the Military Council of the Voronezh Front remarked: "In Shumilov's sector the enemy in strength of two tank and three infantry divisions – a total of 270 tanks – resumed the offensive at 0400 6.7.43, and having pushed back Shumilov's center regained possession of Krutoi Log."[22] Combat Report No. 2 from the commander of the 73rd Guards Rifle Division at 1200 on 6 July 1943 supports this version of events. In it, he requests air support for his troops and asks "to bomb Krutoi Log" together with the bridges.

The quotes cited above are from documents either from very high headquarters, or from divisions that were adjacent to the 78th Guards Rifle Division, so a mistake can't be excluded. Unfortunately, I've been unable to uncover the documents of the 225th Guards Rifle Regiment that would have described the battle for Krutoi Log, and so it isn't possible to ascertain the details of how this anti-tank strongpoint changed from hand to hand, or whether that really happened. There are doubts about Krutoi Log's initial capture by the Germans, or that it was taken for a

---

21 From the personal archive of A.I. Il'iasov, the son of the 8th Rifle Company's commander Captain I.V. Il'iasov.
22 TsAMO RF, f. 203, op. 28423, d. 489, l. 23.

second time by the Germans at 1000 on 6 July. From the 78th Guards Rifle Division's journal of combat operations:

> At 0500 the Germans with a force of 20 tanks and more than three battalions of infantry launched an attack toward Krutoi Log and by 1200 after fierce attacks took Hill 176.0 and the southern slopes of Hill 191.2. The 225th Guards Rifle Regiment was totally encircled. Having received an order over the radio from the division commander: "Fight to the last, but do not abandon Krutoi Log!" the regiment continued to fight in encirclement. At 1320 40 tanks and up to a battalion of infantry reached the northeastern outskirts, and at 1400, suffering heavy losses in men and equipment, at an order from the division commander the regiment fought its way out of the pocket and took up a defense on the western fringe of the woods north of Hill 151.4, with combat outposts on the crest of Hill 176.0.[23]

The reason for the two mutually exclusive decisions regarding the 225th Guards Rifle Regiment (fight to the last – break out) taken by the commander of the 78th Guards Rifle Division over a brief interval of time is explained by the regiment's political chief Colonel B.I. Mutovin. He witnessed how Skvortsov reached his decision for the regiment to break out of encirclement. In his book he categorically asserts that the 225th Guards Rifle Regiment didn't fully emerge from the pocket until the evening of 6 July. The Guardsmen didn't simply slip out of the pocket, but had to fight their way out with heavy losses, including an entire battalion. Mutovin wrote:

> I was at the division headquarters, when the commander of the 225th Regiment Major D.S. Khorolenko reported to General Skvortsov that the fascist tanks had been stopped by the fire of the 158th Artillery Regiment and the corps and army anti-tank forces, and the infantry had been separated from the tanks. The Major requested aid [his regiment] in throwing back the enemy, in order to come out of the encirclement. A.V. Skvortsov was plainly upset.
> "Of course things are hard for Khorolenko, and he needs help, but how? All of the regiments are tied up in fighting in their own sectors of defense," he said, addressing me. "He must hold out. The village of Krutoi Log must be held whatever happens. … Then the division commander issued an order to the regiment commander to take up an all-round defense and not to abandon Krutoi Log before receiving a special instruction.
> I offered a suggestion: "Perhaps it is possible to support the regiment with the fire from the division's artillery group and the corps' anti-tank guns?" Skvortsov thought for a moment.
> "I think that's what we'll do," he agreed. "Pass this along to the corps commander."
> General Safiulin, having heard my report, kept silent for a long time, before ordering: "Tell Khorolenko that he should abandon Krutoi Log under the supporting artillery fire and come out of the pocket. Otherwise, the entire regiment will perish. The fascists are throwing ever increasing forces against him."
> That night, the regiment broke out of the pocket and took up a new line of defense. Staff officers and officers of the Political Department met the elements as they came out. … The regiment suffered considerable losses. Its 2nd Rifle Battalion, which was covering the withdrawal and was the last to come out of the pocket, was hit particularly hard. Its commander Guards Captain I.A. Matsokin was killed.[24]

---

23 TsAMO RF, f. 1225, op. 1, d. 16, ll. 24, 24obr.
24 Mutovin, *Cherez vse ispytaniia*, p. 99.

THE 7TH GUARDS ARMY'S MAIN DEFENSIVE BELT CRUMBLES

If you analyze the available information, including a report from Korps Raus, the following picture emerges. In the course of 5 July, the enemy never took possession of Krutoi Log. On 6 July, between 1000 and 1100 the Germans encircled the village with the forces of two divisions, and in several sectors German infantry infiltrated into the depth of the 225th Guards Rifle Regiment's defense. At the moment of receiving the order to withdraw, Khorolenko's regiment had already been split into several isolated pieces, and thus the order didn't reach all of the companies. A certain number of men managed to reach friendly lines by 1500. Then the Germans, having thrown two battalions of infantry and 15 assault guns at the combat outposts on Hill 176.0, overran them and infiltrated into the woods and toward Hill 151.4. So that the reader can imagine that hell that was going on in the Guardsmen's positions, I'll note that in addition to the tank attacks and volleys of Nebelwerfer rockets, between 1330 and 1430 Krutoi Log (together with the 225th Guards Rifle Regiment) were thoroughly worked over by two groups of our Il-2 ground attack aircraft that had been summoned by Colonel S.A. Kozak, who because of the lack of communications with the headquarters of the 78th Guards Rifle Division didn't know the real situation in the village. The companies of the 2nd Rifle Battalion that had been left behind to cover the withdrawal and other scattered elements engaged in bloody fighting with Infantry Regiment 240 and the right flank of the 7th Panzer Division in the village itself and on Hill 151.4 until late in the evening. Only with the onset of darkness did the survivors of the fighting break out of the ring of encirclement and make their way along a spur of the balka east of Krutoi Log to the line of the 73rd Guards Rifle Division (toward Hill 209.6). On the morning of 7 July, commanders were continuing to assemble and rally the men of Khorolenko's regiment in the overgrown ravine on Hill 209.6.

Returning to the mistake made by the 73rd Guards Rifle Division's commander when calling for a strike by *Sturmoviki* [Il-2s] against Krutoi Log, it must be said that during the defensive operation, communications up and down the chain of command (regiment – division – corps – army) worked rather consistently in the entire 7th Guards Army, with the exception of isolated cases when regiments, under the pressure of a superior foe, were making fighting withdrawals to a new line. However, as concerns lateral communications (division to division and corps to corps), here serious interruptions took place. There were several reasons for this.

In the first place, the primary means of communication in the Soviet rifle division was the telephone and cable lines (main and alternate) that ran to the corps' communication center. The radio was actively used, primarily, only in emergency situations or else to repeat an order. The division headquarters also had telephone lines between each other, but in the course of a battle it was usually the first to be knocked out, because the lines ran through a zone of intensive fire and in sectors of possible breakthroughs by enemy armor. Already on the first day of the German offensive, groups of enemy panzers were operating within the defenses of the two first-echelon divisions, and later the situation became even more complicated. In the second place, on the axis of the enemy's main attack, a number of division headquarters were threatened by encirclement or capture, and so the location of command posts and observation posts had to be changed several times (as in the case of the 73rd Guards, 78th Guards and 81st Guards Rifle Division and the 25th Guards Rifle Corps), and naturally as the first order of business they established communications with their regiments and corps headquarters, but with their neighbors only as it became necessary. There were often cases when the headquarters of one division didn't even know the new location of another division's command post, much less roll out a new telephone line to the neighbor.

In the third place, training played an important role in keeping communications functioning, as did, though it might seem strange, the age of the personnel of the signals battalions. In the spring of 1943, pursuant to the order from the Voronezh Front command about bringing the combat units back up to establishment strength, the division commands directed older enlisted men and junior commanders (under 50 years of age) into service and support units, including the signals battalions, while younger soldiers were sent to the line units. As a result, the qualification of the signalers sharply fell and the efficiency of laying down lines of communication dropped. All this taken together was multiplied by the high density of opposing forces in the sector of the 7th Guards Army, which often led to the fact that division commanders often lacked accurate information about the situation in the neighbor's sector and were forced to send patrols, groups of observers and liaison officers in order to check on the situation there. If a division withdrew to a new line, then after this it took a minimum of 24 hours to scout the new area of defense and to try to establish direct or visual communication with neighbors. Thus it isn't surprising that division commanders directed airstrikes on areas that were being held by a different division's units, and that artillery fired at friendly tanks in a neighbor's sector.

As Raus recalled, his divisions received limited objectives for 6 July. In particular the 106th Infantry Division after taking Krutoi Log was supposed to go over to an active defense; looming over the left flank of the 73rd Guards Rifle Division and the right flank of the 72nd Guards Rifle Division, it was to draw their reserves away from the sector where the panzer groups of the 6th and 7th Panzer Divisions would be launching their attack. Therefore almost simultaneously with the start of the attack against Krutoi Log and the center of the 73rd Guards Rifle Division's defenses, bitter fighting erupted on its left flank as well, while the sector of the 72nd Guards Rifle Division was subjected to an intensive artillery barrage. The deputy commander of the 1st Artillery Battalion of the 155th Guards Artillery Regiment T.Z. Vinogradov recalled:

> At dawn on 6 July, the enemy resumed attacks. The fighting went not at all favorably for us. On the right flank the adversary was striving to exploit the success in the neighbor's sector [the 73rd Guards Rifle Division] and at the boundary with it, and on the left flank the enemy was moving fresh forces into the battle. The Nazis hit the western fringe of the Shebekinskaia Dacha Woods with a powerful artillery barrage, and several shells struck the direct proximity of the artillery regiment's observation post; literally just minutes later reports came that the regiment commander was badly wounded. The division's artillery commander ordered Major Kharchenko to take command of the regiment, having giving the chief of staff Captain Cherednichenko responsibility for directing the artillery fire.
>
> The commander of the 2nd Battalion ... Captain Mikhailovsky reported over the telephone: "I've organized an all-round defense. I'm conducting fire on the northwestern outskirts of Bezliudovka. The enemy is preparing a new attack ... I'm requesting concentrated fire on the area with the coordinates ... Fire – at my command."
>
> Everyone at the observation post was endlessly amazed that Mikhailovsky's telephone line continued to operate without disruption. It turns out that the signalers of the 2nd Battalion were using the barbed wire obstacles that had been placed by the Germans along the Bezliudovka – Churaevo road. The Nazis never suspected the role that the barbed wire beside them was playing. Several minutes passed, and then Savchenko [the commander of the 1st Artillery Battalion] reported: "Neman, ready." A short time later, the voice of the commander of the 3rd Artillery Battalion Pochekutov rang out, "Irtysh, ready." Mikhailovsky requested a registration round to be fired, and after making the necessary adjustments, gave the command: "Three shells, rapid fire!"[25]

At 0640, the 1st Battalion of the 73rd Guards Rifle Division's 211th Guards Rifle Regiment was attacked by a *kampfgruppe* of the 106th Infantry Division's Infantry Regiment 239. Incidentally, the Soviet documents describe this combat rather vaguely. In the division's own account, Kozak indicated that up to a battalion of infantry and 15 tanks attacked, but in the reports of its

---

25 Vinogradov, *Dorogoe – Navsegda*, pp. 89-90.

headquarters, it was up to two companies that attacked with the support of two large-caliber machine guns (possibly, these were self-propelled anti-aircraft guns or halftrack-mounted machine guns). Nevertheless, in one line the "enemy's losses" are given: the regiment knocked out 10 tanks. It isn't clear where these tanks came from. Either the large-caliber machine guns thanks to the "spin" of the staff officers were converted into tanks, or they were actually tanks of Schülz's panzer regiment (or assault guns of the StuG Battalion 905), which took part in the storming of Krutoi Log together with the 106th Infantry Division. Most likely it was the latter. However it went the attack here against the 1/211 Guards Rifle Regiment suggested a reconnaissance-in-force, and likely had the objective to force a dispersal of the division commander's tactical reserve. Thus, having met a stiff rebuff, the Germans were played out after a second attack and spent the rest of the morning shelling the positions of the 211th Guards Rifle Regiment with artillery.

Thus, by mid-day von Funck had succeeded in seizing only the two strongpoints of Krutoi Log and Razumnoe, but his panzer division had been unable to create a breach in the defenses of the 73rd Guards Rifle Division. Nevertheless, this success was rather significant in his difficult situation. In Combat Report No.02/op at noontime, Colonel S.A. Kozak reported:

2. The 209th Guards Rifle Regiment with 1/153 Guards Artillery Regiment and a regiment of the 30th Separate Destroyer Anti-Tank Artillery Brigade is occupying the position indicated in the report for 1900 5.7.43. The regiment destroyed 11 tanks and up to a battalion of enemy infantry. The regiment has lost 15% of its men.
3. The 214th Guards Rifle Regiment with 2/153rd Guards Artillery Regiment and a battery of the 1438th Self-propelled Artillery Regiment fought back an attack by up to 50 enemy tanks and are occupying its former position, locked in bitter fighting with tanks and submachine gunners. In the course of the last attack, 30 enemy tanks struck the right-flank 2nd Rifle Battalion, which suffered large losses; its situation is being ascertained. The regiment destroyed 19 tanks and up to a battalion of infantry, and suppressed the fire of a mortar battery. The regiment has lost up to 60% of its men, and the regiment's 45mm anti-tank battery has been destroyed. The remaining losses are being ascertained.
4. The 211th Guards Rifle Regiment with 3/153rd Guards Artillery Regiment with its left flank has twice repulsed up to two companies of submachine gunners with the support of 2 large-caliber machine guns. The regiment is holding its positions. The regiment destroyed up to 10 tanks, one large-caliber machine gun and up to a company of infantry. It has lost up to 5% of its men.

I've decided:
1. To continue to carry out the assignment to hold the line stubbornly.
2. To give help to the 214th Guards Rifle Regiment with one battalion and to place 12 guns of the 30th Separate Destroyer Anti-tank Artillery Regiment at its disposal.

I request:
A. Hasten the arrival of the anti-tank rifle battalions.
B. Increase the air support and block the approach of enemy reserves from Solomino, Tavrovo and Brodok.
C. I request the bombing of Razumnoe, Dorogobuzheno, Solomino, the bridges across the Northern Donets River in this sector, and Krutoi Log.

> My reserve is in the area of Hill 209.6 and has not yet been committed. I'm with an operational command group in my observation post – Hill 209.6.[26]

A fresh, significantly stronger attack against the line of Safiulin's 25th Guards Rifle Corps, which according to Breith's calculations was to break through the first army-level belt of defenses and create a breach in the second (between Hill 209.6 and Hill 216.1) was launched at 1430 with the forces of three panzer divisions simultaneously. According to Operational Summary No.359 at 1900 on 6 July 1943 from the headquarters of the 7th Guards Army, at 1500 the army's defensive front ran along the line: labor corrective camp – southeastern outskirts of Belinskaia – patches of woods 4 kilometers northeast of Krutoi Log – "Poliana" State Farm – northern portion of the Shebekinskaia Dacha Woods – Maslova Pristan' – Bezliudovka. The III Panzer Corps command intended to launch the main attack on the Belinskaia – Generalovka – Hill 167.4 – Hill 191.2 front, which extended for approximately 6 to 6.5 kilometers. In the process it was planned to attack not only the boundary between the 81st Guards Rifle Division and 73rd Guards Rifle Division, but also the flanks of the units positioned in the center of their combat positions. Thus, Schmidt especially assigned *Kampfgruppe* Köhler to attack the 238th Guards Rifle Regiment in the sector between the labor corrective camp and the "Day of Harvest" collective farm.

By this time, the 6th Panzer Division's panzer regiment, which had been made operationally subordinate to von Funck, had arrived behind the 7th Panzer Division's left flank. I've been unable to locate accurate data about the number of serviceable panzers in Panzer Regiments 11 and 25 on the morning of 6 July 1943. Figures on the condition of the panzers began to appear in the daily summaries of the III Panzer Corps only on 6 July, and at that not for all of the panzer divisions, but only for the 19th Panzer Division. According to a variety of estimates, the number of tanks and assault guns (not including halftracks) in the panzer wedge that was directed to break through the second army-level belt of fortifications of the 7th Guards Army and seize ground up to the line of the Iastrebovo road, Hill 207.9 and the "Batratskaia Dacha" State Farm varies between 220 to 260.

The right flank and center of Kozak's 73rd Guards Rifle Division – the 209th and 214th Guards Rifle Regiment, as well as two battalions of the 78th Guards Rifle Regiment's 223rd Guards Rifle Regiment, were to receive the attack of this armored armada. However, the backbone of the defenses here were nevertheless the army and corps artillery. At 0200 6 July, both combat-ready regiments of Colonel M.G. Sapozhnikov's 30th Separate Destroyer Anti-tank Artillery Brigade that were located in the brigade of the 73rd Guards Rifle Division's artillery commander at a verbal order were moved up into positions that lay 300-400 meters behind the frontline trenches of Slatov's and Davydenko's regiments. However, their batteries weren't positioned compactly, as a massed source of anti-tank fire, but were signficantly dispersed across the front. The 1848th Destroyer Anti-tank Artillery Regiment was deployed on Hill 191.2 with the assignment to prevent enemy tanks from passing through the combat positions of the 214th Rifle Regiment in the "Batratskaia Dacha" State Farm – Miasoedovo direction, while the 1844th Destroyer Anti-tank Artillery Regiment was dug in behind the 209th Guards Rifle Regiment in the woods southeast of Hill 167.1. Unfortunately, the anti-tank brigade had not yet completed its process of forming up and had a significant deficit of authorized weapons and equipment. Because of the lack of prime movers, the two aforementioned anti-tank regiments had left behind 14 of their available 40 anti-tank guns, including six of the feared 76mm ZiS-3 anti-tank guns.[27] Meanwhile, the 1846th Destroyer Anti-tank Artillery

---

26 TsAMO RF, f. 1212, op. 1, d. 28, l. 5.
27 For this reason, the 5th Battery of the 1844th Anti-tank Artillery Regiment wasn't committed into the fighting until the beginning of August 1943.

Regiment, which was equipped with only four 76mm anti-tank guns, took no part in the fighting in the 7th Guards Army's sector on 6 July.

In addition to the above-listed units, a large wooded area northeast of Krutoi Log was in the path of the 6th and 7th Panzer Divisions toward Hill 216.1. It extended from the basin of the Razumnaia River almost up to the road running between the "Poliana" State Farm and the "Batratskaia Dacha" State Farm, and lurking within it was a group of tanks, self-propelled guns and heavy artillery in their prepared positions. Incidentally, the woods also held the command post of the 73rd Guards Rifle Division. On the western fringe of the woods, behind the 209th Guards Rifle Regiment stood Major Prokhorov's 265th Guards Cannon Artillery Regiment of 152mm howitzers. The firing positions of its first two battalions were positioned on the left bank of the Razumnaia River in the 19th Panzer Division's sector of attack (the 1st Artillery Battalion – in the eastern part of Belinskaia, and the 2nd Artillery Battalion between the "Day of Harvest" collective farm and the basin of the Razumnaia River, blocking the path to Belinskaia). Major Orlov's 3rd Battalion/265th Cannon Artillery Regiment was on the right bank of the river, between the northeastern portion of the woods (east of Generalovka) and the basin of the Razumnaia River, covering the exit from Generalovka toward Iastrebovo. As before, the self-propelled guns of Major F.A. Zatylkin's 1438th Self-propelled Artillery Regiment were positioned along the southwestern and southern fringe of the woods behind the 214th Guards Rifle Regiment. In addition to supporting Davydenko's regiment with their fire, they received the order to prevent enemy tanks from breaking through its boundary with the 209th Guards Rifle Regiment. At 1000 Major Zatylkin ordered his reserve howitzer battery (4 SU-122) to move up to the western fringe of the woods east of Generalovka. However, unfortunately not all of the heavy self-propelled howitzers reached the designated area; on the march, two of the self-propelled guns were destroyed by enemy artillery fire. For the number of self-propelled guns and assault guns in the self-propelled artillery regiments of the 7th Guards Army and the separate assault gun battalions of Army Detachment Kempf between 5 and 16 July 1943, see Table 10.

In order to avoid heavy fighting in the woods, where armor would not be very effective and might suffer substantial losses, von Funck decided to bypass the woods on both sides with his panzer regiments and push on further to Hill 216.1, which lay behind the large wooded area. He directed the panzers of his division to the east. Schülz, meanwhile, was supposed to continue his current assignment: breaking the resistance of the 73rd Guards Rifle Division, he was to advance across Hill 191.2 and Hill 187.4 to the dirt road running between the "Poliana" and "Batratskaia Dacha" State Farms, and after capturing Hill 209.6 (which was located on this road), he was to pivot to the northeast, and having seized the "Batratskaia Dacha" State Farm, to arrive at Hill 216.1 from the south.

Von Funck assembled von Oppeln-Bronikowski's *panzerkampfgruppe* (II/Panzer Regiment 11 and II/Panzergrenadier Regiment 114 mounted in halftracks) together with *Kampfgruppe* Gläsemer on the 7th Panzer Division's left flank with the assignment: while supporting the 19th Panzer Division (which would be advancing on the left bank of the Razumnaia River), to penetrate the boundary between the 73rd Guards and 81st Guards Rifle Divisions along the right bank, seize the strongpoints of Generalovka and Belinskaia (northeast of Generalovka) that were located on the river's right bank, after which with its main forces it was to reach Iastrebovo, while its right flank would pivot toward Hill 216.1. Thereby, the knot of resistance in the woods east of Hill 191.2 would be encircled by the two armored groups, and to destroy it subsequently would present no difficult task.

Table 10 Number of operational assault guns in Army Detachment Kempf's separate assault gun units[28] and operational self-propelled guns in the 7th Guards Army's self-propelled artillery regiments from 5 until 16 July 1943

Date	228 Battalion	905 Battalion	393 Battery	1438 SP-artillery Regiment		1529 Heavy SP-artillery Regiment	
	StuG G/ StuG H	StuG G/ StuG H	StuG G/ StuG H	SU-76	SU-122	SU-152	KV-1
5 July (morning)	22/9	23/9	12/-	12	9	12/1[1]	1
6 July				10 (20.00)	3 (20.00)[2]	12/1	1
7 July						11/1[3]	1
8 July (2000)				4/2[4]	-/2	11/1[5]	1
9 July (morning)	23	21	8			12/1	1
10 July (morning)	11	26	8	4 (16.00)	1 (16.00)	12/1	1
11 July (morning)	No report	28	9	4 (16.00)	2 (16.00)[6]		
12 July (morning)	19	29	9	4 (18.00)	1 (18.00)		
13 July (0500)	No report	29	4				
14 July (0500)	No report	27	5				
14 July (evening)	14	-	No report				
15 July (0500)	14	27	4				
16 July (0500)	17	27	5				

Notes
1 In the numerator, all ready for combat; in the denominator, located outside the regiment's dispositions – at tactical exercises in the area of Rzhava Station.
2 According to the regiment's Operational Summary No.94 at 2000, its command was aware of the location of only one of its self-propelled guns – at the bridge in Nekliudovo.
3 One SU-152 was receiving maintenance in the village of Nezhigol'.
4 The numerator indicates the operational tanks, while the denominator gives the number of those under repair.
5 One SU-152 was undergoing maintenance.
6 At this time, all 6 self-propelled guns were under the command of the 262nd Tank Regiment; by 1600 on 11 july, the 1438th Self-propelled Artillery Regiment repaired one more SU-76, but didn't transfer it to the 262nd Tank Regiment.

Schülz's units were the first to go on the offensive, and their attacks were similar to the blows of a battering ram, swinging on enormous chains. Despite the fact that a lot of armor had been activated, the first attempt to penetrate the line of the 214th Guards Rifle Regiment failed; the panzers only made a shallow penetration in its forward edge. Having pulled his tanks back, Schülz concentrated artillery fire on the breakthrough sector. The following general attack by two reinforced panzer regiments against the positions of the 209th and 214th Guards Rifle Regiments began between 1430 and 1450. Committing approximately 100 armored vehicles into the battle simultaneously in the sector between Hill 191.2 and Hill 187.4, it smashed its way forward through the line of Kozak's 73rd Guards Rifle Division by approximately 2 kilometers, and having encircled the 1st and 3rd Rifle Battalions of the 214th Guards Rifle Regiment, the panzers entered the woods 1 kilometer north of Hill 209.7. The 73rd Guards Rifle Division's journal of combat operations lays out the start of the fighting in the following way:

---

28 Zetterling, N. and Frankson, A., Kursk 1943: A statistical analysis (London, Portland: FRANK CASS, 2000), p. 190.

THE 7TH GUARDS ARMY'S MAIN DEFENSIVE BELT CRUMBLES 265

Having regrouped his forces, the enemy at 1310 undertook an even more powerful attack. He threw up to 90 tanks against the center of the division's defense – in the sector of the 214th Guards Rifle Regiment. Having no infantry behind them – the tanks were stopped in the area 1 kilometer north of Point 187.4. After working over the defenses with artillery and up to a regiment of infantry had come up, the enemy managed to penetrate the defenses between the 1st and 3rd Rifle Battalions of the 214th Guards Rifle Regiment; having let the tanks pass, the infantry following behind them was annihilated.[29]

An especially critical situation developed in Captain A.A. Bel'gin's 3rd Rifle Battalion; the main attack of Schülz's panzer regiment struck his 3-kilometer sector of defense. For two hours, an unequal combat went on between his companies and the numerically superior foe. The 80th Separate Destroyer Anti-tank Artillery Regiment and Senior Lieutenant Sh.M. Soselii's 2/153rd Guards Artillery Regiment, which had been moved up to the 214th Guards Rifle Regiment's sector, were buttressing the battalion's line. The battalion commander himself was wounded, but he refused to leave the battlefield. When the enemy armor broke through into the depth of the defenses and were rolling past his command post, Captain Bel'gin continued to direct the battalion's fighting. A short time later, panzers again appeared in front of his semi-demolished command post, but this time escorted by infantry. With the fire from his PPSh submachine gun, the battalion commander cut down some of the advancing Germans and damaged one tank with a grenade, but he himself received a mortal wound. The 73rd Guards Rifle Division command reported: "… in the sectors of the 209th and 214th Guards Rifle Regiments, intoxicated enemy infantry and submachine gunners escorting a group of 50-80 tanks attacked the units' positions 11 times. Only after intense artillery and mortar fire on the area of the 214th Guards Rifle Regiment's 3rd Rifle Battalion did 13 enemy tanks manage to enter the battalion's combat positions, scatter the units of the 2nd and 3rd Rifle Battalions, and approach the bend in the road 2 kilometers southeast of the "Batratskaia Dacha" State Farm."[30]

However, despite the precarious position it found itself in, the 3rd Rifle Battalion continued to cling to its positions tenaciously. After the battalion's senior adjutant[31] Captain P.D. Pereskokov was also killed, Captain I.V. Il'iasov, the 8th Rifle Company's commander, assumed command of the battalion. Despite the fact that enemy armor had split the battalion into several isolated pieces, and its defense had deteriorated from a carefully-arranged system into scattered knots of fierce resistance, the Germans were still unable to break free and capitalize on the success. Those on both sides caught in the fighting were full to overflowing with rage and malice. Hand-to-hand combats were taking place in nearly all the trenches, and it was important that the enemy didn't see any signs of panic or the usual "flight" when under tank attack. As one of the veterans of the Guards division put it to me later in a conversation, "from the side it seemed like fire at the Germans was coming from each and every mound and hillock." However, despite the bitter resistance, some of the German panzers still reached the approaches to Hill 209.6, but the halftracks and vehicles following behind were being destroyed by grenade bundles and the anti-tank riflemen, while the infantry was being cut down by bursts of machine-gun fire and submachine gun fire. This enraged the Nazis who were trying to break the will of the defenders, and the enemy panzer crews responded ferociously, firing their main guns at the anti-tank rifle crews, pouring machine-gun fire into the communication trenches, and spinning on rifle pits, crushing them beneath their tracks, until each tank had sunk like a drill bit up to a half-meter into the ground. One of the

---

29 TsAMO RF, f. 73 gv. sd, op. 1, d. 33, l. 26obr.
30 TsAMO RF, f. 1212, op. 1, d. 28, l. 5.
31 At that time, that was the official name given to the post of battalion chief of staff.

panzers headed straight toward Captain I.V. Il'iasov's bunker, but wounded and covered by log beams, he continued to bark commands over the telephone, which by some miracle continued to operate. As M.S. Shumilov later recalled, when breaking through the line of the 214th Guards Rifle Regiment, the enemy used flamethrower tanks in addition to the regular tanks. However, judging from the archival sources, the 7th Panzer Division didn't have any such tanks; 13 flamethrower tanks were with the 6th Panzer Division. Possibly, some of them had been attached to Schülz's *panzerkampfgruppe* for the breakthrough.

In this most difficult battle, the combat troops of the 73rd Guards Rifle Division demonstrated their highest qualities: valor, resolve in the struggle with the foe, and self-sacrifice in the name of a greater cause – defense of the Motherland. Several times, damaged telephone lines with the 1st Rifle Company that had been cut by the Germans were restored by Sergeant S.P. Zorin, the commander of the telephone squad of the 214th Guards Rifle Regiment's signals company. Twice he encountered the enemy almost face to face, and at critical moments the soldier's wit and strokes of luck helped him out. The soldier dropped prone into a crater and feigned death, and then got back to work. The last time he was almost crushed beneath a tank's tracks, but he managed to roll away in time and toss a grenade. The tank began to emit smoke, and after continuing for 100 meters came to a stop. Combat medics of the 3rd Rifle Battalion gathered soldiers who weren't critically wounded from the battlefield and collected them in a dugout at the entrance to a balka. An enemy panzer crew spotted the activity in this place and steered the tank toward the shelter. Saving his comrades, the battalion's Party organizer Senior Lieutenant V.L. Slushkov grabbed a grenade bundle and darted toward the tank. At the cost of his own life, he saved 28 soldiers and officers.

From the recollections of V.E. Kvashin:

> During the sixth attack, a tank began to attempt to crush Bel'gin's command post beneath its tracks, but quickly became immobilized by a broken track. The battalion commander was beneath the tank, and communications with the regiment were lost. Signal Sergeant Zorin restored it 12 times. Zorin himself at first glance didn't really stand out from others by his appearance, and it was impossible to imagine a hero out of this melancholy fellow. His build was slender, and his neck didn't protrude from the collar of his combat blouse. He even carried a little cross as a good luck charm, which his mother had given to him. However, this young, still physically immature man stood morally above the others and performed miracles in this battle. When fixing the next break in the battalion rear, he damaged a tank with a grenade that he had just scrounged from the body of one of our dead soldiers. Battalion commander Bel'gin had been wounded even before the German tank had clambered on top of his bunker, but never left the battlefield and continued to command the companies. As my war buddies later told me, the regiment commander called him and asked: "Bel'gin, what are you doing there?", and he replied, "I'm beneath a tank and directing the fighting."
>
> Around this time, in the course of the sixth attack, tanks began break through to the battalion rear and overrun our trenches. It seemed that the battalion had already been destroyed, but as soon as the [enemy] infantry appeared, those soldiers still alive blanketed the field with their corpses, and the tanks deprived of infantry support began rolling back.
>
> Next the Germans conducted another artillery preparation. After this they launched tanks that had sleds attached to them with tow cable, upon which were receptacles filled with rags that were saturated with fuel oil and a combustible mixture. The infantry was again advancing behind this wall of flames and black smoke. The Germans began to overrun the battalion's trenches from the left flank to the right. Having crushed the trenches, the tanks again moved off into the battalion rear, but once again the field was blanketed with corpses clad in field gray uniforms. The fighting disintegrated into separate pockets. The Germans were

immolating soldiers with flamethrowers, but our guys continued to resist, their bodies lacerated with wounds, their faces blackened, and lips cracking from thirst.

A tank came up to the tank that was immobilized on Bel'gin's command post, attached a tow line, and hauled it back to the rear for repair. A group of tanks broke through to Il'iasov's command post and began to crush the trenches around it with their tracks. A hatch opened on one of them, and having taken a glance from it, the tank commander suggested Captain Il'iasov surrender, and immediately took a bullet to the forehead. The hatch closed and the tank, having rolled atop the company commander's slit trench, applied the brakes to one track, and began to spin around in place, burying the Captain in his collapsed trench. He just had time to say over the phone line, "I'm dying, kill them …."

Our machine gun had been smashed and tossed 20-30 meters away from us; its jacket had been riddled with fragments and the water had all leaked out. We began to fight off the pressing German infantry at first with our submachine guns, and then with those we collected from the battlefield from dead Germans. In this battle, the machine gunner Polukhin showed envious cool. Skillfully taking advantage of folds in the ground, he killed 40 fascists. However, the battalion's strength was melting away. We had now repulsed 11 attacks, ammunition was running low, we had a lot of wounded, and the [enemy] tanks had not only overrun the battalion rear, they had also reached the regiment's command post. Heavy fighting was going on there, and the artillery was barking.[32]

According to data that still needs clarification, of the 450 soldiers of the 3rd Battalion of the 214th Guards Rifle Regiment that entered the battle on the morning of 6 July, only 93 men were able to break out to friendly lines that evening. For their courage and tenacity, demonstrated in the fighting against a numerically superior foe, many of the battalion's Guardsmen were awarded Orders and medals. Andrei Antonovich Bel'gin, Ivan Vasil'evich Il'iasov and Sergei Petrovich Zorin by a decree of the Presidium of the USSR Supreme Soviet were awarded the title of "Hero of the Soviet Union"; both captains were awarded it posthumously.

Von Oppeln-Bronikowski's *panzerkampfgruppe* advanced at approximately the same rate as Schülz's units, although it went on the offensive somewhat later. This was a tactical subterfuge, intended to give the impression of a strong attack only in one direction and to force the Soviet command to send its main tactical reserves to counter Schülz's attack. After the war, the former commander of Panzer Regiment 11 Colonel H. von Oppeln-Bronikowski recalled:

> Together with Colonel Adelbert Schülz, later Major General and wearer of the Diamonds, I carried out a tank attack on a broad front. It was the biggest I ever experienced. Having 240 tanks, we broke through two deeply-echeloned lines in front of the Pena River [sic] line. The cannon fire seemed like a great lightning storm. Bunkers and Soviet antitank guns were smashed with concentrated fire. German tanks drove over mines and were immobilized. Others were knocked out by antitank guns. Nevertheless, the enemy's deeply-echeloned defense was breached.[33]

---

32 From the personal archive of A.I. Il'iasov, the son of the commander of the 8th Rifle Company I.V. Il'iasov.

33 F. Kurowski, *500 tankovykh atak: Luchshie assy Pantservaffe* [*500 tank attacks: Top aces of the Panzerwaffe*] (Moscow: Iauza, 2007), p. 354. The original German has been translated into English as *Panzer Aces II: Battle Stories of German Tank Commanders of WWII* and originally published in New York by Ballantine Books in 2002. Slight differences exist between the translations, but the main one is the fact that the Russian translation presents von Oppeln-Bronikowski's story in the first person, while the English version puts it in the third person. I have followed the English translation where it matches the Russian, but where

If no attention is paid to the somewhat heroic tone and the author's mistake, probably due to the passage of many years, when he confused the Razumnaia River with the Pena River, then all he said matches the reality. Despite the strong resistance, due to the German superiority in armor, by the end of 6 July the enemy had broken through the 73rd Guards Rifle Division's lines at its boundary with the 81st Guards Rifle Division to their entire depth, and only thanks to the dispatch of reserves by the command of the 7th Guards Army was the German advance stopped in the Iastrebovo area. The reason for such a clean breakthrough was, among other things, a crude blunder committed by Colonel S.A. Kozak, which I'll discuss below.

The defenses of the 25th Guards Rifle Corps on the axis of the main attack by von Oppeln'-Bronikowski's *panzerkampfgruppe* was arranged in two echelons. In the first echelon, the 1st and 2nd Rifle Battalions of Major S.A. Arshinov's 223rd Guards Rifle Regiment (of the 78th Guards Rifle Division) had dug in along the line: 1 kilometer south of Generalovka – Hill 164.7 – (excl.) northeastern outskirts of Krutoi Log – forest ranger's lodge in the southern portion of the woods east of Hill 164.7. Behind them (along the southern fringe of the woods were the trenches of the 2nd Battalion of Captain Minin's 209th Guards Rifle Regiment (of the 73rd Guards Rifle Division), the dug-in positions of the composite company of the 167th Separate Tank Regiment (8 tanks and 5 reserve tanks), and the positions of an anti-tank rifle company. Behind the right flank of the 209th Guards Rifle Regiment stood 14 76mm anti-tank guns of the 1844th Destroyer Anti-tank Artillery Regiment, which were not only to prevent an enemy breakthrough of the 209th Guards Rifle Regiment's positions by enemy tanks, but also to cover with its fire the tank-vulnerable terrain in the direction of Iastrebovo between the woods northeast of Krutoi Log and the basin of the Razumnaia River (at Belinskaia).

By 1200, under the pressure of the 19th Panzer Division, the entire 228th Guards Rifle Regiment had successfully fallen back to a new line, leaving behind a rifle platoon from each of the 1st and 2nd Rifle Battalions as a covering force. The main forces of Major Khitsov's regiment quickly and stealthily withdrew to the right bank of the Razumniaia River and took up positions extending along the bank between (excl.) Razumnoe to (excl.) Generalovka, and deployed scattered mines as an anti-tank obstacle. Due to this successful withdrawal and redeployment on a new line, the 6th and 19th Panzer Divisions after seizing Razumnoe were unable to link their adjacent flanks or mop up the river basin, and were forced to keep a substantial covering force here.

When viewing the course of the combat in this area, the following circumstances must be kept in mind. In the morning, the right flank of the 73rd Guards Rifle Division had successfully repulsed several panzer attacks, but with the approach of von Oppeln-Bronikowski's *panzerkampfgruppe*, it became increasingly difficult to hold the line against the combined German panzer forces. The enemy's superiority in armor was telling here. The Germans launched attacks in a narrow sector with several dozen armored vehicles simultaneously. In addition, the ground on the flanks of the German armored wedge was being systematically worked over by intense fire from the Nebelwerfers and field howitzers. Also, the Soviet anti-tank artillery regiments that were playing an important role here lacked radios for communications within each regiment, and thus command and control had to be implemented over the telephone, which substantially reduced the ability to react efficiently to the situation in the course of a rapidly-flowing combat with tanks. In essence, after the start of the struggle against the enemy armor, because of breaks in the lines, communications became disrupted and the regiment broke into separate pieces, i.e. into batteries, and sometimes isolated guns, depending on the length of the sector of defense. Indeed, from that moment on, each crew could count only on its own efforts. It was unbelievably difficult to withstand such pressure, especially if a regiment was equipped with 45mm anti-tank guns, like for

---

the Russian translation differs, I have used it.

example, the 30th Separate Destroyer Anti-tank Artillery Brigade's 1848th Anti-tank Regiment, which was deployed in the 214th Guards Rifle Regiment's sector.

At the moment when Schülz's armored group after noontime once again attacked Davydenko's battalions, the 73rd Guards Rifle Division commander decided that this regiment had exhausted its resilience and would no longer be able to withstand this massed panzer attack, so Kozak decided to shift the 1844th Destroyer Anti-tank Artillery Regiment to its sector, but this decision came too late. From the 30th Separate Anti-tank Artillery Brigade's account:

> At 1300 06.07.1943 the 1844th Destroyer Anti-tank Artillery Regiment was pulled out of its occupied positions at a verbal order from the commander of the 73rd Guards Rifle Division and sent to Hill 209.6 with the mission to strengthen the 214th Guards Rifle Regiment's anti-tank defense, but by this time enemy tanks were blocking its route with fire and didn't give it the opportunity to deploy on this line. Then the division commander ordered the 1844th Anti-tank Regiment to return to its previous positions in connection with the deteriorating situation in the 209th Guards Rifle Regiment's area of defense and to repel tank attacks against the 209th Guards Rifle Regiment. On the way to Hill 167.1, the 1844th Destroyer Anti-Tank Artillery Regiment encountered the 209th Guards Rifle Regiment as it was retreating to the "Batratskaia Dacha" State Farm – enemy tanks had broken through the 209th Guards Rifle Regiment's combat positions and were moving toward Iastrebovo.[34]

Division commander S.A. Kozak had plainly overreacted. The removal of the destroyer anti-tank artillery regiment from its firing positions substantially weakened the 209th Guards Rifle Regiment's defense east of Generalovka, and in essence worked to the enemy's advantage. However, even though this decision was in fact mistaken, I think it is incorrect to fault the division commander. He was in a most difficult situation; over the previous nine hours, the division had been whittling down the units of two enemy panzer regiments, while the 106th Infantry Division gained a position that was looming over its left flank. The 1844th Destroyer Anti-tank Artillery Regiment was the last and only anti-tank reserve that could block the Germans' path to the road between Gremiachii and the "Batratskaia Dacha" State Farm. Immediately after the anti-tank artillery regiment's withdrawal to Generalovka, however, von Oppeln-Bronikowski's *panzerkampfgruppe* and Gläsemer's panzergrenadiers had gone on the attack against the 209th Guards Rifle Regiment. The story with the 1844th Destroyer Anti-tank Artillery Regiment's movements had its own continuation, but I'll return to it later.

Simultaneously as the 6th and 7th Panzer Division's panzer forces had gone on the offensive, the 19th Panzer Division's artillery opened up with heavy fire against the units of the 73rd and 78th Guards Rifle Divisions from the right bank of the Razumnaia River. In less than an hour of combat, von Oppeln's panzers had made a penetration at the boundary with the 223rd Guards Rifle Regiment, and having created an opening, seized Hill 164.7 and pushed on toward the woods containing the positions of Captain Malinin's 2nd Battalion of the 209th Guards Rifle Regiment. At this time, Gläsemer's *kampfgruppe* was attacking Captain N.K. Zhilin's 2nd Battalion of the 223rd Guards Rifle Regiment in Generalovka. They were met by the fire from the crews of the 167th Separate Tank Regiment. Having been struck by the enemy's armored steamroller, Malinin's battalion lost more than half of its men and began to retreat toward the "Day of Harvest" collective farm in disorganized groups. According to information from the headquarters of III Panzer Corps, already at 1715 Gläsemer's grenadiers, relying on support of tanks, had driven the units of the 223rd Guards Rifle Regiment out of Generalovka and continued to push them back to the

---

34 TsAMO RF, f. 9721, op. 1, d. 5, l. 203.

northeast. However, in the 25th Guards Rifle Corps' report, a different time is given for when the Germans took Generalovka – by 1900, but this isn't reliable. By this time the enemy had not only passed through Generalovka; having seized Belinskaia, the Germans were already closing on Iastrebovo from the south.

After the panzergrenadiers and panzers had reached Generalovka, the resistance of the Guards units crumbled; under the enemy's attack, the infantry began to retreat, leaving the artillery without cover, while groups of enemy tanks were roaming along the entire line of defense, including in the rear of the artillerymen. Thus each gun commander or battery commander had to decide on his own when to withdraw his element and in what direction. In such a situation, the commander of the 30th Separate Destroyer Anti-tank Artillery Brigade Lieutenant Colonel M.G. Sapozhnikov, who was located in his command post on the right bank of the Razumnaia River, could offer little help. Considering that two of his regiments, at the order of division commander Kozak, had been shifting from one sector to another, just like a fire brigade, he had lost communications with them and physically had no possibility to control them. Realizing that the front had been broken and the infantry was retreating, while the German panzer wedge was rolling on toward Sevriukovo, where the headquarters of the 81st Guards Rifle Division was located, Sapozhnikov drove off to see I.K. Morozov, the commander of the 81st Guards Rifle Division, to brief him on the situation and get help. However, unfortunately, as experience shows, at such a tense moment it is rare that any higher-standing commander is in the condition to delve into the problems of subordinates. The Voronezh Front's SMERSH Counterintelligence Department reported, "On 6 July, under the onslaught of enemy tanks, units of the 30th Destroyer Anti-tank Artillery Brigade began to retreat in disorder. The temporarily acting commander of the brigade Sapozhnikov, without taking adequate measures to restore the proper order in the brigade's units, appeared at the command post of the 81st Guards Rifle Division's commander, for which the commander of this division gave him a disciplinary punishment."[35] We don't know all the details of the division commander's discussion with the brigade commander; in the course of an intense battle, everyone's nerves were on edge. Nevertheless, it should be noted that on this day the artillerymen of the 30th Destroyer Anti-tank Artillery Brigade played an important role in the struggle against the enemy's two armored groups, although they themselves suffered substantial losses. From the account of the 7th Guards Army's artillery headquarters: "With the further advance, the enemy was greeted by the fire of the 30th Destroyer Anti-tank Artillery Brigade. In stubborn fighting, the brigade brewed up or knocked out 22 tanks, while losing one 76mm gun and 11 45mm guns, and under the pressure of a superior enemy, it was forced to retreat to the "Batratskaia Dacha" State Farm.[36] For the combat actions on 6-7 July 1943, M.G. Sapozhnikov was put up for the Order of the Red Banner by the command of the 25th Guards Rifle Corps' artillery and the command of the 7th Guards Army, and he was subsequently awarded with it.

At the moment when von Oppeln's tanks had begun to shove Zhilin's rifle battalion and the remnants of Sapozhnikov's anti-tank artillery brigade out of Generalovka, a remarkable episode occurred, which testifies to the fact that division commander Kozak didn't in fact draw any useful lesson from the 167th Separate Tank Regiment's disastrous attack on 5 July. At 1700, when Gläsemer's *kampfgruppe* and von Oppeln-Bronikowski's *panzerkampgruppe* were advancing through Generalovka, he issued an order to Lieutenant Colonel A.A. Verba to counterattack the enemy panzer group in the Generalovka – Razumnoe direction out of the woods east of Generalovka with two of the 167th Tank Regiment's remaining four tanks together with the remnants of the 209th Guards Rifle Regiment. Fortunately, to put it gently, this unrealistic order was cancelled by the 7th

---

35 *"Ognennaia duga": Kurskaia bitva cherez glazami Lubianki*, p. 50.
36 TsAMO RF, f. 7 gv. A, op. 5312, d. 539, l. 145.

Guards Army's commander of the Department of Armored and Mechanized Forces Lieutenant Colonel A.A. Bogdanov. At this moment, he was fortuitously at the command post with Verba and directed instead "to deploy the tanks in ambush positions, dig in, and be ready to meet the enemy with fire from the ambushes."[37]

Throughout the day, Major V.F. Prokhorov's 265th Guards Cannon Artillery Regiment rendered substantial support to the rifle units on the boundary between the 73rd Guards and 81st Guards Rifle Divisions. However, after the seizure of Generalovka, Major Iurlov's 3rd Artillery Battalion fell into a most difficult situation. Its three batteries were conducting intensive fire at the attacking enemy from defilade positions. When the German armor reached the area of the battalion's position, its crews switched the 152mm howitzers to firing over open sights. The deputy commander of the regiment Major I.F. Zherebtsov recalled:

> Engaged in bitter fighting and checking the enemy's offensive, we held out until evening. We had no communications with the regiment commander, and so I independently made the decision to withdraw the battalion to a new line, since the enemy had already reached our rear, expanded through the orchards in the area of the "Batratskaia Dacha" State Farm, and was approaching the village of Miasoedovo. Clearly, it was impossible to remain on the occupied line. So with the onset of darkness, I issued an order for the battalions to assemble quietly on the edge of the woods southwest of Miasoedovo. Simultaneously, I summoned the battalion's chief of staff and ordered him to take a vehicle and some submachine gunners and deliver my briefing, in which I had laid out the situation, our location, my decision and the battalions' losses, and requested authorization to change our combat position.[38]

Unfortunately, the order to retreat arrived too late; von Oppeln's and Schülz's panzer regiments had already bypassed the woods, in which the battalion was positioned, and had reached the area of Iastrebovo and Hill 216.1.

The retreat began by battery and went very slowly, since slow-moving STZ tractors were used to tow the heavy guns. At this difficult moment, the neighboring 161st Guards Cannon Artillery Regiment that was located in Dal'niaia Igumenka rendered valuable assistance. From the commendation list, signed by the 7th Guards Army's artillery commander Major General A.N. Petrov:

> On 6 July 1943, around 250 enemy tanks, having broken through the combat positions of our infantry between Krutoi Log and Razumnoe, headed toward the combat positions of the 265th Guards Cannon Artillery Regiment of the Supreme Command Reserve, bypassed it and began to isolate it from friendly units. The regiment was engaged in heavy fighting with enemy tanks. The situation that developed was exceptionally critical, threatening the existence of the entire regiment.
>
> The commander of the 161st Guards Cannon Artillery Regiment of the Supreme Command Reserve Lieutenant Colonel I.M. Bogushevich, seeing his neighbor's predicament, at his own initiative quickly pivoted his regiment by 180 degrees and opened destructive fire on the enemy tanks that were threatening to isolate the 265th Guards Cannon Artillery Regiment of the Supreme Command Reserve, and in the process 14 tanks were knocked out or set ablaze. The tanks' further advance was brought to a halt.[39]

---

37 TsAMO RF, f. 925 sap, op. 1, d. 3, l. 108.
38 Zherebtsov, I.F., "Pod Belgorodom" ["At Belgorod"], *V ogne Kurskoi bitvy: Iz vospominaniia uchastnikov boev* [*In the fire of the Battle of Kursk: From the recollections of veterans of the fighting*] (Kursk: Kurskoe knizhnoe izdatel'stvo, 1963], p. 356.
39 TsAMO RF, f. 33, op. 686044, depository item 1148, entry number 19877939.

While the 8th and 9th Batteries were moving through the woods in the direction of the "Solov'ev" collective farm, the 7th Battery was covering them, but the foe was pressing. The crews of two of its howitzers were literally shooting up the combat machines at point-blank range. Major I.F. Zherebtsov remembered:

> They were heading directly toward the battery and approaching from the left flank, in order to take it in "pincers", but the battery kept firing until its last shell was expended. It destroyed eleven enemy tanks and several self-propelled guns. Almost all of the battery's fighting men, led by the commander himself, fell bravely in this battle. An order to our regiment on 7 July 1943 had this to say about the 7th Battery's death: "Drop from the regiment's rosters those who were killed in the fighting for the Motherland on 6 July 1943 in the Belgorod area: 7th Battery commander Lieutenant Z.K. Davlikaev, gunnery control platoon commander Lieutenant A.D. Ratnikov, gun commander Senior Sergeant M.I. Sitalo, signals squad leader Sergeant A.K. Mikhalychev, signals squad leader Senior Sergeant V.D. Borzenko, machine gunner Private M.A. Kozlov, armorer Senior Sergeant F.A. Petrov, gun crew member Private Sh.P. Shelest, tractor driver Private V.A. Grabrov, gun crew member Private V. Aiumov, gun crew member Kh. Amangaleev, gun crew member N.M. Laptu, machine gunner Private G.M. Nechepurenko, telephone operator T. Abdurakhmanov, and gun crew members Privates K. Kul'bekov and P.N. Tarshelov.
>
> The gunnery control platoon commander who survived the action later talked about the collective exploit of the Guardsmen of the 7th Battery. Enraged by the heavy losses in tanks and men, the Nazis, having seized the guns that had been damaged in the duel with them, used their submachine guns to execute the wounded soldiers and officers who were still alive. An eyewitness to this atrocity, the badly wounded platoon commander Lieutenant I. Vasil'ev, crawled into a dense patch of bushes near a firing position, where he laid, bleeding, until nightfall. By dawn he had crawled to a brook on the other side of the "Batratskaia Dacha" State Farm, where he was picked up by our soldiers.
>
> …
>
> When the area of the firing positions had been liberated, I and the regiment commander Major Prokhorov visited the place where the 7th Battery perished. There were no words to express our anger at the fascist fiends. The bodies of the soldiers who'd been killed were left where they had fallen for two weeks. They were lying there with riddled heads and chests, inflicted by the bursts of submachine gun fire from the Nazis. The traces of the massacre were distinctly visible on the combat blouses that had faded from the sun. According to local residents' stories, before our units' counteroffensive, fascist sentries had guarded the battery, so that no one could collect and bury the corpses, and the knocked out tanks and guns had been transported away. Only several meters away from one firing position lay the turret of a Tiger tank that had been blown off by a shell. Embedded deeply in the ground, it was testifying to the battery's last-ditch battle with the foe.[40]

When exiting the woods, one more battery of Iurlov's artillery battalion came under an attack by von Oppeln's *panzerkampfgruppe*. Elements of the 223rd Guards Rifle Regiment were also retreating together with the artillerymen of the 265th Guards Cannon Artillery Regiment. At an order from division commander Kozak, an overgrown balka east of Hill 209.6 was designated as the place for the regiment's re-assembly, but by that time the path to it, as well as the hill itself, were already in German hands. Thus the soldiers moved toward the "Batratskaia Dacha" State

---

40   Zherebtsov, "Pod Belgorodom", *V ogne Kurskoi bitvy*, p. 355, 357.

THE 7TH GUARDS ARMY'S MAIN DEFENSIVE BELT CRUMBLES

Farm, across Hill 216.1, to bypass the German positions. Incidentally, some Soviet units remained in the woods northeast of Krutoi Log until the sunrise on 7 July, continuing to defend tenaciously. Their resistance was so stubborn, that the 7th Panzer Division's command was compelled to attack this pocket of resistance with tanks. From the daily report of the subordinate divisions to the headquarters of III Panzer Corps:

> 6th Panzer Division … von Oppeln's panzer regiment, subordinate to the 7th Panzer Division, in cooperation with units of this division, attacked the enemy holding Generalovka, seized this point, and at 1910 (Moscow time) reached the area 1.5 kilometers south of Iastrebovo. Light artillery fire [the remnants of the 167th Separate Tank Regiment] is coming out of the woods 2.5 kilometers east of Generalovka, out of Belinskaia – anti-tank fire [the 30th Destroyer Anti-tank Artillery Brigade], and out of Miasoedovo – enemy artillery fire. At the spearhead of the advance, the adversary is retreating to the western bank of the Razumnaia.
>
> *Kampfgruppe* Unrein has an order to move out from its assembly area at Koloniia Dubovoe and follow in the wake of the panzer group to Generalovka. *Kampfgruppe* Quentin [commander of the 6th Panzer Division's reconnaissance battalion] is grouping in a new assembly area.
>
> Continuous enemy air activity with bomb strikes and strafing attacks.
>
> 7th Panzer Division … In continuation of the breakthrough achieved on 5.7 by *Kampfgruppen* Gläsemer and Schülz, a successful attack has been conducted and the heights northeast of Krutoi Log seized. Schülz's panzer shock group, moving out to the east against the "Batratskaia Dacha" State Farm, broke into the enemy's reserve positions 1.5 kilometers northeast of Point 209.6 and played a decisive role in the success of the neighboring division's attack. Generalovka, which was ferociously defended by the enemy on the left flank, with the heaviest artillery support and ceaseless aerial activity, was taken by an assault at 1715 (Moscow time) by *Kampfgruppe* Gläsemer and von Oppeln's panzer group that has been subordinated to the division from the 6th Panzer Division.
>
> In the continuing offensive toward the main defensive strongpoint in the enemy's reserve position at Batratskaia Dacha, by 1830 the line: State Farm (2 kilometers south of "Batratskaia Dacha" – WW (4 kilometers west) – northwestern corner of the woods (northeast of Krutoi Log) – center of the area 1 kilometer east of Belinskaia has been reached.
>
> The offensive continues with the initial objective of first taking "Batratskaia Dacha" and the hills southwest of it, in order then to strike to the north.
>
> 2) Line of contact: Southwestern corner of the woods (2 kilometers northeast of Krutoi Log) – Hill 164.7 – Generalovka.
> 3) Panzer Regiment 11 has been made subordinate to the division.
> …
> 5) Division command post at Point 205.4 (2 kilometers northwest of Solomino).[41]

Simultaneously with the attacks by the reinforced 7th Panzer Division against the 73rd Guards Rifle Division, the 19th Panzer Division also continued to launch attacks against the positions of the 81st Guards Rifle Division. At the moment of the breakthrough of Kozak's division, to General Breith it was extremely important that on the axis of the III Panzer Corps' main attack, the command of the 7th Guards Army wouldn't be able to reinforce the sector by bringing up reserves (or shifting forces from the flanks). Therefore the 19th Panzer Division was supposed to place as much pressure as possible on the defenders in its sector, but it proved exceptionally

---

41 NARA US, t. 314, r. 197, f. 001098, 0010102.

difficult to carry out this assignment. The Russians' well-fortified defensive belt had taken splendid advantage of the difficult terrain and had abundantly saturated it with obstacles and all kinds of "nasty surprises" that were difficult to detect, and which the assault groups of Schmidt's 19th Panzer Division encountered at almost every step. A summary from the 19th Panzer Division's headquarters stated:

> The second attack by *Kampfgruppe* Becker and Infantry Regiment 442, launched at 1530 (Moscow time) to the north from the Razumnoe – 600 meters southwest of the "Day of Harvest" collective farm sector ran into deep minefields, through which a narrow passage was cleared only by 1910 (Moscow time).
>
> I/Panzergrenadier Regiment 74 at 1925 (Moscow time) took possession of the hill to the west of the "Day of Harvest" collective farm from a strong and well-entrenched enemy.
>
> I/Infantry Regiment 429 at 1430 (Moscow time) crossed to the eastern bank of the Donets in order to comb through the woods to the north, reached the northern fringe of the woods by 1700 (Moscow time) and established contact with Panzergrenadier Regiment 73 within the bridgehead.
>
> … Throughout the day multiple bombing and strafing attacks on the forward edge. Constant activity by our fighters.
>
> 3) Regiment headquarters and II/Panzergrenadier Regiment 74 have been subordinated to *Kampfgruppe* Becker.
> 4) The 1st Battery of Flak Battalion 272 conducted a change of position with two light anti-aircraft platoons to the eastern bank of the Donets River, where they deployed at the railroad south of the Kreida railyard.[42]

One of the most stressful and difficult moments in the course of the entire defensive operation arrived for the commands of both the 7th Guards Army and the Voronezh Front in the latter half of the day of 6 July. Still while repulsing the initial morning panzer attacks on the right flank of the 73rd Guards Rifle Division, our reconnaissance established the movement of II/Panzer Regiment 11 across the bridge in Solomino. M.S. Shumilov was informed that the Germans were preparing to bring up a significant amount of armor opposite the forward edge of Kozak's division. In addition, corps commander Safiulin reported on the increasing attacks by panzer groups against the left flank of the 81st Guards Rifle Division in the direction of Belinskaia and Blizhniaia Igumenka. Realizing that the Germans were trying to draw his reserves toward the sector of Morozov's 81st Guards Rifle Division, while sending their own reserves against the sector of the 73rd Guards and 78th Guards Rifle Divisions in the Iastrebovo – Sevriukovo – Miasoedovo direction or toward the "Batratskaia Dacha" State Farm and Nekliudovo, the 7th Guards Army commander made a number of important decisions. In the first place, he decided to hedge his bets in the event of an enemy breakthrough and to block the enemy's path to the northeast with the 31st Separate Destroyer Anti-tank Artillery Brigade (which N.F. Vatutin had nevertheless subordinated to him). In the second place, he decided to move up his combined-arms reserve – Major General E.I. Vasilenko's 15th Guards Rifle Division – to the line of the Koren' River. From there it would block the enemy's expansion into the rear of the 24th Guards Rifle Corps, and allow the possibility of launching a flank attack to the northeast against the German group attacking through the 73rd Guards Rifle Division's right flank. From the 15th Guards Rifle Division's account:

---

42 NARA US, t. 314, r. 197, f. 001098.

On the night of 5-6.07.1943 the division, having turned over its sector of defense to units of the 111th Rifle Division, conducted a march along the Volchansk – "Pletnevka" State Farm road, assembled in Shebekino by 0800. In connection with the abrupt changes in the situation on the army's front, in the course of 2 hours the division received several combat orders and didn't have time to set out in an indicated direction before one order was changed by another, and only at 1200 6.07.1943 did the division move out from its assembly point in order to take up a defense along the Nekliudovo – Churaevo line with the assignment to prevent a breakthrough by enemy tanks and infantry across the Koren' River. At 1700 the division took up a defense on the (excl.) Nekliudovo – Churaevo line, having its forward edge along the Koren' River.

The 50th Guards Rifle Regiment occupied the (excl. Nekliudovo) – Pentsevo – 1.5 kilometers southeast of Hill 136.3 sector.

The 47th Guards Rifle Regiment: (excl. Pentsevo) – Churaevo – woods 2 kilometers east of Hill 123.2.

The 44th Guards Rifle Regiment: 1.5 kilometers east of Hill 136.8 – 3 kilometers southeast of Pentsevo – Point 201.3.[43]

At mid-day N.F. Vatutin was located in the Front headquarters at the communications center and had a discussion over the Baudot device with Lieutenant General I.M. Chistiakov. It was during this conversation that he received the news from the 6th Guards Army's commander that at 1210, up to two enemy tank divisions (of the II SS Panzer Corps) had created a breakthrough in the vicinity of Iakovlevo on the Prokhorovka axis and were continuing to advance in his army's rear. It became clear to the General of the Army Vatutin that if he couldn't change the situation quickly with the decisive actions of the Front's reserves in this area and was unable simultaneously to back up M.S. Shumilov (who was struggling to contain the enemy's attacks in his sector) that the Germans would finally seize the initiative. Thus he agreed with I.M. Chistiakov's recommendation and authorized him to launch a counterattack with the 5th Guards Tank Corps and the 2nd Guards Tank Corps against the spearhead and right flank of the enemy's penetration. In order to reinforce the 7th Guards Army, Shumilov received the 31st Separate Destroyer Anti-tank Artillery Brigade, and in addition, the commander of the 35th Guards Rifle Corps Lieutenant General S.G. Goriachev, who was at the time subordinate to the 69th Army, received an order to move up two of his divisions into the second army-level belt of defenses at the boundary between the 6th Guards and 7th Guards Army. At 1330 the corps commander signed Special Orders No.1 and No.2, in which he directed the commander of the 92nd Guards Rifle Division Colonel V.F. Trunin "to move immediately to the Verkhnii Ol'shanets – Ol'khovatka area and replace the units of the 89th Guards Rifle Division in the sector: Sabynino – (excl.) Kiselevo – Shliakhovoe – (excl.) Mazikino – Verkhnii Ol'shanets – (excl.) Krivtsovo, and to pay particular attention to the Sabynino – Gostishchevo – Shliakhovoe – Dal'niaia Igumenka – Belgorod direction. Boundary on the left: Razumnaia River;"[44] and directed the commander of the 94th Guards Rifle Regiment Colonel I.G. Russkii "… to move immediately to the Lomovo, Mazikino, Sheino area with the assignment to defend the Mazikino – Sheino – Novo-Troevka – Alekseevka area, and to pay particular attention to the Mazikino – Melikhovo – Belgorod; Mazikino – Miasoedovo – Belgorod; and Novo-Troitskoe – Nekliudovo – Shebekino directions. Boundary on the right: Razumnaia River."[45]

---

43 TsAMO RF, f. 25 gv. sk, op. 1, d. 12, ll. 165-167.
44 TsAMO RF, f. 35 gv. sk, op. 1, d. 26, l. 76.
45 Ibid., p. 77.

The Front Commander-in-Chief planned to use Colonel M.P. Seriugin's 89th Guards Rifle Division jointly with the two Guards tank corps in order to launch a counterattack on the morning of 7 July against the enemy grouping that had broken through into the rear of Chistiakov's Guards army on the Prokhorovka direction. Meanwhile, the two divisions of Goriachev's 35th Guards Rifle Corps were to create a second echelon for the 7th Guards Army in the most vulnerable sector – behind its right flank and the boundary with the 6th Guards Army. Thus, despite the sharply deteriorating situation, N.F. Vatutin persistently continued to adhere to his plan to keep von Manstein's Fourth Panzer Army and Army Detachment Kempf separate. Thus far, he had succeeded in doing this.

In parallel with the creation of a second echelon for the 7th Guards Army, the Front Commander-in-Chief reinforced the army with Major General I.P. Beliaev's 270th Rifle Division. In the middle of the day, it received an order from the headquarters of the 49th Rifle Corps "to make a forced march along the route: Belianka – Malo-Mikhailovka – Voznesenovka – Logovoe – Shebekino route and by the morning assemble with the 973rd Rifle Regiment – Krapivnoe; 975th Rifle Regiment – Ustinka; and the 977th Rifle Regiment – Shebekino. After assembling, pass to the operational control of the 7th Guards Army's 24th Guards Rifle Corps."[46] This decision suggested itself. M.S. Shumilov, having transferred the 15th Guards Rifle Division to the commander of the 25th Guards Rifle Corps, was left with only the 111th Rifle Division in his reserve, which hadn't yet been authorized for use. In order to reinforce the 24th Guards Rifle Corps, which had already committed its first echelon into the fighting, he had nothing left for a second echelon. However, N.F. Vatutin at this moment was also experiencing an acute deficit of forces; he had emptied his reserves on the Front's left flank, and thus he personally directed for Beliaev's rifle division not to to pass to control of the 7th Guards Army commander, but directly to corps commander N.A. Vasil'ev, and at that only temporarily, and for it to be used only with the authorization of the Front's command or as a "fire brigade" in response to a crisis.

In addition, that morning at the request of M.S. Shumilov, the Front Commander-in-Chief had ordered the 17th Air Army to increase its operations east of Belgorod, and to direct a portion of the 2nd Air Army's 1st Ground Attack Aviation Regiment to destroy the German bridges across the Donets River. The commander of the 17th Air Army Lieutenant General V.A. Sudets operationally assigned Colonel A.F. Isupov's 306th Ground Attack Aviation Regiment for operations in the 7th Guards Army's sector. German troops immediately noticed the activation of the pilots' combat work, and at that, not only on the axis of the army detachment's main attack. Both of Kempf's subordinate corps began to report "heavy attacks by enemy aircraft," "bombing of the bridgehead fortifications in Mikhailovka and the eastern portion of Belgorod", etc. However, as Soviet combat documents show, the effectiveness of our aviation formations on this day could have been significantly higher. I'll discuss this a little later.

Now let's return to the events in the sector of the 73rd Guards Rifle Division. The timely reconnoitered route of march to the sector of the 7th Guards Army enabled the commander of the 31st Separate Destroyer Anti-tank Artillery Brigade Lieutenant Colonel S.V. Shmanov to get his units on the march already at 1420 and to send a reconnaissance group of the 1849th Destroyer Anti-tank Artillery Regiment led by its commander and the brigade's chief of staff to the area of Hill 206.9. When this group arrived at Iastrebovo, von Oppeln's and Gläsemer's units were already assaulting Generalovka, while separate groups of tanks were fighting in Belinskaia. The 223rd Guards Rifle Regiment of the 78th Guards Rifle Division and the 209th Guards Rifle Regiment of the 73rd Guards Rifle Division had been defeated and were retreating toward the woods east of Hill 191.2 and further on to the left bank of the Razumnaia River, while some of their companies,

---

46 TsAMO RF, f. 270 sd, op. 1, d, 1, l. 12.

THE 7TH GUARDS ARMY'S MAIN DEFENSIVE BELT CRUMBLES

having lost command and control due to the attack by "rolling waves of tanks" were moving to the east into the rear of Safiulin's corps. The 31st Separate Destroyer Anti-tank Artillery Brigade's chief of staff Major Korshevniuk reported back to S.V. Shmanov about the breakthrough in the line and the rifle units' retreat. In the brigade's report, that moment was described in the following fashion: "At this time, the infantry and its heavy weapons were retreating one way or the other: the cannons and mortars were fleeing in disorder along the road to Sheino. Enemy tanks (more than 70) were advancing along the road from Hill 216.1 to Miasoedovo, often firing at the Iastrebovo – Sevriukovo road."[47]

Having assessed the situation, the commander of the 31st Separate Destroyer Anti-tank Artillery Brigade immediately issued an order to deploy the 1849th Destroyer Anti-tank Artillery Regiment's 2nd Battery, which was already located in Iastrebovo, on its southern outskirts and under its cover to move up and deploy the regiment on the Sevriukovo – "Solov'ev" collective farm line, running across Point 160, with the aim of blocking the enemy's panzer group. Thus, even though there were no longer any troops behind the line of the 73rd Guards Rifle Division, which might have been able to check the two panzer divisions, nevertheless due to the proper assessment of the unfolding operational situation and the timely steps taken by the 7th Guards Army command, Shmanov's anti-tank artillery brigade was already on the approach. It had a real possibility to tie up the 6th and 7th Panzer Division's armored group in battle for several hours, in order to bring up reserves. Fortune favored the anti-tank artillerymen; they managed to achieve much more than had been demanded of them at that moment.

Having broken the organized resistance at the boundary between the 73rd Guards and 81st Guards Rifle Divisions, *Panzerkampfgruppe* von Oppeln was advancing rather rapidly along the road being used by the retreating Guardsmen. Stubborn street fighting was still underway for possession of Generalovka, but the majority of Major Franz Bäke's II/Panzer Regiment 11 had already rolled through Belovskaia and at 1700 was located just 1 kilometer to the south of Iastrebovo. However, at this moment an unpleasant event occurred for the enemy, about which the headquarters of the 6th Panzer Division, judging from its summaries, failed to report to the III Panzer Corps headquarters. Its participants, the German commanders, also "forgot" to mention it in their memoirs. After having lost several tanks disabled by mines, the German panzer crews received an order: if the Russians weren't firing at the tanks, to march in a column formation and to deploy into a combat formation only with the onset of fighting. Von Oppen's *kampfgruppe* was also adhering to this order as it was approaching the line of Senior Lieutenant F.P. Pochtarev's 2nd Battery of 76mm anti-tank guns, which the commander of the 1849th Destroyer Anti-tank Artillery Regiment Major D.I. Zorin had moved out to the Iastrebovo – Point 160 – Sevriukovo line in order to cover the regiment's deployment. From the account of the 31st Separate Destroyer Anti-tank Artillery Brigade's headquarters:

> 70 enemy attacks were moving in march formation, with up to 30 heavy tanks at the head of the column; having encountered heavy flanking fire from the 2nd Battery [the battery joined battle with only 3 anti-tank guns; the fourth had lagged behind and was still on the march at the head of the regiment's column], which was positioned on the hillocks on the southern outskirts of Iastrebovo. The column attempted to deploy, but when deploying the four lead Tiger tanks were set ablaze and two tanks were knocked out by two crews. In the same place, five tanks were knocked out by the No. 3 and No. 4 guns. The lead knocked-out tank formed an artificial roadblock, and in addition the high rate of fire from the gun crews was hampering the observation from the tanks, and thus fire on the battery's firing positions

---

47 TsAMO RF, f. 203 (artillery headquarters), op. 2843, d. 29, l. 109.

began only after an hour of combat. The tanks had no opportunity to turn around and head to the west, because each tank, when turning, entered the cross-sights of the gunners and was quickly knocked out. By 1830 the battery had fully carried out its orders from the regiment commander to screen the deployment of the rest of the batteries, leaving 6 knocked out and 9 burned-out German tanks on the battlefield. Having expended all of its armor-piercing shells, the 2nd Battery under the cover of the 1st Battery was withdrawn from its firing positions to reserve positions.

However, the enemy tanks resumed their movement in the same direction – toward Iastrebovo. At this time, a second column of more than 100 tanks appeared on the horizon on Hill 207.9 [Schülz's Panzer Regiment 25]. The regiment's four remaining anti-tank batteries, having deployed from the march, opened fire simultaneously at the first column [von Oppeln's armored group]. The 1st Battery targeted the head of the column, of which 55 tanks remained, while the 3rd and 4th Batteries targeted the center, and the 5th Battery fired at the column's tail. A portion of the second column, having assessed the strength of the fire that was hitting the first column [the mushroom clouds of smoke, fire and dust], opted to stop and await the outcome of the battle. The fighting lasted for 90 minutes. The first column, having lost a total of 30 tanks knocked out or destroyed, at 2000 turned toward the "Batratskaia Dacha" State Farm and the "Solov'ev" collective farm. On the approaches to the State Farm, the column of tanks ran into the infrequent, but extremely accurate fire of a 76mm anti-tank gun and tank, the identity of which hasn't been established. Five tanks were left burning on the road to the "Batratskaia Dacha" State Farm, and 3 more were knocked out. Nevertheless, up to 13 tanks and 3 self-propelled guns, which had fallen in with the second column, broke into the "Batratskaia Dacha" State Farm at 2100.

It should be emphasized that the success of Zorin's anti-tank regiment was of extremely important significance for the Soviet side. After the capture of the village of Belovskaia by von Oppeln's *panzerkampfgruppe* and the breakthrough to Hill 216.1 by Schülz's *panzerkampfgruppe* (which occurred almost simultaneously), the flanks of the 81st Guards and 73rd Guards Rifle Divisions had been ruptured and a gap had been created with a breadth of 4.5 to 5 kilometers, which the 31st Separate Destroyer Anti-tank Artillery Brigade and the 148th Separate Tank Regiment, which was also located here, had to plug. At the moment there were no other Soviet forces behind the positions of the anti-tank brigade and tank regiment in the direction of Miasoedovo, and if the enemy hadn't been checked, the rampaging panzer columns would have had to have been stopped in the rear by the Front's reserves on an unprepared line.

There are several reasons why Senior Lieutenant F.P. Pochtarev's 2nd Anti-tank Battery was able to achieve such high results. In the first place, the anti-tank crews had reached the indicated line while staying concealed and had carefully camouflaged their firing positions, and they caught the enemy by surprise. In the second place, the battery commander had successfully selected his firing positions. The anti-tank guns were firing at the flanks of the panzer column, while at the same time the crews remained outside the zone of return fire for a considerable amount of time. In the third place, for the anti-tank gun crews, the terrain conditions were favorable for conducting anti-tank gun fire at the road over which the enemy panzer column was moving in march column. Finally, there was the excellent training of the anti-tank gun crews themselves. Indeed, it isn't surprising that in the brigade's documents, it is given notice that during the preparatory period before the start of the battle, according to an order from the Front's artillery command to make genuine tank destroyers out of the gun crews, each day the enlisted men and junior officers went through 10 hours of training, of which two were dedicated to firing over open sights at moving targets. The mid-level command staff (the commanders of platoons and batteries) underwent eight hours of training every two days out of three.[48]

Whenever a breakthrough was noted in a sector, the Soviet command sought to shift whatever could fire to the threatened sector, right down to separate guns and anti-tank rifle crews. The 7th Guards Army's command was operating approximately in the same way in this situation. M.S. Shumilov back on the evening of 5 July had accurately assessed the line of the 73rd Guards Rifle Division as the most dangerous sector, and had brought up all available anti-tank means to back it up. Thus both panzer groups of the 7th Panzer Division, despite all their power, didn't move against the positions of Kozak's division in parade formation, and under the hailstorm of shells, mortar rounds and anti-tank rifle slugs literally wallowed through the artfully prepared multitude of minefields and obstacles. That's why the scene of the combat between the anti-tank gun crews of Major D.I. Zorin's anti-tank regiment and von Oppeln's panzers had no influence on the decision by Lieutenant Colonel A. Schülz's decision to pivot his armored group toward the "Batratskaia Dacha" State Farm; it was completely other factors. Firstly, it was the strong fire coming from the 148th Separate Tank Regiment, which at 0800 on 6 July had arrived in the area of the "Solov'ev" collective farm (on the western fringe of the woods east of Iastrebovo), and by the moment of the German breakthrough, its tank companies had already dug in their combat machines together with submachine gunners and anti-tank riflemen, having thereby created a strong line of defense. Secondly, the commander of Panzer Regiment 25 had a precise order from his superior General Breith: to take the "Solov'ev" collective farm on 6 July and thereby clear a path for Korps Raus to the Razumnaia River. Thus it was decided to take the collective farm with the forces of von Oppeln's *panzerkampfgruppe* that was approaching from the Iastrebovo area, while Shulz turned his units toward the "Batratskaia Dacha" State Farm.

In order to dispel any doubts and to understand who was fighting with whom, and how this happened, we'll turn to the archival documents. From the 148th Separate Tank Regiment's journal of combat operations for 6 July:

> At 0040 on 6 July, Combat Order No.0020/op was received from the headquarters of the 7th Guards Army's Armored and Mechanized Forces about subordinating the 148th Separate Tank Regiment to the 31st Separate Destroyer Anti-tank Artillery Brigade and assembling its units in the area of Hill 206.9 [800 meters north of the "Solov'ev" collective farm]. At 0420 the regiment set out to the indicated area and by 0800 it was assembled along the western fringe of the woods east of Iastrebovo and Sevriukovo. The 3rd Tank Company with two squads of submachine gunners and four anti-tank rifle crews occupied the southeastern outskirts of Miasoedovo. … In the course of the day, the regiment without artillery support and infantry cover engaged the enemy armor successfully, repulsing repeated attacks by German tanks. With the appearance of the German tanks, the 31st Separate Destroyer Anti-tank Artillery Brigade fell back from its occupied sector and took no part in combat operations. By this time the 94th Guards Rifle Division was still on the approach and couldn't take part in the fighting. The headquarters of the 31st Destroyer Anti-tank Artillery Brigade reported to the headquarters of the 35th Guards Rifle Corps that at the moment of its retreat, the enemy had seized its formerly occupied area. As a result of this, the 148th Separate Tank Regiment was twice subjected to attacks by our *Sturmoviki* [Il-2 ground attack aircraft].… In this fighting, tank commander Senior Lieutenant Malin distinguished himself by knocking out 3 tanks.…[49]

---

48 TsAMO RF, f. 203 (artillery headquarters), op. 2843, d. 29, l. 100obr.
49 TsAMO RF, f. 148 otp, op. 661360, d. 3, l. 77.

Now I will cite the combat diary of the 6th Panzer Division's Panzer Regiment 11:

> Under severe enemy artillery fire and tank fire, the *panzerkampfgruppe* reached Point 216.1 and Hill 207.9. The 6th and 8th Companies, supported by the Tigers, established themselves at the "Solov'ev" collective farm, but they came upon strong enemy resistance. Both companies suffered losses. At 2000 hours, contact was established with the advancing right flank regiment of the 7th Panzer Division. During the night, Von Oppeln's *panzerkampfgruppe* occupied a hedgehog position on Hill 207.9. They achieved the day's objective. Achievements: 7 enemy tanks, 10 anti-tank guns, 1 infantry gun, 3 152mm guns, 1 air defense battery (four 76.2mm guns), and 120 enemy dead. Losses: 8 tanks by fire, 3 by mines.[50]

A comparison of the information from the two above-cited entries from the respective combat diaries permits not only a clearer understanding of the events that took place while simultaneously containing a certain amount of reliability and completeness, but also clarifies the losses of the two sides in the course of the Germans' unsuccessful assault on the "Solov'ev" collective farm. It is a rather rare occurrence – the headquarters of both the Soviet tank regiment and the German panzer regiment made almost no attempt to exaggerate enemy losses or understate their own losses. In the evening Lieutenant Colonel L-A. Lifits reported that in the course of the day's fighting, his 148th Separate Tank Regiment had set ablaze 11 enemy armored vehicles, including 6 Tigers and 1 self-propelled gun. Regarding the losses of the Soviet side in tanks cited in Panzer Regiment 11's combat diary, the Germans were unable to calculate the destroyed armored vehicles of the 167th Separate Tank Regiment or the knocked-out tanks in the 148th Separate Tank Regiment, because they were located behind enemy lines. According to the information of the 148th Separate Tank Regiment it lost 8 tanks, including 2 T-34 destroyed, 5 T-34 knocked-out, and one T-70 damaged, as well as having 37 soldiers and officers killed or wounded.[51] I've also managed to clarify the identity of the destroyed 152mm guns and anti-aircraft artillery battery as reported by the Germans. The point is that Major Bäke's panzers caught a column of the 8th Battery of 3/265th Guards Cannon Artillery Regiment on Hill 216.1 that was in the process of retreating from the woods east of Generalovka. The artillerymen didn't even have time to unlimber and deploy their guns, even though the troops of Colonel M.A. Kudriashov's 5th Anti-Aircraft Artillery Battalion that was positioned not far away attempted give them help, and engaged in solitary combat with II/Panzer Regiment 11. The chief of staff of the 7th Guards Army's artillery headquarters Lieutenant Colonel Sanfirov reported: "One battery of the 265th Guards Cannon Artillery Regiment was shot up by enemy tanks while on the march in the area of Point 216.1 [subsequently, when this area was re-taken by our troops, it was established that the prime movers and howitzers had taken direct hits from enemy shells]. A battery of the 743rd Anti-Aircraft Artillery Battalion [85mm guns] was positioned in this area, which managed to destroy 6 tanks while firing over open sights. The battery suffered heavy losses in men. Guns were destroyed and captured by the enemy."[52]

According to the information given in the 265th Guards Cannon Artillery Regiment, on 6 July the regiment had a total of 4 howitzers, 5 ChTZ-65 prime movers and one GAZ-AA destroyed. It had more substantial losses in personnel, with 40 men killed or severely wounded, including, as

---

50   Haupt, W., *Srazheniia gruppy armii "Iug"* [*Battles of Army Group South*] (Moscow: Iauza, 2006), p. 294. This has been translated into English as *Army Group South: The Wehrmacht in Russia* (Schiffer Military History) (Schiffer Publishing, Ltd; First Edition (January 1, 1998).
51   TsAMO RF, f. 148 otp, op. 661360, d. 3, l. 78.
52   TsAMO RF, f. 7 gv. A, op. 5312, d. 539, l. 146.

has been already noted, the commander of the 7th Battery Lieutenant Z.K. Davlekaev, who was killed, and the commander of the 6th Battery Captain Kuriachy, who was wounded.[53]

Thus, summing up the results of the fighting in the afternoon and evening of 6 July, it should be stressed that owing to the well-planned system of defense in the sector of the 25th Guards Rifle Corps; the timely and smoothly implemented decisions to shift reserves; and the tenacity and coordinated actions of the 78th Guards Rifle Division, 73rd Guards Rifle Division, two regiments of the 30th Separate Destroyer Anti-tank Artillery Brigade, the 1849th Destroyer Anti-tank Artillery Regiment of the 31st Destroyer Anti-tank Artillery Brigade, the 148th and 167th Separate Tank Regiments and the 265th Guards Cannon Artillery Regiment; the Soviet command was able to contain essentially two panzer divisions within the second defensive belt in the 7th Guards Army's sector despite all of the German efforts, and prevent its breakthrough to the entire depth. It was a close-run affair, however.

Now let's return to area of the "Batratskaia Dacha" State Farm, where at day's end bitter fighting flared up between a portion of the 7th Panzer Division's armored group and the elements of the 73rd Guards Rifle Division that had fallen back to this place, and the tanks of Verba's and Lifits' tank regiments. Having been unable to drive the Soviet forces back to the "Solov'ev" collective farm, Lieutenant Colonel A. Schülz decided once again to carry out the task that had been set by von Funck to break through in the "Batratskaia Dacha" State Farm – Nekol'skoe direction (along with Nekliudovo), which was connected not only with Kempf's objective for the day to clear a path for Korps Raus to enable it to reach and fortify itself along the western bank of the Koren' River. The point is that in these two large villages of Nekliudovo and Borovskoe, which were situated side by side across the Koren' River, served as the 25th Guards Rifle Corps supply base at the terminus of the highway leading from Shebekino Station. There were also bridges across the Koren' River here, over which ran the movements of supplies for the troops of the 7th Guards Army's right flank. The command of Army Detachment Kempf was aware of this, and Kempf, together with the liquidation of a threat from the flank, was counting upon cutting the artery of supplies feeding the defending forces opposite Breith's III Panzer Corps with an attack toward Nekliudovo, and if not that, then at least seriously complicate keeping them supplied with everything necessary.

The "Batratskaia Dacha" State Farm didn't have a lot of buildings, and they were compactly located at its eastern end, right next to the woods. The wooden huts and threshing barns, covered with straw thatch, had almost all been burned down in the first half of the day by the fire of tanks and artillery. To the west of them stretched several hectares of fruit tree orchards. Before the war the State Farm had been famous for its apples and pears, but on 6 July the orchards became the epicenter of bloody combat. After 1800, the remnants of the 214th Guards Rifle Regiment, the 167th Separate Tank Regiment, the 262nd Separate Heavy Tank Regiment and the 1438th Self-propelled Artillery Regiment were digging in here. From Lieutenant Colonel A.A. Verba's account:

> Toward 2030 6.7.43 enemy tanks numbering 30 machines escorted by up to two battalions of infantry attacked from Hills 216.1 and 207.9 in the direction of the "Batratskaia Dacha" State Farm. The tank regiment [the 167th Separate Tank Regiment] consisting of 5 T-34, 2 T-70 and 4 KV tanks that were attached from the 262nd Separate Heavy Tank Regiment, together with the anti-tank rifle companies greeted the enemy tanks with their fire. As a result of the combat action, the regiment inflicted the following losses to the Germans: 6 Panzer VI, 2 Panzer III, 4 guns and up to two companies of infantry. Three burned-out tanks belong to the credit of Lieutenant Shtango's anti-tank rifle platoon, and the platoon commander himself

---

53　TsAMO RF, f. 265 gv. pap, op. 1, d. 2, l. 8.

killed a German 1st Lieutenant – a company commander who was decorated with two Iron Crosses, 1st and 2nd Class.

Despite the suffered losses, the enemy didn't cease attacking. Our infantry and artillery in the area of the regiment's defense, having abandoned their line during an enemy attack, retreated in the direction of Nikol'skoe [4 kilometers to the east]. By this time, 2 T-34, 1 KV and 1 SU-122 had been destroyed in the regiment, and 3 men had been killed and 1 wounded. As a result of the enemy's large superiority in tanks and infantry, I was compelled to withdraw my remaining tanks to a line 1 kilometer east of the "Batratskaia Dacha" State Farm and took up a defense in the woods 2 kilometers northwest of Nikol'skoe and Nekliudovo.[54]

Thus, although both of Breith's armored groups had reached Hill 216.1, which they had been supposed to take on 5 July, they failed to clear a path fully for Korps Raus to the Koren' River. In addition, the 73rd Guards Rifle Division had retained its combat capabilities and was continuing to loom over the right flank of his formation. On this day its troops had demonstrated exemplary stubbornness and tenacity when fighting to hold its line. Here is what Colonel S.A. Kozak reported about the division's condition at 2200 on 6 July to the corps commander:

a) 209th Guards Rifle Regiment: the 2nd Battalion, having suffered up to 60% casualties, was hurled back to the "Day of Harvest" collective farm. The 1st and 3rd Battalions, attacked by enemy tanks in the flank and rear, were thrown back to the southern section of the "Batratskaia Dacha" orchards, where they rallied and took up a line of defense. It [the regiment] destroyed 82 enemy tanks, knocked out or set ablaze 18 vehicles, and killed up to 300 enemy soldiers and officers. The regiment has lost up to 500 men killed or wounded, and losses in materiel are being ascertained.

b) 214th Guards Rifle Regiment is holding the line: Point "Courtyard" lying 500 meters south of the "Batratskaia Dacha" State Farm's orchards, Point "K", Hill 209.6. The regiment has destroyed 39 enemy tanks, wiped out up to a battalion of infantry, and knocked out 6 vehicles. The regiment has lost: 600 men killed or wounded; 10 guns, 9 82mm mortars, 25 heavy machine guns, 24 anti-tank rifles, and 10 50mm mortars.

c) 211th Guards Rifle Regiment is holding the line: Point "K", 1 kilometer northwest of Koren'skaia Dacha, "Poliana" State Farm. The regiment has destroyed 6 tanks, one vehicle, one self-propelled gun, two mortars, 6 machine guns, and scattered or destroyed up to two battalions of enemy infantry. The regiment has lost 14 dead, 48 wounded (including the commander of the 2nd Battalion Guards Major Chapur); and 3 anti-tank guns, one anti-tank rifle, two heavy machine guns, 2 light machine guns, 6 submachine guns, 8 rifles and 2 horses have been knocked out or lost.

d) 153rd Guards Artillery Regiment is in firing positions in the units' area of defense. The regiment has destroyed 29 enemy tanks and self-propelled guns. The regiment has lost 12 guns, and suffered 8 dead and 12 wounded.

e) 80th Guards Separate Destroyer Anti-tank Artillery Battalion – is in firing positions in the 214th Guards Rifle Regiment's area. The battalion has destroyed 7 enemy tanks. Losses: 4 guns, and 15 dead or wounded.

f) Training battalion – in my reserve in the vicinity of Hill 209.6 and hasn't been introduced into the fighting.

3. I have decided: in connection with the enemy's arrival on the road leading to the "Batratskaia Dacha" State Farm and Nekliudovo, his expansion into the woods south of

---

54 TsAMO RF, f. 925 sap, op. 1, d. 3, l. 109.

THE 7TH GUARDS ARMY'S MAIN DEFENSIVE BELT CRUMBLES 283

the "Batratskaia Dacha" State Farm, and the arising danger of the division's encirclement from the right, as well as the absence of a neighbor [on the right] and the emergence of enemy tanks and submachine gunners near the "Poliana" State Farm – to pull back the division's right flank with a front to the north and to take up for a defense the line: Kashlakovo, northern protrusion of the woods 2 kilometers northeast of Koren'skaia Dacha, Point "Sar" and further to the south to the "Poliana" State Farm.

4. I request:
   a) Urgent measures to eliminate the gap between me and the 81st Guards Rifle Division; with my own strength, I can do nothing.
   b) Urgent measures to close the gap between me and the units operating on the left; the 2nd Rifle Battalion of the 213th Rifle Division's 223rd Guards Rifle Regiment [sic][55] fled under enemy pressure and I can't make contact with it.
5. Transfer to my subordination the 201st Tank Brigade and 7 guns of the brigade's self-propelled artillery regiment.[56]
6. My command post from 0300 7.07.1943 – Hill 190.6, which is 1 kilometer northeast of Koren'skaia Dacha.[57]

In the second half of the day, the situation also changed in the sector of the 19th Panzer Division's offensive, although the results of its efforts by the end of 6 July proved to be rather modest and far from those that the headquarters of the III Panzer Corps was expecting. After the Germans revealed the system of fire and destroyed the primary artificial obstacles fronting Major S.I. Titarenko's 233rd Guards Rifle Regiment, which was defending the sector: (excl.) north of Hill 139.9 – "Day of Harvest" collective farm – Belovskaia, the main burden of the struggle against the enemy armor fell upon the divisional artillery and the 1st and 3rd Tank Companies of the 262nd Separate Tank Regiment, the tanks of which had been dug-in at the Kreida railyard and among the buildings of the collective farm. Starting at 1430, Bäke's armored group in cooperation with a *kampfgruppe* of Infantry Regiment 442, which was advancing on the right, began making slow headway against the 81st Guards Rifle Division's left flank. With great effort, by 1800 these units had finally captured the "Day of Harvest" collective farm. Captain Sh.M. Gakhokidze's 3rd Battalion of the 173rd Guards Artillery Regiment, which had been transferred to this point the night before went through a an extremely severe trial here among the ruins of the former collective farm. Its twelve gun crews left 12 tanks of the 19th Panzer Division smoking on the battlefield. A the 7th Guards Army's artillery headquarters reported, the last few tanks were knocked out by the gunners literally at point blank range: "Being outflanked by infantry, the battalion couldn't limber up and withdraw its guns, and only some of the crews returned fire before retreating to the north. The subsequent advance of the enemy tanks was stopped by the 114th Guards Destroyer Anti-tank Artillery Regiment, which destroyed 6 tanks, including two Panzer VI tanks (which were set ablaze from a range of 300 meters by 76mm armor piercing discarding-sabot shells that struck their flanks).[58] As noted in the 81st Guards Rifle Division's combat diary, despite the strong tank attack and subsequent semi-encirclement, the artillerymen, after exhausting their ammunition, were nevertheless able to blow up their guns and make their way back to friendly lines.

---

55 This is like a mistake and he is referring to 3/222 Guards Rifle Regiment of the 72nd Guards Rifle Division, which was holding Hill 207 (3 kilometers southwest of the "Poliana" State Farm.
56 Kozak has in mind the 1529th Self-propelled Regiment of SU-152 self-propelled guns, which had been attached to the 201st Separate Tank Brigade.
57 TsAMO RF, f. 1212, op. 1, d. 28, l. 6.
58 TsAMO RF, f. 7 gv. A, op. 5312, d. 539, l. 145.

In the course of preparing for the summer campaign, a mutually-supporting and balanced system of fire had been arranged in the 81st Guards Rifle Division, in which each gun, tank and rifle element was not only to conduct fire, but also to cover adjacent firing positions from the flanks and rear. Now after two days of the heaviest fighting and the enemy's breakthrough into the depth of the regiments' positions, this system was disrupted. Now each tank crew and gun crew, and the commanders of the companies and battalions had to think not only of destroying the attacking enemy, but also about protecting their flanks and rears. Because of this, Gakhokidze's artillery battalion was almost completely wiped out. To the left of him, southeast of the "Day of Harvest" collective farm, 5 KV tanks of the 3rd Tank Company were dug-in, but that afternoon the Germans destroyed them, when the infantry of the 81st Guards Rifle Division's 233rd Guards Rifle Regiment that had been covering them retreated. German submachine gunners, entering the breach that had been created, attacked the KV tanks from the flank and rear. The situation in this sector of Morozov's 81st Guards Rifle Division, albeit it sparsely, was laid out with complete reliability in a daily summary for 6 July from III Panzer Corps' headquarters and 19th Panzer Division's morning summary for 7 July. The III Panzer Corps reported:

> 19th Panzer Division, linking up with the 7th Panzer Division's left flank, moved out to the north of the Razumnaia River, captured a collective farm northwest of Generalovka and the "Day of Harvest" collective farm, as well as the woods north of there, and moved on toward Blizhniaia Igumenka. The left-hand *kampfgruppe* is still locked in combat for the fiercely defended Kreida railyard.
>
> 168th Infantry Division, other than enemy harassing artillery and mortar fire, had no events. Reconnaissance showed the lack of changes on the enemy's side.
>
> Infantry Regiment 417, Reconnaissance Battalion 248 and the 1st Battalion of StuG Battalion 228 have again been made subordinate to the 168th Infantry Division [then further by hand] IV [or II] and III/Artillery Regiment 248.

The 19th Panzer Division reported:

> On the evening of 6.7 *Kampfgruppe* Becker on the offensive reached the area 1200 meters north of the church in Belovskaia; Infantry Regiment 442 – the area on both sides of the church in Belovskaia; and *Kampfgruppa* Köhler with elements of Panzergrenadier Regiment 773 – the enemy system of trenches west of the Kreida railyard.
>
> In the early evening hours, high activity of enemy aircraft and bombing strikes in the areas of Pushkarnoe and Krasnoe.[59]

Thus, under heavy pressure from three directions, the 81st Guards Rifle Division's area of defense was gradually shrinking, as if drying out like pebble-grain leather. By the end of the day, all three regiments began gradually withdrawing some of their battalions to the main defensive line's second set of trench works or even partially to the second army-level belt of defenses. The 19th Panzer Division had closed upon the Kreida railyards and was engaged in combat in the center and on the western outskirts of Belovskaia, while the 168th Infantry Division, due to the withdrawal Major G.T. Skiruta's 235th Guards Rifle Regiment and Major T.F. Kriuchikhin's 238th Guards Rifle Regiment to the second set of trenches had somewhat expanded the Mikhailovka bridgehead. However, the enemy hadn't managed to destroy the Guards division; as before, it was stubbornly defending its sector. Nevertheless, Schmidt's panzer division was continuing to smash

---

59 NARA US, t. 314, r. 197, f. 001103, f. 001130.

its way forward like a bull in a china shop toward its assigned objective in the system of the 25th Guards Rifle Corps' first defensive belt, even though its progress into the depth of the defenses, approximately 4.5 kilometers, was noticeably smaller than on the evening before. A number of factors were affecting this, but the primary one was the fact that due to a variety of reasons, Panzer Regiment 27's combat strength had fallen by almost 50% in less than 24 hours. On 4 July, the 19th Panzer Division had a total of 95 tanks, including 81 in its panzer regiment and 14 Pz.Kpfw. VI from the Separate Heavy Panzer Battalion 503. In the summary for 6 July the III Panzer Corps headquarters that the 19th Panzer Division's panzer regiment had 48 operational tanks: "2 Pz.Kpfw. III (short-barreled), 12 Pz.Kpfw. III (long-barreled), 9 Pz.Kpfw. III (with a 75mm gun), 1 Pz.Kpfw. IV (short-barreled), 23 Pz.Kpfw. IV (long barreled), and 1 command tank."[60] Judging from indirect data, this report on the number of tanks was generated at 1300. In addition, it should be added that in Heilman's attached Tiger company, on the evening of 5 July there was only one operational Tiger. Simple computations show that by mid-day on 6 July, which is to say over less than 24 hours of fighting, Becker's Panzer Regiment 27 had already lost 46.3% of its tank pool knocked-out. Indeed, this is without the inclusion of those combat machines that had already been repaired on the night of 5-6 July and had returned to service. Thus, if you consider that the total number of tanks in the regiment included 5 Pz.Kpfw. I and II, which couldn't be employed when attempting to break through such a powerful defensive line, then at that moment the 19th Panzer Division command could use only 47 tanks, or around 52% of the serviceable tanks it had at the start of the fighting (not including the Tigers). Of these, only 23 Pz.Kpfw. IV had the long-barreled 75mm gun; the rest consisted of Pz.Kpfw. III with guns barrels of different lengths and caliber (50mm or 75mm), one Pz.Kpfw. IV with a short barrel, and a certain number of repaired Tigers. Incidentally, in its account of the fighting near Belgorod, the division headquarters not only acknowledged a direct correlation between the division's pace of advance and Panzer Regiment 27's combat strength, but in separate cases (for example in the 81st Guards Rifle Division's sector) also the influence of the high losses in tanks on the possibility of even starting an attack with its *kampfgruppen*. On the fighting of 6 July, this particular document states:

> Having achieved the railroad, the division attacked the subsequent system of fortification on the line: "Day of Harvest" collective farm – Kreida railyard. That night the enemy committed his reserves [3/173rd Guards Artillery Regiment and the 114th Guards Destroyer Anti-tank Artillery Regiment].[61] In the first place both strongly-fortified nests of resistance on the flanks in this new line had to be destroyed. East of the railroad there were again minefields, in which the panzer regiment lost a certain number of tanks [18], which resulted in a serious delay in the attack toward the collective farm. This delay was even more unpleasant because the enemy with flanking fire from the hills at the "Day of Harvest" collective farm was making it impossible for Panzergrenadier Regiment 73 to attack toward the Kreida railyard.[62]

Korps Raus was only able to achieve significantly less results by the end of 6 July, although in general this was embedded in its plan of actions for 6 July from the outset. The 106th and 320th Infantry Divisions were as if in a "holding mode", and while holding a rather narrow sector stretching from the Northern Donets River to the railroad (the main and in part the reserve positions of the 72nd Guards Rifle Division's first-echelon regiments), were poised to go on the attack

---

60 NARA US, t. 314, r. 197, f. 001086.
61 According to a regiment report, in the course of 05.07.1943 it had conducted only light fire against the enemy, because its batteries were located at a significant distance from the line of contact.
62 TsAMO RF, f. 38 A, op. 9027, d. 46, l. 4.

once its stronger neighbor on the left had cleared a path for them to the Koren' River. Postel's division, primarily because of its position, could offer little assistance to III Panzer Corps, and in addition it had suffered painful losses on 5 July. Thus its main task at the moment was to hold the area of Priiutovka and the Bezliudovka bridgehead by conducting an active defense. Forst's division, although it also had gone over to a defense, had nevertheless on this day undertaken attacks at the boundary between the 73rd Guards Rifle Division and 213th Rifle Division. Some of them were in rather large strength and supported by armor, which enabled them to inflict substantial damage to the Soviet side and to create a tense situation in this area. Even so, Korps Raus had not been able to make noticeable progress, and the main reason for this was the relatively even strength of the opposing sides in this area.

N.A. Vasil'ev back on the night of 5-6 July had been forced to issue an order to spread his reserve 27th Guards Tank Brigade company by company along a 12-kilometer sector. This weakened the brigade's shock force and complicated command and control, but at the same time it was serving a very important duty – to strengthen the defense of the 213th Rifle Division (including with respect to morale). Buslaev's rifle division was playing a role as a type of unique gird, which enabled the weakened units of the 72nd Guards Rifle Division to keep possession of the army's main defensive belt. The combat actions here suggested a pendulum: Lacking substantial armor support, Postel and Forst were concentrating significant amounts of infantry (from two battalions to up to a regiment) on a narrow sector, and after a preparatory artillery barrage, they attacked the units of Vasil'ev's Guards rifle corps (usually from two directions) with the support of 5-7 assault guns. As a result, there were times during such attacks when the grenadiers managed to break through to the second set of trenches. The Soviet command would immediately launch a counterattack with the use of tanks. As a result, as a rule the enemy retreated, and then the process would start all over again, sometimes now in a different sector. Thus, a discernible stabilization descended over the front here, although at the same time both sides were suffering attrition and becoming exhausted.

In brief, the course of the combat operations on the 7th Guards Army's left flank took the following shape. Already at dawn, preparing a stable position for the looming offensive by the two panzer regiments of the 7th Panzer Division (its own inherent panzer regiment, plus the one attached from the 6th Panzer Division), Forst launched strong attacks in two directions. His Infantry Regiment 240 in cooperation with Schülz's Panzer Regiment 25 attacked Krutoi Log, and until mid-day was locked in bitter street fighting in this major strongpoint. Meanwhile, Infantry Regiment 239 with the support of StuG Battalion 905 again attempted to win back possession of Rzhavets, which the 213th Rifle Division and 27th Guards Tank Brigade were holding, and emerge in the rear of the Soviet units east of Priiutovka. According to a report from Nevzhinsky's 27th Guards Tank Brigade, with the sunrise up to a battalion of enemy infantry and 15 armored vehicles went on the attack out of Maslova Pristan' at the boundary between the 72nd Guards Rifle Division and 213th Rifle Division. The main attack struck the right-flank regiments of the latter. From the account of the 7th Guards Army headquarters:

> With the sunrise, the enemy after a strong preparatory fire by artillery and six-barreled rocket launchers [Nebelwerfers] went on the attack against the 798th and 702nd Rifle Regiments' sectors, striving to reach the graded road south of Rzhavets. By 0600 the units of the 213th Rifle Division had suffered heavy losses, and in several places the division's right flank, which had been outflanked from the north and overrun, were breached. Covered by the fire of artillery, mortars and the tanks of the 27th Guards Tank Brigade, our units on the right flank broke out of semi-encirclement and reached the line of: Point "Sar" 2 kilometers northeast of Rzhavets. The 213th Rifle Division's left flank [in the area of Bezliudovka] held in place on the line it occupied on the evening of 5 July.

At 1200 units of the 213th Rifle Division, after a short artillery barrage, with a brief, sharp counterattack jointly with the 27th Guards Tank Brigade drove the enemy back out of Rzhavets. The further advance was stopped by strong artillery fire from the southeastern outskirts of Maslova Pristan'. The units of the 213th Rifle Division that were occupying Rzhavets put themselves back into order and worked on improving the defenses; however, at 1800 the enemy with superior forces [up to an infantry regiment] with the support of 5 tanks again attacked Rzhavets and took it. Under the pressure of superior forces of infantry and heavy artillery fire, the units of the 213th Rifle Division were forced to fall back to the line they were occupying at 1200. In the process, they suffered large losses in men and equipment.[63]

To the above I will add that the command of the 106th Infantry Division, having received information that Soviet tanks were operating in the Rzhavets area, concentrated a significant amount of artillery here, primarily assault guns. Thus two regiments of Buslaev's 213th Rifle Division were thrown back 2 kilometers from the village in the morning, and because of their heavy losses they couldn't regain their original position with their inherent forces. The division commander realized this and ordered for the 2nd Battalion of the 585th Rifle Regiment to move quickly from the Shebekino area and to become subordinate to the 793rd Rifle Regiment in order to bolster his left flank and create a continuous line of defense on the boundary between the 793rd and 702nd Rifle Regiments. This helped replenish the two regiments that had been operating at Rzhavets with men, but the absence of the necessary amount of artillery didn't allow the village to be held. The 27th Guards Tank Brigade also proved powerless to help, because its 50 combat tanks[64] had been extended along a front of 12 kilometers.

An even more difficult situation developed on the right flank of the 24th Guards Rifle Corps. The defenses of the 72nd Guards Rifle Division already by the middle of the day on 6 July had lost their operational resilience. Indeed, the enemy quickly tried to take advantage of this; right after 1200, up to two companies of submachine gunners of the 320th Infantry Division almost destroyed the operational command group that was accompanying Major General A.I. Losev in a forward observation post.

After the encirclement of Krutoi Log, the command of the 106th Infantry Division attempted to destroy the 3rd Battalion of the 222nd Guards Rifle Regiment, which was saddling the road from Maslova Pristan' to the "Poliana" State Farm, and the 1st Battalion of the 229th Guards Rifle Regiment which had fallen back on the evening of 5 July to the northwestern fringe of the Shebekinskaia Dacha Woods at the road running between Maslova Pristan' and Hill 207. Having accomplished this and having seized Hill 207, the Germans were to breakthrough to the "Poliana" State Farm. At 1100 up to two infantry companies with the support of 18 armored vehicles shoved the Guardsmen back to the hill and took the first trench line. After this, with a decisive lunge they took the patch of woods west of Hill 207, opening a path to the State Farm. At the same time, the weakened 1/229th Guards Rifle Regiment was thrown back from the Maslova Pristan' – "Poliana" State Farm road to the southeast. However, the adversary couldn't completely carry out his plan. The 73rd Guards Rifle Division's 211th Guards Rifle Regiment blocked the approach of reserves from Maslova Pristan' with its heavy fire and after two hours of intense fighting, 3/222nd Guards Rifle Regiment drove the Germans out of the trenches. According to the estimates of the 211th Guards Rifle Regiment's command, the foe left up to 100 dead or severely wounded men on the battlefield, as well as 6 tanks. Two batteries of Lieutenant Colonel P.I. Gotsak's 1669th Destroyer

---

63 TsAMO RF, f. 7 gv. A, op. 5312, d. 268, ll. 5-6obr.
64 In addition, on this day 5 T-34 were out of action due to mechanical breakdowns.

Anti-tank Artillery Regiment (equipped with ZiS-3 76mm guns) rendered great assistance to the infantry in this battle. From Order No.68 to the regiment:

> On 06.07.1943 the crew of the No. 4 gun of the 3rd Battery in combat against the German-fascist aggressors in the area of the intersection of the Maslova Pristan' and "Poliana" State Farm roads [at the woods there] with the fire of their gun set ablaze two Panzer VI tanks. I am expressing my gratitude to all the members of the crew. The gun commander Guards Senior Sergeant Putivsky, and the platoon's acting commander Guards Senior Sergeant M.A. Bokholdin distinguished themselves in the battle and have been put up for decorations. The regiment's paymaster on the basis of Order No.38 is to give cash awards in the size indicated in this order:
> To gun commander Guards Senior Sergeant M.A. Putivsky – 1,000 rubles
> To the gunner Junior Sergeant N.S. Uchaikin – 1,000 rubles
> To crewmen N.N. Dubin, F.K. Markov, S.F. Kobiakov, G.K. Iskhakov and P.F. Semershinov – 400 rubles each.[65]

The above-cited document is evidence of one of the first cases of the application of Order No.38 from 24.06.1943 in the Voronezh Front about awarding cash payments to the personnel of units and formations for the destruction of enemy armor. Gotsak's anti-tank regiment actually did fight heroically. Its crews not only destroyed several German armored vehicles, but their main achievement was to help hold the occupied line and still saved their guns. In the course of this combat action, a number of artillerymen received severe wounds, including the commander of the 4th Battery's headquarters platoon Junior Lieutenant V.V. Kolubin, a driver of the 4th Battery Private M.Kh. Anan'ev, a gun commander of the 3rd Battery Private F.N. Markov and gun commander of the 3rd Battery Senior Sergeant M.A. Putivsky, who were all evacuated to the medical-sanitation battalion. Only the claim that the knocked-out tanks were Tigers prompts doubt. Judging from the archival sources, on this day all of the companies of Separate Heavy Panzer Battalion 503 were located in the divisions of III Panzer Corps, while the Tiger company attached to 7th Panzer Division was operating at the spearhead of its attack, in the sector of the 73rd Guards Rifle Division's 209th Guards and 214th Guards Rifle Regiments.

Nevertheless, Major General Losev felt first-hand the consequences of the breakthrough by the *kampfgruppe* of the 106th Infantry Division in this area already at 1400. From the 24th Guards Rifle Corps' journal of combat operations: "By 1400 small groups of enemy submachine gunners numbering up to 200 men in total infiltrated to the area of the 72nd Guards Rifle Division commander's observation post and gained a foothold beyond the western fringe of the Shebekinskaia Dacha Woods, enveloping the observation post of the division commander. With reserve forces /training battalion and reconnaissance company/, by evening the enemy's group of submachine gunners had been scattered and repulsed. The western fringe of the Shebekinskaia Dacha Woods was fully mopped up."[66]

By the end of the day, the front in the sector of the 73rd Guards and 213th Guards Rifle Division had become stabilized along the line: western fringe of the Shebekinskaia Dacha Woods – barn, 2 kilometers northeast of Rzhavets – western fringe of the woods east of Priiutovka – 500 meters east of Bezliudovka – mouth of the Nezhegol River. Both Soviet divisions had suffered heavy losses, in particular Losev's division. According to documents from his headquarters, according to preliminary data over two days of fighting it had lost 2,828 soldiers and commanders killed, wounded

---

65 TsAMO RF, f. 1669 iptap, op. 275953, d. 1, l. 52obr.
66 TsAMO RF, f. 24 gv. sk, op. 1, d. 21, l. 23.

or missing-in-action, while Buslaev's division had lost 637 men on 6 July.[67] For more details, refer back to Tables 7 and 8.

The regiments that were fighting for possession of Rzhavets suffered the greatest damage; in the 793rd and 702nd Rifle Regiments, a total of 589 men were killed or hospitalized with severe wounds. The headquarters of the 27th Guards Tank Brigade also reported on the losses of men and knocked-out tanks, but they proved to be significantly lower: one T-34 was left burned-out, and six T-34 tanks received combat damage. All of the disabled tanks were evacuated and collected at field repair shops by the maintenance service and support unit. In addition, another 5 T-34 tanks were disabled by mechanical problems outside the field of battle.[68] On the condition of the materiel of the tank regiments and brigades by the end of day 6 July, refer back to Table 9.

For the command of the Voronezh Front, the second day of the enemy's offensive was no less stressful than the preceding one. The results of the combat operations on 5 July 1943 had been, in general, successful. Even though the Fourth Panzer Army had broken through the 6th Guards Army's main defensive belt, it was only in one place, on the left flank, while on the right flank the German XXXXVIII Panzer Corps was bogged down in the defenses of Chistiakov's army. On 6 July, the situation here significantly deteriorated and was unfolding very rapidly. Hoth's two panzer corps had overrun the forward edge of the second army-level defensive belt. The XXXXVIII Panzer Corps was continuing to bull its way through the defenses in the direction of Oboian', while the II SS Panzer Corps, having reached the Prokhorovka direction, was heading toward the rear defensive belt. The breakthrough gap began gradually to widen. By midnight not one of the commands of the three Soviet armies (1st Tank, 6th Guards and 69th Armies), nor did the Voronezh Front command have any reliable knowledge about what was really happening on the Prokhorovka direction. According to information of the 6th Guards Army headquarters, a group of German tanks was already approaching the village of Kochetovka (several of them had supposedly been spotted on the distant approaches), where the 6th Guards Army headquarters was located. In reality, two of the three panzergrenadier divisions of the SS Corps had already entered the breach, and the 5th Guards "Stalingrad" Tank Corps that had been moved up as reinforcement had fallen into encirclement. Having no accurate information and fearing the worst, N.F. Vatutin sent M.E. Katukov an order that placed the responsibility of destroying the panzer grouping and defending this area on his tank army. However, the most alarming thing was the fact that by the end of 6 July, the General of the Army no longer had any full-value reserves, which is to say troops that hadn't already been committed into the fighting or that were holding quiet sectors. Thus, the Voronezh Front's Military Council appealed to I.V. Stalin with a request, which was supported by the Chief of the General Staff, to reinforce the Front quickly with several tank and aviation corps.

At this exceptionally difficult moment, in order to stabilize the situation it was important for the Front's left wing to hold its line securely and prevent a deep penetration by von Manstein's auxiliary grouping, and especially to prevent it from linking up with the main grouping. The 7th Guards Army on 6 July had carried out this task completely, and moreover virtually with its own inherent forces, if you don't consider the transfer of the 31st Separate Destroyer Anti-tank Artillery Brigade, even though the III Panzer Corps had essentially committed its reserve – 6th Panzer Division's panzer regiment – into the fighting on the main axis of advance.

Analyzing the decisions made by M.S. Shumilov, it is impossible not to praise the fact that each step he had taken was deeply and thoroughly pondered. He superbly grasped the operational situation both in the sector of his 7th Guards Army and on the entire Voronezh Front, which enabled him, using his rich combat experience and knowledge acquired at Stalingrad, to

---

67 TsAMO RF, f. 24 gv. sk, op. 1, d. 16, ll. 62-64.
68 TsAMO RF, f. 3108, op. 1, d. 10, l. 61, 62.

predict the enemy's actions quickly and accurately and to assemble his reserves rapidly on the most dangerous directions. The defensive arrangements he made on the night of 5-6 July opposite the assault wedge of Army Detachment Kempf proved its resilience and strength. The 25th Guards Rifle Corps' counterattack grouping assembled on the evening before, although unable to launch a counterattack because of the fact that its troops were already tied up in fighting, nevertheless in the final analysis played a key role and decided the outcome of the day's combat operations. If you compare the forces that Breith activated on the afternoon of 6 July in the Generalovka – Batratskaia Dacha State Farm sector (which extended for 4 to 8.5 kilometers) with the results it achieved, the impression forms that the "mountain brought forth a mouse". The efforts expended by von Funck's enormous armor machine proved not at all comparable with the results obtained.

Once III Panzer Corps, having seized Razumnoe and Krutoi Log and having crossed von Oppeln's panzer regiment to the eastern bank of the Northern Donets River, launched its offensive toward Hill 216.1, opposite the reinforced 7th Panzer Division approximately 1.5 rifle divisions (73rd Guards Rifle Division and the battered 78th Guards Rifle Division) were defending, reinforced by the equivalent of one full destroyer anti-tank artillery brigade (two anti-tank regiments of the 30th and one anti-tank regiment of the 31st Separate Destroyer Anti-tank Artillery Brigades), one fresh tank regiment (the 148th Separate Tank Regiment), one incomplete tank company (of the 167th Separate Tank Regiment) and one regiment of howitzers. These were relatively modest forces, if you consider that the right flank and center of Kozak's and Skvortsov's divisions were struck by a grouping of more than 200 panzers with the support of the artillery of two divisions and the III Panzer Corps, while throughout the day the 106th Infantry Division reinforced with assault guns loomed over the left flank of the 73rd Guards Rifle Division. At the start of the fighting, there were not less than 50 German panzers per kilometer of front. If you discount the 211th Guards Rifle Regiment, which repulsed the attack by Forst's division, and add the two full-strength battalions of the 78th Guards Rifle Division's 223rd Guards Rifle Regiment, then on average each panzer regiment of von Funck's panzer division, which were reinforced by 1-2 battalions of infantry and artillery, was met by 4 rifle battalions, two destroyer anti-tank artillery regiments, 1.5 battalions of a divisional artillery regiment, 1.5 artillery battalions of a howitzer regiment, up to 25 tanks, and two batteries of a separate destroyer anti-tank artillery battalion equipped with 45mm anti-tank guns. Given such a correlation of strength, a breakthrough of the defenses was unavoidable and it did take place. Von Funck's forces broke through two lines of defenses of the 73rd Guards Rifle Corps and overran the 78th Guards Rifle Division, but despite every effort, could advance no further. Indeed, the Germans stopped not because they had carried out the day's tasks, as some sources in foreign archives maintain. It is difficult to conceive a situation where if the Guardsmen of Safiulin's Guards rifle corps had in fact scattered in defeat, von Oppeln's and Schmidt's panzer regiments would have stayed on the line they had achieved in the area of Hill 209.7.

Incidentally, when you read the combat documents of the Wehrmacht formations or the recollections of German participants in the Battle of Kursk, you will be involuntarily struck by the high degree of self-confidence, even the arrogance of their authors, which literally jumps from the pages. In any situation, when describing the events, in the course of which all the previously-prepared plans plainly came to ruins, the German officers and generals stick to an iron principle – "We followed our orders precisely". It is irrelevant if the combat plan or conceived operation went awry. That is exactly how III Panzer Corps described its situation. Breith's panzer corps on 6 July failed in fact to accomplish its main objective and didn't link up with the right flank of the Fourth Panzer Army, while the area of Hill 216.1 that it seized on 6 July was supposed to have been taken the day before, on 5 July; the 7th Panzer Division took this hill with great difficulty, and not by itself, but with the 6th Panzer Division, only a day later than planned. Thus, owing to strenuous efforts and great sacrifices, after 48 hours of the heavy fighting, von Hünersdorff's and von Funck's

THE 7TH GUARDS ARMY'S MAIN DEFENSIVE BELT CRUMBLES

panzer divisions managed to break through only the main belt of defenses and make a shallow, narrow penetration into the second belt of defenses, while Schmidt's 19th Panzer Division was still fully bogged down in the 81st Guards Rifle Division's main defensive belt. With each passing day of the offensive, the objective given to III Panzer Corps seemed to recede, more than approach, since its strength was inexorably ebbing. Failure was obvious, but in the documents of its headquarters and those of Army Detachment Kempf, this conclusion isn't at all noticeable. The ordinary routine of war runs through the summaries and reports: "We've attacked in some direction, reached this or that line, and pursuant to orders took the hill lying in front of us", and if you read the account of the 19th Panzer Division, you won't find any description of the fact that the division was failing to reach one objective after another, but you will find commendations for decorations after the grandiose victory that had been achieved. Possily, that is how German commanders were supposed to act in hard moments by downplaying setbacks and thereby support the troops' combat morale. However, when you read the interrogations of German prisoners, seized by Shumilov's army in July 1943, you sense that the mettle that the Germans had demonstrated even before the start of Citadel, not to mention how the prisoners had conducted themselves a year before, had plainly faded.

In reality the enemy, at the very least, was perplexed, and there was a reason for this. Operation Citadel wasn't going at all as the German command had anticipated, particularly in Army Detachment Kempf's sector. Thus the thought that this grand undertaking might end in failure began to creep into the minds not only of open pessimists. A line from a Soviet wartime poster relates to the mood of the troops in Army Detachment Kempf after 48 hours of the heaviest fighting: "It was smooth on paper, but they forgot about the ravines we'd have to cross!" After the war, the former chief of staff of the Fourth Panzer Army F. Fangohr gave the following description of his impressions regarding the actions of the Voronezh Front's troops and their mood in the initial days of his army's offensive:

> Red Army officers and noncommissioned officers had been briefed in detail about Russian responses in case of a German attack. This conclusion is supported by the fact that a sand table was discovered in the woods where the headquarters of a major Russian unit had placed its command post. Besides, we could easily tell that Soviet operations had been meticulously prepared by the absence of any sign of disorder and no indications of hasty or panicked retreat by the units in the defensive system. There were no radioed "SOS" calls, which had been so frequently intercepted in the past. **The enemy, like us, felt confident in the first few days of the battle that everything was unfolding according to plan.**[69] [Emphasis the author's]

Relying not only on the above-cited statement, but also on a number of published memoirs written by the defeated Wehrmacht commanders, it is possible to assert with confidence that only a few representatives of the Wehrmacht's high command staff were distinguished by modesty or self-criticism. As for the generals who commanded the corps and armies headed by the headquarters of Army Group South during the Battle of Kursk, in my view such characteristics were completely lacking. It is difficult to appreciate the tenacity of a foe's troops and the faith in their own strength, because these are inherent qualities that aren't transferrable. As for the meticulous preparation of the troops and the defensive lines, then on the Soviet-German front no one (including the Wehrmacht) had ever yet erected such a defensive system like the one built by the Voronezh and Central Fronts by July 1943. Yet Vatutin's and Rokossovsky's troops in the

---

69 Newton, *Kurskaia bitva: Nemetskii vzgliad*, pp. 121-122.

springtime had only been given a minimum amount of time for mission planning and to prepare for their tasks in training exercises, so that they could demonstrate their skill.

Fangohr's indication that the German command was attentively watching and waiting impatiently for the moment when the Soviet troops would take to flight, as had happened previously in the war, was actually the case. In the messages from Luftwaffe reconnaissance aircraft intercepted by the Voronezh Front's radio intelligence in the first days of the Battle of Kursk, any signs of this were particularly stipulated. Here is an excerpt from only two such transmissions found in Report No.80 from the 313th Separate Radio-Reconnaissance Battalion for 5 July 1943:

> 0715: Along the Oboian' – Mikhailovka road, no signs of an enemy retreat. In the Oboian' – Cherkasskoe sector, no enemy movement is observable. In the Belgorod – Gostishchevo – Alekseevka sector [of the 6th Guards Army], no enemy movement to the east or west has been spotted.
>
> 1755: Along the Dal'niaia Igumenka – Staryi Gorod – Belgorod – Igumenka road, the Belgorod – Belovskaia road or Belgorod to Sevriukovo, no traffic.[70]

Here is information from Vororonezh Front's SMERSH counterintelligence command about the resolve of the Front's personnel at the start of the Battle of Kursk. On 9 July Major General N.A. Osetrov reported:

> From the start of active combat operations in the sector of the Voronezh Front, the troops that have made contact with the enemy are behaving tenaciously; signs of panic haven't been identified. However, incidents have taken place on the part of individual servicemen, who showed cowardice and fled from the battlefield. In the sector of the 7th Guards Army, over the period between 5 and 6 July, 15 men have been detained by blocking detachments and the operational staff of the counterintelligence departments [in the rear of all four divisions of the first echelon], of which 8 showed cowardice and fled the battlefield, 2 were deserters, 3 had self-inflicted wounds, and 2 were German accomplices. Among those who fled the battlefield, one was a platoon commander.[71]

If however you turn to the interrogation transcripts of prisoners of war captured by troops of the 7th Guards Army, the apathetic mood of the soldiers is plainly discernible, especially among those from Raus' divisions. This is due to two factors. First, it stemmed from the prolonged war and as a consequence of the high level of casualties (in particular in the 320th Infantry Division). Second, there was the alarming news from home; letters and soldiers returning from leave talked of the systematic bombing by American bombers not only of industrial targets, but also civilian residential areas and the deaths of a significant number of civilians. There were also food shortages in Germany. In the Wehrmacht there was a rule that in the case of a home's destruction during an air raid or if relatives were killed, a soldier was granted an unscheduled leave of absence. One such soldier of the 320th Infantry Division was taken prisoner by the 72nd Guards Rifle Division. He wrote eloquently about his comrades and their morale. Incidentally, a bit later (after two or three days), reports about German deserters began to appear in the 7th Guards Army's combat documents, though not many, and it was still too early to talk about any complete collapse of morale among Army Detachment Kempf's troops. Nevertheless, these initial reports were the first "alarm bell", and the more heavy and intense the fighting, the more the Army Detachment

---

70 TsAMO RF, f. 203, op. 2843, d. 452, l. 15.
71 *Ognennaia duga: Kurskaia bitva glazami Lubianki*, p. 38.

Kempf command had a reason for concern. Already on 14 July 1943 south of Prokhorovka, an entire panzergrenadier squad of the 6th Panzer Division came across the lines in the 5th Guards Tank Army's sector, and in August 1943 during the fighting for Belgorod, Raus would announce to Kempf that the mood of the troops of separate divisions of his was such that not even the threat of the use of a weapon could get them to fight.[72]

Turning to figures, the results achieved by Army Detachment Kempf in the course of the first 48 hours of Operation Citadel were as follows: By the end of 6 July, both of its assault formations, having forced a crossing of the Northern Donets River, had penetrated into the defenses of the Voronezh Front east of Belgorod by approximately 14.5 kilometers. Breith's panzer corps with great difficulty had fully broken through the main army-level defensive belt with the forces of the 6th and 7th Panzer Divisions, and had penetrated the forward edge of the second army-level defensive belt in the Hill 209.6 – Hill 207.9 sector. Von Oppeln's *panzerkampfgruppe* had pushed just 1.3 kilometers into the second defensive belt, while Schülz's *panzerkampfgruppe* had formed a penetration of approximately 3 kilometers. Thereby, over 48 hours of the offensive, Kempf's shock formation had seized a section of the 7th Guards Army's most heavily fortified lines with a total area of 126-130 square kilometers, having driven a corridor through them that suggested a rectangle with a base of 9 kilometers (along the eastern bank of the river) and a depth of approximately 14 kilometers (on the right flank). In the process, significant damage had been done to the 73rd Guards and 78th Guards Rifle Divisions, but they hadn't been completely destroyed. They continued to hold defensive sectors with means of reinforcement, and as before posed a serious threat to the right flank of the III Panzer Corps while blocking Korps Raus' path to the Koren' River.

There is little doubt that III Panzer Corps' relative success was primarily due to the use of a relatively large number of armored vehicles in its sector. However, the panzer divisions that were sent forth to break through a prepared defense began to suffer conspicuous losses after the first several hours of the offensive even before entering combat. Therefore already in the first days of Operation Citadel, the Soviet side noticed changes in the tactics of the enemy's panzer units and in the behavior of their panzer crews as a reaction to the altered conditions and the Red Army's new combat methods. Below is an observation from the artillerymen of the 31st Separate Destroyer Anti-tank Artillery Brigade about the details of the tactics employed by the panzer crews of Breith's III Panzer Corps:

> The defensive system and patterns of fire are deeply studied by the enemy, even at the cost of heavy losses and the loss of time. His interest in taking up a line from concealed approaches is becoming apparaent, with the aim of aggregating forces and means for the exploitation of further successes. The enemy hasn't rejected the tactic of seizing roads, but is paying particular attention to level terrain for open combat with infantry. The enemy tanks in these combat actions and in the fighting observed in the sector of the 81st Guards Rifle Division [19th Panzer Division] don't deploy into a combat formation, but are attacking in a column of march, while paying special attention to placing fire on [anti-tank] artillery targets with the tanks, if artillery or mortars are lacking. Given the absence of anti-aircraft cover, [the enemy] is making wide use of tactical reconnaissance aircraft in order to reveal and suppress artillery targets.

The heavy Pz-VI tanks, in addition to tank attacks, are being used as scouts in order to reveal artillery positions and the density of artillery means.

---

72 NARA US, t. 312, r. 54, f. 7569802.

As a rule, the column's lead tank doesn't open fire, but scans ahead. Only tanks in the middle of the column fire at positions. During tank attacks cases have been observed when the gun commanders seek to knock out the lead tank, and upon opening fire, the lead tank stops and seems to catch fire. In actual fact, it has mounted smoke dischargers on it, and it givese the appearance that a fire has started, while its crew continues to observe, after which [the German tanks] begin to fire.

When opening fire at the attacking column of tanks, the latter don't deploy, but continue movement at the previous speed. In this case, when knocked out or ignited tanks come to a stop, the rest continue their movement, bypassing the immobile or burning tanks on either side, from whence they continue to engage in combat [i.e., cover the knocked-out tanks].[73]

To this I will add that the well-laid network of artificial obstacles and the system of fire in all three defensive belts, as well as the tenacity of the men of the Guards divisions already after the first 48 hours of Operation Citadel curbed the enthusiasm of the commanders of the German panzer units and their panzer crews. They forced them to take another look at the capabilities of the Soviet forces and to reexamine their approaches to meet the objectives they'd been given. This is especially noted in the documents of a number of the 7th Guards Army's tank, anti-tank and artillery units. Here is one of the typical assessments of the enemy, taken from an account from the 167th Separate Tank Regiment's headquarters: "It is characteristic that the German tankers don't have last year's audacity."[74]

Concerning the novelties employed by the panzer divisions of Breith's III Panzer Corps, I want to point the reader's attention to one detail. Previously it has already been noted that prior to the start of the Battle of Kursk, a new type of artillery had arrived in the 6th Panzer Division, self-propelled howitzers, the Hummel and Wäspe. These guns, though organizationally part of 6th Panzer Division's panzer artillery regiment, were to be used to provide direct support for panzer attacks with the aim of demolishing anti-tank strongpoints. In addition to this, the III Panzer Corps' panzer divisions received Nebelwerfer battalions as reinforcement. Soviet troops that came under their fire considered them to be a very effective weapon. However, regarding the self-propelled howitzers, even the Germans weren't terribly impressed by them. Considering that the authors of some books on the Great Patriotic War regard this type of weapon rather highly, I think the reader will be interested to know the opinion of those who directly used them in battle. From an account by the commander of SS Panzergrenadier Division *Das Reich*'s panzer artillery regiment:

> The 1943 offensive provided rich material for study in the area of the experience of providing artillery support to a tank attack. The question, "Will the further development of self-propelled carriages, given the availability of 150mm rocket launchers on self-propelled carriages[75] be sensible?" stands out particularly sharply. In my opinion, this is easy to explain if the question is asked: "What task stands before the artillery during a tank attack, and which weapon at your disposal can resolve it in the best way?"
>
> These tasks are the following:

---

73 TsAMO RF, f. 31 oiptabr, op. 1, d. 29, l. 114, 114obr.
74 TsAMO RF, f. 925 sap, op. 1, d. 3, l. 110.
75 Ed. note: He is referring to the German Sd.Kfz.4/1 Panzerwerfer 42, a self-propelled rocket launcher that mounted 10 Nebelwerfer rocket tubes. It could fire both explosive and smoke rockets out to a maximum range of 7,000 meters. They first appeared in the spring of 1943 as an answer to the Russian Katiusha rocket launchers.

THE 7TH GUARDS ARMY'S MAIN DEFENSIVE BELT CRUMBLES

1. The suppression or destruction of enemy anti-tank guns, especially if they are deeply echeloned, in order to facilitate a breakthrough by the tanks.
2. The blinding of the anti-tank gun crews in order to launch an attack with tanks, bypassing pockets of resistance and enemy observation posts.
3. The breaking up of enemy tank attacks.
4. The saturation of areas with barrages to destroy enemy-held villages and woods [which was something very pertinent in the 7th Guards Army's sector]

In order to carry out these tasks, at present time there are available the self-propelled howitzers *Hummel* and *Wäspe*, and the self-propelled 150mm mortars. A thorough comparison of all the shortcomings and advantages of the above indicated weapons should bring clarity to the question about their use.

Hummel self-propelled howitzer

Advantages:
1. Ample caliber of the gun
2. Ability to open fire rapidly
3. Long range of fire
4. The gun is adaptable for the struggle against small targets
5. The gun is suitable for the counter-artillery struggle

Shortcomings:
1. The chassis from the point of view of the gun's weight is totally inadequate for it.
2. Extreme vulnerability to attacks from the air because of the gun's large dimensions.
3. All the howitzers of the artillery battalion must be placed in one position, one next to the other, so that fire can be quickly concentrated on a target. Thus the topographically precise positioning for combat gunnery is slow, and this isn't always desirable for dynamic combat actions.
4. The gun's angle of traverse is insufficient.
5. The gun is cumbersome on the march and in combat.
6. The number of gun tubes is too small for the effective placement of smoke. In addition, in the majority of cases the supply with smoke shells is insufficient.
7. There is a large need for technically qualified personnel.
8. On the defense, due to the limited traverse, the guns are only relatively useful. Especially in winter, the engines must be started up day and night, so that at any time the gun can be turned.

Wäspe self-propelled gun

Given the availabitily of a large quantity of 75mm and 88mm guns, during a tank attack the 105mm *Wäspe* doesn't justify its name. Experience shows that the caliber of these guns is inadequate for placing smoke screens and countering attacking tanks.

From the mechanical point of view, in contrast to the *Hummel*, the *Wäspe* is totally reliable.

150mm self-propelled rocket launcher

Advantages:
1. The possibility of concentrating the fire of a battery's 60 tubes more rapidly.
2. Saturation fire on areas, as well as blinding and suppressing anti-tank guns.
3. Powerful smoke screen generating capabilities.
4. The fire's powerful effect on the enemy's morale.
5. An adequate countermeasure when massed against a tank attack.

6. The low vulnerability to air attacks in view of the rocket launcher's low visibility.
7. The production of 150mm rocket launchers is several times easier than the production of heavy howitzers. In addition, a battalion of 150mm rocket launchers requires less manpower.

Shortcomings:
1. The 150mm rocket launcher cannot be used against small targets
2. It has a small range of fire and widely scatters
3. It cannot be used for the counter-artillery battery struggle
4. The delivery of ammunition for the 150mm rocket launchers is not always ensured to a sufficient level.

The comparison of the advantages and shortcomings shows that the self-propelled 150mm rocket launchers best correspond to the tasks that stand before the artillery in the area of supporting tank attacks; one battalion with two batteries of 6 rocket launchers each is fully sufficient for combat. This corresponds to the firepower of 7 battalions of 18 self-propelled 150mm howitzers *Hummel* each.[76]

Already after the Battle of Kursk, in the course of the marches and fighting, the *Hummel* revealed more weaknesses in addition to the shortcomings listed above. In particular, this related to its small ammunition load, just 14 shells. After they were expended, shells had to be brought up aboard special transporters, and when situated on the defense in wintertime, its engine had to be kept running day and night in order to be able to turn the gun in the needed direction at any moment. This led to a significant expenditure of fuel and rapid wear on the engine. The running gear of both self-propelled howitzers caused a lot of problems. The same artillery officer of the SS Panzergrenadier Division *Das Reich* noted:

> Each disabled self-propelled carriage means the loss of one howitzer, which in the artillery is a rare happenstance when using mechanized tow. In the event of this, the guns can be immediately hitched to other vehicles. Experience … plainly demonstrates the superiority of vehicle-towed artillery over self-propelled artillery. After six months of incessant fighting with heavy strain on the artillery units, those using mechanized-tow still had 95% of the guns' tow vehicles in good running order and were combat-ready. At the same time, in the battalion of self-propelled howitzers, only 25% of all the guns were still combat-ready. If in these battles our regiment had been equipped with two battalions of self-propelled artillery, that would meant in the majority of cases, the divisions' sectors wouldn't have been supported with artillery.[77]

In the Central Archives of the Russian Federation's Ministry of Defense, there are a number of other captured documents, in which the officers of the German panzer divisions share their experience with using various types of self-propelled artillery in the course of the Battle of Kursk. They are united in their critical assessment of the weaknesses of the self-propelled carriages and the methods of employing self-propelled guns in the panzer units, including the assault guns in the infantry divisions (which had much less firepower than the panzer divisions). Here is an excerpt from a report given by the commander of II/103rd Artillery Regiment of the 4th Panzer Division, which operated in the Army Group Center's sector in the summer of 1943:

---

76 TsAMO RF, f. 236, op. 2673, d. 324, l. 35-38.
77 Ibid., l. 39.

Since the tanks being used today in large numbers by both sides are the decisive offensive means, they (or better the self-propelled guns) must absolutely take part in any offensive if we want it to be successful. It has been noted that in an offensive by a regular infantry regiment, which is operationally attached to our division, in every case the attack bogs down given the appearance of just 2-3 enemy tanks, which with the fire of their superior guns from a range of 2-3 kilometers disrupt the attack even before our anti-tank guns using mechanized tow have time to take part in it. In such situations, self-propelled guns operate more efficiently and with great effect. In essence, self-propelled guns are a means of basic defense on the forward edge. They should be used as a mobile reserve, in order to undertake a counterattack with them from the depth of the positions given an enemy breakthrough in one or another sector. There were cases when only a few self-propelled guns positioned on reverse slopes of hills immediately behind the forward edge of defense checked an offensive by enemy tanks and infantry. Owing to such use of the self-propelled guns, a high degree of effectiveness of fire was achieved given only a small number of them. In those cases when there were no self-propelled guns on the forward edge, the enemy almost always achieved a breakthrough, which later could be eliminated by counterattacks only with great difficulty.

Since the Russians on their part use the same tactics as we do with anti-tank guns by allowing our tanks onto hilltops in order to then knock-them out [from reverse slope positions] … this clearly demonstrates that self-propelled guns, which form an important means of supporting an offensive, can quickly turn into a decisive means of defense against any enemy. Fearing that the movement of self-propelled guns up to the forward edge might deprive them of mobile attack reserves in this sector, our command left them in the depth of the defense, which as a result meant that when the Russians swiftly penetrated the forward edge, and the tanks and self-propelled guns would be introduced into the fighting in order to localize the breakthrough only after a certain amount of time had passed. It would have been more useful to have several self-propelled guns positioned immediately behind the forward edge, in order immediately after the start of an enemy tank attack to prevent a breakthrough with their assistance.[78]

Although these assessments relate to the events in the sector of Colonel General Model's Ninth Army, they are similar with those that took place in the sector of attack of Army Detachment Kempf's infantry divisions.

Now let's return to the 7th Guards Army's sector of defense and take a look at the results that Korps Raus's troops were able to achieve on 6 July. Their successes were much more modest than those achieved by their stronger neighbor, III Panzer Corps. Korps Raus was unable to fight its way through the first belt of Russian defenses. The place of its penetration into the defenses of the 24th Guards Rifle Corps suggested an irregular triangle, at the corners of which were three major Russian strongpoints: Krutoi Log, Nizhnii Ol'shanets and Bezliudovka. Of its two infantry divisions, the 106th Infantry Division achieved the more prominent successes. The maximal advance make by its *kampfgruppen* amounted to 8 kilometers, while the 320th Infantry Division pushed forward only 2 to 4 kilometers. I've already talked about the reason for this above: the close cooperation of the 7th Panzer Division with the 106th Infantry Division and the reliance on its armor when storming the villages of Nizhnii Ol'shanets and Krutoi Log.

However, the progress made by Kempf's troops came at a high price. Over two days of fighting, Korps Raus lost 5,851 men, including 820 killed, 4,628 wounded and 403 missing in action.[79]

---

78 TsAMO RF, f. 203, op. 2673, d. 324, l. 21.
79 Frankson, N. and Zetterling, A., *Kursk: A statistical analysis* (London: Frank Cass, 2000), p. 199.

At the very least, if the losses in men of the Fourth Panzer Army when breaking through the 6th Guards Army's main defensive belt on 5 July (a situation very similar to that of Kempf's forces by the end of 6 July) are compared with those of Army Detachment Kempf, then the losses of Hoth's panzer army proved much lower, by 3,324 men. (For more detail on the losses of Army Detachment Kempf and the Fourth Panzer Army between 5 and 16 July 1943, see Table 11):

Table 11 Casualties of Army Detachment Kempf and the Fourth Panzer Army during Operation Citadel (5 to 16 July 1943)[80]

Day	Army Detachment Kempf				Fourth Panzer Army			
	Killed	Wounded	Missing in action	Total	Killed	Wounded	Missing in action	Total
5 July	275	3111	98	3484	365	2129	33	2527
6 July	545	1517	305	2367	310	1511	23	1844
7 July	142	512	34	688	262	1301	19	1582
8 July	184	920	70	1174	136	685	27	848
9 July	171	1092	14	1277	315	1613	68	1996
10 July	414	1326	49	1789	136	734	30	900
11 July	73	481	0	554	157	651	9	817
12 July	108	558	8	674	330	1499	44	1873
13 July	102	566	25	693	261	1112	87	1460
14 July	116	739	15	870	184	908	42	1134
15 July	118	593	14	725	148	532	51	731
16 July	65	288	21	374	82	367	8	457
Total:	2313	11703	653	14669	2686	13042	441	16169

The units and formations of the 7th Guards Army also suffered heavy losses in the course of the first two days of fighting. As already noted, the 72nd Guards Rifle Division and its attached 4th Anti-tank Rifle Battalion alone lost 2,828 soldiers and officers, while the 213th Rifle Division and the 27th Guards Tank Brigade that launched the counterattack lost correspondingly 1,391 and 18 men over this same period of time.[81] Accordingly, when fighting to hold the first army-level belt of defenses, the 24th Guards Rifle Corps alone had no less than 4,261 killed or hospitalized with wounds, including 34 men of the 36th Guards Rifle Division (11 killed and 23 wounded) when eliminating the groups of German submachine gunners who had infiltrated to the Titovka area on 5 July.[82]

In addition, there was one more category of losses that Soviet commanders were usually unwilling to report, and that is the category of men taken prisoner by the enemy and deserters. According to information received by the Intelligence Department of Army Group Center from Army Group South through channels of mutual information, over 5-6 July 1943 Army Detachment Kempf captured 1,310 military prisoners, including 16 officers, while another 177 Red Army servicemen and 3 officers voluntarily came over to the German side.[83] To me, as a Russian, it is bitter to read

---

80 Zetterling, N. and Frankson, A., Kursk 1943: A statistical analysis (London, Portland: FRANK CASS, 2000), p. 199.
81 TsAMO RF, f. 3108, op. 1, d. 10, l. 59, 61.
82 TsAMO RF, f. 36 gv. sd, op. 1, d. 16, l. 108.
83 TsAMO RF, f. 500, op. 12472, d. 797, l. 34.

these lines, especially about the deserters, but there are always weak-willed men in every army of the world, and it is difficult to do anything about them. However, if you compare these figures with the data from the first days of Wehrmacht offensive operations in 1941 or 1942, then they seem miserly, and unquestionably, they testify to the high combat qualities that the Red Army's troops had acquired by that time, and about their great faith in achieving ultimate victory over the aggressors.

So, despite all the efforts and sacrifices made by Army Detachment Kempf, it failed to achieve two of its main objectives: to cover the right flank of the Fourth Panzer Army and to crush the resistance of the 7th Guards Army. The consequences of these failures began to affect the actions of von Manstein's main attack grouping right away. In addition to the fact that on 5 July Hoth had been forced to leave the SS Panzergrenadier Division *Totenkopf* on his right flank, which had been unable to breach the lines of the 375th Rifle Division, on 6 July, immediately after the SS Panzergrenadier Divisions *Leibstandarte Adolf Hitler* and *Das Reich* had been able to reach the Prokhorovka direction, it had also been forced to repulse a counterattack by the 2nd "Tatsinskaia" Tank Corps here.

Problems also arose for the commander of the II SS Panzer Corps P. Hausser, the troops of which were positioned on the right flank of Fourth Panzer Army (in the center of Army Group South's combat formation). Disturbed by the appearance of a Soviet mobile formation (2nd Guards Tank Corps) on his extended right flank and the tense situation that arose here, already on 6 July in a conversation with Hoth, he placed particular emphasis on this alarming fact. In addition, having collided with the Russians' well-prepared field defenses, Hausser understood that with two panzergrenadier divisions, it was virtually impossible to achieve tangible results. Thus he asked the Fourth Panzer Army commander to assign forces to screen the II SS Panzer Corps' right flank, so that he could regroup the SS Panzergrenadier Division *Totenkopf* to the center of his combat formation for an attack in the direction of the Psel River bend, but received a refusal. Neither Hoth nor von Manstein had any operational reserves. Therefore, while sharing Hausser's concern, they didn't have the forces to influence the situation in any cardinal way.

It nevertheless proved possible to resolve this problem, but only with great difficulty, and only by the afternoon of 9 July. However, the time for a dash across the bend in the Psel River would be irretrievably lost. On 7-8 July, when the Voronezh Front command was only pulling together the forces in order to seal the area of breakthrough by the SS troops and block their path to the northeast and east, the introduction of the third SS panzergrenadier division in the area of the bend of the Psel River might have placed the Soviet side in a critical situation, since the reserves promised to N.F. Vatutin by the *Stavka* of the Supreme High Command were still on the march. At the very least, on these two days P. Hausser had a real opportunity not only to emerge in operational space by at least making a forced crossing of the Psel River significantly sooner than it was done by his troops (10-11 July) and create a breach in the rear army-level belt of defenses, and also, perhaps, to break through it to its entire depth. By 9 July, the Soviet side would bring up two separate tank corps and General P.A. Rotmistrov's fresh tank army to the Prokhorovka axis, and by 11 July – the 5th Guards Army as well. As a result, the SS troops' chances for a breakthrough would sharply fall, or to put it more accurately, would drop to zero.

The German participants after the war would write openly about Army Detachment Kempf's failure, which had a significantly negative influence on the entire Operation Citadel, although rather gently (and how else, if this was an intrinsic failure?). Friedrich Fangohr, the Fourth Panzer Army's chief of staff: "Resolute enemy resistance and heavy defensive artillery fire against *Armeeabteilung* Kempf allowed the Soviets to maintain heavy pressure against Fourth Panzer Army's right wing.

Elements of II SS Panzer Corps, as a result, still remained on the defensive immediately north of Belgorod, which diminished SS Lieutenant General Hausser's strength for the main effort."[84]

The chief of staff of Army Group South T. Busse repeated Fangohr's words: "The SS advance was especially hampered by the flanking threat from the east that had developed when *Armeeabteilung* Kempf's left wing had been halted. Continuous enemy attacks – first by infantry and, starting 7-8 July, by tanks – tied down the SS *Totenkopf* Panzergrenadier Division until the 167th Division arrived, setting back the corps' schedule."[85]

Thus, not only the heroism of the soldiers of the 1st Tank and 6th Guards Armies prevented Hoth from realizing the real opportunities of a breakthrough to the entire depth of the defenses of Voronezh Front's armies that appeared in the first days of the offensive, but also to a significant degree the stubborn resistance of Lieutenant General M.S. Shumilov's Guardsmen. From the first hours of Army Group South's offensive, his divisions resolutely held Kempf's almost 100,000-strong grouping in the system of army-level defensive belts while inflicting substantial damage to the foe, even greater than those inflicted by the Front's forces on the Oboian' – Prokhorovka direction. However, the defensive operation had only begun, and the 7th Guards Army had even more difficult and dramatic events lying in front of it, the story of which lies ahead.

---

84 Newton, *Kurskaia bitva: Nemetskii vzgliad*, p. 111.
85 Ibid., p. 37.

5

Breith's III Panzer Corps reaches the line of the 69th Army, 7-8 July 1943

By the end of 6 July, the situation in Army Detachment Kempf's sector for its command was not only quite complex, but also in part murky. At this moment, of its three main tasks: forcing a crossing of the Northern Donets River; screening the right wing of the Fourth Panzer Army; and creating a solid front along the west bank of the Koren' River; only the first had been carried out. At the same time, Raus' forces, despite the assistance given to them by III Panzer Corps with an entire panzer division, were not only continuing to make little headway, but in some sectors had even fallen back under the Russians' pressure. Moreover, neither the corps' headquarters nor did Kempf himself have information on the 7th Guards Army's real strength and reserves, or its system of fortifications in front of Korps Raus and the right flank of III Panzer Corps. Thus, having failed to clarify the situation or to resolve the matter of establishing a strong screen for the right flank of Breith's strongest formation at that moment – the 7th Panzer Division – it had been risky to pivot it to the west in order to resolve the key task, a link-up with the II SS Panzer Corps, about which Army Group South was persistently reminding Kempf. Especially if you consider that the Soviet side from the first day of the operation was conducting counterattacks in the sector of Korps Raus with the use of tanks. General H. von Funck recalled:

> There was no success in reaching the Koren' River, as the higher command had planned. Thus, the pre-requisites for establishing a screen, which was supposed to keep sliding slowly to the north, hadn't been created. Coming up with the plan for combat actions on 7 July, it was necessary to pay heed to this situation. The division [7th Panzer Division] would have to clarify for itself the completely unclear situation on the right flank and take whatever measures to turn its forces to the east.[1]

Besides that, at this time German intelligence still hadn't established either the approach or the commitment into the battle of Soviet operational reserves (including the 31st Separate Destroyer Anti-tank Artillery Brigade, a regiment of which had turned back von Oppeln's *panzerkampfgruppe* on the approaches to Iastrebovo). Therefore the German command believed that the Russians were holding the front opposite Army Detachment Kempf with those same forces that had been assigned directly to hold the main defensive belt. Indeed, this led to alarming thoughts: If the first-echelon forces were defending so tenaciously, then what would it be like when the operational reserves approached, much less the strategic reserves?

---

1 TsAMO RF, f. 15, op. 11600, d. 1539, l. 25.

At the same time, the line of resistance running from (excl.) Mikhailovka through Belovskaia to Iastrebovo hadn't yet been broken, and thus the III Panzer Corps' path to the northeast remained blocked. The 19th Panzer Division and 168th Infantry Division plainly didn't have the strength to breach it, and there was nothing with which to reinforce their attack. However, the command of Army Detachment Kempf still hadn't lost hope for success. The II SS Panzer Corps after two of the heaviest days of combat had been forced to pause to bring itself back to order and to resolve a number of important tactical tasks, in particular establishing shoulder-to-shoulder contact between its attacking panzergrenadier divisions. As a result of this, on 7 July its divisions, other than the SS Panzergrenadier Division *Totenkopf* were given no offensive missions. Thus Kempf was supposed to use this pause in order to rectify the situation with respect to screening the right flank of the Fourth Panzer Army and to give a nudge with the forces of III Panzer Corps' right wing to break the standstill in the sector of Korps Raus. The plan of actions for Breith's panzer corps was quite similar to what it had been for 6 July, only in mirror-like reverse. The 7th Panzer Division was given the task to smash the Russians opposite the left wing of Korps Raus and to drive them back beyond the Koren' River, although Raus wasn't relieved of the full responsibility for resolving this problem. Together with von Funck's *panzerkampfgruppe,* his 106th Infantry Division was supposed to play a key role in this matter, while the 320th Infantry Division received the order to keep strong possession of the major villages of Maslova Pristan' and Bezliudovka and to conduct an active defense on the right flank of the army detachment's shock wedge and thereby tie down the Russian's opposing forces. Postel's division was no longer capable of doing anything more.

Parallel with the resolution of the 7th Panzer Division's main task, the *kampfgruppen* of its panzergrenadier regiments were to break through in the Miasoedovo – Melikhovo direction and drive back the Soviet forces to the east, in order to secure the left flank of Korps Raus and clear a path for its main forces, in the event they began to pivot to the northeast. At the same time, they were to draw the Russians' operational and tactical reserves upon themselves.

The day before, the 19th Panzer Division and 168th Infantry Division had failed to accomplish a similar task. Now, Breith reinforced these divisions with the 6th Panzer Division and gave them the mission to crush the 81st Guards Rifle Division; in other words, they were to seize the key strongpoints in its defenses of Staryi Gorod, Blizhniaia Igumenka, Iastrebovo and Sevriukovo in order to create the conditions together with the panzergrenadiers of the 7th Panzer Division for a breakthrough to the Fourth Panzer Army's right flank. Thus, the direction of III Panzer Corps' main attack and consequently that of the entire Army Detachment Kempf was to shift from the east to the northeast. This decision was plainly dictated by Hoth's request to von Manstein to cover the right flank of his Fourth Panzer Army as had been planned, which meant Kempf had finally begun to recognize the full seriousness of the situation east of Belgorod and the degree of its negative influence on the course of Army Group South's offensive.

The tasks for III Panzer Corps' panzer divisions were spelled out in detail in Corps Order No.1417/43. Its final version was delivered to their subordinate headquarters rather late, between 0208 and 0300 on 7 July. This also provides evidence that the determination of the plan of actions for 7 July wasn't a simple matter. Here is the full document itself:

1) The enemy is continuing to defend fiercely in the depth of his positions and is using a growing number of tanks, including assault guns mounting 122mm guns on the chassis of T-34 tanks.[2] The commitment of operational reserves wasn't detected on 6.7.

---

2   The document is pointing to the SU-122s of Major F.A. Zatylkin's 1438th Self-propelled Artillery Regiment, which was operating against the combat wedge of the 6th and 7th Panzer Divisions.

2) III Panzer Corps on 7.7 continues the offensive to the north and takes the Miasoedovo and Blizhniaia Igumenka high ground, and launches an attack toward the Mazikino – Sabynino line.
3) Tasks:
   a) 7th Panzer Division in cooperation with Korps Raus occupies the sector of woods southwest of Hill 215.1 and launches an attack to the east from the Razumnaia River to Mazikino. Infantry Regiment 442 remains with the 19th Panzer Division; the IV and V Battalions of Artillery Regiment 248 remains as before subordinate to the 7th Panzer Division.
   b) 6th Panzer Division again subordinates von Oppeln's *panzerkampfgruppe*; it launches an attack in the sector of the Razumnaia River near Sevriukovo through Melikhovo toward the hills north of Ol'khovatka.
   c) 19th Panzer Division destroys the enemy in the area of Blizhniaia Igumenka, takes the Kreida railyard, and subsequently captures Dal'niaia Igumenka and Sabynino. Together with Infantry Regiment 442, which remains subordinate to the division, mop up the western bank of the Razumnaia as far as the southern end of Serebriakovo; the regiment remains there at the corps' disposal; the order will be transmitted through the 19th Panzer Division. After taking the Kreida railyard, I/Infantry Regiment 429 and I/Infantry Regiment 428 are returned to the 168th Infantry Division, which by this time takes over the sector as far as the Kreida railyard.
   d) 168th Infantry Division defends its position and after the 19th Panzer Division's capture of the Kreida railyard assumes this sector as well. Upon the cessation of enemy resistance, the division joins the breakthrough together with the 19th Panzer Division and the SS Division *Totenkopf*. [Further the handwritten lines are indecipherable.]
4. Artkommando 3 together with the bulk of the corps' artillery early on the morning of 7.7 changes position across the bridge over the Donets in southern Pushkarnoe and supports the offensive by the 6th and 19th Panzer Divisions toward Blizhniaia Igumenka and the hills to the northeast. Confirm activity in the sector of woods northeast of Krutoi Log. Agree upon the time of the river crossing directly with the 19th Panzer Division.
5. Flak artillery:
   a) The chief of the corps' flak artillery ensures protection of the bridges across the Donets with the key point in the Solomino – Dorogobuzheno sector, and supports the 19th Panzer Division's attack with the assistance of II/Flak Regiment 38 by operating against ground targets in the Belgorod area.
   b) I/Flak Regiment 38 and II/Flak Regiment 43 continue cooperation together with the 6th and 7th Panzer Divisions.
   c) Luftflotte IV tentatively attacks enemy targets in the Miasoedovo – Iastrebovo – Blizhniaia Igumenka around 0757 to 0800 with large formations of Stukas and fighter-bombers. The divisions and Artkommando 3 provide information about separate targets by telephone and telegraph from 0500 7.7. Preparations for the attack must be done so that <u>after the final bomb drops,</u> the attacks gets underway immediately [emphasis in the original]. I emphasize the accurate identification of the forward line.
7) Traffic control is assigned:
   7th Panzer Division – bridge across the Donets in Solomino
   6th Panzer Division – bridge across the Donets in Dorogobuzheno
8) The corps command post remains in Novo-Nikolaevka.[3]

---

3   NARA US, rg. 242, t. 314, r. 197, f. 001113, 001114.

Thus, two panzer divisions and one infantry division were assigned to resolve the main task – a breakthrough to the northeast to the right flank of the Fourth Panzer Army, while with one panzer division and two infantry divisions (Korps Raus) Kempf was trying to shatter the 7th Guards Army's defenses in the eastern direction (toward Miasoedovo) and drive back Safiulin's and Vasil'ev's forces (73rd Guards Rifle Division and elements of the 78th Guards, 72nd Guards and 213th Rifle Divisions) back beyond the Koren' River, in order to form a firm defensive barrier.

The line that Hünersdorff's and von Funck's panzer divisions were to reach (the Ol'khovatka – Mazikino line) lay at a distance of 17-18 kilometers from the jumping-off positions of their *kampfgruppen*. Accordingly, on 7 July Breith's forces were not only to overcome completely the 7th Guards Army's second belt of defenses, but also to penetrate the defenses of the 6th Guards Army's left flank and the center of the 69th Army. Considering the level of resistance put up by the Soviet troops and the strength of their lines, the ambitiousness of the day's objectives is surprising. As an option, it can be assumed that when preparing the order it was understood that in the event that not all of the objectives were reached on 7 July, they would remain in force on 8 July, since the direction of the corps' movement didn't change fundamentally. Nevertheless, when reading this document, it is difficult to separate from the thought that the people who prepared it, and especially those who signed it, were either very large optimists, or as a result of the situation that was forming, were forced to demonstrate their unbending faith in their own forces, paying no attention to the reality as it was.

A distinguishing feature of III Panzer Corps' plan for 7 July was that, prior to the kick-off significant forces of Luftflotte XIII were to be employed for the first time on the axis of its main attack. It is possible, considering the preceding combat experience in the Battle of Kursk, it was this circumstance that gave the corps command a certain confidence in the success of the forthcoming attack. Over the preceding two days it had become obvious that thus far the Soviet command had little armor in this sector, so German command was planning with the airstrikes primarily to silence the main means of struggle of Shumilov's troops – the artillery, and pulverize the artificial obstacles and fortifications in their positions.

The 7th Guards Army headquarters staff was also working with extreme exertions on that night. There was much to do over those short summer nights. Considering that the Germans' main panzer forces were operating opposite the 25th Guards Rifle Corps, M.S. Shumilov gave it only one task – to prevent a deep German breakthrough of its front. The army commander's main worry was strengthening its sector in the eastern and northeastern directions. On the evening of 6 July, von Funck's two panzer regiments under his command had crashed through the boundary between the 81st Guards and 78th Guards Rifle Divisions, as a result of which a gap of approximately 5 kilometers had been created between their flanks. The gap was plugged by the 31st Separate Destroyer Anti-tank Artillery Brigade and the 148th Separate Tank Regiment. According to Special Order No. 3 from the commander of the 35th Guards Rifle Corps, by 0300 on 7 July (based on a directive from N.F. Vatutin), Colonel I.G. Russkikh's 94th Guards Rifle Division was supposed to arrive on the Sevriukovo – "Solov'ev" collective farm line and take up a defense there. Prior to this it had been located in the Voronezh Front reserve and hadn't taken part in the fighting, and thus it had on 5 July 1943 its establishment amount of men (9,385) and heavy weapons (a total of 287 45mm, 76mm and 122mm guns) and mortars (526 50mm, 82mm and 120mm).[4] After taking up its line, the 31st Separate Destroyer Anti-tank Artillery Brigade and the 148th Separate Tank Regiment were made subordinate to it. On the afternoon of 6 July, M.S. Shumilov had informed G.B. Safiulin that the division was already on the march and would come under his operational control together with its means of reinforcement.

---

4 TsAMO RF. f. 203, op. 3843, d. 426, l. without number.

Although by the end of the day the situation on the right flank of the 7th Guards Army had become somewhat stabilized, nevertheless the Voronezh Front command believed that the enemy, by introducing reserves, would be able to break through at the village of Belovskaia to the northeast. Thus before midnight, at 2330, the 35th Guards Rifle Corps commander Lieutenant General S.G. Goriachev signed a new order, in which he made a change to the task of the 94th Guards and 92nd Guards Rifle Divisions. The latter had already started to replace the 89th Guards Rifle Division, which was preparing to take part in a counterattack on the morning of 7 July against the II SS Panzer Corps' right flank: "In view of the 94th Guards Rifle Division's movement to the line: Severiukovo – "Solov'ev" collective farm – Nekliudovo, the 92nd Guards Rifle Division should expand its front and also occupy the Sheina – Novo-Troevka sector. Cover the Sheina – Miasoedovo direction particularly strongly."[5] This decision enabled a substantial strengthening of the 7th Guards Army's important sector of defense in front of the villages of Nikol'skoe and Nekliudovo. The left-flank regiment of the 94th Guards Rifle Division was moved into the second echelon behind the positions of the 73rd Guards Rifle Division, and with its left flank was to tie in with the right-flank regiment of the 15th Guards Rifle Division in the Nekliudovo area. Thus, on the dangerous "Batratskaia Dacha" State Farm – Nikol'skoe direction, along which the 7th Panzer Division's *panzerkampfgruppe* had been stubbornly trying to break through on the afternoon and evening of 6 July, there was now a defense in depth arranged in two echelons.

If the army commander had given the 25th Guards Rifle Corps only the task to hold its line, he was viewing the situation in the 24th Guards Rifle Corps somewhat differently. M.S. Shumilov realized that here the enemy was operating with weaker forces than those opposite Safiulin; in the estimates of his headquarters, the Germans here had two infantry divisions, which had also already been battered. Their trump card was powerful artillery and armor reinforcement, although the latter was still in small numbers. Thus possessing substantial firepower, they had been able to pin down Vasil'ev's two Guards divisions, and he'd been also forced to hold one division at a minimum in the second echelon here. So a certain balance in the strength of forces on the opposing sides had settled into place here. However, considering that on the right flank and center of Shumilov's army the heaviest fighting was going on with three panzer divisions while under a strict limit of artillery means, this situation was more advantageous to the Germans. Therefore Shumilov, having no way to change the situation on the left flank markedly and quickly with one attack, decided to "probe Raus' sensitive point" and attack the bridges, thereby complicating the process of keeping his forces supplied.

It was obvious that the enemy troops in this area, holding only a small bridgehead, were forced to keep needed supplies – ammunition, food and replenishments – moving across the river over the bridges in a constant stream, although a limited amount of supplies was probably stockpiled on the eastern bank. The largest bridges had been built by the Germans in Maslova Pristan' and Bezliudovka. Therefore N.A. Vasil'ev was ordered to focus his corps' efforts to seize precisely these conduits of supply. Shumilov also promised to direct the combat aircraft that the Voronezh Front would assign to the army to these same bridges. Considering that the 72nd Guards Rifle Division's left-flank regiment and almost the entire 213th Rifle Division were already located near the outskirts of Bezliudovka, Vasil'ev demanded of their command staffs to take this village first. The 224th Guards and 585th Rifle Regiments and one artillery battalion of the 213th Rifle Division's 671st Artillery Regiment were initially designated for the assault. Both rifle regiments over the preceding days had suffered considerable losses and the shock power of their battalions had fallen, but the corps didn't have any reserves. Therefore N.A. Vasil'ev contacted the commander of the 36th Guards Rifle Division and ordered him to transfer two rifle companies to the 224th Guards

---

5 TsAMO RF, f. 35 gv. sk, op. 1, d. 26, l. 80.

Rifle Regiment. On the night of 6-7 July, a submachine-gun company and a rifle company of the 36th Guards Rifle Division's 108th Guards Rifle Regiment made their way across the Nezhegol River and by dawn they were already occupying their jumping-off positions in the 224th Guards Rifle Regiment's sector.

Significantly more effort was required in order to capture Maslova Pristan'. Here the enemy was firmly holding the former reserve position of the first-echelon Soviet Guards regiments along the line of the railroad embankment and in the hamlet of Rzhavets, blocking the path to Maslova Pristan'. A powerful artillery grouping was deployed in the hamlet itself, and assault guns had been spotted there. Therefore at first it was important to take the hamlet and drive the German infantry out of the trenches along the railroad embankment. Only after this was accomplished would the attack toward Maslova Pristan' get going. To accomplish this, the 24th Guards Rifle Corps commander assigned the 213th Rifle Division's commander I.E. Buslaev to take on the task, and attached a tank battalion of the 27th Guards Tank Brigade to his division.

Opposite the 7th Panzer Division's *panzerkampfgruppe* and the *kampfgruppen* of the 106th Infantry Division in the first echelon of the 24th Guards Rifle Corps was the 73rd Guards Rifle Division with two regiments that were blocking the way to the eastern bank of the Koren' River. The 214th Guards Rifle Regiment was holding a sector with its right flank 500 meters south of the "Batratskaia Dacha" State Farm and its left flank at Point "K". The 211th Guards Rifle Regiment's sector ran from Point "K" to the "Poliana" State Farm. It was tied in with the right-flank 1st Battalion of the 213th Rifle Division's 793rd Rifle Regiment, which was defending the sector from (excl.) "Poliana" State Farm to (excl.) Hill 202.9. As before, the 3rd Battalion of the 72nd Guards Rifle Division's 222nd Guards Rifle Regiment was saddling the road that ran from Maslova Pristan' to the "Poliana" State Farm in the vicinity of Hill 207. The 73rd Guards Rifle Division's 209th Guards Rifle Regiment, which had fallen under the steamroller of von Oppeln's armored group on 6 July, was continuing to rally its scattered men in the woods east of the hamlet of Gremiachii, and on 7 July it was still not fit for combat. Two regiments of the 78th Guards Rifle Division (the 223rd Guards and 225th Guards Rifle Regiment), which had fallen back from their positions after the heavy fighting on 6 July, were now among the combat positions of Kozak's 73rd Guards Rifle Division. The 223rd Guards Rifle Regiment was digging in somewhere around the road in the area of Hill 209.6, while the 225th Guards Rifle Regiment was somewhere in the Gremiachii area. It is difficult to establish their precise locations because of mistakes in the operational documents and their failure to match most of the information about the real situation as given in the documents. The point is that when issuing the orders, the commander of the 78th Guards Rifle Division A.V. Skvortsov was unaware that after receiving the strong attack on 6 July, two of his regiments had fallen back to the positions of the 73rd Guards Rifle Division and were now intermingled among its regiments and battalions. Thus, Skvortsov gave orders as if nothing had happened and were based on the situation as it had existed before the 223rd and 225th Guards Rifle Regiments had retreated.

M.S. Shumilov also considered it important to disrupt the III Panzer Corps' main supply artery, the bridges in Dorogobuzheno and Solomino. His howitzer artillery was no longer sufficient to accomplish this. In the first place, there was too little of it. In the second place, some of the batteries had already been knocked-out. Thirdly, the howitzer crews were primarily accustomed to acting against targets that were directly on the battlefield. Thus, Shumilov was persistently asking N.F. Vatutin's help with air support: at night with bombers, and in the day time with Il-2 ground attack aircraft. The *Stavka* had a detailed knowledge of the situation in the sectors of the Central and Voronezh Fronts, including the fact that in the skies above the southern face of the Kursk bulge, it was the Luftwaffe that had superiority, not the 2nd Air Army. Thus on the night of 6-7 July, the Chief of the General Staff Marshal of the Soviet Union A.M. Vasilevsky issued a directive to draw upon the Southwestern Front's air force – Lieutenant General V.A. Sudets' 17th

Air Army – in order to destroy the attacking enemy in Voronezh Front's sector. Its forces were primarily directed to support the 7th Guards Army. On the evening of 6 July and on the night of 6-7 July, in addition to the rumbling cannonade at Staryi Gorod and Kreida, the entire Northern Donets erupted in flashes of explosions. It was the Bostons [Lend-Lease Douglas A-20 Havoc light bombers] of Major General V.I. Klevtsov's 244th Bomber Aviation Division of the 17th Air Army that were targeting the bridges and the southwestern and southern outskirts of Belgorod, where significant aggregations of vehicles had been spotted.

At an order from Moscow, General A.E. Golovanov's long-range bombers significantly increased their activity around Belgorod. At an order from the *Stavka*, on the first two days of the German offensive, they had operated primarily against Army Group Center. On the night of 6-7 July, the 3rd Guards Aviation Corps of Golovanov's Long-Range Aviation, which was based in Lipetsk, worked particularly actively in the sector of the 7th Guards Army. The overwhelming majority of the crews of its aviation divisions carried out two missions against the bridges across the Northern Donets in Dorogobuzheno, Solomino and Toplinka during this night, and also targeted force aggregations in Razumnoe and Krutoi Log. In the latter village and in the woods east of it, the Germans had set up a refueling point for motorized vehicles and tanks. Here is how the former chief of staff of the 9th Guards Aviation Regiment Major D.K. Peremont, who on that night led the regiment while flying aboard the lead bomber, recalled the strike on this area in his memoirs *Na dal'nikh marshrutakh* [*On distant flight paths*]:

> I was leading the Il-4 to the target, toward the woods to which we had been directed, where enemy tanks stretched out in a column. They were hurrying to take cover from the air strike, while simultaneously topping up their engine with fuel. We had 1,500-kilogram bombs on board. We approached the woods. I dropped my load. Behind us, the entire regiment went to work. As we turned, we saw roaring flames above the woods. Combat machines, fuel drums, mobile shops – all were enveloped in flames. Even the ground, which had been saturated with leaking fuel, was burning.[6]

It is difficult to say how effective the combat work of General Sudets' and Golovanov's pilots and crews were. It is only known that in the morning summary reports, almost all of the III Panzer Corps' divisions reported intensive airstrikes by the Russians:

> 19th Panzer Division. In the early evening hours, high activity of enemy aircraft and bomb strikes in the areas of Pushkarnoe and Krasnoe.

> 6th Panzer Division. Persistent activity of enemy aircraft with bombing attacks on the battlefield and against troop aggregations.

> 168th Infantry Division. The night passed quietly with artillery fire, especially on the bridgehead area and the eastern portion of Belgorod. Stronger enemy air raids in the evening hours with bomb strikes against bridgehead positions and installations in the rear of the division's sector.[7]

---

6   Peremont, D.K., *Na dal'nikh marshrutakh* [*On distant flight paths*] (Minsk, 1982), p. 89.
7   NARA US, reg. 242, t. 314, r. 197, f. 001130.

For its part, the III Panzer Corps command, using the information from the morning summary reports, reported to Speidel's headquarters at 0625 (Moscow time) on 7 July: "Enemy aircraft are continuously and heavily bombing the bridges."[8]

At the same time, it is impossible not to notice that already from 6 July and on subsequent days, the attacks by Soviet aircraft in the sector of the Voronezh Front began to diminish and not only because of the high losses. The point is that after 5 July, a significant portion of the 2nd Air Army – Colonel I.S. Polbin's 1st Bomber Aviation Corps – was grounded (ostensibly because of the lack of fighter cover as asserted by the 2nd Air Army command) and didn't resume participation in the fighting until 12 July. This perceptibly reduced the strength of the air strikes by Krasovsky's air army and prevented it from rendering the necessary help to the ground forces. This was especially so in the initial, most intense period of the Kursk defensive operation, including in the sector of the 7th Guards Army as well. With only Il-2 *Sturmoviki*, it was impossible to respond effectively to the tasks that arose in pace with the enemy's advance into the depth of the Front's defenses, even with the involvement of the 17th Air Army. At this time, there was an acute shortage of Soviet bombers in the region.

Even so, if you compare the operations of Luftflotte IV at this moment on the Oboian' and Prokhorovka directions with the combat performance of its forces east and northeast of Belgorod, then a statement from on Soviet document can serve as the most accurate assessment: "They weren't much of a nuisance." Here Fliegerkorps VIII primarily conducted reconnaissance missions on behalf of Kempf's attacking forces and launched targeted airstrikes in groups of 15-20 aircraft against knots of resistance on the axis of the panzer divisions' main attack. This allowed the 7th Guards Army, more than the 6th Guards Army and 69th Army, to retain the artillery and destroyer anti-tank units that comprised the backbone of their defenses. Even so, as we'll see below, at separate critical moments, the crews of the 17th Air Army's *Sturmoviki* would render substantial assistance to Shumilov's troops.

At dawn on 7 July, the 6th and 7th Panzer Divisions were conducting intensive preparations for the morning resumption of the offensive. Only the *kampfgruppen* of the 19th Panzer Division and 168th Infantry Division were grinding themselves and the Guardsmen down practically without stop while hammering away at the line of the 81st Guards Rifle Division at the Kreida railyard and the village of Belovskaia.

Von Hünersdorff's 6th Panzer Division at this moment was mustering his forces; his two panzergrenadier regiments were assembling around the village of Belinskaia on the western bank of the Razumnaia River. In order to reinforce von Oppeln's *panzerkampfgruppe*, Unrein's *kampfgruppe* (based on Panzergrenadier Regiment 4) and von Bieberstein's *kampfgruppe* (Panzergrenadier Regiment 114, minus its II Battalion, which was already subordinate to von Oppeln's *panzerkampfgruppe*) were operationally attached to it. In addition to this mustering and reorganization, at dawn units of the 6th Panzer Division had to take part in a brief, but very bitter combat action. At this moment, the 73rd Guards Rifle Division command had decided to launch a reconnaissance-in-force in the direction of Hill 207.9. The attack was accompanied by strong artillery fire, and was driven back by the grenadiers of I/Panzergrenadier Regiment 114 only thanks to the panzers of Panzer Regiment 11 that were positioned on the hill. This episode, in the opinion of 6th Panzer Division's headquarters, was so significant that it received mention in the morning summary to III Panzer Corps: "An enemy breakthrough from the southeast in the force of a company was repulsed by a group of panzers that had penetrated to Hill 207.9." The reason for such fixed attention to this area was simple. At the time, von Oppeln's *panzerkampfgruppe* was supposed to turn over the hill and the sector adjacent to it to the 7th Panzer Division, after which it was supposed to advance to

---

8 NARA US, t. 312, r. 54, f. 7569621.

Belinskaia and launch two attacks, one in the directions of the Kreida railyard and the other in the Iastrebovo – Sevriukovo direction. On its part, at this time *Kampfgruppe* Gläsemer was moving to the assembly area of the 7th Panzer Division's main forces. Thus, a calm situation here at this moment was very important for the enemy.

Alongside the ordinary concerns when preparing an offensive, the 7th Panzer Division command before sunrise was occupied with an analysis of the situation on its flanks. In addition to the absence of information about the Russians' strength and intentions opposite the panzer division's entire front, the encircled group of Soviet forces on the division's right flank that were still tenaciously defending in the woods northeast of Krutoi Log was quite annoying. Attempting to clarify the situation facing him, von Funck back during the night had sent Panzer Reconnaissance Battalion 37 on a deep foray into the 24th Guards Rifle Corps' defenses (from the area of "Batratskaia Dacha" State Farm in the direction of Shebekino). The recon troops were to clarify the situation, first and foremost on the right flank, and when encountering significant Russian forces, they were to call in artillery fire on them using the information from the artillery spotters. Simultaneously he had ordered Schülz's Panzer Regiment 25 to begin to pivot to the left flank for an attack against the woods between Generalovka and the "Batratskaia Dacha" State Farm, and to initiate the formation of a blocking group out of the specialized elements, including non-combat ones. After the war when in Soviet captivity he recalled:

> A composite group was created out of units of the panzerjäger battalion, the signal battalion and the division's rear service and support units, which was to fight to secure the protection of the division's right flank on the line of the road leading from Hill 209.6 and in the area of the "Batratskaia Dacha" State Farm [the 73rd Guards Rifle Division's sector]. To the north it was also necessary to take some sort of measures in order to prevent the possibility of surprise attacks on the enemy's part. Such a possibility wasn't excluded and raised concern, since in the area to the west of the woods [the wooded area north and east of the "Solov'ev" State Farm], numerous artillery firing positions that had registered fire to the north, as well primarily on the fringe of the woods; and the positions of combat machines [the 167th Separate Tank Regiment] and motorized infantry that had come up in a hurry, had been detected.[9]

In addition to the elements listed by Von Funck in the above excerpt, units of the 106th Infantry Division were also already operating on the 7th Panzer Division's right flank. During the night, a regrouping had been conducted and the sector as far as the "Batratskaia Dacha" State Farm had been assumed by Forst's division. In the morning, in order to strengthen the boundary with the 106th Infantry Division, von Funck moved up some of his armor to the right flank (behind the front line).

After sunrise, information from Panzer Reconnaissance Battalion 37 about the situation opposite the corps' boundary still hadn't arrived, and in order not to lose any more time, von Funck, approximately after 0700, decided at first to attack out of the area of Hill 216.1 toward Miasoedovo, where the situation was still unknown. Simultaneously he issued an order for a group of panzergrenadiers to launch an attack against the encircled forces in the woods northeast of Krutoi Log. According to some information, elements of Lieutenant Colonel G.P. Slatov's 209th Guards Rifle Regiment (of the 73rd Guards Rifle Division), Major S.A. Arshinov's 223rd Guards Rifle Regiment (of the 78th Guards Rifle Division) and scattered anti-tank rifle teams and anti-tank gun crews were located in these woods. Possibly, the forces of other units might have been operating here as well. The first attack here demonstrated that the Guardsmen were still stubbornly

---

9   TsAMO RF, f. 15, op. 11600, d. 1539, l. 27.

holding their positions, and so it was difficult to predict when this pocket of resistance would be successfully eliminated. A bit later, *kampfgruppen* of the 7th Panzer Division launched a powerful attack against the "Batratskaia Dacha" State Farm, and having taken it around 0900, continued advancing into the depth of the 25th Guards Rifle Corps' defenses.

The 106th Infantry Division went on the attack toward the Koren' River a bit earlier than its neighbor, 7th Panzer Division, back at twilight, before the sun had even risen. Its main forces were assembled in the Hill 209.6 – Machine Tractor Station – Hill 207 sector (that extended for 5 kilometers), which was being held by two divisions of Safiulin's 25th Guards Rifle Corps. The defenders there had been arranged into two echelons. In the first echelon, the 73rd Guards Rifle Division had the 211th Guards Rifle Regiment holding the line from Point "K" (1 kilometer northwest of Koren'skaia Dacha) to the "Poliana" State Farm, while in the second echelon the 78th Guards Rifle Division had the 223rd and 225th Guards Rifle Regiments holding a sector from the crossroads south of the "Batratskaia Dacha" State Farm to the "Poliana" State Farm. The backbone of the defense here was Colonel I.A. Taranov's 201st Separate Tank Brigade. Out of its units, two strongpoints had been created: one at the boundary between the 211th and 214th Guards Rifle Regiments in the woods 800 meters north of Hill 209.6 consisting of Senior Lieutenant Kozhar's 2nd Tank Company of the 296th Tank Battalion and Lieutenant Koliad's 2nd Tank Company of the 295th Tank Battalion with a company of submachine gunners; and the second among the positions of 2/211th Guards Rifle Regiment in the area 1 kilometer west and northwest of Gremiachii, consisting of Captain D.A. Dziuba's 201st Motorized Rifle Battalion, the 3rd Tank Company of the 295th Tank Battalion (11 Mk-III Valentine tanks), and the 1669th Destroyer Anti-tank Artillery Regiment.

At first it was important for Forst to take the strong knot of resistance at the boundary between the 73rd Guards and 72nd Guards Rifle Divisions, which included three small settlements that had been prepared by Soviet troops according to the scheme of anti-tank strongpoints: Gremiachii, the hamlet of the Machine Tractor Station,[10] and the "Poliana" State Farm. The boundary between the 7th Guards Army's two subordinate Guards rifle corps also lay here. The Germans were aware of this, and thus it was here that the main attack of two divisions (the 106th Infantry and 7th Panzer Divisions) was directed, while an auxiliary attack was directed toward Hill 209.6 (in the center of the 73rd Guards Rifle Division) and Hill 207.0 (on the right flank of the 72nd Guards Rifle Division).

At 0400 after "a heavy barrage from six-barreled rocket launchers and artillery", more than a regiment of infantry from the 106th Infantry Division with the support of 13 panzers attacked the line of the 72nd Guards Rifle Division from the southwest in the Maslova Pristan' – "Poliana" State Farm and the Maslova Pristan' – Hill 192.8 directions, as well as the left flank of the 73rd Guards Rifle Division's 211th Guards Rifle Regiment in the Hill 209.6 – Koren'skaia Dacha and the Hill 207 – "Poliana" State Farm – Machine Tractor Station – Gremiachii direction. Approximately an hour later the Germans fell back from Hill 207 on the main axis, leaving behind 4 knocked-out tanks on the battlefield. However, this was only the first round of the offensive. Bringing his units back into order, at 0700 Forst again struck the boundary between the Guards rifle corps. More than three battalions of infantry moved against the positions of 3/222nd Guards Rifle and 1/793rd Rifle Regiments (a battalion of which had been made operationally subordinate to the commander of the 72nd Guards Rifle Division A.I. Losev) along the road running from Maslova Pristan' to the "Poliana" State Farm, while artillery placed intense fire on the State Farm.

---

10 The hamlet of the Machine Tractor Station was a small settlement, which prior to the war held the machine tractor station's office and where the tractor drivers lived with their families. It also had garages for the tractors and repair shops.

By approximately 0730 Forst's troops had reached the line: "Poliana" State Farm – Hill 209.6 – woods north of it, and by 0900, having crushed 3/222nd Guards Rifle Regiment and a bit later the right-flank 1st Company of 1/793rd Rifle Regiment, they took the "Poliana" State Farm and continued to surge toward the Machine Tractor Station and Gremiachii, but they were finally brought to a stop before reaching them, and with great difficulty approximately an hour later thrown back beyond the State Farm. Meanwhile Forst's units were exerting strong pressure on the sector in front of Koren'skaia Dacha, which was located south of the "Poliana" State Farm, but here the Germans made practically no headway.

After the capture of the "Poliana" State Farm, the enemy's two main assault wedges became distinctly clear: from out of the "Poliana" State Farm area and from out of the area northwest of Hill 209.6 and both attacks were aiming toward the villages of Kashlakovo and Pentsevo. The strength of the attackers and defenders at the "Poliana" State Farm and the village of Gremiachii that was located behind it was approximately even. The 106th Infantry Division was attacking simultaneously with three infantry battalions, and their advance suggested a tidal movement. The attacks came at short intervals of time and were accompanied by artillery and Nebelwerfer fire. Tanks of the 7th Panzer Division and assault guns of StuG Battalion 909 served as a battering ram, and their numbers increased with each attack.

The 73rd Guards Rifle Division's 211th Guards Rifle Regiment and the 78th Guards Rifle Division's 225th Guards Rifle Regiment that were defending here were also relying on armor – the Matildas and Valentines of the 201st Separate Tank Brigade. In addition A.I. Losev, apprehensive about a tank attack against his right flank (from the "Poliana" State Farm) brought up the 1st Tank Battalion of the 27th Guards Tank Brigade that was subordinate to him to a point northwest of the State Farm. Thus the fighting here became extremely savage. The opposing sides suffered heavy losses in men and equipment, and the "Poliana" State Farm, Gremiachii and the Machine Tractor Station changed hands several times. As soon as the enemy broke into these settlements, the commanders of both Guards rifle corps, Safiulin and Vasil'ev, would immediately launch fierce counterattacks, which transformed into hand-to-hand struggles, and at times even fistfights. Everything at hand was thrown into the fighting here – units of Kozak's, Skvortsov's and Buslaev's divisions, elements of Taranov's and Nevzhinsky's tank brigades, and the 1529th Heavy Self-propelled Artillery Regiment. The combat diary of the 201st Tank Brigade for 7 July conveys the intensity and drama of the combat for Gremiachii and the "Poliana" State Farm to us today:

> At 0800 out of the eastern outskirts of Krutoi Log and from Point 176.0, the enemy launched an attack in strength of up to 300 submachine gunners supported by 20 tanks in the direction of 1/201st Motorized Rifle Battalion (company commander Senior Lieutenant Afanas'ev), which was occupying a defense 1 kilometer northwest of Gremiachii. Fire from four batteries of the 1669th Destroyer Anti-tank Artillery Regiment and two batteries of the 1529th Self-propelled Artillery Regiment was called down on the attacking infantry and tanks. After the opening of the artillery fire, the attack's pace slowed. The attack was finally stopped by tank fire from the position of the 3rd Company/296th Tank Battalion out of the area of the northeastern fringe of woods lying west of Gremiachii, mortar fire from the 201st Motorized Rifle Battalion's mortar company, and rifle and machine-gun fire from 1st Company/201st Motorized Rifle Battalion and the 73rd Guards Rifle Division's 3/211th Guards Rifle Regiment. The enemy, suffering heavy losses, was thrown back to the jumping-off positions. In this combat, submachine gun company commander Lieutenant Pervushin was wounded.
>
> At 0920 the brigade commander directed two platoons of submachine gunners from his reserve to support the 296th Tank Battalion. At 0930 the Germans again launched a fierce attack. Despite the enemy's numerical superiority in this sector, they were driven back with

large losses for them. The commander of the 296th Tank Battalion Senior Lieutenant A.S. Kuksin fell heroically in this battle.

Despite the losses suffered and the stubborn resistance of our units, the adversary, having brought up a battalion of infantry and 20-25 tanks, resumed the offensive. The attack took on a savage nature; drunken Germans were advancing at full height, wildly firing from their submachine guns. Several attacks were beaten back, one after the other, but the enemy kept coming. An order from the brigade commander said, "Not one step back!" The arriving chief of staff Colonel Pisarevsky issued a directive to the commander of the 296th Tank Battalion: "Fire at the enemy at point blank range, hold out and don't retreat."[11]

At 1130 up to 600 infantry and 60 armored fighting vehicles again went on the attack in the direction of the "Poliana" State Farm and Gremiachii. This attack was also driven back by the active defense of the 201st Separate Tank Brigade and the 3rd Battalion of the 211th Guards Rifle Regiment, supported by the 1669th Destroyer Anti-tank Artillery Regiment and the 1529th Heavy Self-propelled Artillery Regiment. However, the Soviet units and formations that had gathered here also suffered losses, particularly the regiments of the 78th Guards Rifle Division. Its decimated rifle companies were often unable to withstand the attack of German tanks and retreated without warning neighbors beforehand; in individual sectors, there were also manifestations of panic. In such a troubled situation, it was very difficult to figure out who was the first to shake and who let down whom, and thus in the heat of combat the division commanders were accusing each other of faltering and abandoning tactically important lines. It reached the point where at one such critical moment, A.V. Skvortsov didn't trust a report from the commander of his 223rd Guards Rifle Regiment Major S.A. Arshinov that his regiment was holding Gremiachii, and sent him the following Order No.85: "Draw up a document with a combat report that is countersigned by the commanders on your right and left, as proof that the regiment is holding its occupied line."[12]

However, there were no justifications for the distrust. At 0900 Arshinov's regiment together with units of the 73rd Guards Rifle Division was holding a line extending from the crossroads south of the "Batratskaia Dacha" State Farm to Hill 209.6, and had driven back an attack by 22 armored vehicles and a battalion of infantry, in the course of which the Germans left 9 smoking tanks on the battlefield. The 223rd Guards Rifle Regiment continued to hold its position tenaciously until the day's end.

Twice on this day, the commander of the 225th Guards Rifle Regiment Major D.S. Khorolenko personally inspired the battalions (and not only his) to launch a counterattack toward Gremiachii. He was not only directing the battle, but remained up among the men until the moment they had consolidated their grip on the hamlet. Of course, it isn't the job of a regiment commander to lead units in combat; that is for platoon and company commanders to do, or in an extreme case, a battalion commander. The major wasn't a totally unseasoned guy at the front; he had taken part in the Battle of Stalingrad, and he himself understood his role perfectly well. But he also knew something else: that there were such moments when "it was impossible to raise your head from the ground" because of the intense enemy fire, but also impossible to wait the situation hunkered down in the trenches – a counterattack was the only way to hold the line and to save a unit from annihilation. It was at such times that even a regiment commander couldn't be faulted for "going over the top" and leading a counterattack. In conversations with me, veterans have recalled that at the front, the example and personal courage of a commander who appeared at a critical moment was always highly valued by the men. Not flashy displays just for show, but deliberate actions that

---

11 TsAMO RF, f. 3256, op. 1, d.7, ll. 48-49.
12 TsAMO RF, f. 1225, op. 1, d. 13, l. 86.

brought real results and turned around a difficult situation. Denis Semenovich more than once demonstrated these qualities in combat, which is why his Guardsmen respected and valued him.

I repeat – the "Poliana" State Farm was located next to the hamlets of Gremiachii and the Machine Tractor Station and was part of a single anti-tank strongpoint. The Soviet command saw this as an important line in front of the Koren' River, and thus was striving at any cost to prevent the Germans from taking it. Forst, on the other hand, having met stubborn resistance from the offensive's first minutes, decided to smash the forces of the 24th Guards Rifle Corps' divisions that were defending here. Thus, parallel with the attack in the direction of the State Farm and the hamlets on the morning of 7 July, as soon as the Soviet troops abandoned the "Poliana" State Farm for the first time, he immediately launched another attack against the right flank of Losev's 72nd Guards Rifle Division. In the preceding days it had suffered heavy losses, and in addition one of its regiments was located outside its zone of defense, and thus the division was in a most difficult situation. Its 222nd Guards and 229th Guards Rifle Regiments were holding the "Poliana" State Farm – Hill 192.6 – Hill 192.8 sector, while its 224th Guards Rifle Regiment was fighting for Bezliudovka together with the 213th Rifle Division. A *kampfgruppe* of the 106th Infantry Division split the 2/222nd Guards Rifle Regiment that was saddling the Maslova Pristan' – "Poliana" State Farm road into two pieces, while its main forces advanced toward the crossroads of the "Poliana" State Farm and Hill 202.9, which were being held by the 1st Battalion of the 793rd Rifle Regiment. Meanwhile, up to two infantry companies which had deployed on Hill 207 were attacking in the direction of the Shebekinskaia Dacha Woods, trying to get behind the 2/222nd Guards Rifle Regiment. However, the 2nd Battalion commander reacted in time and bent back his right flank to face the north. At this same time, several assault guns and up to two battalions of the 320nd Infantry Division's Infantry Regiment 586 were engaged in combat for Hill 192.6. As soon as Soviet forces abandoned Gremiachii at 1400, the attacking Germans grabbed Hill 192.6, and having consolidated their grip on it, continued to push the Guardsmen back toward the Shebekinskaia Dacha Woods.

A.I. Losev, who was attempting to restore the situation on his division's right flank and simultaneously guard against a new possible attack out of the area of the "Poliana" State Farm wound up in a very difficult predicament. In the first place, he lacked the strength to take back the State Farm, because here the enemy had an advantage in artillery and tanks. In the second place, he had to reinforce the defense of Hill 192.8 quickly. With each passing hour, the situation on his right flank was deteriorating. The enemy was gathering strength, while the infantry of 2/222nd Guards Rifle and 1/793rd Rifle Regiments were unable to withstand the tank attacks and was withdrawing, albeit slowly, leaving their positions to the enemy.

Nervous tensions grew. The division commander Losev began to lose composure and snap at subordinates. Instead of retaining his poise and discussing the situation calmly with the commander of the sole unit that had the possibility to turn the situation around – the 1st Tank Battalion of the 27th Guards Tank Brigade – he instead gave him what was essentially a suicidal order: to attack the "Poliana" State Farm with tanks without any support. When the battalion commander reasonably raised the question about infantry and artillery support, Losev threatened to shoot him. From Operational Summary No.56 of the 27th Guards Tank Brigade headquarters at 2100 on 7 July 1943:

> At 1200 the enemy in strength of up to a battalion of infantry with the support of artillery and tanks attacked the "Poliana" State Farm and Gremiachii. The tanks of the 1st Tank Battalion from their jumping-off positions 1 kilometer southeast of the "Poliana" State Farm were monitoring the enemy in the direction of the "Poliana" State Farm. By 1300, overcoming the enemy's stubborn fire resistance, our tanks reached a line 200 meters southeast of the "Poliana" State Farm, where they were counterattacked by 5 Pz-VI and up to a battalion of

enemy infantry, and also met by strong anti-tank artillery fire from the direction of the woods 1 kilometer south of the "Poliana" State Farm. Our tanks exchanged fire with the enemy's tanks and infantry. At 1400 the battalion's tanks, being hit by intense artillery fire and the fire of heavy tanks, fell back to their jumping-off positions to friendly infantry, where they exchanged fire with the enemy's tanks and infantry until the onset of darkness.[13]

Yet here is how brigade commander N.V. Nevzhinsky laid out the situation in his brigade after two days of fighting in the sector of the 72nd Guards Rifle and 213th Rifle Divisions in a combat report at 1500 on 8 July 1943:

> From the sunrise on 6.7.43, the 27th Guards Separate Tank Brigade on the basis of a special order from the commander of the 24th Guards Rifle Corps was operating on the front: (excl.) "Poliana" State Farm – Point 192.6 – Point 192.8 – Point 140.1 – railroad bed southeast of Rzhavets. The brigade was cooperating with one tank battalion on the right with the 72nd Guards Rifle Division, and with one tank battalion on the left with the 213th Rifle Division. The combat actions of the brigade as a result of operating on a front of 12 kilometers were executed in a piecemeal fashion, as a consequence of which very difficult conditions were created for commanding the brigade, organizing cooperation with other types of troops, as well as implementing evacuation and supply services.
>
> 2. The piecemeal actions of the brigade on a broad front don't yield such effectiveness in shock power and maneuver, or its use in more important sectors.
> 3. The brigade received its combat tasks verbally, without confirmation by written orders. There were cases when commanders personally gave orders about executing a combat mission to take a point without artillery support or infantry support with the warning: "If you fail to take it, I will shoot you." In an incident on 7.7.43, the commander of the 72nd Guards Rifle Division declared as much to the commander of the 1st Tank Battalion (supplement – report of the 1st Tank Battalion command). Thus, as a result of such use, the brigade suffers heavy losses in men and materiel.[14]

Likely, the reader already understands that the resolution of immediate tasks by any means, with no regard for the capabilities of the involved forces and despite any losses, was a widespread and even commonplace matter in the Red Army. In the situation with the attack on the "Poliana" State Farm, the tankers it might be said were lucky. If to judge from the actions of the 27th Guards Tank Brigade throughout the course of the defensive phase of the Battle of Kursk, then it should be said that its crews were well-trained, and to a great extent this was what helped the 1st Tank Battalion in particular get out of a jam. A frontal attack across open ground against a village, where enemy anti-tank guns and tanks were already deployed could result in nothing other than losses. However, the tanks crews advanced at high speed, and maneuvering, managed to cover an entire 800 meters of open ground without losing all of the battalion's tanks. According to the 27th Guards Tank Brigade's report, on this day 4 T-34 tanks were knocked-out, including two that were left burned-out and two that were damaged by anti-tank artillery. In addition, at 2100 the brigade headquarters reported that one more T-34 had taken combat damage – its turret had been jammed by a shell, but the crew continued to fight. In addition to the tanks, two guns of an anti-tank battery that was supporting the attack toward the State Farm were knocked out. The

---

13   TsAMO RF, f. 3108, op. 1, d. 10, l. 60.
14   TsAMO RF, f. 3108, op. 1, d. 7, l. 103.

combat losses in men amounted to 15, of which 3 were killed, 10 wounded, and 2 concussed.[15] If you consider that the 2nd Tank Battalion on this day only exchanged fire from fixed positions together with units of the 213th Rifle Division while keeping in check a German attack out of the Maslova Pristan' – Rzhavets area, then with a great amount of probability one can assert that the losses given in the report relate only to the 1st Tank Battalion of the 27th Guards Tank Brigade.

The peak of the struggle at the boundary between the 72nd and 73rd Guards Rifle Divisions occurred at mid-day. At 1300 the next and very strong attack of the 106th Infantry Division out of Maslova Pristan' toward the "Poliana" State Farm began. According to Major D.S. Khorolenko's report, up to a regiment of infantry with the support of two groups of armor totaling 17 tanks took part in it. The 2nd Battalion of the 73rd Guards Rifle Division's 211th Guards Rifle Regiment, suffering significant losses and unable to withstand the attack by superior forces, began to retreat in the direction of Churaevo (4 kilometers to the southeast on the western bank of the Koren' River), thereby exposing the flank of the 225th Guards Rifle Regiment. Striving to prevent the Germans from rolling up the regiment's left flank, D.S. Khorolenko decided to bend it back and issued an order to the battalions to fall back to the eastern outskirts of Gremiachii and to dig in there. At 1400, the grenadiers of the 106th Infantry Division took full possession of the hamlet and continued to attack in the direction of Kashlakovo and Churaevo.

At 1230 on 8 July 1943, a report with the following contents was sent to the commander of the 7th Guards Army's Armored and Mechanized Forces:

> Up to 200 submachine gunners have infiltrated into the hamlets of Gremiachii and the "Poliana" State Farm. Two companies of 2/211th Guards Rifle Regiment were smashed; the rest retreated to the west, which left the brigade's left flank exposed [as well as the 225th Guards Rifle Regiment]. The 296th Tank Battalion and the motorized rifle battalion are engaged in combat with the submachine gunners, holding a defense of their current lines. The 3rd Battalion of the 211th Guards Rifle Regiment has been sent to the Gremiachii area. The enemy, having brought up fresh forces of up to a regiment of infantry supported by 45 tanks resumed the attack in the direction of Gremiachii and the "Poliana" State Farm. The 296th Tank Battalion and the 201st Motorized Rifle Battalion, supported by attached self-propelled guns [of the 1529th Heavy Self-propelled Artillery Regiment] and the 1669th Destroyer Anti-tank Artillery Regiment drove back the enemy attack. The enemy withdrew into the woods west of Gremiachii.
>
> At 1500 the enemy, bringing his troops back to order, resumed the attacks. Separate groups of submachine gunners infiltrated through the combat positions of the 296th Tank Battalion and 201st Motorized Rifle Battalion, but were also eventually thrown back. The brigade's personnel in these battles demonstrated their readiness to conduct combat in contemporary conditions, making maximal use of all available weapons and equipment. Suffering relatively light losses, the brigade inflicted significant damage to the foe.[16]

Archival documents testify that practically the entire personnel of Taranov's 25th Guards Tank Brigade demonstrated courage and heroism in the combat for these three settlements, but Captain D.A. Dziuba's 201st Motorized Rifle Battalion showed particular tenacity. His main forces (rifle companies, mortar company and anti-tank rifle company) were arrayed in two echelons: in the woods west of Gremiachii and in the hamlet itself. In the course of 7 July 1943 Dziuba's battalion repelled 12 fierce attacks. More than once the Germans drove his companies from a line, but the

---

15 TsAMO RF, f. 3108, op. 1, d. 10, l. 60.
16 TsAMO RF, f. 3256, op. 1, d. 7, ll. 47-48.

positions were again regained with counterattacks. Five times, the battalion commander personally inspired the second echelon to attack. An interesting detail – when I was looking through the communiques of the Sovinformburo, in one of them (for 13 July 1943) I discovered a report about the unparalleled fortitude of the 201st Motorized Rifle Battalion. The surname of the battalion commander is mentioned in it. After the end of the Battle of Kursk, for his skillful command of the unit when repelling the attacks of a numerically superior foe and for the personal courage he displayed when defending Gremiachii, Captain Dem'ian Afanas'evich Dziuba at an order from the commander of the 7th Guards Army was awarded the Order of the Red Banner.

In order to regain the positions in this sector, G.B. Safiulin personally, having assembled a group of units (1st and 2nd Battalion/211th Guards Rifle Regiment, the 225th Guards Rifle Regiment and 1st Battalion/793rd Guards Rifle Regiment) at approximately 1600 launched a counterattack toward Gremiachii and the hamlet of the Machine Tractor Station with fire support from the 201st Tank Brigade and the 1529th Heavy Self-propelled Artillery Regiment. After a 10-minute artillery preparation, the Guardsmen, going on the counterattack, after an hour had driven the Germans from the hamlet, or more accurately from the place where it had once stood; by this time, all that remained of it were ashes and several orphaned chimney stacks. As the veterans recalled who took part in the fighting, it was hard to imagine that several days before there had been life on this blackened clump of earth. The fighting here continued until late in the evening with the same bitterness that it had before. The account of the 7th Guards Army headquarters states: "The fighting repeatedly dissolved into hand-to-hand combat." Both sides took heavy losses. For example, in the 1st Company of the 1st Battalion of the 213th Rifle Division's 793rd Rifle Regiment, which entered the fighting on the morning of 7 July, by noon only 8 men remained in action. Other units also reported high casualty rates. Striving to retain combat effectiveness and command and control over the troops, the 24th Guards Rifle Corps commander subordinated the remnants of companies and battalions of the 72nd Guards Rifle and 213th Rifle Divisions that had been defending Gremiachii to the 211th Guards Rifle Regiment of the 73rd Guards Rifle Division and the 225th Guards Rifle Regiment of the 78th Guards Rifle Division. In particular, 1/793rd Rifle Regiment was made operationally subordinate to the commander of the 225th Guards Rifle Regiment.

Around 1800 the Guardsmen, continuing to push back the enemy slowly, once again took possession of the hamlets of Gremiachii and the Machine Tractor Station. However, the 106th Infantry Division's command, having quickly brought up reserves, once again launched a strong attack in the direction of Gremiachii a short time later. In the course of the heaviest five-hour combat, the Soviet troops managed to retain the hamlet, and according to report from the 73rd Guards Rifle Division commander S.A. Kozak, they even mopped up the "Poliana" State Farm of enemy submachine gunners once again, but later it turned out that this information wasn't accurate.[17]

Although by the end of the day the enemy, having pushed back the 24th Guards Rifle Corps' right flank, had gained possession of two important knots of resistance (the "Poliana" State Farm and Hill 192.6), this didn't hinder N.A. Vasil'ev from successfully carrying out the order given by the army commander to destroy Korps Raus' bridges. In the reports of its headquarters, the evacuation of the units of the 320th Infantry Division from the Bezliudovka area because of the strong pressure of the 24th Guards Rifle Corps' forces are presented as if it was a measure contained in the plan, and not as a failure of the preliminary calculations because of the underestimation of the Soviet side. From the morning briefing of Korps Raus at 0625:

---

17   TsAMO RF, f. 1212, op. 1, d. 28, ll. 8-9.

The night passed quietly. The bridgehead at Bezliudovka remains screened as planned by weak rear guard detachments. Enemy pressure is imperceptible. At present the regrouping of the last units is underway. At dawn the enemy aviation conducted powerful airstrikes.[18]

However, already within a short time, the situation sharply changed. Early in the morning after a short artillery barrage by 3/671st Artillery Regiment on Bezliudovka, two battalions of the 213th Rifle Division's 585th Rifle Regiment and a battalion of the 72nd Guards Rifle Division's 224th Guards Rifle Regiment went on the attack toward Bezliudovka from three directions. By 0920 units of the 224th Guards Rifle Regiment were the first to break into the village and gradually pushed forward toward its center. Grenadiers of the 320th Infantry Division's Infantry Regiment 585, supported by several assault guns, were putting up stubborn resistance, but at 1130 their opposition was broken. The Germans hastily retreated at first toward the bridges, and then to the western bank of the Donets River. From the 24th Guards Rifle Corps' combat diary:

> In Bezliudovka the enemy left behind up to 500 corpses of soldiers and officers.[19] In addition, the following booty was seized: 2 knocked-out tanks, 1 knocked-out self-propelled guns; 2 75mm guns, 1 45mm gun, 1 37mm gun, all damaged; and 20 light machine guns, 1 81mm mortar, 1 50mm mortar, 2 flamethrowers and 2 submachine guns have been picked up; and an ammunition stockpile, one motorcycle, one bicycle and other military items have been seized.[20]

In addition, the victorious Russians took four prisoners from Infantry Regiment 585 in Bezliudovka, and under interrogation they reported that from a conversation with an officer, they learned that on that day (other information give 6 July as the date) the commander of the 320th Infantry Division Major General G. Postel had been wounded and transported to a hospital.[21] At 1205 the headquarters of Korps Raus reported:

> In Bezliudovka the enemy is continuing pursuit, and thus far not all of our units have crossed to the right bank of the Donets. The front along the Donets in this area is being held by reserve battalions of the 320th and 106th Infantry Divisions. From out of the woods east of Rzhavets [the 320th Infantry Division's right flank], the enemy attacked with 7 tanks but was driven back. One tank was knocked out. No changes on the 320th Infantry Division's left flank.[22]

However, the attempt to drive the Germans out of Maslova Pristan' wasn't crowned with success. The units of two rifle regiments of the 213th Rifle Division and tanks of 2/27th Guards Tank Brigade that were activated here were unable to break the resistance offered by the 320th Infantry Division, although several times the Germans had to launch strong counterattacks. By the evening of 7 July (at 1800) the situation even in Rzhavets was not fully clear to the command of the 24th Guards Rifle Corps, so it took measures to clarify it. In the operational summary of the 213th Guards Rifle Division, it is indicated that "2/585th Rifle Regiment is operationally

---

18   NARA US, t. 312, r. 54, f. 7569621.
19   It is possible to consider this figure rather complete, because at first the 72nd Guards Rifle Division reported on 650 German dead, but then a special team was assigned for counting the German dead.
20   TsAMO RF, f. 24 gv. sk, op. 1, d. 21, l. 25.
21   According to Western sources, Major General Georg-Wilhelm Postel formally left his post as commander of the 320th Infantry Division on 10 July 1943.
22   NARA US, t. 312, r. 54, f. 7569622.

subordinate to the commander of the 793rd Rifle Regiment, and is engaged in combat on the line of the northwestern fringe of the woods near Rzhavets. At 1600 an attempt to attack with two battalions toward Rzhavets had no success."²³ At the same time, the headquarters of the 27th Guards Tank Brigade at 2100 reported: "At 1700 the enemy took Rzhavets and by the end of the day reached the line: spur of the woods west of Hill 192.6 – Point 140.1 – southern outskirts of Rzhavets – Point 106.6. The 2nd Tank Battalion in cooperation with units of the 213th Rifle Division throughout the day was stubbornly defending its occupied line and engaged in combat to repulse enemy attacks out of Maslova Pristan' toward Rzhavets."²⁴ Probably, Rzhavets, which was blocking the Soviets' path to Maslova Pristan', still remained in enemy hands.

At the same time as Korps Raus launched the offensive on its left flank with the forces of the 106th Infantry Division in order to drive back Kozak's, Buslaev's and Losev's divisions to the Koren' River, and the 320th Infantry Division was evacuating its units out of Bezliudovka, the situation on the axis of Army Detachment Kempf's main attack remained rather calm, and judging from captured German documents, even stable. From the morning report of the III Panzer Corps:

> 7th Panzer Division launched an attack at 0715 into the woods northeast of Krutoi Log. 6th Panzer Division assembled southeast and south of Iastrebovo. 19th Panzer Division on the evening of 6.7 took the western portion of Belovsksaia and the hill 1.5 kilometers to the north of it. In the sector of the 168th Infantry Division, enemy artillery fire on the bridgehead and eastern section of Belgorod. At night, enemy air attacks focused on the bridges across the Donets.²⁵

However, this impression is deceptive. The documents don't convey the intensity of the fighting taking place on the right flank of the 7th Guards Army. On the night of 6-7 July, the fighting in the sector of defense of Safiulin's 25th Guards Rifle Corps almost never subsided. All three *kampfgruppen* of the 19th Panzer Division with bitter and improbable persistence were grinding their way through the lines of the 81st Guards Rifle Division. After Fourth Panzer Army had emerged on the Prokhorovka direction and its right flank had become extended by up to 25 kilometers, the seizure of the Staryi Gorod – Blizhniaia Igumenka – Belovskaia area had key significance for the further advance of Army Group South's main assault grouping. Instead of a maximal concentration of force on the spearhead of II SS Panzer Corps' main attack, Hausser had been forced to keep one-third of his available strength – the SS Panzergrenadier Division *Totenkopf* – in a position to cover his exposed right flank. In a briefing to Army Group South at 0625, the headquarters of III Panzer Corps had reported on the situation of its neighbor to the left: "The SS Division *Totenkopf* hasn't succeeded in launching an attack across the Donets; it was occupying a defense 2-3 kilometers west of it."²⁶ Thus, there was still a gap between von Manstein's two attack groupings, and Hoth's panzer army in essence had been marking time for 24 hours. Kempf recognized that this was leading to the offensive's failure, but his troops thus far had not been able to resolve the problem. That is why Breith was conducting attacks almost around the clock against the 81st Guards Rifle Division. These efforts were yielding results, albeit slowly. With great difficulty, Schmidt's 19th Panzer Division was nevertheless making headway, pushing the Guardsmen out of their fortified positions and constricting the knot of resistance in the Staryi Gorod – Kreida area,

---

23 TsAMO RF, f. 213 sd, op. 1, d. 15, l. 225.
24 TsAMO RF, f. 31078, op. 1, d. 10, l. 60.
25 NARA US, rg. 242, t. 314, r. 197, f. 001130.
26 NARA US, t. 312, r. 54, f. 7569621.

and on 7 July the 6th Panzer Division was also supposed to link up with it. The 81st Guards Rifle Division commander I.K. Morozov remembered:

> On the night of 6-7 July: 238th Guards Rifle Regiment had dug into the second line of trenches and the reserve positions with a front to the southeast; 233rd Guards Rifle Regiment was dug into the second line of trenches and occupying the battalion resistance nest in Blizhniaia Igumenka, with a front to the east and northeast; 235th Guards Rifle Regiment had fallen back to the second line of trenches with its left flank, with a front to the southwest, while holding Staryi Gorod and the road leading to Shishino and Khokhlovo with two battalions, with a front to the west. The KV tanks had been pulled back to Blizhniaia Igumenka.[27]

I will remind that the battalion resistance nest of Blizhniaia Igumenka was constructed according to the scheme of a fortified area with an outer ring of works, anti-tank ditches, a strong system of anti-tank defense, etc. The forward observation post of the 25th Guards Rifle Corps was also located here. Because of this, an assault on Blizhniaia Igumenka was not a simple matter and the troops of the 19th Panzer Division alone proved insufficient. Thus, in order not to waste time and strength, Breith ordered to bypass and encircle it with the two *panzerkampfgruppe* and to leave behind a screen of panzergrenadiers on the outskirts to seal it, while the tanks were to press on with the advance to the east, into the rear of the 81st Guards Rifle Division. Executing this order, Becker's *panzerkampfgruppe* (of the 19th Panzer Division) at sunrise was preparing to attack out of Belovskaia in the direction of a Machine Tractor Station hamlet and Andreevskie, while von Oppeln's (of the 6th Panzer Division) was preparing to attack out of the Iastrebovo area toward Hill 125.5, Hill 212.4 and Postnikov. However, first Unrein's panzergrenadiers with the support of tanks were to take Iastrebovo, then Sevriukovo, and after von Oppeln's *panzerkampfgruppe* crossed to the western bank of the Razumnaia River, they were to screen its right flank. At the same time Köhler's units (19th Panzer Division's Panzergrenadier Regiment 73) with the support of the 6th Panzer Division were to resume the offensive from the Kreida railyard toward Staryi Gorod, with the aim of covering the left flank of Becker's *panzerkampfgruppe*. The 168th Infantry Division received the order to fix the Guardsmen's forces in Staryi Gorod with systematic attacks out of the Mikhailovka bridgehead. Thereby, Breith by the end of 7 July was planning with Schmidt's and Hünersdorff's panzer divisions and Chales de Beaulieu's infantry division to split the 81st Guards Rifle Division's front to its entire depth in at least two places and to emerge with an armored group on the boundary between the 7th Guards and 6th Guards Armies in the Postnikov, Andreevskie, Chernaia Poliana area (on the left flank of the 375th Rifle Division).

It is difficult to lay out the course of combat operations in the 19th Panzer Division's sector of the offensive on the night of 6-7 July and the morning of 7 July. The summary reports of the divisions of III Panzer Corps and its own reports to the headquarters of Army Group South for this day have only been partially preserved. Only information concerning 7 July that was mistakenly entered in the daily summary for 8 July remains, which somewhat clarifies the situation, although unfortunately not completely so. The operational documents of the 81st Guards Rifle Division for this period are also almost completely lacking in the Ministry of Defense's Central Archives. Judging from the information I've been able to find, which is far from complete, *Kampfgruppe* Köhler, which was advancing toward the Kreida railyard from the south along the railroad was engaged in particularly heavy fighting. After a short pause to rest, at 0330 on 7 July its units continued to attack and after five hours of intense fighting, broke into this powerful strongpoint.

---

27 TsAMO RF, personal files of Major General I.K. Morozov; autobiography, ll. 47-48.

The positions of Major T.F. Kriuchikhin's 238th Guards Rifle Regiment, which was operating here, had been well-prepared for a lengthy defense. A particular feature of the construction of its positions and the system of fire at the Kreida railyard was that when building the shelters and bunkers, rails and rail ties were used, and in addition all the brick structures (the repair shops, railroad depot and two semi-demolished elevators) had been converted into pillboxes. Moreover, at first three, and then two companies of KV tanks of the 262nd Heavy Tank Regiment were located on the loading platforms, and emplacements had been made along the railroad embankment for BM-13 rocket launchers with reserve positions for the 81st Guards Rifle Division's separate anti-tank battalion. Something that was very important was that the entire system of weapons had been tied in with artificial obstacles. This circumstance together with the tenacity of the division's combatants and the difficult ground for the employment of tanks was the main reason that made the line of Morozov's division one tough nut to crack.

In addition, back on 6 July Morozov had reinforced Kriuchikhin's 238th Guards Rifle Regiment by shifting the 1st and 3rd Battalions of the 233rd Guards Rifle Regiment to the Kreida area from their positions near Blizhniaia Igumenka and the hamlet of the Machine Tractor Station. Thus, the 19th Panzer Division's *kampfgruppen* encountered bitter resistance here and made slow headway with great difficulty. A tactic employed already on the second day of the offensive proved to be effective: Assault teams would encircle a bunker while combat engineers blew them up, and if this wasn't successful, they would be destroyed by specially assigned heavy weapons. However, all of the firing positions in this area were covered by deep minefields and mortar and artillery fire; in particular, the approaches to the railyard from the south and southwest were controlled by a mortar company of the 238th Guards Rifle Regiment and the full 2nd Battalion of the 290th Mortar Regiment. In addition, captured German documents show that after two days of extremely heavy fighting, the 19th Panzer Division began to experience an acute shortage of artillery means. Two main factors were affecting this. First, there was the sharp decrease in the number of operational tanks in the panzer regiment because of losses, particularly caused by minefields. Second, the breakthrough tactic, when each of the *kampfgruppen* was supposed to have subordinate guns for placing direct fire on bunkers and pillboxes was a rather extravagant use of them. Besides this, the division command was supposed to have sufficient artillery both to support the offensive on the main axis and as a reserve. The artillery battalion that had been transferred to it from the 168th Infantry Division wasn't sufficient to ameliorate the acuteness of the problem and it wasn't a coincidence that in the order for the corps for 7 July, the command of the Flak units were given a special assignment: to support the 19th Panzer Division's attack with II/Flak Regiment 38, which (as was especially stipulated) was to conduct fire at ground targets northeast of Belgorod.

Thus, while penetrating into the depth of Morozov's division, Schmidt's units were leaving behind a bloody trace: hundreds of dead and wounded daily, and dozens of destroyed or knocked-out tanks and vehicles. As reported by the headquarters of the 19th Panzer Division, the loss of men in Panzergrenadier Regiment 73, which was fighting for possession of the Kreida railyard, was particularly high. I've been unable to establish accurate data on the daily manpower losses of the 19th Panzer Division, but according to the daily report of its headquarters for 8 July, after the Kreida railyard and its adjacent area would be fully taken under German control, I/Panzergrenadier Regiment 73 alone was missing half its personnel. In German documents, the line of the 81st Guards Rifle Division is often called none other than "an unprecedented system of fortifications". In his book I.K. Morozov cites an excerpt from a document of the 19th Panzer Division, which listed several problems with which the enemy collided in the course of this fighting: "In addition to all else, the Russians obstructed the roads with fallen trees, and mined all the ravines and balkas and filled them with fuel, so whenever our tanks attempted to bound across them, they exploded, burned, sank to the bottom or were shot up by Russian heavy artillery."[28]

In reality, it was the first time for the Germans to encounter such elaborate defenses and skillfully-led troops. I.K. Morozov recalled one of the morning attacks on 7 July:

> Twenty German tanks, 10 self-propelled guns and up to one and a half infantry regiments were advancing from the south toward Mikhailovka and the Machine Tractor Station; 60 tanks and self-propelled guns and up to two infantry regiments of the Germans were attacking through the "Day of Harvest" collective farm toward Kreida. Flame-throwing tanks and infantry advancing in their wake had already broken through to the railyards and were pushing toward the commander's observation post [in one of the semi-destroyed grain elevators]. However, two battalions of Katiusha rocket launchers with thermite rockets that had been deeply dug into the ground at the railroad embankment had been patiently waiting for them for a long time. Not far to the east of them stood our famous anti-tank battalion led by the bravest gunner Captain Georgii Sushitsky [the 87th Guards Separate Destroyer Anti-Tank Artillery Battalion], whom our Guardsmen called "The War Hawk" for his energy and dash, ready to fire over open sights. … The tanks, emitting black smoke and fire, crawled toward the railroad embankment; self-propelled guns were accompanying them. Some were carrying submachine gunners on their armor. Now the group had crossed the low ground in front of the railroad, and the tanks began to climb upward. At this moment a volley of our anti-tank artillery and a salvo from our Guards mortars rang out. Everything became jumbled together, explosions and flames … The Katiusha thermite warheads were shattering on the tanks' armor and sending out billowing streams of fire. Machines and Nazi soldiers were being consumed in the flames. The self-propelled guns were bumping into the tanks and running over their own infantry. The battalions of Captains Kachanov,[29] Antonov,[30] Akimov,[31] Iarko[32] and Zavodsky[33] rose on the counterattack. The infantry finished off the work of the artillery gunners with bayonets. A sudden silence descended on the Kreida railyard.[34]

Morozov's memoirs came out in the early 1960s, and thus like the majority of publications of that time, it is overflowing with heroic pathos, but rather sparse in details. They only show the outline of the events, although with respect to facts, the author rarely sinned (there is the sense that Morozov relied not only on his own memory, but also worked with documents); practically all of the events described in his memoirs actually took place. For this reason, this source is valuable.

The rocket launchers weren't intended to counter tanks; however, in the course of the Battle of Kursk the Soviet side had to resort to them in order to repel tank attacks, including in the 7th Guards Army's sector, and they proved to be rather effective. The aggregation and analysis of such experience probably wasn't conducted after the battle, because so far no such documents have been found. Therefore the examples of the use of Katiusha rockets that are cited in the books by veterans of the battle are quite interesting. They brightly testify that the strength of the Voronezh Front's defense rested also on the initiative and creative approach to combat work of the soldiers and officers. So that the reader might become convinced of this, I'll cite the recollections of a

---

28 Morozov, I.K., *Polki srazhalis' po-gvardeiski* [*Regiments fought like Guards*] (Volgograd, 1962), p. 134.
29 Captain I.P. Kachanov – commander of 3/233rd Guards Rifle Regiment
30 Captain A.N. Antonov – commander of 2/233rd Guards Rifle Regiment
31 Major I.A. Akimov – commander of 1/235th Guards Rifle Regiment
32 Captain N.M. Iarko – commander of 1/233rd Guards Rifle Regiment
33 Captain Ia. Zavodsky – commander of 1/238th Guards Rifle Regiment
34 Morozov, *Polki srazhalis po-Gvardeiski*, pp. 136-137.

former commander of a BM-13 rocket artillery battery of the 79th Guards Mortar Regiment M.P. Ivanikhin:

> We knew that the fascists would be using a large quantity of tanks, and so it was necessary to learn to conduct direct fire from open firing positions at approaching enemy tanks. I immediately want to stipulate that the Katiusha couldn't really place targeted fire; it wasn't tube artillery. Its minimal range of fire at targets is just 400 meters, because of the fact that the guide rails are angled upwards. In order to place direct fire, it was necessary to point the guide rails directly at a target, and for this reason it was necessary dig the ground beneath the wheels of the truck so that they settled into this pit and the guide rails became parallel to the ground, which means they were pointing directly at a target.
>
> On 30 June 1943 test firing was conducted in our battery, which demonstrated that it was possible to fire in this manner. We drove out into a balka – a deep ravine that was overgrown with woods here and there, and set out targets. We dug the pit, which the forward wheels of the Studebakers would be entering, carefully aimed the weapon at a target, and fired one rocket. However, our rocket launchers and shells were designed for firing at area targets, so the scattering of the rockets is quite high. Thus, the rocket exploded 50 meters to the right of the target. We didn't fire any more rockets; it was clear that it would be possible to hit a tank in this way only if all 16 rockets were fired in a salvo. The attacking tanks would unquestionably stop if a warhead struck the tank itself, a track was broken or if fragments would hit the engine. This experience was later very beneficial in the course of the Battle of Kursk, when we often had to fire from open firing positions.[35]

I will add that the rocket launching crews also worked out, and then employed a means of firing a Katiusha so the shell would ricochet. At a certain angle of incidence with the ground it would ricochet upward by 8-12 meters, and if the detonator triggered at that height, the area of damage would significantly increase. Although all of the above-listed techniques were not in the manuals or part of the training curriculum, they often bailed the Guardsmen out when in a pinch.

> In the course of the Battle of Kursk, not only the largest BM-13 rocket launcher was used widely, but also the BM-8 and other rocket launchers. For example, in order to damage or destroy enemy armor on the Central Front, the BM-30 rocket launcher was used rather widely.[36] They equipped three brigades of the 5th Guards Mortar Division of the 4th Guards Artillery Breakthrough Corps of the Supreme Command Reserve. According to Soviet data, between 7 and 12 July this Guards mortar division brewed up 58 German tanks.[37] Even so,

---

35 Ivanikhin, M.A., Ivanikhin, P.P., *Kurskaia bitva* [*Battle of Kursk*] (Moscow: MGF "Veteran of Moscow, 2004), p. 79.
36 The BM-30 rocket launcher's main component was a 300mm rocket. It had been devised and accepted by the Red Army in 1942 and was intended for use against enemy firing positions and destroying enemy fieldworks in the tactical zone. It was launched from a wooden container, in which it was also transported. The rocket weighed 72 kilograms, including a warhead that weighed 28.9 kilograms. When exploding, the warhead would create a crater 8-meters in diameter and more than 2 meters deep. The rocket had a short range (2,800 meters) and low accuracy, and thus in March 1943 it was updated by a new model. With the new engine, its flight range almost doubled in distance. In combination with the large explosive charge, it proved to be a fully effective artillery weapon. It entered the troops under the code designation "M-31". In the spring of 1944 it appeared mounted on Studebaker trucks, which were used to launch the M-31 rockets.
37 *Sbornik No.11 po obobshcheniiu opyta voiny* [Manual No. 11 for analyzing the war's experience] (Moscow: Voenizdat, 1944), p. 127.

because of their construction and low mobility, it was difficult to use these systems for defensive fighting on tank-vulnerable directions.

However, let's return to the situation in the sector of the 7th Guards Army's right flank. Already by 0700 on 7 July, *Kampfgruppe* Köhler with the support of the 6th Panzer Division's armor had managed to force back Kriuchikhin's, Khitsov's and Titarenko's regiments, and having gained complete possession of the Kreida railyard, it had reached a line running from the crossroads in the southern section of Mikhailovka through the Kreida railyard to the western outskirts of Belovskaia. Officers of the 19th Panzer Division's headquarters wrote:

> Up to four battalions of the enemy with a large quantity of mortars and anti-tank rifles had fortified themselves in the railroad pits at Kreida that had been converted into pillboxes and in a fruit orchard that was located along both sides of the railroad south of Kreida that was completely riddled with fighting positions. At the least, 70-80% of these battalions were Asians [from Central Asia], the majority of which were superb shots. Taking many casualtiese and frequently bringing assault guns into action against isolated hardened positions, in close cooperation with the artillery and Nebelwerfers, Panzergrenadier Regiment 73 managed to take Kreida by the morning of 7 July. Often, the battle descended into hand-to-hand fighting. … The enemy suffered large losses. From Kreida, which had been transformed into ruins by the German artillery fire, the surviving remnants of two Russian divisions [81st Guards Rifle Division and the 228th Guards Rifle Regiment of the 78th Guards Rifle Division] withdrew to Blizhniaia Igumenka to prepared positions and into positions on the hills and in the woods located to the south of us.[38]

In this citation there are a lot of emotions, but few concrete details, so let's turn to a different source. Even when the Germans captured Kreida itself, the 81st Guards Rifle Division's system of fortifications remained viable; despite a strong attack from the railyard along the railroad bed to Staryi Gorod, the Germans failed to split the 81st Guards Rifle Division. From a report of the headquarters of III Panzer Corps for 8 July:

> The reinforced Panzergrenadier Regiment 73 at 0845 on 7.7 broke into strongly-fortified settlement and railroad yard of Kreida from two directions. After a northward advance to breakthrough the defenses of this settlement by units of Infantry Regiment 429, the regiment pivoted to the northwest, but despite the support of heavy weapons, stopped on a hill at a small patch of woods north of the "Day of Harvest" collective farm in front of a deeply-constructed and stubbornly defended system of positions west of the woods to the north of Belovskaia. Repeated attacks made no headway.[39]

With no less stubbornness *Kampfgruppe* Becker with Richter's Panzergrenadier Regiment 74 was putting pressure on the line of Captain A.N. Antonov's 2/233rd Guards Rifle Regiment in Belovskaia, striving to break through to Blizhniaia Igumenka. By the morning of 7 July, its panzers reached the western outskirts of Belovskaia and consolidated their grip on them. Between Becker's *kampfgruppe* and Panzergrenadier Regiment 73, Reconnissance Battalion 19 was slowly and stealthily making its way from the "Day of Harvest" collective farm to the hamlet of the Machine Tractor Station. Bypassing knots of resistance and infiltrating through the combat positions of

---

38 TsAMO RF, f. 38 A, op. 0927, d. 46, l. 4.
39 NARA US, rg. 242, t. 314, r. 197, f. 001205.

the Guardsmen, this unit managed to penetrate to an area just 3 kilometers short of the southern outskirts of Blizhniaia Igumenka. However, the 81st Guards Rifle Division's system of defense was so complex and multi-tiered that even having found itself within them, the 19th Panzer Division's reconnaissance battalion was unable to crack it.

Between 0830 and 0930 as had been planned by the headquarters of Army Detachment Kempf, German bombers of VIII Fliegerkorps appeared above the 25th Guards Rifle Corps' right flank. Twenty-six Ju-87 Stukas struck positions in Staryi Gorod, Blizhniaia Igumenka, Iastrebovo, Miasoedovo and on Hill 207.8. Major General I.K. Morozov was an experienced division commander who had passed through the furnace of Stalingrad; thus, when studying how the enemy was behaving from his observation post before the air raid, he guessed the enemy's intentions and issued an order for the troops in Staryi Gorod and Dal'niaia Igumenka to evacuate the trenches and get into shelters. On the entire forward edge of Major G.T. Skiruta's 235th Guards Rifle Regiment, there remained only a rifle company of the 2nd Battalion and approximately two dozen Maksim machine-gun crews along the eastern bank of the Donets in the special wells that had been dug into the earth almost to the level of the river's surface. Just as soon as the German air raid ended and the dust began to settle, the Guardsmen of Captain A.F. Goshtinar's 2nd Rifle Battalion and Captain I.Ia. Sokolenko's 3rd Rifle Battalion returned to their positions.

A short time later, combat groups of the 168th Infantry Divisions Infantry Regiments 417 and 429 moved out of the Kreida railyard and Mikhailovka toward their positions. The battalions met the enemy with heavy fire. I.K. Morozov recalled:

> Attacking the Staryi Gorod center of resistance, the Nazis were simultaneously striving to divert our attention and forces from the axis of their main attack in the direction of the Kreida railyard, the village of Belovskaia, and Sevriukovo. By 0900 on 7 July 1943, the division had been compressed into the shape of a horseshoe, the right arm of which comprised the Staryi Gorod center of resistance and Mikhailovka. Here the fascists with remnants of the 168th Infantry Division undertook ceaseless, but already weakening attacks. The Kreida railyard at this time was the center of the horseshoe, and German tanks, self-propelled guns and infantry were also attacking it. A mortal threat was hanging over the left arm of the horseshoe from the "Day of Harvest" collective farm to the villages of Belovskaia and Sevriukovo – an enemy breakthrough into the rear. An enemy that had broken through from the southeast might cause our defenses to collapse and press us back toward Staryi Gorod and Mikhailovka, and then with a simultaneous attack from the west – out of Belgorod, and from the east – toward Sevriukovo and Belovskaia, smash the division into pieces.[40]

The events were developing according to just this scenario. Immediately after the Stuka strikes, the 19th and 6th Panzer Divisions moved out once again on the attack. Becker's *panzerkampfgruppe* together with Infantry Regiment 442 and Reconnaissance Battalion 19 launched an attack out of Belovskaia in the direction of the hamlet of the Machine Tractor Station and the southern outskirts of Blizhniaia Igumenka, while von Oppeln's *panzerkampfgruppe* and Unrein's panzer grenadiers attempted to force a crossing of the Razumnaia River at Iastrebovo, which was located on the river's western bank. In order to execute a dash into the rear of the 81st Guards Rifle Division, tanks were necessary, so it was important for von Oppeln-Bronikowski to seize Iastrebovo as quickly as possible and create a bridgehead there for crossing the armor. In the process, while seizing Iastrebovo he ordered to preserve the bridges there, in order to save time from building new bridges.

---

40 Morozov, *Polki srazhalis' po-Gvardeiski*, p. 135.

On the evening of 6 July, considering the possibility of a panzer division emerging on the deep left flank of his division, I.K. Morozov decided to reinforce the villages along the Razumnaia River. Major I.A. Khitsov's 228th Guards Rifle Regiment of the 78th Guards Rifle Division, which had fallen back into the sector of the 81st Guards Rifle Division, was extended along the (excl.) Belovskaia – Iastrebovo – Sevriukovo sector. He moved up the 161st Guards Cannon Artillery Regiment and the 114th Guards Destroyer Anti-tank Artillery Regiment to the areas of Iastrebovo and Sevriukovo from their positions near Blizhniaia Igumenka and Staryi Gorod. Both regiments had the slow-moving S-60 tractors to tow their guns, and in addition to this the anti-tank artillery regiment was experiencing an acute deficit of motorized transport for delivering ammunition and food. Therefore their shift in location went slowly, all through the night, and despite the great exertions made by the artillerymen, by the start of the 6th Panzer Division's offensive they hadn't fully had time to assemble the artillery in their designated positions. Striving to carry out the order in time, the crew of one 76mm gun of the 1st Battery of the 114th Guards Destroyer Anti-tank Artillery Regiment was forced, as noted in the regiment's account, "to haul the gun through their own efforts"[41] from the area of the "Day of Harvest" collective farm to Iastrebovo. Simply speaking, seven artillerymen spent all night manhandling a gun that weighed more than 1-tonne plus the shells for it to Iastrebovo, which was located approximately 5.5 kilometers from their previous firing positions. The dawn of 7 July found the crews of the 114th Destroyer Anti-tank Artillery Regiment in the area of four villages: the 4th Battery with two guns was deployed 1 kilometer northwest of Iastrebovo; the 3rd Battery in full and the 1st Battery with 1 gun (and one on the way) were on the eastern outskirts of Sevriukovo; the 5th Battery with two guns (and two on the way) was on the northern outskirts of Miasoedovo; and the 2nd Battery with three guns was on the southwestern outskirts of Sheino. At this same time, howitzers of the 1st and 3rd Battalions of the 161st Guards Cannon Artillery Regiment were beginning to unlimber in open firing positions in Iastrebovo, while the 2nd Battalion was still on the march between Sevriukovo and Sheino. Nevertheless, it was these two regiments that became the backbone of the defense of Iastrebovo, Sevriukovo and Miasoedovo, and it was thanks to the resolve of their soldiers and officers that the 6th and 7th Panzer Divisions failed to push beyond Miasoedovo on this day.

From the early morning of 7 July, the artillery of III Panzer Corps and the 6th Panzer Division conducted strong, concentrated fire on all the villages along the Razumnaia River where the Guardsmen of Safiulin's 25th Guards Rifle Corps had taken up a defense. Under the cover of this barrage, small groups of German submachine gunners began to move out. They'd been given the task to cross the river and in the first place to wipe out the groups of Soviet sappers that were ready to blow up the bridges and the artillery crews. However, Major I.A. Khitsov anticipated the enemy's intentions and thwarted them. Right after the German artillery opened up, at the agreement of I.K. Morozov, he blew up the bridge in Iastrebovo. Thereby, he delayed the 6th Panzer Division's advance by several hours, though panzergrenadiers of its two panzergrenadier regiments started to force a crossing of the river at a ford immediately after the explosion and became tied up in combat with the battalions of the 228th Guards Rifle Regiment. From the report of the 6th Panzer Division:

> After a preparatory Stuka attack on enemy targets in and around Iastrebovo, von Oppeln's *panzerkampfgruppe* began to attack out of the Hill 207.9 area and Unrein's *kampfgruppe* out of the Belinskaia area to the north against the enemy located in Sevruikovo and Iastrebovo. The panzer group, with the II/Grenadier Regiment 114 and Unrein's *kampfgruppe* [I/ Panzergrenadier Regiment 4], quickly crossed the Razumnaia River, pushed the enemy out of

---

41 TsAMO RF, f. 114 gv. aiptap, op. 10873, op. 8808ss, d. 4, l. 328.

the village, and captured the high ground directly west of the northern edge of Sevriukovo. All of the bridges leading to the roads on the eastern bank were destroyed. While the bridges on the southern edge of Iastrebovo were repaired in three hours' time, tank attacks were launched from the north, but they were all repulsed. Because of them, a bridge hasn't been laid down to allow the tanks to cross the Razumnaia. *Kampfgruppen* Bieberstein and Unrein did cross over the bridge.[42]

It is hard to say anything about the tank attacks mentioned in the report from Hünersdorff's panzer division. At this moment in the sector of the 81st Guards Rifle Division there were 6 operational KV tanks of the 262nd Separate Heavy Tank Regiment; there were no other tank units present. Four of the KV tanks (the 1st Tank Company) were located on loading docks in Blizhniaia Igumenka (from which they never left) and 1 KV tank was on the southern outskirts of Miasoedovo. When I.K. Morozov received information from the commander of the 228th Guards Rifle Regiment about German attempts to build a bridge in Iastrebovo, he ordered the chief of staff of the 262nd Separate Heavy Tank Regiment Captain Kostin, who was constantly located at its command post, to send the last KV tank (the headquarters KV) to the western outskirts of Iastrebovo. According to Operational Summary No.140, the crew of this KV tank engaged in combat with German tanks that had broken through from the Belinskaia area, and set two of them ablaze. The KV tank also took a hit that set it on fire, but the crew managed to abandon the tank; however, by 1800 7 July only the driver-mechanic had made it back to the regiment.[43] It is possible that during the crossing of the 6th Panzer Division's panzergrenadiers, Major I.A. Khitsov launched a counterattack with the participation of this KV and the Germans took this as something more. However, this is just a supposition that hasn't yet been confirmed by documents.

Von Bieberstein's submachine gunners, having driven back the companies of the 228th Guards Rifle Regiment from the outskirts did in fact break into Iastrebovo, but there became bogged down in heavy street fighting. At this time Unrein's *kampfgruppe* began to break through to Sevriukovo along the river valley (along the right bank), where the headquarters of the 81st Guards Rifle Division was located, while on the left bank the 6th Panzer Division's reconnaissance battalion, reinforced with two panzer companies, including one of Tigers, was trying to break through to the same village while under fire from the 31st Separate Destroyer Anti-tank Artillery Brigade. After the units of the 81st Guards Rifle Division had become tied up in fighting in Iastrebovo and Sevriukovo, Hünersdorff launched an attack with his *panzerkampfgruppe* to the northeast in order to reach Melikhovo. However, he was unable to break the resistance of the Guardsmen that were defending here quickly, despite the fact that at a minimum half of the 6th Panzer Division had concentrated here.

After the 19th Panzer Division took Belovskaia, the significance of Iastrebovo and Blizhniaia Igumenka for the enemy increased. These two strongpoints were located practically side by side and were blocking the path to the boundary between the 7th Guards and 6th Guards Armies. Therefore on that morning Breith committed two panzer divisions simultaneously in order to seize them, hoping for a quick success. Iastrebovo was being defended by only meager forces: a battalion of the 228th Guards Rifle Regiment, the 1st and 3rd Battalions of the 161st Guards Cannon Artillery Regiment (12 122mm howitzers), the 4th Battery of the 114th Guards Destroyer Anti-tank Artillery Regiment and one KV tank of the 262nd Separate Heavy Tank Regiment. When under enemy pressure the infantry of the 228th Guards Rifle Regiment began to retreat from the village center around 1000, the 8th and 2nd Batteries of the cannon artillery regiment wound up

---

42 Haupt, *Srazheniia gruppy armii "Iug"*, pp. 294-295.
43 TsAMO RF, f. 72 gv. otp, op. 27453, d. 1, l. 107.

in a difficult situation. German tanks approached within direct fire distance to their firing positions. However, the howitzer crews didn't flinch and lowered their gun muzzles for direct fire, and in a fleeting combat action they knocked out or destroyed 9 enemy tanks, forcing the enemy to withdraw. Unfortunately, in the course of this clash the artillerymen suffered heavy casualties. According to information from the regiment's headquarters, of the howitzer crews 7 were killed and 11 wounded. In addition, the chiefs of staff of both artillery battalions that took part in the battle, Senior Lieutenants V.N. Gorshkov and A.M. Nikitin suffered serious wounds, as did the cannon artillery regiment's deputy commander Major Fokin. Shell fragments damaged the sight and pivot mechanism on one howitzer, and the recoil mechanism of another howitzer. Two Ford cars and a GAZ-AA were left burned out by direct hits from a tank, while an S-60 tow tractor took damage to its radiator. Nevertheless, both artillery battalions abandoned their line only after the Germans had almost fully taken Iastrebovo. In the process, despite the fire, they managed to take with them all their materiel and the bodies of their fallen comrades. From a report of the 6th Panzer Division on the evening of 7 July:

> During the occupation of … Iastrebovo and Sevriukovo on 7 July the enemy offered tenacious resistance, supported by tanks. The withdrawal, which was also observed from the air and which was taken at first as the sign of a general retreat, was contrary to the continuing resistance and the contents of an intercepted radio signal, in which they were ordered to hold on. The enemy's air force made its presence felt with bombs and aircraft weapons.[44]

Judging from captured German documents, the alarm in both Army Detachment Kempf and Army Group South because of the inability to screen the Fourth Panzer Army's flank was growing with each day. So from the morning of 7 July, their commands were demanding great efforts with the aim of fundamentally changing the situation in this area. Breith's panzer corps was making such little headway because his forces were approximately equal to those of the defenders. Understanding this, the headquarters of Army Group South attempted to help him, not with additional forces and equipment, but by means of a regrouping. Von Manstein's headquarters believed that the 168th Infantry Division was being used ineffectively, having been split up among the panzer divisions, and so it decided to gather it together and assign it an independent sector of the front. Thus, Breith's panzer forces would be freed from tasks for which they were unaccustomed, like destroying the Russians' deeply-echeloned defenses, and the infantry would take over this job. In addition, hoping that on 7 July, or in the extreme case on 8 July the panzer corps would nevertheless overcome the 7th Guards Army's defensive belts, the command of Army Group South decided to ensure that the panzer divisions would have an opportunity for a dash into the depth of the Voronezh Front's defenses by having previously readied forces for tying up Shumilov's troops in combat on the flanks of Army Detachment Kempf's breakthrough. Responsibility for this would be given to the 168th Infantry Division, Korps Raus, and the 198th Infantry Division that was already approaching for it. Incidentally, Speidel personally informed Raus about this at 1155 and let him know that the earliest arrival of this division would be on 9 July.[45] Even if a breakthrough wasn't achieved on 7 July, it was assumed that the 168th Infantry Division would take on the encirclement of the center of resistance in Staryi Gorod, while the main forces of the 6th and 19th Panzer Divisions that had been activated here would be relieved of this task and would join the corps' assault wedge in order to reinforce it.

---

44 Haupt, *Srazheniia gruppy armii "Iug"*, p. 295.
45 NARA US, t. 312, r. 54, f. 7569622.

At 1045 the Chief of Staff of the Army Group Theodor Busse called the command post of the 168th Infantry Division and asked if there was a practical chance to pull the division together efficiently and how much time this would require. Having received an affirmative reply, he emphasized that in the meantime the division had to act according to III Panzer Corps' plan, but just a short time later III Panzer Corps received a directive: no later than 8 July to gather all of the division's regiments under the command of the 168th Infantry Division headquarters.[46] Thus, despite the complete disruption in the offensive's timetable, the high losses, the obvious inability of Kempf to implement the plan of Operation Citadel with his available forces and the operation's unclear prospects, the command of Army Group South didn't "throw in its hand" and persistently tried to execute the plan in its existing form, making no changes, relying on the calculation of the Wehrmacht's superiority on a tactical level and its advantage in command and control over the troops.

Around this same time (at 1200) Speidel was also having an intensive conversation, but with the command of the 10th Flak Division, the chief of staff of Luftflotte IV and the chief of staff of Flak Corps I, with the same objective of increasing the effectiveness of command over the troops and arranging closer cooperation with the air forces, which thus far hadn't been on a high level. As Army Group South's combat journal notes: "The chief of staff of the Army Group established that in fact, cooperation with the Flak units during attacks is impossible. Requests being sent up the line of command aren't reaching the Flak Corps."[47] Nevertheless, Speidel gained the understanding of the Luftflotte IV command, which promised to give as much effective support as possible to the ground forces of Army Group South.

Kempf was also completely absorbed with the complicated situation in III Panzer Corps. At 1200 he drove out to visit Breith, and then traveled together with him to the area north of Generalovka to have a discussion with the commander of the 6th Panzer Division Major General W. von Hünersdorff, get his opinion about the prospects of a breakthrough, and try to anticipate the subsequent actions of his *panzerkampfgruppe*. The journey over the chewed-up roads in the frontal zone wasn't simple, and thus Kempf returned to his command post in Dolbino only at 1600, even though he hadn't had to cover much distance. Judging from the captured German documents, Army Detachment Kempf's commander was out of contact during his trip and was unable to receive any new information while on it. Speidel also didn't communicate anything other than the results of his conversations with the Luftwaffe and his order to the army detachment regarding the 168th Infantry Division. Thus, neither of them was promising any reinforcements; the panzer division commanders therefore had to act as before with their available forces, so there was only one way out of the jam in order to resolve the main task: Crush the enemy while there was still enough strength to do so, and this was clearly apparent in their efforts.

The course of the 25th Guards Rifle Corps' combat with the 6th Panzer Division for possession of the villages along the Razumnaia River, which by the middle of the day went with the greatest success among all the divisions of III Panzer Corps, is described sparsely and not completely understandably in the Soviet documents, while judging from everything, the summary reports of Breith's subordinate divisions have been lost. In Combat Report No.60 of the 81st Guards Rifle Division for 1500 on 7 July 1943, it is indicated that "the enemy, having superiority in tanks at 1100 shoved back the units that were defending Belovskaia, Sevriukovo and Iastrebovo and took the latter. The division command post moved to the hamlet of Postnikov. ... The division's

---

46 Ibid.
47 NARA US, t. 312, r. 54, f. 7569622.

communications with the rear services has been interrupted, and there are difficulties in bringing up food and ammunition."[48]

The account of the 25th Guards Rifle Corps states:

> 81st Guards Rifle Division with attached assets and the 228th Guards Rifle Regiment of the 78th Guards Rifle Division from 0400 7 July engaged in bitter fighting with the attacking enemy. <u>At 1130 the enemy</u> in strength of up to five battalions of infantry with the support of 150 tanks and aircraft broked through the forward edge of defense of the 233rd Guards Rifle Regiment and <u>reached the line: eastern outskirts of Sevriukovo</u>, Point 215.5, Point +1.0, Hill 212.1, northern outskirts of Blizhniaia Igumenka, thereby turning the left flank of the 81st Guards Rifle Division ... 228th Guards Rifle Regiment, which was operating in the 81st Guards Rifle Division's sector, after the enemy breakthrough of the 81st Guards Rifle Division's left flank, was withdrawn into the second echelon and took up a defense on the western outskirts of Nikol'skoe.[49]

The hills mentioned in the above account are located 3 to 4 kilometers northwest of Iastrebovo. Thus according to the information available to the 25th Guards Corps headquarters, already by around noontime the 19th and 6th Panzer Divisions had taken complete possession of Belovskaia and Iastrebovo, and a portion of Sevriukovo. The information in the 81st Guards Rifle Division's account says approximately the same thing.

However, the situation probably unfolded more rapidly than that. The 94th Guards Rifle Division didn't reach the sector of the 7th Guards Army in time (by 0300 7 July); its regiments were moving 6-7 hours behind schedule and entered combat with the 6th Panzer Division's *kampfgruppen* from the march. Here is an excerpt from Operational Summary No.0100/op at 2000 on 7 July: "2. At 1000 7.7.43 the 94th Guards Rifle Division, having replaced the units of the 81st Guards Rifle Division, made contact with the enemy. The enemy took Sevriukovo and broke into the southern half of Miasoedovo before the division could take up a defense."[50]

Today it is difficult to determine which headquarters is closer to the truth and the exact time when the 6th Panzer Division took the two key villages of Iastrebovo and Sevriukovo, because the majority of Soviet commanders were governed by one main principle: "When we fight, it is each to his own." This is plainly seen in operational documents. Almost all of the headquarters reported to higher headquarters only about their own troops and only very rarely mentioned neighbors, even though the manuals about the work of headquarters of the Red Army made it obligatory to indicate neighbors on the flanks and the situation there. Thus, for example, if an operational summary states that a regiment retreated from some village, this still doesn't mean that the enemy had taken it. It is fully possible that the troops of a neighboring division were still continuing to fight there. More than once when working with the archival documents, I've encountered such a situation. In addition, certain commanders seemingly "by mistake" deliberately omitted key moments and mention of the neighbors in their reports, thereby creating confusion in order to shrug off responsibility for a failure.

However, let's return to the events in the Iastrebovo – Sevriukovo – Miasoedovo sector. Here, at first units of the 81st and 78th Guards Rifle Division and elements of at least one tank regiment and four artillery regiments were defending on that morning, but later the 94th Guards Rifle Division began to arrive from the march, as did the 148th Separate Tank Regiment and the 31st

---

48 TsAMO RF, f. 81 gv. sd, op. 1, d. 7, l. 288.
49 TsAMO RF, f. 25 gv. sk, op. 1, d. 27, l. 5.
50 TsAMO RF, f. 1269, op. 1, d. 9, l. 125.

Separate Destroyer Anti-tank Artillery Brigade from the area of the "Solov'ev" collective farm. Relying on their information, the situation is seen as follows. First, in the middle of the day (1200 to 1300) the Germans attacked through Iastrebovo, emerged on the lines of communication of Morozov's 81st Guards Rifle Division and continued to spread like locusts in the depth of the 25th Guards Rifle Corps' defenses. Already at 1000, panzergrenadiers of the 7th Panzer Division also entered the major center of resistance of Miasoedovo, which was located next to Sevriukovo, while German tanks were engaged on the eastern outskirts with artillery of the 94th Guards Rifle Division that was arriving from the march. However, we'll discuss this a bit later. Thereby, a breach had been created on the boundary between the 81st and 73rd Guards Rifle Divisions, which began gradually to expand, while Morozov's division wound up in semi-encirclement. Its only escape route was to the north, but no one in the division was even thinking about retreating. Second, even after mid-day Sevriukovo didn't come under the control of the enemy; at this time, Unrein's panzergrenadiers and a company of Tigers were stilled locked in combat on its outskirts.

I was able to find one interesting document – a description of the combat of two batteries of the 114th Guards Destroyer Anti-tank Artillery Regiment with the Tigers of the Heavy Panzer Battalion 503 that was attached to the 6th Panzer Division, which was prepared for the artillery headquarters of the 7th Guards Army by an eyewitness, the anti-tank artillery regiment's chief of staff Captain Lutov:

> 7.7 In the area of Sevriukovo the battery commanded by Senior Lieutenant Zykov was attacked by enemy tanks. The tanks moved [obliquely] with their flanks exposed to the battery. First an echelon of Tigers, then medium tanks. Having allowed them to approach to within 600 meters, the crews opened fire at vulnerable spots: tracks, the running gear and the rear hull. Fire was conducted with armor-piercing – incendiary shells. With 13 hits, 3 Pz-VI were left burning. Then the enemy opened up intensive artillery fire on the battery's position. The soldiers were crouched and resolutely waiting for when the barrage would end. However, now the tanks shifted and attacked the battery head-on. Two Tiger tanks were knocked out 70 meters from the firing positions, one after five hits; the other after four. Fire was concentrated on the running gear and the drive sprocket. An armor-piercing shell doesn't penetrate the tank's frontal armor, but easily penetrates the turret's side armor. It has been noticed that if the tank crew spots an anti-tank gun, the tank pivots and strives to approach it by any means while only presenting its frontal armor.[51]

As soon as von Oppeln's *panzerkampfgruppe* began moving into jumping-off positions for the attack against Major D.I. Zorin's regiment, the army commander contacted I.K. Morozov and warned him that in the nearest time, enemy tanks would be in the village where at that moment the headquarters of the 81st Guards Rifle Division was still located, and issued an order for the bridge to be blown. Recalled I.K. Morozov:

> The enemy went on the attack simultaneously from the west and the east. Army commander Shumilov called: "A major enemy tank formation is approaching. It will be necessary to blow up the bridges in Sevriukovo and Iastrebovo within an hour or an hour and a half. Otherwise …." We understood ourselves what would happen if "otherwise" took place. I summoned the commander of a demolition team Sergeant Nikolai Krasiukov. He was informed that within an hour or less, a Nazi tank formation would emerge in our rear and might rout us. [His] task was to blow up the bridge in Sevriukovo.

---

51   TsAMO RF, f. 114 gv. aiptap, F. 10873, op. 8808ss, d. 4, l. 351.

Within 30 minutes, a squad of sappers crawled up to the bridge, dragging a demolition charge. Although the bridge had been prepared for demolition, Krasiukov grabbed a spare one just in case.

Bullets were kicking up dust on the dirt road; it seemed that the earth was smoking under the heat of the sun. Krasiukov's men kept crawling forward. One Guardsman was wounded. The rest, tightly hugging the earth, went into a belly crawl.

They attached the additional demolition charge to a bridge support, and Krasiukov gave a signal. The sappers crawled back and Krasiukov lit the fuse. After this he dropped to the ground and kept an eye on the burning fuse. Thirty enemy tanks, deployed in a column, were approaching the bridge. The Germans wanted to extinguish the fuse and prevent the bridge from blowing up.

Krasiukov realized this, abruptly turned around and quickly crawled back to the bridge. He gave a long burst from his submachine gun at the Germans. Two or three Nazis toppled into the water, and the rest began to fall back at a crawl.

The lead tank approached the bridge at a great speed. It was already on the middle of the bridge when there was a large explosion. The steel monster – the tank – flew into the air, and then plummeted downward. The order had been carried out. The bridge had been demolished; the tanks didn't make it across.[52]

Sergeant N. Krasiukov received a severe wound when the bridge exploded, but his combat comrades dragged him away out from under enemy fire and took him to a medical-sanitation battalion. From there, Krasiukov went to a hospital.

After the strike by Stuka dive bombers of Fliegerkorps VIII (between 0845 and 0915), the bitterest fighting developed in and around Blizhniaia Igumenka and to the south. Approximately from 0930 and until mid-day, Becker's *panzerkampfgruppe* and Reconnaissance Battalion 19 persistently attacked the positions of the 233rd Guards Rifle Regiment and the 262nd Heavy Tank Regiment in the vicinity of this village and the hamlet of the Machine Tractor Station. Around 1200 enemy tanks broke through to the southern outskirts of Blizhniaia Igumenka, and at that moment a tragic mistake took place which cost the lives of several dozen of our soldiers and officers. The point is that Major S. Titarenko's regiment and one company of Colonel I.I. Azenberg's[53] heavy tank regiment were conducting a withdrawal on the night of 6-7 July from the

---

52 Morozov, *Polki srazhalis' po-Gvardeiski*, pp. 138-139.
53 Isaak Il'ich Aizenberg (Colonel, 30.01.1943) was born in April 1900 in Belaia Tserkva (Ukraine). He completed four years in a city school, and then took up a job as a buyer and seller of gold. Aizenberg joined the Red Army in 1919 and participated in the Russian Civil War. He passed through training in the 2nd Moscow Infantry School in 1923. He served in rifle units until the early 1930s, but in 1932, after completing the Moscow Armor Courses he switched to the tank troops. In 1938 he completed the evening school of the Frunze Military Academy. For his successful study in the academy, he was awarded a monthly salary, a set of dress suits and a silver watch. Aizenberg fought in the Winter War with Finland. On 23.3.1941 he became the operations chief in the headquarters of Odessa Military District's 47th Tank Division. On 9.9.1941 he was transferred to take the post of chief of combat training of the Khar'kov Military District's Armored and Mechanized Forces, before becoming chief of this department on 7.01.1942. Aizenberg returned to the acting army on the Voronezh Front in January 1942. On 24.01.1942 he became the chief of staff of the 4th Tank Corps' 47th Tank Brigade, and on 26.06.1942, the commander of the 18th Tank Corps' 110th Tank Brigade. On 16.09.1942 Aizenberg was dismissed from this post "due to inability to cope with his responsibilities". On 30.09.1942 he became the deputy commander of the 25th Tank Corps' 162nd Tank Brigade. From November 1942, Aizenberg served as the commander of the 14th Separate Training Tank Regiment of the Voronezh Front. On 09.04.1943, he took command of the 262nd Separate Tank Regiment. Between December 1943 and April 1944, he attended the High Command Courses in the Red Army's Military Academy of Motorized and Mechanized Forces.

area of the "Day of Harvest" collective farm. The divisional artillery regiment was never informed of this, so when word came about a breakthrough of enemy tanks to the southern outskirts the division commander demanded to increase the artillery fire, but the crews of the 173rd Guards Artillery Regiment mistook the KV tanks as enemy machines and opened fire at them. From the 262nd Heavy Tank Regiment's report:

> At 2100 6.7.43 because of the absence of the 81st Guards Rifle Division's infantry, the tanks of the 1st Tank Company, numbering 4 KV switched their line of defense and moved to the area of Blizhniaia Igumenka. At 1200 7.7.43 the artillery of the 81st Guards Rifle Division opened fire at the tanks of the 1st Tank Company. As a result of concentrated anti-tank artillery fire on the part of the enemy and our own artillery, 3 tanks of the 1st Tank Company were destroyed. Killed: tank commander Lieutenant Gurov, tank commander Lieutenant Pinarsky, Senior Sergeant Kovalev and Guards Sergeant Major Diubin. Severely wounded: Lieutenant Shamarov, Sergeant Major Elin and a junior driver-mechanic. Missing: Company commander Senior Lieutenant Belov with his tank, and company commander Senior Lieutenant Kosenov.[54]

According to the 7th Guards Army's Operational Summary No.360, at 1300 the Germans seized the southern outskirts of Blizhniaia Igumenka, while Infantry Regiment 442, which was attached to the 19th Panzer Division, was attempting to break through to its northeastern outskirts from the direction of Belovskaia.[55] At the same time, striving to divert 81st Guards Rifle Division's forces onto themselves, units of Major General Chales de Beaulieu's 168th Infantry Division again launched an attack at 1300 out of the vicinities of Mikhailovka and Kreida toward Staryi Gorod. From the morning report of the 168th Infantry Division on 8 July: "The attack, conducted in the afternoon hours by a reinforced company to the north along both sides of the road was stopped south of the road fork 700 meters to the northwest of the Kreida railyard after advancing just 300 meters due to heavy mining on the east side of the road and growing enemy resistance in the vicinity of the hamlet of the Machine Tractor Station. At the same time, strong mortar fire was suddenly opened from the area of Staryi Gorod."[56]

With systematic attacks by the *panzerkampfgruppe* and infantry units, Breith's III Panzer Corps was persistently attempt to shatter the defense of Morozov's division, but it was tenaciously clinging to its line. The division commander recalled:

> Three kilometers southeast of Belovskaia, approximately 40 tanks, 20 self-propelled guns and up to a regiment of infantry of the enemy's emerged in our rear. The division's rear elements were cut off and connection with the neighbor on the left [the 73rd Guards Rifle Division] was lost. Only the news from the right-hand neighbor [the 375th Rifle Division], which was still strongly holding on to its positions, was positive. We reported to the Front's deputy commander General of the Army I.P. Apanasenko about our situation and assured him that we would fight to the last man, and if things were difficult on other sectors of the front, we would try to get by without any assistance. We requested only one thing – water.

After returning to the front, Aizenberg resumed command of the same tank regiment, but in August 1944 he was transferred to take command of the 40th Engineer Tank Regiment. He ended the war in this post. Between 1940 and 1945, he received four concussions and two wounds. On 08.05.1946, he was discharged from the ranks of the Red Army due to illness.

54 TsAMO RF, f. 7 gv. A, op. 5330, d. 60, l. 13.
55 TsAMO RF, f. 7 gv. A, op. 5312, d. 239, l. 162.
56 NARA, rg. 242, t. 314, r. 197, f. 001175.

The Northern Donets was filled with enemy corpses, so it was impossible to drink the filthy, contaminated water.[57]

The absence of not only drinking water, but also water for the Maksim heavy machine guns was a serious problem, especially for the soldiers of the 233rd Guards Rifle Regiment. Having taken Kreida and Belovskaia, the enemy had cut the regiment off from its main water sources: the drilled wells of the railyard, from which pipes ran to street hand pumps and to the main gander for refilling the tenders of the steam engines and the wells in the village.

I.P. Apanasenko arrived in the Voronezh Front from the Far East not long before the start of the Battle of Kursk as an "apprentice" to N.F. Vatutin, and at the Front Commander-in-Chief's behest during the battle he would drive out to the most-threatened sectors of the front in order to monitor the execution of orders and to lend a hand to the army commanders. On the morning of 7 July he arrived at the command post of the 35th Guards Rifle Corps in Zaiach'e, in order to assess how the moving out of its divisions was going. After this he arrived in Postnikov together with the corps commander S.G. Goriachev, to where the headquarters of the 81st Guards Rifle Division was in the process of moving. Having heard I.K. Morozov's report, he directed immediate help from the corps' rear services. With great difficulty the command of the 35th Guards Rifle Corps organized the delivery of water to the division, but even so the shortage of it was felt over all the following days. In addition, having familiarized himself with the situation in the Staryi Gorod – Blizhniaia Igumenka area and obtained information about the available forces at the disposal of the division commander, the General of the Army Anapasenko promised help with artillery. At the same time, he made it clear that they couldn't count on much.

In the morning, information from the reconnaissance battalion had arrived in the headquarters of the 7th Panzer Division. It had moved out of the area of the "Batratskaia Dacha" State Farm and approached the positions of the 25th Guards Rifle Corps' second echelon. The scouts informed that on the right bank of the Koren' River from Nikol'sky to the south, there was a strong defensive line that was being occupied by fresh troops (the 15th Guards Rifle Division). Thus, a further advance toward Shebekino was impossible. Von Funck wrote: "A report arrived from the reconnaissance battalion that just 2 kilometers east of the "Batratskaia Dacha" State Farm it had run into major enemy forces with artillery, which might not only give a check to our offensive to the east, but were also on their part showing offensive intentions. In addition, aerial reconnaissance was reporting intense enemy movements along the Koren' River."

In this situation, the III Panzer Corps allowed von Funck to improvise, which meant it was up to him to devise a plan of subsequent actions. The 7th Panzer Division headquarters sent Reconnaissance Battalion 37 an order: to conduct a reconnaissance-in-force and to attempt to envelop the opposing forces from the flanks.

Meanwhile, von Funck himself concentrated on preparing a breakthrough of the second army-level defensive belt. He decided to use the standard approach – a double envelopment. He directed his main forces to seize the woods southwest of Miasoedovo, in order to break through them to Arkad'evka, and then having pivoted to the left, to seize Hill 210.3 northeast of Miasoedovo. As a result, his forces, having bypassed the strongly-fortified point of Miasoedovo, were to link up with the 6th Panzer Division, which was attacking along the Razumnaia River to the northeast through Sevriukovo, and therefore take Miasoedovo in a ring. Consequently, the opportunity would appear to attack the exposed right flank of the 73rd Guards Rifle Division. In the event that this plan worked and the 7th Panzer Division would reach the Borovskoe – Nikol'skoe area while the 106th Infantry Division broke through Gremiachii to Pentsevo, the threat of the encirclement

---

57 Morozov, *Polki srazhalis' po-Gvardeiski*, p. 136.

of the entire grouping of Soviet forces opposite the 106th Infantry Division and on the right flank of the 7th Panzer Division would arise. Given further pressure, there would be the chance to force it to withdraw from the western bank of the Koren' River to the eastern bank. If this happened, Korps Raus would receive the opportunity, as had been determined in the plan for Operation Citadel, to start to construct a defensive front along the Koren' River.

In order to resolve this task, von Funck that morning assembled Gläsemer's panzergrenadiers in the area of Hill 207.9 and to the west of there, and positioned his *panzerkampfgruppe* behind them. The panzergrenadiers' first attack was directed at the "Solov'ev" collective farm and the woods around it, which were being held by the 148th Separate Tank Regiment. Recalled von Funck:

> Simultaneously with the defensive measures, preparations were underway to form a strong combat group that consisted primarily of motorized infantry for an attack against the strongly-fortified positions in the Miasoedovo area. The terrain conditions were unsuitable for the use of tanks. Thus, several panzer companies were assigned to support the attack. Despite the enemy's powerful artillery and mortar fire and the stubborn resistance of his infantry, the first attack went off successfully. It was necessary to take immediate advantage of the favorable situation that had developed. The division brought up another group of motorized infantry to the northern section of the large wooded area [southeast of Miasoedovo], while the panzer regiment and a battalion of self-propelled guns were standing ready to the west of the woods. Artillery positions were selected with the calculation that the artillery might provide support to the combat even in the area of the wooded hill 2-3 kilometers northeast of Miasoedovo [Hill 210.3].[58]

The fighting in the Hill 207.9 – "Solov'ev" collective farm area lasted for several hours. As a result a group of von Funck's tanks and panzergrenadiers broke through to Miasoedovo, seized the southern and southwestern outskirts of the village, and between 1000 and 1030 entered combat with two battalions of the 94th Guards Rifle Division's artillery regiment. It isn't clear where this clean breakthrough took place; in the documents of the 148th Separate Tank Regiment and the 31st Separate Destroyer Anti-tank Artillery Brigade, there is no mention of it. However, according to the information of the 94th Guards Rifle Division headquarters, the 2nd and 3rd Battalions of Lieutenant Colonel G.S. Burnazian's 199th Guards Artillery Regiment at the indicated time joined combat with a large group of tanks in the sector 1.5 kilometers northeast of Miasoedovo. This took place even before the forward 2nd Battalion/288th Guards Rifle Regiment of this same division arrived. In the artillery regiment's documents, it is given that 23 German armored vehicles were knocked out in the action, after which the enemy fell back to Miasoedovo.[59] Thus, even before the 7th Panzer Division struck the positions of the 31st Separate Destroyer Anti-tank Artillery Brigade and the 148th Separate Tank Regiment around noontime, its *panzerkampfgruppe* was already operating in the rear of the 25th Guards Rifle Corps' units, at the boundary between the 78th Guards and 81st Guards Rifle Divisions.

The German activity in the morning hours in just this sector was very unpleasant for M.S. Shumilov. The enemy had taken the Belovskaia – Iastrebovo line, tanks had emerged near Blizhniaia Igumenka, and panzergrenadiers were fighting in Sevriukovo. Safiulin's 25th Guards Rifle Corps was holding on, but in several places breakthroughs had already been already been noted. At the same time, there was nothing behind the two regiments of the 31st Separate Destroyer Anti-tank Artillery Brigade and the 148th Separate Tank Regiment that were deployed between (excl.)

---

58   TsAMO RF, f. 15, op. 11600, d. 1539, l. 28.
59   TsAMO RF, f. 199 gv. ap, op. 1, d. 5, l. 8.

Iastrebovo and the "Solov'ev" collective farm. The main forces of the 94th Guards Rifle Division were still on the march. Only the forward battalions of its 288th Guards Rifle Regiment had neared the sector stretching from Miasoedovo to northeast of Sevriukovo. Realizing that the Germans were forming two assault wedges for the attack in the direction of Miasoedovo, and having no way to hinder this, the army commander got in touch with the command of the 17th Air Army and requested that it quickly strike the areas of Generalovka and Hill 216.1 with bombers and ground attack aircraft. His request was granted. Because of the fact that Breith's panzer divisions were operating in narrow sectors of the front with their main forces, the Il-2 attacks had a substantial effect. The panzergrenadiers took particularly painful losses. Even so, the enemy's panzer wedges were seriously protected by both the Luftwaffe and Flak units; the latter were moving out directly among their combat formations.

Unfortunately, during these air strikes, because of the highly fluid combat operations and because of the approach of the Front's significant operational reserves to the area of the enemy breakthrough, they didn't go by without mistakes. The headquarters of the 148th Separate Tank Regiment reported: "At 1100 our ground attack aircraft with the support of fighters bombed and strafed our troops that were located west of Point 191.8."[60] This attack was made by crews of Colonel A.F. Isupov's 306th Storm Aviation Regiment of the 9th Composite Air Corps. The Soviet pilots attacked both artillery positions and Lifts' tanks, which were retreating from the "Solov'ev" collective farm. This ChP [a Russian acronym for "extraordinary incident", used for any accident, unfortunate coincidence or snafu] became one of the first of a long list of fratricidal incidents that took place on the Voronezh Front during the Battle of Kursk. Already just several hours later, the Il-2s of the 17th Air Army would once again pound the positions of the very same 148th Separate Tank Regiment.

According to Operational Summary No.360 of the 7th Guards Army headquarters, the situation by 1400 in its sector had taken the following shape:

> Troops of the army's right flank and center were continuing to conduct stubborn fighting with the enemy in the strength of three infantry and two tank divisions, which were exploiting the offensive to the north and east; on the left flank, the troops are holding their occupied lines. The enemy, continuing the offensive, at 1300 took the southern portion of Blizhniaia Igumenka, Sevriukovo and the "Solov'ev" collective farm; individual submachine gunners have reached the northwestern fringe of the woods 2 kilometers southeast of Miasoedovo; up to two regiments of infantry with tanks have seized the Machine Tractor Station on the western outskirts of Gremiachii.
>
> Enemy aircraft were supporting the units' offensive with groups of 22-23 Ju-87, which bombed the area of Miasoedovo, the "Solov'ev" collective farm and the "Batratskaia Dacha" State Farm. Solitary aircraft conducted reconnaissance.[61]

M.S. Shumilov, striving to operate proactively, was alertly following the course of the combat operations, in order to grasp the evident tendency in the development of the operational situation. After it became clear that the defense in the (excl.) "Poliana" State Farm – (excl.) "Batratskaia Dacha" State Farm – Miasoedovo sector had started to crumble, and the enemy, albeit slowly, had begun to make progress against the 25th Guards Rifle Corps, he reached a number of important decisions. Fearing a German breakthrough into the rear of the forces on the army's left flank, he set about creating a fully-fledged second echelon along the eastern bank of the Koren' River,

---

60 TsAMO RF, f. 7 gv. A, op. 5330, op. 1, d. 60, l. 12.
61 TsAMO RF, f. 7 gv. A, op. 5312, d. 239, l. 162.

and also attempted to get air support for the 81st Guards Rifle Division, which was in a difficult situation.

First, Lieutenant General Shumilov at 1430 issued an order to the commander of the 111th Rifle Division Colonel M.A. Bushin to shift to the north from its occupied line between Shebekino and Volchansk, and to take up a defense in the (excl.) Churaevo – Shebekino sector, thereby creating a second echelon behind the 72nd Guards Rifle and 213th Rifle Divisions. Second, he directed for the Major General I.P. Beliaev to hasten the movement of his 270th Rifle Division to the eastern bank of the Koren' River and to replace the units of the 15th Guards Rifle Division in the (excl.) Nikol'skoe – Churaevo sector in order to create a second echelon behind the 73rd Guards Rifle Division. At this time, the 270th Rifle Division's main forces had already assembled in the Krapivnoe – Ustinka – Shebekino area, and were waiting for their lead rear elements to finish coming up. However, having received word about the 94th Guards Rifle Division's delay, Shumilov realized that already within a matter of 2-3 hours G.B. Safiulin would require forces in order to plug the breach between the "Batratskaia Dacha" State Farm and Miasoedovo, since the battered 31st Separate Destroyer Anti-tank Artillery Brigade and the 148th Separate Tank Regiment had been unable to stop the enemy's panzer battering ram. It was possible to move up a regiment from the second-echelon 15th Guards Rifle Division, but considering the heavy German pressure against the sector of the 73rd Guards Rifle Division, this was undesirable and even dangerous. Thus the army commander once again insistently demanded Beliaev's 270th Rifle Division, which hadn't yet fully gathered, to move up into the sector of the 25th Guards Rifle Corps. At 1500 several of its battalions went on the march, but the main forces got underway only after a three-hour delay. After the replacement of Major General E.I. Vasilenko's 15th Guards Rifle Division by units of the 270th Rifle Division, it was supposed to take up prepared positions along the Novo-Troevka – Nekliudovo line, but skipping somewhat ahead of the events I will note that the rotation of the divisions became dragged out and would finish only by the evening of 8 July. Thus E.I. Vasilenko would all the same be forced to send some of his strength into the first echelon on the evening of 7 July in order to counter the German breakthrough.

After the seizure of the "Solov'ev" collective farm and the breakthrough to Iastrebovo, Hünersdorff and von Funck introduced their division's *panzerkampfgruppen* into the fighting. Their commanders decided to repeat the successful tactic on 6 July with two parallel panzer wedges attacking to the northeast. However, prior to jumping off, between 1100 and 1200 three aerial attacks were conducted against the positions of the 31st Separate Destroyer Anti-Tank Artillery Brigade. Right after 1300, von Oppeln's *panzerkampfgruppe*, which had been marking time in Iastrebovo, moved out along the Razumnaia River toward Sevriukovo, while Schülz's *panzerkampfgruppe* attacked out of the area of the "Solov'ev" collective farm side by side with von Oppeln's panzers in the direction of the eastern outskirts of Miasoedovo and through the woods east of the collective farm. According to the 25th Guards Rifle Corps' headquarters, by 1300 the enemy had committed up to 300 armored vehicles against the 73rd Guards Rifle Division (on its entire front) in the 5-kilometer sector running between the "Solov'ev" collective farm and Iastrebovo. However, it should be mentioned that both panzer wedges consisted not only of tanks, but also assault guns and halftracks. Two regiments of Shmanov's anti-tank brigade and Lifits' tank regiment were the first to meet the German attack. From the account of the 31st Separate Destroyer Anti-tank Artillery Brigade:

> At 1330 both groups of tanks, being led by heavy Pz-VI tanks, began advancing with brief halts in order to fire at the firing positions of our guns. Enemy mortars from out of the low ground west of Iastrebovo opened concentrated fire on the right-flank batteries, and then steadily walked the rounds along the line to the left flank.

The first tank column [Schülz's *panzerkampfgruppe*], being led by up to 20 Pz-VI, slowly advanced in a column formation in the direction of Hill 206.9.

The second tank column [von Oppeln's *panzerkampfgruppe*], led by up to 35 Pz-VI, advanced in the direction of Sevriukovo at a pace of 8-10 kilometers per hour with short halts.

The columns were striving to envelop both flanks of the brigade. The German infantry at this time was heading toward Hill 206.9 in a deployed formation, advancing at full height in a line, striving to block the path of retreat and the delivery of ammunition to the regiments' batteries. The batteries opened fire as soon as the tanks of the second column drew even with Iastrebovo and entered the swale east of Iastrebovo. Fire was opened at the first column and the infantry at a range of 600-900 meters. Neither the tanks nor the infantry stopped coming, despite the ever growing losses.

Of the 1,000 infantrymen that went on the attack, only 200-300 remained, which then broke into a run, striving to encircle the 3rd Battery of the 1849th Destroyer Anti-tank Artillery Regiment, which was placing destructive fire on the infantry. The battery's rate of fire picked up; the infantry at 300-400 meters was forced to hit the earth but continued bellycrawling forward. The tanks of the second column, having lost 9 tanks knocked out and 13 tanks left burning, became confused and stopped, stood motionless for 10-15 minutes, then bypassing the burning tanks to the left, resumed advancing and the head of the column reached Sevriukovo. Not stopping, losing knocked out and burned out tanks, they continued pushing on to Miasoedovo. The firing positions of the right-flank batteries were overrun by tanks from the left. The first column [7th Panzer Division], attacking in bounding advances, accelerated once the second column reached Sevriukovo, and the tanks began firing while on the move.

Fifteen tanks were left burning in the swale and 13 were knocked-out; they looked like a railroad train, intermingled with platform cars and boxcars. It was impossible to conduct targeted fire at the tanks that were bypassing the knocked out and burning machines, because the tanks moved into an obscuring zone of heavy smoke. When the enemy's lead tanks reached the bend in the road leading to Sevriukovo from the left, all of the communications with the batteries was lost. Command and control became impossible.

Up to a company of enemy infantry moved out of the northern outskirts of Iastrebovo at full height and also headed toward the bend in the road. It was impossible to fire at them, because the tanks were pressing so hard. Shells were running low. At the moment communications became disrupted, we'd already lost (destroyed) 4 76mm anti-tank guns, 2 45mm anti-tank guns and 4 prime movers. In this situation, it was decided to fall back to the reserve firing positions in the area 1.5 kilometers northeast of Hill 206.9.

It became impossible to leave the battlefield by battery. The commanders of the 1853rd and 1849th Destroyer Anti-Tank Artillery Regiments ordered to cover the withdrawal with the 3rd and 4th Batteries. The withdrawal started with the 1st Battery. The commanders of the batteries that were covering the retreat of the rest were ordered to fight in encirclement until the last shell and bullet had been expended, and to fight their way out with rifle butts and grenades.[62]

Thus, between 1500 and 1600 Schülz's panzers and the panzergrenadiers of Panzergrenadier Regiment 6, having crushed the line of Shmanov's anti-tank brigade, took full possession of the "Solov'ev" collective farm, Hill 206.9, and had penetrated the woods lying next to the Solov'ev collective farm along the first firebreak from the collective farm. Earlier that morning,

---

62 TsAMO RF, f. 203 (artillery headquarters), op. 2843, d. 29, ll. 112, 112obr.

panzergrenadiers of the 7th Panzer Division mounted on halftracks, bypassing the positions of our anti-tank artillery and tanks, broke into Miasoedovo and got a grip on the southern end of the town. However, two artillery battalions of the 94th Guards Rifle Division that had come up from on the march were blocking the Germans' path into the depth of the 25th Guards Rifle Corps' defenses, while at 1300 the 2nd Battalion of Lieutenant Colonel M.P. Aglitsky's 288th Guards Rifle Regiment that had come up joined combat with the Germans in the northwestern portion of Miasoedovo and prevented them from taking complete possession of it. Nevertheless, having taken control of the southern and southeastern outskirts, already that morning the German panzergrenadiers had secured the left flank of Schülz's *panzerkampfgruppe*, which was trying to break through in the direction of Hill 206.9 through the corridor between this village and the woods lying to the southeast.

Accordingly, because of the delay in the arrival of Russkikh's 94th Guards Rifle Divsion in the sector of the 25th Guards Rifle Corps and Safiulin's lack of the necessary forces, by 1600 von Funck's and Hünersdorff's panzer divisions had created a breach on the boundary between the 81st Guards Rifle Division and 73rd Guards Rifle Division, taken full possession of Sevriukovo and Iastrebovo, and gained a foothold in Miasoedovo. After this, the 7th Panzer Division, making combat contact with the 94th Guards Rifle Division's elements that were coming up, was forced to halt its advance, but the 6th Panzer Division was rapidly advancing through the line of the 81st Guards Rifle Division toward the village of Melikhovo, which was situated already behind the boundary between the 7th Guards and 6th Guards Armies.

The remnants of the 31st Separate Destroyer Anti-tank Artillery Brigade began to come out of encirclement by 1700, and at the order of the 7th Guards Army's deputy artillery commander, immediately took up positions in front of the southwestern outskirts of Miasoedovo – "in the narrow neck of woods that are 1.5 kilometers northeast of Hill 206.9." Altogether, 11 guns (5 45mm guns of the 1853rd Destroyer Anti-tank Artillery Regiment and 6 76mm guns of the 1849th Destroyer Anti-tank Artillery Regiment) deployed here.

On its part the command of the 7th Panzer Division attempted to make use of the situation that had developed for an attack in the direction of the village of Sheino, which was located 7 kilometers northeast of Miasoedovo (and in the meantime in order to seize the large area of woods northeast of Miasoedovo). Von Funck recalled:

> In connection with this, the capture of Hill 210.3 became a new possibility. With the support of a large amount of artillery, the *kampfgruppe* [Panzergrenadier Regiment 6] set out on a broad front toward Miasoedovo; its left, northern flank gradually drew in toward the village during the advance. This was done in order to give the impression that the main attack was being launched against the southwestern and western fringe of the [Miasoedovo] woods. Then suddenly the panzer regiment moved out. Reinforced by one battalion of panzergrenadiers in halftracks and accompanied by the self-propelled artillery battalion, it quickly bounded across the interval between the large wooded area [east of the "Solov'ev" collective farm] and Hill 210.3. Heavy fire was placed on the southern fringe of the woods on Hill 210.3 with the aim of blinding the enemy and suppressing the anti-tank guns and observation posts. Reaching the open ground southwest of Arkad'evka, the panzer regiment pivoted to the north in order to envelop the wooded Hill 120.3 from the east, and then from the north [meanwhile, Panzergrenadier Regiment 6 was breaking through the eastern outskirts of Miasoedovo toward the northern fringe of the woods on Hill 210.3]. During this maneuver, which filled the atmosphere with fire, smoke and dust, panzergrenadiers advanced from the northern fringe of the large wooded area directly to the southwestern fringe of the woods on Hill 210.3. Thereby, all three *kampfgruppen* were able to break into the woods on Hill 210.3, which were being heroically defended by the enemy, from different directions. Meanwhile,

elements of the panzer regiment and the self-propelled artillery battalion were screening the eastern flank.[63]

At this time, the headquarters of the 94th Guards Rifle Division reported that the Germans had assembled up to a regiment of infantry and 150 armored vehicles in the area of Miasoedovo on Hill 206.9 and to the south of there, and were firing on the division's defenses with artillery and mortars.[64] In order to blind the crews of our guns, which were located in Miasoedovo and the woods to the northeast, as the moment the *panzerkampfgruppe* pivoted to the east, the Germans used Nebelwerfers to blanket their positions with a smoke screen.

As a result, by the evening Panzergrenadier Regiment 6 had seized the southern and eastern portions of Miasoedovo, while *Kampfgruppe* Gläsermer and Schülz's panzer regiment took the woods northeast of the village, except for its northern section, after which the *panzerkampfgruppe* managed to break through even to the southwestern slopes of Hill 213.7 (0.5 kilometer southwest of Arkad'evka), before being rebuffed by units of the 94th Guards Rifle Division. Von Funck, striving to arrange a covering screen in order to free Panzer Regiment 25 for resolving further tasks, issued an order for a battered battalion of Panzergrenadier Regiment 7 to move up to the area south and southwest of Arkad'evka. The regiment commander Colonel von Steinkeller personally led his regiment toward the assigned area, but the Germans didn't manage to consolidate their hold here. The Guardsmen of Russkikh's 94th Guards Rifle Division threw back Steinkeller's panzergrenadiers to the woods southwest of Miasoedovo, and the *panzerkampfgruppe* was forced to fall back to the same place from Hill 213.7.

By the end of 7 July, the 94th Guards Rifle Division was occupying a defense arranged in two echelons: the 288th Guards Rifle Regiment in the sector stretching from the northern half of Miasoedovo to a point 2 kilometers east of Miasoedovo; the 286th Guards Rifle Regiment was occupying Hills 205.5, 206.9, 191.8 and 202.3; 3rd Battalion/283rd Guards Rifle Regiment was on the northeastern outskirts of Sheino; 1st Battalion/283rd Guards Rifle Regiment was north of Miasoedovo and east of the Razumnaia River with a front to the northwest; 2nd Battalion/283rd Guards Rifle Regiment was on the southern fringe of the woods 2 kilometers west of Miasoedovo. Thus, panzergrenadiers of the 7th Panzer Division were still holding a portion of Miasoedovo. This was the first populated point on the forward edge of the second army-level belt of defenses that the troops of III Panzer Corps entered.

After Russkikh's division had dug in and repulsed several attacks, the intensity of the fighting in this sector subsided somewhat, and the 25th Guards Rifle Corps commander Safiulin had the opportunity at last to get busy with strengthening the 73rd Guards Rifle Division's right flank and two "sore spots" in the defenses – the "Solov'ev" collective farm and the "Batratskaia Dacha" State Farm. Here, the 7th Panzer Division's Reconnaissance Battalion 37, reinforced with several tanks, artillery and halftracks, was embedded just like a thorn in the Soviet defenses. Both of these places were adjacent to woods, and using the natural cover, the reconnaissance battalion throughout the day not only conducted reconnaissance, but also launched several attacks at the boundary between units of the 73rd Guards Rifle Division, and even attempted to infiltrate on its right flank into the rear. In addition, considering that German tanks were already located east of Hill 206.9, the enemy had the possibility to encircle part of the 25th Guards Rifle Corps in the woods west of Nikol'skoe through meeting attacks and emerge in the rear behind the 73rd Guards Rifle Division.

Thus, with the aim of neutralizing the activity of Reconnaissance Battalion 37, and then driving it out of the "Batratskaia Dacha" State Farm, in the evening Safiulin issued an order in response to

---

63 TsAMO RF, f. 15, op. 11600, d. 1539, l. 28.
64 TsAMO RF, f. 1269, op. 1, d. 9, l. 125.

an alarm to the 15th Guards Rifle Division to send Lieutenant Colonel I.A. Usikov's 44th Guards Rifle Regiment to the "Solov'ev" collective farm and the "Batratskaia Dacha" State Farm. At 2300, before reaching its indicated jumping-off sector (1 kilometer east of the "Solov'ev" collective farm and 2 kilometers east of the "Batratskaia Dacha" State Farm), the regiment from the march bumped into and attacked a large group of submachine gunners which was caught advancing in the direction of Nikol'skoe. The fighting continued all night; the reconnaissance battalion's operational area was firmly sealed, but there was no success in destroying it or actually pushing it back from its hastily-occupied positions. At dawn E.I. Vasilenko reported: "By the morning of 8 July the regiment reached the line: Hill 202.3 and Point "K" in the area of the Batraskaia Dacha State Farm, where it went over to the defense."[65]

The 7th Panzer Division command was actually viewing its reconnaissance battalion as both an outpost for holding the "Batratskaia Dacha" State Farm and as an auxiliary force for the possible encirclement of the 73rd Guards Rifle Division's forces. Thus throughout the day of 7 July it supported the reconnaissance battalion with artillery fire, and for the next day was planning to augment its firepower.

Hünersdorff's 6th Panzer Division achieved even more substantial results on 7 July. By the end of the day, after three days of the heaviest fighting, having overcome the line of the 81st Guards Rifle Division, it was the first of Army Detachment Kempf's divisions to break through the boundary line on the right flank of the 7th Guards Army and reach a line now belonging to the 6th Guards Army, and enter combat with its troops and those of the 69th Army. Thereby III Panzer Corps had seized a springboard for the capture of the tactically-important corridor between the Northern Donets and Razumnaia Rivers. Control over it would give it the possibility to plan the encirclement of Soviet forces (the 69th Army's 48th Rifle Corps) that were defending on the joint flanks of the Fourth Panzer Army and Army Detachment Kempf in the interfluvial area between the Northern Donets and Lipovyi Donets Rivers. Heavy fighting was still going on in Sevriukovo when von Oppeln's *panzerkampfgruppe* launched an attack out of Iastrebovo in the direction of Melikhovo. Behind it, panzergrenadiers of the 19th Panzer Division (Lieutenant Colonel Helmut Richter's Panzergrenadier Regiment 74), bypassing Blizhniaia Igumenka, were moving along the Belyi Kolodez' ravine toward Dal'niaia Igumenka; a bit later it began to force a crossing of the ravine in the Postnikov area. Approximately between 1400 and 1500 the *kampfgruppen* of the 6th and 19th Panzer Divisions, having fully overrun the 81st Guards Rifle Division's sector, emerged on the left flank of Colonel P.D. Govorunenko's 375th Rifle Division (of the 6th Guards Army) at the boundary between the 6th and 7th Guards Armies. Already in Operational Summary No.238 at 1500, the chief of staff of this division Lieutenant Colonel Lozhko reported that a rifle company and two platoons of submachine gunners were exchanging fire with Germans in Dal'niaia Igumenka.[66] Considering the time it took for the information to travel from the regiment to the division, at a minimum the enemy submachine gunners had made their way through the 81st Guards Rifle Division's defenses to their entire depth at least an hour and half before this and had joined combat with outposts of the left-flank regiment of Govorunenko's 375th Rifle Division.

Even though the commander of the 1241st Rifle Regiment Major N.A. Karklin had in fact been briefed previously about the possibility of an enemy breakthrough out of the Blizhniaia Igumenka – Sevriukovo area, the appearance of German tanks on the regiment's left flank (or more accurately, almost in the division's rear) came as a complete surprise to him. At this moment the 375th Rifle Division was occupying a defense along the following line: woods, east of Visloe – Hill 209.5

---

65 TsAMO RF, f. 1526, op. 1, d. 8, l. 158.
66 TsAMO RF, f. 375 sd, op. 1, d. 36, l. 237.

– Shopino (West) – ravine, 1 kilometer north of Hill 211.6 – Pokrovka – Dal'niaia Igumenka, and had been repulsing heavy attacks by units of the SS Panzergrenadier Division *Totenkopf* and the 168th Infantry Division along its entire line. Combat had also taken place on the front of the 1241st Rifle Regiment, which was holding the (excl.) Belomestnaia – (excl.) Chernaia Poliana sector. After the report arrived from the 1241st Rifle Regiment, P.D. Govorunenko realized that the 81st Guards Rifle Division was no longer able to hold its entire sector of defense, and that the 35th Guards Rifle Corps' 92nd Guards Rifle Division had not yet arrived in this area from the march, so he could only rely on his own inherent forces. Therefore at the alarm he got his reserve moving toward the positions of the 1241st Rifle Regiment – a company of the 137th Anti-tank Rifle Battalion. Thus, in the afternoon hours, while the *panzerkampfgruppen* of the 6th and 19th Panzer Divisions had been breaking through to Dal'niaia Igumenko and Melikhovo, there were only weak forces on the left flank of Karklin's regiment along the "Main Fruit and Vegetable" State Farm – Postnikov – Dal'niaia Igumenka line: an anti-tank rifle company, a rifle company, and two platoons of submachine gunners. The situation began to change for the better only around 1600 when the 92nd Guards Rifle Division's 280th Guards Rifle Regiment began to assemble here; at approximately 1530, one of its rifle companies began to take up positions in Dal'niaia Igumenka.

The march of Colonel V.F. Trunin's 92nd Guards Rifle Division had been difficult. At 1900 on 6 July, Lieutenant Colonel N.I. Novikov, the commander of the 280th Guards Rifle Regiment, had summoned his battalion commanders and informed them since the morning of 6 July, an enemy grouping numbering up to 300 armored vehicles with infantry support had been continuing to develop an attack on the boundary between the 81st Guards Rifle and 73rd Guards Rifle Divisions, striving to break through to the Belgorod – Korocha highway. The division commander had received an order from the 35th Guards Rifle Corps to move out quickly and occupy the Blizhniaia Igumenka – Hill 216 – Sevruikovo line. Next Lieutenant Colonel Novikov turned to issuing orders. His regiment was to become the division's forward detachment, and by 1600 on 7 July it had moved up to the indicated line in order to screen the deployment of the rest of the division. When issuing this order to the regiment command, the division commander had particularly emphasized that the operational situation was changing very quickly and it had to be ready to meet enemy tanks. Thus Colonel Trunin had transferred Lieutenant Colonel I.I. Shapovalov's 197th Guards Artillery Regiment (minus the 2nd Artillery Battalion) and one battery of the 99th Separate Destroyer Anti-tank Artillery Battalion to N.I. Novikov's operational control. Given favorable conditions, the 280th Guards Rifle Regiment was to occupy the designated line and wait for the rest of the division's approach, and in the event of an enemy breakthrough in the direction of the Belgorod – Korocha highway, it was to repel the attack on the Dal'niaia Igumenka – Razumnaia River line and dig in there.

Immediately after receiving the order, the regiment headquarters sent out a reconnaissance and lead forward detachment (1/1st Rifle Battalion and a battery of 1/197th Guards Artillery Regiment), which given the enemy's appearance was to occupy (or seize) the line running from the western outskirts of Dalniaia Igumenka through the woods, 2 kilometers west of Melikhovo, to Shliakhovoe. The regiment commander, considering that the march would be conducted partially in the evening and nighttime hours, strove to gain time and ensure the unhindered movement and deployment of the main forces. Thus he decided to conduct the march in a single march column, but before moving out he sent a strong advance guard (the 1st Rifle Battalion (minus one company, which had departed earlier, and the rest of 1/197th Guards Artillery Regiment) to the Blizhniaia Igumenka – Sevruikovo – Andreevskie line, capable of securing the deployment and subsequent wide maneuvering with the main forces. In addition, the Lieutenant Colonel issued an order for the immediate formation of a mobile anti-tank reserve out of artillery and sapper elements (a battery of the regiment's anti-tank battalion and a squad of combat engineers), which were to follow behind the advance guard in readiness to deploy on the southwestern outskirts of

Shliakhovoe. The regiment would have to make a march of 35 kilometers. Considering that the column would have a length of approximately 13 kilometers, it might be subjected to attacks from the air, so N.I. Novikov directed for there to be an interval of 500 meters between the battalions in daylight hours, and 300 meters once the sun had set. All of his decisions would play an important role in the subsequent events.

Just as the division commander had anticipated, the situation was very fluid and at the moment the regiment's vanguard was approaching Melikhovo, von Oppeln's *panzerkampfgruppe* was already nearing its southern outskirts. At 1620, reconnaissance patrols that were located in the woods northeast of Andrevskii and to the south of the "Kalinin" collective farm reported to the regiment about the enemy's appearance south of Melikhovo. At the same time, the regiment's chief of staff received word from a reconnaissance aircraft about the approach of an enemy column of tanks to within just 3-4 kilometers from Melikhovo. These messages were quickly passed by N.I. Novikov to the division headquarters, which allowed it to move out the division's anti-tank reserve quickly from Kazach'e to the "Comintern" collective farm (northeast of Mazikino). At the moment, there was not the necessary strength and means to hold the defense along the Dal'niaia Igumenka – Melikhovo – Sheino line. Only artillery units were located in these villages; in particular, the 161st Guards Cannon Artillery Regiment was in movement from Iastrebovo to Sheino, while the 1st Artillery Battalion of the 193rd Cannon Artillery Regiment was deploying on the northwestern outskirts of Dal'niaia Igumenka under the cover of a small quantity of rifle elements (including of the 375th Rifle Division). Further to the northeast, there were no Soviet forces at all in the 17-18 kilometers between the Northern Donets and the Razumnaia River that separated the 375th Rifle Division and the positions of the 69th Army's 305th Rifle Division, if you exclude the 92nd Rifle Division's 276th Guards and 282nd Guards Rifle Regiment that were in the process of moving up.

At 1620 the 280th Guards Rifle Regiment's lead mobile detachment ran into grenadiers of the 6th Panzer Division on the southern outskirts of Melikhovo. The regiment's vanguard commander (the commander of the 1st Rifle Battalion) decided to take the heights south of the village and thereby pin down the enemy with combat until the arrival of the regiment's main forces. For this purpose he gave an order to the commander of the attached 1/197th Guards Artillery Regiment Captain D.A. Prokop'ev to deploy his battery quickly and to open fire at the enemy infantry and the sector where the enemy armor was concentrating. Meanwhile, he ordered the commanders of the 2nd and 3rd Rifle Companies to attack and drive the enemy from the heights 2-3 kilometers south of the village under the cover of the artillery fire. A short time later, a howitzer battery that was deployed north of Shliakhovoe opened up concentrated fire that hindered the deployment of Colonel von Oppeln's *panzerkampfgruppe* into a combat formation for the attack, while two batteries of 76mm guns of 1/197th Guards Artillery Regiment, which had moved up to within close range opened fire at the German tanks.

It must be recognized that the breakthrough by von Opplen's *panzerkampfgruppe* to this area was an unpleasant surprise for the Soviet command. In contrast, the rapid advance made by General Hünersdorff's *kampfgruppen* generated optimism in General Breith. He therefore attempted to squeeze as much advantage as he could out of the situation, and decided to crush the center of resistance as quickly as possible in order to push the *panzerguppen* as far as they could go into the depth of the Russian defenses. The Soviet command was also quickly reacting to the situation. The 6th Panzer Division's *panzerkampfgruppe* hadn't yet jumped-off on the attack toward Melikhovo, when aircraft from both sides appeared in the skies above this area. At 1620 eight Ju-88 bombers pounced on the Russian howitzer battery, but the artillerymen avoided serious losses. Just a half hour later, a squadron of Il-2 ground attack aircraft struck the German tanks with anti-tank bomblets and rockets.

N.I. Novikov, who arrived in Melikhovo with some of his command staff, approved the decision taken by the vanguard commander and ordered to carry out the designated plan at whatever the cost and cover the deployment of the regiment's main forces. For reinforcement he gave the commander of the 1st Rifle Battalion operational control of the 148th Separate Tank Regiment's 3rd Tank Company, which had just arrived from the 94th Guards Rifle Division at the order of the 35th Guards Rifle Corps. Having received the asset, the battalion commander decided first of all to interfere with the enemy's deployment of his main forces. Thus, anticipating that the Germans would attack from the south, he immediately directed the 3rd Tank Company into the woods southwest of the village. The tankers received an order: with fire from fixed positions, and in the event of an attack with a maneuver onto the German flank, to prevent the Germans from reaching the outskirts of Melikhovo or from bypassing the village to the west. So Prokop'ev's artillery battalion and the company of T-34 tanks promptly set out to carry out the vanguard commander's scheme, which could not be said about the rifle companies. Their commanders, fearing to come under enemy tank attack on a level piece of ground that hadn't been prepared for defense, were in no hurry to attack the heights south of Melikhovo.

I will remind the reader that according to N.F. Vatutin's order from back in April, a number of the larger villages in the system of the army-level defensive belts had been converted into fortified areas, including Dal'niaia Igumenka as well. In the 6th Guards Army's 23rd Guards Rifle Corps, the village was referred to as "Battalion Strongpoint 7", and it had an outer ring of fieldworks. It was being defended by the 2nd Battalion of the 375th Rifle Division's 1241st Rifle Regiment, 15 T-34 tanks and 10 anti-tank guns. Next to it on its outskirts, three lines had been dug for the deployment of the 375th Rifle Division's anti-tank artillery reserve. Two kilometers to the southwest was the anti-tank strongpoint of Postnikov, in which positions had been prepared for an anti-tank gun battery and 14 T-34, as well as a network of trenches for a rifle company. Melikhovo hadn't been so well-prepared for defense as far as fieldworks, even though the village and its outskirts had a network of trenches sufficient for a rifle battalion, emplacements with ramps for 15 T-34 and positions for 10 anti-tank guns, and some, but not all, of the tank-vulnerable ground in front of it had been mined. However, the village had no outer ring of fieldworks, nor did it have serious anti-tank obstacles like anti-tank ditches and scarps, which would substantially reduce the defensive strength of the village and make it easier for the enemy to take it. Thus, the Germans would be able to take Melikhovo already on 8 July, while the fighting for Dal'niaia Igumenka continued for an additional 24 hours.

However, let's return to the events on 7 July. Already at 1700, despite the attempts made by the Soviet side to disrupt the attack with artillery fire, after a 10-minute preparatory artillery barrage, a *kampfgruppe* of the 6th Panzer Division went on the attack in two directions: 18 tanks and up to two companies of infantry attempted to bypass Melikhovo on its eastern side, and 17 tanks and up to a company of infantry attempted to outflank it on the west. It should be noted that the firepower of the 280th Guards Rifle Regiment's vanguard was equal to the assigned task; they almost simultaneously entered combat (the tanks opened fire first) and secured the deployment of the regimental columns that were arriving from the march. The tankers, getting a jump on the enemy, had taken up up advantageous positions in the woods southwest of Melikhovo and opened a heavy fire on the enemy. Almost simultaneously, the two batteries of 1/197th Guards Artillery Regiment opened fire over open sights at the enemy's group that was advancing somewhat to the west. Emboldened by the friendly firepower, the vanguard's 2nd and 3rd Rifle Companies also stepped off and began to take positions on the heights to the south of the village.

The 280th Guards Rifle Regiment's reconnaissance and intelligence service was working well, so N.I. Novikov received timely information that up to a battalion of halftracks escorted by several tanks was attempting to breakthrough out of the area northwest of Sevriukovo. This was Major F. Quentin's Reconnaissance Battalion 6 of the 6th Panzer Division, which had received an order to launch a reconnaissance-in-force through Sheino in the direction of Mazikino.

Bitter fighting flared up along the entire front stretching from Postnikov, Dal'niaa Igumenka and Melikhovo to Sevriukovo and Miasoedovo. The entire horizon became enshrouded with smoke and ashes from the burning woods, and all around there was the howling of shells and booming explosions. The regiment commander understood that the situation was precarious. The enemy was operating with large groups of panzers on a broad front, and judging from everything, the regiment had no continuous line of defense on the left flank. In the meantime, the main efforts of its units were focused on defending Melikhovo. There was still adequate force in order to hold the village and allow the division to deploy, but the situation regarding the enemy group that was attacking out of Sevriukovo (Panzer Reconnaissance Battalion 6, but the regiment commander didn't know this) was totally unclear. The ground toward which it was presumably attacking was supposed to have been occupied by the 280th Rifle Regiment's left-flank units and units of the 94th Guards Rifle Division, which were marching toward the front side-by-side with the 92nd Guards Rifle Division. However, at the moment the enemy's attack stepped off, it wasn't clear whether or not the neighbor had come up (in fact, the 94th Guards Rifle Division's 288th Guards Rifle Regiment was already fighting on the northern outskirts of Miasoedovo, but no shoulder-to-shoulder contact had yet been established between the 92nd and 94th Guards Rifle Divisions), but the battalion of the 280th Guards Rifle Regiment was still on the march toward this area.

It was obvious that both enemy panzer groups that were operating south of Melikhovo and north of Miasoedovo were striving to expand the gap between his regiment and the 73rd Guards Rifle Division (or possibly that of the 94th Guards Rifle Division if it had come up) and break through Shliakhovoe and Mazikino to the line of the large villages of Nizhnii Ol'shanets and Zaiach'e. The regiment commander decided to prevent this and organize a semi-ring of fire out of artillery units in the path of Quentin's reconnaissance battalion and von Oppeln's *panzerkampfgruppe*. As soon as the regiment's anti-tank artillery reserve arrived from the march in the area of Shliakhovoe (approximately after an hour of fighting), N.I. Novikov sent it to repulse a possible attack from Miasoedovo toward Mazikino. The artillerymen and combat engineers deployed east of Melikhovo (2 kilometers southeast of Shliakhovoe). Around the same time Lieutenant Colonel Novikov created an anti-tank barrier in the regiment's rear. Striving to preclude any advance by German tanks along the road to Shliakhovoe and further on toward Lomovo, in case the Germans broke through the vanguard's line, he ordered the commander of the 197th Guards Artillery Regiment to get in touch with the 2nd Artillery Battalion and to deploy it on the southern fringe of the woods southwest of the "Comintern" collective farm (5 kilometers northeast of Melikhovo) with the assignment to block the Shliakhovoe – Lomovo road. Meanwhile, the division's anti-tank artillery reserve that had come up was immediately sent to the Hill 222 – southern outskirts of Gremiachii line with a front to the southwest, in order to block the path of the German tanks in the (excl.) Shliakhovoe – Zaiach'e sector. In addition, Captain S.S. Smorzh's 3/197th Guards Artillery Regiment was sent to Dal'niaia Igumenka with the task to prevent the Germans from crossing the Belyi Kolodez' ravine and taking that village.

While the regiment commander was putting together his anti-tank defenses on the directions of a possible breakthrough by the 6th Panzer Division, the regiment vanguard was holding back the onslaught of von Oppeln's *kampfgruppen* with great difficulty, because of the Germans' numerical superiority. Even though the first attack left 16 tanks smoking on the battlefield, its pressure didn't cease. At 1830 Colonel von Oppeln-Bronikowski shifted his *kampfgruppe*'s main efforts to the southwest of Melikhovo (into the sector of the 148th Separate Tank Regiment's tank company) and attacked here with 30 panzers simultaneously. At the same time from the south, 20 panzers were moving toward the village through the line of the vanguard's rifle companies.

Only a regiment could withstand such substantial forces, not a single battalion, even a reinforced one; however, the 280th Rifle Regiment's 2nd and 3rd Battalions were still on the march. Thanks to aerial reconnaissance, the enemy knew that a column of Russian troops was approaching the village, so with the start of the panzer attacks, 12 German bombers appeared above it. With great difficulty and suffering losses, between 1830 and 1930 both battalions finally began to assemble in Melikhovo, and a new problem arose in front of N.I. Novikov: how to provide covering fire for them while they took up positions south of the village; after all, all of the artillery had already been activated in the combat with the German tanks. Striving to prevent high casualties as the battalions were deploying, the regiment commander ordered the approaching battalions to split quickly into platoons while they were still on the march, after which they gradually began to move into the lines of defense, including the network of trenches.

Judging from the archival sources, both battalions took up their positions without any particular difficulties over a period of about 2.5 hours and entered the fighting. The arrival of Novikov's entire regiment in Melikhovo substantially strengthened this line of defense. Nevertheless, persistently launching several successive panzer attacks against one and the same sector, the enemy managed all the same to break through the regiment's defense. Already late in the evening, several times von Oppeln's tanks passed through the combat positions of the 280th Guards Rifle Regiment and were even reaching the outskirts of Melikhovo. However, under heavy anti-tank fire, they would again fall back to their jumping-off positions, but now in fewer numbers. By the end of the day, the units of the 94th Guards Rifle Division's right flank using artillery fire also managed to thwart the attempt by Panzer Reconnaissance Battalion 6 to break through to Mazikino.

In several publications of the Soviet era, the meeting battle for Melikhovo was presented as a model of the organization of a rifle regiment's march in anticipation of a battle, and also as an example of its commander's professional approach to planning and shaping the battle in unfavorable conditions when engaging with a major enemy tank grouping. Indeed, Lieutenant Colonel N.I. Novikov demonstrated exceptional professional skill and fine organizational abilities in this battle. On 7 July his Guardsmen accomplished a very important job: they were able to hold the 6th Panzer Division's *panzerkampfgruppe* south of Melikhovo, thereby allowing the command to bring forces up to the corridor between the Northern Donets and Razumnaia Rivers, and in the process inflicted substantial damage to the enemy.

The events that took place in this sector of the Voronezh Front haven't yet been studied in detail by domestic scholars; only the recollections of participants in the fighting have been left behind, in which it is difficult to find connection between times and locations where the events took place. Unfortunately, the authors of these memoirs as a rule describe their own individual perceptions of endless attacks and a series of heroic feats by their comrade peers. Thus it is extremely difficult to lay out the course of combat actions in detail. Only owing to the few preserved archival documents is it possible to understand how the events were unfolding at one or another moment of time. For example, in some publications one encounters the assertion that the timely arrival of the two other regiments of the 92nd Guards Rifle Division helped the 280th Guards Rifle Regiment withstand the German attack and hurl the Germans back from the village. However, this doesn't correspond with reality. I will refer to the account of the 35th Guards Rifle Corps about the combat operations on the Belgorod axis:

> Pursuant to orders, the 92nd Guards Rifle Division ceased to relieve the 89th Guards Rifle Division's units and set off in the direction of Staryi Gorod with the assignment to take up a defense on the line: woods 1 kilometer northeast of Chernaia Poliana, Staryi Gorod, Blizhniaia Igumenka, (excl.) Sevriukovo, tying in with the line of the 94th Guards Rifle Division, and to prevent a breakthrough by enemy tanks and infantry on the indicated line.
>
> The division, moving with the 276th Guards and 282nd Guards Rifle Regiments along the Shinino – Staryi Gorod route and the 280th Guards Rifle Regiment on the Shliakhovoe – Melikhovo – Blizhniaia Igumnka route at 1900 became engaged with the vanguard battalion

of the 280th Guards Rifle Regiment in combat against up to two battalions of enemy infantry accompanied by 35 tanks on a line 2 kilometers south of Melikhovo.

Having driven back two enemy attacks, the vanguard battalion enabled the 280th Guards Rifle Regiment to deploy and tank up a defense on the line: ravine east of Dal'niaia Igumenka – patch of woods south of Melikhovo.

The 276th and 282nd Guards Rifle Regiments, having lost contact with the division headquarters, by [the following] morning reached the area of Staryi Gorod, where at the directive of the 81st Guards Rifle Division's commander they took up a line of defense on the line: "Main Fruit and Vegetable" State Farm, Staryi Gorod, Blizhniaia Igumenka with a front to the west and southeast.[67]

The Voronezh Front received word about the German breakthrough to the sector of the 6th Guards Army and the main results of the fighting at Melikhovo approximately around midnight. However, the messaged contained no detailed information about how this had happened, because only the 280th Guards Rifle Regiment of Trunin's entire division reached the Melikhovo area, and the location of the other two regiments was unknown. When the situation finally became clear, it became understood that the division commander and headquarters had lost command and control over their units, and the sector had been held only because of the decisive and intelligent actions of the 280th Guards Rifle Regiment's commander; this prompted N.F Vatutin to rebuke the corps commander S.G. Goriachev for his weak oversight when moving out his troops to the forward edge. The commander of the 35th Guards Rifle Corps knew that Colonel V.F. Trunin was a young division commander who had just assumed his post, and moreover had little experience as a combat commander.[68] At the end of June 1943, when characterizing him, S.G. Goriachev

---

67 TsAMO RF, f. 35 gv. sk, op. 1, d. 44, ll. 1, 2.
68 Vasilii Fedorovich Trunin, Colonel. Born on 12.02.1906 in Tula Oblast's village of Mar'tem'ianovka; a Russian. After completing seven years of schooling, he worked in village cooperatives. From October 1928 to March 1931, he served in the Red Army, and after de-mobilization worked as a physical plant manager in the Thermal Engineering Institute. In October 1931, as part of a mobilization of Party members, Trunin was again called up into the Red Army and was directed into political work as a political instructor at the "Vystrel" ["Shot"] tactical courses. He worked in this post, then as a propaganda instructor of a battalion, until 1935. In October 1935 Trunin was assigned to enroll in the Lenin Military-Political Courses, but after one and a half months he was summoned before the Communist Party's Central Committee for a review of his political documents. In April 1937 he was appointed as an instructor in the Political Department of the Stalin Military Academy of Mechanization and Motorization, and in 1938 he was selected as an independent secretary of the Academy's Party Commission. On 28.06.1941, Trunin was appointed as a Party investigator as part of a Party commission of the Reserve Front's Party Board, and from the end of July 1941, Trunin was appointed as a commissar of this Front headquarters's Intelligence Department. On 13.10.1941 he was transferred to become a secretary in the 60th Reserve Army's Party commission (subsequently this army became the Northwestern Front's 3rd Shock Army). On 25.4.1942, he became the commissar of the 154th Separate Motorized Rifle Brigade. He took part in the fighting near Demiansk and Stalingrad (64th Army). In September 1942 after the brigade commander was wounded, he assumed command of the brigade. After the fighting in a suburb of Stalingrad and in Beketovka, Trunin was awarded with the Order of the Red Banner. Between 18.11.1942 and 10.01.1943, he served as the commander of the 64th Army's 66th Separate Motorized Rifle Brigade, and between 10.01 and 28.04.1943, Trunin commanded the 64th Army's 93rd Separate Rifle Brigade. In this post he took part in the fighting to destroy the German Sixth Army, after which he for the second time was awarded with the Order of the Red Banner. On 28.04.1943, he was appointed as the commander of the 92nd Guards Rifle Division, which he formed out of two rifle brigades. On 13.07.1943, he was removed from his post for his poor command over the division by the 69th Army's Military Council. On 29.08.1943 Trunin was sent to accelerated courses in the Frunze Military Academy. Subsequently he commanded the 71st Rifle Division, but once again he was dismissed from his post because of his professional incompetence and reduced in rank to deputy division commander. He ended the war as a commandant of the 208th Camp for Liberated

had written: "As one of the former political workers, his military training for the occupied post is inadequate. It is extremely desirable to give him more military training to assume a command post through short-term courses, after which he will make a fine general officer."[69]

Because it was Trunin's division that was moving out to meet an enemy panzer division that had broken through, and considering the above-listed circumstances, the corps commander was obliged to oversee this personally, or at least to send to the division some operational group of officers to assist the 92nd Guards Rifle Division's command staff. During a discussion over the Baudot device that evening with the commander of the 69th Army Lieutenant General V.D. Kriuchenkin, N.F. Vatutin had applied just one word to describe the situation in the 35th Guards Rifle Corps – "disgraceful". The General of the Army was different from the overwhelming majority of his service peers and a number of other Front commander-in-chiefs by his rather proper attitude toward subordinates, and the word "disgraceful" can be considered the penultimate stage of indignation before he would begin to get enraged, and with good reason. The corps command, in favorable conditions according to the standards of the acting army, had been unable to get two divisions moved into prepared positions within 14 hours. Moreover, one division en route had lost track of its units, and at a critical moment its headquarters didn't know where two of its rifle regiments were located.

I will note regarding V.F. Trunin that according to the documents available today, one can say that this man by his background and training was simply unable to command a division. Even a year later, after the colonel had received a certain amount of experience and knowledge, he continued all the same to make elementary mistakes, just like he did near Belgorod when he had paid no heed to advice and instructions from senior officers. Here is just one more example, from a memorandum written by the commander of the 13th Army's 24th Rifle Corps Lieutenant General N.I. Kiriukhin on 31 July 1944:

> Despite a great desire to work, integrity and dedication in work, despite a number of other positive qualities as a man, Comrade Trunin doesn't have the necessary traits and knowledge of a general officer. The experience and knowledge to shape a battle and the ability to forge cooperation among different types of forces are lacking. This was particularly shown in the fighting for Kristopol' [sic – Kostopol] on 18 and 19 June 1944, in which his lack of cooperation with the 11th Tank Corps and his unskilled use of artillery means led not to success, but to heavy losses. The same situation took place in the fighting to force a crossing of the San River. His excessive egalitarianism and weak exactingness toward subordinates leads to the fact that his subordinates don't show any motivation or "personal drive" in work, and this leads to failure when carrying out a combat assignment. For example, despite the fact two days had been given to preparations, the division failed to form a forward detachment for seizing a bridgehead on the San River.
>
> Forgetfulness regarding previously-issued orders and the successive issuing of orders that are completely contrary to each other [are characteristic for him]. During the march from the San River to the Vistula River, Comrade Trunin once again lost track and didn't know where the regiments were located from 2000 on 28 July to 29 July 1944, and this was despite the fact that I had personally warned him that it was necessary to make sure that he didn't let command and control lapse.[70]

Soviet Prisoners of War and Civilians. Trunin retired from active service on 30.04.1955. He passed away on 11 September 1958.
69   Author's personal archive.
70   Author's personal archive.

The bitter fighting between the 92nd Guards Rifle Division's 280th Guards Rifle Regiment with the 6th Panzer Division's *kampfgruppen* and elements of the 19th Panzer Division ended before midnight, and by this time the tension had somewhat subsided. However, skirmishes in isolated sectors continued all night long. There is evidence that Lieutenant Colonel N.I. Novikov formed a combat raiding party out of two rifle companies, which on the night of 7-8 July was to infiltrate the German-held territory from out of the area northeast of Dal'niaia Igumenka and destroy an enemy headquarters in Miasoedovo. Moreover, subsequently the results of the work of this group were assessed as successful, but so far I haven't found any detailed information about this raid in the archives of the Russian Ministry of Defense. There is justification to assume that this attack was conducted somewhat later, because at the indicated time, Miasoedovo was under dual control: in the northern section were troops of the 94th Guards Rifle Division, and in the southern and southeastern sections was the 7th Panzer Division, and thus no one would have permitted the positioning of a major headquarters in such close proximity to the front.

However, let's return to the results of the fighting for Melikhovo. Considering the large significance of this village for the stability of the defense on this axis, as well as the fact that the fighting ended very late in the day, it is important to understand where the frontline stabilized. According to accounts of the 92nd Guards Rifle Division, by the end of the day its units had stopped the enemy, and then pushed the Germans back to the line: (excl.) southeastern outskirts of Dal'niaia Igumenka – southwestern slopes of the hills south of Melikhovo – Kalinin. In a report from the 7th Guards Army's artillery headquarters, an adjustment has been made as to where von Oppeln-Bronikowski's panzers were stopped: "… By 2000 the group of enemy tanks reached the bend in the road (2 kilometers west of Kalinin)."[71] However, if we check a map, the division's information and that of the artillery headquarters indicate one and the same place, even though they are giving it different names. Nevertheless, it is difficult to determine the area where the 6th Panzer Division's *panzerkampfgruppe* reached by the end of 7 July with any great certainty. At that moment, not even Breith's III Panzer Corps had such information. The point is that Hünersdorff's panzer division, like incidentally all of III Panzer Corps' divisions that were locked in heavy fighting in the system of Voronezh Front's second army-level belt of defenses, had lost contact with its units. The information arriving at the corps headquarters from their headquarters was sparse and often contradictory. Moreover, mistakes in the reports were multiplying because of the highly fluid combat operations among other reasons. At times, a line that had been reported as captured was taken back by Soviet troops (as happened on the night of 7-8 July in Dal'niaia Igumenka). There were incidents when in the course of an attack, the troops of one division, having successfully found a weak spot in the Guardsmen's defenses, exploited it and conducted active combat operations in a sector of one of III Panzer Corps' other divisions. If in the process communications were spotty, then a division, in which for example there was a strongpoint that had been seized by a neighbor, would unintentionally report that it had been captured by its own forces (people are always thinking first about one of their own successes), and say not a word about its neighbors.

An analogous situation took place as well during the breakthrough by 6th Panzer Division's *panzerkampfgruppe*. I will remind the reader that exploiting the success of the 19th Panzer Division, which had first seized the center of Blizhniaia Igumenka, and then toward evening having completely driven units of the 81st Guards Rifle Division out of this village Colonel von Oppeln-Bronikowski had launched an attack directly to the north out of Iastrebovo. By 2000 his panzers had split the line of Morozov's division practically to its entire depth and reached the area 2 kilometers west of Kalinin (2 kilometers north of Miaseodovo). However, from Schmidt's 19th Panzer Division, information arrived at the III Panzer Corps headquarters that it was its

---

71 TsAMO RF, f. 7 gv. A, op. 5312, d. 539, l. 146.

panzerkampfgruppe that had scored such a notable success, and not the adjacent 6th Panzer Division. In the course of the fighting for Blizhniaia Igumenka, the commander of the 19th Panzer Division's Panzer Regiment 27, Colonel Becker, had received a wound and been transported to a field hospital; Westhofen assumed command of the panzer regiment. It is possible that the confusion was connected with this change in commanders. The situation was clarified only by the middle of 8 July. On a typewritten daily report to the headquarters of Army Group South there is a handwritten note that the supplied information was mistaken, and that the panzers that made this striking advance belonged not to the 19th Panzer Division, but to the 6th Panzer Division. It isn't clear who wrote this note, but most likely it was a staff officer in Breith's headquarters after a detailed analysis of the situation that developed in this area.

For the 81st Guards Rifle Division commander, it wasn't important to which enemy division the *panzerkampfgruppe* belonged that had cut off his division from its rear services and was surging toward his command post (the Germans were approximately 4 kilometers from the division headquarters in Sevriukovo). The threat of the encirclement of his entire division and the Germans' emergence in the rear of the 6th Guards Army's and 2nd Guards Tank Corps' left-flank forces had arisen. The situation of the 81st Guards Rifle Division sharply changed only toward midnight. At that moment, the two stray regiments of the 92nd Guards Rifle Division began to arrive in its sector. Later I.K. Morozov recalled:

> By 2300 two regiments of the 35th Guards Rifle Corps' 92nd Guards Rifle Division arrived that were at my disposal. With one regiment [the 276th Guards Rifle Regiment] I reinforced the defense of the Dal'niaia Igumenka – Andreevskie – Postnikov sector with a front to the northeast with the mission to prevent an enemy breakthrough to Postnikov. The second regiment [282nd Guards Rifle Regiment] was placed in echelon behind the 238th Guards and 233rd Guards Rifle Regiments, in readiness to counterattack toward Belovskaia and Sevriukovo.[72]

Of course, having received operational control of two fresh rifle regiments, the division commander was elated. However, if the situation is assessed objectively, such a quantity of troops was already excessive for that diminutive area now being held by the 81st Guards Rifle Division, and no one had been expecting or preparing for their arrival. Therefore whereas the 276th Guards Rifle Regiment was quickly assigned a sector and rapidly (in the course of a night) and smoothly merged into the division's combat positions, the same could not be said for the 282nd Guards Rifle Regiment. From the account of this regiment's commander Lieutenant Colonel I.I. Samoilenko:

> 7 July and the night of 7-8 July were passing, when the vanguard and the main forces came under a bombing attack. At dawn on 8.7.43, the regiment arrived at its designated place of assembly and began to move out toward a defensive line. Mortar fire was opened on our combat formations. We took up a position: the northern outskirts of Staryi Gorod on the right, Point 12 on the road from Staryi Gorod to Dal'niaia Igumenka on the left, with the calculation of an all-round defense. We began to reconnoiter with reconnaissance patrols, with elements on foot and mounted scouts, and by means of observation, in order to locate where the enemy was and locate his firing positions. The area of the regiment's defensive sector had been previously mined without prior notification and without cleared passages, as a result of which there were incidents of needless sacrifices as a result of triggering our own

---

72   TsAMO RF, personnel file of Major General I.K. Morozov, autobiography, l. 49.

mines. Throughout the day of 8 July the enemy conducted concentrated artillery and mortar fire on our right flank, because of which the regiment had losses of up to 10% of its men and equipment.[73]

Let's dwell upon this in a bit more detail. In the operational summaries for 7 and 8 July, the 81st Guards Rifle Division's command reported that the division was located in encirclement.[74] Later this information migrated over into account material, and from there, already after the war, into the studies of historians. As a result, a legend about the operational encirclement of the 81st Guards Rifle Division near Belgorod arose, and then about its breakout from the pocket. It was also advantageous to the enemy to support the myth about a "pocket", and the poorly organized evacuation from it by Morozov's division on 10 July 1943 to a new line. The legend stipulates that a lot of weapons were left in the positions, and approximately two battalions of infantry of the 81st Guards Rifle Division and 92nd Guards Rifle Division were taken prisoner. Owing to this, the myth had a grip for a long time. However, in reality the events that unfolded in this area are far from that given in the majority of publications. If you look at the operational maps of the Voronezh Front, as well as those of the 6th Guards and 7th Guards Armies between 5 and 9 July inclusively, then the falsehood becomes obvious. In reality the main forces of Morozov's division (the combat units) were in a difficult situation, and after the breakthrough by the 6th Panzer Division's *panzerkampfgruppe* on the evening of 7 July in the Blizhniaia Igumenka – Kalinin sector, they wound up isolated from their rear services. However, there was no complete encirclement; a path to the north through the combat positions of the 375th Rifle Division was open. Incidentally, the Guardsmen made use of it, when they were forced to abandon their positions and retreat to a new line beyond the Donets.

The authorship of this canard belongs to the commander of the 81st Guards Rifle Division. It was part of his nature as a person to exaggerate the achievements of his subordinates, which served to place himself in an advantageous light as an on the ball leader. Unquestionably, for five days of the hardest and bloodiest fighting the Guardsmen of his division had held on tenaciously. Thanks to their courage and heroism, the division fully carried out the assignment it had been given, and this in turn played an important role in the success of the plan of the defensive operation of the entire Voronezh Front. The real actions of the combatants of the 81st Guards Rifle Division speak for themselves, while the "heroic" fables only interfere with the exhibition of their genuine contribution to the overall cause of victory in the Battle of Kursk.

The breakthrough by the forces of III Panzer Corps to Melikhovo substantially complicated the situation of the Soviet troops on the boundary between the 6th Guards and 7th Guards Armies. Real prospects arose for a further exploitation of Army Detachment Kempf's offensive in the direction of Korocha along the corridor between the Northern Donets and Razumnaia Rivers. In addition, the distance between the forces of Hoth's and Kempf's shock groupings had noticeably decreased. On the morning of 7 July, the SS Panzergrenadier Division *Totenkopf* also began to show high activity; its attacks against the right flank of the 375th Rifle Division out of the Soshenkov – Visloe area in the direction of Gostishchevo noticeably increased. The SS troops were striving to seize this junction of dirt and railroads, in order to reach the highway that connected the major villages of Gostishchevo, Sabynino, Melikhovo and Dal'niaia Igumenka. By the end of the day, the 6th Panzer Division and SS Panzergrenadier Division *Totenkopf* were separated by just 17-18 kilometers as the crow flies.

---

73 TsAMO RF, f. 282 gv. sp, op. 349903, d. 2, l. 39.
74 TsAMO RF, f. 81 gv. sd, op. 1, d. 7, l. 289.

The fact alone of the breakthrough of the 25th Guards Rifle Corps' line by von Oppeln-Bronikowski's *panzerkampgruppe* over a relatively short interval of time (between morning and 1600), and the haste with which the Soviet side was organizing a defense along the Dal'niaia Igumenka – Melikhovo line showed the German command that the most heavily fortified, and thus most difficult sector of the Russians' defenses had finally been overcome. In addition, the 81st Guards Rifle Division, the line of which was the cornerstone of Vatutin's plan to keep the Fourth Panzer Army and Army Detachment Kempf separate, had been placed in a very difficult situation. The movement into its sector of the 92nd Guards Rifle Division, a significant portion of the commanders of which (primarily of the units and headquarters) lacked a large amount of combat experience in command of the division and its units (their arrival at the front in a disheveled condition is a vivid confirmation of this assertion), was unable to strengthen the line reliably as had been planned by the Front command. It had been necessary to reinforce the 81st Guards Rifle Division, but in fact the "fragmentation" of the 92nd Guards Rifle Division, which eventually wound up struck by the spearhead of III Panzer Corps' attack, negatively influenced the strength of the defense on the boundary between the 6th Guards and 7th Guards Armies. Indeed, this became clear to everyone already on the next day, 8 July, but it was impossible to correct the situation. The supposition arises that the Soviet side (primarily N.F. Vatutin) simply didn't expect such a swift advance by the Germans on the operation's third day. In the opposite case, the 305th Rifle Division, which the Front Commander-in-Chief ordered only on the morning of 8 July to move out urgently in order to cover the boundary between the two Guards armies, might have already been positioned in the Dal'niaia Igumenka – Melikhovo – Shliakhovoe sector already on 7 July. Incidentally, N.F. Vatutin himself didn't pass along the assessment of the situation that came together northeast of Belgorod on 7 July, even though, for example, in a later conversation with P.A. Rotmistrov, he expressed his regrets about the decisions that were taken to launch a number of counterattacks on the Oboian' – Prokhorovka axis in the first days of Operation Citadel. From the archival documents, only one thing is clear: the General of the Army Vatutin believed that the command of the 92nd Guards Rifle Division and that of the 35th Guards Rifle Corps had proved to be unable to carry out an elementary task – to move troops to a designated area in a timely manner and without any snags or hitches.

In the situation that had developed by 7 July, the stubbornly defending 81st Guards Rifle Division was for Kempf like a bone in the throat. The unbending resistance of this division very much obstructed his troops from covering the Fourth Panzer Army's right flank. In the documents of the German divisions, the staff officers with plain irritation were calling its line "a wasps' nest". However, with each passing day it became ever more difficult for the Guardsmen to hold on, and a particularly hard situation arose on the evening of 7 July. Indeed, this was not only because of the large losses suffered thus far, although they were painful. By the end of the day, the division commander had been deprived of the possibility to use virtually any of his assets. Back on 6 July, under enemy pressure and because of large losses, the 265th Cannon Artillery Regiment had been transferred to a different sector. On the night of 6-7 July, because of the threat that the enemy would capture its howitzers, he withdrew the 161st Cannon Artillery Regiment from the area of Blizhniaia Igumenka to Iastrebovo. The 114th Guards Destroyer Anti-tank Artillery Regiment had been transferred to him in order to reinforce the Iastrebovo, Sevriukovo and Miasoedovo area of defense, but the 97th Guards Mortar Regiment was withdrawn from his operational control back on 5 July. In addition, virtually all of the tanks of the 262nd Separate Heavy Tank Regiment had been knocked out of action, while the 290th Mortar Regiment had lost half of its materiel. I will remind the reader also that one battalion of the 81st Guards Rifle Division's 173rd Guards Artillery Regiment had been completely destroyed on 6 July at the "Day of Harvest" collective farm. It is easy to imagine the situation of a division commander who'd been deprived of such a significant amount of heavy weapons and who was still facing the pressure of a superior foe.

However, even though it was at the limit of its strength, the 81st Guards Rifle Division was continuing to repulse the attacks of three of the III Panzer Corps' divisions. The arrival of two fresh regiments from the 92nd Guards Rifle Division not only blunted the advance of the 6th Panzer Division's tanks, it also rallied the defenders of the "Belgorod bastion", as General Raus called this area in his memoirs.

The headquarters of III Panzer Corps succinctly summed up the situation of affairs in the sector of its divisions by the end of 7 July in an operational briefing at 2125 (Berlin time):

> 7th Panzer Division with its reconnaissance battalion is advancing from the Batratsakaia Dacha State Farm to the north through the "Solov'ev" collective farm, and with part of its strength to the east of the State Farm. Fighting still continues in the northern portion of Miasoedovo. There is concern about the eastern flank, because fresh enemy units have openly taken position in the woods to the east. The sector of woods northeast of Miasoedovo and around Kalinin have been strongly occupied [by the 94th Guards Rifle Division].
>
> 6th Panzer Division has been stopped 4 kilometers north of Sevriukovo because of strong flanking fire from Kalinin.
>
> 19th Panzer Division remained east of Postnikov; Panzergrenadier Regiment 73 is fighting in the woods between Belovskaia and Blizhniaia Igumenka.[75]

Judging from the documents that show the line being held by the 7th Guards Army's units at the end of 7 July, which have been found in the Russian Federation's Central Archives of the Ministry of Defense, the troops of Army Detachment Kempf were halted on the following line:

a. 81st Guards Rifle Division's sector: 235th and 238th Guards Rifle Regiments – Staryi Gorod – railroad hut (4 kilometers north of the Kreida railyard); 233rd Guards Rifle Regiment – Blizhniaia Igumenka; 276th Guards Rifle Regiment of the 92nd Guards Rifle Division – (excl.) Blizhniaia Igumenka – (excl.) Postnikov; and 280th Guards Rifle Regiment in reserve.
b. 94th Guards Rifle Division's sector: northern part of Miasoedovo – northern section of the woods 2 kilometers east of Miasoedovo.
c. 44th Guards Rifle Regiment of the 15th Guards Rifle Division: 1 kilometer north of the "Solov'ev" collective farm – 2 kilometers east of the "Batratskaia Dacha" State Farm; and the 167th Separate Tank Regiment (5 T-34 and a company of anti-tank rifles[76]) was 1 kilometer west of Nikol'skoe, saddling the road between there and the "Batratskaia Dacha" State Farm.
d. 73rd Guards Rifle Division: 214th Guards Rifle Regiment (intermingled in its combat positions with the 223rd Guards Rifle Regiment of the 78th Guards Rifle Division) – road fork 500 meters south of the "Batratskaia Dacha" State Farm – Point "K"; 211th Guards Rifle Regiment: Point "K" to the Machine Tractor Station; 209th Guards Rifle Regiment – assembled on the western fringe of the woods 1 kilometer east of Gremiachii; the 78th Guards Rifle Division's 225th Guards Rifle Regiment was digging in within the village itself, along with the attached 1/793rd Rifle Regiment of the 213th Rifle Division.
e. 72nd Guards Rifle Division: 229th Guards Rifle Regiment – Hill 190 to Hill 192.6; 222nd Guards Rifle Regiment – (excl.) Hill 192.6 to a point 500 meters southeast of Hill

---

75 NARA US, t. 312, r. 54, f. 7469626.
76 At this time, 2 T-34 were on th eastern bank of the Koren' River, guarding the bridge in Nikol'skoe.

192.8; 224th Guards Rifle Regiment: 1st Rifle Battalion – woods 1 kilometer southeast of Priiutovka; 3rd Rifle Battalion – Bezliudovka; 2nd Rifle Battalion – with two rifle companies along the railroad bed at the railroad hut 1 kilometer north of the Kar'ernaia railyard; 585th Rifle Regiment of the 213th Rifle Division – (excl.) Bezliudovka – Nezhegol River.

In the sector: (excl.) "Poliana" State Farm – (excl.) Rzhavets – Bezliudova – Nezhegol River, troops of the 72nd Guards Rifle Division were intermingled with the 213th Rifle Division and it is difficult to determine precisely where its units were located. It is known that at 1800, the 793rd Rifle Regiment (minus the 1st Rifle Battalion) was holding the Hill 192.8 – (excl.) Rzhavets sector, while the 702nd Rifle Regiment was holding the sector running from (excl.) Rzhavets to the eastern fringe of the woods east of Rzhavets. With the onset of darkness, the 585th Rifle Regiment turned over its sector to the 6th Rifle Company of the 72nd Guards Rifle Division's 224th Guards Rifle Regiment.

Now let's take a look at the results that the entire Army Group South achieved on this day and how they affected the performance of Army Detachment Kempf's troops. By the end of 7 July, no fundamental changes had taken place in the offensive sector of Field Marshal von Manstein's main grouping. The situation of both of his subordinate armies that were directed toward Kursk was gradually worsening. The Fourth Panzer Army, having broken though the first army-level defensive belt completely, had entered the second belt of defensive fortifications and there became engaged in heavy fighting with two Soviet armies – the 6th Guards Army and the 1st Tank Army. In addition to the multitude of current problems, two more major problems that had been poorly anticipated in his plan arose before Hoth during the attack against deeply-echeloned lines. First, having in fact broken through half of the Voronezh Front's army-level fortified defensive belts, XXXXVIII and II SS Panzer Grenadier Corps hadn't been able to forge a continuous front; on their adjacent flanks, a powerful wedge had been created that was being held by the forces of the 1st Tank Army with the support of the 6th Guards Army, which stood just like a breakwater that was splitting the Fourth Panzer Army's entire attack grouping. Thus in the course of 7 July, both of Hoth's panzergrenadier corps had stubbornly, but slowly ground their way forward through the Voronezh Front's defenses, striving to create the conditions for the destruction of Katukov's tank army on their adjacent flanks. In addition, the two SS panzergrenadier divisions of the II SS Panzer Grenadier Corps that were advancing on the Prokhorovka direction hadn't been able to link their flanks. This forced Hausser to allow the commanders of the SS Panzergrenadier Divisions *Das Reich* and *Liebstandarte Adolf Hitler* throughout the day to pause in their offensive in order to put themselves back into order, bring up their rear services, and take care of the situation on their flanks after two days of the heaviest fighting imaginable. A similar, but more significant problem that was affecting the situation had erupted on the right flank of the Fourth Panzer Army. The analysis of captured German documents show that the leadership of Army Group South and that of the Fourth Panzer Army began to consider the inability of Kempf's army detachment to cover the flank of Hoth's panzer army as a very serious problem only on 7 July. The chief of staff of the Fourth Panzer Army General F. Fangohr confirms this.

Secondly, the hopes that had been placed on the Führer's armored battering ram – Panzer Brigade 10 of Panthers – had collapsed. It had proved totally unable to carry out the task of serving as a powerful steamroller, which was to lay down a path toward Kursk through the Russian defenses for the rest of the Fourth Panzer Army. Already by the evening of 7 July, mostly due to mechanical breakdowns and mines, only a fifth of its Panthers was still operational (at 2030, there were 40 Pz.Kpf.wg V serviceable),[77] but the struggle with the 1st Tank Army in which it had been supposed to play a key role had only started. In addition, the offensive by Colonel General W. Model's Ninth Army north of Kursk had also sharply slowed.

All these signs of the pending failure of Operation Citadel were becoming obvious in Berlin as well. However, the OKH could find nothing better to do at the moment than to take 30% of the bombers, 40% of the fighters, and 50% of the Stukas of VIII Fliegerkorps from the most successfully operating Army Group South and transfer them to Army Group Center.[78] This decision was erroneous. It couldn't help Model get his army moving, and at the same time complicated von Manstein's ability to resolve the accumulating problems connected with the approach of the Soviet operational and strategic reserves.

Thus, having become enmeshed in the powerful and many-layered system of defenses of the Voronezh Front with its armored wedges, which were beginning to move in diverging directions, the enormous machine of Army Group South by the end of the third day of the offensive began to stall. In this exceptionally complex situation, a decisive lunge forward by the Army Detachment Kempf was extremely important for von Manstein, but despite the encouraging results of 7 July in III Panzer Corps' sector, it was still too early to talk about a clean breakthrough by his divisions into operational space.

The third day of the German offensive showed that the 7th Guards Army commander M.S. Shumilov was confidently handling the task that the Voronezh Front's Military Council had laid upon him. He had managed to contain the forces of the albeit auxiliary, but still rather powerful enemy grouping and prevented them from emerging out of the main army-level fortified zone throughout the initial, hardest days of the defensive operation. A number of important factors had helped him conduct a successful struggle with the enemy.

In the first place, he and his headquarters (of course, not without the help of the Front headquarters), had accurately determined the enemy's objectives and tasks well before the enemy had launched the offensive. Thanks to this, a balanced plan of combat operations, relying on a powerful system of defense and a minimum of needed forces, had been prepared, which included several possible variants for how the situation might develop, including those negative for his 7th Guards Army.

In the second place, the forces and means with which the enemy was striving to attain his objectives had been rather quickly determined. For example, already on the evening of 6 July, it was precisely indicated in the army's Operational Briefing No.358 that the enemy was trying to crush its defenses with two panzer and three infantry divisions.[79] There was confusion over the identification of the divisions; the summary cited the Divisions *Leibstandarte Adolf Hitler* and *Totenkopf*, but the German strength was determined rather accurately. On the next day, the headquarters of the 7th Guards Army again reported the presence of the same five German divisions, even though the 6th Panzer Division had already been introduced into the fighting.

This mistake was connected with the fact that the Soviet command was still unaware of the change in the number of armored vehicles of a Werhmacht panzer division under a new Table of Organization and Equipment that had been adopted. By the middle of 1943, their establishment strength was no longer 200 panzers, as it had been in 1941 and 1942, but now 141. Thus when taking guidance from the total number of tanks that was operating on this axis, it seemed comparable with the strength of two panzer divisions equipped according to the old TO&E, which meant 200 tanks each. There had been no success in capturing a military serviceman of all three panzer

---

77   NARA US, t. 313, r. 368, f. 8654312.
78   Newton, *Kurskaia bitva: Nemetskii vzgliad*, p. 247.
79   TsAMO RF, f. 7 gv. A, op. 5312, d. 239, l. 157.

divisions in the initial days of the operation, because the density of troops was very high, and the places where the fighting was going on were constantly under the enemy's control. Even so, already on 6 July in the Krutoi Log area, a search patrol when investigating a knocked-out tank found the documents of a member of the 7th Panzer Division, but the scouts incorrectly identified the number of the field post office. The situation began to become clear only on 8 July, when on this day a reconnaissance patrol of the 78th Guards Rifle Division's 228th Guards Rifle Regiment in the area of the "Batratskaia Dacha" State Farm came upon the documents of a Lieutenant Müller of the 7th Panzer Division's Engineer Battalion 58; a reconnaissance patrol of the 81st Guards Rifle Division in the woods southeast of Blizhniaia Igumenka took the identification papers off the body of Lieutenant Adorf of the 19th Panzer Division's panzer reconnaissance battalion; and information arrived from the 94th Guards Rifle Division that the 6th Panzer Division was operating in the Kalinin area. In Operational Briefing No.190, the headquarters of the 7th Guards Army's Armored and Mechanized Forces at 1800 on 8 July would clearly indicate that the Germans were operating with the 6th, 7th and 19th Panzer Divisions in the northern and northeastern directions.[80] However, the previous misidentifications didn't influence the assessment of the enemy's strength, and the calculations made by the 7th Guards Army's command to assign forces (of those that it had) to hold one or another line proved correct. Even though the enemy was continuing to make progress through the army's defenses, it wasn't a rapid advance. The offensive of the enemy's divisions resembled more the work of a woodpecker, when it is pecking out a hole in a strong tree trunk.

In the fourth place, the army commander's main decisions in the course of the combat operations relied on the accurate prognosis of the enemy's intentions and the assessment of the capabilities of his forces, both in terms of firepower and speed of movement. M.S. Shumilov was flawlessly determining the right moment for shifting rifle divisions with the aim of bolstering vulnerable sectors, even though the timetable of their march wasn't always properly observed; nevertheless, there wasn't a single case of a German breakthrough because of the untimely movement of the army's forces to one or another area. All this testifies to the high professional skill and combat experience of this military commander, and knowledge of both the strengths and weaknesses of his own troops and those of the enemy. Serious hitches began to occur only when the army's precise plan of combat actions began to depend directly on the arrival of reserves from the Voronezh Front. As far as he was able, the army commander made sure of this. The situation with the 31st Separate Destroyer Anti-tank Artillery Brigade plainly demonstrated this, when only thanks to the efficiency of the staff officers of the 7th Guards Army's headquarters, this anti-tank brigade at the last possible moment arrived on the axis of the III Panzer Corps' main attack and stopped von Oppeln-Bronikowski's *panzerkampfgruppe*. However, even in such difficult moments, when for example the 92nd and 94th Guards Rifle Divisions were still on the march, and the line of the 25th Guards Rifle Corps was being held only with great difficulty against the strong attacks made by von Funck's and Hünersdorff's *panzerkampfgruppen*, fortune didn't turn its back on M.S. Shumilov. However, the word "fortune" is more suitable for artistic films and novels. Primarily, success in the course of such large-scale battles is instead a matter of deep knowledge, combat experience and accurate calculations.

Thus, owing to the energetic countermeasures adopted by the 7th Guards Army that accurately corresponded to the operational situation, not a single one of the daily plans of Army Detachment Kempf was realized in the course of the first three days of the offensive. All of the efforts of its shock formation – III Panzer Corps, not to mention those of Korps Raus, boiled down to a slow advance through the system of the 7th Guards Army's defenses and rather high losses. Not even Kempf's daily order for 7 July, despite the obvious progress, was completely realized by all his

---

80 TsAMO RF, f. 341, op. 5312, d. 246, l. 58.

subordinate forces. Only the 6th and 7th Panzer Divisions achieved clear successes. However, even they only made an advance of 9 kilometers on this day from the line they had occupied that morning, and they were supposed to cover a distance twice that far. Even so, this more modest advance proved sufficient in order at last to penetrate the second army-level belt of defenses to its entire depth.

Yet this day brought another, more substantial, unpleasant surprise to the 7th Panzer Division; in addition to the reinforced 73rd Guards Rifle Division that was looming on the right flank and the 15th Guards Rifle Division that was located in reserve, opposite von Funck's 7th Panzer Division the full-strength 94th Guards Rifle Division appeared in its path. Back on the morning of 7 July, having received information from his panzer reconnaissance battalion about the presence of a defense of two-echelons on his right flank, von Fuck had already started to think about a menacing danger there; even so, counting on the stability of the 106th Infantry Division and his Panzer Reconnaissance Battalion 37, he had moved his tanks toward Miasoedovo. Now, however, the appearance of Russkikh's division completely tied down his division's forces in this area. In the documents of the 7th Panzer Division it is noted:

> The approach of the enemy's operational reserves toward the front and flanks of the corps was not detected by aerial reconnaissance. In the 7th Panzer Division's area alone two new divisions were discovered in addition to tank and anti-tank regiments. In order to continue the attack on 8 July, the 7th Panzer Division is to guard the deep right flank. The 6th and 19th Panzer Divisions are to break through the ridge of hills northeast of Blizhniaia Igumenka, concentrating on Melikhovo and Dal'niaia Igumentka respectively with panzers to the forefront.[81]

Skipping ahead of the events, I'll note that the corps' plan to use Schmidt's 19th Panzer Division for launching an attack to the northeast along the basin of the Northern Donets came to naught. The troops of the 19th Panzer and 168th Infantry Division became bogged down in exhausting and bloody fighting with the 81st Guards Rifle Division, and in the nearest time they were unable to get out of this pitfall, which had been prepared for them by Morozov's Guardsmen. In the course of the past 24 hours, both divisions had succeeded in fully taking and consolidating their grip only on the Kreida railyard and Belovskaia. Elements of the 81st Guards Rifle Division's 233rd Guards Rifle Regiment that night would again stealthily re-enter Blizhniaia Igumenka, which the Germans had taken the previous evening, and fighting there would erupt with renewed intensity with the sunrise.

An alarming situation was also forming on Army Detachment Kempf's right flank. As a result of the high casualties, and because of the need to cover the flank of III Panzer Corps, which was continuing to become stretched, albeit slowly, Kempf was forced to keep the troops of the 106th Infantry Division gradually moving along in the wake of the 7th Panzer Division, and in the process the front of the entire Korps Raus was beginning to be stretched thin. On the morning of 7 July after regrouping the 106th Infantry Division, its Infantry Regiment 240 took up a line in the vicinity of the "Batratskaia Dacha" State Farm. Thus, Korps Raus' front now extended for almost 25 kilometers. The calculations that Forst's division would not only securely cover III Panzer Corps' flank with active operations, but also take part in the 7th Panzer Division's attack to the east with a portion of its strength, while the 320nd Infantry Division, reinforced with artillery and StuG Battalion 905, would be able to repel the Russian attacks against its front without any particular difficulty, were only partially justified. There was no use even thinking about using Forst's

---

81 Haupt, *Srazheniia gruppy armii "Iug"*, p. 295.

kampfgruppen in the sector of the 7th Panzer Division's attack. Because of the dogged Russian resistance east of the "Batratskaia Dacha" State Farm and their ferocious attacks at Gremiachii and the "Poliana" State Farm, Raus and Breith were forced not only to concentrate all of the 106th Infantry Division here, but also to dispatch the 7th Panzer Division's panzer reconnaissance battalion, reinforced with armor, to this area, as well as to divert a significant portion of its Panzer Regiment 25. The 320th Infantry Division was also struggling to hold onto its positions on the eastern bank of the Donets. Noticeably weakened by the preceding fighting, the division had been forced already on the morning of 7 July to abandon the major strongpoint of Bezliudovka under the pressure of Soviet troops, and to withdraw its right-flank hastily to its jumping-off positions.

In his memoirs, E. Raus acknowledged the high losses of his troops in the course of the fighting in the Bezliudovka area, but explained the reason for the 320th Infantry Division's retreat to the western bank of the Donets in a very original manner – this, supposedly, was a premeditated withdrawal. He wrote, "The initial success of the first day required immediate exploitation of the breach at Krutoi Log, where the 7th Panzer Division had punched through. All our forces were concentrated to this end, and the *Armeeabteilung* even abandoned the nonessential and costly Bezliudovka bridgehead on the southern flank."[82]

If this was a planned withdrawal, then it is difficult to see why the 320th Infantry Division, which was supposed to cover the flank of Army Detachment Kempf's shock grouping, which meant first of all organizing a strong defense, withdrew from a major village that it had already occupied. In reality, because of the strength of the 24th Guards Rifle Corps' grouping, the bridgehead in this area proved to offer no prospects for developing an attack in the direction of Shebekino. However, considering that Army Detachment Kempf at the time of the withdrawal held only an insignificant amount of territory on the eastern bank, this village was one of the three key strongpoints (Nizhnii Ol'shanets, Maslova Pristan' and Bezliudovka) that were adding strength to its defense. Raus' words also sound strange because already on the night of 7-8 July and then on following day, suffering no small losses, the 320th Infantry Division would again make attempts to force a crossing of the river and regain possession of this sector. Moreover, it is difficult to call the abandonment of Bezliudovka by its troops on 7 July a planned withdrawal; it looked more like panicked flight: weapons and ammunition were abandoned, and piles of corpses of its officers and soldiers were left behind, even though usually one never saw such things after a planned evacuation of Wehrmacht troops.

Like nothing else, the casualty figures cast a bright light on the difficult situation confronting Army Detachment Kempf and the illusionary nature of its divisions' plans. In the West, facts that testify to the failures of the Wehrmacht have been rarely published or get published today. In addition, even today it is extremely difficult for Russian scholars to gain access to the archival materials of the German Army for various reasons. Finally, a significant portion of the documents, including those covering casualty figures, were irretrievably lost back in the war years. Nevertheless, even that sparse amount of available information that appears in certain publications helps partially pull back the curtain of dissembly and heroic pathos regarding the Wehrmacht's stalwart warriors, which the surviving Wehrmacht generals and mass media drew over the events of the summer of 1943 back in the Cold War years.

The former Wehrmacht General Gotthard Heinrici cites interesting data on this subject in his research on Operation Citadel: "In the 320th Infantry Division up to 1600 men were wounded on 7 July [1943]. Four battalions of this division now had 200 men each."[83] Here's the clear answer

---

82 Raus, *Tankovye srazheniia na Vostochnom fronte*, p. 241.
83 Glantz, D. and House, J., *Kurskaia bitva: Reshaushchii povorot punkt vtoroi mirovoi voiny*, p. 439.

why this division retreated from Bezliudovka so hastily. The enemy simply had nothing left by which to hold the bridgehead at the village.

Even so, it should be noted that on 7 July, the total manpower losses of Army Detachment Kempf relative to the preceding days of combat fell sharply and amounted to a total of 688 men, which was almost 3.5 times less than on 6 July, and 5 times less than on 5 July. The main reason for this was the change in tactics. The Germans suffered most of their casualties when forcing a crossing of the Donets, when assaulting fortified anti-tank strongpoints (which as a rule consisted of villages, in the capture of which infantry played the main role) in the main belt of the 7th Guards Army's defenses and during the counterattacks by the troops of the 24th Guards Rifle Corps against the 320th Infantry Division, which at that time didn't have a sufficient number of anti-tank guns and hadn't been able yet to consolidate its gains on the eastern bank. By 7 July, the situation had changed; a continuous breakthrough front had been created, all of the stubbornly defended centers of resistance in the rear of the III Panzer Corps had been destroyed, and the German command was now relying on tanks and concentrated artillery fire on a narrow sector of the front.

After two days of the offensive it had become obvious that the method used in 1942, when the Germans would launch powerful panzer attacks simultaneously, concentrated on 2-3 points in the Soviet defenses, which would then shatter like a glass vase and allow the German tanks to break into operational space, wasn't working in this operation. The breakthrough of the 7th Guards Army's line was made substantially more difficult, especially in the first stage, by the absence of adequate air support. The tenacity of the infantry and the artfully devised cobweb of fire by the Soviet command led to the fact that the *kampfgruppen* became enmeshed in caldrons of fire and suffered heavy losses. Therefore the division commands were forced to resort to a different technique. They began concentrating a significant quantity of heavy weapons on a narrow sector, owing to which with dense artillery fire paths were literally burned through the defensive belts, then flattened by the tanks; only after this would infantry be committed into the fighting. Not without justifications, the enemy was assuming that in the end, this method would lead to the ultimate collapse of the 7th Guards Army's robust scaffold. During such an attack, the grenadiers would go into action already after the bulk of the defender's firing weapons had been suppressed, and the minefields had been revealed. Primarily, the panzergrenadiers were busy consolidating the hold on seized territory, mopping up small pockets of enemy resistance, and also fighting in villages and settlements located in narrow defiles and wooded areas that were difficult for the tanks to enter, but at that only when supported by intense artillery fire and tanks. Thus, the infantry were now suffering fewer casualties relative to the two previous days of combat.

In addition, on 7 July the aircraft of VIII Fliegerkorps made significantly more appearances over the sector of Army Detachment Kempf. This also substantially affected the level of casualties among the men, since the airstrikes were focused on knots of resistance, which were putting out heavy fire and were seriously obstructing the advance. At the same time, the use of supplementary types of weapons immediately on a relatively narrow sector of the front allowed the command of the panzer divisions to increase the intensity of fire on the defenders' positions. Now prior to an attack by a Panzerkeil, two waves of fire would pass over the Guardsmen's positions one after the other – first an airstrike, followed by an artillery barrage, which naturally adversely affected the level of resistance offered by a defensive line once the attack got underway.

This approach wasn't new; the enemy had used it previously, and so the Soviet side before the start of the summer campaign, anticipating that it might be used, came up with several effective antidotes and introduced them among the troops. This first included the elaborate system of trenches in combination with a large quantity of dugouts for the men of the rifle elements and the crews of the artillery units directly in the combat positions: trench shelters, foxholes, anti-fragmentation shelters and so forth. Second was the more widespread use in the tactical zone than previously of infantry support tanks and self-propelled guns, including armored firing points that were dug into the ground, in order to increase the staying power of the infantry on the axis of the main attack (in the 7th Guards Army, these were the 201st Tank Brigade, the 262nd Heavy Tank Regiment, the 167th Separate Tank Regiment, the 1529th Self-propelled Artillery Regiment and the 1438th Self-propelled Artillery Regiment).

Thirdly, there was the significantly larger scale of deploying mines than in 1942, not only in the main defensive belt, but also in the depth of the second army-level belt, and also between the second and third army-level defensive belts. To this one should add the artificial obstacles that were quickly emplaced in sectors where German Panzerkeils might attempt to attack. They were especially effective in difficult terrain, since it was more obvious where the enemy tanks might go, and where it was easier to camouflage the obstacles.

With the change in breakthrough tactics, the loss of armor in Breith's panzer divisions sharply grew. Naturally this wasn't widely advertised, but it was also impossible to keep it hidden. In captured German documents relating to 7 July, this problem has been crisply delineated. Here are just a couple of lines from the III Panzer Corps' combat diary: "Friendly losses correspondingly reflected the severity of the combat. Thousands of mines had to be removed."[84] From the diary of the Wehrmacht's Supreme Command: "Our panzer losses because of mines are most significant in Kempf's operational group."[85]

When assessing the results of the combat work of any military formation, in addition to the success or failure of combat missions, the loss figures have paramount importance. How much manpower did Shumilov's army lose in the first three days of the Battle of Kursk? In Operational Summary No.00376 from the headquarters of the Voronezh Front at 1000 on 8 July it is stated that "over the period between 5 and 7.7, the forces of the 7th Guards Army had 6,782 killed and wounded, and 443 missing in action."[86] Accordingly, by the end of 7 July 1943 a total of 7,225 soldiers and officers had been put out of action. Army Detachment Kempf had approximately the same losses; its headquarters reported over this same period of time that its two corps had 6,539 killed, wounded or missing. Considering that the 7th Guards Army over these three days was keeping in check an enemy grouping, the nucleus of which was a panzer corps, these losses can be considered commensurate.

Unfortunately, it is still impossible to determine the daily rate of casualties in all the divisions of the 7th Guards Army. Documents with such information are almost absent in the files of the Ministry of Defense's Central Archives. One can assume that during the fighting they weren't even tracked, because the battalion commanders didn't always know the casualty rates for specific days. However, even if the casualty figures can be found in operational documents, doubts arise regarding their accuracy. Nevertheless, such figures always prompt increased interest, since they provide a certain image of both the level of losses and the severity of the fighting in one or another area, which is something no less important. Summary No.363 from the headquarters of the 7th Guards Army for 0700 9 July 1943 and Combat Report No.057/op from the 25th Guards Rifle Corps for this same day at 1800 have been preserved, which present casualty figures for certain divisions for 7 and 8 July. An elementary mathematical calculation yields the casualty figures for 7 July. Thus, in the operational summary there is the note that "… the losses of the 81st Guards Rifle Division over 7 and 8 July: Killed – 584, wounded or missing – 2,643."[87] Accordingly, over the two-day period the division lost a total of 3,227 men. That evening, corps commander G.B.

---

84 Haupt, *Srazheniia gruppy armii "Iug"*, p. 295.
85 KTV/OKW, Bd. 111, s. 757.
86 TsAMO RF, f. 203, op. 2843, d. 459, l. 312.
87 TsAMO RF, f. 7 gv. A, op. 5312, d. 239, l. 168.

Safiulin reported adjusted data for 8 July: 69 killed, 140 wounded.[88] Thus, if we rely on these two documents, it turns out that on 7 July 1943, the casualties of the 81st Guards Rifle Division amounted to 3,018 men or almost 35% of the division's strength on the morning of 5 July 1943.

Of the total number of casualties suffered by the 81st Guards Rifle Division over five days of combat near Belgorod, a significant number (prior to the start of the counteroffensive in the latter half of July 1943) were recorded as missing-in-action. I'll remind the reader that in the Red Army, a military serviceman was considered missing in action in two cases: if he didn't return to his unit and wasn't found dead on the battlefield, or if none of his fellow soldiers were able to confirm his death. The combat reports of the 19th Panzer and 168th Infantry Divisions over this period of time note that not a significant number of Guardsmen of Morozov's 81st Guards Rifle Division were taken prisoner in their sectors. For example, a morning briefing of 8 July from the headquarters of the 168th Infantry Division announced that on 7 July "… when mopping up the area southwest of Kreida, 15 prisoners were captured."[89] On 8 July, the same division captured a total of 40 men. Thus, this means that the majority of men missing in action in the 81st Guards Rifle Division were soldiers and officers who honorably carried out their duty and were killed in their positions: piled up in trenches, craters or demolished works; or consumed in bunkers by the fiery streams of flamethrowers. At the same time I'll let slip that today it still isn't known whether or not the number given in the army's operational summary cited above includes the 107 men of this division, who in the course of 7 and 8 July had left the battlefield without an order and were picked up behind the lines by blocking detachments of the 92nd NKVD Regiment, and subsequently turned over to the 81st Guards Rifle Division's SMERSH Counterintelligence Department.

Relying on the two documents already mentioned and the same sort of computations, the losses of the 73rd Guards Rifle Division for 7 July also become clear. On this day, it lost a total of 974 men, including 142 killed and 832 wounded.

Thus far, the defensive operation of the 7th Guards Army was proceeding in a fully acceptable fashion for the Voronezh Front command, although the threat of a breakthrough in this area was no longer only faint; on the contrary, it was becoming more tangible with each passing day. Army commander M.S. Shumilov had skillfully handled his forces and was carrying out his orders with the same amount of forces that had been planned to activate here from the beginning. This becomes particularly apparent when you compare them with the enormous resources that were committed to repulse the Fourth Panzer Army's attack on the Oboain' and Prokhorovka directions, though Hoth's strength was greater. Nevertheless, the operation had only just started when N.F. Vatutin, who knew firsthand the Germans' cunning and their capacity to overcome hardships, exerted maximum efforts in order to reveal E. von Manstein's intentions. Vatutin thought von Manstein did so so primarily in one way – by massing his reserves. Despite the fact that reconnaissance and intelligence had not yet identified the appearance of any new German divisions, including opposite the 7th Guards Army, Vatutin still had his doubts. In the first place, the adversary could artfully conceal a regrouping. In the second place, even if reserves hadn't yet been introduced into the fighting, it was extremely important to anticipate the approximate time of their appearance.

Vatutin's analysis of the operational situation both in the entire German breakthrough sector and to the east and northeast of Belgorod made it clear that even though the enemy's offensive was going with great difficulty, it was still making headway. This meant that while the Germans were suffering losses that needed to be replenished, the front was also gradually extending, and so the minimal forces required for covering the flanks of the penetration on the first two days of

---

88 TsAMO RF, f. 25 gv. sk, op. 1, d. 28, l. 59.
89 NARA US, rg. 242, t. 314, r. 197, f. 001203.

the offensive would have to be augmented. Accordingly, the appearance of fresh enemy divisions should be anticipated, including in the sector of the 7th Guards Army as well, and this means that N.F. Vatutin had to give some thought beforehand as to how to contain them. After all, the Germans had also inflicted substantial damage to the Voronezh Front. Considering that the Germans were breaking through the defenses with large tank formations, it was necessary for both the Voronezh Front command and the 7th Guards Army command to have a constant stream of anti-tank reserves.

According to documents of the Front's Intelligence Department and the Front's chief of staff Lieutenant General S.P. Ivanov, who was personally responsible for keeping the commander informed, that was just how they were viewing the situation would develop in the next couple of days. Thus already in Intelligence Summary No.194 at 0700 on 7 July it had been indicated that it should be expected that the enemy would introduce one fresh panzer division (in order to restore the shock potential) and one fresh infantry division (in order to cover the flanks) to reinforce the Belgorod grouping.[90] It had in mind the entirety of Army Group South. At the time this supposition wasn't based on objective data (prisoner statements, documents and so forth), but only on the assessment of the enemy's losses in armor, the extending length of the breakthrough front, as well as the combat experience of the Voronezh Front command. It must be said that in general, the Soviet generals' intuition didn't let them down.

N.F. Vatutin was an experienced professional with a solid academic background. His estimates and calculations in the course of the Battle of Kursk relied on deep knowledge and a broad base of the leading theoretical works of contemporary military science. However, in order to grasp the sequential nature Operation Citadel's plan (first the destruction of the Soviet reserves, and only then turning to the breakthrough to Kursk), in addition to his knowledge and experience Vatutin also had to have extensive information about the overall condition of Germany's economy and armed forces. However, Vatutin didn't possess such information, and thus he believed the German forces had the main and sole task of a breakthrough to Kursk and a link-up with the Ninth Army that was operating against the Central Front. So far not a single document has been found that might show that he was considering that the German command had a different strategic goal in the summer campaign, which was to grind down and bleed white both Soviet *fronts*, in order to avoid being steamrolled by the Soviet strategic reserves that had accumulated by the spring of 1943, though it is possible to assume that he had such thoughts. Nevertheless it needs to be understood that Vatutin was making important decisions in the course of the Kursk defensive operation only on the basis of such a conceptualization of the enemy's main tasks that were confirmed by intelligence (and not on the basis of conjecture and suppositions).

Meanwhile the situation with armored vehicles in von Manstein's forces really was becoming problematic. Archival documents show that on the afternoon of 7 July, of the more than 300 tanks which the Fourth Panzer Army's Panzergrenadier Division *Grossdeutschland* had serviceable on the morning of 5 July (112 tanks in its panzer regiment[91] and 200 Panthers in Panzer Brigade 10), only 85 were still operational.[92] As of 2030 on 7 July, it only had 45 tanks in its own panzer regiment, including 12 flame-throwing tanks and 2 Tigers; the rest were in the brigade of Panthers. Meanwhile 47% of its tanks and assault guns in the II SS Panzer Corps had been knocked out of action by the morning of 8 July.[93] Naturally, neither N.F. Vatutin nor the Front headquarters knew these figures. Nevertheless, on aerial reconnaissance photographs taken by the 2nd Air Army

---

90 TsAMO RF, f. 203, op. 2843, d. 452, l. 42.
91 Zetterling and Frankson, *Kursk 1943: a statistical analysis*, Table A6.3.
92 NARA US, t. 313, r. 368, f. 8654312.
93 Zetterling and Frankson, *Kursk 1943: a statistical analysis*, Table A6.4-A6.6.

and during trips to the front, he personally observed fields that were strewn with burned-out or knocked-out enemy armor. Being professionals and having served at the front for more than two years, it was hard for them to believe that having such losses, they wouldn't in the nearest future introduce fresh reserves into the fighting, assuming the Germans were still striving to break through to Kursk. Possibly, the Voronezh Front command might have been surprised to know that von Manstein at that moment had only a single panzer corps in reserve, which he couldn't even use without Hitler's personal consent.

However, the Front's intelligence was continuing to warn that the enemy would augment his shock grouping with reserves, and as proof it was offering reports from aerial reconnaissance about increased traffic on the roads from Khar'kov leading to Belgorod and Tomarovka. Thus, in an intelligence briefing at 0700 on 8 July there was the statement that aerial reconnaissance had spotted "between 0530 and 1530 from Akhtyrka to Tomarovka, separate columns of up to 300 tanks and 700 vehicles; from Maksimovka and Khar'kov to Tomarovka and Belgorod, separate columns of up to 1,000 troop-laden vehicles and up to 150 tanks."[94] Subsequently in the document there is the following conclusion:

> In the course of 7.07, the enemy unsuccessfully attempted to develop the offensive in the direction of Oboian' and in the area northeast of Belgorod with the aim of linking up the flanks of the shock groupings operating to the northwest and northeast of Belgorod. The enemy <u>brought up reserve tanks (!)</u> from Akhtyrka and <u>not less than a tank division (!)</u> from the area of Belgorod, which on the morning of 8 July 1943 might be introduced into the battle in order to develop the offensive. The possibility of shifting the 88th Infantry Division that has been withdrawn into the reserve on the Sumy direction, to the Tomarovka direction, can't be excluded. [Emphasis the author's]

Just like in the entire flow of information that arrived on N.F. Vatutin's desk during the battle, in the intelligence information he had to separate the wheat from the chaff. Reading such briefings and reports, he probably realized that a large amount of information in them wasn't accurate. Nevertheless, it was impossible to ignore the high activity on the enemy's lines of communication. There were also objective reasons for heeding the intelligence reports. Despite their evident losses, the Germans were continuing to launch strong attacks along the entire front of Army Group South. From where were they drawing these forces? The Front Commander-in-Chief, like any far-sighted military commander, understood the level of his responsibility and striving to reduce the risk did everything that depended on him in order to adhere to the principle "An ounce of prevention is worth a pound of cure." When sharing his thoughts with the *Stavka* regarding the course of the enemy offensive, he gave a succinct assessment of the situation facing the Voronezh Front, with no needless dramatization: The Germans, despite their high losses in tanks, were continuing to attack actively. From a combat report from the Front command to the General Staff of the Red Army about the results of the fighting on 7 July:

> The enemy in strength of nine tank divisions and seven infantry divisions after a powerful preparation with airstrikes on the morning of 7.7 resumed the offensive, focusing his main efforts on the Oboian' – Kursk direction. On the Dmitrieevka – Luchki line the enemy has deployed up to 700 tanks, and opposite the 7th Guards Army 250-300 tanks …
>
> In three days of fighting our troops have shown exceptional tenacity and resolve, and have inflicted great damage to the enemy in manpower and equipment. Our infantry, as a rule,

---

94 TsAMO RF, f. 203, op. 2843, d. 452, l. 53.

allows the enemy tanks to pass through their combat positions, separates the infantry from them, and inflicts heavy losses to them.[95]

The circumstance that the Voronezh Front had already exhausted its reserves was substantially complicating the situation. Therefore N.F. Vatutin, in addition to the two Guards armies that were already on the march to the Front's sector, on 7 July requested one more army in order to cover the Korocha direction. He wasn't anticipating the need to introduce it quickly into the fighting; this was just a precautionary step. It must be said that Moscow was dissatisfied by the way that the Voronezh Front was conducting the defensive operation. More than once the members of the State Defense Committee had expressed their reservations personally to the Front's Commander-in-Chief in telephone conversations. N.F. Vatutin was not one of those generals who generated slag heaps of lies and fabrications, but it was also hard to call him a scrupulously honest man. He wasn't able to afford such a luxury in the role of a Front commander-in-chief.

Thus when discussing the course of combat operations while making the request, he indicated the early signs of the enemy troops' reduced activity. Possibly this was in fact a mistaken supposition, but the Germans would hardly able to keep attacking for a long time at such a high tempo, and by the moment the requested army arrived in the army's sector, it would be in time for the designated counteroffensive after the enemy was halted. The 5th Guards Army and 5th Guards Tank Army that were on their way to the Voronezh Front were under the same sort of orders, i.e., preparations for the future counteroffensive. However, it is difficult to believe that such an experienced commander like General of the Army Vatutin didn't realize that the final defeat of the enemy's offensive was still something distant. Unfortunately, today the transcripts of I.V. Stalin's discussions with the Voronezh Front command are still inaccessible to scholars. So there is still no way to find out the arguments that N.F. Vatutin offered to the Supreme Commander-in-Chief when requesting one more army. Even so, the documents of his headquarters found in the Ministry of Defense's Central Archives show just such logic.

The General Staff confirmed that the situation on the southern face of the Kursk salient was unstable; the Front's troops were putting up tough resistance, but the enemy still hadn't run out of steam, so there was still the threat of a breakthrough. Based on such an assessment, it recommended that the Steppe Front's 47th Army under Lieutenant General P.P. Korzun move up to the Khmelovoe – Korocha – (excl.) Budanovka area on the night of 7-8 July.

It should be noted that the information from the Front's Intelligence Department already mentioned above about the enemy's readiness to commit fresh reserves (the 88th Infantry Division) into the battle on 8-9 July was unfounded. During the preparations for Citadel, Berlin had rejected von Manstein's request about strengthening his group with one or two additional infantry divisions. Understanding that infantry was catastrophically short, the Field Marshal back at the end of June (according to some information, on 29 June) directed the replacement of Major General H. von Horn's[96] 198th Infantry Division in the Izium area and to prepare it to move to Army

---

95 TsAMO RF, f. 203, op. 2843, d. 431, l. 48.
96 Hans Joachim von Horn (Lieutenant General, 01.10.1943) was born on 23 October 1896 in Koenigsberg. He joined the army in 1914. He received his first officer's rank on 22.05.1915. In the inter-war period he served in headquarters of infantry units and formations, and engaged in military-diplomatic work. Between 02.06.1936 and 05.11.1938 von Horn was the chief of operations of the XII Army Corps. From 15.11.1938 to 08.09.1939 he served as the military attaché to France, then Portugal. Between 08.09.1939 and 01.06.1940 he returned to the Wehrmacht and was appointed chief of staff of XII Army Corps. From 01.06.1940 to 15.7.1942 he served as the chief of staff of X Army Corps. Subsequently he spent time in the reserve command pool and in Army Group Don. On 07.02.1943 he became the acting commander of the 198th Infantry Division, before taking command of the division between 1 April 1943 and 1 June 1944. On 01.12.1943 he was awarded the German Gold Cross. Between 1 June and 1 July 1944 he was

Detachment Kempf's sector. On 6 July 1943 the division's combat units loaded onto trucks and began rolling toward the Belgorod area. According to the information of its headquarters, two days later the main forces of its Infantry Regiment 326 were assembling southwest of the city, but according to a prisoner's testimony, on 7 July its combat units were already located in the vicinity of Krutoi Log. The following message sent by the III Panzer Corps headquarters to the commander of the 7th Panzer Division on 8 July has been preserved: "The division most provide transport with a load capacity of 150 tons under the direction of an energetic officer for a regiment of the 198th Infantry Division. Set out at 0700 on 9.7 along the Brodok – Tavrovo road; the commander reports upon arrival in Tavrovo to the commander of the 198th Infantry Division's regiment."[97] Although von Horn's division was being transferred to Korps Raus, it was experiencing an acute deficit of transport, so Kempf ordered Breith to detach vehicles for it. Judging from the fact that the message specified the load-capacity of the trucks, they were needed to carry military equipment and ammunition. On the night of 9-10 July, the Army Group South Command planned to replace 7th Panzer's right (southern) flank with this regiment, so as to allow von Funck to concentrate his division's dissipating strength into an assault wedge and to continue the offensive.

When analyzing the orders and instructions of Shumilov's and Kempf's corps for the fighting on 8 July, it is impossible not to note that the scale of the planned combat operations were sharply reduced in comparison with the preceding days. Both sides were preparing to operate primarily in the sectors of the 25th Guards and 35th Guards Rifle Corps, which is to say on the axis of III Panzer Corps' main attack. At the same time, both Korps Raus and Vasil'ev's 24th Guards Rifle Corps, in essence, went over to positional fighting.

A main task stood before the Soviet side: prevent the further expansion of Army Detachment Kempf into the depth of the Front's defenses. To achieve this, the 7th Guards Army's command and the Front's reserves urgently had to find solutions to a number of pressing problems. First, it was necessary to strengthen the defenses around the narrow penetration made by 6th Panzer Division's *panzerkampfgruppe* in the Kalinin – Melikhovo – Dal'niaia Igumenka area, which meant fleshing out the rifle units and reinforcing the anti-tank defense. Second, they had to regain complete control over the two important centers of resistance, Blizhniaia Igumenka and Miasoedovo, and the ground surrounding them. Third, a firm defense on the left flank of the 25th Guards Rifle Corps had to be formed, and the 7th Panzer Division had to be held by an active defense before the front of the 73rd Guards and 94th Guards Rifle Divisions.

The Front command was seeing that by the end of 7 July, the axis along which the Germans would be launching their next main attacks was plainly conspicuous: Dal'niaia Igumenka – Melikhovo – Shliahkhovoe. It was obvious the Germans had reached a point when the further advance toward Kursk would be impossible without creating a continuous front of breakthrough by Fourth Panzer Army and Army Detachment Kempf. The lagging of the auxiliary grouping behind the main grouping was costing von Manstein's troops dearly. It was forcing them to divert forces on the main axis that were so necessary for a decisive attack. Therefore the Soviet side was anticipating that in the immediate future, the Germans would make an effort to link the adjacent flanks of Hoth's and Kempf's two attack groupings, and for this purpose would bring up reserves to the boundary between Chistiakov's 6th Guards Army and Shumilov's 7th Guards Army. If not panzer divisions, then infantry divisions – it was mandatory in order to relieve the 7th Panzer

---

again in the reserve command pool of the German High Command, before serving as a military attaché to Switzerland between 01.07.1944 and the end of the war. Between 10.05.1945 and 17.09.1947 he was imprisoned by the British. From 1956 to 1961 von Horn served in the German Bundeswehr, and achieved his final officer's rank of Lieutenant General on 01.12.1958. He passed away in Wiesbaden (FRG) on 10 January 1994.

97 NARA US, rg. 242, t. 314, r. 197, f. 001099.

Division that was already committed on the eastern flank of the breakthrough and shift it to III Panzer Corps' main grouping in the area of Melikhovo.

Thus on the afternoon of 7 July and morning of 8 July, all of the efforts of the Soviet side were directed at strengthening just this sector, which was being held by the forces of three armies: the 6th Guards Army (375th Rifle Division), the 69th Army (92nd and 93rd Guards Rifle Divisions) and the 7th Guards Army (94th and 81st Guards Rifle Divisions). Even though the Front was experiencing an acute deficit of reserves, two fresh rifle divisions were located in the rear army-level belt of defenses on this direction: The 48th Rifle Corps' 305th and 107th Rifle Divisions of the 69th Army were occupying a defense along the Vypolzovka – Kazach'e line (19 kilometers from the line of contact with the enemy), ready at any moment to move up in order to cover the boundary between the 6th and 7th Guards Armies. However, both the armies and the Front were experiencing great difficulties finding anti-tank means.

By the end of 7 July, the Voronezh Front's artillery headquarters had withdrawn five anti-tank artillery regiments that had lost all their guns for refitting; another five anti-tank artillery regiments had lost 35 to 45% of their guns and prime movers. At the same time, the *Stavka* had not sent a single anti-tank artillery regiment as a replacement. Thus, it was necessary to make do without them and make use of combat experience creatively. For example, various types of weapons that were not directly designated for attacks against tanks were used, in particular rocket launchers, and on 9 July the Front's Military Council went even further and officially authorized the use of howitzers to combat enemy armor by firing over open sights. This decision was in fact not a new one; the authorization only gave legal cover to the orders of commanders who were already rather widely practicing these techniques at critical moments in the fighting. However, if when repelling tank attacks a heavy gun received serious damage or God forbid was captured by the enemy, the commanders who'd given such orders faced serious charges. Now, however, such an order might be given on an authorized basis, which unquestionably strengthened the troops' anti-tank capabilities.

However, let's return to the events near Belgorod. After midnight, the following units were occupying the defenses in front of III Panzer Corps: 81st Guards and 92nd Guards Rifle Divisions on the line: Staryi Gorod – hamlet of the Machine Tractor Station (276th Guards Rifle Regiment of the 92nd Guards Rifle Division) – Blizhniaia Igumenka (233rd Guards Rifle Regiment of the 81st Guards Rifle Division) – Postnikov – Melikhovo (280th Guards Rifle Regiment of the 92nd Guards Rifle Division); the 94th Guards Rifle Division: northern portion of Miasoedovo – Hill 213.7 – Hill 206.9 – (excl.) "Solov'ev" State Farm; 73rd Guards and 78th Guards Rifle Divisions: "Solov'ev" State Farm – 1.5 to 2 kilometers east of the "Batratskaia Dacha" State Farm – Hill 209.7 – "Poliana" State Farm.

Already on the afternoon and evening of 7 July, N.F. Vatutin began to build a second line of defense behind the boundary between 81st Guards and 94th Guards Rifle Divisions (and accordingly the boundary between the 6th Guards and 7th Guards Armies). As already noted, in the sector of the 6th Panzer Division's offensive (on the left flank of the 6th Guards Army), there were several villages that had been converted into anti-tank strong points. After the arrival of the 92nd Guards Rifle Division, it regiments were to take up positions in these villages. The 197th Guards Artillery Regiment's 1st and 3rd Battalion together with two rifle regiments of the 92nd Rifle Division were made operationally subordinate to Morozov, but there was nothing with which to reinforce the remaining units of the 92nd Guards Rifle Division in the anti-tank strong points, since the commander of the 35th Guards Rifle Corps Lieutenant General S.G. Goriachev had no artillery left.

Thus, the Front Commander-in-Chief first decided to give Goriachev help and began to gather whatever bits and pieces of anti-tank means he could find in the troops. At 1750 on 7 July he issued an order to the commander of the 6th Guards Army to transfer Major General V.G. Lebedev's

96th Separate Tank Brigade to the 35th Guards Rifle Corps. Some anti-tank units had to be taken from the 2nd Guards "Tatsinskaia" Tank Corps, which was operating not far away in the Novye Lozy – Nepkhaevo area (6th Guards Army). At 2000 Major Zotov, the commander of the 1500th Anti-tank Artillery Regiment (19 45mm guns) received an assignment from the corps commander A.S. Burdeinyi to take up firing positions on the outskirts of Khokhlovo and in cooperation with Lieutenant Colonel M.T. Shevchenko's 47th Guards Separate Breakthrough Heavy Tank Regiment to prevent the capture of the village and bridges in it across the Northern Donets in the event of an enemy breakthrough with tanks at Dal'niaia Igumenka or Shishino. By dawn on 8 July the regiment arrived in the indicated area and deployed with its 1st Battery on the southern outskirts of Khokhlovo, its 2nd and 3rd Batteries at the crossroads southeast of the village, and the 4th and 5th Batteries 1 kilometer southwest of Dal'niaia Igumenka. From the account of the 47th Guards Separate Heavy Tank Regiment:

> At 2300 7 July the regiment commander received an order from the commander of the 2nd Guards Tank Corps to take up a defense in Dal'niaia Igumenka and together with the 1500th Destroyer Anti-tank Artillery Regiment defend the Khokhlovo – Dal'niaia Igumenka line. At 0100 8.7.43 the regiment reached Dal'niaia Igumenka with 4 Churchill tanks and by 0400 it had taken up a defense on the southwestern outskirts. The 1500th Destroyer Anti-tank Artillery Regiment's 5th Battery was occupying a defense on the southern outskirts of Khokhlovo and along the road to Dal'niaia Igumenka. By 0600 only the 47th Guards Heavy Tank Regiment and a company of riflemen of the 92nd Guards Rifle Division were holding Dal'niaia Igumenka. The closest battery of the destroyer anti-tank artillery regiment was on a hill 1.5 kilometers away from Dal'niaia Igumenka. A medical-sanitation battalion was located in Dal'niaia Igumenka, but upon the appearance of enemy tanks at 0530 it left to go to Khokhlovo.[98]

At the order from the chief of staff of the 7th Guards Army's artillery headquarters, at dawn on 8 July the remaining 76mm anti-tank guns of the 114th Guards Destroyer Anti-tank Artillery Regiment arrived in Melikhovo and moved into firing positions on its southwestern outskirts. In addition, on the afternoon of 7 July the commander of the Front's subgrouping of Guards mortars Colonel I.S. Iofa began to bring up some rocket launchers to this area. The 97th Guards Mortar Regiment moved two battalions into Melikhovo and one battalion into Postnikov, while the 218th Battalion of the 314th Guards Mortar Regiment and 447th Battalion of the 315th Guards Mortar Regiment were in Shishino. In addition, as before the 1/93rd Cannon Artillery Regiment (6 152mm howitzers) of the 6th Guards Army's 27th Separate Heavy Cannon Artillery Brigade remained in Dal'niaia Igumenka.

However, by 8 July the process of bringing up forces to strengthen the Dal'niaia Igumenka – Melikhovo sector in time as had been planned had failed. The 92nd Guards Rifle Division, which according to the original scheme had been supposed to have deployed behind the boundary between the 81st Guards and 94th Guards Rifle Divisions, already on the afternoon of 7 July wound up in the first echelon, and from the march had gone into battle that continued until the morning of 8 July. This division was one of only two fresh rifle divisions in front of the III Panzer Corps' assault wedge (the other being the 94th Guards Rifle Division). In addition, by the morning of 8 July it regiments weren't occupying a single, compact sector, but had wound up in the sectors of two divisions, with the 276th Guards and 282nd Guards Rifle Regiments in the north of Staryi Gorod – hamlet of the Machine Tractor Station – Postnikov sector (which extended for 10 kilometers)

---

98   TsAMO RF, f. 2 gv. Ttk, op. 1 d. 24, l. 203.

under the command of division commander Morozov, and with the 280th Guards Rifle Regiment in the Melikhovo area, under the command of division commander Trunin. Thus, by the moment they were called upon to try to repulse the attack of the 6th and 19th Panzer Divisions, one can't speak about any combat formation echeloned in depth or an integrated system of fire (including of the anti-tank guns) in the 92nd Guards Rifle Division. At the same time, the units and formations that had been assigned to counter the German tanks in this sector hadn't fully assembled in it, and those that had arrived by the morning of 8 July did so without much of their equipment (for example, of the 21 tanks in the 47th Guards Separate Breakthrough Tank Regiment, only 5 were operational). Each of the regiment and brigade commanders were operating according to his own plan, while the commander of the 35th Guards Rifle Corps, even when the battle started, didn't know where they were located, so naturally he couldn't rely on them.

As is known in war, any combat plan is in essence only a prediction of how the command intends to operate over a certain amount of time, relying on the available information and the conclusions made on its basis. Of the entire multitude of factors that can substantially affect the commander's decision, one is primary – the enemy's actions, which are very difficult to predict. In order to avoid miscalculations in the majority of cases when planning a battle or operation, as a safeguard the command considers the main ways the operational situation might go and comes up with measures to be taken in one or another situation. When though the operational situation is suggesting or compelling some major measure in the nearest time, but it either needs a certain amount of time to prepare it or the moment for conducting it hasn't yet arrived, higher headquarters send preliminary orders to the commanders of units and formations. These documents lay out the basic intent of the plan, and also that circle of problems that each commander must resolve in order to prepare his troops to carry out the probable order.

By the end of 7 July the Soviet side was assessing the situation that had developed in the sector of defense of the 1st Tank Army and 6th Guards Army on the Oboian' direction as very dangerous and unstable. The enemy pressure here was exceptionally strong and there were not yet signs that it would weaken; on the contrary, every sign pointed to the fact that the enemy in the next several days would continue attempts to breakthrough to Oboian'. N.F. Vatutin didn't have the possibility to strengthen substantially Katukov's or Chistiakov's armies, but it was also intolerable to permit a breakthrough. Thus, in order to divert some of the Fourth Panzer Army's strength from this area, he planned to launch a counterattack against the II SS Panzer Corps with the forces of five tank corps (including two fresh ones) with the support of rifle divisions of the 69th Army's right wing. On this same day, M.S. Shumilov was also planning to conduct a counterattack with the aim of reducing the pressure on the 92nd Guards Rifle Division's front that the enemy was placing at the boundary between the 81st Guards and 94th Guards Rifle Divisions. However, the conditions for conducting both counterattacks were unfavorable.

Nevertheless, because of the difficult situation in the sector of Katukov's and Chistiakov's armies, a Soviet counterattack southwest of Prokhorovka did take place, but there was not one east of Belgorod. In the files of the Russian Ministry of Defense's Central Archives, a preliminary order from the commander of the 25th Guards Rifle Corps has been found, in which the intentions of the 7th Guards Army's leadership has been laid out rather clearly. Although the order has been labeled "Preliminary", nevertheless the details touching upon the preparations for it show that this wasn't a rough draft, but a fully-prepared document resulting from a lot of work, which was directed from the beginning toward a concrete result. This means a counterattack had been prepared, moreover conscientiously so, but its implementation had been disrupted, probably by the difficult situation that had developed in the sector of the 35th Guards Rifle Corps already on the morning of 8 July. A number of details testify to this. First, the document is type-written (and not written out by hand), registered as No.0011/op, and it contains the genuine signatures of the corps commander and chief of staff. Second, it was issued to the troops (the copy cited below was found in the files for the 262nd Heavy Tank Regiment). Here is an excerpt from this document:

...

2. On the right the 35th Guards Rifle Corps with units of reinforcement launches a counterattack out of the Miasoedovo and the woods southeast of Miasoedovo area in the direction of Miasoedovo and the Kreida railyard.
3. 25th Guards Rifle Corps consisting of the 73rd Guards Rifle, 78th Guards Rifle and 270th Rifle Divisions; the 161st Guards Cannon Artillery Regiment, the 30th Destroyer Anti-tank Artillery Brigade and the 97th Guards Mortar Regiments; as well as the 201st Tank Brigade, 1529th Self-propelled Artillery Regiment and 262nd Heavy Tank Regiment; conducts a counterattack in the sector: on the right (excl.) Batratskaia Dacha, (excl.) Gremiachii in the direction of the northern outskirts of Krutoi Log, Razumnoe and Dal'nie Peski.
4. 73rd Guards Rifle Division with the 30th Destroyer Anti-tank Artillery Brigade, the 309th Guards Mortar Regiment, the 161st Guards Cannon Artillery Regiment and 1/158th Guards Artillery Regiment launches a counterattack on the right: (excl.) "Batratskaia Dacha" State Farm, (excl.) Hill 209.6 in the direction of Generalovka and the labor corrective camp.
5. 270th Rifle Division with the 265th Guards Cannon Artillery Regiment, the 97th Guards Mortar Regiment, the 201st Tank Brigade, the 1629th Self-propelled Artillery Regiment, and 2 and 3/158th Guards Artillery Regiment launches a counterattack in the sector on the right: Hill 209.6, on the left: (excl.) Gremiachii in the direction of the northern outskirts of Krutoi Log and Dal'nie Peski.
6. 78th Guards Rifle Division after its relief by the 270th Rifle Division and 111th Rifle Division [24th Guards Rifle Corps] and after the regrouping of the 73rd Guards Rifle Division reaches the area: Pentsevo, Kashlakovo, where it brings itself back to order and gets ready to exploit a success and a counterattack in the corps' indicated directions.
7. 262nd Heavy Tank Regiment, 167th Separate Tank Regiment and the 1438th Self-propelled Artillery Regiment under the overall command of the commander of the 262nd Heavy Tank Regiment are in the Nekliudovo area as my reserve.
8. 78th Guards Rifle Division seizes the "Batratskaia Dacha" State Farm with one regiment and covers the right flank of the 25th Guards Rifle Corps.
9. 81st Guards Rifle Division with the 114th Guards Destroyer Anti-tank Artillery Regiment and the 315th Guards Mortar Regiment strongly holds the line: Staryi Gorod, and with two regiments launches a counterattack in the direction of the Kreida railyard.
10. Formation commanders conduct the regrouping and relief of forces at a special order. Bring the men back to order and replenish stocks of ammunition. Give all the personnel a day's worth of dry rations. Reconnoiter the indicated sectors and directions of the counterattacks. Formation commanders are to keep the directions of the counterattacks in the strictest secrecy.
11. The formation commanders when planning the counterattacks are to have in mind in the event of success the forcing of the Northern Donets River and the seizing of the western bank of the Northern Donets River.
12. Establish and prepare recognition sheets for communication with aircraft and marking your forward edge, and obtain flares and rockets of various colors.[99]

---

99 TsAMO RF, f. 262 ttp, op. 32956, d. 2, l. 98.

As we see, the plan gave the troops of the 25th Guards Rifle Corps rather ambitious tasks – reaching the eastern and even the western banks of the Northern Donets. That means the plan intended to cut off III Panzer Corps from its rear services and points of supply on the western bank. Unfortunately, on the original pages there is only the date "8.7.1943", but no time is given for when it was signed off or received by the 262nd Heavy Tank Regiment, so it is hard to say when the work on the preliminary plan of the counterattacks ended. On the basis of a number of indirect indications, it is possible to assume that this document was prepared on the night of 7-8 July as a safeguard measure in case the III Panzer Corps succeeded in breaking through Melikhovo into the depth of the 69th Army's defenses.

It must be acknowledged that the command of Army Detachment Kempf was following with great attention even what seemed at first glance to be insignificant steps by the Soviet side, professionally analyzing them, and drawing appropriate conclusions on their basis. Thus the possibility of a counterattack against its right flank wasn't a surprise for it. Already on the evening of 7 July Army Detachment Kempf's headquarters reported to Army Group South:

> The foe already today was bitterly resisting the breakthrough defending deeply articulated, fortified and occupied positions on the hills. He made an attempt to reinforce the still-standing cornerposts of his system of positions with local reserves and newly arrived forces, to gather scattered units and again take up rear positions. Probing attacks and the shifting of tanks in the after-dinner hours in the wooded area north of Shebekino and in the area on both sides of the Koren' River, primarily between Pentsevo and Borovskoe, indicate the creation of a grouping for an attack against the army detachment's eastern flank.[100]

Now let's take a look at how the planning of combat actions on 8 July was going in the German headquarters. For the command of Army Detachment Kempf, the tasks for this day relative to the preceding days had practically not changed. Even though the 6th Panzer Division had managed to reach the second army-level belt of defenses, for the enemy the situation had not fundamentally changed – Kempf's forces still hadn't linked flanks with the II SS Panzer Corps and reached a position where they could cover the Fourth Panzer Army's lengthening right flank. At the same time, the troops of Korps Raus were still 5-8 kilometers short of the Koren' River and making no headway, and considering the Russians' ferocious resistance, the prospects for creating a solid covering front along the river remained illusory. Thus, the 7th Guards Army was still containing Kempf's forces within its defenses, which substantially restricted the possibility of the German command to conduct sweeping maneuvers with its forces.

The command of Army Detachment Kempf considered the primary task for 8 July was to ensure the conditions for the development of the 6th Panzer Division's success to the northeast. For this, it was necessary to resolve two problems. The first was to destroy the "flanking cornerposts" – the Soviet strongpoints of Miasoedovo and the line of the 81st Guards Rifle Division, or in the extreme case, at least take Blizhniaia Igumenka. The gap torn into the Soviet lines by von Oppeln-Bronikowski's *panzerkampfgruppe* was rather narrow and didn't exceed 6 kilometers. Thus, considering the Russians' bitter resistance and their employment of tanks in this area, for a further advance it was necessary to take these centers of resistance on 8 July, or, at the very least, create strong flanking blocking positions in front of them. However, because of the paucity of forces in III Panzer Corps, it was difficult to realize this option. Secondly, it was extremely important to strengthen the assault wedge of Breith's panzer corps substantially, since 6th Panzer Division after two days of hard fighting had suffered significant losses.

---

100 NARA US, t. 312, r. 54, f. 7569627.

It was extremely important to address these problems, but also very difficult. The 198th Infantry Division which was to relieve the 7th Panzer Division on the right flank within two days was still on the march. Kempf had no other reserves, and at the same time the heavy pressure of the Soviet forces along the entire front of Army Detachment Kempf's breakthrough made it impossible for him to remove even a single battalion from other divisions. On the evening of 7 July Kempf decided to leave the 7th Panzer Division in place in order to help the 106th Infantry Division take full possession of Miasoedovo and its surrounding territory and dig in on it. Only after this was accomplished was he planning to launch an attack against the Sheino – Ushakovo sector with Schülz's *panzerkampfgruppe*, believing this would also aid the 6th Panzer Division's further advance.

Meanwhile, the command of III Panzer Corps was to engage in finding ways to carry out the mission to destroy the "flanking cornerposts". However, Breith also had no reserves, so he had no other option than to demand Generals Chales de Beaulieu (168th Infantry Division) and Schmidt (19th Panzer Division) to increase their pressure on the 81st Guards Rifle Division's defenses. Accordingly, it was left to the grenadier regiments of these same divisions with the support of just a single battery (6 assault guns) of StuG Battalion 228 and one panzer company of the 19th Panzer Division's Panzer Regiment 27 to break the Guardsmen's resistance in the "Belgorod bastion". Simultaneously, Breith began to form a combat wedge for taking Melikhovo and a further advance into the depth of the 69th Army's defenses. Sensing that the Russian strength in the Staryi Gorod was gradually waning, and at the same time experiencing an acute deficit of tanks, Breith set about carrying out the army detachment's order about gathering the 168th Infantry Division into a fist and turning over the Mikhailovka – Blizhniaia Igumenka sector (the panzer corps' right flank) to it, in order to withdraw all of Schmidt's forces from there in the next day or two. So his first decision for 8 July was an order to bring up Westhofen's panzer regiment of the 19th Panzer Division out of Blizhniaia Igumenka in order to join von Oppeln-Bronikowski's panzer regiment; even though by the end of 7 July Westhofen's *panzerkampfgruppe* was in a battered condition, nevertheless in those circumstances it would become a substantial reinforcement for III Panzer Corps' combat wedge.

Simultaneously Breith ordered a portion of the 168th Infantry Division's artillery to return to it, including as compensation for the withdrawal of the panzers of the 19th Panzer Division, and to reinforce 7th Panzer Division with artillery and Flak units, so that it could not only organize a solid anti-tank screen, but after Miasoedovo fell and the 106th Infantry Division went over to a defense, the possibility would appear to add some of its panzers to III Panzer Corps' assault wedge, having replaced them in the defense with howitzers and anti-aircraft guns serving in a ground role. On the evening of 7 July, a radio message arrived in the headquarters of von Funck's 7th Panzer Division, which informed him of the corps' following instructions:

1) IV and V Battalions of Artillery Regiment 248 [of the 168th Infantry Division] are re-subordinated to the 168th Infantry Division. Immediately after Razumnoe, they should move to Mikhailovka. A bridge across the Razumnaia River should be ready by 2000.
2) II/Artillery Regiment 62 [of 105mm howitzers] is made subordinate to 7th Panzer Division. Brought to the attention of Artkommando 3.
3) Flak Artillery 99 with I and II/Regiment 38 from 8.7 cooperates with 7th Panzer Division.[101]

---

101 NARA US, rg. 242, t. 314, r. 197, f. 001158.

After three days of the offensive, in addition to the combat tasks, the command of Army Detachment Kempf had substantial concerns about keeping the troops supplied. On 7 July, the line of combat contact was already 15-16 kilometers from the bridges on the Northern Donets. Thus when planning the further offensive, it was necessary to begin building a system of logistics on the eastern bank of the river, not according to a temporary scheme, but on a continuous basis. This was made necessary by other substantial circumstances – the 198th Infantry Division was approaching, for which it would be necessary ahead of time to provide space for the deployment of its rear services and support elements, as well as to erect new bridges and to improve and expand the road network. According to Soviet aerial reconnaissance there were seven operational crossing sites in the Mikhailovka – Maslova Pristan' sector on the afternoon of 7 July. Up to this moment, the headquarters of III Panzer Corps was marking the Repnoe – Tavrovo – Dorogobuzheno road as its main artery of supplies, and further along the eastern and western bank of the Razumnaia River. The primary 50-tonne bridge across the Donets was located in Dorogobuzheno, and further along the route there was a 24-tonne bridge in Razumnoe, 50-tonne and 8-tonne bridges in Belovskaia, and a 24-tonne bridge in Sevriukovo. However, with the approach of the 198th Infantry Division, a 24-tonne bridge was under construction in the southern end of Pushkarnoe for augmenting the transiting capacity of the bridge in Dorogobuzheno. The new bridge was planned to be ready on the morning of 9 July, which is to say, by the arrival of von Horn's forces. In the meantime the forward Infantry Regiment 326 of the 198th Infantry Division was using the 7th Panzer Division's bridge in Solomino to cross the river and was assembling in Krutoi Log. The expansion of the volume of bridge and road work required a regrouping of the specialized units. From a directive of Army Detachment Kempf's headquarters:

1) Pioneer Battalion 651 (motorized), which to this point has been subordinate to III Panzer Corps, by 0600 8.7 withdraws and assembles in the Bolkhovets area, southwest of Belgorod, at the disposal of Army Detachment Kempf.
2) Gruppe Trisk (headquarters of Pioneer Regiment 601 with the subordinate Pioneer Battalion 127 and Motorized Bridge-building Battalion 531) remains subordinate to III Panzer Corps for ensuring military bridges across the Donets and the construction of auxiliary bridges. Gruppe Trisk is not to be used east of the Donets without the agreement of Army Detachment Kempf.
3) In order to construct approaches to the bridges suitable for use, the headquarters of Pioneer Regiment 601 is given operational control over 1/Special Road-building Battalion 538. The company is now located in the village of Griaznoe, 10 kilometers southwest of Belgorod. The headquarters of Pioneer Regiment 601 immediately summons it.[102]

The combat activity on the axis of Army Detachment Kempf's main attack ceased after midnight. As before, intense fighting was still going on only in two places: at the "Batratskaia Dacha" State Farm and in Blizhniaia Igumenka. In both areas, the Soviet side was showing activity. Late in the evening, the panzer company of Panzer Regiment 27 that was attached to *Kampfgruppe* Köhler finally pushed the battalion of the 81st Guards Rifle Division's 233rd Guards Rifle Regiment out of Blizhniaia Igumenka, but it was unable to consolidate its grip on the village, because the panzers were weakly covered by panzergrenadiers. After von Oppeln-Bronikowski's *panzerkampfgruppen* had created a narrow penetration at the boundary of the two Guards armies, the significance of Blizhniaia Igumenka as a strongpoint on the flank of the 6th Panzer Division had grown. It was extremely important for Safiulin to hold the shoulders of the narrow penetration made by a

---
102 NARA US, rg. 242, t. 314, r. 197, f. 001167.

panzerkampfgruppe of Breith's III Panzer Corps. To contain it was only possible with the retention of a serious threat to its flanks, and for this the control over the two adjacent strongpoints – Blizhniaia Igumenka and the anti-tank region 5 kilometers northeast of Miasoedovo – was necessary. Blizhniaia Igumenka was also important for the durability of the 81st Guards Rifle Division's system of defense. Its line rested on three strongpoints – Staryi Gorod, the hamlet of the Machine Tractor Station, and Blizhniaia Igumenka. So after Infantry Regiment 442 with the support of the 19th Panzer Division's panzers pushed the 233rd Guards Rifle Regiment's battalion out of the village on the evening of 7 July, regaining possession of the village became the first order of business for Morozov. Having been reinforced with two rifle regiments of the 92nd Guards Rifle Division, I.K. Morozov decided under cover of night, using the system of communication trenches that allowed him to close on the village stealthily with all of his units, to re-occupy the positions in the center of Blizhniaia Igumenka and to the south of there. He issued an order to Major S.I. Titarenko: to assemble the units of his 233rd Guards Rifle Regiment, move them into the village, and having linked up with Major M.E. Simonov's 276th Guards Rifle Regiment that was holding the (excl.) Staryi Gorod – (excl.) north of the Kreida railyard – hamlet of the Machine Tractor Station sector, to create a solid line of defense. At the same time the commander of the 94th Guards Rifle Division Colonel I.G. Russkikh received an order from the corps commander: firmly hold the northern portion of Miasoedovo and if possible drive the Germans out of the southern portion of the village.

I.K. Morozov knew that his regiments had suffered heavy losses, including in anti-tank weapons, and that the men were worn out after three days of exhausting fighting, so in the future he decided to rely chiefly on minefields and massed mortar fire. He ordered for the damaged artificial obstacles to be repaired over the course of the night and to check the condition of the minefields, which still hadn't been stumbled over by the Germans. In addition, he ordered Major M.E. Simonov to prepare a counterattack with the forces of his regiment by morning in the direction of Blizhniaia Igumenka, in case the enemy attempted to breach the line of Major S.I. Titarenko's 233rd Guards Rifle Regiment. These steps yielded fruit already in the middle of the night of 7-8 July. From the morning reports of the divisions to the headquarters of III Panzer Corps:

> 19th Panzer Division: Panzergrenadier Regiment 73 at 0330 began to mop up the woods north of Belovskaia and at 0430 ran into the first line of bunkers with a strong garrison on the western edge of the woods. Panzer Reconnaissance Battalion 19 is advancing to the south 2 kilometers south of Blizhniaia Igumenka. When mopping up the terrain southwest of Kreida, 15 prisoners were taken.

> 168th Infantry Division: The reconnaissance probe conducted with major forces out of the area of the Kreida railyard toward the hamlet of the Machine Tractor Station encountered a stubbornly defended enemy system of trenches to the south of it. The positions of four mortars and many machine guns have been identified.[103]

At the same time as the Guardsmen were engaging in night combat on the left flank of the 81st Guards Rifle Division with elements of the 168th Infantry and 19th Panzer Divisions, in the woods east of the "Batratskaia Dacha" State Farm and the "Solov'ev" collective farm, a fierce clash was continuing between the 7th Panzer Division's Panzer Reconnaissance Battalion 37 and Lieutenant Colonel I.A. Usikov's 44th Guards Rifle Regiment of the 15th Guards Rifle Division.[104]

---

103 NARA US, rg. 242, t. 314, r. 197, f. 001174.
104 On the evening of 04.07.1943, the 15th Guards Rifle Division had 8,684 men, including 4,602 active

The forward element of von Funck's panzer division had been strongly reinforced with armor and had the possibility to call down artillery fire quickly on Russian firing positions with the aid of artillery spotters that were assigned to the panzer reconnaissance battalion. Thus, the Guardsmen had to endure a very difficult fight.

There were a lot of firebreaks in the woods east of the State Farm, but primarily they were full of fallen tree entanglements and had been partially mined. Thus knowing that the Germans in this sector had tanks, the regiment commander was striving to block the primary tank-vulnerable axis – the road between the "Batratskaia Dacha" State Farm and Belovskaia, having moved up to this point a battery of 45mm anti-tank guns under the command of Captain Tiapkov before dawn. The woods were burning in several places, filling the fire breaks with smoke and ashes. Even before the anti-tank gun crews had time to camouflage their positions a German halftrack appeared on the road. With the very first shot, the gun layer of the No. 1 gun Sergeant Danchenko knocked the halftrack out; immediately after the shell exploded, a dozen submachine gunners leaped out of the halftrack. Concealed by the underbrush, they opened up a heavy fire from their submachine guns, which killed the breech operator Private Belousov and wounded the platoon commander Lieutenant Lukinin. Captain Pavlov's arriving rifle company helped the artillerymen repulse the panzergrenadiers' attack. Just as soon as the exchange of fire ended, the silhouettes of two tanks materialized among the trees out of the twilight gloom. Having waited several minutes, gun commander Podkorytov with rapid fire knocked out both tanks. However, their crews managed to fire several rounds. As a result, one 45mm anti-tank gun was damaged, and a second was destroyed. Several Red Army soldiers that were covering the battery received wounds. Taking advantage of the enemy's evident confusion, the regiment launched a counterattack.

In his report on the attack, the division commander E.I. Vasilenko indicated that going on the offensive from the line: 1 kilometer east of the "Solov'ev" collective farm – 2 kilometers east of the "Batratskaia Dacha" State Farm, by the morning of 8 July the regiment reached a line 300 meters west of a point (in the area of the "Batratskaia Dacha" State Farm) and 200 meters southeast of the "Batratskaia Dacha" State Farm. Thus, in the course of the night the 44th Guards Rifle Regiment made approximately a 1 kilometer advance. Its headquarters reported knocking out or capturing two tanks, two halftracks, a 75mm gun and four machine guns; in addition, the enemy left behind more than 100 bodies of dead soldiers and officers on the ground that its units had been occupying. The regiment also managed to capture a serviceable truck that was loaded with uniforms and one motorcycle. I'll immediately state that the knocked out equipment and vehicles could not only be seen, but also touched; as concerns the piles of dead bodies, then I consider this information dubious, especially when you look at the losses suffered by Usikov's regiment. In such a lengthy and bitter clash, they proved to be extremely few: just 2 men killed and 68 wounded; both guns of Tiakov's battery were knocked out, and two Maksim machine guns were destroyed by shells.[105]

A difficult situation also arose in the Gremiachii – "Poliana" State Farm area that night, where the enemy in the course of 7 July had launched strong counterattacks with the use of tanks. Bitter fighting went on here until midnight. Under the onslaught of the tanks, the infantry of the 73rd Guards Rifle Division fell back from their line several times, but the sector was held thanks to the crews of the 201st Tank Brigade and the gun crews of the 1669th Destroyer Anti-tank Artillery Regiment. With the onset of darkness, a continuous line of defense couldn't be set up here. Fearing that during the hours of darkness enemy submachine gunners would infiltrate into the rear of his tank brigade, Colonel I.A. Taranov at 0130 sent the following report to the commander of the 73rd Guards Rifle Division:

---

bayonets, 2,213 artillerymen, and 1,869 service personnel. (TsAMO RF, f. 15 gv. sd, op. 1, d. 10, l. 45.
105 TsAMO RF, f. 15 gv. sd, op. 1, d. 8, l. 158.

> The enemy is occupying the fringe of woods north of the Machine Tractor Station (1 kilometer west of Gremiachii) as far as the "Poliana" State Farm in front of the 201st Tank Brigade.
>
> 1/211th Guards Rifle Regiment after an attack toward Gremiachii reached the line: 500 meters west of Gremiachii – fringe of woods east of the "Poliana" State Farm. On the left, remnants of the 78th Guards Rifle Division's 225th Guards Rifle Regiment are operating.
>
> The tanks of the 2nd Battalion of the 201st Tank Brigade are occupying positions on the northern fringe of the woods lying 2 kilometers northwest of Gremiachii (at the bend in the road leading to the "Batratskaia Dacha" State Farm. The battalion's positions are being subjected to the constant fire of German submachine gunners.
>
> I request immediate steps be taken to move up the infantry of the 211th Guards Rifle Regiment to the line of the narrow patch of woods (Point 201), which is 2.5 kilometers west of Gremiachii. In the event that the infantry of the 211th Guards Rifle Regiment doesn't arrive, I'll be forced to withdraw my tanks to the Gremiachii area. I request that you inform me of the steps taken.[106]

The division commander understood the concerns of the tank brigade commander, and by morning his infantry were already digging in along the tank brigade's line of defense.

So, with the dawn on 8 July, von Oppeln-Bronikowski's and Westhofen's panzer regiments were preparing for an attack. In the first stage, they had to break the resistance at the boundary between the 25th Guards and 35th Guards Rifle Corps and seize two strongpoints: Melikhovo (6th Panzer Division) and Dal'niaia Igumenka (19th Panzer Division). Then, they were to launch an attack in the direction of an important road hub, the village of Shliakhovoe. The approach to the first two strongpoint villages was being protected by units of two battalions of the 92nd Guards Rifle Division's 280th Guards Rifle Regiment. The positions of the 94th Guards Rifle Division's rightflank units rested on two smaller villages, Postnikov and Kalinin, but they also had been seriously prepared for an all-round defense; anti-tank riflemen were lying in concealment between these two villages. Behind them, the entire expanse of level ground (south of Melikhovo and east of Dal'niaia Igumenka) had been densely mined. Thus, the artillery, sappers and three panzergrenadier *kampfgruppen* (Unrein's, von Bieberstein's and Richter's) were supposed to clear a path for the panzers. The combat engineers and panzergrenadiers were supposed to crush Novikov's regiment and open the way to Melikhovo through the multiple layers of mines and obstacles for von Oppeln-Bronikowski's panzer crews. The way forward included a lot of bottlenecks and a significant amount of natural cover, which allowed the anti-tank rifle crews to let the enemy tanks to approach within close range to ensure accuracy of their fire. Thus, the Germans were counting very much on their Nebelwerfers. This type of weapon had already demonstrated its effectiveness when breaking through an echeloned defense, primarily in the struggle against Soviet artillery and when laying down smoke screens.

In addition to the immediate preparations of the troops of Breith's panzer corps to penetrate into the depth of the 69th Army's defenses, the command of Army Detachment Kempf was continuing to take special measures in the tactical zone as well with the aim of helping its *kampfgruppen* shatter the Russian defenses on this axis from within. The use of diversionary groups in order to destroy battalion and regiment command posts here was now not very effective, because there was no longstanding system of command and observation posts with developed telephone communications here, and few prisoners had been taken. The Soviet forces were in constant movement, new units and formations were taking up positions on unprepared lines, so often the battalion commanders had no special bunkers for command posts and were using ordinary trenches as command posts,

---

106 TsAMO RF, F. 3256, op. 1 d. 6, l. 177.

while regiment headquarters were setting up in any more or less suitable ravine or patch of woods. Thus it was extremely difficult to locate them quickly and destroy them in the course of a battle. Because of this, the commando teams of Abwehr Kommando 204 went more deeply behind the Soviet lines, into the rear of Kriuchenkin's army, beyond Prokhorovka and toward Korocha, and once there they reconnoitered, launched diversionary attacks against targets of opportunity, and killed senior command staff.

Emphasis was also placed on mass propaganda with the aim of undermining the morale of the Soviet troops, targeting chiefly the sergeants and privates who were shouldering the main burden of the war. Back in May 1943, on the basis of OKW Order No.13 from 21 April 1943[107] "On the military servicemen of the Red Army who have voluntarily come over to the German side", the Wehrmacht began to execute Operation "Silver Ribbon", which was supposed to stimulate desertions, and accordingly reduce the fighting spirit of the Red Army's combat units. For this purpose, in the course of the next three months the Soviet tactical rear area was strewn with a variety of leaflets, which described the "heavenly" conditions of prisoners-of-war to the Red Army soldiers in a language that was rather awkward, but fully understandable. According to the data of V.G. Krysko, in May 1943 alone German aircraft dropped more than 32,000,000 copies of leaflets over the area of the Kursk salient.[108] This method of undermining the combat capabilities of the Soviet formation was actively used not only in the period of lull, but also directly in the full swing of the Battle of Kursk, including actively on the Korocha direction as well. A number of operational documents testify to this. For example, in the summaries of the headquarters of the 305th Rifle Division for 8 July (at 0200 and 1400), it is reported: "Enemy aircraft are conducting separate flights over the division's sector and scattering leaflets, which the units and specialized elements are collecting and burning."[109]

However, let's return to the Melikhovo – Dal'niaia Igumenka area on the morning of 8 July. At this time Major General von Hünersdorff's 6th Panzer Division had been reinforced with StuG Battalion 228 (minus one battery), III/Nebelwerfer Regiment 54, a company of the Heavy Panzer Battalion 503, and the Separate Artillery Battalion 857 of 210mm mortars, while Major General G. Schmidt's 19th Panzer Division as before had the 168th Infantry Division's Infantry Regiment 442, Nebelwerfer Regiment 54 (minus III Battalion), a Tiger company of the Separate Heavy Panzer Battalion 503, and II/Artillery Regiment 71 (150mm howitzers). *Panzerkampfgruppe* Westhofen had attached to it only one battalion of Panzergrenadier Regiment 74, and two battalions of Nebelwerfers and howitzers. The rest of the division (troops of Panzergrenadier Regiments 73 and 74, Panzer Reconnaissance Battalion 19, a panzer company, 6 flame-throwing tanks of the 6th Panzer Division, the main forces of artillery and so forth) were to continue to attack the 81st Guards Rifle Division's lines in the Blizhniaia Igumenka – hamlet of the Machine Tractor Station sector.

Initially, the attack toward Melikhovo was set for 0700, but the heavy mortar battalion was late moving into its firing positions so von Hünersdorff, who had personally driven in his command armored car out to the area of jumping-off positions of von Oppeln-Bronikowski's *panzerkampfgruppe*, postponed the attack by an hour. Three hours before this moment, the 6th Panzer Division had conducted an hour-long reconnaissance-in-force in the direction of Melikhovo with up to a battalion of panzergrenadiers and 30 armored vehicles. It demonstrated that the village couldn't be taken with a frontal attack because of heavy harassing artillery fire out of the Kalinin – Sheino

---

107 Khristoforov [chief ed.], *Velikaia Otechestvennaia voina: 1943 god – Issledovaniia, dokumenty, kommentarii* [*Great Patriotic War: 1943 – Research, documents and commentary*] (Moscow, 2013), pp. 660-661.
108 Krysko, V.G., *Sekrety psikhologicheskoi voiny* [*Secrets of the psychological war*] (Minsk, 1999), p. 122.
109 TsAMO RF, f. 48 sk, op. 1, d. 17, l. 27.

area and artificial obstacles on the approaches to Melikhovo, which were being covered by intense infantry fire. Thus, it was decided to take Kalinin first.

At 1000 (Moscow time) after a strong artillery barrage on the positions of the 280th Guards Rifle Regiment (initially on the left flank, and then in the depth of the combat positions), in which all of the artillery of the 6th Panzer Division and the attached heavy mortar battalion took part, the panzergrenadiers and assault guns of StuG Battalion 228 moved out on the attack toward the hamlet. From the daily report of the 6th Panzer Division's headquarters:

> The start of the attack set for 0700 (Moscow time) was postponed to 1000 (Moscow time), because only by this time could the supporting mortar battalion be ready in their firing positions. The formation at the start of the attack:
>
> On the right, *Kampfgruppe* Bieberstein, which was supposed to jump off from the western slope of a branch of the Razumnaia River, and attack through Kalinin toward Melikhovo.
>
> Further to the left, *Kampfgruppe* Unrein
>
> Between it and the panzers of the 19th Panzer Division -- von Oppeln's panzer regiment
>
> The attack of the grenadiers launched later at 1100 was stopped by an anti-tank ditch that was located on a hill on the northern outskirts of Kalinin. After collapsing the walls with demolition charges in order to get across, it was necessary to sweep two belts of mines that were located one after the other. *Kampfgruppe* Bieberstein advanced to a point near Kalinin, but still couldn't take the hamlet because of heavy flanking fire from the direction of the northern portion of Miasoedovo [the 94th Guards Rifle Division] and the hills to the east of it.[110]

Simultaneously Westhofen's *panzerkampfgruppe* of the 19th Panzer Division went on the attack toward Dal'niaia Igumenka. Panzergrenadier Regiment 74 that was attached to it had already taken heavy losses, so the *panzerkampfgruppe* was acutely short of supporting panzergrenadiers. Thus, aware of the presence of the anti-tank ditch and minefields, which would naturally be covered by fire, Westhofen was forced to issue an order: until special instructions otherwise arrived, to escort the tanks only with combat engineers. Meanwhile, Richter's panzergrenadiers (Panzergrenadier Regiment 73 of the 19th Panzer Division) were supposed to drive the Russians out of the patches of woods east and southeast of Postnikov and thereby screen the left flank of the *panzerkampfgruppe*. Just like in its neighbor's sector, the start of the attack by the 19th Panzer Division was preceded by heavy artillery fire on Postnikov and Dal'niaia Igumenka, which shifted into the depth of the 92nd Guards Rifle Division's defenses several minutes before the panzers appeared on the battlefield. Let's take a glance at this attack through the eyes of staff officers of the 47th Separate Heavy Tank Regiment:

> At 0800 on 8.7.1943 up to 60 enemy tanks went on the attack toward Dal'niaia Igumenka out of the area east of Postnikov. By this time the fifth Churchill tank of our regiment had arrived in Dal'niaia Igumenka, which was being held by our regiment at the directive of Guards Major Leonenko. The German tanks, unsupported by infantry, were moving in the combat formation of a wedge with great depth. Enemy mortars and artillery at 0800 opened up concentrated fire, striving to disrupt the staying power of our defense and ensure the breakthrough of tanks into the village. Despite the lack of means of reinforcement and the enemy's large advantage in tanks (60 against 5), the fascists' attack was beaten back.[111]

---

110 NARA US, rg. 242, t. 314, r. 197, f. 001204.
111 TsAMO RF, f. 2 gv. Ttk, op. 1, d. 24, l. 203.

The desire of the officers to confirm their crews' tenacity with the given figures is understandable, but it is impossible to take them seriously given an analysis of the operational situation in this area. Westhofen's *panzerkampfgruppe* was stopped not by five Churchill tanks, but primarily by a deep anti-tank ditch and the broad minefields in front of them and on the approaches to Dal'niaia Igumenka, and by the intense fire of 1/93rd Cannon Artillery Regiment out of Dal'niaia Igumenka and two battalions of Katiusha rocket launchers of the 97th Guards Mortar Regiment firing out of Melikhovo.

As I've already noted, information on the number of operational tanks in the III Panzer Corps prior to 9 July hasn't yet been found in archival sources. Prior to 9 July, the summaries of the divisions that contained such information were sent to the corps headquarters only once every 24 hours, but they are missing. Only after a special directive was released on the morning of 9 July that stated "… in these decisive days of combat, it has been ordered to submit reports on the status of tanks twice a day for keeping the higher command informed; staff officers are responsible for the accurate submission of these reports over the radio"[112] did summaries appear with relatively complete information about the condition of the tank pool. According to the information from the Soviet side, in the triangular (excl.) Postnikov – (excl.) Dal'niaia Igumenka – (excl.) Kalinin area, up to 220 German tanks, assault guns and halftracks were spotted on the morning of 8 July, though only a total of 160 armored vehicles took direct part in the initial morning attacks toward Kalinin and Dal'niaia Igumenka. The concentration of such a significant force of tanks was quickly reported to Voronezh Front headquarters. A transcript of the discussions between corps commander S.G. Goriachev and the Front headquarters' deputy chief of operations Colonel F.I. Gorlachev at 0940 on 8 July have been preserved, in which he also reported the start of the attack by III Panzer Corps' group of armor:

> **S.G. Goriachev:** … 93rd Guards Rifle Division with two rifle regiments has taken over two-thirds of Burdeinyi's sector [of the 2nd Guards Tank Corps] while one rifle regiment has taken position directly west and southwest of Gostischevo. The enemy today is showing no activity in its sector. The 92nd Guards Rifle Division upon moving out to the indicated area with one rifle regiment since 1900 yesterday evening has been engaged in combat on the hills 2 kilometers east of Melikhovo. The enemy's combined attack has been repulsed. The remaining two regiments of the 92nd Guards Rifle Division reached the indicated area and linked up with the 81st Guards Rifle Division …. I've been searching all night and still haven't found the 96th Separate Tank Brigade and the Churchill tanks. I've now received information from [garbled in text] that a group of approximately 50 tanks, having encountered stubborn resistance from Truninsky's regiment [280th Guards Rifle Regiment] at Melikhovo pivoted toward Dal'niaia Igumenka; we are taking measures to repel the attack. I request that you compel Burdeinyi to carry out the boss's [N.F. Vatutin's] order and to occupy Khokhlovo and Dal'niaia Igumenka. Over.
>
> **F.I. Gorlachev:** At what time did Burdeinyi leave the old place and do you know where he is now? Today at 0600 the enemy resumed the offensive out of the Luchki, Bol'shie Maiachki, Pokrovka, Krasnaia Dubrava area in the general Kochetovka – Sukho-Solomino direction. Altogether up to 200 tanks are operating in this sector; in other sectors, the enemy isn't conducting active operations.
>
> **S.G. Goriachev:** I'm speaking myself from the new place, I left yesterday at 2200. I request that you urgently report the situation to Ivanov [the Front's chief of staff], since the movement of the group of tanks toward Dal'naia Igumenka creates a definite threat.

---

112 TsAMO RF, f. 203, op. 2843, d. 461, l. 38.

F.I. Gorlachev: I'm reporting the situation; I request your information about Burdeinyi.

S.G. Goriachev: I don't have accurate information now; as soon as I get some through to the 93rd Guards Rifle Division, I'll report it.[113]

As we see, even the senior commanders of the Red Army had large problems not only with performance discipline, but also with elementary knowledge of their duties and understanding the significance of operational information for higher headquarters, especially in stressful moments. Five Churchills of the 47th Guards Breakthrough Heavy Tank Regiment were already at dawn standing in Dal'niaia Igumenka next to the positions of Lieutenant Colonel N.I. Novikov's 280th Guards Rifle Regiment. Both regiments were awaiting the Germans' tank attack while being totally unaware of each other's presence. Meanwhile, one lieutenant colonel (Shevchenko), who had arrived in the sector didn't get around to setting up an observation post or doing reconnaissance as the field manual demanded, or bother to report to his superior, the commander of the 35th Guards Rifle Corps, while a second lieutenant colonel (Novikov) had already spent a day and night in this sector, having never established contact or cooperation with neighbors, not to mention report to the division about the arrival of tanks on his right flank. Thus even though the 47th Guards Breakthrough Heavy Tank Regiment was in fact positioned on the defense at 0530, no one knew about this but the tankers' themselves and perhaps the artillerymen of the 1500th Destroyer Anti-tank Artillery Regiment. Meanwhile Lieutenant General S.G. Goriachev had been searching all night for the tankers, who had been standing close beside him, and was rebuking the commander of the 2nd Guards Tank Corps Colonel A.S. Burdeinyi for irresponsibility. This episode testifies again to the fact that the command of the 35th Guards Rifle Corps, which I'll remind had just been formed in April 1943, hadn't yet managed to forge an effective chain of command over the troops. As a result, it more than once would cause a failure in the course of the intense fighting on the Korocha axis.

As for the 96th Separate Tank Brigade, the situation here isn't quite clear. Prior to the evening of 7 July it had been located under the control of the 6th Guards Army and had been operationally subordinate to the commander of the 375th Rifle Division. The order from the Front Commander-in-Chief about transferring it to the 35th Guards Rifle Corps arrived in the headquarters of Chistiakov's army at 1750 on 7 July. Why it didn't reach the tank brigade until almost a day later isn't clear.

The report about the start of an attack by an enemy tank group at the boundary between the 6th Guards and 7th Guards Armies alarmed N.F. Vatutin. At this moment on the Oboian' highway, the Germans were also advancing with significant amounts of armor to the north and under their onslaught the 6th Guards Army and 1st Tank Army had begun to fall back slowly. In the morning hours the Front headquarters assessed the situation here in a report sent over the Baudot device to the communications hub of the 7th Guards Army by the deputy Front commander General of the Army I.P. Apanasenko:

> I am reporting: at 1000 the enemy in strength of up to 220 tanks with infantry from the Lukhanino – Oboian' highway (2 kilometers southeast of Krasnaia Dubrava) is attacking in the direction of Verkhopen'e. Up to 40 tanks at 1030 neared the southern outskirts of Syrtsevo, lying 6 kilometers south of Verkhopen'e. Up to 120 tanks with infantry were attacking, and of them, 50 tanks broke through to the Veselyi area (3 kilometers west of Griaznoe). As a result of the combat, the tanks suffered losses and fell back to the Griaznoe area. The enemy's

---
113 TsAMO RF, f. 203, op. 2843, d. 461, l. 38.

situation and the actions of our troops – of the tank group on the Teterevino – Visloe front [the Front's counterattack grouping] is being ascertained.[114]

From a report from the Front's chief of staff Lieutenant General S.P. Ivanov, who was at the headquarters of the 69th Army in Korocha, N.F. Vatutin knew that the tank corps that had been designated for the counterattack from the Prokhorovka direction had already assembled (although this wasn't actually the case), and accordingly would be introduced into the battle as had been planned. Thus the General of the Army wasn't especially concerned about the start of the counterattack. However, the defense on the Front's left flank was weak, and it was in need of urgent reinforcement. Between 1000 and 1130 N.F. Vatutin reached a number of important decisions and sent orders to the commander of the 69th Army over the Baudot apparatus, in which he gave him several important tasks. First, he was to reinforce quickly the vulnerable Melikhovo – Dal'niaia Igumenka sector with anti-tank means and groups of mine-laying engineers. Second, he was to form a second echelon on the axis of Army Detachment Kempf's main attack by moving up two of his army's divisions to take position behind the 92nd Guards Rifle Division.

From a coded telegram of the Front's Commander-in-chief General of the Army Vatutin sent at 1030:

> … Pass this quickly to Lieutenant General V.D. Kriuchenkin, with copies to Generals M.S. Shumilov and S.G. Goriachev.
> The enemy began an offensive on Shumilov's front at 0800 on 8.7.1943, launching the main attack in the Sevriukovo, Melikhovo direction. For today, this direction is the most important. Goriachev is late.
> I am ordering you to allocate a portion of the means of struggle against tanks and infantry and deliver them on trucks to the Melikhovo area for Goriachev. Inform Goriachev and Shumilov about this. Always keep a mobile anti-tank reserve.[115]

For V.D. Kriuchenkin, the order from the Front Commander-in-Chief was difficult to carry out. At that moment, he had hardly any anti-tank means in reserve. The only thing he could do quickly to carry out the order was to send Captain Bogachev's 122nd Anti-tank Rifle Battalion, which consisted of 107 anti-tank rifle crews, aboard one-and-a-half ton trucks to the Melikhovo – Shliakhovoe area. So that is what he did.

At 1118 a new order arrived from the Voronezh Front headquarters. It was addressed to the same generals, but this time a copy went to the Red Army's Chief of the General Staff:

1. 305th Rifle Division is to move immediately into the line previously prepared by us: Sabynino, Melikhovo, Sheino, Ushakovo.
2. Tie right flank of the 107th Rifle Division in with the left flank of the 305th Rifle Division at Ushakovo. A rifle regiment of the 305th Rifle Division with its left flank is in the Krivtsovo area.
3. Report on the execution [of this order] by 2000 8.7.1943.[116]

While information about the start of tank attacks toward Melikhovo and Dal'niaia Igumenka was traveling up the chain of command and decisions were being reached about creating a second echelon on the axis of the enemy's attack, division commanders Morozov, Trunin and Russkikh,

---

114 TsAMO RF, f. 7 gv. A, op. 5312, d. 294, l. 76.
115 TsAMO RF, f. 7 gv. A, op 5312, d. 294, l. 77.
116 TsAMO RF, f. 7 gv. A, op. 5312, d. 294, l. 78.

as well as corps commander Goriachev, were trying to strengthen their lines by shifting remnants of reserves and forces from quieter sectors. The command post of the 94th Guards Rifle Division was located on the southern outskirts of Sheino, while its observation post was to the southwest, in the combat positions of the second-echelon 288th Guards Rifle Regiment. From the morning, the division commander had been located at his command post. On the basis of arriving intelligence and the reports of observers, he was following how things were going on the front of his neighbor on the right, the 92nd Guards Rifle Division. In the middle of the battle, he drove out to his observation post, and having made a quick assessment of the strength of the forces that the Germans had committed against the elements of the 92nd Guards Rifle Division that were positioned in front of his right-flank 283rd Guards Rifle Regiment in the direction of Kalinin, he decided to reinforce his right flank. At 1030 he issued an order to L.A-M. Lifits to move up his 148th Separate Tank Regiment (minus the 3rd Tank Company) to Sheino, and to be ready to repulse an enemy attack toward Sheino and in the direction of Melikhovo. Then Russkikh issued preliminary instructions to bring up the 100th Separate Destroyer Anti-tank Artillery Battalion to the division's right flank in order to join the artillery battalion of the 199th Guards Artillery Regiment that was positioned here. At this moment Lieutenant General S.G. Goriachev arrived to see him in his observation post. After getting a short briefing from I.G. Russkikh, he announced that V.F. Trunin's situation was very difficult and that he was being attacked by large German forces. He then ordered the division commander to send an anti-tank rifle company of the 100th Separate Destroyer Anti-tank Artillery Battalion and a submachine company of the 288th Guards Rifle Regiment aboard trucks to a hill 2 kilometers east of Melikhovo, in order to block the path to Shliakhovoe in the event that the Germans took Melikhovo.

While the pioneers were making passages across the anti-tank ditches and through the minefields at Kalinin, Hünersdorff was receiving reconnaissance reports and briefings from the commanders of his *kampfgruppen* and analyzing the current situation. He then got in touch with Breith and offered him a detailed proposal for continuing the offensive. It consisted of four points. First, the general decided to take personal command over the forces that were fighting their way toward Melikhovo. Second, he planned to combine *Kampfgruppe* von Bieberstein and *Kampfgruppe* von Oppeln-Bronikowski into a single fist, and to place the commander of Panzer Regiment 11 in command over the composite group. Third, Hünersdorff requested authorization to transfer *Kampfgruppe* Unrein to Westhofen's *panzerkampfgruppe* (of the 19th Panzer Division) and to direct it as well toward Melikhovo. Meanwhile Richter's panzergrenadiers (of the 19th Panzer Division) were to continue to attack in the direction of Postnikov with the support of Panzergrenadier Regiment 74's artillery; simultaneously one Nebelwefer battery would continue to pound the revealed Soviet positions in Postnikov and on the outskirts of Dal'niaia Igumenka. After both panzer wedges neared Melikhovo, *Kampfgruppe* Westhofen was to reach the Dal'niaia Igumenka – Shliakhovoe road and outflank the former village with its main forces from the northeast, while Unrein's attached panzergrenadiers struck the northeastern outskirts of Dal'niaia Igumenka. The panzer crews had no previous opportunity to deploy near this village, because the approaches to it from the south and the east were blocked by a swampy ravine. Finally, Hünersdorff planned to assemble all of the available artillery for a barrage on a narrow sector directly in front of von Oppeln-Bronikowski's and Westhofen's *panzerkampfgruppen*, in order to flatten the artificial obstacles and blow up the minefields in the course of an hour with strongly concentrated fire, before shifting it to the flanks of the breakthrough and on to Melikhovo itself. Thus, the general was intending to create a dead zone that extended up to 3.5 kilometers. Breith approved the scheme and feverish work to implement it got underway.

From the moment that the 6th Panzer Division's offensive temporarily halted (at 1000) and for the ensuing three to four hours, the entire sector of the 280th Guards Rifle Regiment was subjected to a heavy barrage from artillery and Nebelwerfers, and only after 1200 did the Germans begin to test the Soviet lines with a reconnaissance-in-force. Thus in the majority of Soviet operational documents, it is difficult to determine the precise time when Colonel von Oppeln-Bronikowski's *panzerkampfgruppe* launched its decisive attack toward Melikhovo. Only in the 35th Guards Rifle Corps' account is there a rather detailed description of this moment. The information in this source is similar to the information found in other documents, so I believe that it describes the main stages of the battle for this major strongpoint rather accurately:

> At 1400 in strength of up to two battalions of motorized infantry with the support of 60 tanks, the enemy launched an attack toward Melikhovo, and by 1700 at the cost of heavy losses (40 tanks knocked-out) the Germans entered the village, and reached its northeastern outskirts by 1800. The surviving elements of the 280th Guards Rifle Regiment made a fighting withdrawal to Shliakhovoe, and together with the training battalion, the reconnaissance company, a submachine gun company of the 282nd Guards Rifle Regiment and the 122nd Separate Anti-tank Rifle Battalion by 2100 took up a defense on the Machine Tractor Station – Shliakhovoe – Orlov ravine line, preventing the enemy from expanding to the north in the direction of Shliakhovoe.[117]

For approximately the first two hours, the artillery of the 92nd Guards Rifle Division, 1/93rd Cannon Artillery Regiment, and crews of the 47th Guards Separate Tank Regiment played the main role in resisting the massed attack by two panzer regiments. In addition, rocket launchers of the 97th Guards Mortar Regiment offered fire support out of Melikhovo both prior to the attack and during it. However, the Germans' numerical superiority made itself known, and approximately after one hour, the forward edge of the 280th Guards Rifle Regiment began to crack. German armor broke into the Guardsmen's positions and combat began to heat up with new intensity now in the depth of their lines.

After 1600, tankers took on the main burden of struggle against the enemy. When the Germans began to work over the positions of the 280th Guards Rifle Regiment with artillery, S.G. Goriachev, who was as before at the 94th Guards Rifle Division's observation post, deciphered the Germans' intentions and issued an order to I.G. Russkikh to block the approaches to Shliakhovoe from the direction of Melikhovo with the 20 tanks of the 148th Separate Tank Regiment; in other words, to take up a defense in the path of the 6th Panzer Division in the event it made a breakthrough.

At 1530, N.F. Vatutin's instructions finally reached the 96th Separate Tank Brigade (46 T-34 and 5 T-70[118]) as well. The brigade commander Major General V.G. Lebedev received an order to counterattack the enemy between Melikhovo and Dal'niaia Igumenka (the 19th Panzer Division), and to hold the latter place until the rifle units arrived. Accordingly, by approximately 1600 the path of von Oppeln-Bronikowski's and Westhofen's panzer regiments was to be blocked by the 74 tanks of the 148th Separate Tank Regiment and 96th Separate Tank Brigade. If we add the five Churchill tanks of the 47th Guards Separate Breakthrough Heavy Tank Regiment and the five batteries of the 1500th Destroyer Anti-tank Artillery Regiment (in the Dal'niaia Igumenka area), as well as the Katiusha rocket launchers and the 1/93rd Cannon Artillery Regiment, augmented by the numerous artificial obstacles, then the 280th Guards Rifle Regiment had real chances to hold its positions in Melikhovo. However, unfortunately the tankers were late in arriving and began to approach this area at a time when a portion of Novikov's 280th Guards Rifle Regiment had already been driven back from the main line and were falling back to the northeast and east under the pressure of superior forces. The first to join battle (approximately 40 minutes after receiving

---

117 TsAMO RF, f. 35 gv. sk, op. 1, d. 44, l. 5.
118 TsAMO RF, f. 96 otbr, op. 1, d. 3, l. 15obr.

the order) with Westhofen's left-flank units (his anti-tank screen) were the crews of Lebedev's tank brigade. The main forces of *Kampfgruppe* Westhofen had been drawn into the village, and were engaged in street fighting in its center, but had exposed their left flank to an attack by the 96th Separate Tank Brigade. By this time von Oppeln-Bronikowski's panzers had reached the southern outskirts of Melikhovo and were attempting to break through to the large village of Shliakhovoe that was located nearby.

Brigade commander Lebedev launched the first attack at 1610 with the forces of Captain Kul'kov's 228th Tank Battalion (24 T-34), which attacked in the direction of Point 217.4 and the woods west of Melikhovo, striving to pin down the enemy's forces (Westhofen's panzer regiment) between Melikhovo and Dal'niaia Igumenka. Meanwhile Captain Shcheglov's 331st Tank Battalion moved up into the positions previously occupied by the brigade in the Shishino area (west of Dal'naia Igumenka) with the aim of creating a threat to the 19th Panzer Division's flank, and at a suitable moment attack in the direction of Postnikov and Blizhniaia Igumenka. When passing over Hill 217.4 Kul'kov's tank battalion deployed into a wedge-shaped combat formation and moved off in two directions, since at that moment a report arrived that the Germans were not only fighting in Melikhovo, but had also already broken into the eastern outskirts of Dal'niaia Igumenka and were even approaching Postnikov. From the report by the 96th Separate Tank Brigade's headquarters:

> 3/228th Tank Battalion went on the attack toward the woods west of Melikhovo, and having broken the resistance of a deployed blocking force [Westhofen], reached the vicinity of the woods south of the village. During the attack, the company destroyed or damaged 8 tanks, 6 guns, 7 vehicles and up to a company of infantry. 2/228th Tank Battalion at this time drove back an attack by enemy infantry from the eastern outskirts of Dal'niaia Igumenka and reached the hamlet of Postnikov, thereby securing the arrival and deployment of the 331st Tank Battalion for the counterattack. 1/228th Tank Battalion supported the actions of the attacking tank companies with fire from fixed positions.
>
> The enemy [von Oppeln-Bronikowski], becoming aware of the flank attack, halted the offensive toward Shliakhovoe and was forced to return, in order to take Dal'naia Igumenka. He committed up to 50 tanks, 12 self-propelled guns and up to a regiment of infantry in order to take the village.
>
> The 228th Tank Battalion was forced to fall back from the woods south of Melikhovo in the direction of Dal'naia Igumenka and take up a defense along the eastern fringe of the woods at Hill 217.4. The enemy from the march attempted to take Dal'naia Igumenka, but was stopped by the fire of our tanks and forced to stop in the patch of woods west of Melikhovo.[119]

The flank attack by the tank battalions of the 96th Separate Tank Brigade was swift and unexpected for the enemy, although the tanks weren't properly supported by artillery fire or accompanied by infantry, which was one of the reasons they failed to carry out the assignment.[120] As to why Westhofen left behind such an insignificant force in order to cover his left flank, it is clear that he overlooked the approach of enemy tanks from this direction. Incidentally, the German aerial reconnaissance was also not reporting anything threatening. Here is an intercepted radio message from a reconnaissance aircraft of VIII Fliegerkorps:

---

119 TsAMO RF, f. 203, op. 2851, d. 24, ll. 421obr, 422.
120 TsAMO RF, f. 96 otbr, op. 1, d. 14, l. 51.

1045: 2 enemy tanks on the southern outskirts of Dal'naia Igumenka, moving to the west. Along the road from Dal'naia Igumenka to the northwest, 30-40 wagons. From Dal'niaia Igumenka to the southwest, an enemy motorized column.

1300: On the eastern outskirts of Melikhovo, 120 enemy soldiers are dug in. Anti-tank ditches to the south of Melikhovo; no tanks observed.

1510: 5 tanks and 2 guns [the 148th Separate Tank Regiment] on the Melikhovo – Mazikino road. Our panzers are 1.5 kilometers southeast of Dal'niaia Igumenka. On the southern outskirts of Melikhovo, 5 enemy tanks and 2 enemy guns.

1825: 8 enemy tanks presumably in Shliakhovoe. Our panzers are in Melikhovo.

1850: At the crossroads west of Melikhovo, our panzers are engaged in combat with enemy tanks.[121]

Between 1900 and 2000 the organized resistance by the units of the 92nd Guards Rifle Division and the 96th Separate Tank Brigade in the center of Melikhovo and on its northern and northeastern outskirts collapsed. Soldiers and officers of the 280th Guards Rifle Regiment began to retreat in groups and alone in the direction of Shliakhovoe and Sabynino. Corps commander S.G. Goriachev wound up in a precarious situation. On the axis of the enemy panzer group's main attack, a 4-kilometer gap had been torn into the corps' defenses. Moreover, to the northeast beyond Melikhovo in the direction of Sabynino, there was still no line being occupied by Soviet troops; the 305th and 107th Rifle Divisions had just moved out of their previous areas of defense. There was only one promising thing – two tactically-important strongpoints on the shoulders of the breach, Dal'niaia Igumenka and Shliakhovoe, remained in our hands, but each had few troops holding them. For some time, they would be unable to pose a serious threat to the flanks of the enemy penetration. Relying on the tanks of the 148th Separate Tank Regiment, the battered units of the 280th Guards Rifle Regiment might be able to defend Shliakhovoe for some time, albeit with difficulty. Dal'niaia Igumenka was being held by a wing and a prayer and the heroism of the tankers of the 96th Separate Tank Brigade, the 47th Separate Breakthrough Heavy Tank Regiment and the crews of the 93rd Cannon Artillery Regiment. There was little infantry in the village.

Goriachev was running out of reserves and it was impossible to weaken the line of the 94th Guards Rifle Division further; the 7th Panzer Division was operating in front of its left flank and center, and the regiment that had been sent to reinforce his right flank was already engaged in heavy combat in Kalinin. It was possible to consider the shifting one of the regiments of the 92nd Guards Rifle Division that had been transferred to the 81st Guards Rifle Division's control to the Dal'niaia Igumenka – Shliakhovoe sector as an option. However, the enemy was also exerting strong pressure in the Staryi Gorod – Blizhniaia Igumenka area, so with no other alternative Major General I.K. Morozov had been forced at 2000 to bring up the 282nd Guards Rifle Regiment to his left flank in order to reinforce the (excl.) Blizhniaia Igumenka – Postnikov sector.

Fearing that the enemy might try to break through to Sabynino on the boot heels of the retreating infantry, S.G. Goriachev at 2030 issued an order to tank brigade commander Lebedev through the headquarters of the commander of the 35th Guards Rifle Corps' Armored and Mechanized Forces to withdraw the 331st Tank Battalion, the motorized rifle battalion and the destroyer anti-tank artillery battalion to Hill 211.5 (on the road from the Shliakhovoe Machine Tractor Station to Sabynino) and to the woods east of Sabynino with the task to prevent an enemy tank breakthrough to Sabynino. Just 30 minutes later the corps commander issued an order for all of the corps' 76mm guns to be deployed to fire over open sights at enemy tanks. However, unfortunately

---

121 TsAMO RF, f. 203, op. 2843, d. 452, l. 61.

there was little sense in this order, because by evening the rifle and artillery units were experiencing an acute ammunition shortage. Trunin's and Russkikh's divisions had been moved out to the line hastily and had joined combat from the march 24 hours earlier, so the division commanders hadn't had the physical possibility to bring up ammunition. In Special Combat Order No.5 signed at 2100, Goriachev had demanded: "Throughout the night, using all motorized transport available, right down to the prime movers of guns, organize the delivery of ammunition, bringing up the bullets for soldiers and the artillery shells to a single standard combat load."[122]

The main thing that S.G. Goriachev had been able to achieve by launching the counterattack with the 96th Separate Tank Brigade was the splitting of the III Panzer Corps' shock wedge. Westhofen's *panzerkampfgruppe* had been forced to turn toward Dal'niaia Igumenka, and without its assistance it had been beyond the strength of von Oppeln-Bronikowski's *panzerkampfgruppe* to break through to Shliakhovoe, while on the penetration's right flank problems had arisen. First, the 148th Separate Tank Regiment had appeared in its path, and units of the 94th Guards Rifle Division (the anti-tank rifle company and submachine gun company) had been moved up by the division commander even before midday. From the combat diary of Lifits' 148th Separate Tank Regiment:

> Upon the regiment commander's arrival at the command post of the 94th Guards Rifle Division in Shliakhovoe, the regiment had been given an assignment by division commander Colonel Russkikh to prevent enemy tanks from reaching Shliakhovoe. By 1700 the regiment had assembled in Shliakhovoe with 17 T-34 and 5 T-70, but didn't have time to take up a defense, and thus met the advancing enemy tanks from the march.
>
> By 1700 enemy infantry supported by 60 tanks had already gone on the offensive toward Melikhovo, and having seized the latter attempted to exploit the success toward Shliakhovoe. However, the enemy's tank attack was repulsed, after which a portion of the enemy armor began moving in the northeastern direction, while up to 15 tanks turned back to Melikhovo.[123]

Secondly, approximately at this same time, somewhere after 1700, when von Oppeln-Bronikowski's panzers had begun to advance from Melikhovo toward Shliakhovoe, *Kampfgruppe* von Bieberstein (of the 6th Panzer Division) had driven the Guardsmen out of Kalinin. Having received a report about this, I.G. Russkikh got in touch with commander of the 283rd Guards Rifle Regiment Major A.A. Ignat'ev and demanded that he quickly retake the hamlet. Approximately three hours later, the 1st and 2nd Rifle Battalions with the fire support of an artillery battalion of the 199th Guards Artillery Regiment launched a counterattack, and took the hamlet after a hard fight by 2200, having thrown the enemy back 1 kilometer to the west. By the end of the day, the division's chief of staff Lieutenant Colonel G.N. Shostatsky reported that over the day, the division had lost 35 killed and 215 wounded, while enemy tank fire had knocked out 10 76mm guns and 4 vehicles. In addition to the assault on the hamlet of Kalinin, units of the 94th Guards Rifle Division on this same day had taken part in repulsing several strong attacks by the 7th Panzer Division against the Miasoedovo – Hill 206.9 line. According to Operational Summary No. 0101 for 1500 8 July, by this time the division had suffered 7 killed and 46 wounded.[124] Thus, the recapture of Kalinin had cost the division a total of 294 soldiers and officers, including 25 killed and 269 wounded, which is evidence of the stiff resistance put up by the Germans.

---

122 TsAMO RF, f. 35 gv. sk, op. 1, d. 26, l. 81.
123 TsAMO RF, f. 148 otp, op. 661360, d. 3, l. 78, 79.
124 TsAMO RF, f. 148 otp, op. 661360, d. 3, l. 78.

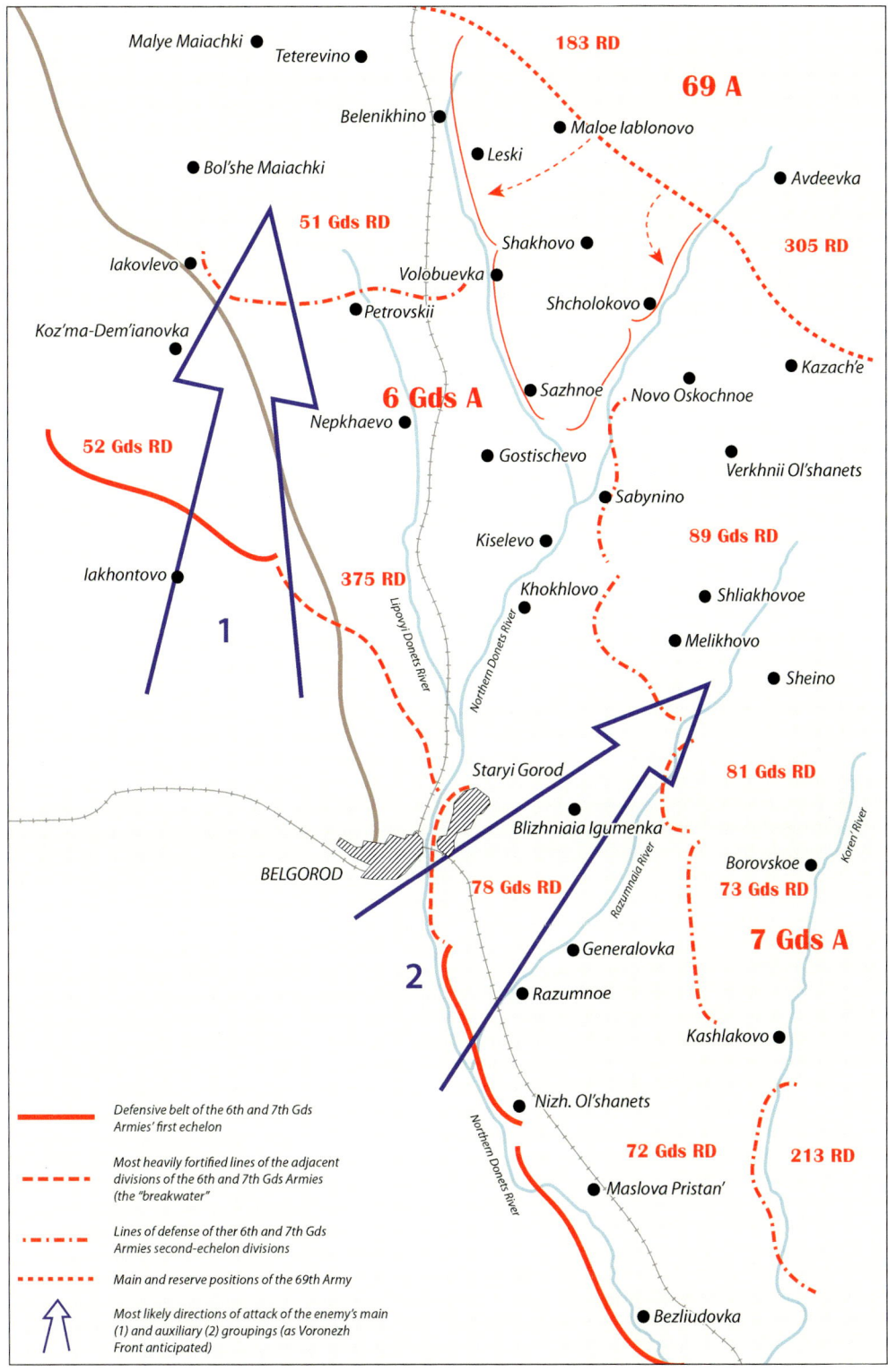

Map 1 "Vatutin's Plan": The 7th Guards Army in the system of the Voronezh Front's defense and the anticipated directions of the enemy's attack.

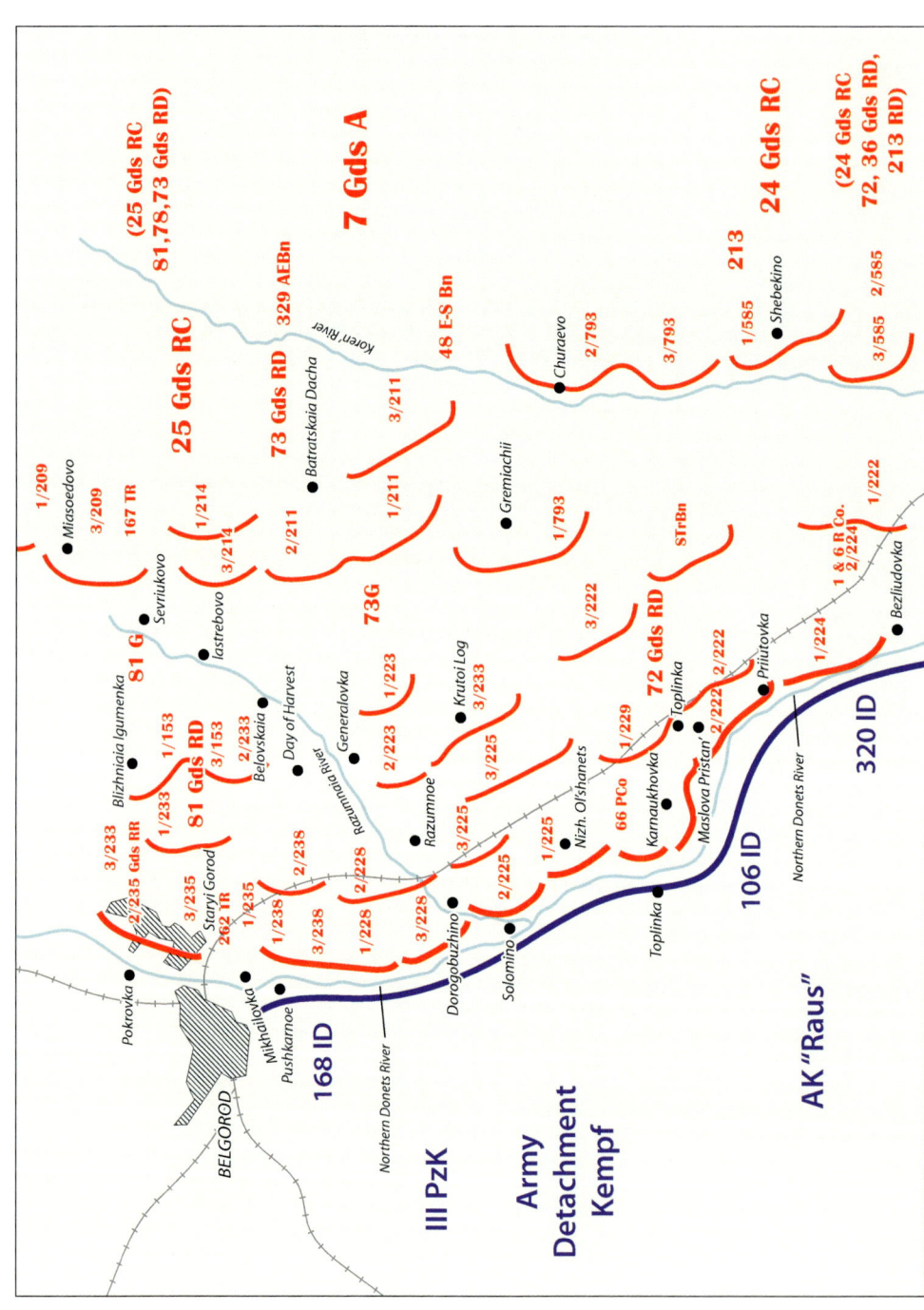

Map 2 The sector of the 7th Guards Army's main and second defensive belts on 1 July 1943 (minus the 15th Guards and 36th Guards Rifle Divisions).

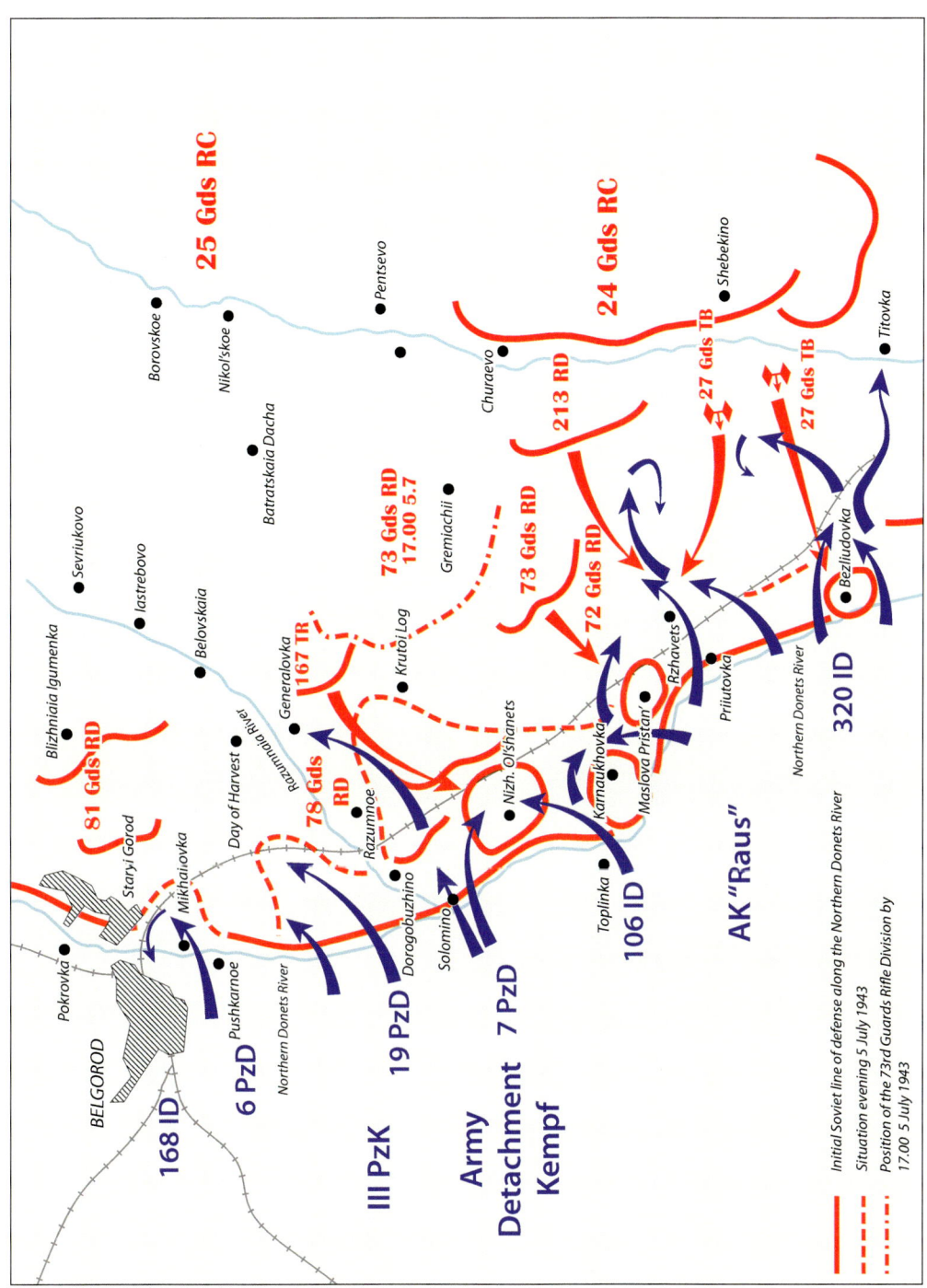

Map 3 Combat operations in the 7th Guards Army's sector, 5 July 1943.

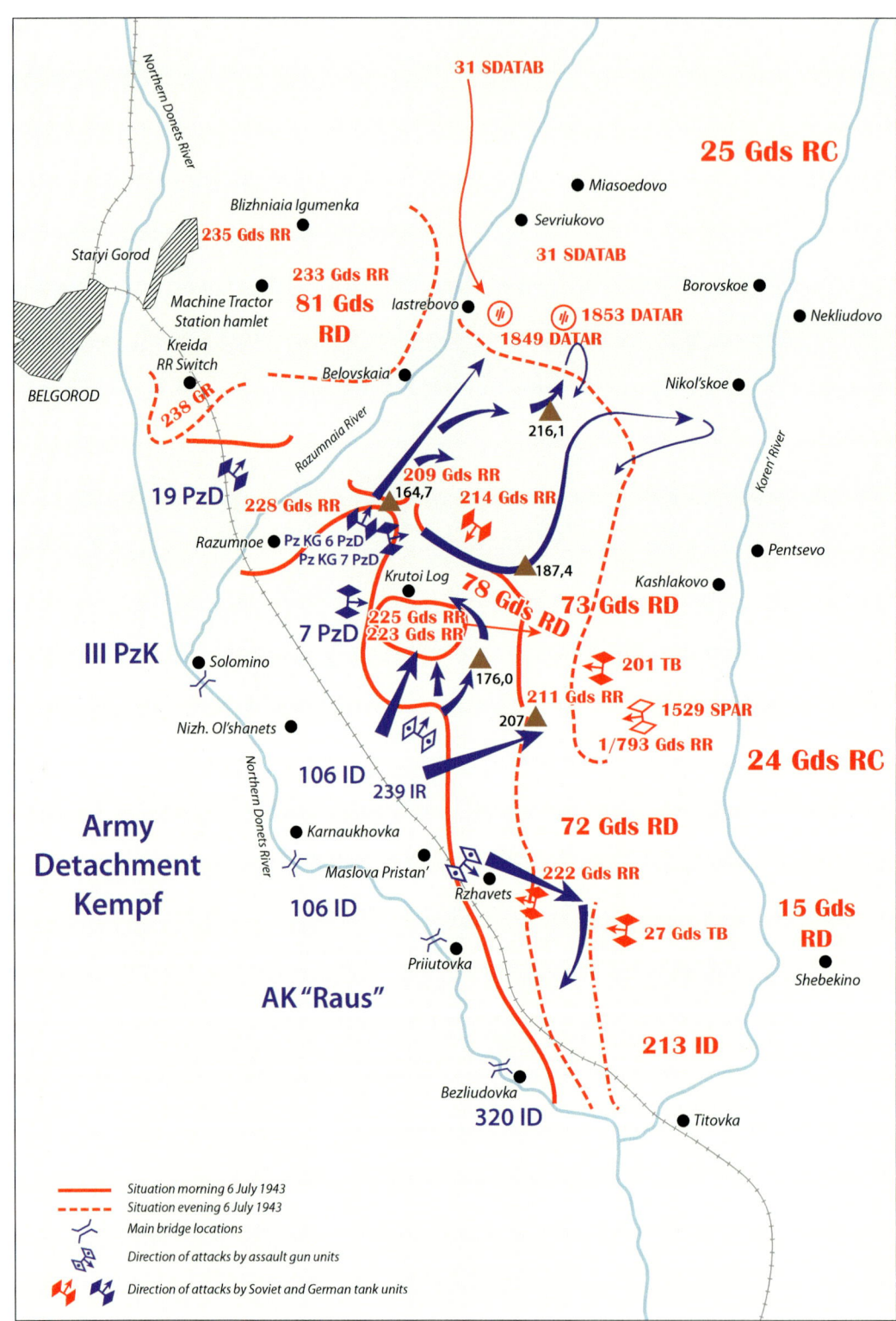

Map 4 The course of combat operations in the 7th Guards Army's sector on 6 July 1943.

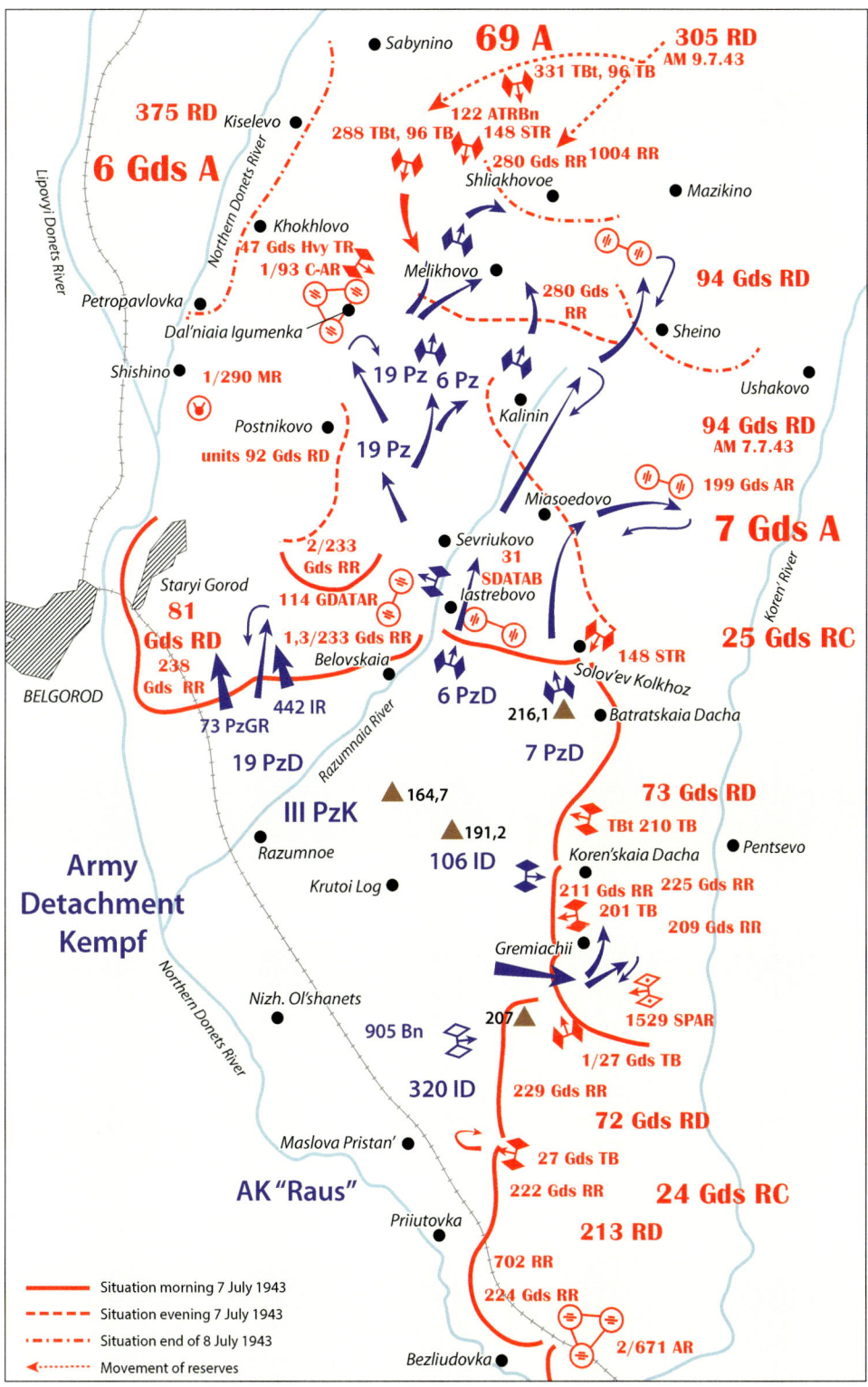

Map 5 III Panzer Corps' breakthrough at the boundary between the 6th Guards and 7th Guards Armies on 7 July 1943 and the combat in the Melikhovo area on 8 July 1943.

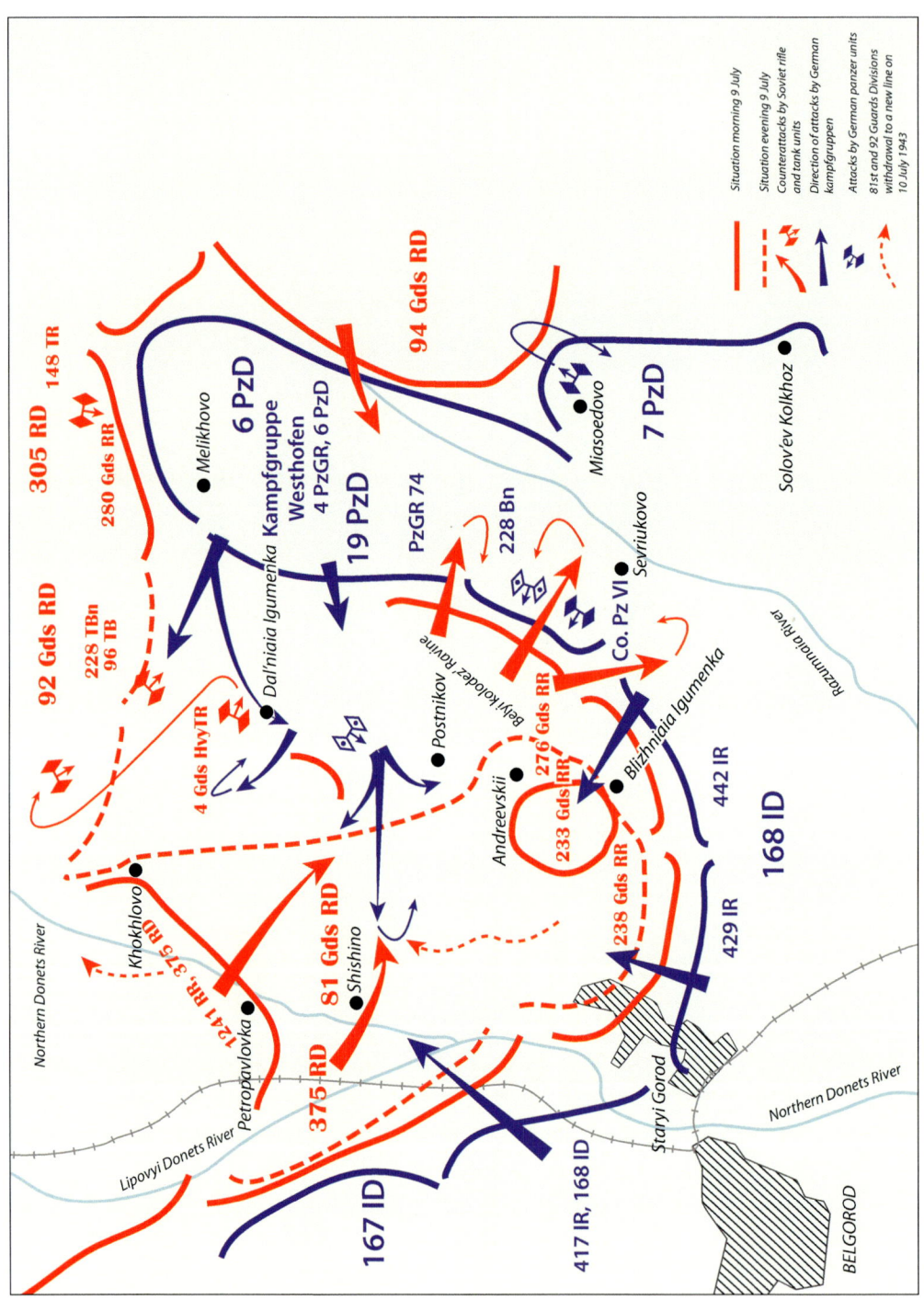

Map 6 The 81st and 92nd Guards Rifle Divisions' combat against III Panzer Corps, 9 July 1943.

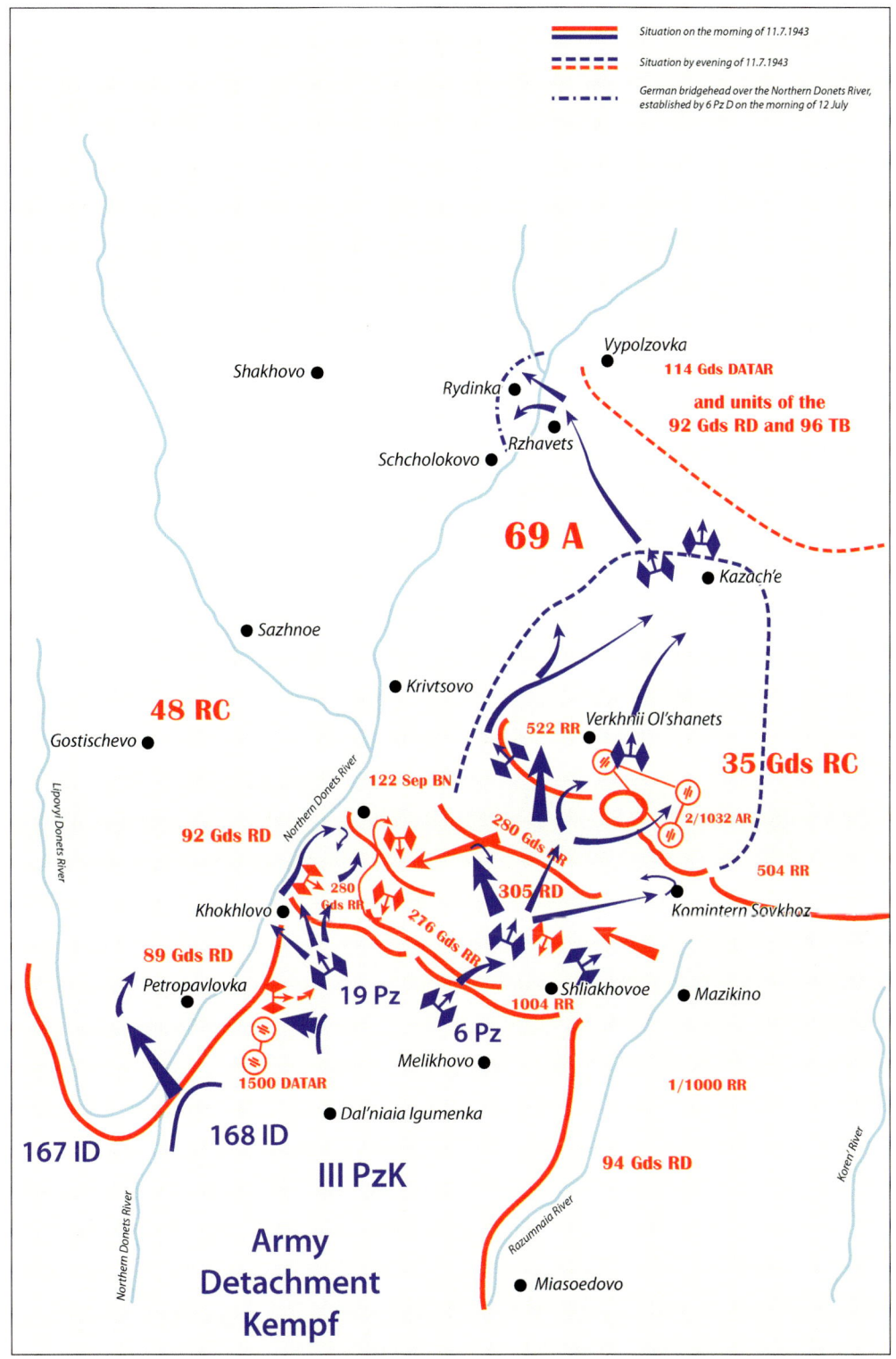

Map 7 Breakthrough of the 69th Army's second army-level defensive belt by III Panzer Corps in the course of 11 July and the night of 11-12 July 1943.

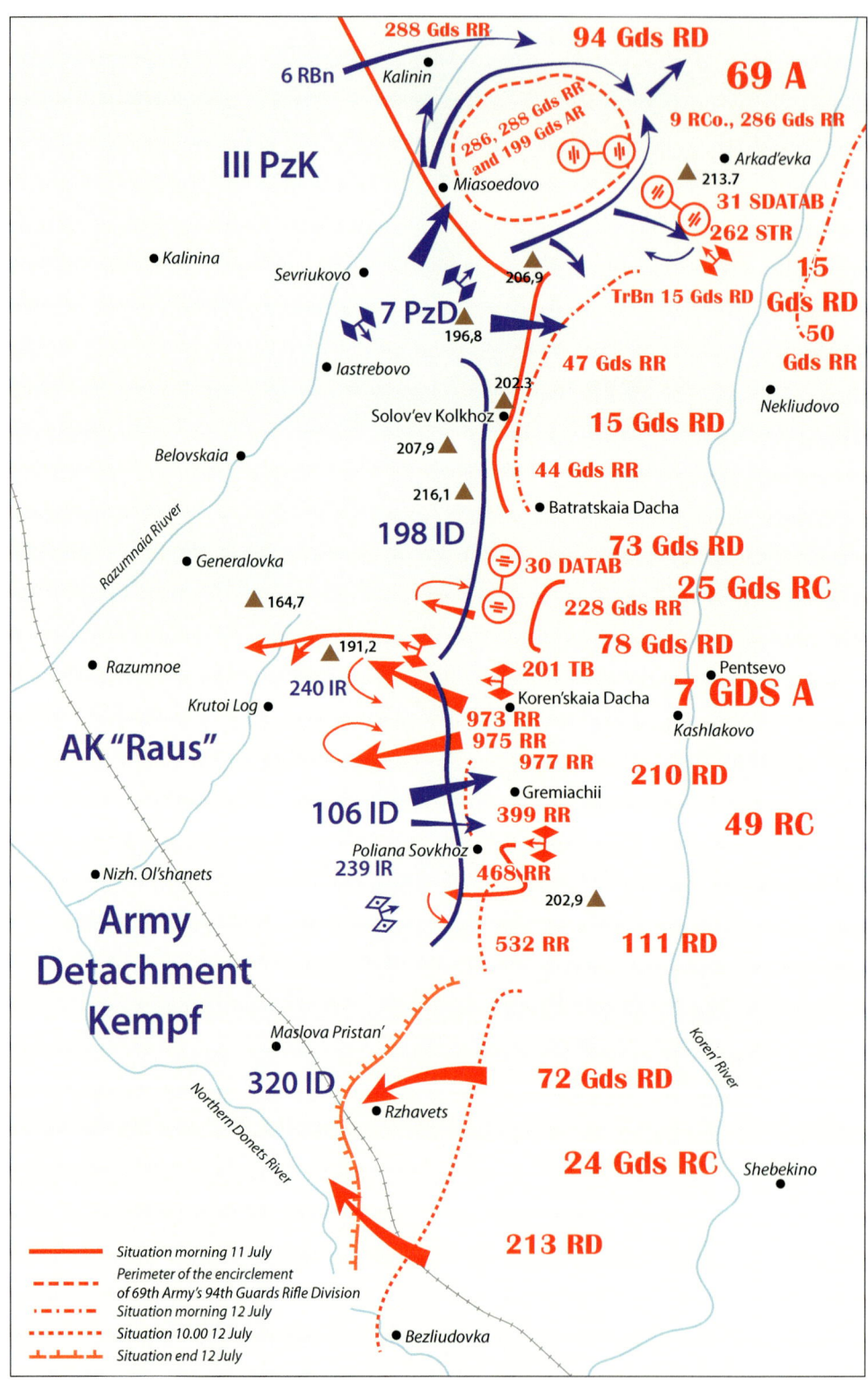

Map 8 Encirclement of the 35th Guards Rifle Corps' 94th Guards Rifle Division on 11 July 1943 and the 7th Guards Army's participation in the 12 July 1943 counteroffensive.

The defense of Shliakhovoe, which had been reinforced with armor; the fierce Russian counterattacks in the Kalinin area and the attacks by the 96th Separate Tank Brigade between Dal'niaia Igumenka and Melikhovo, as well as the intensive fire by heavy howitzers and "Stalin's organs" on the combat formations of the attacking panzer wedges forced Hünersdorff, who as before was leading both of the *panzerkampfgruppen* of the 19th and 6th Panzer Divisions, to halt the offensive between 2100 and 2200 and go over to fortifying the ground that had been gained. The headquarters of III Panzer Corps reported: "6th Panzer Division attacked to the north out of the area north of Sevriukovo, overcame a mined anti-tank ditch to the northwest of Kalinin, and with a decisive lunge took Melikhovo and reached the road 1 kilometer north of it. The enemy was defending with exceptional ferocity, with the support of tanks and powerful artillery and rocket-launcher fire."[125]

Combat actions on the left flank of III Panzer Corps' panzer wedge continued somewhat longer. Here, Westhofen's *panzerkampfgruppe* made repeated attempts to take Postnikov and Dal'niaia Igumenka after 2200. However, it could achieve no success. It lacked the strength to take two fortified strongpoints simultaneously, and in front of his panzers there was a large natural obstacle, the swampy Belyi Kolodez' ravine, the slopes of which had been densely mined, while the approaches to it had been registered by howitzer fire. The forcing of this ravine proved to be significantly more complicated than crossing an ordinary anti-tank ditch. Having blown up the edges of an anti-tank ditch, it was possible to create passages for armor rather quickly across it, but in a swampy ravine it was also necessary to build an embankment or lay down a corduroy road while under enemy fire. Thus the fighting in front of Dal'niaia Igumenka was just as heavy and bloody as in the Melikhovo area. In the course of it both sides – the troops of III Panzer Corps and those of the 35th Guards Rifle Corps – were models of resolve, tenacity and singleness of purpose in achieving their objectives. Late in the evening, General Schmidt reported: "*Kampfgruppe* Westhofen under the heaviest enemy anti-tank and artillery fire closed upon Dal'niaia Igumenka at 1525 (Berlin time), and after overcoming an anti-tank ditch and clearing the minefield situated to the north of it is now located on the approaches to the settlement."[126]

The Guardsmen were resisting savagely, especially the artillery crews and tank crews. At the hardest moment, when Westhofen's armor, having passed through the minefield and outflanked the ravine from the north, broke into the village's outskirts, the commander of the 3rd Battery of the 93rd Cannon Artillery Regiment's 1st Battalion Senior Lieutenant K.K. Golovash deployed his 152mm howitzers to fire over open sights at the enemy tanks. Even the high-explosive 46 kilogram shells of the howitzer had an effect when striking an enemy tank. According to the regiment's report, the battery repelled two attacks, wiped out up to a company of infantry, and destroyed four tanks and two assault guns. However, during the second attack a misfortune took place. Sensing the damaging fire from the southwestern outskirts, the enemy concentrated heavy fire on the battery. One of the shells hit a stockpile of 36 shells, which detonated. In the explosion several of the artillerymen were wounded or concussed, but remained at their posts. After the Germans fell back, the crews withdrew their howitzers out from under enemy fire, before redeploying and opening fire once again. For the successful fulfillment of a combat assignment and for the personal courage displayed in the fighting, K.K. Golovash was awarded the Order of the Red Star.[127]

I want to call attention to the following detail. In certain publications that have come out recently, there is the assertion that with the capture of Melikhovo, the second army-level defensive belt had been breached to its entire depth. This isn't so. Possibly, this mistake crept in because of the fact that the documents concerning the fortification of the Voronezh Front's defensive belts

---

125 NARA US, rg. 242, t. 314, r. 197, f. 001203.
126 NARA US, rg. 242, t. 314, r. 197, f. 001204.
127 TsAMO RF, f. 33, op. 686044, ed. khr. 3232, entry number 19709021.

are still classified, and thus it is difficult to pinpoint the trace of the forward edge of the second and rear army-level belts using the available sources. Let's turn to a document of the Voronezh Front headquarters entitled "Condition of the fortification of the Voronezh Front's defense as of 5.7.1943" – it indicates that the sector of the forward edge of the second-army level belt of defense, which is of interest to us, ran along the Petrovskii – Sazhnoe – Miasoedovo line, while the rear defensive belt ran along the Zhimolostnoe – Novoselovka – Vypolzovka – Mazikino – Sorokovka line. Accordingly, the fighting in this area on 8 July took place primarily within the main army-level defensive belt (which included Postnikov and Dal'niaia Igumenka) and on the forward edge of the second army-level defensive belt (Melikhovo).[128]

It must be said that on 8 July, both the 96th Separate Tank Brigade and the 148th Separate Tank Regiment played a very important role in frustrating the plan of III Panzer Corps' command to break through into the depth of the 69th Army's defenses through Melikhovo. The intense fire of the tank crews of the 148th Separate Tank Regiment in combination with anti-tank gun crews slowed the pace of the attack by von Oppeln-Bronikowski's *panzerkampfgruppe*, which by advancing along the outskirts of Melikhovo was attempting to break through to a hub of dirt roads at the Shliakhovoe Machine Tractor Station. Meanwhile the swift maneuver by Lebedev's 96th Separate Tank Brigade into the flank of Westhofen's *panzerkampfgruppe* made not only the enemy command nervous, it forced it to turn around the tanks that were poised to attack Shliakhovoe. No less important, during these actions the brigade and regiment were operating with relatively small forces and suffered small losses. In a report of the 19th Panzer Division, it is indicated that its units over the day knocked out 21 T-34 and KV tanks. This information is dubious, because in the sector of the 69th Army and 7th Guards Army, only one unit was equipped with KV tanks – the 262nd Heavy Tank Regiment, but on 8 July it wasn't anywhere near the 19th Panzer Division's sector of attack, and moreover took no part in fighting on this day. According to information from the 148th Separate Tank Regiment's combat diary, in the fighting on 8 July it had 9 killed and 17 wounded among its tank crews and lost 3 T-34 that were left burned-out.[129] In the 96th Separate Tank Brigade, 3 T-34 were destroyed and 3 were disabled, but were evacuated from the battlefield to the rear for repairs.[130] All five Churchill tanks of the 47th Guards Separate Heavy Tank Regiment positioned in Dal'niaia Igumenka were lost, including two left burned out, but the other three were turned over to a mobile repair shop.[131] One driver-mechanic of this regiment perished in the flames of his burning tank, and 10 tankers received wounds of varying degrees of severity. Thus, over the day of fighting in this area, a total of 14 Soviet tanks were knocked out, of which 8 were destroyed.

However, at this moment the Front command was still unaware of all of the problems and hitches I've talked about above, and it wouldn't be informed of the situation in this area until after 2200. So that the reader might take a glance at how the Front and armies' headquarters were functioning on the tensest days of the Battle of Kursk, get a sense of rhythm of the combat work of their staff officers, and understand the complexities standing in front of them, in particular on the evening of 8 July, I'll cite a transcript of the conversations between the Front's deputy chief of staff Major General S.I. Teteshkin and the operations chief of the 69th Army Colonel D.N. Surzhits, which took place between 1900 and 1930 on 8 July:

---

128 TsAMO RF, f. 203, op. 2845, d. 227, l. 1.
129 TsAMO RF, f. 148 otp, op. 661560, d. 3, l. 79.
130 TsAMO RF, f. 96 otbr, op. 1, d. 3, l. 29.
131 TsAMO RF, f. 2 gv. Ttk, op. 1, d. 24, l. 204.

Major General S.I. Teteshkin on the line. Greetings. Report how the units of Bazhko and units of Danilovich[132] arrived on the indicated lines. What's the situation on Kostitsyn's right flank?[133] Do you have contact with Burkov, Popov and Kravchenko?[134] What's the situation opposite their front and the approximate line that they've reached? What's the enemy grouping and the nature of the fighting over today in front of the commanders I've mentioned? Over.

D.N. Surzhits: I am reporting. Danilovich's and Bezhko's[135] units left at 1930 today. The commanders are requesting extended air cover until the onset of darkness.

Second. No changes have taken place yet on Kostitsyn's right flank to the present time. At 2000 my liaison officer will arrive from him with a detailed report on the situation; I will report immediately upon his arrival.

Third: The situation regarding Kravchenko's and Popov's outfits and the one equivalent to Popov's [Burkov's], as well as regarding Goriachev has been reported to you in code. Burdeinyi is engaged in combat with tanks on the eastern bank of the Lipovyi Donets River. Kravchenko is engaged in combat directly to the south of Kostitsyn. A group of officers has been sent to Popov's and Kravchenko's outfits in order to organize communications and gather information on the situation; I'm expecting to receive information from them by 2100-2200. I will report immediately upon receipt. Regarding Goriachev, the exact location of his outfit was reported to you by code at 1915. Over. Surzhits.

S.I. Teteshkin: Comrade Surzhits, as far as I recall, the two outfits indicated by you should have been in place by 2000. But you are saying that they were only leaving their former positions at 1930. What's going on, why the delay? I gave an order for you to keep in touch with their outfits. Burkov, Popov and Kravchenko reported the situation to me in their sectors this evening.

I will report to Comrade Ivanov about your foot dragging and poor job of keeping us informed. Give me the situation on the front of these three outfits not only regarding the enemy, but also the position of their units, and briefly outline the combat dynamics over the day no later than 2130; now I'm waiting for an explanation regarding the delay of Comrades Bezhko and Danilovich. That's all I have. I'm waiting by the device. Prepare to transmit your operational summary immediately upon the completion of these talks. That's all I have.

D.N. Surzhits: I'm reporting. First, I'll now give you an explanation for Bezhko's and Danilovich's delay.

Second. Popov and the outfit similar to his [the 10th Tank Corps], which are in the area of Kostitsyn's dispositions, still haven't taken part in any combat actions at all (their positions have been reported to you in code); they are located in the area of one of your outfits. Thus even in the future (before restoring direct communications between us and

---

132 The general is mistaken. After 2 May 1943, Colonel I.A. Danilovich was no longer commanding the 305th Rifle Division. It was now being led by Colonel A.F. Vasil'ev.
133 Major General A.S. Kostitsyn, who was commanding the 183rd Rifle Division. Its right-flank 285th Rifle Regiment was covering an important sector that was vulnerable to tanks: (excl.) Vasil'evka – Komsomolets State Farm – Ivanovskii Vyselok. This sector was guarding the approaches to the Prokhorovka Station railroad.
134 Lieutenant General V.G. Burkov commanded the 10th Tank Corps. Major General A.F. Popov commanded the 2nd Tank Corps. Major General A.G. Kravchenko commanded the 5th Guards "Stalingrad" Tank Corps. On 8 July 1943, all of these tank corps were located on the right flank of the 69th Army (on the Prokhorovka direction) and had taken part in a counterattack against the SS II Panzer Corps.
135 Major General M.P. Bezhko, the commander of the 107th Rifle Division.

them) we will be communicating through you. Thus it is desirable to make it possible to use their outfits' devices where they are located, and you, on your part, must also take interest in the situation on their front.

Teteshkin: It is clear that it is necessary for you to take steps in order to obtain a situation report from them in order to transmit it to us. I will be waiting by the device for you and your information about the situation on the front of these three outfits at 2100 – 2200. Teteshkin 1840 8.7.1943.

D.N. Surzhits: I am reporting: Everything has been done on our part in order to have reliable communications with them. Steps have been taken. The situation will be reported to you.[136]

The late arrival of the 305th Rifle Division in the Shliakhovoe area was complicating the situation in this area and created a real threat of a German breakthrough. The main reason for the delay was the low mobility of the Soviet rifle divisions and the absence of high-quality communication devices in the troops. On the example of the regrouping of the 305th and 107th Rifle Divisions, one can plainly trace the speed at which urgent information traveled up the lines of communication from their headquarters to the army command and from there back to the rifle corps and division. For example, N.F. Vatutin issued the order for the regrouping at 1100-1110 and it immediately went to the Front's communications hub, from whence via the Baudot device it was received at the headquarters of the 69th Army (which was located in Korocha) at 1118. After the passage of a certain amount of time the order was sent by the army to the 48th Rifle Corps. Less than an hour later, at 1215 its commander Major General Z.Z. Ragoznyi prepared and sent (in the course of 15-20 minutes) his order with a liaison officer to the commander of the 305th Rifle Division Colonel A.F. Vasil'ev, which was delivered at 1620. Thus, the urgent document signed by N.F. Vatutin that was sent according to the customary scheme reached its designated recipient, who was located approximately 60 kilometers from the Front headquarters, only after a passage of six hours.

There were other options, for example, the radio or mobile means of communication (a liaison officer aboard an aircraft or in a car). However, this type of order, because of its special importance, was transmitted over the radio only in exceptional cases, and went more often over the Baudot device or with liaison officers. In normal conditions (when a division was located in reserve), a division commander required (if there had been no preliminary instructions) clarification of the task, and time to prepare his order for the troops, gather the regiment commanders, inform them of the tasks (both general and individual), send out the division's forward detachment (or a reconnoitering group), and finally, get the first battalion columns on the march. This entire array of steps took approximately 5.5 to 6 hours until the moment when the first units moved out on the march, and if the division was sallying in response to an alarm, no less than 3.5 hours were required to get moving.

Both the 305th and the 107th Rifle Divisions met these minimal periods of time when moving out to screen the Korocha direction. Accordingly, to accuse the commanders of the 69th Army in dragging their feet is unjustified, putting it gently. Everything that depended on them had been done. At the same time, one must also understand the situation in which the officers and generals of the Front headquarters were located at that moment. On the third day of the operation, combat operations were going not at all as had been planned; on the main axis the enemy was already in front of the rear army-level defenses and continuing to push back the Soviet forces, albeit slowly. The situation demanded composure, promptness and accuracy in carrying out orders, and only

---

136 TsAMO RF, f. 203, op. 2843, d. 461, l. 37, 37obr.

this could influence the outcomes of the fighting. Thus, the commands at every level were putting pressure on subordinates, striving to increase the pace of their work substantially, and thereby take the initiative back from the enemy. However, experience was demonstrating that demands alone rarely helped the matter. For example, three headquarters – Front, army and corps – were simultaneously persistently demanding the commander of the 305th Rifle Division Colonel A.F. Vasil'ev to take "prompt and immediate action to fulfill an order", but not one of them had anything to do with the manner in which he carried it out, because no one bothered to look into his needs and problems. Even so, everyone knew that the divisions of the 69th Army had been equipped on a lower-priority basis, and so the 305th Rifle Division, like its neighbors in the 69th Army, lacked transportation (the shortage of horses amounted to approximately 70%)[137] even for moving its most vital supply – ammunition. So that its regiments didn't enter combat with empty stocks, the division headquarters had been forced to order each soldier to carry a shell.[138] Weighed down by this, the Red Army soldiers had to march dozens of kilometers on foot, and each of them was also carrying his weapon, entrenchment tool, gas mask, cartridges, grenades, dry rations and personal items that were rolled up in a tent half and carried over the shoulder. I think that it isn't hard to picture the physical condition in which they arrived at the end of the march. It was a desperate measure, but there was simply no other way to transport the shells.

Nevertheless, despite all the difficulties, the efforts of the Soviet side yielded a certain result, even though it was unable to form a second line of defense at Shliakhovoe, as N.F. Vatutin had planned. However, by the start of III Panzer Corps' attack, the village's defense had been substantially strengthened. By dawn on 9 July, the incomplete 1004th Rifle Regiment of the 305th Rifle Division had deployed here together with the battalions of the 280th Guards Rifle Regiment that had fallen back to here from the Melikhovo area.

However, now let's return to the sector of the 81st Guards Rifle Division and take a look at how events were developing here on 8 July. By the morning, the division and two attached regiments were holding a front along the line: mouth of the Northern Donets – southern outskirts of Staryi Gorod – orchard north of the Kreida railyard – southern outskirts of Blizhniaia Igumenka – Hill 212.1 – Hill 207.8 – Hill 192.5.[139] Throughout the day, *kampfgruppen* of Schmidt's 19th Panzer Division and Chales de Beaulieu's 168th Infantry Division undertook 15 attacks against its positions. Primarily they were attacking in two directions: Panzergrenadier Regiment 73 and the panzer reconnaissance battalion of the 19th Panzer Division out of the southwestern outskirts of Kreida and Infantry Regiment 442 from the eastern outskirts of Blizhniaia Igumenka into the center of that village, while Infantry Regiment 429 was attacking out of the Kreida railyards along the railroad toward the southern outskirts of Staryi Gorod. Both groups had been reinforced with artillery and armor. A battery (6 assault guns) of StuG Battalion 228 was supporting Infantry Regiment 429, and 6 flame-throwing tanks were supporting Panzergrenadier Regiment 73. In addition, one panzer company of Panzer Regiment 27 was still located in this area in Schmidt's reserve.

The 276th Guards and 233rd Guards Regiments were defending in Blizhniaia Igumenka and south of it at the Machine Tractor Station. Bitter fighting here erupted before sunrise, and continued with only short pauses until late in the evening. From a daily report of III Panzer Corps:

---

137 TsAMO RF, f. 426, op. 10753, d. 43, l. 13.
138 Ibid., l. 13obr.
139 Hills 207.8 and 192.5 were located in the woods east of Postnikov. Postnikov itself was located on the western side of the swampy Belyi Kolodez' ravine, and the command post of the 81st Guards Rifle Division that had relocated from Sevriukovo was located in it.

With joint actions of Panzergrenadier Regiment 73 and Panzer Reconnaissance Battalion 19 against the enemy positions 3 kilometers south of Blizhniaia Igumenka, separate sectors of the system of positions were rolled up at 1030; bunkers were blown up and enemy's casualty lists grew longer. The enemy's main bulk was able to hold their positions. Panzer Reconnaissance Battalion 19 fell back to its jumping-off positions.

I/Panzergrenadier Regiment 73 suffered heavy losses in hard offensive and defensive fighting and has two combat-capable companies.

Lieutenant Adorf of Panzer Reconnaissance Battalion 19 fell in the fighting for the trenches and was left in the enemy's hands.

Throughout the day and previous night, numerous attacks by enemy bombers and ground attack aircraft in the sector of the 19th Panzer Division. Our fighters and reconnaissance aircraft are operating.[140]

The 19th Panzer Division headquarters' account described the combat actions in this area more emotionally:

On the defensive line north of the "Day of Harvest" collective farm, the enemy in strength of up to two battalions, assembled from several regiments, was offering bitter resistance with a large quantity of anti-tank rifles. Our attack against these positions out of the Kreida area developed very slowly in view of the open terrain that climbed toward the enemy's positions, and was ultimately stopped north of the "Day of Harvest" collective farm. The enemy's narrow trenches were largely untouchable by artillery fire, and thus the attack was launched with a group of 6 *Flammpanzers* in cooperation with assault groups from Pioneer Battalion 12, Panzergrenadier Regiment 73 and Panzer Reconnaissance Battalion 19.

Despite the large losses that the defending enemy suffered, and in spite of the fact that entire sectors of trenches and dugouts were left completely burned out by the *Flammpanzers*, we were in fact unable to drive the Russians numbering more than a battalion out of the northern portion of the defended sector. The Asians that were dug into the system of trenches were knocking out our *Flammpanzers* with fire from anti-tank rifles and putting up fanatic resistance to the grenadiers, who had to attack across open ground.[141]

In the daily summary of the 168th Infantry Division it is noted that at 1700, Infantry Regiment 442 launched an attack with two battalions supported by 20 panzers toward Dal'niaia Igumenka from the southeast and "simultaneously the foe launched a meeting attack out of the village." Such a thing sometimes happens when both sides, not planning a deliberate attack, launch an attack at one and the same time. In such cases the outcome boils down to who flinches first, and if both sides are in a determined mood, then the attack transforms into a hand-to-hand combat and suggests not an encounter between military formations, but a wild bar fight. One of the veterans of the 92nd Guards Rifle Division in a conversation with me said that "somewhere near Belgorod" he took part in one such fight. It is possible that this was the very same attack mentioned in the German document. The old soldier recalled that at some moment the fury of the attackers reached such a boiling point that around 30 men of both sides (which he saw nearby, "but there might have been even more") threw down their rifles and went into an ordinary brawl. My conversation partner was unlucky; a Fritz head and shoulders taller than him leaped on him. The Guardsman's toughness and "a tremendous desire to live" saved him. When the German knocked him off his

---

140 NARA US, rg. 242, t. 314, r. 197, f. 001204.
141 TsAMO RF, f. 30A, op. 9027, d. 46, l. 153.

feet, then took a seat on top of him and continued to batter him with his "sledgehammer fists", he became so distracted by the effort that he didn't notice it when the Russian pulled a Finnish knife out of his boot top and with one blow struck down the "thug".

At veterans' reunions of Morozov's 81st Guards Rifle Division, I had the opportunity to hear a lot about rather unusual combat encounters with the panzers of Schmidt's division. Here is just one of them. In the vicinity of Blizhniaia Igumenka and the hamlet of the Machine Tractor Station there was one panzer crew of the 19th Panzer Division that was distinguished by the fact that during an attack they didn't destroy Russian firing positions with shots from their main gun, but instead opted to pick one out and overrun it, methodically spinning in circles atop it until the emplacement was level with the ground. In the process, all the defenders in it would suffer an agonizing death, as if falling into a meat chopper. The tank crew was openly ignoring the danger, exposing their tank to flanking fire while they used the tracks of their tank grind the emplacement into the ground. The Guardsmen took notice of this and organized a hunt for the "Black Hans", as they began calling the German tank among themselves. They assembled a special team of six brave hearts, gave each of them three special Molotov cocktails filled with potassium nitrate, and began to wait for the German tank's next appearance. The "villainous" panzer crew didn't take part in each attack, and at the same time the special tank-hunting team didn't reveal their presence. When the "Black Hans" finally made another appearance, the six men calculated roughly where the tank was heading and converged on that place simultaneously from several directions. They were calculating that if the Germans opened machine-gun fire from the tank, one or two of them would still get through and destroy it. The plan worked, and several bottles struck it simultaneously, while in the process three Guardsmen were wounded, one mortally. The "Black Hans" erupted like an enormous torch, and having rolled on for another 50 meters, came to a stop. However, the most terrible thing was, as the veterans said, no one leaped out of the hatches. The Germans inside didn't even make an attempt to open them. So the entire crew burned up in the conflagration within the tank.

This story by former defenders of the "Belgorod bastion" came to mind when I was reading an appendix to an Order No.6 of the 167th Infantry Division's Infantry Regiment 315 from 7 July 1943 that I found in the Russian Ministry of Defense's Central Archives. In the document Lieutenant Colonel (in some documents, Major) Grau openly and with military precision instructed his soldiers: "The Russian has always been and still remains our most cunning and wiliest foe. The German soldiers is too proud to mess around with these creatures more than is necessary."[142] Possibly, the crew of "Black Hans" also felt that they weren't simply Wehrmacht soldiers, but ancestors of the "Great Aryans", so thought it was a pity to waste even shells on these "creatures", though it is also possible to regard this episode as a manifestation of vengeance.

In the already cited account of the 19th Panzer Division's headquarters about the combat operations between 5 and 18 July 1943, it is mentioned that on 10 July, during the thrust into Blizhniaia Igumenka, "very few prisoners were taken, because our score with the Russians still hadn't been settled over the preceding days, after the commander of Panzergrenadier Regiment 73 had been killed by a bullet fired by a Russian officer."[143] Presumably this quote is talking about the death of Colonel Köhler in the area of Blizhniaia Igumenka. Schmidt's panzergrenadiers continued to perpetrate massacres on following days as well, even of captured Soviet soldiers and officers. For example, on the night of 14-15 July 1943, when the 375th Rifle Division was coming out of encirclement in the Shakhovo area, the 6th Company of the 1243rd Rifle Regiment's 2nd Rifle Battalion was left behind as a covering force. At dawn the enemy managed to capture 40 of its

---

142 TsAMO RF, f. 1 TA, op. 3109, d. 13, l. 73.
143 TsAMO RF, f. 38A, op. 9027, d. 46, l. 153obr.

soldiers, which the Germans then shot, before grinding the bodies into a pulp beneath the treads of their tanks. It isn't clear why this was done, out of blind hatred or in order to erase all traces of the crime, but it still became known to the Soviet side. Private Bashkov, who managed to escape before the mass shooting reported about it; a bit later the mutilated bodies were found in the place that he indicated.[144]

It must be said that a lot of Soviet soldiers were also full of feelings of fury and revenge during this battle, but judging from revealed documents, they released them not on defenseless adversaries, but in open battle. Reading the archival documents, at times I've encountered acts that are surprising and difficult to understand from the point of view of a rational mind, which in general each military man should always have. Here is one such account, related to the combat work of Lieutenant A.F. Usmanov, a deputy squadron commander with the 17th Air Army's 94th Storm Aviation Regiment in the sector of the 7th Guards Army:

> In the operation south of Belgorod between 7.07 and 9.07.1943, 5 successful individual combat sorties were conducted that destroyed 3 tanks and 5 vehicles and wiped out up to 100 enemy soldiers and officers. When carrying out a combat mission in the Razumnoe, Krutoi Log area, Guards Lieutenant Usmanov displayed exceptional courage and heroism. Destroying fascist tanks and infantry, Guards Lieutenant Usmanov's Il-2 dove to strafing altitude and with cannon and machine-gun fire shot up an aggregation of fascist troops. During the attack, his squadron commander Captain Petukhov's Sturmovik was shot down. Guards Lieutenant Usmanov, seeking revenge, dove again to nap of the earth flight and after a barrage of cannon and machine-gun fire, began to chop up fascist infantry with his propeller. According to the observation of other crews, Guards Lieutenant Usmanov began to cut down dozens of the fascist scoundrels. Upon landing back at his airfield … his armored turret and propeller screw were spattered with blood.[145]

Possibly there is an element of exaggeration in this description, but it was found in documents that had been signed off by the command of the 94th Guards Storm Aviation Regiment, thus I think it shouldn't be shrugged off as a piece of fiction. In conclusion, I will add that for his role in the fighting at the Kursk salient, already on 9 July 1943 A.F. Usmanov was put up for the Order of the Red Banner, and he was awarded it on 21 July 1943.

Now let's return to the combat operations on 8 July near Belgorod. In the sector of Major G.G. Skiruta's 235th Guards Rifle Regiment, up until 1400 the enemy only conducted combat reconnaissance and intensively shelled revealed firing points and the positions of our artillery with guns and heavy mortars. From a daily summary of the 168th Infantry Division:

> In the morning hours, traffic in both directions was observed between Staryi Gorod and Dal'niaia Igumenka. There was movement of up to two companies of infantry from the fruit orchards of the "Main Fruit and Vegetable" State Farm. One company moving from the orchards dug in on the slope of a hill 2 kilometers west of Andreevskie with a front to the southwest and southeast. Reconnaissance conducted toward Kreida through Staryi Gorod and the hamlet of the Machine Tractor Station along the Staryi Gorod – Blizhniaia Igumenka road ran into occupied enemy positions south of the Machine Tractor Station. The situation is quiet on the division's left flank [on the western bank of the Donets]. Conducted reconnaissance showed the absence of changes in the enemy positions. An attack conducted by units

---

144 TsAMO RF, f. 375 sd, op. 1, d. 143, l. 17, 17obr.
145 TsAMO RF, f. 33, op. 682526, ed. khr. 767, entry number 16584719.

of Infantry Regiment 429 at 1500 from the Kreida railyards along the road to Staryi Gorod despite bitter resistance reached a line 300 meters to the southeast of the southern entrance to Staryi Gorod. The enemy line stretched across the road leading back to Staryi Gorod.

To this point 25 prisoners have been taken. I/Panzerjäger Battalion 248, which had already been withdrawn from Infantry Regiment 247's sector [on the western bank of the Donets] for operations on the eastern side of the river, had to return again in readiness behind Infantry Regiment 417's sector, because in the morning hours aerial reconnaissance reported and our own observation confirmed the movement of enemy tanks in the Ternovka area toward the Belgorod – Kursk railroad. Continous activity in the air on the part of both sides.[146]

The second "sore spot" in the sector of the 81st Guards Rifle Division, where extremely heavy fighting went on, was the Blizhniaia Igumenka – Postnikov sector. The pressure being exerted by the 19th Panzer Division's significant armor forces forced division commander Morozov at 2000 to move Lieutenant Colonel I.I. Samoilenko's 282nd Guards Rifle Regiment to this point; previously, this regiment had been positioned north of Belgorod with a front to the northwest. By the end of 8 July there'd been no substantial changes in the sector of the 81st Guards Rifle Division. Despite considerable exertions, the enemy was in fact unable to break the resistance of Morozov's Guardsmen and make any significant headway (excluding the small sectors that passed from the control of one side to the other). However, the introduction of the 282nd Guards Rifle Regiment on the deep left flank of the division, while it did reinforce this line, weakened the density of forces in the Staryi Gorod – Blizhniaia Igumenka sector, which the enemy would exploit the next day.

There were no noticeable changes in the operational situation on the left flank of the 25th Guards Rifle Corps on this day either, although both sides showed a high amount of activity. After sunrise the situation for the 7th Guards Army command was still not quite clear. Reconnaissance patrols reported the approach of enemy reserves in the Krutoi Log – Maslova Pristan' area, while at the same time the Germans were actively conducting combat reconnaissance out of the Kalinin area and bringing up approximately 200 armored vehicles south of Melikhovo. In this situation, it was decided to cancel the counterattack with the forces of both Guards Rifle Corps that had been worked out by the 7th Guards Army headquarters. Even so, G.B. Safiulin back on the evening of 7 July, having issued an order to the 73rd Guards Rifle Division's commander to hold the division's line with his own inherent forces, directed him to conduct a number of counterattacks jointly with the 15th Guards Rifle Division's 44th Guards Rifle Regiment in the direction of the "Batratskaia Dacha" and "Solov'ev" State Farms in order to hinder the regrouping of the enemy's forces to the Melikhovo area and ease the situation in the sector of Kozak's 73rd Guards Rifle Division. Colonel S.A. Kozak conducted preparations for the counterattacks throughout the night, and just an hour after Hünersdorff's and Schmidt's panzers moved out on the attack against the positions of the 92nd Guards Rifle Division, two regiments of the 73rd Guards Rifle Division and the 44th Guards Rifle Regiment launched a counterattack. Almost simultaneously, with the same purpose, the 94th Guards Rifle Division struck the positions of the 7th Panzer Division in the sector: southern outskirts of Miasoedovo – Hill 206.9. From Combat Report No.5/op from the headquarters of the 73rd Guards Rifle Division at midnight on 8 July 1943:

> At 1030, the 214th Guards Rifle Regiment with the 30th Destroyer Anti-tank Brigade and the 131st Anti-Tank Rifle Battalion went on the counterattack in the direction of the "Batratskaia Dacha" State Farm and the woods 2.5 kilometers southwest of the State Farm. As a result of six hours of fighting, 1/214th Guards Rifle Regiment with the support of the

---

146 NARA US, rg. 242, t. 314, r. 197, f. 001204.

30th Destroyer Anti-tank Artillery Brigade advanced to the north as far as the pond on the "Batratskaia Dacha" State Farm, while the 131st Anti-tank Rifle Battalion, which had previously occupied a defense along the "Batratskaia Dacha" State Farm – "Poliana" State Farm road, by 1700 had advanced 500 meters to the west. Lacking the support of neighbors and met by powerful enemy artillery and mortar fire, the battalions, suffering significant losses in men, were forced to halt the attack.

At 1705 12 enemy tanks attempted to counterattack the 131st Anti-Tank Rifle Battalion's positions, but having been met by the fire of our artillery, were forced to retreat in the direction of Point 199.1.

In the course of the day, units of the 214th Guards Rifle Regiment destroyed two tanks and killed up to 200 enemy men. Losses: 214th Guards Rifle Regiment – 81 men killed or wounded; 131st Anti-tank Rifle Battalion – 85 men.

...

2 and 3/209th Guards Rifle Regiment are occupying a defense in the division's second echelon on the western fringe of the woods lying 1 kilometer east of Koren'skaia Dacha. 1/209th Guards Rifle Regiment, having moved up into the fringe of the woods east of the "Poliana" State Farm by 0900, drove enemy submachine gunners out of the woods. At 1000 following a barrage by six-barreled rocket launchers the enemy launched a counterattack in strength of up to a company of infantry and two tanks against the area of defense occupied by 1/209th Guards Rifle Regiment. However, greeted by heavy fire, the enemy was thrown back to the "Poliana" State Farm. By 1500 8.7.43, 1/209th Guards Rifle Regiment was occupying a line in the woods 300 meters east of the "Poliana" State Farm.[147]

At the "Batratskaia Dacha" State Farm, the Guardsmen with the help of Lieutenant Colonel M.G. Sapozhnikov's 30th Destroyer Anti-tank Artillery Brigade, after an hour-long combat, had noticeably pushed back the units of the 106th Infantry Division's Infantry Regiment 241 and even managed to take the State Farm for a certain time. However, von Funck quickly brought up his reserve and at 1200 threw 30 panzers into a counterattack. As a result, the battalions of the 214th Guards Rifle Regiment were forced to abandon the State Farm. The headquarters of III Panzer Corps reported: "7th Panzer Division repulsed strong enemy attacks from the east and northeast toward Hill 206.9 and Miasoedovo, having again met there the 94th Guards Rifle Division. At 1100 with the support of heavy artillery and salvoes of rockets, the enemy [15th Guards Rifle Division] attacked the "Batratskaia Dacha" State Farm. Local penetrations were quickly eliminated by a counterattack with the support of panzers."[148]

A second attempt by the 15th Guards Rifle Division's 44th Guards Rifle Regiment to drive the Germans out of the area of the two farms failed. The attack by Usikov's regiment against the "Batratskaia Dacha" State Farm late on the evening of 7 July from the beginning hadn't been planned and was a compulsory measure. For the command of the 25th Guards Rifle Corps at that moment it was important to stop the advance of German panzergrenadiers through the woods west of Nikol'skii. The 44th Guards Rifle Regiment had been moved up hastily; its commander, even though he anticipated a meeting battle, didn't have time to organize the attack in proper fashion. However, the regiment had coped with its task, but the combat actions on 8 July demanded a different approach to shaping the battle and substantial artillery support. Although both the "Batratskaia Dacha" and "Solov'ev" collective farm had been converted by the Germans into strong centers of resistance that included the presence of panzer units, Lieutenant Colonel I.A.

---

147 TsAMO RF, f. 1212, op. 1, d. 28, l. 10.
148 NARA US, rg. 242, t. 314, r. 197, f. 001203.

Usikov continued to operate as he did the evening before. In the course of the attack, he dispersed his own forces and underestimated the enemy's strength. Three of his battalions attempted to attack both farms simultaneously. At the same time, he conducted no reconnaissance and not only failed to bring up the regimental artillery, but also the battalion artillery and mortar companies. In addition, when organizing the battle the regiment commander showed himself to be not so much a prudent organizer as he did a penny-pinching handler. Usikov made no attempt to organize cooperation between his units and the attached 1848th Destroyer Anti-tank Artillery Regiment, but acted according to the principle "I'll save my own tobacco and borrow some from my neighbor". From the account of the 30th Separate Destroyer Anti-tank Artillery Brigade:

> The brigade was used not as a single compact anti-tank fist; instead its regiments were allocated to rifle regiments and even battalions, the commanders of which used the batteries as if they were their own artillery and deployed the crews without infantry cover. The guns were standing in firing positions in dense woods out in front of their own infantry, and the crews had to defend their positions against pressuring German submachine gunners, suffering losses in men and guns. Meanwhile the commanders of the divisions were keeping their own destroyer anti-tank artillery battalions in reserve, while the commander of the 15th Guards Rifle Division's 44th Guards Rifle Regiment in the course of the fighting on 8 July for the "Batratskaia Dacha" State Farm moved up the brigade's batteries that were attached to it into the combat positions of the infantry, while keeping his own regimental battery and even the battalion 45mm guns in concealed positions.[149]

There can't be any talk about massed fire support, if even the regimental and battalion artillery were essentially standing inactive. I think that the reader can clearly understand it, if the regiment late on the evening of 7 July was moved out to a new area in response to an alarm and left its artillery in place, so the artillery couldn't support the rifle battalions that were advancing toward the farms, because it didn't know where they were located or where it should fire. In Combat Order No.173 at 1530, division commander Vasilenko wrote, "I decided to halt the attack by the 44th Guards Rifle Regiment until 1920 or the onset of darkness, in order to bring up fire support and prepare concentrated fire from all the guns on the "Solov'ev" collective farm and "Batratskaia Dacha" State Farm."[150] Despite the implemented measures, by the end of the day the situation in the sector of Usikov's regiment hadn't fundamentally changed.

Incidentally, the fact that throughout the day two divisions of the 7th Guards Army had unsuccessfully attempted to drive the units of Army Detachment Kempf from out of these two farms was unknown in the Red Army General Staff, and there, they believed both farms were now in our hands. Back on the morning of 8 July, the Voronezh Front's deputy chief of staff Major General S.I. Teteshkin had signed Operational Summary No.00376 and sent it to Moscow by 1000, in which it was succinctly stated, "… troops of the 7th Guards Army throughout the night were defending their current lines and with counterattacks by the 72nd and 73rd Guards Rifle Divisions drove the enemy out of the "Solov'ev" collective farm, the "Batratskaia Dacha" State Farm, the Machine Tractor Station on the western outskirts of Gremiachii, and the "Poliana" State Farm."[151]

Of the four listed places in the document, three were not only not taken or at least switched hands in the course of see-saw fighting; the troops of Shumilov's 7th Guards Army hadn't even reached their outskirts. For several more days, they would be the focus of bitter and bloody fighting. Even

---

149 TsAMO RF, f. 9721, op. 1, d. 5, l. 203.
150 TsAMO RF, f. 15 gv. sd, op. 1, d. 8, l. 158.
151 TsAMO RF, f. 203, op. 2843, d. 442, l. 313.

the Front Commander-in-Chief had to be aware of this. However, people are people everywhere; even having donned uniforms with shoulder boards, by any means they sought as far as possible to avoid unpleasantries. Thus in the Red Army there existed a practice of lying when passing information up the chain of command. The essence of it consisted in the fact that when a situation wasn't going well and the enemy was gaining ground, then the real situation wouldn't be reported, only "adjustments": yesterday evening we gave up the village, but already that night we won it back, but unfortunately the Germans took it back again by dinnertime. All the commanders were well aware of this "spinning", but as a rule they shut their eyes to it, since to one or another extent they employed it themselves. Today, already more than 70 years after those events, in order to reveal the essence of these petty fibs it is necessary to dig through mountains of bogus reports and slag heaps of "victorious" accounts, "deep" dissertations and memoirs filled with heroics that were written on their basis. I don't want to be a pessimist, but picturing that volume of tales (both large and small) that the headquarters at every level were feeding each other each and every day, great doubts arise whether we'll ever know the real, and not conceived history of that Great and terrible Patriotic War.

However, let's return to the combat operations. So, during the attack by the 73rd Guards Rifle Division on 8 July and when repelling the enemy counterattacks, the 1529th Heavy Self-propelled Artillery Regiment and the 97th and 309th Guards Mortar Regiments that had been assigned to division commander Kozak from out of the army's reserve, played a major role. The headquarters of both rocket-launching regiments and their units were located in Pentsevo (3 kilometers east of Korenskaia Dacha). Their Katiusha battalions were primarily firing on Krutoi Log and the balkas and patches of wood to the east of there. According to the reports from our aerial reconnaissance, this village contained not only concentrations of infantry reserves (including the 198th Infantry Division) that had arrived there from the western bank of the Donets, but also a supply base. On the western outskirts pilots of the 2nd Air Army had spotted several dozen fuel drums, and intelligence analysts believed that they betrayed the location of "fuel tank trucks and refueling stations for motorized transport and armored fighting vehicles." Thus, in the course of the relatively quiet hours of 8 July alone, the 422nd and 423rd Guards Mortar Regiments fired 253 M-13 rocket shells at the area east of Krutoi Log. Here's how K. Behr, a grenadier of III/Infantry Regiment 308 of the 198th Infantry Division described his impressions of the activity of the Soviet rocket launchers in a letter home, after witnessing the effects of its combat work:

> Katiusha already visited us four times today; this is a most nasty weapon. It drives up on a truck and after firing a volley, it drives away again. When Katiusha fires a salvo of 38-40 rockets, they fall one right next to each other, and the impression is created as if they're playing an organ [the Germans called the Soviet rocket launchers "Stalin's organ"]. In fact, whoever winds up in the zone of its barrage will be silenced forever. When I get home, I'll have something to say. This is a second Stalingrad, but I still have hope [probably, to survive it].

The cases were not rare when in order to break up an attack, the Guardsmen fired heavy M-20 rocket shells even at attacking tanks. Judging from the operational documents of the Voronezh Front's rocket artillery group, primarily the 97th Guards Mortar Regiment resorted to such practice. It is possible that this was connected with the fact that this regiment had only M-20 rocket shells available.

The 1529th Heavy Self-propelled Artillery Regiment was assembled on the left flank of Kozak's 73rd Guards Rifle Division and primarily fired from reverse slope positions at aggregations of enemy troops in the area of the "Poliana" State Farm and Gremiachii, and the woods west of them, but also took part in repulsing enemy attacks. The second half of the day of 8 July proved especially successful for the self-propelled gunners. Even the army commander arrived to see for himself the results of their combat work. From the regiment's Operational Summary No.39 for 8 July:

> The regiment had action … At 1600 the assault guns conducted successive fire by battery on the southern outskirts of the "Poliana" State Farm. Seven self-propelled guns were knocked out or destroyed and 2 earth-and-timber bunkers were smashed; 12 high-explosive shells were expended. At 1700 the assault guns fired at enemy tanks (up to 10 of them) that had emerged on the graded road 2 kilometers southwest of Batratskaia Dacha; 2 tanks were set ablaze and 2 were knocked out by the 3rd Battery's SU-152 firing over open sights; one of the German tanks was a Pz VI. Fifteen high-explosive shells were expended. At 1800 the commander of the 7th Guards Army Lieutenant General Shumilov visited the 3rd Battery and expressed his gratitude to the crews for their excellent gunnery at the tanks. At 1900 the assault guns fired on a column of vehicles and wagons loaded with infantry on the road south of the "Poliana" State Farm; 2 vehicles and 6 wagons with infantry were smashed. Up to a company of infantry was scattered and partially destroyed; 6 high-explosive shells were expended.[152]

From the side it might seem that the exhausting fighting in the sector of the 73rd and 78th Guards Rifle Divisions brought no results other than heavy casualties and had no influence on the overall course of the army's defensive operation. However, this isn't so; the influence was quite substantial and immediate. In fact Colonel S.A. Kozak on this day, just like on 7 July, proved unable to push the enemy back in a single sector. His division was unable to retake a single village or hamlet that had been seized by the Germans, even though it had undertaken numerous attempts for this purpose, including in cooperation with the 15th Guards Rifle Division. It is also true that the *kampfgruppen* of von Funck's 7th Panzer Division and Forst's 106th Infantry Division inflicted considerable casualties on the Guardsmen. However, it mustn't be forgotten that two German divisions, one of them a panzer division, were operating against them. The main point was not the capture of any particular settlement, but the fact that they tied up these two German divisions in front of them with their available means. While experiencing an acute deficit of strength on the axis of main attack, especially with respect to panzers, because of the active defense of two battered Russian rifle divisions (Kozak's and Skvortsov's), the command of Army Detachment Kempf had been unable to regroup the 7th Panzer Division. The chief of staff of Army Group South General T. Busse openly writes about this in his recollections: "Employing mobile defensive tactics during this period, the 7th Panzer Division – adjoining XI Corps [Korps Raus] – repulsed strong attacks from the east in the area southeast of Melikhovo; though successful, the division was thus tied down in this area."[153]

For his part Breith, having no other way to cover the flanks of his III Panzer Corps, was forced to commit panzer divisions to take fortified villages and hamlets in the sector of Morozov's, Trunin's and Russkikh's divisions, thereby dissipating his assault wedge. In addition, judging from everything, the enemy's losses were substantial. So far concrete figures for the daily manpower losses haven't been found for the 7th Panzer Division or 106th Infantry Division, but a quite a bit of indirect information testifies to the fact that they were high. For example, von Funck already on 7 July was forced to commit special units into action on the front line, which under normal conditions were kept out of action. First our divisional reconnaissance returned from the battlefield on the "Batratskaia Dacha" State Farm on 7 July with the papers of members of the 7th Panzer Division's Panzerjäger Battalion 42 and the soldier's booklet of a Lieutenant Müller, and then on 8 July, that

---

152 TsAMO RF, f. 1529 tsap, op. 27736, d. 3, l. 29.
153 Newton, *Kurskaia bitva – nemetskii vzgliad*, p. 38.

of a soldier of Pioneer Battalion 58. A bit later a private of one of the pioneer units was captured alive, who under interrogation in the headquarters of the 15th Guards Rifle Division revealed, "His company consisting of 120 men has been operating as an infantry unit. In the words of the prisoner, the company has suffered 50% losses."[154] As concerns the 106th Infantry Division, even though in the most difficult period of the offensive between 5 and 10 July 1943 it was relying on its more powerful neighbor, its losses in Operation Citadel proved to be the highest among the infantry divisions – 3,277, which was even higher than in the 320th Infantry Division, which lost 3,038 men.[155]

An unusual calm settled over the sector of the 24th Guards Rifle Corps on this day. The reason for this is the fact that both sides had suffered substantial losses over the preceding three days and were bringing their troops back to order. In addition, the Germans were still preparing to replace the 7th Panzer Division with the 198th Infantry Division on the boundary between III Panzer Corps and Korps Raus, so for them there was no reason to kick up trouble here. Throughout the day, intense exchanges of fire periodically erupted only in three places: the "Poliana" State Farm, Hill 192.6 and Rzhavets. Only in the sector of the 72nd Guards Rifle Division did a full-scale battle flare up. Here at 1700 the Germans with the forces of the 320th Infantry Division's Infantry Regiment 586 were tempted into conducting a human wave attack. Up to two companies of grenadiers, plainly intoxicated, without the usual artillery barrage in such cases, moved out at full height against the positions of the 3rd Company of 1/222nd Guards Rifle Regiment in the vicinity of Hill 196.2, and before closing within 300 meters of the first trenches opened fire. The Guardsmen realized the condition of the attackers, and having waited a bit, machine-gunned several ranks. According to the division's Operational Summary No.0224, up to 80 German soldiers and officers were killed or wounded.[156] Major General N.A. Vasil'ev reported on the situation in the corps' sector for the evening of 8 July in Combat Report No.053 at 1800:

1. In the course of the past 24 hours the enemy had undertaken no active operations, placing artillery and mortar fire on the combat positions of the corps' divisions. With infantry weapons the enemy conducted random fire at the forward edge.

    In strength of up to two battalions (remnants of the 106th Infantry Division's Infantry Regiment 241) and 22 tanks the enemy continues to hold the "Poliana" State Farm. In strength of up to two infantry battalions (remnants of Infantry Regiment 586 with replacements from the reserves) and 5 tanks are holding the line: Hill 192.6, Point "Sar". Up to two battalions are fortifying the line: Rzhavets, Priiutovka, conducting work on trenches in small groups and setting up barbed wire.

    Aggregations of infantry have been spotted in the Maslova Pristan', Volkovo, Ivanovka area. Movement of motorized transport, infantry, artillery and motorcyclists since the morning of 8.7.43 from the area of Maslova Pristan' in the direction of the "Poliana" State Farm and Krutoi Log.

    Enemy aviation with solitary aircraft and groups of 2-5 aircraft throughout the night bombed Gastishche-1, Volchansk, Logshovoe, Shebekino, Krapivnoe, Ustinka, Rzhevka and especially the Shebekinskaia Dacha Woods. Altogether they dropped 400 high-explosive and incendiary bombs.

    The corps exchanged fire with the enemy on the line: Point 202.9, Hill 192.6, 192.8, barn, northwestern fringe of the Shebekinskaia Dacha Woods, woods west of Bezliudovka and further along the eastern bank of the Northern Donets River.

---

154 TsAMO RF, f. 15 gv. sd, op. 1, d. 8, l. 159.
155 Zetterling and Frankson, *Kursk 1943: a statistical analysis*, p. 114.
156 TsAMO RF, f. 72 gv. sd, op. 1, d. 17, l. 405.

> The 72nd Guards Rifle Division is holding the line: Point 202.9, Point 192.6, Point 192.8, woods north of Bezliudovka, Bezliudovka. On the night of 7-8.7.43, 3/224th Guards Rifle Regiment occupied the sector of 1 and 3/585th Rifle Regiments (southeastern portion of Bezliudovka, woods east of Bezliudovka).
>
> The 213th Rifle Division engaged in an exchange of fire with the enemy on the line: Point 190.0, (excl.) Point 202.9, 1 kilometer southeast of Rzhavets.
>
> On the night of 7-8 July, 3/585th Rifle Regiment yielded its combat sector to the 224th Guards Rifle Regiment and left for the area of the "Poliana" State Farm.
>
> 36th Guards Rifle Division – situation without changes.
>
> 111th Rifle Division on the night of 7-8.7.43 occupied the sector of defense: (excl.) Churaevo, Krapivnoe, Ustinka, Shebekino (north). Forward edge along the eastern bank of the Koren' River.[157]

The fact that the Germans had begun throwing up fieldworks wasn't news to M.S. Shumilov. He had been waiting impatiently for this moment. The first to inform him of this fact was Major General A.I. Losev when he reported that the Germans were strengthening the defenses of the "Poliana" State Farm, and at 1200 approximately a battalion of motorcycle troops had arrived here. It had become obvious that after three heavy days of fighting, the adversary had finally exhausted his abilities for an offensive in this sector. Reconnaissance intelligence was also testifying to this. In the woods on Hill 192.6, a reconnaissance patrol of the 72nd Guards Rifle Division's 222nd Guards Rifle Regiment had captured a Lance-Corporal Walther Hess of the 9th Company of III/Infantry Regiment 586. His interrogation revealed the difficult situation in the 320th Infantry Division and the low combat effectiveness of its units because of the substantial casualties. From his interrogation transcript:

> In the company 60 men, 4 light machine guns and 2 heavy machine guns remain; the same applies to the battalion's 10th, 11th and 12th Companies. The task of the 9th Company: occupy a defense. According to soldiers' talk, on the left, in the direction of the "Poliana" State Farm, units of the 106th Infantry Division are operating. It is known to the prisoner that the remaining units of the 320th Infantry Division have suffered large losses in men and equipment, and a lot of the command staff has been killed or wounded. The age composition of the 9th Company: the majority is of 30-35 years of age; there are very few older soldiers left. The commander of III Battalion is replacing 1st Lieutenant Pohl. Headquarters Sergeant Lorenz is temporarily carrying out the duties of company commander. In the 9th Company he saw 5 Ukrainians serving in the supply train. From their talk he understood that some Liberation Army is forming (in Khar'kov). In Ziborovka the prisoner saw a lot of gendarmes and Russian prisoners. The morale of the company's soldiers is depressed in connection with the prolonged war. He has received letters from home that talk about frequent raids primarily by British and American bombers.[158]

Signs of fatigue and the unsteadiness of units were also appearing in the 7th Guards Army. In the course of the heaviest fighting on 5-6 July, 15-20 soldiers and commanders who had left the battlefield without an order were being detained each day by the army's blocking detachments, pickets and mobile groups of NKVD troops that were securing the Front's rear beyond the tactical zone. On the third day of the battle, the number of those who abandoned their positions

---

157 TsAMO RF, f. 24 gv. sk, op. 1, d. 14, l. 56.
158 TsAMO RF, f. 72nd gv. sd, op. 1, d. 60, l. 7.

without an order grew to almost 200 over the day, but the majority of them were being held in the corps' sectors. On 8 July, the number detained by the 92nd NKVD Rifle Regiment[159] alone multiplied. According to the operational summary of its headquarters, on this day 758 military servicemen were detained, including 734 who were retreating in disorder from the front – practically the equivalent of one and a half rifle battalions. These were those soldiers and commanders who managed to pass through the line of the divisional and army blocking detachments. Here is more information from this same regiment: "In the sector of the 3rd Rifle Battalion in the area of the villages of Zaiach'e, Lomovo, Iutanovka, Strelitsa, Bol'shoe Gorodishche, Aleksandrovskii and Tsepliaevka,[160] the large movement to the rear of small groups of men and solitary men retreating disorderly from the battlefield is being noted, especially on the part of units of the 78th Guards, 73rd Guards and 81st Guards Rifle Divisions. Over the period of 7 and 8 July, 339 men of the 78th Guards Rifle Division, 332 men of the 73rd Guards Rifle Division and 107 men of the 81st Guards Rifle Division have been detained. All of the detained men have been transferred to division's counterintelligence departments."

Nevertheless, the day of 8 July proved fully successful for the Soviet side, even though it didn't bring around the results anticipated by N.F. Vatutin. On the Oboian' direction, the enemy was unable to make any headway. Despite the fact that the situation here was fundamentally unchanged (both panzer corps of the Fourth Panzer Army were still enmeshed in the second army-level belt of defenses), the danger of a German breakthrough to the third army-level belt of defenses and beyond remained high. At the same time, the attempt to divert significant enemy forces from the front of the 1st Tank Army and 6th Guards Army to the right wing of the 69th Army had failed. The planned counterattack on the Prokhorovka direction had been disorganized; the tank corps' attacks were uncoordinated, and the 10th Tank Corps hadn't even budged from its start line. Even so, their actions had a certain effect. As is known in war, a commander must base his decisions not so much on the enemy's intentions as on his potential capabilities. Thus the commander of the SS II Panzer Corps SS Lieutenant General P. Hausser, having received information on the afternoon about the approach of a significant force of Russian tanks on the corps' right flank and their introduction into combat decided to take no risks. By evening he issued an order to the *kampfgruppen* of the SS Panzergrenadier Divisions *Leibstandarte Adolf Hitler* and *Das Reich* to abandon approximately 5 kilometers of the ground they had already seized and pull back to the Bol'shie Maiachki – Greznoe – Luchki area. This somewhat weakened the pressure on the 1st Tank Army and 6th Guards Army and gave their commands a chance to conduct a regrouping in order to strengthen weak sectors.

Near Belgorod an unstable situation was also developing. Even though the enemy here, as before, had made little headway, his persistence and determination were gradually undermining the defenses of Shumilov's and Kriuchenkin's armies. Thus the situation on the Korocha direction was gradually taking a turn for the worse. The halting of the German offensive on the 7th Guards Army's left flank and the observed facts that the Germans were fortifying their sectors, contrasted with the high activity of the panzer divisions on the right flank (the German capture of Melikhovo), plainly showed that III Panzer Corps was persistently attempting to break out of the defenses of the 7th Guards Army in the northeasterly direction (Shliakhovoe – Verkhnii Ol'shanets – Kazach'e). However, strength for a decisive lunge was plainly lacking; Shumilov's army was still tying up Breith's main forces opposite its front, although the 7th Guards Army

---

159 Officially, this regiment was called the "92nd Red Banner Border Regiment of the NKVD".
160 The above-listed places are located behind the right flank of the 7th Guards Army and behind the boundary between the 7th Guards and 6th Guards Armies.

had suffered substantial losses. The enemy, though, obviously had no intention to halt the strong attacks by the panzer groups in the 35th Guards Rifle Corps' sector.

Once again the question arose in front of the Voronezh Front command: "Where was the source of the enemy's strength?" It was exceptionally important to reveal this, since on the main (Oboian') direction the second army-level defensive belt had effectively already been breached and the German offensive here showed no sign of flagging. On the night of 8-9 July, this question came up at a meeting of the Front's Military Council. Usually, a verbatim record of a Military Council meeting where the latest 24 hours an operation was discussed wasn't made. Everything that happened there is known to us only from the decisions made by N.F. Vatutin: his orders, directives, instructions, as well as the preserved transcripts of his conversations with the army commanders over the Baudot device. Yet the intelligence that provided the rationale for the Military Council's decisions has been preserved in the summaries of the Intelligence Department and is accessible today to scholars. On their basis, it is possible to understand the logic of the decisions and to reconstruct the course of the discussions regarding the results of the operation. From Summary No.196 of Voronezh Front's Intelligence Department for 0700 9 July:

> An aggregation of up to a regiment of infantry and 80 tanks has been spotted on the northern outskirts of Krutoi Log. Between 0900 and 1500 aerial reconnaissance has established the movement of up to 80 tanks and 100 vehicles from Khar'kov to Maslova Pristan'. Up to 40 tanks are in the area of Krutoi Log and the "Poliana" State Farm, and 20 tanks in Iastrebovo.
>
> A captured lance-corporal of the 19th Panzer Division's Panzergrenadier Regiment 74, seized in the area of Postnikov (3 kilometers southwest of Dal'naia Igumenka) on 7.7 under preliminary interrogation revealed that the 7th and 6th Panzer Divisions are operating to the right of the 19th Panzer Division. The prisoner heard from a sergeant that nine tank divisions are operating on the Belgorod direction, which includes the Panzer Division *Wiking* (the interrogation is still under way).
>
> According to the testimony of a prisoner taken from the 320th Infantry Division, units of the 330th Infantry Division on the night of 7-8.7 replaced the 320th Infantry Division's 587th and 585th Infantry Regiments in the Rzhavets – Bezliudovka sector. From a conversation with a lance-corporal of the 320th Infantry Division, it is known to the prisoner that the 330th Infantry Division on 9 or 10.7.43 is to go on the attack in order to take the Shebekinskaia Dacha Woods with an enveloping maneuver from the south (the information requires checking).
>
> With the taking of prisoners and papers from the dead, the actions of the 106th Infantry Division in the area of the "Batratskaia Dacha" State Farm, the 6th Panzer Division in the area of the "Batratskaia Dacha" State Farm and Gremiachii, the 320th Infantry Division (586th Infantry Regiment) in the area of the "Poliana" State Farm and the 55th Regiment of rocket launchers in the Grafovka area is confirmed.
>
> Conclusions: In order to reinforce the Belgorod grouping, the enemy is continuing to bring up reserves taken from other fronts. From 9.7 one can expect the introduction of two fresh divisions into the fighting on the axis of the main attack.[161]

On the basis of information available to us today from the documents of both sides related to the entire period of the Battle of Kursk, one can assert that the information given in the summary is in the first place a collection of rumors or deliberate disinformation (this concerns primarily the supposed attack by the 330th Infantry Division), and in the second place only evidence of ordinary

---

161 TsAMO RF, f. 203, op. 2843, d. 452, l. 70.

routines in the combat units – nothing more. The information regarding the assembly of up to 80 tanks on the northern outskirts of Krutoi Log can be verified. On the evening and early morning, the panzer regiment of the 7th Panzer Division together with the armored vehicles of other units (assault guns, halftracks) were undergoing refueling here; in Soviet documents, they usually made no distinctions between the types of armored vehicles and called them all tanks. The approach of almost 100 tanks to Maslova Pristan' is either a mistake or an inaccurate interpretation of aerial reconnaissance photographs. Army Detachment Kempf never used daylight hours to move up so many tanks to the forward edge in order not to disclose the Germans' intentions and because of the absence of reliable air cover. If a lengthy column had been spotted in this area, then instead of tanks moving to the front (possibly from the Khar'kov Tractor Factory, where the Germans had set up repair facilities), the pilots might have been counting halftracks or something that resembled tanks. One must also consider such an important factor as disinformation on the part of the enemy.

The command of Army Detachment Kempf understood that the Soviet means of gathering intelligence were similar to its own, and thus tried to take advantage of this. For example, the III Panzer Corps (just like the XXXXVIII Panzer Corps) had a certain quantity of artfully crafted dummy tanks and used them at a moment of need. For example, on 12 and 13 July 1943 the command of III Panzer Corps deployed several dozen wooden tanks in the area of Kazach'e and Verkhnii Ol'shanets, and also while redeploying genuine tanks dragged wooden dummy tanks behind them in order to create the image of a much large force. As a result the 2nd Air Army reported the assembly here of a new enemy panzer division over a short period of time. N.F. Vatutin didn't believe this (although he was presented with the aerial reconnaissance photographs) and ordered the information to be rechecked. The command of the 69th Army sent reconnaissance patrols, including engineers, to this area, which in fact discovered this subterfuge.[162] One can grant that by 8 July the Germans had already begun to move up these dummy tanks to the forward edge, and possibly the 2nd Air Army's aerial reconnaissance had spotted this movement.

If you don't know all these nuances, then from the side it might seem that the enemy was actually redeploying major reserves, including panzer divisions. However for a professional like N.F. Vatutin, the main criterion was information that could be checked objectively: papers collected on the battlefield and taken from prisoners, but at that time he didn't have any. Therefore the supposition about the approach of reserves and the commitment into the battle of fresh divisions was viewed only as a possibility. Until the latest moment the German grouping near Belgorod had been stable, so there was a reason why the intelligence document let slip that the information about the appearance of the 330th Infantry Division needed verification. At the same time the increased traffic and the redeployment of troops from the area of Maslova Pristan' and Krutoi Log to the left flank of the 25th Guards Rifle Corps, where panzers were operating (according to the intelligence report, the 6th and 7th Panzer Divisions), in combination with the reduced enemy combat activity in the Maslova Pristan' – Krutoi Log area prompted the thought that a reserve division was being brought up, ready to replace these panzer divisions in order to free up forces and shift them to the grouping that was directed to the northeast.

Analyzing the documents of the Voronezh Front headquarters, I formed the impression that N.F. Vatutin was seemingly of two minds regarding the question of the approach of enemy reserves. The first was based on official intelligence information, which maintained that the Germans really were bringing up increasing amounts of fresh forces. This was convenient for Vatutin in every respect, especially during conversations with Moscow; the General of the Army always brought up such information, especially if the conversation revolved around where the Soviet strategic

---

162 TsAMO RF, f. 69 A, op. 10765, d. 13, l. 10.

reserves should go. The second point of view was his personal opinion, which was formed on the basis of his own experience, intuition, and one can express it so, his "feel" for the situation. Vatutin probably thought that it was likely the Germans had brought up (or was just bringing up) reserves, but so far they weren't very substantial. If the reserves had been substantial, they probably would have already broken free into operational space. The enemy was achieving success only in separate sectors, primarily whereever he concentrated high amounts of artillery, heavy mortars and Luftwaffe support. In contrast, in those places where our divisions were making full use of their fortifications, exploiting favorable terrain and arranging proper coordination, the enemy was suffering heavy losses and making little headway.

However, in the Voronezh Front's daily life Vatutin often encountered the helplessness, laziness and elementary evasions of corps and division commanders, and their inability to organize even something basic, like marching a division to the front for example, as happened in the case of the 92nd Guards Rifle Division. Thus Vatutin's orders, preserved in the transcripts of his conversations with army commanders, chiefs of staff and other high-ranking generals are festooned with constant demands to improve command and control, arrange cooperation, and more diligently ready the system of fire.

Considering that the Voronezh Front had already exhausted its reserves on 7 July, and seeing no real evidence that the Germans were introducing fresh divisions into the battle, N.F. Vatutin decided that V.D. Kriuchenkin had the minimum strength necessary to block III Panzer Corps' advance into the depth of the 69th Army's defenses. However, this wasn't really quite the case, especially with respect to anti-tank means, but there were not enough of those even in the Voronezh Front. The main thing now was the ability of the commander to handle the resources he had available correctly. Thus, the question about strengthening the Korocha direction evidently didn't come up in the meeting of the Voronezh Front's Military Council on the evening of 8 July.

For 9 July 1943 the command of the 69th Army was given a primary task: having gathered the 92nd Guards and 94th Guards Rifle Divisions into a compact force, as well as having deployed the 305th and 107th Rifle Divisions, to strengthen the Dal'niaia Igumenka – (excl.) Melikhovo – Shliakhovoe – Miasoedovo line securely, and relying on the system of fortifications and artificial obstacles in this area, whittle down the enemy tank strength. Meanwhile, the 7th Guards Army in parallel was to conduct an active defense, and by threatening the right flank of the enemy's grouping opposite the left flank of the 69th Army, divert as much enemy strength as possible onto itself.

N.F. Vatutin himself decided to take up the matter of improving the command and control in the three armies of the Front's left wing. For this purpose, based on the configuration of the lines of defense at the boundary between the 69th Army, 7th Guards and 6th Guards Armies, he decided to redistribute the divisions and corps between these armies and establish new boundary lines for them.

6

The fall of the Belgorod bastion, 9-10 July 1943

Formally speaking, 8 July 1943 became the last day when Army Detachment Kempf's shock formation, Breith's III Panzer Corps, conducted large-scale combat operations directly against the 7th Guards Army in the positions that had been prepared for it. On the night of 8-9 July, the 81st Guards Rifle Division became subordinate to the 69th Army together with the sector it was holding, and the 35th Guards Rifle Corps' 94th Guards Rifle Division returned to take up a position behind it. Meanwhile, the 7th Panzer Division began gradually to turn over its sector to the units of the 198th Infantry Division, in order to re-join the two other panzer divisions of III Panzer Corps for a breakthrough along the corridor between the Northern Donets and Razumnaia Rivers. Thus, the main phase of the defensive operation of Shumilov's 7th Guards Army was coming to an end. Nevertheless, the "Belgorod bastion" (the Staryi Gorod – Blizhniaia Igumenka – Postnikov – Dal'niaia Igumenka area) – Shumilov's brainchild – continued to be defended, but the main command consideration was the fact that new boundary lines between the 7th Guards Army and the 69th Army's 35th Guards Rifle Corps hadn't yet been drawn. In addition, as archival documents testify, on 9 July communications (which means as well command and control) between the 81st Guards Rifle Division and the 25th Guards Rifle Corps continued to function continuously right up until evening, or more precisely until the moment Morozov had to evacuate his command post out of Shishino, but it had no communications at all with the headquarters of the 35th Guards Rifle Corps prior to midnight. It is unknown whether or not Major General I.K. Morozov ever received the order about subordinating his division to the 35th Guards Rifle Corps. In combat dispatches and operational summaries over this day, G.B. Safiulin believed the 81st Guards Rifle Division was still under his command, and he tried to help it as far as he was able. Even the Voronezh Front command out of inertia in Combat Report No.00214 for 2400 on 9 July addressed to I.V. Stalin assigned the Staryi Gorod – Dal'niaia Igumenka area to the 7th Guards Army. The point is that although bitter fighting went on here throughout the day of 9 July, formally it was being conducted now by the 35th Guards Rifle Corps of Kriuchenkin's 69th Army; in reality these hours were the "final chord" of the 7th Guards Army's battle against Army Detachment Kempf within the framework of the Kursk defensive operation (excluding the counterattack on 12 July 1943).

The penetration made by Breith's III Panzer Corps on the left flank of the 6th Guards Army and the capture of Melikhovo meant that it had breached the Front's main army-level defensive belt in this area and represented a substantial tactical success. However, Breith wasn't able to exploit it fully, because he hadn't obtained freedom of maneuver. The breach was still narrow, and thus by the end of 8 July his *kampfgruppen* were still as before tightly cramped between the 7th Guards Army's 25th Guards Rifle Corps and the 69th Army's 35th Guards Rifle Corps. Despite strenuous efforts made on 8 July by the 6th and 19th Panzer Divisions, they were unable to break free and at least take the Shliakhovoe area under control. According to archival records, by the end of 8 July the Germans had taken a portion of Shliakhovoe, but on the night of 8-9 July they'd been driven back out of there. The assault wedge of the two panzer divisions was stuck in the hastily constructed, but sufficiently firm line of Goriachev's 35th Guards Rifle Corps, having exposed their flanks to the fire of Soviet artillery out of three anti-tank strongpoints: Postnikov (81st Guards Rifle Division), Dal'niaia Igumenka (92nd Guards Rifle Division) and Sheino (94th Guards Rifle Division). Without their elimination, a further advance was risky and threatened the encirclement of the 6th and 19th Panzer Divisions' forward units. By its outline, the pocket that they had entered suggested a crack at the tip of a sword blade that was 5 to 6.5 kilometers wide and had a depth of up to 7 kilometers. Three important factors were hindering their ability to break the Russian resistance on the shoulders of the penetration and to expand the breach: the restricted terrain that was filled with fortified villages and artfully arrayed fortifications; the tenacity of the Guards rifle divisions; and the heavy losses in both panzer divisions. Kempf understood Breith's difficult situation, and despite the persistent demands of Army Group South's command to increase the attacks against the 35th Guards Rifle Corps' front, he decided to halt the attack into the depth of the 69th Army's defenses until the moment that III Panzer Corps reached the basin of the Northern Donets River and the Belgorod bastion fell. In order to accomplish this, he decided to direct his main forces against the Dal'niaia Igumenka – Blizhniaia Igumenka sector.

Alongside the problems listed above, on the evening of 8 July one more problem presented itself to Kempf. Army Group South's intelligence, relying on intercepted radio messages, reported that the Russians were concentrating large operational reserves on the flanks of the army group – at a minimum, four tank and cavalry corps. There was the large possibility that on 9 July they would launch a counterattack into both of its flanks. If you recall the counterattacks made by Burdeinyi's and Kravchenko's tank corps on 6 and 8 July 1943 against Fourth Panzer Army's right flank and didn't know the situation in the Voronezh Front with respect to reserves, then there would be nothing unusual about this apprehension.

The Soviet side was using all of its available possibilities with great skill in order to conceal its forces, including the active use of counterintelligence measures employing the corps and army radio networks. The spoofing of the Germans relative to the plans of the Voronezh Front command for 9 July can serve as an example of their effectiveness. Parallel with the work of the main radio stations, in several Voronezh Front formations a number of specially prepared radio nets were operating according to a special scheme (as if part of an army radio network). Because of this, the enemy was disoriented about where individual Soviet corps were located and under the control of which armies. As a result of the analysis of the collected information (or more accurately, the information specially prepared by Soviet counterintelligence), the intelligence organs of Army Group South came to the mistaken conclusion that the Voronezh Front command had brought up the 3rd Tank Army to the forward edge, consisting of the 2nd Guards, 5th Guards and 3rd Guards Tank Corps and the 1st Guards Cavalry Corps. It was these forces, in their opinion, that were poised to conduct a counterattack on 9 July. The Abwehr officers didn't know the Voronezh Front's precise composition, and so when determining the nature of a signals hub (assigning it to an army or a corps), they used logic (their own, not ours) and in fact assigned it by guess to a formation that they had previously identified in this area, believing that it was still located there. This is what happened with respect to Major General I.A. Vovchenko's 3rd Guards Tank Corps, which in March 1943 had fought in the Belgorod area. Army Group South's intelligence believed that it was still located in N.F. Vatutin's reserve, and together with Major General S.V. Sokolov's 6th Guards Cavalry Corps, which had also been in this area back in March, was ready to strike the right flank of Army Detachment Kempf. This was the same approach used with respect to General P.S. Rybalko's 3rd Tank Army. The enemy still didn't have any information about its conversion into the 57th Army, but knowing that the above-listed tank corps were Guards formations, the Germans combined them into one army (supposedly the 3rd Tank Army) and added the Guards title to its designation, even though as is known, not all the formations in a Guards army had to have the Guards title, nor did an army have to have the Guards title to have Guards formations under its control.

Kempf had to take into account such serious intelligence information, given that the peculiar configuration of the frontlines made it convenient for a Soviet counterattack. Therefore he issued an order to Breith to go over to a temporary defense on the spearhead of the main attack (in the Melikhovo – Shliakhovoe area) until the problem of the "Belgorod bastion" was resolved, and to strengthen the sector of the 7th Panzer Division, having turned over the area of the "Batratskaia Dacha" State Farm to the 198th Infantry Division's Infantry Regiment 326. Meanwhile the 106th Infantry Division, having withdrawn Pioneer Battalion 58 into the reserve, was supposed to hold in place until the matter regarding the Russian counterattack and the situation in the Staryi Gorod – Postnikov – Dal'niaia Igumenka sector became clear.

Under the influence of the threat of a counterattack, Breith began to "scrape the bottom of the barrel" in order to form some sort of corps reserve, and unable to find anything better, called back the Tiger company from the 19th Panzer Division and placed it under his personal control. Meanwhile he directed the forces of the 6th and 19th Panzer Divisions to seize the line of the 81st Guards Rifle Division and formed two assault groups out of them, placing personal command of them on Generals von Hünersdorff and Schmidt. The III Panzer Corps' order for July 9 1943, which was already transmitted after midnight (at 0255 Moscow time), said:

1) The foe today launched numerous attacks against the corps' eastern flank with tanks supported by strong artillery and rocket fire, while at the same time two fresh divisions were detected. The enemy also offered fierce resistance to our successful attack against Melikhovo. Stronger attacks out of the wooded terrain north of the "Batratskaia Dacha" State Farm should also be anticipated.
2) III Panzer Corps, holding the previously seized ground, on 9.7 destroys the enemy in the area between the Razumnaia and Donets as far as Shishino.
3) Tasks:
   a) 7th Panzer Division on 9.7 defends today's line. After the replacement of its southern flank by units of the 198th Infantry Division, the division's freed up forces assemble behind its left flank.
   b) *Sturmgruppe Nord* (commander – commander of the 6th Panzer Division, composition – 6th Panzer Division with its present make up, minus the Flammpanzers; Westhofen's *panzerkampfgruppe*; and a battalion of light field howitzers of the 19th Panzer Division and II/Artillery Regiment 71[1]) assembles early on the morning of 9.7 in the area of hills north of Shliakhovoe, destroys enemy tanks in Dal'niaia Igumenka, breaks through to the Donets at Shishino, and together with the 168th Infantry Division mops up the enemy from the terrain in the Postnikov – Shishino – Staryi Gorod area. 6th Panzer Division transfers 5 Flammpanzer to the 19th Panzer Division.
   c) *Sturmgruppe Sud* (commander – commander of the 19th Panzer Division in its present composition (minus Westhofen's *panzerkampfgruppe* and one light artillery battalion), with the Infantry Regiment 442 and IV, V/Artillery Regiment 248 subordinate to it, and also the 5 Flammpanzer from 6th Panzer Division takes the area from Blizhniaia Igumenka to the woods to the south of it. Subsequently it must destroy the enemy in the sector of woods 3 kilometers northeast of Blizhniaia Igumenka.

---

1 As before, there remained one company of Tiger tanks of Heavy Panzer Battalion 503 and Artillery Battalion 857 in the 6th Panzer Division.

Start of the attack: 0600

d) 168th Infantry Division (minus the units attached to 19th Panzer Division) continues the advance of *Sturmgruppe Nord* to Staryi Gorod, and in cooperation with *Sturmgruppe Nord* mops up the ground between the Belyi Kolodez' ravine and the Donets. Given the weakening of enemy resistance, it should also break through west of the Donets to the crest of Hills 190.5 and 211.6 (west of Belomestnoe).

4) After carrying out these tasks, *Sturmgruppen Nord* and *Sud* are disbanded and the units of the divisions reunite in their previous organization in the following areas: 6th Panzer Division – Melikhovo; 19th Panzer Division – Blizhniaia Igumenka and to the north; 168th Infantry Division – in the Dal'niaia Igumenka sector to the corps' left boundary line.

5) The Tiger company, located to this point in the 19th Panzer Division, again becomes subordinate to Heavy Panzer Battalion 503 and transits through Tavrovo and across the 50-tonne bridge in Dorogobuzheno to Generalovka for the corps' use. The commander of the Tiger company makes contact with the 7th Panzer Division.

6) The corps' command post remains in the wooded area 300 meters west of the southern outskirts of Iastrebovo.[2]

By placing command of the assault groups directly on the commanders of the panzer divisions, as well as by setting tasks to destroy the "Belgorod bastion" as the day's primary and sole objective shows that Breith was not only supposed to secure the flanks of the corps' assault groups when breaking through the 35th Guards Rifle Corps' sector, but also, at last, by any means possible, finally resolve the problem of establishing contact with the II SS Panzer Corps and covering the Fourth Panzer Army's extended right flank. The assignment was not only long-standing and important, but also extremely difficult. In the first place, in front of the northern and southern assault groups was a sector of defense that consisted of a line of well-fortified centers of resistance: the hamlet of the Machine Tractor Station – Blizhniaia Igumenka – Andreevskie – Postnikov – Dal'niaia Igumenka line. Moreover, only the first two were on the eastern bank of the deep and swampy Belyi Kolodez' ravine; the rest were on the western side of this ravine, which served as an anti-tank ditch. This was not only a powerful natural obstacle, but also simultaneously a structure that bound the strongpoints together into a single, strong line. In the second place, the commander of III Panzer Corps possessed rather a rather modest amount of mechanized forces. By the morning of 9 July, there were a total of 178 panzers and 23 StuG assault guns operational in his panzer divisions, with which he was simultaneously supposed to hold a 10-kilometer front on his right flank and conduct a difficult offensive on his left flank. The 6th Panzer Division had the most combat-ready tanks – 70, but in order to break through the defenses of the 81st Guards Rifle Division, only 50 of them were suitable; the rest (the command tanks, flame-throwing tanks and Pz.kpf.wg II) might be employed only after knocking out or suppressing anti-tank guns as an auxiliary means of struggle and command. The 19th Panzer Division had the fewest operational tanks – just 36, of which one was a command tank. The 7th Panzer Division was also facing an extremely difficult situation with tanks; on the morning of 9 July, it had just 39 operational tanks, including 3 command tanks and 4 Pz.kpf.wg II light tanks. Only Separate Heavy Panzer Battalion 503, despite its high losses on the first two days of Operational Citadel, retained a rather high combat capability. Of the 45 Tigers that it had at the start, 33 remained operational. Thus, in order to carry out the day's main mission, Breith could theoretically use 130 panzers and 23 assault guns. (For the number of tanks and assault guns in the panzer divisions of III Panzer

---

2 NARA US, rg. 242, t. 314, r. 197, f. 00216.

Corps, Separate Heavy Panzer Battalion 503 and the assault gun battalions of Army Detachment Kempf between 9 and 16 July 1943, see Tables 10 and 12.) As noted above, he had already received tentative information on the evening of 8 July from the headquarters of Army Detachment Kempf about the Russians' intention to launch a strong tank counterattack against III Panzer Corps' flanks. Even though his own intelligence service hadn't detected a large aggregation of enemy armor directly on the flanks, nevertheless Breith couldn't ignore this information. Thus on the morning of 9 July he was forced to begin to form a personal mobile reserve, in which he included all of *Kampfgruppe* Unrein and a portion of von Oppeln's *panzerkampfgruppe*. Considering that the main combat actions were to unfold in a small arena, in his opinion these forces were sufficient to keep the situation under control in the event of a Russian counterattack until the panzers that were to launch an attack against the Mikhailovka fortified area arrived.

The combat actions of both of III Panzer Corps' assault groups were to unfold according to the principle of a blacksmith's work. The troops of Schmidt's *Sturmgruppe Sud* were to act as the anvil. The three infantry regiments of the 168th Infantry Division under Schmidt's command were positioned in a semi-ring along the line: eastern outskirts of Blizhniaia Igumenka (Infantry Regiment 442) – hamlet of the Machine Tractor Station – (excl.) southern outskirts of Staryi Gorod (Infantry Regiment 429) and further across the Donets as far as the woods north of Pokrovka (Infantry Regiment 417). Panzer Reconnaissance Battalion 19 and Panzergrenadier Regiment 73 (reinforced with the Flammpanzer from 6th Panzer Division) were also available, but they were in a noticeably battered condition. For example, in all of the panzergrenadier regiment's companies, there were a bit more than 400 men, but there was no other option; at this moment, each of Breith's soldiers counted.

Sturmgruppe Nord was to act as the hammer; it included a company of Heavy Panzer Battalion 503, *Kampfgruppe* Bieberstein (which had already been reinforced during the battle with approximately 60 panzers of Panzer Regiment 11), Westhofen's *panzerkampfgruppe* with Panzergrenadier Regiment 74, and Quentin's panzer reconnaissance battalion of the 6th Panzer Division with StuG Battalion 228. The panzergrenadiers of Colonel M. Unrein and the tankers of Colonel von Oppeln-Bronikowski were instructed to hold the Melikhovo – (excl.) Shliakhovoe – Kalinin – Sevriukovo line by way of an active defense, while simultaneously serving as the bulk of the corps reserve. The 2nd Company of Separate Heavy Panzer Battalion 503, which had been withdrawn from subordination to the 19th Panzer Division, was also in Breith's reserve, but on the morning of 9 July an additional *panzerkampfgruppe* under the command of Major Graf Kageneck would be hastily formed on its basis, first in order to repulse a counterattack by the 92nd Guards Rifle Division's 276th Guards Rifle Regiment, and then for an auxiliary attack toward Postnikov. Thus, 75% (151) of Breith's operational armor vehicles were assigned to the northern and southern assault groups, of which 86% would take part in the fighting.

Meanwhile, how was the Soviet defense arranged on the axis of Army Detachment Kempf's main attack? In order to hold the enemy's offensive to the north and northeast, the leadership of the 69th and 7th Guards Armies was prepared to use two primary methods: a passive defense based on strengthening the anticipated breakthrough sector (the 81st and 92nd Guards Rifle Divisions) with all available means, and short flanking counterattacks against the wedge of Breith's panzer corps. Judging from captured German documents, the Germans didn't view the Soviet infantry as a serious force in the struggle with their panzer divisions; they correctly believed that the individual training of a Red Army soldier was poor, while his equipment and individual weapon didn't meet the demands of contemporary combat. However, at the same time they recognized that if the rifle units were occupying a prepared line and sensing support from even a small quantity of artillery and tanks, then they defended fiercely. Combat operations in the first days of the Battle of Kursk showed that the most important element of the Soviet infantry positions, which substantially strengthened them, were mines. In their level of density, the 7th Guards Army's sector yielded only to the 6th Guards Army. Moreover, the density of the minefields was significant not only on the forward edge of the main defensive belt, but also in the depth of the defenses. They were girding villages and hamlets and covering all tank-vulnerable directions. Even in combination with a small amount of artillery (in some cases only anti-tank rifle battalions), the rifle units were not only able to slow the pace of German panzer attacks, but also repulse them. An account of Voronezh Front's engineer troops notes:

> Minefields were primarily knitted in with the organization of rifle, artillery and tank fire. However, there were cases when they were also deployed in isolation, and the combat engineers with the fire of their anti-tank rifles, machine guns and rifles provided cover for these obstacles. For example, in one minefield Red Army soldier Pechenkin's anti-tank rifle crew destroyed 4 enemy tanks with the fire from their anti-tank rifle.[3]

If in the sector of attack an impressive artillery grouping had been assembled alongside the artificial obstacles, then the infantrymen's faith in their own defensive strength multiplied. It often happened when an entire panzer division without Luftwaffe support proved unable for entire days to take a more heavily fortified strongpoint like Krutoi Log, for example, which was being held by only 1.5 to 2 rifle battalions and 1 to 1.5 artillery battalions. The Soviet side knew the weaknesses and strengths of their own forces and sought not only to fortify important directions with artificial obstacles, but also to concentrate anti-tank guns and heavy artillery on them. This yielded an impressive result. To wit, after four days of bitter fighting in the sector of the 7th Guards Army, the number of combat machines in Breith's panzer divisions fell by 49.3%. On the morning of 9 July, 44% of the 6th Panzer Division's panzers were deemed unserviceable; in the 7th Panzer Division, 65.2% of its tanks had been knocked out, while this figure amounted to 55% of the 19th Panzer Division's tanks and 25.8% of StuG Battalion 228's assault guns. In essence, this was the cost of breaking through the main belt of defenses of Shumilov's troops.

Therefore the task for the troops of the 7th Guards Army and 69th Army was to hold the enemy's main forces in the Staryi Gorod – Melikhovo – Miasoedovo for as long as possible; as before this had been its primary task, but it was becoming increasingly more difficuld to achieve this. The enemy's mobile divisions had reached the line of the 69th Army, which hadn't been as diligently prepared with fortifications and obstacles as the 7th Guards Army's positions stood of on the morning of 5 July, and the 69th Army's troops lacked the necessary amount of anti-tank weapons. The army had only one full-strength anti-tank artillery regiment (the 1076th Destroyer Anti-tank Artillery Regiment) and several battalions of anti-tank rifles. Moreover, and this was very important, by this time the Voronezh Front no longer had any reserves. Thus both Kriuchenkin and Goriachev were making every effort to improve command and control over the troops and regroup the available means to create a relatively high density of them on the most vulnerable directions. The 81st Guards Rifle Division's strength was also melting away, especially in its own rifle regiments.

The scheme according to which the Soviet side sought to arrange its defenses between the Northern Donets and Razumnaia Rivers on the evening of 8 July and morning of 9 July looked as follows. In the Blizhniaia Igumenka – Postnikov – Dal'niaia Igumenka – (excl.) Melikhovo – Shliakhovoe Machine Tractor Station – flood basin of the Razumnaia River sector, the troops of two rifle divisions (the 305th Rifle Division – from the march and the 92nd Guards Rifle Division – after combat) began to occupy positions in two echelons. The first echelon was the 92nd Guards Rifle Division along the Blizhniaia Igumenka – Postnikov – Dal'niaia Igumenka

---

3 TsAMO RF, f. 203, op. 2845, d. 227, l. 14.

– (excl.) Shliakhovoe – basin of the Razumnaia River line. The second line, held by the 305th Rifle Division, stretched from Khokhlovo to Ushakovo through Shliakhovoe and Mazikino. In the key strongpoints of Shliakhovoe and Dal'niaia Igumenka, the crews of 19 T-34 and 8 T-70 of the 148th Separate Tank Regiment,[4] and 5 Mk-IV Churchills of the 47th Guards Separate Heavy Tank Regiment (3 that had arrived from the repair shop and 2 that had been repaired by the crews over the night of 8-9 July)[5] were supposed to dig in their tanks. The 35th Guards Rifle Corps commander Goriachev directed his most combat-capable mobile formation (his reserve 96th Separate Tank Brigade, which consisted of 45 T-34 and T-70 tanks)[6] to assemble in the rear of the 305th Rifle Division's units. He planned to reinforce the most dangerous Dal'niaia Igumenka – Postnikov – (excl.) Andreevskie sector, where the Germans had already launched strong attacks with panzers on 7 and 8 July, with batteries of the 92nd Guards Rifle Division's artillery regiment, a portion of the infantry subordinate to the 81st Guards Rifle Division, anti-tank rifle elements and artificial obstacles.

Now let's take a look at how this scheme was put into practice, and whether or not it had been fully realized. At 2100 on 8 July, when heavy fighting was still going on in the Melikhovo area, the commander of the 35th Guards Rifle Corps signed Special Combat Order No.5, in which Colonel V.F. Trunin was given a directive to regain the positions that had been lost by the 280th Guards Rifle Regiment and to stabilize the front in the Melikhovo – Dal'niaia Igumenka area. The document demanded:

> The 92nd Guard Rifle Division with the 96th Separate Tank Brigade, the 148th Separate Tank Regiment and the 122nd Anti-Tank Rifle Battalion in the course of the night of 8-9 July are to regain the original position of the 280th Guards Rifle Regiment and prevent the expansion of enemy infantry and tanks in the Melikhovo – Shliakhovoe direction. Withdraw the 276th Guards Rifle Regiment from the Staryi Gorod area and use it to plug the gap between the 282nd Guards Rifle Regiment and 280th Guards Rifle Regiment on the line of the northwestern bank of the Belyi Kolodez' ravine with the mission to prevent enemy tanks and infantry from reaching the Staryi Gorod – Dal'niaia Igumenka highway.[7]

To plug the gap between the regiments of Trunin's division at that moment was exceptionally important and most importantly had to be done quickly. After the German capture of Melikhovo, a gap, albeit a narrow one, had been created in the corps' defense, because beyond this village there was no continuous line of defense, nor had trenches been dug everywhere. After the withdrawal of the units of Novikov's regiment to Shliakhovoe, the surge made by von Oppeln's *panzerkampfgruppe* beyond Melikhovo had been disrupted only by the fire of the 280th Guards Rifle Regiment's and 92nd Guards Rifle Division's artillery and the minefields, but these means couldn't work for long without the cover of rifle units. The evening advance by a group of German panzers to Shliakhovoe had been stopped only by the intense fire of the 148th Separate Tank Regiment.

As concerns "regaining the original position of the 280th Guards Rifle Regiment", this is more likely wishful thinking than an order that a regiment that had been worn out by two days of fighting with enemy mechanized forces might in principle be able to carry out. According to revealed documents, when the corps commander signed the order, he didn't have any clear understanding of what had happened at Melikhovo and what forces the enemy had called upon in order

---

4　TsAMO RF, f. 341, op. 27453, d. 1, l. 110; f. 148 otp, op. 661360, d. 3, l. 79.
5　TsAMO RF, f. 2 gv. Ttk, op. 1, d. 24, l. 204.
6　Before the combat on 8 July, the brigade had 51 tanks, but by the end of the day 3 tanks had been left burned out and 3 had been knocked out. (TsAMO RF, f. 96 otbr, op. 1, d. 3, ll. 15obr, 16.)
7　TsAMO RF, f. 35 gv. sk, op. 1, d. 26, l. 81.

to capture it. What talk could there be about regaining the position, if the units of the 280th Guards Rifle Regiment had been driven from the line by the *kampfgruppen* of two enemy panzer divisions and had retreated across exposed ground, under enemy fire, toward positions that were unknown to them in Shliakhovoe? In what way would Lieutenant Colonel N.I. Novikov be able in that situation to regain the lost line? Hypothetically there was only one – with a counterattack, but in reality there was no way; after all, the German panzers had crushed his regiment! Moreover, at this particular moment he didn't know exactly where his battalions were and the condition they were in. The combat was already taking place in the rear, on the outskirts of Shliakhovoe and even in the village itself. After the heavy day of fighting, ammunition was running low (even Goriachev knew about this, because in the order he gave a directive to replenish it). Thus the first order of business it was necessary to rally the men and deploy them on new lines, while simultaneously conducting reconnaissance, mining vulnerable sectors and bringing up the rear services.

Thus, the situation in the Dal'niaia Igumenka – Shliakhovoe sector on the evening of 8 July was extremely murky and fraught with heavy consequences. Only the arrival of Colonel A.F. Vasil'ev's 305th Rifle Division might stabilize it.[8] However, at the time indicated by the Front command, 2000 8 July, it still hadn't appeared there. In fact, its columns had only just set out on the march from its former area.

By the start of the Battle of Kursk, the 305th Rifle Division was an ordinary, average rifle division for the Voronezh Front, having a total strength of 7,778 men, 334 light and heavy machine guns, 219 anti-tank rifles, 157 mortars (50mm to 120mm) and 80 guns (45mm to 122mm).[9] I think that to the majority of readers, these figures say little and don't provide an opportunity to take a look at the division "from the inside": to assess its level of preparation at the moment of entering combat and the level of its soldiers' and commanders' level of training. Therefore in order to fill this gap, let's turn to archival sources although there are very few of them. I will cite an excerpt from a report from Colonel Sereda, a member of the 69th Army's Political Department who was accompanying the division during the march:

> Vasil'ev's outfit at 2000 8.7.43 set out on the march to the new line. I was moving with it during an overnight stop; the march was organized and conducted not badly. It is necessary to note a shameful fact in the 2nd Battalion. The battalion commander Captain Poliakov, his senior adjutant Kozlitin and the counterintelligence agent got drunk and lost all control over the battalion.
>
> The field outfit [the combat units] reached its line at 0500 and occupied it; bare ground without a single foxhole, and occupied Ushakovo, Mazikino and Sheino. The outfit during the night was subjected to aerial bombing, as a result of which more than 50 men were wounded or killed.

---

8 Vasil'ev, Aleksandr Fedorovich (1909-1984), Major General (1945). He joined the Red Army in 1928. On 8.05.1942 he was sent into the acting army and was appointed chief of staff of Voronezh Front's 75th Fortified District (field type). On 26.07.1942 Vasil'ev became the deputy commander of Voronezh Front's 305th Rifle Division. Between April 1943 and the end of the war, he commanded the 305th Rifle Division. In the course of Operation "Polkovodets Rumiantsev", the 305th Rifle Division distinguished itself during the liberation of Belgorod. On 05.08.1943 its units were the first to break into it western outskirts (simultaneously with units of the 89th Guards Rifle Division that were operating from the east) and within 24 hours had fully mopped it up of German aggressors. For this success, the division was deemed worthy of the honorific title "Belgorod". Between 1946 and 1953, Vasil'ev was under investigation and imprisoned. He was fully rehabilitated after Stalin's death. Upon his release, he went into teaching work. In 1963 with a resolution of the Belgorod Council of People's Deputies, he was awarded the title "Honorary citizen of Belgorod".

9 TsAMO RF, f. 203, op. 28432, d. 426, l. 165.

The foursome [the 1004th Rifle Regiment] took up a defense of Shlaikhovoe and at 0600 became engaged in combat, repulsing enemy attacks out of Melikhovo. [The enemy] has Tiger tanks which are now firing on Shliakhovo.

In connection with the fact that Vasil'ev's outfit has a 70% shortage of authorized horses, it was forced to leave 6 76mm guns and 2 howitzers in its former place,[10] as well as a lot of ammunition.

The enemy is operating exclusively with tanks and has a large amount of artillery and mortars; it is interesting that the enemy's anti-aircraft means is being kept directly on the forward edge. Our air force is operating actively.

I want to note that the division headquarters is not working as a team, is not operating smoothly, and lacks the necessary guidance. Vasil'ev is an old partisan, and in the old way is hauling around a wench [a frontline girlfriend].

The outfit's combat supply needs have been met in the following combat loads: rifle cartridges – 0.95; PPSh – 0.8; D'iakonov hand grenades – 2.0; anti-tank grenades – 0.4; rounds for 50mm mortars – 1.2; for 82mm mortars – 1.6; for 120mm mortars – 1.5; ammunition for 45mm guns – 1.4; for 76mm guns – 1.4; for 76mm field guns – 2.0; for 122mm howitzers – 1.4; for anti-tank rifles – 0.8. Of these ammunition supplies – one-fourth was left behind on the former line and couldn't be brought up, even though every measure was adopted, right down to giving each soldier one shell to carry.

I believe it is very bad that the outfit took position on bare ground, where there isn't a single foxhole. I'm hurrying to write, the liaison officer is leaving, I will write in more detail later. 9.07.1943, 0530.[11]

Nevertheless, despite the delay and hard march, at 0400 on 9 July the 305th Rifle Division began to take up a defense. Its 1002nd Rifle Regiment with 2/830th Artillery Regiment deployed behind the combat positions of the 92nd Guards Rifle Division in the Sabynino – along the highway north of Melikhovo – (excl.) Shliakhovoe Machine Tractor Station. The 1004th Rifle Regiment and 1,2/830th Artillery Regiment took up the Shliakhovoe – sector of the Razumnaia River basin – northwest of Sheino line, while the 1000th Rifle Regiment moved into position on the Ushakovo – Sheino – Mazikino – Komintern line (and had no contact with the enemy).

In addition to the problems mentioned above, a system of command and control hadn't been ironed out in the troops that were operating in front of Kempf's assault wedge. Because of the complex configuration of the front lines, certain divisions wound up noticeably distant from the headquarters of their corps and armies, or any headquarters at all and were located in semi-encirclement. Communications were working poorly. All of this complicated command and control and didn't allow quick reactions to a rapidly changing situation, or to keep the troops fully supplied with everything necessary. Primarily this concerned the 81st Guards Rifle Division and the 35th Guards Rifle Corps, which were operating in a narrow sector in close cooperation, but were subordinate to different armies. Colonel P.D. Govorunenko's 375th Rifle Division of the 6th Guards Army was in a similar situation.

Therefore on the morning of 9 July N.F. Vatutin, striving to simplify the command arrangements, transferred a number of divisions of the 7th Guards Army to the 69th Army and set up new boundary lines between Kriuchenkin's corps. According to his order, the 81st Guards Rifle

---

10 In addition, the 385th Separate Destroyer Anti-tank Artillery Battalion instead of its establishment number of 12 45mm anti-tank guns had only 10. On 09.07.43 2 guns were guarding the command post of the 35th Guards Rifle Corps in the Raevka area.
11 TsAMO RF, f. 426, op. 10753, d. 43, l.13, 13obr. Translator's note: This message was obviously written in a hurry and featured very poor grammar. It has been cleaned up to make it more understandable.

Division became subordinate to the 35th Guards Rifle Corps, and a bit later an order arrived about returning the 94th Guards Rifle Division to Goriachev and transferring the 375th Rifle Division. In its Operational Summary No.0241 for 0300 on 9 July, the headquarters of the 375th Rifle Division reported:

1. The division with the attached assets (93rd Cannon Artillery Regiment, 263rd Mortar Regiment, 16th Guards Mortar Regiment, 137th Anti-tank Rifle Battalion, 1647th Destroyer Anti-tank Artillery Regiment and the 192nd and 88th Flamethrower Companies), having turned over its sector of defense: Vodnianoi ravine woods, 2 kilometers east of the "Bold for Labor" collective farm, Hill 209.5, Hill 192.3, 4 kilometers northeast of Shopino to the 89th Guards Rifle Division, is holding the line: Shopino (west), Hill 211.6, Hill 195, woods north of Pokrovka, having screening element in the "Main Fruit and Vegetable" State Farm, Postnikov, Dal'niaia Igumenka area.
2. The 1243rd Rifle Regiment is holding the line: Shopino (west), ravine 1 kilometer north of Hill 211.6.
3. The 1245th Rifle Regiment is holding its current line; the positions of the 1st and 3rd Rifle Battalions are unchanged. The 2/1245 Rifle Regiment has taken up the defense of Petropavlovka.
4. The 2 and 3/1241st Rifle Regiment are defending their current line. The 1/1241st Rifle Regiment, having turned over its defense of the area west of Ternovka, took up a line in the area of Belomestnaia. The 1st Rifle Company, two platoons of submachine gunners, and a company of the 137th Separate Anti-tank Rifle Battalion are screening the regiment's left flank in the area of the "Main Fruit and Vegetable" State Farm, Postnikov and Dal'niaia Igumenka.
5. Neighbor on the right – 89th Guards Rifle Division (Visloe – Ternovka); on the left – 35th Guards Rifle Corps is engaged in stubborn fighting in the area of Blizhniaia Igumenka and Melikhovo.[12]

Thus, by the morning of 9 July Goriachev's situation noticeably improved in comparison with the preceding days, although it continued to remain very complicated. His 35th Guards Rifle Corps was supposed to hold the only corridor suitable for tanks on the left flank of the 69th Army (between the Northern Donets and Razumnaia Rivers), having four rifle divisions that were stretched out in a single line that extended for 48-50 kilometers, with only one incomplete tank brigade in reserve. At the same time, the main forces of the battered, but still combat-capable panzer divisions of III Panzer Corps were operating opposite his front. The corps' line formed a zig-zag that ran along broken ground that was cut by deep ravines, the flood basins of two rivers and full of large villages, but hadn't been fully-prepared for a defense. The sector in the center of his combat positions (the [excl.] Chernaia Poliana – Staryi Gorod – Postnikov – Dal'niaia Igumenka – Shliakhovoe) was considered to be the vulnerable, and was being held chiefly by the 81st Guards Rifle Division and the two regiments of the 94th Guards Rifle Division that were attached to it. In order to strengthen it, the corps headquarters prepared a separate plan that was laid out in Order No.6 at 0430 on 9 July:

> Units of the 81st Guards Rifle Division jointly with the 276th Guards Rifle Regiment are to take up a defense on the line: woods, 1.5 kilometers northeast of Chernaia Poliana, Staryi Gorod, Andreevskie, Postnikov with the task to prevent a breakthrough by enemy infantry

---

12 TsAMO RF, f. 375 sd, op. 1, d. 37, l. 240.

and tanks to the north and northeast. Chernaia Poliana is to have no less than two artillery battalions in readiness to conduct fire to the southeast.

The commander of the 35th Guards Rifle Corps' 282nd Guards Rifle Regiment is to assemble in the Postnikov area with the assignment to occupy a defense along the northwestern bank of the Belyi Kolodez' ravine in the sector: (excl.) Andreevskie, Dal'niaia Igumenka, (excl.) Shliakhovoe with a front to the southeast, with the task to prevent a breakthrough of enemy infantry and tanks along the highway to the north and northeast.[13]

Probably, close to sunrise S.G. Goriachev received detailed information about the situation in the Melikhovo area, so in Order No.6 he substantially adjusted his decision regarding the arrangement of the defense in the (excl.) Chernaia Poliana – Staryi Gorod – Postnikov – Dal'niaia Igumenka – Shliakhovoe sector. With this order he introduced the fresh 282nd Guards Rifle Regiment, which in essence hadn't yet seen combat, on the axis of III Panzer Corps' main attack, while the 280th Guards Rifle Regiment was supposed to hold only Shliakhovoe. This scheme was more prudent and took greater consideration of the details of the situation that had developed here by the end of 8 July.

It should be noted that even though S.G. Goriachev signed the above-mentioned orders for the 81st Guards Rifle and 375th Rifle Divisions, this doesn't mean that throughout the day of 9 July he would be actually directing Morozov's and Trunin's divisions or substantially affecting the course of combat actions in their sector. In the first place, the corps headquarters and the corps commander himself were in fact unable to establish communications with the divisions until the very end of this day. Secondly, judging from everything, Major General I.K. Morozov received Order No.6 late and aligned his actions with the 25th Guards Rifle Corps' combat plan for 9 July. Meanwhile Colonel P.D. Govorunenko found out about it only at 1700 on 9 July over the telephone from his chief of staff. However, this document could neither help him or change anything fundamentally: the combat in the Dal'niaia Igumenka – Postnikov sector would be approaching its peak in intensity, and his division even without this order fought tenaciously to repel panzer attacks against its line. Relying on combat documents found in the TsAMO RF, it is possible to assert that only the 7th Guards Army's 25th Guards Rifle Corps would exert centralized command over the troops in this area throughout 9 July to any degree, while division commanders Morozov, Govorunenko and Trunin would take personal command of the combat units in the course of the fighting, while at its most difficult moments, only the regiment commanders would be directing the combat.

Now let's return to the problem of strengthening the 35th Guards Rifle Corps' center with artillery and anti-tank guns. On the night of 8-9 July, although not very significant, extremely necessary anti-tank forces and heavy artillery would be brought up to the Postnikov[14] area and north of there. At the direction of the 81st Guards Rifle Division's artillery commander, three batteries of Major Kazarinov's 114th Guards Separate Destroyer Anti-tank Artillery Regiment began to arrive here from Melikhovo on the evening of 8 July. In the preceding fighting the regiment lost almost half its guns, and now had only 11 76mm Model 1942 anti-tank guns still in action.[15] By morning the 5th Battery (4 guns) was digging in on the northwestern outskirts of Postnikov, the 4th Battery (4 guns) – on the southwestern outskirts of the hamlet, and the 2nd Battery – 1 kilometer northeast of Shishino. For his part, in addition to the artillery of the three regiments (the 276th Guards

---
13 TsAMO RF, f. 35 gv. sk, op. 1, d. 26, l. 82.
14 The hamlet of Postnikov held the command posts of the 81st Guards Rifle Division and the 92nd Guards Rifle Division's 197th Guards Artillery Regiment.
15 TsAMO RF, f. 10873, d. 8808ss, d. 4, l. 341.

Rifle, 282nd Guards Rifle and 1241st Rifle Regiment) and the 137th Separate Anti-tank Rifle Battalion that were positioned in the area, the division commander of the 92nd Guards Rifle Division moved up the 1st and 3rd Battalions of Lieutenant Colonel I.I. Shaposhnikov's 197th Guards Artillery Regiment to the hamlet. In addition, at the instructions of the Front's artillery headquarters, two battalions of Lieutenant Colonel V.I. Melnikov's 27th Separate Heavy Cannon Brigade began to move into positions here. The 1st Artillery Battalion of the 142nd Cannon Artillery Regiment of the Supreme Command Reserve was left in its firing positions in the sector of the 6th Guards Army and received the order to conduct fire on targets in the Dal'niaia Igumenka area, while 1/93rd Cannon Artillery Regiment was withdrawn from this village. Concerned that in the event of a panzer breakthrough the artillerymen wouldn't have time to bring their heavy howitzers out from under enemy fire and treads, the commander of the 93rd Cannon Artillery Regiment of the Supreme Command Reserve Major S.F. Evtushenko had requested the brigade commander's authorization to redeploy the 1st Artillery Battalion out of Dal'niaia Igumenka to the eastern outskirts of Kiselevo (5 kilometers north of Dal'niaia Igumenka) and to give him the assignment to render assistance to the infantry with blocking fire when fighting to repel the Germans' attacks toward Dal'niaia Igumenka, and if the German tanks did breakthrough toward Kiselevo, to deploy his howitzers to fire over open sights. His superior approved this suggestion and without hesitation gave him the OK. By dawn the howitzer crews were already in their new positions. Thus, before Assault Group "North" the Soviet side had assembled 53 guns alone of the divisional and army artillery with a caliber ranging between 76mm and 152mm.

Taking into attention the large tactical significance of the Dal'niaia Igumenka area, as well as considering the small number of tanks left in Lieutenant Colonel M.T. Shevchenko's 47th Heavy Tank Breakthrough Regiment, which was positioned in the village, S.G. Goriachev ordered to leave the 331st Tank Battalion of the 96th Separate Tank Brigade in the Sabynino area, while the 228th Tank Battalion of this same tank brigade was to assemble in the woods north of Dal'niaia Igumenka. The approaches to the basin of the Northern Donets from the directions of Postnikov and Dal'niaia Igumenka, as before, were being covered by Major Zotov's 1500 Destroyer Anti-tank Artillery Regiment of the 2nd Guards Tank Corps. It had 19 45mm anti-tank guns and was subordinate to the command of the 47th Guards Separate Heavy Tank Regiment. Its batteries had set up firing positions in the areas: 1st Battery – on the southern outskirts of Khokhlovo; 2nd and 3rd Batteries – at the crossroads southwest of Khokhlovo; the 4th and 5th Batteries – 1 kilometer southwest of Dal'niaia Igumenka.[16] Considering that the enemy was operating with tanks at Melikhovo, the commander of the 375th Rifle Division also reinforced his left flank, having moved up to there a number of units, including a battalion of the 932nd Artillery Regiment and the entire 383rd Separate Destroyer Anti-tank Artillery Battalion. In addition, as before, 1/290 Mortar Regiment (18 heavy 120mm mortars) was in firing positions 1 kilometer northwest of Postnikov.

Finally, the 148th Separate Tank Regiment was still positioned in Shliakhovoe together with units of the 92nd Guards Rifle Division's 280th Guards Rifle Regiment and the 305th Rifle Division's 1004th Rifle Regiment. They were serving as Colonel V.F. Trunin's mobile reserve.

Especially for the struggle against enemy mechanized forces, special groups of the Front's and 69th Army's engineer units were also sent to this area: mobile blocking detachments and combat engineer tank hunters. They were prepared for active work directly in the rear of the enemy's attacking groups of panzers in order to mine ground that had already been cleared by German sappers and passages across anti-tank ditches; to block the most likely routes of the tank's movements and roads that saw the traffic of motorized transport; and to blow up bridges.

---

16 TsAMO RF, f. 2 gv. Ttk, op. 1, d. 115, l. 158.

In addition, the Front command ordered M.S. Shumilov to render assistance to the 69th Army and to launch a counterattack with the 25th Guards Rifle Corps' right flank into the flanks of the enemy grouping that was advancing toward Shliakhovoe. On the morning of 9 July, the 25th Guards Rifle Corps actually included (and had communications with them): the 81st Guards, 94th Guards, 73rd Guards, 78th Guards, 15th Guards and 270th Rifle Divisions; the 30th and 31st Separate Destroyer Anti-tank Artillery Brigades; the 201st Tank Brigade, the 262nd Heavy Tank Regiment and the 1438th and 1529th Self-propelled Artillery Regiments; the 1667th Destroyer Anti-tank Artillery Regiment, the 265 Guards Cannon Artillery Regiment, and the 97th, 309th and 315th Guards Mortar Regiments; the 2nd and 4th Anti-tank Rifle Battalions; the 329th Engineer Battalion and the 191st Flamethrowing Company.

Despite this lengthy list of formations and units, the 25th Guards Rifle Corps had little strength. The 15th Guards and 270th Rifle Divisions were only operationally attached, so the corps commander could use them only with the authorization of the army commander, and only then, in extreme cases. Secondly, the remaining formations and units were badly understrength after the previous days of fighting. For example, the 73rd and 78th Guards Rifle Divisions, which were holding that stretched for 10 kilometers from a point 200 meters east of the "Solov'ev" State Farm past the "Batratskaia Dacha" State Farm (excl.) to the "Poliana" State Farm, had a combat strength that was actually equivalent to a single rifle division. At this moment they had respectively 5,985 and 4,981 men, and a combined strength of 64 mortars (including 17 50mm mortars), 24 45mm guns, and 56 76mm and 122mm guns.[17] The 31st Separate Destroyer Anti-tank Artillery Brigade had 17 45mm and 11 76mm anti-tank guns left, while the 201st Tank Brigade had 36 tanks (3 T-34, 18 Mk-II[18] Matilda and 14 Mk-III Valentine tanks).[19] The 25th Guards Rifle Corps' mobile reserve had 18 tanks (6 serviceable KV-1 tanks in the 262nd Heavy Tank Regiment,[20] 5 T-34 and 2 T-70 in the 167th Separate Tank Regiment, and 4 SU-76 and 1 SU-122 in the 1438th Self-propelled Artillery Regiment[21]). The 315th Guards Mortar Regiment, although subordinate to G.B. Safiulin, had moved on the night of 8-9 July in order to conduct fire on targets in the 92nd Guards Rifle Division's sector. Thus the 25th Guards Rifle Corps commander had been forced to shift all of his available fire support to strengthen the 73rd Guards Rifle Division's sector and its boundary with the 94th Guards Rifle Division, so for the counterattack (if the resulting action could even be called that) had only crumbs left – the 276th Guards Rifle Regiment (of the 81st Guards Rifle Division) and 1/283rd Guards Rifle Regiment (of the 94th Guards Rifle Division). These forces were to attack toward the hamlet of Kalinin from two directions: Simonov's 276th Guards Rifle Regiment out of the area of Postnikov to the east, and the battalion of Russkikh's 94th Guards Rifle Division out of the northern outskirts of Miasoedovo to the north.

In the publications of certain Western authors, it is maintained that on the morning of 9 July the weather in the sector of Army Group South sharply deteriorated and "torrential rains weakened the momentum of the German attack".[22] This is far from the case. There actually were rain showers, but not so abundant to stop the offensive. According to combat documents of the opposing sides, on 9 July the roads were fully trafficable for vehicles, not to mention for infantry. From Operational Summary No.363 of the 7th Guards Army at 0700 9.07.1943: "The weather at night: Low cumulus clouds with 40% coverage of the sky, calm, temperature 12-15 C. The dirt

---

17 TsAMO RF, f. 878, op. 1, d. 32, l. 137obr. Data for the 73rd Guards Rifle Division are for 08.07.1943, and for the 78th Guards Rifle Division – 09.07.1943.
18 One of these Mk-II was not located in the sector of defense and was on assignment elsewhere.
19 TsAMO RF, f. 341, op. 5312, d. 246, l. 59.
20 TsAMO RF, f. 72 gv. sd, op. 27453, d. 1, l. 110.
21 TsAMO RF, f. 341, op. 5312, d. 246, l. 60obr.
22 Haupt, *Srazheniia gruppy armii "Iug"*, p. 298.

roads are suitable for traffic."²³ Here are several excerpts from reports from III Panzer Corps' divisions: "partly cloudy, humid" (168th Infantry Division; "partly cloudy, warm, roads are good" (7th Panzer Division); "sunny, warm, evening rain, temperature at 1200 – 31 C." (III Panzer Corps report to Army Detachment Kempf).²⁴ For the weather conditions in the sector of the Voronezh Front and the 7th Guards Army between 1 and 16 July 1943, see Table 12.

Secondly, on this day the forces of Army Group South were able to achieve rather impressive results. By the evening XXXXVIII Panzer Corps, having breached the line of the 1st Tank Army's 3rd Mechanized Corps to its entire depth on the Oboian' direction, and advancing another 8 kilometers, was able to take the tactically important village of Novoselovka and push another 1.5-2 kilometers beyond it to the north. Then its strongest division *Grossdeutschland* began to pivot to the left flank of the Fourth Panzer Army for an attack into the bend of the Pena River against the left flank of 1st Tank Army's 6th Tank Corps (Group Getman). At the same time, III Panzer Corps, despite the bitterest opposition of the 35th Guards Rifle Corps, with strong attacks forced the Soviet command to issue an order to retreat from the "Belgorod bastion" to two Guards divisions. Thus, it is difficult to agree with the statement that the momentum of the German attack on 9 July was "greatly weakened".

Now on the basis of documents let's return to near Belgorod to the forces of the opposing sides in order to take a look at how events developed here before dawn. In the reports from the divisions of Breith's III Panzer Corps, it was noted that the night of 8-9 July had passed rather quietly across the entire front. This is understandable – a regrouping of forces was underway across the entire front of Army Detachment Kempf's breakthrough. From the morning reports:

> 7th Panzer Division: The division commander is conducting a relief by the units of the 198th Infantry Division in the "Batratskaia Dacha" State Farm – edge of the woods 2 kilometers south of Miasoedovo sector. The replacing units of the 198th Infantry Division are subordinate to him. Transfer command to the 198th Infantry Division's commander after the completion of the rotation, on the morning of 10.7.

> 19th Panzer Division: … Infantry Regiment 442 after repulsing an enemy counterattack in the evening hours reached the center of Blizhniaia Igumenka and is digging in with a front to the west and northwest.

> 6th Panzer Division: The night went quietly, with light activity by enemy aircraft.

> 7th Panzer Division: Throughout the night, local attacks from both sides of the "Solov'ev" collective farm, which were repelled by a counterattack. Enemy aerial activity is less than on preceding days.

> 168th Infantry Division: Throughout the night only light harassing enemy artillery and mortar fire. Around 0400 the enemy, with approximately two companies, attacked the positions at the railroad embankment to the northwest of Kreida from out of the southern portion of Staryi Gorod. The attack was driven back. Only overflights by enemy aircraft with the release of a bomb in the area of the Belgorod – Kursk highway.²⁵

---

23 TsAMO RF, f. 7 gv. A, op. 5312, d. 239, l. 169.
24 NARA US, rg. 242, t. 314, r. 197, f. 001255.
25 NARA US, rg. 242, t. 314, r. 197, f. 001225, 001233.

Table 12 Information on meteorological conditions in the sector of the Voronezh Front between 1 and 16 July 1943

Day of the week, date	In the Voronezh Front's sector (data from its headquarters' operational summaries)					Sector of the 7th Guards Army (info from operational summaries of its headquarters and formations)
	Temperature, C. 1000/2200	Rain, 1000/2200	Cloudiness, 1000/2200	Wind, 1000/2200	Visibility 1000/2200	
Friday, 1 July	12–14/18–22	Scattered rain/ downpours and thunderstorms	50–100%/60–100%, altitude of 400–600 meters			
Saturday, 2 July	11–14/18		40–90%/50–80%	Out of the west, 0 to 2 meters a second	Bad visibility	In the daytime, roads were passable for vehicles
Sunday, 3 July	/19–23	–/local light rains; brief scattered showers	–/60 to 70%, altitude of 500–800 meters	Out of the southwest, 3–7 meters a second		Roads were passable for vehicles
Monday, 4 July	10–14/20–24	–/in the afternoon and evening, local light rains	40–70%/60 to 100%, altitude of 600–1000 meters	Calm/out of the southwest, 2–5 meters a second	?/out to 10 km	In the morning, partly cloudy with showers; roads were passable for vehicles/in the daytime, clear weather
Tuesday, 5 July	10–15/18–22	–/–	–/60 to 100%	Out of the west, 1–3 meters a second	Clear, fine/–	In the daytime, small cumulus clouds, 20–40% coverage, wind out of the southwest at 1–3 meters/second. Roads passable for vehicles.
Wednesday, 6 July	–/13–21	–/–	50 to 100%, altitude of 600–1000 meters	Out of the southwest		Up to 90% cloud cover with brief light showers, wind out of the west at 4 meters/second; up to 20C., visibility out to 10 kilometers, roads passable for vehicles
Thursday, 7 July	10–14/20–26	In the first half of the night, rain on the left flank/–	In the first half of the night, 10 to 15%/–	Out of the southwest at 1–5 meters a second/out of the southwest	Clear	Partly cloudy, wind out of the northwest at 4 meters a second; visibility out to 10 kilometers; roads passable for vehicles
Friday, 8 July	11–14/21–27	–/–	–/70 to 100%	–/out of the south	Clear, fine/–	Mostly cloudy, gusty wind out of the south at up to 7 meters a second; 28 C., visibility out to 10–12 kilometers; roads passable for vehicles
Saturday, 9 July	12–16/?	Local showers at night/?	70 to 100%/?	Out of the southwest at 0–5 meters a second	Poor/?	At night, partly cloudy, 12–15C., roads passable for vehicles. In the daytime, clear, roads passable for vehicles
Sunday, 10 July	16–18/18–24	Light rain in the first half of the night	70–90%/70–100%	Out of the south at 1–3 meters a second/out of the south, 3–8 meters a second	Fine/out to 10 kilometers	At night, cloudy (overcast), with showers, wind out of the southwest, 15 C., roads passable for vehicles

THE FALL OF THE BELGOROD BASTION, 9-10 JULY 1943 419

Day of the week, date	In the Voronezh Front's sector (data from its headquarters' operational summaries)					Sector of the 7th Guards Army (info from operational summaries of its headquarters and formations)
	Temperature, C. 1000/2200	Rain, 1000/2200	Cloudiness, 1000/2200	Wind, 1000/2200	Visibility 1000/2200	
Monday, 11 July	12–16 C.	Light rains at times	60 to 100% at approximately 10 kilometers of altitude/	Out of the southwest at 2–6 meters a second	At intervals of sunshine, fine/	At night, cloudy, in the morning, a thundershower, wind out of the southeast at 1-3 meters a second, 14-17 C., unsurfaced roads were passable for vehicles. In the daytime, overcast with showers.
Tuesday, 12 July	12–18 C.	–/–	50 to 100%	Out of the southwest, 2–6 meters a second	–/?	At night, stratus clouds, wind out of the southeast at 2 meters a second, up to 14 C., roads drying out after the rains
Wednesday, 13 July	11–14/17–20	–/–	80 to 100%/70 to 100%, altitude of 400–800 meters	East winds at 2–5 meters a second/out of the south at 4–7 meters a second	/ Visibility out to 10 kilometers	At night, stratus clouds, wind out of the southeast at 2 meters a second, 14 C., roads passable for vehicles. In the daytime, cloudy, winds out of the southwest at 3 meters a second, 17 C., visibility out to 5 kilometers, roads passable for vehicles
Thursday, 14 July						At night, stratus clouds, 80 to 100% coverage, wind out of the south at 0–3 meters a second, 13–15 C., roads passable for vehicles
Friday, 15 July	19–25 C.	–/	50–90%/	South, southwestern at 3–7 metes a second		In the daytime, weather overcast, periodic sprinkles; condition of the roads satisfactory
Saturday, 16 July	17–20 C (day) 11–13 C (night)	In the daytime and evening, rain	60–100%/	Out of the northwest, 2–5 meters a second		In the daytime, partly cloudy, winds out of the northwest at 3 meters a second, visibility of 5–7 kilometers; by evening, showers, roads passable for vehicles

However, already after sunrise the situation began to change. The offensive by the III Panzer Corps' assault groups wasn't planned to begin simultaneously, because the forces of Assault Group "North" still hadn't fully gathered in the designated area. The 19th Panzer Division still needed several more hours in order to yield its sector and shift its troops from Blizhniaia Igumenka. Thus the first to go over to active operations would be Assault Group "South". However, the German command wasn't counting on its forces. That small tactical success achieved by Infantry Regiment 442 on the evening of 8 July by breaking through to the center of Blizhniaia Igumenka was evaluated as the beginning of the Russian defense's collapse in this sector, but this was only a misleading appearance of this. Despite every effort, by the morning of 9 July the Germans had been unable take full possession of the strongpoints of Blizhniaia Igumenka and Miasoedovo on the flanks of the German penetration. The sector of the 6th and 19th Panzer Divisions' penetration suggested the neck of a bottle that extended up to 8 kilometers, at the base of which Breith was forced to keep rather strong "buttresses" (in the Sevriukovo – Melikhovo sector alone, Unrein's full *kampfgruppe* reinforced with von Oppeln's panzers), fearing the encirclement of Assault Group "North" by meeting attacks at the base of the penetration. However, the Soviet side lacked the necessary forces here (especially tanks) for this purpose.

The order from the Front command addressed to army commanders Shumilov and Kriuchenkin was to use all available forces to prevent with an active defense the enemy's further advance at the boundary between the 6th and 7th Guards Armies. Therefore I.K. Morozov issued an order to Major M.E. Simonov and Lieutenant Colonel I.I. Samoilenko that night to ready their 276th and 282nd Guards Rifle Regiments for a counterattack against III Panzer Corps' left flank in the Blizhniaia Igumenka – Postnikov sector, in order to relieve pressure on the 280th Guards Rifle Regiment's line at Shliakhovoe and the units in front of Dal'niaia Igumenka. Everything that the division commander was able to assemble was ready to support their attack: the 1st and 3rd Artillery Battalions of Lieutenant Colonel I.I. Shapovalov's 197th Guards Artillery Regiment (92nd Guards Rifle Division), the 1st Battalion of Major Makarov's 290th Mortar Regiment, remnants of Major K.Ia. Poliakovsky's 173rd Guards Artillery Regiment (81st Guards Rifle Division), and the regiments' mortar companies.

On the morning of 9 July, the Soviet side was the first to go over to active operations. At first, the 276th Guards Rifle Regiment went on the attack in Blizhniaia Igumenka. The attack proved to be so strong and unexpected for the enemy that grenadiers of Infantry Regiment 442, instead of taking the Guardsmen's positions, fled in panic from their own lines. Moreover, it is possible that panic enveloped the entire regiment of the 168th Infantry Division, since even the headquarters of III Panzer Corps received a report about this event. From the daily summary of the 19th Panzer Division:

> At 1000 (Moscow time) Infantry Regiment 442 again moved up to the southeastern portion of Blizhniaia Igumenka for an attack against this village. However an enemy counterattack in strength of a regiment hurled back our infantry to the southern and southeastern outskirts of this village. Only after using every effort and catching [rallying] fleeing infantrymen (!) was it possible to block the enemy's planned breakthrough to the southeast. In the afternoon after re-assembling, Infantry Regiment 442 once again took up its line.[26]

Almost simultaneously with the start of the attack by Simonov's regiment, 1/283rd Guards Rifle Regiment (94th Guards Rifle Division) went on the attack toward Kalinin from the northern outskirts of Miasoedovo. With heavy support from the divisional artillery, with one lunge of its

---

26 NARA US, rg. 242, t. 314, r. 197, f. 001251.

companies, having thrown back *Kampfgruppe* Unrein (I/Panzergrenadier Regiment 4), it seized the hamlet. Tied up in fighting with the 276th Guards Rifle Regiment, the Germans were unable to bring up armor quickly and again win back their abandoned positions. When a counterattack was launched an hour later, the 1st Battalion of the 283rd Guards Rifle Regiment had already firmly dug in and without any particular difficulties repulsed the Germans.

Approximately one and a half hours after the start of the attack, units of the 276th Guards Rifle Regiment broke into the center of Blizhniaia Igumenka (to the church square) and reached the southern outskirts. At this time, at 1100, the 282nd Guards Rifle Regiment stepped off on the attack out of Postnikov with two battalions and struck the boundary between the 6th and 19th Panzer Divisions at Hill 212.1 (600 meters northeast of Blizhniaia Igumenka). The Soviet battalions drove a company of grenadiers in halftracks (which was covering the left flank of Reconnaissance Battalion 6) off the hill, and despite the heavy fire, two companies cut the road 1 kilometer to the northwest of Hill 207.8 (on the southeastern fringe of the woods east of Postnikov).

Although the attack was unexpected, Hünersdorff was quickly able to deploy Major Kageneck's Tiger company with an attached company of the reconnaissance battalion mounted in halftracks on the flanks of the 282nd Guards Rifle Division (in the direction of Hill 212.1), and sent a portion of *Kampfgruppe* Bieberstein (up to two battalions and 15 panzers) from Melikhovo to the left flank (in the direction of the woods northeast of Postnikov). With the appearance of several dozen tanks and halftracks on the flanks of the regiment's attacking wedge, the Guardsmen didn't flinch, and repelling counterattacks, continued to advance. However, using their advantage in mechanization, the enemy then cut off some of the companies from the regiment's main forces. Lieutenant Colonel I.I. Samoilenko, commander of the 282nd Guards Rifle Regiment, reported:

> On the night of 8-9 July the regiment switched to a new defensive line: on the right – the western outskirts of Blizhniaia Igumenka, on the left – the northern fringe of the woods 1 kilometer north of Postnikov. The left flank was exposed, and at 0500 the enemy shoved back the right-hand neighbor [276th Guards Rifle Regiment] out of Blizhniaia Igumenka to the Belyi Kolodez' ravine, and thus the regiment's right flank became exposed. The enemy was preparing for an offensive and conducted devastating artillery fire on our combat positions. By this time ammunition was running low. In response to our queries about a resupply, no answer came from the division.
>
> At 1030 the enemy went on the offensive against the regiment's left flank from out of the area of the Belyi Kolodez' ravine and the woods southeast of the Belyi Kolodez' ravine. With submachine gunners the enemy managed to drop into the lengthy ravine, but the intensive fire of our artillery, mortars and rifle weapons forced him to fall back (with losses) and to reveal his precise dispositions. At 1100 with the support of mortar and artillery fire, Senior Lieutenant Maksimushkin's 1st Rifle Battalion went on the attack. From directly out of the patch of woods, the Germans opened up intensive fire from heavy machine guns against the attackers. However, the enemy didn't break the will of the 1st Rifle Battalion's commander; our anti-tank riflemen knocked out 4 enemy firing positions and the battalion continued to attack. With the outstanding coordination of fire between the companies, the battalion seized the "Round" woods east of Postnikov and continued to exploit the success toward the ravine 2 kilometers southwest of Kalinin. Already during the attack against the "Round" woods, the Germans initiated a counterattack along a gully on the left, but it was repulsed.
>
> Striving to stop the regiment's units, the enemy launched a second counterattack, but it was also thwarted. In the process 2 of their vehicles loaded with infantry were destroyed, 4 tanks were knocked out and approximately 70 soldiers and officers were killed. Enemy tanks emerged to the left and to the right. Having no support on the part of the mortar units, or from the artillery units, Maksimushkin continued to advance. However, after a certain

amount of time the Germans undertook a third counterattack. Even though it was brought to a stop, companies wound up in encirclement. The situation was becoming critical: the battalion was exhausted, ammunition was running low, and the battalion commander decided the companies would fight their way out of encirclement.

Captain Serov's 2nd Rifle Battalion, having started to move out via the ravine to Blizhniaia Igumenka, was met on the march by the fire of heavy machine guns and mortars. The companies began to advance by bounds, while the regiment's automatic weapons suppressed the fire of one mortar battery and a heavy machine gun on the eastern slopes of Hill 212.1. The enemy, leaving behind their tanks to cover the withdrawal, began to retreat. In this combat action Serov's battalion knocked out 9 tanks and killed up to 300 soldiers and officers.

Senior Lieutenant Novozhilov's 3rd Rifle Battalion received an assignment on the night of 8-9 July to move from Staryi Gorod to a new defensive line in the Postnikov area. As the regiment was moving out, the enemy was firing on his combat formation with six-barreled rocket launchers. Novozhilov began to attack in the sector: on the right the Kolodez' ravine, on the left – the "Round" woods at the bend in the road. In this battle the battalion encountered superior enemy forces of infantry and tanks. In a heated clash, the Guardsmen knocked out a light vehicle, a self-propelled gun, 3 motorcycles and suppressed the fire of a mortar battery. The Germans launched a counterattack which was repulsed with losses for them. Having broken the resistance, the battalion continued to advance, but came under another counterattack. I n order to bring the companies back to order and bring up supplies, Navozhilov ordered the battalion to dig in, but enemy tanks struck the battalion directly from the front and rear, through the regiment's command post. As a result, the 3rd Rifle Battalion wound up encircled.[27]

Unfortunately, because of the poor preparation and the weak fire support, the attack of a fresh, almost fully manned and equipped Guards regiment didn't bring the anticipated result and had heavy consequences for it. In the TsAMO RF, the list of the names of the soldiers and commanders of the rifle regiments of Trunin's Guards rifle division who went missing in action are kept, along with copies of death notices sent to the families of the fallen soldiers and commanders. They are plainly incomplete; a significant portion of them are timeworn and faded, and not all of the handwritten lines are decipherable. Only a portion of the lists of the non-commissioned officers and rank and file of the 282nd Guards Rifle Regiment are suitable for work. An analysis of these documents yields an approximate image of how many men in which units didn't answer the roll calls after this attack. According to these records, those missing after the battle "for unknown reasons" amounted to 111 men in the 1st Rifle Battalion, 291 men in the 2nd Rifle Battalion, 41 men in the 3rd Rifle Battalion, and 157 men in the specialized units.[28] The regiment's total losses for this category of military servicemen alone amounted to 610 men, though according to other information these losses were at a minimum 33% greater, but about this later.

A diversionary attack by Assault Group "South" in the Kreida – Staryi Gorod area had a substantial influence on the enemy's repulse of the 282nd Guards Rifle Division's attack. Because of the enemy's heavy pressure in this area, the 81st Guards Rifle Division commander wasn't able to support Samoilenko's regiment with artillery fire has had been originally planned. The headquarters of the 19th Panzer Division reported:

---

27 TsAMO RF, f. 282 gv. sp, op. 349903, d. 3, ll. 39-40.
28 TsAMO RF, f. 282 gv. sp, op. 349905s, d. 11, ll. 1-23

At 1015 Reconnaissance Battalion 19 with several assault groups began to roll up the system of enemy positions west of the edge of woods 3 kilometers to the south of Blizhniaia Igumenka. In the bitterest close combat, suffering high losses, the battalion managed to mop up the enemy positions right up to an enemy strongpoint that was built like a fortress in the northeastern corner of the woods, blew up a lot of bunkers, including some that were occupied, and in the process wiped out approximately an enemy battalion. Flammpanzers that came up in the evening successfully completed the undertaken venture.[29]

If you take a look at the configuration of the front line, then the decision to attack an enemy panzer division with an infantry regiment on a broad front (3 to 3.5 kilometers) without the support of armor looks at the very least unpromising. A simultaneous attack by the 276th Guards and 282nd Guards Rifle Regiments to meet the entire 286th Guards Rifle Regiment of the 94th Guards Rifle Division with the use of the 25th Guards Rifle Corps' mobile reserve (the 262nd Heavy Tank Regiment, the 167th Separate Tank Regiment and the 1438th Self-propelled Artillery Regiment) at the base of the 6th and 19th Panzer Divisions' penetration seems more sensible. However, even then the rifle regiments didn't have the strength to overcome the 6-kilometer sector between Blizhniaia Igumenka and Miasoedovo and cut off Assault Group "North" – an entire enemy panzer division (the 6th Panzer Division) and a portion of another (the 19th Panzer Division) were already located in the breakthrough salient. Nevertheless, a converging attack by three regiments into the flanks of the enemy might have diverted more of the enemy's strength in this area. It is hard to believe that the Soviet command didn't take a close look at the situation. It was obvious, but at this moment in essence only the 81st Guards Rifle Division's commander took careful consideration of what was happening. That morning his division formally passed to the control of the 69th Army, but in reality it was caught suspended between the 25th Guards Rifle Corps and 35th Guards Rifle Corps – one corps commander (G.B. Safiulin) had seemingly (in response to an order) yielded it, but the other (S.G. Goriachev) still hadn't received it (even communications hadn't been established with it). G.B. Safiulin decided to keep his mobile reserve at hand. Moreover, just in front of Nekliudovo, where his mobile reserve was positions, the Germans had panzers, and the village itself was located behind the boundary between his corps and the 35th Guards Rifle Corps and had a large bridge across the Koren' River, over which his corps' supply line ran. Therefore instead of one large, but extremely difficult task, like attempting to sever the German penetration at its base, he issued two smaller ones: to the commander of the 94th Guards Rifle Division to drive the Germans out of Kalinin, and for the 81st Guards Rifle Division to conduct a frontal attack at the base of the enemy's penetration in the Blizhniaia Igumenka – Postnikov sector. Given the fulfillment of this order, Russkikh's 94th Guards Rifle Division might be able to improve the situation on his right flank somewhat, while Morozov's division diverted German forces from Shliakhovoe and Dal'niaia Igumenka onto itself. Taken together, they would carry out the army commander's order to conduct a counterattack.

It is possible that to the reader it might seem that the 25th Guards Rifle Corps commander's somewhat self-centered order only harmed the situation by bringing about excessive losses. However, this isn't quite the case. War has its own irrefutable and cruel logic. After all, the general was responsible not only for the lines of the 81st Guards Rifle Division and 94th Guards Rifle Division, but for his corps' entire sector of defense, so he was obliged to weight his available forces and think not only of the immediate problems, but also take into account the future and what he would have left after the counterattack was completed. In addition, the area where the

---

29 NARA US, rg. 242, t. 314, r. 197, f. 001251.

counterattack was conducted had already passed to the responsibility of a different army, even though his subordinate units, just as before, were continuing to fight there.

How were events then going on the main axis of attack of Assault Group "North"? The 6th Panzer Division's panzer regiment with a portion of *Kampfgruppe* Unrein by morning had assembled in Melikhovo and on the hills north of there. Back on 8 July, having ran into the tanks of the 148th Separate Tank Regiment in the Shliakhovoe area, and also recalling Breith's warning that the Russians were planning to launch a major counterattack in this area, Major General W. von Hünersdorff cautioned Colonel von Oppeln to be ready to repel Russian tank attacks, including from the direction of Shliakhovoe. Thus while Kageneck's group of Tigers and the portion of von Bieberstein's panzergrenadiers together with Infantry Regiment 442 were attempting to beat back the onslaught of the attacking Russians, the commander of Panzer Regiment 11 decided to conduct reconnaissance out in front of the entire sector of his *panzerkampfgruppe*, and in addition at 0830 undertook a strong reconnaissance probe toward Shliakhovoe. The combat generated by this probe didn't last long; having received a decisive repulse by the 148th Separate Tank Regiment and the 280th Guards Rifle Regiment, his reconnaissance group returned to its jumping-off positions.[30] The acquired information indicated that the Soviet side was setting up a powerful strongpoint in the woods north of Dal'niaia Igumenka (Hill 217.1), which contained both tanks and anti-tank rifle teams. Understanding that in the event of an attack toward the village, the flanks of this *panzerkampfgruppe* would come under Russian fire from these woods, and also attempting to accelerate the forthcoming offensive, Hünersdorff decided not to waste time while waiting for the approach of the 19th Panzer Division's units, but to breach the defenses of the 92nd Guards Rifle Division west of Melikhovo and to destroy the revealed Russian strongpoint on Hill 217.1. One of the two tank battalions of the 96th Separate Tank Brigade was located here along with one company of the motorized rifle battalion and an anti-tank artillery battalion. After midday, the units of *Kampfgruppe* Bieberstein that had been left in Melikhovo with the support of von Oppeln's *panzerkampfgruppe* launched an attack at the boundary between the 282nd Guards and 280th Guards Rifle Regiments. After an hour-long combat with the infantry, approximately 150 tanks and self-propelled guns closed within direct fire range to the positions of the 228th Tank Battalion and began to approach the northwestern outskirts of Dal'niaia Igumenka. The combat outposts of the 375th Rifle Division supported by the division's artillery and the crews of Lebedev's tank brigade were offering stubborn resistance. From the "Account of the combat operations of the 96th 'Cheliabinsk Komsomol' Tank Brigade over the period from 5 to 14.7.1943":

> At 1330 up to 60 enemy tanks and a regiment of infantry with the support of a large amount of artillery began to attack the woods on Point 217.4. The 228th Tank Battalion consisting of 13 T-34 over the next four hours repulsed furious enemy attacks. By 1800 the battalion had lost 6 machines, and having expended all of its ammunition, was forced to fall back to the villages of Kiselevo.[31] The battalion, having lost one more tank during the retreat, took up a defense with six tanks on the eastern outskirts of the village of Kiselevo.[32]

The freed-up units of the 19th Panzer Division began moving out from the Blizhniaia Igumenk area between approximately 1030 and 1100 and continued until 1300. The regrouping being conducted was spotted by reconnaissance by both the 94th Guards and 92nd Guards Rifle

---

30 TsAMO RF, f. 148 otp, op. 661360, d. 3, l. 70.
31 The village of Kiselevo, one of the largest villages in the district, was located on the left bank of the Northern Donets River (5 kilometers north of Dal'niaia Igumenka), while on the opposite right bank a hamlet with the same name of Kiselevo was located.
32 TsAMO RF, f. 203, op. 2851, d. 234, l. 422.

Divisions, and with Operational Summary No.64 the headquarters of the 197th Guards Artillery Regiment reported: "It has been established by observation that groups of 7-8 tanks and covered vehicles apparently containing infantry are moving along the road from Blizhniaia Igumenka to Melikhovo. The movement of light vehicles is being observed."[33]

The attack by von Oppeln's *panzerkampfgruppe* at the boundary between the 282nd Guards and 280th Guards Rifle Regiments (between Melikhovo and Dal'niaia Igumenka) in essence marked the beginning of the III Panzer Corps' offensive, although the main forces didn't join the attack until 90 minutes later. Thus in the documents of its headquarters it is indicated that both Assault Groups "North" and "South" went on the attack at 1500. By this time the counterattack made by the 276th Guards Rifle Regiment had been repulsed and a breach had been created at the boundary between the 280th Guards and 276th Guards Rifle Regiments. Battalion-sized groups of Infantry Regiment 429 were also located in their jumping-off positions; they were to launch two attacks: a pinning attack from the Kreida railyards toward Staryi Gorod, and a main attack toward the hamlet of the Machine Tractor Station. Then they were to break through across the Belyi Kolodez' ravine to the north to the Andreevskie – Postnikov area, where they were supposed to link up with *Sturmgruppe Nord*. Thus, the Germans were striving to catch the 81st Guards Rifle Division and two regiments of the 92nd Guards Rifle Division in pincers.

The command of III Panzer Corps at that moment was located in a very difficult position. On the one hand Army Group South's leadership was putting pressure on it because of its inability to screen the Fourth Panzer Army's extended right flank, but on the other hand, its battered divisions were still facing a Soviet defense that was still standing like a granite boulder on a serpentine mountain road, which was impossible to bypass and couldn't be penetrated. Therefore when planning to seize the lines of two Guards divisions, from the beginning Breith was anticipating that Schmidt's 19th Panzer Division and Hünersdorff's 6th Panzer Division would experience heavy panzer losses on this day. There was no other option: they had to take a line that had been prepared in an anti-tank respect, without Luftwaffe support and with an acute deficit of infantry and artillery.

In reality the commanders of the two assault groups were in something of a quandary, especially the commander of *Sturmgruppe Nord*. He had to take into account the danger of counterattacks by the 2nd Guards and 5th Guards Tank Corps, about which Army Group South's intelligence had warned him. Probably it was under their influence that Hünersdorff had significantly changed his plan. He decided to leave behind significant strength in the Melikhovo – Sevriukovo sector: Unrein's full *kampfgruppe*, a portion of von Bieberstein's *kampfgruppe*, and up to 20 panzers of Panzer Regiment 11 and Marder self-propelled anti-tank guns. He was planning to resolve the task standing before him with von Oppeln-Bronikowski's *panzerkampfgruppe* (the remaining portion and two Tiger companies), the bulk of *Kampfgruppe* Bieberstein, Westhofen's *panzerkampfgruppe*, Quentin's panzer reconnaissance battalion and StuG Battalion 228, with the support of artillery. Moreover, the detached group of armor was supposed to remain in the Melikhovo area during the first stage of the offensive, in order to screen the right flank of *Sturmgruppe Nord* (from the Kiselevo – Khokhlovo direction), after which it would break through to Dal'niaia Igumenka and begin movement to the southwest (along the Belyi Kolodez' ravine). Meanwhile its crews were engaged in combat with a tank battalion of the 96th Separate Tank Brigade. In the operational documents I've been unable to find accurate data on the numerical strength of the artillery possessed by both of the III Panzer Corps' assault groups. Only the number of anti-tank artillery pieces of the 19th Panzer Division for mid-day 9 July is known. At that moment it had 26 medium anti-tank guns,

---

33 TsAMO RF, f. 11046, op. 1, d. 5, l. 21

7 76.2mm guns mounted on self-propelled carriages (Marders), and 2 76.2mm guns with mechanized tow (including Infantry Regiment 442 and Westhofen's *panzerkampfgruppe*).[34]

At 1500 the entire front of the 81st Guards Rifle Division's defense and that of its attached two regiments, which extended for approximately 15-16 kilometers, was attacked simultaneously by the forces of 5-6 battalions supported by more than 130 panzers and assault guns. Although the German armor was distributed almost evenly across the front and directed toward the same objective – Staryi Gorod – the strongest attack was launched out of Melikhovo toward Dal'niaia Igumenka, against the left flank of Lieutenant Colonel I.I. Samoilenko's 282nd Guards Rifle Regiment. At this time the 25th Guards Rifle Corps headquarters received a radio message from the 81st Guards Rifle Division's commander, in which he reported:

> The enemy has gone on the offensive toward Staryi Gorod with the forces:
> a) 5 tanks and three infantry battalions from out of the Kreida railyard;
> b) 30 tanks and an infantry battalion from out of the "Day of Harvest" collective farm;
> c) 40 tanks and two infantry battalions from out of Blizhniaia Igumenka;
> d) 50 tanks and three infantry battalions from out of Melikhovo toward Dal'niaia Igumenka.[35]

Before 1600 *Sturmgruppe Nord* undertook not one attack (toward Dal'niaia Igumenka), but two attacks simultaneously: with the forces of Panzer Reconnaissance Battalion 6 and *Kampgruppe* Kageneck at the boundary between the 282nd and 276th Guards Rifle Regiments through the woods east of Postnikov, and with *Kampfgruppe* Bieberstein (reinforced with units of the 19th Panzer Division) toward the northeastern outskirts of Dal'niaia Igumenka. The attack against the boundary between the two rifle regiments was driven back by anti-tank artillery and tank fire, but von Bieberstein's panzergrenadiers with the support of a company of Tigers from the 6th Panzer Division and assault guns, having overrun 1/282nd Guards Rifle Regiment, broke into the center of Dal'niaia Igumenka at 1600. Combat began to flare up in the depth of the defenses of Morozov's division. Taking advantage of the German armor superiority, and considering that Quentin's panzer reconnaissance battalion with Kageneck's companies of Tigers and halftracks had tied up 3/282nd Guards Rifle Regiment with combat in the Postnikov area, Hünersdorff didn't begin to wait for when the panzergrenadiers would take full possession of Dal'niaia Igumenka and quickly introduced Westhofen's *panzerkampfgruppe* (the 19th Panzer Division's Panzer Regiment 27) into the battle. At 1630 20 panzers escorted by a battalion of infantry was moving along the Dal'niaia Igumenka – Staryi Gorod road toward Hill 185.7. Simultaneously 5 combat machines with a company of infantry were directed from the northwestern outskirts toward the Northern Donets River basin in order to probe the Soviet defenses in the direction of Khokhlovo. Approximately an hour later, having driven in the combat outposts (blocking detachment) of the 375th Rifle Division's 1241st Rifle Regiment on the road (the 1st Rifle Company, submachine gunners and company of anti-tank rifles, which retreated toward Shishino), the enemy reached the hill and became tied up in combat in a fruit orchard of the "Main Fruit and Vegetable" State Farm with units of the 1241st Rifle Regiment and the 137th Anti-tank Rifle Battalion. As a result, the 282nd Guards Rifle Regiment wound up isolated almost along the axis of the defense from the northeast to the southwest. The bulk of the 1st Rifle Battalion retreated toward Postnikov, while approximately a bit more than a company continued to fight in the western and southwestern portions of Dal'niaia Igumenka.

---

34 NARA US, rg. 242, t. 314, r. 197, f. 001251.
35 TsAMO RF, f. 878, op. 1, d. 33, l. 24.

Thus, around 1700 four regiments of the 81st Guards and 92nd Guards Rifle Divisions (the 233rd Guards, 238th Guards, 276th Guards and 282nd Guards Rifle Regiments) fell into semi-encirclement, which was marked by the line: Hill 185.7 – Dal'niaia Igumenka – woods northeast of Postnikov – Hill 212.1 – church in Blizhniaia Igumenka – (excl.) southern portion of Staryi Gorod. Only the 235th Guards Rifle Regiment was outside the forming pocket, occupying the Staryi Gorod – (excl.) Chernaia Poliana sector. Now the distance between the forward units of *Sturmgruppe Sud* (south of Staryi Gorod) and *Sturmgruppe Nord* at the neck of the forming pocket was just 7.5 kilometers as the crow flies. From the daily report of the 6th Panzer Division:

> The units of the 19th Panzer Division with I/Panzergrenadier Regiment 114 and StuG Battalion 228 (minus one battery) that were made subordinate today joined *Kampfgruppe* Bieberstein. Because of the necessary regrouping, the start of the attack could be set only at 1500 as agreed upon with the panzer division. The main forces of the *kampfgruppe* moved out from the northeast out of the woods west of Melikhovo toward the southwest through Dal'niaia Igumenka, while I/Panzergrenadier Regiment 114 was deployed echeloned to the right as a flanking screen. Panzer Reconnaissance Battalion 6 received an order to tie up the enemy in Dal'niaia Igumenka and on the eastern slope of the Belyi Kolodez' ravine with simultaneous fire and an attack, and force him to regroup. Thus we managed to break through quickly to the southern outskirts of this village. There, a further attack was again undertaken to cross the anti-tank ditch and the wide minefield adjacent to it.
>
> After a passage was made across the anti-tank ditch and the belt of mines south of Dal'niaia Igumenka, *Kampfgruppe* Bieberstein, Quentin's panzer reconnaissance battalion and *Kampfgruppe* Kageneck (the Tigers and a panzergrenadier battalion in halftracks) resumed the attack. The two latter groups closed to destroy the enemy on the eastern edge of the Belyi Kolodez' ravine, while *Kampfgruppe* Bieberstein attacked Andreevskie with grenadiers and, together with the *panzerkampfgruppe* became engaged in vicious fighting in a fruit orchard east of the "Main Fruit and Vegetable" State Farm.
>
> The enemy aerial activity is very persistent; the activity of our fighters is quite insignificant.[36]

Colonel Govorunenko's units intercepted the enemy's attempt to reach the basin of the Northern Donets in the Khokhlovo area, though even here the situation was deteriorating. By 1800, the two Churchill tanks of the 47th Guards Separate Breakthrough Heavy Tank Regiment (of the initial five), around which the defense of the remnants of 1/282 Guards Rifle Regiment in Dal'niaia Igumenka was organized, had been knocked out. Meanwhile the 228th Tank Battalion of Lebedev's 96th Separate Tank Brigade that was defending in the woods to the north (on Hill 217.1), having lost half of its T-34s, began to withdraw toward Kiselevo. Von Bieberstein's panzergrenadiers, relying on the tank fire (from the southeastern and southern portions of the village) began to push the Guardsmen out of Dal'niaia Igumenka. Simultaneously von Oppeln-Bronikowski's panzers attempted to outflank Dal'niaia Igumenka from the north (across Hill 217.1), in order to strike the defenders in the village from the rear. From the account of Shevchenko's regiment:

> Not risking to remain in the German rear, 3 operational tanks and one knocked-out tank (under tow) retreated to the hill 0.5 kilometers northwest of Dal'niaia Igumenka and took up a defense, shooting up the attacking enemy tank [of von Oppeln-Bronikowski's panzer regiment] from the flank. Of the support units, only the 1st Battery of the 1500th Destroyer Anti-tank Artillery Regiment was left, while the others, according to an order

---

36   NARA US, rg. 242, t. 314, r. 197, f. 001250.

from the corps commander, were shifted to a different direction. The enemy, having seized Dal'niaia Igumenka by 1930 9.07.1943, launched an attack toward Chernaia Poliana, Shliakhovoe and Sabynino, while not displaying any active offensive operations toward Khokhlovo and Kiselevo, but only conducting methodical artillery and mortar fire.[37]

It is impossible to agree with the assertion that after the capture of Dal'niaia Igumenka, the German activity in the direction of the Northern Donets River basin decreased. On the contrary, the pressure on the left flank of Major N.A. Karklin's 1241st Rifle Regiment noticeably grew. At some moment a unit of Westhofen's *panzerkampfgruppe* (I/Panzer Regiment 27) broke through to the regiment's positions on Hill 176.3 (on the Dal'niaia Igumenka – Khokhlovo road). The chief of the 375th Rifle Division's Political Department Colonel S.Kh. Ainutdinov recalled:

> The nerves of some of the soldiers, who had just arrived at the front the night before, gave out. Some of the soldiers ran away. Some of the artillerymen also abandoned their guns. A critical moment had arrived. Located in his observation post, the deputy commander of an anti-tank gun battery Lieutenant Evgenii Putintsev leaped out of the trench and took off at a run to meet the fleeing soldiers. He rushed over to an anti-tank gun that had been abandoned by its crew, loaded it and with the first shot set fire to the lead enemy tank. In our division, Putintsev was considered a sniper-artilleryman. The Lieutenant reached for the next shell and caught sight of the returning crew coming up at a run. Just 80-100 meters were now separating Putintsev from the advancing enemy tanks and infantry. He loaded the gun and knocked out a second tank. At this time a cannon shot thundered somewhat to the right. Not far from him, submachine guns and heavy and light machine guns began to chatter. It was coming from the soldiers who had returned in order to kill the enemy together with the officer. The Lieutenant disabled another tank, but was mortally wounded. The courage and personal example of Lieutenant Evgenii Vladimirovich Putintsev salvaged the situation, having prevented a panic. … Altogether in this action, 21 enemy tanks were knocked out and more than 200 Nazis were killed; several dozen more were captured, including the commander of a tank company.[38]

Striving to prevent a German breakthrough to Khokhlovo, Major N.A. Karklin at 2000 launched a counterattack with the forces of 2nd Battalion/1245th Rifle Regiment with the support of 4 T-34 tanks of the 96th Separate Tank Brigade and 3 Mk-IV Churchill tanks of the 47th Guards Separate Breakthrough Heavy Tank Regiment. Even though the rifle battalion didn't advance any further than the western outskirts of Dal'niaia Igumenka, the regiment's situation was salvaged. After this, the Churchill tanks fell back to the hill 2 kilometers south of the southern outskirts of Khokhlovo, while the T-34s of the 96th Separate Tank Brigade returned to Kiselevo. In the course of this counterattack, the regiment's soldiers dragged the commander of the 3/I/Panzer Regiment 27 Senior Lieutenant P. Sonntag and two of his panzer crew members out of a knocked-out tank on the western outskirts of Dal'niaia Igumenka. This was the first German officer (not including captured pilots) captured alive by Soviet troops over five days of fighting in the sector of Army Detachment Kempf's offensive. For purposes of comparison, according daily report for 9 July from the headquarters of the 7th Panzer Division, over four days of the offensive its units alone captured 17 Soviet commanders and 511 soldiers, and 33 commanders and 50

---

37 TsAMO RF, f. 2 gv. tk, op. 1, d. 24, ll. 203-205.
38 Ainutdinov, S.A., *U oboianskogo shosse* [*At the Oboian' highway*] (Sverdlovsk: Sredne-ural'skoe knizhnoe izdatel'stvo, 1973), p. 87.

soldiers voluntarily came over to the German side.[39] The command of the enemy's divisions was very sensitive to facts of officers going missing in action, even down to the company level. Thus, it was compulsory to make these incidents known not only to corps headquarters, but also to army headquarters. In its daily summary, the 19th Panzer Division reported: "Knight's Cross recipient 1st Lieutenant Sonntag and 2 men of Panzer Regiment 27 went missing on 9.7; they probably fell into enemy hands dead or wounded."[40]

In the 124st Rifle Regiment's Operational Summary No.0243 it is noted that both of the attacks, the one toward Khokhlovo and the one toward the orchard, had been completely repulsed by 2050 and the penetrating panzergrenadiers had been destroyed. In both areas, "… 20 tanks have been destroyed, knocked out or disabled by mines, and up to 100 infantry men were killed."[41]

When battling to eliminate the attacking enemy in the sector of the 276th Guards and 282nd Guards Rifle Regiment, and then in the depth of their defenses, the Soviet side employed Katiusha rocket launchers. However, their number was small in comparison, for example, with the number of Guards Mortar regiments that had been shifted to the 69th Army's right wing on this day (near Prokhorovka). Even though the rifle units in both areas were experiencing an acute deficit of supporting weapons, near Prokhorovka in addition to the Guards Mortar Regiments, the brigades of two tank corps were also activated. According to the information of the headquarters of Voronezh Front's Guards Mortar units, on 9 July 1943 the 218/16th Guards Mortar Regiment was working most intensively in the sector of the 35th Guards Rifle Corps. Between 1200 and 1800 its batteries launched 136 M-13 rockets at the enemy tanks and infantry that had gone on the offensive in the Postnikov – Dal'niaia Igumenka area, while one rocket launcher of the 217th Battalion of this same regiment at 1650 fired on an aggregation of tanks and infantry southwest of Dal'niaia Igumenka.

The success of Goriachev's 35th Guards Rifle Corps, which prevented the Germans from breaking through to the channel of the Northern Donets River and into the depth of the 81st Guards Rifle Division, although obvious, was achieved not by the tenacity of the defending soldiers and commanders alone. A number of other objective factors played a role in this. In the first place, the 1241st Rifle Regiment of the 375th Rifle Division had been occupying its positions here for a long time; its companies had prepared them and importantly, had organized the system of fire, while its artillery had pre-registered targets with consideration for the minefields and anti-tank obstacles. None of this had been done, for example, on the line where the 92nd Guards Rifle Division's forces deployed. In the second place, P.D Govorunenko on the morning of 9 July reinforced his left flank by moving up 2/1245th Rifle Regiment to the line east of Khokhlovo – Kiselevo, which was used actively on this day by the commander of the 1241st Rifle Regiment as a reinforcement. Finally, although *Sturmgruppe Nord* was attacking the "Main Fruit and Vegetable" State Farm and Khokhlovo with panzers, these weren't its main forces; in total, it was operating here with just 25-30 panzers and assault guns. Meanwhile Hünersdorff, striving to link up with Schmidt's 19th Panzer Division as quickly as possible, concentrated his main efforts on destroying the powerful strongpoints along the Belyi Kolodez' ravine and in Dal'niaia Igumenka, Postnikov and Andreevskie. Thus after the panzergrenadiers took Dal'niaia Igumenka, the defending Guardsmen had to hold out in a particularly heavy and bloody combat in the Postnikov area. Here, *Kampfgruppe* Bieberstein (reinforced by von Oppeln-Bronikowski's freed-up panzers), Quentin's panzer reconnaissance battalion and Kageneck's Tigers were simultaneously advancing, opposed by a portion of the companies of the 282nd Guards Rifle Regiment that had

---

39 NARA US, rg. 242, t. 314, r. 197, f. 001251.
40 NARA US, rg. 242, t. 314, r. 197, f. 001392.
41 TsAMO RF, f. 375 sd, op. 1, d. 36, l. 242.

come out of encirclement and two batteries of the 114th Destroyer Anti-tank Artillery Regiment. In addition, all of the combat-capable batteries of the 197th Guards Artillery Regiment's 1st and 3rd Artillery Battalions were deployed in the hamlet. It was these two artillery battalions that were the backbone of its defense.

The artillerymen fought bravely and even desperately. From the award commendation for Senior Sergeant N.I. Tokarev, a gun commander of the 7th Battery of 3/197th Guards Artillery Regiment:

> On 9.07.1943, fighting to repel German tank attacks, he knocked out 7 tanks, including one Pz-VI. When firing, after each shot N.I. Tokarev stood on the gun carriage behind the gun layer and observed the result of the fire, demonstrating cool composure and bravery while doing so. In the process of firing at German tanks, he was severely wounded. After his first moderate wound, he had continued to command the gun.[42]

However, the enemy had superiority in equipment and heavy weapons. The Guardsmen suffered particularly heavily from the Nebelwerfer fire. After approximately 90 minutes of struggle, having launched a third attack both across the front and against the right flank of 1/197th Guards Artillery Regiment, the Germans broke into its firing positions and wiped out the artillery battalion. The panzers crushed all of the guns and the battalion's observation post, killing its commander Captain Prokop'ev and a lot of the gun crew members, especially the gun layers. Having overrun the defenses on the northeastern outskirts, enemy armor broke into hamlet, where it was greeted by intense fire from Captain S.S. Smorzh's 3/197th Guards Artillery Regiment. Not only its 12 gun crews joined battle with the enemy, but also officers of the 197th Guards Artillery Regiment's command staff headed by its commander Lieutenant Colonel I.I. Shapovalov. German submachine gunners broke through to the hut that was holding the artillery regiment's headquarters. However, before taking up an all-round defense in it, the staff officers burned all of the operational documents as required by orders. Unfortunately, today without the lost documents it is hard to figure out not only the events that took place here on 9 July, but also the course of fighting in this sector over the preceding three days, in which the 197th Guards Artillery Regiment played a very important role. Thus it is necessary to resort to the archival files of higher-standing headquarters, but even they don't provide a full image. I will cite only one excerpt from the 35th Guards Rifle Corps' account of the combat operations:

> The commanders and soldiers of the 197th Guards Artillery Regiment together with the 282nd Guards Rifle Regiment fought bravely to hold the line of defense, shooting up tanks and infantry at pointblank range. Being encircled by tanks and submachine gunners, the men of the 3rd Battalion took up an all-round defense and alternately conducted fire from the guns and automatic weapons, and launched counterattacks. Many crews were firing at tanks from ranges of 20-30 meters, dying under the treads of tanks but refusing to abandon their guns. As a result of bitter fighting, units of the 92nd Guards Rifle Division knocked out or set ablaze up to 50 enemy tanks, in the process taking heavy losses in personnel and materiel (17 guns alone were lost). In the combat for Postnikov, Lieutenant Colonel I.I. Shapovalov, the commander of the 197th Guards Artillery Regiment, deputy commander Major Gorin, and commander of the 3rd Artillery Battalion Guards Captain S.S. Smorzh fell bravely in the battle.[43]

---

42 TsAMO RF, f. 33, op. 682526, ed. khr. 1825, entry number 17224098.
43 TsAMO RF, f. 35 gv. sk, op. 1, d. 44, l. 7.

Fortunately, as recently uncovered documents testify, Captain Smorzh was lucky; he not only survived the battle, he made it all the way to Berlin and greeted the grand VE-Day, and in the mid-1970s he visited the places of former battle in the Belgorod area with fellow veterans. Yet the commander of the 1st Artillery Battalion Captain D.A. Prokop'ev, whose batteries together with the 280th Guards Rifle Regiment had been the first to engage the *kampfgruppen* of Breith's III Panzer Corps at Melikhovo on 8 July, was killed on this day while fighting to repulse a German panzer attack against one of his batteries.

The crews of two batteries of the 114th Guards Destroyer Anti-tank Artilery Regiment fought valiantly with Kageneck's *kampfgruppe* and the panzer reconnaissance battalion of the 6th Panzer Division in front of the southwestern outskirts of Postnikov. The guns were standing in a field of rye, which made it hard for the enemy to detect them. The commander of the 4th Battery Sergeant Andrianov allowed the enemy to close within 500 meters before opening fire. Three minutes later, three Pz.kpfw. III were burning and one was knocked out. The crews of the other enemy tanks quickly determined the location of the "impudent" gun and concentrated the fire of several tanks at it, and then Tiger tanks moved out toward its position. Two shells fired by the gun crew ricocheted off one Pz.kpfw. VI tank's turret. Then the gunners targeted its running gear. With the first shot they severed a track and the heavy tank spun in place, exposing its flank to the fire of the gun; in a matter of seconds, the gun crew planted two 76mm shells into its flank. The "monster" began smoking. Altogether, during two attacks 8 German tanks and 12 vehicles loaded with infantry and cargo were knocked out by the crews of the 4th Battery. However, the artillerymen also suffered losses; under heavy enemy fire, they managed to tow away only one of the four 76mm anti-tank guns and bring out two STZ-5 tractors. The remaining guns together with two tractors and two ZiS-5 and GAZ-AA trucks were blown apart by the Germans. For those readers who regard with distrust the figures of knocked-out tanks, especially Tigers, that were reported by the headquarters of our units after the fighting, I'll note that the information on the loss of approximately 10 Pz.kpfw. VI Tigers, in particular in the Postnikov area, is close to the truth. It should be considered that artillery units that were equipped with 76mm and 122mm guns were deployed here. I'll remind the reader that altogether in *Sturmgruppe Nord* by the start of the general attack there were two companies numbering a total of 30 Tiger tanks (possibly several of these tanks had already been knocked out when repulsing the counterattack by the 282nd Rifle Regiment). One company was operating in the Dal'niaia Igumenka area, and the second (in Kageneck's *kampfgruppe*) was attacking Postnikov from the west through the Belyi Kolodez' ravine.

The crews of the 5th Battery of the 114th Guards Destroyer Anti-tank Artillery Regiment also achieved high results on this day while operating at Postnikov; on this day they tallied 8 tanks and 14 vehicles knocked out by them. The 5th Battery also suffered heavy losses. All of its materiel and motor transport were destroyed. As it says in the regiment's account, "Only when all the guns were destroyed did the crews and commanders abandon their firing positions. Moving out of Postnikov, Junior Lieutenant Bal'taziuk caught sight of one regimental cannon in a rye field. Taking position behind the gun layer, he opened fire from it at the enemy tanks from a range of 400 meters and knocked out two medium tanks."[44]

An analysis of the archival documents of the various units and formations that were operating in the 7th Guards Army's sector and on the Korocha direction show the important role played by the combat engineers of the 69th Army and Voronezh Front in the struggle against the enemy armor and in destroying motorized transport carrying men and ammunition, especially the one played by the so-called "tank hunters". These were a group of engineers who had been specially selected and who had undergone a special program of training. The principal feature of their actions was

---

44 TsAMO RF, f. 10873, op. 8808ss, d. 4, l. 352.

the active search and destruction of enemy armor. Each group of tank hunters (2-7 men each) was given a sector of 3-4 kilometers, in which through personal reconnoitering and the questioning of commanders of defending units, they were to find aggregations of enemy tanks; points of their refueling; and also knocked out tanks that hadn't blazed up to which enemy recovery and evacuation units might approach, and then block these sectors, routes and places with implanted mines. Considering that the primary target of the "hunters" was tanks and motorized transport, which were most vulnerable when moving along roads that had already been checked by the engineers, the tank-hunting groups were primarily directed to penetrate into the enemy's tactical rear. In the accounts and operational documents of the engineer headquarters of the 69th and 7th Guards Armies, cases are mentioned when separate groups of "hunters" spent several days behind enemy lines. They were indentifying roads and bridges with an average amount of traffic, and determining suitable approaches to them. They would then block them with planted mines. On average during one trip, a group would destroye 2-3 vehicles loaded with cargo or men, or one armored vehicle. In the process, even though it was a problematic matter to destroy tanks on the roads, it also had a secondary effect. Enemy vehicles in the rear usually moved in small groups of 2-4 trucks, unescorted by engineers (if one truck struck a mine engineers were rarely summoned either), and traffic resumed after 15-20 minutes. Yet engineers always accompanied a column of armored vehicles, and if one panzer or assault gun struck a mine, the column would stop, anti-aircraft weapons would deploy, and the sweeping of the road and the entire area adjacent to it would begin. In this case, traffic in this sector would be halted at a minimum for an hour or more.

However, tank hunters believed the most widespread method of use was dragging anti-tank mines under tanks from concealed positions and re-emplacing mines on ground over which tanks had already passed. In conversations with veterans, I happened to hear about one rather unique, but according to my conversation partner, very simple and effective way to conceal mines, which worked almost 100% of the time, but only in the course of combat. This was camouflaging anti-tank mines under corpses, and scattering mines on roads and likely routes of enemy tank movement. This was usually done after the first combat, and the bodies of animals or enemy soldiers were selected. Former minelayers who participated in the Battle of Kursk recalled one strange characteristic of the drivers of German tanks that they noticed in the battles – they almost always sought to avoid objects in their way (like crates, clothing, etc.), but rarely paid any attention to corpses. Thus the "tank hunters" often placed mines not under objects themselves, but in the ground next to them, onto which a tank or halftrack might turn.

In captured German sources I managed to uncover one more interesting method used by Soviet engineer units in the course of repelling Army Detachment Kempf's attack in the sector of the 24th Guards Rifle Corps, which I'd never heard before. From an order of the commander of the 198th Infantry Division dated 18 July 1943, which analyzed the experience of fighting in the 7th Guards Army's sector in the course of Operation Citadel:

> In one of the divisions, the enemy [most likely, it was the 15th Guards or 94th Guards Rifle Division] set up signs carrying the German inscription "Cleared of mines" on the western side of minefields. Owing to this, troops and especially machines were falling into the trap that had been set by the enemy. Forbid the use of signs with the inscription "Cleared of mines" in the division. Detected minefields must be marked by barbed wire or charts. Any type of sign with a German inscription must prompt caution. Immediately report to the division headquarters the location of the latter.[45]

---

45 TsAMO RF, f. 500, op. 12480, d. 13, ll. 102, 103.

THE FALL OF THE BELGOROD BASTION, 9-10 JULY 1943

Despite the fierce resistance, by 1900 the defense of the 69th Army's troops in the Dal'niaia Igumenka – Postnikov sector had been completely overrun. The remnants of the 282nd Guards Rifle Regiment of the 92nd Guards Rifle Division and eight guns of two regiments, having left their screening position in the Postnikov area, began slowly to retreat in the direction of Andreevskie, where they took up a new position and fought to repulse enemy attacks until the end of the day, while a portion of the regiment's forces were continuing to fight in encirclement east of Postnikov; the rumble of the combat here was audible until dawn. I've been unable to establish the identity of the units that were trapped here, but apparently it was the two companies that had been saddling the road 1 kilometer northwest of Hill 207.8 on the morning of 9 July. The 276th Guards Rifle Regiment, that was holding Blizhniaia Igumenka, was engaged in heavy fighting there until the last twilight.

Thus, by approximately 1930 *Sturmgruppe Nord* had seized only the two strongpoints of Dal'niaia Igumenka and Postnikov with great difficulty, and its main forces had reached the line: Andreevskie – orchard of the "Main Fruit and Vegetable" State Farm – 1.5 kilometers east of Shishino. From that moment until sunrise on 10 July, the situation here remained principally unchanged. On 9 July, Breith had been unable to reach the Northern Donets River channel with a decisive attack, not to mention complete the encirclement of the 81st Guards and 92nd Guards Rifle Divisions. From the document "Description of the combat operations of the 19th Panzer Division from 5 to 18 July 1943":

> The available forces here were hardly sufficient. Dal'niaia Igumenka was taken only once the anti-tank ditch and numerous minefields were overcome, and the resistance of the enemy's vastly numerically superior force was broken. The powerful minefields in the Postnikov – Shishino area, as well as the thinned ranks of the panzer grenadier regiment (up to 400 men with attached assets and the headquarters company) didn't give Westhofen's *panzerkampfgruppe* the possibility to achieve its assigned objective – Shishino – by the end of 9.7. The enemy exerted every effort to hold the high ground east of Shishino. The units of two Guards rifle divisions (92nd and 81st) were operating here.[46]

Even so, nevertheless, by around this time (1930-2000) a fundamental turning point took place in the sector of the 81st Guards and 92nd Guards Rifle Divisions, which led to the fall of the "Belgorod bastion". At this time, *Sturmgruppe Sud* broke into the depth of the 81st Guards Rifle Division's positions from two directions (from Dal'niaia Igumenka and the Kreida railyard toward the hamlet of the Machine Tractor Station), having ruptured its front in this area and having encircled a portion of its forces. In the 35th Guards Rifle Corps' account, there is the statement:

> Thus, having taken heavy losses the 276th Guards Rifle Regiment and 282nd Guards Rifle Regiment, and units of the 81st Guards Rifle and 375th Rifle Divisions, having wound up in semi-encirclement at 2200, began to retreat along the route: northern outskirts of Staryi Gorod, Shishino, Khokhlovo, Kiselevo, Sabynino while covering themselves from the flanks and rear. The 276th Guards and 282nd Guards Rifle Regiments assembled in the woods southwest of Verkhnii Ol'shanets. The 280th Guards Rifle Regiment, continuing to defend the Shliakhovoe Machine Tractor Station – Orlov ravine line, having turned it over at 2100 to the 305th Rifle Division's 1004th Rifle Regiment and according to order, took up a defense on the Kiselevo, (excl.) Shliakhovoe Machine Tractor Station line.[47]

---

46 TsAMO RF, f. 38A, op. 9027, d. 46, l. 153obr.
47 TsAMO RF, f. 906, op. 1, d. 44, l. 7.

Despite the difficult situation, the Guardsmen were continuing to defend stubbornly; the combat in the sector of the 81st Guards Rifle Division was of an extremely bitter nature. The positions here periodically changed hands in see-saw fighting, and often counterattacks ended in hand-to-hand fighting. Both sides suffered heavy casualties, and communications with higher headquarters were maintained only by radio, and even then with interruptions. Thus the situation in the offensive sector of *Sturmgruppe Sud* (in the Staryi Gorod – hamlet of the Machine Tractor Station – Blizhniaia Igumenka area) was unclear at the end of the day, and didn't become clear even to the headquarters of Breith's III Panzer Corps on the following day. From the 9 July daily report of the 168th Infantry Division to the corps:

> At 1500 Infantry Regiment 429 from out of the Kreida railyard undertook an enveloping attack toward the hamlet of the Machine Tractor Station, having III Battalion on the right and II Battalion on the left. Enemy bunkers and 2 machine-gun nests were destroyed on Point 153.2 [600 meters south of the hamlet]. From 1730 the battalions were rolling up the enemy positions in the hamlet of the Machine Tractor Station. Our panzers, having moved out at 1630 from Dal'niaia Igumenka, were stopped 1.5 kilometers east of Shishino [in the vicinity of Hill 185.7]. Three enemy tanks were set ablaze in the northeastern vegetable plots of the "Main Fruit and Vegetable" State Farm. Our artillery struck 4 enemy rocket launchers in Shishino. Insignificant enemy aerial activity.[48]

I'll note that the information about the destruction of tanks and Katiushas mentioned in the report isn't confirmed by Soviet documents. According to the operational summaries of the headquarters of the Voronezh Front's Guards Mortar regiments, not a single one lost so many BM-13 rocket launchers on this day, including the 16th Guards Mortar Regiment that was firing on the attacking troops of *Sturmgruppe Nord* in the Dal'niaia Igumenka and Postnikov area.

When analyzing the documents of the 81st Guards Rifle Division the impression forms that I.K. Morozov also didn't know the real situation of affairs in this area on the evening of 9 July. The situation in its general outlines became clear to him, probably, by midnight (if at all). However, in his Order No.057 that I found in the TsAMO RF it is indicated that the commander of the 35th Guards Rifle Corps issued an order about withdrawing to a new line on the night of 9-10 July 1943 precisely after receiving the division commander's report.

The capture of the two important strongpoints on the left flank of Morozov's division and the breakthrough to the hamlet of the Machine Tractor Station cost Breith's panzer corps dearly. According to the documents of its headquarters, the Guardsmen knocked out a total of 92 tanks and assault guns in his two assault groups, or approximately 61% of those available at the start of the attack, and approximately 70% of those that took part in the fighting in the sector of the 81st Guards and 92nd Guards Rifle Divisions. This figure shouldn't be viewed as conclusive. The real losses of Westhofen's and von Oppeln's panzer regiments were clearly less, because throughout that night the repair shops returned a certain number of lightly-damaged tanks and assault guns to service. Even so, the number is impressive. There wasn't such a loss of armor even in the two panzer corps of the Fourth Panzer Army when breaking through the 6th Guards Army's main defensive belt on 5 July 1943. Back then, the six divisions of the XXXXVIII and II SS Panzer Corps lost on 78 panzers and assault guns (not including the Panthers).

On the morning of 10 July of the 70 panzers in the 6th Panzer Division that had been counted as operational the day before, only 32 (45.7%) were left, and of the 36 in the 19th Panzer Division, only 13 (36%) were left. Of the 33 Tigers in the Heavy Panzer Battalion 503 on the day before,

---

48 NARA US, rg. 242, t. 314, r. 197, f. 001254.

only 14 remained combat-ready. The Pz.kpfw. VI company that was attached to the 7th Panzer Division was held out of the fighting on 9 July; it had just 3 Tigers still operational.[49] Thus, the 19 Tigers that had been knocked out of service on 9 July belonged to the two other Tiger companies that took part in the offensive against the line of the 81st Guards and 92nd Guards Rifle Divisions. More than half of the assault guns of StuG Battalion 228 were knocked out on 9 July; of the 23 that were operational on the morning of 9 July, there remained only 11. For more details on the losses, see Tables 10 and 13.

In connection with this I should note one important detail. The battlefield remained behind enemy lines on the evening of 9 July, which means the Germans had the opportunity to evacuate all of their repairable panzers and assault guns and return them to service within a certain amount of time. However, it you take a look at the number of Pz.kpfw. IV that returned to service in the 19th Panzer Division (20 of the 23 had been knocked out) after having assumed the main burden of the fighting, then approximately half of them were irreparably knocked out on 9 July. The fact that 5-9 tanks of this type were daily counted as operational in this division between 10 and 18 July, and the 10 machines that were ready for combat between 19 and 21 July each day, speaks to this. It is understandable that a rotation of tanks was going on: some were being knocked out and being sent for repairs, while others were being returned to service after being repaired. However, over a short period of time all the tanks couldn't have gone through the full cycle. In addition, a similar situation was observed with the Pz.kpfw. IV tanks in the 6th Panzer Division. Of the 14 Pz.kpfw. IV tanks in it that were introduced into the fighting on 9 July, by morning there were 7 still operational, while between 11 and 21 July, the division never had more than 6 serviceable machines of this type. Accordingly, at a minimum all the rest were undergoing repairs.

The situation in the 6th Panzer Division's Panzer Regiment 11 particularly stands out with respect to the knocked out Pz.kpfw. III tanks with the 50mm guns. Of the 24 tanks of this type that were ready for combat on the morning of 9 July, the regiment lost 12, but on the morning of 19 July, it now had 18 Pz.kpfw. III tanks with the 50mm gun in service. The bulk of the machines of this type had been disabled in minefields when pursuing retreating infantry or by undetected mines located in already seized terrain. Why? In the first place, it is known that the Soviet anti-tank mines were not very powerful; when a German tank detonated one most of the damage was done to their rolling assembly – treads or rollers. In the second place, when analyzing the situation regarding knocked out enemy armor in the first several days of the defensive operation, the Voronezh Front's Military Council came to the conclusion that when fighting to repel a German panzer attack, the anti-tank gunners frequently only immobilized a target, and didn't finish them off conclusively. The enemy took full advantage of this. As a rule, when controlling a battlefield, the Germans efficiently evacuated disabled tanks and assault guns to the tactical rear (at a distance of up to 3 kilometers from the front), and quickly repaired them. Thus on 7 July 1943 N.F. Vatutin's order went out to the troops: damaged enemy armored vehicles on the battlefield should be continued to be targeted by anti-tank guns and anti-tank rifles until they were set ablaze or exploded. In the files of the 35th Guards Rifle Corps and 375th Rifle Division kept in the TsAMO RF, there are documents that note that a telegram containing this order arrived in their units and elements on 7 and 8 July. So on 9 July the anti-tank crews were already aware of this order, and sought not only to stop tanks and assault guns by firing at their running gear, but also tried to finish them off, since strict monitoring over the implementation of this order had been established. This is clear from the situation with the Pz.kpfw. IV tanks. Indeed, the troops of the 69th Army had the main conditions to achieve this – expansive mine fields and fortified villages, which the enemy took with massed panzer attacks. The data on the knocked out Pz.kpfw. III tanks

---

49 NARA US, rg. 242, t. 314, r. 197, f. 001250.

Table 13 Availability of tanks in the panzer divisions of Army Detachment Kempf's III Panzer Corps on 5 July and between 9 and 21 July 1943[1]

Date, time	6th Panzer Division								7th Panzer Division									19th Panzer Division								505 Separate Heavy Panzer Battalion
	Pz-II	Pz-III 50mm L42	Pz-III 50mm L60	Pz-III 75mm	Pz-IV L43/L48	Command/ Flamethrower	Total		Pz-II/Command	Pz-III 50mm L42	Pz-III 50mm L60	Pz-III 75mm	Pz-IV L24	Pz-IV L43/L48	Total			Pz-III 50mm L42	Pz-III 50mm L60	Pz-III 75mm	Pz-IV L24/ Command	Pz-IV L43/L48	Total		
5.7 morning	13	52	24	12	28	-/13	106		12	62			38					38			38		81[2]		33
9.7 morning	7	0	24	12	14	3/10	70		4/3	0	16	1	3	12	39			2	5	4	1/1	23	36		33
10.7 morning	–	–	12	1	7	2/?	22/?		7/6	?	21	4	1	17	49/?			1	3	3	2/1	3	13		14
11.7 morning	2	2	11	?	6	3/7	24/?		0/4	0	19	5	1	25	54			1	6	5	2/2	0	16		23
12.7 morning	No reports								0/3	0	24	2	1	9	39			0	7	4	0/1	3	15		?
13.7 (0500)	In service, 12 tanks of all marks and modifications								0/3	0	28	0	1	9	41			1	15	0	1/1	7	25		?
14.7 (0500)	0	0	9	?	3	2/?	14/?		0/2	0	11	0	1	10	24			2	13	0	3/1	9	28		?
14.7																									6
15.7 (0500)	0	0	7	?	6	2/?	16/?		0/2	0	11	?	?	10	23/?			2	13	0	3/1	9	28		9
16.7 (0500)	0	0	2	?	2	?/?	4/?		0/1	3	10	?	?	9	23/?			0	16	0	1/2	6	25		8
17.7 (0500)	0	0	5	?	3	2/?	10/?		No data available in the source									3	9	0	1/2	5	20		13
18.7 (0500)	0	0	8	?	4	2/?	15/?											13							
19.7 (0500)	0	0	18	?	4	4+1 T-34	27/?											14							
20.7 (0500)	0	0	7	?	5	4/?	16/?											15							
21.7 (0500)	0	0	8	?	4	4/?	16/?											4							

Notes
1 Zetterling, N. and Frankson, A., Kursk 1943: A statistical analysis (London, Portland: FRANK CASS, 2000), pp. 188, 189, 190.
2 In addition to the listed tanks, the 19th Panzer Division had 3 Pz-I and 2 Pz-II.

also confirm this. If after eight days of fighting, 18 of the original 24 Pz.kpfw. III tanks were still operational (I'll assume that these were tanks that had been knocked out back on 5-8 July), then the reason for such small irreparable losses suggests itself – they weren't irreparably destroyed by artillery, because in this stage of the battle the crews were striving primarily to slow the enemy offensive, firing at the enemy tank's running gear, and paying little regard to how dependably they had neutralized the combat machine. I'll acknowledge that everything I've said with respect to the losses of the Pz.kpfw. III and IV tanks in III Panzer Corps may not seem very convincing, but I've introduced these ideas to the readers' judgement as a possibility, which flows out of these available facts and figures.

As concerns the reasons for such high operational losses in armor in Breith's panzer corps, they aren't hard to plumb. In the first place, and this is one of the main reasons, the enemy didn't use his forte in the fighting on 9 July – strong airstrikes out in front of the attacking *panzerkampfgruppe*. The enemy's weak air support in this area to a significant extent helped the Soviet side conserve its artillery. At the same time, attacking aircraft were its main enemy, since the level of losses from bombings was as a rule higher than from artillery or tank fire. A barrage of its positions only by heavy mortars was nearly as effective as an airstrike, especially if the batteries were standing in exposed firing positions.

In the second place, Westhofen's Panzer Regiment 27 and von Oppeln-Bronikowski's Panzer Regiment 11 were weaker than at the start of Operation Citadel, and they were trying to break through a line of defense that had been prepared in an anti-tank respect, which was being covered by anti-tank guns, heavy artillery and tanks. Moreover, both before the battle and during it, the Soviet anti-tank defenses were supplemented by the actions of the "tank hunting" groups of combat engineers, which deployed additional mines behind the tanks on the designated directions of the panzer wedges' attacks. The commander of the panzer company of the 19th Panzer Division's Panzer Regiment 27 who'd been captured in Dal'niaia Igumenka later acknowledged under interrogation, "Our losses in tanks are enormous, primarily from your mine fields. We didn't anticipate that the Russians could place so many mines. The tankers are operating timidly because of the minefields, and this is restraining our offensive to a significant extent."[50]

The documents of our combat units that were defending in this area confirm the fact that the crews of the German panzers and StuGs were operating indecisively even in the depth of the Soviet defenses. For example, the account of the 47th Separate Guards Breakthrough Heavy Tank Regiment stated, "… in the fighting for Dal'niaia Igumenka, Khokhlovo and Kiselevo the enemy conducted the offensive fumblingly, conducting thorough prior reconnaissance, and didn't throw large groups of tanks into the battle against the anti-tank defenses."[51]

In the third place, divisional artillery regiments, destroyer anti-tank artillery regiments with 76mm anti-tank guns, and tanks comprised the bulwark of the defense in this area. Moreover, on the axis of advance of the *kampfgruppen*, units moved up (both to the forward edge and to the knots of resistance in the woods on Hill 217.1, Dal'niaia Igumenka and Postnikov) that were equipped primarily with tanks that had an average caliber of 57mm and 76mm (T-34 and Mk-IV Churchill tanks), while the artillery crews had anti-tank guns and field artillery with a caliber of 76mm and greater, even howitzers. In addition, the howitzer crews played a key role in sealing several panzer breakthroughs in the infantry positions. Even rifle companies that were armed with 45mm anti-tank guns actively took part in the fighting to repel the German panzer attacks. Their crews, like the anti-tank riflemen, made a definite contribution to the overall job of holding the defenses, but played an auxiliary role in the struggle with enemy armor.

---

50   TsAMO RF, f. 203, op. 2845, d. 227, l. 11.
51   TsAMO RF, f. 2 gv. tk, op. 1, d. 24, l. 205.

Finally, the German *panzerkampfgruppen* launched attacks on villages that had been prepared according to the scheme of fortified regions. So here once again it is necessary to recall General of the Army N.F. Vatutin, who not only proposed this idea, but also made a great personal contribution to implementing it.

Nevertheless, it must be recognized that despite the failure to meet the day's objectives and the high losses of armor, by the end of 9 July Breith's subordinate divisions still managed to turn the situation to their favor. Having seized two tactically significant centers of resistance and having destroyed the main Soviet artillery forces in this area (primarily the girding 197th Guards Artillery Regiment and the 114th Guards Separate Destroyer Anti-tank Artillery Regiment), they took full control of the initiative and forced S.G. Goriachev (with the agreement of the Voronezh Front headquarters) to initiate the withdrawal not only the 81st Guards and 92nd Guards Rifle Divisions to new lines of defense on the night of 9-10 July, but also the 375th Rifle Division.

In the first three days of fighting, the 35th Guards Rifle Corps headquarters, like in general the majority of the corps commands of the Voronezh Front, didn't show its best side. This was for its staff the first experience of combat work. Moreover, the formation was not simply holding a quiet sector of the front, but had to operate on the axis of the main attack of an enemy panzer corps, albeit one already weakened by combat. Unfortunately, at the most stressful moments, its officers were unable to get even the gathering, verification and transmission of operational information in the necessary amounts to the army up and running smoothly. From the moment that the main forces of III Panzer Corps went on the attack on 9 July, the corps command didn't have complete control over the situation in its sectors, not to mention any consistency and precision in command and control over the troops, nor did it know in detail how the operational situation was developing. As already noted, the corps commander himself was having a negative effect on it with his irresponsible approach to carrying out his direct responsibilities. Even by day's end, S.G. Goriachev had no contact with the 81st Guards Rifle Division, nor any reliable information on how things were going in the sector of Morozov's division and on the right flank of Trunin's division.

When fighting to repel the attack by superior enemy forces, command over the troops was executed primarily by I.K. Morozov and P.D. Govorunenko in person from the divisions' forward observation posts and regimental command posts. As concerns Colonel V.F. Trunin, then his role as a division commander in this fighting and his influence on its outcome are still unclear. The documents revealed in the TsAMO RF show that a lot of just and unjust accusations were lodged against him, which today are difficult to weigh. One thing is clear – he wasn't ready to command such a major combat formation as a division, and the Front leadership, when appointing him as a division commander, should have realized this. It also should be noted that V.F. Trunin at that moment differed little from the majority of senior officers who took command of divisions on the Voronezh Front in the spring of 1943. His superiors must have taken notice of his personal drive, and his absence of any passion for alchohol, which was a widely distributed flaw among the command staff. This doesn't mean that he was an absolute tee-totaller, but during a battle he was always sober and he never processed tons of grain and sugar designated to feed the troops into moonshine, like for example the commander of his neighboring division Colonel I.G. Russkikh did. I assume that if Trunin's 92nd Guards Rifle Division hadn't fallen into the meat grinder at Melikhovo on 7 July, but had instead been smoothly introduced into battle on a secondary direction, Colonel Trunin might have been added to the list of heroes, rather than be removed from his post already on 14 July 1943 with the harsh admonition of "twice allowing the division's flight from the field of battle." I've happened to come across no few such examples of this type. However, I repeat, this is just my speculation.

In the documents of both the Voronezh Front and the 69th Army for the period of the Battle of Kursk, kept in the files of the TsAMO RF, Lieutenant General S.G. Goriachev[52] is also presented not in the most favorable light: he is depicted as a man with little initiative, who worked in fits and starts ("lackadaisically"). Despite adequate experience in command of a corps, he was slow to get the work of his headquarters up and running properly. Explaining the enemy's success in one sector or another, the general was inclined to exaggerate the enemy's strength. For example, when briefing the army headquarters on the results of the fighting on 9 July, Goriachev indicated that up to 350 tanks were operating opposite his corps' front in the Chernaia Poliana – Dal'niaia Igumenka – Melikhovo area, even though at this time there were only 201 armored vehicles in the entire III Panzer Corps. Knowing this corps commander's trait, the commander of the 69th Army Kriuchenkin was forced to verify the information in Goriachev's reports. Understandably, given such an attitude toward work and responsibility on the part of its leader, there was little point counting on quality combat work from the corps. Located in Korocha,[53] the Voronezh Front's chief of staff Lieutenant General S.P. Ivanov, tired of the corps commander's foot dragging and "sleights of hand" when his troops were holding an important axis, reported about this to N.F. Vatutin on the morning of 10 July: "Goriachev works without sufficient energy, the army commander is always goading him; only by the morning [of 10 July] did he establish contact with all of his divisions, and prior to this matters were disgraceful and his two reports that were received by us, after checking them through the division commanders, proved to be at variance with the facts."[54] The Front Commander-in-Chief ordered to give an admonition to the corps commander: "Warn Goriachev that he'd better fundamentally improve his work and command over the forces entrusted to him."[55]

However, as later events show, this didn't have any effect on Goriachev. Two days later, inflicting heavy losses to the defenders, Breith's III Panzer Corps would roll through (in the literal sense of

---

52 Goriachev, Sergei Georgievich, Lieutenant General (24.04.1943) was born in St. Petersburg on 20 September 1893 and after four years of schooling worked on a railroad. In 1916-1918 he served in the Imperial Army, ending the war in the rank of chief warrant officer. Goriachev joined the Red Army in 1919 and took part in the Soviet campaign against Poland. In 1927 Goriachev completed the "Shot" courses. Until the end of the 1930s he served in the infantry and advanced through all the levels of a career combat commander, and on 04.05.1939 was appointed as the commander of the Belorussian Military District's 50th Rifle Division. In this post he took part in the annexation of the western regions of Belorussia. On 29.11.1939 he was transferred to the post of the commander of the 5th Rifle Division (of the 16th Special Rifle Corps), which was located in Lithuania, but already on 29.04.1941 he became commandant of the Kovno Fortified District. The war found him in this post. From 28.06.1941 he served as the commander of the 23rd Division, which was fighting in the Baltics as part of the 11th and 27th Armies, near Polotsk and on the Northwestern Front. On 21.08.1941 as an officer who was familiar with the system of fortified districts, he was transferred to take command of the Valdai Fortified District. However, already on 06.09.1941 Goriachev became the commander of the 256th Rifle Division. He took part in the counteroffensive near Moscow with this division. For the liberation of Kalinin he was awarded the Order of the Red Banner. On 17.03.1942 Goriachev took command of the 185th Rifle Division, but on 02.05.1942 he was directed into the short-term courses at the Voroshilov Military Academy. Upon returning to the active forces, he formed the 7th Rifle Corps of the Volga Military District, with which he was sent to Stalingrad on 17.09.1942, where the corps became part of the 64th Army, which was fighting in the southern portion of the city. After the fighting ended on the Volga, he was awarded the Order of the Red Banner. In April 1943 the 35th Guards Rifle Corps was formed on the basis of the 7th Rifle Corps and Goriachev would command it until the end of the war. For his participation in the Battle of Kursk, on 27.08.1943 Goriachev was deemed worthy of the Order of Suvorov, 2nd Class. He was discharged into the reserve on 02.08.1958 and took up residence in Kiev.
53 The headquarters of the 69th Army was in Korocha.
54 TsAMO RF, f. 203, op. 2843, d. 461, l. 56.
55 TsAMO RF, f. 203, op. 2843, d. 461, l. 56obr.

the words) the entire second belt of the 69th Army's defenses in the sector of the 35th Guards Rifle Corps and penetrate to its rear defensive belt, while only Colonel V.F. Trunin would be made the scapegoat for this.

So that the reader can picture what information the leadership of the 69th Army and the Voronezh Front possessed about the situation of affairs on the Korocha direction by the end of the day and how they planned to build a defense against Army Detachment Kempf's assault wedge (III Panzer Corps), I'll give an excerpt from the transcripts of N.F. Vatutin's discussions with V.D. Kriuchenkin and S.P. Ivanov at 2240 on 9 July:

> **V.D. Kriuchenkin:** I've just received fresh information. The enemy with up to 200 tanks attacked from the direction of Razumnoe, Belovskaia and the woods north of Belovskaia, and had up to two infantry regiments operating together with the tanks. As a result of the attack, the enemy took Staryi Gorod and the "Main Fruit and Vegetable" State Farm; units of the 81st Guards and 92nd Guards Rifle Division fell back to the line: Northern Donets, Petropavlovka, Khokhlovo. I've taken steps to stop and take up a defense of Belomestnoe, Petropavlovka, Khokhlovo, Hill 211.8 and on the southern outskirts of Shliakhovoe.
>
> **N.F. Vatutin:** What does the enemy have on the rest of the front and how do you assess the enemy's strength and intentions? What steps are you taking? Report.
>
> **V.D. Kriuchenkin:** I will reply: opposite the front of the 183rd Rifle Division are units of the SS *Das Reich* and *Totenkopf* Divisions with a total of 200-250 tanks, while the 19th and 7th Panzer Divisions and units of the 168th Infantry Division are in front of the 35th Guards Rifle Corps. There is information that a fresh division, the 330th Infantry Division has come up with around 250 tanks. The 168th Infantry Division and two regiments of the 330th Infantry Division are fully taking part in the battle, launching their main attack: Melikhovo, Dal'niaia Igumenka, Staryi Gorod, Chernaia Poliana.
>
> The enemy is launching an attack [from] Belgorod [toward] Korocha. My conclusion is that the enemy will continue to attack to the north, rolling up combat positions, thereby freeing his hands for an offensive toward Oboian'.
>
> **S.P. Ivanov** at the device: I am reporting that I managed to have a talk with Comrade Goriachev over the telephone. For me it is clear that Goriachev had no contact at all with the 81st Guards Rifle Division, and it is possible that the events in this sector have been exaggerated, or perhaps even worse – the 250 enemy tanks about which he reported have have already crushed the 81st Guards Rifle Division. Thus it is necessary to believe that the sector from the direction of Staryi Gorod to the northeast is simply open and a new front has to be built here. Their 96th Separate Tank Brigade today has only 36 tanks.[56]

The cited excerpt from the transcript plainly demonstrates that the Soviet generals were pulling the wool over each other's eyes with poppycock about hundreds of German panzers that were supposedly storming their lines, and then working out grandiose plans to destroy them. For example, S.G. Goriachev reported to his immediate superior V.D. Kriuchenkin on the evening of 9 July that 350 enemy tanks were operating against his 35th Guards Rifle Corps. The army commander, naturally, didn't believe this (and he himself was guilty of similar fables), and ordered his chief of staff to re-check the information. Yes, even the Front's chief of staff, dissatisfied with the corps commander, also demanded that this information be verified. Without waiting for updated information from the army commander, guessing that 350 tanks after almost a week of

---

56 TsAMO RF, f. 203, op. 2843, d. 461, ll. 92-94.

fighting was too much, he reduced them to 250 and reported this opinion to his own immediate superior N.F. Vatutin.

Where were they finding these murky figures regarding the number of enemy tanks? As for the 35th Guards Rifle corps commander everything was clear: he extracted the information about 200 tanks in the Chernaia Poliana – Shishino sector from the interrogation of a prisoner, a grenadier of the 7th Company of the 168th Infantry Division's Infantry Regiment 442 who was captured in Blizhniaia Igumenka on 9 July at 1400 (the frightened soldier blurted out everything he knew, and things that he could not have known in principle), while his reconnaissance and intelligence had rather accurately counted up 150 German tanks in the Postnikov – Melikhovo sector. As concerns the 69th Army commander, then here things are even simpler – General Kriuchenkin came up with his figure by guesstimate. In order to dispel the readers' doubts, I'll discuss the metamorphosis of that same 330th Infantry Division in Kriuchenkin's report, which incidentally at the time was part of Army Group Center's Third Panzer Army.[57] This information that this division had appeared in the sector of the 7th Guards Army was first obtained from a grenadier of the 320th Infantry Division who was captured on 8 July in the sector of the 24th Guards Rifle Corps (or who voluntarily came across the lines as the prisoner maintained). The prisoner asserted that "… units of the 330th Infantry Division on the night of 7-8 July replaced the 320th Infantry Division's Infantry Regiments 587 and 585 in the Rzhavets – Bezliudovka sector."[58] This was a new division, which hadn't previously been identified on the Voronezh Front. Thus intelligence at every level of command (including that of the Front, the summaries of which were signed by S.P. Ivanov personally, and which V.D. Kriuchenkin was supposed to read) regarded this information with caution, considering it unreliable until a prisoner of this division was captured. I will note that subsequently no one took the information about this German infantry division seriously. The fact this information hadn't been verified didn't trouble the commander of the 69th Army, and he personally reported it to his superior N.F. Vatutin, while moreover adding that this infantry division had up to 250 tanks!

When all these nuances become known, the impression is created that in the transcript cited above, we're not talking about the report of an army commander – a man with prominent authority who was responsible for the lives of tens of thousands of men – to his direct superior at a very difficult moment of the battle, but a conversation among senior residents in a home situation. Such discussions are so densely strewn with all types of speculation, conjectures and unsubstantiated assertions, and the events at the front as laid out by generals are so distant from reality that it is impossible to read them without astonishment. Unfortunately, this goes not only for the 69th Army commander.

So that it doesn't seem to the reader that I am prejudiced against the commanders of the Voronezh Front and I'm deliberately pointing out uncharacteristic details about their conduct and character in minute particulars, I'll note that many of the generals of the Red Army to one or another degree engaged in open lying and spinning in order to create a positive image of themselves in the eyes of superiors at the expense of the overall cause. Moreover they sinned in large and small ways, showing no fear of Stalin or the NKVD. As an illustration of this, I'll cite Message No.30137 that was prepared by the General Staff and personally signed by the Supreme Commander-in-Chief at 0335 on 9 July 1943. It was addressed to the Commander-in-Chief of the Red Army's Air Force Colonel General A.A. Novikov and to the Commander-in-Chief of the PVO TS [Anti-aircraft defense of the Country's Territory][59] Lieutenant General M.S. Gromadin:

---

57 TsAMO RF, f. 500, op. 12451, d. 79, l. 3.
58 TsAMO RF, f. 203, op. 2843, d. 452, l. 70.
59 That how it was stated in the document, but according to other information, on 29.06.1943 he

After repulsing a raid on 2.6. by German aircraft on Kursk, reports arrived in the General Staff about the number of aircraft shot down and number of pilots and aircrew members captured: From the Commander-in-Chief of the Western Front that 50 enemy aircraft had been shot down by the Front's means and 76 enemy aircraft shot down by the anti-aircraft guns of the PVO TS, and from Lieutenant General Gromadin that 86 enemy aircraft had been shot down by the anti-aircraft guns of the PVO TS.

In addition, on 3.6 Lieutenant General Gromadin reported the capture of 42 German pilots and aircrew members, while the chief of staff of the Voronezh – Borisoglebsk Anti-Aircraft Divisional Area Colonel Gavrilov reported that 61 German pilots and aircrews were captured. A re-checking of the reports established that a total of 123 German aircraft were shot down, but only 5 German pilots and aircrew members were captured, 4 of them on the Voronezh Front in the vicinity of Oboian'.

Thus, the reports on the number of German aircraft shot down were generally correct [Author's note: Nonsense, they added an extra 92 aircraft alone to the total score!], while the reports about the German aircrew members that were captured turned in by Lieutenant General Gromadin and Colonel Gavrilov were unverified and didn't correspond with the facts [the extra 92 aircraft is taken as something normal, but the exaggeration by 99 men is bad].

I am calling the attention of the Lieutenant General, commander in chief of the PVO TS to the poorly organized monitoring and verification of the reports received by him.

I am formally rebuking the chief of staff of the Voronezh-Belogrebsk Anti-aircraft Divisional Area Colonel Gavrilov for giving false information.

I am limiting the charges with respect to Comrade Gavrilov to this only because I am taking into account his preceding excellent work record.

Announce this order to all the Front chiefs of staff and the commanders and chiefs of staff of the air armies, as well as the commanders and chiefs of staff of the zones and areas of the country's anti-aircraft defense.[60]

Possibly, it might seem to someone that I.V. Stalin treated liars too leniently. However, one should compare the influence of the unverified information on the number of pilots and aircrews taken prisoner with the reports on the attack by a German panzer grouping, the strength of which was exaggerated exponentially. In addition, it is necessary to take into account the scale of the calamity, because after all I'll repeat that such false information was given at every level of the army's command structure, and if everyone who submitted it was removed from their post or something similar, then who would be left to fight? The Commander-in-Chief of the Voronezh Front was in a similar situation.

As concerns the commander of the 69th Army, as was noted in his qualification documents, Kriuchenkin wasn't distinguished by a "broad operational outlook"; to put it gently, he struggled to carry out his duties. Here is what the deputy chief of the NKVD Special Department of the Stalingrad Front V.M. Kosopalov wrote in an internal memo to the Security Commissar V.S. Abakumov[61] about the style of work of the commander of the 4th Army Major General V.D. Kriuchenkin in August – September 1942:

---

was occupying the post of Commander-in-Chief of the Western Front's Anti-aircraft Defenses (*Komandarmy:Voennyi biograficheskii slovar'* [*Army commanders: Military biographical dictionary*] (Moscow-Zhukovskii: Kuchkovo pole, 2005), p. 342.

60 I am citing a copy of the document from the files of Colonel General D. Volkogonov in the US Library of Congress. The original copy is in the CPSU Central Committee Archives, Case No.24, 1943, ll. 158, 159.
61 At the time, V.S. Abakumov was the Deputy People's Commissar of the USSR NKVD.

The headquarters of the army and the acting units are not engaged in the continuous reconnaissance of the enemy's strength, as a result of which they don't know which enemy units are facing them, the number of enemy units, and don't know what the enemy's objectives are; in general, they have no information at all about the enemy. A statement made by commander Kriuchenkin on 25 August in the presence of the deputy commander-in-chief of the Stalingrad Front Major General Kovalenko is characteristic: "The devil only knows what the enemy is doing over there, nothing is known for certain: what the enemy has up his sleeve, what the 62nd Army is doing, where our units that are in contact with the enemy are located. ... The enemy might outflank us on the left; in general, the situation is unclear."[62]

It is possible that the year that had passed since that time had increased General Kriuchenkin's professional skills. However, if the date of the memo given above wasn't known, then it can be fully accepted as a report on the 69th Army commander's style of work in July 1943. Unfortunately, practically nothing had changed. In the course of the Kursk defensive operation, "his overseer Lieutenant General S.P. Ivanov" had to redo and correct a lot for the 69th Army commander. An interesting detail: N.F. Vatutin had previous knowledge of V.D. Kriuchenkin and his style of work and level of training, so he regarded Kriuchenkin's reports suspiciously and relied more on S.P. Ivanov. Nevertheless, the General of the Army Vatutin submitted approximately the same information to Moscow, and used it in his conversations with his subordinate army commanders. Why? In the first place, it was obtained through official channels from a high-posted general. In the second place, information like this was advantageous when dealing with the *Stavka*. The circle was unbroken – the cover stories conceived by the generals began to affect their real decisions and actions. This would become particularly obvious in the course of III Panzer Corps' fighting with the troops of the 69th Army between 11 and 14 July.[63]

The day of 9 July 1943 became the day of crisis for the enemy's offensive on the southern face of the Kursk salient. Over five days of constant, bloody fighting, von Manstein's two assault groupings had been unable to achieve any decisive successes. The heavy losses suffered over this time and the absence of perceptible results in the sector of Army Detachment Kempf forced the leadership of Army Group South to agree with Hoth's proposal and to pivot both of his panzer corps to the east toward Prokhorovka, in order to resolve an important, but now tactical success – the liquidation of the threat to its flanks. On the significantly extended left flank of the Fourth Panzer Army, the divisions of the 6th Guards Army and 1st Tank Army were defending with great stubbornness, backed by Lieutenant General K.S. Moskalenko's fresh 40th Army, while on the right flank Lieutenant General P.A. Rotmistrov's 5th Guards Tank Army was already beginning to assemble in the Prokhorovka area. The threat of the encirclement of Army Group South's assault wedge was beginning to grow. H. Hoth saw the danger, and thus proposed to break through to Prokhorovka with the forces of II SS Panzer Corps and III Panzer Corps in the next day or two and to encircle the 69th Army, and thereby create the conditions for repulsing the attack by the Russian mobile reserves that were approaching Prokhorovka. The plan was a good one and no less important, conformed to the thoughts of E. von Manstein himself, who was skeptical of the possibility to break through to Kursk, but believed that the "operation to destroy Russian forces" that had been set in motion by his forces in the course of this offensive still hadn't run out of steam.

However, there was still one important question which was difficult for H. Hoth to answer: "Was there enough strength to realize this scheme, when both panzer corps had already suffered

---

62 Central Archive of the FSB, f. 14, op. 4, d. 222, l. 69.
63 This situation has been laid out in detail in my book *Zasekrechennaia Kurskaia bitva* [*Classified Battle of Kursk*] (Moscow: Iauza, 2008), pp. 692-694.

substantial losses, especially III Panzer Corps?" The preliminary calculations that the Russians would hurl significant reserves against Army Detachment Kempf and it would be able to crush them in the first few days of the offensive had already been proven unjustified. Army Detachment Kempf's three panzer divisions and three infantry divisions had diverted onto themselves only six rifle divisions (92nd Guards, 94th Guards, 107th, 111th, 270th and 305th Rifle Divisions), one destroyer anti-tank artillery brigade and one tank brigade out of Voronezh Front's operational reserves. Moreover, up until 9 July inclusively, only three of these divisions had taken a direct part in the fighting. This of course wasn't insignificant, but not a single Soviet tank corps had been transferred here, yet the main point was that the diversion of these forces to the Korocha direction hadn't affected the strength of the Front's defenses on the whole; just as before, it was sufficiently tough and hadn't collapsed under the strong blows of the panzer attacks like a house of cards, which had been part of the calculations from the outset when preparing for Operation Citadel.

Indeed, at the same time Korps Raus had been forced to go over to the defensive already on 7 July because of the high losses and the lack of prospects for a continued offensive, while the losses of III Panzer Corps in armored fighting vehicles by the morning of 10 July had exceeded 70%; it now had 116 panzers and 11 assault guns operational, or 31.2% of those it had available at the start of the offensive. Meanwhile the Russians were fighting just as fanatically, tying down all of Kempf's available forces. Despite the powerful attack undertaken on 9 July against the area north of Belgorod, the breakthrough corridor that the 6th and 19th Panzer Divisions had entered on 8 July had expanded somewhat, but not so much as to allow the continuation of the offensive to the north and northeast without concerns for the flanks of Army Detachment Kempf. Indeed, the losses in these two panzer divisions over the day of fighting on 9 July had been frightening: von Hünersdorff had only 22 panzers still serviceable; Schmidt had only 13, and the Tiger battalion had only 14. At this moment Breith's strongest panzer regiment was the 7th Panzer Division's Panzer Regiment 25, which had 49 operational panzers. However, von Funck's division was covering III Panzer Corps' right flank, containing the Russian pressure in the Miasoedovo – "Batratskaia Dacha" State Farm area, and only on the evening of 9 July had the 198th Infantry Division begun the process to take over this sector. Therefore the road to Prokhorovka, which Hoth was already planning to seize, was still lengthy and difficult for Kempf's forces.

Nevertheless the intelligence analysts of both Fourth Panzer Army and the Ninth Army, and those of their subordinate assault groups, were reporting that the Russians were continuing to assemble mobile reserves on the flanks. I will cite an excerpt from a message sent by Army Group South's intelligence chief at 2100 to Army Group Center in accordance with an exchange of operational information:

> The expected offensive on the flanks of Army Detachment Kempf didn't take place. The supposed operational reserves here, it seems, aren't being confirmed. The 3rd Guards Tank Corps and 1st Guards Cavalry Corps thought to be here, together with the 2nd Guards and 5th Guards Tank Corps are working in a single radio network (presumably of the 3rd Tank Army). According to this it can be assumed that the 3rd Tank Army is located in front of the Fourth Panzer Army.
>
> The 6th Panzer Division is attacking through Melikhovo to the north and is engaged in combat with enemy tanks, which are attacking out of Sabynino to the southeast [units of the 96th Separate Tank Brigade and 47th Guards Breakthrough Heavy Tank Regiment]. The 19th Panzer Division seized Dal'niaia Igumenka and from there went on the offensive to the west and south with the aim of clearing the enemy from the area north of Belgorod.
>
> The enemy is behaving inactively in front of the II SS Panzer Corps' eastern flank. Attacking, the SS Panzer Corps with its right flank reached the area 2 kilometers southeast of Hill 244.8. The *Grossdeutschland* Division attacked out of the area north of the settlement of Verkhopen'e

to the west. Significant enemy forces were attacking along both sides of Dmitrievka against the western flank of the Fourth Panzer Army and managed to make a penetration. Here the 161st and 309th Rifle Divisions were revealed [the 40th Army's reserve], as well as a tank regiment. No changes opposite the LII Army Corps.

The general impression is such that enemy resistance as a result of losses yesterday has become weaker.[64]

Counterattacks were one of the most dangerous steps taken by the Soviet command for the enemy in the course of the defensive operation, since usually significant forces were called upon in order to conduct them, primarily tanks. Therefore it wasn't hard to understand that the revelation of a concentration of Soviet mobile forces was an important indicator that the Soviet side was preparing to undertake active operations. The command of the Fourth Panzer Army didn't fully share the point of view held by Army Detachment Kempf's officers on the matter of the withdrawal of operational reserves from the flanks of Kempf's forces. It believed that the Russians had decided to send them to the south. In the summary of the events of 9 July, the headquarters of Hoth's Fourth Panzer Army stated:

> Situational assessment: The panzer clash south of the Psel River is continuing even today. The 2nd Guards Tank Corps on the eastern bank of the Lipovyi Donets River undertook numerous attacks against the Fourth Panzer Army's eastern flank and <u>seemingly intends to join battle with Army Detachment Kempf's vanguard</u>. Units of the 5th Guards Tank Corps and 2nd Tank Corps, which were resisting south of Prokhorovka, can be considered shattered, since they've ceased combat actions in this area.[65]

In fact by this time Major General A.G. Kravchenko's 5th Guards Tank Corps had suffered serious losses in materiel, and even by the standards of the Red Army, its condition was assessed as "badly battered". However, the adversary was hasty in writing off the Guardsmen; Major General A.F. Popov's 2nd Tank Corps, which on the morning of 10 July possessed more than 100 combat machines, hadn't been shattered. As for Colonel A.S. Burdeinyi's 2nd Guards Tank Corps, this formation could have been used effectively in order to reinforce the defenses in front of III Panzer Corps. However, N.F. Vatutin decided differently. By the end of 9 July he had already reached the decision to launch a frontal attack and sent a request to I.V. Stalin to grant his approval for it. N.F. Vatutin was planning to launch the strongest possible attack against the enemy on 12 July, and thus sought to conserve his tank corps. However, his subordinate force's strength was melting away with each passing day, and he couldn't count upon the enemy to call off his offensive. The 69th Army had essentially just entered the fighting, so it had had a sufficient amount of infantry, but it was catastrophically short of anti-tank artillery, especially after the heavy fighting on 9 July. By the morning of 10 July V.D. Kriuchenkin had gathered just two incomplete anti-tank artillery regiments numbering a total of 27 anti-tank guns and had sent them to the Shliakhovoe area. Thus, the positioning of the 2nd Guards Tank Corps on this axis would have been very fortunate, especially since its main forces didn't engage in any large-scale fighting on 11 July.

N.F. Vatutin was a focused man, and having given himself an objective, he exerted every effort to achieve it, but at the same time didn't always take into account the rapidly changing situation or the enemy's possibilities. An obvious example of this is the case of the 2nd Guards "Tatsinskaia"

---

64 TsAMO RF, f. 500, op. 12462, d. 790, ll. 25, 26.
65 Emphasis the author's. Stadler S., *Die offensive gegen Kursk 1943 II SS – Panzerkorps als Stoskeil im Grosskampf* (NATION EUROPA Verlag GmbH. Coburg, 1998), p. 82.

Tank Corps. When preparing for the 12 July frontal counterattack (on 10 and 11 July) he believed that it was extremely important to conserve its strength, but also for it to resolve two major problems: to hold the line of deployment set for the main forces of the 5th Guards Tank Army near Prokhorovka and to prevent a breakthrough of the forward edge of the 35th Guards Rifle Corps by the forces of the III Panzer Corps, and in the extreme case to contain the Germans within the system of the second belt of defensive fortifications, which meant within the "corridor" between the Northern Donets and Razumnaia Rivers. In the current situation, this task could have been carried out either by a portion of the 5th Guards Tank Army that was approaching from out of the strategic reserve or by the 2nd Guards Tank Corps on the flanks of the 69th Army (in order to create a mobile defense, first on the left flank on 10 July, and then a counterattack on the right flank on 11 July). However, the 5th Guards Tank Army was the *Stavka*'s reserve, which meant it was necessary to secure Moscow's approval in order to commit it into combat here, while the Voronezh Front Commander-in-Chief himself forbade the use of the 2nd Guards Tank Corps in Goriachev's sector. He realized his mistake only on the evening of 11 July, when the SS troops arrived on the outskirts of Prokhorovka. Unfortunately, the great hopes that the Soviet side placed both on the counterattack and on the 2nd Guards Tank Corps' participation in it were unjustified. Within just two days, Burdeinyi's and Rotmistrov's Guardsmen would nevertheless have to join combat with Breith's III Panzer Corps, but now in more difficult conditions, when the German panzers would break through to the rear defensive belt and emerge directly on the flanks of the 69th Army's 48th Rifle Corps. These dramatic events unfolded a bit later, although they were directly connected with what happened on 9 July in the sector of the 35th Guards Rifle Corps and with the decisions taken by the Soviet side on the night of 9-10 July.

The capture of Dal'niaia Igumenka and Postnikov didn't expand the breakthrough corridor by much; the depth of the penetration was 3 to 3.5 kilometers, while its breadth was 9-10 kilometers. Even so, Breith was hoping that a fissure had formed in the Russian defenses north of Belgorod, and had hope for the offensive's success into the depth of the 69th Army's lines (to the north across the Northern Donets) and to the northeast between the basins of the Donets and Razumnaia Rivers. Only one, but substantial factor was troubling him – the low combat strength of the panzer regiments of all three panzer divisions. So he decided to have a talk with Kempf about this and to request Luftwaffe support for the forthcoming attack. On 10 July Breith was proposing to destroy the remaining knots of resistance held by the units of the 81st Guards and 92nd Guards Rifle Divisions, which meant to take the Andreevskie – Staryi Gorod – Chernaia Poliana – Shishino area and to reach the channel of the Northern Donets River, in order there to ready the divisions for a further offensive. The plan's details and the tasks for each division were laid out in the order, which his corps headquarters transmitted to the divisions between 0115 and 0245 10 July. Let's turn to this document:

1. The enemy had moved up a Guards rifle corps with three fresh divisions to the front and flanks. Units of the 81st Guards and 92nd Guards Rifle Divisions are concentrated east of Belgorod.
2. III Panzer Corps on the morning of 10.7 destroys enemy forces assembled in the Blizhniaia Igumenka – Staryi Gorod area, and proceeds with a further breakthrough to the north.
3. Tasks:
    a) 7th Panzer Division hands over the "Batratskaia Dacha" State Farm – corner of the woods 2 kilometers south of Miasoedovo to the commander of the 198th Infantry Division before noon on 10.7; after the completion of the rotation on 10.7, in the afternoon it breaks through to the woods northeast of Miasoedovo, in order subsequently to launch an attack to the north.

b) 6th Panzer Division in cooperation with the 168th Infantry Division mops up the Shishino – (excl.) Staryi Gorod – (excl.) Blizhniaia Igumenka – sector of woods 2 kilometers north of Andreevskie area. Then the division must assemble in the Melikhovo area. Given the possibility, destroy the enemy units located between Kalinin and Komintern, west of the Razumnaia River. The passage at Komintern must be screened. After eliminating the pocket (the line of the 81st Guards Rifle Division), the subordinated units of the 19th Panzer Division are to return to their command.

c) 19th Panzer Division 10.7 at 0200 passes command in the Blizhniaia Igumenka sector to the 168th Infantry Division. By this moment of time, Infantry Regiment 442 and 4 and 5/Artillery Regiment 248 return to their division. Panzergrenadier Regiment 73 and the panzer reconnaissance battalion early on the morning of 10.7 are replaced by units of the 168th Infantry Division. The division assembles in the area of Dal'niaia Igumenka and given the opportunity still on 10.7 takes Sabynino and the bridge across the Northern Donets.

d) 168th Infantry Division on 10.7 at 0200 takes control of the Blizhniaia Igumenka sector. Regarding the subordination of the units, see Point "b".

e) Early on 10.7 the division mops up Blizhniaia Igumenka, Staryi Gorod and the eastern bank of the Donets as far as Shishino. West of the Donets given weaker enemy resistance it advances to the north in order to seal the enemy forces defending the "Day of Harvest" collective farm and prevent a breakout. Free up the units of the 19th Panzer Division positioned there on the opposite bank early on the morning of 10.7.

4. Units:
   a) After the mopping-up of the pocket before midday on 10.7, the headquarters of Artillery Regiment 62, Heavy Artillery Battalion 87, Headquarters Battery 19 and 76, II/Artillery Regiment 71 and II/Artillery Regiment 62 (the battalion remains subordinate to the 7th Panzer Division until the evening of 10.7) become subordinate to Artkommando 3. Artkommando 3 with the forces of the corps artillery supports the further advance of the 6th and 19th Panzer Divisions out of the Melikhovo – Dal'niaia Igumenka area to the north, primarily by countering the enemy artillery fire on the Korocha – Belgorod road in the direction of Zaiach'e; the requested neutralization of enemy flanking fire from the wooded hills north of Petropavlovka is being confirmed.
   b) Nebelwerfer Regiment 54 (minus III Battalion) on the morning of 10.7 is subordinate to 7th Panzer Division and transfers to the 19th Panzer Division after reaching Sevriukovo. The commander must appear at the command post of the 7th Panzer Division.
   c) The headquarters and 1st Company of the Separate Heavy Panzer Battalion 503 is at the corps' disposal in the area of Hill 215.5.
   d) The commander of the corps engineers prepares to lay down a bridge across the Donets at Sabynino with the delivery of the necessary means.
5. Corps' command post – 300 meters west of the southern exit from Iastrebovo.[66]

Kempf was in a hard spot; von Manstein was extremely alarmed by the slow pace of his army detachment's advance and had expressed his dissatisfaction to him more than once. Thus, as is obvious from the document cited above, he was persistently prodding his subordinates. In the

---

66 NARA US, rg. 242, t. 314, r. 197, f. 001263.

course of the day of 10 July alone, III Panzer Corps was supposed to create the conditions for the breakthrough of the second army-level belt of defenses being held by the 69th Army on 11 July. For this it was necessary to take complete possession of the fortified area near Belgorod, which had cost it enormous efforts and losses; replace the 7th Panzer Division and gather the 19th Panzer Division and 168th Infantry Division; break through to the Northern Donets in the Shishino – Khokhlovo – Kiselevo sector and if possible seize Sabynino; and finally rupture the adjacent flanks of the 15th Guards and 94th Guards Rifle Divisions, and through the breach at their boundaries, reach the woods east of Miasoedovo. The number of tasks for a corps, which after five days of the heaviest fighting was in woeful condition, was plainly excessive. At dawn on 10 July there were a total of 109 serviceable panzers and assault guns in Breith's panzer corps (just 29% of those it had available on 5 July). The most numerous was the 7th Panzer Division's Panzer Regiment 25, which had 49 panzers, of which 6 were command tanks. The rest of the panzer formations had fewer machines: 6th Panzer Division had 22 panzers, 19th Panzer Division had 13 (including 1 command tank), Separate Panzer Battalion 503 had 14 Pz.kpwf. VI, and StuG Battalion 228 had 11 StuGs. Their panzergrenadier regiments had also suffered heavy casualties, especially in Schmidt's 19th Panzer Division. In the daily summary for 10 July, his headquarters reported that Panzergrenadier Regiment 73 had only around 300 active bayonets, and his Panzergrenadier Regiment 74 had approximately 100 more.[67]

What steps did the Soviet command take, after S.G. Goriachev had reported late on the evening of 9 July to the Front's chief of staff that the Germans had seemingly driven the 81st Guards and 92nd Guards Rifle Divisions from their positions near Belgorod and that they were hastily retreating to the north? This wasn't exactly the case, so thereby the corps commander himself (intentionally or not) was calling upon the Front's leadership to reach a decision about withdrawing both divisions across the Northern Donets River.

For the Soviet side, with each passing day the enemy's plans were becoming clearer: Army Detachment Kempf was not only striving to divert the Front's forces from the Oboian' direction onto itself, but also probably had the task, advancing in parallel with the II SS Panzer Corps, to penetrate as deeply as possible into the Front's defenses and close the ring around the 69th Army's forces. There was no doubt that the headquarters of both German groupings that were attacking on the Oboian' and Korocha directions were striving to coordinate their actions. In this situation it was important to wear down and deplete both enemy panzer corps as much as possible and prevent them from joining up. This difficult task was given to V.D. Kriuchenkin on the evening of 9 July as a priority, while M.S. Shumilov, even though his army was now playing a secondary role, also received an order to increase the pressure on Army Detachment Kempf's right flank.

The command of Army Group South was aware of the fact that its offensive plans were no secret to the Soviet side. Thus it was anticipating additional steps to strengthen the defensive lines and to reinforce the troops both on the Korocha direction in general and opposite Korps Raus in particular. Let's return to the transcript of the conversations between N.F. Vatutin and V.D. Kriuchenkin on the evening of 9 July:

> **N.F. Vatutin**: What do you plan to do then in order to block the enemy's offensive to the north? Keep in mind that the enemy may simultaneously launch an attack on the Vasil'evka – Belenikhino front or the Belenikhino – Teterevino front. How do you plan to parry this attack?
> **Kriuchenkin**: I believe it necessary to occupy a line strongly with a front to the southeast on the line: 375th Rifle Division – Shopino, Belomestnoe; 35th Guards Rifle Corps

---

67 NARA US, rg. 242, t. 314, r. 197, f. 001307.

with the 92nd Guards, 93rd Guards and 81st Guards Rifle Divisions – Petropavlovka, Khokhlovo, Kiselevo, Shliakhovo, Mazikino, having assigned to it the 305th Rifle Division and 96th Separate Tank Brigade; and coordinating their actions with Comrade Shumilov. Simultaneously I request that you leave the 2nd Guards Tank Corps and 2nd Tank Corps under my command; then I will shift Burdeinyi's tank corps to the Gostishchevo, Sabynino, Krivtsovo area in readiness for actions to the south, while I will assemble Popov's tank corps in the Pravorot', Malo-Iablonovo area in readiness to operate to the west and southwest.

N.F. Vatutin: Comrade Kriuchenkin, from the morning of 10 July it is necessary to expect a continuation of the enemy's offensive out of the Dal'niaia Igumenka, Melikhovo area to the north.

On the other hand, judging from the assembly of enemy tanks on the Vasil'evka – Belenikhino front, it is necessary to expect an offensive by this grouping to the east, and with part of its strength to the southeast, with the intention to encircle units of your army. Thus, your main assignment, upon which you must concentrate your attention, is to prevent the enemy's further advance to the north from the Dal'niaia Igumenka, Melikhovo area. On the other hand keep a very strong defense on the Vasil'evka – Belenikhino front, and on this front you must absolutely repulse the enemy's attack, in no case allowing an enemy breakthrough. This task must be resolved in the following manner.

First. On the Petropavlovka – Shliakhovoe – Sheino – Ushakovo front, organize in the most thorough manner a defense and an especially strong anti-tank defense with the use of artificial obstacles and intense fire from anti-tank artillery. Here you have enough troops. You need to use them skillfully. Ensure as well the stubbornness and resilience of the troops on the defense, while liquidating those disgraces that happened with Goriachev. Make capable use of the 96th Separate Tank Brigade.

Second. It is necessary to ensure an absolutely firm defense on the right flank, in the Vasil'evka – Belenikhino – Teterevino sector. For this I am subordinating the 2nd and 2nd Guards Tank Corps to you on 10 July. The 2nd Tank Corps must be left in its place as it is, otherwise you'll have no one to stand on the defense here. At the same time ensure, in case of necessity, the maneuverability of the 2nd Tank Corps, at least with part of its strength. Pull the 2nd Guards Tank Corps out of the first line of defense, having replaced it with rifle units, and after this assemble it in the Belenikhino – Leski – Shakhovo – Dal'nii Dolzhik area.

Considering that the 5th Guards Tank Corps' tanks have moved out toward a different position, for the meantime the commander of the 5th Guards Tank Corps is ordered to leave his motorized infantry on the sector they occupy. However, you must in the future replace this motorized infantry. Organize the replacement of the 2nd Guards Tank Corps in the most careful manner and keep an eye on it, so that the system of defense isn't disrupted on the forward edge and in the depth. Keep in mind that Kravchenko's tanks have already left, so you must hurry. The 10th Destroyer Brigade[68] will come up to the Korocha area on the morning of 10 July, which will remain here in my reserve. On both of the aforementioned directions, our aircraft will be supporting you well. Do you or Comrade Ivanov have any questions or suggestions? (2347 9.7.43)

V.D. Kriuchenkin: All is clear, I will get to work.

---

68 This is a mistaken reference to the 10th Separate Destroyer Anti-tank Artillery Brigade, which the *Stavka* transferred to N.F. Vatutin from the Southwestern Front.

Ivanov at the device: The following solution suggests itself, and I request your instructions on this matter.

First. Move the 183rd Rifle Division's 227th Rifle Regiment, which is positioned on the Volobyevka – Sazhnoe – Krivtsovo line, to the right flank under the control of the commander of the 183rd Rifle Division and position it on the Vinogradovka – Ivanovka – Leski line, thereby strengthening the sector from which Kravchenko departed.

Second. The 89th Guards Rifle Division, which is occupying a defense on the Kalinin – (excl.) Petropavlovka line should bend back its defensive front along the Northern Donets River. Remove the 375th Rifle Division from the western bank of the Lipovyi Donets River and position it on the Petropavlovka – Khokhlovo – Shliakhovoe line. Assemble the 81st Guards Rifle Division somewhere in the Krivtsovo, Novo-Oskochnoe, Kazach'e area and subsequently "implant" it on the previously prepared line held by the 305th Rifle Division.

Third. Shouldn't Burdenyi be left in the Shakhovo, Sazhnoe, Krivtsovo, Ryndinka area, and all of his equipment and resources, which have been prepared to the south on the Gostishchevo – Sabynino line be left untouched?

Fourth. Unquestionably, it isn't normal that communications haven't been established with all the nearby units here; on this matter Kriuchenkin and his headquarters must show greater resourcefulness.

N.F. Vatutin: Comrade Ivanov, leave Burdeinyi there, where I've indicated. As for the other questions, it is good and proper that you look into them together with Comrade Kriuchenkin. Accurately indicate where whatever units are located, and report Kriuchenkin's decision to me with your comprehensive suggestions. Have in view that the troops have time to settle into the line by morning. Let Kriuchenkin issue the high-priority order right away. Everyone get to work, if there are no questions. (0015).

Ivanov: There are no questions, right away we'll once again clarify and look into everything and will make a decision.

N.F. Vatutin: Be healthy, I wish you success.[69]

Before continuing to lay out the course of events, I want to bring the reader's attention to the Front Commander-in-Chief's phrase about the capable use of the 96th Separate Tank Brigade. It testifies to the fact that he knew well that in order to block the enemy grouping that had penetrated the boundary between the 6th Guards and 7th Guards Armies that armor would be the backbone of the defense, and tanks were very necessary. He also knew that the line of Kriuchenkin's army in this area hadn't been prepared similarly everywhere with respect to fortifications and obstacles, and most importantly, there was little anti-tank artillery here, so only a major tank (or anti-tank) formation could quickly stabilize the situation. However, from the analysis of the revealed documents the impression forms that the idea of a "major attack" at Prokhorovka, which at this time fully pre-occupied N.F. Vatutin, and as it seemed gave hope for a sharp turning point in the situation and the complete regaining of the initiative, prevented him from fully realizing the level of danger lurking within the situation in the 35th Guards Rifle Corps' sector on the evening of 9 July. Therefore he didn't add adequate measures for addressing it to the formulation of a plan, and turned over the solution of the problems of defending this direction to S.P. Ivanov and V.D. Kriuchenkin, who didn't possess sufficient anti-tank means in order to block firmly the path into the depth of the 69th Army's defenses for Breith's panzer corps.

---

69 TsAMO RF, f. 203, op. 2843, d. 461, ll. 92-94.

The Commander-in-Chief of the Voronezh Front General of the Army N.F. Vatutin on a trip to the front; July 1943. (RGAKFD)

The chief of staff of the Voronezh Front Lieutenant General S.P. Ivanov discusses a document with the Front's Military Council member Lieutenant General N.S. Khrushchev (on the left) outside the Front headquarters; area of Rzhava Station, July 1943. (Photography by F. Kislova, RGAKFD)

The commander of the 35th Guards Rifle Corps Lieutenant General S.G. Goriachev; a July 1943 photograph. (RGAKFD)

The commander of the 92nd Guards Rifle Division Colonel V.F. Trunin; a 1945 photograph. (TsAMO RF)

The commander of the 94th Guards Rifle Division Colonel I.G. Russkikh; a June 1943 photograph. (TsAMO RF)

A truck carrying infantry of one of Army Detachment Kempf's infantry divisions moving through the captured village of Sevriukovo; July 1943. (A captured photograph, RGAKFD)

The commander of the 6th Panzer Division Major General W. von Hünersdorff (in a Sd.Kfz.250/3 halftrack) listens to a report from the commander of II/Panzergrenadier Regiment 114 Captain Necknauer in the vicinity of Belinskaia in the valley of the Razumniaia River; 7 July 1943. (Bundesarchiv, Bild 101I-022-2923-29A, photo: Kipper)

Near Belinskaia, the commander of the 6th Panzer Division Major General W. von Hünersdorff (second from the left) together with a group of his officers observing the fighting in the area of the villages of Sevriukovo and Miasoedovo; 7 July 1943. (Bundesarchiv, Bild 101I-022-2923-19A, photo: Kipper)

Colonel A. Schulz, the commander of the 6th Panzer Division's Panzer Regiment 11 (in the foreground on the left) issues an order to a subordinate commander in the Sevriukovo area. In the background is a Pz.Kpf. III command tank. 7 July 1943. (Bundesarchiv, Bild 101I-022-2922-13, photo: Kipper)

Colonel A. Schulz, commander of Panzer Regiment 11 at a crossing site on the Razumniaia River. In front of him is the armor skirt of a passing tank. 8 July 1943. (Bundesarchiv, Bild 101I-022-2922-09, photo: Kipper)

German trucks of one of Army Detachment Kemp's divisions move toward the front across a rebuilt bridge in the village of Iastrebovo. In the foreground is the remnants of the previous bridge that had been blown up by retreating troops of Shumilov's army. 8 July 1943. (Bundesarchiv, Bild 101I-022-2925-15, photo: Wolff/Altvater)

An RSO prime mover tows a 50mm anti-tank gun. On the left front of the vehicle is the tactical insignia of the 168th Infantry Division, painted in white. Area of Iastrebovo, 8 July 1943. (Bundesarchiv, Bild 101I-022-2925-06, photo: Wolff/Altvater)

A panzerjäger unit of one of Army Detachment Kempf's divisions rolls past a destroyed Soviet prime mover that had been towing a 76mm ZiS-3 M1939 divisional gun. Area of Sevriukovo, July 1943. (Bundesarchiv, Bild 101I-022-2924-15, photo: Kipper)

Mark II Matilda tanks of one of the 201st Separate Tank Brigade's companies moving out with tank riders aboard toward the front.

A group of soldiers and officers of the 201st Separate Tank Brigade aboard a captured German Sd.Kfz.8 Daimler Benz heavy half-tracked prime mover moving toward the area of combat operations in the 7th Guards Army's sector on 9 July 1943. (Files of the "Stalingradskaia bitva" State Historical Park Museum)

The commander of the 201st Separate Tank Brigade's 201st Motorized Rifle Battalion Captain D.A. Dziubin; a 10 July 1943 photograph. (TsAMO RF)

Junior Lieutenant V.A. Vlasov, an anti-tank rifle platoon commander of the 201st Separate Tank Brigade's 201st Motorized Rifle Battalion; a 10 July 1943 photograph. (TsAMO RF)

Senior Lieutenant A.S. Kuskin's bloody Party card. He was the commander of the 201st Separate Tank Brigade's 296th Tank Battalion.

A German aerial reconnaissance photograph of the two major villages in the interfluvial area between the Northern Donets and Razumniaia Rivers, Melekhovo and Shliakhovoe, through which Army Detachment Kempf's assault wedge broke through toward Prokhorovka; a July 1943 photograph. (NARA US)

The commander of the 69th Army Lieutenant General Kriuchenkin (on the right) and his chief of operations Colonel D.N. Surzhits at a forward observation post on the Korocha axis; a July 1943 photograph. (Photograph by I. Ozersky, RGAKFD)

The commander of a rifle company (second from left in foreground, with binoculars) observes the start of an attack. To his right, the crew of a 50mm mortar prepares to support the attack; a July 1943 photograph. (RGAKFD)

A dug-in Red Army soldier awaits the completion of an attack by Il-2 ground assault aircraft against German positions; Voronezh Front, July 1943. (RGAKFD)

Elements of the 69th Army taking up new positions in the basin of the Northern Donets River; Korocha axis, July 1943. (RGAKFD)

Medic V. Kameneva of one of the Guards rifle divisions dragging a wounded soldier from the battlefield; Voronezh Front, July 1943. (Given the cleanliness of her uniform and face, this is likely a staged photograph). (RGAKFD)

The commander of the 305th Rifle Division Colonel A.F. Vasil'ev (in the center) discusses recent combat results with a group of subordinate commanders at his forward outpost in Shliakhovoe. Judging from the smiles, the news was good. Korocha axis, July 1943. (RGAKFD

An armored group of one of the panzer divisions of Breith's III Panzer Corps waits for the start of an attack. On the left in the background are Pz.Kpfw. VI Tigers, and on the right are Pz.Kpfw. III and IV tanks. In the foreground is the gun barrel of another Tiger tank. Sector of the 69th Army, July 1943. (Bundesarchiv, Bild 101I-022-2950-15A, photo: Kipper)

A column of prisoners, consisting of soldiers and officers of the 69th Army captured by troops of Army Detachment Kempf, moving to the rear. July 1943. (Bundesarchiv, Bild 101I-022-2925-05, photo: Wolff/Altvater)

Army Detachment Kempf's chief of staff Major General H. Speidel (on the left) meets with the commander of the 198th Infantry Division's Grenadier Regiment 305 Major J. Grassman in the area east of Belgorod. July 1943. (Bundesarchiv, Bild 101I-022-2933-05, photo: Heinz Mittelstaedt)

The commander of the 6th Panzer Division Major General W. von Hünersdorff (in the center) in a Sd.Kfz.250/3 halftrack in the area of Rzhavets. July 1943. (Bundesarchiv, Bild 101I-022-2912-13A, photograph: Horster)

The commander of the 111th Rifle Division Colonel M.A. Bushin; a 1945 photograph. (TsAMO RF)

A tank-riding company of the 7th Guards Army's 27th Guards Tank Brigade waits for the signal of attack; 12 July 1943. (RGAKFD)

Soldiers of the 73rd Guards Rifle Division in combat in the area of the "Batratskaia Dacha" State Farm; a July 1943 photograph. (Author's personal archive)

Senior Lieutenant G.M. Kozhar (third from left and in the inset), the commander of the 1st Tank Company of the 201st Separate Tank Brigade's 295th Tank Battalion, stands together with his crew in front of his Matilda tank; a May 1943 photograph. (TsAMO RF)

The burial ceremony for fallen soldiers and commanders of the 7th Guards Army's 73rd Guards Rifle Division; July 1943. (Author's personal archive)

What decisions were made in the headquarters of the 69th Army after the conversation with the Front Commander-in-Chief? S.P. Ivanov had roughed out a future defensive plan on the Korocha direction already during the conversation, but he was relying on shaky information that hadn't been checked adequately, so he was unable to implement it in the form in which he had reported to N.F. Vatutin. At 0145 10 July, the commander of the 35th Guards Rifle Corps signed off on a coded telegram to the commander of the 375th Rifle Division:

1. The enemy in strength of up to 250 tanks around 1430 attacked units of the 81st Guards Rifle Division in the Blizhniaia Igumenka, Postnikov area and by the end of the day took Dal'niaia Igumenka and Shishino.
2. I am ordering: immediately fall back in the direction of Kiselevo, and by 0600 10.7.1943 occupy a defense: Kiselevo along the southwestern slopes of Hill 211.5, (excl.) Machine Tractor Station, west of Shliakhovoe, Sabynino. Assignment: Prevent a breakthrough by enemy infantry and tanks to the northwest. Command post of the division headquarters – wooded area 2 kilometers southeast of Sabynino.

    Prior to your arrival, remnants of the 92nd Guards Rifle Division and 96th Separate Tank Brigade are defending the indicated line.[70]

The 375th Rifle Division chief of operations Lieutenant Colonel N.V. Zhulanov didn't receive this order until dawn at 0435, when it was already quite dangerous to move such a large mass of troops at the front without reliable cover, but as is known, orders aren't for discussion, so division commander Govorunenko was forced to get his troops moving whatever the current conditions. At this moment the 35th Guards Rifle Corps' third and final division began to retreat from the Belgorod area to new lines of defense. Colonel S.Kh. Ainutdinov, the chief of the 375th Rifle Division's Political Department, recalled:

Unfortunately, we received this order after a lengthy delay, and in combat a delay in carrying out an order not only for several hours, but even for several minutes threatens mortal danger. Executing the corps commander's order, the division began to move out to the new line in daylight hours, in full view of the enemy. Our withdrawal from the "pocket" was supported by our own fire and the combat actions of the 89th Guards Rifle Division's units. We still hadn't had time to reach the Sabynino area, when a new order came in: to take up a defense on the Zhimolostnoe – Malo-Iablonovo – Shakhovo line and prevent a breakthrough by enemy tanks to the east.[71]

In fact the division's withdrawal did begin at an unsuitable time, within the enemy's eyesight. However, this wasn't connected with a delay in receiving the order (from the moment of signing it until it was delivered only a little more than two and a half hours had passed); rather, the difficult operational situation required this. The 92nd Guards Rifle Division had in fact been shattered, and a significant number of its men had been widely scattered, the bulk of its artillery regiment's guns had been destroyed, and the command and control over it had lapsed. V.F. Trunin and his headquarters retreated into the woods southwest of Verkhnii Ol'shanets, and at dawn he sent out officers in order to rally the men coming out the closing pocket near Belgorod. Thus it was exceptionally important not only to cover the line that had been left abandoned by the 92nd Guards Rifle Division, but also considering that enemy panzer divisions were operating here, simultaneously strengthen the boundary between the 89th Guards Rifle Division, which was extended

---

70 TsAMO RF, f. 375, op. 1, d. 23, l. 39.
71 Ainutdinov, *U oboianskogo shosse*, p. 88.

along the right bank of the Northern Donets River (railroad hut northwest of the woods, west of Kiselevo, village of Kiselevo, southern outskirts of Sabynino), and the 305th Rifle Division, which was holding the (excl.) Sabynino – Shliakhovoe – Sheino line, with a full-strength division. As for S.Kh. Ainutdinov's assertion that "we had only started to arrive, when we were immediately removed", this is nothing more than the author's far-fetched explanation. In its headquarters' Operational Summary No.0244 at 1500, the situation was described differently:

1. 375th Rifle Division has taken up a line: northeastern outskirts of Kiselevo, Point 211.5, (excl.) Shliakhovoe Machine Tractor Station.
2. 1243rd Rifle Regiment screened by rearguard units left its former line and has occupied a new one: northeastern outskirts of Kiselevo, Point 211.5, and is busy setting up firing positions.
3. 1245th Rifle Regiment has taken up the line: (excl.) Point 211.5, (excl.) Shliakhovoe Machine Tractor Station. It is setting up positions.
4. 1241st Rifle Regiment is in the second echelon in the Sabynino area. Up until 0600 it was engaged in fighting with enemy infantry on its previous line. At 0420 after an artillery preparation the enemy with the forces of up to two battalions of infantry went on the attack out of the area of the Invalid Home and the woods west of Pokrovka in the direction of Hill 193.6 and attacked our units three times; having lost up to 100 men, the enemy retreated. [This counterattack was launched by the 168th Infantry Division's Infantry Regiment 417 after reconnaissance had detected the withdrawal to the north of the 81st Guards Rifle Division's columns]. The regiment's losses were 7 killed and 3 wounded.[72]

The 375th Rifle Division continued remain in this new sector for almost another 24 hours. In the course of 10 July its first echelon units actively took part in fighting off attacks by the 19th Panzer Division toward Kiselevo. In fact it left for the right bank of the Northern Donets into the reserve of the 69th Army only at 0600 on 11 July, without turning over its defenses to the rallied units of the 92nd Guards Rifle Division and the left-flank regiment of the 89th Guards Rifle Division.

In exchange for the shattered 81st Guards Rifle Division and 92nd Guards Rifle Division, S.G. Goriachev was given two fresh divisions: the 305th and 107th Rifle Divisions. The former was supposed to occupy the Sabynino, Shliakhovoe, Orlov ravine, Mazikino, Sheino, Ushakovo sector. On its right flank, the 92nd Guards Rifle Division's 280th Guards Rifle Regiment was continuing to stand on defense together with remnants of the 96th Separate Tank Brigade. The 107th Rifle Division received the order to take up positions in the second echelon along the line: Novo-Oskochnoe; Verkhnii Ol'shanets; "Komintern" Association of Collective Farms; woods, 1 kilometer northeast of Shukhovtsovo; lake, 1.5 kilometers northeast of Shukhovtsovo; Hill 221.0; southern outskirts of Gremiachii; Popovka.

In addition, the 35th Guards Rifle Corps received as reinforcements an impressive grouping of artillery and mortar units: the 122nd and 130th Anti-tank Rifle Battalions; the 114th Guards Destroyer Anti-tank Artillery Regiment; the 1667th Destroyer Anti-tank Artillery Regiment; the 263rd and 290th Mortar Regiments; the 16th and 315th Guards Mortar Regiments; and the 27th and 31st Separate Anti-tank Artillery Brigades. However, all of these units had already taken part in the fighting and had suffered painful losses; several of them were in fact no longer combat-capable. For example, the 114th Guards Destroyer Anti-tank Artillery Regiment had only four

---

72 TsAMO RF, f. 375 sd, op. 1, d. 36, l. 243.

76mm anti-tank guns still serviceable, and two more damaged guns that had been sent back to the regimental repair shop,[73] while only the 1st Battalion of the 290th Mortar Regiment was in firing positions in the sector of the 81st Guards Rifle Division with 18 120mm mortars (the 2nd Battalion had been withdrawn into the reserve of the 7th Guards Army's commander because of the loss of all of its mortars).[74] In the two regiments (the third hadn't yet been equipped) of the 31st Separate Anti-tank Artillery Brigade, which was covering the boundary between the 94th Guards and 15th Guards Rifle Divisions, there remained only 17 45mm anti-tank guns and 11 76mm anti-tank guns.

Now let's turn to one more transcript of conversations conducted by N.F. Vatutin on the evening of 9 July, so we might hear from M.S. Shumilov's "own lips" how he was now assessing the situation of affairs in the sector of his 7th Guards Army and the results of the combat work of his troops:

> **Stepnoi [Shumilov]** at the device: Greetings! I am reporting: at 0800 the enemy with up to a division of infantry and tanks began to attack out of Sevriukovo and Iastrebovo in the direction of the "Solov'ev" collective farm and "Batratskaia Dacha" State Farm; suffering losses from artillery, they were pinned down on Hill 160.8, and then with a second salvo from two battalions of rocket launchers, they rolled back to Sevriukovo and Iastrebovo.

At 1630 up to a regiment of infantry and 40 tanks and self-propelled guns attacked Gremiachii. The attack was repulsed. Two fully operational self-propelled guns were captured. No more attacks were conducted anywhere on the army's front; [the Germans] conducted a regrouping and at 1830 an enemy assembly of up to two battalions of infantry and 30 tanks was spotted in the wooded area west of Point 207.9 (on the 1:10000 scale map), up to a regiment of infantry and 50 tanks on the eastern fringe of the woods south of Hill 216.1 and up to 50 tanks on the eastern outskirts of Krutoi Log. In the area of Point 176.0 there is up to a regiment of infantry with tanks in the patch of woods west of Gremiachii, and a large aggregation of motorized transport in the Razumnoe, Krutoi Log, Maslova Pristan' area.

Units of the army conducted a regrouping in connection with the new boundary lines. The 15th Guards Rifle Division with two regiments is moving into and occupying: Point 206.9, "Solov'ev" collective farm, "Batratskaia Dacha" State Farm, one regiment of which is replacing the regiment of the 94th Guards Rifle Division in the Point 206.9, "Solov'ev" collective farm area, and will be the occupying Krasnyi Mai, (excl.) Nekliudovo area; the army's remaining units are still occupying their previous positions, with the exception of the 270th Rifle Division, which is occupying the Nekliudovo, Pentsovo and Churaevo area, while its right flank is extended along the Koren' River as far as Nekliudovo.

I've ascertained the corps' composition … I request that you confirm it. In addition, I request that you approve the following: the 262nd Heavy Tank Regiment, 167th Separate Tank Regiment and 1438th Self-propelled Artillery Regiment have suffered losses and only have a handful of machines each, therefore I'm asking for the 8 tanks of the 262nd Heavy Tank Regiment, 4 self-propelled guns of the 167th Separate Tank Regiment, the 1438th Self-propelled Artillery Regiment and 6 T-34 from out of my reserve to be consolidated under control of the commander of the 262nd Heavy Tank Regiment, and to withdraw the headquarters and crews of the 167th Separate Tank and 1438th Self-propelled Artillery Regiment.

---

73   TsAMO RF, f. 10873, op. 8808ss, d. 4, l. 332.
74   TsAMO RF, f. 290 mp, op. 20928s, d. 6, l. 173.

> Third. I assess the enemy's actions today in the following way; the enemy, having conducted four days of stubborn fighting, having suffered losses and moreover having placed great strain on his tanks, is today bringing himself and his materiel back into order, so tomorrow I expect his active operations:
>
> 1. To the north against Goriachev.
> 2. Against the "Batratskaia Dacha" State Farm and to the south of there.
> 3. In the area of Gremiachii, "Poliana" State Farm.
>
> On the two latter directions the enemy has given itself the task to reach the Koren' River and dig in along the western bank of the Koren' River, thereby securing maneuver to the north.
>
> I request that you confirm my decision for tomorrow to continue to defend on the line occupied by the army, preventing the enemy from reaching the Koren' River.
>
> Over the present day of fighting, up to 2,000 enemy soldiers and officers have been killed, 23 tanks and 10 machine guns have been destroyed, and 5 aircraft shot down. Booty: 2 self-propelled guns, from which immediately after their capture, opened fire at the enemy.
>
> Among the prisoners are an officer and two NCOs who belong to the 8th Aviation Corps [Fliegerkorps VIII], who were seized in the following circumstances: They were driving from Khar'kov to Krutoi Log in an armored car, carrying air mail, but failing to find their unit in Krutoi Log, drove on further and fell into our ambush. The armored car was knocked out and they were captured. These prisoners are confirming the presence of six tank divisions opposite the army's front.
>
> **Vatutin**: Comrade Stepnoi, I am approving your proposals. Operate as you've decided and absolutely prepare active operations on 11 July. Report your ideas to me. Keep in mind that the enemy has concentrated major tank forces on Kriuchenkin's flank. I have great concerns for Kriuchenkin, so for tomorrow have your right flank very strong in order to help Kriuchenkin with heavy fire; if necessary, then with counterattacks and the maneuver of your anti-tank means.
>
> Closely tie the actions of your right flank with Kriuchenkin's left flank, and do not in any event allow the enemy to break through at your boundary with Kriuchenkin.[75]

In the above excerpt, two interesting episodes have been mentioned – the capture of the intact, operational self-propelled guns and the prisoners together with their mailbag. It is interesting that both of these events happened in the sector of the 73rd Guards Rifle Division. As its combat report states, at 1240 members of the training battalion, which was serving as the commander's reserve and was entrenched in the area of Hill 209.6, spotted a car (not an armored car) moving from Krutoi Log in the direction of Hill 191.2 and knocked it out. The 1st Lieutenant, Staff Sergeant and Senior Lance-Corporal that were riding in it attempted to hide, but were caught. Under preliminary interrogation they testified that they belonged to Flak Regiment 38 of Fliegerkorps VIII and had accidentally bumped into the Guardsmen's line – they had lost direction and become confused.[76] As for the two self-propelled guns, the information given by Shumilov can't be confirmed in the archives. Documents of the 7th Guards Army show that the sole enemy self-propelled gun captured by its troops was a "self-propelled gun on the chassis of a Pz-IV tank". Tankers of the 201st Separate Tank Brigade came across it on the battlefield on 17 July, and having repaired it, the German self-propelled gun became part of the brigade's inventory of armored vehicles.

---

75 TsAMO RF, f. 203, op. 2843, d. 461, l. 7.
76 TsAMO RF, f. 1212, op. 1, d. 28, l. 12.

By the morning of 10 July, in the first echelon of the 7th Guards Army (that extended for approximately 49 kilometers) were as before two of its own inherent corps consisting of six rifle divisions, which had a combined total of 38,779 soldiers and commanders. The 25th Guards Rifle Corps was holding the line: 15th Guards Rifle Division (47th Guards and 44th Guards Rifle Regiments) – Hill 206.9, (excl.) "Solov'ev" collective farm, (excl.) "Batratskaia Dacha" State Farm, Hill 209.6; the 78th and 73rd Guards Rifle Divisions – Nikol'skoe (78th Guards Rifle Division's 228th Guards Rifle Regiment), Hill 209.6, Korenskaia Dacha, 0.5 kilometers south of Gremiachii. The 24th Guards Rifle Corps: 1/793rd Rifle Regiment of the 213th Rifle Division – (excl.) "Poliana" State Farm, (excl.) Hill 202.9; the 72nd Guards Rifle Division, 27th Guards Tank Brigade and 2,3/793rd Rifle Regiment of the 213th Rifle Division – 1 kilometer northwest of Hill 187.0, 0.5 kilometers south of Rzhavets, (excl.) northern outskirts of Bezliudovka; 1, 3/586th Rifle Regiment of the 213th Rifle Division – western and southern outskirts of Bezliudovka, right bank of the Nezhegol River at Timovka; the 36th Guards Rifle Division – Timovka, Novaia Tabalzhanka, Gastishche-2, Prilipka, (excl.) Oktiabr'skoe.

The boundary line between the 25th Guards and 24th Guards Rifle Corps ran along the line: Repnoe (25th Guards Rifle Corps) – "Poliana" State Farm (25th Guards Rifle Corps) – Maslova Pristan' (25th Guards Rifle Corps), while the boundary between the 7th Guards Army and 69th Army ran along the line: Novoselovka, Arkad'evka, Miasoedovo (all belonging to the 35th Guards Rifle Corps), Iastrebovo.

According to M.S. Shumilov's Order No.00285/op, which was agreed upon with N.S. Vatutin in the course of the discussions on 9 July, both corps had the following combat roster of units:

25th Guards Rifle Corps: 15th Guards, 73rd Guards and 78th Guards Rifle Divisions, 201st Separate Tank Brigade, 30th Separate Destroyer Anti-tank Artillery Brigade, 1669th Destroyer Anti-tank Artillery Regiment, 1529th Heavy Self-propelled Artillery Regiment, 161st Cannon Artillery Regiment, 97th Guards Mortar Regiment, four battalions of anti-tank rifles and the 329th Engineer Battalion.

24th Guards Rifle Corps: 36th Guards, 72nd Guards Rifle Divisions and the 213th Rifle Division, 27th Guards Tank Brigade, 115th Guards Destroyer Anti-tank Artillery Regiment, 109th Guards Cannon Artillery Regiment, 265th Guards Cannon Artillery Regiment, 309th Guards Mortar Regiment, 131st and 132nd Anti-tank Rifle Battalions and the 176th Separate Maintenance and Repair Battalion. (See Table 14 for the combat and total strength of the 7th Guards Army on 10 July 1943.)

In addition to Safiulin's and Vasil'ev's two Guards rifle corps, Major General G.N. Terent'ev's 49th Rifle Corps (111th and 270th Rifle Divisions without means of reinforcement) was still operationally subordinate to the 7th Guards Army. It was occupying a defense in the army's second echelon, behind the 25th Guards Rifle Corps, along the eastern bank of the Korocha River in the sector: (excl.) Nekliudovo – Pentsevo – Charaevo-Shebekino, while the 50th Guards Rifle Regiment of the 15th Guards Rifle Division was on its right flank in the (excl.) Nekliudovo – Krasnyi Mai – (excl.) Novoselovka sector.

Now let's return to the events of 9 July in the sector of the 81st Guards Rifle Division and try to figure out who made the decision to withdraw from the Staryi Gorod – hamlet of the Machine Tractor Station – Andreevskie sector to a new line without the authorization of the Front Commander-in-Chief (about which N.F. Vatutin's conversations with V.D. Kriuchenkin and S.P. Ivanov on the evening of 9 July testifies), and how its units carried out this order. I will say right away that it is impossible today to give an unambiguous answer to these questions. Only one official document has been preserved – the commander of the 81st Guards Rifle Division's Order No.057, which explains who gave him the order to withdraw his division and two attached regiments beyond the Northern Donets River, and the reasons for this decision. Here is the complete text:

Table 14 Manpower and combat equipment of the 7th Guards Army as of 10 July 1943[1]

Formation and unit	Manpower					Total horses	Total number of rifles	PPSh and PPD submachine guns	Machine guns		Anti-aircraft	Mortars		Guns			76 mm divisional artillery[2]	76 mm regimental artillery[3]	45 mm	Anti-tank rifles	Vehicles	Tanks of all types	BM-13, BM-8 rocket launchers	37 mm/25 mm and 20 mm A-A guns	Armored cars
	Command staff	Junior commanders	Enlisted men	Total					Light	Heavy		120 mm	82 mm	50 mm	152 mm	122 mm									
									Rifle forces																
15 GRD	832	2444	5384	8660		995	3778	2408	420	138	5	27	85	14	–	12	27	12	47	252	153	–	–	–	–
36 GRD	864	2448	5122	8334		496	5500	2425	436	139	–	28	92	58	–	12	23	12	48	242	164	–	–	–	–
72 GRD	690	1132	4410	6232		790	2980	1581	138	39	–	14	30	15	–	6	23	6	20	104	89	–	–	–	–
73 GRD	694	1491	3800	5985		937	2215	1300	142	47	1	16	31	17	–	11	13	11	15	100	103	–	–	–	–
78 GRD	620	1248	3113	4981		704	2505	923	103	31	2	3	19	13	–	3	15	3	6	100	833	–	–	–	–
213 RD	782	2236	4469	7487		605	4072	2009	239	94	–	21	83	56	–	15	16	15	38	212	55	–	–	–	–
111 RD	692	1617	3404	5713		966	5074	2003	426	111	–	19	55	48	–	10	16	10	36	213	92	–	–	–	–
270 RD	780	1942	4769	7491		657	5215	2025	259	72	–	21	91	68	–	12	20	12	40	226	56	–	–	–	–
Total for Rifle forces	**5954**	**14558**	**35571**	**54983**		**6051**	**31339**	**14744**	**2163**	**671**	**8**	**149**	**486**	**289**	–	**81**	**153**	**81**	**250**	**1449**	**795**	–	–	–	–
									Tank forces																
27 GTB	203	520	460	1183		–	424	228	24	4	–	–	6	–	–	–	1	–	–	21	122	39/13	–	6/4	–
201 TB	217	395	477	1089		–	415	257	15	1	1	–	8	–	–	–	1	–	–	35	46	37/7	–	–	–
262 TR	58	121	32	206		15	36	34	–	–	1	–	–	–	–	–	–	–	–	–	32	6/3	–	–	–
167 TR	75	185	204	464		–	164	113	2	–	–	–	–	–	–	–	–	–	–	18	71	15	–	0/1	–
Separate Armored Train Bn	26	99	82	207		–	125	3	14	8	5	–	–	–	–	–	4	3	–	–	–	–	–	–	–
	21	85	68	174		–	73	40	26	8	5	–	–	–	–	–	6	3	–	–	–	–	–	–	–
Total for Tank forces	**595**	**1405**	**1323**	**3323**		–	**1237**	**675**	**81**	**21**	**11**	**14**	–	–	–	–	**12**	**6**	–	**74**	**271**	**97/23**	–	**0/5**	–
									Artillery forces																
1669 DATAR	46	103	92	241		–	–	48	10	–	–	–	–	–	–	–	20	–	–	10	26	–	–	–	–
1670 DATAR	48	109	315	472		–	241	48	10	–	–	–	–	–	–	–	8	–	–	10	18	–	–	–	–
265 GCAR	96	222	697	1015		–	635	69	3	–	–	–	–	–	14	–	–	–	–	18	29	–	–	–	–
162 GCAR	91	177	471	739		–	436	66	3	–	–	–	–	–	18	–	–	–	–	21	37	–	–	–	–
109 GCAR	98	224	628	950		–	501	159	13	–	1	–	–	–	18	–	–	–	–	18	87	–	–	–	–
114 GDATAR	50	166	231	447		–	299	52	8	–	–	–	–	–	–	–	20	–	–	12	33	–	–	–	–
115 GDATAR	52	153	270	475		3	206	69	–	–	3	–	–	–	–	–	–	–	–	–	34	–	–	–	–

THE FALL OF THE BELGOROD BASTION, 9-10 JULY 1943

Formation and unit	Manpower				Total horses	Total number of rifles	PPSh and PPD submachine guns	Machine guns			Mortars			Guns					Anti-tank rifles	Vehicles	Tanks of all types	BM-13, BM-8 rocket launchers	37 and 25mm/20 mm A-A guns	Armored cars
	Command staff	Junior commanders	Enlisted men	Total				Light	Heavy	Anti-aircraft	120 mm	82 mm	50 mm	152 mm	122 mm	76 mm divisional artillery[2]	76 mm regimental artillery[3]	45 mm						
12 CAR	101	240	729	1070	15	693	74	-	8	3	-	-	-	17	-	-	-	-	21	30	-	-	-	-
30 DATAB	60	75	231	366	-	180	164	10	-	-	-	-	-	-	-	-	-	-	-	25	-	-	-	-
290 AMtrR	63	190	393	646	-	415	73	-	-	-	13	-	-	-	-	-	-	-	-	38	-	-	-	-
1 SATR Bn	18	75	124	217	-	63	72	-	-	-	-	-	-	-	-	-	-	-	31	15	-	-	-	-
3 SATRBn	25	67	190	281	6	49	100	3	1	-	-	-	-	-	-	-	-	-	70	2	-	-	-	-
4 SATRBn	14	30	116	160	9	65	58	1	-	-	-	-	-	-	-	-	-	-	22	4	-	-	-	-
5 SATR Bn	26	79	155	260	3	82	100	-	-	-	-	-	-	-	-	-	-	-	71	1	-	-	-	-
Total for artillery	787	1910	4642	7339	51	3865	1152	61	9	7	13	-	-	67	-	48	-	-	304	379	-	-	-	-
Guards Mortar units																								
97 GMtrR	81	212	447	740	-	373	16	7	-	-	-	-	-	-	-	-	-	-	21	70	-	20	-	-
Anti-Aircraft units of the Supreme Command Reserve																								
670 A-AR, 5th A-AD	38	87	219	344	-	70	20	-	-	15	-	-	-	-	-	-	-	-	-	22	-	-	-	-
743 A-AR	26	108	270	414	-	54	13	-	-	13	-	-	-	-	-	-	-	-	-	35	-	-	-	-
1119 A-AR	39	99	232	370	-	69	22	-	-	16	-	-	-	-	-	-	-	-	-	24	-	-	-	-
1181 A-AR	39	69	217	325	-	60	22	-	-	14	-	-	-	-	-	-	-	-	-	23	-	-	-	-
162 GAA-AR	36	98	182	316	-	139	29	-	-	17	-	-	-	-	-	-	-	-	-	49	-	-	-	-
258 GAA-AR	41	115	219	375	-	114	41	-	-	36	-	-	-	-	-	-	-	-	-	33	-	-	-	-
Total for A-A units	229	576	1339	2144	-	506	147	-	-	101	-	-	-	-	-	-	-	-	-	186	-	-	-	-
Grand total for the 7th Guards Army	7646	18661	42222	68529	6102	37320	16764	2312	701	127	167	500	289	67	880	213	81	256	1850	1701	97/23	20	0/5	-

Notes
1 TsAMO RF, f. 203, op. 2843, d. 426, unnumbered page.
2 These were the famous ZIS-3 light artillery pieces, which also served as potent anti-tank guns.
3 These were the short-barreled 76mm guns for direct infantry support. At Kursk, these were likely primarily M1923 guns, though the documents don't specify.

The enemy by 1800 9.7.1943 reached Staryi Gorod along the road from Blizhniaia Igumenka, as well as from out of the area of the "Day of Harvest" collective farm and north of the Kreida railyard, as a result of which the 238th and 233rd Guards Rifle Regiments were cut off from the 235th Guards Rifle Regiment.

1. On the basis of an order from the 35th Guards Rifle Corps commander, with the aim of preserving combat capability, the division's units began to withdraw to the north and by the morning of 10 July had assembled in the northeastern portion of the woods lying 1.5 kilometers northwest of Khokhlovo. The 89th Guards Rifle Division is occupying a defense along the southern fringe of these woods.
2. Report to me on the arrival of the units at their place of assembly in a combat message.[77]

Unfortunately, on the document there is no time given when it was signed, only the date – "10.7.1943", which doesn't allow us to track the process of reaching the decision in detail. Judging from the document's contents, and also taking into consideration that a similar order regarding a change of lines was issued by the 35th Guards Rifle Corps commander to the neighboring 375th Rifle Division at 0145 on 10 July, it is possible to assume that Order No.057 was signed by him prior to 0200 10 July. However, a number of facts allow us to surmise that the document itself (which as we know carried no time) and the assertion that it was initiated personally by Lieutenant General S.G. Goriachev, appeared already after the withdrawal of the division from the Belgorod area had been completed, or more likely even after the end of the defensive phase of the Battle of Kursk. What facts support this conclusion?

First, the document's appearance gives the impression that the order was prepared not during a combat situation for transmission to the troops, but to be filed away and forgotten (because it was so crisply written and so clean). It was produced by a typewriter, on white paper, like all the operational summaries over this time period (even though the headquarters under the threat of capture had already changed location twice); signed only by the chief of staff Major B.Iu. Svetnik; and on it there are no indications that it was received or carried out. In contrast, several days later Morozov's division again wound up in encirclement in the Shakhovo area, and its units would have to emerge from the pocket at night under the pressure of superior enemy forces. However, the order for this was plainly prepared on the night of 14-15 July 1943 in its headquarters in Shakhovo, written out by hand, and on it is the precise time when the commander of the 48th Rifle Corps Major General Z.Z. Ragoznyi gave the order to the division commander to begin pulling out of the pocket. In addition, there are various margin notes and signatures testifying to the fact that the order was being carried out, and not being prepared for submission to an archive.

Second, in the account of the 35th Guards Rifle Corps it is precisely indicated that the division and its two attached regiments began to retreat to the north at 2200 9 July, which other sources confirm, but Order No.057 was dated 10 July. Who then took on the responsibility and issued the order for the division to retreat from the Belgorod area on 9 July? The following scenario is possible: the units that had been bled white began to abandon their positions under enemy pressure on their own accord and retreat toward Staryi Gorod. The division commander understood that the situation could no longer be salvaged and got in touch with the corps commander (possibly through a liaison officer). Having laid out the situation, he received approval to change lines and issued the order to the units that very day about a retreat to the northeast, while the chief of staff, who was located in a different place, formally enshrined this decision by the corps commander with an order to the division, and because of the absence of I.K. Morozov, signed it himself. This scenario is

---

77 TsAMO RF, f. 81 gv. sd, op. 1, d. 5, l. 290.

fully plausible, if not for the existence of one "but". Judging from S.P. Ivanov's report to the Front Commander-in-Chief around 2300 on 9 July, Goriachev had no contact with Morozov (although it might have stopped suddenly after issuing the order), and so he didn't know what was happening at that moment in the sector of the 81st Guards Rifle Division. Thus it isn't clear whether the corps commander even had the possibility to issue orders to the division to retreat. As a possible variant, I.K. Morozov and S.G. Goriachev may have previously agreed upon an approximate time and the circumstances for the division's withdrawal to a new line, but so far I haven't been able to find any documentary evidence of this.

Thirdly, in the 25th Guards Rifle Corps' combat diary for 9 July there is an entry that at 1500 the corps headquarters received a radio message from the headquarters of the 81st Guards Rifle Division about the enemy's launching of a decisive offensive simultaneously along the entire line of its defense. Moreover, in the history of this same corps, prepared by its headquarters and kept today in the TsAMO RF, there is the note: "In the course of 4-5 hours, the division [the 81st Guards Rifle Division] conducted heavy defensive fighting in semi-encirclement against superior enemy forces, fighting to repel their tank attacks. Indeed only that night [night of 9-10 July], having repulsed all the attacks, <u>at the order of the commander of the 7th Guards Army it retreated to the northeast into the sector of the 69th Army and became no longer subordinate to the corps</u> [Author's emphasis]." A document from the 7th Guards Army's Operations Department under the title "Description of the 7th Guards Army's combat operations in the defensive operation between 5.7.1943 and 25.7.1943" also testifies to this.[78] Relying on these sources it is possible to assume that even though the 81st Guards Rifle Division on the night of 8-9 July had formally become subordinate to the 35th Guards Rifle Corps, it maintained more stable communications only with the 25th Guards Rifle Corps and at a critical moment it was namely M.S. Shumilov who gave the order for it to retreat, even though it was no longer subordinate to him. Only later, based on the formal orders from the Front command about its transfer to the 35th Guards Rifle Corps, was the typewritten Order No.057 prepared by its headquarters on 10 July (for the record), in which S.G. Goriachev's role when making the decision about withdrawing the troops to a new line explicitly stated.

Judging from S.P. Ivanov's report to N.F. Vatutin on 10 July at 1115, S.G. Goriachev learned the details of what had happened in the 81st Guards Rifle Division's sector on the evening of 9 July, yet in his version it came out of the forming pocket only on the afternoon of 10 July. Here is an excerpt from this transcript: "… 81st Guards Rifle Division is assembling in Krivtsovo and to the north of there, in the area of the two lakes; according to preliminary information, only 30% of the division is present. Now contact has been made with division commander Morozov, who is being summoned by Goriachev, and upon receiving information, everything regarding this sector will be reported to you."[79]

It would seem everything is now clear, but not quite. The alternative that M.S. Shumilov ordered the retreat can also not be considered fully substantiated. The 25th Guards Rifle Corps' Operational Summary No.0125/op for 0400 on 10 July 1943, which was signed by the chief of staff Colonel A.A. Funtikov, stated:

> The 81st Guards Rifle Division with attached assets was engaged in defensive fighting on its current lines. At 2000, a half hour after the enemy launched an attack, communications over the radio became interrupted, and there's been no success in restoring it to the present time.

---

78 TsAMO RF, f. 5312, d. 268, l. 14.
79 TsAMO RF, f. 203, op. 2843, d. 461, l. 56.

The last message from Shishino about the attack launched by the enemy was transmitted by radio under submachine gun fire.[80]

How could the 7th Guards Army commander have issued the order, if the last message from the division was received by the headquarters of Safiulin's 25th Guards Rifle Corps, not by the 7th Guards Army headquarters, and then all communications with the division lapsed until the next morning?

Here again we can only speculate. Hence, following the quickly deteriorating situation near Belgorod, M.S. Shumilov realized that the 81st Guards Rifle Division could no longer hold its line, so earlier in the day when communications were still working he gave authorization to Morozov at a critical moment to act at his own discretion. Thus, later that day the division commander independently issued an order to retreat at 2200. At the same time, after midnight, somehow S.G. Goriachev nevertheless established contact with I.K. Morozov, and having received a briefing about the situation at hand, approved his decision. Thereby he gave it legal authority. After all, there was still no complete encirclement as such, and the division still had enough strength to "fight to the last cartridge". No one had cancelled I.V. Stalin's Order No.227, which demanded: "Unconditionally remove commanders of corps and divisions from their posts, who have allowed the voluntary retreat of troops from occupied positions."[81] On the contrary, even though this order was rarely used during the Battle of Kursk, nevertheless at critical moments both N.F. Vatutin and his army commanders more than once reminded their subordinates about it.[82]

In this connection I will note that the Voronezh Front Commander-in-Chief was not always such a thoughtful and just commander with respect to subordinates, as his peers would make him out to be in their memoirs, including those who fought under his command at the Battle of Kursk.[83] At stressful moments he was not only susceptible of adopting a harsh tone when addressing subordinates, but also displayed totally unjustified (except for arrogance) cruelty in his decisions. Although he never struck a subordinate who was negligent in his view, as I.V. Stalin recommended to his generals to do, nevertheless, he could without bothering to look into the situation ruin a combat officer's career, rattle rattles his nerves, and wreck his health. I've already written about his unseemly role in the situation regarding the dismissal of the commander of the 18th Tank Corps Major General B.S. Bakharov from his post in early 1943 and the subsequent unjust investigation of him.[84] It is possible to cite other cases as well, testifying to the fact that the General of the Army was a man of his times and at times dealt badly with people. For example, in 1941 as the chief of staff of the Northwestern Front, Vatutin had ordered for the operations chief of the 4th Shock Army Colonel I.I. Lednev to be prosecuted for the fact that he was unaware of the situation on the army's left flank, where the Germans had driven back our forces, because at the time, with the permission of the chief of staff General V.V. Kurasov, Lednev was resting, and documents from the divisions that confirmed the German breakthrough hadn't yet arrived at the headquarters.

However, this didn't perturb N.F. Vatutin and he didn't cancel his decision. The tribunal sentenced Colonel Lednev to be shot "for losing control over the troops". Colonel Lednev spent the next two weeks in a bunker under arrest, waiting for the sentence to be carried out, and when

---
80 TsAMO RF, f. 878, op. 1, d. 32, l. 137.
81 As cited by Samsonov, A.M., *Stalingradskaia bitva* [*Battle of Stalingrad*] (Moscow: Nauka, 1989), p. 602.
82 For example, N.F. Vatutin's discussion with the commander of the 5th Guards Army Lieutenant General A.S. Zhadov on 13 July 1943 (TsAMO RF, f. 203, op. 2843, d. 461, l. 64, 64obr.).
83 For example, see K.S. Moskalenko, *Na iugo-zapadnom napravlenii: Vospominaniia komandarma* [*On the southwest direction: Recollections of an army commander*], Vol. 2 (Moscow, 1973), p. 36.
84 Zamulin, V.N. *Prokhorovka: Neizvestnye podrobnosti ob izvestom srazhenii* [*Prokhorovka: Unknown details about a well-known battle*] (Moscow: Veche, 2013), pp. 273-274.

he emerged from incarceration his hair had gone completely gray. The army's chief of staff had saved him; he had gotten in touch with Moscow, laid out the essence of the case, and obtained a reversal of the sentence, even though Colonel Lednev was reduced in rank to a private. However, justice eventually prevailed and his rank was restored. He ended the war as a major general in the post of chief of staff of the 11th Guards Army, and after the war's conclusion he headed the headquarters of the Tauric Military District.[85] I've related all this so that the reader can understand that the fate of the commanders in that terrible war wasn't so easy, even for those who occupied high posts in the acting army, for whom it could cost them a career or even their lives under the colossal pressure of responsibility and danger in which they were constantly located. For I.K. Morozov the situation on 9 July and the night of 9-10 July was not simply problematic for a corps commander, but also quite dangerous for a general, fraught with big risks. After all, he had lost contact with higher headquarters, and being unable to hold his line, Morozov assumed a serious responsibility by deciding to withdraw his corps out of a very precarious situation to the other side of river.

However, let's return to the events near Belgorod on the night of 9-10 July. I cannot fail to mention two more documents, discovered in the archives of the TsAMO RF, which might tip the balance in favor of the argument that the commander of the 35th Guards Rifle Corps prior to the 81st Guards Rifle Division's retreat had nevertheless managed to make contact with its headquarters. Even so, they also don't bring any clarity. In the first, not only in Order No.057 but also in the division's subsequent combat reports, there is evidence that the order was issued in fact by S.G. Goriachev. However, these combat documents, just like Order No.057, were plainly printed after the battle, and the information that they contain might have been entered on a later date. Two copies of a combat report by the commander of the 81st Guards Rifle Division dated 11 July 1943 that I found in the files of the TsAMO RF might serve as confirmation of this: a handwritten copy (sent with a liaison officer), and a typewritten copy of the same document that was plainly done later.[86] In the second place, Morozov himself in his autobiography, which is kept in his personal file in the TsAMO RF, writes that "… at 2400 9 July I received an order to withdraw the units during the night and by 0800 take up a defense on the front: Shakhovo, (excl.) Chursino, along the western bank of the Donets."[87] However, as is known, a person's memory is unquestionably an important source of information, but one that is not always reliable, and after all, Morozov wrote his autobiography in 1947; moreover the order originally read differently: "Assemble in the northeastern portion of the woods lying 1.5 kilometers northwest of Khokhlovo." This document might only confirm the version that M.S. Shumilov initially gave the order to retreat earlier that day, and S.G. Goriachev only confirmed it at midnight, as I.K. Morozov's immediate superior.

As for the commander of the 35th Guards Rifle Corps himself, Goriachev's agreement with the division commander's decision also might have been viewed by the Front's Military Council as a case of fear mongering and weakness, so he probably gave it relying not only on the authority of the army commander, but also that of the Front's deputy commander in chief General of the Army I.P. Apanasenko, who arrived at the 35th Guards Rifle Corps around mid-day on 9 July and remained with it until 10 July.[88] So naturally Goriachev took this step with Apanasenko's knowledge and approval.

Now we'll make an attempt to figure out whether or not the 81st Guards Rifle Division really found itself in a pocket and why the Soviet command decided nevertheless to withdraw its troops

---

85 Sverdlov, F.D., *Neizvestnoe o sovetskikh polkovodtsakh* [*Unknown about Soviet military commanders*] (Moscow, 1995), p. 116.
86 TsAMO RF, f. 1232, op. 1, d. 7, ll. 291-293.
87 TsAMO RF, personal file of Major General I.K. Morozov, l. 49.
88 According to his report, he left the headquarters of the 7th Guards Army at 1030 on 9 July (TsAMO RF, f. 7 gv. A, op. 5312, d. 294, l. 100).

beyond the Northern Donets River. Once again I must stress that the base of sources of the opposing sides is sparse. Judging from the reports of the headquarters of the 19th Panzer Division and 168th Infantry Division, Blizhniaia Igumenka and the hamlet of the Machine Tractor Station were fully occupied by their units only on the morning of 10 July, when the main forces of the 81st Guards Rifle Division and the 276th Guards Rifle Regiment had pulled out of this sector. Prior to that moment, these locations had seen bitter fighting. Like Order No.57, German sources also refer to an encirclement, but vaguely so; they mention "mopping up the pocket" in this area. At the same time, not a single enemy division ever reported about a breakthrough to Staryi Gorod on the evening of 9 July. There is no basis to doubt the language in I.K. Morozov's order about the encirclement of Titarenko's 233rd Guards Rifle Regiment and the regiments of Kriuchenkin's 69th Army, but so far unfortunately no documents have been found to confirm his words. So thus far, there is no such confirmation. The 81st Guards Rifle Division's headquarters all the while was located outside the supposed "pocket" (until the middle of 7 July – in Sevriukovo, and on the evening of 8 July it moved to the command post of the 276th Guards Rifle Regiment in Shishino); all of its operational summaries and orders have been preserved, but they are very superficial, and the information in them doesn't give a clear answer about the disposition of its units, nor any details of the operational situation on the evening of 9 July.

On the basis of the information I've collected, it seems that as of 1800 9 July there was no encirclement of the entire 81st Guards Rifle Division in the literal sense of that word. Units of Schmidt's 19th Panzer Division (Panzergrenadier Regiment 73 and Panzer Reconnaissance Battalion 19) that were breaking through out of the area south of Blizhniaia Igumenka toward Staryi Gorod were stopped on the eastern outskirts of the hamlet of the Machine Tractor Station, where together with the grenadiers of the 168th Infantry Division's Infantry Regiment 429 they fought with the hamlet's defenders all through the night. Only elements of the 233rd Guards and 238th Guards Rifle Regiments between the southwestern and southern outskirts of Blizhniaia Igumenka and the hamlet of the Machine Tractor Station fell into a pocket that night between 2000 and 2100, but it was not a solid ring of encirclement. In addition, a few of the rifle companies of the 92nd Guards Rifle Division's 282nd Guards Rifle Regiment located east of Postnikov were caught in a pocket. Considering that by this time German panzers were already located in Andreevskie (5 kilometers northeast of the hamlet of the Machine Tractor Station), which is to say essentially in the rear of the 233rd Guards and 238th Guards Rifle Regiments, it would have been extremely difficult for these regiments to hold their positions, and in essence, senseless to try to do so.

Likely, by that time I.K. Morozov, who had already received prior approval earlier that day from higher command (of the 25th Guards Rifle Corps or Shumilov himself) about abandoning the line, had already sent his order to the unit commanders through messengers: prepare to withdraw the remaining forces beyond the Donets River on the night of 9-10 July. As subsequent events demonstrated with the encirclement of a portion of his regiments' strength, this decision proved far-sighted, helped avoid needless sacrifices, and saved the lives of several thousand soldiers and commanders who had endured the harshest trials in the heaviest of fighting. Even so, it must be acknowledged that the fall of the "Belgorod bastion" wasn't very favorable to the Soviet side. It became the first major event that predetermined the failure of Vatutin's plan to keep separate von Manstein's two assault groupings, which up until this moment had been working successfully. I'll remind the reader that the sector of the 81st Guards Rifle Division and 375th Rifle Division was playing the role of a "breakwater" that divided the offensive front of the Fourth Panzer Army and Army Detachment Kempf. Now however both flanks of the 69th Army's 48th Rifle Corps, which was holding the wedge of ground between the Northern Donets and Lipovyi Donets Rivers, were exposed. In addition, the withdrawal of the forces from out of the Belgorod area also had an adverse effect on the execution of the frontal counterattack against the II SS Panzer Corps that would be launched on 12 July 1943.

So far, no detailed description or any sort of account documents have been found in the TsAMO RF about how the units of the 81st Guards Rifle Division pulled out of their positions in the Belgorod area to a new line in the interfluvial area between the Lipovyi Donets and Northern Donets. I've been able to find only the recollections of those events of the commander of the 235th Guards Rifle Regiment Colonel G.T. Skiruta, which were published in a small number of copies already after the war in a collected volume. His recollection isn't large in size, so I will cite it in full:

> The division commander's order said: pull out of combat tonight. However, by this time we faced pulling not out of combat, but out of encirclement, and this is much more difficult. Having received the order to retreat, we began to weight how best to carry out the mission. My deputy combat commander Guards Lieutenant Colonel Aleksandr Vasil'evich Chernov proposed withdrawing to the east. There, he said, was our division, and if we did so, it could support us with a little fire – and we had the strength to advance 6-8 kilometers with fighting if we had to do so.
>
> The chief of staff remarked, "But we have a lot of wounded and little transport. Our movement will be slow."
>
> "We'll break out!" Chernov insisted.
>
> From the expressions on the faces of those present, it was clear that they didn't agree with Chernov. I also felt that way, and here is why: Of course it isn't so difficult for a fresh unit to fight its way forward for 6-8 kilometers, even though this isn't always accomplished. We, however, had been fighting for several days without either sleep or rest. Ammunition was low. There were a lot of wounded men, and we had almost no transport.
>
> Say what you will, but the Germans had been attacking our positions for four days already. Since we hadn't dug in our vehicles, prime movers and wagons, most of them had been destroyed or damaged. In such a situation you won't achieve any speed or maneuverability, and a unit that has lost mobility in the enemy rear, as a rule, is threatened with heavy losses.
>
> By this time, according to our reconnaissance patrols' information, the Nazis had a lot of tanks and artillery blocking our path. They plainly were only waiting for when sooner or later we would begin to break out precisely along this, the shortest route. However in war, as is known, one must never do what the enemy is expecting you to do. War is rich with contradictions, I would say, even paradoxes. One of them that the commander encounters frequently when making a decision is expressed by the formula: "It is possible, but impossible". Chernov, when choosing a path to the east plainly didn't consider this detail and hadn't thought deeply about the possible course of events. His "We'll break out!" would have plainly led to a lot of casualties. But it was difficult to say otherwise how we would be able to break out.
>
> Having heard the reports of other deputy commanders, I made the decision to move to the northwest along the left bank of the Northern Donets River in the overall direction of the hamlet of Iablonevyi [sic – there is no hamlet with such a name in this area; he was likely talking about the village of Malo-Iablonovo]. This was a somewhat longer route, but on the other hand made it less likely that we would run into major enemy forces. In order to confuse the fascists about our real intentions, we decided to feign a breakout by a vanguard in the Kreida railyard, "Day of Harvest" collective farm, Belovskaia direction.
>
> I gave the assignment to the battalion commanders. I set a time for when it would begin, gave the route of march and determined the sequence in which the battalions would pull out of combat. I paid particular attention to ensuring movement off the roads and to the organization of masking all lights and sounds. I demanded that they constantly show concern for the wounded. I ordered lightly-wounded men to be freed of carrying any load, and for the rest of the wounded to be carried on stretchers or transported in wagons or on gun carriages.

The sun still hadn't dropped below the horizon, but clouds began to cover the sky. It quickly became dark, and we were happy for this: possible rain and a pitch-black night were our closest allies. At the indicated time, scouts set out along the designated route. Then all the weapons of Guards Senior Lieutenant Said Turaev's company opened up in order to give the appearance of a breakout attempt. It raised such a ruckus that the enemy began to feel uneasy. Cannons and mortars responded with fire. Lurid explosions erupted on our former positions. However, this didn't trouble us; the regiment's companies by this time had already begun moving.

We stayed off the roads. A gentle, fine rain was falling. One doesn't quickly get tired of such. It was of benefit to us. However, it was hard to walk; now and then we kept stumbling over the detritus of battle and craters, which a recent battlefield always has in full. When the head of the column had already reached Chernaia Poliana, German aircraft began to "hang lanterns" (as we said whenever they dropped flares overhead) over the Kreida railyard – "Day of Harvest" collective farm – Belovskaia line. We sighed with relief: that meant the enemy had jumped at our bait.

Behind the regimental scouts, Aleksandr Fedorovich Goshtenar's battalion was next in the column. I was located with it. We'd already been marching for more than an hour, when a scout came running up to me.

"On the right, a column of Germans is moving beside us along a ravine", he reported.

"A large one?" I asked.

"Possibly a regiment."

"More precisely?"

"It is hard to say in the darkness."

"But maybe it's a battalion?" my intelligence chief Cherevichko interceded in the discussion. "In the darkness even a cat sometimes appears to be a tiger. How did you determine the size?"

"By the column's length."

"Then it's completely possible you're not mistaken."

Taking along several cars, Vladimir Ivanovich Cherevichko and I set out behind the scout. After going approximately 150 meters, we spotted the moving column. Neither its head nor its tail was visible. Sometimes far out in front or somewhere in the rear, we could see the flicker of little lights: plainly, the Germans were turning flashlights on and off. The rumble of engines rose above the ravine.

The sharp eyes of the intelligence chief quickly took everything in. We had no reason to get tied up in combat. I ordered the battalion commanders to increase their flank security and pick up the pace of the march. At whatever the cost, we had to break away from our totally undesirable neighbor. Soon the rumble of engines began to recede to the right. A short time later, scouts reported that the Germans had stopped.

By now we'd already been marching for three hours. It was time to think about rest. However, the absence of news from Guards Junior Lieutenant Grigorii Mitin's forward reconnaissance group, which had been sent out in the direction of Iablonevyi [sic], was troubling me.

Fortunately, Mitin soon made himself known. A messenger reported:

"In the hamlet itself it is quiet. Six trucks with field kitchens have been discovered. A captured sergeant revealed that they were preparing breakfast for the men of one of the regiments of the III Panzer Corps. The regiment was 2-3 kilometers to the north of Iablonevyi [sic]. The tanks had moved up that evening. They are expecting the infantry by morning."

The last sentence particularly stuck in my mind.

I called for a halt. I had to let the men rest and get ready for combat: plainly, we still hadn't avoided contact with the enemy, though thus far he was behaving calmly. This was confirmed by a new message from the scouts: "North of Iablonevyi [sic], tanks are standing in single file in a cornfield. There are 25-30 meters between each tank. However, there are some gaps that are even larger. The barrels of the tanks' main guns are pointed away from us."

That meant the fascists weren't expecting us at this place and time!

Having issued an order to the chief of staff to prepare a battalion for a breakout, I and Cherevichko and several vehicles moved ahead in order to assess the situation on the spot. In reality, the tanks were seemingly slumbering in the cornfield. The gun barrels had been lowered and no movement of men was noticeable. Captain Cherevichko was standing next to me, lost in thoughts.

Suddenly he quietly asked, "What if we …?" I attentively listened to the captain and fully agreed with his proposal, even though it contained a certain amount of risk.

Yes, there was risk, and no small amount of it. But what officer can assert that there is not an element of risk when making even the safest decision? True, the bolder and more extraordinary the order, the greater the risk. But in war it is impossible to exclude it entirely. After all, combat is not a unilateral action. The commander of the opposing side also strives to anticipate your plan, pinpoint your actions, and grab the initiative from the very first minute of combat.

Therefore it is impossible not to agree with the assertion that combat is like a duel between the minds of the two opposing commanders, their energy in action, and their audacity in command. Indeed, this duel begins long before the first shot is fired. Here the main thing is that your actions in the search for a way out of a situation and your reliance on risk are not based on unfounded intuition, but on the ability to see an opening opportunity instantly, grasp it, and make correct use of it without delay. In general, if you want to achieve success with little blood, you must think and operate more quickly than the enemy…

So, it was decided. We took advantage of the Germans' respose and made an attempt to slip Akimov's and Gostenar's battalions quietly through the tank barrier in the cornfield. Meanwhile Ivan Sokolenko's rearguard battalion and Vasilii Kovalenko's battery would launch an attack against the tanks with every possible means. Then Sokolenko's 3rd Battalion, covered by the 1st and 2nd Battalions, would pull out of the combat.

I gave an order for the 1st and 2nd Companies to deploy into company columns and without any noise pass through the intervals between the tanks. Each company would be led by an assault group. More anti-tank grenades would be allocated to them. If the Nazis stirred, they were to clear a path with the grenades.

The rain stopped. The sky brightened a bit. Dawn was approaching. Guards Captain Aleksandr Goshtenar's battalion led the way. Behind him, echeloned to the left, was Ivan Akimov's battalion. Guards Senior Lieutenant Petr Simonenko's anti-tank battery was on the right flank. If necessary, it would quickly deploy and cover the battalions with fire.

The Guardsmen had already been picking their way forward for several minutes, and in the enemy's position everything was quiet. Now the assault groups were among the tanks and had taken cover in places of concealment, in order to let the companies pass through them. Suddenly here and there hatches opened on the turrets, and the silhouettes of men appeared. Showing no alarm, they were looking at the approaching columns. Apparently, they took us as their own men.

The battalions in accelerated step were disappearing into the pre-dawn twilight. Another minute passed, and then the silence exploded with a dozen grenade explosions and the chattering of machine guns and automatic weapons. Hoarsely and in a drawn out manner, as if coughing from the damp morning air, cannons barked: ours and those of the German tanks.

However, the half-asleep Germans were firing randomly, unsure of their targets. Cannons from the defenders out in front of the Soviet troops also fired. The shells landed close to the tanks and in the area of our 3rd Battalion.

Having broken through to friendly lines, the mortar crews of the 1st and 2nd Battalions and the artillery crews of Senior Lieutenant Petr Grigor'evich Simonenko pivoted by 180 degrees and together with elements of the 92nd Guards Rifle Division which was defending on this line opened fire at the enemy, securing the way out for our 3rd Battalion.

At dawn even Guards Senior Lieutenant Said Turaev's company gained separation from the enemy. Moving along the designated route, the soldiers watched as more than 150 German aircraft bombed the regiment's former positions.

Cannons and mortars spoke up after the aircraft flew away. They were especially working over the hills in the vicinity of the Machine Tractor Station, which is southeast of Staryi Gorod, and the woods north of the Kreida railyard.

After this storm of fire, the Germans advanced against our abandoned positions. They were attacking from three directions. The soldiers didn't know how the attack ended: with an accelerated march, they were moving forward.

They came out of encirclement in an organized manner. No one floundered. Each man was ready to overcome any obstacle in our path. The first of my colleagues that I met after coming out of encirclement was our division's chief of staff Guards Lieutenant Colonel B.Iu. Svetnik, who had joined our division after the Stalingrad fighting. Boris Iur'evich not only knew staff work well, he was also an exceptionally brave man, a fact which I more than once had the opportunity to convince myself. Having shared the latest news, Svetnik congratulated me upon the successful completion of the fighting on the former line and my awarding with the Order of the Red Banner.[89]

In these recollections, two events – the withdrawal to the new line and the decoration – have been merged in time. I will allow that the author's memory betrayed him, although it is possible that this was done by an editor or censor intentionally (there were such cases), with the aim of showing the command's special concern for their soldiers and subordinate commanders: the regiment had just come out of battle, and the division headquarters had not only already prepared the medal recommendations, the army headquarters had already approved them. In reality, everything went somewhat differently. For his meritorious behavior, Major G.T. Skiruta really was considered worthy of the Order of the Red Banner, but I.K. Morozov signed his letter of commendation only 10 days later, on 20 July (the letter particularly mentions the heavy casualties inflicted on the enemy by the 235th Guards Rifle Regiment over the period of fighting between 5 and 16 July 1943), but the 7th Guards Army's Military Council approved it only on 21 August 1943.[90] On the morning of 10 July, the command of the 81st Guards Rifle Division was in no mood for filling out award papers. The defensive operation was in full swing and the higher command was now sending out orders to take up a defense on a new line and hold it, even though at that moment no one had any clear knowledge of the forces the division still had or where they were located. Around mid-day I.K. Morozov received Special Order No.5 from the commander of the 48th Rifle Corps, in which Major General Z.Z. Ragoznyi demanded:

1. In accordance with Order No.00979/op from the 69th Army's Military Council, the 81st Guards Rifle Division has been operationally subordinated to me.

---

89 Skiruta, G.T., "Soldaty velikoi pobedy" ["Solders of the great victory"], in *Na zemle, v nebesakh i na more* [*On the ground, in the air and on the sea*] (Moscow: Voenizdat, 1982), pp. 42-46.
90 TsAMO RF, f. 33, op. 686044, ed. khr. 1559, entry number 19757032.

2. 81st Guards Rifle Division with attached assets is to occupy and stubbornly defend a prepared line of defense: Hill 147.0, Volobuevka, Sazhnoe, Krivtsovo, Novo-Oskochnoe, Shcholokovo. Mission: in no case allow a breakthrough by enemy tanks and infantry in the direction of Shakhovo from the southwest and southeast. Be ready to operate together with the 2nd Guards "Tatsinskaia" Tank Corps for counterattacks in the Belenikhino, Malye Maiachki direction and in the overall Melikhovo – Staryi Gorod direction. Be ready for the defense by 0700 11.07.1943.
3. Immediately bring the troops to order and replenish stockpiles of ammunition and food.[91]

As can be seen from this document, on 10 July V.D. Kriuchenkin was still nurturing the hope to obtain the 2nd Guards Tank Corps from N.F. Vatutin and to use it for containing Breith's panzer corps between the Northern Donets and Razumnaia Rivers and had already made plans for when he would be reinforced with it. However, unfortunately the difficult operational situation on the Prokhorovka direction didn't allow the Front Commander-in-Chief to take advantage of this, in general, reasonable proposal from the commander of the 69th Army and his chief of staff.

The situation with the units of the 92nd Guards Rifle Division is presented completely differently in the archives. In the TsAMO RF, a number of documents have been uncovered that testify to the destruction of this division over two days of fighting near Belgorod. The first of them – "Information on the losses of the 92nd Guards Rifle Division's units from 9 June to 9 July 1943" – was filled out in the form of a table. According to it, between 29 June and 6 July inclusively, the division's total loss of men amounted to 21. On 9 July, the division lost 1,038 soldiers and commanders, including 391 killed and 644 wounded or concussed. Moreover, the table doesn't give the losses of all the units and elements, only: "280th Guards Rifle Regiment, a decrease of 980 men (380 killed); 282nd Guards Rifle Regiment – 22 men (1 killed); 197th Guards Artillery Regiment – 29 men (8 killed); 99th Guards Separate Destroyer Anti-tank Artillery Battalion – 7 men (2 killed)." Below the document there is a comment: "Submitted at 1800 9.7.1943 over the telephone from the command post of Osipov's division to Staroverov's corps."[92] As for the data on the losses of the 282nd Guards Rifle Regiment for 9 July, they must be woefully incomplete. Several of its battalions were located in encirclement in the Postnikov area, so neither their regimental headquarters nor the division headquarters could know what their casualty figures were.

Below this note, the casualty figures now for 10 July are given, but once again not for all the regiments:

In the 282nd Guards Rifle Regiment (senior commanders – 5, junior commanders – 20, rank and file – 31) – 56 killed; wounded, concussed (13, 36, 110) – 159; missing in action (93, 608, 752) – 1,453; Total (111, 664, 893) – 1,668.
In the 276th Guards Rifle Regiment: killed (14, 86, 122) – 222; wounded, concussed (42, 304, 391) – 737; missing in action (18, 65, 321) – 404; Total (74, 455, 834) – 1,363.
197th Guards Artillery Regiment: killed (command staff – 2) – 2; wounded or concussed – (6, 8) – 14; missing in action – (4, 6, 19) – 29; Total (12, 14, 19) – 45.
Training battalion: killed (-, 3, 1) – 4; wounded, concussed (-, -, 4) – 4; Total (-, 3, 5) – 8.
Engineer battalion: wounded (-, -, 1) – 1; missing in action (-, 4, 10) – 14; Total – (-, 4, 11) – 15.

---

91 TsAMO RF, f. 48 sk, op. 1, d. 17, l. 19.
92 TsAMO RF, f. 92 gv. sd, op. 1, d. 13, l. 41. Osipov and Starovetov were staff officers in the respective division and corps, but their posts are unknown.

99th Guards Separate Destroyer Anti-tank Artillery Battalion: killed (2, 6, 12) – 20; wounded (3, 10, 43) – 56; Total (5, 16, 55) – 76.

Reconnaissance company: a total of 4, including wounded (0, 1, 3) – 4.

Total for the division for 10 July 3,131 military personnel.

However, I believe both dates given in this document are incorrect; they should be one day earlier. On 8 July the 280th Guards Rifle Regiment, a battalion of the 197th Guards Artillery Regiment and the 99th Guards Separate Destroyer Anti-tank Artillery Battalion took on the main attack by the 6th and 19th Panzer Divisions, and by 1800 on 9 July, when the fighting was at its height, the regiment headquarters were able to report to the division headquarters only those figures known to them. The results for the day were usually totaled at night, thus the losses for 9 July given in the first part of the table were the losses suffered when defending the villages of Melikhovo, Dal'niaia Igumenka and Shliakhovoe on 8 July, while the casualties given for 10 July were the figures for the losses in the course of 9 July, when holding attempting to hold the Blizhniaia Igumenka – Postnikov – Dal'niaia Igumenka line and during the division's withdrawal beyond the Northern Donets River on the night of 9-10 July. I will remind the reader that the 280th Guards Rifle Regiment, which had suffered significant losses, retreated to Shliakhovoe on the evening of 8 July and on the following day of 9 July took no active part in the fighting. The entire burden of the effort to repulse *Sturmgruppen Nord* and *Sud* rested on the 81st Guards Rifle Division's units and elements, which were listed at the end of the document. As is obvious from the figures given in it, the 282nd Guards and 276th Guards Rifle Regiment suffered the greatest damage on 9 July, because the former attacked the units of the 19th Panzer Division and 168th Infantry Division which were deployed in their firing positions, and thus suffered a lot of dead or wounded commanders and soldiers, while the number of missing in action was relatively not so high. The situation in the latter regiment was different. It went on the attack against a line that was being held by *kampfgruppen* of a panzer division. Using their high mobility and firepower, the Germans rather quickly cut off the forward attacking troops from the regiment's main forces east of Postnikov, as a result of which over a short period of time more than two rifle battalions were partially destroyed or partially taken prisoner. These are terrible figures – the outcome of poorly conceived and poorly prepared frontal assaults by infantry against tanks, which was so frequently practiced by the Soviet command, including during the Battle of Kursk.

From the figures cited above it is obvious that the majority of the losses were men who went missing in action. In the practical work of the headquarters of the Red Army's formations and units, these three words simultaneously meant three categories of manpower losses: the first – prisoners, the capture of which by the enemy could only be assumed; the second – those dead, badly wounded or concussed left on the battlefield controlled by the enemy; and the third – men who eventually came out of the depth of enemy-held territory. The last category were the Red Army men and commanders who after a certain amount of time reappeared in their units or were delivered by blocking detachments to collection points, before again being returned to their units. Judging from archival records (including captured German ones), the majority of the missing in action in the 92nd Guards Rifle Division were men taken prisoner during the elimination of the pockets of resistance on 10 July east of Postnikov and in the area of Dal'niaia and Blizhniaia Igumenka. Moreover, they proved to be significantly more than was reported by the division headquarters in the immediate aftermath of the battle. Standing in second place by number were the killed and mortally wounded men who were left on the battlefield, died in their trenches, burned to death by flamethrowers in bunkers, and buried by captured Soviet prisoners of war at the order of the Germans at the spot where their bodies were found.

Now let's turn to two other documents, which will allow us to ascertain the number of missing in action for the entire 92nd Guards Rifle Division and determine the division's condition after a week of fighting. In a table of losses according to the results of the fighting between 7 and 17 July 1943, submitted by the division headquarters to the corps on 23 July 1943, it is especially noted that "in the total number of men who went missing in action there are 2,577 men, the fate of which is unknown since the moment of encirclement of the division's units in the Belgorod area."[93] A report from the new division commander Colonel A.N. Petrushin addressed to the Red Army's Chief of the General Staff on the number of casualties and the reasons for the high loss of men over this period states:

> Over the period of combat operations the division lost 924 killed, 2,212 wounded, 2,499 missing in action and 5 sick for a total of 5,640 men, including 343 killed, 1,030 wounded and 366 missing in action in the 276th Guards Rifle Regiment; 233 killed, 459 wounded, 1,004 missing in action and 2 sick in the 280th Guards Rifle Regiment; 172 killed, 407 wounded and 915 missing in action in the 282nd Guards Rifle Regiment; 98 killed, 118 wounded, 120 missing in action and 3 sick in the 97th Guards Artillery Regiment. The rest of the losses are among the division's specialized elements.[94]

As a rule, even when coming out of a closing pocket, the troops have a certain number of missing in action. In the first place they've been taken prisoner or killed when fighting off the enemy until the last bullet; soldiers and commanders who covered the withdrawal, as well as those whom the order to retreat never reached. As concerns the cases when units and elements were located in full encirclement, as happened with Trunin's 92nd Guards Rifle Division, their losses are as a rule even greater. However, one can say the 92nd Guards Rifle Division was lucky in this respect, since only an insignificant amount of its strength wound up in a pocket – two rifle companies that failed to come out, who were located in the woods near Postnikov, and a portion of the scattered units that the order never reached. Moreover, on the afternoon of the day, the 168th Infantry Division, which was mopping up to ground in the 81st Guards Rifle Division's former sector, reported the capture of prisoners equivalent to two full-strength rifle companies. Likely, among these prisoners were soldiers who belonged to the two divisions, the 81st Guards and 92nd Guards Rifle Divisions.

The morning of 10 July on almost the entire sector of the Voronezh Front proved to be gloomy. In the area of Belgorod and to the north of there, rain periodically fell from sun-up until almost the middle of the day. It sometimes ended and the skies would clear, or it lightly sprinkled, but in places the rain turned into a downpour, which washed the charred soil and extinguished isolated pockets of fires. However, already around noon the sun came out and the air became sweltering and humid above the fields that had seen fighting: the evaporation of the rainfall, thickly intermingled with the stench emitted by thousands of rotting corpses and dead animals and the smoke rising from buildings and knocked-out armor. If you take into account the time required for the order to travel from the division headquarters to the regiments and lower, then the 81st Guards Rifle Division and the two regiments of the 92nd Guards Rifle Division probably began to retreat across the Donets River between 0200 and 0300 on 10 July. Several rifle companies (with a total strength of up to a battalion) were left behind in the Andreevskie, Blizhniaia Igumenka, hamlet of the Machine Tractor Station, Staryi Gorod area as a rearguard, which were being supported by the regiments' artillery and mortar companies. In isolated sectors, in particular from out of the woods southwest of Chernaia Poliana in the direction of Belgorod the Guardsmen launched an entire series of nighttime counterattacks. They had the aim of first of distracting the enemy's attention

---

93 TsAMO RF, f. 92 gv. sd, op. 1, d. 13, l. 129.
94 TsAMO RF, f. 92 gv. sd, op. 1, d. 13, l. 134.

from the initiation of the retreat by the main forces of Morozov's division, and then to help isolated groups come out of the encirclement, which had been found by the enemy. The Germans were assuming that the Soviet command might pull its troops out of this area, but their reconnaissance and intelligence couldn't spot the moment the withdrawal began. In the morning the divisions of Breith's III Panzer Corps reported to its headquarters:

> 6th Panzer Division. The night, according to the reports that have arrived up to the given moment, passed quietly, with harassing artillery fire on the forward line and the ground lying in front of it. Continuous aerial activity with the dropping of bombs.
>
> 19th Panzer Division. Attempts by enemy units, which attacked on 9.7, to break out have been repulsed by the reconnaissance battalion [repeated counterattacks by the 276th Guards Rifle Regiment from out of the hamlet at the Machine Tractor Station]. After the onset of darkness, assault units of Panzergrenadier Regiment 73 broke into the enemy's system of trenches from the south and took more than 20 combat positions and bunkers [probably east of the Machine Tractor Station hamlet]. In the course of the night, continuous enemy activity in the air. Numerous bombs were dropped on the sector. Losses were taken. Contact with the 168th Infantry Division thus far only by radio.
>
> 168th Infantry Division. Having broken through from the Kreida railyard as far as the Blizhniaia Igumenka – Staryi Gorod road, units of Infantry Regiment 429 in the course of the night were attacked by separate enemy groups, both from the east and the west. So far more detailed reports haven't arrived. A wounded prisoner captured in the sector of Infantry Regiment 417 when repulsing an enemy assault group informed us that the enemy forces located in front of the regiment's sector intended to break through to Belgorod. An attack undertaken by units of Infantry Regiment 417 at 0245 against the sector of woods 600 meters southwest of the Chernaia Poliana church and the ravine northwest of it ran into fierce enemy resistance and provoked strong enemy artillery and mortar fire. Thus far the attack has been able to reach the edge of the woods. The commander of Infantry Regiment 417 was severely wounded by the explosion of a mortar round.[95]

Likely, a rifle battalion, which Colonel P.D. Govorunenko at the directive of the commander of the 35th Guards Rifle Corps was supposed to hand to the operational control of I.K. Morozov earlier that day, was trying to fight its way from out of Chernaia Poliana through Pokrovka to Belgorod, but the attack failed.

Prior to sunrise the command of the 168th Infantry Division and 19th Panzer Division were supposed to conduct a rotation of units and sectors of defense. Afterward, a general attack was designated by the now fully-gathered division of Chales de Beaulieu to the north from the Blizhniaia Igumenka – Staryi Gorod – area southwest of Chernaia Poliana. However, this plan couldn't be fully implemented, because Schmidt's units throughout the short summer night were engaged in bitter fighting with units of the 238th Guards and 233rd Guards Rifle Regiments in the vicinity of the hamlet of the Machine Tractor Station, gradually pushing them back toward Staryi Gorod. The headquarters of the 19th Panzer Division reported: "In the course of the night, assault units of Panzergrenadier Regiment 73 and Reconnaissance Battalion 19 took the positions of the enemy that is retreating, 3 kilometers south of Blizhniaia Igumenka. Prisoners, weapons

---

95 NARA US, rg. 242, t. 314, r. 197, f. 001282.

THE FALL OF THE BELGOROD BASTION, 9-10 JULY 1943

and various items of gear were captured here. Infantry Regiment 442 in the morning hours took Blizhniaia Igumenka."[96]

After sunrise, the 6th Panzer Division went on the attack from the east. From the daily summary of its headquarters:

> *Kampfgruppe* Bieberstein in its previous composition set out today from the Postnikov – Andreevskie area and took the "Main Fruit and Vegetable" State Farm, as well as north and south of Shishino. Reconnaissance Battalion 6 wiped out the enemy encircled in the woods 2 kilometers to the northeast of Andreevskie [units of the 276th Guards Rifle Division]. *Kampfgruppen* Oppeln and Unrein were in a defensive posture in Melikhovo. Enemy activity in the air is less than on preceding days. Our own Luftwaffe with large formations of bombers and dive bombers were striking targets in front of our forward units.[97]

The main events within the "Belgorod bastion" and around it began to unfold approximately between 0700 and 0800. At this time the 168th Infantry Division went on the attack along the entire front, and a bit later a portion of Fliegerkorps VIII's strength was sent to this area in order to destroy the retreating divisions of the 35th Guards Rifle Corps and help the troops of Army Detachment Kempf quickly snuff out embers of resistance, and if things went well break into the defenses between the Northern and Lipovyi Donets Rivers on the boot heels of the Guardsmen. However, the Nazi forces didn't manage to achieve this. The Soviet platoons that had been left behind here to screen the withdrawal and the groups that had been scattered in the course of the night fighting put up desperate resistance for as long as they had bullets and grenades, though there were some who surrendered without stubborn opposition after being worn out by five days of heavy fighting. The details of these events have been laid out in a daily report from the headquarters of the 168th Infantry Division:

> The planned attack by the reinforced Infantry Regiment 429 against the Blizhniaia Igumenka – Staryi Gorod ravine proceeded on 10.7.43 and in the mid-day hours reached the paved road in the outer orchards of the "Main Fruit and Vegetable" State Farm. The enemy was thrown out of the field positions they occupied or taken prisoner. Staryi Gorod was captured at 1030 (Berlin time) with air support. Infantry Regiment 429 is presently pursuing the enemy toward Shishino. The attack foreseen in the morning hours on the regiment's left flank against the sector of woods 600 meters southwest of the Chernaia Poliana church ran into the heaviest enemy opposition and had only insignificant success. A reconnaissance-in-force at 1235 (Berlin time) showed that a weak enemy garrison was occupying the sector of woods. A resumed attack led to the capture of the woods. The regiment's units set out from Chernaia Poliana to the north.
>
> Reconnaissance on the regiment's left flank revealed that the enemy positions there are occupied by the same forces. The Infantry Regiment 442 that was again returned to the division is linking up with the division's right flank. Around 300 prisoners have been taken. Spoils of war (according to initial calculations): 91 light machine guns, 14 heavy machine guns, 71 anti-tank rifles, 75 submachine guns, 115 rifles, 21 heavy and 20 light mortars, and 8 45mm anti-tank guns. The division's command post – since 1400 in Blizhniaia Igumenka.[98]

---

96 NARA US, rg. 242, t. 314, r. 197, f. 001307.
97 NARA US, rg. 242, t. 314, r. 197, f. 001306.
98 NARA US, rg. 242, t. 314, r. 197, f. 001306.

In the middle of the day there occurred an event in the area of the village of Shopino, which by this time wasn't so very important, but nevertheless represented a significant event for the enemy. Having driven screening elements of Morozov's and Govorunenko's divisions from the village, the forces of the Fourth Panzer Army and Army Detachment Kempf (the right-flank regiment of the 167th Infantry Division and the left-flank regiment of the 168th Infantry Division) finally linked up. The commander of the 167th Infantry Division Lieutenant General W. Trierenburg, whose units were now occupying the positions once-held by the 375th Rifle Division that had gradually retreated beyond the river, rather prosaically laid out how this happened in his Order No.28:

> The enemy: Given weak enemy opposition, by the middle of the day of 10.7.43 the settlement of Shopino was taken by Infantry Regiment 339. Units of Infantry Regiment 315 entered the western side of Visloe. There was no enemy in Shoshenkovo. Since 0700 the enemy has been retreating to the east and northeast. The enemy is conducting artillery, mortar and rocket launcher fire on the center and northern sectors of the forward edge of defense [the left flank].
>
> Neighbors: Near Shopino contact was established with the left flank of the 168th Infantry Division; other units of Army Detachment Kempf are attacking to the north and northeast. With its left flank, the SS Division *Das Reich* reached the area east of Iasnaia Poliana.[99]

It must be said that if the 375th Rifle Division's change in positions was being covered by fire and counterattacks by the neighboring 89th Guards Rifle Division, then during the withdrawal of Morozov's and Trunin's divisions, not a single counterattack was launched in order to help them because of the lack of communications with both the 7th Guards Army and the 35th Guards Rifle Corps. Even though the divisions that had been bled white and worn out by the heaviest fighting were in great need of this, there can be no talk about any organized withdrawal, if it isn't clear who issued the order to retreat.

Morozov's 81st Guards Rifle Division and attached regiments of the 92nd Guards Rifle Division spent approximately a day pulling out of the Belgorod area, and by the end of 10 July the bulk of their men had assembled in the areas designated for them. An excerpt from Combat Report No.063 from the 81st Guards Rifle Division's headquarters at 0300 on 11 July 1943 reveals the condition it was in:

> Units of the division retreated to the Verkhnii Ol'shanets – Novo-Oskochnoe assembly area and by 2000 10.07.1943 arrived in the following composition:
> a) Personnel: Up to 3,500-4,000 men according to questionable data;
> b) 40-50% of materiel according to preliminary calculations;
> c) Divisional artillery has been completely destroyed in the fighting;
> e) Anti-tank artillery has also been almost completely destroyed;
> f) Regimental artillery has been completely destroyed, only the 235th Guards Rifle Regiment has any;
>
> 4. All communications equipment with the exception of radios has been destroyed.
> 5. The division has no means of reinforcement.
> 6. In order to bring the division's units back to combat-readiness, the following are necessary:

---

99 TsAMO RF, f. 500, op. 12462, d. 729, l. 146.

a) Replenishment with weapons and equipment (rifles, motorized transport, machine guns, anti-tank rifles, etc.);
b) Divisional and regimental artillery;
c) Bring the personnel back to order and provide them with uniforms and weapons;
d) Provide communications equipment.[100]

Judging from the further steps the command of the Voronezh Front highly evaluated the actions of both the division commander and his subordinates in the five days of defensive fighting, deciding that despite the heavy losses, the division had fully carried out its mission. For his successful leadership of the troops near Belgorod, on 27 August 1943 Major General I.K. Morozov was awarded the Order of Kutuzov, 2nd Class.

However, the "mopping up" of the former positions held by Morozov's and Trunin's divisions wasn't the main task for III Panzer Corps on 10 July. Its command had been primarily directed to prepare for a further advance to the north and northeast. The leadership of Army Detachment Kempf was running out of time, and Breith was aware of this. He understood perfectly well that the lack of success of his panzer corps' offensive to this point was to a great extent constraining the initiative of Hoth's Fourth Panzer Army. Thus, the breakthrough of his panzer corps to Prokhorovka in the next day or two was extremely important not only for the operation, but also personally for Kempf. In order to achieve this, already by the evening of 10 July it was necessary to resolve two clusters of extremely important tasks. First, he had to gather the 19th Panzer Division back together and bring it back to order, and transfer the 7th Panzer Division's sector to the 198th Infantry Division. Second, it was necessary to take three tactically important sectors:, the Kalinin area (4.5 kilometers southwest of Sheino) and the woods southeast and east of Miasoedovo with the forces of the 7th Panzer Division (in order then to crush the right flank of the 94th Guards Rifle Division with its panzers); and the Shishino – Khokhlovo – Kiselevo sector along the channel of the Northern Donets River by *kampfgruppen* of the 19th Panzer Division. The resolution of these tasks would secure the flanks of the next phase of the offensive and create a satisfactory "start line" for III Panzer Corps' assault wedge for a lunge into the depth of the Russian defenses through the Sabynino – Shliakhovoe – Sheino line. However, Breith was unable to execute this scheme on 10 July.

Before talking about how the 7th Panzer Division attempted to break through the boundary between the 7th Guards Army and 69th Army in the Miasoedovo – Hill 206.9 – Hill 205.5 sector, I want to dwell upon one puzzling event that took place on the right flank of Shumilov's army at the fault of a number of commanders of the 94th Guards Rifle Division and almost ended with tragic consequences. According to Combat Order No.0282/op of the 7th Guards Army from 9 July 1943, the 25th Guards Rifle Corps' 81st Guards Rifle Division and 94th Guards Rifle Division passed to the 69th Army's control, while in return it received operational control over the full 15th Guards Rifle Division. On the night of 9-10 July its 47th Guards Rifle Regiment was to replace the 94th Guards Rifle Division's 286th Guards Rifle Regiment in the northern portion of the woods southeast of Miasoedovo in the area of Hills 205.5, 206.9, 191.8 and 202.3.

The hand-over of defensive sectors on the forward edge is always an extremely delicate and dangerous matter, since it could provide a suitable opportunity for an enemy breakthrough of the line. Thus the side conducting a rotation in the line always thoroughly prepared it. As a rule, the replacement of units took place at night, and it was required that this sector be covered by no less than a battalion of mortars or artillery, in case the enemy got a whiff of

---

100 TsAMO RF, f. 81 gv. sd, op. 1, d. 7, l. 293.

what was going on. On the other hand, reconnaissance patrols and intelligence officers of the opposing side always strive to determine the moment a rotation takes place. On the night of 9-10 July, fortune smiled upon the reconnaissance patrols of the 7th Panzer Division. Because of the irresponsible attitude to their duties, a number of commanders of the 94th Guards Rifle Division left a gap at the boundary between the two armies for several hours, which the 7th Panzer Division's panzer reconnaissance battalion discovered and quickly moved in to occupy the area of the former positions of the 286th Guards Rifle Regiment. Let's turn to Order No.00194 of the Voronezh Front Commander-in-Chief dated 21 July 1943:

> The commander of the 94th Guards Rifle Division Guards Colonel I.G. Russkikh, having received an order from the commander of the 35th Guards Rifle Corps Lieutenant General S.G. Goriachev to secure the replacement of a portion of the division on his left flank with units of the 7th Guards Army, regarded the execution of this order formally and didn't follow how it was being carried out.
>
> The commander of the 286th Guards Rifle Regiment of this same division Guards Captain Chuev, having crudely violated the procedure established for yielding a line, assigned a commander with insufficient authority to carry out this task: Guards Senior Lieutenant Belik, the commander of a submachine gun company. The latter, not waiting for the arrival of the commander of the 15th Guards Rifle Division's 47th Guards Rifle Regiment, left to rejoin his regiment. The document regarding the receiving and handing over of a line was never signed.
>
> At the moment of the replacement of one regiment with another, the enemy attacked the sector of defense, where the exchange in units was taking place, and seized important points. This to a significant degree contributed to the circumstance that the commander of the 47th Guards Rifle Regiment, who still hadn't formally taken over the sector and not being factually responsible for it, made no effort to direct the fighting. Only after several hours was the enemy driven out of the occupied positions by a counterattack of units of the 15th Guards Rifle Division and the situation restored.[101]

The "important points" mentioned were three of the four hills (with the exception of Hill 202.3) that were being held by the 286th Guards Rifle Regiment, including Hill 206.9 that was exceptionally important in a tactical sense, which was located on the fringe of the wooded area southeast of Miasoedovo. The fighting to win back the hills taken by Panzer Reconnaissance Battalion 37 lasted for a long time. It started even before sunrise, but Lieutenant Colonel P.I. Gremaiko's 47th Guards Rifle Regiment finally managed to drive the German units from the hills only just before noon. One must give the enemy his due; despite the fact that they took the line they held from the march, the grenadiers fought stubbornly. To a significant extent the fact that they were being supported by several panzers contributed to this. According to Combat Order No.0020/op from division commander E.I. Vasilenko, in the area of the hills five medium tanks and one Tiger of a company of the Separate Heavy Panzer Battalion 503 that was attached to the 7th Panzer Division were knocked out, and up to two platoons of infantry were destroyed.[102] These are relatively meager numbers for enemy losses and they were probably taken from the reports of the 47th Guards Rifle Regiment after examining the battlefield, which remained in the Guardsmen's possession. I will note that both Captain D.S. Chuev and Colonel I.G. Russkikh were treated rather gently according to the frontline standards for their negligence – with rebukes announced

---

101 Personal archive of the author.
102 TsAMO RF, f. 15 gv. sd, op. 1, d. 8, l. 140.

in an order from the Front Commander-in-Chief. As concerns Senior Lieutenant F.V. Bezik, he also didn't suffer, but on the contrary on 19 July 1943 for the successful actions by the regiment's command between 7 and 15 July was put up for the medal "For Courage".[103] One shouldn't be surprised at this; in war, even stranger things happen.

On the afternoon the 15th Guards Rifle Division with two regiments fully moved into the first echelon of the 25th Guards Rifle Corps' defenses and had dug in on the line: 47th Guards Rifle Regiment – (excl.) woods, 2.5 kilometers east of Miasoedovo, Hills 205.5, 206.9, 191.8; 44th Guards Rifle Regiment – Hill 202.3, "Solov'ev" collective farm, "Batratskaia Dacha" State Farm (as far as the lake inclusively); the 50th Guards Rifle Regiment was holding a sector of defense in the second echelon: Novo-Troevka, (excl.) Nekliudovo. Boundary lines: (right flank) with the 35th Guards Rifle Corps' 94th Guards Rifle Division: Hill 244.9, 205.5, (excl.) Sevriukovo; (left flank) with the 73rd Guards Rifle Division – Aleksandrovskii, (excl.) Nikol'skoe, "Batratskaia Dacha" State Farm, Hill 191.2, Nizhnii Ol'shanets.

While the 47th Guards Rifle Regiment and Panzer Reconnaissance Battalion 37 fought for possession of the hills on the right flank of Safiulin's 25th Guards Rifle Corps, the yielding by von Funck's units of the "Batratskaia Dacha" State Farm – Hill 206.9 sector to the arriving Infantry Regiment 326 of the 198th Infantry Division went actively throughout the night and the first half of the day of 10 July. The Germans were hurrying, and thus made no particular effort to conceal the process. Nevertheless, a significant portion of the 25th Guards Rifle Corps' right-flank division was tied up in combat, while the main forces of the 7th Panzer Division's Panzer Regiment 25 were assembled in a patch of woods 2.5 kilometers northeast of Krutoi Log, serving as an operational reserve in the event of possible Russian counterattacks.

The reconnaissance of the 25th Guards Rifle Corps was working rather effectively and already that morning reported: "40 vehicles set out to the west from the "Batratskaia Dacha" State Farm; the large movement of up to a battalion of infantry from Krutoi Log to the woods east of there was spotted. Observation has established a large concentration of infantry and tanks in the woods, which lie 2.5 kilometers northeast of Krutoi Log."[104] G.B. Safiulin assumed that the increased activity in this sector was nothing other than the rotation of units and decided to take advantage of it. His 25th Guards Rifle Corps had already been given a task for the day; with a stubborn defense, to hold its line and prevent the enemy from breaking through to the right bank of the Korocha River. On the night of 9-10 M.S. Shumilov, after a discussion with N.F. Vatutin, contacted the commander of the 25th Guards Rifle Corps and ordered him to maintain continuous pressure on the enemy on the corps' right flank throughout the entire day, in order for the forces of the second echelon, with the support of the 15th Guards Rifle Division that was moving up into the first echelon, to launch powerful counterattacks in the direction of the "Batratskaia Dacha" State Farm and the "Solov'ev" collective farm. Thus an opportunity had appeared for G.B. Safiulin not only to carry out the order, but also to disrupt the enemy's plan for a regrouping.

Despite the "mishap" that had occurred on the right flank, he ordered the commander of the 78th Guards Rifle Division to move up the 228th Guards Rifle Regiment toward the "Batratskaia Dacha" State Farm from out of the second echelon (from Nikol'skoe), and at 1000 to move out to storm it. The battle began on time, but went unsuccessfully for the Guardsmen. The Germans opened up a hailstorm of fire from Nebelwerfers and pinned the attacking infantry down in front of the fruit orchard. An attempt to rally the men and resume the attack had no success. Realizing that Khitsov's regiment was being bled white and having no possibility to offer it fire support,

---

103 TsAMO RF, f. 33, op. 686044, ed. khr. 2996, entry number 20167662.
104 TsAMO RF, f. 878, op. 1, d. 33, ll. 25-26.

within an hour the corps commander ordered E.I. Vasilenko to form an assault group quickly out of the 44th Guards Rifle Regiment and go to the assistance of his neighbor.

The 15th Guards Rifle Division's commander immediately contacted Lieutenant Colonel I.A. Usikov and directed him to leave one battalion on the defense, and with the remaining two battalions to attack the "Solov'ev" collective farm and the "Batratskaia Dacha" State Farm, which were located less than 1.5 kilometers from each other. By 1200 the regiment's artillery had been brought up to the forward edge and had began to deploy there, and one and a half hours later the 1st and 2nd Rifle Battalions attacked in the Hill 202.3, lake, (excl.) "Batratskaia Dacha" State Farm direction (which extended for 2 kilometers). The attack started well; the Guardsmen quickly closed with the enemy in order to prevent him from bringing down directed mortar fire. The attack proved not only strong, but also very untimely for the enemy, because the exchange in line of the 7th Panzer Division's units still hadn't been finished. In particular, its combat engineer battalion was overrun on the "Batratskaia Dacha" State Farm. This became clear to the Soviet side when a prisoner was brought back to the division headquarters. In the course of an hour, the elements of two rifle regiments had driven the grenadiers out of the fruit orchard and semi-demolished buildings on the eastern outskirts, having pushed the defenders back 300-500 meters into the depth of the State Farm. However, the enemy was clinging to every structure and foxhole. Having been pushed back to the network of trenches in the center of the village and having occupied them, the panzergrenadiers now offered strong fire resistance.

Attentively following the developing situation on the corps' right flank, G.B Safiulin saw that Khitsov's and Usikov's regiments were running out of steam, but the knot of resistance had to be taken as quickly as possible, before the Germans moved up panzers and rendered all the sacrifices to be in vain. He contacted A.S. Kozak and ordered him to support the attack against the State Farm with the forces of the 214th Guards Rifle Regiment, which together with remnants of the 30th Separate Destroyer Anti-tank Artillery Brigade was occupying defensive positions to the south. A short time after the conversation with A.S. Kozak, Safiulin ordered the commander of the 97th Guards Mortar Regiment to work over the concentrations of enemy troops in front of the attacking regiments quickly with Katiusha rocket launchers.

From Operational Summary No.00190 from the headquarters of Voronezh Front's Guards Mortar regiments:

> 388/97th Guards Mortar Regiment was assembled in Nekliudovo. At 1700 10.7.43 it fired a battery salvo at an aggregation of enemy tanks on the "Solov'ev" collective farm. Two tanks were knocked out. 16 M-20 rockets were expended. At 1810 if fired a salvo with one rocket launcher at enemy tanks in the same area. 8 M-20 rockets were expended. At 1855 it fired a salvo with five rocket launchers at a concentration of enemy infantry and tanks in the vicinity of the woods 1 kilometer west of the "Batratskaia Dacha" State Farm. The target was blanketed. 78 M-13 rockets were expended.[105]

How subsequent events went was briefly laid out in the 73rd Guards Rifle Division's journal of combat operations: "At 1830 the 1 and 3/214th Guards Rifle Regiment, in cooperation with the 228th Guards Rifle Regiment, went on the attack with the task to mop up the "Batratskaia Dacha" State Farm of the enemy. Having met concentrated artillery and mortar fire, the units were unable to make headway. For the rest of the day, the regiment continued to exchange fire with the enemy."[106]

---

105 TsAMO RF, f. 203, op. 920412, d. 21, l. 449.
106 TsAMO RF, f. 73 gv. sd, op. 1, d. 33, l. 29.

While the 7th Panzer Division's artillery was busy with repulsing the attack of the two neighboring regiments, Usikov's Guardsmen again launched a counterattack against the "Batratskaia Dacha" State Farm. However, almost immediately the left flank of the 2nd Battalion of the 44th Guards Rifle Regiment was counterattacked by a German company north of the State Farm. The regiment commander smoothly introduced the 8th and 9th Companies of the 3rd Rifle Battalion, which overran the panzergrenadiers. The 15th Guards Rifle Division's commander reported: "The units with a decisive charge burst into the enemy trenches and tied the Germans up in hand-to-hand combat. The Germans, unable to withstand the hand-to-hand combat, retreated to the road junction 1 kilometer east of Hill 216.1. The regiment by 2300 reached the patch of woods on Point 216.1 and the western outskirts of the "Batratskaia Dacha" State Farm."[107] Continuing the pursuit, the Guardsmen by the end of the day had driven the enemy back by 1.5 kilometers and had reached the western outskirts of the State Farm, but they were unable to take complete possession of it. The fighting on its western and southwestern outskirts continued all night. The main reason for the incomplete success was the fact that during the afternoon, the fresh Infantry Regiment 326 of the 198th Infantry Division entered the fighting here.

Before dawn, Lieutenant Colonel I.A. Usikov reported that in the course of the counterattack the regiment had lost 20 killed and 120 wounded. Two enemy guns, two vehicles and 4 machine guns were destroyed, while two machine guns, 12 submachine guns, 23 rifles and 500 81mm mortar rounds were captured intact.[108] Meanwhile the commander of the 73rd Guards Rifle Division reported that the 214th Guards Rifle Regiment had 78 men killed or wounded, two Maksim heavy machine guns knocked out, and 4 horses killed.[109]

Major General von Funck realized that the Russians were attacking, albeit fiercely, in a narrow sector and without armor support, and therefore he had little concern about a breakthrough. Therefore he decided not to postpone the offensive with the aim of breaking through to the woods east of Miasoedovo (through the boundary of the 7th Guards and 69th Armies), and in the first phase to take not only the northern portion of the large forested area southeast of Miasoedovo (the right flank of the 25th Guards Rifle Corps) with an attack, but also to launch a flank attack against the units of the 15th Guards Rifle Division that had taken possession of most of the "Batratskaia Dacha" State Farm. Getting in touch with the III Panzer Corps headquarters, he reported the strong pressure of Russian infantry on the State Farm, briefly laid out his plan of actions, and checked to see whether or not he would receive air support as had been previously planned. Breith approved his plan and confirmed that according to plan bombers would strike the designated areas for 30 minutes, starting at 1750. At first the bombers would bomb the woods east of Miasoedovo and Hill 210.3 for 10 minutes, and then would bomb the northern portion of the woods southeast of Miasoedovo for 20 minutes.

From the operational summary of the 25th Guards Rifle Corps at 0400 on 11 July: "Enemy aircraft were on patrol and at 1800 44 Junkers-88s bombed the northern portion of the woods that lie 2 kilometers southeast of Miasoedovo. At 1820 after the attack by the bombers on the positions of the 47th Guards Rifle Regiment [15th Guards Rifle Division], the enemy went on the attack in strength of up to two battalions and 50 tanks in the Point 191.8, Hill 206.9, Hill 205.5 sector."[110] This attack struck the 47th Guards Rifle Regiment's 2nd Battalion, which had just finished repelling Panzer Reconnaissance Battalion 37's attack in the middle of the day against the positions on Hill 206.9 and to the south. However, the battalion stood firm even during this attack as well,

---

107 TsAMO RF, f. 15 gv. sd, op. 1, d. 8, l. 159.
108 Ibid.
109 TsAMO RF, f. 1212, op. 1, d. 28, l. 13.
110 TsAMO RF, f. 878, op. 1, d. 32, l. 143.

even though it suffered significant losses; the attack of the 7th Panzer Division's *kampfgruppe* was accompanied by heavy artillery fire from II/Artillery Regiment 62 and Nebelwerfers of I/Nebelwerfer Regiment 54. In response, the artillery batteries of Lieutenant Colonel Bogushevich's 161st Cannon Artillery Regiment, the firing positions of which were located to the east in the woods south of Nikol'skii, attempted to work over the attackers. However, their fire was relatively ineffective. Because of uncertainty about the location of our units' positions, the artillery regiment only fired 84 122mm shells at previously identified targets. The neighboring howitzer batteries of the 94th Guards Rifle Division, which were deployed in the woods east of Miasoedovo, gave more effective assistance to the defending rifle battalion. The enemy had made approximately a 1.5-2 kilometer advance from their jumping-off positions and came within visible range of the howitzer batteries, so their fire proved to be more effective.

The flanking 94th Guards Rifle Division's fire strongly hindered 7th Panzer Division's *kampfgruppe*, so von Funck personally requested a Luftwaffe liaison officer to call upon Stukas to strike the firing Russian batteries' positions quickly. At 1940 13 Ju-87s appeared above the woods and for the next several minutes formed a carousel over the howitzer positions to drop their bombs. However, judging from archival records, the results of their attacks proved low. According to Operational Summary No.0106 from the headquarters of Russkikh's division, in the course of 10 July four airstrikes were delivered against its line, in the course of which the losses amounted to 2 killed and 5 wounded in the 283rd Guards Rifle Regiment, 9 wounded in the 288th Guards Rifle Regiment, and no losses at all in the artillery regiment.[111]

The Guardsmen of Vasilenko's 15th Guards Rifle Division were not only tenaciously holding on to their positions against Schülz's *kampfgruppe* in the area of Hill 206.9, but were also continuing to exert strong pressure on the "Batratskaia Dacha" State Farm. A short time after the start of the offensive, 7th Panzer Division headquarters sent a daily summary to the III Panzer Corps, which stated:

1) In the course of the night a rotation in force was conducted, first with a regiment of the 198th Infantry Division in the sector extending from the "Batratskaia Dacha" State Farm (incl.) to the western spur of the woods (incl.). Throughout the night and the entire day, [there was] persistent pressure on the division's entire front. Throughout the night, lively enemy air activity. After the regrouping and bringing the units freed-up by the replacement to readiness, at 1800 the division, with powerful artillery and air support, launched an attack with the aim of capturing the northern portion of the woods. After taking the northern portion of the woods the division's objective consists of moving moving with the attacking panzer groups to the east, to attack and seize the sector of woods and commanding heights 2 kilometers southwest of Miasoedovo, and then to outflank it from the northeast in cooperation with units of the 6th Panzer Division.

b) The situation with panzers: 4 command tanks, 4 Pz.kpfw. II, 5 Pz.kpfw. III with 75mm guns, 19 Pz.kpfw. III with the long barrel 50mm gun, 1 Pz.kpfw. IV /with the short barrel/, 25 Pz.kpfw. IV /with the long barrel/, 3 Pz.kpfw VI. The situation with anti-tank guns: 6 75mm Pak 40 on mechanized tow, 6 76.2mm self-propelled guns, 15 medium anti-tank guns, 5 captured 76.2mm anti-tank guns.[112]

---

111 TsAMO RF, f. 1269, op. 1, d. 9, l. 131.
112 NARA US, rg. 242, t. 314, r. 197, f. 001302. Note that this report contained muddled figures and typos, and the correct figures were derived with the assistance of other sources. To wit, this report stated the 7th Panzer Division had 6 command tanks, just 1 (instead of 19) Pz.kpfw. III with the long-barrel 50mm gun, and 3 Pz.kpfw. IV [sic] at the end of the tank inventory listing.

Between 1820 and 2100 Lieutenant Colonel P.I. Grimailo's 47th Guards Rifle Regiment repulsed three panzer attacks launched by the 7th Panzer Division, but after the fourth, under the pressure of superior enemy strength, its battalion commanders began to withdraw their companies to reserve positions to the east, along the line: 1.5 kilometers south of Hill 205.5, 2.5 kilometers east of Hill 191.8, (excl.) Hill 202.3, where they consolidated.

The capture of the woods southeast of Miasoedovo was necessary for Breith for the following reason: control over the village itself, which was a Soviet strongpoint on the eastern bank of the Razumnaia River, was extremely important in order to continue 7th Panzer Division's attack to the northeast. Von Funck's panzer division back on 7 July had already tried to take it in cooperation with von Hünersdorff's *kampfgruppen*, but unsuccessfully. Now after turning over its sector to the 198th Infantry Division, it was decided to take the anti-tank strongpoint with enveloping pincers: with right-flank units of the 6th Panzer Division out of the area southwest of Kalinin in the direction of Hill 210.3, and with the forces of the 7th Panzer Division out of the area southwest of Hill 206.9 in the direction of Arkad'evka and further on toward Hill 210.3. However, the hill with the designation of 206.9, through which Schülz's *panzerkampfgruppe* had been trying to break through all day, was positioned right on the northern edge of the large wooded area held by the 47th Guards Rifle Regiment. Accordingly, in order for the 7th Panzer Division's *kampfgruppe* to attack Arkad'evka without concern over its right flank, it was important to throw Gremailo's regiment off the hill toward Borovskoe, thereby expanding the corridor between the southwestern outskirts of Miasoedovo and the Guards regiment's forward edge.

The units of Vasilenko's division were fully tying up the forces of the 7th Panzer Division and didn't allow them to achieve the given objective. Its *kampfgruppen* spent all night engaged in heavy combat with the Guardsmen in the large wooded area, and they failed to break through to Hill 210.3 (east of Miasoedovo). Only by morning, having driven back the 47th Guards Rifle Regiment the minimum distance necessary, they nevertheless managed to create enough room to assemble Schülz's *panzerkampfgruppe* for an attack against the 94th Guards Rifle Division's left flank. In the process, very substantial damage had been inflicted on the defending Guardsmen. Before sunrise P.I. Gremailo didn't know the location of his 2nd Rifle Battalion, which had received the main attack by the 7th Panzer Division's *kampfgruppe*. Therefore the 15th Guards Rifle Division commander hastily moved up his reserve – the training battalion – to the right flank of Gremailo's regiment. By 0700 on 11 July, communications was restored with the 2nd Rifle Battalion. The battalion commander reported that the situation in the subordinate companies was serious: the whereabouts of more than half the personnel was still unknown, panzers had crushed four 45mm anti-tank guns, and almost all the machine guns had been knocked out. According to Report No.059 from the headquarters of the 25th Guards Rifle Corps, over 10 July the 15th Guards Rifle Division lost a total of 540 men (180 killed, 360 wounded), 4 45mm anti-tank guns, 40 machine guns (32 RPD light machine guns and 7 Maksim heavy machine guns).[113] Considering that the 50th Guards Rifle Regiment took no part in combat operations that day, and the 44th Guards Rifle Regiment lost 140 men, then the remaining 400 casualties likely were those of the 47th Guards Rifle Regiment. This figure included the killed and wounded lost in the course of the nighttime attack to retake the line that Bezik's rifle company (of the 94th Guards Rifle Division) had abandoned, without waiting for its replacement to show up. The regiment's rather high casualties were connected primarily with the strong, well-planned fire of artillery and panzers on a small sector of terrain.

In addition, both regiments of the 15th Guards Rifle Division lacked any artillery assets, so the struggle against the enemy armor was conducted by the establishment anti-tank means: anti-tank

---

113 TsAMO RF, f 25 gv. sk, op. 1, d. 28, l. 61obr.

rifles, 45mm anti-tank guns and 76mm regimental guns M1923 or M1943, which were intended to destroy light fortifications and had limited anti-tank capabilities using HEAT [high-explosive, anti-tank] shells because of their insufficient range and low muzzle velocities. This was the main reason why Schülz's panzer regiment didn't suffer significant panzer losses in this sector. Over the day the 7th Panzer Division lost 6 tanks knocked-out, including 2 command tanks. Likely, in the course of the night the division's repair service restored a certain number of these tanks back to service, so one can assume that in the course of this fighting, no more than 1-2 were destroyed or rendered combat-ineffective for any length of time. This didn't substantially affect the combat-capability of von Funck's 7th Panzer Division, which numbered 53 tanks by the morning of 11 July (not including the attached Tigers), including 8 more long-barreled Pz.kpfw. IV than it had available on the morning of 10 July.[114]

I will note that judging from subsequent events, which led to the encirclement of the main forces of Russkikh's division near Miasoedovo on 11 July, at this moment the Soviet side (primarily the command of the 35th Guards Rifle Corps and 94th Guards Rifle Division) underestimated the degree of danger that was hanging over the left flank of this division at this moment. The enemy, operating with groups of panzers, and already driven back or shoved aside the neighboring 15th Guards Rifle Division and was assembling forces for an attack against Russkikh's division, but its command had no thought of deploying an infantry screen (of at least one rifle company) for the two incomplete regiments of the 31st Separate Destroyer Anti-tank Artillery Brigade, which were emplaced 1 kilometer southwest of Hill 213.7 and were the sole serious anti-tank means that were covering its flank.

The attempts by the 19th Panzer Division to reach the basin of the Northern Donets River and the 6th Panzer Division to break through to Shliakhovoe also ended in complete failure on 10 July. All day their artillery conducted increased artillery fire, especially on Kiselevo and Sabynino, while the Fliegerkorps VIII's bombers struck the positions and regrouping forces of the 35th Guards Rifle Corps between the Northern Donets and Razumnaia River, hindering the work to throw up fortifications and obstacles, as well as the deployment of the artillery that was arriving here. Especially heavy aerial bombing began in the evening. According to the 35th Guards Rifle Corps' Operational Summary No.109, from 1800 until the onset of twilight, the enemy conducted a total of 160 individual combat sorties of Ju-88 in the Kiselevo, Shliakhovoe, Mazikino and Sheino sectors. According to the combat diary of the 148th Separate Tank Regiment, which was in defensive positions in the Shliakhovoe area (together with the 305th Rifle Division's 1004th Infantry Regiments), at 1810 up to 51 bombers dropped their death-dealing loads over the regiment's forward edge.[115] Next, the German bombers switched their attention to Kiselevo and Sabynino. The main purpose of these airstrikes was unquestionably to disrupt the system of the Soviet defenses (communications, fire, etc.) before the onset of 11 July, but at the same time, von Hünersdorff and Schmidt were seeking to use this as well to check the strength of the 305th Rifle Division's and a portion of the 92nd Guards Rifle Division's forward edge. I will remind the reader that their regiments were holding the following sectors: 92nd Guards Rifle Division's 280th Guards Rifle Regiment – Kiselevo, Hill 211.5, (excl.) Shliakhovoe Machine Tractor Station; 305th Rifle Division's 1002nd Rifle Regiment – Sabynino, Hill 211.5, (excl.) Shliakhovoe Machine Tractor Station; and the 305th Rifle Division's 1004th Rifle Regiment – Shliakhovoe Machine Tractor Station, Orlov ravine, Razumnaia River.

Thus throughout the day units of the 6th and 19th Panzer Divisions conducted several reconnaissance-in-force, attacking the forward edge of the Soviet defense with 3-5 panzers supported

---

114 Zetterling and Frankson, *Kursk 1943: a statistical analysis*, p. 189.
115 TsAMO RF, f. 906, op. 1, d. 32, l. 171.

by 1 to 1.5 companies of panzergrenadiers, but in the evening both panzer divisions made an effort nevertheless to achieve the day's objectives. Very strong attacks by the *kampfgruppen* of both panzer divisions began, staggered somewhat in time. Around 1900 von Oppeln-Bronikowski's *panzerkampfgruppe* [22 panzers and up to a battalion of panzergrenadiers] covered by intense mortar fire moved out of Melikhovo in the direction of the Shliakhovoe Machine Tractor Station toward the positions of the 305th Rifle Division. A half hour later Westhofen's units attempted to breach the line of the 280th Guards Rifle Regiment in the direction of Kiselevo and Sabynino. From the daily summary from the headquarters of III Panzer Corps' headquarters:

> III Panzer Corps on 10.7 destroyed the encircled enemy forces northeast of Belgorod [the 81st Guards and 92nd Guards Rifle Divisions], and after a regrouping, again undertook a breakthrough to the north. The number of prisoners continues to increase. The quantity of captured guns and military equipment is significant, but hasn't been calculated so far. Smaller enemy groups, having abandoned their heavy weapons, fell back across the Donets at Staryi Gorod to the north and west.
>
> 6th Panzer Division occupied the "Main Fruit and Vegetable" State Farm and the southern [outskirts] of Shishino and destroyed the encircled enemy in the woods 2 kilometers northeast of Andreevskie. **Enemy attacks toward the hamlet of Kalinin and to the west were driven back by a meeting attack. Hill 230.3 north of Melikhovo that was being defended by panzers had to be yielded as a consequence of the heaviest artillery and anti-tank fire, in order to avoid the unnecessary loss of panzers. The crossroads west of Melikhovo is being firmly held in our hands.** [Emphasized and crossed out in the text.]
>
> 19th Panzer Division in the course of the day was assembling in the area of Dal'niaia Igumenka and at 1930 the panzer group set off in the direction of Kiselevo and the bridge in Sabynino. Sabynino and Kiselevo are occupied by strong enemy garrisons.[116]

The fighting at Shliakhovoe lasted for approximately two hours, but unable to withstand the withering fire of the anti-tank guns, the Germans retreated. It isn't clear why the announcement regarding the withdrawal of the panzers from Hill 230 was stricken out in the document, but in reality it fell back to Melikhovo that evening together with von Oppeln-Bronikowski's main forces. The losses in Vasil'ev's division weren't very high; throughout the day, from the bombing attacks and in the course of repulsing the panzer attacks, it suffered 26 killed and 72 wounded, while one 45mm anti-tank gun, one 120mm mortar, two 82mm mortars and one Maksim heavy machine gun were destroyed.[117]

Having up to 700 active bayonets in the two panzergrenadier regiments and 15 operational panzers in Panzer Regiment 27, at 1930 the 19th Panzer Division attacked in two directions: toward Kiselevo and Sabynino, while the main forces of Westhofen's panzer regiment advanced in the direction of the river channel. The attack was accompanied by airstrikes and strong artillery and mortar fire, which was organized by the corps' artillery headquarters. In the evening the 19th Panzer Division headquarters reported:

> Before mid-day the employed units [in the margin there is a handwritten comment that states "except for Infantry Regiment 442"] were assembled and throughout the rest of the day used

---

116 NARA US, rg. 242, t. 314, r. 197, f.001303.
117 TsAMO RF, f. 906, op. 1, d. 32, l. 171.

in mass in the area of Dal'niaia Igumenka and to the north of there. Two artillery regiments and the troop Flak battalions are ready to open fire in the new area.

The reconnaissance battalion established that Kiselevo was strongly occupied, but Khokhlovo is being held by a weaker enemy garrison. Heavy flanking fire from the heights southeast of Sabynino. Ground reconnaissance identified enemy movement from the west in the direction of the eastern and southern ends of the ravine south of Hill 211.5, to the Shpaki ravine and to the woods north of there.

At 1930 a panzer breakthrough together with the remaining panzers and a panzer grenadier battalion toward Kiselevo and the bridge in Sabynino succeeded.[118]

Novikov's Guards regiment that was defending in front of Westhofen's *panzerkampfgruppe* had been bled white in the preceding fighting. Thus already in the first hour of the attack, after the powerful, combined preparation by artillery and Fliegerkorps VIII, the enemy's panzergrenadiers, supported by panzers, drove back the battalion defending in front of Kiselevo and broke through into the depth of its defenses. The heavy fire coming from Hill 211.5 that was mentioned in the report from the 19th Panzer Division was being laid down by the 305th Rifle Division's artillery group (two battalions of the 830th Artillery Regiment) and 2/93rd Cannon Artillery Regiment. The appearance of German tanks in the depth of the positions in separate sectors created confusion; the companies wavered and began to retreat toward the village, where batteries of 1/93rd Cannon Artillery Regiment were located. The howitzer crews had to undergo a severe trial on this day. Several of its batteries dueled with the tanks in front of their positions, having rolled out their howitzers to fire over open sights. From the account of the headquarters of the 27th Separate Heavy Cannon Artillery Brigade:

> On 10 July the enemy began an offensive in the Kiselevo, Sabynino direction, throwing fresh reserves into the battle. Our infantry, engaging in heavy, stubborn fighting with the superior enemy, retreated. At 1500 an order was received personally from the Voronezh Front's artillery commander about the brigade's inclusion in the Voronezh Front's Long-Range Artillery Group; it was supposed to assemble on the Verkhnii Ol'shanets, Novo-Oskochnoe, and Rzhavets direction. The regiments were compelled to prepare for and begin a march to the new area while covering themselves with their own fire, keeping in check the pressing enemy.
>
> On this day 1/93rd Cannon Artillery Regiment of the Supreme Command Reserve, conducting fire at the enemy's attacking tanks and infantry, drove back two attacks, destroying 5 tanks, one self-propelled gun, up to 20 vehicles and up to a company of infantry. 2/93rd Cannon Artillery Regiment knocked out two tanks and up to 40 vehicles.
>
> 4/93rd Cannon Artillery Regiment was left behind to cover the brigade's maneuver. The battery carried out its given assignment with honor. Its crews knocked out 9 tanks, of which 5 were Pz VI, and wiped out a large quantity of infantry. In the process the battery lost only one cannon, which was knocked out by the direct hit of two shells. Sergeant Nochevkin's crew, having lost 4 men killed and 2 wounded, heroically dueled with the Tigers until the final minute, when the cannon was blown up. In this clash the commander of the 4th Battery Senior Lieutenant Pastushenko distinguished himself by helping the heroic crew until the final minute.[119]

---

118 NARA US, rg. 242, t. 314, r. 197, f. 001302.
119 TsAMO RF, f. 27 otpabr, op. 1, d. 9, l. 53, 54.

Despite all the efforts, before the onset of twilight, the enemy fell back from Kiselevo without having achieved any real results. Now, in order to give a picture of the fighting, I will cite a captured German document "Description of the combat actions of the 19th Panzer Division between 5 and 18 July 1943", in which officers of Shmidt's panzer division gave their assessment of the events that took place north and northeast of Belgorod:

> The enemy sensed the encirclement that was threatening him in the area northeast of Belgorod, and therefore on the night of 9-10.7, withdrew his forces to the north, along the valley of the Donets River, leaving behind a large quantity of arms, ammunition and military equipment (the division couldn't examine these trophies, since it was pushing forward). This [the withdrawal] was done in order to hold the bridges across the Donets River in the Kiselevo, Rzhavets area, which means in the final account to hold the Verkhnii Ol'shanets – Sabynino line, with all the withdrawn and brought up forces under his control.
>
> Judging from the forces which the enemy brought up to the Kiselevo – Rzhavets line, the advance of the German troops along the Donets River [the attack by the 19th Panzer Division] was particularly dangerous for him [!?]. The enemy didn't withdraw all his forces located between the Donets River and the SS Panzer Corps. For this purpose he needed the bridges that were now under the threat of capture. In any case, he had to hinder the link-up between the units of III Panzer Corps that were attacking from the southeast in the direction of the Donets River and the SS Panzer Corps, as a result of which his divisions operating on the Donets might become encircled.
>
> What regroupings the Russians were doing in order to hold the Kiselevo – Hill 211.5 – Ol'shanets line! They committed remnants of the 81st Guards and 73rd Guards Rifle Divisions; units of the 375th Rifle Division, 89th Guards Rifle Division, two regiments of the 107th Rifle Division, one regiment of the 305th Rifle Division, remnants of the 92nd Guards Rifle Division, remnants of the 4th Motorized Rifle Brigade [of the 2nd Guards Tank Corps], and judging from the evidence of the SS Panzer Corps – one battalion of anti-tank rifles (112 such rifles). Facing them was the 19th Panzer Division consisting of two panzergrenadier regiments (with a total of just 400 active bayonets), a weakened panzer reconnaissance battalion and 17 combat-ready panzers.[120]

The excerpt cited above plainly shows how the command of the 19th Panzer Division sought to touch up its "image" by "demonstrating a fine play during a bad game". In the document, the events have been especially compressed in time somewhat: the officers merged what had happened by 10 July with what would occur 2-4 days later, in particular the regrouping of the 89th Guards Rifle Division, the 107th Rifle Division, the 4th Guards Motorized Rifle Brigade and so forth. Up until this moment, the listed Soviet formations didn't take part in repulsing the attacks of the 19th Panzer Division. It is clear why this was done: How could such a disgrace be left behind in the division's history? Over five days of the offensive, just one reinforced rifle division of the Russians had made such scraps of the panzer division? That explains the multiplicity of units and formations gathered by the Soviet side – "Look how we brave few stood up against the hordes of slant-eyed Asians!" As for the assertion that supposedly the main danger for the Russians was the axis along the river channel (where the 19th Panzer was attempting to break through), and not the attacking sector of its neighbor the 6th Panzer Division, is far from true.

All of this was very distant from reality. By this time, the failure of Operation Citadel had become obvious to everyone who was associated with it, and moreover to a significant degree

---

120 TsAMO RF, f. 38A, op. 9027, d. 46, l. 154.

precisely because of the fact that Army Detachment Kempf couldn't carry out the main task that had been given to it. Therefore by the end of 10 July, the command of Army Group South was already concerned with how it could withdraw the Fourth Panzer Army's forces from the "mouse trap" into which they themselves had chased it. For this purpose it was exceptionally important, at last, to destroy the powerful Russian grouping in the wedge-shaped center of opposition between the adjacent flanks of the Fourth Panzer Army and Army Detachment Kempf (the 69th Army's 40th Rifle Corps in the narrow interfluvial area between the Northern and Lipovyi Donets Rivers). However, the prospects for even carrying out this task still remained rather murky. Moreover, having given so much time to analyzing the situation, primarily in Army Detachment Kempf's sector, on the morning of 11 July 1943 von Manstein felt compelled to summon the commanders of the Fourth Panzer Army and of Army Detachment Kempf, as well as their chiefs of staff, to a conference at Dolbino Station (on the Belgorod – Khar'kov rail line), in order to address the question: "What to do next, and was it possible at all for both formations – II SS Panzer Corps and III Panzer Corps – to reach Prokhorovka?"

An excerpt from the transcript of the ensuing discussion describes a cheerless picture, which had formed after six days of the offensive by the Wehrmacht's most powerful grouping on the Eastern Front:

> **W. Kempf:** Today 7th Panzer is to take the woods east of Sheino. After this, the plan for it and 6th Panzer Division will be as follows: to break through the final enemy defensive position to the south of Sabynino, with the order to continue their advance to the north to meet the Fourth Panzer Army. The commander of III Panzer Corps had promised that the attack will be successful.
>
> **E. von Manstein:** The task for Army Detachment Kempf is the following: to protect the right flank of Fourth Panzer Army against enemy attacks. For this the panzer corps [Breith's] must advance to the area southeast of Prokhorovka. The question is as follows: Will the III Panzer Corps' offensive to the north be successful, or will Fourth Panzer Army have to pivot for an attack to the south?
>
> **W. Kempf:** The answer to this question will be known after the heights to the east of Sabynino are taken – no sooner than this evening.
>
> **Fangohr [Chief of Staff of Fourth Panzer Army]:** The situation this morning is as follow [in the Fourth Panzer Army's sector]: All the panzer divisions are on the attack. *Das Reich* – to the east, through Ivanovka and in the area north of it, against the 2nd Tank Corps; *Leibstandarte Adolf Hitler* is advancing toward Prokhorovka with the assignment: to secure a defense to the north and east. *Totenkopf* is west of the Psel River, advancing to the northeast, with the task to cover *Leibstandarte Adolf Hitler* left flank against enemy attacks.
>
> To the north, in front of the XXXXLVIII Panzer Corps, the enemy isn't ready for offensive operations. The corps is pushing the 11th Panzer Division to the north; *Grossdeutschland* and the 3rd Panzer Division are successfully attacking in the western direction, but they have a strong enemy opposite their flank. It is presumed that on our western flank, in the Kruglik area, the 6th Tank Corps is operating. The 332nd Infantry Division is attacking across the Pena River.
>
> It is necessary to free up the *Grossdeutschland* Division as quickly as possible, and send it across the Psel River to the Peresyp' area. It will be able to arrive there no sooner than 12 July, so it can attack no earlier than 13 July. 3rd Panzer Division must attack the 6th Tank Corps and force it to retreat.
>
> **E. von Manstein:** The pivot to the south and the advance in the southern direction must be implemented by more than one division. The offensive to the northeast (toward

Prokhorovka) is now still possible, but will be impossible later, because the enemy is assembling fresh tank forces in this area [in the vicinity of Prokhorovka]. If III Panzer Corps' attack proves unsuccessful, then it should go over to a defense, so its divisions can be used on the right flank [of Fourth Panzer Army] or to the north of Oboian' in order to develop an offensive in the western direction [into the rear of 40th Army]. XXIV Panzer Corps will arrive no sooner than 17 July and it is being planned to use it for an offensive in the western direction, if III Panzer Corps still can't be used for this.

Fangohr: It would be good if II SS Panzer Corps continued its offensive to the northeast [toward Prokhorovka], since everything previously planned was based on this calculation. So it might be better to use XXIV Panzer Corps for an attack to the southeast or south, and not the II SS Panzer Corps.

E. von Manstein: XXIV Panzer Corps will arrive too late, so I propose to the commander of Fourth Panzer Army to examine the option in which 167th Infantry Division might be used to assist III Panzer Corps that is attacking in the northern direction.[121]

Thus, by the end of 10 July 1943, Army Detachment Kempf had converted from being the main assistant of Hoth's Fourth Panzer Army to von Manstein's primary headache. Its forces had ended up being pinned down by the Soviet armies' powerful defense on Voronezh Front's left wing and had been bled so white that it was no longer in the condition not only to resolve its former tasks, but even great doubts had arisen in their capability to advance even to a point southeast of Prokhorovka. Therefore, as is clear from the conference proceedings, the question about diverting a portion of Fourth Panzer Army's strength in order to aid them was discussed. This despite the fact that it was Kempf, not Hoth, who had already received one fresh infantry division (198th Infantry Division) as reinforcement. This (the maximum bleeding of the Army Detachment Kempf) and the diversion of reserves to it (the 198th Infantry Division) was the main outcome for which M.S. Shumilov and the Guardsmen of his 7th Army had been striving and achieved.

We should tip our hats to them, and honor forever all those who fell in the struggle. Thus it is even more bitter and painful to acknowledge that N.F. Vatutin's brilliant idea to sever von Manstein's two primary assault groupings from each other with a thoroughly prepared and well-conducted defensive operation in the first stage was in fact botched during its conclusion (including because of the General of the Army's own decisions that were not fully considered).

Concluding this tale of the events near Belgorod on 9-10 July 1943, I want to bring the reader's attention to two very important aspects, which by this time began to appear and seriously and adversely affected the results of the combat work of the command and troops of the Voronezh Front. The first was the losses in personnel and heavy weapons, as well as the overall exhaustion and stress on the men after almost a week of uninterrupted fighting, which began to reduce noticeably the combat capabilities and tenacity of its troops. After 10 July 1943 the situation regarding the resilience of the defense on all three directions, the Oboian', Prokhorovka and Korocha directions, became substantially complicated. Problems began to accumulate like a snowball, gradually undermining the idea that had formed for the frontal counterattack, set for 12 July 1943, which the Soviet side was counting upon to halt the advance of Army Group South into the depth of the Front's defenses once and for all, and to seize the initiative from von Manstein.

In the second place, the eviction of Morozov's and Trunin's divisions from the "Belgord bastion" on 10 July, followed by the defeat of Group Getman (the 6th Tank Corps) in the bend of the Pena River on 11 July, were together an important tactical success for the enemy, which had a very serious and negative influence on the failure of the counterattack plan on 12 July, since both

---

121 NARA US, t. 313, r. 366, f. 000421.

Morozov's and Getman's groupings up until this moment had been looming on the flanks of the Fourth Panzer Army's XXXXVIII Panzer Corps and Army Detachment Kempf's III Panzer Corps, diverting their main forces onto themselves and thereby fettering the German initiative. Now these problems had been eliminated. Skipping somewhat ahead in the events, I'll note that the command of Voronezh Front didn't succeed in restoring the situation in the sector of the 1st Tank Army and 6th Guards Army, which would have forced Hoth to return Panzergrenadier Division *Grossdeutschland*, which had already begun to regroup in the direction of Peresyp', to the bend of the Pena River, nor did it stop the III Panzer Corps, which although battered, still had some penetrative power. Breith's persistent and professional actions in the final account would lead to heavy consequences: the dispersion of the main counterattack grouping (the 5th Guards Tank Army), which had assembled on the morning of 12 July in the vicinity of Prokhorovka, and two days later the encirclement of half of the 69th Army as well.

7

"The beast is badly wounded, but still very dangerous." Breith's III Panzer Corps' dashing foray into the 69th Army's rear

The day of 11 July 1943 became one of the hardest and most dramatic for Vatutin's troops in the course of the Kursk defensive operation. By day's end, von Manstein's Army Group South managed to make noticeable progress in every direction. The Fourth Panzer Army's XXXXVIII Panzer Corps smashed Group Getman in the bend of the Pena River. Its neighbor the II SS Panzer Corps reached the outskirts of Prokhorovka, thereby depriving the Voronezh Front's shock army, the 5th Guards Tank Army, of the last suitable line for deploying its forces for the counterattack. Meanwhile, III Panzer Corps' *kampfgruppen* in the course of the day penetrated the 69th Army's line to its entire depth at the boundary of its two corps, encircled the main forces of the 94th Guards Rifle Division, and on the night of 11-12 July, having forced a crossing of the Northern Donets, created a bridgehead on its northern bank at Rzhavets. This means they had finally penetrated into the defenses of the 69th Army's 48th Rifle Corps, which was holding the interfluvial area between the Northern and Lipovyi Donets Rivers. There had been days when Army Group South made more significant progress into the depth of the Front's defenses, but its successes on 11 July had a more substantial influence on the further plans of the two sides not because of the capture of territory, but because of the fact that they forced N.F. Vatutin to disperse his primary counterattack grouping at Prokhorovka, and thereby to a certain degree predetermined its failure.

How the events developed on this day on the right flank (near Prokhorovka) and in the center (Kiselevo – Shliakhovoe) had been described in detail in my preceding works.[1] Therefore below I will touch upon only the circumstances of the breakthrough of the 69th Army's 35th Guards Rifle Corps' line, the encirclement of the 94th Guards Rifle Division, and dwell briefly on the results of the day. So, in the course of the discussions between N.F. Vatutin and M.S. Shumilov that took place on the evening of 9 July, the General of the Army had expressed the idea that within two days the Germans would likely launch a decisive attack with the aim of crushing the line of Kriuchenkin's 69th Army and reaching Prokhorovka from the south. Based on this supposition, he gave the army commander a task: "Absolutely prepare for active operations on 11 July … the enemy has assembled major tank forces on Kriuchenkin's flanks. Thus you are to have your right

---

1 Zamulin, V.N., *Prokhorovka* (Moscow: Veche, 2013) and Zamulin, V.N., *Zasekrechennaia Kurskaia bitva* [*Classified Battle of Kursk*] (Moscow: Iauza, 2013). In English, see his *Demolishing the Myth. The tank battle at Prokhorovka, Kursk 1943: An operational narrative* (Helion & Company, Ltd, Solihull UK, 2011), translated by Stuart Britton.

flank be very strong, in order to assist Kriuchenkin with heavy fire, if necessary, or by counterattacks and the maneuver of your anti-tank means."[2] Pursuant to this order, M.S. Shumilov ordered G.B. Safiulin on 11 July to continue counterattacks on the right flank and center of his 25th Guards Rifle Corps, in order to tie up enemy strength and thereby prevent the Germans from concentrating maximum strength for an attack against 69th Army's left flank. However, after Major General H. von Horn's 198th Infantry Division partially replaced the 7th Panzer Division opposite the 25th Guards Rifle Corps' sector of defense, the corps commander no longer had the possibility to keep the 7th Panzer Division tied down on his front. Nevertheless, an order is an order and it must be carried out. That night the commanders of the 44th Guards and 47th Guards Rifle Regiments of the 15th Guards Rifle Division received an order to attack the Hill 205.5 – Hill 202.3 – "Solov'ev" collective farm – "Batratskaia Dacha" State Farm at 1000.

N.F. Vatutin's calculations proved to be accurate. Despite the fact that III Panzer Corps had not succeeded in breaking through even to the woods east of Miasoedovo, much less close on Sheino from the south, Kempf presented Breith with a much more sizeable task for 11 July: with simultaneous attacks against the flanks of the 25th Guards Rifle Corps along the basins of the Northern Donets and Koren' Rivers to crush it, and having reached the Verkhnii Ol'shanets – Kazach'e area, to prepare the conditions for seizing crossing sites on the Donets River in the Sholokovo – Rzhavets sector. Thereby, over the day the III Panzer Corps had to overcome the Front's second army-level belt of defenses, where half of the 69th Army was deployed.

These tasks were given to Breith on the evening of 10 July. But that morning Kempf, located in his command post in Dolbino, at 1020 (40 minutes after the conference with von Manstein) called Breith, in order to receive the latest information first-hand about the operational situation, and to clarify his point of view as to whether or not the III Panzer Corps could handle the day's task. Among the captured documents of the headquarters of III Panzer Corps, there is a staff memorandum that lays out the essence of this discussion:

> In the existing situation the commander of Army Detachment Kempf believes that it is now impossible to detain the panzer corps. The corps commander doesn't share his point of view. He considers that the day's forthcoming fighting (7th Panzer Division in the area of the fringe of the woods, 6th Panzer Division in the Shliakhovoe and Verkhnii Ol'shanets area, 19th Panzer Division – Sabynino) will be very hard. These sacrifices are necessary in order to destroy completely the enemy's rear positions. ... It is known that the SS Panzer Corps, which is actively advancing in the direction of Prokhorovka, has gradually weakened the enemy's resistance on the [III Panzer] corps' western flank. If the [Breith's] corps carries out its given mission, it will thereby conclusively receive freedom of actions in the northeastern and northern directions.[3]

From the document it is clear that Breith understood the importance of the success of his panzer corps' offensive for the overall cause, but in his words it is hard to find any notes of the optimism that Kempf expressed at the conference. Well, from where could he get such optimism, if by the morning of 11 July III Panzer Corps had only 33% of the operational tanks that it had on the morning of 5 July?

The Operations Department of the headquarters of Breith's III Panzer Corps issued the order to his divisions for the fighting on 11 July over the telephone back on the evening of 10 July. It was significantly shorter and more laconic than such documents in the preceding days and said:

---

2 TsAMO RF, f. 203, op. 2843, d. 461, l. 50.
3 NARA US, rg. 242, t. 314, r. 197, f. 001363.

1. III Panzer Corps 11.07.1943 is to destroy the enemy encircled in the "pocket" east of Belgorod and early in the morning to continue to advance to the north.
   Tasks:
   a) 7th Panzer Division consolidates its positions in the large wooded area northeast of Miasoedovo and is to be ready either to continue the offensive further to the northeast, or after turning over its positions to the units of the 198th Infantry Division is to advance west of the Razumnaya River across the bridges in Sevriukovo and Belovskaia to the north.
   b) 6th Panzer Division is to take Shliakhovoe and Nizhnii Ol'shanets, to destroy the enemy located in the area between Kalinin and the "Komintern" State Farm, west of the Razumnaia River. Isolate the "Komintern" State Farm.
   c) 19th Panzer Division is to take Sabynino, as well as the bridge across the Northern Donets.
   d) 168th Infantry Division is to take Khokhlovo, Belomestnoe and the hills to the west and to be ready after the 19th Panzer Division's advance to guard the corps' left flank as far as Sabynino (incl.). Conduct active reconnaissance against the wooded hills north of Petropavlovka and further on to the Lipovyi Donets.
4. The chief of Artkommando 3 retains his previous order. II/Artillery Regiment 62, first of all, comes under the command of Artkommando 3 after the 7th Panzer Division takes the wooded hills northeast of Miasoedovo.
5. Heavy Panzer Battalion 503 (minus one company) is attached to the 6th Panzer Division.[4]

Thus, in the first stage of the fighting Army Detachment Kempf's shock formation was to unleash all of its strength against the line of one of the two corps of Kriuchenkin's 69th Army – the 35th Guards Rifle Corps. Breith's three panzer divisions were to destroy four powerful centers of resistance (in the second army-level belt of defenses), upon which the 35th Guards Rifle Corps' forward edge of defense was relying. Subsequently, the *panzerkampfgruppen* of Schmidt, von Hünersdorff and von Funck were to continue the offensive with a united front against the positions of Goriachev's 35th Guards Rifle Corps in the corridor between the Northern Donets and Razumnaia Rivers.

Two infantry divisions were to operate on the flanks of III Panzer Corps. The 168th Infantry Division received the task: covering the left flank of III Panzer Corps' assault wedge, and having overcome the line of the 48th Rifle Corps' 89th Guards Rifle Division, to emerge in the depth of the 48th Rifle Corps' defenses. Meanwhile von Horn's 198th Infantry Division from Korps Raus received the order to reinforce the 7th Panzer Division's attack and given its advance into the depth of the 69th Army's lines, to take over defense of the captured ground from Miasoedovo and further to the northeast.

By sunrise 11 July, the defense of Goriachev's 35th Rifle Corps was arranged in two echelons. In the first, the 94th Guards Rifle Division was dug in on the line: Hill 206.9 (excl.), northern portion of Miasoedovo, Kalinin, and along the basin of the Razumnaia River as far as the Orlov ravine (excl.). Its rifle regiments were arrayed in a single line, and on the left flank, covering the boundary with the 7th Guards Army (in the area of Hill 213.7) was the 31st Separate Destroyer Anti-tank Artillery Brigade. On the left flank, considering that the 92nd Guards Rifle Division had suffered heavy losses, and the 305th Rifle Division was experiencing an acute deficit of anti-tank means and was positioned in hastily prepared positions, the command of the 69th Army made the decision to firm up the forces of the first echelon (in a sector of 10 kilometers) by not only arraying

---

4   NARA US, rg. 242, t. 314, r. 197, f. 001313, 001314.

their regiments in a single line, but also at the expense of their units to create a second echelon within the divisions, as well as a strong reserve. After 0330 on 11 July, the 92nd Guards Rifle Division's 280th Guards Rifle Regiment together with the 2nd and 3rd Battalions of the 305th Rifle Division reached the Orlov ravine – Kiselevo – Hill 211.5 sector, and the 92nd Guards Rifle Division's 276th Guards Rifle Division together with the 1st and 3rd Battalions of the 305th Rifle Division's 1002nd Rifle Regiment moved into the sector: (excl.) Hill 211.5 – (excl.) Shliakhovoe Machine Tractor Station. In the division's second echelon, the 92nd Guards Rifle Division's 282nd Guards Rifle Regiment was dug in along a line from the bend of the road leading from Sabynino to Znamenka across Hill 224.4 to (excl.) western edge of the Dubrova ravine. Meanwhile in order to stand ready for a counterattack in case of a breakthrough of the forward edge, a reserve had been formed out of two battalions of the 305th Rifle Division: 2/1002nd Rifle Regiment in the Znamenka area, and 1/1004th Rifle Regiment in the Dubrova ravine, Hill 220.1 area.

By 1000 10 July, the still practically unbloodied 89th Guards Rifle Division under Colonel M.P. Seriugin's command was occupying a line running from the western fringe of the woods west of Kiselevo through Kiselevo to the southern outskirts of Sabynino.[5] It was thereby covering two large villages (and bridges) in the 19th Panzer Division's sector and saddling the road from Melikhovo to Sabynino and further across the Donets River to Gostishchevo.

The tankers of Lebedev's and Shevchenko's tank brigades comprised the backbone of the defense of the villages on the left bank of the Northern Donets River. The 96th Separate Tank Brigade (28 T-34, 5 T-70, 2 T-60, 3 76mm guns and an anti-tank rifle company[6]) had the 228th Tank Battalion, three 76mm anti-tank guns and an anti-tank rifle company deployed on a line running from the southwestern outskirts of Kiselevo to (excl.) Hill 211.5, and the 331st Tank Battalion and motorized rifle battalion positioned on a line running from Hill 211.5 to the patch of woods 1 kilometer southeast of Sabynino, while a company (3 Mk-IV and one armored car) of the 47th Guards Separate Heavy Breakthrough Tank Regiment and 5 batteries (4 45mm anti-tank guns each) of the 1500th Destroyer Anti-tank Artillery Regiment in Khokhlovo (1 kilometer southwest of Kiselevo). In addition, on the southwestern outskirts of Shliakhovoe and the Machine Tractor Station (on the road to Dal'niaia Igumenka) 18 tanks of the 148th Separate Tank Regiment, a submachine gun company, an anti-tank rifle company and the 122th Anti-tank Rifle Battalion (107 anti-tank rifles) were dug in.

In the second echelon of the 35th Guards Rifle Corps was Major General M.P. Bezhko's 107th Rifle Division. From Operational Summary No.0201 of the division headquarters for 0500 11 July:

2. 107th Rifle Division with the 496th Mortar Regiment of the Supreme Command Reserve and the 130th Anti-tank Rifle Battalion has occupied and is defending the Verkhnii Ol'shanets – Shukhovtsevo – Gremiachee – Ploskoe sector. Work is being done to fortify the sector, and units in their sectors are studying the terrain and the enemy.
3. The 522nd Rifle Regiment with 2/1032nd Artillery Regiment is defending the sector: Verkhnii Ol'shanets, Shukhovtsevo, quadrangular woods 2 kilometers east of Verkhnii Ol'shanets, fortifying the positions and emplacing the available mines on tank-vulnerable directions [emphasis added].
4. The 504th Rifle Regiment with 1/1032nd Artillery Regiment, 1/496th Mortar Regiment of the Supreme Command Reserve, the 130th Anti-tank Rifle Battalion minus one company and one battery of the 409th Destroyer Anti-tank Artillery Battalion is

---

5   TsAMO RF, f. 48 sk, op. 1, d. 15, l. 67.
6   TsAMO RF, f. 96 otbr, op. 1, d. 3, l. 16obr.

defending the sector: (excl.) Shukovtsevo, Gremiachee, northern outskirts of Lomovo. Defensive works are being thrown up.

5. The 516th Rifle Regiment with 3/1032nd Artillery Regiment, one company of the 130th Anti-tank Rifle Battalion and one battery of the 409th Destroyer Anti-tank Artillery Battalion is defending the sector: (excl.) Gremiachee, Ploskoe, Peshchanoe. Defensive work is being conducted.[7]

The command of the 35th Guards Rifle Corps did everything possible to strengthen the defense based on its available forces and means. However, it was no longer in the condition to resolve a number of substantial problems, which ultimately became the reason for the enemy's rapid breakthrough of the divisions' lines.

In the first place, the divisions of its right flank didn't possess the necessary amount of anti-tank artillery to counter enemy armor, while the units and formations attached to the corps had a large deficit of weapons, prime movers and transport. I will remind the readers that in the 92nd Guards Rifle Division's 197th Guards Artillery Regiment, its 1st Artillery Battalion and almost half of the 3rd Artillery Battalion had been completely wiped out, while the regiment itself was leaderless; in the preceding fighting, its commander and deputy commander had been killed, and its headquarters had been destroyed. In addition, in the 114th Guards Destroyer Anti-Tank Artillery Regiment attached to the division, there remained only a single battery, and it had been sent to the rear (to the Krasnoe Znamia area) into the corps commander's reserve. The tank units that were positioned among the infantry positions undoubtedly strengthened their anti-tank defense, but unfortunately, they were acting on their own, poorly tying their actions together with the infantry. Moreover, there was little time to get close cooperation functioning, because the neighbors were changing every day or two, and sometimes even more frequently.

In the second place, the 92nd Guards Rifle Division's 276th Guards and 282nd Guards Rifle Regiment had just come out of encirclement the day before. In the preceding fighting they had incurred heavy losses, and the men were exhausted by four days of fighting and the nighttime withdrawal from the pocket. Their battalions took up their positions also at nighttime, and in the morning they were already engaged in combat with enemy panzers. The 280th Guards Rifle Regiment with respect to setting up a defensive line was in a more favorable position, but its losses in men were also heavy and the condition of its remaining men was also poor. Thus the regiments had no possibility or time to arrange a system of fire, establish communications and get cooperation running smoothly.

The 305th Rifle Division that had arrived here from the march in the early morning hours of 9 July was also not in very good shape; as already noted, it "took position in an unprepared place". Therefore, although its men had dug trenches, they were not everywhere of standard profile and their network, naturally, was not as elaborate as, for example, in the 7th Guards Army.

In the third place, the minefields and other artificial obstacles in front of the forward edge and in the depth of the 35th Guards Rifle Corps' sector were poorly developed. A portion of the available minefields had been removed in order to allow the passage of their own troops, and another portion had been destroyed or detonated in the course of bombing raids and artillery barrages. The divisions that had arrived here (92nd Guards, 107th and 305th Rifle Divisions) had a limited number of anti-tank mines and they were unable to block all the vulnerable directions. In addition, Goriachev's entire 35th Guards Rifle Corps as before was experiencing an acute deficit of ammunition.

---

7   TsAMO RF, f. 1396, op. 1, d. 20, l. 209.

In the fourth place, the level of training and discipline of the men (including the commanders), the teamwork of the headquarters staff, and the efficiency of command over the units, was rather low in the 92nd Guards and 305th Rifle Divisions. The command of the 94th Guards Rifle Division as well, including Colonel I.G. Russkikh in person and his regiment commanders, weren't distinguished by a responsible attitude to carrying out their duties, or ensuring that their orders were carried out properly. There were also large problems with the personal discipline of the commanders, as we'll see below, and in some of the units that arrived here from out of the 69th Army's reserve as reinforcements. Thus, Trunin's, Vasil'ev's and Russkikh's divisions, which were located on the direction of III Panzer Corps' attack, weren't completely ready to receive it on the morning of 11 July.

The enemy spent the entire night of 10-11 July feeling out and simultaneously eroding the defense of the 35th Guards Rifle Corps, but the first to launch powerful attacks at the boundary between the 15th Guards Rifle Division and 94th Guards Rifle Division was the 7th Panzer Division. This sector was subjected to particularly strong pressure after sunrise. Considering that these Guards divisions were occupying a prepared line of defense, and Schülz's panzer regiment no longer had a large quantity of operational armor, when planning the breakthrough von Funck placed an emphasis on an intensive, prolonged artillery preparation and airstrikes on the centers of resistance, primarily on artillery positions. Meanwhile during the intervals between the artillery fire and airstrikes, the *kampfgruppen* were to feel out the most vulnerable sectors that had been revealed by the 7th Panzer Division's reconnaissance, which it must be recognized was operating very actively here. So, for example, at 0730 up to 400 submachine gunners supported by artillery in the sector 2.3 kilometers east of Hill 191.8 attempted to infiltrate into the depth of the 47th Guards Rifle Regiment, but the attempt was repulsed. A half-hour later an artillery spotter appeared above the area of the boundary between Russkikh's 94th Guards Rifle Division and Vasil'enko's 15th Guards Rifle Division, and almost immediately the 7th Panzer Division's heavy artillery and mortars blanketed the positions of the units on the right flank of the 15th Guards Rifle Division and left flank of the 94th Guards Rifle Division. The staff officers of the 31st Separate Anti-tank Artillery Brigade wrote in an account: "The enemy was constantly keeping the entire area of the regiments' defense under heavy rocket artillery fire. Meanwhile a FW-189 was correcting the fire of the batteries right up to the start of the general attack, which took place around 1130." The barrage continued for approximately 40 minutes, and then the grenadiers against moved out toward the positions of the 47th Guards Rifle Regiment. However, the Guardsmen stood firm once again. Up until 1000, combined attacks were repeated two more times, but now with the support of 12-15 panzers. Having received a sharp rebuff, the enemy resumed a lengthy aerial bombing now of the positions of the 31st Separate Anti-tank Artillery Brigade (on Hill 213.7 and in Akadev'ka); before noontime, Luftwaffe formations of up to 30 Ju-88 each bombed its combat positions three times.

At 1000 the Soviet side opened up fire on the "Solov'ev" collective farm and the area west of the "Batratskaia Dacha" State Farm, but it wasn't as intense as the enemy's artillery fire, and then rifle companies of the 47th Guards Rifle Regiment rose on the counterattack. The headquarters of the 25th Guards Rifle Corps reported before noon: "The regiment … at 1030 went on the offensive, but advanced only 100-200 meters before falling under a storm of fire and became pinned down."

Having received a preliminary report about the 15th Guards Rifle Division's failed attack, G.B. Safiulin contacted the army commander, and having briefed him of the situation on the corps' right flank, emphasized that according to his intelligence, the Germans, using the concealment of the woods in the area of Hill 191.8 and Hill 206.9, were assembling significant armor forces. Considering their high activity on the flank of Vasil'enko's 15th Guards Rifle Division and the intensive artillery barrage on the boundary with the 35th Guards Rifle Corps, by mid-day it was necessary to expect a panzer attack in the direction of Hill 213.7 in the corridor between Miasoedovo and the woods to the southeast that the Germans had cleared the day before. Therefore the corps commander requested assistance to strengthen the 15th Guards Rifle Division's training battalion, which was defending on the boundary with the 94th Guards Rifle Division. M.S. Shumilov agreed with his proposal and promised to provide immediate assistance with tanks. Around 1100 the chief of staff of the Armored and Mechanized Forces Major Krygin sent the following message to the 262nd Heavy Tank Regiment: The Commander-in-Chief of the army's Armored and Mechanized Forces has ordered: "urgently detach six tanks to be made subordinate to the commander of the 25th Guards Rifle Corps Guards Major General Safiulin. Position the assigned tanks on the defense, having dug them into the ground at the indication of the 25th Guards Rifle Corps commander. Report on the execution of this order by 1300 11.7.1943 over the telephone."[8] At 1310 Colonel I.I. Aizenberg was now signing his Directive No.3, which precisely designated the positions for the tanks and instructed his combat deputy Lieutenant Colonel Lozhkin to monitor the positioning of the tanks and the preparation of their emplacements. According to this document, by 1400 four T-34 tanks were supposed to reach the area of Hill 213.7 and with fire from fixed positions support the infantry in the struggle against the 7th Panzer Division's panzers, while the two other T-34 tanks were to assemble on the northeastern slopes of a nameless hill on the "Batratskaia Dacha" State Farm. The tank regiment's remaining armor (KV-1 and SU self-propelled guns), which at this time were located in Nekliudovo, were ordered by Colonel Aizenberg to prepare for a counterattack in the direction of Hill 213.7 and the State Farm. Already within three and a half hours, under the influence of the enemy's actions, this order would be substantially changed. However, it was namely the first four T-34 tank crews who together with the 47th Guards Rifle Regiment would serve as the backbone of the defense on the left flank of the 7th Guards Army, and until late in the evening would repulse all attempts by the 7th Panzer Division's *kampfgruppen* to break through into the rear of the 25th Guards Rifle Corps and reach the channel of the Koren' River in the Novo-Troevka – Nekliudovo sector.

Nevertheless, all of the main burden of combat with the 7th Panzer Division's panzer regiment, which had prepared since early morning to overrun the boundary between the divisions of Russkikh (the left-flank 283rd Guards Rifle Regiment) and Vasil'enko (the training battalion and right-flank 47th Guards Rifle Regiment) fell upon Lieutenant Colonel S.V. Shmanov's 31st Separate Destroyer Anti-tank Artillery Brigade. Its 29 gun crews were located in open firing positions southwest of Hill 213.7. Moreover, the brigade's area of defense wasn't adequately screened by the infantry of the 94th Guards Rifle Division. At 0200 on 11 July, division commander Russkikh had personally instructed Captain D.S. Chuev to move out the 9th Company of his 286th Guards Rifle Regiment and an anti-tank rifle company to Arkad'evka and the boundary with the 15th Guards Rifle Division in order to reinforce the left flank of the 283rd Guards Rifle Regiment. However, these units arrived already once the fighting was underway and didn't deploy in the firing positions of the anti-tank artillerymen, but 1 kilometer to the east of them (on the southwestern outskirts of Arkad'evka), in part because they had also been ordered to "cover the flank of the 283rd Guards Rifle Regiment". According to division commander Russkikh's logic, the fact that the anti-tank crews would be fighting off enemy submachine gunners was brigade commander Shmanov's problem, even though I'll remind the reader that Shmanov's anti-tank artillery brigade was subordinate to the 94th Guards Rifle Division. From the account of the 31st Separate Destroyer Anti-tank Artillery Brigade:

> At 1130, 16 tanks, the majority of which were heavy Pz-VI, emerged from out of the woods that lie south of the "corridor", and moved toward the fringe of the woods north of the "corridor". Up to 15 enemy aircraft dropped their bomb loads on the regiments' firing positions.

---

8   TsAMO RF, f. 262 ttp, op. 32956, d. 2, l. 104.

Simultaneously with the appearance of the 16 tanks on the fringe of the woods, east of Hill 206.9 more than a battalion of infantry emerged at full height, and firing on the move, headed toward the ravine. After this a second group of 45 tanks emerged from the woods, the majority of them medium tanks, of which 20 were light tanks that were bringing up the rear; 25 headed down the road along the woods toward Sheino, and 20 turned onto the road toward Borovskoe.

The emergence and the advance of the tanks and infantry [Schülz's *panzerkampfgruppe*] were accompanied by strong mortar fire on the anti-tank artillery's firing positions of the brigade's regiments. Of the first 16 tanks, gunners of the 1849th Destroyer Anti-tank Artillery Regiment set 4 ablaze and knocked out 7 more; the rest took cover in the woods. The 45 tanks (of the second column) had submachine gunners aboard them, and as the tanks closed on the firing positions, they leaped off and opened fire at the direction of the anti-tank artillery's firing positions, covering the movement of the tanks. However, the fire of the submachine gunners proved to be completely ineffective, since the gun crew casualties weren't struck by bullets from submachine guns, but were killed and wounded by the explosions of mortar rounds and tank shells.

At 1115 heavy combat flared up; 17 45mm anti-tank guns and 11 76mm anti-tank guns opened destructive fire at the tanks simultaneously. To counter the enemy infantry and submachine gunners, each crew specially detached one submachine gunner, and each battery was given a light machine gun. The German infantry and submachine gunners, having lost up to 50% of their men, became pinned down. More than ten tanks were burning; 15 tanks of the tanks that were moving toward Borovskoe were knocked out. The anti-tank guns increased their rate of fire, but the overall effect of the batteries weakened, since the majority of the crews, or more accurately the guns, had been damaged.

When the attack of the second column faltered, and there remained only several tanks on the battlefield, at 1205 34 more tanks emerged out of the same woods, led by four Pz-VI tanks. The submachine gunners and machine gunners of the majority of crews had been wounded or killed. The rate of the anti-tank fire lessened. Infantry simultaneously with the tanks again surged forward on the attack, advancing at full height. Communications with the regiments was lost at 1218. The radios also fell silent.

Five times the brigade commander requested infantry support from the commander of the 94th Guards Rifle Division; initially he promised to send a battalion, which was occupying a defense in the woods on the right of the passage, on the counterattack, but then answered "Hold out!" The brigade couldn't wait for the counterattacks, and by themselves, they couldn't hold out: 14 guns of the 1853rd Destroyer Anti-tank Artillery Regiment were knocked out of action, and 10 of the 11 guns of the 1849th Destroyer Anti-tank Artillery Regiment were destroyed. Infantry broke into the firing positions of the batteries of the first line, and then outflanked the left-flank batteries from the right. The company that had been standing on the defense behind the batteries' firing positions fell back beyond Arkad'evka at the height of the battle. The remnants of the anti-tank gun crews, having lost their guns, began to retreat in the direction of Arkad'evka. The collecting point for those retreating from the battle was set up in the ravine northeast of Arkad'evka. As a result of the combat, 70 enemy tanks were knocked out or destroyed, of which the 1829th Destroyer Anti-tank Artillery Regiment claimed 28 and the 1853rd Anti-tank Artillery Regiment claimed 42. More than 400 enemy soldiers and officers were killed, and 5 armored cars and 5 trucks were knocked out.

In the fighting, the commander of the 1849th Destroyer Anti-tank Artillery Regiment Major Zorin, who had trained the regiment's men for such tenacious fighting, and had organized them well for a meeting battle with tanks, as well as for combat from a previously prepared line, distinguished himself. Zorin's regiment stood out for its exceptional crispness, organization and high discipline in combat, and to fight even when encircled became a principle of each commander and soldier. Of the battery commanders, Senior Lieutenant Pochtarev stood out, whose battery knocked out or set ablaze 34 tanks. Being concussed in the second combat action, Pochtarev continued to command his battery and destroyed enemy tanks with even greater success.[9]

The clash between Shmanov's anti-tank brigade and Schülz's *panzerkampfgruppe* has been laid out in detail and with complete accuracy in the document, save for one thing: the very high enemy losses in tanks. According to the information from the headquarters of 7th Panzer Division, over the day of fighting it lost 20 panzers, though this is also quite a few. Even if you consider that because of the smoke on the battlefield and the high physical and mental stress, the artillerymen mistakenly took assault guns and halftracks as tanks, nevertheless the claim of 70 armored vehicles knocked out or destroyed can be considered with complete confidence a "paper claim", as they said at the front, or in other words, an exaggeration. It should be noted that the 7th Panzer Division command rated rather highly the level of organization of the Soviet anti-tank defense and the tenacity of the men of the anti-tank artillery and tank units, even though they were operating in rather meager forces.

Between 1400 and 1430, the enemy fully crushed the line of the 31st Separate Destroyer Anti-tank Artillery Brigade, and von Funck quickly moved a panzer company out to his division's right flank in order to contain the 15th Guard Rifle Division with an active defense, while the main forces of Schülz's Panzer Regiment 25 and Panzergrenadier Regiment 7 launched an attack against the left-flank regiment of the 94th Guards Rifle Division. From a daily summary of the 7th Panzer Division headquarters:

1. The division's offensive, launched in the afternoon hours of 10.07 against the northern portion of the large wooded area [the right flank of the 15th Guards Rifle Division], after stubborn fighting with alternating success led to the seizure of the northern portion of the woods, which was important for the further offensive. In the course of this attack, the grenadiers were suddenly attacked from the south by a prepared enemy regiment-sized group [the 44th Guards Rifle Regiment]. After regrouping and bringing the troops back to order, as well as delivering ammunition and other types of supplies, at 1515 the division with strong artillery support resumed the offensive against the sector of woods 3 kilometers northeast of Miasoedovo.

    The attack by the panzer shock group [Schülz's Panzer Regiment 25] with exemplary support of heavy weapons, first of all the artillery and Nebelwerfers, at 1530 led to the quick attainment of the southeastern corner of the woods. The panzers were attacking here under heavy flanking fire from dug-in tanks and anti-tank guns on Hill 213.7 [the 31st Separate Destroyer Anti-tank Artillery Brigade and the T-34s of the 262nd Separate Tank Regiment]. Strong artillery barrages forced the enemy tanks to abandon their positions. A panzer battle is still continuing.

    The forward units then launched an attack to the north and by 1545 reached Hill 210.3, which is to say the northern corner of the woods. The retreat of prominent enemy forces in the direction of Sheino and out of the valley of the Razumnaia River was spotted. The attack by the two panzergrenadier regiments through the woods is continuing.
2. Hill 210.3 (3 kilometers south of Sheino) – the extreme point of advance in the north – woods (3 kilometers northeast of Miasoedovo).[10]

---

9 TsAMO RF, f. 203 (artillery headquarters), op. 2843, d. 29, l. 112obr, 113.
10 NARA US, rg. 242, t. 314, r. 197, f. 001340.

The retreat from the Razumnaia River mentioned in this daily summary – this was the panicked flight of Senior Lieutenant Leonov's company of 1/288th Guards Rifle Regiment of the 94th Guards Rifle Division, which was prompted by the attack of Quentin's panzer reconnaissance battalion of the 6th Panzer Division and the panzergrenadiers of Panzergrenadier Regiment 6 against the right flank of Major M.P. Aglitsky's 288th Guards Rifle Regiment (through the northern and northeastern outskirts of Miasoedovo toward Sheino). The reconnaissance battalion had been reinforced with 20 armored vehicles, and the rifle company's soldiers couldn't withstand the onslaught and retreated to Sheino in disorder, which was one of the main reasons for the Germans' rapid emergence in the regiment's rear from this direction, and then its complete encirclement as well. The account of the 35th Guards Rifle Corps notes:

> The attacks were accompanied by a large airstrike with the support of strong artillery and mortar fire. The enemy managed to drive back the units of the 94th Guards Rifle Division at the boundary with the 15th Guards Rifle Division and by 1700 to reach the northeastern fringe of the woods located 1.5 kilometers south of Sheino. Simultaneously a group of tanks, operating along the Miasoedovo – Sheino road, having breached the defenses of the 288th Guards Rifle Regiment, reached the northeastern fringe of this same patch of woods. By this time, Kalinin had been taken by the enemy in strength of up to a regiment of infantry and up to 40 tanks [units that included the 6th Panzer Division's Panzer Reconnaissance Battalion 6]. Thus, the 283rd Guards and 288th Guards Rifle Regiments wound up encircled and went over to an all-round defense on the line: 283rd Guards Rifle Regiment – southwestern fringe of the patch of woods 1.5 kilometers south of Sheino; 288th Guards Rifle Regiment – northern half of Miasoedovo, where it was continuing to fight off enemy attacks.[11]

Skipping somewhat ahead in the events, I'll call the reader's attention to the following important aspects. Over almost six days of the defensive operation, this was the fifth operational encirclement of a large group (two rifle regiments and an artillery regiment) of the Voronezh Front's forces. On 11 July alone, the enemy completed two encirclements: in the bend of the Pena River around Group Getman and in the area of Miasoedovo around the 94th Guards Rifle Division. However, the latter encirclement relative to the others had two important details. First of all, even though the 7th Panzer Division crushed the 35th Guards Rifle Corps' left flank, no decisive dash into the depth of its lines followed. Von Funck's panzer division, reinforced by von Horn's units, became tied up in heavy fighting in the area of Miasoedovo and the woods southeast of that village and was unable to develop this tactical success into a complete operational breakthrough. Nor did it succeed in doing this even after the units of the 94th Guards Rifle Division slipped out of the pocket and took up a new line that still wasn't ready to repulse an attack. Secondly, the encirclement didn't last very long; the Guardsmen were able to make it back to friendly lines in a fully organized fashion and without significant losses.

Now let's return to the combat positions of the troops of the left flank of Goriachev's 35th Guards Rifle Corps. The "ring" of encirclement wasn't a single one. The two rifle regiments not only wound up encircled, but isolated from each other within the pocket, and the 199th Artillery Regiment had also been split into two pieces. Despite the heavy bombing and artillery barrages, their headquarters continued to have radio communications both with the division commander and with each other. Subsequently this would play a very important role. Striving to prevent the piecemeal destruction of the units, Colonel I.G. Russkikh issued an order to the commander of the 283rd Guards Rifle Regiment Major A.A. Ignat'ev to prepare a counterattack in the direction of

---

11 TsAMO RF, f. 35 gv. sk, op. 1, d. 44, l. 10.

The Commander-in-Chief of the Voronezh Front General of the Army N.F. Vatutin on a trip to the front; July 1943. (RGAKFD)

The chief of staff of the Voronezh Front Lieutenant General S.P. Ivanov discusses a document with the Front's Military Council member Lieutenant General N.S. Khrushchev (on the left) outside the Front headquarters; area of Rzhava Station, July 1943. (Photography by F. Kislova, RGAKFD)

The commander of the 35th Guards Rifle Corps Lieutenant General S.G. Goriachev; a July 1943 photograph. (RGAKFD)

The commander of the 92nd Guards Rifle Division Colonel V.F. Trunin; a 1945 photograph. (TsAMO RF)

The commander of the 94th Guards Rifle Division Colonel I.G. Russkikh; a June 1943 photograph. (TsAMO RF)

A truck carrying infantry of one of Army Detachment Kempf's infantry divisions moving through the captured village of Sevriukovo; July 1943. (A captured photograph, RGAKFD)

The commander of the 6th Panzer Division Major General W. von Hünersdorff (in a Sd.Kfz.250/3 halftrack) listens to a report from the commander of II/Panzergrenadier Regiment 114 Captain Necknauer in the vicinity of Belinskaia in the valley of the Razumniaia River; 7 July 1943. (Bundesarchiv, Bild 101I-022-2923-29A, photo: Kipper)

Near Belinskaia, the commander of the 6th Panzer Division Major General W. von Hünersdorff (second from the left) together with a group of his officers observing the fighting in the area of the villages of Sevriukovo and Miasoedovo; 7 July 1943. (Bundesarchiv, Bild 101I-022-2923-19A, photo: Kipper)

Colonel A. Schulz, the commander of the 6th Panzer Division's Panzer Regiment 11 (in the foreground on the left) issues an order to a subordinate commander in the Sevriukovo area. In the background is a Pz.Kpf. III command tank. 7 July 1943. (Bundesarchiv, Bild 101I-022-2922-13, photo: Kipper)

Colonel A. Schulz, commander of Panzer Regiment 11 at a crossing site on the Razumniaia River. In front of him is the armor skirt of a passing tank. 8 July 1943. (Bundesarchiv, Bild 101I-022-2922-09, photo: Kipper)

German trucks of one of Army Detachment Kemp's divisions move toward the front across a rebuilt bridge in the village of Iastrebovo. In the foreground is the remnants of the previous bridge that had been blown up by retreating troops of Shumilov's army. 8 July 1943. (Bundesarchiv, Bild 101I-022-2925-15, photo: Wolff/Altvater)

An RSO prime mover tows a 50mm anti-tank gun. On the left front of the vehicle is the tactical insignia of the 168th Infantry Division, painted in white. Area of Iastrebovo, 8 July 1943. (Bundesarchiv, Bild 101I-022-2925-06, photo: Wolff/Altvater)

A panzerjäger unit of one of Army Detachment Kempf's divisions rolls past a destroyed Soviet prime mover that had been towing a 76mm ZiS-3 M1939 divisional gun. Area of Sevriukovo, July 1943. (Bundesarchiv, Bild 101I-022-2924-15, photo: Kipper)

Mark II Matilda tanks of one of the 201st Separate Tank Brigade's companies moving out with tank riders aboard toward the front.

A group of soldiers and officers of the 201st Separate Tank Brigade aboard a captured German Sd.Kfz.8 Daimler Benz heavy half-tracked prime mover moving toward the area of combat operations in the 7th Guards Army's sector on 9 July 1943. (Files of the "Stalingradskaia bitva" State Historical Park Museum)

The commander of the 201st Separate Tank Brigade's 201st Motorized Rifle Battalion Captain D.A. Dziubin; a 10 July 1943 photograph. (TsAMO RF)

Junior Lieutenant V.A. Vlasov, an anti-tank rifle platoon commander of the 201st Separate Tank Brigade's 201st Motorized Rifle Battalion; a 10 July 1943 photograph. (TsAMO RF)

Senior Lieutenant A.S. Kuskin's bloody Party card. He was the commander of the 201st Separate Tank Brigade's 296th Tank Battalion.

A German aerial reconnaissance photograph of the two major villages in the interfluvial area between the Northern Donets and Razumniaia Rivers, Melekhovo and Shliakhovoe, through which Army Detachment Kempf's assault wedge broke through toward Prokhorovka; a July 1943 photograph. (NARA US)

The commander of the 69th Army Lieutenant General Kriuchenkin (on the right) and his chief of operations Colonel D.N. Surzhits at a forward observation post on the Korocha axis; a July 1943 photograph.
(Photograph by I. Ozersky, RGAKFD)

The commander of a rifle company (second from left in foreground, with binoculars) observes the start of an attack. To his right, the crew of a 50mm mortar prepares to support the attack; a July 1943 photograph.
(RGAKFD)

A dug-in Red Army soldier awaits the completion of an attack by Il-2 ground assault aircraft against German positions; Voronezh Front, July 1943. (RGAKFD)

Elements of the 69th Army taking up new positions in the basin of the Northern Donets River; Korocha axis, July 1943. (RGAKFD)

Medic V. Kameneva of one of the Guards rifle divisions dragging a wounded soldier from the battlefield; Voronezh Front, July 1943. (Given the cleanliness of her uniform and face, this is likely a staged photograph). (RGAKFD)

The commander of the 305th Rifle Division Colonel A.F. Vasil'ev (in the center) discusses recent combat results with a group of subordinate commanders at his forward outpost in Shliakhovoe. Judging from the smiles, the news was good. Korocha axis, July 1943. (RGAKFD

An armored group of one of the panzer divisions of Breith's III Panzer Corps waits for the start of an attack. On the left in the background are Pz.Kpfw. VI Tigers, and on the right are Pz.Kpfw. III and IV tanks. In the foreground is the gun barrel of another Tiger tank. Sector of the 69th Army, July 1943. (Bundesarchiv, Bild 101I-022-2950-15A, photo: Kipper)

A column of prisoners, consisting of soldiers and officers of the 69th Army captured by troops of Army Detachment Kempf, moving to the rear. July 1943. (Bundesarchiv, Bild 101I-022-2925-05, photo: Wolff/Altvater)

Army Detachment Kempf's chief of staff Major General H. Speidel (on the left) meets with the commander of the 198th Infantry Division's Grenadier Regiment 305 Major J. Grassman in the area east of Belgorod. July 1943. (Bundesarchiv, Bild 101I-022-2933-05, photo: Heinz Mittelstaedt)

The commander of the 6th Panzer Division Major General W. von Hünersdorff (in the center) in a Sd.Kfz.250/3 halftrack in the area of Rzhavets. July 1943. (Bundesarchiv, Bild 101I-022-2912-13A, photograph: Horster)

The commander of the 111th Rifle Division Colonel M.A. Bushin; a 1945 photograph. (TsAMO RF)

A tank-riding company of the 7th Guards Army's 27th Guards Tank Brigade waits for the signal of attack; 12 July 1943. (RGAKFD)

Soldiers of the 73rd Guards Rifle Division in combat in the area of the "Batratskaia Dacha" State Farm; a July 1943 photograph. (Author's personal archive)

Senior Lieutenant G.M. Kozhar (third from left and in the inset), the commander of the 1st Tank Company of the 201st Separate Tank Brigade's 295th Tank Battalion, stands together with his crew in front of his Matilda tank; a May 1943 photograph. (TsAMO RF)

The burial ceremony for fallen soldiers and commanders of the 7th Guards Army's 73rd Guards Rifle Division; July 1943. (Author's personal archive)

Miasoedovo, in order to link up with the 288th Guards Rifle Regiment. Next at 1830 the division commander got in touch with Captain D.S. Chuev and ordered him to undertake a counterattack quickly with the 2nd Rifle Battalion from Sheino toward the northern fringe of the woods (south of the village), in order to divert some of the enemy's strength while within the pocket the regiments would attempt to break out, and then help them escape encirclement.

In the account of the 35th Guards Rifle Corps headquarters on the results of the defensive phase of the Battle of Kursk there is the remark that the regiments located within the pocket already by 2030 broke through the thin enemy crust separating them and linked up, and then, covered by two battalions from the northwest, broke though in the direction of Kalinin and by 2400 came out of the encirclement, where at the order of the 35th Guards Rifle Corps commander they took up a line in the area of the two large villages of Sheino and Ushakovo: "the 288th Guards Rifle Regiment along the Mazikino, northwestern outskirts of Sheino line, and the 286th Guards Rifle Regiment along the western and southwestern outskirts of Shieno to the orchard south of Sheino, while the 283rd Guards Rifle Regiment occupied a line running from the orchard south of Sheino (inclusively) to Ushakovo (inclusively)."[12]

However, in reality everything went far from as smoothly as laid out in the 35th Guards Rifle Corps' account. The command of Captain D.S. Chuev's 286th Guards Rifle Regiment was unable to organize a counterattack with the 2nd Rifle Battalion quickly. Its preparation stretched for 3 hours, as noted in Order No.0117 from the division commander: "The headquarters of this regiment headed by its chief criminally regarded the carrying out of the given order, and also failed to monitor the carrying out of it, which might have led to needless sacrifices. Indeed, it was only after the interference of the division's chief of staff that this order was executed."[13] In the course of the defensive fighting near Belgorod, the command at every level (including that of the Voronezh Front) more than once justly criticized Captain D.S. Chuev for his poor executive discipline and the careless regard for his duties. However at this particular moment, judging from indirect information, the regiment commander simply lost his head and was not in the condition to deal quickly with the complex assignment, while his headquarters, which had been formed only two months previously, proved not to be his full-value assistant, even though it was headed by an officer senior in rank to the regiment commander – Major Beksak. The regiment, though positioned in the second echelon, became engaged in combat with the Germans on the southern approaches of Shcino after the encirclement of the 283rd Guards and 288th Guards Rifle Regiments, thus it was unable to organize a counterattack with the 2nd Rifle Battalion right away. Nevertheless, this delay enabled the enemy to apply heavy pressure on the encircled regiments. The Germans tried to consolidate the ring around the pocket as quickly as possible and prevent the Guards regiments within the pocket from linking up with each other.

In the second half of the day, von Funck's possibility to do this substantially grew. Von Horn's fresh units had neared Miasoedovo and joined the fighting together with the 7th Panzer Division's *kampfgruppen*. From the daily summary of Korps Raus:

> The 198th Infantry Division, continuing to move up to the front lines on the evening of 10 July, on the morning of 11 July on the left flank with Grenadier Regiment 326 reached the woods southeast of Miasoedovo and the area in front of the "Solov'ev" State Farm [sic] north and northeast of the highway. The mopping up of enemy remnants from the woods and the fringes of it was still continuing. Grenadier Regiment 308 supported the 7th Panzer Division's attack and together with Grenadier Regiment 326 is occupying positions as far as

---

12 TsAMO RF, f. 906, op. 1, d. 44, l. 10.
13 TsAMO RF, f. 199 gv. ap, op. 1, d. 4, ll. 29-30.

the southern edge of the woods northeast of Miasoedovo. Grenadier Regiment 305 on the afternoon shifted from the woods northeast of Krutoi Log to the vicinity of Miasoedovo and linked up there with Grenadier Regiment 308 and units of the 7th Panzer Division. By midday almost all of the units of the 198th Infantry Division arrived at the front with the exception of the 5th Battery of Artillery Regiment 235, a squadron of armored cars of Motorized Battalion 235 [sic], the 13th and 14th Companies of Grenadier Regiment 235 and rear echelon units, which remained in the Iastrebovo area, and the arrival of which is expected on 12 July.[14]

The pressure on Aglitsky's and Ignat'ev's encircled regiments was growing, but the artillerymen of Lieutenant Colonel Burnazian's 199th Guards Artillery Regiment were giving them great assistance. Within the pocket, two of its artillery battalions were positioned in firing positions in the woods 3 kilometers northeast of Miasoedovo (in the area of Hill 210.3), which after the German breakthrough, took up an all-round defense and defended ferociously. Junior Lieutenant N.I. Kolbasov and Junior Lieutenant R.N. Kushliansky, the commanders of gun platoons, particularly distinguished themselves. Kolvbasov's platoon knocked out three tanks, but perished in the fighting. Remaining alone, Nikolai Illarionovich from close range managed to knock out four more enemy armored vehicles, after which he took up an all-round defense with a group of infantrymen. When ammunition ran low, he raised the troops on the counterattack and broke out to friendly lines. Meanwhile R.N. Kushliansky personally knocked out three tanks in this battle and also led his platoon out of the encirclement. For the personal courage and heroism displayed in the area of Sheino, by a Decree of the Presidium of the USSR Supreme Soviet both officers were awarded the title "Hero of the Soviet Union".

Approximately an hour before the main forces of the 7th Panzer Division went on a decisive attack at the boundary between Goriachev's 35th Guards and Safiulin's 25th Guards Rifle Corps, III Panzer Corps' other two panzer divisions simultaneously struck the right flank of the 35th Guards Rifle Corps. On the morning of 11 July, the panzer regiments of the 6th and 19th Panzer Divisions had a total number of 38 panzers fit for combat (23 in the 6th Panzer Division, 15 in the 19th Panzer Division), while 23 Tigers were now operational in the three heavy panzer companies of Separate Heavy Panzer Battalion 503 (including those located with the 7th Panzer Division). There is no precise data for StuG Battalion 228 on 11 July; on the morning of 10 July it had 11 StuG fit for combat in it, and on 12 July it would now have 19 combat-ready StuG.[15] Accordingly, for the breakthrough in the corridor between the Northern Donets and Razumnaia Rivers (in the 69th Army's sector), Schmidt's and von Hünersdorff's panzer divisions might have activated a total of 55-65 armored vehicles on this day, 6 of which would have been command tanks and light Pz.kpfw. II tanks.

Considering the greatly reduced combat strength of his units and the absence of shoulder to shoulder contact with the neighboring 168th Infantry Division on the left, Lieutenant General G. Schmidt at 0930 connected with Breith over the telephone and proposed:

> Launch the offensive toward Sabynino only after both neighboring divisions [the 168th Infantry and 6th Panzer Divisions] come up, because the opposing enemy is situated in well-fortified positions in the Kiselevo area and the hills to the east, as well as in Sabynino. At the same time he reported on the low strength of his division and the absence of support from other ground troops [assets]. The corps commander believes that the Russians are retreating

---

14 NARA US, t. 312, r. 59, f. 7574638.
15 Zetterling and Frankson, *Kursk 1943: A statistical analysis*, pp. 188-189.

from the Belomestnoe area and the wooded heights north of Petropavlovka in a northern direction, in order to avoid the threat of encirclement by units of III Panzer Corps and the 167th Infantry Division, which are already in the Donets River – Shopino – Visloe area. In the area south of Sabynino the enemy is attempting to hold out with all available forces and means in order to cover the retreat of his forces. Thus 19th Panzer Division must quickly launch an attack toward Sabynino and take this village and its bridge across the Donets, paying no regard to the departure of the neighboring units from the right flank. Success is necessary for the corps' further use in the next day or two. Not only preemptive artillery attacks, as before, but the entire shock strength of the division and the full use of artillery must be considered the components of success. In addition, the division will be offered support by the corps' artillery. Cover for the 19th Panzer Division's left flank and rear rests upon the 168th Infantry Division, which advances in the direction of Khokhlovo in the area east of the Donets River.[16]

Breith perfectly understood Schmidt's difficult situation, but was unable to change it in any fundamental way. He had Kempf's categorical order: Make every effort to break through to Prokhorovka from the south in the next day or two. Thus there could be no talk about any delay. After all, von Hünersdorff's 6th Panzer Division was also just a shadow of its former self, and thus success could be achieved only through combined efforts by all of the corps' divisions simultaneously.

The 6th and 19th Panzer Divisions launched an attack against the 35th Guards Rifle Corps at 1030. After a three-hour artillery preparation and Luftwaffe strikes on Kiselevo, Shliakhovoe and the northern portion of Miasoedovo, up to two panzergrenadier battalions with the support of 30 panzers moved out toward the positions of the 280th Guards and 276th Guards Rifle Regiments. From the 19th Panzer Division's account:

> At night, the concentration of artillery in the area southeast of Dal'niaia Igumenka was completed. The support of dive bombers during the attack was also secured. On 11.07 the division commander personally directed the offensive of the full division for the first time. The attack was conducted with two assault groups out of the area northwest of Hill 217.4 (north of Dal'niaia Igumenka) in the direction of Khokhlovo and Kiselevo along the valleys leading to the north. The panzer regiment was with the group that was attacking on the right. The very active Flintz [a Luftwaffe liaison officer] was operating next to the general in his command vehicle, working to transmit by radio the latest requests from the forward units to the overhead Stuka formations. Communications were functioning irreproachably.[17]

However, the first attack faltered. The Germans discovered a large minefield on the road from Khokhlovo to Kiselevo, and were forced to stop and go over to an exchange of fire while covering the combat engineers. The three *kampfgruppen* of the 6th Panzer Division also failed to penetrate the forward edge of the 305th Rifle Division; they were stopped by intense artillery fire. At 1400, Schmidt's and von Hünersdorff's panzer divisions launched another attack: Westhofen's *panzerkampfgruppe* (with 20 panzers and self-propelled guns and a company of panzergrenadiers) out of the woods north of Dal'niaia Igumenka attacked in the direction of Kiselevo, while von Oppeln-Bronikowski's panzer regiment attacked out of Melikhovo toward Shliakhovoe. However,

---

16 NARA US, rg 242, t. 314, r. 197, f. 001362.
17 TsAMO RF, f. 38A, op. 9027, d. 46, l. 154.

under the fire of Russian tanks and artillery, both groups were forced to halt the attack once again and fall back to their jumping-off positions.

At 1500, for the next 30 minutes the divisional and corps artillery pounded the defenses of Trunin's and Vasil'ev's units, after which the attacks by the 6th and 19th Panzer Divisions were resumed, and this time they succeeded in making penetrations. Von Oppeln-Bronikowski's panzer regiment and Unrein's panzergrenadiers attacked the boundary between Major S.E. Simonov's 276th Guards Rifle Regiment of the 92nd Guards Rifle Division and Lieutenant Colonel I.D. Govorunenko's 1004th Rifle Regiment of the 305th Rifle Division from out of Melikhovo. Tigers of the Heavy Panzer Battalion 503 led the way, followed by two panzer companies of Major Bäke's II/Panzer Regiment 11, which included all of the regiment's remaining tanks. After breaking through, the panzer battalion commander ordered the Tiger crews and 1st Lieutenant Spiekermann's 8th Panzer Company to advance along the road over Hill 230 (northeast of the village) in the direction of Ol'khovatka, and 1st Lieutenant Reutemann's 6th Panzer Company to support Unrein's panzergrenadiers, which had the task to break through the southern outskirts of Shliakhovoe to the village center together with assault guns. Soviet archival records speak to how subsequent events unfolded. From the combat diary of the 148th Separate Tank Regiment for 11 July 1943:

> At 1530 up to a battalion of infantry with the support of 50 tanks went on the attack out of Melikhovo toward Shliakhovoe. At 1600 enemy tanks cut the road from Shliakhovoe to Dal'niaia Igumenka, and at 1630 20 enemy tanks reached the eastern outskirts of Shliakhovoe in the vicinity of the church. This thereby placed the regiment's tanks in an unfavorable situation, having created a semi-circle of tanks around them. The only remaining road toward the southern outskirts of Shliakhovoe proved impassable because of a deep ravine. The regiment's only exit was completely blocked.
>
> With the appearance of the enemy's tanks and vehicles carrying infantry in Shliakhovoe, some units of the 305th Rifle Division began to flee in disorder in the direction of Kazach'e. The German tanks that had broken through were met by the dense fire of our combat machines and anti-tank rifle crews, while the regiment's submachine gunners that were covering the tanks were also engaged in combat. The enemy's tanks were painted in a green color with streaks [of a different color], and the crosses (swastikas) on several of them were covered by shelter halves. Our crews were continuing to exchange fire with the enemy armor. In the combat in the Shliakhovoe area, the regiment's battalions knocked out or set ablaze up to 10 tanks and wiped out up to a platoon of infantry.
>
> By 2100, in the course of the fighting with the superior enemy, all of the regiment's tanks that were located in Shliakhovoe (14 T-34 and 3 T-70) were left burned out, but without an order from the regiment commander, not a single crew left the battle. The crewmen showed themselves to be courageous and resolute in the struggle with the fascist Germans. The personnel of the submachine gun company, anti-tank rifle company, headquarters company and the remaining crewmen on the night of 11-12 July began to make their way out of the pocket and by dawn on 12 July reassembled in Zaiach'e, where the regiment's first echelon was located.[18]

Let the reader not be confused by the figures regarding the destroyed enemy tanks given in this excerpt – this is a falsehood; even in a prayer there weren't so many. Such an impressive number of "kills" appeared in the first place in order to offset the enemy's successful dash into the depth of the 35th Guards Rifle Corps' defenses, and in the second place, in the confusion and chaos of

---

18 TsAMO RF, f. 148 otp, op. 661360, d. 3, l. 79.

combat, to the event's participants all of the armored vehicles seemed to be tanks; moreover, as almost every single Soviet operational combat document notes, "in the majority they were Tigers".

Incidentally, the dozens and even hundreds of enemy machines "materialized" not only to the commanders of the 69th Army's tactical level, but also to the senior staff officers at its headquarters. For example, at 2200 the army's intelligence chief Colonel Domoratsky reported in Intelligence Summary No. 4 that "… as a result of the most bitter fighting from 1100 to 1450 11.7, the enemy in strength of up to 90 tanks seized Kiselevo and Khokhlovo", and the acting chief of staff Colonel S.M. Protas agreed with this.[19] Of course, the villages indicated in the statement were attacked by the 19th Panzer Division alone, which had on the morning just a total of 15 serviceable tanks. I'll note that whereas the journal of combat operations was "a document for history", then the operational information contained in the army's intelligence summaries was necessary for combat work and making decisions. Thus without any particular difficulty it is possible to imagine how many command decisions might have been made on the basis of such erroneous information.

The disordered flight of the soldiers of the 305th Rifle Division noted in the 148th Separate Tank Regiment's combat diary actually did take place. However, this occurred later; the first to abandon their combat positions, even without having engaged in combat, were the 2nd and 3rd Companies of the 122nd Separate Anti-tank Rifle Battalion, which was positioned in Shliakhovoe on the right flank of the 148th Separate Tank Regiment, which is to say, on the axis of the 6th Panzer Division's main attack. The wild flight of more than a hundred soldiers and commanders in front of the attacking enemy worked like a catalyst for the other units. The mob, pursued by the German tanks and panzergrenadiers in half tracks, hurriedly retreating to the rear of the 305th Rifle Division, accumulated more and more soldiers with each passing minute. The former front-line soldier, the artilleryman I.G. Kobylansky writes:

> We try to imagine the condition and conduct of men on the forward edge at the moment when the enemy began an attack. Even the bravest and most resolute soldiers, who are firing at the attackers, monitor with their peripheral vision what is happening on the left and right of them: Are the comrades there still armed? Have their trenches emptied? Will I be left all alone, doomed to a certain death or imprisonment? … Just how should a soldier behave, having discovered that his neighbor, or maybe two, has fled in the direction of the rear? With very rare exceptions, he took off after them. That is how the chain reaction of a panicked retreat begins, which, can't be stopped other than at the clear threat of death. Very often a "skedaddle", which arose from the cowardice of one or a few men resulted in the death of an incomparably large number of men. I'm convinced that there is nothing more terrible (and shameful) than a panic that has started (not only at the front), if it might potentially envelop a multitude of men.[20]

The panic that started in the battalion managed to be extinguished only thanks to the tenacity of Colonel Lifts' tankers. The reason for the shameful conduct of the anti-tank riflemen was banal – the complete moral dissolution of the unit's command and, as a consequence, the absence of discipline and command and control in the unit. I will cite Lieutenant General V.D. Kriuchenkin's Order No.035 from 17 July 1943, in whose reserve this anti-tank rifle battalion was located right up until it was sent to the Shliakhovoe – Melikhovo area on 8 July:

---

19 TsAMO RF, f. 426, op. 10765, d. 13, l. 6.
20 See Rubtsov, Iu.V., *Shtrafniki Velikoi Otechestvennoi: V zhizni i na ekrane* [*Penal soldiers of the Great Patriotic: In life and on the screen*] (Moscow: Veche, 2008), p. 240. Incidentally, Kobylyanskiy's memoirs have been translated into English and published by the University Press of Kansas in 2008 as *From Stalingrad to Pillau: A Red Army Artillery Officer Remembers the Great Patriotic War*.

The commander of the 122nd Separate Anti-tank Rifle Battalion Captain Bogachev doesn't direct the battalion's fighting and never visited the combat positions of the companies. After an enemy airstrike on 11 July 1943 in the area of Shliakhovoe, he abandoned the battalion to its fate, shamefully fled to the rear, and wound up in the village of Podkopaevka on 12 July. Having arrived in Podkopaevka, Comrade Bogachev calmly spent his time there engaged in binge drinking until 15 July. On 15 July he sent his adjutant to Novyi Oskol in order to search for the army headquarters, which according to him had supposedly moved there.

The battalion's deputy political commander Lieutenant Puzanov didn't conduct any Party or political work to support the combat actions, never spent any time at all in the battalion's combat positions, all the while sitting in the rear at the field kitchen, but on 11 July he was the first, having abandoned the battalion, who shamefully fled to Podkopaevka, where he spent all the time getting drunk. Having lost all face of a Communist and political worker, Puzanov on the night of 14-15 July with the threat of a weapon raped Ch., a female resident of Podkopaevka, engaged in debauchery and the wild firing of a pistol and carbine, beat up a 70-year-old senior Chernikov and two Red Army soldiers, and knocked out the windows and frames in the apartment of two of the village's collective farmers, thereby discrediting the army in the eyes of the people.

The battalion's assistant commander for logistics Lieutenant Parshin spent all the time in the rear. He placed all the responsibility for keeping the battalion supplied on the shoulders of Sergeant Major Vasil'ev, didn't ensure the normal feeding of the soldiers with hot meals, and on 11 July the 2nd and 3rd Companies were completely left without food. Having acquired 100 liters of vodka at an army warehouse, Parshin began to play around with it. When the battalion was in combat, he didn't distribute the vodka to the troops, whereas on 13 and 14 July, when the battalion's remnants were located in the deep rear, vodka was distributed to the Red Army men, but not to everyone. The majority of the vodka had been bargained away, and the lion's share of it went to the battalion's command staff.

As a result of the absence of requisite leadership over the battalion in battle, in the battalion there were facts of the mass abandonment of weapons to the enemy. Of the 107 anti-tank rifles available in the battalion, on 17 July only 17 had been collected. The men of the 1st and 4th Anti-tank Rifle Companies, who knocked out 8 tanks [on 11.7] behaved well, but the Red Army men and commanders of the remaining companies, refusing combat and tossing aside their weapons, fled in panic and did a disappearing act in other units.[21]

To the above I will add that the tankers of the 148th Separate Tank Regiment in the difficult conditions of a struggle against a numerically (and qualitatively) superior foe, which prompted a panic in the rifle units, and then in the ensuing encirclement fought heroically. This slowed the advance of the 6th Panzer Division's *panzerkampfgruppe*, allowing the rifle units of the 1002nd Rifle Regiment that were retreating from the breakthrough location toward Mazikino sufficient time to consolidate on its eastern outskirts, where trenches had already been dug; it also prevented the Germans from taking complete possession of Shliakhovoe until after midnight. However, the knot of resistance based around Lifits' tankers didn't have flank cover, and so after the retreat by the two anti-tank rifle companies of the 122nd Separate Anti-tank Rifle Battalion from the positions on their left, the Germans quickly isolated the 148th Separate Tank Regiment. Indeed the encircled tankers in the village together with the remaining elements of the 92nd Guards and 305th Rifle Divisions did in fact divert some enemy strength onto themselves, but not a significant amount. The bulk of von Oppeln-Bronikowski's *panzerkampfgruppe* already within an hour

---

21 TsAMO RF, f. 290 mp, op. 20928s, d. 4, l. 239.

continued a rapid advance to the northeast in the Ol'khovatka – Znamenka – Verkhnii Ol'shanets direction, although by this time, taking advantage of the confusion and loss of command in the retreating troops of the 35th Guards Rifle Corps, a small group of panzers and panzergrenadiers in halftracks had already broken into its rear. According to the information of the 148th Separate Tank Regiment's headquarters, in the course of defending Shliakhovoe, the regiment lost a total of 38 men, including 9 killed and 20 missing in action.[22]

The daily report of the 6th Panzer Division complained:

> As a result of the absence of the anticipated Luftwaffe support, Unrein's and von Oppeln's *kampfgruppen* got held up by the enemy tanks remaining in Shliakhovoe, since there was no change in orders. As *Kampfgruppe* Unrein was breaking into Shliakhovoe from the northeastern edge of Melikhovo and from the south, von Oppeln's panzer regiment was stepping off from the road fork 1.5 kilometers north of Melikhovo, and after overcoming a minefield pushed to the north 1 kilometer to west of the road fork. Since the enemy by this time was already showing the first signs of retreating, the panzers were not used to support *Kampfgruppe* Unrein in Shliakhovoe, but instead attacked in the general direction to the northeast in order to destroy the enemy units that had started to retreat.
>
> *Kampfgruppe* Quentin when reconnoitering the woods southwest of Kalinin and the Shipov ravine detected defending enemy units [elements of the 94th Guards Rifle Division's 288th Guards Rifle Regiment]. Further reports haven't come in. Above the battlefield are the constant activity of our Luftwaffe and the rare activity of the enemy's air force, dropping bombs and strafing.[23]

The 19th Panzer Division's attack in the Khokhlovo – Kiselevo sector went significantly less well. I'll remind the reader that here its *kampfgruppen* were faced not only by the thoroughly battered units of the 92nd Guards Rifle Division, but also Colonel M.P. Seriugin's fully combat-capable 89th Guards Rifle Division, reinforced by the tanks of the 96th Separate Tank Brigade and the 47th Guards Separate Heavy Breakthrough Tank Regiment. From the panzer division's daily report to the III Panzer Corps headquarters:

> Panzergrenadier Regiment 74 after overcoming an extensive minfield at 1630 burst into a strongly-built system of enemy positions east of Kiselevo and at the present time is mopping up the area.
>
> Panzergrenadier Regiment 73 together with the panzer regiment broke through to the northern end of Khokhlovo, destroyed the enemy on the southern outskirts of Kiselevo, made a further advance through the village, mopped it up, and after the tanks took on ammunition, is ready for a subsequent attack toward Sabynino. … <u>Two Churchill tanks that were standing in the rear were shot up in the process</u>.
>
> Reconnaissance Battalion 19 advanced as far as the northern outskirts of Kiselevo and received the assignment to create a bridgehead together with Panzergrenadier Regiment 73. On the road from Khokhlovo to Kiselevo and along both sides of it, up to 800 mines were lifted.
>
> In the course of the entire attack, strong flanking fire struck all three *kampfgruppen* from the northeast and from the heights to the west, and continues to the present time. The enemy

---

22 TsAMO RF, f. 148 otp, op. 661360, d. 3, l. 80.
23 NARA US, rg. 242, t. 314, r. 197, f. 001340.

batteries were impossible to destroy either with dive bombers or artillery. The Luftwaffe supported the attack with good results.[24]

The assault against these two strongpoints on the left bank of the Donets River was laid out in more detail in the account of the headquarters of Schmidt's 19th Panzer Division regarding the results of the offensive:

> More serious resistance was offered in Kiselevo. Hill 211.5, which was positioned on the flank and behind which there was strong Russian artillery, proved to be a genuine fortress with an elaborate network of trenches. Only small forces could be sent on the attack against this hill in view of the overall low numerical strength. Dive bombers conducted an attack on the hill and reported that they were observing nothing on it. In fact, a reinforced regiment was crouched in the trenches there, which was impossible to see even from a distance of 5 meters. In the majority, the regiment consisted of Asians, against which it is impossible to count upon an effect on morale, and moreover in their slit trenches they suffered almost no losses from our dive bombers. To make matters worse, all of the ravines and the outskirts east of Kiselevo had already been mined, to the panzers attempted to bypass the minefields from the left, southeast of Kiselevo, but blundered into a swamp and became bogged down there 1 kilometer northeast of the outskirts of Khokhlovo.
>
> Despite the heavy fire of at least a hundred anti-tank rifles of the 122nd Anti-tank Rifle Battalion [in the sector of the 19th Panzer Division, its 1st and 4th Companies were defending, which didn't abandon their positions] and from heavy tanks, the division's assault group continued to attack and took Kiselevo, almost at the same time the left-hand group took Khokhlovo. At this moment two British Churchill tanks suddenly appeared on the outskirts of Khokhlovo. Probably, they were intending to get behind our tanks that were located in Kiselevo. Their crews had no inkling about the two bogged-down panzers, in front of which they found themselves to be sitting as if in the palm of the hand. One Pz.kpfw. IV immediately dealt with both of them.[25]

The "heavy tanks" and the two Lend-Lease Churchill tanks mentioned in the document belonged to Lieutenant Colonel Shevchenko's 47th Guards Separate Heavy Breakthrough Tank Regiment, which as before was positioned in this area. In the documents of its headquarters, this counterattack by the Churchill tanks in the course of the fighting for Khokhlovo is laid out in more detail, but somewhat differently:

> At 1530 11.07.1943 the enemy in groups with a total number of 25 tanks supported by up to a company of infantry conducted an attack toward Kiselevo. Our units that were defending the village had set out in the direction of Sabynino [the 280th Guards Rifle Regiment], and the bridges in Khokhlovo and Kiselevo had been blown up by sappers. Three combat machines under the command of Guards Lieutenant Riazantsev in response to a command given over the radio by Lieutenant Colonel Shevchenko moved out from Khokhlovo toward Kiselevo with the task to strike the flank of the enemy tanks from the left, repulse the attack and link up with the units defending Kiselevo, in order not to be cut off from the bridges and their own units. Two more tanks had been sent from the direction of Sabynino in order to assist the regiment's three combat machines. However, having no support of artillery or tanks, which

---

24 NARA US, rg. 242, t. 314, r. 197, f. 001340.
25 TsAMO RF, f. 38A, op. 9027, d. 46, ll. 154-154obr.

had been located previously in Kiselevo's defenses [the 228th Tank Battalion had already departed by this time], the attack had no success and the enemy took complete possession of Kiselevo, while the 3 Mk-IV and armored car wound up cut off from their units, and having no possibility to cross to the right bank of the Northern Donets, engaged with German tanks from out of an ambush position. As a result, over 11.07.1943 the regiment lost: 2 Mk-IV left burned out, 3 – knocked out and the armored car. Of the crews, 4 men were killed and 4 wounded. The rest of the men on the night of 11-12 July 1943 came out and rejoined the unit. During this action, up to 50 enemy soldiers and officers were killed.[26]

One interesting detail: the two tanks of Shevchenko's regiment that undertook the attack out of Sabynino against the 19th Panzer Division's right flank were knocked out not by its units, but by elements of the 6th Panzer Division. This episode was noted in a daily report from its headquarters.

The combat actions of all the divisions of Breith's III Panzer Corps on this day were complicated by one general, basic problem – the large losses incurred over the preceding days, which weakened their most important element, the panzer regiments. However, 6th Panzer Division was in a more difficult situation than its neighbors. For example, the 7th Panzer Division had also suffered heavy attrition in armor, but in the course of the encirclement of part of the 94th Guards Rifle Division, it received substantial assistance from the 198th Infantry Division. Meanwhile, Gustav Schmidt, who commanded the 19th Panzer Division, the weakest in III Panzer Corps, had been given a significantly simpler task than the one given to von Hünersdorff. His troops only had to seize the two villages of Kiselevo and Sabynino, which were situated just 1 kilometer apart from each other. Thus he had the possibility to concentrate all of his forces on a very narrow sector. For the same reason, the Luftwaffe's strikes in the sector of the 19th Panzer Division, judging from the reports of its command, proved to be very effective. In addition, in the morning the Nebelwerfers of the 198th Infantry Division's 52nd Mortar Regiment arrived to reinforce it and joined in the 19th Panzer Division's attacks.

In the 6th Panzer Division everything was different. In the first place, its front extended up to 9 kilometers, and von Hünersdorff had been compelled to shift his reconnaissance battalion to the right flank in order to take Kalinin and screen the boundary with the 7th Panzer Division. In the second place, his panzer division had to make a 10-kilometer penetration into the depth of the Russian defenses, and in order to accomplish this it was necessary to take at least five villages and hamlets along the Melikhovo – Verkhnii Ol'shanets (the day's objective) axis alone, all of which had been prepared for a defense and were occupied by divisions of the 35th Guards Rifle Corps. This doesn't include the company-sized strongpoints that had been set up by the Soviet units in this sector (on hilltops and in patches of woods). Therefore Unrein's and Von Oppeln-Bronikowski's *kampfgruppen* were forced to implement a breakthrough attack on a rather wide front that extended up to 6 kilometers, and the systematic accompaniment of the panzers by dive bombers was required for this. At the very least, prior to the taking of Shliakhovoe and the breakthrough, the *kampfgruppen* would have to chew through 3.5 to 4 kilometers of the heavily fortified ground into the depth of the 35th Guards Rifle Corps' defenses. However, at this moment Fliegerkorps VIII was no longer able to render such support. The groups of Junkers and Heinkels weren't always overhead above the defenders, but appeared only periodically, bombing only major centers of resistance, after which they immediately departed. Thus in the messages of the 6th Panzer Division on 11 July, its headquarters complained about the "absence of the anticipated Luftwaffe support". With their own strength, von Oppeln-Bronikowski's and Unrein's forces were still unable to achieve a decisive breakthrough.

---

26 TsAMO RF, f. 2 gv. tk, op. 1, d. 24, ll. 203,204.

While Westhofen's tankers were still engaged in fighting at Kiselevo, his panzergrenadiers in halftracks, bypassing Kiselevo, were surging toward the outskirts of Sabynino. At 1530 V.F. Trunin, who was located in the division's command post in Sabynino, hurled Lieutenant Colonel I.I. Samoilenko's 282nd Guards Rifle Regiment into a counterattack along the Sabynino – Kiselevo axis. However, the counterattack failed; the documents of the 35th Guards Rifle Corps' headquarters notes: "The counterattack was disrupted by a large aerial attack and a group of enemy tanks that were attacking Sabynino from the direction of Kiselevo. The regiment suffered heavy losses and the remnants went over to a defense on the line: Sabynino Machine Tractor Station, woods 2 kilometers east of the Machine Tractor Station, where it checked the enemy until 2300."[27] Having broken through the line of the 1002nd Rifle Regiment's 1st Battalion, the panzergrenadiers broke into Sabynino, but they were unable to take it from the march – units of the 280th Guards Rifle Regiment with a counterattack drove them back out of the village. Meanwhile 1/1002 Rifle Regiment and the 276th Guards Rifle Regiment, which were holding the ground between Kiselevo and Shliakhovoe, after the breakthrough by the 6th Panzer Division and its emergence in Shliakhovoe, wound up semi-encircled; however, they didn't flinch, and having taken up an all-round defense of a sector that stretched from the western slopes of Hill 230 along the Shpaki ravine, continued to fight stubbornly.

Thus, by 1600 the forward edge of the 35th Guards Rifle Corps' line in the Kiselevo – Shliakhovoe – Sheino sector had been penetrated in several places, but the defense still hadn't collapsed, and the 92nd Guards and 305th Rifle Divisions with attached assets were defending tenaciously. Their command was continuing to search for forces and means in order to counter the German penetrations. As soon as a report arrived that German tanks were now attacking Ol'khovatka, Trunin ordered the commander of the 106th Engineer Battalion Major M.M. Arustamov to load trucks with two platoons of minelayers and mines and get them headed toward the village. The battalion commander personally led the blocking detachment of 50 men. Having set out promptly to the area northeast of Ol'khovatka, the tiny force for a certain amount of time blocked von Oppeln-Bronikowski's *panzerkampfgruppe* at this village. The headquarters of Voronezh Front's engineer troops noted: "Skillfully using the terrain and the situation, Arustamov's engineers, operating in small teams, in the course of the fighting blew up 11 enemy tanks, thereby disrupting the attack that had started."[28]

However, von Hünersdorff realized that the Russian defense was beginning to crack, and striving to take advantage of the moment, paying no particular attention to losses, he stubbornly continued to launch attacks in the depth of the 35th Guards Rifle Corps' defenses. Three hours after the start of the day's attacks, the main forces of 6th Panzer Division's panzer regiment (its 8th Company was still located in Shliakhovoe), having advanced approximately 7 kilometers from the attack's jumping-off positions, completely broke through the defenses of the 92nd Guards and 305th Rifle Divisions, and were now attacking the troops of the second echelon of Goriachev's 35th Guards Rifle Corps on this direction, the positions of the 522nd Rifle Regiment, which was on the right flank of Colonel P.M. Bezhko's 107th Rifle Division and in front of the large village of Verkhnii Ol'shanets. From the operational summary of the headquarters of the 107th Rifle Division at 0100 on 12.7.1943:

> Up until 1830 the 522nd Rifle Regiment and one company of the 130th Anti-tank Rifle Battalion were defending the Novo-Oskochnoe – Verkhnii Ol'shanets – Shukhovtsevo sector. From 1840 they began fighting to repulse enemy tank attacks on the approaches to the

---

27 TsAMO RF, f. 35 gv. sk, op. 1, d. 44, l. 9.
28 TsAMO RF, f. 203, op. 2845, d. 277, l. 14.

forward edge with every available anti-tank weapon. Five enemy tanks were set ablaze and 7 more were knocked out. The regiment was subjected to an intense aerial bombing, and unable to withstand the enemy's onslaught, proved unable to prevent the enemy tanks' capture of Verkhnii Ol'shanets. Up to 10 enemy tanks entered a patch of woods east of the village and began firing at the regiment's command post. The 1st and 2nd Battalions throughout the course of this battle continued to hold their lines stubbornly. The situation with the battalions (with which there are now no communications) is being ascertained.

The 504th Rifle Regiment with 1/496th Mortar Regiment of the Supreme Command Reserve, one company of anti-tank rifles from the 130th Separate Anti-tank Rifle Battalion, and one battery of the 409th Separate Destroyer Anti-tank Artillery Battalion have been defending its previous sector and the 1st Rifle Battalion is engaged in combat with enemy tanks that were advancing toward the 522nd Rifle Regiment.[29]

Together with the 522nd Rifle Regiment, the division commander's reserve, the 305th Rifle Regiment, joined combat with the units of the 6th Panzer Division at Znamenka. However, A.F. Vasil'ev was still unaware of everything that had happened, and so he even tried to organize a counterattack with two rifle battalions toward Shliakhovoe, where a panzer company of the Panzer Regiment 11 was operating. At 1900 he signed his Order No.103, which demanded first to move out his reserve, 2/1002nd Rifle Regiment, from Znamenka toward Ol'khovatka, and for 1/1000th Rifle Regiment to make a forced march from Sheino to the area 2 kilometers northeast of Shliakhovoe. Relying on archival documents one can assert that even if the Germans were located at this moment not in Verkhnii Ol'shanets, but in front of Ol'khovatka, the division commander's plan would have resulted in heavy losses and there would have been little sense in this. The two rifle battalions were supposed to attack out of the Ol'khovatka – Dubovoi ravine area toward the northwestern and southeastern outskirts of Shliakhovoe, which is to say, to launch a head-on attack against 6th Panzer Division's *panzerkampfgruppe* across level terrain, and also be ready (as an option) for a counterattack toward Sabynino. However, this scheme was disrupted by the rapidly changing operational situation and the ensuing tragic events now in the rear of Vasil'ev's division. At the moment when von Oppeln-Bronikowski's panzer regiment broke through to Verkhnii Ol'shanets, a portion of *Kampfgruppe* Unrein crushed the left flank of the 522nd Rifle Regiment together with 2/1002nd Rifle Regiment and encircled the 305th Rifle Division's command post in the woods near Raevka (2 kilometers southeast of Verkhnii Ol'shanets). The headquarters' security and men of the specialized units took up an all-round defense, while the commander of the 1000th Rifle Regiment Lieutenant Colonel N.P. Davydov, having received information about the surrounding of the division's headquarters, cancelled the 1st Rifle Battalion's previous order and issued it a new order to pivot toward Ol'khovatka and from the march counterattack it with the aim of freeing the command post. Meanwhile, 2/1002nd Rifle Regiment continued to operate according to Vasil'ev's designated plan. From the 305th Rifle Division's combat diary:

> 1/1000th Rifle Regiment given the encirclement of the division's command post by the enemy launched a counterattack, wiped out up to a company of enemy soldiers and officers, took Ol'khovatka, and then being almost surrounded, at the order of the division commander fell back to Lomovo.

---

29 TsAMO RF, f. 1296, op. 1, d. 10, l. 213.

2/1002nd Rifle Regiment, battling superior enemy forces of tanks and motorized infantry, suffered heavy losses and retreated in scattered groups to Novo-Oskochnoe, where they linked up with friendly units.[30]

That evening, the division headquarters and the 1st Battalion of the 1000th Rifle Regiment made a fighting withdrawal to Lomovo, and that night with the authorization of the corps commander, assembled in Kolomitsevo (13 kilometers northeast of Lomovo).

Von Hünersdorff, who was personally directing the combat operations of his division's *kampfgruppen* on this day, having an insufficient amount of armor in order to break the resistance of the 522nd Rifle Regiment, which was stubbornly defending Verkhnii Ol'shanets and Novo-Oskochnoe, from the march, decided to isolate them with a portion of Colonel M. Unrein's Panzergrenadier Regiment 4 and to bring up flamethrowers, flame-throwing panzers and several regular panzers. Meanwhile, the general kept the main forces of von Oppeln-Bronikowski's *panzerkampfgruppe* (7./Panzer Regiment 11, the Tiger company, and a company of panzergrenadiers mounted in halftracks) advancing to the northeast. Incidentally, on the following day, reporting on the situation in the 522nd Rifle Regiment, the division commander M.P. Bezhko particularly emphasized that the regiment had suffered its greatest number of casualties from flamethrowers. The 6th Panzer Division's *panzerkampfgruppe*, which had Major Bäke's II/Panzer Regiment 25 leading the advance, bypassing Verkhnii Ol'shanets from the west, advanced another 5 kilometers between 2130 and 2230 and before the onset of twilight took Kazach'e. However, sensing the taste of victory, Colonel von Oppeln-Bronikowski decided not to stop on what had been achieved and undertook a night attack, in order to take intact bridges across the Northern Donets in the village of Rzhavets (6 kilometers north of Kazach'e). He gave this mission to Major F. Bäke immediately after the last pockets of resistance by Soviet troops had been liquidated in Kazach'e.

Thus, by the end of 11 July, approximately after nine hours of a constant advance, 6th Panzer Division had fully carried out the day's mission. By this time, a deep (13 kilometers) but rather narrow (5-6 kilometers) penetration had been made in the center of the 69th Army's combat positions, at the boundary between its two corps, which on the night of 11-12 July von Oppeln-Bronikowski's *panzerkampfgruppe* would extend another 4-5 kilometers. Even though this striking advance was no longer able to save Operation Citadel from failure (on 13 July it would be officially cancelled by Hitler), nevertheless this was an impressive success by Breith's III Panzer Corps, even though the capture of Kazach'e didn't mean that by this time von Hünersdorff's and Schmidt's panzer divisions had taken full control over all the ground they had advanced across in the corridor between the Northern Donets and Razumnaia Rivers. They had several villages in their hands, albeit not fully so: Khokhlovo, Kiselevo, Shliakhovoe, Ol'khovatka, Raevka and Kazach'e, while heavy street fighting was continuing in Verkhnii Ol'shanets and Novo-Oskochnoe. Along the entire sector of the 6th Panzer Division's breakthrough, its panzergrenadier regiments were engaged in bitter fighting on the hills and in the hamlets, ravines and patches of wood with isolated units and elements of three Soviet divisions (92nd Guards, 305th and 107th Rifle Divisions). Meanwhile, the 19th Panzer Division, having taken Kiselevo with great difficulty, was unsuccessfully trying to take Sabynino and create a bridgehead on the right bank of the Northern Donets River. Despite every effort exerted by Schmidt's panzer division, the Soviet units here, backed by armor, were continuing to fight tenaciously. After losing 6 T-34 tanks, the 96th Separate Tank Brigade's 228th Tank Battalion and a portion of the 89th Guards Rifle Division's 267th Guards Rifle Regiment fell back from Kiselevo to Sabynino, which noticeably bolstered the line of the 280th Guards Rifle Regiment, which had been positioned here since 9 July. Only after midnight did the 280th Guards

---

30 TsAMO RF, f. 305 sd, op. 1, d. 5, l. 28.

Rifle Regiment abandon this area pursuant to orders, and Panzergrenadier Regiment 74 reached and dug in on the tactically important Hill 211.5. However, even after this, Schmidt's units were unable to create a firm line in the area of Kiselevo, because the manpower in the regiments' companies had fallen to 20 grenadiers each. Documents of the 19th Panzer Division headquarters note: "In order to repel night attacks and the actions of Russian assault groups, the division's regiments took up an all-round defense on the hills they had captured, since it was impossible to create a continuous front. Even so it must be recognized that the Soviet side as well, because of high casualties, also lacked the strength to take advantage of their enemy's weakness."

From a briefing given by the operations chief of III Panzer Corps at 0610 (Moscow time):

> 6th Panzer Division' last evening at 2100 reached Kazach'e and is engaged in heavy fighting there with enemy tanks. The bulk of the division is deployed in the Verkhnii Ol'shanets – Shliakhovoe area.
>
> 19th Panzer Division, which was attacked by large infantry forces and approximately 20 tanks, had to give up the southern portion of Sabynino again. The division will step off again at 0745 (Moscow time) with the support of Ju-87s, all of the corps' artillery and the 52nd Mortar Regiment [of Nebelwerfers].
>
> 168th Infantry Division yesterday evening passed through Petropavlovka and B.V. from the west and entered the woods south of Gostishchevo. Other units were mopping up the terrain east of Kiselevo and south of Sabynino of isolated pockets of enemy. Enemy activity in the air is moderate.[31]

Reading the combat documents of the opposing sides that were operating in the corridor between the Northern Donets and Razumnaia Rivers, it is impossible to get a sense how high the degree of bitterness in the fighting was. The ground between the two rivers, or as it was sometimes called in Soviet documents, the "breakthrough sleeve", was like a seething cauldron, in which an intermingled mass of opposing troops were trying to kill each other in an unbelievable frenzy. The 35th Guards Rifle Corps was in the most difficult situation. The commanders of its divisions and attached assets were paying no attention to the fact that the enemy had seized the initiative and had penetrated deeply into the defenses. Given the slightest opportunity, they were raising their units on the counterattack, even when caught in a hopeless situation.

It should be stressed that in the second half of the day, and especially close to evening, the Luftwaffe nevertheless gave the 6th and 19th Panzer Divisions substantial help by destroying the more or less major pockets of resistance in their paths and inflicting heavy blows on communication hubs and points of command and control of the divisions of both of 69th Army's corps. For example, at 1900 up to 200 Luftwaffe aircraft leveled the command post of the 89th Guards Rifle Division and hammered the positions of its regiments on the right bank of the Northern Donets opposite the 168th Infantry Division and 19th Panzer Division.[32] As a result, a number of officers were wounded, some badly so, vehicles were destroyed, and communication equipment knocked out, so the division commander Colonel M.P. Seriugin made the decision to move the division headquarters. However, he wasn't able to do this smoothly, as a result of which communications were temporarily lost with the units, and on the night of 11-12 July, during the march, the headquarters' column between Rzhavets and Kazach'e came under an attack by von Oppeln-Bronikowski's *panzerkampfgruppe*, which was roaming through the 69th Army's rear.

---

31 NARA US, t. 312, r. 54, f. 7569656.
32 TsAMO RF, f. 89 gv. sd, op. 1, d. 22, l. 11.

At the same time, the Soviet 2nd Air Army was showing passivity. A large number of documents of the ground formations and units have been preserved that show they sought its assistance. Our commanders were persistently asking higher headquarters for air cover, but unfortunately their requests went unanswered. At 0200 on 12 July Major General M.P. Bezhko sent Report No.00121 to the commander of the 35th Guards Rifle Corps, in which he bitterly commented, "My repeated calls for airstrikes on the enemy tanks and the scattering of his aircraft haven't been satisfied."[33] Indeed, this wasn't a case of unjustified finger pointing; throughout the day of 11 July and the morning of 12 July, the 6th Panzer Division headquarters was also reporting rare enemy activity in the air.

To compound matters, at the same time throughout the Voronezh Front's entire area of defensive combat, the number of fratricidal bombing and strafing attacks by crews of the 2nd and 17th Air Armies sharply increased. Those divisions that were operating in the German breakthrough corridor and on the flanks it noted a particularly large number of fratricidal attacks by ground attack aircraft. On the evening of 11 July the commander of the 69th Army with his Special Order No.00984/op repeated an order from the Voronezh Front command, which stated:

> In recent days incidents of dropping bombs by our own aircraft in the vicinity of friendly forces has increased. The reason for this is the insufficient experience of the pilots and their inadequate knowledge of the forward edge of our forces.
>
> I am ordering elements of the forward units to make it known immediately to the pilots where the forward edge their own troops runs and to mark it by laying down cloth strips that point toward the enemy, or given the absence of specialized means, to identify themselves with miscellaneous signaling or the waving of helmets or other articles of the uniform [!]. Other than these signals, fire a series of green flares, including out of open tank hatches. The pilot must thoroughly study his area of operations. Assign more highly trained pilots to crews of the lead aircraft. Immediately put those guilty of [fratricidal] bombings on trial. Make this order known to each pilot.[34]

It is one thing if the *Sturmoviki* were pounding the rear areas flat, but was it really possible to carry out the demands of this order at the front by waving off pilots and taking off your combat blouse to do this, when the enemy is firing at your from every gun barrel?

We won't call excessive attention to such petty matters. Lieutenant General V.D. Kriuchenkin at that moment really had no time to ponder each and every word of the order; it was important by any means to cease this mayhem that was happening in the skies above the 69th Army. There wasn't a day when the "Red Star falcons" didn't pounce on their own troops several times. The attacks struck both rear areas and the front. On 11 July, judging from the messages of division commanders Trunin, Vasil'ev and Bezhko, friendly bombs rained down on the heads of their units as if out of the horn of plenty. The commander of the 69th Army himself came under them. At a point 5 kilometers south of Korocha, his Willys jeep and the vehicles of the officers of the operational command group that were following it were fired upon by two Il-2 aircraft. Unfortunately, neither this order, nor the directives that came after it fixed this problem. A day later, on 12 July 1943, over a short period of time crews of the 1st Storm Aviation Corps worked over the command post of the 48th Rifle Corps several times in succession, nearly killing its commander Major General Z.Z. Ragoznyi.[35]

---

33   TsAMO RF, f. 1296, op. 1, d. 9, l. 113.
34   TsAMO RF, f. 199 gv. ap, op. 1, d. 4, l. 27.
35   TsAMO RF, f. 426, op. 10753, d. 43, l. 9.

However, the Luftwaffe's superiority in the skies above the battlefield and the mistakes made by their own pilots weren't the main problem for the Soviet side at this moment. Two important factors were seriously complicating the situation in the 69th Army's sector: the lack of even minimal reserves at the army commander's disposal, or available to the division commanders; and the divisions' loss of communications with their subordinate regiments and the headquarters of the 35th Guards Rifle Corps. Already after the first 2 to 2.5 hours of the enemy's offensive, the command posts of the 96th Separate Tank Brigade ("Amalgamated" State Farm), the 92nd Guards Rifle Division (Sabynino), the 305th Rifle Division (Raevka area) and the 107th Rifle Division came under enemy attack, as did the headquarters of their regiments and battalions. The headquarters of the 35th Guards Rifle Corps, which had been located on the morning of 11 July in Raevka, with the start of the 6th Panzer Division's attack moved to the eastern outskirts of Kazach'e, and after von Oppeln-Bronikowski's *panzerkampfgruppe* broke through to the forward edge of the 107th Rifle Division, hastily departed to Dal'nii Dolzhik (on the western bank of the Northern Donets River), which was located in the sector of defense of the 69th Army's 48th Rifle Corps. Communications became disrupted, forcing the use of runners to relay information and commands, which because of the rapidly changing operational situation, the relocation of divisional command posts and the lack of a continuous line of defense, were unable timely to deliver orders and directives. In addition, the operational information arriving from the front was sparse and not always accurate (often because they no longer corresponded to the situation). The acting chief of staff of the 69th Army Colonel S.M. Protas wrote to the subordinate corps commanders: "Despite the repeated directions and demands, the operational summaries and combat reports continue to arrive from you with a delay of 3-9 hours, fail to reflect accurately and completely the actions and position of the units, and have nothing to say about the enemy's losses or your own losses."[36]

Therefore after the enemy reached Verkhnii Ol'shanets, the 69th Army's defenses in front of the assault wedge of the III Panzer Corps no longer existed as a unified whole, and Goriachev, like Kriuchenkin, had no way to block the enemy's combat groups that had broken through into the depth of his lines. Lieutenant General S.G. Goriachev later recalled this tragic moment in the defensive operation:

> The headquarters of our corps also wound up in a most difficult situation on this day. In the morning the headquarters was located in Raevka. When a message arrived that a large group of enemy tanks had broken through to the vicinity of Shliakhovoe and was moving toward Ol'khovatka, I gave a command for the headquarters to relocate to Kazach'e, where a reserve command post had been previously set up. Despite all the demands of the regulations and situation, we had to move the headquarters not at night, but in daylight hours. We moved it in small groups of vehicles and wagons. The first to set out with some of the officers of the Operations Department was the corps chief of staff Colonel D.S. Tsalai. He managed to get underway safely, and about 20 minutes later he reported that he had arrived at the destination; the command post had been set up; and communications with all the divisions and units was working without interruption.
>
> Having temporarily turned over command to him, I headed out in my vehicle along with the rest of the headquarters. We successfully made it past the dangerous spots. But about an hour after our arrival, enemy aircraft in two groups of approximately 100 each attacked the village in which we were located. The ground shook from the explosions of hundreds of bombs. Buildings collapsed and fires began. However, we had no casualties, thanks largely to

---

36 TsAMO RF, f. 48 sk, op. 1, d. 2, l. 18.

the engineer battalion. The engineers had dug deep slit trenches with excellent overhead cover near the location of the headquarters and the communications post, adequate to hold all of the personnel of the headquarters and service elements. As a result, just one female operator, who was on duty at the central telephone switchboard, was wounded, and only lightly so. Just a few of the vehicles took any damage. There were almost no residents left in the village by this time – they had departed as the front drew nearer.

The heavy bombing did completely disrupt the lines of communication. There weren't enough radios at this time, and their range of effective operation was extremely short. Therefore, left without telephone communications, we had no information about the course of the fighting of our units and formations.

Immediately after the enemy air attack, I called together the staff officers in order to resolve the problem with getting communications up and running again. At this time we were hearing some thudding noises: once, twice, three times … At first no one paid any attention to them, but the sounds were being persistently repeated and approaching us. Having taken a look around, we discovered that on the western outskirts of Kazach'e, a group of approximately 50 enemy tanks were firing at us with armor-piercing rounds from a small hill. Fortunately, they apparently didn't have any high-explosive shells; otherwise things would have been bad for us. The armor-piercing rounds were penetrating the walls of huts and landing without exploding. However, we had to take shelter even from this fire. What saved us was the fact that the village was split from north to south by a deep ravine, at the bottom of which a small stream flows. The tanks weren't able to cross this ravine, and evening was already approaching.

I had no units or elements at all in order to cover this direction. The headquarters had only a signals battalion and engineer battalion. It was also impossible to summon help from neighbors because of the lack of communications. We quickly had to form a mobile blocking detachment out of the engineer battalion with a supply of anti-tank mines, and ordered it to mine all possible approaches and hold the line until relieved. Meanwhile I and my headquarters set off for Aleksandrovka. Along the road we encountered a "Katiusha" battalion standing in firing positions; the Guards mortar men then fired at the aggregation of enemy tanks.

As became clear later, the enemy tanks didn't advance any further, since they didn't have any infantry with them – they had been separated from the tanks by our own troops. The German tankers didn't dare operate without infantry, especially as night was falling. This is what saved us. To remain in Kazach'e without any communications made no sense. We retreated to Aleksandrovka and got busy with restoring communications with the divisions. The majority of the staff officers and political officers headed out in vehicles, on motorcycles and on horseback in order to find the headquarters of the divisions and units, and give them on the spot combat orders to fall back and take up new lines of defense in the Vypolzovka, Aleksandrovka, Sviridovo area, and to the south along the elevated banks of the Razumnaia River.

On this difficult day for us, the assistant chief of operations Guards Major Georgii Fillipovich Pominov distinguished himself with his bravery and administrative ability in organizing a defense and re-establishing communications. During the breakthrough of the 50 tanks to a point near the corps command post in the village of Kazach'e, the valiant major under enemy fire and bombing attacks quickly and capably organized the evacuation of the men to a safe place and took measures to preserve the staff documents. He carried out all of his assignments from the command quickly and successfully. The fact of the re-establishment of communications at the new command post, thanks to which we were able to deliver new assignments promptly to the formation and unit commanders; smoothly implement the withdrawal to new lines; and get command over the troops up and running, resulting in the stopping of the enemy's offensive, are to the great merit of G.F. Pominov. The corps command recommended the awarding of Communist Pominov with the Order of the Red Banner.[37]

When a breakthrough by a tank group occurs, it can be stopped either by a very strong line in the depth of the defenses, saturated with anti-tank guns or by a counterattack with tanks. The commander of the 35th Guards Rifle Corps had neither one nor the other. The 148th Separate Tank Regiment fell into encirclement in Shliakhovoe. Both battalions of Lebedev's 96th Separate Tank Brigade were engaged in heavy fighting at Sabynino, though this to a great extent helped the 92nd Guards Rifle Division hold this village. Moreover, the headquarters of the 96th Separate Tank Brigade had no radio or telephone communications and didn't know where either battalion was precisely located, so by any stretch of the imagination it was impossible to organize a counterattack, all the more so because the 96th Separate Tank Brigade's command post, which had come under an attack by enemy panzers, had to pack up hastily and move to a new location.

The sector of the second echelon 107th Rifle Division was not a strong anti-tank line. Not even all of the tank-vulnerable ground out in front of its forward edge had been mined, not to mention that the division had no assets other than one mortar regiment and a battalion of anti-tank rifles. I'll remind the reader that after 1800 the left flank of the 35th Guards Rifle Division had also been crushed, and the 94th Guards Rifle Division had wound up encircled. The corps commander had no reserves, and also had poor knowledge of the situation in the latter half of the day. The circumstance that beyond the village of Kazach'e to the northeast there were no other units, not to mention divisions, if you exclude separate artillery elements (like for example the 4/114th Guards Destroyer Anti-tank Artillery Battalion, which the 92nd Guards Rifle Division commander had deployed in the area of Vypolzovka "just in case"), added to the urgency of the situation.

Thus, the command of both the 69th Army and of the Voronezh Front around 2100 had no detailed knowledge about how events were developing within the breakthrough corridor, not to mention any ability to react to them adequately. Likely, on the night of 9-10 July S.P. Ivanov and V.D. Kriuchenkin were concerned about just such a turn in events, when during the discussions that night with N.F. Vatutin they had requested to redirect the 2nd Guards Tank Corps from Prokhorovka Station to the south. However, at that time the situation didn't allow the Front Commander-in-Chief to authorize its lateral movement into the sector of the 69th Army. The situation on the Prokhorovka direction was prompting greater alarm than the one on the Korocha direction. Vatutin was worried about the capture of the station by the SS troops from the march, and accordingly, the line of deployment for the 5th Guards Tank Army, and the 2nd Guards Tank Corps was his sole, substantial mobile reserve here. Indeed, it must be said that the General of the Army's concerns were justified. On the evening of 11 July the commander of the 2nd Guards Tank Corps Colonel A.S. Burdeinyi received an order from Vatutin to launch an attack into the flank of the II SS Panzer Corps' units that had reached the outskirts of the station. Later it became clear, however, that the forces of the 5th Guards Army had succeeded on their own in localizing the German breakthrough.

Now however, having received a report on the evening of 11 July about the deep penetration made by the Germans at the boundary between the 69th Army's two corps, Vatutin hastily began to direct to this point not only the forces of the 2nd Guards Tank Corps, but now also significant forces of the 5th Guards Tank Army, which had been planned to take part in the counteroffensive.

---

37 Goriachev, S.G., *Ot Volgi do Al'p* [*From the Volga to the Alps*] (Kiev: Politizdat Ukrainy, 1982), pp. 59-62. By order of the 69th Army's Military Council on 25.08.1943, Lieutenant Colonel G.F. Pominov was awarded the Order of the Patriotic War 2nd Class (TsAMO RF, f. 33, op. 686044, ed. khr. 657, entry number 18145541).

At first N.F. Vatutin transferred the 10th Separate Destroyer Anti-tank Artillery Brigade, which had already been attached to the 5th Guards Tank Army as reinforcement, to V.D. Kriuchenkin. Then he would be forced to take P.A. Rotmistrov's reserve from him – a forward detachment, which at this time was positioned near Oboian'. Already at 0300 12 July 1943, an order was sent to its commander Major General K.G. Trufanov through the Military Council member N.S. Khrushchev about making a forced march to the area of III Panzer Corps' breakthrough. Three hours later, right after sunrise, the commander of the 5th Guards Tank Army, who was located in a forward observation post near Prokhorovka, would receive an order to move the 2nd Guards Tank Corps' 26th Guards Tank Brigade from out of the army's first echelon and two mechanized brigades of the 5th Guards Mechanized Corps, which had been planned to stand ready to exploit a success of the 5th Guards Tank Army's shock formation, to this area.[38] Thus, Breith's breakthrough on the evening of 11 July had substantially reduced the chances that Rotmistrov's Guardsmen would be able to split the II SS Panzer Corps with a head-on attack and reach the area of Iakovlevo, as N.F. Vatutin had been assuming. The counteroffensive hadn't even been launched, but in order to parry the threat of a breakthrough into the rear of the 5th Guards Tank Army from the south, 161 tanks (almost 20% of the total number of tanks in the 5th Guards Tank Army), 11 self-propelled guns, 36 armored cars, 2 artillery regiments and 2 anti-tank batteries, as well as the 10th Separate Destroyer Anti-tank Artillery Brigade would leave the 5th Guards Tank Army. As a result, its first echelon would be weakened (by the departure of the 2nd Guards Tank Corps and the 10th Separate Destroyer Anti-tank Artillery Brigade), and its second echelon would be cut in half (the 5th Guards Mechanized Corps),[39] leaving Vatutin with only two brigades of the 5th Guards Mechanized Corps (92 tanks) in order to exploit a success and act as a reserve.[40] In such circumstances, it would now be difficult to count upon fulfilling the ambitious tasks that had been set in the plan for the counteroffensive.

Judging from the documents the situation in the sector of the 35th Guards Rifle Corps became clear to the leadership of the 69th Army, but not fully so, approximately between 2200 and 2300. So that the reader might understand what information it had then, and how its command was planning to rectify the bad situation, here is an excerpt from the transcript of the discussions between N.F. Vatutin and S.P. Ivanov that took place at 2130 on 11 July 1943:

> **N.F. Vatutin:** What do you have new on your left flank? Have you managed to stop the enemy? What additional steps are you taking? Keep in mind that Shumilov's KV tank regiment is located 3 kilometers east of Miasoedovo. Directly south of Korocha there is one regiment each of the 30th and 31st Separate Destroyer Anti-tank Artillery Brigade, each of which has 4 guns. Urgently take them and send them with the 10th Separate Destroyer Anti-tank Artillery Brigade to any other axis at your decision.
>
> **S.P. Ivanov, V.D. Kriuchenkin:** We are reporting. Reconnaissance and prisoner statements completely confirm that up to 250 enemy tanks are operating on this direction; according to the latest information approximately 100 enemy tanks have been deployed and are engaged in combat south of Verkhnii Ol'shanets, Raevka and Komintern. Up to 20 enemy tanks bypassed the Verkhnii Ol'shanets strongpoint on its west side and are heading toward Kazach'e [Major Bäke's II/Panzer Regiment 11] and at the given time are located 1.5 kilometers north of Verkhnii Ol'shanets. Goriachev and his headquarters have left the place. According to the reports of commanders who are observing the battle,

---

38 TsAMO RF, f. 332, op. 4948, d. 70, l. 132.
39 TsAMO RF, f. 332, op. 4948, d. 75, l. 10.
40 Ibid.

the 92nd Guards Rifle Division retreated in disorder to the north. In addition, the enemy air force attacked Kazach'e with approximately 100 aircraft, and Verkhnii Ol'shanets and Lomovo with 30 aircraft each.

Measures taken: The 10th Separate Destroyer Anti-tank Artillery Brigade has already been raised in response to an alarm and is already in motion; at 2130 it headed out of Korocha with its last gun, with the assignment to arrive in the 69th Army's main line of defense along the line: Vypolzovka, Novo-Aleksandrovskii Vyselok-1, Sviridovo, Podsumki and to block the main directions toward Aleksandrovka and Podsumki.

Goriachev has been given an instruction: if it isn't too late, to send one regiment to Verkhnii Ol'shanets and to accomplish this in the course of the night.

305th Rifle Division is to be withdrawn to a line of defense that it previously occupied and was prepared by it: Vypolzovka, Podsumki, Alekseevka, Ploskoe.

94th Guards Rifle Division is to have one regiment for the defense at Razumnoe on the Shukhovtsevo – Mazikino – Sheino front, a second regiment there, where it is standing on the Sheino, Ushakovo line, and the third regiment on the Koren' River on the (excl.) Ploskoe, Novoselovka front.

31st Separate Destroyer Anti-tank Artillery Brigade: We are assigning half of the brigade to the 94th Guards Rifle Division, and half to the Alekseevka, Ploskoe line; 8 guns, which are in the stage of forming up, are being positioned for the direct defense of Korocha.

The retreating 92nd Guards Rifle Division will be assembled in the Ryndenka – Rzhavets – Gnezdilovka – Kireev area.

Now the entire headquarters will be divided into groups and be sent tonight to the troops in order to carry out this exact decision.

81st Guards Rifle Division has received an order to occupy the Krivtsovo, Verkhnii Ol'shanets, Novo-Oskochnoe line; it has available one composite regiment of infantry and just 6 guns, only 2 of which are divisional guns.

In addition, perhaps, something can be detached from other formations.

89th Guards Rifle Division is stretched along the Northern Donets as far as Sabynino.

That is all. We have no requests. We will take every measure in order to execute this decision; toward the evening today, there were complaints coming in from all the divisions about the incessant aerial bombing of their combat positions. There is a request for air cover from tomorrow morning.

N.F. Vatutin: Act more energetically, in order to carry out the decision you've made. Don't expose Shumilov's flank. Keep in mind that by the morning of 12 July Rotmistrov's mechanized corps will reach the Krasnoe area [5 kilometers southwest of Prokhorovka]. Aviation will provide cover. Rotmistrov has begun to operate in the Prokhorovka area. These operations will continue early in the morning. Demand discipline from the troops.[41]

At this moment when the discussions were going on between the Front and 69th Army headquarters, bitter fighting was continuing on the right flank of the 35th Guards Rifle Corps, which had been virtually crushed, but their intensity gradually subsided. At 2330 S.G. Goriachev signed an order about withdrawing the 92nd Guards Rifle Division to the Vypolzovka – southern outskirts of Aleksandrovka (4 kilometers northeast of Kazach'e) line, which was part of the system of the

---

41 TsAMO RF, f. 203, op. 2843, d. 461, l. 57, 57obr.

rear army-level defensive belt. Under the cover of gathering darkness, large groups of soldiers and commanders, exhausted by the heavy fighting, and the remaining tanks of the 96th Separate Tank Brigade were moving out of Kiselevo, Sabynino and Shliakhovoe to the northeast. However by the morning of 12 July only 2/280th Guards Rifle Regiment, the training battalion and the reconnaissance company had assembled in the indicated area together with the headquarters of the 92nd Guards Rifle Division. The men of the remaining regiments and specialized elements were making their way out of enemy-occupied territory and reassembling in the Novo-Slabodka, Dolgoe, Novo-Khmelevoe area until 14 July. Incidentally, the 280th Rifle Regiment by this time had been virtually destroyed. Already after the war, on 21 January 1949, a report arrived at the Department of Personnel of the Officers Staff with the USSR Armed Force's Main Cadre Department from the 108th Guards Mechanized Regiment (formerly the 280th Guards Rifle Regiment), which in particular stated:

> 10-12 July 1943 the regiment's units were fighting while remaining in their occupied positions, but the enemy broke through with tanks on the flanks, as well as partially through their combat positions, as a result of which the units continued to fight in encirclement. That night, when coming out of battle the regiment commander Lieutenant Colonel Novikov and the chief of staff Major Komarov disappeared. On 18.07.1943 when the regiment was withdrawn after taking heavy losses for refitting, Major Komarov showed up and said that he had crawled away alone, and he didn't know where Comrade Novikov was. The enemy was conducting devastating artillery and small arms' fire. Thus it was difficult to establish whether Comrade Novikov had been killed, or whether he was left on the battlefield wounded, since not all of the regiment's command staff had returned. Thus, Comrade Novikov never returned to the regiment and no one saw him alive or his corpse.[42]

Lebedev's 96th Separate Tank Brigade also began to arrive in the same place, in the Aleksandrovka – Sviridovo sector. From its journal of combat operations:

> At 2200 at an order from the brigade commander, a reconnaissance squad mounted on a T-70 tank set off to the battalions with the task to bring them out to the Aleksandrovka area. During the battle 12 enemy tanks were either set ablaze or knocked out. Our losses are 13 T-34 and 2 T-60. At 2300 the brigade headquarters, the headquarters company, 3 T-70 and 1 T-34 took up a defense southwest of Aleksandrovka, and together with a rocket-launching battalion repulsed one tank attack.[43]

The brigade's main forces had reassembled by 0500 on 12 July, having 14 T-34 and 3 T-70, plus one 76mm anti-tank gun in the headquarters company.[44]

Before midnight, the 107th Rifle Division's commander also received an order from the army headquarters to defend the (excl.) Sviridovo, Razumnaia balka, lake, Gremiachee, Ploskoe line with the forces of the 514th and 594th Rifle Regiments, and to reassemble the shattered 522nd Rifle Regiment in the Zaiach'e area. However, S.G. Goriachev's main joy arrived late in the evening, when a powerful anti-tank formation – the three regiments of the 10th Separate Destroyer Anti-tank Artillery Brigade – began to arrive under his operational control. The corps commander remembered:

---

42 TsAMO RF, f. 33, op. 594261, d. 65, l. 121.
43 TsAMO RF, f. 96 otbr, op. 1, d. 3, l. 16obr.
44 Ibid.

The situation remained critical. I had no full confidence that the officers of the headquarters would be able to make their way back to the command post. There was also no confidence that the soldiers, after such debilitating, heavy fighting would have time to conduct the march and take up new lines of defense by morning. But how we all rejoiced, when around midnight an anti-tank artillery commander showed up and reported that he had arrived with his anti-tank brigade under my operational control! Unfortunately, time has erased his family name from my memory.[45]

This was the 10th Separate Anti-tank Artillery Brigade's commander himself, Lieutenant Colonel A.F. Antonov. In addition, it must be said that despite the extremely tense atmosphere that was reigning in the headquarters of the Soviet forces on the Korocha axis at this time, as well as in the headquarters of the 69th Army itself, the command staff of this brigade worked efficiently and very professionally. The brigade's journal of combat operations for 11 July testifies to this:

> At 1800 the brigade commander drove to the Voronezh Front's artillery headquarters in order to receive a new combat assignment [to take part in the counteroffensive as part of the 5th Guards Tank Army].
>
> At 2000 the assistant chief of staff Captain Serdiuk drove to the headquarters of the 5th Guards Tank Army in order to receive a combat order (on the basis of a directive from the headquarters of the 69th Army). By 2100 the brigade's units were ready for a march in the direction of Oboian' [to Prokhorovka] in order to move into jumping-off positions.
>
> At 2100 a verbal order was received from the 69th Army's artillery commander: the brigade's regiments were to move to the Novo-Oskochnoe, Kazach'e, Lomovo, Gremiachee line, where it was to take up a strong anti-tank defense. The brigade's units immediately set out to carry out this combat order: the 522nd Destroyer Anti-tank Artillery Regiment to Novo-Oskochnoe, the 1245th Destroyer Anti-tank Artillery Regiment to Kazach'e, and the 1243rd Destroyer Anti-tank Artillery Regiment to Lomovo and Gremiachee.
>
> Despite the series of contradictory orders and the sharply changing operational situation, which created extreme difficulties in commanding the brigade its headquarters nevertheless dealt with the task. The brigade's units while on the march were turned around and at 0200 on 12 July 1943 took up an anti-tank defense on the indicated line: 522nd Destroyer Anti-tank Artillery Regiment – in the Aleksandrovka area; the 1245th Destroyer Anti-tank Artillery Regiment – in the Sviridovo – southwestern outskirts of Novo-Slobodka area; the 1243rd Destroyer Anti-tank Artillery Regiment in the Podsumki – Zaiach'e – Lomovo area. The brigade headquarters remained in Korocha, the rear services – in their previous location. In order to ensure command and control over the units, the brigade commander drove to the 1245th Destroyer Anti-tank Artillery Regiment, and the chief of staff drove to the 522nd Destroyeer Anti-tank Artilley Regiment.[46]

To this it should be added that from the moment Antonov's anti-tank brigade deployed in this area, it became the bulwark of the 35th Guards Rifle Corps' defense in the interfluvial area between the Northern Donets and Razumnaia Rivers. In the following days it would play an important role in repulsing the attempts by the III Panzer Corps to push toward Korocha.[47]

---

45   Goriachev, *Ot Volgi do Al'p*, p. 61.
46   TsAMO RF, f. 10 oiptabr, op. 1, d. 28, l. 8, 8obr.
47   For the successful resolution of combat tasks during the Battle of Kursk on the Belgorod direction, the command of the 69th Army's artillery recommended Lieutenant Colonel A.V. Antonov for the Order of the Patriotic War 1st Class on 29 August 1943, and he was subsequently awarded with this honor.

Thus, already after midnight the shattered forces of the 35th Guards Rifle Corps and the forces arriving from the Front's reserve started to occupy positions along the Vypolzovka, Aleksandrovka, Sviridovo, western bank of the Razumnaia River, Mazikino, Sheino, Ushakovo line. Here, they began to work to their utmost to set up a strong defense.

Meanwhile, on the left flank of Goriachev's 35th Guards Rifle Corps, with the onset of twilight the fighting between the encircled units of the 94th Guards Rifle Division and von Funck's and Horn's divisions flared up with renewed intensity. In the previously cited account of the 35th Guards Rifle Corps it was noted that two rifle regiments and a portion of the artillery regiment of Russkikh's 94th Guards Rifle Division had emerged from the pocket by midnight and were occupying a defense stretching from Mazikino to Ushakovo, but this isn't the case. According to Report No.09 from its headquarters at 0700 on 12 July, the main forces of the two rifle regiments had not yet come out of the pocket by midnight, but already after sunrise on 12 July (between 0400 and 0600), and had started to reassemble in the immediate vicinity of the villages of Sheino and Ushakovo. The 288th Guards Rifle Regiment's own combat diary states:

> At 2400 the regiment consisting of the 1st, 2nd and 3rd Battalions, and 2/283rd Guards Rifle Regiment began to break out of the enemy encirclement to their own units along a ravine on the right bank of the Razumnaia River in the direction of Sheino. The regiment commander and the headquarters of the 1st Rifle Battalion were moving in front with the reconnaissance. At 0400 the regiment arrived in the Sheino area and was assembling in the Ushakovo area in order to receive further instructions. Along the way out, the regiment's deputy combat commander Captain Karpov and a propaganda instructor Captain Sharov were killed by a mine explosion.[48]

In this same report the commander of the 94th Guards Rifle Division reported that he had decided "to hold the Hill 174.1 – Sheino – Ushakovo line with his available forces."[49] However, by this time the village of Mazikino was already in the 6th Panzer Division's hands and it was only a day later, by 0600 13 July that the 288th Guards Rifle Regiment would drive the Germans out of it. Only after this was the division able to build out a continuous defense on the line: (excl.) Komintern Kolkhoz – Mazikino – Sheino – Ushakovo. However, on the morning of 12 July, judging from the documents of the 94th Guards Rifle Division, there was no firm defense opposite the right flank of the III Panzer Corps in the Mazikino – Sheino – Ushakovo sector, with the exception of the village of Sheino itself. There were a lot of troops here that when coming out of battle began to take up positions in this area, although at this moment there was a lot of confusion among the regiment commanders and the division commander over the exact line along which the division's defense should be arranged. For example, the 288th Guards Rifle Regiment over the day received three contradictory orders: between 1000 and 1300 it reached and took up a defense along the Hill 193.0 – western outskirts of Ushakovo line, whereupon it received an order to abandon this sector and move to the Hill 215.3 – western outskirts of Nelidovo – western fringe of the woods southeast of Mazikino sector, but on the night of 12-13 July it was shifted to the eastern bank of the Razumnaia River, where it started to build positions along the line between (excl.) Komintern Kholkoz – (excl.) Mazikino line.

Breith was aware of the fact that on the morning of 12 July, the Soviet positions in the Sheino – Mazikino area were being weakly held, and undoubtedly would have tried to exploit the weakness,

---

(TsAMO RF, f. 33, op. 68604, ed. khr. 1553, entry number 19606565.
48 TsAMO RF, f. 288 g. sp, op. 318884, d. 1, l. 4obr.
49 TsAMO RF, f. 1269, op. 1, d. 9, l. 9.

but he lacked the strength to take advantage of this favorable situation and launch an attack in this sector. For him, the primary task at this moment was to withdraw the 7th Panzer Division and move it to join the III Panzer Corps' assault wedge, which is to say to the Rzhavets – Aleksandrovka – Verkhnii Ol'shanets area. However, von Funck's division together with Horn's infantry were tied up in fighting with the 94th Guards Rifle Division throughout the night of 11-12 July, and right after sunrise they were continuing to mop up pockets of stubborn resistance of the Guardsmen in Miasoedovo itself and in its surrounding area. It was only late in the morning that the 7th Panzer Division began to turn over its lines to the 198th Infantry Division, and this continued until mid-day, after which its main forces finally began moving to the northeast. Thus, during the hardest period for the Soviet side from the moment of the German breakthrough on 11 July to well into the following day, when V.D. Kriuchenkin and N.F. Vatutin were "scraping the bottom of the barrel" trying to restore the 69th Army's shattered front, one of Breith's three panzer divisions was locked in fighting with the 94th Guards Rifle Division. This was one of the main reasons for the fact that even though the 6th Panzer Division already by sunrise on 12 July had created a bridgehead across the Northern Donets River at Rzhavets that was fully suitable for an attack toward Prokhorovka from the south, while the defending Soviet forces here were very sparse, a rapid dash on 12 July in order to link-up at last with the II SS Panzer Corps didn't ensue.

There is one significant detail, to which it is necessary to pay attention. Despite the heavy fighting, the enemy's superiority in heavy weapons and the operational encirclement, the losses of the 94th Guards Rifle Division didn't actually prove to be very high. For example, on 11 July the 288th Guards Rifle Regiment lost 420 men.[50] However, and this was very important, the regiment's rifle battalions retained their combat capability. To wit, on the morning of 11 July 430 men reported for duty in the 1st Rifle Battalion, but on the next day 344 men reported for duty; in the 2nd Rifle Battalion these figures were correspondingly 368 and 308, and in the 3rd Rifle Battalion – 351 and 273.[51]

Around midnight on 11 July, von Oppeln-Bronikowski's *panzerkampfgruppe* set off to carry out an order to break through to the bridges across the Northern Donets in Rzhavets. The division command realized that a rapid march through the tactical belt of the 69th Army's significantly disorganized forces would still be extremely risky and dangerous because the area was crowded with them. Therefore it decided to activate collaborationists. Some scholars believe this was a unit of *Eingriffgruppe* [Attack group] Tietjen,[52] which was attached to the 6th Panzer Division prior to Operation Citadel[53] and consisted of 7 T-34 tanks. At the head of his panzer battalion's column, Major Bäke placed two captured T-34 tanks, crewed by former Soviet tankers who had gone over to the German side. Exploiting the twilight and confusion that was reigning in the rear of Kriuchenkin's army, the group advanced several kilometers from Kazach'e to Rzhavets, and having taken the bridges that were wired for demolition but weren't blown up, reached the northern bank of the Northern Donets River. From the morning and daily summary of the 6th Panzer Division to the headquarters of III Panzer Corps:

> Oppeln's panzer group is fighting in the Kazach'e area with enemy heavy tanks [there were no heavy Soviet tanks there]. *Kampgruppe* Unrein from its latest message is located with a portion of its strength in the area south of Verkhnii Ol'shanets, while another portion is engaged in bitter fighting to mop up Shliakhovoe [the southeastern portion of it]. *Kampfgruppe* Quentin

---

50 TsAMO RF, f. 288 gv. sp, op. 47024s, d. 6, l. 164, 166.
51 Ibid.
52 In the latter half of July 1943, *Eingriffgruppe* Tietjen was reformed into the 709th Regiment zbV.
53 Chuev, S., *Prokliatye soldaty: Predateli na storone tret'ego Reikha* [*Condemned soldiers: Traitors on the side of the Third Reich*] (Moscow: EKSMO, 2004), p. 84.

[the panzer reconnaissance battalion plus attached assets] with part of its force is on the march in order to take up a line east of Shliakhovoe, while the other part is still in Kalinin. Weak enemy aerial activity.

... The bridgehead northeast of Rzhavets seized in the course of the resolute pursuit on the night of 11-12 July is being held on 12.7 by von Oppeln's *panzerkampfgruppe* under artillery and tank fire. The division's forces in the course of the day are assembling in the Kazach'e – Kurakovka area.[54]

I've been unable to find any Russian archival materials that contain a description of the combat of Major Bäke's II/Panzer Regiment 11 between Kazach'e and Rzhavets; its details are known from Western publications, some of which cite documents as well. Here is an excerpt from one of them, Frank Kurowski's *500 tankovykh atak: Luchshie assy Pantservafee* [*500 tank attacks: Top aces of the Panzerwaffe* – the Russian translation of Kurowski's *Panzer Aces: German Tank Commanders of WWII*]:

> The attack continued toward Kasatchje [Kazach'e] and the Soviet antitank ditches there … After reaching the antitank ditches, Colonel von Oppeln-Bronikowski received orders to take Rshvets [Rzhavets] in a surprise night attack and establish a bridgehead across the Ssewernyi-Donets [Northern Donets]. Hermann von Oppeln-Bronikowski described the raid in his personal diary: "I greeted the commanders as they arrived at a provisional command post outside Kasatchje [Kazach'e]: 'Gentlemen, we will carry out our mission by night. The terrain lends itself to such an attack. Bäke, you and the 2nd Battalion take the lead. I will join you in my command vehicle.'"
>
> Major Bäke nodded in agreement and noted something on his map board. The battle group commander continued: "We will try to pass the Russian truck columns moving along the same road in the same direction unrecognized."
>
> The nocturnal advance began. Now and then the tanks and the Soviet truck columns were only meters apart. Everything appeared to be going as planned. Leading the way were two captured T-34s under Lieutenant Huchtmann. It was hoped that these would fool the enemy into believing this was a Soviet column.
>
> Suddenly, however, a Soviet armored column with mounted infantry was spotted coming the other way. The Germans kept their nerve and tried to pass unnoticed, but then one of the captured T-34s developed a mechanical problem and pulled off to the side. There was momentary confusion among the approaching group of Soviet T-34s, but then they opened fire, having recognized the German ruse. This action has been reconstructed from entries in Bäke's war diary:
>
>> Leading the way was a captured T-34. I had ordered radio silence and no firing. Silently we passed the first enemy barricade, moving by the deadly anti-tank guns which remained silent, believing us to be one of their own units.
>>
>> When the T-34 broke down with engine trouble, a Panzer-IV was forced to assume the lead. Rshvets [Rzhavets] appeared in front of us. At the edge of town was a row of T-34s. They readily made way for what they obviously believed to be their own tanks returning from the front. Then a column of tanks appeared heading in the opposite direction.

---

54 NARA US, rg. 242, t. 314, r. 197, f. 001340, f. 001341.

> Lieutenant Huchtmann in the lead tank reported twenty-two T-34s. These passed my unit, almost track to track. But then six or seven pulled out of the column, turned, rolled back and pulled in behind us.
>
> I order the rest to continue and placed my command tank, which was equipped only with a dummy gun, across the road in order to force the enemy tanks to halt. Seven T-34s rolled up and formed a semi-circle around me.
>
> I instructed my operations officer to break out the hollow charges. Then the two of us left the tank. We slid out of the field of view of the T-34 to our right. Reaching the tanks, we placed the hollow charges on two T-34s and jumped into cover.
>
> The detonations rang through the night. The T-34s were put out of action. We fetched two more hollow charges and put them in place. Two more T-34s were blown up. The fifth T-34 was destroyed by one of my tanks.[55]

The facts laid out in this text, given careful scrutiny, raise questions and doubts. Why, given the breakdown of the first T-34, was it necessary to bring up a Pz.kpfw. IV to the head of the column, thereby unmasking it, if there was a second T-34? In the second place, from the description of the events the impression forms that on the night of 11-12 July the rear of the 35th Guards Rifle Corps was simply teeming with tanks, which were moving in large columns to the rear from the front, and in the reverse direction. It is possible to say this only if a major Soviet tank grouping was deploying at this time in the rear of the 69th Army. In reality on the night of 11-12 July, only two battered battalions of the 96th Separate Tank Brigade were in this area, which according to the brigade's documents, joined combat with II/Panzer Regiment 11 at Rzhavets before dawn. Major Bäke's assertion (or Huchtmann's) that after their column passed the outskirts of Rzhavets, a column of 22 Soviet tanks rolled past them raises doubt. There were no T-34 tanks here before sunrise. The two mechanized brigades of the 5th Guards Tank Army would approach the Shipy area only after 0900 12 July, when Rzhavets was already in the 6th Panzer Division's possession, and once the German panzers had already created a bridgehead on the northern bank of the river. In the third place, it is hard to believe that the crews of the Soviet T-34 tanks formed a semi-circle around one Pz.kpfw. IV (why a semi-circle, when this would hinder movement?), and waited patiently as two bold Germans blew them up with hollow charges. Moreover, these munitions were supposedly stored in their tank, so the remaining T-34s waited while they returned to get more in order to blow up the next T-34s? Not much here makes any sense.

Undoubtedly, this incident is interesting and indicative first of all of the fact that it demonstrates the lack of cooperation and the absence of command and control both in the headquarters of the 35th Guards Rifle Corps and in the headquarters of its subordinate divisions. In addition, the cited information forces us to treat more carefully the memoirs of war veterans. As is known, for each soldier the main events of a battle, and for some, of the entire war, take place in the vicinity of his foxhole, and no farther. Major Bäke wasn't an ordinary soldier; he commanded a panzer battalion, but this fundamentally doesn't change anything. Describing this action, he first of all wanted to show his valor and that of his comrades, and not describe the historical events as they really happened, if they didn't seem so impressive. The major didn't take on this group of T-34s with hollow-charge anti-tank mines. First his panzers shot up the column of the headquarters of the 89th Guards Rifle Division that was on the march, and only later joined combat with a group of not more than 6-7 tanks in Rzhavets, where it is possible the T-34s of the 96th Separate Tank Brigade were knocked out by hollow charges as well, although this action started with an exchange of fire. However, I'll go through this action in sequence.

---

55 Kurowski, *Panzer Aces: German Tank Commanders of World War II* (Stackpole Books, 2004), pp. 53-54.

So, after the capture of Kazach'e, it was late in the evening, but not yet twilight and the situation seemed prime for exploitation: there was no continuous line of defense in front of the 6th Panzer Division, the Russians were in retreat, and thus von Hünersdorff decided, taking advantage of this opportunity, to take the bridges in Rzhavets. Approximately around midnight or shortly thereafter, *Kampfgruppe* Bäke, which included II/Panzer Regiment 11 and panzergrenadier battalions of Panzergrenadier Regiment 114 mounted in halftracks, set out.

By sunrise, it was supposed to not only breakthrough to the village; the main objective was to take the bridge there intact and create at least a small bridgehead on the opposite bank of the Northern Donets River. Special significance was given to carrying out this order. Breith not without justification believed that if he couldn't take a bridge from the march now, when the Russians were stunned and reeling, then a forced crossing of this river barrier might become a prolonged process.

At this time the 168th Infantry Division and 19th Panzer Division were advancing, albeit slowly. Breith understood that if the Russians that were bitterly defending Kiselevo weren't destroyed, then given the panzer corps' subsequent advance, a threat of a flank attack from out of this strong point would only grow. In addition, he was striving to create a bridgehead on the opposite bank of the river as quickly as possible and penetrate as deeply as possible into the system of defense of the 69th Army's 48th Rifle Corps in the interfluvial area between the Northern and Lipovyi Donets Rivers. Thus, as soon as it became clear that the 19th Panzer Division's attack had begun to bog down, he urgently requested Luftwaffe support. At 1900, Fliegerkorps VIII struck the area of the villages of Kiselevo and Sabynino, and the hamlet of Kiselevo, heavily. The headquarters of the 89th Guards Rifle Division was located in that hamlet at that moment. From the division's operational summary at 2200 on 12 July:

> At 1900 more than 200 enemy bombers bombed the combat positions and the division's command post. During the attack on the command post, the PNO-1 [Assistant Chief of Operations-1] Guards Major [illegible] and the division commander's adjutant Popyk were severely wounded, four officers were lightly wounded, and three men were killed; in addition, two cars were destroyed. Simultaneously, the enemy attacked our line.
>
> At an order from the division commander, the headquarters moved to the area of Novo-Oskochnoe, and at 0200 12.07.43, the jeep carrying the division commander, the chief of staff, and the deputy combat commander, as well as a vehicle carrying other staff officers, were cut off by a column of up to 300 enemy tanks. The command team and the headquarters staff had time to abandon the vehicles before they were knocked out or destroyed by the tanks.[56]

Retreating under the guard of the training battalion, the command of Seriugin's Guards division in the twilight gloom had bumped into Bäke's *panzerkampfgruppe*, which at that moment was advancing from Kazach'e, and engaged it in battle between the villages of Rzhavets and Kurakovka. Panzers were moving in the vanguard, followed by the halftracks of Captain Roempke's II/Panzergrenadier Regiment 114. Captain N.V. Riabtsev's training battalion of the 89th Guards Rifle Division was the first to engage the enemy. The memoirs of a participant in those events, the battalion's deputy commander Major M.G. Boev, have been preserved:

> The night of 11-12 July was exceptionally dark. The march was being conducted from the forward positions, and it seemed that there was nothing that should prompt an alarm; however, the situation was putting us on guard. Riabtsev and I were moving at the head of the

---

56 TsAMO RF, f. 89 gv. sd, op. 1, d. 22, l. 11.

column, peering into the impenetrable darkness and taking heed of every sound. A messenger came running up and communicated the division's order to me: "Wider step!" Just as soon as the messenger left, we could hear the rumble of motors coming from out in front of us. The battalion commander listened intently: "Tanks. Only whose, that's the question."

He promptly sent the chief of staff to report to the division commander about the tanks and ordered the commander of the lead company to send out a patrol squad.

… The returning chief of staff, who came running up, reported, "The division commander said that there could only be our tanks in Kurakovka."

Nevertheless, we strained our vision until our eyes hurt. About 50 meters in front of us, a silhouette of a tank dimly emerged out of the darkness. It was one of our T-34s. The lead tank was cautiously rolling forward at low speed with open hatches. A head stuck out from the turret hatch. "*Priniat' vpravo!* [*Bear to the right!*] – We could hear from the tank. That meant it was one of ours. The tension instantly fell away. We were marching side by side with the tank column, glancing at the first, the second, and then the third T-34. Then suddenly:

"Germans!"

Everyone turned their heads to the left and caught sight of white crosses on the sides of the tank, just two paces away. The bitter realization flashed through my thoughts like lighting: the fascists had placed traitors of the Motherland – Vlasovites – at the head of the column.

The battalion commander leaped to one side: "Battalion, to battle! Use grenades!"

The command was drowned in the clatter of the tracks and the explosions of grenades. The "pocket artillery" dashed against the fascist armor, submachine guns began to chatter, and the German tankers slammed close their hatches. The battalion shook out into a combat formation, taking up a position on the roadside, warding off the Germans with grenades.

The early sunrise was melting away the night, and now everyone could clearly see the white crosses and predatory beasts painted on the armor of the enemy tanks. Several tanks and halftracks stopped and from fixed position opened fire at the trainees' defensive positions, while in the distance motorized infantry spilled out of halftracks – the main force of the tank column, bypassing the knocked out machines, continued moving in the direction of Rzhavets. Trainee Kulakov wound up between the tanks, unable to understand what was happening. It was the war's third year, and such a thing hadn't happened yet. Only when the long barrel of a Tiger wavered in front of his eyes did everything become clear. He grabbed an anti-tank grenade and hurled himself after the rear of a Tiger that was moving away. It was impossible to take a look back or to see how the grenade worked – other tanks were moving toward him. Now they were moving in a deployed formation, several tanks each in a row. Little distance remained to the nearest tank, and the trainee, swinging his arm, tossed another grenade beneath a track and dropped to the ground. The tank pivoted on a single track. Kulakov didn't have any more grenades, and the tanks kept coming and coming. He picked his way between enemy machines, firing from a submachine gun at the tank riders.[57]

Colonel M.P. Seriugin had lost his composure, and having no information about the situation in front of his division, made an incorrect assessment of the situation. It was necessary to move the headquarters to a new location at that moment, but he should have moved it to the northeast toward the villages of Chursino or Shakhovo, and not to the south, toward the enemy panzers. This would have enabled him to keep control over the division, to maintain the lines occupied by it, and would have prevented it from becoming intermingled with enemy tanks. As a consequence, his rash action proved tragic. The 168th Infantry Division, which was operating on the left flank

---

57 Boev, M.G., *Zvezdnyi chas Belgoroda* [*Belgorod's star hour*] (Belgorod: Vezelitsa, 1998), pp. 72-73.

of the 19th Panzer Division, taking advantage of the blunder, pushed across the Northern Donets with insignificant forces and took Gostishchevo that night – a major village in the depth of the 48th Rifle Corps' defenses. From Order No.00194 dated 21 July 1943 from the Commander-in-Chief of the Voronezh Front:

> The commander of the 89th Guards Rifle Division Guards Colonel Seriugin, without contacting his neighbors and the corps command, and being because of this insufficiently informed about the situation, made an incorrect decision and voluntarily abandoned the Kalinin, Kiselevo line along the Northern Donets River, which was being held by the 267th Guards Rifle Regiment.
>
> Taking advantage of the departure of the 267th Guards Rifle Regiment, the enemy took the woods that were being defended by this regiment, and then Gostishchevo as well, as a result of which the implementation of a combat assignment given to a different division was disrupted.
>
> Having received information about the appearance of enemy tanks in the Verkhnii Ol'shanets area, Colonel Seriugin lost control over the division's units, and having taken command of the training battalion, left together with it to go to the Kazach'e area, where he intended to set up a new command post. En route to Kazach'e, Seriugin bumped into enemy tanks and was shoved aside to the Rzhavets area, where he again encountered enemy tanks and was forced to retreat. Winding up isolated from the division's units, he was unable to command them for 14 hours.[58]

The 6th Panzer Division's *panzerkampfgruppe* encircled the 89th Guards Rifle Division's column. Division commander Seriugin ordered to take up an all-round defense. The combat lasted for several hours; only by morning was the division headquarters able to break out of the pocket and retreat to Plota. From here, the headquarters sent a message to the commander of the 48th Rifle Corps:

> At an order from the division commander, the division headquarters was moving to the Novo-Oskochnoe area, and at 0200 on 12.07.43 the staff car that was carrying the division commander, his deputy, and the chief of staff, as well as a vehicle that was carrying staff officers, was cut off by a column of up to 300 enemy tanks. The command and headquarters managed to abandon the machines before they were knocked out by the tanks.
>
> By dawn the division command, with the exception of the assistant chief of operations Guards Captain Lebedenko and the staff topographer Senior Lieutenant Shevchenko, came out of encirclement in the Plota area and returned to normal work …
>
> The division's specialized units, which were moving with the headquarters particularly suffered and are being brought back to order … Losses are being ascertained.[59]

According to the documents of Lebedev's 96th Separate Tank Brigade, while the training battalion and headquarters of the 89th Guards Rifle Division were engaged in their unequal struggle north of Kurakovka, before dawn on 12 July remnants of the 96th Separate Tank Brigade's 331st Tank Battalion clashed with Bäke's panzer column in the Rzhavets area. Six T-34 tanks and a crew with one anti-tank gun of a destroyer anti-tank artillery battery that were leaving the Kiselevo area ran into the enemy on the outskirts of Rzhavets. According to the report, in the

---

58 Records of the Federal State Institute of Culture "State Military Historical Museum 'Prokhorovka Field'.
59 TsAMO RF, f. 89 gv. sd, op. 1, d. 22, l. 11

nocturnal action the tankers managed to knock out 9 panzers of the 6th Panzer Division, and by 0400 12.07.43 the battalion, having passed through Bol'shshie Pod'iarugi reached Aleksandrovka, where it took up a defense.

The dark night, the unfamiliar ground and other such clashes with the retreating elements of the 35th Guards Rifle Corps, as well as the minefields and artificial obstacles in their way – all this prevented the adversary from exploiting the morning success and making rapid progress to the northeast into the depth of the lines of Kriuchenkin's army. Bäke's *panzerkampfgruppe* reached the village of Rzhavets around 0300 on 12 July. By this time the 69th Army's headquarters had managed to strengthen the defenses in this area somewhat. From the "Description of combat operations of the 19th Panzer Division from 5 to 18 July 1943":

> On 11.07 units of the 6th Panzer Division attacked out of the Melikhovo area toward Rzhavets and seized it that night. It also managed to create a small bridgehead. In connection with this, the enemy felt squeezed between the 19th Panzer Division and 6th Panzer Division. Mining the paths of retreat and leaving strong covering detachments on them, consisting primarily of anti-tank rifles, he began to withdraw his units on the night of 11-12.07 out of the Sabynino, Sheliakovo area to the western bank of the Donets River, in order from there to hamper our further advance at Rzhavets and Sheliakhovo across the Donets.[60]

The forcing of the Northern Donets River by the Germans, their capture of Gostishchevo, and especially the 6th Panzer Division's emergence on the north bank of the river north of Rzhavets had very important significance for both sides. As a result of these events, the potential threat of the encirclement of the 48th Rifle Corps began to take on real outlines. After the loss of Rzhavets, Major General Z.Z. Ragoznyi's corps fell into semi-encirclement, and because of the German capture of the two bridgeheads at Gostishchevo and Rzhavets, the corps' defense on the left flank lost operational resilience. Owing to the great mobility of the III Panzer Corps' *kampfgruppen*, Breith had placed the Soviet command in a very awkward position. At the moment when von Hünersdorff's panzers and panzergrenadiers reached the river in the sector running from the fishing cooperative (north of Krivtsovo) through Sholokovo to Rzhavets, there was no continuous line of defense here. After all, back on the afternoon of 11 July, this was the divisional rear area of the 69th Army's first echelon, which had been holding the Shishino, Khokhlovo, Kiselevo, Shliakhovoe, Sheino, Miasoedovo line.

As documents uncovered today show, the leadership of the 48th Rifle Corps was the first to react to the information about the German breakthrough. Already at 2245, its chief of staff Colonel Shcheglov sent Colonel P.D. Govorunenko, whose division had been occupying a defense on the Zhimolostnoe, Malo-Iablonovo, Shakhovo line since 1300 11 July, the following directive: "The corps commander has ordered to send one battalion with two anti-tank guns to Ryndinka quickly in order to cover Shakhovo from the Kurakovka, Rzhavets direction. Conduct reconnaissance in the direction of Kazach'e. Report from Shakhovo. According to unverified information, tanks have broken through to Kazach'e. Report the results of the reconnaissance of Shakhovo and the Vasil'eevka ravine."[61] There is a note on the document: "Sent at 0100 with a staff officer."

Subsequent events developed quickly; the 69th Army command began to bring up forces in order to localize the breakthrough. At 2300 Lieutenant S.G. Goriachev, having received information of the movement of enemy tanks toward Rzhavets, withdrew a portion of the 92nd Guards

---

60 TsAMO RF, f. 38 A, op. 9027, d. 46, l. 154obr.
61 TsAMO RF, f. 375 sd, op. 1, d. 23, l. 41a.

Rifle Division to the Vypolzovka, southern outskirts of Aleksandrovka line across the bridge in the Shchelokovo area, and the 305th Rifle Division – to the Kolomytsevo, Novo-Slobodka line.

At 2330 the commander of the 81st Guards Rifle Division Major General I.K. Morozov issued Order No.060:

1. The enemy with the support of large air formations and tanks broke through the line of defense and by 2100 11.07.43 reached the Kiselevo, Khokhlovo, 1 kilometer south of Verkhnii Ol'shanets line.
2. The 235th Guards Rifle Regiment by 0600 12.07.43 with two battalions (1st and 2nd) is to take up and strongly defend the prepared line in the Krivtsevo – road leading to Verkhnii Ol'shanets – northwest fringe of the woods 500 meters southwest of Verkhnii Ol'shanets sector.
   Task: In no event allow a breakthrough of tanks and infantry in the direction of Novo-Oskochnoe. Command post – Chursino. Operational command group – Novo-Oskochnoe.
3. The 238th Guards Rifle Regiment by 0600 12.07.43 is to take up and strongly defend the prepared line in the sector: eastern fringe of the woods (Point 294.5), southern outskirts of Verkhnii Ol'shanets, having reinforced the left flank on the eastern outskirts of Verkhnii Ol'shanets.
   Task: Prevent a breakthrough of enemy tanks and infantry in the direction of Novo-Oskochnoe. Command post – Novo-Oskochnoe.
   On the right, the 235th Guards Rifle Regiment is defending, on the left – the 305th Rifle Division.
   Pay attention to organizing reconnaissance once the units move into their defensive sectors.[62]

The General Staff of the Red Army was attentively following the situation in this area. At 0115 on 12 July Stalin signed *Stavka* Directive No.01815 that was sent to General I.S. Konev, the Commander-in-Chief of the Steppe Front:

> On the Belgorod direction the enemy in strength of up to 200 tanks and infantry drove back the units of the 69th Army and, attacking in the direction of Korocha, reached the Kiselevo, Mazikino, Sheino area by the end of 11.7.
> The *Stavka* of the Supreme High Command has ordered:
>
> 1. Destroy the enemy grouping that is moving in the Korocha direction and further on toward the Oskol River with a combined attack by Ryzhov [the commander of Steppe Front's 47th Army] and Obukhov [commander of Steppe Front's 3rd Guards Mechanized Corps] from the southeast, and by Solomatin [commander of Steppe Front's 1st Mechanized Corps] from the north, for which Ryzhov and Obukhov are to assemble their forces in the Novyi Oskol, Velikomikhailovka, Sidirovka, Bulanovka, Slonevka area by the end of 13.07. Solomatin by the morning of 13.07 is to move from the Solntsevo area to the Viazovoe, Skorodnoe, Bobrovo-Dvorskoe area.
> 2. Report over the high-frequency radio to Antonov [General of the Army A.I. Antonov, the First Deputy Chief of Staff of the Red Army between May 1943 and February 1945] about the time of your receipt of the present order.[63]

62　TsAMO RF, f. 81 gv. sd, op. 1, d. 5, l. 275.
63　TsAMO RF, f. 148 a, op. 3763, d. 130, l. 190.

However, this directive talks about the assembly of the counterattacking groupings by the end of July 13, and prior to this time the enemy had to be contained by the forces of the Voronezh Front. Vatutin had no more reserves: all of his forces were engaged in defensive fighting or committed to the counterattack at Prokhorovka on 12 July, so Kriuchenkin could only rely on his own forces. In addition, there was one more, substantial circumstance. In the text of the *Stavka* Directive, there is mention that the area of the villages of Kiselevo, Mazikino, Sheino was the line that the enemy reached by the end of 11 July, whereas in fact III Panzer Corps had already fully broken through the second army-level defensive belt and had reached the third and final army-level belt in the Rzhavets, Vypolzovka area. This information still hadn't reached Moscow.

Thus, Breith had kept his promise to Kempf, and then to von Manstein personally. The progress made by his divisions was impressive. In the course of a 12-hour, virtually ceaseless attack, two of his battered panzer divisions had penetrated approximately 18 kilometers into the depth of the Voronezh Front's defenses and had created two vital bridgeheads for Army Detachment Kempf on the opposite bank of the Donets, into which already by the morning of 12 July von Hünersdorff would smoothly bring up artillery and two companies of I/Panzergrenadier Regiment 114 and give them the mission to advance in the direction of Krasnoe, which was positioned already east of Prokhorovka.[64] One must pay due credit to the resolve and professionalism of Breith and his subordinates. Not once over the entire course of Operation Citadel did a German panzer corps, having such a miserly amount of armor, a total of just 62 tanks (23 in the 6th Panzer Division, 16 in the 19th Panzer Division, 23 in the Separate Heavy Panzer Battalion 503)[65] achieve such impressive results. In addition, I'll remind the reader that by the end of 11 July, the II SS Panzer Corps, having broken through the defenses of the 69th Army, and of the 5th Guards Army that had arrived from out of the *Stavka* Reserve, had reached the outskirts of Prokhorovka, thereby depriving the last suitable line of deployment for the 5th Guards Tank Army's subordinate corps in order to launch the counterattack on 12 July 1943. Without exaggeration one can say that for the command of the Voronezh Front, the situation had become critical.

The Soviet generals knew perfectly well the essence of their own failures, but in the messages and reports to the Front leadership they placed the main emphasis not on the real reasons for the failures, but on the staggering amount of armor that the enemy had supposedly committed into the fighting at that moment. In the opinion of the 69th Army commander, at that moment the Germans had 250-300 tanks in the Verkhnii Ol'shanets – Kazach'e – Rzhavets area, while the command of the 35th Guards Rifle Corps put the size of the enemy grouping at 350 armored vehicles, while the aerial reconnaissance of the 2nd Air Army on the morning of 12 July reported to the commander of the 5th Guards Tank Army Lieutenant General P.A. Rotmistrov that 500 to 700 enemy tanks were operating here. Rotmistrov himself believed that there could not be more than 350-400 tanks in the indicated area.[66] Indeed, this entire wave of figures that were so distant from fact together with the stunning enemy advance late on the evening of 11 July fell on N.F. Vatutin like a ton of bricks. The General of the Army was skeptical of numbers of such magnitude, so when assessing the events he primarily relied on his own intuition and view of the operational situation. His estimate of the size of the enemy grouping that had broken through, which he reported to the *Stavka*, was a little closer to the truth – up to 200 tanks, but that figure was also far from reality.

V.D. Kriuchenkin's and S.G. Goriachev's positions are understandable: by reporting about several hundred German tanks south of Prokhorovka (whereas in the three panzer divisions of the III Panzer Corps there were not more than 100-120 operational armored vehicles), they were

---

64 NARA US, t. 312, r. 54, f. 7569657.
65 Zetterling and Frankson, *Kursk 1943: a statistical analysis*, Tab. A6.7, A6.9, A 6.10.
66 TsAMO RF, f. 203, op. 2843, d. 461, l. 63.

striving first of all to offer a convincing explanation as to why their troops had been unable to hold their positions and to offer a rationale for assigning reserves to them.

For the Front command the situation in which Kriuchenkin's army wound up gave rise to a more significant problem. By itself, the appearance of Breith's III Panzer Corps just 18 kilometers south of the area of deployment for the Front's main counterattack grouping was unexpected to N.F. Vatutin. However, he didn't view this as a catastrophe. There were forces available for localizing the penetration – two Guards armies in the Prokhorovka area. The question was, how best to use them: To conduct the planned counterattack, or to continue to hold the rear army-level defensive belt using the previous methods? If the latter plan was adopted, then a portion of the 5th Guards Tank Army's strength should immediately be sent to the 69th Army's sector, and the rest should hold in place to strengthen the 5th Guards Army's defense at Prokhorovka Station. However, Rotmistrov's tank army was still part of the *Stavka* Reserve, and therefore Stalin's decision was necessary. In fact, judging from everything, Vatutin received it. According to the testimony of the Front's former first deputy chief of communications Colonel V.V. Zvenigorodsky, on the night of 11-12 July 1943 a discussion took place between I.V. Stalin on the one hand, and N.F. Vatutin and the Chief of the General Staff A.M. Vasilevsky, who was located on the Voronezh Front, on the other.[67] The discussion included the fate of the counterattack and how best to use Zhadov's and Rotmistrov's Guards armies. The Supreme Commander-in-Chief ordered to conduct the counterattack as planned, despite the unfavorable situation. However, just in case, as already noted above, at A.M. Vasilevsky's suggestion, the 53rd Army's 1st Mechanized Corps would be moved out of the Steppe Front to the Korocha direction, together with some of the 5th Guards Army's and 5th Guards Tank Army's strength.

---

67 Copy of V.V. Zvenigorodsky's manuscript "Nekotorye voprosy organizatsii sviazi shtaba Voronezhskogo fronta v Kurskoi bitve letom 1943" ["Certain questions on the organization of communications within the headquarters of the Voronezh Front in the Battle of Kursk in the summer of 1943"], p. 43. Author's personal archive.

8

The pinning counterattack: 7th Guards Army and the events of 12 July

In this chapter, the mission that was given to the 7th Guards Army for 12 July 1943 by the Voronezh Front command will be discussed. In addition, the course of the combat operations in its sector on this day will be covered, and an attempt will be made to determine the role that Shumilov's troops actually played in the course of the Soviet frontal counterattack.

By dawn on 12 July, the 69th Army commander V.D. Kriuchenkin was facing a very difficult situation. In addition to restricting a German breakthrough that morning, his troops were to launch a counterattack. Of the 48th Rifle Corps' five rifle divisions, three (the 183rd, 375th and 93rd Guards Rifle Divisions) had been planned to take part in it, and N.F. Vatutin was no longer in a position to change anything – the matter was in Moscow's control. His two other rifle divisions, the 81st Guards and 89th Guards Rifle Division, having extended their front along the right bank of the Lipovyi and Northern Donets, were holding the line opposite the stubbornly attacking 19th Panzer Division and 168th Infantry Division. Moreover, Morozov's 81st Guards Rifle Division had by now been reduced to nothing more than a composite regiment and 8 guns.

In the 35th Guards Rifle Corps, of the four divisions, one (92nd Guards Rifle Division) had just come out of encirclement and no one knew how many men it had left (by the morning of 12 July, two full battalions and its headquarters had been reassembled with difficulty); in the second (305th Rifle Division), two of its regiments had suffered losses and their units were filtering out of enemy-occupied territory all night long in isolated groups of men; in the third (107th Rifle Division), one rifle regiment had been scattered and the division command didn't know where it was located or its condition; and in the fourth (94th Guards Rifle Division), after repulsing six attacks by the 7th Panzer Division and 198th Infantry Division, two of its rifle regiments and a large portion of the artillery regiment had ended up encircled, while the third rifle regiment was making desperate counterattacks in order to free them.

The attached units of reinforcement had also been bled white. Just 12 tanks and one gun remained in the 96th Separate Tank Brigade, while the 148th Separate Tank Regiment had four operational tanks (3 T-34 and 1 T-70), four combat-ready anti-tank rifle teams, and a platoon of submachine gunners. In the 31st Separate Destroyer Anti-tank Artillery Brigade, the men of two of its regiments were coming out of battle up until the end of 12 July and at 1000 it was known that only one gun and 50% of the men were left, while the third regiment was still forming up in Korocha (receiving materiel). Only four anti-tank guns were left in the 114th Guards Destroyer Anti-tank Artillery Regiment.

Neither the army commander nor the corps commanders had any reserves. In order somehow to reinforce the 81st Guards Rifle Division, V.D. Kriuchenkin was forced to send division commander Morozov one regiment from the 375th Rifle Division and move it to the Plota area.

In the counterattack plan, which had begun to be prepared back on 9 July, 7th Guards Army had also been included. Originally two of its corps were given the mission to launch an attack at the base of III Panzer Corps' penetration, with the aim of keeping it in the Staryi Gorod – Dal'niaia Igumenka area. By the end of 11 July, the situation had changed sharply. Therefore several changes were made to the assignments of Shumilov's forces. They were now to keep the forces of Army Detachment Kempf in front of them and not allow the enemy the opportunity to shift forces from the right flank to a point south of Prokhorovka, but because of this their significance for the results of the frontal counterattack (especially when considering the reports of 300-500 tanks south of Prokhorovka) only grew. Even so, it must be recognized that neither on 9 July nor on 11 July did M.S. Shumilov have any possibility of tying down significant enemy forces (especially the III Panzer Corps).

How did the plan of his army's counterattack look, and what objectives was it pursuing? Let's take a look at recently de-classified documents in the TsAMO RF. The cornerstone of Shumilov's scheme was the encirclement of the enemy's major strongpoint in Krutoi Log with two converging attacks. The village was not only a strong center of enemy resistance, but was also serving as a major forward supply base, and the forward observation post of the 106th Infantry Division was also located there. It was planned that 7th Guards Army's right wing would launch the strongest attack. The divisions that formed it (the 270th and 73rd Guards Rifle Division with the 201st Tank Brigade and artillery reinforcements) received an order to attack toward the eastern and northeastern outskirts of the village. The left wing forces (the 111th Rifle Division and the 27th Guards Tank Brigade) were to break through to the southwestern outskirts. After taking Krutoi Log and the destruction of the enemy forces in this area, the army's shock forces were to continue to advance to the bridges on the Northern Donets in the vicinities of Solomino and Dal'nie Peski, and were also to capture Generalovka. From the account of the 7th Guards Army's Operations Department:

> The commander decided to conduct a force regrouping and on 12.7.43 go over to a counter-offensive, launching the main attack in the general Krutoi Log, Razumnoe, Dal'nie Peski direction. The primary objective of the indicated operation consisted of preventing the enemy from digging in on the achieved lines; to remove combat units and use them to reinforce other directions, while simultaneously launching a flank attack in order to cut off the path of retreat toward the bridges across the Northern Donets in the Solomino area; and to emerge in the rear of the enemy grouping that was operating southeast of Belgorod. (Order No.00286 from 11.7.1943)
>
> On the basis of Order No.0015/op from the Front Commander-in-Chief on 9.7.43, the 49th Rifle Corps (the 270th and 111th Rifle Divisions) joined the 7th Guards Army, and on the night of 11-12.7.1943 set out to take up the jumping-off position for the attack on the line: Point 209.6, Machine Tractor Station, Point 202.3.
>
> According to the army commander's scheme, the main attack would be launched with the army's center (49th Rifle Corps, 73rd Guards Rifle Division of the 25th Guards Rifle Corps) in the general Krutoi Log, Razumnoe, Dal'nie Peski direction with the task to destroy the enemy that was occupying the area between Krutoi Log and Gremiachii, and to reach the line: (excl.) Hill 164.7, southwestern outskirts of Krutoi Log.
>
> Subsequent task: take the eastern bank of the Northern Donets in the (excl.) Pushkarnoe, Solomino sector, having taken the line of heights 2 kilometers west of Dal'nie Peski, Kolodezek woods, Hill 205.5 with a forward detachment.
>
> Launch an auxiliary attack on the right flank with the 25th Guards Rifle Corps' 15th Guards Rifle Division and on the left flank with the 72nd Guards and 213th Rifle Divisions.

The remaining formations and units should contribute to the offensive with their artillery and mortar fire, as well as rifle and machine-gun fire.[1]

If we rely on the information available to scholars today, then at first glance it might seem that it was fully within the power of the assigned forces to execute this plan. For example, the line from which they were supposed to launch the main attack – (excl.) Batratskaia Dacha, Hill 209.6, Machine Tractor Station, Hill 202.9 – had a total length of 9 kilometers, so accordingly, each of the three attacking divisions had a 3-kilometer sector. In the first phase, having broken through the defenses of the 198th and 106th Infantry Divisions, they were to reach the line: southeastern outskirts of Krutoi Log – Hill 164.7 – western fringe of the woods 2 kilometers east of Krutoi Log, and thereby drive the Germans back 5.5 kilometers from their jumping-off positions. The three other divisions were supposed to cover the flanks of the assault wedge and simultaneously pin down the enemy's forces. If to compare even this information, for example, with the plan of the counterattack of the two Guards armies at Prokhorovka, then it seems rather convincing, if not for one "however". The 7th Guards Army's main problem consisted in the lack of serious firing means.

According to the Front leadership's plan, the main role was to be played by Major General G.N. Terent'ev's[2] 49th Rifle Corps, which had formed up just before the start of the Battle of Kursk and still hadn't taken part in any fighting, and the 25th Guards Rifle Corps' 73rd Guards Rifle Division. Alongside the problem of a lack of cohesion and teamwork which was acutely felt by each of the Front's rifle corps at this time, Terent'ev's rifle corps had a large deficit of men and weapons. On 10 July 1943 the 111th Rifle Division had a total of 4,141 men (or approximately 43.8% of its authorized manpower),[3] while the 270th Rifle Division had 7,792 men (82.5% of establishment strength).[4] In addition, if you exclude the rear-echelon personnel and artillerymen then these two divisions had a total fighting strength of just 3,915 active bayonets. The 73rd Guards Rifle Division was in a similar situation. At 2200 on 11 July it had a total 4,593 men reporting for duty (48.6%).[5] Thus, the three divisions of the assault grouping had a total number of 16,526 soldiers and commanders, including 5,325 artillerymen and approximately 6,301 service personnel.[6]

---

1   TsAMO RF, f. 7 gv. A, op. 5312, d. 268, l. 9.
2   Terent'ev, Gurii Nikitich (Lieutenant General from 20.04.1945) was born on 11 January 1898 in the village of Ivanovo in Kalinin Oblast. He joined the Red Army in 1918 and served in the Russian Civil War. In 1921 he completed the "Shot" courses, and in 1923 the 8th Infantry School in Petrograd. In 1924 he graduated from the Unified Kiev Infantry School, and five years later from the Frunze Military Academy. After a short period of work in unit staffs, he switched to instruction work in 1934 and led the Tactics Department of the Frunze Military Academy. In June 1940 Terent'ev was appointed as the chief of combat training in the headquarters of the Far Eastern Front, and from May 1941 served as the deputy commander of the Far Eastern District's 40th Rifle Division. In August 1941 Terent'ev became the chief of staff of the Far Eastern District's 25th Army, before being transferred to serve as the deputy logistics commander of the Western Front's 10th Army in November 1941. Less than a month later Terent'ev was transferred to the post of commander of the 322nd Rifle Division that was defending Tula, and in January 1942 it took part in the enemy's defeat in the Mikhailov and Epifan' area, then conducted defensive fighting on the Zhizdra direction. From February 1943 he served as the deputy commander of Voronezh Front's 38th Army, which at that moment was taking part in the Khar'kov offensive. On 25 June 1943 Major General G.N. Terent'ev assumed command of the 49th Rifle Corps (first of the 69th Army, then of the 7th Guards Army). On 18.06.1944 he left the post for medical treatment. Upon returning from the hospital on 05.07.1944, he again took command of the 49th Rifle Corps, which after Germany's retreat, took part in the war with Japan as part of the 53rd Army. In August 1953 Terent'ev was retired and went into the reserve.
3   TsAMO RF, f. 7 gv. A, op. 5312, d. 539, l. 122.
4   Ibid.
5   TsAMO RF, f. 73 gv. sd, op. 1, d. 30, l. 16.
6   The number of service personnel in the 73rd Guards Rifle Division is a tentative number.

Moreover, the rifle regiments of the 111th Rifle Division still lacked their 76mm batteries and had a deficit of several dozen mortars (of all calibers), while the 270th Rifle Division's divisional artillery regiment was short 10 76mm anti-tank guns and one 76mm field gun. In addition, not one of the divisions had a single anti-aircraft machine gun, and the 49th Rifle Corps had no additional assets, which were usually added before conducting such attacks. (The number of men and weapons in the rifle divisions of the main and auxiliary attack groupings of the 7th Guards Army formed for the counterattack on 12 July 1943 can be seen in Table 15).

The 7th Guards Army's own three divisions, which had been planned to cover the flanks of the attacking divisions, had also suffered substantial losses. In the 213th Rifle Division there remained just 4,903 active bayonets (including 984 artillerymen), and in its 793rd and 702nd Rifle Regiments, which were called upon directly for the counterattack, had a total of 2,484 active bayonets (including 279 artillerymen). The 15th Guards Rifle Division was in better shape; by 0400 11 July it had a total of 8,440 men, but just as in the case of the 213th Rifle Division, only two of its regiments were to be activated in the counterattack.

Realizing that the 49th Rifle Corps had arrived "emaciated and famished", Shumilov sought to augment its firepower as far as he was able. Over the 24 hours before the scheduled counterattack, he made the following units operationally subordinate to G.N. Terent'ev: the 27th Guards Tank Brigade (50 tanks) and the 201st Tank Brigade (33 tanks); the 265th Guards Cannon Artillery Regiment (13 152mm howitzers), the 1669th Destroyer Anti-tank Artillery Regiment, the 309th Guards Mortar Regiment of rocket launchers, the 132nd Anti-tank Rifle Battalion, and 2/47th Separate Rifle Battalion of the 60th Engineer Brigade. The 73rd Guards Rifle Division also received operational control of a number of artillery units: the 97th Guards Mortar Regiment (20 BM rocket launchers), the 161st Guards Cannon Artillery Regiment (16 152mm howitzers), and the 131st Anti-tank Rifle Battalion.

The division commander gave the regiments and units their tasks in divisional orders, which had been prepared by the end of 11 July 1943; Colonel Kozak signed the last such document, Order No.0013, at 2300. It stated:

> The 73rd "Stalingrad" Guards Rifle Division with the 30th Destroyer Brigade,[7] the 161st Guards Cannon Artillery Regiment, the 97th Guards Mortar Regiment and the 131st and 132nd Anti-tank Rifle Battalions has the task, attacking in the sector: on the right – (excl.) lake on the "Batratskaia Dacha" State Farm, on the left – (excl.) Hill 209.6 to seize the line: western fringe of the woods northeast of Krutoi Log, and with a forward detachment, to take Generalovka.
>
> I've decided: Launching the main attack with the left flank, outflanking from the north and south, to encircle and destroy the enemy in the woods northeast of Krutoi Log, and prevent the enemy's retreat to the west.
>
> H-hour is set for 1000 12.07.1943. Signal for the attack – a salvo of rockets.
>
> a) 214th Guards Rifle Regiment with one battery of 76mm guns, the 30th Destroyer Brigade and the 131st and 132nd Anti-tank Rifle Battalions is to attack in the direction of Hills 199.1 and 167.1, destroying the enemy in the woods south of the hills. Immediate task: to reach the ravine 500 meters west of Point 199.1 and subsequently to capture Point 167.1.

---

7   It would have been correct to write "Separate Destroyer Anti-tank Artillery Brigade", but at that time this term had just entered the ordinary army lexicon. Thus, not only in the discussions between commanders, but also in the documents, the destroyer anti-tank artillery brigades were called according to the old style "Destroyer Brigades".

Table 15 Amount of personnel and weapons in the rifle divisions of the 7th Guards Army's shock and auxiliary groupings, formed for the counterattack on 12 July 1943

Division	Manpower			Weapons			Machine guns			Mortars			122 mm howitzers	76mm division artillery	76mm regiment artillery	Anti-tank rifles	Anti-aircraft guns
	Active bayonets	Artillerymen	Service personnel	Total	Rifles	PPSh submachine guns	Light	Heavy	A-A	50 mm	82 mm	120 mm					
Shock grouping																	
49th Rifle Corps[1]																	
111 RD	1091	1200	1850	4141	5998	1926	284	95	–	46	76	16	8	26	–	196	35
270 RD	2824	2578	2400	7792	6081	2157	243	81	–	56	83	21	8	16	15	282	38
25th Guards Rifle Corps[2]																	
73 GRD	2051[3]	1547	?	4593	2251	1480	194	52	–	12	41	14	10	12	10	?	14
Total	5966	5325	4250	16526	14330	5563	721	228	–	114	200	51	26	54	25	408	87
Auxiliary Grouping																	
25th Guards Rifle Corps																	
15 GRD	No data available																
24th Guards Rifle Corps																	
72 GRD	No data available																
213 RD[4]	4903	984															

Notes
1 TsAMO RF, f. 7 gv. A, op. 5312, d. 539, l. 122.
2 TsAMO RF, f. 73 gv. sd, op. 1, d. 30, l. 16.
3 Figure taken conditionally.
4 TsAMO RF, f. 213 sd, op. 1, d. 15, l. 233.

Jumping-off position for the offensive: (excl.) lake on "Batratskaia Dacha" State Farm, (excl.) fork in the dirt path 500 meters west of the point marked "Sar" [on the map].

Regiment command post remains in place. Forward artillery group: 1/153rd Guards Artillery Regiment and a battalion of the 97th Guards Mortar Regiment, plus a battery of 120mm mortars.

b) 209th Guards Rifle Regiment plus a regiment of 45mm anti-tank guns of the 30th Destroyer Brigade is to attack the enemy in the direction of the nameless hill with sparse patches of woods, 800 meters northwest of Hill 209.6, and the forest ranger's hut, 1 kilometer northeast of Krutoi Log, and destroying the enemy in the woods northeast of the forest ranger's hut, to take the line: southwestern fringe of the woods northeast of Krutoi Log, Hill 164.7.

Immediate task: Reach the fire break that leads north from the forest ranger's hut, and subsequently take Hill 164.7. Jumping-off position for the offensive: (excl.) fork in the path, 1 kilometer north of Hill 209.6.

Regiment command post – northern corner of the woods 2 kilometers north of Koren'skaia Dacha. Forward artillery group: 3/153rd Guards Artillery Regiment and a rocket artillery battalion of the 97th Guards Mortar Regiment. The commander of the forward artillery group is the commander of 3/153rd Guards Artillery Regiment.

c) 211th Guards Rifle Regiment is to attack in the direction of the ravine in the center of the woods northeast of Krutoi Log, and exploiting the success of the 209th Guards Rifle Regiment from behind its right flank, is to seize the southwestern spur of the woods northeast of Krutoi Log. Be ready with one rifle battalion (a forward detachment) to seize Generalovka.[8]

Operating in the sector of Kozak's division was the 78th Guards Rifle Division, which according to an order from Shumilov, was withdrawn into his reserve. Its 233rd Guards and 225th Guards Rifle Regiments were to take up defensive positions in the 25th Guards Rifle Corps' second echelon along the Nekliudovo – Pentsevo – Churaevo line, while its 228th Guards Rifle Regiment and a battery of the 158th Guards Artillery Regiment were to continue to hold positions along the eastern outskirts of the "Batratskaia Dacha" State Farm, guarding the boundary between the 15th Guards Rifle Division and 73rd Guards Rifle Division. The remaining units of the 158th Guards Artillery Regiment were to support the attack of the 25th Guards Rifle Corps' and 49th Rifle Corps' units with fire.

In the center of the army's attacking formations (on the left flank of the 73rd Guards Rifle Division), Major General I.P. Beliaev's full-strength 270th Rifle Division was to attack. From its journal of combat operations:

Combat Order No.2/op from 2200 11.07.1943 from the headquarters of the 49th Rifle Corps has been received:

270th Rifle Division by 2300 11.07.1943 is to replace the units of the 25th Guards Rifle Corps on the line Point 209.6, (excl.) Gremiachii and is to be ready from the morning of 12.07.1943 to attack in the Krutoi Log – Razumnoe – Dal'nie Peski direction.

Combat task: To attack in the sector: on the right – Krasnaia Poliana, (excl.) Repnoe, Pentsevo, Point 209.6, (excl.) Generalovka, (excl.) Pushkarnoe, Boliasovets Station; on the left – Kupino, Koshlakovo, (excl.) Gremiachii, (excl.) Point 176.0, (excl.) Razumnoe railyard, Point 205.4. At 1000 the 270th Rifle Division with the attached assets of the 201st Tank

---

8 TsAMO RF, f. 25 gv. sk, op. 1, d. 12, l. 138.

Brigade, the 132nd Anti-tank Rifle Battalion and one company of the 47th Separate Rifle Battalion of the 60th Engineer Brigade undertakes an offensive, launching the main attack with its right flank in the direction: Koren'skaia Dacha, Hill 190.2, Hill 176.6.

The division commander's order:

    973rd Rifle Regiment attacks on the right in the direction of Hill 191.2 and takes it.

    975th Rifle Regiment (2nd Rifle Battalion) together with one platoon of the 549th Separate Rifle Battalion with an attack in the direction of Koren'skaia Dacha and the southern slopes of Hill 191.2 is to seize them.

    977th Rifle Regiment with one engineer platoon by an attack in the direction of the nameless hill 2 kilometers east of Krutoi Log and Hill 176.0 is to seize them.

    201st Tank Brigade attacks in the direction: Hill 191.2, church in Krutoi Log. Jumping-off positions: western fringe of the woods east of Hill 209.6.

Division commander's reserve: 1 and 3/975th Rifle Regiment, the training company, the penal company and the chemical company advances behind the center of the 975th Rifle Regiment from jumping-off positions: woods east of Koren'skaia Dacha. Anti-tank reserve – the 321st Separate Destroyer Anti-tank Artillery Battalion and the 132nd Separate Anti-tank Rifle Battalion attacks in the direction of Hill 131.2.[9]

Possibly, the reader has already noted two odd details in the cited documents. In the first place, the 132nd Separate Anti-tank Rifle Battalion was simultaneously attached to two divisions, not by companies, but as a whole. In the second place, a person, even distant from the military, will be at the least surprised by how one division can replace a second division by 2300, if the order was signed at 2200. At the very least it was first necessary to deliver the document to the headquarters and for the command staff to become familiarized with it, not to mention conceive of some way to move several thousand soldiers and officers with their equipment and weapons across several kilometers within eyesight of the enemy in just one hour. In fact in both the first instance and the second, no mistake was made on paper. Simply because of the lack of means of reinforcement, each unit was worth its weight in gold, and the 132nd Anti-tank Rifle Battalion was literally caught in an unspoken tug of war. The anti-tank rifle battalion was the army commander's reserve, but prior to this it had been part of the 25th Guards Rifle Corps. So naturally G.B. Safiulin transferred it to "his" 73rd Guards Rifle Division, even though M.S. Shumilov in his order directed it to be sent to the 270th Rifle Division. When this contradiction was figured out, the battalion returned to Beliaev's 270th Rifle Division, but this already happened in the course of the counterattack. As for the time given to carry out an order, this was a fully normal occurrence in the acting Red Army. The cited excerpt is a clear example how on the one hand higher headquarters covered itself (by getting its orders on the way more quickly, which means shifting responsibility for it to the division commander), but on the other hand cared less about how subordinates would extricate themselves when carrying out senseless directives.

Now let's return to the counterattack plan. On the 270th Rifle Division's left flank, Colonel M.A. Bushin's 111th Rifle Division was supposed to attack. From the division commander's Order No.007 from 11 July 1943:

  2. 111th Rifle Division with the 27th Guards Tank Brigade, the 1669th Destroyer Anti-tank Artillery Regiment, and the 2nd Platoon of the 60th Engineer Brigade's 47th Separate Rifle Battalion launches an attack with its left flank, takes possession of the line

---

9   TsAMO RF, f. 270 sd, op. 1, d. 1, l. 13obr, 14.

of the northwestern fringe of the woods west of Gremiachii and with an attack in the direction of Hills 156.2 and 137.7, in cooperation with the 270th Rifle Division encircles and destroys the enemy in Krutoi Log, and subsequently advances in the direction of Solomino. With the division's arrival on the eastern bank of the Northern Donets River, a reinforced battalion of it seizes a bridgehead on the western bank of the river in order to ensure a river crossing.

Boundary line with the 270th Rifle Division: (excl.) Koshlakovo, Gremiachii, (excl.) Point 176.0, Razumnoe railyard, (excl.) Hill 212.3. On the left, the 73rd Guards Rifle Division seizes the line: Hill 146, Maslova Pristan', Point 205.5.

3. I've decided to launch the main attack with the left flank in the direction of the road junction south of the "Poliana" State Farm, Point 167.7, Point 156.2, and Point 137.7, and in cooperation with the 270th Rifle Division to encircle and destroy the defending units of the enemy's 106th Infantry Division in the wooded area west of the "Poliana" State Farm, and subsequently – in Krutoi Log.
4. 399th Rifle Regiment with 1/267th Separate Destroyer Anti-tank Battalion attacks toward Point 137.7. Infantry artillery support – a battery of 120mm mortars and 3/286th Artillery Regiment after execution of the immediate assignment. Boundary on the left: quadrangular patch of woods 600 meters southwest of Point 203.6. Command post: eastern fringe of the woods northwest of Churaevo.
5. 532nd Rifle Regiment with 3/267th Separate Destroyer Anti-tank Battalion and an engineer platoon of the 181st Separate Rifle Brigade is to take the eastern fringe of the woods southwest of the "Poliana" State Farm, and is to attack subsequently in the direction of Points 156.2 and 122.3, and the center of Solomino.

   Infantry support artillery: 532nd Rifle Regiment [inherent artillery], 2/286th Artillery Regiment and a battery of 120mm mortars.

   Boundary on the left: southern fringe of the woods on the northwestern outskirts of Churaevo – road junction south of the "Poliana" State Farm – Point 156.2 – (excl.) Point 122.3. Command post: eastern spur of the woods west of Churaevo.
6. 468th Rifle Regiment with 2/267th Separate Destroyer Anti-tank Battalion and two platoons of engineers of the 181st Separate Rifle Brigade is to take Point 207.9 and subsequently advance in the direction of Points 167.7, 157.1, 122.3 and the southern portion of Solomino.

   Infantry support artillery: 1 and 3/286th Artillery Regiment and a battery of 120mm mortars, led by the commander of the 286th Artillery Regiment.[10]

When analyzing the documents of the 7th Guards Army, I formed an impression that even though the army commander had received a preliminary order for a counterattack back on 9 July, the decision that was made to include the army in it (the written order for this) had taken too long, and that is likely why it is clear that the operation was prepared in great haste. Possibly that was the reason why the regrouping of forces on the level of the divisions was poorly organized and why there was a number of unjustified delays with the replacement in line of the tank brigades and artillery units. These circumstances, which rested on a number of other objective and subjective problems, substantially affected the results of the counterattack. How the preparations went for the counterattack in the 49th Rifle Corps was laid out in sufficient detail in the account of its headquarters:

---

10 TsAMO RF, f. 111 sd, op. 1, d. 15, l. 23.

4. Nature of the terrain: Rough ground from the enemy's direction, with a lot of large ravines, hills and patches of wood; good dirt roads, which support the stubbornness with which the enemy is holding the line and communications with the rear. From our direction: there are woods, ravines and hills, which allow us to approach the enemy, conduct reconnaissance with observation of his actions, and make it possible for us to conceal maneuvers and regroupings of our forces.

...

7. Time calculations: The commander's order for the offensive was received on 11.07.1943 at 1700. There are 14 hours before the start of the operation. The units are located in the army's second echelon in Kashlakovo, Churaevo, Shebekino area. Time is fully adequate to cover the 4-kilometer distance to the start line for the offensive. Use the time:
   a) To clarify the task standing before the corps as given by the commander of the 7th Guards Army and to issue preliminary instructions – 30 minutes;
   b) To reconnoiter the ground with the division commanders in the corps' sector of offensive – 3 hours;
   c) For the commanders of the attached and supporting units to get reports [briefings] – 40 minutes;
   d) For the paperwork and delivering orders to their executors – 3 hours.[11]

However, judging by a report from Major V.P. Liukshin, a General Staff officer with the headquarters of the 7th Guards Army, who personally drove out to the staging area of the of the army's counterattack grouping on the morning of 12 July, the corps command wasn't able to make sensible use of its available possibilities. His report lays out a sorry picture of the movement of its division up into the jumping-off positions. Here is a short excerpt from Liukshin's report:

Through a personal inspection it was established that the 111th and 270th Rifle Divisions hastily took up the new line. At 0300 12.7.43 the units of the 270th Rifle Division had been fully brought up, but the division commander still had no communications with the new command post. The 111th Rifle Division spent the nighttime hours assembling, and conducted the rotation of units and separate elements in the line already during daylight hours. By 0800 12.7.43 the 111th Rifle Division's guns still hadn't unlimbered and been emplaced; soldiers were traipsing around the field, disclosing their assembly. The enemy took advantage of this condition of the 111th Rifle Division and partially of the 270th Rifle Division, and opened intense rocket artillery fire. The element of surprise was lost. Units of the rifle divisions until the very moment of launching the counteroffensive were located under heavy mortar shelling and rifle and machine-gun fire. Just 40-50 minutes were left before the designated hour of the attack (1000), and the divisions of the 49th Rifle Corps still hadn't assembled their attached units. Thus, the assembly for the attack of the 49th Rifle Corps' divisions and of several of the units of reinforcement was extremely hasty and disorganized, which didn't bring about the desired success.[12]

The basic responsibility for the poor organization of the regrouping and the preparation of the troops should be assigned first of all to the division commanders. In their actions, one can see foot dragging, a lack of purpose and basic egoism. For example, the journal of combat operations of the strongest 270th Rifle Division, which was to operate in the center of the army's attack formation,

---

11 TsAMO RF, f. 7 gv. A, op. 5312, d. 539, ll. 116-117.
12 TsAMO RF, f. 7 gv. A, op. 5312, d. 183, ll. 11-12.

observed that "… at 0900 the division commander drove out to the operational area together with staff officers, unit commanders and the commanders of attached assets for a reconnaissance."[13] That is to say, Major General I.P. Beliaev with his subordinates drove up to the front in order to figure out where and how his regiments and attached assets would be operating just an hour before his troops were to go on the attack and just 20 minutes before the start of the artillery preparation. Just when then did the battalion commanders receive their final orders, and when did they in turn ready their units for the attack? Having received the preliminary order between 1800 and 1900 on 11 July, the division commander could have reconnoitered, at the very least, right after sunrise (around 0500-0600). It is understandable that the troops spent all night moving up to the front, taking up their assigned sectors, bringing up artillery and supplies, but the senior officers of the headquarters weren't lugging shells.

In this situation, things went particularly hard for the tankers and artillerymen of the units and formations that were attached to the divisions as reinforcement. In addition to assembling in their jumping-off positions, they had to have time to conduct reconnaissance, determine the enemy's patterns of fire, study the terrain, identify sectors passable for tanks and minefield obstacles (their own and the enemy's), and prepare data for firing. For example at 2300 on 11 July the commander of the 201st Separate Tank Brigade, which was located in the first line of defense in the sector of the 73rd Guards Rifle Division sent a message to division commander S.A. Kozak: "A combat order has been received from the commander of the 270th Rifle Division about removing the brigade from the defense and assembling it by 1000 12.07.1943 in jumping-off positions in the vicinity of the western fringe of the woods lying east of Hill 209.6. Thus, the brigade's sector of defense will remain uncovered. Is the brigade's relocation known to the commander of the 7th Guards Army's Armored and Mechanized Forces?"[14] Indeed, in this situation how was the tank brigade commander supposed to act? However, there is the impression that the commanders of the 49th Rifle Corps' divisions didn't understand this or didn't want to delve into other people's problems. In the course of the night and even by the start of the counterattack, not all of the 201st Tank Brigade's units were in fact replaced. Considering that the Germans in its sector were conducting daily counterattacks with the use of tanks, Colonel I.A. Taranov simply couldn't leave the line without a reliable screen. Moreover, by this time having probably sensed that the Russians were preparing for an attack, the Germans launched several preemptive attacks against the positions of the brigade's motorized rifle battalion and 296th Tank Battalion, trying to tie them down in combat. Major V.P. Liukshin, the General Staff officer with the 7th Guards Army, wrote: "The brigade required a necessary minimal amount of time in order to bring it back to order, but these elementary rules weren't followed, because no time was left."[15]

As a result of all this, the tank crews moved their combat machines into their jumping-off positions literally just several minutes before the start of the attack, and the artillery opened fire not at revealed enemy firing positions and troops concentrations, but at general areas. V.P. Chibisov, who at this time was commanding a Matilda tank in the 295th Tank Battalion, wrote emotionally about how the process of issuing orders to the tank battalions in the 201st Tank Brigade went:

> The battalion moved past some devastated little village, where there was a burned-out machine that had been destroyed by a bomb, then along a sloping bank of some river [the Koren' River], at which point we turned left, the river receded behind us, and the tanks entered some woods while it was still quite dark. The column continued rolling another 10 minutes or so,

---

13 TsAMO RF, f. 270 sd, op. 1, d. 1, l. 13obr.
14 TsAMO RF, f. 3256, op. 1, d. 7, l. 49.
15 TsAMO RF, f. 7 gv. A, op. 5312, d. 183, l. 12.

and stopped before exiting the woods. No one in the platoon knew where we had just been on the march, where we were now, where the enemy was, or where our own side was, since in the battalion they hadn't assembled us and didn't brief us regarding the situation in this sector of the front, the disposition of the German forces, and who our neighbors were on the right and left.

Finally a command ran down the column: the tank platoon commanders and tank commanders were to report to the battalion commander. Battalion commander Major A.S. Semenov issued his order; I remember this extremely short order almost word for word: "The enemy is in front of us in the hamlet of Krutoi Log. Move into your jumping-off positions by company. … Take into account that there is a minefield in front of us. … Fight to the last drop of blood! Any questions?"

Everyone was silent for several seconds, but then I asked, "How are we to pass through the minefield?" The major explained: "Lanes have been marked with birch tree branches. Clear? No one has anything else to say?"

Behind our backs in the pre-dawn twilight, the powerful combat machines were still quietly rumbling, ready to set off into the unknown. Together with my bewilderment, other questions flashed through my mind: Why hadn't there been any reconnoitering of the ground before the battle, and what had our intelligence reported?

The command "To your machines!" followed, and we each ran off to our own tank. First I informed the driver-mechanic about the minefield, but now we were on our own to pass through it along the lanes that had been marked by birch branches.[16]

Colonel N.V. Nevzhinsky's 27th Guards Tank Brigade was in a more advantageous situation. It was located in the 24th Guards Rifle Corps' reserve, and several days before this it had been fully moved up into the second echelon of defense, so it was completely ready for the pending counterattack and its assembly in the jumping-off area went without any hitches. Moreover the brigade had conserved practically all of its armor; by the morning of 12 July, it had 50 operational tanks, including 45 T-34 and 5 T-70.[17] In its motorized rifle battalions, two rifle companies, the submachine gun company, the mortar company and the anti-tank rifle company were still combat-capable, and 3 76mm guns remained in its anti-tank gun battery. Nevertheless, prior to the attack even its battalion commanders didn't know the location of the enemy's minefields on the axis of the forthcoming attack, nor had the system of the 106th Infantry Division's anti-tank defenses been revealed.

For its part, the command of Korps Raus, having received information from aerial reconnaissance and ground observers about the assembly of significant Russian forces opposite the 106th and 198th Infantry Divisions, including tanks, brought up several additional Flak artillery batteries to the Maslova Pristan' – Krutoi Log area. Having subordinated them to the 106th Infantry Division, it created a powerful anti-tank line on the path of advance of Taranov's and Nevzhinsky's tank brigades. Thus, there could be only one outcome of the attack on the axis of the 7th Guards Army's main attack – high losses and the failure to reach assigned objectives.

In addition, units of the 15th Guards Rifle Division were ready to launch secondary attacks against the left flank of the 198th Infantry Division, while the full 72nd Guards Rifle Division and two rifle regiments of the 213th Rifle Division were to launch diversionary attacks against the

---

16 Chibisov, V.P., *Angliiskie tanki v Krutom Logu* [*English tanks in Krutoi Log*] (Novosibirsk: Avion, 1996), p. 112.
17 TsAMO RF, f. 3108, op. 1, d. 10, l. 66.

entire 320th Infantry Division and the right flank of the 106th Infantry Division. From the 15th Guards Rifle Division's division commander's Order No.019 from 11 July 1943:

2. The Division's training battalion, 44th Guards and 47th Guards Rifle Regiments attack in the sector: on the right – Novoselovka, Arkadeevka, (excl.) Miasoedovo; on the left – Nekliudovo, "Batratskaia Dacha" State Farm's lake (incl.), "Day of Harvest" collective farm, Mikhailovka with the task by day's end to take Hill 160.8 and seize Belovskaia with a forward detachment.
3. The training battalion by 0500 12.7.43 with the support of three KV tanks of the 262nd Heavy Tank Regiment, a battalion of the 97th Guards Mortar Regiment, the 161st Guards Cannon Artillery Regiment, and 1/43rd Guards Artillery Regiment is to take Hill 205.5, and subsequently with the advance by division's units, screen the flank: Hill 205.5, Hill 206.9.
4. 47th Guards Rifle Regiment: on the right – Hill 122.4, Hill 191.8, Hill 124.5; on the left – (excl.) brick building in Nekliudovo, (excl.) Hill 202.3, (excl.) Point K, southern outskirts of Nekliudovo, has the task to seize the western slopes of Hill 191.8, northwestern slopes of Hill 202.3, and to prevent the enemy's infiltration into the woods. Infantry artillery support group: 1/43 Guards Artillery Regiment.
5. 44th Guards Rifle Regiment, screening the Hill 202.3, "Solov'ev" collective front, with an attack in the direction: Hill 216.1, Hill 207.9, is to take Hill 207.9 and the farmyards 1.5 kilometers southwest of Hill 207.9; subsequently with an attack to the west, by the end of the day it is to seize Hill 160.8, western fringe of the woods 2 kilometers southwest of Hill 160.8, and to take Belovskaia with a forward detachment. Infantry artillery support group: 2 and 3/43rd Guards Artillery Regiment.[18]

It should be noted that the favorable terrain, in particular where Safiulin's corps was defending, gave the Soviet side a certain amount of assistance in preparing the counterattack. To a certain degree it offset the shortcomings in organizing the regrouping of forces, which were tolerated by the division commanders. The 25th Guards Rifle Corps' account noted:

The enemy was occupying a line that ran along the northwestern and western slopes of hills. The entire sector between Hill 205.5 (the enemy's left flank on the corps' front) and the "Batratskaia Dacha" State Farm was clearly visible and kept under fire by our side. Between the "Batratskaia Dacha" State Farm to the south as far as Hill 209.6, the enemy line was screened by intervening woods, but further to the south, as far as the woods 1 kilometer west of Gremiachii (the enemy's right flank on the corps' front), it was again exposed. This circumstance allowed our side to conduct observation from the front and the flank along the entire sector, as well as in the depth as far as the Razumnaia River. Almost across the entire corps' sector, the enemy was occupying the trenches and earth-and-timber bunkers of the corps' former second echelon. The completely exposed terrain with ground that sloped in the enemy's direction didn't allow the Germans to conduct stealthy regroupings, bring up reserves, and keep his troops supplied with everything necessary.

The line of defense occupied by the 25th Guards Rifle Corps' units ran along the western fringe of the woods stretching from Hill 205.5 to the south as far as the "Batratskaia Dacha" State Farm. Further to the south as far as the "Poliana" State Farm, the defensive line traveled across open ground. The entire line ran along heights and allowed us to monitor the enemy's

---

18 TsAMO RF, f. 15 gv. sd, op. 1, d. 8, l. 142.

line. The presence of the sharply cut ground and woods behind our forward line allowed our units to conduct regroupings, bring up reserves directly to the front, and keep our units supplied with ammunition and food in concealment. The line was not fortified and the units had to strengthen their line with trenches, communication trenches and earth-and-timber bunkers simultaneously while conducting stubborn fighting with the enemy.[19]

Two main tasks were given to the 24th Guards Rifle Corps. In the first place, it had to screen the left flank of the 111th Rifle Division securely against possible enemy counterattacks. Secondly, it had to attack the enemy across the line: (excl.) southwestern outskirts of Krutoi Log, Maslova Pristan' and Priiutovka, and capture all the villages on the eastern bank of the Northern Donets River. The 72nd Guards Rifle Division received the order to drive the Germans out of Nizhnii Ol'shanets and Karnaukhovka, while the 213th Rifle Division was to take possession of Rzhavets and Priiutovka. Maslova Pristan', because of the particular strength of its defenses, was to be assaulted by both divisions with the units that were positioned on their adjacent flanks. The length of the attack sector allocated to Vasil'ev's corps and the depth of its objectives were such like its neighbor, the 25th Guards Rifle Corps had, 9 and 5 kilometers respectively, but the 24th Guards Rifle Corps' strength was much more modest: it had all of Losev's battered division, and two rifle regiments of Buslaev's division. On 10 July 1943 the 72nd Guards Rifle Division had a total of 6,232 men, while the 213th Rifle Division had a total of 7,487, but their combined fighting troops totalled 4,903 (refer to Table 14).[20] The 24th Guards Rifle Corps also had modest means of reinforcement: the 115th Guards Destroyer Anti-tank Artillery Regiment, the 109th Guards Cannon Artillery Regiment (18 152mm howitzers), two anti-tank rifle battalions and the 176th Separate Flamethrower Company. Meanwhile, however, its 265th Guards Artillery Regiment, 309th Guards Mortar Regiment and 27th Guards Tank Brigade were transferred to the 49th Rifle Corps.

Rain fell all night long on the night of 11-12 July, not in downpours, but across the entire front, and dawn proved to be cloudy. On the Soviet side of the lines, the men were glad for this – it meant that they wouldn't come under heavy Luftwaffe attacks. From the middle of the night onward, all the roads, forest firebreaks and paths were jammed with troops in the sector between the Koren' River and the line of defense of 7th Guards Army's first echelon; thousands of soldiers and officers and hundreds of vehicles, wagons, guns and tanks were moving in various directions – the large-scale regrouping was underway.

Intensive movements were observed on the enemy side as well. At this time the 198th Infantry Division was completing the process of replacing the units of the 7th Panzer Division, which Breith was striving to send to the Kazach'e area as quickly as possible in order to consolidate the success achieved by the 6th Panzer Division. The forces of the other divisions of the III Panzer Corps were also moving to assemble in new areas. From the morning report of the divisions to its headquarters:

> 6th Panzer Division: "The assault *panzergruppe* back on the evening of 11 July reached Kazach'e and is engaged in combat there with heavy tanks [there were no heavy Soviet tanks in this area at the time]. The division is concentrating south of Verkhnii Ol'shanets. Light enemy aerial activity."[21]

---

19 TsAMO RF, f. 25 gv. sk, op. 1, d. 27, l. 12.
20 The active bayonets were tabulated on 11 July 1943.
21 The information for 6th Panzer Division was taken from a message from the III Panzer Corps headquarters to the headquarters of Army Detachment Kempf.

7th Panzer Division: The division set out from the northern outskirts of Miasoedovo for the offensive late in the evening. At 0200 contact was established with the battalion that was operating in the southeastern portion of the village. The area is still in the process of being mopped up. Over the night, enlivened enemy activity in the air."

19th Panzer Division: "The reinforced Panzergrenadier Regiment 73 and Panzer Reconnaissance Battalion 19 throughout the night defended the captured territory. Constant harassing artillery, anti-tank and mortar fire on the positions. Our artillery without interruption conducted harassing fire on Sabynino. During the night, enemy aerial activity noted."

168th Infantry Division: "Grenadier Regiment 417 in the afternoon hours of 11.7 attacked Petropavlovka, reached the brushy area north of Petropavlovka from south and west, and set about destroying the strong enemy opposition in the southwestern portion of the woods. The offensive will be resumed in the early morning. The enemy lost 28 men taken prisoner, and a verified 25 killed and 25 wounded. The number of prisoners taken during the attack toward Khokhlovo also rose. Captured on 11.7 – 6 light machine guns, 2 heavy machine guns, 2 trucks, 14 machine pistols and 35 rifles. The night in the division's sector passed quietly, despite active bombing of the division's disposition. Movement to the designated assembly area is underway. The division command post [will be] in the sector of woods north of Dal'niaia Igumenka from 0900."[22]

When the dawn began to break on the morning of 12 July, in the staging areas of the troops of the 7th Guards Army's counterattack grouping, field kitchens and vehicles carrying food began to turn up with uncustomary frequency. The commanders were seeking to feed men before the attack and distribute the authorized cheap tobacco and "People's Commissariat norm [of vodka]". For example, the 15th Guards Rifle Division commander back on the evening of 11 July had signed Special Combat Order No.058/op, which alongside the other aspects of preparing the division for the counterattack, touched upon questions of food supply: "Ready all the men for battle. Give the men breakfast; cook the breakfast and lunch together and hand them out simultaneously. Give the men their authorized shot of vodka at breakfast."[23]

The rear area personnel were being guided by professional intuition when this large amount of work began. Thus the level of supplying the troops at this moment improved somewhat; the logistics personnel were striving to deliver to the "frontline troops" all that they needed in the shortest amount of time, in order as one of the veterans of the 27th Guards Tank Brigade expressed to me in a conversation, "not to chance a punch from any shell-shocked battalion commander." However, this was a rule that didn't get by without exceptions. There were enough slouches and deadbeats everywhere. Nevertheless, as veterans recalled, for example, the tankers of the 295th Tank Battalion of Taranov's tank brigade, which arrived from the march in the area of its jumping-off positions 15 minutes before the attack (but the rest of the units somewhat later), they found cooks already standing at the ready: "The field kitchen team had brought up fresh bread and distributed it among each crew. We took up our positions in our tanks, broke the aromatic loaf into pieces, and hastily munched on the bread."[24]

Before 0600 a breeze was blowing; the skies began to clear, and already at 0620 the first *rama* ["frame" – the nickname given to the twin-boomed Focke-Wulff 189 reconnaissance aircraft]

---

22 NARA US, rg. 242, t. 314, r. 197, f. 001365.
23 TsAMO RF, f. 15 gv. sd, op. 1, d. 1, l. 141.
24 Chibisov, *Angliiskie tanki v Krutom Logu*, p. 113.

appeared in the sky above Safiulin's and Terent'ev's corps, and approximately at 0700 the German artillery, having received the first target coordinates, opened fire. The German artillery barrage by guns and Nebelwerfers continued incessantly right up the start of the counterattack at 1000, but not across the entire front, but only in separate sectors where the enemy had likely spotted the active movement of Soviet troops. Between 0910 and 0920 (according to various data), the artillery of the 7th Guards Army and of its subordinate divisions spoke up. In the sky, the fiery streaks of rockets appeared. The roaring and screeches intensified, the ground beneath the feet quaked, and a thin, bluish-grey caustic haze from exploding shells and uplifted earth spread across the battlefield. However, considering how the regrouping of the forces had been conducted, it was out of the question to expect any sort of substantial results from the artillery's work, since the artillery crews were conducting area fire; thus the enemy's system of fire remained intact virtually everywhere. This had a negative effect on the course of the counterattack from the first minutes.

The first to go on the counterattack were units of the 111th, 73rd Guards and 15th Guards Rifle Divisions. Within several minutes after the haze over the battlefield and woods cleared and the contours of groves and trees standing in the distance reappeared, the voices of company and platoon commanders rang out: "Guardsmen, forward, into the attack!" Then the ground riddled with foxholes, trenches and field works was covered by hundreds of soldiers, advancing and firing on the move. However, not a single one of the divisions was able to make an advance of more than 300-400 meters in the first half hour. For example, the divisions of the 49th Rifle Corps didn't have even an elementary picture of the enemy's system of defense, and on separate sectors the commanders of the forward battalions didn't know exactly where the first line of enemy entrenchments ran. The chief of staff of the 49th Rifle Corps Colonel Polkovnikov wrote self-critically in a report, "The regimental and battalion reconnaissance didn't do adequate work before the start of the offensive, and failed to disclose the enemy's forward edge of defense, fortifications, system of fire or artificial obstacles. As a result of this the 111th Rifle Division from the very start of its attack came under unexpected enemy artillery and machine-gun fire and its further advance was stopped."[25]

To put it more precisely, the battalions of Bushin's division became pinned down just 300 meters from their jumping-off positions. However, whereas for the 111th Rifle Division the German fire was "unexpected", division commanders Kozak and Vasil'enko were fully aware that already within the first several minutes, the Germans would force their lead battalions to hug the earth. They also knew how and from which firing positions the Germans would lay down a murderous fire, but they were unable to change anything, because they didn't have the means to suppress the enemy's elaborate, multi-layered and well-planned system of fire. The first attack of Safiulin's two Guards divisions (15th Guards and 73rd Guards) was already halted in its tracks by 1030-1040. The regiments literally melted away in the first 200-300 meters. Kozak's division suffered particularly heavy casualties. The terrible fire from the units of the 198th Infantry Division forced its battalions to hug the ground several times, while the Soviet artillery weakly placed light methodical fire on the German positions. From Combat Dispatch No. 125 from the headquarters of the 73rd Guards Rifle Division on 12 July 1943:

> The 214th Guards Rifle Regiment with one battery of 76mm guns from the 30th Destroyer Brigade and the 131st and 132nd Anti-tank Rifle Battalions, which were attacking in the direction of the barn (2 kilometers west of the "Batratskaia Dacha" State Farm) and Point 191.2 made slow progress up until 1230. However, incessantly blanketed with the fire of six-barreled rocket launchers and swept by the fire of heavy-caliber machine guns, suffering

---

25 TsAMO RF, f. 7 gv. A., op. 5312, d. 539, l. 121.

significant losses in men, the regiment was forced to stop. According to preliminary information, the regiment's losses amounted to 393 men killed or wounded.[26]

The 73rd Guards Rifle Division's 209th Guards and 211th Guards Rifle Regiments wound up in similar situations; over two hours, the division gained approximately 400 meters of ground.

However, this was just the beginning, and at 1015 a fresh wave of attackers surged toward the enemy – the 270th Rifle Division and Taranov's brigade went on the counterattack. This attack proved to be stronger and more successful, primarily due to the decisive actions of Major A.S. Semenov's 295th Tank Battalion, which moved out from Hill 209.6 in the direction of Hill 187.4. The tanks' appearance threw the enemy into panic, and the shaken grenadiers of the 106th Infantry Division began hastily to abandon their occupied positions, but the confusion in the enemy ranks didn't last long. The command of the German army corps was aware of the forthcoming counterattack by Soviet troops, and was ready to repulse it. General E. Raus early that morning had visited the command post of the commander of the 106th Infantry Division Lieutenant General W. Forst in Maslova Pristan', and personally observed the start of the Guards divisions' attack. Not only was strong mortar fire opened on Beliaev's attacking division, but already within 15 minutes up to three battalions of infantry of the 106th Infantry Division's 241st Grenadier Regiment launched a counterattack against its right flank from out of the woods 2 kilometers east of Krutoi Log. However, the tanks of the 295th Tank Battalion located in the 973rd Rifle Regiment's combat formations with their fire and tracks crushed the grenadiers and continued to push on toward Hill 187.4.

Albeit gradually and with great difficulty, Terent'ev's 49th Rifle Corps began to make progress. At this moment, a dilemma arose before the crews of the 201st Separate Tank Brigade: in order to make a rapid breakthrough into the depth of Forst's division, it was necessary to accelerate, but in order not to be deprived of infantry support, it was necessary to destroy the machine-gun nests and mortar batteries, and this would correspondingly slow the pace of the advance and divert them from a strike into the depth. It made no sense to attempt to place targeted fire on the move from the gun, so the tankers, operating on a rather broad front, began to place fire from their machine guns on the German positions and crush their crews beneath their tracks. However, this tactic gave the enemy gunners the opportunity of concentrating anti-tank fire on the combat machines.

V.B. Chibisov recalled:

> One after another, the tanks emerged from the woods and deployed with a front toward an open field, which had been mined by our sappers. Turning my periscope, I took a close look: Just where were those damned birches branches, but I didn't see any birch at all. It seemed we had passed them! The level ground came to an end, and the tank began increasingly to rock and even bounce. Up ahead, one had to suppose, loomed the Nazi's first belt of fortifications. But where was Krutoi Log?!
>
> About 5 meters to the left of my machine, the Matilda of Junior Lieutenant Makhiaddin Guseinov, a valiant Azerbaidzhanian from Baku, who'd seen fighting since 1941, was moving. Somewhat further to the left was the tank of the company commander, Senior Lieutenant G.M. Kozhar. A long stream of tracer bullets was coming from his turret, and there was the flash of a shot from his cannon. Suddenly all the machines on my right, firing more from machine guns than the main guns, began to close on my own. In my headset I wasn't hearing the voice of the company commander; probably, I had forgotten connect to him through the UKV radio. I shouted to my driver Gerasimov over the tank's intercom to choose a course toward a patch of woods out in front of us. He muttered something in response.

---

26 TsAMO RF, f. 1212, op. 1, d. 28, l. 15.

We were rolling over trenches and foxholes, because the tank was really being jolted. In one place the machine slowed, and having come to a stop, pivoted to the left and then back again to the previous direction. I understood and agreed with the driver's maneuver. It seemed that the tank had nearly settled on its hull, and a moment later clouds of dust rose in front and along the sides of the machine. Likely, a bunker had just collapsed. The engine howled, and the tank now surged toward the nearby woods. The company's tanks were now moving very closely bunched together, probably because of the rough terrain. Already on the approach to the woods, there was suddenly a sharp blow against the turret and a rattling sound on the armor, as if a handful of small stones that had been tossed against it were tumbling down the armored plate. Everything went silent in my headset. It was as if I'd taken a cold splash of water in the face, but I turned the periscope, trying to identify the source of the shell that had struck our tank. All of the company's machines were stopping, continuing to fire. Through the periscope I saw the commander's cupola on the tank of our company commander wagging back and forth, most likely in order to attract attention. Then the hatch opened on the company commander's machine, and the commander thrust his arm out of the turret, his hand clenched into a fist. The fist sternly rocked forward, back, then forward again, and everyone understood – forward, through the woods. The woods [the grove east of Hill 187.4], though, was stuffed with enemy dugouts and stockpiles.

At this moment I caught sight of the battalion's nurse, Ania Dunaeva, who had appeared from somewhere, as she ran up to the hatch of the driver-mechanic of the tank next to the company commander's machine. She said something to the driver, then bent over, she ran up to a second, then a third tank, while from the turrets continued to come bursts of machine-gun fire or shots from the cannon. When she ran up to our tank, however, and bent over the hatch, the turret gunner Gavrilo, not seeing her beneath the cannon, fired a round before I could warn him. Ania grabbed her ears and collapsed out of sight in front of the nose of the tank. Several seconds later I watched as she stood back up, and still holding her hands over her ears, she laboriously ran further, skipping the machine standing next to us on the right. So I never learned what Ania Dunaeva was saying and where she went after this momentary mishap. Years later I found out that she was captured, just like I'd been.[27]

Trying to overcome the Germans' stubborn resistance, the divisions of Beliaev and Bushin with the support of the tank battalions of the two brigades, began gradually to drive back the enemy in the entire sector where they had gone on the attack. Even so, this came with great difficulty and a lot of blood. The officers of the 27th Guards Tank Brigade's headquarters remarked:

The artillery preparation was weakly conducted; the artillery fire struck not previously studied and detected enemy targets, but fell on general areas, as a consequence of which the enemy's system of fire during the artillery preparation wasn't suppressed, so during the tanks' attack, the tanks had to combat not enemy infantry, but his artillery, as a result of which the tanks suffered large losses. As a result of the enemy's previously prepared system of fire, our infantry during the attack became cut off from the tanks, and suffering large losses, the tanks fought independently without infantry support. The terrain in the sector of operations (woods, ravines) presented great difficulties for the maneuvering of the tanks.[28]

---

27 Chibisov, *Angliiskie tanki u Krutogo Loga*, p. 113.
28 TsAMO RF, f. 3108, op. 1, d. 1, l. 17.

In full measure this also applied to the sector where the crews of the 201st Tank Brigade were attempting to break through. By 1200 the right-flank units of the 270th Rifle Division with the 295th Tank Battalion took Hill 187.4, though with great difficulty, and penetrated 2 kilometers into the defenses of the 106th Infantry Division. A bit earlier, around 1130, despite the intense artillery fire coming from the "Poliana" State Farm, the 27th Guards Tank Brigade was breaking through with the 1st Tank Battalion to the southern outskirts of the State Farm, and with the 2nd Tank Battalion to a point 100 meters south of Hill 207.0. Three regiments of the 111th Rifle Division were stretched out behind the tanks, and they reached the eastern fringe of the woods west of Gremiachii, the eastern outskirts of the Poliana State Farm, and a point 200 meters west of the fringe of woods on Point 190.0. Thus, the tank battalions of Nevzinsky's brigade made an advance of 800 meters to up to 2000 meters from their jumping-off positions. I will emphasize that it was just the tanks, because the rifle companies of the brigade's motorized rifle battalion and the infantry of the 111th Rifle Division became pinned down 400 meters or even 500 meters behind the combat machines that had pushed ahead.

In addition to the intense fire of artillery and mortars, Bushin's division was met by counterattacks by elements of the 106th Infantry Division's 239th and 241st Grenadier Regiments across the entire sector. Considering the failure of the first counterattack against the 270th Rifle Division (when it was crushed by the Matildas), Forst reinforced the infantry with several tanks of the panzer company, which was left behind by the 7th Panzer Division, but as before he kept StuG Battalion 905 in reserve at Maslova Pristan' (it was located in a patch of woods 1.5 kilometers east of that village). The reason for this was obvious; at this time units of the 213th Rifle Division were already engaged in street fighting in Rzhavets, plainly aiming to break through to Maslova Pristan'. From the 111th Rifle Division's combat journal:

> At 1130 units of the division reached:
> - 532nd Rifle Regiment, having gained the eastern outskirts of the "Poliana" State Farm, was counterattacked by 5 tanks with a group of submachine gunners from the northeastern fringe of the woods west of the State Farm. The regiment was engaged in heavy fighting with the enemy.
> - 468th Rifle Regiment was counterattacked by the enemy from the "Poliana" State Farm – up to a company of infantry, as well as from out of the woods south of the Poliana State Farm. The regiment, having repulsed the enemy's counterattack, took the woods south of the "Poliana" State Farm.
> - 399th Rifle Regiment reached the eastern fringe of the woods northwest of Gremiachii, where it encountered strong enemy resistance from Hill 201.0 and from the northeastern fringe of the woods west of the "Poliana" State Farm.[29]

Thus, by mid-day only a modest success began to be noted in the sector of the 270th Rifle Division alone. By 1200 its regiments, having advanced approximately 3 kilometers, reached the area of Hill 191.2. The 973rd Rifle Regiment had reached the ravine 800 meters southeast of Hill 191.2; the 975th Rifle Regiment – the ravine 1.5 kilometers west of the same hill; the 977th Rifle Regiment – the ravine 1.5 kilometers northwest of the Gremiachii Machine Tractor Station; 1/975th Rifle Regiment and the 321st Separate Destroyer Anti-tank Artillery Battalion were saddling the road running between Hill 209.6 and the "Poliana" State Farm.

However, enemy fire from Hill 191.2 was greatly interfering with further progress. The account of the 49th Rifle Corps' headquarters noted: "Given the partial success of the 270th Rifle Division,

---

29 TsAMO RF, f. 111sd, op. 1, d. 12, l. 12, 12obr.

the units of the 111th Rifle Division didn't support its advance into the depth of the enemy's defenses, and the neighbor on the right – the 73rd Guards Rifle Division – didn't place fire on the enemy's firing positions 1.5 kilometers north of Hill 191.2, which hindered the further advance by units of the 270th Rifle Division, as result of which the division came under a flanking attack from the right and left and its progress was brought to a halt."[30]

Trying to resolve the situation, I.P. Beliaev at 1230 sent Combat Order No.022 to the commander of the 975th Rifle Regiment, in which he directed that the regiment, while continuing to attack toward Krutoi Log, detach a portion of the right-flank's forces in order to take Hill 191.2. On his part, the division commander additionally moved up 3/975th Rifle Regiment from out of his reserve to the sector of the 973rd Rifle Regiment in order to seize the hill. The 295th Tank Battalion was supposed to support the infantry. The attack by the battalions of the two regiments simultaneously toward the hill was set for 1300.

By the middle of the day, small headway began to be made on secondary directions. At 1235, having overcome the strong fire resistance from Horn's division, the 44th Guards Rifle Regiment of the 15th Guards Rifle Division took the "Solov'ev" collective farm and continued the attack in the direction of Hill 160.8. However, its neighbors the 47th Guards Rifle Regiment and the 15th Guards Rifle Division's training battalion were unable to strengthen the attack and they continued to exchange heavy fire with the Germans in the woods on the approaches to Hills 202.3 and 205.5.

Even though the command of both Army Group South and Korps Raus, which received the main attack of the 7th Guards Army, were expecting active operations by Shumilov's troops, nevertheless they came as a surprise for them, and on separate sectors the attacks were viewed as dangerous. At 1140 E. von Manstein headed out along the road to Kempf's command post in Dolbino, in order to obtain the latest operational information. Twenty minutes later, an alarming report arrived from the headquarters of Hoth's panzer army: "Across the entire front, the enemy has attacked with large forces. South of Prokhorovka, the enemy is shifting numerous tank forces from the east to the west, and savage panzer battles are taking place there. Even SS Panzer Grenadier Division *Totenkopf*'s bridgehead has been subjected to a strong attack."[31]

Just 25 minutes later, a call rang out in the Operations Department from General E. Raus, which only confirmed that the day was being noted as very difficult. Raus reported:

> Starting at 1000 (Moscow time), the enemy is attacking the corps' sector on a front of up to 20 kilometers with infantry and tanks, and more precisely from both sides of Rzhavets and across the open field to the east of it in the direction of Maslova Pristan'; to the north of it against the 586th Grenadier Regiment with tanks; in the sector of the 106th Infantry Division from the wooded terrain north of Hill 202.9; at the fringe of the woods south of the "Poliana" State Farm, where there was a small penetration; and the "Poliana" State Farm has been attacked as well with the support of tanks. In the center of the division's dispositions to the southwest of Hill 219.6, 12 enemy tanks broke through in the direction of Krutoi Log. Yet another enemy attack took place toward the "Batratskaia Dacha" State Farm and to the south of there. The enemy achieved a third breakthrough in the vicinity of the Solov'ev collective farm. Counter-measures are being taken. Out of the reserves 2/III/585th Grenadier Regiment and a battalion of assault guns stand ready, and there are 16 Flak guns in front of Krutoi Log in order to repulse tanks.[32]

---

30 TsAMO RF, f. 7 gv. A., op. 5312, d. 539, l. 121.
31 NARA, t. 312, r. 54, f. 7569658.
32 Ibid.

After this G. Speidel came to the telephone and E. Raus asked him to support the corp's northern flank at the Solov'ev collective farm with forces of the 7th Panzer Division, which at this time was assembled at Iastrebovo for a march to the sector of 6th Panzer Division. Army Group South's chief of staff promised help, and on his part reported that Fliegerkorps VIII had already given its agreement to launch a strike against the enemy opposite his corps. Wrapping up the discussion, Speidel sent a radio message to Breith about the complex situation in the sector of Korps Raus and an order: his 7th Panzer Division should for the meantime hold at Iastrebovo because of the possibility that it would have to be used in order to block a possible breakthrough. This was the first and only order from Army Group South about deferring the movement of forces from out of the sector of the 7th Guards Army to the area south of Prokhorovka, which was directly connected with the counterattack by Shumilov's forces. Even though this delay didn't last for long – a little more than 2 hours – because of it von Funck's panzer division on this day would in fact not be introduced into the fighting south of Prokhorovka Station.

After mid-day, promising information of all kinds began to arrive at the command post of the 7th Guards Army. At 1300, the chief of staff Major General G.S. Lukin received a message over the Baudot device from the 24th Guards Rifle Corps: "At 1200 Losev's units took the woods south of the 'Poliana' State Farm and Point 171.8, and are fighting for Priiutovka."[33] A little later, yet another message arrived: At 1330 the 72nd Guards Rifle Division, continuing to develop the success, drove the enemy out of the northwestern spur of the Shebekinskaia Dacha Woods (1.5 south of Hill 207). In the course of the fighting, two German corporals were captured: Wernand Zücker and Ludwig Körgster from the 106th Infantry Division's I/Grenadier Regiment 239. On the basis of their interrogation, the division's intelligence chief Captain Kalmykov quickly composed a report, in which he wrote:

> In front of the division's sector, up to a regiment of infantry from the 106th and 320th Infantry Divisions is defending. The I and III Battalions of the 106th Infantry Division's 239th Grenadier Regiment are holding the sector northwest of the Shebikinskaia Dacha Woods, Hill 207.9, "Poliana" State Farm. Artillery – up to a battalion, in the woods east of Maslova Pristan'. Anti-tank artillery is positioned in the area 1.5 kilometers northeast of Maslova Pristan'.
>
> There are large losses in I Battalion; in each company there remain up to 40 men. A company commander, a 1st lieutenant, has been killed. In III Battalion there are 180 men. The 106th Infantry Division's 239th Grenadier Regiment has large losses from the very first day of the offensive, which for it began at 0900 on 5.7.1943.
>
> The prisoners indicated that there is a large amount of artillery in the Grafovka, Volkovo area. Tanks of the 6th Panzer Division are supporting the 106th Infantry Division. A prisoner saw three tanks in the woods north of Shebekinskaia Dacha. The headquarters of the 239th Grenadier Regiment is located in Maslova Pristan', and up to a battalion of infantry is assembled there; evidently, this is II/239th Grenadier Regiment. To the left of the 239th Grenadier Regiment, the 106th Infantry Division's 241st Grenadier Regiment is defending. Nationality composition: 80% Germans, 20% Poles.
>
> The prisoners are also aware of a bridge being constructed on the Northern Donets in the vicinity of Maslova Pristan' with a load-bearing capacity of 25 tonnes, and another in the Pristen' – Toplinka area with a load-bearing capacity of up to 40 tonnes.

---

33 TsAMO RF, f. 7 gv. A, op. 5312, d. 294, l. 1.

The [German] soldiers say that four Russian armies have already been encircled in the Belgorod area, and their task is to hold the defense and destroy the attacking Russian units. The prisoners hear soldiers' talk that two Cossack armies are forming up in Khar'kov.[34]

At noontime, Buslaev's division, enveloping the hamlet of Rzhavets with the 793rd Rifle Regiment from the northeast and the 702nd Rifle Regiment from the southeast, drove the grenadiers of Infantry Regiment 320 from it and reached the line: southeastern outskirts of Maslova Pristan' and Priiutovka. Accordingly, the 73rd Guards Rifle Division and the 213th Rifle division were advancing at approximately the same pace as their neighbor on the main axis of attack – 2.5 kilometers over 3.5 hours.

Thus, although all three of Shumilov's corps were continuing to make progress, over 3.5 hours they'd been unable to achieve any substantial success. The enemy's defenses had been ruptured in three locations to a depth of 1.5 to 2.5 kilometers. The 270th Rifle Division made the deepest penetration, since its units exploited the decisive actions of Taranov's tank brigade, but the 111th Rifle Division was unable to help and made no significant advance. There were two primary reasons for this: first, the strong anti-tank defenses at the "Poliana" State Farm and on Hill 207.0 (which now consisted of assault guns as well), which had been left virtually untouched during the 40-minute artillery preparation; second, at the start of the attack the tanks didn't have enough escorting artillery fire, and as a result, the actions of the tank crews and infantry were indecisive. Skipping somewhat ahead in the events I'll note that the Soviet troops here in fact never reached the further line, achieved by other Soviet forces by 1400, and on the left flank of the 25th Guards Rifle Corps, the enemy even managed to push back the 15th Guards Rifle Division and recapture lost ground.

Nevertheless, both M.S. Shumilov and the Front's deputy commander General of the Army I.P. Apanasenko, who was located at Shumilov's command post, believed that matters were going pretty well. At 1430 the General of the Army sent a message to N.F. Vatutin through the signals hub of the 7th Guards Army, in which he stated:

1. The offensive of the 7th Guards Army that started at 1000 is flowing smoothly, as Shumilov has been reporting to you.
2. Our air force started combat work at 1230. Cooperation is good. At 1430 they are attacking: Maslova Pristan', Krutoi Log and Nizhnii Ol'shanets, where the enemy supply trains are heading. I'm driving out to Maslova Pristan'. When I return, I'll report.[35]

The generals' logic was understandable. The army was not operating on its own, but within the framework of the Front's general plan. Its main task was to tie the enemy down with fighting and not allow the Germans to maneuver with forces and means. If their troops, albeit slowly, were making progress, then the enemy wouldn't risk removing units from this sector and using them to reinforce other areas, and first of all, the Prokhorovka direction. It was this that N.F. Vatutin had achieved by organizing a "pinning" counterattack against the right flank of Army Detachment Kempf. Indeed, this calculation in general was proper, but the Soviet side underestimated the enemy's possibilities. The Russians' strong pressure across the entire front had alarmed E. Raus, but Seidemann kept his promise. Already at 1340, several dozen bombers from the VIII Fliegerkorps, in rotation, struck the assault wedge of the 49th Rifle Corps. At 1455 (Moscow time), Raus reported to H. Speidel:

---

34 TsAMO RF, f. 72 gv. sd, op. 1, d. 60, l. 14, 14 obr.
35 TsAMO RF, f. 7 gv. A, op. 5312, d. 294, l. 102.

The situation has eased somewhat. All attacks have been repulsed in the sector of the 320th Infantry Division. 106th Infantry Division: "Poliana" State Farm is in our hands, as well as the recently-acquired forward edge of defense in front of the division's center and the Batritskaia Dacha State Farm. A counterattack is underway against the enemy that has broken through to the Solov'ev collective farm. So far 15-17 tanks have been knocked out. I believe that there is no longer a need to hold the 7th Panzer Division at the ready.[36]

Analyzing the situation, the 49th Rifle Corps commander General G.N. Teret'ev came to the conclusion that a "a continuation of the offensive made no sense and that it was necessary to regroup the forces and conduct a new attacking maneuver."[37] Afterward he issued a number of directives to the subordinate commanders of his divisions. On the basis of them, the commander of the 111th Rifle Division signed Combat Order No.003 at 1600, in which he assigned the following tasks to his units:

1. The enemy opposite the division's front is offering stubborn resistance, especially keeping hold of the woods west of the "Poliana" State Farm.
2. I've decided: Carry out the given task to envelop the woods from the north and south and take them.
3. The commander of the 399th Rifle Regiment at 1700 on 12.07.43, being covered on the left, is to attack with the entire regiment toward the nameless hill north of the Machine Tractor Station via the ravine leading toward Krutoi Log.
4. The commander of the 532nd Rifle Regiment at 1700 on 12.07.43 with a decisive attack from the flanks is to take the "Poliana" State Farm, and subsequently the western fringe of the woods and Point 167.7.
5. The commander of the 468th Rifle Regiment together with the 27th Guards Tank Brigade at 1700 on 12.07.43 is to take Hill 207.9 with a decisive attack and in the future is to attack along the southern slopes of Hill 207.9 and to reach Hill 156.2.[38]

However, the regrouping of the forces without additional fire support didn't yield the desired results. Indeed, how could it have otherwise? Colonel M.A. Bushin was planning to capture the "Poliana" State Farm, which was a well-fortified knot of resistance, with the forces of just one regiment, and yet prior to this the State Farm had been attacked for several days by the units of two rifle divisions and the 201st Separate Tank Brigade, supported by the 1529th Self-propelled Artillery Regiment.

The commander of the 270th Rifle Division also received an order to change the initial plan of actions. All of the attempts to drive the Germans off of Hills 176.0 and 191.2, which were located on the flanks, had proved fruitless. The latest attack by the 973rd Rifle Regiment, reinforced with elements of the 975th Rifle Regiment, just like all the others before it, had been disrupted by intense Nebelwerfer fire coming from this same area. The division commander got in touch with the corps commander and requested assistance in taking the two tactically important hills on the flanks. However, Major General Terent'ev could offer him no assurance: Bushin had halted the offensive of all his entire division and was organizing a new assault on the "Poliana" State Farm, and the 73rd Guards Rifle Division had virtually made no headway, nor did the corps have any reserves. Having received no support, the division commander Beliaev was forced to halt the fruitless attacks of the 973rd Rifle Regiment toward Hill 191.2, and at 1400 issued a combat directive

---

36 NARA US, t. 312, r. 54, f. 7569659.
37 TsAMO RF, f. 7 gv. A, op. 5312, d. 539, l. 121.
38 TsAMO RF, f. 111 sd, op. 1, d. 15, l. 24.

to the commander of the 975th Rifle Regiment to screen his left flank from a possible counterattack out of the woods west of the Gremiachii Machine Tractor Station, and with his main forces take Hill 176.0 (the eastern outskirts of Krutoi Log), after which he was to set up a blocking force on the regiment's left flank and cooperate with the 973rd Rifle Regiment in capturing Hill 191.2 with an attack to the north.

At this time, a message arrived, stating that German tanks were counterattacking the neighbor on the left (the 111th Rifle Division) in the area of Gremiachii. Thus, the division commander was to set up an anti-tank barrier in the depth of his division's combat formations, in the event that the enemy turned his armor along the road running to Korenskaia Dacha from Gremiachii. The division headquarters "at 1430 has issued Order No. 024: the commander of the 132nd Separate Anti-tank Rifle Battalion is to become subordinate to the chief of the anti-tank reserve – the commander of the 321st Separate Destroyer Anti-tank Artillery Battalion and is to take up a defense from Point 'K' to the western outskirts of Korenskaia Dacha."[39] A half-hour later, at 1500, I.P. Beliaev issued another order in order to screen the division's right flank against a possible attack from out of the woods 2 kilometers east of Krutoi Log: "By 1600 1/975th Rifle Regiment (the division's reserve) is transferred to the separate patches of woods northwest and northeast of Hill 209.6, where it is to take up a defense."[40]

Now let's return to the events in the sector of the 270th Rifle Division. Around 1400, the progress made by its regiments had been stopped by intense airstrikes. Then the unit commanders began to prepare for a fresh attack in accordance with the received orders. At this time the forward battalions were exchanging fire on the achieved lines, and at 1500 a new assault began on Hills 176.0 and 191.2. In the course of the attack toward the latter hill, the infantry was being supported by the 295th Tank Battalion, which had 10 serviceable tanks (5 Mk. II, 4 Mk. III and one T-34).[41] Taking advantage of the folds in the ground, the crews of the Matilda and Valentine tanks with a decisive attack at great speed broke through the line of the 106th Infantry Division's Grenadier Regiment 239, and bypassing the hill, penetrated into the depth of Forst's division (to the northeastern outskirts of Krutoi Log). An hour later, by 1600, Major Semenov's tank battalion, having made a penetration of 4.5 kilometers, reached the valley northeast of the village, but in the process lost contact with the brigade and became deprived of the support from the infantry of the 270th Rifle Division, which means essentially it had fallen into encirclement, so this charge ended in tragedy. Already during the breakthrough, the Germans unleashed concentrated fire from Flak artillery at this cluster of combat machines. A participant in this action, V.P. Chibisov, recalled:

> All the tanks made a dash like restive horses, their engines howling. … Having broken out into an open clearing, I thought that it here was likely the reason, more than any other, that our battalion had been launched toward the hamlet of Krutoi Log – a fortified area of the Nazis. However, lacking reconnaissance information, we were rolling almost half-blind into targeted, pre-registered German fire. Our smoking tanks were already visible here and there in a different sector.
>
> About a half-kilometer in the distance ahead of us and a bit to the left ran a level embankment of either a railroad or a wagon road [the Krutoi Log – Generalovka road], which disappeared on the right into a little patch of woods on a hillock with dense brush fronting it. Most likely, it was most likely here the German camouflaged guns were firing, since in front

---

39 TsAMO RF, f. 270 sd, op. 1, d. 1, l. 14.
40 Ibid.
41 TsAMO RF, f. 3256, op. 1, d. 6, l. 182.

of them opened the valley through which our tanks were penetrating. Several more of our knocked-out tanks were visible in front of the embankment.

About 100 meters or less to the left of our tank, a Matilda appeared out of some bushes, jouncing along on the dips and bumps like a steel automaton, moving directly toward the side of our tank. Doubtlessly, the driver of this tank, and likely the rest of the crew had been killed, but the engine continued to work, and the machine was rolling along unguided, its cannon lodged at a setting of maximum elevation, until it either bottomed out in a trench or toppled into a crater. Now only a dozen meters or so remained before it hit us, but my driver still hadn't seen the approaching danger. Hoping that my voice would rise above the howl of the engines and thunder of the guns, I began to shout at him: "A tank from the left! Gerasimov! A tank from the left … from the left!"

The gunner, hearing my shouts, thought this was a German tank and instantly began to pivot the gun in order to fire at the Germans. … Without tearing myself away from the periscope, I managed to shout now at Gavrilov: "It is one of ours!" The gunner realized that he was about to set one of our tanks ablaze. … My tank smoothly came to a stop and began to pivot to the right – probably Gerasimov had by now noticed the looming collision, but it was already too late to avoid it, and now it might only be possible to avoid being overturned by it. Fortunately, we received a glancing blow against the front left corner of our hull, without damaging our idler sprocket. I never in fact found out who these dead tankers were – comrades in arms, who had taken on a share of the general brunt of the combat for the village.

Now my tank was moving significantly to the right of the embankment. Two Valentines were rolling approximately 70-100 meters to the left of us. Then suddenly there was a blow against our tank, which seemingly jolted it backwards; a dull red flame erupted in the turret, and there was an acrid, bitter smell in the nose … The radio operator Kolia Kubarev suddenly slumped in his seat, doubled over, and it felt like a club had struck me in the right elbow. In the following seconds there was another blow against the tank, the turret became filled with fire and acrid smoke, the cannon gave a sharp jerk, and the gunner Sergeant Gavrilov collapsed. The rumbling of the engine stopped suddenly, and in the ensuing silence a thought flashed through my mind – the next shell would be for me, and it would come at any second! I literally swam through the stinking smoke, but managed to give a jerk to the lock release on the hatch, gave it a push with my cracked skull and tumbled out of the hatch.

I came to on the ground next to the tank's mangled right side. In the silence I could hear bullets whistling past the tank. Blood was flowing from my head, covering my eyes and the entire right side of my face; the flesh had been torn away from my right palm, and my ring finger was broken. Glancing at my damaged hand, with sadness I was thinking that I would never again play the accordion, and it never came to my cracked head that cold lead and steel were still whistling all around, and that somehow I'd still have to make my way out of the depth of the German fortified area.

I glanced at my tank: the track was broken in several places, the bogie wheels were damaged, the armored side skirt was mangled, and there were six through and through shell penetrations in the tank. It seemed that the Nazis were firing from Flak cannons aimed horizontally from accurately registered positions, and that is likely why the hits had followed almost one after the other in a matter of seconds. However, these considerations came to my head only several days later.[42]

---

42 Chibisov, *Angliiskie tanki u Krutogo Loga*, pp. 115-120.

At 1608 a German observer, seated in a reconnaissance aircraft located above the battlefield, sent the message: "I see 7 burning tanks in Krutoi Log."[43] These were the tanks of the 201st Separate Tank Brigade.

This breakthrough by the combat machines of the 295th Tank Battalion to the area of Krutoi Log was akin to the charge made by the 15 T-34s of the 1st Company of Major Ivanov's 32nd Tank Battalion of the 29th Tank Corps to the Komsomolets State Farm in the course of the famous clash at Prokhorovka between Rotmistrov's tank army and Hausser's SS corps, which happened on the same day. This is due not only to the fact that they made deeper penetrations in the adversary's defense than other units in their armies, but also, unfortunately, by the tragic fate of the participants. Of the 49 crew members (14 officers and 35 sergeants and privates) in the 10 T-34, Mk. II and Mk. III tanks, not one of them returned to the brigade. The Germans took prisoner some of the wounded tankers, but the majority of them died in their tanks, while the machines were left burned out. On this same day, the headquarters of the 201st Separate Tank Brigade reported, "A reconnaissance patrol was sent in search of the heroic crews of the 295th Tank Battalion with the task to determine their location and establish contact with them; all attempts by the patrol to find and make contact with the 295th Tank Battalion were unsuccessful."[44] Only on 22 July 1943 at 1900 did the next group of scouts, which had returned from the area of Hill 191.2, report that "8 tanks of the 295th Tank Battalion were spotted, 7 of which were burned-out and 1 knocked-out; on one of the machines, the radio and machine gun had been removed, and three charred corpses were found."[45] Although this was the bulk of Major Semenov's group, it was still only part of it (1 T-34, 7 Matildas and Valentines). The crews of the remaining two machines, attempting to bypass the positions of the enemy 88-mm batteries, began to withdraw to the woods northwest of the village, but they were also destroyed on its western fringe. On 23 July these two machines were found by a reconnaissance group of the 201st Separate Tank Brigade headed by Lieutenant Shcherbakov. There were no crew members in them; one tank was evacuated by a repair team and subsequently restored to service.

The penetration made by the group of tanks of Taranov's tank brigade to the area of the hamlet of Krutoi Log had no effect on the operational situation in the sector of the 270th Rifle Division. Its infantry had been cut off by intense fire and continued to engage in fighting for Hills 176.0 and 191.2 until late in the evening. Before twilight, as a result of the latest counterattack, Beliaev's division managed to take only the latter hill. By 2100 his regiments reached the following line:

> 973rd Rifle Regiment is on Hill 191.2, with its right flank screened by the division's penal company from the direction of the woods lying 1.5 kilometers northeast of Krutoi Log; 975th Rifle Regiment – on the southwestern slopes of a nameless hill, 1.5 kilometers southeast of Hill 191.2; 977th Rifle Regiment – on the knoll, 1 kilometer northeast of Hill 176.0, covering its left flank with one rifle battalion in the direction of the triangular woods, where in fact they've dug in.[46]

Until the end of the day, a certain success accompanied only the 468th Rifle Regiment; relying on the tanks of the 27th Guards Tank Brigade, it managed to advance approximately another 400 meters, having driven the Germans out of a small patch of woods 700 meters south of the "Poliana" State Farm. M.S. Shumilov recalled:

---

43 NARA US, t. 312, r. 54, f. 7569660.
44 TsAMO RF, f. 3256, op. 1, d. 7, l. 49, 49 obr.
45 TsAMO RF, f. 3256, op. 1, d. 7, l. 55 obr.
46 TsAMO RF, f. 270 sd, op. 1, d. 1, l. 15.

It must be said that the soldiers and commanders on this day fought heroically. During the attack against the woods south of the "Poliana" State Farm, a tank platoon of 2/27th Guards Tank Brigade under the command of Senior Lieutenant I.A. Konorev against heavy Nazi fire swiftly broke into their positions. When two of our tanks were knocked out, the officer and Communist Konorev was left alone to face the adversary. However, he kept his cool and having joined unequal combat with five self-propelled guns, he knocked out three of them, and the other two took to flight. Pursuing them, Konorev's tank struck a mine, as a result of which the engine stopped working. Even in these circumstances the commander didn't abandon his machine. Being wounded, he continued to fire at the enemy. The ammunition on board was running low. Making sure each remaining shell counted, Konorev was selecting the most important targets and firing at them. Then the fascists rolled out an anti-tank gun in order to fire over open sights. The hero was killed, but didn't surrender to the foe. The Motherland highly noted the tanker's exploit; Senior Lieutenant I.A. Konorev was posthumously awarded the title "Hero of the Soviet Union."[47]

Although Nevzhinsky's 27th Guards Tank Brigade, continuing the attack, advanced another 2 kilometers beyond this patch of woods and even broke through to the western slopes of Hill 207.0, because of the intense fire of enemy anti-tank guns and assault guns, as well as the absence of support on the part of the infantry, it was forced to retreat. All the remaining units of the 111th Rifle Division virtually made no headway at all. The 27th Guards Tank Brigade's journal of combat operations described the conclusion of the fighting on 12 July and its results in the following way:

> Up until 1700 the brigade's combat machines, maneuvering on the battlefield, exchanged fire with enemy firing positions and infantry. By 1710 the tanks under the effect of the intense anti-tank artillery fire fell back to their infantry and continued to fire from fixed positions at revealed enemy firing positions.
> At 1715 the tanks together with the infantry [the 111th Rifle Division] launched a second attack. The enemy offered stubborn resistance with fire, but by 1830 the tanks reached the western slopes of Hill 207.0, where they met strong enemy anti-tank artillery fire, and also broke through to an area of minefields, where they engaged in combat until the onset of darkness and the approach of their infantry. With the arrival of darkness, the brigade's combat machines marched to an assembly point in the vicinity of Hill 202.9 for topping up with fuel and lubricants and for replenishing ammunition. Over the day of combat, the following damage was inflicted on the enemy: Destroyed – 45 anti-tank guns and pieces of field artillery, 3 self-propelled guns, 25 mortars, 2 soft vehicles, 1 command post and 735 soldiers and officers; in addition, with the fire of the anti-tank gun battery and mortars of the motorized rifle battalion, up to a company of enemy infantry was scattered and partially destroyed.
> Over the day of combat the brigade has losses:
> a) In materiel – 4 T-34 burned out, 15 T-34 knocked out by enemy artillery fire, 3 T-34 disabled by mines;
> b) In men – 4 mid-level commanders and 8 junior commanders killed; 4 mid-level commanders, 12 junior commanders and 4 enlisted men wounded.[48]

---

47 *Ognennaia duga: Belgorod-Kursk – Orel* [*Bulge of fire: Belgorod, Kursk and Orel*] (Moscow: "Zvonnitsa-MG", 2003), pp. 288-289.
48 TsAMO RF, f. 3108, op. 1, d. 14, l. 16, 17.

The disabling of the tanks occurred already in the course of the attack, which started at 1715. Several T-34s on the move stumbled upon an undetected minefield east of Hill 207.0. It in fact was the primary obstacle in the brigade's path, because it immediately slowed the pace of its battalions' advance. In addition, in the divisions' Operational Summary No. 61 at 2200 on 12.07.43 it is indicated that during the day's combat, 2 tanks broke down with mechanical problems.[49] Thus, over the course of this day, the 27th Guards Tank Brigade lost a total of 24 combat machines or 48% of its available tanks.

Throughout the entire day of the combat, Colonel M.V. Nevzhinsky personally led the formation. According to his nature the brigade commander was a cautious man, and immediately after receiving the order he didn't rush at full tilt to carry it out. In the complex situation he tried to act sensibly, as require by the book and manuals, while relying on his own combat experience. It was just this trait that superior commanders frequently didn't like. For example, during the Battle of Stalingrad his brigade (at the time, the 121st Tank Brigade) was subordinate to General I.M. Chistiakov's 21st Army. Just as soon as it arrived in the army's sector, the army commander immediately ordered it to launch an attack. The brigade commander's request to be given time to conduct elementary engineer analysis of the terrain was regarded by the army commander as indecisiveness and he temporarily removed N.V. Nevzhinsky from command of the brigade. Without revealing the brigade commander's identity, I.M. Chistiakov talked about this case in his memoirs. It is hard to judge who was right without knowing the details of that unpleasant episode, although it is hard to call a request to familiarize oneself with the terrain a personal whim. At the same time, when analyzing the actions of the 27th Guards Tank Brigade in the course of the defensive phase of the Battle of Kursk one can say that Nevzhinsky gave thought to the planning of the combat, seeking to avoid expending men and materiel in vain. Therefore with a great deal of confidence it is possible to assume that the loss of almost half of the brigade's tanks on 12 July 1943 was a consequence primarily of the persistent demands of Nevzhinsky's superiors to increase the pressure on the foe without regard for the strength of the enemy's anti-tank defense.

As concerns the enemy losses indicated in the document, here the officers of the 27th Guards Tank Brigade gave free reign to their imagination to the utmost. It is impossible not to note that the subject of enemy losses is a fruitful field for all types of fictions and exaggerations in any army. After all, these figures have no effect on the practical work of the troops, and it was difficult to check their accuracy. Mainly, however, if they proved to be large (even on paper), then unquestionably they gave the command of a combat formation both weight and respect. The Wehrmacht officers were also guilty of exaggeration, but not on the same scale as a significant portion of the Soviet commanders. Even so, in our headquarters there were their own, unwritten rules: in operational documents – be circumspect (lie to the extent necessary, considering the situation), but in accounts – lie to your heart's desire.

So that the reader can picture the difference in these approaches, I will cite the numbers that the commanders of the 27th Guards Tank Brigade reported on German losses on 12 July 1943 in Operational Summary No.22 (for comparison, in the parentheses are the numbers from the account document – the journal of combat operations): Destroyed: guns – 19 (45); self-propelled guns – 2 (3); mortars – 9 (25); soft vehicles – 2 (2); soldiers and officers – 440 (735); command posts – 1 (none). As we see, exaggeration was no sin in the account, and the operational summary granted the possibility that the figure of enemy losses would increase; its Point 4 indicates: "Losses inflicted on the enemy are being confirmed." It would be interesting to know how the brigade's headquarters was confirming these losses. After all, the battalions reported straightaway what was visible on the battlefield (corpses, knocked out tanks), and after 2200 they made no advance. To

---

49 TsAMO RF, f. 3108, op. 1, d. 10, l. 66.

send out reconnaissance patrols in order to confirm enemy losses in the enemy rear is an absurdity; such wasn't practiced in the troops. I doubt the enemy shared the number of their losses with the brigade's command.

The units of the 73rd Guards Rifle Division over 10-12 hours made an advance from their jumping-off positions of 400 meters to 1.4 kilometers. The left-flank 209th Guards Rifle Regiment commanded by Major G.P. Slatov made the deepest penetration into the enemy's defenses. His battalions, having crossed the road running between the "Batratskaia Dacha" State Farm and the Gremiachii Machine Tractor Station, burst into the patch of woods 2 kilometers northeast of Krutoi Log, and having met bitter resistance, spent the rest of the day engaged in heavy combat here. Here's how the results of the division's counterattack are described in its combat journal:

> The 214th Guards Rifle Regiment, having advanced up to 400 meters, ran into strong artillery and mortar blocking fire and was forced to dig in along the attained line.
>
> The 209th Guards Rifle Regiment by 1200 took the nameless wooded hill 800 meters northwest of Hill 209.6. The 2nd Rifle Battalion by 1400 drove the enemy out of the southern corner of the woods lying 2 kilometers northeast of Krutoi Log. At 1700 the enemy counterattacked 2/209th Guards Rifle Regiment with eight tanks and up to a company of infantry. The battalion, having an exposed left flank, took heavy losses from enemy fire and was forced to retreat to the southeastern spur of these same woods.
>
> The 2nd and 3rd Battalions of the 211th Guards Rifle Regiment, attacking from behind the right flank of the 209th Guards Rifle Regiment, by 1700 reached a line 400 meters east of the woods and Point 199.1. Having met intense fire resistance – exclusively from six-barreled rocket launchers and heavy projectile apparatuses of the type "D" [likely, the report speaks here about the same *Nebelwerfers* but of a larger caliber – 210mm], the battalions took up a defense 200 meters west of the "Batratskaia Dacha" – Machine Tractor Station road. The 1st Rifle Battalion continued to defend the Machine Tractor Station, and in the course of the day repulsed two enemy counterattacks in strength of up to two infantry companies. The division's losses amounted to 800 men killed or wounded.[50]

The 15th Guards Rifle Division was also unable to develop the counterattack. Lieutenant Colonel I.A. Usikov's 44th Guards Rifle Regiment, having taken the "Solov'ev" collective farm at mid-day, continued to engage in heavy fighting there until late in the evening. The headquarters of Korps Raus reported:

> At 1700 [Moscow time]: "At the present time 24-25 enemy tanks have been knocked out across the entire front. The main line of defense, except the 'Solov'ev' collective farm, is in our hands."
>
> At 1845 [Moscow time]: "Stubborn fighting is continuing in the spur of the woods south of the 'Poliana' State Farm with 15 enemy tanks, which undertook a second attack. One battalion of the Grenadier Regiment 585 and StuG Battalion 905 of the 320th Infantry Division are taking part in our counterattack.
>
> Combat is continuing at the 'Solov'ev' collective farm. In total, the enemy in the sector between Priiutovka and the collective farm set up approximately 10 defensive positions [a line of trenches]. A particularly high density of defensive lines is in the area of [the hamlet of] Rzhavets, south of the 'Poliana' State Farm, on Hill 209.6 and on the 'Solov'ev' collective farm."[51]

---

50   TsAMO RF, f. 73 gv. sd, op. 1, d. 33, l. 30.
51   NARA US, t. 312, r. 54, f. 7569660.

Nevertheless, before sunset the Guardsmen were forced to fall back to their previous positions on the line between Hill 202.3 and the "Batratskaia Dacha" State Farm.

According to Operational Summary No. 371 from the headquarters of the 7th Guards Army, all three of its corps, the troops of which took part in the counterattack, by the end of day on 12 July 1943 had dug in on the line: 25th Guards Rifle Corps – northern section of the woods 2 kilometers southeast of Miasoedovo, Point "Sar" (1 kilometer west of the "Batratskaia Dacha" State Farm), 1250 meters east of Point 191.2; 49th Rifle Corps – Hill 191.2 to [excl.] 'Poliana' State Farm; 24th Guards Rifle Corps – northwestern portion of the Shebekinskaia Dacha Woods, southeastern outskirts of Maslova Pristan', [excl.] Priiutovka.[52]

Thus almost the entire territory that Safiulin's and Terent'ev's corps had seized at the outset of the attack by the end of the day had again been left to the enemy. The only exception was the ground that Buslaev's 213th Rifle Division and partially Losev's 72nd Guards Rifle Division had won from Korps Raus. The evening summary from the headquarters of Korps Raus also testifies to this:

> The corps is holding its positions against enemy attacks on its entire front, and there, where the foe has made local penetrations, it was able to restore the main line of combat with counterattacks.
>
> At 0900 the adversary began persistent attacks to the north in the Rzhavets area. The attacks were conducted in separate places with the forces of approximately a battalion with the support of numerous tanks. By the present time, 28 tanks have been destroyed and approximately 80 prisoners have been taken.
>
> Tomorrow, a repeat of the attacks should be expected on the entire front. In the 320th Infantry Division's sector, at 0900 the enemy attacked both sides of Rzhavets through unoccupied terrain to the east, in the direction of Maslova Pristan'. The attack was timely spotted and stopped by concentrated artillery fire. To the north the adversary, with the armor support, attacked Grenadier Regiment 586. After the destruction of 2 tanks, the Russians fell back to their jumping-off positions.
>
> In the sector of the 106th Infantry Division, the enemy attacked out of the woods northwest of Point 202.9 against the spur of the woods south of the "Poliana" State Farm in strength of one battalion with the support of tanks. The attack was repulsed, and individual tanks were knocked out. A lot of tanks broke through in the division's center [the main line of resistance south of the positions of Grenadier Regiment 248], followed by a small amount of infantry [the 201st Tank Brigade's 296th Tank Battalion and the 270th Rifle Division]. Some of the combat machines were able to break through to Krutoi Log, but were destroyed. Meanwhile the accompanying infantry became pinned down under the fire from our main line of defense.
>
> The enemy, having launched an attack in the afternoon hours with the support of 15 tanks toward the spur of the woods south of the "Poliana" State Farm, reached the eastern fringe of the woods. In order to liquidate the breakthrough, a counterattack began with a battalion from the corps reserve and StuG Battalion 905.
>
> An attack of the Russians toward the "Batratskaia Dacha" State Farm and to the south toward the boundary line between the 106th and 198th Infantry Divisions, which started simultaneously, was stopped in front of the main line of resistance despite the strong support of artillery, mortars and rocket salvoes. To the north the adversary managed to take the

---

52 TsAMO RF, f. 7 gv. A, op. 5312, d. 239, l. 191, 192.

"Solov'ev" collective farm. The breakthrough was stopped, and the old main combat line was restored with a counterattack in the afternoon hours.[53]

What, according to the opinion of the 7th Guards Army's Military Council, were the main reasons for the fact that the actions of its troops on 12 July, as "diplomatically" expressed in the materials of the 25th Guards Rifle Corps' headquarters, "didn't have adequate success"? Unfortunately, documents haven't been found in the files of the TsAMO RF in which the army command staff analyzed in detail the failure of the fighting on this day. Only the account of the 25th Guards Rifle Corps for the period of combat operations between 11 and 27 July 1943 has been discovered, in which its chief of staff briefly touched upon just one problem – the poor organization of coordination between the rifle and artillery units. Colonel A.A. Funtikov wrote:

> In the period of preparation for the offensive, the divisional artillery was situated along the roads, fire breaks and eastern fringe of the woods west of Borovskoe, Nikol'skoe and Kashlakovo. A portion of it was located directly in the combat formations of the infantry. The artillery observation posts were located in the woods, which made observation difficult, and the artillery was unable to affect the enemy in full measure. The infantry frequently didn't inform the artillery crews about their progress or else gave them incorrect information. For example, they indicated one or another line that was supposedly already occupied by our infantry at a time when our infantry still hadn't reached it. Despite the fact that artillery commanders were located at the infantry's command posts, these manifestations were observed because the information that flowed up the chain of command suffered from inaccuracy. Cooperation signals were absent, and if there were any, they weren't used; there were no rockets [likely, for signal flare pistols]. Repeatedly the artillery chiefs had to drive in person to the front line in order to ascertain it. One can cite the following fact as an example of the inadequate communication between the infantry and artillery. During the offensive of our units toward the patch of woods at Point 200.0 [northwest of Belovskaia], the artillery crews received word about an aggregation of infantry in these woods. When attempting to clarify this question, no one was able to say whether the concentration of infantry was ours or the enemy's. When it became clear that retreating enemy infantry was collecting in these woods and our artillery opened fire, it turned out that the woods were empty – the enemy had been given time to retreat further.[54]

If to judge from one more document, Combat Order No. 0046/op, which was signed by G.B. Safiulin already at 0600 on 13 July, this problem stood very acutely in front of his troops during the fighting on 12 July. This document notes that the artillery in the dynamic flow of the fighting lagged behind the infantry and gave it weak support; the corps commander assessed this problem alongside the poorly arranged cooperation between the commanders of the rifle and artillery units as "a major shortcoming". He demanded during attacks to have artillery observers in the infantry's combat formations, in order to suppress enemy resistance quickly with artillery fire, and to conduct the artillery's change of position during a battle in such a way, so that 1/3 of it continued to escort the infantry "with fire and wheels". In addition, the corps commander paid particular attention to the poor consolidation of the occupied ground, and obligated the commanders in the future, when resolving these tasks, to organize anti-personnel and anti-tank fire quickly, while

---

53   NARA US, t. 314, r. 197, f. 001340.
54   TsAMO RF, f. 878, op. 1, d. 27, l. 13.

combining it with artificial obstacles.[55] Unquestionably, for professionals all of these, in general, are fundamental maxims, but unfortunately, very often in the Red Army they were recalled only when analyzing failures.

How did the 7th Guards Army's counterattack affect Kempf's plans, and primarily Breith's III Panzer Corps? Let's turn to the daily summary for 12 July of its headquarters:

> 19th Panzer Division: The division at 0845 attacked to the north out of the area that had been seized the night before by the reinforced Panzergrenadier Regiments 73 and 74. The reinforced Panzergrendier Regiment 73, covered on the right by the Panzer Reconnaissance Battalion 19, in the face of weak enemy resistance, after overcoming the numerous minefields at Sabynino, reached Sabynino and Strel'nikov, and at 1515 – Rzhavets [18 kilometers south of Prokhorovka Station], where it established contact with units of the 6th Panzer Division. Panzergrenadier Regiment 74, after mopping up the woods southeast of Sabynino, attacked to the east and followed behind the left-hand group. Panzergrenadier Regiment 73 and I/Panzergrenadier Regiment 74 at this time moved into the bridgehead and expanded it. Early in the morning and at mid-day, there were repeated attacks on our batteries by enemy ground attack aircraft. The activity of our own fighters and reconnaissance aircraft is weak. Nebelwerfer Regiment 52 was subordinated to the division.
>
> 6th Panzer Division: The division's forces throughout the day were assembling in the Kazach'e – Kurakovka area. As a consequence of the delay in the arrival of units of the 7th Panzer Division, which had been designated to replace the panzer reconnaissance battalion in the area east of Shliakhovoe, their departure was delayed. Panzer Reconnaissance Battalion 6, which had been moved up to screen the left flank, discovered that the ground that had been cleared of the enemy that morning along the line between Novo-Aleksandrovskii Vyselok and Aleksandrovka had been re-occupied by the enemy. Reinforcements, including 25 tanks, were constantly moving up to it. In order to exclude the danger of a flank attack, panzers, assault guns and the unengaged elements of Panzer Reconnaissance Battalion 6 were attached to *Kampfgruppe* Unrein, which was assembled in the Kazach'e – Kurakovka area. It received an order to attack the enemy holding Novo-Aleksandrovskii Vyselok and Aleksandrovka and take this ground. Combat is still underway. The command post – sector of woods 1 kilometer west of Kazach'e.
>
> With the arrival of the 19th Panzer Division's units in the bridgehead and the freeing up of its own forces, it has been decided to create a bridgehead on the Northern Donets northwest of Vypolzovka. Aerial activity with bombers and strafing is moderate.
>
> 2) The corps' forward line: Kazach'e – Kurakovka – Vypolzovka – south of Ryndinka. Command post is in Novo-Oskochnoe.
> 3) Again subordinate: Headquarters and II/Nebelwerfer Regiment 54, II/Artillery Regiment 62, Light Flak Artillery Battalion 91 and the *Abwehr* [Intelligence] unit 204.
>
> 168th Infantry Division: The attack started by Grenadier Regiment 417 on 11.7 toward the thickets of brush was continued in the early morning hours. In separate places of the thickets, strong enemy resistance was broken in close combat. After reaching the northern edge, a battalion launched an attack to the northeast against the woods 2 kilometers southeast of Gostishchevo and seized hostile field positions and bunkers that were located in front of the

---

55 TsAMO RF, f. 878, op. 1, d. 33, l. 31.

forest edge [the defenses of the 89th Guards Rifle Division]. Enemy units fled in disorder from the northern edge of the woods toward Gostishchevo. In the course of rapid pursuit of the enemy, Gostishchevo was taken. During our attack into the bushy woods [the area of Hill 223.3], the enemy lost 200 prisoners and a lot of dead, the number of which hasn't been determined.

Sectors of the woods east, west and northwest of Znamenka were mopped up by Reconnaissance Battalion 248; in places it met bitter resistance. A lot of prisoners were taken.

Current measures: Replacement of Grenadier Regiment 442 in the Komintern – Kazach'e sector. Movement of the bulk of Grenadier Regiment 417 from the western bank of the Northern Donets in order to occupy the eastern bank in the Krivtsovo – Sabynino – Kiselovo sector. Replacement of Grenadier Regiment 429 in the Verkhnii Ol'shanets area and to the southwest of there; it has been planned to use it further on the left flank of Grenadier Regiment 442 on both sides of Aleksandrovka.

Prisoners: More than 400.

Situation with anti-tank guns: 6 assault guns are ready for use.

7th Panzer Division: The division by mid-day was replaced by units of the 198th Infantry Division. The bulk of the division is moving through Melikhovo toward Kazach'e; a regimental group, a company of medium panzers and a battalion of artillery are being held at the disposal of the corps in the Iastrebovo area. I/Nebelwerfer Regiment 54 is subordinate to the division.[56]

Accordingly, if one discounts Funck's setting aside of one regimental *kampfgruppe* and a panzer company in Iastrebovo as a form of insurance, and the delay of his units that had been planned to replace Panzer Reconnaissance Battalion 6, there were no other changes in the plans of III Panzer Corps on this day. On the contrary, two of Breith's divisions continued to make progress: the 19th Panzer Division along the left bank of the Northern Donets, while 168th Infantry Division on the right bank shoved back Kriuchenkin's units and took the three large villages of Gostishchevo, Sabynino and Krivtsovo. In addition, Schmidt's panzer division closed flanks with the 6th Panzer Division and began to take over its bridgehead on the right bank of the Donets in the Rzhavets area. Thus, active preparation for a further offensive toward Prokhorovka from the south, in the Rzhavets – Vypolzovka sector, was going on in von Hünersdorff's 6th Panzer Division without any particular interruptions. Kempf's order for 13 July testifies to his intention to launch his attack on that day:

13 July 1943 … Korps Raus: screen the eastern flank.

III Panzer Corps: With its main forces launches an attack with the objective of destroying the enemy opposing the SS Panzer Corps at the bend in the road south of Prokhorovka, and throws the enemy tank forces back beyond the Northern Donets to the north and northwest on the both sides of Rzhavets. One panzer division screens this operation along the eastern bank of the Northern Donets; it also has the task to capture a bridge across the Razumnaia River in the Komintern area. The 168th Infantry Division must make the withdrawal of enemy forces across the Northern Donets impossible.[57]

---

56 NARA US, rg. 242, t. 314, r. 197, f. 001392, 001393.
57 NARA US, t. 312, r. 54, f. 7569661.

Thus, the "pinning" counterstroke by Shumilov's 7th Guards Army had no substantial effect on the plans of III Panzer Corps to link up with the II SS Panzer Corps at Prokhorovka. If one looks at the modest means of fire, primarily howitzer artillery and tanks, that were assigned to conduct it, then there was nothing surprising about this.

However, besides a direct effect, the 7th Guards Army's counterattack did have an indirect influence on the events in this area, which should also receive mention. In the first place this concerns Korps Raus. Despite the fact that its troops had retained full possession of their line, their combat effectiveness had significantly declined. Around 1900 (Moscow time) the following discussion took place in the headquarters of Army Detachment Kempf: "General Raus, having concluded the conversations with the divisions, announced that as a result of the heavy losses in personnel, both divisions have insufficient strength for such an extended front. As a result of the Russian attacks today, the situation has deteriorated to the extent that the enemy will have no problem breaking through the attenuated front and it will be impossible for us to throw him back."[58]

Considering that Raus wasn't distinguished by modesty and often "muddied the waters", I will emphasize that this statement was not an exaggeration. I will remind the reader that his corps was located on the right flank of the overall attack by von Manstein's grouping, while the left flank was being held by General E. Ott's LII Army Corps of the Fourth Panzer Army, the situation of which was also extremely difficult. It had already committed its last infantry reserve into the fighting – the 198th Infantry Division, which the command of Army Group South had obtained prior to Operation Citadel. Therefore I believe that the difficult situation on the flanks of the breakthrough which had arisen by the start of the counterattack and had become extremely acute after the fighting on 12 July 1943 played a significant role in Hitler's decision to curtail Operation Citadel, about which von Manstein would find out already on the following day.

Incidentally, the Field Marshal highly regarded the tenacity of Army Detachment Kempf when repulsing the 7th Guards Army's counterattack. Having arrived from Hoth's headquarters at the command post of Army Detachment Kempf around 1900 and having familiarized himself with the operational situation, he ordered Speidel to express his personal gratitude to Raus's troops.[59] Only Hausser's SS Panzer Corps also earned such a high esteem by the Army Group South Commander-in-Chief on this day. It one considers the formations and strength that the Soviet command hurled against them on this day, von Manstein's words are not a common formality, but sincere admiration at their combat skill.

In this connection, the data on the losses of both sides on 12 July 1943 are of special interest. So far, the total number of casualties of the troops of the 7th Guards Army that took part in the counterattack hasn't been established. In the revealed combat documents of the divisions, casualty figures differ. For example, according to Report No. 061/op from the commander of the 25th Guards Rifle Corps at 1800 on 13 July, 15 men were killed and 125 wounded in the 15th Guards Rifle Division.[60] However, the 7th Guards Army's Operational Summary No. 371 at 0700 on 13 July greatly increases these numbers: 146 killed and 881 wounded.[61] On its part, in the army's documents the losses of the 73rd Guards Rifle Division on the contrary have been plainly understated. For example, at 2400 on 12 July Colonel S.A. Kozak reported that over the day of fighting, he'd lost a total of 840 soldiers and officers killed, wounded or missing-in-action, but on the morning of 13 July the headquarters of the 7th Guards Army reported that this division had lost just a total of 90 men.

---

58 NARA US, t. 312, r. 54, f. 7569660.
59 NARA US, t. 312, r. 54, f. 7569661.
60 TsAMO RF, f. 25 gv. sk, op. 1, d. 28, l. 63.
61 TsAMO RF, f. 7 gv. A, op. 5312, d. 239, l. 191.

It is possible to understand the situation of the headquarters of the divisions that went on the counterattack; even by midnight, it wasn't simple to ascertain the number of casualties for the entire division. Usually the situation became clear the next morning, and even then, not always. For example, the reconnaissance patrol of the 201st Separate Tank Brigade, which had been sent out to search for the 10 missing crews of Semenov's tank battalion, returned on 13 July without having found them. But what can explain the "play in figures" for divisions that stood on the defense? Thus, in Operational Summary No. 217 of the 36th Guards Rifle Division at 0400 on 13 July, it was reported that the division exchanged fire with the enemy and over the day of 12 July lost a total of 5 servicemen wounded and 1 killed. But the 7th Guards Army's operational summary cited above for the morning of 13 July gives the number of men killed in the division as 4, and the number of wounded as 22.

Unfortunately, there are still no other aggregate data than those found in Operational Summary No. 371, so we will rely on the figures given in it, but keep in mind that they show only an approximate level of the divisions' losses. Thus, in total the 7th Guards Army lost 3,359 soldiers and commanders on 12 July, including 1,121 men (199 killed, 922 wounded) in the divisions of the 25th Guards Rifle Corps; 1,438 men in the 49th Rifle Corps; and 804 men in the 24th Guards Rifle Corps. These figures only lead to bitter thoughts, especially if one compares them to the cited casualty figures of Army Detachment Kempf over this same day of 12 July. According to Western sources, two of its corps lost a total of 674 men, including 116 killed or missing-in-action, and 558 wounded. The total correlation of losses in personnel thus amounts to 5 to 1 in the German favor. Even if we assume that the distortion in the Soviet sources in the direction of exaggeration amounted to 15-20% (missing-in-action; wounded, but evacuated to other units; etc.), then even in this case the numbers are shocking.

Nevertheless, the Voronezh Front command believed that the events of 12 July, even though they didn't achieve the desired results, had a serious effect, including on the stabilization of the situation south of Prokhorovka. Despite the fact that on the following day the troops of the 69th Army would be compelled to abandon a number of defended sectors, there were no large German breakthroughs, as had happened the day before. Indeed, the enemy's activity on 13 July proved relatively small. They believed that the reasons for this were first, the high German casualty rate in the course of combat operations on 12 July, and secondly, the results of the efforts of the 7th Guards Army to divert upon itself the reserves of von Manstein's auxiliary grouping that were operating on the Korocha direction. Thus at a conference, which was conducted in the presence of the Deputy Supreme Commander in Chief Marshal of the Soviet Union G.K. Zhukov, who arrived at the Voronezh Front on the morning of 13 July, regarding the continuation of the counterattack, it was decided that all of the Front's armies, including the 7th Guards Army, were to exert heavy pressure on the enemy to one degree or another.

All of this was happening against the backdrop of increasing Red Army activity beyond the Kursk bulge, and the Allied landing in Sicily. On 13 July 1943 Hitler summoned the commanders-in-chief of Army Group Center and Army Group South to his headquarters, where he announced that the Allies had landed on Sicily on 10 July. Likely, it would be impossible to hold the island, and so there was an urgent need to create a strong grouping in order to guard Italy and the western Balkans. For this purpose, the II SS Panzer Corps was to be transferred from the Eastern Front to Europe. In addition, at this conference the Commander-in-Chief of Army Group Center Field Marshal G. von Klüge reported that he lacked the strength to continue Operation Citadel, because his troops were holding the Orel salient only with great difficulty against a a Russian offensive that had started on 12 July. E. von Manstein's declaration that the Battle of Kursk had entered its culminating stage; that the Russians were running out of mobile reserves; and now it was necessary to lean a little bit more on the enemy in order to achieve a maximal effect, fell on deaf ears.⁶² Hitler ordered to wrap up the operation at Kursk, although he also partially satisfied von Manstein's request, allowing his group, as the Field Marshal supposed, to complete the process of finishing off the troops of the Voronezh Front. However, this supposition was far from reality.

Robert Cross writes:

> Although Zitadelle had not fulfilled OKH's expectations, about which the Führer had always harbored doubts, he nevertheless derived some comfort from the damage it appeared to be inflicting on the Russian reserves. A few days more punishment might ensure that these reserves would be burned away, leaving the Red Army in no shape to mount another winter offensive. This qualified optimism, however, failed to take into the attrition suffered by the Ostheer at Kursk. The oversight was to draw this observation from the OKW war diarist:
>
> > *After the bloody struggle for the city of Stalingrad there followed another struggle for strongly fortified field positions, a second 'Verdun', followed by a third, which was supposed to make the enemy exhaust his 'last forces' at a strategically important point. However, this 'Verdun' swallowed up even more of our divisions in an ever more horrifying whirlpool.*
>
> The fighting continued in the Kursk salient although it was now shifting in favour of the Red Army.⁶³

---

62 Von Manstein, *Uteriannye pobedy* [*Lost victories*] (Smolensk: Rusich, 2003), p. 539.
63 Cross, R., *Operatsiia Tsidadel* [*Operation Citadel*] (Smolensk: Rusich, 2006), p. 251, 253. This is the Russian translation of Cross' book *Citadel: The Battle of Kursk* which was published in 1993 by Sarpedon Publishers.

9

"The operation's failure turned into a tragedy"

That is how General W. Kempf, who led his army detachment in the Wehrmacht's general summer offensive in the area of the Kursk salient, assessed its results. General T. Busse, the chief of staff of Army Group South, seconded his opinion:

> Operation Citadel did not produce the results desired by Hitler. The battle neither denied the Soviets a base of operations around Kursk nor destroyed sizeable enemy forces, nor even eliminated the STAVKA's intention to conduct a major offensive in 1943. The German Army did not achieve freedom of action, could not establish a shorter line designed to conserve its waning strength, and – quite the contrary – the operation exhausted almost all reserves on the Eastern Front.[1]

What in the assessment of the army detachment command fundamentally affected the lack of success of its troops in the course of the large-scale Operation Citadel that had been prepared? In Kempf's opinion, the main reasons for the offensive's failure were:

a. The offensive's repeated postponement, which allowed the Soviet side to build back up its battered divisions and create a powerful system of defense;
b. Berlin's inability to equip its group with forces and means up to the level of the Voronezh Front, which was "able to make gains in strength greatly exceeding our own thanks to … a considerably greater economic war potential."[2]
c. Army Detachment Kempf's acute lack of the latest equipment and weapons, in particular the Panther and Tiger tanks;
d. Army Detachment Kempf's strict adherence to an offensive plan, which didn't take into account improvements in the Soviet defenses in the designated breakthrough sectors in May and June: "Either we should have refrained from attacking at all, or the operation should have been carried out to strike the enemy not at his strongest but at his weakest point – in this case the front sector east of Sumy. Our panzer divisions would have received freedom of maneuver much earlier, unlike the actual battle, in which they were hamstrung in fighting through the Soviet defensive system against a numerically superior enemy."[3]
e. The shortage of infantry forced the panzer divisions to take on unfamiliar roles, such as assaulting fortified points and screening flanks, even before reaching operational space.

---

1   Newton, S., *Kurskaia bitva: Nemetskii vzgliad* [*Kursk: The German View*] (Moscow: Iauza, 2006), p. 42.
2   Ibid., p. 83.
3   Raus,

Kempf wrote: "Our plans also suffered from the diverging commitment of the forces in the attacking armies [which is in fact what N.F. Vatutin planned and achieved]. This led to the breakup of the operation into a series of individual battles and … caused our command to forfeit freedom of action … What was to have been a 'smooth operation' degenerated into a 'slugging match'."[4]

Virtually all of the Wehrmacht generals who participated in the Battle of Kursk, when giving their opinions regarding the failure, even if in only a few lines of text emphasize that the military leadership and the troops weren't responsible for it. Even Kempf didn't refrain from this when he flatly declared: "The failure of the operations is not to be ascribed to the frontline leadership or to the troops", who he believed showed no lack of desire to fight. However, how can then one assert that the operation was "meticulously planned" (who devised it, if not the military men?), while at the same time maintaining that the enemy's possibilities weren't considered, which forced the diverging commitment of the armies, the panzer divisions to carry out unfamiliar tasks, and so on and so forth? Where is the logic here? The answer is obvious; the factors listed by General Kempf undoubtedly brought about the failure of Operation Citadel, but this is only part of the explanation.

The defeated Nazi military chiefs persistently avoid mentioning the main reason. As is known, memoirs are the author's personal view of the historical events. None of the participants in the battle wanted to look like lame ducks. Yet objectively the German side, having put together this "dish", ended up making a hash of things. Despite the Red Army's previous huge losses in personnel, equipment and weapons and the Wehrmacht's capture of an enormous expanse of land, which even in the spring of 1943 had more than 64 million people, including hundreds of thousands of draft-age men, the political leadership of the Soviet Union managed over a short period of time both to restore and greatly augment the combat potential of the *fronts* that were holding the defenses in the area of the Kursk salient. For their part the Soviet military command, despite an active German disinformation campaign, was able to determine the German intentions accurately and to plan a defense in such a way that given any course of events, Army Group South would be unable to reach operational space and implement its far-reaching aims. In contrast, Germany, despite all the propagandistic slogans of the type "total mobilization" or "wonder weapons", which were supposedly ready for Operation Citadel, proved unable to rebuild its troop strength on the Eastern Front after Stalingrad and provide them with the necessary means for such a massive operation.

For Germany, Operation Citadel was an already an impossible undertaking, and it was conducted primarily in order to achieve political, not military goals. Several key men in Hitler's immediate circle in fact didn't hide this.[5] After Germany's defeat in the war, the Third Reich's top brass, however, or at least the majority of it, persistently maintained that back in the spring of 1943 they foresaw the tragedy, but instead of coming together and presenting a unified, professional, informed opinion, they were in fact unable to come to an agreement among themselves whether it was better to launch a summer offensive, or to go over to an active defense. The lack of unity among key figures of the Wehrmacht to a significant extent prompted Hitler to draw the Wehrmacht into this risky venture. Not one of its leaders in their books wanted to take responsibility in front of history and the German people for their participation in making this fatal

---

4 Newton, *Kurskaia bitva: Nemetskii vzgliad*, p. 83.
5 Guderian, H., *Vospominaniia nemetskogo generala: Tankovye voiska Germanii vo Vtoroi mirovoi voine 1939-1945* [*Memoirs of a German general: Germany's panzer forces in the Second World War 1939-1945*] (Moscow: Tsentrpoligraf, 2009), p. 340. This is the Russian translation of Guderian's memoirs, published in English under the title of *Panzer Leader* and reissued by Da Capo Press in 2001.

decision for the German Army, so they emphasized tactical aspects of the fighting, of which there are plenty in any combat operation.

As concerns the drawing up of the offensive plan for the armies and corps, which wasn't the job of politicians, but for the generals, even here no sound reasoning and meticulous detail are visible. It is hard not to agree with S. Newton, who writes:

> The stunning lack of oversight by army group headquarters over the assault plans for 5 July calls many aspects of German tactical and operational planning into question. In the case of XLVIII Panzer Corps, von Manstein and Busse allowed the entire success of the *Schwerpunkt* to depend on the recently arrived, completely inexperienced, and technically unprepared brigade of Panthers. With respect to III Panzer Corps, von Manstein himself had voiced objections to Breith's plan of attack, but he did not insist on its being changed … It is worth reiterating that had XLVIII and III Panzer Corps planned as carefully as Hausser and company [the command of II SS Panzer Corps], then the outcome of Operation Citadel might have been different.[6]

However, it is difficult to agree that it was just these two problems that decided the outcome of the German Kursk offensive; at the very least, this isn't obvious to me, but this is a large subject for a different conversation.

Now let's return to the assessment of the 7th Guards Army's combat performance in the course of repelling Operation Citadel and briefly dwell on the main reasons for its troops' successful actions and the shortcomings that led to the fact that they weren't able to achieve completely the army's objectives within the framework of the defensive operation. I'll note straightaway that the Voronezh Front command had rather high regard for the results of the 7th Guards Army's combat work and the courage and heroism of all of its men. Even though its troops were in fact unable to prevent the Germans from breaking through in their sector of defense, they inflicted substantial damage to Breith's III Panzer Corps, and by tying down all three divisions of Korps Raus before their front, they ultimately frustrated von Manstein's plans. Just as N.F. Vatutin was counting upon, the assault wedge of Army Group South from the very first minutes of the start of Citadel was split into two disjointed groupings. Indeed, even despite the great efforts that it made, Army Detachment Kempf was in fact unable to screen the Fourth Panzer Army's right flank, which was one of the main reasons for the failure of its offensive. From 5 to 10 July 1943, at the most intense moment of combat against the Wehrmacht's most powerful assault grouping, of the two Guards armies that were activated in this sector of the Kursk salient (the divisions of the 7th Guards Army together with the troops of the 6th Guards Army's left flank and the frontal reserves) managed to engage six of the Wehrmacht's panzer and infantry divisions and hold them within the system of the first two army-level defensive belts.

At the same time, the Guardsmen conducted the bitter fighting with rather modest means – only those, that had been planned ahead of time by the Front leadership in order to resolve the given tasks and even fewer (for example, the 2nd Guards "Tatsinskaia" Tank Corps wasn't engaged in the sector). Thus, up until 10 July in the sector of the 7th Guards Army, six (of eight) rifle divisions, two tank and two destroyer anti-tank artillery brigades, and five tank and self-propelled artillery regiments took direct part in the fighting with Army Detachment Kempf. Meanwhile, Shumilov's army received only one rifle division, one destroyer anti-tank artillery brigade and a Katiusha rocket-launcher regiment out of the Front reserve (the 94th Guards Rifle Division, the 31st Separate Destroyer Anti-tank Artillery Brigade, and the 309th Guards Mortar Regiment),

---

6   Newton, *Kurskaia bitva: Nemetskogo vzgliad*, p. 508.

which took direct part in holding its lines. In contrast, during the battle one rifle division, one tank regiment, two destroyer anti-tank artillery regiments and a Guards Mortar regiment was withdrawn from it and transferred to the 69th Army. The 49th Rifle Corps that became subordinate to the 7th Guards Army on 11 July was called upon to resolve tasks that weren't related to holding the army's sector of defense (the army was capable of this even without this reinforcement), but in order to take part in the pinning counteroffensive to aid the Front's main counterattack grouping at Prokhorovka. In addition to those units already sent to the 69th Army, simultaneously with the receipt of the 111th and 270th Rifle Divisions, on 11 July M.S. Shumilov sent his 1529th Heavy Self-propelled Artillery Regiment to reinforce the 5th Guards Tank Army, even though he himself was experiencing an acute deficit of artillery.

In addition to carrying out an assigned task, casualty figures are an important indicator of success. What were they? If to rely on the course of combat operations, then the army's divisions were operating to meet the objective of splitting Army Group South's assault wedge primarily in the first (active) phase of the defensive operation, which came to an end on 10 July 1943. According to a report from the 7th Guards Army's Personnel Department, over the six days from the start of the operation it lost 15,796 men. For more detail, see Table 16.

However, these data are incomplete; they don't include the losses of the 148th Tank Regiment, the 94th Guards Rifle Division (between 7 and 9 July) and the 81st Guards Rifle Division for the categories of killed and severely wounded. According to incomplete data, in addition to the 1,520 missing-in-action in the fighting near Belgorod shown in the table, the 81st Guards Rifle Division lost 815 men killed. Considering this, as well as the fact that, for example, in the 213th Rifle Division alone 358 men who had been listed as missing-in-action returned to it after 16 July, it is possible to assume that with respect to the losses of Russkikh's and Morozov's divisions and Lifitz's regiment, the total casualty figure might vary between 17,400 and 17,600 men. Over this same period Army Detachment Kempf lost 10,779 men.[7]

As is known, casualty figures in a battle testify not only to the intensity of the fighting and the firepower of the opposing sides, but also the accuracy of the approaches taken by their command, in particular with respect to the manners and methods of conducting combat operations. In the course of my search work in the TsAMO RF, I found an account from Voronezh Front's Personnel Department on the losses of its armies between 5 and 16 July 1943, which was prepared on 20 October 1943. The casualty figures presented in it are only for the formations (divisions and brigades), although to judge from the summary figures, the armies' losses in it correspond to those that were announced by their headquarters after 23 July 1943, which is to say immediately after the front became stabilized. Nevertheless, this source is interesting by the fact that it allows firstly to determine the 7th Guards Army's level of losses relative to the Front's other armies in the course of defeating Army Group South's summer offensive, and secondly to follow the fluctuation in the casualties during the first (5-10 July) and second (11-16 July) phases of the Kursk defensive operation. In Tables 17 and 18 data are given for the three armies that operated on the main and auxiliary directions and which received the main attack by von Manstein's forces.

As follows from these numbers, the 7th Guards Army stands in third place, losing 23,390 men, the 6th Guards Army in second place, losing 24,921 men, and in first place is the 69th Army; its formations lost 29,267 soldiers and officers.

If to compare these figures with the data in Table 16, then it turns out when defending the main and second army-level belts, which is to say in the period when Shumilov's army was fighting with two of Kempf's fresh corps, including one panzer corps, its losses relative to the total loss of personnel over 12 days amounted to 67.5%. Even so, in the concluding phase of the operation,

---

7   Zetterling, N. and Franksen, A., *Kursk: A statistical analysis*, p. 199.

Table 16 Casualties of the 7th Guards Army between 1 and 10 July 1943[1]

Unit	Killed or died during evacuation to hospital			Wounded, concussed or burned with evacuation to hospital			Hospitalized with illness			Missing in action			Taken prisoner			Other causes			Summary casualties			Total
	Command staff	Junior commanders	Enlisted men	Command staff	Junior commanders	Enlisted men	Command staff	Junior commanders	Enlisted men	Command staff	Junior commanders	Enlisted men	Command staff	Junior commanders	Enlisted men	Command staff	Junior commanders	Enlisted men	Command staff	Junior commanders	Enlisted men	
24 GRC Headquarters	3	3		1		2												1	1		2	3
36 GRD	25	76	33	6	20	87	1	6	46		1	6		1	4				10	31	177	218
72 GRD	25	206	242	97	406	877				47	301	396					1		170	783	1515	2468
213 RD	24	206	699	70	687	1395	1			1		3	1				1		96	893	2097	3086[2]
25 GRC Headquarters						4			6										2		10	12
15 GRD	2	27	74	14	44	172		1	19						5				16	72	270	358
73 GRD	19	142	296	43	155	473	1	14	21	88	459	898			1				151	770	1689	2610
78 GRD	60	226	719	115	533	1097	1	3	6	71	313	512							247	1075	2334	3656
81 GRD												1520									1520	1520
270 RD		1		2		6	2	2	28						2				2	3	36	41
62 Penal Co.	2	13	43	1	6	142			1			6							3	19	192	214
63 Penal Co.	2	5	26	5	13	97					6	31							7	24	154	185
65 Penal Co.	2	12	46	3	27	178													5	39	224	268
66 Penal Co.	5	4	10		1	30			1	1	23	193							6	28	234	268
5 Penal Co.				2	3														2	3		5
82 S BD Co.			3			1															1	1
85 S BD Co.						2															2	2
86 S BD Co.						3						3									9	9
27 GTB	5	5	4	6	10	16		1	1										11	16	21	48
201 TB	8	6	9	17	42	48					4	9							25	2	66	143
167 TR	8	20	1	14	19	2		1											22	39	3	64
262 TR	3	7		10	10		1			2	4								16	21		37
1438 SPAR	2	7	4	2	4	3		1											4	11	7	22
290 AMtrR	3	4	16	1	4	43	1	1	1										5	9	60	74
109 GCAR	1		1	3	2	1													4	2	2	8
161 GCAR		1	2	2		6		1	3										2	2	14	18
265 GCAR	2	7	7	4	7	6					4	3							6	18	33	57
1669 DATAR				2	1	4			2			20							2	1	4	7
1670 DATAR						1												2			5	5

"THE OPERATION'S FAILURE TURNED INTO A TRAGEDY"

Unit	Killed or died during evacuation to hospital			Wounded, concussed or burned with evacuation to hospital			Hospitalized with illness			Missing in action			Taken prisoner			Other causes			Summary casualties			Total
	Command staff	Junior commanders	Enlisted men	Command staff	Junior commanders	Enlisted men	Command staff	Junior commanders	Enlisted men	Command staff	Junior commanders	Enlisted men	Command staff	Junior commanders	Enlisted men	Command staff	Junior commanders	Enlisted men	Command staff	Junior commanders	Enlisted men	
114 GDATAR[3]			11	1		20				2									3		31	52
115 GDATAR		1	1																	1	5	6
838 S ARA Bn		1	1						3											1	1	2
1 S ATR Bn		2	12	8	13	13													9	15	25	49
4 S ATR Bn	2	4	16	2	8	32				3	10	34							7	22	82	111
5 S ATR Bn			1			1			1											2	3	5
30 S DATAB		4	14	3	4	26	1		4										4	8	44	56
5 A-AR	3	2	9		3	4	17				2	6							6	8	32	46
162 GA-AR																					6	6
176 Backpack FT Co.			4			2															13	17
191 S FT Co.	1		2		1	3				1	1	3						5	1	3	13	17
128 Signals Rgt.								2	3											2	3	5
60 S Eng Bn				1		1			4										1		5	6
175 A Eng Bn						2		1	15											1	17	18
329 A Eng Bn						1	1		2										1		3	4
185 Auto Bn			1																		1	1
578 Aviation Recon Squadron							1	1											1	1		2
190 ARRR						1															1	1
328 S Wagon Co.	1					1													1		1	2
Total:	183	787	2296	435	2023	4797	9	35	170	214	1128	2123	1	1	4	2		16	844	3974	9406	15796

Notes

1 TsAMO RF, f. 7 gv. A, op. 5317, d. 11, l. 341, 342.
2 According to the information of the 213th Rifle Division, after the fighting ended 358 men who had been counted as missing in action returned to the 702nd Rifle Regiment, thus the casualty figures over all the days were later corrected.
3 Information for the 114th Guards Destroyer Anti-tank Artillery Regiment is from TsAMO RF, f. 114, op. 8808, d. 4, l. 329, and in the last line of the given table, only single figure was given for the summary casualties.

THE FORGOTTEN BATTLE OF THE KURSK SALIENT

Table 17 Casualties of the 7th Guards Army between 5 and 16 July 1943

Army and unit	Killed or mortally wounded			Wounded, concussed with evacuation to hospital			Hospitalized with illness			Missing in action			Taken prisoner			Other causes			Summary casualties			Total
	Command	Junior command	Enlisted	Command	Junior command	Enlisted	Command	Junior command	Enlisted	Command	Junior command	Enlisted	Command	Junior command	Enlisted	Command	Junior command	Enlisted	Command	Junior command	Enlisted	
7th Guards Army																						
36 GRD	4	9	47			154	1	6	73		2	7		1	4				21	57	290	368
72 GRD	51	107	355	117	905	1501		1	4	49	322	551				2		1	229	1043	2412	3684
213 RD	36	314	852	101	648	1796	3	3	21	7	43	121							155	1219	2652	4026
15 GRD	25	124	251	122	505	1115	1	15	33	88	484	965						5	134	818	1507	2459
73 GRD	45	182	441	137	639	1341	1	4	8	71	313	512						9	258	1186	2789	4233
78 GRD	68	275	843	97	64	1460			4									2	278	1232	2825	4335
111 RD	40	185	232	102	457	931		2	29									2	146	713	1169	2028
270 RD	23	120	156	6	10	983		1	1		4		8					6	128	609	1172	1909
27 GTB	5	5	4	17	42	16													11	16	21	48
201 TB	8	6	9	1	19	48						9							25	52	66	143
167 TR	8	20	1	14	10	2				2	4								22	39	3	64
262 TR	3	7	–	10	10		1												16	21		37
30 DATAB		4	14	3	4	26	1		4										4	8	44	56
Total	296	1456	3205	726	3333	9373	8	32	177	218	1172	2169	1	1	4	10		25	1427	7013	14950	23390
69th Army																						
107 RD		11	30	7	18	76	1	12	28										72	339	856	1267
183 RD																			37	136	503	676
305 RD	5?		97	25	132	201	2	9	75	24	187	483	2	7		21		3	138	457	1270	1865
375 RD	2?	41														12		2	207	1350	3280	4897
81 GRD																			279	1088	2996	4363
89 GRD																			128	874	2638	3640
92 GRD	49?	231	434	96	402	1030			21	115	683	1104							305	1511	2912	4728
93 GRD																			396	1859	3341	5596
94 GRD	8?	50	133	47	275	588	2	7	33	1	7	20			6				130	643	1368	2141
96 TB	6?	16	9	10	24	25					2	1							16	43	35	94
Total	60?	349	703	185	941	2924	5	28	157	140	879	1608	2	13	34			5	1768	8300	19199	29267

Table 18 Casualties of the 6th Guards Army between 5 and 16 July 1943[1]

Unit	Killed or mortally wounded			Wounded, concussed with evacuation to hospital			Hospitalized with illness			Missing in action			Taken prisoner			Other causes			Summary casualties			Total
	Command	Junior command	Enlisted	Command	Junior command	Enlisted	Command	Junior command	Enlisted	Command	Junior command	Enlisted	Command	Junior command	Enlisted	Command	Junior command	Enlisted	Command	Junior command	Enlisted	
51 GRD	50	74	283	75	230	693	15	1	45	48	258	712	1	3	14	3		23	192	590	1820	2602
52 GRD	48	169	507	142	468	1436	4	20	47	65	336	639		2	11	1			260	995	2640	3895
67 GRD	64	136	368	92	552	1371	4		79	50	281	1201							212	969	3019	4200
71 GRD	48	134	741	139	306	1379	5	20	105	10	79	542							202	539	2767	3508
90 GRD	44	142	415	138	273	758	3	1		82	564	1538							267	980	2711	3958
184 RD	9	36	100	49	100	621	5		14	84	560	881							147	695	1616	2458
204 RD	17	35	132	56	151	636				26	78	287							99	264	1055	1418
219 RD	9	42	106	29	187	380													38	229	486	753
309 RD	32	121	246	30	367	808	2	10	49	6	54	266						2	70	552	1371	1993
245 STR	12	53	6	1	28	22				5	5	9							13	86	37	136
Total for the 6th Guards army	333	941	2094	751	2662	8104	38	52	339	371	2215	6075	3	5	25	4		25	1500	5899	17522	24921

Note
1 TsAMO RF, f. 203, op. 2843, d. 427, l. 19.

when III Panzer Corps had exited its defensive belts and Korps Raus had gone over to a defense, the army still suffered painful damage, losing 7,594 men. A significant portion of them were losses for 12 July 1943 resulting from the "pinning counterattack".

Now let's turn to the losses of the 7th Guards Army's divisions. Judging from the data presented in Table 16, the 78th Guards Rifle Division, which received an attack made in colossal strength – essentially that of two panzer and partially two infantry divisions – had the greatest losses. From 5 to 10 July the division lost 3,656 men, of which 67% were lost irrecoverably (1,005 killed and 1,445 missing in action). This is a very high figure. Although in comparison with the casualties 6th Guards Army's divisions over the period between 5 and 9 July (see Table 18), especially those that were located at the focal point of Fourth Panzer Army's main attack – the 67th Guards and 52nd Guards Rifle Divisions (in the first echelon) and the 51st Guards Rifle Division (in the second echelon), they were significantly higher: 5,495, 6,456 and 4,750 men respectively.[8]

In second place on this doleful list is the 213th Rifle Division; it lost 2,757 soldiers and commanders. It entered battle only on the afternoon of 5 July and operated together with units of the 72nd Guards Rifle Division, which was located in the first echelon and over this same period lost 2,468 men. There are several reasons for such heavy losses, but we've already talked in detail about the main ones above. Now I will dwell only on one of the reasons: the character of its commander Colonel I.E. Buslaev, since I believe that the division suffered such painful losses (primarily in the rifle battalions) not only because of objective factors, but also because of his bungling, poorly considered actions. By the start of the Battle of Kursk, at the time of his arrival in his new post, he was the youngest division commander in the 7th Guards Army, as well as the least prepared for this work. He didn't manage to acquire either a normal civilian education (having completed 5 grades of a village school) or military education (only the Vystrel [Shot] courses); in practice he had never commanded a battalion, and immediately from the post of commander of a machine-gun company (in 1938 at the height of Stalin's terror) he was promoted to take command of a rifle regiment. The following excerpt is a performance review of Major I.E. Buslaev as commander of the 603rd Rifle Regiment of the Belorussian Special Military District's 161st Rifle Division at the end of October 1940:

> A large minus of Comrade Buslaev is his low general education training and general cultural level, as a result of which he labors to lead staff work and doesn't know how to control it. For the same reason, he doesn't engage in training the headquarters staff. His organizational capabilities are inadequately developed. He strives to do everything himself. The personnel in the regiment are cohesive. He knows how to organize and conduct exercises with the command staff, but his command language is unpolished and his expressions are unclear. He doesn't understand mobilization work and doesn't know how to direct it. He enjoys authority among subordinates and comrades. He is healthy, and fit for campaign life. For carrying out a special assignment of the Party and government, he has been awarded with the Order of the Red Banner.[9] He plainly does insufficient work on increasing his general education. He knows well how to handle a gun and is a superb shot with all types of weapons.[10]

It must be said that the Major wasn't timid and at difficult moments he knew how to buck up his subordinates' resolve, which was something very important, especially in the first months of the war. In August 1941 for courage and heroism his regiment received the "Guards" title, and

---

8   Zamulin, V., *Kurskii izlom* [*Kursk turning point*] (Moscow: Iauza, 2007), pp. 956-957.
9   Buslaev was on special assignment to Spain during the Spanish Civil War.
10 TsAMO RF, personal files of Major General I.E. Buslaev.

Buslaev was considered worthy of the Order of Lenin. After recuperating in a hospital (due to a wounding), on 25 February 1942 he was appointed deputy commander of the 7th (Estonian) Rifle Division. However, having served not even three months in this post, he was transferred to take command of the 6th Destroyer Brigade (even though he never had anything whatsoever to do with the artillery), and just two weeks before the start of the Battle of Kursk, on 22 June 1943 Buslaev became the commander of the 213th Rifle Division.

Such a winding path up the career ladder didn't enable him to acquire either the necessary training or the practical experience in commanding such a large tactical formation as a rifle division. In addition to the aforementioned shortcomings, Ivan Efimovich had a full array of negative qualities. In a review given to him already after the Battle of Kursk, it is noted:

> Operationally and tactically at the division level, he is fair to middling prepared. He has experience in commanding a division in offensive and defensive battles; prone to passivity – he doesn't like to take risks …. He orients himself in a situation with difficulty and does so somewhat primitively. He labors to grasp all the situational information, gives attention to only some of its elements and completely misses the most important point. He comes to conclusions with difficulty and isn't always right. He makes decisions without considering all the situational information, as a consequence of which they are frequently incomplete.[11]

Major General N.A. Vasil'ev knew full well all of the blunders and miscalculations made by the division commander, but on paper he accented his positive qualities and even exaggerated them. The reason for this is obvious. In the first place, he understood that a division commander isn't made in a short period of time, and so he believed that in reviews, which had no particular effect on practical matters (there were few who bothered to read personnel files), it was simply stupid and even harmful to pull no punches. In the second place and this was the main thing, in the acting army the prestige of a division played an important role. It took a long time to accrete and grow, very gradually, but it had a substantial influence, both on the career of the corps commander personally (honors, titles) and on the decisions made by higher command about using it, reinforcing it, and so forth. Therefore each commander strove by every possible means to present his troops (and naturally his subordinate commanders) in the best possible light (as long as there were no personal conflicts), both in front of his immediate superior, and in front of Moscow. In the process, of course, fetched arguments and excess couldn't be avoided. More than once, I happened to hear the stories of veterans that in the chase after "inflated" prestige, individual formation commanders artificially "piled up" the number of decorated soldiers and officers in their formation, including those with Gold Stars as well. Or take another example: In the course of the Battle of Stalingrad, a number of commanders (including V.I. Chuikov) displayed great jealousy whenever a team of writers and journalists from Moscow gave more attention to rival commanders, or even worse, met directly with subordinates, or if they didn't stand out on the pages of the central press so often.[12] Because of this, even very serious conflicts arose between generals. At the height of the Battle of Kursk, General of the Army K.K. Rokossovsky and his headquarters, using their connections among Moscow's brotherhood of writers, sent a group of photojournalists and film operators to capture the results of the fighting (knocked out armor) at Ponyri Station and on the Ol'khovatka direction. He did so, despite the fact that those results, in general, were rather modest. N.F. Vatutin at that moment had no time for a publicity stunt; with great strain, he was attempting to contain the enemy's most powerful grouping. However, as further events showed,

---

11   TsAMO RF, personal file of Major General I.E. Buslaev.
12   *Stalingradskaia epopeia* [*Stalingrad saga*] (Moscow: "Zvonnitsa-MG", 2000), pp. 390-391.

the Commander-in-Chief of the Central Front proved to be more far-sighted. Now more than 70 years later, documentary films and television programs continue to use just these scenes, where knocked out Ferdinands and Tigers are shown burning, as visible evidence of the more successful combat work done by Rokossovsky's troops, than Vatutin's men did.

M.S. Shumilov to a certain extent also took part in similar "chases for honors", but as it seems to me, he wasn't sick with the "competitive fever". Instead, he participated in them like all army commanders, whenever the need arose, which is to say he didn't try to change the system, but tolerated it. Whenever he had the opportunity, he rated his subordinates with complete objectivity. Thus on 24 July 1943, when allocating the honors and award for Kursk defensive operation, at his recommendation N.F. Vatutin gave I.E. Buslaev a lower honor than the other division commanders of the 7th Guards Army, but one Buslaev deserved, the Order of the Red Banner. Although Shumilov had the right to award this honor, he didn't make use of it in order to raise the status of the award (a medal given in accordance to an order from the Front Commander-in-Chief was considered prestigious). Nevertheless, at the same time he made it clear to the division commander that even though he had indeed passed his first competency examination, he still had much to learn.

Up until the moment Army Detachment Kempf's shock formation, Breith's III Panzer Corps, exited the defensive belts of the 7th Guards Army, its defensive operation went through two stages: 5-7 July – the combat at the crossing sites and defense of the main defensive belt; and 8-10 July – holding the second army-level defensive belt. As can be assumed, the artillery became the weapons that took on the enemy's main attack from the first minutes of his offensive, and throughout the entire course of the operation, the firmness of the 7th Guards Army's line depended on its fire. The first stage began with an important and successful measure for the Guardsmen, in which the artillery and mortar units played first violin – with the counter-artillery preparation. It was a constituent part of the unified plan for the Kursk defensive operation of both *fronts* that were holding the salient. In the planning of the Central Front command, the counter-battery struggle was laid at its foundation, and the other tasks, including striking local aggregations of enemy troops, were viewed as secondary. N.F. Vatutin proposed to go after different objectives. He considered that in the course of the counter-artillery preparation, it was first of all necessary to target enemy troops and equipment in their jumping-off positions. This point of view was based not only on the general's experience and intuition; he was primarily considering Voronezh Front's possibilities. With respect to artillery, his forces had more than 2,000 pieces of artillery less than the Central Front. For example, in the 6th Guards and 7th Guards Armies, the average density of guns in the divisions of the first echelon was less than half that in the 13th Army, which was also positioned on the axis of an enemy main attack. Experience showed that this approach proved to be more effective than the one taken on the Central Front.

Among all the armies of the Voronezh Front's first echelon, the counter-artillery preparation went most successfully in the sector of the 7th Guards Army. Very favorable circumstances came together for conducting it. A very serious natural obstacle, the Northern Donets River, ran in front of the line of almost all of its divisions that were defending the main line of resistance, except the 81st Guards Rifle Division. It didn't allow Army Detachment Kempf to launch an attack against the Guardsmen's positions with all of its *kampfgruppen* simultaneously, as happened in the sector of the 6th Guards Army. This forced the commanders of the German divisions to create special assault groups and to concentrate men and equipment at the designated crossing sites in eight sectors of the line. The leadership of the 7th Guards Army took advantage of this fact. Naturally, the 40-minute barrage at revealed targets in principle couldn't foil the planned offensive of Kempf's two corps, even though formally this was the task given to the preemptive artillery barrage. Nevertheless, the artillery opened fire not only just at the moment when Breith's and Raus's troops were in their jumping-off positions, but even started 15 minutes before they began to force a crossing of the river (by constructing bridges and fording the channel with grenadiers). Thus the counter-artillery preparation inflicted considerable damage to the assault groups, engineer units and bridge-building teams, destroyed a portion of the bridge-building park, disrupted communications, and had a serious effect on the Germans' morale.

The barrage that started next on the areas where Breith's and Raus's divisions were trying to build bridges or had already created small bridgeheads not only inflicted substantial casualties on the forward battalions, but also completely frustrated the crossing of one of the five divisions, the 6th Panzer Division, designated for the initial attack. For the same reasons, the crossing of the 19th Panzer Division, especially of its panzer regiment, also went with considerable trouble. In addition, the 320th Infantry Division, because of the fact that the defending Guardsmen had destroyed several bridges as troops were crossing them, before day's end was unable to cross a sufficient amount of anti-tank guns to the eastern bank, which played a substantially negative role when fighting to repel the counterattacks made by the 213th Rifle Division and 27th Guards Tank Brigade. Besides this, it should be stressed that the 2nd and 17th Air Armies also made large contributions by inflicting casualties on the enemy troops when forcing the river on 5 July. Despite the unsuccessful strikes against the German airfields in the region, their aviation formations rather quickly began combat operations in the sector of the 7th Guards Army.

So, let's now briefly summarize the results. As is known, the main reason for the enemy's penetration into the depth of the Voronezh Front's defenses on 5 July and over subsequent days was the significant superiority in forces and means over the defenders that the Germans concentrated on rather narrow sectors of the front. On the direction of the main attack, the Soviet command was able to turn the situation around and change the correlation of strength in its favor only several days later, by means of moving up reserves. In the sector of the 7th Guards Army on the first day of Operation Citadel, the Soviets were able to avoid a sharp superiority on the side of the enemy thanks to the fact that as a result of the counter-artillery preparation and struggle for the bridges, M.S. Shumilov prevented the rapid build-up of a significant amount of Kempf's forces on the eastern bank, and the divisional *kampfgruppen* that managed to cross were not strong enough and lacked the necessary assets to breach the 7th Guards Army's main line of resistance from the march, as happened in the 6th Guards Army's sector. Only the situation in the 78th Guards Rifle Division was an exception; there, because of characteristics of the layout of its line, the III Panzer Corps command was able to cross the significant armor forces of the 7th Panzer Division, thanks to which the Germans created a high concentration of force on an insignificant breakthrough sector. However, even this was just a tactical success, because of the previous, correctly prepared and quickly implemented plan of maneuver with the divisions of the army's second echelon. Because of this, the Germans were unable to exploit this success straightaway.

A second important factor, which seriously affected the strength of the main line of resistance of both Vatutin's Front and Shumilov's 7th Guards Army, was the accurate distribution of firepower and the correct planning of its anti-tank defenses, which were built around an artful combination of artificial obstacles and anti-tank regions. The anti-tank areas were prepared for all-round defense and were echeloned in depth, which allowed an escape from a linear distribution of artillery along the front and the creation of a sufficient concentration of fire on directions that were vulnerable to tanks.

The decision to appoint artillery officers in command of the anti-tank regions and to organize their system of fire on the principle of an anti-tank artillery nest, which amplified the fire of the assigned means of fire (anti-tank guns, anti-tank rifles, mortars and rifle elements) completely justified itself. The enemy's most powerful and numerous panzer attacks fell apart against these anti-tank strong points in the main defensive belt of the Voronezh Front in the first days of the Battle of Kursk. In the process of eliminating them, the Germans suffered their first painful losses in armor. One can see this particularly plainly through the example of the 19th Panzer Division.

From the very first minutes of the offensive up until 10 July inclusively, together with the 168th Infantry Division it struggled to take the positions held by the 81st Guards Rifle Division, the defense of which rested on four such hubs of resistance. As a result, over the five days of fighting Schmidt's panzer division suffered the highest losses of all the divisions of III Panzer Corps in men and tanks. On the morning of 11 July, its panzer regiment had only 16 operational combat machines, or around 20% of the number with which it had started the offensive.

The anti-tank areas became a serious obstacle in the sector of the offensive of Kempf's other divisions. I will mention that on the first day of Operation Citadel, of the 12 anti-tank areas in the 7th Guards Army's main defensive belt, the enemy managed to capture only three: Nizhnii Ol'shanets, Maslova Pristan' and Bezliudovka. The rest continued to hold out and carry out their assignments. The corrective labor camp, and the villages of Razumnoe and Krutoi Log, which were located on the flanks of Army Detachment Kempf's advance particularly hampered Breith's and Raus' troops. Schmidt's, von Funck's and Forst's *kampfgruppen* were forced to expend 1.5 to 2 days assaulting these fortified villages.

To a significant degree, the enemy's deficit in air strength enhanced the resilience of both the hubs of resistance and the entire system of defense as a whole on the direction of Army Group South's auxiliary offensive. When analyzing the course of combat operations, in particular those of III Panzer Corps, the strict correlation between a successful attack by the *kampfgruppen* of its panzer divisions and Luftwaffe activity sharply stands out. If you lay out the order of the main reasons why the artillery and destroyer anti-tank artillery units, which were the main antagonist of the enemy's panzer units, suffered the greatest damage, then airstrikes stand in third or even fourth place. As a rule, the main loss of men and equipment of the artillery regiments was caused by tank fire and Nebelwerfer fire. This is followed by artillery barrages and airstrikes. This also relates to the situation with losses in tanks and self-propelled guns. In the account of the 7th Guards Army's Chief of Armored and Mechanized Forces Colonel A.A. Bogdanov, he wrote: "The tank troops of the 7th Guards Army had no losses in combat materiel due to enemy aircraft … the tanks' main damage came from artillery fire, including that of tanks, followed by damage due to mines."[13]

As concerns the artificial obstacles, both on the forward edge and in the depth of both army-level defensive belts, they not only proved effective in knocking out enemy armor (in isolated cases in the course of one attack, up to 14 German panzers became disabled by mines), but also according to interrogated prisoners, gave rise to "mine fright" in the German tankers, which perceptibly reduced their activity and decisiveness in battle. The significance of the minefields particularly rose when breaking into the depths of the 69th Army, where the other elements of its system of defense weren't as developed as in the positions of the 7th Guards Army.

A third factor, which even though it appeared as early as 5 July seriously and adversely affected the situation in the sector of Army Detachment Kemp's offensive right up until its very conclusion, was the successful counterattack launched by the 213th Rifle Division and 27th Guards Tank Brigade. Counterattacks by operational-tactical reserves with the aim of smashing enemy that had broken through into the depth of the defenses were an important element of any Red Army defensive operation. Thus they were diligently prepared ahead of time. First, alternative scenarios for the most likely development of the operational situation were determined. Then several different plans would be devised for them, and they would be allocated the necessary forces, which were assembled in the second echelon of the army's dispositions, and as a rule, be directed toward the most endangered sectors. The 7th Guards Army headquarters conducted just such preliminary work before the Battle of Kursk with its subordinate corps. However, on the axis of Army Detachment

---

13 TsAMO RF, f. 341, op. 5312, d. 246, l. 175.

Kempf's main attack, because of III Panzer Corps' divisions and because of the significant amount of armor that the Germans committed into the fighting, 7th Guards Army's command was forced in the first days of the operation to reject the idea of launching counterattacks (for example, with the reinforced 73rd Guards Rifle Division).

The situation on the army's left flank received much better prior consideration. One of the scenarios of the development of the enemy offensive in the sector of the 24th Guards Rifle Corps, envisioned by the 7th Guards Army command, proved to be extremely accurate, which allowed M.S. Shumilov in a complex situation to make an accurate decision quickly and to launch an attack against the weakest point in Army Detachment Kempf's attack formation; this enabled N.A. Vasil'ev to move up the divisions planned for the counterattack smoothly and in a short period of time to accomplish a significant portion of his mission. Although not one division of Korps Raus was completely destroyed (it even retained possession of all the bridgeheads it had seized on the eastern bank of the river), the counterattack achieved its main purpose – the pace of Korp Raus' advance into the depth of the 24th Guards Rifle Corps' lines was abruptly curtailed. This allowed by the end of day 5 July not only the stabilization of the situation on the army's left flank to a significant degree, but also, having thrown back the 320th Infantry Division a substantial distance, to seize the initiative here and to retain it until the end of the defensive operation.

By keeping Korps Raus within the system of the main belt of defenses, M.S. Shumilov fundamentally disrupted W. Kempf's plans. In addition to Raus' two infantry divisions, he also drew practically a third of III Panzer Corps' strength to the left wing of his army from the axis of Army Detachment Kempf's main attack and compelled Breith to address a problem arising outside of his sector of responsibility by detaching an entire panzer division (7th Panzer Division) in order to screen his panzer corps' right flank.

Unfortunately, although the conditions for launching a counterattack in the sector of the 24th Guards Rifle Corps proved to be quite favorable (during the march and in the ensuing combat, the enemy aircraft seldom made an appearance; the counterattack was launched out of the second echelon against a sector, where the 72nd Guards Rifle Division's front line units hadn't yet been completely overrun by the enemy; and the Germans had no panzers opposite the 24th Guards Rifle Corps's front), Buslaev's division and Nevzhinsky's tank brigade weren't able to take advantage of these circumstances in full measure, and as noted in documents of the 7th Guards Army headquarters, while incurring unjustified losses. Good organization, cohesion and a sense of purpose were absent in their actions. Cooperation both within the 213th Rifle Division itself and with the 27th Guards Tank Brigade was poor, even though their headquarters had been working on this matter right up until the start of the counterattack. As already noted above, the regiment commanders failed to organize proper reconnaissance and security on the march, units lost contact with each other frequently, and entire battalions were late in arriving in the combat zone. Moreover, the 213th Rifle Division command was unable to identify the critical sectors accurately and failed to mass strength on these directions. As a result, having struggled to throw back the forward units of the 320th Infantry Division from the ground they had just taken, and having driven them back to the fortified villages on the eastern bank of the Northern Donets River, Buslaev's troops even with the support of tanks proved unable to take even one major strong point in the river's basin. In contrast, at the same time the enemy actually managed to encircle a number of the division's units and inflicted significant damage to them. For example, according to the information from 7th Guards Army's Personnel Department, in the 793rd and 702nd Rifle Regiments alone, during the encirclement and when coming out of the pocket between 5 and 8 July, they respectively had 125 and 69 soldiers and officers who went missing in action.[14]

---

14 TsAMO RF, f. 7 gv. A, op. 5317, d. 11, l. 379.

Colonel A.A. Bogdanov commented rather critically on the actions of their subordinates during the counterattack and the cooperation between the tank crews and rifle units. In his account on the results of the Kursk defensive operation, he wrote:

> The infantry's attack was not always vigorous, because of which the tanks became separated and lost cooperation with them. The infantry, being cut off from the armored vehicles by enemy fire, failed to support the actions of our tanks with their own fire while the enemy artillery was active. As a result, the tanks suffered unjustified losses. The tankers didn't adequately maneuver on the battlefield, failed to use the terrain for making sneak approaches into the enemy's flank and rear, and sometimes launched frontal attacks.[15]

In the course of the struggle with III Panzer Corps' armored *kampfgruppen* in the depth of the defensive belt, success was achieved due to the following factors. First was the correct determination of the direction of the enemy's main attack. Second was the creation in this sector of a strong anti-tank artillery and artillery grouping in this sector, which was echeloned in depth (particularly in the sector of the 81st Guards Rifle Division). Third was the dispatch of the 7th Guards Army's and Voronezh Front's reserves to this axis. Even though all of the artillery and mortar units of the divisions of the first echelon, as well as the corps artillery, took part in the fighting to repulse the enemy's massed attacks on the morning of 5 July, even so already that afternoon M.S. Shumilov was forced to activate his mobile and anti-tank reserve in the sector of Breith's panzer corps. Throughout the extent of the entire operation, these units meritoriously shouldered the responsibilities they'd been given. The destroyer anti-tank artillery regiments and brigades played an important role in the defense, even though there were not many of them in the 7th Guards Army's sector – two brigades and three separate regiments. However, they proved to be highly effective and without exaggeration, together with the divisional artillery regiments, were the main means of struggle against the enemy tanks, especially those equipped with the ZiS-3 76mm gun.

In addition, in those places where the use of the tank and artillery units was planned and executed by the headquarters of the artillery and the armored and mechanized forces (which is to say, as a rule whereever the regulations and precepts of combat field manuals were employed), they not only yielded high results, they also didn't suffer heavy losses in return. The swift maneuver of the 31st Separate Destroyer Anti-tank Artillery Brigade to the axis of the 6th Panzer Division's main attack at a critical moment on 7 July, as well as the successful use of ambush tactics and a mobile defense by the command of the 201st Separate Tank Brigade when holding the line of the 73rd Guards Rifle Division, can serve as examples of this. In general, the 27th Guards Tank Brigade was also properly used in the fighting. Throughout the entire defensive operation, in essence it served as the backbone of Buslaev's and Losev's divisions. Owing to the professional skill of brigade commanders Taranov and Nevzhinsky, these formations not only carried out their assigned missions, they also preserved the combat readiness of 81 tanks (75% of their tank park) over six days of the heaviest fighting, having started with 108 operational armored fighting vehicles on the morning of 5 July. In addition, their command paid great attention and showed initiative with respect to not only conserving tanks, but also putting tanks back into service. For example, despite the fact that the tanks of the 27th Guards Tank Brigade were badly worn out, its men maintained the high combat readiness of the battalions through hard work and a well-organized repair service in the field repair shops. In the 201st Separate Tank Brigade, the repair teams were not only busy with repairing their own disabled tanks, but also enemy assault guns. The men of the tank brigades showed tenacity, prepared to counter large enemy tank formations in a professional

---

15 TsAMO RF, f. 341, op. 5312, d. 246, l. 170.

manner, and they made an enormous contribution to turning back Army Detachment Kempf's offensive.

However, unfortunately, this was far from true everywhere. Experience demonstrated that even some rifle division commanders of the 7th Guards Army not only showed they were unable to plan the use of the attached units properly, but also went against all orders and directives, paying no heed to the recommendations of specialists. The commanders of the 72nd Guards and 73rd Guards Rifle Divisions acted most ignorantly in this respect. I will remind the reader that already on 5 July, striving to halt 7th Panzer Division's armored *kampfgruppe*, Colonel S.A. Kozak launched a head-on attack against it with only the forces of the 167th Separate Tank Regiment. As a result of this swashbuckling attack, the objective wasn't reached and the regiment lost 62% of the tanks with which it had started on the morning of 5 July. On the evening of 7 July, instead of merging the battered units of the 30th Separate Destroyer Anti-tank Artillery Brigade that had been attached to him, which had already suffered large losses, into a single composite regiment and using it as a solid fist, the division commander split its anti-tank artillery regiments up and parceled their guns out to the rifle battalions. He did this, even though this practice had been categorically banned. In comparison, the 201st Separate Tank Brigade, which operated in the sector of the 73rd Guards Rifle Division and was used according to the manual on defense, over 6 days of fighting (6-11 July) conserved 64% of its tanks and kept possession of all of the positions it occupied. This, despite the fact that combat actions in its sector over this period were no less bitter than they had been on 5 July in the sector of the 73rd Guards Rifle Division.

The 7th Guards Army's leadership was aware of the ineptitude, and at times even incapability of senior officers at the division and even corps level to organize the combat of attached units together with their formations. Colonel A.A. Bogdanov reported: "The combined-arms commanders, particularly the division commanders, just as before are striving to throw their tanks into combat hastily or are chopping the tank units into small groups of 3-5 combat machines with the aim of covering separate directions."[16] However, as in the case with the 213th Rifle Division commander, higher brass drew no serious conclusions whatsoever about this. Everyone understood – with tongue lashings and performance reviews, which were conducted from case to case, you couldn't make a cardinal change in the situation. Only the basic training of the divisional command staff and increasing the firepower of the rifle units, which the division commanders on their own sought to augment by splitting the tank and artillery regiments up and parceling them out in spite of strict orders and good sense, could change the situation. However, prior to the summer of 1943 and immediately after it, the Red Army command and the country's political leadership were not in a condition to solve these two problems. The Battle of Kursk became the catalyst for positive change; it was the victory there, in combination with the enormous losses suffered by the troops in men and equipment over 49 days that would force the *Stavka* to give more fixed attention to these problems. Therefore already by the start of 1944, for example, the situation with the firepower of the mobile formations and the quality of tanks and self-propelled guns began to change for the better.

Now let's turn our attention to the factors that contributed to the breakthrough to the boundary between the 7th Guards and 6th Guards Armies and the emergence of Breith's panzer corps from the defensive belts of Shumilov's army. The defense of the boundary between Safiulin's and Vasil'ev's corps began gradually to crumble from the first minutes of Army Detachment Kempf's offensive. It was already penetrated to its entire depth on the afternoon of 7 July, and by the end of this day 6th Panzer Division's *kampfgruppen* emerged on the left flank of the 6th Guards Army's 375th Rifle Division. The primary reasons for the breach was the high concentration of III Panzer Corps' armor and artillery targeting the designated breakthrough sector in the defenses of the

---

16 TsAMO RF, f. 341, op. 5312, d. 246, l. 170.

25th Rifle Corps, and M.S. Shumilov's lack of the necessary strength to contain Kempf's assault formation. I'll remind the reader that the evening before, when the armored steamroller of Schülz's and von Oppeln-Bronikowski's two panzer regiments, which had more than 250 armored fighting vehicles in total, overran the 73rd Guards Rifle Division and the 78th Guards Rifle Division, which had previously fallen back to the former's positions, their units retreated to the corps' left flank and took up a defense along the line: (excl.) "Poliana" State Farm – (excl.) "Batratskaia Dacha" – (excl.) "Solov'ev" collective farm. The main artillery and tank units from the corps' and army's reserve were drawn to this line: the 265th Guards Cannon Artillery Regiment; the 1669th Destroyer Anti-tank Artillery Regiment and the 30th Separate Destroyer Anti-tank Artillery Brigade; the 97th Guards and 309th Guards Mortar Regiments; the 167th, 148th and a portion of the 262nd Tank Regiments; and the 1438th and 1529th Self-propelled Artillery Regiments. This grouping had the task for 7 July by means of an active defense to keep the 7th Panzer Division and a portion of the 106th Infantry Division in front of themselves. Their retreat to the southeast left the 81st Guards Rifle Division, which was positioned on the 25th Guards Rifle Corps' right flank and was covering the left flank of the 6th Guards Army and the boundary with it, all alone to face the 19th and 6th Panzer Divisions, which by this time had been reinforced with two regimental groups of the 168th Infantry Division as well. Having as reinforcements 19 76mm ZiS-3 guns (of the 114th Guards Destroyer Anti-tank Artillery Regiment), 4 KV tanks (of the 262nd Heavy Tank Regiment's 1st Tank Company), 18 152mm howitzers (of the 161st Guards Cannon Artillery Regiment and 18 120mm mortars (of 1st Battalion/270th Mortar Regiment), on the third day of the operation it proved unable to withstand the blow of such a force.

A second important factor that negatively affected the situation in this area was the mistake made when planning the 7th Guards Army's system of defense – the planners didn't foresee the need for switch positions between the main and second army-level defensive belts, which might have covered the deep left flank of the 81st Guards Rifle Division. Because of this, the 19th and 6th Panzer Divisions, having fully breached the main line of resistance, pivoted to the north and began to roll up the Guardsmen's defenses in the direction of the boundary between the two armies. As a result, already on 7 July they managed to drive a "corridor" through the defenses of the 81st Guards Rifle Division and reach the sector of Chistiakov's 6th Guards Army. The arrival of the 94th Guards Rifle Division played an important role in reinforcing the line of the 25th Guards Rifle Corps, especially in the sector where the 7th Panzer Division was operating, and thereby prevented a widening of the breach to the south, but it was unable to stop the 6th Panzer Division or at least to divert part of its strength.

Miscalculations also could not be avoided on the following days, though at the same time one has to admit that the subsequent decisions taken then by the Front command regarding the reinforcement of this direction proved mistaken. In fact, N.F. Vatutin's desire to block Breith's panzer corps only with rifle divisions (the 92nd Guards, 94th Guards and 305th Rifle Divisions) wasn't justified. In the first place, it was obvious that it would be extremely difficult for their units to counter the panzer corps only with their inherent artillery means, and if their artillery suffered substantial losses (as happened with the 92nd Guards Rifle Division's 197th Guards Artillery Regiment), then the divisions would immediately collapse. In order to bolster the defenses in this sector, it was necessary to give each division at least one full-strength destroyer anti-tank artillery regiment. In the second place, the Front Commander-in-Chief knew that the fortifications in the 69th Army's sector were unfinished, including in the area of Kiselevo, Sabynino, Melekhovo and Sheino; the network of trenches and the density of the artificial obstacles were significantly lower than in the sectors of the 6th Guards and 7th Guards Armies. So he was obliged to address this weakness somehow. One cannot say that the Front leadership wasn't aware of these problems. The Voronezh Front's Military Council had full knowledge of the operational situation across the entire extent of the 80-kilometer sector, where at this moment defensive fighting was raging. There is evidence of this: both the shifting of the 96th Separate Tank Brigade from the Oboian' direction, and the detachment of artillery from the 7th Guards Army headquartrs to the 25th Guards Rifle Corps. However, N.F. Vatutin didn't have an anti-tank artillery reserve, while the units of the 40th and 38th Armies that were coming up were directed to the main axis against the Fourth Panzer Army. Therefore the decision to attempt to withstand the blows of Breith's armored group only with the infantry of Kriuchenkin' rifle corps until 10 July was a compulsory measure, taken, to put it bluntly, because he had no other real choice.

Was it even possible to hold the III Panzer Corps on the Kiselevo – Sabynino – Shliakhovoe – Ushakovo line at least until the morning of 12 July after the retreat of the 81st Guards and 92nd Guards Rifle Divisions from the Staryi Gorod area? I believe it might have been possible, but only in the event that the 2nd Guards "Tatsinskaia" Tank Corps or at least two of its tank brigades had been shifted to this sector from the Prokhorovka area, as the 69th Army command had proposed. After all, by the morning of 11 July there were only 116 panzers still operational in the three panzer divisions and Separate Heavy Panzer Battalion 503, and the 7th Panzer Division, the most combat capable with 54 serviceable panzers and assault guns, was still located to the south opposite the 7th Guards Army. If Burdeiny's 2nd Guards Tank Corps had arrived in this breakthrough sector, with great likelihood N.F. Vatutin wouldn't have had to dispatch a forward detachment, the mechanized brigades of the 5th Guards Tank Army, and a portion of the very same 2nd Guards Tank Corps on 12 July in order to block a German breakthrough, but now not at Melikhovo, but at Rzhavets, and send them to Belenikhino and Leski in order to contain SS Panzer Grenadier Division *Das Reich*. Even so, it mustn't be forgotten that this conclusion flows from hindsight analysis of both the situation in the sector of the Voronezh Front by the end of 10 July and the subsequent events. N.F. Vatutin, however, was not only making decisions based on the operational situation and his capabilities; the *Stavka*, which at this time was reacting very nervously to Vatutin's inability to stop the SS Panzer Corps, also had a substantial influence on his thinking. It was in fact near Prokhorovka Station where the most threatening situation had developed by that moment, so General of the Army Vatutin decided not to take any chances and left Burdeinyi's tank corps at the station as a reserve.

At the same time, it is hard to explain a number of decisions made by the Soviet side at this time (8 July and later). According to the combat records of the 17th Air Army, which the *Stavka* initially assigned to the 7th Guards Army's sector, and then to the 69th Army's sector, its forces showed the greatest activity over the first three days of the German offensive. In this period its aviation formations conducted on average up to 200 individual combat sorties a day, but then their activity began to decrease sharply, down to around 75 sorties a day. This, it would seem, was in circumstances when it was hard to find other means of helping the divisions that were defending in the Belgorod area. This air army should have been operating intensively, dumping tons of death-inflicting metal on the enemy. I will remind the reader that at this time, the intensity of the air strikes launched by the 2nd Air Army noticeably slackened as well. The reasons for this were not only the high loss of aircraft, but also the poor organizational work of its command. For example, the entire 1st Bomber Aviation Corps remained idle at a time when the Front's ground forces were in acute need of its support.

As for the 7th Guards Army, by the end of 10 July it ability to contain Breith's III Panzer Corps in its defensive works had also noticeably decreased. There are three reasons for this. First, the enemy had taken under control the entire ground that the 25th Guards Rifle Corps had prepared and fortified for the summer fighting, and had captured all the most heavily fortified centers of resistance, on which the defense was based, including the largest – the combat sector of the 81st Guards Rifle Division. Second, M.S. Shumilov transferred a substantial portion of his artillery and tanks to the 69th Army, while 7th Guards Army's remaining units had suffered high losses. For example, by 2000 on 10 July, of the 84 tanks and self-propelled guns in the 1438th Self-propelled

Artillery Regiment, the 167th Tank Regiment and the 262nd Heavy Tank Regiment that started the operation, there were now only 20 (23.8%) left in service.[17] Its artillery and anti-tank artillery had also been substantially weakened. Thirdly, by 10 July Kempf had started to bring up the 198th Infantry Division to the sector of Safiulin's 25th Guards Rifle Corps. Even though immediately a Nebelwerfer regiment had been withdrawn from it in order to reinforce III Panzer Corps' assault wedge, in exchange it received a panzer company of the 7th Panzer Division and two infantry battalions. As a result, by 12 July the enemy had created a strong defensive line opposite the 7th Guards Army, one that was saturated with weapons, and the commanders of the infantry divisions that were holding this line received mobile reserves of panzer units and assault guns of the Separate StuG Battalion 905. This enabled Raus to defend his corps sector confidently only with his own forces (even on 12 July), while Breith calmly completed the process of turning over his sector to Horn.

At the concluding stage of the Kursk defensive operation, the most noticeable measure taken by the Voronezh Front command, in which the 7th Guards Army took active part, was the counterattack on 12 July, which with the deft touch of journalists came to be known as a "pinning counterattack". In fact, Shumilov's troops did have one main objective for it: to prevent Kempf from shifting of units and formations from this sector to the area south of Prokhorovka, but this it failed to do. The activity of Shumilov's 7th Guards Army on this day had no substantial influence on the plans of the command of both Army Detachment South and the Fourth Panzer Army, while at the same time his divisions suffered painful losses. In general, there were no particular reasons for this failure. The offensive was conducted within the framework of a single frontal counterstroke according to a unified, previously prepared plan, and so the mistakes made in it where in principle the same everywhere. When assessing the work done by the command of the 7th Guards Army when preparing for the operation and in the course of carrying it out, then one can say with confidence that the army commander sought to find a balance between the tasks that had been given to him and his own modest capabilities to carry them out. However, he was unable to achieve noticeable results, because his army was forced to launch an attack against a prepared German line that was saturated with a significant amount of firing means with minimal forces and little time for preparation.

So in conclusion I will briefly dwell on how the contributions made by the main participants in the events that are described in this book were evaluated and the fate of these men in the following two years of the war. For the 7th Guards Army, the preparation for the Battle of Kursk became a most important reference point. Having suffered enormous losses at Stalingrad, in essence the army over these three months began to be re-born. Serious organizational and restructuring changes took place in it; the corps level of command was reconstituted and the majority of the subordinate divisions transferred to new Guards tables of organization and equipment. Its command staff changed substantially, in essence, just before the events at Kursk, a nucleus of officers and generals was formed which was fated to lead it successfully to final victory through the trials of the second stage of the Great Patriotic War.

Lieutenant General M.S. Shumilov played a key role in all these transformations. From April 1943 his special concern became putting together the headquarters of the rifle corps. As a rule, they were formed in the rear out of officers who had been called back from the front for promotions, who'd been discharged from hospitals, and from the reserve command pool. The leadership of the *fronts* and armies were intensely interested that "one of their own trusted men" commanded each corps. There were cases when the USSR People's Commissariat of Defense's Main Personnel Directorate took into account the requests and recommendations of the *fronts*, which were to

---

17   TsAMO RF, f. 341, op. 5312, d. 246, l. 57.

assume command of the corps headquarters, and accommodated their requests by appointing generals to command the corps that had been recommended by the Front command. In addition to subjective factors (whether they could work together or not), which often dominated, purely practical considerations affected the decisions. For a superior chief, it was important to know the capabilities of a subordinate (whether or not he could handle the work), as well as his personality, temperament, and weaknesses. It was important that the commander was known among the Front's (and army's) command staff, which means that he had well-established connections and respect. This relieved the superior commander of the need to keep a close eye on the newcomer from the outset and helped the new corps commander quickly find his bearings and get cooperation (teamwork) with the rest of the headquarters staff up and running in daily, practical work.

Understanding that the level of training of the majority of the Red Army's command cadres was pretty much the same, M.S. Shumilov adhered to the rule to promote officers to independent command posts who'd come up in his own army. He kept an attentive watch on the commanders of his corps and divisions, strove to increase their professional level, and in the case of failures didn't hurry to remove an officer from his post, but looked into the matter and used it as the basis of instruction; he also didn't forget to commend an officer for successes and by every possible means strove for stability in the subordinate command staff at the corps and divisional level. So, at his recommendation and personal request, in April 1943 Generals G.B Safiulin and N.A. Vasil'ev, whom Shumilov knew personally and had checked in the furnace of the fighting back at Stalingrad, took charge of the army's two Guards rifle corps. According to the standards of the acting army, they were fully prepared commanders, who shared the normal experience of commanding rifle divisions in combat conditions. Both had emerged from the NKVD's interior troops and prior to the war lacked a sufficient general army training, but having wound up at the front in the first months of the war, by the spring of 1943 they'd been able to acquire a certain level of professional skill, which enabled them to adapt quickly to their new posts.

G.B. Safiulin arrived in the Kalinin Front's 22nd Army at the end of June 1941. At first he commanded the 256th Rifle Division's 930th Rifle Regiment, and then became the deputy commander of the Southwestern Front's 38th Rifle Division. In October 1942 he assumed command of this division. It fought at Stalingrad, including as part of the 64th Army. More than once M.S. Shumilov noted his resourcefulness, personal drive and initiative. On 29 June 1943 the army commander signed a performance review, which stated:

> Commanding a division, he showed himself to be a capable, tactically astute commander, who knows how to assess a situation quickly and take the correct decisions. The division was always combat ready and carried out difficult orders in the fighting to defeat the enemy at Stalingrad.
>
> Comrade Safiulin forged his headquarters into an organ of command. He devotes a lot of work and combat experience to training and to strengthening the defensive capabilities of the corps' units.
>
> As for practical work, the corps commander is young and does not have sufficient experience in commanding the corps' forces in battle, but he is a blossoming and capable commander. He fully corresponds to the duties of corps commander.[18]

Judging by the preserved attestation documents, during the first major operation that G.B. Safiulin conducted in his post of corps commander, he didn't let down the army commander. M.S. Shumilov wrote on 24 July 1943:

---

18 TsAMO RF, personal files of Lieutenant General G.B. Safiulin.

Having assumed command of a corps, he exerted a lot of effort and energy to the fortification of the corps' defensive sector. He worked out the question of cooperation ahead of time with the entire command staff. He properly positioned his weapons and created a mobile anti-tank reserve. During the fighting between 5 and 10.7.43, he proved to be a bold and decisive commander, and capably maneuvered his artillery, tanks and infantry with fire and movement. Owing to a correct assessment of the situation, he coolly commanded the troops. The enemy, with superiority in force, was unable to breach the corps' defenses completely, while suffering heavy losses. Further enemy attacks to the east were decisively repulsed by the corps, with high losses for the enemy. The corps' units between 5 and 18.7.1943 launched counterattacks, thereby drawing enemy reserves against them. Then, going on the offensive, they regained their former line.[19]

Until the start of 1945, Lieutenant General (as of 2.11.1944) G.B. Safiulin served in the 7th Guards Army, but on 18 March he took command of the 57th Rifle Corps of the 2nd Ukrainian Front's 53rd Army, which had been transferred to the Far East, where it took part in the defeat of Japan's Kwantung Army as part of the Trans-Baikal Front. After the war, like the majority of generals at his level, he underwent training in courses at the Voroshilov Military Academy, and up until his discharge into the reserve in 1957 he served as deputy commander of a rifle division and corps. Safiulin passed away on 14 October 1973.

Before his appointment as commander of the 24th Guards Rifle Corps, the army commander knew the 42-year-old Major General N.A. Vasil'ev better. On 26 June 1941, he was appointed chief of staff of the forming 250th Rifle Division. Already on 20 July this division joined combat with the Germans near Belyi from the march as part of the 30th Army. After spending two months in the acting army, he was called back to the USSR People's Commissariat of Defense's Main Personnel Directorate and sent to Kuibyshev to the Frunze Military Academy. However, because of the deteriorating situation at the front, a month later he was called back to the Siberian Military District in order to form the 298th Rifle Division. From the end of February to the beginning of August 1942, the division under his command operated on the Western Front, and from 23 August already engaged in fighting on the Stalingrad direction as part of the 4th Tank Army, and subsequently the 24th and 21st Armies. It took part in the destruction of Paulus's Sixth Army. On 5 February 1943 the general became the deputy commander of the 64th Army, and on 25 April Vasil'ev was appointed as the commander of the 24th Guards Rifle Corps.

A lot of documents have been conserved in the TsAMO RF, in which superior commanders, to which Vasil'ev was subordinate, including M.S. Shumilov, constantly emphasized such qualities as his high cultural level, good professional training, exactingness, prompt fulfillment of the orders given to him, initiative, "vivacity" and simultaneously his diligence in work. From his performance review of 29 June 1943:

> From his first days of assuming command of the corps he demonstrated fine organizational capabilities regarding forging combat teamwork and the organization of training in the corps' divisions, into which a new contingent of replacements was flowing, which had no experience in fighting against the German aggressors.
>
> He has sufficient combat seasoning – he commanded a division up until January 1943, made it stand out among the best, and the division was converted into a Guards division. In a combat situation he is brave, calm and quick-witted. He makes rapid decisions depending on the course of the fighting and firmly implements them. He doesn't lose poise in a difficult

---

19 Ibid.

combat situation. He is able to instruct and bring up soldiers and subordinate commanders in the light of the demands of a combat situation. The headquarters is forged as an organ of command, he has experience in staff work, highly appreciates it, and gives a lot of help to his staff, and through them to the division headquarters. With his command he has full control of the divisions, but sometimes permits inadequate exactness to subordinates, as a result of which there are shortcomings in the corps, which show up in the tardiness in fortifying ground and poor discipline at the front in separate units.[20]

The 7th Guards Army's Military Council highly valued the combat work of both generals during the Battle of Kursk. Both corps commanders were deemed worthy of command honors – the Orders of Kutuzov 2nd Degree. A year later, in May 1944 Lieutenant General Vasil'ev transferred to the 1st Baltic Front to take command of the 1st Rifle Corps. The corps under his command took part in forcing a crossing of the Western Dvina River, the encirclement of Vitebsk and the eventual defeat of the German Courland grouping. After the war he completed academic courses with the Voroshilov Military Academy, commanded a rifle corps in the Baltics, and then served in various posts with the Soviet Army's General Staff until his retirement in 1964.

In the spring of 1943, the command cadres chosen by Shumilov also arrived in the army's rifle divisions. As a result of the army commander's purposeful and systematic work with the command staff, a rather rare situation for the Red Army emerged in the 7th Guards Army: in the assessments of senior leadership, both commanders of its rifle corps and all of the division commanders for the following two years performed fully successfully and not a single one of them was removed from a post until the end of the war. In addition, three division commanders (A.I. Losev and A.V. Skvortsov in 1945, and S.A. Kozak in 1944) became rifle corps commanders and successfully led them.

It is no secret that in the acting army, there were quite a few senior chiefs, who adhered to the principle: "Until I become a Hero of the Soviet Union or a general, there won't be any in the division (corps or so forth)." M.S. Shumilov regarded incentives without any particular qualms. He viewed both awards and personal ranks not as manna from heaven, but as a way to stimulate further growth in a man and a desire to achieve new heights in the military profession. At his recommendation, G.B. Safiulin, N.A. Vasil'ev and five of the eight division commanders who participated in the Battle of Kursk (A.I. Losev, A.V. Skvortsov, S.A. Kozak, I.E. Buslaev and M.I. Denisenko) were awarded the title Hero of the Soviet Union, and all of them became generals. A number of regiment commanders of the 7th Guards Army were awarded Gold Stars, including Majors G.T. Skiruta and G.M. Batalov, whose battalions heroically fought at Staryi Gorod and Maslova Pristan'.

For Army Detachment Kempf, the Battle of Kursk ended tragically. Its troops not only failed to carry out the tasks of Operation Citadel, in the course of it they suffered substantial losses. From 5 to 16 July 1943, the army detachment lost 14,669 servicemen, including 2,966 killed and missing-in-action. In comparison over this same period, the three German corps (II SS Panzer Corps, XXXXVIII Panzer Corps and the LII Corps) of the Fourth Panzer Army lost a combined 16,169 men.[21] So far, detailed information for each division hasn't yet been found. In his book, E. Raus gives the casualty figures for the period between 5 and 20 July only for three infantry divisions. According to his data, they lost a total of 8,754 men, including 3,244 (46 officers) in the 106th Infantry Division, 2,839 (30 officers) in the 320th Infantry Division, and 2,671 (27 officers) in the

---

20 TsAMO RF, personal file of Lieutenant General N.A. Vasil'ev.
21 Zetterling and Franksen, *Kursk 1943: A statistical analysis*, p. 199.

168th Infantry Division.[22] In the opinion of scholar D. Ellis, whom British historian R. Cross cites in his book, this corresponds to 38, 29 and 27% of their combat strength respectively.[23]

So far it hasn't been possible to establish the precise number of panzers and assault guns lost by III Panzer Corps, but the data that has been presented in Table 12 testify to the destruction of the army detachment's shock grouping. According to incomplete data, of the 344 combat machines of the III Panzer Corps that were assembled in the Belgorod area on the morning of 5 July, at 0500 on 16 July only 61 panzers (including 8 Tigers) were still operational – just 18%. However, the losses of assault guns turned out to be relatively low, and the greatest number of them were knocked out in StuG Battalion 228, which was employed exclusively in the sector of Breith's III Panzer Corps. In the three assault gun units that took part in Operation Citadel, a bit less than a third (32%) of their assault guns had been destroyed or were under repair on the morning of 16 July, including 5 in StuG Battalion 905, 14 in StuG Battalion 228 and 5 in StuG Battery 393.

Great damage was done to Breith's panzer corps in the course of the Battle of Kursk in terms of manpower, especially at the command level. For example, according to the information available today, in Hoth's panzer corps of the Fourth Panzer Army, not a single division commander was killed or evacuated to a hospital after being wounded. In contrast III Panzer Corps was deprived of two division commanders. General W. von Hünersdorff was mortally wounded south of Prokhorovka in the course of Operation Citadel,[24] while Lieutenant General G. Schmidt was killed on 5 August 1943 during the Soviet Belgorod – Khar'kov offensive operation. The British historian R. Cross writes:

> On 14 July, while returning to his advanced headquarters after inspecting the bridgehead, he [von Hünersdorff] was shot in the head by a Russian sniper. Hünersdorff was taken to the military hospital at Kharkov where surgery failed to remove the bullet fragments in his brain. He died on the 17th without regaining consciousness, tended to the end by his wife who was in charge of the forward forces' convalescent centre of the German Red Cross. Had von Hünersdorff woken from his coma he would have learnt that the offensive – about which he had so robustly expressed doubts – had failed.[25]

The commander of the 6th Panzer Division enjoyed great esteem in the Wehrmacht; both Kempf and von Manstein regarded him highly. The leading German neurosurgeon Professor Tennis had been urgently brought to the area from Berlin especially for Operation Citadel. Key figures of both the command of Army Group South and of Army Detachment Kempf attended von Hünersdorff's funeral, and his former commander in *Panzergruppe* 3 Colonel General H. Hoth gave the eulogy. There is one more not insignificant detail that emphasizes E. von Manstein's personal special order on behalf of von Hünersdorff. Already after his death, post-dated back to 1 July 1943, von Hünersdorff was promoted to the rank of lieutenant general.

Several versions exist about the circumstances of Lieutenant General G. Schmidt's death. The most well-known one in Russia is the version presented in Sovieet director N. Ozerov's motion picture film *Osvobozhdenie* [*Liberation*]. According to it, the commander of the 19th Panzer Division supposedly shot himself at his forward command post after hearing from von Manstein that the offensive had failed. In reality everything happened somewhat differently. The general was killed on 5 August 1943 near Tomarovka in the course of the encirclement of units of the

---

22 Raus, *Tankovye srazheniia na Vostochnom fronte* (Moscow: AST, 2005), p. 309.
23 Cross, *Operatsiia "Tsitadel"* (Smolensk: Rusich, 2006), p. 264.
24 On 1.08.1943 Major General Hasso-Eccard Freiherr von Manteuffel assumed command of the 7th Panzer Division.
25 Cross, *Operatsiia "Tsidadel"*, p. 238.

19th Panzer Division by forces of the 5th Guards Army and the 1st Tank Army.[26] According to the recollections of Lieutenant General M.E. Katukov, his body was discovered and brought to his army's auxiliary command post. After the war Mikhail Efimovich talked about this episode with a group of officers, among which was Colonel G.A. Sereda, who during the Battle of Kursk commanded the 267th Guards Rifle Regiment of 6th Guards Army's 89th Guards Rifle Division. In his own book, he passed along the army commander's story as follows:

> By 1200 the army had completely destroyed the encircled units of the fascists' 19th Panzer Division. Tankers brought in the body of its commander, Lieutenant General Schmidt – who'd been killed – on a canvas tent half. They also brought in several captured officers. At this time General of the Army I.P. Apanasenko arrived and began to interrogate the prisoners. Krivoshein, a mechanized corps commander, called Katukov. He jumped down into a trench and began to listen to the corps commander's report. At this moment a squadron of Heinkels began to bomb the command post. The army commander asked Apanasenko to enter the trench, but he continued to stand on the trench's parapet. Two bombs exploded not far away, the fragments of which struck the General of the Army, who passed away quickly from the wounds.[27]

According to Western historians, G. Schmidt was killed together with his adjutant Lieutenant Körne during the destruction of a column of tanks and equipment of the 19th Panzer Division by Katukov's tank army on 7 August 1943, and was buried in the village of Berzovka on that same day by surviving members of the command tank's crew, who'd been captured by the 1st Tank Army.

Fate smiled upon the commander of the third panzer division of Breith's III Panzer Corps, Lieutenant General H. von Funck. He survived not only Operation Citadel, but also the following retreat from Ukraine, and on 5 December 1943 he received a promotion and was temporarily placed in command of XXIII Corps; three months later, on 5 March 1944, he transferred to the same post in the XXXVII Panzer Corps. In the autumn of 1944 he was sent into the reserve, and on 15 February 1945 he was discharged from the Wehrmacht. However, this didn't prevent Soviet troops from taking the general prisoner. He was held in a Soviet prison camp until 1955, when he was released and handed over to West Germany, where he died on 14 February 1979.

More commanders at the regimental level were also killed or wounded in the III Panzer Corps, than for example in the adjacent Fourth Panzer Army. During the offensive toward Kursk, only the commander of SS Panzer Grenadier Division *Totenkopf*'s panzer regiment was killed, while in the XXXXVIII Panzer Corps, the commanders of a panzergrenadier regiment and of a panzer regiment (and simultaneously of the brigade of Panthers) were severely wounded. Meanwhile in Breith's panzer corps, altogether six regiment commanders were lost: Köeller (19th Panzer Division's Panzergrenadier Regiment 73) and von Bieberstein (6th Panzer Division's Panzergrenadier Regiment 114) were killed; and Becker (19th Panzer Division's Panzer Regiment 25), Richter (19th Panzer Division's Panzergrenadier Regiment 74), von Oppeln-Bronikowski (6th Panzer Division's Panzer Regiment 11)[28] and Barkmann (168th Infantry Division's Grenadier Regiment 417) were

---

26 On 18.08.1943, Major General Hans Källner assumed command of the 19th Panzer Division
27 Sereda, G.A., *Pervyi saliut Rodiny* [*Motherland's first salute*] (Saransk: Mordovskoe knizhnoe izdatel'stvo, 1993), pp. 126-127.
28 After the wounding of the commander of the 6th Panzer Division's Panzer Regiment 11 Colonel von Oppeln-Bronikowski, his duties were carried out by the commander of the II Panzer Battalion Major von Bäke. The latter was also wounded during an attack on 13 July, but it was only a light wound and therefore he remained at his post.

badly wounded. This fact is one more piece of evidence of the extremely bitter and bloody combat on the Korocha axis.

In the course of Operation Citadel, the command staff of infantry divisions also suffered losses. According to captured sources in the TsAMO RF, two infantry division commanders with Army Group South were hospitalized with wounds: General Schaeffer, commander of LII Corps' 332nd Infantry Division, and General Postel, commander of the 320th Infantry Division (Korps Raus). Incidentally, Major K.R. von Bieberstein, Colonel H. von Oppeln-Bronikowski, as well as a number of other commanders with the 6th Panzer Division and the attached StuG Battalion 228 were killed or wounded on 13 July 1943 during a mistaken Luftwaffe attack on the division's advanced command post, where at the time von Hünersdorff was holding a meeting. In total, 15 men were killed and 49 wounded during this heavy fratricidal airstrike. According to some information, the 19th Panzer Division also suffered during this attack, but so far no detailed information on this division has been found. The Luftwaffe's attack on a friendly command post became known to the Voronezh Front's leadership just an hour after it took place. In the TsAMO RF, I managed to find a message sent by General of the Army I.P. Apanasenko to N.F. Vatutin from the 7th Guards Army's signals hub. Here are several lines from this document: "At 1145 a report came in from Kriuchenkin's headquarters that the enemy attacked friendly forces in the Kazach'e – Rzhavets area with 8 aircraft, and later 60 of our Il-2 ground attack aircraft attacked the same enemy. This is great!"[29] It isn't difficult to understand the general's joy, and what satisfaction the Soviet command might have had, having found out that Seidemann's subordinates didn't only work over the III Panzer Corps' forces so methodically and diligently in the German style, but in a matter of minutes also beheaded one of its three panzer divisions.

In comparison I will give data on the command staff losses of the Soviet side. In the course of the Kursk defensive operation, not a single commander of a rifle formation with the Voronezh Front was killed, and only Colonel I.M. Nekrasov, the commander of the 6th Guards Army's 52nd Guards Rifle Division, which was defending on the axis of II SS Panzer Corps' main attack, was wounded and evacuated to a hospital. On the regimental level, the loss of command staff proved higher: the commanders of two divisional artillery regiments (of the 69th Army's 92nd Guards Rifle Division and of the 5th Guards Army's 95th Guards Rifle Division) and of two rifle regiments (of the 6th Guards Army's 92nd Guards Rifle Division and 375th Rifle Division) were killed. One regiment commander with the 375th Rifle Division was captured, but survived and returned in 1945; and two regiment commanders (of 6th Guards Army's 52nd Guards Rifle Division and 67th Guards Rifle Division) were wounded badly enough to require hospitalization. The command staff of the Front's armored and mechanized forces suffered the highest losses: the deputy commander of the 1st Tank Army's 10th Tank Corps was captured and died in imprisonment, the commander of the 170th Tank Brigade (of the 5th Guards Tank Army's 18th Tank Corps) and the commander of the 5th Guards "Stalingrad" Tank Corps' 48th Guards Separate Heavy Tank Regiment) were killed in action, while one corps commander (Lieutenant General V.G. Burkov, 10th Tank Corps), three brigade commanders (of the 29th Tank Corps' 31st and 25th Tank Brigades and of the 2nd Guards "Tatsinskaia" Tank Corps' 4th Guards Tank Brigade) and two regiment commanders (of the 15th Guards Heavy Tank Regiment of 69th Army's 2nd Tank Corps and of the 36th Guards Heavy Tank Regiment of the 5th Guards Tank Army's 18th Tank Corps) were wounded.

The situation with the loss of command staff in the 7th Guards Army was completely different: not a single unit or formation commander was killed, badly wounded or captured, even though as

---

29 TsAMO RF, f. 7 gv. A, op. 5312, d. 294, l. 103.

I will remind the reader, that it was here that the enemy managed to execute an operational encirclement of units of the 94th Guards Rifle Division and the semi-encirclement of the 81st Guards Rifle Division. To a significant extent, this was due to the well-organized system of command in the regiments and divisions (a successfully arranged network of command posts, observation posts and signals); the enemy's lower aerial activity than on the axis of Army Group South's main attack; and also the professional abilities of the command staff when breaking out of encirclement or escaping a pocket.

The Germans were forced to recognize that Operation Citadel, which had been presented by Germany's leadership as a turning point in the war, had failed. So Hitler coyly expressed his gratitude to his generals for conducting it, but neither von Manstein, nor Hoth, nor especially Kempf were awarded with any Orders or medals. Of the five commanders of Army Group South's panzer and infantry corps that took part in the Kursk offensive, only P. Hausser was bestowed with the Knight's Cross with Oak Leaves on 28 July 1943. Of the 15 division commanders that took direct part in the fighting, only Major General von Hünersdorff received the Oak Leaves to his Knight's Cross; his award documents were signed on 14 July 1943, on the day he was mortally wounded.

Officers at the tactical level from the regiment on down were decorated. Thus, the commanders of the two panzer regiments of Breith's III Panzer Corps that had performed most successfully, Colonel A. Schülz and H. von Oppeln-Bronikowski respectively received the "Crossed Swords" (6.8.1943) and "German Cross in Gold" (7.8.1943). However, this didn't have any immediate effect on their careers. Only on 1 January 1944 would A. Schülz become a division commander (of the 7th Panzer Division), and on this same day be awarded with his first general's rank, while von Oppeln-Bronikowski would take command of the 24th Panzer Division even later – in October 1944. He passed through Germany's defeat rather successfully; although he was taken prisoner by British troops, already on 4 July 1947 he would be released, and he would die in West Germany on 19 September 1966. Schülz's fate was much more tragic. He would be killed in a battle with Soviet forces on 28 January 1945.

One more German participant in the Battle of Kursk, who I've come across more than once in my research on the battle, had a pretty good career until the end of the war. This was the 42-year old Colonel Martin Unrein, the commander of the 6th Panzer Division's Panzergrenadier Regiment 4. Even though he wasn't noted for the Battle of Kursk, already on 10 September 1943 he was awarded the Knight's Cross, and on 5 November 1943 he took command of the 14th Panzer Division. With this panzer division he would take part in the bitter fighting at Cherkassy and in Courland. For his successful command of the division, on 26 June 1944 he was bestowed the Oak Leaves to the Knight's Cross, and already on 1 July 1944 he received the rank of lieutenant general. Between 11 February and 5 March 1945, M. Unrein would lead the III SS (Germanische) Panzer Corps, and on 1 April he would take command of Panzer Division Clausewitz. At the end of this month he would be taken prisoner by the Allies, but already in 1947, like many of his fellow Wehrmacht officers, he would be released from prison and would survive to old age in West Germany. Unrein passed away on 22 January 1972.

Hitler would remind the Commander-in-Chief of Army Detachment Kempf of its failure in the offensive approximately a month later. On 3 August 1943, the offensive by the Voronezh and Steppe Fronts would begin, and already within 10 days their forces would reach the approaches to Khar'kov, and the second stage of combat for this Ukrainian major industrial center would begin. At this time, it was being defended by Kempf's forces. There was no possibility to hold the city and the command of Army Group South understood this well, so it prepared to withdraw from the city. Hitler however insisted on holding it unconditionally. In this situation, Kempf became the scapegoat. On 16 August 1943, he was removed from his post and sent to take command of

Wehrmacht troops in East European countries.[30] This appointment proved to be the last one in his career. After the war, von Manstein wrote in regard to Kempf's dismissal from command of Army Detachment Kempf: "Although I had got on well with General Kempf, I didn't oppose the change – the proposal from which came from Hitler ...." I believe that Army Detachment Kempf's failure in the offensive toward Kursk had substantial influence on taking this decision.

Of all the commanders of Army Detachment Kempf's subordinate corps that took part in the fighting near Belgorod, after the Battle of Kursk the 44-year-old E. Raus would climb most successfully up the career ladder. He not only kept his post as commander of XI Corps [formerly Korps Raus] after the abandonment of Khar'kov, but on 22 August 1943 he also became one of the few who received a high honor for the August fighting around Khar'kov – the Oak Leaves to his Knight's Cross. In October 1943 he assumed command of the XXXXVII Panzer Corps, and on 3 November of the same year there would follow a big promotion – after H. Hoth's dismissal, Raus became the Commander-in-Chief of the Fourth Panzer Army. Before the war ended, Raus would go through two changes in post, but this movement would be only horizontal: on 1 May 1944 he became the Commander-in-Chief of the First Panzer Army, and less than four months later (on 16 August), already in the course of the Soviet offensive in Belorussia, he took charge of the Third Panzer Army. As a result of the Red Army's East Prussian offensive, his troops would suffer very heavy losses, and on 5 March 1945 he would be replaced in this post by General von Manteuffel. Over a year before Germany's downfall, E. Raus would manage to receive a promotion to the rank of colonel general. He would be captured by the Americans, but would avoid a trial and a lengthy incarceration. After the creation of a study group in 1947 for the US Army under the leadership of T. Busse, which was to provide an inside look on the Wehrmacht while analyzing major events of the Second World War, including the Battle of Kursk, he would be recruited to make a contribution to the work. He would write several articles, his memoirs, and would pass away on 3 April 1956 in the FRG.

So, Operation Citadel foundered. After nineteen days of the bloodiest fighting in the center of the European portion of the Soviet Union, the final strategic offensive by Nazi Germany in the East was stopped. Both von Manstein's and Model's assault groupings were played out and began to retreat. R. Cross writes:

> Conceived, planned and executed by the heirs of the Great General Staff, Zitadelle had been a complete failure on the part of the professional military class which Hitler so despised. ... A *Materialschlacht* – clash of machines – had been sought at Kursk in the full knowledge that the attacking forces were inferior to the enemy and that there were insufficient reserves to exploit any success to the hilt. The operation seems to have been planned on the assumption that, as had inevitably happened before, the Russians would collapse at the first impact. Little thought was given to what might happen if they did not, although Model had a pretty clear idea of the consequences. Dash, and the dismissal of the enemy as Slavic *Untermenschen*, was no longer enough. When the enemy stubbornly refused to disintegrate, and then began to pick apart both Hoth's and Model's weakly held flanks, the folly of the exercise was starkly revealed. Poor German intelligence at every stage of the operation and the masterly placing and handling of the Russian strategic reserve had ensured the failure of Zitadelle.[31]

---

30 W. Kempf replaced O. Weller, Erich von Manstein's former chief of staff, when he took command of the Eleventh Army.
31 Cross, *Operatsiia "Tsitadel'"*, pp. 264-265.

However, the thwarting of the enemy's general offensive was only half the job. For the Red Army command, it was important to alter the course of the war conclusively and clear the country from the occupiers. Indeed, it didn't miss the opportunity to make full use of this success that was achieved in the heavy July fighting, which was consolidated in the course of Operations Kutuzov and Polkovodets Rumiantsev. Over two summer months, the Wehrmacht not only exhausted their formations in the East, while losing a large amount of armor and trained personnel; it was also forced to abandon significant Soviet territory. The German forces were thrown back by 200 kilometers across the entire Soviet-German front, which by this time extended for 1,200 kilometers. As Colonel General Heinz Guderian wrote in his book, from this moment on for the German command there were to be "… no more periods of quiet on the Eastern Front."

Index

INDEX OF PEOPLE

Adorf, Lieutenant 355, 390
Aglitsky, Major/Lieutenant Colonel M.P. 338, 496, 498
Ainutdinov, Colonel S.Kh. 428, 451-452
Aizenberg, Colonel I.I. 70, 205, 493
Antonov, Captain A.N. 321, 323
Apanasenko, General I.P. 332-333, 378, 461, 549, 587-588
Arshinov, Major S.A. 64, 171, 254, 268, 309, 312

Bäke, Major Franz 141, 277, 280, 283, 500, 508, 514, 519-522, 524-525, 587
Barkmann, Ernst 141, 160, 249, 587
Batalov, Major G.M. 174-175, 585
Beaulieu, Major General Chales de 110, 249, 319, 332, 389
Becker, Lieutenant Colonel H. 141, 199, 207-209, 212-213, 218, 252-253, 274, 284-285, 319, 323-324, 331, 349, 587
Bel'gin, Captain Andrei Antonovich 254-255, 265-267
Beliaev, Major General I.P. 276, 336, 534-535, 538, 544-545, 547, 550-551, 553
Bezhko, Major General M.P. 387, 490, 506, 508, 510
Bezik, Senior Lieutenant F.V. 475, 479
Bieberstein, K.R. von 141, 158-160, 182, 211-212, 308, 326, 374, 376, 380, 384, 408, 421, 424-427, 429, 471, 587-588
Bogachev, Captain 379, 502
Bogdanov, Lieutenant Colonel A.A. 204, 215, 271, 576, 578-579
Bordzilovsky, Major General Iu.V 144-145
Borisov, Senior Lieutenant 75-76
Breith, General Hermann xv-xvi, 111-115, 119-120, 124, 133, 140, 142-143, 150, 155, 158, 160-161, 170, 172, 183, 186, 188, 191, 199, 201, 206, 208-211, 215, 221, 231, 236-239, 242, 247, 249, 252, 262, 273, 279, 281-282, 290, 293-294, 301-302, 304, 318-319, 326-328, 332, 335, 342, 348-349, 357, 359, 364, 369-370, 372, 374, 380, 397, 400, 404-409, 417, 420, 424-425, 431, 433-434, 437-439, 444, 446, 448, 450, 467, 470, 473, 477, 479, 484, 486-489, 498-499, 505, 508, 514, 518-519, 522, 525, 527-528, 541, 548, 559-560, 566, 574-582, 586-587, 589
Burdeinyi, Colonel A.S. 153-154, 366, 377-378, 387, 405, 445-446, 449-450, 513, 581
Burnazian, Lieutenant Colonel G.S. 334, 498
Bushin, Colonel M.A. 225, 336, 535, 550

Buslaev, Colonel I.E. 189, 194-195, 197-199, 286-287, 289, 306, 311, 318, 541, 549, 557, 572-574, 577-578, 585
Busse, General Theodor xviii, 118, 136, 210, 221, 234, 300, 328, 397, 564, 566, 590

Cherevichko, Captain Vladimir Ivanovich 464-465
Chernov, Lieutenant Colonel Aleksandr Vasil'evich 463
Chibisov, V.P. 538, 551
Chistiakov, Lieutenant General I.M. 25-27, 29, 65, 93, 97, 149, 154, 182, 223, 225, 275-276, 289, 364, 367, 378, 555, 580
Chuev, Captain D.S. 474, 493, 497
Chuikov, V.I. 30, 573

Davydenko, Lieutenant Colonel V.I. 255, 257, 262-263, 269
Denisenko, Major General M.I. 31, 59, 81, 99, 194, 199, 226, 585
Dvoinyi, Senior Lieutenant V.A. 175, 177, 180, 228
Dziuba, Captain Dem'ian Afanas'evich 310, 315-316

Fangohr, General Friedrich 210, 291-292, 299-300, 353, 484-485
Forst, Lieutenant General W. 143, 170, 173, 197, 236-237, 286, 290, 309, 311, 356, 397, 544, 551, 576
Funck, Major General H. von xviii, 49, 112-113, 121, 123-124, 128-129, 137, 142-143, 163, 169-170, 183-186, 201-209, 221-222, 234, 238, 242, 247, 249-250, 253-254, 257, 261-263, 281, 290, 301-302, 304, 309, 333-334, 336, 338-339, 355-356, 364, 370, 373, 394, 397, 444, 475, 477-480, 489, 492, 495-497, 518-519, 548, 576, 587
Funtikov, Colonel A.A. 55, 147, 459, 558

Gakhokidze, Captain Sh.M. 212, 283-284
Gläsemer, Colonel W. 142, 186-187, 204, 250, 253-254, 263, 269-270, 273, 276, 309, 334
Goriachev, Lieutenant General S.G. 28-29, 95, 225, 275-276, 305, 333, 346, 365, 377-381, 383-384, 387, 405, 409-411, 413-415, 423, 429, 438-440, 446, 448-449, 452, 454, 458-461, 474, 489, 491, 496, 498, 506, 511, 513-518, 525, 527
Goshtenar, Guards Captain Aleksandr Fedorovich 82, 324, 464-465

Gotsak, Lieutenant Colonel P.I. 287-288
Govorunenko, Lieutenant Colonel P.D. 55, 340-341, 412, 414, 429, 438, 470, 500, 525
Grimailo, Lieutenant Colonel P.I. 474, 479
Gromadin, Lieutenant General M.S. 441-442

Hausser, P. 299-300, 318, 353, 400, 553, 561, 566, 589
Heilmann, Captain 206-207, 215
Hitler, Adolf xiv, 24, 29, 66, 107-108, 111, 116-120, 126, 136-137, 234, 240, 299, 353-354, 362, 400, 484, 508, 561-565, 589-590
Horn, Major General H. von 363-364, 371, 488-489, 496-497, 510, 518-519, 547, 582
Hoth, Colonel General H. xii-xiii, 107-112, 115, 125, 133-134, 139, 152, 191, 210-211, 223, 237, 289, 298-300, 302, 318, 350, 353, 360, 364, 443-445, 473, 485-486, 547, 561, 586, 589-590
Huchtmann, Lieutenant 520-521
Hünersdorff, Major General W. von 112, 140, 159, 182, 190, 202, 209, 211, 222, 234, 237, 247, 249-250, 253, 290, 304, 308, 319, 326, 328, 336, 338, 340, 342, 348, 355, 375, 380, 385, 393, 406, 421, 424-426, 429, 444, 479-480, 489, 498-499, 505-506, 508, 522, 525, 527, 560, 586, 588-589

Iastrebov, Captain P.G. 163, 168, 186
Ignat'ev, Major A.A. 384, 496
Il'iasov, Captain Ivan Vasil'evich 255, 257, 265-267
Isupov, Colonel A.F. 276, 335
Iurlov, Major 271-272
Ivanov, Lieutenant General S.P. 60-61, 97, 102, 226, 245, 361, 377, 379, 387, 439-441, 443, 449-451, 455, 459, 513-514, 553

Jeschonnek, General 114-115

Kageneck, Captain Graf von 75, 141, 161, 207, 408, 421, 424, 426-427, 429, 431
Karklin, Major N.A. 160, 340, 428
Katukov, Lieutenant General M.E. 25-26, 90, 244-245, 289, 353, 367, 587
Kazarinov, Major 244, 414
Kempf, General W. xii, xviii, 21, 25-27, 32, 41, 49, 51, 63, 67, 73, 92, 94, 107-121, 125, 127-129, 133-134, 136-137, 139-140, 148-153, 155, 157-159, 161, 172, 178, 182-183, 186, 188-192, 209-210, 221, 223-224, 226, 231, 234, 236-240, 242, 249, 252-253, 263-264, 276, 281, 290-293, 297-302, 304, 308, 318, 324, 327-328, 340, 350-359, 364, 369-371, 374, 379, 395, 397, 402, 404-406, 408, 412, 417, 428, 432, 436, 440, 443-448, 462, 471-473, 484-486, 488-489, 499, 527, 530, 541, 547, 549, 559-562, 564-567, 574-577, 579-580, 582, 585-586, 589-590
Khitsov, Major I.A. 64, 162, 165, 168, 186, 203, 208, 254, 268, 323, 325-326, 475-476
Khorolenko, Major D.S. 64, 166, 254, 258-259, 312, 315

Khrushchev, Lieutenant General N.S. 56, 100
Khusanov, Sergeant Ziiamat Ustinovich 163-165
Köhler, Colonel Rudolf 163, 165, 199, 206-207, 209, 212-214, 252-253, 262, 284, 319, 323, 371, 391
Kozak, Colonel S.A. 31, 52, 55, 67, 99, 190, 205-206, 216-218, 220, 222, 242, 244, 246-247, 251, 254, 257, 259-262, 264, 268-270, 272-274, 279, 282-283, 290, 306, 311, 316, 318, 393, 396-397, 476, 532, 534, 538, 543, 561, 579, 585
Kozhar, Senior Lieutenant G.M. 310, 544
Krasiukov, Sergeant Nikolai 330-331
Krasovsky, Lieutenant General S.A. 190, 192, 308
Kriuchenkin, Lieutenant General V.D. xv, 24, 26, 28-29, 347, 379, 403, 440-443, 445, 448-450, 455, 467, 501, 510, 513-514, 519, 527, 529
Kriuchenkin, Major T.F. xv, 24, 26, 28-29, 52, 61, 211, 214, 252-253, 284, 320, 323, 347, 375, 379, 400, 403-404, 409, 412, 420, 439-443, 445, 448-450, 454-455, 462, 467, 487-489, 501, 510-511, 513-514, 519, 525, 527-529, 560, 581, 588
Kvashin, V.E. 254, 256, 266

Lebedev, Major General V.G. 365, 381-383, 386, 424, 427, 490, 513, 516, 524
Lednev, Colonel I.I. 460-461
Lifits, Lieutenant Colonel L.A-M. 70, 248, 280, 380
Liukshin, Major V.P. 537-538
Losev, Major General A.I. 31, 63, 79-80, 99, 174-176, 178, 180, 189, 193, 215, 224, 227, 229-232, 287-288, 310-311, 313, 318, 399, 541, 548, 557, 578, 585
Lozhko, Lieutenant Colonel 340, 493
Lukin, Major General G.S. 98, 100, 184, 548

Malinin, Captain V.M. 221, 255, 269
Manstein, Field Marshal E. von xii-xv, 25-26, 29, 65, 107, 109-110, 113-114, 116-119, 127, 133, 136, 210-211, 224, 234, 237, 276, 289, 299, 302, 318, 327, 353-354, 360-364, 443, 447, 462, 484-485, 487-488, 527, 547, 561-563, 566-567, 586, 589-590
Matsokin, Captain I.A. 166, 170-171, 187, 258
Morozov, General I.K. 31, 52-54, 56-57, 81, 99, 150, 153, 156, 158-159, 182-183, 187, 189-190, 202, 212, 224, 231, 244, 246, 248, 251, 270, 274, 284, 319-321, 324-326, 330-333, 348-350, 356, 360, 365, 367, 372, 379, 383, 391, 393, 397, 404, 414, 420, 423, 426, 434, 438, 458-462, 466, 470, 472-473, 485-486, 526, 529, 567
Moskalenko, Lieutenant General K.S. 26, 443, 460
Müller, Lieutenant 355, 397
Mutovin, Colonel B.I. 202, 208, 258

Nevzhinsky, Colonel M.V. 70-71, 195, 197-198, 286, 311, 314, 539, 554-555, 577-578
"Nikolaev", see General A.F. Vatutin
Novikov, Lieutenant Colonel N.I. 341-345, 348, 378, 411, 516

Oppeln-Bronikowski, Lieutenant Colonel Hermann von 141, 211, 249, 252, 263, 267-273, 276-280, 290, 293, 301, 303, 306, 308, 319, 324-325, 330, 336-337, 340, 342, 344-345, 348, 351, 355, 369-371, 374-376, 380-382, 384, 386, 408, 410, 420, 424-425, 427, 429, 434, 437, 481, 499-500, 502-503, 505-509, 511, 519-520, 580, 587-589
Orlov, Major 255, 263
Osetrov, Major General N.A. 177, 179, 292
Osis, Captain V.T. 207, 212, 214

Petrov, Major General A.N. 49, 80, 95, 97, 148, 254, 271-272
Pliaskin, General V. 41, 45
Pochtarev, Senior Lieutenant F.P. 277-278, 495
Polbin, Colonel I.S. 191, 308
Pominov, Major Georgii Fillipovich 512-513
Popov, Major General A.F. 180, 387, 445, 449
Postel Major General G. 143, 173, 176-178, 197, 227, 236-237, 286, 302, 317
Prokhorov, Major V.F. 97, 263, 271-272
Prokop'ev, Captain D.A. 342-343, 430-431
Protas, Colonel S.M. 501, 511

Quentin, Major F. 273, 343-344, 408, 425-427, 429, 496, 503, 519

Ragoznyi, Major General Z.Z. 28, 388, 458, 466, 510, 525
Raus, General Erhard xiv, xvii, 51, 108, 110, 112, 116, 119-123, 125, 130-132, 136-138, 140, 142-144, 151-152, 155, 170, 172-173, 175-178, 188-189, 191-193, 197-198, 214-215, 228, 231, 233-235, 237-239, 242, 247, 249-250, 259-260, 279, 281-282, 285-286, 292-293, 297, 301-305, 316-318, 327, 334, 352, 355-357, 364, 369, 397-398, 444, 448, 489, 497, 539, 544, 547-549, 556-557, 560-561, 564, 566, 572, 574-577, 582, 585-586, 588, 590
Razgel'deev, Captain V.I. 255-256
Richter, Lieutenant Colonel Helmut 141, 160, 165, 183, 199, 209, 211, 252, 323, 340, 374, 376, 380, 587
Rokossovsky, General K.K. 67, 107, 146, 291, 573-574
Rotmistrov, Lieutenant General P.A. xv, 299, 351, 443, 446, 514-515, 527-528, 553
Russkikh, Colonel I.G. 94-95, 275, 304, 338-339, 356, 372, 379-381, 384, 397, 416, 423, 438, 474, 478, 480, 492-493, 496, 518, 567
Rybalko, General P.S. 29, 405

Safiulin, Major General G.B. 31, 54, 63, 140-141, 147-149, 164-165, 185, 190, 202, 204, 206-207, 244, 246-248, 251, 258, 262, 274, 277, 290, 304-305, 310-311, 316, 318, 325, 334, 336, 338-339, 359-360, 371, 393, 404, 416, 423, 455, 460, 475-476, 488, 492-493, 498, 535, 540, 543, 557-558, 579, 582-585

Samoilenko, Lieutenant Colonel I.I. 349, 393, 420-421, 426, 506
Sannikov, Major S.P. 213-214
Sapozhnikov, Lieutenant Colonel M.G. 205, 244, 262, 270, 394
Savchenko, Sergeant I.P. 138, 179, 208, 260
Savchenko, N.I. 138, 179
Schmidt, Major General Gustav 110, 112, 141, 163, 165, 199, 206-207, 215, 234, 251-253, 262, 274, 284, 290-291, 318-320, 348, 356, 370, 375, 385, 389, 391, 393, 406, 408, 425, 429, 444, 448, 462, 470, 480, 489, 498-499, 504-505, 508-509, 560, 576, 586-587
Schülz, Lieutenant Colonel Adelbert 142, 185-187, 203-204, 206, 208, 216, 220, 238, 250, 253-255, 257, 261, 263-267, 269, 271, 273, 278-279, 281, 286, 293, 309, 336-339, 370, 478-480, 492, 494-495, 580, 589
Semenov, Major A.S. 539, 544
Sereda, Colonel G.A. 93, 411, 587
Seriugin, Colonel M.P. 276, 490, 503, 509, 522-524
Shapovalov, Lieutenant Colonel I.I. 341, 420, 430
Shevchenko, Lieutenant Colonel M.T. 366, 415, 504
Shmanov, Lieutenant Colonel S.V. 62, 245, 276-277, 493
Shumilov, Lieutenant General M.S. xiii-xv, xvii-xviii, 21, 25, 27, 29-30, 32, 40-43, 46, 51-53, 57-62, 65, 67-71, 77, 80, 82, 96, 99, 101-102, 105, 120, 130, 139-140, 146, 148-149, 153-156, 172, 178, 182, 188-189, 203-204, 215, 223-226, 230-232, 242, 244-248, 251, 257, 266, 274-276, 279, 289, 291, 300, 304-306, 308, 327, 330, 334-336, 354-355, 359-360, 364, 367, 379, 395, 397, 399-400, 404, 409, 416, 420, 448-449, 453-455, 459-462, 473, 475, 485, 487-488, 493, 514-515, 529-530, 532, 534-535, 547-549, 553, 561, 566-567, 574-575, 577-585
Simonenko, Senior Lieutenant Petr Grigor'evich 465-466
Simonov, K.M. xvii, 372, 416, 420, 500
Simonov, Major M.E. 372, 420
Skiruta, Major G.T. 52, 82, 158, 284, 324, 466
Skvortsov, Major General A.V. 31, 63, 65, 81, 151, 153, 171, 181, 185, 187, 189-190, 202-204, 216, 222, 231, 254, 258, 290, 306, 311-312, 397, 585
Slatov, Lieutenant Colonel G.P. 255-257, 262, 309, 556
Smorzh, Captain S.S. 344, 430
Sokolenko, Major Ivan Ia. 82, 324, 465
Sonntag, Senior Lieutenant P. 428-429
Speidel, Major General H. 111, 117-118, 150, 159, 166, 179, 183, 192, 236-238, 308, 327-328, 548-549, 561
Stalin, I.V. 21, 23, 28-29, 32, 58, 70, 91, 126, 135-136, 162, 168, 202, 221, 245-246, 257, 289, 346, 363, 385, 396, 404, 411, 441-442, 445, 460, 526, 528, 572
"Stepnoi", see Lieutenant General M.S. Shumilov
Sudets, Lieutenant General V.A. 190, 276, 306-307
Surzhits, Colonel D.N. 386-388

Sushchitsky, Captain Georgii 212, 321
Svetnik, Lieutenant Colonel/ Major B.Iu. 458, 466

Taranov, Colonel I.A. 70-71, 216, 246, 248, 310-311, 315, 373, 538-539, 542, 544, 549, 553
Tatiev, Junior Lieutenant Sarsibai 181-182
Terent'ev, Major General G.N. 28, 455, 531-532, 550
Teteshkin, Major General S.I. 153, 184, 386-387, 395
Titarenko, Major S.I. 52-53, 283, 323, 331, 372, 462
Trekhglazov, Junior Lieutenant N.I. 217, 255
Trunin, Colonel V.F. 275, 341, 346-347, 367, 379-380, 384, 397, 410, 414-415, 422, 438, 440, 451, 469, 472-473, 485, 492, 500, 506, 510
Turaev, Senior Lieutenant Said 464, 466

Ulosovets, Major A.I. 179-180, 193
Unrein, Colonel Martin 141, 273, 308, 319, 324-326, 330, 374, 376, 380, 408, 420-421, 424-425, 471, 500, 503, 505, 507-508, 519, 559, 589
Usikov, Lieutenant Colonel I.A. 340, 372-373, 394-395, 476-477, 556
Ustanovich, Ziiamat 163-164

Vasil'ev, Colonel A.F. 387-389, 411-412
Vasil'ev, Lieutenant I. 41, 272
Vasil'ev, Major General N.A. 31, 58, 143, 148, 153, 178, 180, 184, 188-189, 194, 226, 232, 247, 276, 286, 304-305, 311, 316, 364, 398, 455, 481, 492, 500, 502, 507, 510, 541, 573, 577, 579, 583-585
Vasilenko, Major General E.I. 31, 99, 131, 248, 274, 336, 340, 373, 395, 474, 476, 478-479

Vasilevsky, Chief of General Staff A.M. 22, 25, 136, 211, 306, 528
Vatutin, General N.F. xii, xiv, 21-29, 32, 43, 51, 55-58, 60-62, 65-67, 69, 76, 89, 97-99, 101-102, 107, 127, 135, 138, 146, 148, 154-155, 211, 223, 225-226, 231, 245, 247, 274-276, 289, 291, 299, 304, 306, 333, 343, 346-347, 351, 360-363, 365, 367, 377-379, 381, 388-389, 400-403, 405, 412, 435, 438-441, 443, 445, 448-451, 453-455, 459-460, 462, 467, 475, 485, 487-488, 513-515, 519, 527-529, 549, 565-566, 573-575, 580-581, 588
Verba, Lieutenant Colonel A.A. 70, 204-205, 215, 217-221, 218, 244, 246, 248, 255, 270-271, 281
Vinogradov, T.Z. 138, 173, 179, 260
Vovchenko, Major General I.A. 29, 405

Westhofen, 1st Lieutenant Heinrich 349, 370, 374-377, 380-382, 384-386, 406, 408, 425-426, 428, 433-434, 437, 481-482, 499, 506

Zatylkin, Major F.A. 205, 217, 263, 302
Zhadov, Lieutenant General A.S. 460, 528
Zherebtsov, Major I.F. 271-272
Zhukov, Marshal G.K. 22, 25, 29, 51, 57-58, 61-62, 70, 136, 225, 231, 562
Znamensky, Major S.K. 156, 213-214
Zorin, Major D.I. 277, 279, 330, 494
Zorin, Signal Sergeant Sergei Petrovich 266-267
Zotov, Major 366, 415

INDEX OF PLACES

Akhtyrka 28, 135, 362
Aleksandrovka 512, 515-519, 525-526, 559-560
Aleksandrovskii 48, 400, 475, 515, 559
Alekseevka 22, 27, 48, 275, 292, 515
Andreevskie 44, 319, 341, 349, 392, 407, 410, 413-414, 425, 427, 429, 433, 446-447, 455, 462, 469, 471, 481
Arkad'evka 333, 338-339, 455, 479, 493-494
Arkhangel'skoe 127, 145, 147-149

Batratskaia Dacha 55-56, 67, 73, 140, 190, 204-205, 217, 221, 262-263, 265, 269-274, 278-279, 281-283, 290, 305-306, 309-310, 312, 333, 335-336, 339-340, 352, 355-357, 365, 368, 371-374, 393-395, 397, 401, 406, 416-417, 444, 446, 453-455, 475-478, 488, 492-493, 531-532, 534, 540, 543, 547, 556-557, 580
Belenikhino 448-449, 467, 581
Belgorod viii, xi-xv, xviii, 21-22, 24-26, 28-30, 40-43, 45, 51-53, 64, 66, 75, 77-78, 88, 101, 105, 107-108, 118, 122, 126, 129, 132, 134-135, 137-138, 140-141, 144-148, 150, 152, 155, 157, 159-161, 163-165, 167, 170, 173, 175, 182-183, 189, 194, 206, 209, 221, 223-224, 226, 228, 231, 235-236, 245, 249, 271-272, 275-276, 285, 292-293, 300, 302-303, 307-308, 318, 320, 324, 341, 345, 347, 350-352, 360-362, 364-365, 367, 370-371, 390-393, 400-402, 404-407, 411, 417, 431, 433, 440, 444, 446-448, 451, 458, 460-463, 467, 469-473, 481, 483-485, 489, 497, 517, 523, 526, 530, 549, 554, 567, 581, 586, 590
Belianka 27, 276
Belinskaia vi, 52, 54, 212-213, 215-218, 220, 224, 230, 244, 251-252, 262-263, 268, 270, 273-274, 276, 308-309, 325-326
Belomestnaia 341, 413
Belomestnoe 407, 440, 448, 489, 499
Belovskaia 244, 277-278, 283-284, 292, 302, 305, 308, 318-319, 323-326, 328-329, 332-334, 349, 352, 356, 371-373, 440, 463-464, 489, 540, 558
Belyi Kolodez 27, 32, 45, 60, 98, 340, 344, 385, 389, 407, 410, 414, 421, 425, 427, 429, 431
Berezovka 22, 126, 154
Berlin 24, 107, 117-119, 136, 141-142, 151, 235, 352, 354, 363, 385, 431, 471, 564, 586
Bezliudovka 31, 41, 51, 58, 140, 143, 154, 156, 172, 176, 178, 180, 189, 191, 193, 198-199, 223, 226-228, 235-236, 249, 260, 262, 286, 288, 297,

302, 305, 313, 316-318, 353, 357-358, 398-399, 401, 441, 455, 576
Blizhniaia Igumenka xv, 22, 52, 55, 70, 149, 152, 159, 209, 224, 239, 241-242, 244, 251, 274, 284, 302-303, 318-320, 323-326, 329, 331-335, 340-341, 345-346, 348-352, 355-356, 364-365, 369-372, 375, 382-383, 389-393, 404-409, 413, 417, 420-423, 425-427, 433-434, 441, 446-447, 451, 458, 462, 468-471
Bobrovo 90, 526
Bochkovo 60, 70
Bogodukhovo 109, 127, 135
Bol'she-Troitskoe 27, 48, 73
Bol'shie Maiachki 377, 400
Bolkhovets 160, 371
Borovskoe 281, 333, 369, 479, 494, 558
Brodok 31, 137, 146, 261, 364
Bulgaria 164-165

Central Asian republics 100, 123, 182
Cherkasskoe 223, 240, 292
Chernaia Poliana 31, 44, 140-141, 159-160, 234, 242, 319, 341, 345, 413-414, 427-428, 439-441, 446, 464, 469-471
Chuguev 30, 118, 125
Churaevo 44, 58, 78, 260, 275, 315, 336, 399, 453, 534, 536-537
Chursino 461, 523, 526
"Comintern" collective farm 342, 344

Dal'niaia Igumenka 48, 55-56, 71, 78, 140, 239, 241, 271, 275, 292, 303, 324, 340-344, 346, 348-351, 364, 366, 374-386, 390, 392, 403-407, 409-411, 413-415, 420, 423-429, 431, 433-434, 437, 439-440, 444, 446-447, 449, 451, 468, 481-482, 490, 499-500, 530, 542
Dal'nie Peski 41, 63, 141-142, 150, 155, 157, 160, 163, 165-166, 169, 171, 186, 189-190, 199, 202, 204, 206, 208, 212, 226, 230, 234, 252, 368, 530, 534
Dal'nii Dolzhik 449, 511
Dalniaia Igumenka 55, 341
"Day of Harvest" collective farm 163, 212, 215, 221-222, 241, 244, 251-253, 262-263, 269, 274, 282-285, 321, 323-325, 332, 351, 390, 426, 447, 458
Dolbino 183, 328, 484, 488, 547
Don River 23-24
Donets River xv, xviii, 27, 56, 108, 122, 125, 128-129, 137-138, 141-143, 150, 152, 155, 159, 161-162, 166-167, 172-173, 175, 183-184, 189, 192, 206, 209-210, 215-216, 228, 235-236, 241-242, 249-250, 274, 276, 303, 317-318, 324, 350, 357-358, 371, 392-393, 396, 406-408, 446-447, 461-462, 469, 481, 483, 488, 490, 499, 504, 525, 527, 560
Dorogobuzheno 41-42, 44, 64, 111, 150, 163, 166, 168-170, 172, 184-187, 189-190, 201-202, 206-208, 211, 225-226, 241-242, 250, 261, 303, 306-307, 371, 407

Dragunskoe 22, 154

Generalovka 44, 64, 183, 190, 202-204, 206, 208, 212, 215-216, 218-221, 224, 237-238, 241, 244, 246, 252-255, 262-263, 268-271, 273, 276-277, 280, 284, 290, 309, 328, 335, 368, 407, 530, 532, 534, 551
Gostishchevo 48, 224, 275, 292, 350, 449-450, 490, 509, 524-525, 559-560
Grafovka 127, 146, 401, 548
Gremiachii 44, 190, 202, 205, 216, 220, 244, 269, 306, 310-313, 315-316, 333, 335, 344, 352, 357, 368, 373-374, 395-396, 401, 452-455, 490-491, 516-517, 530, 534, 536, 540, 546, 551, 556
Gremiachii Machine Tractor Station 546, 551, 556
Griaznoe 371, 378

Hill 108.9 168-171, 185-186, 201
Hill 126.3 163, 170-171, 199, 207, 211-212, 226
Hill 139.9 209, 212, 230, 252-253, 283
Hill 145.4 179, 195
Hill 146 175, 536
Hill 151.4 258-259
Hill 156.2 536, 550
Hill 160.8 203-204, 220, 453, 540, 547
Hill 164.7 64, 216, 218, 220-221, 230, 238, 254-255, 268-269, 273, 530-531, 534
Hill 167 58, 70
Hill 167.1 262, 269, 532
Hill 167.4 217, 262
Hill 167.7 224, 236
Hill 171.8 58, 59, 70
Hill 176.0 258-259, 535, 550-551, 553
Hill 184.4 58, 70
Hill 185.7 426-427, 434
Hill 187.4 257, 263-264, 544-546
Hill 190 283, 352, 535
Hill 191.2 220, 254, 256, 258, 262-264, 276, 454, 475, 535, 546-547, 550-551, 553, 557
Hill 191.8 67, 339, 473, 475, 479, 492, 540
Hill 192.6 313, 316, 318, 352, 398-399
Hill 192.8 310, 313, 316, 318, 352-353, 398-399
Hill 202.3 339-340, 473-476, 479, 488, 540, 547, 557
Hill 202.9 306, 313, 455, 531, 547, 554
Hill 205.5 67, 339, 473, 475, 477, 479, 488, 530, 540
Hill 206.9 276, 279, 337-339, 365, 384, 393-394, 455, 473-475, 477-479, 489, 492, 494, 540
Hill 207 143, 173, 175, 235, 287, 306, 313, 548
Hill 207.0 310, 546, 549, 554-555
Hill 207.8 324, 389, 421, 433
Hill 207.9 144, 262, 278, 280-281, 293, 308, 325, 334, 540, 548, 550
Hill 209.5 340, 413
Hill 209.6 205, 216, 220, 238-239, 244, 246, 259, 262-263, 265, 269, 272, 282, 293, 306, 309-312, 368, 454-455, 531-532, 534-535, 538, 540, 544, 546, 551, 556
Hill 209.7 264, 290, 365

INDEX

Hill 210.3 333-334, 338, 477, 479, 495, 498
Hill 211.5 383, 451, 480, 482-483, 490, 504, 509
Hill 211.6 341, 407, 413
Hill 212.1 56, 329, 389, 421-422, 427
Hill 213.7 339, 365, 480, 489, 492-493, 495
Hill 216.1 142, 144, 238-239, 250, 262-263, 271, 273, 277-278, 280-282, 290, 309, 335, 453, 477, 540
Hill 217.4 382, 499
Hill 230 481, 500, 506

Iablonevyi 463-465
Iakovlevo 28, 275, 514
Iastrebovo 44, 55, 62, 67, 78, 140, 224, 239, 246, 251-252, 262-263, 268-271, 273-274, 276-279, 301-303, 309, 318-319, 324-330, 334-338, 340, 342, 348, 351, 401, 407, 447, 453, 455, 498, 548, 560
Ivanovka 146, 148, 174, 191, 193, 398, 450, 484
Izium 125, 363

Kalinin 103-104, 146, 193, 342, 348, 350, 352, 355, 364, 374-377, 380, 383-385, 393, 408, 416, 420-421, 423, 439, 447, 450, 473, 479, 481, 489, 496-497, 503, 505, 520, 524, 531, 583
Kar'ernaia 58, 193, 197, 227, 353
Karnaukhovka 41, 143, 146, 153-154, 170, 172, 174-175, 180-181, 188-189, 191-193, 226-228, 235-236, 541
Kashlakovo 283, 311, 315, 368, 537, 558
Kazach'e 342, 365, 400, 402, 450, 488, 500, 508-509, 511-515, 517, 519-520, 522, 524-525, 527, 541, 559-560, 588
Khar'kov xii, xiv, 21-22, 28-29, 31, 68, 77, 88, 90, 95, 110, 118, 126-127, 135, 138, 152, 170, 176, 183, 195, 236, 331, 362, 399, 401-402, 454, 484, 531, 549, 586, 589-590
Khokhlovo 55, 319, 366, 377, 410, 415, 425-429, 433, 437, 440, 448-450, 458, 461, 473, 482, 489-490, 499, 501, 503-504, 508, 525-526, 542
Kiselevo 275, 415, 424-425, 427-429, 433, 437, 448-449, 451-452, 473, 480-483, 487, 490, 498-499, 501, 503-506, 508-509, 516, 522, 524-527, 580-581
Kochetovka 289, 377
Koloniia Dubovoe 199, 206-207, 249, 273
Komintern 412, 447, 452, 489, 514, 518, 560
Komsomolets State Farm 387, 553
Koren' River 173, 194, 274-275, 281-282, 286, 293, 301-302, 304, 306, 310, 313, 315, 318, 333-336, 352, 369, 399, 423, 453-454, 493, 515, 538, 541
Koren' 220, 282-283, 310-311, 394, 534-535
Koren'skaia Dacha 220, 282-283, 310-311, 394, 534-535
Korocha River 107, 110, 455, 475
Korocha xi-xii, xiv, 24-25, 28, 32, 43, 48-49, 61, 69, 71, 76, 101, 107-110, 144, 149, 154, 225, 245, 341, 350, 363, 375, 378-379, 388, 400, 403, 431, 439-440, 444, 447-449, 451, 455, 475, 485, 510, 513-515, 517, 526, 528-529, 562, 588

Krapivnoe 276, 336, 398-399
Krasnaia Dubrava 377-378
Krasnaia Poliana 69, 126, 534
Krasnianskii State Farm 70, 73
Krasnoarmeiskoe 58, 60
Krasnyi Mai 453, 455
Kreida 51-52, 54, 147, 186, 212, 222, 241, 244, 251-253, 274, 283-285, 303, 307-309, 318-321, 323-324, 332-333, 352, 356, 360, 368, 372, 389-390, 392-393, 417, 422, 425-426, 433-434, 458, 463-464, 466, 470
Krivtsovo 275, 379, 449-450, 459, 467, 515, 525, 560
Kruglik 90, 484
Krutoi Log 30, 44, 48, 64, 140, 144, 183, 187, 191, 201-206, 208, 216-221, 224, 226-227, 230, 234-235, 237-238, 241, 244-246, 250-251, 253-254, 256-263, 268, 271, 273, 286-287, 290, 297, 303, 307, 309, 311, 318, 355, 357, 364, 368, 371, 392-393, 396, 398, 401-402, 409, 453-454, 475, 498, 530-532, 534-536, 539, 541, 544, 547, 549-551, 553, 556-557, 576
Kupino 69, 534
Kurakovka 520, 522-525, 559
Kursk Bulge xii-xiii, 129, 137, 195, 306, 562
Kursk Oblast 22, 88-89, 132
Kursk xi-xix, 21-25, 27, 29-30, 32, 40, 42-43, 45-46, 51-52, 55, 58-59, 62-63, 66-68, 73, 75-78, 82-84, 86, 88-91, 95, 97, 99-100, 102, 104, 106-109, 111-113, 116, 119-121, 127-132, 134-135, 137, 146, 149, 151-152, 155, 165, 170, 178, 194-196, 211, 214, 223-224, 228, 232, 234, 245, 250, 264, 271, 290-292, 294, 296-298, 304, 306, 308, 314, 316, 321-322, 333, 335, 350, 353-354, 359, 361-364, 375, 386, 392-393, 398, 401, 404, 408, 411, 417, 432, 436, 439, 442-443, 445, 457-458, 460, 468, 480, 487, 497-498, 517, 527-528, 531, 554-555, 562-567, 572-576, 578-579, 582, 585-590
Kursk salient xii, xv, 21-24, 40, 42-43, 45, 66, 104, 107-109, 128, 135, 146, 170, 363, 375, 392, 443, 563-566

Leski 449-450, 581
Lipovyi Donets River xii, 25, 27, 340, 462, 471, 484, 487, 522
Logovoe 58, 276
Lomovo 48, 245, 275, 344, 400, 491, 507-508, 515, 517
Luchki 362, 377, 400

"Main Fruit and Vegetable" State Farm 341, 392, 413, 426-427, 429, 433-434, 440, 471, 481
Malo-Iablonovo 449, 451, 463, 525
Mazikino 275, 303-304, 342-345, 383, 386, 410-412, 449, 452, 480, 497, 502, 515, 518, 526-527
Melikhovo 56, 241, 275, 302-303, 326, 338, 340-346, 348, 350-351, 356, 364-367, 369-370, 374-377, 379-386, 389, 393, 397, 400, 403-404, 406-410, 412-415, 420-421, 424-427, 431,

438-441, 444, 447, 449, 467-468, 471, 481, 490, 499-501, 503, 505, 525, 560, 581
Miasoedovo 31, 44, 48, 55, 70, 78, 142, 205, 218, 224, 239, 241-242, 262, 271, 273-275, 277-279, 302-305, 309, 324-326, 329-330, 333-339, 344, 348, 351-352, 356, 364-365, 368-370, 372, 376, 384, 386, 393-394, 403, 409, 416-417, 420, 423, 444, 446, 448, 455, 473-475, 477-480, 488-489, 492, 495-499, 514, 519, 525, 540, 542, 557
Mikhailovka xv, 25, 29-30, 41-42, 49, 52-54, 67, 101, 111-112, 114, 130, 134, 137, 140-141, 145, 148-151, 153-160, 165, 172, 182, 184, 186, 190, 199, 207-212, 226, 249, 251-252, 276, 284, 292, 302, 319, 321, 323-324, 332, 370-371, 408, 540
Moscow xi, xiii-xiv, 21, 28, 30-31, 43, 46, 56, 60, 62, 65-67, 78, 87, 91, 104, 107, 113, 119-121, 135, 138, 148-153, 158-159, 164-165, 169, 174-175, 178-179, 183-184, 186, 191, 193, 197-198, 201, 203-204, 211, 216, 221, 228, 235, 238, 245-246, 250, 252-254, 267, 273-274, 280, 307-308, 322, 331, 363, 375-376, 395, 402, 406, 420, 439, 441, 443, 446, 460-461, 466, 487, 501, 509, 519, 527, 529, 547, 549, 554, 556, 561, 564-565, 572-573, 586
Murom 78, 127

Nekliudovo 248, 264, 274-275, 281-282, 305, 336, 368, 423, 453, 455, 475-476, 493, 534, 540
Nezhegol 44, 48, 59, 62, 107-108, 140, 144, 152, 176, 179, 248, 288, 353
Nezhegol River 58, 62, 108, 110, 158, 176, 179, 288, 306, 353, 455
Nikol'skii 394, 478
Nikol'skoe 44, 78, 127, 282, 305, 329, 333, 336, 339-340, 352, 455, 475, 558
Nizhnii Ol'shanets 31, 44, 63-64, 68, 140, 143, 166, 170-172, 174-176, 181-182, 184, 186-190, 201, 203-204, 206, 220, 224, 226, 230, 235-236, 245, 297, 344, 357, 475, 489, 541, 549, 576
Northern Donets River xi-xii, xv, 22, 24, 27, 29-30, 40-42, 45, 49, 52, 57, 60, 63, 78, 82, 96, 110-113, 123-124, 127, 129, 133-134, 137, 139-140, 142, 144-145, 149, 152, 154-158, 163, 166, 168, 171-173, 176-177, 184, 190-191, 193-194, 198, 201, 206, 208, 224-225, 227, 230, 232, 252, 261, 285, 290, 293, 301, 307, 333, 340, 342, 345, 350, 356, 366, 368-369, 371, 389, 398, 404-405, 409, 413, 415, 424, 426, 428-429, 433, 446-448, 450, 452, 455, 462-463, 467-468, 473, 480, 487-490, 498, 505, 508-508, 511, 517, 519, 522, 524-525, 530, 536, 541, 548, 559-560, 574, 577
Novaia Gorianka 126, 154
Novaia Tavolzhanka 58, 146, 194, 455
Noven'koe 90, 109
Novo-Aleksandrovskii 515, 559
Novo-Dmitrievka 22, 126
Novo-Nikolaevka 242, 303
Novo-Oskochnoe 450, 452, 467, 472, 482, 506, 508, 515, 517, 522, 524, 526, 559
Novoselovka 73, 386, 417, 455, 515, 540

Novo-Troevka 275, 305, 336, 475, 493
Novyi Oskol 23-24, 502, 526

Oboian' xi-xii, 21, 24-26, 32, 40, 48, 66, 90, 107-109, 183, 245-246, 289, 292, 300, 308, 351, 362, 367, 378, 400-401, 417, 440, 442, 448, 485, 514, 517, 581
Oktiabr'skoe 58-60, 455
Ol'khovatka 275, 303-304, 500, 503, 506-508, 511, 573
Orel 24, 28, 40, 77, 88, 107, 134, 167, 228, 554, 562
Orlov ravine 381, 433, 452, 480, 489-490
Oskol River 23, 526

Pena River 25, 267-268, 417, 484-487, 496
Pentsevo 31, 143, 245, 248, 275, 311, 333, 368-369, 396, 455, 534
Peresyp' 484, 486
Petropavlovka 55, 413, 440, 447, 449-450, 489, 499, 509, 542
Ploskoe 490-491, 515-516
Plota 524, 529
Podsumki 515, 517
Point "K" 282, 306, 310, 340, 352
Point "Sar" 283, 286, 398, 557
Point +1.0 277, 314, 318, 399, 546
Point 133.6 59-60
Point 140.1 314, 318
Point 156.2 45, 536
Point 167.7 536, 550
Point 176.0 216, 311, 453, 534, 536
Point 190.0 399, 546
Point 191.2 543, 557
Point 191.8 335, 477
Point 191.8 335, 477
Point 192.6 314, 399
Point 192.8 314, 399
Point 199.1 394, 532, 556
Point 202.9 398-399, 557
Point 205.4 273, 534
Point 207.9 453, 536
Point 209.6 244, 273, 530, 534
Point 216.1 280, 477
Pokrovka 126, 145, 249, 341, 377, 408, 413, 452, 470
"Poliana" State Farm 180, 194, 224, 242, 247, 263, 283, 287-288, 306, 310-316, 357, 374, 394-399, 401, 416, 536, 540, 546-547, 549-550, 553-554, 557
Postnikov 55, 70-71, 205, 319, 328, 333, 340-341, 343-344, 349, 352, 365-366, 374, 376-377, 380, 382-383, 385-386, 389, 393, 401, 404-410, 413-416, 420-423, 425-427, 429-431, 433-434, 437, 441, 446, 451, 462, 467-469, 471
Priiutovka 146, 154, 173-177, 197, 226-227, 232, 235, 286, 288, 353, 398, 541, 548-549, 556-557
Prilipy 58-59
Pristen' 127, 548
Prokhorovka Station 48, 108-109, 387, 513, 528, 548, 559, 581

INDEX

Prokhorovka xii-xiii, xv, 25-26, 28, 40, 48, 66, 108-110, 116, 133, 225, 244, 275-276, 289, 293, 299-300, 308, 318, 351, 353, 360, 367, 375, 379, 387, 389, 400, 429, 443-446, 450, 460, 467, 473, 484-488, 499, 513-515, 517, 519, 524, 527-528, 530-531, 547-549, 553, 559-562, 567, 581-582, 586
Psel River 209, 299, 445, 484
Puliaevka 127, 146, 155
Pushkarnoe 41, 145, 148-150, 155, 157, 160-161, 163, 182, 184, 186, 191, 231, 284, 303, 307, 371, 530, 534

Raevka 412, 507-508, 511, 514
Razumnaia River 24, 49, 64-65, 142, 208, 224, 239, 244, 246, 252-254, 263, 268-270, 275-276, 279, 284, 303, 308, 319, 324-325, 328, 333, 336, 339, 340-342, 345, 350, 370-371, 376, 404, 406, 409-410, 412-413, 446-447, 467, 479-480, 489, 495-496, 498, 508-509, 512, 517-518, 540, 560
Razumnoe 48, 51, 55-56, 62, 64-65, 78, 140-142, 163-165, 167-169, 171, 183, 185-187, 190-191, 201-208, 211-212, 216-221, 226, 234, 237-239, 241, 245, 250-254, 261, 268, 270-271, 274, 290, 307, 368, 370-371, 392, 440, 453, 515, 530, 534, 536, 576
Razumnoe Station 142, 169, 201, 208
Repnoe 28, 31, 371, 455, 534
Rzhava Station 73, 264
Rzhavets 49, 143, 173, 175-178, 180, 189, 192-199, 223, 227, 230, 235, 248, 286-289, 306, 314-315, 317-318, 353, 398-399, 401, 441, 455, 482-483, 487-488, 508-509, 515, 519-525, 527, 541, 546-547, 549, 556-557, 559-560, 581, 588

Sabynino 28, 68, 275, 303, 350, 379, 383, 412, 415, 428, 433, 444, 447-452, 473, 480-484, 488-490, 498-499, 503-509, 511, 513, 515-516, 522, 525, 542, 559-560, 580-581
Sazhnoe 386, 450, 467
Sevriukovo 52, 239, 246, 270, 274, 277, 279, 292, 302-304, 309, 319, 324-330, 333-338, 340-341, 343-345, 349, 351-352, 371, 379, 385, 389, 408, 420, 425, 447, 453, 462, 475, 489
Shakhovo 48, 391, 449-451, 458, 461, 467, 523, 525
Shebekino 29-31, 44-45, 48, 58, 78, 89, 101, 172, 194, 247-248, 275-276, 281, 287, 309, 333, 336, 357, 369, 398-399, 455, 537
Shebekino Station 58, 281
Shebekinskaia Dacha Woods 149, 172, 178, 180, 189, 194-195, 199, 224, 239, 260, 262, 287-288, 313, 398, 401, 548, 557
Sheino 44, 48, 56, 275, 277, 325, 338-339, 342-343, 370, 375, 379-380, 405, 411-412, 449, 452, 473, 480, 484, 488, 494-498, 506-507, 515, 518, 525-527, 580
Shishino 55, 319, 366, 382, 404, 406, 414, 426, 433-434, 441, 446-448, 451, 460, 462, 471, 473, 481, 525
Shliakhovoe viii, 28, 48, 275, 341-342, 344-345, 351, 374, 379-386, 388-389, 400, 403-406, 408-416, 420, 423-424, 428, 433, 440, 445, 449-452, 468, 473, 480-481, 487-490, 499-503, 505-509, 511, 513, 516, 519-520, 525, 559, 581
Shliakhovoe Machine Tractor Station 383, 386, 409, 412, 433, 452, 480-481, 490
Shopino 341, 413, 448, 472, 499
Sinel'nikovo 58, 60
Skorodnoe 24, 43, 98, 107-111, 133, 526
Soldatskii 67, 126
Solomino 41-42, 95-96, 111, 127-128, 138, 142, 145, 148-149, 151, 154-155, 157, 163, 166-171, 173, 181, 184-191, 201-203, 206, 208-209, 225, 241-242, 250, 261, 273-274, 303, 306-307, 371, 377, 530, 536
"Solov'ev" collective farm 246, 272, 278-281, 330, 334-340, 352, 372-373, 394-395, 417, 453, 475-476, 492, 547, 556-557
Stalingrad iv, xiii-xiv, xvi, 22, 29, 31, 52, 59, 66, 87, 91, 95, 100, 105, 110, 136, 151, 156, 158, 174, 195, 216, 232, 245, 289, 312, 324, 346, 387, 396, 439, 442-443, 460, 466, 501, 532, 555, 563, 565, 573, 582-584, 588
Staritsa 58, 147
Staryi Gorod xv, 22, 31, 44-45, 47, 52, 54-56, 65, 71, 134, 140-141, 153-154, 158-160, 162, 183, 201, 209, 212, 224, 234, 242, 249, 292, 302, 307, 318-319, 323-325, 327, 332-333, 345-346, 349, 352, 365-366, 368, 370, 372, 383, 389, 392-393, 404, 406-410, 413-414, 417, 422, 425-427, 433-434, 440, 446-447, 455, 458, 462, 466-467, 469-471, 481, 530, 581, 585
Staryi Oskol 22, 24
Sumy 135, 362, 564
Suprunovka 145, 149-150, 157
Sviridovo 214, 512, 515-518

Tavrovo 261, 364, 371, 407
Ternovka 393, 413
Teterevino 109, 379, 448-449
Tim 24, 107, 132
Timovka 44, 58, 455
Titovka 49, 51, 53, 59, 64, 73, 163, 173, 175, 179, 189, 192, 194, 206, 223, 235, 248, 298
Tomarovka 22, 24, 28, 107, 362, 586
Toplinka 127, 130, 138, 145-146, 149, 151, 155-156, 173-174, 189, 193, 196, 235, 307, 548
Tula 28, 216, 346, 531

Urals 83, 120, 195
Ushakovo 31, 370, 379, 410-412, 449, 452, 497, 515, 518, 581
Ustnika 247-248

Velikaia 101, 104, 152, 375
Verkhnii Ol'shanets 171, 275, 400, 402, 433, 451-452, 472, 482-483, 488, 490, 503, 505-509, 511, 514-515, 519, 524, 526-527, 541, 560

Verkhopen'e 90, 378, 444
Visloe 340, 350, 379, 413, 472, 499
Vitebsk 174, 585
Volchansk 22, 24, 28, 31, 44-46, 48-49, 51, 58-60, 69, 78, 101, 105, 247, 275, 336, 398
Volchanskie Vyselki 59-60, 69
Volga River 31, 92, 103, 156, 439, 513
Volkovo 146, 148-149, 176, 191, 398, 548
Volobuevka 450, 467
Volokonovka 22, 24, 31, 40, 49, 64
Voronezh Oblast xii-xv, xvii, 21-29, 31-32, 34, 40-41, 43-44, 47, 50-52, 54-56, 58, 62, 65-68, 73-78, 83, 86-90, 92, 94, 97-103, 105, 107, 109-110, 125-127, 129, 131, 133, 135-136, 138-139, 144-145, 149, 152-153, 156, 164, 176-177, 179, 184, 189-190, 193, 210, 213-214, 223, 225-226, 245-246, 257, 259, 270, 274, 288-289, 291-293, 299-300, 304-308, 321, 327, 331, 333, 335, 345-346, 348, 350, 353-355, 359-363, 365, 377, 379, 385-386, 395-396, 401-405, 409, 411, 417-418, 429, 431, 434-435, 438-442, 444, 446, 460, 469, 473-474, 476, 482, 485-487, 496-497, 506, 510, 513, 517, 524, 527-529, 531, 562-564, 566-567, 574-575, 578, 580-582, 588-589
Voznesenovka iv, 28, 48, 58, 70, 276
Vypolzovka 27, 365, 386, 512-513, 515, 518, 526-527, 559-560

Zaiach'e 241, 333, 344, 400, 447, 500, 516-517
Zavody-2 48, 59
Zhimolostnoe 386, 451, 525
Ziborovka 228, 399
Znamenka 490, 503, 507, 560

INDEX OF SOVIET MILITARY UNITS & FORMATIONS

Fronts:
Briansk Front 28, 104, 174,
Central Front 22, 28, 40, 46, 75, 104, 148, 322, 361, 574,
Kalinin Front 104, 583
Reserve Front 23, 346
Southwestern Front 22, 30-31, 45, 58, 69, 77-78, 88, 108, 135, 152, 174, 189-190, 306, 449, 583
Steppe Front xii, 21, 40, 46, 146, 363, 526, 528, 574
2nd Ukrainian Front 94, 221, 584
Voronezh Front xii-xiv, xvii, 21-23, 24-29, 31-32, 34, 40-41, 43-44, 47, 50-52, 54-56, 58, 62, 65-68, 73-78, 83, 86-90, 92, 94, 97-103, 105, 107, 109-110, 125-127, 129, 133, 135-136, 138-139, 144-146, 149, 152-153, 164, 176-177, 179, 184, 189-190, 193, 210, 213-214, 223, 225-226, 245-246, 257, 259, 270, 274, 288-289, 291-293, 299-300, 304-308, 307, 321, 327, 331, 333, 335, 345-346, 348, 350, 353-355, 359-363, 365, 377, 379, 385-386, 395-396, 401-405, 409, 411, 417-418, 429, 431, 434-435, 438-442, 444, 446, 460, 469, 473-474, 476, 482, 485-487, 496-497, 506, 510, 513, 517, 524, 527-529, 531, 562-564, 566-567, 574-575, 578, 580-582, 588
Western Front 28, 30, 142, 146, 246, 441-442, 531, 584

Armies:
1st Tank Army 25-26, 29, 31, 90, 109, 225, 245, 289, 353-354, 367, 378, 400, 417, 443, 486, 587-588
2nd Air Army 144, 152, 190-192, 276, 306, 308, 361, 396, 402, 510, 527, 575, 581
3rd Tank Army 29, 405, 444
5th Guards Tank Army xv, 293, 363, 443, 446, 486-487, 513-514, 517, 521, 527-528, 553, 567, 581, 588
6th Guards Army xiii-xv, 22, 25-28, 31-32, 40, 43, 45, 48-49, 55-56, 62, 65-69, 71, 76, 78, 84, 88, 90, 93, 97, 99-100, 126-127, 134, 139-141, 145, 148, 152, 160, 223-224, 225, 240, 275-276, 289, 292, 298, 304, 308, 319, 326, 338, 340, 343, 346, 349-351 353, 364-367, 378, 400, 403-404, 409, 412, 415, 434, 443, 450, 486, 566-567, 571-572, 574-575, 579-580, 587-588
7th Guards Army xiii-xviii, 21-22, 25-29, 31-36, 38-49, 51-53, 55-63, 65-73, 75-77, 79-80, 82, 84-86, 88-89, 92-95, 98-100, 102, 105-106, 110, 112, 115-116, 120, 125, 127-131, 133-134, 137, 139-140, 144-146, 148-149, 152-153, 155, 163-164, 169, 173, 176, 178-179, 183-184, 188-192, 194-195, 202, 204-205, 209, 211, 214-215, 223-226, 228, 230-231, 241-246, 248, 250-251, 257, 259-260, 262-264, 268, 270-271, 273-277, 279-281, 283, 286, 289, 292-295, 297-301, 304-305, 307-308, 310, 315-316, 318-319, 321, 323, 326-327, 329-330, 332, 335, 338, 340, 348, 350-352, 354-355, 358-362, 364-367, 369, 378, 386, 392-393, 395, 397, 399-400, 403-404, 408-409, 412, 414, 416-418, 431-432, 441, 450, 453-457, 459-461, 466, 472-474, 477, 489, 491, 493, 529-533, 536-539, 541-543, 547-549, 557-559, 561-562, 566-568, 570, 572, 574-582, 584-585, 588
13th Army 40, 46, 174, 347, 574
17th Air Army 152, 190-192, 250, 276, 306-308, 335, 392, 510, 575, 581
21st Army xiv, 22, 29-30, 89-90, 555, 584
38th Army 22, 40, 89, 100, 102, 139, 531, 581
40th Army 22, 26, 32, 40, 88-90, 98-99, 101, 139, 443, 445, 485, 581
47th Army 363, 526
53rd Army 528, 531, 584
57th Army 22, 29, 31, 58-60, 68-69, 156, 189, 405
60th Army 22, 104
64th Army 22, 29-31, 41, 89, 174, 216, 346, 439, 583-584

INDEX

69th Army xii, xv-xvi, 22, 24, 26-30, 42-43, 48, 56, 89, 94, 100, 102, 133, 180, 214, 225, 243, 245, 275, 289, 301, 304, 308, 340, 342, 346-347, 365, 367, 369-370, 374, 379, 386-389, 400, 402-405, 408, 409, 411-413, 415-416, 423, 429, 431-432, 433, 435, 439-443, 445-446, 448, 450-452, 455, 459, 462, 466-467, 473, 477, 484, 486-489, 492, 498, 501, 508-511, 513-515, 517, 519, 521-522, 525-529, 531, 562, 567, 570, 576, 580-581, 588

Rotmistrov's Tank army see 5th Guards Tank Army

Groups:
Group Getman 417, 485, 487, 496

Corps:
1st Bomber Aviation Corps 191-192, 308, 581
1st Guards Cavalry Corps 246, 405, 444
1st Mechanized Corps 526, 528
1st Storm Aviation Corps 191, 510
2nd Guards "Tatsinskaia" Tank Corps 29-30, 32, 71, 153, 245, 275, 299, 349, 366, 377-378, 387, 405, 415, 445-447, 449, 467, 483-484, 513-514, 566, 581, 588
3rd Guards "Stalingrad" Tank Corps 29, 405, 444
5th Guards "Stalingrad" Tank Corps 245, 275, 289, 387, 405, 425, 444-445, 449, 588
6th Guards Cavalry Corps 30, 405
9th Composite Aviation Corps 191, 335
10th Tank Corps 387, 400, 588
18th Tank Corps 331, 460, 588
23rd Guards Rifle Corps 40, 55, 149, 343
24th Guards Rifle Corps 31-32, 44, 49, 51, 58-59, 63, 70, 99, 130, 143-144, 148, 153, 156, 173, 175, 177-178, 180, 188-189, 192, 195, 197-199, 215, 224-228, 235-236, 239, 247-248, 274, 276, 287-288, 297-298, 305-306, 309, 313-314, 316-317, 357-358, 364, 368, 398, 432, 441, 455, 533, 539, 541, 548, 557, 562, 577, 584
25th Guards Rifle Corps 31, 44, 49, 51, 55, 63, 67, 69, 76, 130, 140, 147-149, 151, 153, 157, 162, 164-165, 184-185, 190, 202, 205-206, 210, 215, 218-219, 222, 224, 226, 230, 242, 244-245, 247, 250-251, 257, 259, 262, 268, 270, 276, 281, 285, 290, 304-305, 310, 318-319, 324-325, 328-330, 333-336, 338-339, 351, 355, 359, 364, 367-369, 374, 393-394, 402, 404, 414, 416, 423, 426, 455, 459-460, 462, 473, 475, 477, 479, 488, 492-493, 498, 530-531, 533-535, 540-541, 549, 557-558, 561-562, 580-582
35th Guards Rifle Corps xvi, 28, 83, 92, 94-95, 102, 225, 275-276, 279, 304-305, 333, 341, 343, 345-347, 349, 351, 364-368, 374, 378, 381, 383, 385, 401, 404-405, 407, 410, 412-414, 417, 423, 429-430, 433-435, 438-441, 446, 448, 450-452, 455, 458-459, 461, 470-472, 474-475, 480, 487, 489-492, 496-500, 503, 505-506, 509-511, 513-515, 517-518, 521, 525, 527, 529
48th Rifle Corps 28, 340, 365, 388, 446, 458, 462, 466, 487, 489, 510-511, 522, 524-525, 529
49th Rifle Corps 28, 247, 276, 455, 530-532, 534, 536-538, 541, 543-544, 546, 549-550, 557, 562, 567

Divisions:
15th Guards Rifle Division 31, 44-45, 51, 56, 58-61, 65, 68, 70, 99, 130-131, 189, 225-226, 245, 247-248, 274, 276, 305, 333, 336, 340, 352, 356, 372, 393-395, 397-398, 416, 448, 453, 455, 473-480, 488, 492-493, 495-496, 530, 532, 534, 539-540, 542-543, 547, 549, 556, 561, 588
19th Rifle Division 31, 68-69
36th Guards Rifle Division 31, 44, 49, 51, 58-62, 65, 67-71, 81, 98-99, 102, 140, 145, 149, 179, 189, 194, 199, 216, 226, 298, 305-306, 399, 455, 562
38th Rifle Division 31, 174, 583
52nd Guards Rifle Division 65-66, 223, 572, 588
67th Guards Rifle Division 65, 223, 572, 588
72nd Guards Rifle Division 31, 44-45, 59, 62-63, 67-68, 79-80, 85, 92, 95, 99, 127, 130, 137-138, 140, 142-143, 145, 149, 153, 155, 173-177, 179, 181-182, 185, 188-189, 192-194, 198-199, 214-215, 223-224, 226-233, 239, 255, 260, 283, 285-288, 292, 298, 304-306, 310, 313-317, 336, 352-353, 395, 398-399, 455, 530, 539, 541, 548, 557, 572, 577, 579
73rd Guards Rifle Division 30-31, 42, 44, 51-53, 55-56, 66, 68, 70, 88, 99-100, 102, 151, 190, 202, 205, 215-219, 221-224, 239, 244-248, 251-252, 254, 256-257, 259-266, 268-269, 271, 273-274, 276-277, 278-279, 281-282, 286-288, 290, 304-306, 308-312, 315-316, 330, 332-333, 336, 338-341, 344, 352, 356, 360, 364-365, 367-368, 373, 393, 395-397, 400, 416, 454-455, 475-477, 483, 530-532, 534-536, 538, 543-544, 547, 549-550, 556, 561, 577-580
78th Guards Rifle Division xvii, 31, 44, 52, 63-64, 66-69, 81, 92, 100, 102, 140-141, 149, 151, 160, 162-163, 166, 168-174, 176, 180-181, 184-190, 199, 202-207, 209, 214-216, 218-219, 221-222, 224, 226-227, 230-231, 238, 242, 244, 252-254, 257-259, 268-269, 274, 276, 281, 290, 293, 304, 306, 309-312, 316, 323, 325, 329, 334, 352, 355, 365, 367-368, 374, 397, 400, 416, 455, 475, 534, 572, 575, 580
81st Guards Rifle Division xiii, xv, xvii, 27, 31, 44-45, 47, 49, 51-56, 63, 65-71, 78, 81, 84, 88, 99, 102, 130, 134, 140-141, 145, 147, 150-151, 153, 157-158, 160-162, 183, 187, 189-190, 202, 205-207, 209, 211-212, 214-216, 218-220, 223-224, 231, 239, 242, 244-246, 251-253, 259, 262-263, 268, 270-271, 273-274, 277-278, 283-285, 291, 293, 302, 308, 318-320, 323-326, 328-330, 332-334, 336, 338, 340-341, 346, 348-352, 355-356, 359-360, 365-372, 375, 377, 383, 389, 391, 393, 400, 404-407, 409-410, 412-414, 416, 420, 422-423, 425-427, 429, 433-435, 438, 440, 446-449, 450-453, 455,

459-463, 466-469, 472-473, 481, 483, 515, 526, 529, 567, 574, 576, 578, 580-581, 589
89th Guards Rifle Division 55, 93, 275-276, 305, 345, 411, 413, 450-452, 458, 472, 483, 489-490, 503, 508-509, 515, 521-522, 524, 529, 560, 587
92nd Guards Rifle Division xv-xvi, 29, 56, 92, 225, 275, 305, 341, 344-352, 365-367, 372, 374, 376-377, 379-381, 383, 390, 393, 403, 405, 408-410, 412, 414-416, 420, 424-425, 427, 429-430, 433-435, 438, 440, 444, 446, 448, 451-452, 462, 466-469, 472, 480-481, 483, 489-492, 500, 502-503, 506, 508, 511, 513, 515-516, 525, 529, 580-581, 588
93rd Guards Rifle Division 29, 83, 225, 365, 529
94th Guards Rifle Division 29, 83, 94-95, 225, 246, 279, 304-305, 329-330, 334-336, 338-339, 343-345, 348, 352, 355-356, 364-367, 372, 374, 376, 380-381, 383-384, 393-394, 404-405, 413, 416, 420, 423-424, 432, 444, 448, 453, 473-475, 478-480, 487, 489, 492-496, 503, 505, 513, 515, 518-519, 529, 566-567, 580, 589
107th Rifle Division 28, 56, 365, 379, 383, 387-388, 403, 444, 452, 483, 490-491, 506, 508, 511, 513, 516, 529
111th Guards Rifle Division 28, 225-226, 247-248, 275-276, 336, 368, 399, 444, 455, 530-532, 535, 537, 541, 543, 546-547, 549-551, 554, 567
161st Rifle Division 89, 445, 572
183rd Guards Rifle Division 28, 30, 42, 387, 440, 450, 529
198th Infantry Division 327, 363-364, 370-371, 396, 398, 404, 406, 417, 432, 444, 446, 473, 475, 477-479, 485, 488-489, 497-498, 505, 519, 529, 531, 539, 541, 543, 560-561, 582
213th Rifle Division 30-31, 42, 44, 51, 61, 64, 68, 70, 92, 100, 131, 151, 179, 189, 194-200, 205, 215, 219, 222-223, 225-227, 231, 247-248, 283, 286-287, 298, 304-306, 313-318, 336, 352-353, 399, 455, 530, 532, 539, 541, 546, 549, 557, 567, 569, 572-573, 575-577, 579
244th Bomber Aviation Division 191, 250, 307
270th Guards Rifle Division 28, 59, 276, 336, 367-368, 416, 444, 453, 455, 530-532, 534-538, 544, 546-547, 549-551, 553, 557, 567
276th Guards Rifle Division 471, 490
305th Rifle Division 28, 56, 342, 351, 375, 379, 365, 383, 387-389, 403, 409-412, 415, 433, 444, 449-450, 452, 480-483, 489-492, 499-502, 506-508, 511, 515, 526, 529, 580
306th Storm Aviation Division 191-192
375th Guards Rifle Division 27, 31, 55, 65, 68, 140, 145, 149, 160, 210, 223, 299, 319, 332, 340, 342-343, 350, 365, 378, 391, 412-415, 424, 426, 428-429, 433, 435, 438, 448, 450-452, 458, 462, 472, 483, 529, 579, 588

Brigades:
10th Separate Destroyer Anti-tank Artillery Brigade 61, 449, 514-516

27th Guards Tank Brigade 58, 60, 70-71, 189, 194-198, 205, 222-223, 227-228, 243, 247, 250, 286-287, 289, 298, 306, 311, 313-315, 317-318, 455, 530, 532, 535, 539, 541-542, 545-546, 550, 553-555, 575-578
30th Separate Destroyer Anti-tank Artillery Brigade 32, 61, 69, 205, 218, 220, 244-245, 255, 261-262, 269-270, 273, 281, 368, 393-395, 455, 416, 476, 532, 534, 543, 579-580
31st Separate Destroyer Anti-tank Artillery Brigade 61-62, 245-246, 274-279, 281, 289, 293, 301, 304, 326, 329, 334, 336, 338, 355, 416, 452-453, 480, 489, 492-493, 495, 514-515, 529, 566, 578
60th Engineer Brigade 532, 535
96th Separate Tank Brigade 55, 71, 160, 366, 377-378, 381-386, 410, 415, 424-425, 427-428, 440, 444, 449-452, 490, 503, 508, 511, 513, 516, 521, 524, 529, 581
201st Separate Tank Brigade 60, 70-71, 216, 242-244, 246, 283, 310-312, 316, 359, 368, 373-374, 416, 454-455, 530, 532, 534-535, 538, 544, 546, 550, 553, 557, 562, 578-579

Regiments:
16th Guards Mortar Regiment 55, 413, 429, 434, 452
30th Separate Destroyer Anti-tank Artillery Regiment 56, 261
43rd Guards Artillery Regiment 59, 68, 248, 540
44th Guards Rifle Regiment 59, 248, 275, 340, 352, 372-373, 393-395, 455, 475-477, 479, 488, 495, 540, 547, 556
47th Guards Rifle Regiment 247, 275, 455, 473-475, 477, 479, 488, 492-493, 540, 547
47th Guards Separate Breakthrough Heavy Tank Regiment 366-367, 376, 378, 381, 386, 410, 415, 427-428, 444
50th Guards Rifle Regiment 248, 275, 455, 475, 479
97th Guards Mortar Regiment 32, 53, 68-69, 150, 202, 244, 256, 351, 366, 368, 377, 381, 396, 416, 455, 469, 476, 532, 534, 534, 540, 580
108th Guards Rifle Regiment 98, 306
114th Guards Separate Destroyer Anti-tank Artillery Regiment 32, 53, 55, 68, 86, 151, 244, 283, 285, 325-326, 330, 351, 366, 368, 414, 430-431, 438, 452, 491, 513, 529, 569, 580
115th Guards Destroyer Anti-tank Artillery Regiment 32, 58, 68, 455, 541
148th Mortar Regiment 61-62
148th Separate Tank Regiment 59, 68, 70-71, 192, 245-246, 248, 278-281, 290, 304, 329, 334-336, 343-344, 380-381, 383-384, 386, 410, 415, 424, 480, 490, 500-503, 513, 529, 580
153rd "Urazovo" Guards Artillery Regiment 31, 53, 68, 151-152, 218, 220, 245-246, 255-256, 261, 265, 282, 534
155th Guards Artillery Regiment 138, 173, 179, 227, 260

INDEX   603

158th Guards Artillery Regiment 64, 151, 204, 206-207, 256, 368, 534

161st Guards Cannon Artillery Regiment 32, 53, 55, 68-69, 150, 160, 190, 205, 220, 246, 271, 325-326, 342, 351, 368, 455, 478, 532, 540, 580

167th Separate Tank Regiment 48, 56, 70-71, 204-205, 217-223, 226, 242-244, 246, 268-270, 273, 280-281, 290, 294, 309, 352, 359, 368, 416, 423, 453, 579-580

173rd Guards Artillery Regiment 55, 212, 244, 283, 285, 332, 351, 420

197th Guards Artillery Regiment 341-344, 365, 414-415, 420, 425, 430, 438, 467-468, 491, 580

199th Guards Artillery Regiment 334, 380, 384, 498

209th "Abgonerovo" Guards Rifle Regiment 31, 205, 217, 220-221, 246, 254-256, 261-265, 268-270, 276, 282, 288, 306, 309, 352, 394, 534, 544, 556

211th "Bassargino" Guards Rifle Regiment 31, 217, 220, 224, 254-256, 260-261, 282, 287, 290, 306, 310-312, 315-316, 352, 374, 534, 544, 556

214th "Voroponovo" Guards Rifle Regiment 31, 205, 217, 220, 246, 254-257, 261-267, 269, 281-282, 288, 306, 310, 352, 393-394, 476-477, 532, 543, 556

222nd Guards Rifle Regiment 174, 177, 180-181, 233, 287, 306, 310-311, 313, 352, 398-399

223rd Guards Rifle Regiment 64, 171-172, 186-187, 226, 254, 262, 268-269, 272, 276, 283, 290, 306, 309-310, 312, 352

224th Guards Rifle Regiment 45, 79-80, 95, 177-180, 193, 198-199, 227-228, 233, 305-306, 313, 317, 353, 399

225th Guards Rifle Regiment 64-65, 102, 151, 166, 168, 170-172, 174, 181, 185, 187, 190, 203-204, 216, 220-221, 226, 230, 254, 256-259, 306, 310-312, 315-316, 352, 374, 534

228th Guards Rifle Regiment 64-65, 162-163, 165-166, 168-169, 151, 171, 186, 202, 204, 207-208, 212-215, 220, 253-254, 268, 323, 325-326, 329, 355, 455, 475-476, 534

229th Guards Rifle Regiment 85, 173-175, 177, 179-181, 193, 228, 232-233, 287, 352

233rd Guards Rifle Regiment 45, 52, 57, 212, 215, 244, 283-284, 319-321, 323, 329, 331, 333, 349, 352, 356, 365, 371-372, 389, 427, 458, 462, 470, 534

235th Guards Rifle Regiment 52-54, 57, 81, 158-159, 211-212, 284, 319, 321, 324, 352, 392, 427, 458, 463, 466, 472, 526

238th Guards Rifle Regiment 52-53, 57, 104, 130, 156-157, 160-162, 183, 211-214, 244, 252-253, 262, 284, 319-321, 349, 352, 427, 458, 470, 526

262nd Separate Heavy Tank Regiment 54, 68, 70-71, 205, 212, 221, 243-244, 264, 281, 283, 320, 326, 331-332, 351, 359, 368-369, 386, 416, 423, 453, 493, 495, 540, 580, 582

263rd Mortar Regiment 413, 452

265th Cannon Artillery Regiment 32, 190, 220, 263, 351

265th Guards Cannon Artillery Regiment 32, 53, 68, 95, 97, 149, 206-207, 218, 244, 246, 255, 263, 271-272, 280-281, 368, 455, 532, 580

267th Guards Rifle Regiment 93, 508, 524, 587

276th Guards Rifle Regiment 342, 345, 349, 352, 365-366, 372, 389, 408, 410, 413, 416, 420-421, 423, 425, 427, 429, 433, 462, 467-470, 491, 499-500, 506

280th Guards Rifle Regiment 341-346, 348, 352, 365, 367, 374, 376-378, 380-381, 383, 389, 410-411, 414-415, 420, 424-425, 431, 433, 452, 467-469, 480-481, 490-491, 499, 504, 506, 508, 516

282nd Guards Rifle Regiment 342, 345-346, 349, 366, 381, 383, 393, 410, 414, 421-423, 426-427, 429-430, 433, 462, 467-469, 490-491, 506

283rd Guards Rifle Regiment 339, 380, 384, 416, 420-421, 478, 493, 496-497, 518

286th Guards Rifle Regiment 339, 423, 473-474, 493, 497

288th Guards Rifle Regiment 334-335, 338-339, 344, 380, 478, 496-497, 503, 518-519

290th Mortar Regiment 32, 53, 55, 65, 68-69, 76, 95, 149-150, 160, 165, 190, 207, 213-214, 320, 351, 420, 452-453

309th Guards Mortar Regiment 155, 190, 244, 368, 396, 416, 455, 532, 541, 566, 580

315th Guards Mortar Regiment 32, 68, 205, 220, 256, 366, 368, 416, 452

399th Rifle Regiment 247, 536, 546, 550

468th Rifle Regiment 536, 546, 550, 553

496th Mortar Regiment 490, 507

522nd Rifle Regiment 490, 506-508, 516

532nd Rifle Regiment 536, 546, 550

585th Rifle Regiment 194-195, 197, 199-200, 227, 287, 317, 353, 399

586th Rifle Regiment 200, 455

671st Artillery Regiment 64, 68, 151, 173, 199-200, 231, 305, 317

702nd Rifle Regiment 194-195, 197, 198, 199-200, 286-287, 289, 353, 532, 549, 569, 577

793rd Guards Rifle Regiment 131, 194-200, 287, 289, 306, 310-311, 313, 316, 318, 352-353, 455, 549, 532, 577

830th Artillery Regiment 412, 482

932nd Artillery Regiment 55, 415

973rd Rifle Regiment 276, 535, 544, 546-547, 550-551, 553

975th Rifle Regiment 276, 535, 546-547, 550-551, 553

977th Rifle Regiment 276, 535, 546, 553

1000th Rifle Regiment 412, 507-508

1002nd Rifle Regiment 412, 480, 490, 502, 506-508

1004th Rifle Regiment 389, 412, 415, 433, 480, 490, 500

1032nd Artillery Regiment 490-491

1241st Rifle Regiment 160, 340-341, 343, 413, 415, 426, 428-429, 452

1243rd Rifle Regiment 391, 413, 452

1245th Rifle Regiment 413, 428-429, 452
1438th Self-propelled Artillery Regiment 56, 67, 70-71, 204-205, 217-220, 223, 244, 246, 255-257, 261, 263-264, 281, 302, 359, 368, 416, 423, 453, 580-581
1500th Destroyer Anti-tank Artillery Regiment 366, 378, 381, 427, 490
1529th Heavy Self-propelled Artillery Regiment 59-60, 67, 70-71, 242, 244, 247, 311-312, 315-316, 359, 368, 396, 416, 455, 550, 567, 580
1667th Destroyer Anti-tank Artillery Regiment 416, 452
1669th Destroyer Anti-tank Artillery Regiment 32, 69, 86, 247, 287, 310-312, 315, 373, 455, 532, 535, 580
1670th Separate Destroyer Anti-tank Artillery Regiment 32, 59, 69
1844th Destroyer Anti-tank Artillery Regiment 262, 268-269
1848th Destroyer Anti-tank Artillery Regiment 262, 269, 395
1849th Destroyer Anti-tank Artillery Regiment 276-277, 281, 337-338, 494
1853rd Destroyer Anti-tank Artillery Regiment 337-338, 494

Battalions:
2nd Anti-tank Rifle Battalion 68, 416
4th Anti-tank Rifle Battalion 64, 68, 228, 231, 298, 416
34th Separate Armored Train Battalion 32, 59, 68
47th Separate Rifle Battalion 532, 535
80th Separate Destroyer Anti-Tank Artillery Battalion 64, 220
87th Guards Separate Destroyer Anti-tank Artillery Battalion 253, 321
99th Guards Separate Destroyer Anti-tank Artillery Battalion 467-468
101st Anti-tank Rifle Battalion 63, 173
122nd Separate Anti-tank Rifle Battalion 381, 452, 490, 501-502
130th Anti-tank Rifle Battalion 452, 490-491, 506
131st Anti-tank Rifle Battalion 393-394, 455, 532, 543
132nd Separate Anti-tank Rifle Battalion 455, 532, 535, 543, 551
137th Anti-tank Rifle Battalion 341, 413, 426
201st Motorized Rifle Battalion 310-311, 315-316
295th Tank Battalion 310, 538, 542, 544, 546-547, 551, 553
296th Tank Battalion 310-312, 315, 538, 557
321st Separate Destroyer Anti-tank Artillery Battalion 535, 546, 551
331st Tank Battalion 160, 382-383, 415, 490, 524
409th Destroyer Anti-tank Artillery Battalion 490-491

Other Formations/Organisations
65th Separate Penal Company 52, 161
66th Separate Penal Company 63, 130, 174-175
622nd Aerial Surveillance Company 75-76

General Staff xviii, 22, 25-26, 29, 46, 66, 91, 131, 135, 152, 174, 211, 289, 306, 362-363, 379, 441-442, 469, 526, 528, 538

NKVD 90, 101, 132, 214, 360, 399-400, 441-442, 583

SMERSH counterintelligence department 84, 87, 129, 131, 177, 179, 193, 213, 270, 292, 360
Soviet Supreme High Command xii, 21, 66, 77, 222, 299, 526
Stavka xii, 21, 23, 28, 31, 66, 77, 82-83, 86, 135, 155, 222-223, 299, 306-307, 362, 365, 443, 446, 449, 526-528, 564, 579, 581
Steppe Military District xii, 21, 23, 28
Supreme Command Reserve 97, 221, 271, 322, 415, 457, 482, 490, 507

Volga Military District 103, 439
Voronezh Front's Military Council 24, 28, 43, 47, 88-89, 98, 100, 104, 126, 257, 289, 354, 401, 403, 435, 514, 580

INDEX OF GERMAN MILITARY FORMATIONS & UNITS

Army Groups:
Army Group Center 107, 296, 298, 307, 354, 441, 444, 562
Army Group South xi-xiii, xv, xviii, 24-28, 41, 107, 110-118, 120-121, 124, 133-134, 136, 138-139, 145, 209-211, 223-224, 226, 234, 238, 240, 280, 291, 298-302, 318-319, 327-328, 349, 353-354, 361-362, 364, 369, 397, 405, 416-417, 425, 443-444, 448, 484-485, 487, 547-548, 561-562, 564-567, 576, 586, 588-589

Armies:
Third Panzer Army 441, 590
Fourth Panzer Army xii-xiii, xv, 25-27, 41, 51, 107-111, 113-115, 121, 125-126, 133-134, 182, 190, 209-211, 225, 234, 237, 239, 242, 245, 276, 289-291, 298-299, 301-302, 304, 318, 327, 340, 351, 353, 360-361, 364, 367, 369, 400, 405, 407, 417, 425, 434, 443-445, 462, 472-473, 484-487, 561, 566, 572, 581-582, 585-587, 590
Sixth Army 111, 346, 584
Ninth Army 107-109, 297, 354, 361, 444
Army Detachment Kempf xi-xiii, xv-xviii, 21, 25-27, 32, 41, 51, 63, 67, 73, 92, 94, 107-108, 110-121, 127-129, 133-134, 137, 140, 149, 151-152, 155, 159, 172, 178, 182-183, 186, 188-189, 192, 209-210,

INDEX 605

224, 226, 231, 234, 236-237, 239-240, 249, 253, 263-264, 276, 281, 290-293, 297-302, 318, 324, 327-328, 340, 350-359, 363-364, 369-371, 374, 379, 395, 397, 402, 404-405, 408, 417, 428, 432, 436, 440, 443-445, 448, 462, 471-473, 484-486, 488-489, 527, 530, 541, 549, 561-562, 564, 566-567, 574, 576-577, 579, 585-586, 589-590

Groups:
Sturmgruppe Nord 406-408, 425-427, 429, 431, 433-434
Sturmgruppe Sud 406, 408, 427, 433-434

Corps:
II SS Panzer Corps 108, 434
III SS Panzer Corps xv, xvii-xviii, 49, 51, 54, 62-63, 108, 110-116, 119-124, 127, 133-134, 139, 141-143, 152, 155, 157, 159, 163, 165-166, 169, 172, 182-184, 186, 199, 201, 207, 209-210, 219, 231, 234, 236-239, 241-242, 244-245, 247, 249, 251-252, 254, 262, 269, 273, 277, 281, 283-286, 288-291, 293-294, 297, 301-304, 306-308, 318-319, 323, 325, 328, 332-333, 339-340, 348, 350-352, 354-356, 358-359, 364-366, 369-372, 377, 384-386, 389, 394, 397-398, 400, 402-408, 413-414, 417, 420, 425, 431, 434, 436-440, 443-446, 448, 464, 470, 473, 477-478, 481, 483-489, 492, 498-499, 503, 505, 508-509, 511, 514, 517-519, 525, 527-528, 530, 541, 559-561, 566, 572, 574-579, 581-582, 586-589
XI Corps xvii, 110, 119, 397, 590
LII Army Corps 108, 445, 561
XXXXII Army Corps 108, 110, 116, 118-119, 140, 151-152, 179, 226
XXXXVIII Panzer Corps xi, xv, 29, 108-109, 111, 113, 128, 234, 289, 402, 417, 434, 486-487, 585, 587
VIII Fliegerkorps 114, 134, 152, 183, 231, 234-235, 308, 324, 331, 354, 358, 382, 454, 471, 480, 482, 505, 522, 548, 549
Korps Raus xvii, 51, 108, 110, 112, 116, 119-123, 138, 140, 142-143, 151-152, 155, 170, 172-173, 175, 178, 188-189, 191, 197-198, 214-215, 228, 231, 233-235, 237-239, 242, 247, 249-250, 259, 279, 281-282, 285-286, 293, 297, 301-304, 316-318, 327, 334, 355-356, 364, 369, 397-398, 444, 448, 489, 497, 539, 547-548, 556-557, 560-561, 566, 572, 577, 588, 590
SS Panzer Corps xv, 66, 108-111, 113-114, 134, 140-141, 160, 176, 209, 234, 244, 275, 289, 299-302, 305, 318, 361, 367, 369, 407, 434, 443-444, 448, 462, 483-485, 487-488, 513-514, 519, 527, 553, 560-562, 566, 581, 585, 588

Divisions:
3rd Panzer Division 111, 134, 484
6th Panzer Division xv, 108, 110-115, 125-127, 137, 139-141, 143, 149-151, 155, 157-160, 172, 180, 182-183, 186, 190, 199, 201-202, 208-211, 231, 234, 237-239, 240-242, 249, 250-253, 260, 262-263, 266, 268, 273, 277, 280, 286, 289-290, 293-294, 302-303, 307-308, 318-319, 323, 324-330, 333, 338, 340-345, 348-350, 352, 354-356, 364-365, 367, 369-371, 374-376, 380-381, 384-385, 401-402, 404-409, 417, 420-421, 423-427, 431, 434-436, 444, 447-448, 468, 470-471, 478-481, 483-484, 488-489, 496, 498-503, 505-511, 518-519, 521-522, 524-525, 527, 541, 548, 559-560, 575, 578-580, 586-589
7th Panzer Division xviii, 49, 111-113, 115, 121-122, 124-128, 138-144, 151, 155, 163, 165-172, 181, 183, 185-186, 188-189, 201-204, 206, 208-211, 214, 216, 218-222, 230-231, 234, 236-239, 241-242, 244, 246, 249-251, 253-254, 259, 260, 262-263, 266, 269, 273, 277, 279-281, 284, 286, 288, 290, 293, 297, 301-303, 305-306, 308-311, 318, 325 327, 330, 333-334, 337-340, 348, 352, 355-357, 364, 370-372, 383-384, 393-394, 397-398, 401-402, 404, 406-407, 409, 417, 428, 435-436, 440, 444, 446-448, 473-480, 488-489, 492-493, 495-498, 505, 519, 529, 541-542, 546, 548, 550, 559-560, 575, 577, 579-582, 586, 589
10th Flak Artillery Division 192, 328
11th Panzer Division 111, 126-127, 250, 327, 484
19th Panzer Division xviii, 21, 110, 111-113, 115, 127, 140-141, 143, 149-151, 155, 158, 160-161, 163, 165, 170, 172, 182, 185-186, 190-191, 199, 201-202, 206-209, 211-212, 214-215, 221, 231, 234, 237, 239, 241-242, 244, 251-253, 262-263, 268-269, 273-274, 283-285, 291, 293, 302-303, 307-308, 318-320, 323-324, 326-327, 329, 332, 340-341, 348-349, 352, 355-356, 367, 370, 372, 374-376, 380-382, 385-386, 389-391, 393, 401, 404-409, 417, 420-421, 422-427, 429, 433-437, 444, 447-448, 452, 462, 468, 470, 473, 480-483, 488-490, 498-501, 503-505, 508-509, 522, 524-525, 527, 529, 542, 559-560, 575, 580, 586-588
57th Infantry Division 108, 126
88th Infantry Division 362-363
106th Infantry Division 111-112, 127, 130, 140, 143-144, 151, 170-177, 180-181, 185, 188, 197, 203, 223-224, 233, 235-236, 254, 260-261, 269, 285, 287-288, 290, 297, 302, 306, 309-311, 313, 315-318, 333-334, 356-357, 370, 394, 397-399, 401, 406, 530-531, 536, 539-540, 544, 546-548, 550-551, 557, 580, 585
167th Infantry Division 126, 391, 472, 485, 499
168th Infantry Division 48, 56, 70-71, 97, 101-102, 110-113, 124, 126, 134, 139-143, 145, 147, 150, 159-161, 182, 201, 204-205, 217-223, 226, 233-234, 241-244, 246, 249, 251, 255, 268-270, 273, 280-281, 284, 290, 294, 300, 302-303, 307-309, 318-320, 324, 327-328, 332, 341, 352, 356, 359-360, 368, 370, 372, 375, 389-392, 406-408, 416-417, 420, 423, 434, 440-441, 447-448, 452-453, 462, 468-472, 485, 489,

498-499, 509, 522-523, 529, 542, 559-560, 576, 579-580, 582, 586-587
198th Infantry Division 327, 363-364, 370-371, 396, 398, 404, 406, 417, 432, 444, 446, 473, 475, 477-479, 485, 488-489, 497-498, 505, 519, 529, 539, 541, 543, 557, 560-561, 582
255th Infantry Division 108, 126
330th Infantry Division 401-402, 440-441
332nd Infantry Division 126, 484, 588
Panzergrenadier Division *Grossdeutschland* 110, 240, 361, 417, 444, 484, 486
SS Panzergrenadier Division *Das Reich* 29, 110, 126, 294, 296, 299, 353, 400, 440, 472
SS Panzergrenadier Division *Leibstandarte Adolf Hitler* 29, 110, 126, 299, 353-354, 400, 484
SS Panzergrenadier Division *Totenkopf* 110-111, 126, 140-141, 160, 209-210, 299-300, 302-303, 318, 341, 350, 354, 440, 484, 547, 587

Brigades:
Panzer Brigade 10 353, 361

Regiments:
Artillery Regiment 62 119, 251, 370, 447, 478, 489, 559
Artillery Regiment 71 375, 406, 447
Artillery Regiment 248 141-142, 159, 284, 303, 370, 406, 447
Flak Regiment 7 119, 191-192
Flak Regiment 38 242, 303, 320, 370, 454
Flak Regiment 43 242, 303
Flak regiments 119, 138, 143-144, 188
Grenadier Regiment 114 158, 325
Grenadier Regiment 239 143, 546, 548, 551
Grenadier Regiment 241 544, 548
Grenadier Regiment 417 141, 158, 160, 542, 559-560, 587
Grenadier Regiment 429 141-142, 560
Grenadier Regiment 585 143-144, 556
Grenadier Regiment 586 143-144, 557
Grenadier Regiment 587 143-144
Infantry Regiment 160, 417 249, 284, 393, 408, 452, 470
Infantry Regiment 239 127, 174-175, 235, 260, 286
Infantry Regiment 240 127, 170, 174-176, 185, 193, 235, 254, 257, 259, 286, 356
Infantry Regiment 241 127, 174-176,235, 394, 398
Infantry Regiment 247 249, 393
Infantry Regiment 315 391, 472
Infantry Regiment 326 364, 371, 406, 475, 477
Infantry Regiment 429 161, 249, 251-252, 274, 303, 323, 389, 393, 408, 425, 434, 462, 470-471
Infantry Regiment 442 166, 206, 274, 283-284, 303, 324, 332, 372, 375, 389-390, 406, 408, 417, 420, 424, 426, 441, 447, 471, 481
Infantry Regiment 585 127, 176, 178, 227, 235, 317, 441
Infantry Regiment 586 176-177, 227, 235, 313, 398-399
Infantry Regiment 587 176-177, 197, 235, 441
Mortar Regiment 52 [Nebelwerfers] 54, 251, 375, 447, 478, 505, 509, 559-560
Panzer Regiment 11 112, 141, 211, 249, 263, 267, 273-274, 277, 280, 308, 380, 408, 424-425, 435, 437, 500, 507-508, 514, 520-522, 587
Panzer Regiment 25 142, 166-167, 185, 234, 238, 250, 254, 278-279, 286, 309, 339, 357, 444, 448, 475, 495, 508, 587
Panzer Regiment 27 141, 199, 208, 215, 231, 234, 252, 285, 349, 370-371, 389, 426, 428-429, 437, 481
Panzergrenadier Regiment 4 141, 180, 308, 325, 421, 508, 589
Panzergrenadier Regiment 6 142, 168, 206, 208, 337-339, 496
Panzergrenadier Regiment 7 142, 168, 186, 206, 208, 339, 495
Panzergrenadier Regiment 73 160, 163, 185, 252, 274, 285, 319-320, 323, 352, 372, 375-376, 389-391, 408, 447-448, 462, 470, 503, 542, 559, 587
Panzergrenadier Regiment 74 141, 160-161, 165, 199, 252, 274, 323, 340, 375-376, 380, 401, 408, 448, 503, 509, 559, 587
Panzergrenadier Regiment 114 141, 159, 263, 308, 427, 522, 527, 587
Pioneer Regiment 601 242, 371

Battalions:
Engineer Battalion 57 141, 158
Engineer Battalion 248 141-142
Heavy Panzerjäger Battalion 560 116-118
Motorized Engineer Battalion 58 142, 166
Panzer Reconnaissance Battalion 6 343-345, 421, 426-427, 471, 496, 559-560
Panzer Reconnaissance Battalion 19 324, 331, 372, 375, 390, 408, 423, 462, 470, 503, 542, 559
Panzer Reconnaissance Battalion 37 309, 333, 339, 356, 372, 474-475, 477
Panzer Reconnaissance Battalion 248 141, 284, 560
Panzerjäger Battalion 42 142, 397
Pioneer Battalion 58 398, 406
Separate Heavy Panzer Battalion 503 75, 115, 139, 141-142, 159, 161, 167, 186, 206-207, 215, 285, 288, 330, 375, 406-408, 434, 447-448, 474, 489, 498, 500, 527, 581
StuG Battalion 228 141, 159-160, 284, 370, 375-376, 389, 408-409, 425, 427, 435, 448, 498, 586, 588
StuG Battalion 905 119, 172, 188, 197, 235, 261, 286, 356, 546, 556-557, 582, 586

Other Formations/Organisations:
Artillerie Kommando 153 119
Artillerie Kommando 3 241-242, 303, 370, 447, 489
Kampfgruppe Becker 252-253, 274, 284, 323

INDEX

Kampfgruppe Bieberstein 141, 158, 160, 211-212, 308, 376, 408, 421, 424-427, 429, 471
Kampfgruppe Gläsemer 250, 253-254, 263, 273, 309
Kampfgruppe Köhler 163, 165, 199, 206-207, 209, 212-214, 252-253, 262, 319, 323, 371
Kampfgruppe Quentin 273, 503, 519
Kampfgruppe Unrein 273, 308, 325-326, 376, 380, 408, 421, 424, 471, 503, 507, 559
Luftflotte IV 153, 303, 308, 328
Luftwaffe 32, 125, 127, 143, 192, 224, 306, 328, 335, 504-505, 509, 511, 588
OKH 116-119, 134, 354, 563
OKW 141, 359, 375, 563

Panzerkampfgruppe Oppeln-Bronikowski 210, 263, 267-269, 272, 278-280, 293, 301, 303, 308, 319, 324-325, 330, 336-337, 340, 342, 344, 351, 355, 369, 375, 381, 384, 386, 408, 410, 424-425, 471, 481, 502, 506, 508-509, 511, 519-520
the SS 29-30, 110, 126, 176, 209, 289, 296, 299-300, 302-303, 318, 341, 350, 353, 387, 400, 440, 444, 446, 472, 483, 488, 513, 560, 581
StuG Battery 393 119, 586
Wehrmacht xi-xiii, xvii-xviii, 21, 75, 107, 110-111, 113, 115, 118-119, 122, 128-129, 131, 135-136, 176, 180, 183, 240, 280, 290-292, 299, 328, 357, 359, 363, 375, 391, 484, 555, 564-566, 586-587, 589-591

INDEX OF WAR MATERIÉL

Aircraft:
Fw 189s 492, 542
Heinkels 505, 587
Il-2 *sturmoviki* 191-192, 153, 259, 279, 306, 308, 335, 342, 392, 510, 588
Junkers 477, 505
Ju-87 Stukas 324, 335, 478, 509
Ju-88s 342, 477

Guns & Rocket Launchers
Anti-tank guns 49, 53-54, 60, 64, 67, 69, 83-86, 93, 124, 163, 176-177, 187, 215, 218, 220, 230-231, 233, 245, 253, 255-256, 258, 262-263, 268, 277-278, 280, 282, 290, 295, 297, 314, 337-338, 343, 358, 366-367, 373, 407, 409, 412, 414-416, 425, 431, 435, 437, 445, 453, 457, 471, 478-481, 490, 494-495, 513, 520, 525, 529, 532, 534, 554, 560, 575
Anti-tank rifles 32-33, 49, 53-54, 63, 79, 83-85, 93, 100, 168-169, 208, 213, 255, 282, 323, 352, 390, 409, 411-412, 426, 435, 455-456, 471, 473, 479, 483, 490, 502, 504, 507, 513, 525, 533, 575
BM-8 rocket launcher 322, 456
BM-13 rocket launcher 53, 320, 322, 434, 532
Howitzers 28, 32, 50, 53, 67-68, 83, 86, 115-116, 119, 124, 142, 150, 152, 158, 173, 176, 199, 202, 205, 207, 218, 230, 251, 256, 263, 268, 271-272, 280, 290, 294-296, 306, 325-327, 342, 351, 365-366, 370, 375, 385, 406, 412, 415, 437, 478, 482, 532-533, 541, 561, 580
Katiusha rocket launchers ("Stalin's organs") 53, 68, 83, 87, 155, 168, 202, 255-256, 294, 321, 377, 381, 385, 429, 476
M-13 rocket launchers/shells 202, 309, 396, 429, 476
Machine guns 27, 33, 35, 40, 45, 47, 54, 56-57, 79, 81-82, 85, 93, 149, 161, 168-169, 178-179, 181, 229-230, 233, 254-255, 261, 282, 317, 333, 372-373, 399, 409, 411, 421-422, 428, 454, 456, 465, 471, 473, 477, 479, 533, 542-544
Maksim machine guns 230, 254, 333, 373, 477, 479

Marder self-propelled anti-tank guns 120, 254, 425-426
Mortars 27, 33, 36, 49, 53-54, 60, 67, 83, 85, 100, 146, 148-150, 158, 161, 165, 169-170, 173, 189-190, 192, 202, 207, 213-214, 230, 233, 251, 277, 282, 286, 293, 295, 304, 321, 323, 336, 339, 366, 372, 375-376, 392, 403, 411-412, 415-416, 421-422, 437, 453, 456, 464, 466, 471, 473, 481, 492, 532-534, 536, 546, 554-555, 557, 575, 580
Nebelwerfer rocket launchers 120, 142, 158-159, 177, 201, 208, 251, 254, 259, 268, 286, 294, 311, 323, 339, 374-375, 380, 430, 447, 475, 478, 495, 505, 509, 543, 550, 556, 559-560, 576, 582
PPSh submachine guns 45, 214, 229, 265, 533
SU self-propelled guns 493
SU-76 33, 243, 257, 264, 416
SU-122 33, 243, 263-264, 282, 416
SU-152 73, 264, 283, 397
ZiS-3 anti-tank guns 53, 262, 288

Tanks:
Churchills 366, 376-377, 381, 386, 410, 427-428, 437, 490, 503-505
Flammpanzers 390, 406, 423
KVs 50, 53-54, 70, 100, 205, 212, 244, 281, 284, 319-320, 326, 332, 386, 416, 540, 580
Matildas ("Mk. II") 100, 311, 538, 546, 551, 553
Panzerjäger Hornisse [Hornet]/Nashorn [Rhinoceros] 116-119
Pz.Kpfw. II 115, 285, 407, 498
Pz.Kpfw. III 115, 215, 219, 285, 431, 435, 437, 478
Pz.Kpfw. IV 115, 126, 160, 168, 186, 215, 219, 255, 285, 431, 435, 437, 478, 480, 504, 521
Pz.Kpfw. V Panthers 115, 117-118, 136, 240, 353-354, 361, 434, 566, 587
Pz-VI Tigers 68, 112-113, 115-116, 123-124, 139, 141, 155, 159-161, 167-168, 183, 185-186, 188, 199, 206-207, 215, 219, 243, 251, 256, 277, 280-281, 283, 285, 288, 293, 313, 326, 330, 336-337, 361, 406-407, 412, 424, 426-427, 429-431, 434-436,

454, 480, 482, 493-494, 498, 500-501, 564, 574, 586
T-34s 59, 70-71, 100, 186, 195, 197, 218, 243, 246, 255, 289, 302, 314, 343, 427-428, 493, 495, 508, 519-521, 523-524, 553, 555
T-60s 33, 59, 72-73, 100, 243, 490, 516
T-70s 33, 59, 72-73, 100, 201, 217-218, 243, 246, 280-281, 381, 384, 410, 416, 490, 500, 516, 529, 539
Valentines ("Mk. III") 71, 100, 310-311, 416, 551, 553

INDEX OF MISCELLANEOUS & GENERAL TERMS

Baudot device 146, 153, 190, 275, 347, 378-379, 388, 401, 548

Cold War xiii-xiv, xviii, 132, 357
Communist Party xiii, xvii-xviii, 97, 174, 346
Cossacks 123, 180

"Hero of the Soviet Union" (title) 30, 59, 158, 164-165, 174, 194, 196, 216, 232, 267, 498, 554, 585

Operation Citadel (Zitadelle) xi, xiii-xv, xviii, 21, 24, 28, 48-49, 53, 82, 107-112, 114, 117-121, 123, 125, 133-134, 136-137, 139-140, 144, 183, 186, 206, 209-211, 223, 234, 240, 291, 293-294, 298-299, 328, 334, 351, 354, 357, 361, 363, 398, 407, 432, 437, 444, 483, 508, 519, 527, 561-566, 575-576, 585-590
Order of the Red Banner 30, 151, 156, 214, 221, 270, 316, 346, 392, 439, 466, 513, 572, 574
Order of the Red Star 174, 179, 385

Panzerkeil formation 358-359
People's Commissariat of Defense 31, 216, 582, 584